Introduction to AutoCAD 2014 for Civil Engineering Applications

Nighat Yasmin
Clemson University

ISBN 978-1-58503-789-6

SDC
Publications

SDC Publications
P.O. Box 1334
Mission KS 66222
(913) 262-2664
www.SDCpublications.com

Publisher: Stephen Schroff

Preface

A picture is worth a thousand words! This is an old saying that an engineer describes every idea with a drawing. With the advance in computer technology and drawing software, the academia is aware of teaching students computer aided design. The main purpose of this book is to provide civil engineering students with a clear presentation of the theory of engineering graphics and the use of AutoCAD 2014 (CAD software). The illustrations used in this book are created using *AutoCAD 2014* and the *Paint* software.

Several improvements are made to the fifth edition. The most important improvement is the usage of ribbon interface. The major contents of the book are based on the ribbon interface. A new chapter titled as *AutoCAD 2014 – Classics Interface* is created to introduce the classic interface. The index is improved. The chapter titled as *Suggested In-Class Activities* provides in-class activities (or ICA). For some of the initial ICAs, it explains the drawing with the help of step-by-step instruction. Also, new problems are added to the homework's chapter. Furthermore, the contents and the drawings of every chapter are improved.

Each chapter starts with the chapter objectives followed by the introduction. The bulleted objectives provide a general overview of the material covered. The contents of each chapter are organized into well-defined sections that contain detailed step-by-step instruction with graphical illustrations to carry out the AutoCAD commands.

This book has been categorized into 10 parts.

Part 1:	Chapters 1-8:	Introduction to AutoCAD2014 ribbon interface
Part 2:	Chapters 9-10:	Use of AutoCAD in land survey data plotting
Part 3:	Chapters 11-12:	The use of AutoCAD in hydrology
Part 4:	Chapters 13-14:	Transportation engineering and AutoCAD
Part 5:	Chapters 15-17:	AutoCAD and architecture technology
Part 6:	Chapters 18:	Introduction to working drawing
Part 7:	Chapters 19:	Introduction to AutoCAD classics interface
Part 8:	Chapters 20-21:	Suggested drawing problems
Part 9:	Chapter 22:	Bibliography
Part 10:	Chapter 23:	Index

1. The 1st chapter, *Introduction to Engineering Graphics*, provides a relationship between an engineering problem and engineering graphics.

2. The 2nd chapter, *Getting started with AutoCAD 2014*, explains the basics of AutoCAD 2014. The emphasis is on the drawing area (save or delete), ribbons, tabs (add, remove, and relocate), panels (add, remove, and relocate), command line, and file operations (open, close, save, and plot). The chapter also explains the basic features of a new file and provides their default values. Furthermore, the

chapter explains how the grid and snap points in the x-y plane help a user during the drawing creation process.

3. The 3rd chapter, *Basics of 2-Dimensional Drawings*, begins with the details of the dynamic input capabilities. The major part of this chapter is devoted to the commands description for 2D objects, such as point, lines, circles, ellipse, rectangles, polygons, polylines, arcs, appearance of object (color, line thickness, and line style). The remaining part of the chapter focuses on creating tables and multiline text objects. The chapter also explains the concept of hatching.

4. The 4th chapter, *Basics of 2-Dimensional Editing* begins with object selection and de-selection methodology. The chapter discusses object snap facility, a fast and easy access to the strategic points on a 2D object. The major emphasis of the chapter is the explanation of the commands (erase, mirror, copy, move, rotate, offset, trim, extend, fillet, scale, break, and explode) to modify 2D objects. An alternate method, the use of grips points, to modify an object is also discussed. This chapter also explains the process of creating rectangular, polar, and path arrays. Finally, the last topic of the chapter explains the use of the property sheet for object editing.

5. The 5th chapter, *Layers*, explains the art of creating, using, and modifying layers.

6. The 6th chapter, *Blocks*, explains how to create and insert different types of blocks.

7. The 7th chapter, *Layouts and Template files* explains how to manipulate layouts and how to create a template files.

8. The 8th chapter, *Dimensioning Techniques*, explains the art of creating and reading a dimensioned drawing. The chapter provides the basics of dimensioning techniques, placement of dimensions, and choice of dimensions.

9. The 9th chapter, *Land Survey*, describes parcel, deed, display angles (azimuth and bearing), open and close traverse, and different types of survey systems.

10. The 10th chapter, *Contours*, introduces the basic terminology used in contour maps. It also provides step-by-step instructions to draw and label contour maps.

11. The 11th chapter, *Drainage Basin*, explains the characteristics of a drainage basin. At the end, it provides step-by-step instructions to delineate channels and their drainage basins on a contour map.

12. The 12th chapter, *Floodplains*, explains characteristics of a channel and its floodplain. At the end, it provides step-by-step instructions to delineate a channel and its floodplain on a contour map.

13. The 13th chapter, *Road design*, explains how to draw PnP (plan and profile) and cross-sections drawing for a proposed road on a contour map.

14. The 14th chapter, *Earthwork*, explains how to use a PnP (plan and profile) drawing for the excavation and embankment delineation on a given contour map.

15. The 15th chapter, *Floor Plan*, explains how to create an architectural drawing of a residential building using simple commands such as point, polyline, circle, trim, extend, offset, and hatch. It also makes use of the blocks from the design center.

16. The 16th chapter, *Elevation*, describes the techniques used to create basic elevation by projecting lines from a floor and roof plans. It also provides step-by-step instruction to create side elevation by projecting lines from a floor and roof plans and from front elevation using 45 degrees miter lines. It provides step-by-step instruction to create hip and gable roofs used in the elevation, too.

17. The 17th chapter, *Site Plan*, provides step-by-step instructions to draw and label a site map of the residential building created in Chapter #15.

18. The 18th chapter, *Construction Drawings*, briefly describes a family of drawings.

19. The 19th chapter, *AutoCAD 2014 – Classics Interface*, explains the basics of AutoCAD 2014's classics interface. The emphasis is on the toolbars (add, remove, and relocate) and pull down menus. It also explains how to save or delete drawing area, command line, and file operations (open, close, save, and plot) using the toolbars and menus. This chapter also explains how to access drawing, editing, layers, block, and dimensioning commands using the toolbars and menus.

20. The 20th chapter, *Suggested In-Class Activities*, provides a list of design problem for the in-class activities or labs.

21. The 21th chapter, *Homework Drawings*, provides a list of design problem for the homework assignments.

22. The 22nd chapter, *Bibliography*, provides a list of the books and papers referenced in the preparation of the manuscript.

23. Finally, the 23rd chapter, *Index*, provides an alphabetical list of the major topics discussed in the book.

Acknowledgment

I wish to acknowledge the patience and continuous support of my husband, Abdul, and my children Nayel, Haaris, and Kirin during the countless hours I spent in preparation of the manuscript.

I would greatly appreciate hearing your comments and suggestions to improve the future editions, or any problem related to this edition.

Nighat Yasmin

yasmin@clemson.edu

Dedication

This book is dedicated to
my parents Shamim and Wajid
my Family and
my siblings and
my students.

TABLE OF CONTENTS

4.   BASICS OF 2-DIMENSIONAL EDITING **195**

10. CONTOURS 405

11. DRAINAGE BASIN 419

12. FLOODPLAINS 433

13. ROAD DESIGN 451

1. Introduction to Engineering Graphics

1.1. Objectives

- What is a computer graphic?
- What is a technical drawing?
- How can a drawing can be enlarged or reduced?

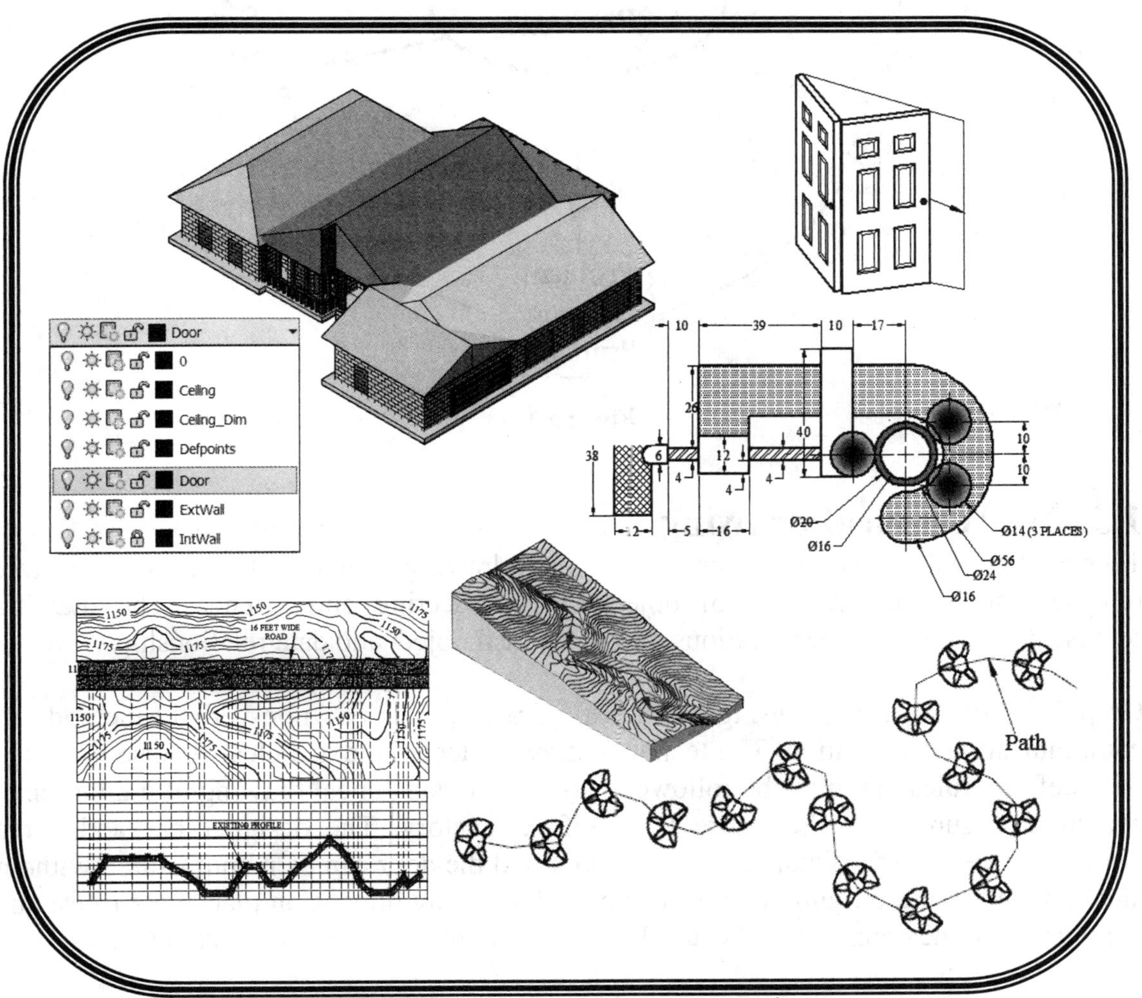

1.2.   Engineering problem

Extensive studies have shown that engineering problem solving techniques are complicated processes. A solution to most of the engineering problems requires a combination of organization, analysis, problem solving principles, communication skills, and/or graphical representations of the problem. The concept map shown in Figure 1-1 represents a simplified version of the interaction and complexities involved in the solution process. The focus of this book is the graphical techniques used to create technical drawings that can be used to find a solution.

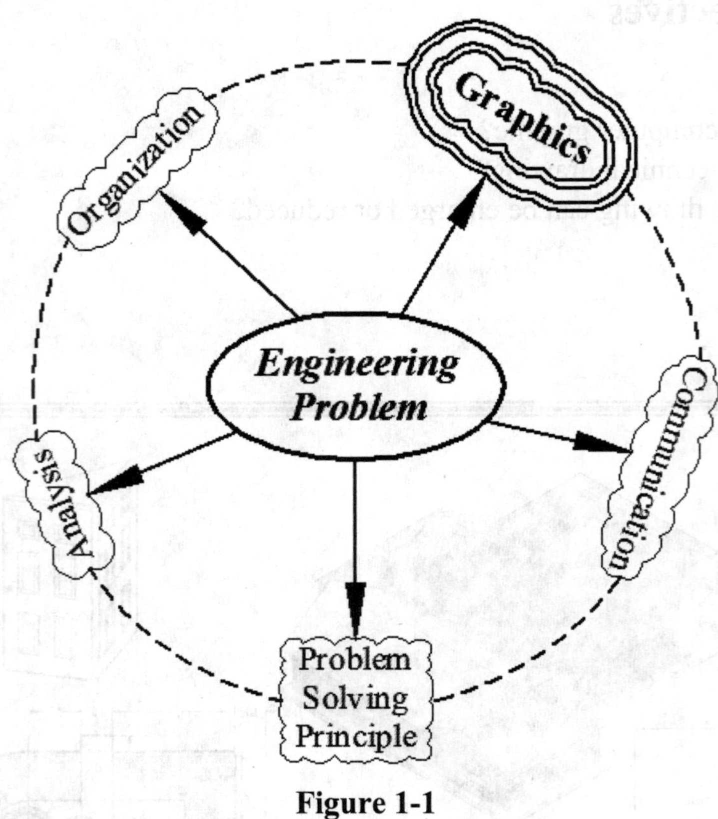

Figure 1-1

1.3.   Technical drawing

Technical drawing, also known as drafting, is a drawing technique that creates accurate representations (the drawing) of objects in engineering and science. The drawing represents designs and specifications of the physical object and data relationships.

Graphic communication using technical drawings is a non-verbal method of communicating information. The technical drawing technique is a clear precise language with definite rules that must be followed. Consider the technical drawing of a door panel shown in Figure 1-2. The figure is a self-explanatory. The designer has added the dimensions necessary to manufacture the door and the door can be manufactured without any confusion. In the figure, dimensions are added using dimension placement rules; and the plus and minus numbers indicates the maximum and minimum acceptable errors.

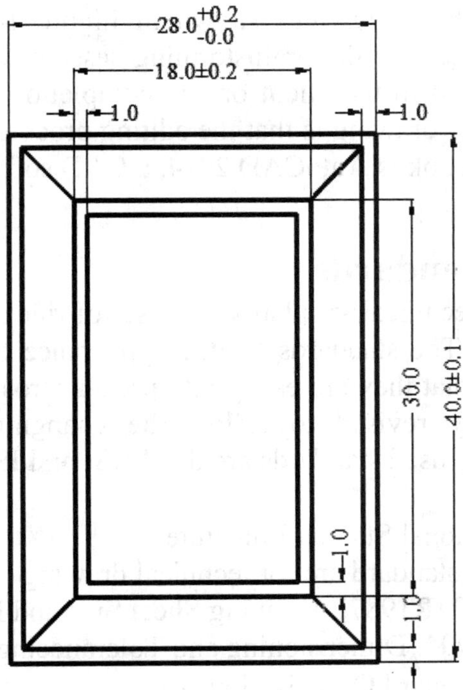

Figure 1-2

1.4.   Drawing methods

A drawing can be made manually (that is freehand or by using mechanical tools) and/or on a computer screen using Computer Aided Design (CAD) software. For example, drawing a line between two points can be done by hand (freehand method), by using compass, protractor, rulers, etc. (mechanical method), or on a computer using a software (CAD software). Figure 1-3a shows a freehand sketch and Figure 1-3b shows the mechanical drawing of a door panel, respectively. Figure 1-3c is the drawing of the same door created using CAD software.

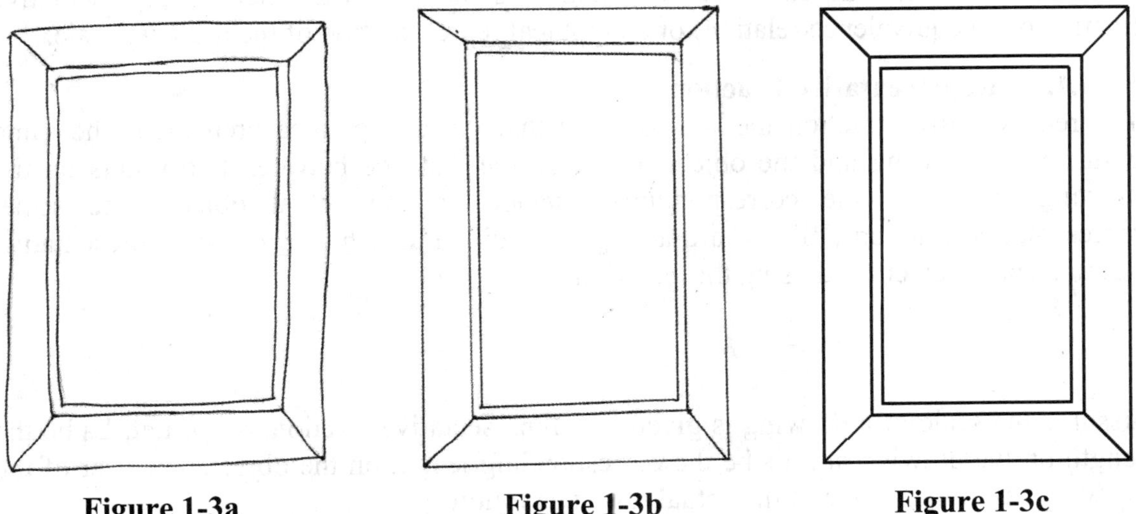

Figure 1-3a   **Figure 1-3b**   **Figure 1-3c**

The appearances of the three drawings shown in Figure 1-3 indicate that free hand sketches are good candidates for the brainstorming session. On the other hand, a CAD drawing should be delivered to the client on the completion of the project. One of the major advantages of a CAD drawing is that the editing process is fast compare to manual method. The focus of this book is AutoCAD 2014, a CAD software.

1.5. Drawing standards

The drawing standard or technical standards are a set of rules that govern how technical drawings are represented. The standards for the appearance of technical drawings have been developed to ensure that they are easily interpreted across the nation and the world. Standards are periodically revised to reflect the changing needs of industry and technology. The commonly used standards are the ANSI and ISO.

- ANSI: American National Standard Institute
    - Y series of ANSI standard are for technical drawing
    - ANSI Y14.1-1980 (R1987): Drawing Sheet Size and Format
    - ANSI Y14.5M-1994: Dimensioning and Toleranceing
- ISO: International Standard Organization
    - Metric standard
    - System is called International System of Units or System Internationale, abbreviated SI

1.6. Scale

The size of a drawing representing an object depends on the sizes of the object and the drawing paper. The ratio of the two sizes is known as the drawing's scale or simply the scale.

1.6.1. Type of scale

The scale of a drawing can be represented as a mathematical relation (representative fraction or an equivalence relation) or a graphical representation of the drawing scale.

1.6.1.1. Representative Fraction

The representative fraction method assumes that the unit of measurement is the same both on the drawing and the object. Let, a is the distance between two points on the drawing and b is the corresponding distance on the actual object. The scale, representative fraction (RF), of a drawing is specified as _a:b_ or _a/b_. The representative fraction can be calculated using the equation:

$$RF = a : b$$

Assume the scale of a drawing is given as a representative fraction, a / b. Let, L_d be the length on the drawing and L_o be the corresponding length on the object. The user of the drawing can find the size of the actual object as follow.

1. <u>Measure the distance of an object on the drawing (L_d)</u>: If the object is straight then ruler can be used to find distance between two points. If the object is not straight then take a string and place it on top of the drawing and then measure the length of the string.
2. <u>Calculate the object distance (L_o)</u>: Calculate the object distance using the equation:

$$L_d/L_o = a/b \qquad\qquad \text{Implies} \qquad\qquad L_o = (b/a) * L_d$$

- <u>Example #1</u>: Let the scale is 1:240 (that is $a = 1$ inch and $b = 240$ inches), $L_d = 25$ inches then
$$L_o = (240/1) * 25 = 6000 \, inches$$

- <u>Example #2</u>: Let the scale is 50:1 (that is $a = 50$ inches and $b = 1$ inch), $L_d = 250$ inches then
$$L_o = (1/50) * 250 = 5 \, inches$$

1.6.1.2. Equivalence relation

The equivalence relation method assumes that the units of measurement are different on the drawing and the object. The equivalence relation is also known as an engineer's scale. Assume, *a inches* is the distance between two points on the drawing and *b feet* is the corresponding distance on the actual object. The scale, equivalence relation (ER), of a drawing is specified as <u>$a'' = b'$</u>.

Assume the scale of a drawing is given as an equivalence relation. Let, L_d be the length on the drawing and L_o be the corresponding length on the object. The user of the drawing can find the size of the object as follow.

1. <u>Measure the distance on the drawing (L_d)</u>: If the object is straight then ruler can be used to find distance between two points. If the object is not straight then take a string and place it on the top of the drawing and then measure the length of the string.
2. <u>Calculate the object distance (L_o)</u>: Calculate the object distance using the equation:

$$a'' = b' \text{ and } L_d \text{ inches} = L_o \text{ feet}$$
$$\Longrightarrow \quad L_d/a = L_o/b$$
$$\Longrightarrow \quad L_o \text{ feet} = (b \text{ feet}) * [(L_d \text{ inches})/(a \text{ inches})]$$

- <u>Example #1</u>: Let the scale is 1" = 240' (that is $a = 1$ inch, $b = 240$ feet), $L_d = 25$ inches then
$$L_o = 240 * 25 = 6000 \, feet$$

- <u>Example #2</u>: Let the scale is 50" = 1' (that is $a = 50$ inches, $b = 1$ foot), $L_d = 250$ inches then
$$L_o = (1/50) * 250 = 5 \, feet$$

1.6.1.3. Converting RF to ER

A representative fraction (RF) scale can be converted into an equivalence relation (ER) and vice versa. A RF scale can be converted into an ER using the methodology explained in the following example.

<u>Example #1</u>: Let RF scale is 1:600 and the units of measurement are inches. Find the corresponding ER.

1. Convert the right side of the scale into feet. The conversion of inches of the scale into feet is shown here.

$$600 \text{ inches} = (600/12) \text{ feet} = 50 \text{ feet}$$

2. Hence, the RF scale of 1:600 can be written in ER format as 1" = 50'.

1.6.1.4. Graphical representation

The graphical representation is knows as graphical or bar scale. Generally, the graphical scales are used for large scale map. In this representation a ruler is drawn on the map as shown in Figure 1-4. In this representation, the bar is divided into two parts; the left and right part. In the left part (*Part 1* in Figure 1-4) the scale is divided into tenths and in the right part (*Part 2* in Figure 1-4) the scale is marked in full units. This representation assumes that the unit of measurement is the same both on the drawing and the object. For the current example, assume that the unit of measurement is inch.

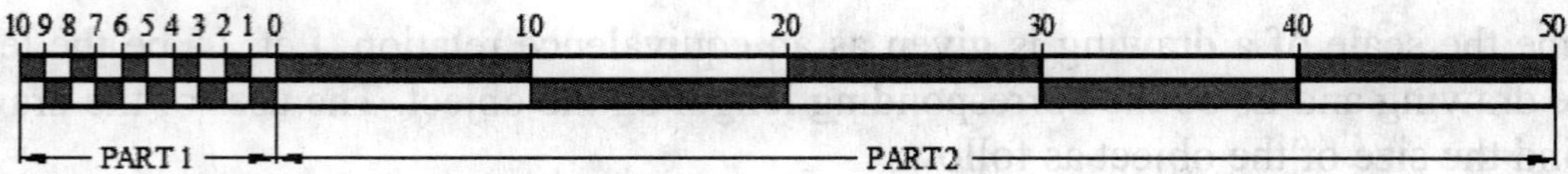

Figure 1-4

<u>Example #1</u>: Assume the scale of a drawing is given as a ruler shown in Figure 1-4. Let, L_m be the distance between two points on the map and L_G be the corresponding distance on the ground. The user of the map can find the distance on the ground as follow.

1. <u>Measure the distance of an object on the drawing (L_m)</u>: If the path is straight then any straight edge object can be used to find the distance between two stations. If the path is not straight then take a string and place it on the top of the path and then measure the length of the string Assume the user of the map (Figure 1-5a) desired to measure the straight line distance between two points A and B. The user will use a piece of paper and will mark two points on the straight edge, one point at the starting station (A) and the second point at the destination station (B), Figure 1-5b. For the demonstration purpose, the marks at A and B are represented as small line segments; the segments are highlighted by displaying their grip points.

2. <u>Find the object distance of the drawing (L_G)</u>: Now place the straight edge on the graphical scale as shown in Figure 1-5c. The distance between the stations A and B is 11.3 inches.

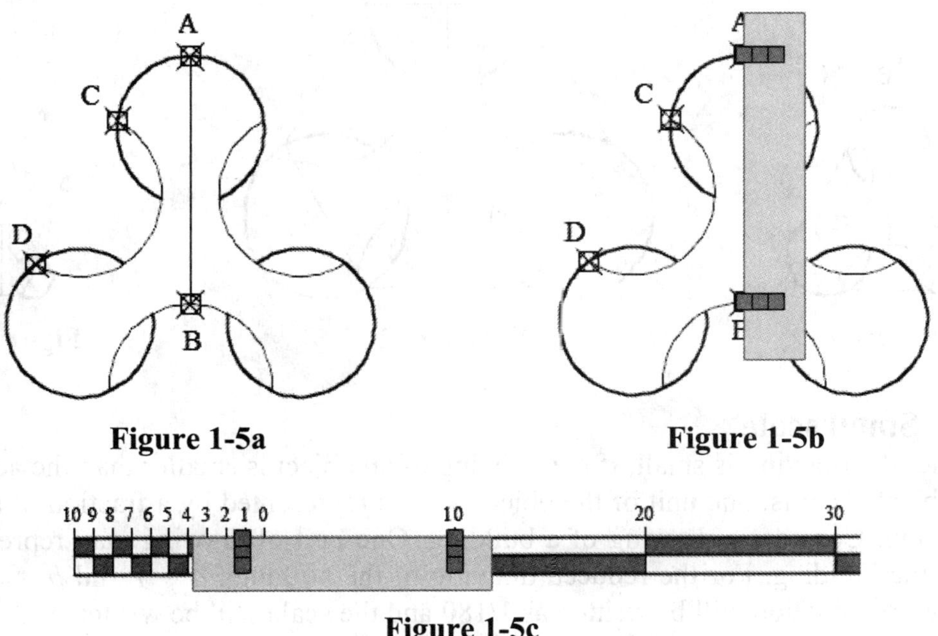

Figure 1-5a   **Figure 1-5b**

Figure 1-5c

1.7.   Scale of a drawing

Generally, drawings are drawn to a scale, because either the object is too large or too small to draw on a drawing sheet. Hence, a drawing can be smaller or larger than the object itself.

1.7.1.   Full scale

The scale of a drawing is full, if the drawing of an object is of the same size as of the object. That is, one unit on the drawing will represent one unit on the object. For example, a drawing of an average calculator (which is 6 inches long and 2.75 inches wide) can be a full scale drawing. For a full scale drawings, $a = 1$ and $b = 1$. The representative fraction will be written as 1/1 and the scale will be written *1:1* or *FULL*. Figure 1-6a shows a drawing of a plate drawn at full scale.

1.7.2.   Large scale

The scale of a drawing is large, if the drawing of an object is larger than the actual size of the object. That is, one unit on the drawing will represent a fraction of a unit on the object. For example, a printed circuit board of a computer chip may be 36 times the actual size; that is, 36 units on the drawing is actually 1 unit on the circuit board. For the enlarged drawing of the computer chip, $a = 36$ and $b = 1$. The representative fraction will be written as 36/1 and the scale will be written as *36:1*. The equivalence relation will be written as *3' = 1"*. Figure 1-6b shows a drawing of a plate drawn at a representative factor of 2 (Scale 2:1).

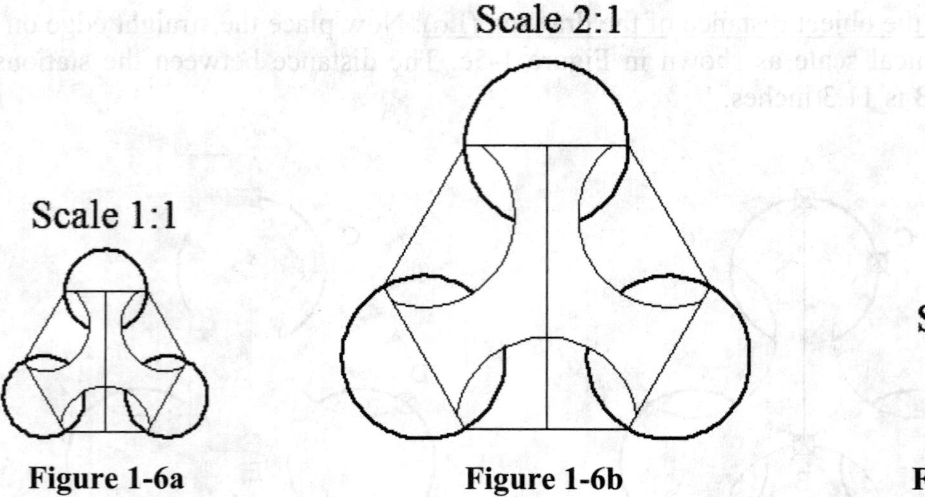

Scale 2:1

Scale 1:1

Scale 1:2

Figure 1-6a   Figure 1-6b   Figure 1-6c

1.7.3. Small scale

The scale of a drawing is small, if the drawing of an object is smaller than the actual size of the object. That is, one unit of the object will be represented by a fraction of a unit on the drawing. Consider a drawing of a building. One unit of drawing may represent 180 units of the building. For the reduced drawing of the building, $a = 1$ and $b = 180$. The representative fraction will be written as 1/180 and the scale will be written as *1:180*. The equivalence relation will be written as *1" = 15'*. Figure 1-6c shows a drawing of a plate drawn at a representative factor of 0.5 (Scale 1:2).

1.8. Computer Aided graphics

Computer Aided Design (commonly abbreviated as CAD) software provides the capability to create graphics, hence, the name computer graphics. The graphics created can be used to analyze, modify, and finalize a graphical solution for the problem being studied. The focus of this book is AutoCAD 2014.

1.8.1. AutoCAD 2014

AutoCAD is a suite of popular CAD software products for 2- and 3-dimensional design and drafting. It is developed and sold by Autodesk.

1.8.2. AutoCAD and drawing scale

A draftsman creating a drawing on a drawing sheet using mechanical equipment needs to decide about the drawing scale before starting the drawing. The selected scale will depends upon the size of the object and the paper, such that the drawing will fit on the drawing sheet. On the other hand, in AutoCAD, every drawing is drawn to full scale (that is 1:1). Generally, a draftsman starts a drawing in AutoCAD without thinking about the scale and chooses the scale when s/he decides to print the drawing. However, it is important to think about the plotting scale early in the drawing process, because, the text size, lineweight, and linetype scale will be effected by changing the drawing scale.

AutoCAD provides both the representative factors and the equivalence relation techniques. The software provides a long list of scale factors, Figure 1-7. Also, the user can make more entries in the list or can delete the existing scale factors. This dialog box is discussed in details in Chapter #7.

The user can create graphical scale using Line, Hatch, and Text commands. These commands are discussed in details in Chapter #3.

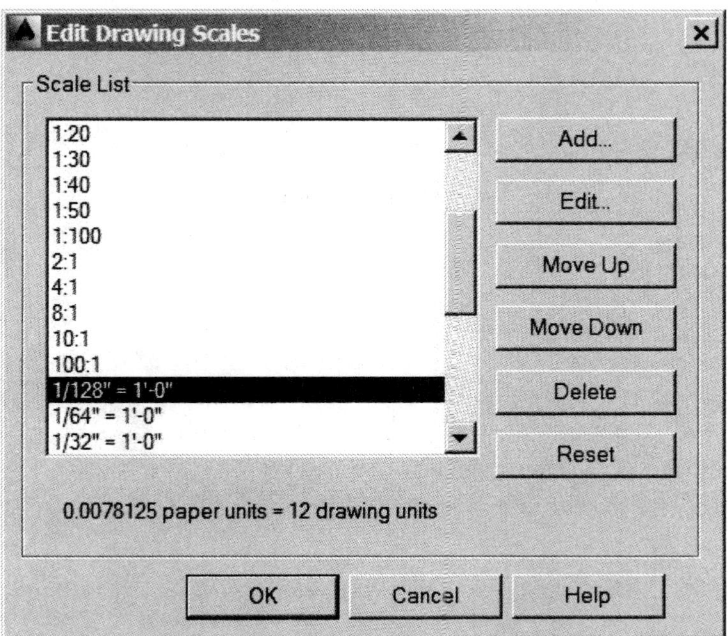

Figure 1-7

Notes:

Figure 1-7

2.   Getting started with AutoCAD 2014

2.1.   Objectives

- Learn the features of the AutoCAD 2014 interface
- Learn to use the drawing area
- Learn to use the ribbon
- Learn to use tabs and panels of ribbon
- Learn to add and/or remove a tab and panel of ribbon
- Learn the features of the command line
- Learn to save and/or delete a workspace
- Learn to open a new file and save a new file
- Learn the basic features of a new file
- Learn the grid and snap commands
- Learn to plot the drawing from model space

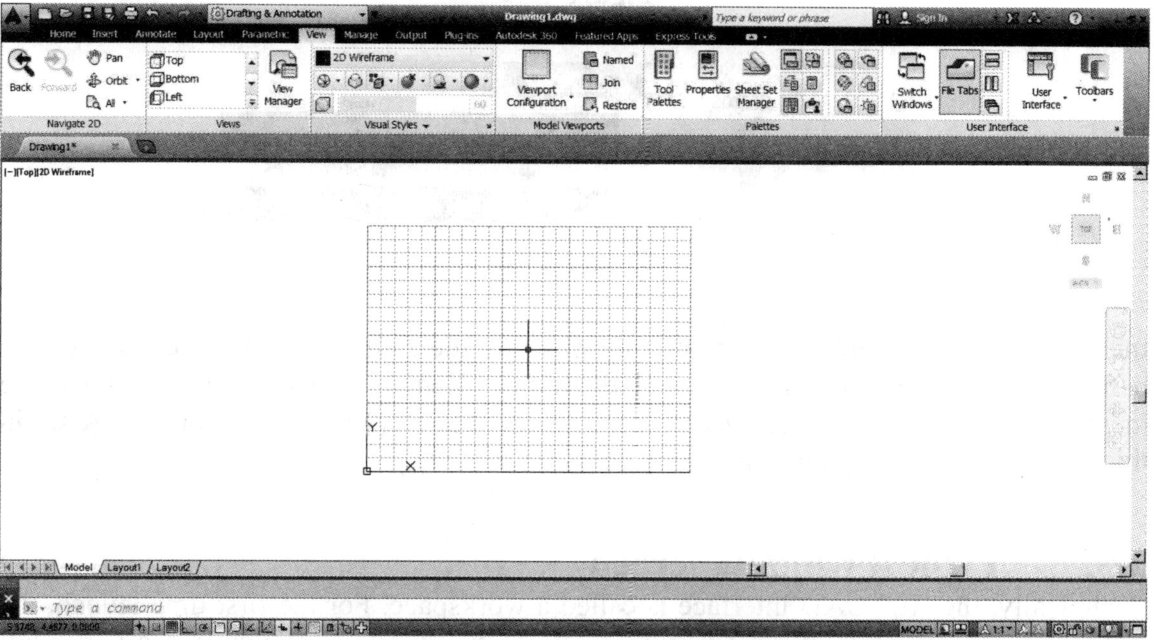

2.2.   Introduction

Initially a general-purpose 2D drafting program, AutoCAD has evolved into a family of products that provides a platform for 2D and 3D computer aided design (CAD). Currently, it is used by civil engineers, land developers, architects, mechanical engineers, interior designers, and medical and other design professionals.

AutoCAD's native/standard file format is DWG; that is, files are saved with the extension '.dwg'. For example, the file *My_First_Drawing* will be saved as *My_First_Drawing.dwg*. AutoCAD allows file interchange to (and/or from) other CAD applications. The commonly used formats are DXF (Drawing Exchange Format), DWF (Design Web Format), and WMF (Window Metafile Format). DXF is an ASCII or binary file for exporting/importing drawings to/from other applications. DWF is a compressed file created from a DWG file for faster publishing and viewing on the Web. WMF files are commonly used to produce clip art.

AutoCAD can be launched by either double clicking on the AutoCAD icon (Figure 2-1a) on the desktop or by clicking *Start* → *All Programs* → *Autodesk* → *AutoCAD 2014*→ *AutoCAD 2014*, Figure 2-1b. If the path of the software is different on your computer, then follow that path. Either of the two launching process will result in opening a new drawing. For the first launch of the software, the AutoCAD interface will be in the *Drafting & Annotation* mode, Figure 2-2a.

Figure 2-1a

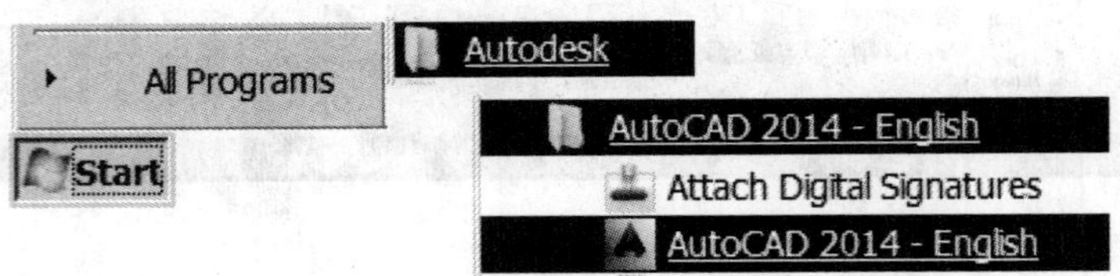

Figure 2-1b

In AutoCAD, commands are executed by pressing the *Enter* key on the keyboard, left button of the mouse, and right button of the mouse. Hence, in this text, unless otherwise mentioned, the terms *click* or *clicking* mean press the left button of the mouse. Also, in this text "a → b" means click "a" followed by clicking at "b".

2.3.   Typical window screen

Technically, the AutoCAD interface is called a workspace. For the first time launch, the AutoCAD workspace is in the *Drafting & Annotation* mode as shown in the upper left corner of the Figure 2-2a and Figure 2-2b.

Figure 2-2a

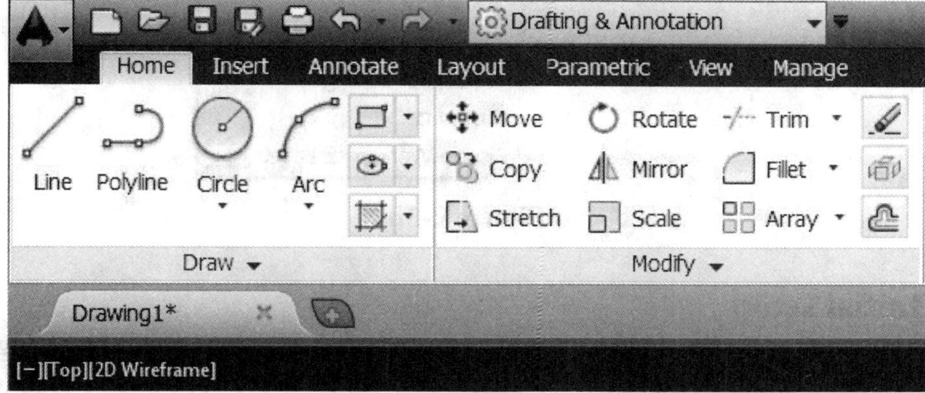

Figure 2-2b

2.3.1.   Focus of the book

The focus of this book is the two dimensional drawing using *Drafting and Annotation* workspace. However, a user can switch to the other environment using one of the following methods.

- (i) Click the small downward arrow to the right of the *Drafting and Annotation* in the upper left corner of the interface, Figure 2-3a. A small window displaying the *Workspace* options will appear on the screen. (ii) Click on the desired option (for example *AutoCAD Classic*) and the interface will be switched to the selected format.
- (i) Click on the small downward arrow on the wheel in the lower right corner of the interface, Figure 2-3b. A small window displaying the *Workspace* options will

appear on the screen. (ii) Click on the desired option and the interface will be switched to the selected format.

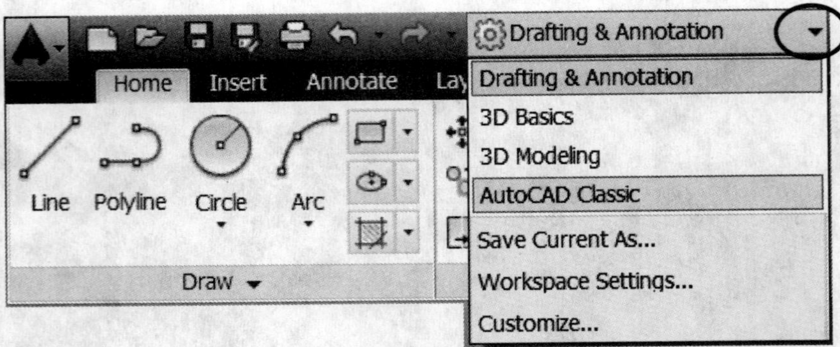

Figure 2-3a

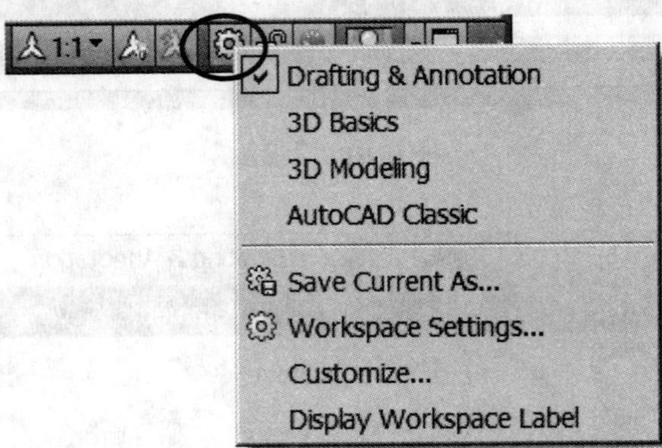

Figure 2-3b

2.3.2. Initial setup

For the demonstration, the background color (of the drawing area) is changed. The drawing area and the color change are discussed in the later sections of this chapter.

- Turn *Off* the grid by clicking the grid box in the lower left corner as shown in Figure 2-4a.
- The interface is updated to a typical 2D *Drafting and Annotation* workspace, Figure 2-4b and Figure 2-4c.

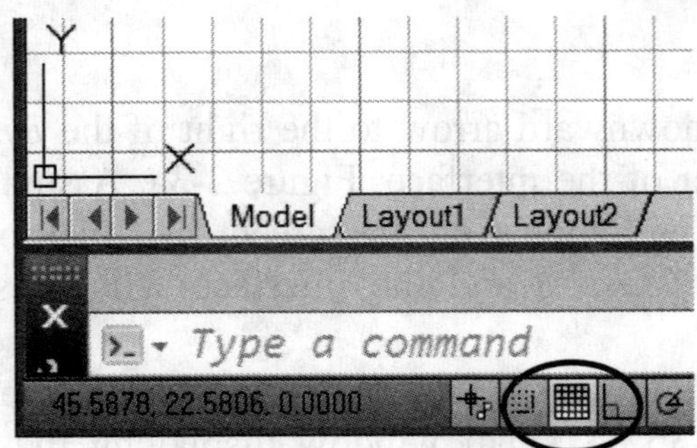

Figure 2-4a

A typical (*Drafting and Annotation*) window screen (Figure 2-4b and Figure 2-4c) is a display of the drawing area, cursor, World coordinate system, viewcube, navigation bar, drawing display format, scroll bars, command line, status bar, ribbon and its tabs and panels, and dockable windows (not shown in the figure), etc. These features are grouped and organized based on the drawing environment and the user requirements.

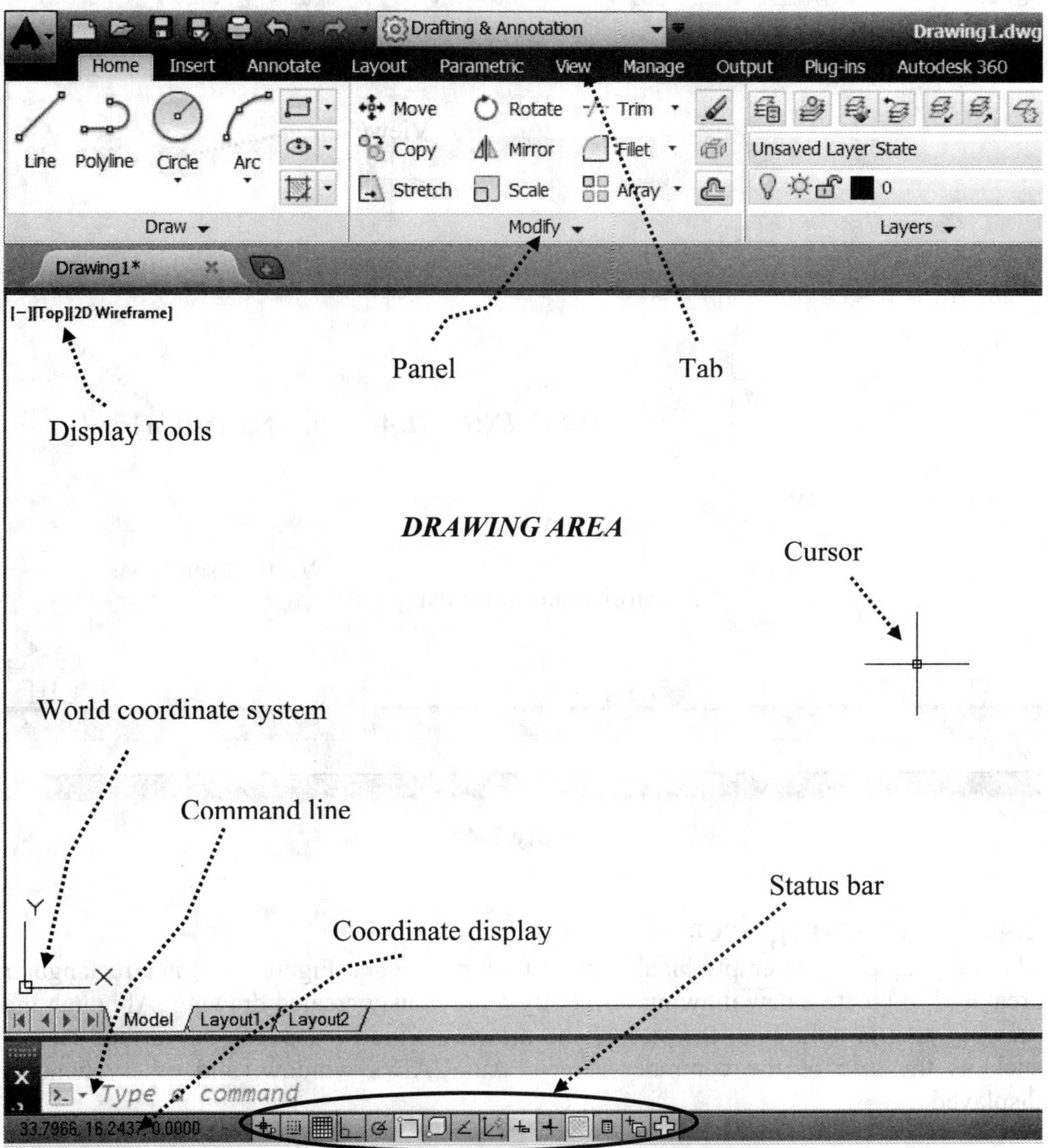

Figure 2-4b

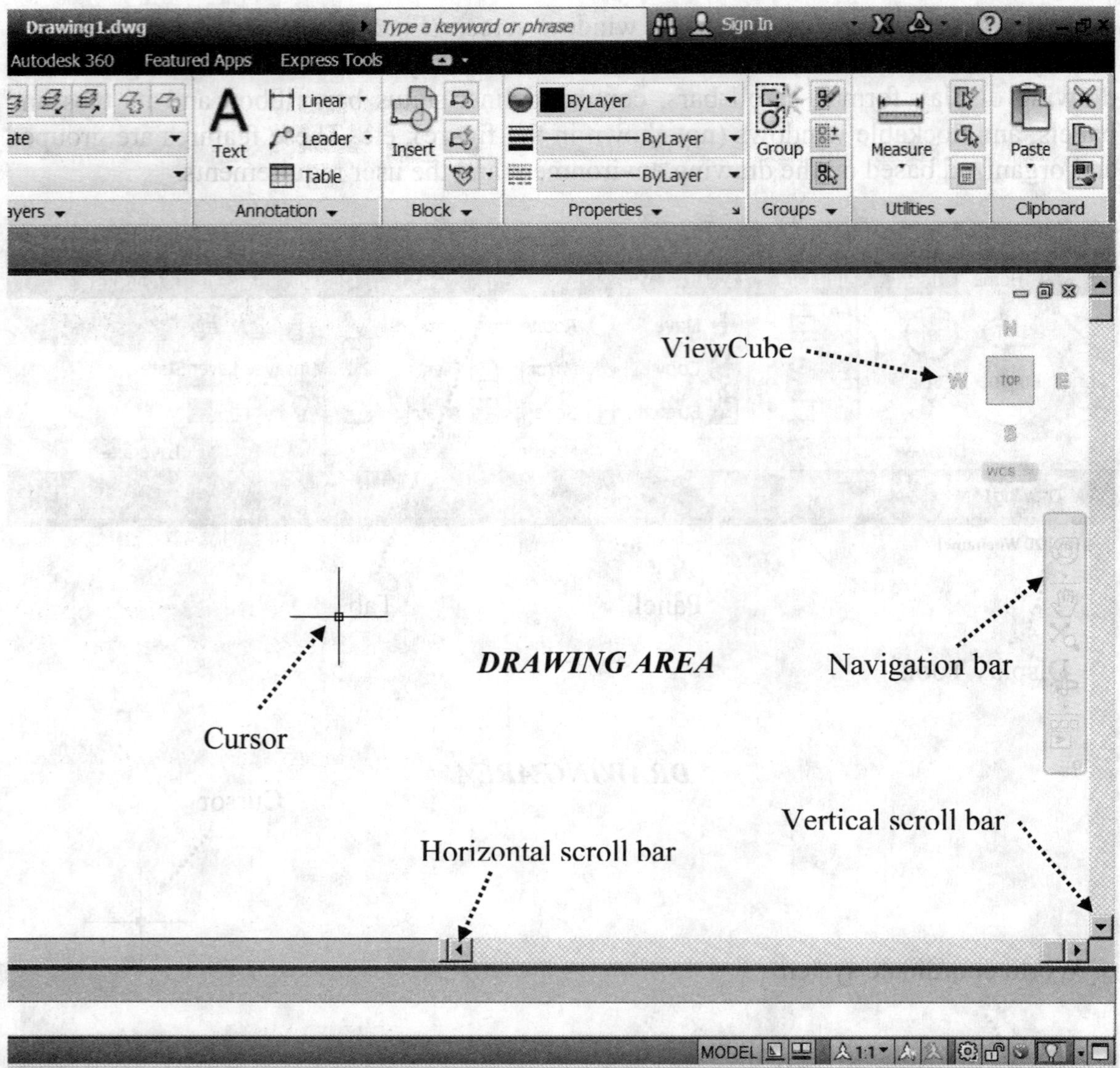

Figure 2-4c

2.4.   Drawing area

The drawing area (the empty blank area in Figure 2-4b and Figure 2-4c) is a rectangular area used to create a new drawing or modify a previously created drawing. Although the drawing area is unlimited, the size of the drawing window depends on various factors such as the size of the computer screen, AutoCAD's window, and other elements displayed.

The drawing area is classified as the model space or layout. The user can switch to the model space or a layout by selecting the *Model* or *Layout* (*Layout1* or *Layout2*) tabs, respectively, from the lower left corner of the drawing area, Figure 2-4b and Figure 2-5.

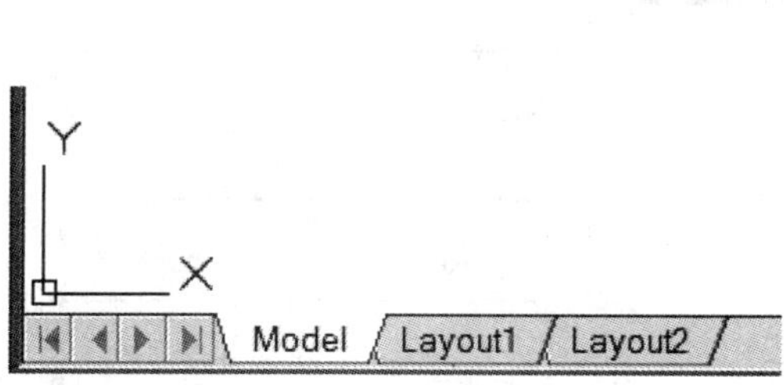

Figure 2-5

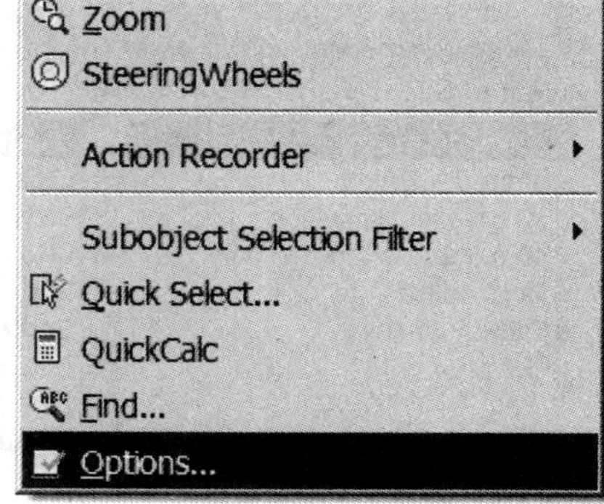

Figure 2-6a

2.4.1.   Model space

A model is a 2D or 3D drawing of an object. Generally, a model is created in the model (workspace) space. The default color of the model space can be changed as follows:

- Click with the right button in the *Drawing area* and select the *Options* option, Figure 2-6a or type *Options* on the command line and press the *Enter* key. The *Options* dialog box (Figure 2-6b) will appear on the screen.
- Select the *Display* tab of the *Options* dialog box by clicking on it.
- Press the *Color* button in the *Window Elements* panel to open the *Drawing Window Colors* (Figure 2-6c) dialog box.

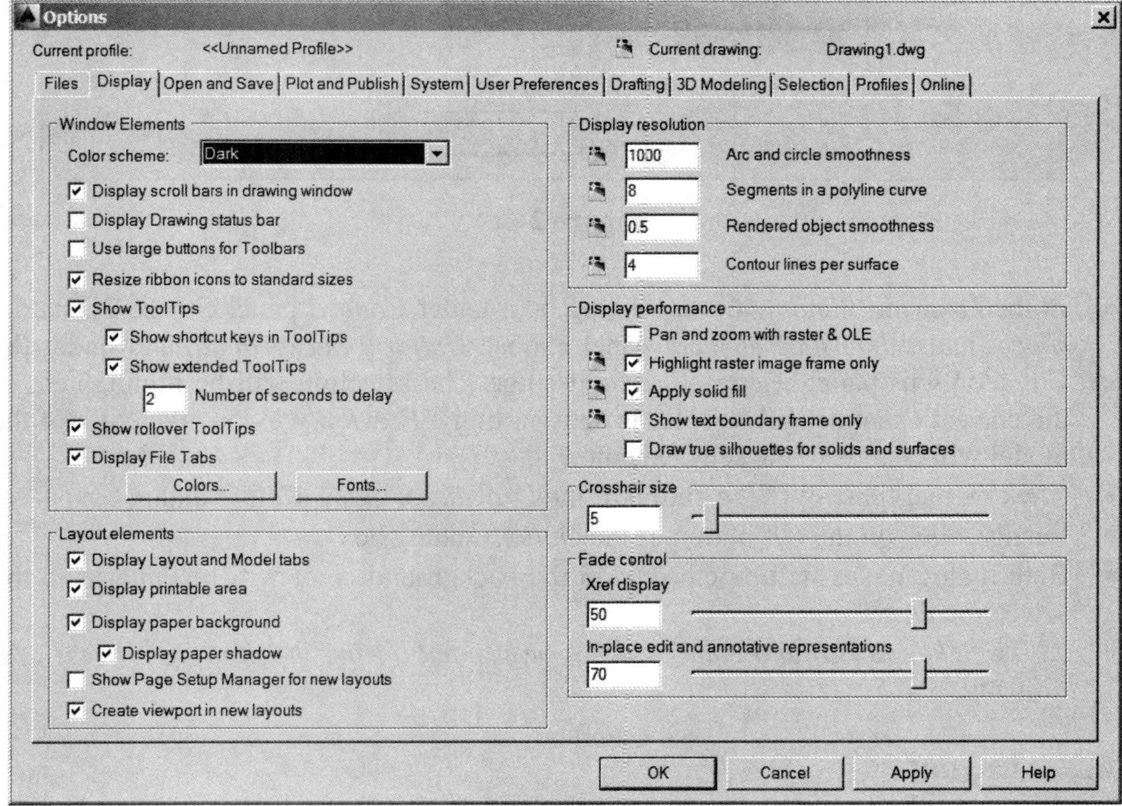

Figure 2-6b

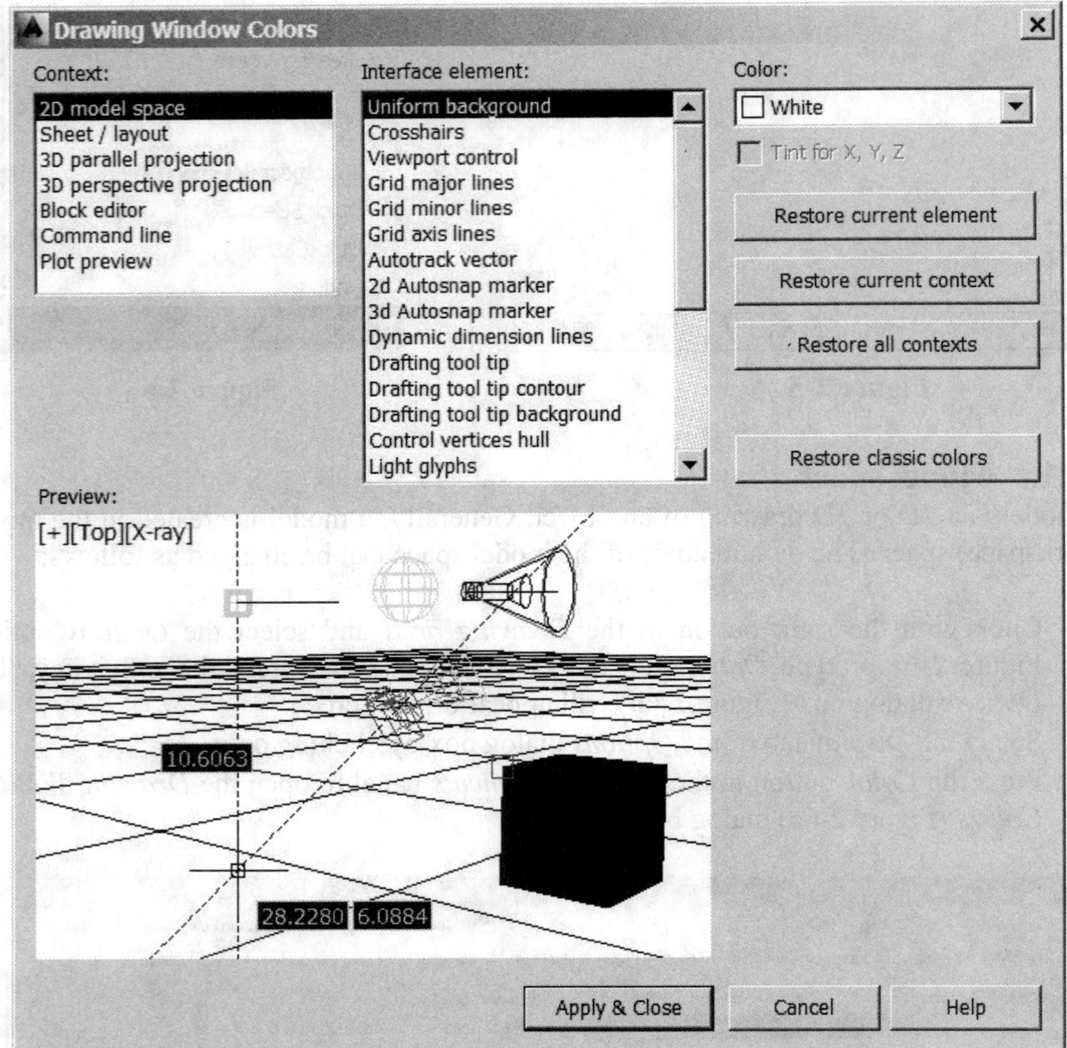

Figure 2-6c

- In the *Drawing Window Colors* dialog box, under *Context* panel choose *2D model space*, under *Interface element* panel choose *Uniform background*, and under the *Color* options panel select the desired color. The selection will be highlighted. In the current example, *White* color is chosen. In the *Preview* window, the color of the model will change to the selected color.
- Click on the *Apply & Close* button of the *Drawing Window Colors* dialog box.
- Finally, click on the *OK* button of the *Options* dialog box.
- Both dialog boxes will be closed and the background color will be updated to the selected color.
- *NOTE: The background color will not be printed during the plotting process of a drawing.*

2.4.2. Layout

Layouts are also known as paper space. When a user clicks on a layout tab, the drawing area will appear as shown in Figure 2-7a. Usually, layouts are not used for drafting or design work. Generally, layouts are used for printing or plotting the drawing. The self-explanatory options for a layout are shown in the *Layout elements* of Figure 2-7b (the lower left quarter of the Figure 2-6a). By default, AutoCAD creates two layouts; however, more layouts can be created for each drawing. Layouts are discussed in details in Chapter #7.

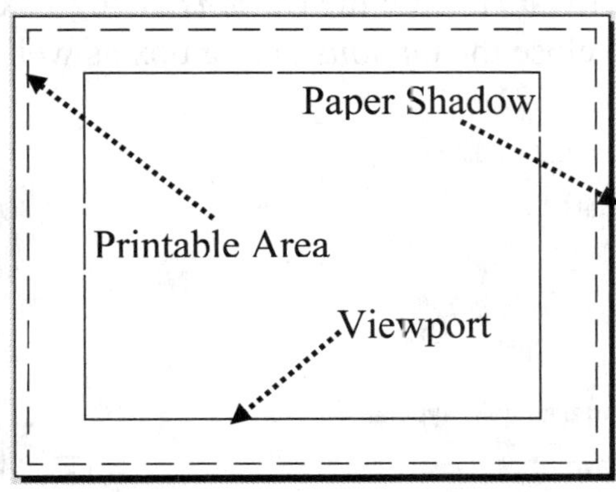

Figure 2-7a

2.4.3.   Hide Model/Layout tabs
A user can hide the *Model* and *Layout* tab using one of the following methods.

Method #1:
- Click with the right button of the mouse in the *Drawing area* and select the *Options* option or type *Options* on the command line and press the *Enter* key.
- The *Options* dialog box will appear on the screen.
- Select the *Display* tab of the *Options* dialog box by clicking on it.
- Clear the *Display Layout and Model tabs* box shown in the *Layout elements* panel, Figure 2-7b.
- Click the *Apply* or *OK* button.
- The *Apply* button will NOT close the *Options* dialog box but will hide the tabs.
- The *OK* button will close the *Options* dialog box and hide the tabs.

Method #2:
- Bring the cursor on the model or layout tab.
- Press the right button of the mouse; the option box shown in Figure 2-7c will appear.
- Highlight the *Hide Layout and Model tabs* by bringing the cursor over it.
- Press the *Enter* key or the left or right button of the mouse.
- This will close the option box and hide the tabs.

2.4.4.   Display Model/Layout tab
A user can display, in a workspace, the model and layout tabs as follow.

- Click with the right button of the mouse in the *Drawing area* and select the *Options* option or type *Options* on the command line and press the *Enter* key.

- The *Options* dialog box will appear on the screen.
- Select the *Display* tab of the *Options* dialog box by clicking on it.
- Check the *Display Layout and Model tabs* box shown in the *Layout elements* panel, Figure 2-7b.
- Click the *Apply* or *OK* button.
- The *Apply* button will NOT close the *Options* dialog box, but will display the tabs.
- The *OK* button will close the *Options* dialog box as well as display the tabs.

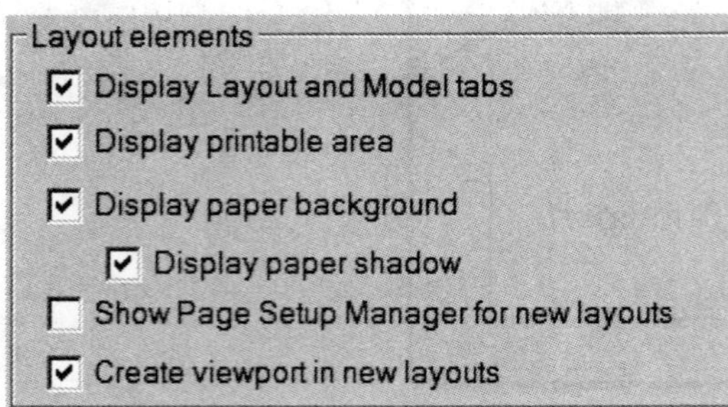

Figure 2-7b

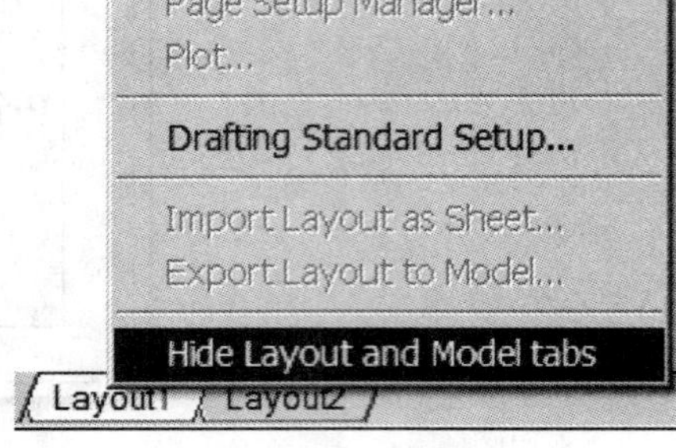

Figure 2-7c

2.5.   Cursor and pointer

In AutoCAD, cursor appears in different format based on the location and status of the cursor. The cursor appears as an arrow head outside the drawing area (if it is on top of a ribbon's panel) and is called a pointer. It appears as crosshairs (two intersecting lines and a small square surrounding the intersection point) in the drawing area if none of the command is active, Figure 2-8a. The small square at the intersection of the crosshairs is called an aperture. If the cursor is waiting for object selection then it appears only as an aperture, Figure 2-8b. However, if a command is active then the cursor appears as a cross-hair without the aperture, Figure 2-8c.

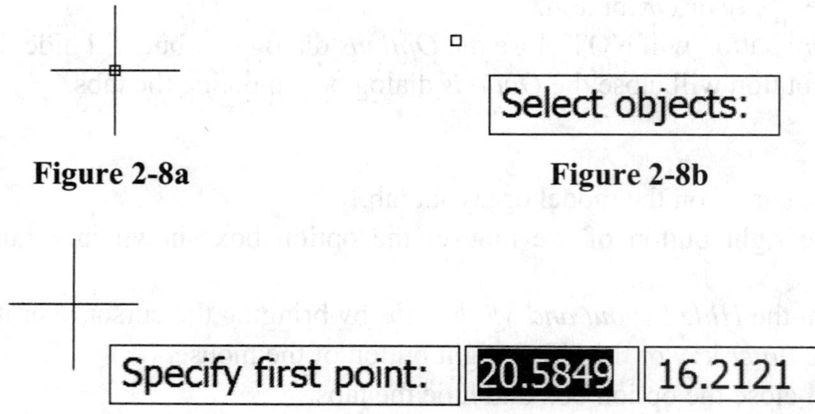

Figure 2-8a   **Figure 2-8b**

Figure 2-8c

2.5.1.   Change the size of the intersecting lines

The size of the intersecting lines of the crosshairs of the cursor can be changed from the *Options* dialog box as follow.

- Click with the right button of the mouse in the *Drawing area* and select the *Options* option or type *Options* on the command line and press the *Enter* key.
- The *Options* dialog box will appear on the screen.
- Select the *Display* tab of the *Options* dialog box by clicking on it.
- To increase the size of the intersecting lines, move the slider of the *Crosshair size* to the right, Figure 2-8d. The slider is in the lower right quarter of the dialog box. Enter the desired value (1 - 100) in the small box.
- Press the *Apply* or *OK* button or press the *Enter* key. The *Apply* button will make the change permanent and the dialog box will remain open. The *OK* button or the *Enter* key will make the change permanent and will close the dialog box, too.
- The accuracy of the drawing is not influenced by the size of the crosshair, however, it is not a good practice to keep the crosshair's size larger than 10.

Figure 2-8d

2.5.2. Change the size of the aperture

A user can change the size of the aperture of the crosshairs of the cursor as follow.

- Click with the right button of the mouse in the *Drawing area* and select the *Options* option or type *Options* on the command line and press the *Enter* key.
- The *Options* dialog box will appear on the screen.
- Select the *Drafting* tab of the *Options* dialog box by clicking on it.
- To increase the size of the aperture, move the slider of the *Aperture Size* to the right, Figure 2-8e. The slider is in the right side of the dialog box.
- The accuracy of the drawing is not influenced by the aperture size, but, it is not good practice to keep the aperture's size too large or too small.
- Press the *Apply* or *OK* button or press the *Enter* key. The *Apply* button will make the change permanent and the dialog box will remain open. The *OK* button and the *Enter* key will make the change permanent and will close the dialog box, too.

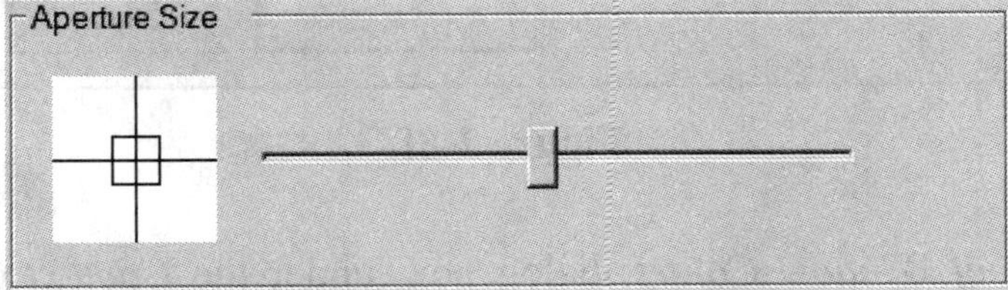

Figure 2-8e

2.5.3. Change the color of the cursor

A user can change the color of the crosshairs of the cursor as follow.

- Click with the right button of the mouse in the *Drawing area* and select the *Options* option or type *Options* on the command line and press the *Enter* key.
- The *Options* dialog box will appear on the screen.
- Select the *Display* tab of the *Options* dialog box by clicking on it.
- Press the *Color* button in the *Window Elements* panel (Figure 2-8f) to open the *Drawing Window Colors* dialog box.

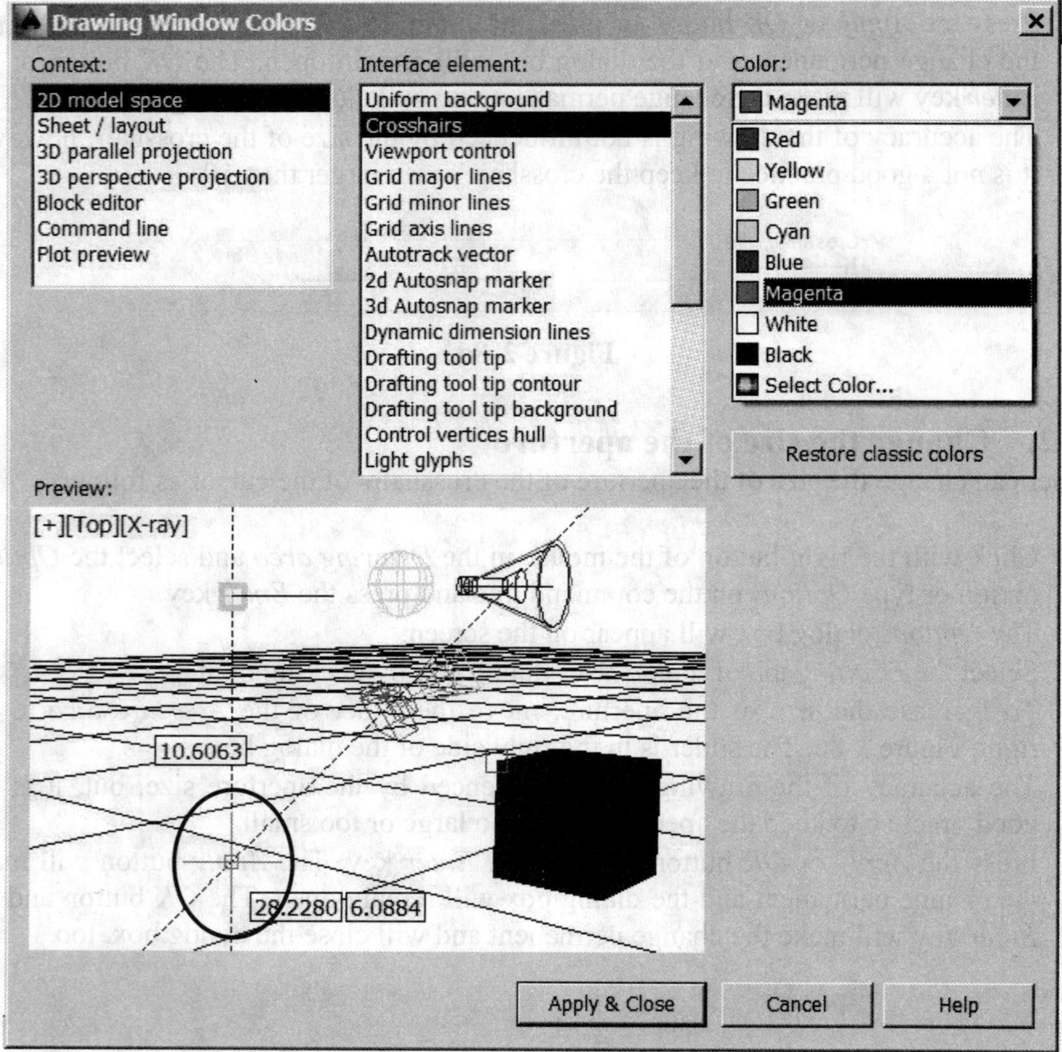

Figure 2-8f

- In the *Drawing Window Colors* dialog box, under the *Context* choose *2D model space*, under the *Interface element* choose *Crosshairs*, and under the *Color* option choose the desired color. The selection will be highlighted. In the current example, the *Magenta* color is selected. In the *Preview* window, the color of the cursor will change to the selected color.
- Finally, click on the *Apply & Close* button to close the dialog box.
- In the 2D model space, the color of the cursor will change to the selected color.

- Similarly, the color of the cursor could be changed in the 3D model space and layouts.

2.6.   World Coordinate System (WCS)

In AutoCAD, there are two types of coordinate systems. The first is a fixed, Cartesian system called as the *World Coordinate System* (WCS). The WCS is used as the basis for defining the drawing object. The second is a movable Cartesian coordinate system and is called as the *User Coordinate System* (UCS). A UCS is defined relative to the WCS. In both the WCS and UCS, the Z-axis is always perpendicular to the XY-plane. In the default setting for 2D drawings, the WCS's X-axis is horizontal, the Y-axis is vertical, and the origin is located at the intersection of the X- and Y-axes (Figures 2-9a and 2-9b). **Note the box at the origin; this box indicates that the coordinate system is WCS.**

The coordinates (x, y, z) of the cursor location are displayed in the lower left corner of the interface as shown in Figure 2-9b.

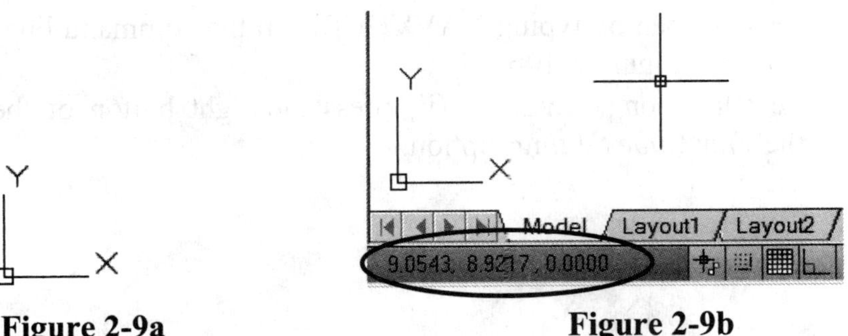

Figure 2-9a   **Figure 2-9b**

2.7.   ViewCube

The *ViewCube* is a navigational tool. It is displayed in 2D or 3D visual style, both in model space and layouts. By default, the tool is on, inactive, and semi-transparent. The *ViewCube* tool contains coordinate system (WCS) and compass (NSWE), Figure 2-10a. By default, it is located in the upper right corner of the drawing area. In 2D model space, the default view is the top view as shown in Figure 2-10a.

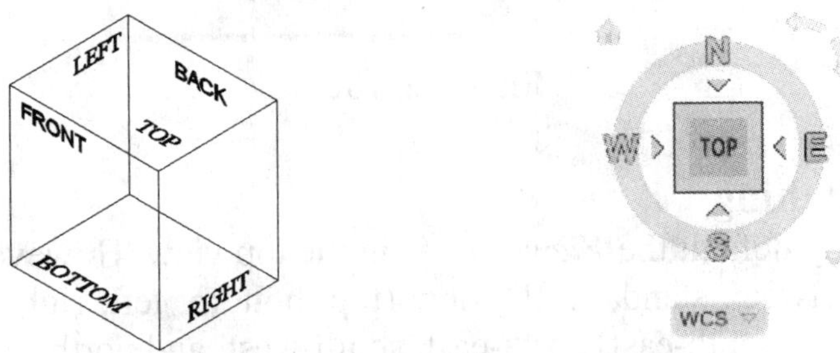

Figure 2-10a

The *ViewCube* can be turn *On/Off* by typing NAVVCUBE on the command line and choosing the desired option, Figure 2-10b.

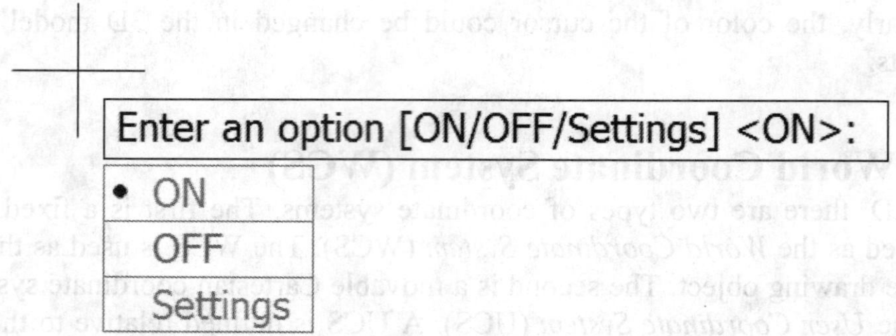

Figure 2-10b

2.7.1. ViewCube settings

The various features of the ViewCube can be changed from the *ViewCube Settings* dialog box. The self-explanatory dialog box is shown in Figure 2-10d. The dialog box can be open sing one of the two methods.

- The dialog box is open by typing NAVVCUBE on the command line and selecting the *Settings* option, Figure 2-10b.
- (i) Bring the cursor on *ViewCube*, (ii) press the right button of the mouse, and (iii) select the *ViewCube Settings* option.

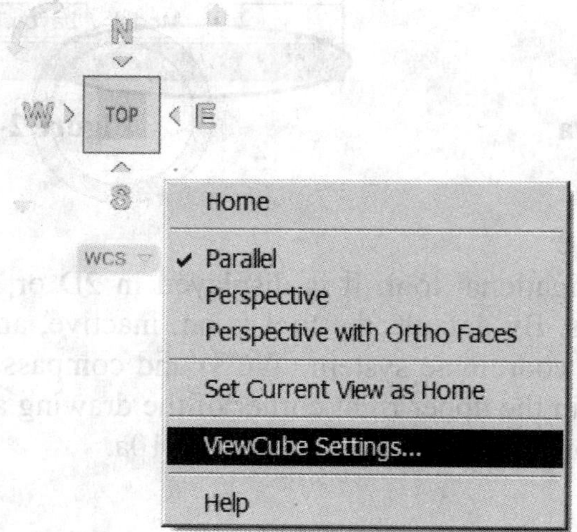

Figure 2-10c

2.7.2. View switching

In 2D model space, by default the *ViewCube* is in the top view. However, this tool allows the user to switch between standard 2D view (top, bottom, left, right, front, and back), and 3D isometric view (south-east, north-east, south-west, and north- west). The user can also switch between any combinations of the six 2D standard views.

The *ViewCube* can be activated by placing the cursor on any part of the tool. The coordinate system can be changed by pressing the down arrow to the right of WCS and selecting the desired option. The other features are discussed in the remaining of this section.

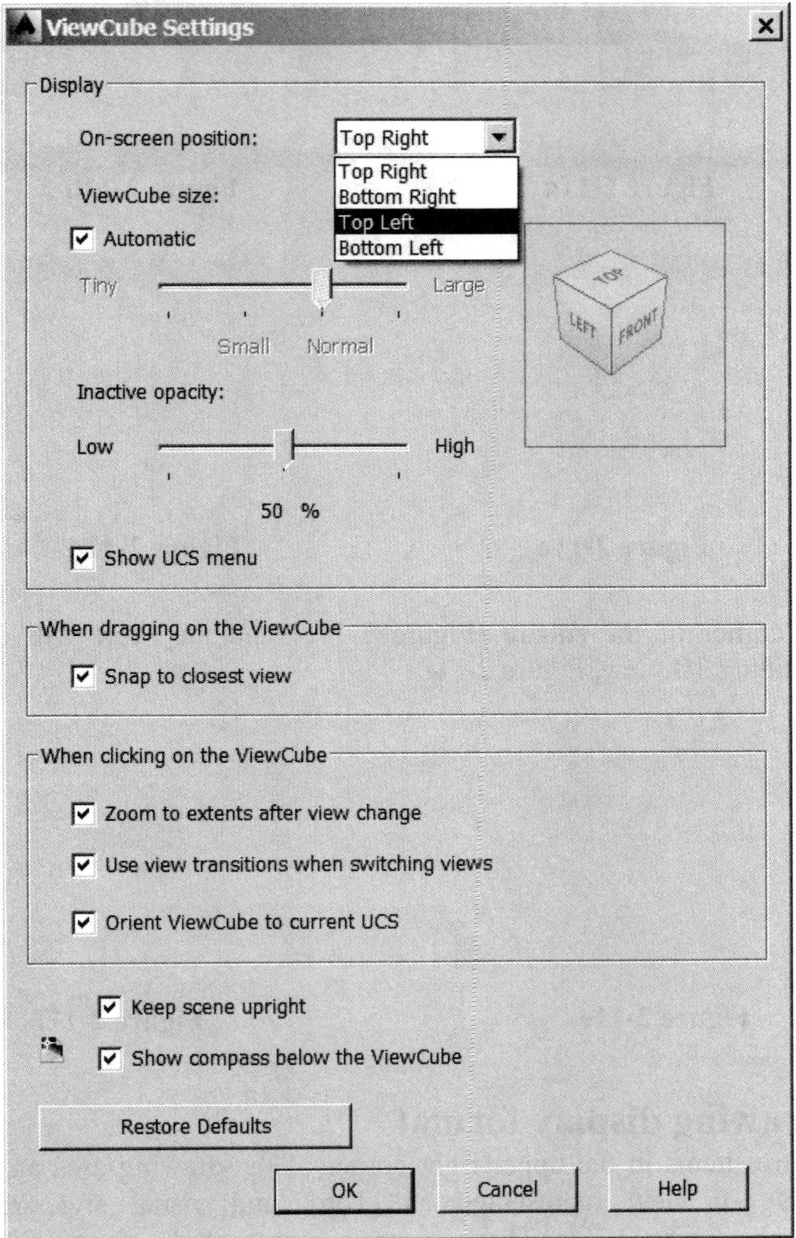

Figure 2-10d

The user can switch from one view to the other as follow.

- Click on a quadrant of the compass (W is selected in Figure 2-11a) or a face of the square and the view will change to the corresponding standard view, Figure 2-11b.
- Click an edge of the square (Figure 2-11c) and the view will change to the corresponding standard view, Figure 2-11d.

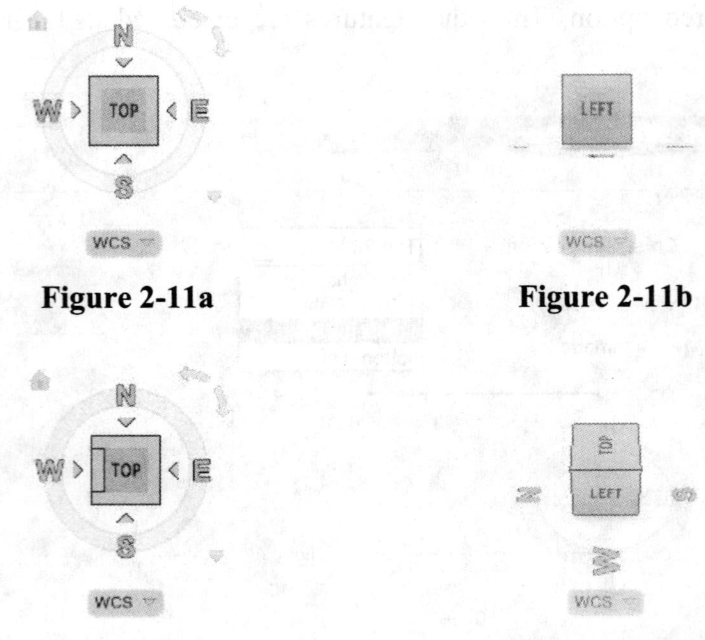

Figure 2-11a   Figure 2-11b

Figure 2-11c   Figure 2-11d

- Click a corner of the square (Figure 2-11e) and the view will change to the corresponding 3D view, Figure 2-11f.

Figure 2-11e   Figure 2-11f

2.8.   Drawing display format

The three control items in the upper right corner of the drawing area are the viewport represented as [-], view represented as [Top], and visual style represented as [2D Wireframe], Figure 2-12a. These controls represent the format of the drawing appearance and discussed briefly.

- Viewport control: The *Viewport control* allows the user to manipulate the viewports in model space and layouts, Figure 2-12b. Viewports are discussed in details in Chapter #7.
- View control: The *View control* allows the user to switch between standard 2D view (top, bottom, left, right, front, and back), and 3D isometric view (south-east, north-east, south-west, and north- west), Figure 2-12c. Generally, the 2D drawings are looked from top and other styles are used to display the 3D drawings.

- Visual style control: The *Visual style control* allows the user to switch between various visual styles, Figure 2-12d. Generally, the 2D drawing are in 2D Wireframe style and the other styles are used to display the 3D drawings.

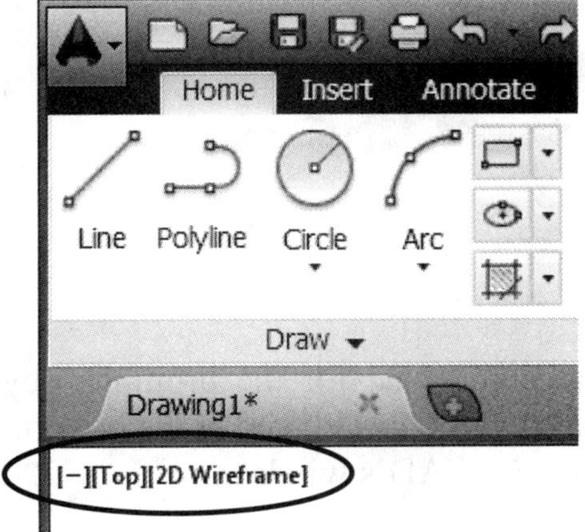

Figure 2-12a

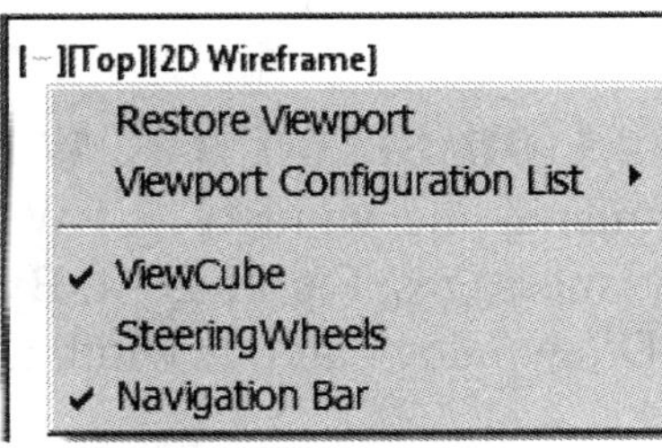

Figure 2-12b

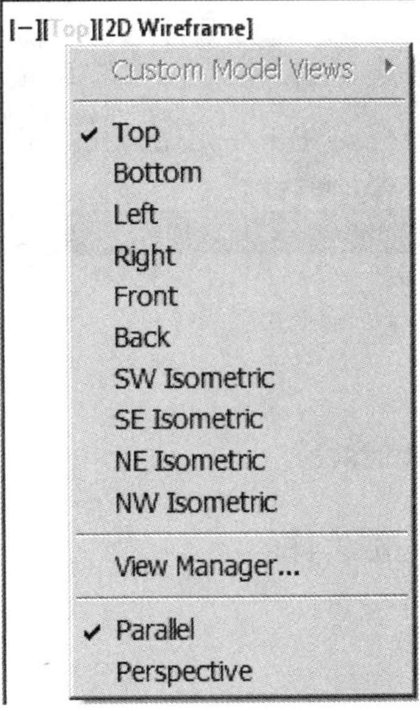

Figure 2-12c

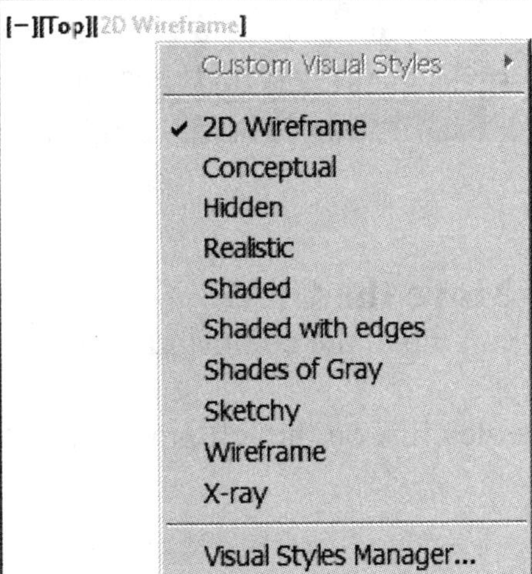

Figure 2-12d

2.9.   Scroll bars

The scroll bars can be added or removed from the workspace as follows.

- Open the *Options* dialog box. The *Options* dialog box (Figure 2-6a) can be opened by clicking with the right button of the mouse in the *Drawing area* and selecting the *Options* option.
- Select the *Display* tab of the *Options* dialog box by clicking on it.
- Check (or clear) the first box (*Display scroll bars in drawing window*) in the *Window Elements* panel to display (or hide) the scroll bars, respectively.

Figure 2-13

2.10.   Command line window

The command line window (CLW) is a text area reserved for the prompts, keyboard input, and messages, Figure 2-14. By default, the CLW is *On*, located at the bottom of the AutoCAD's window, and its width is same as the AutoCAD's window.

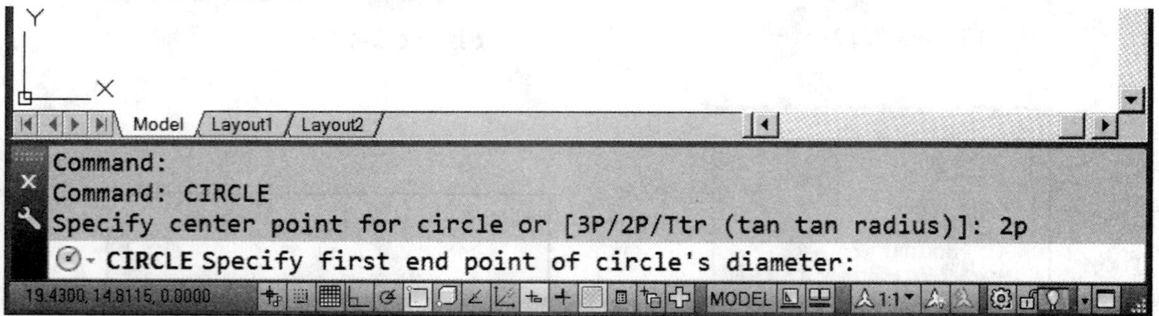

Figure 2-14

2.10.1. Move the CLW

The user can move the command line window on the interface.

- Double click on the left gray end of the CLW, Figure 2-15a.

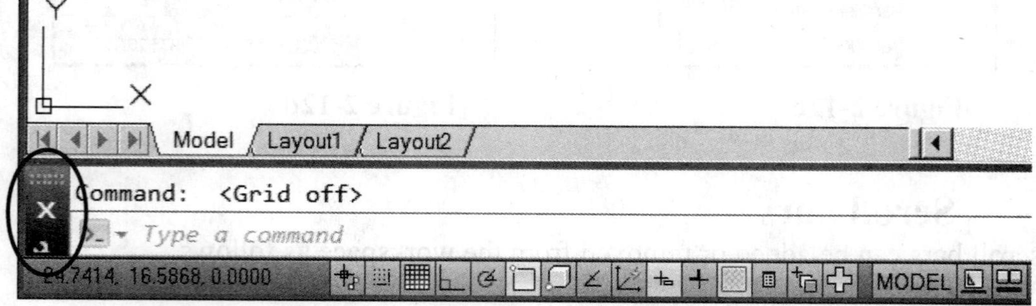

Figure 2-15a

- Select the CLW by placing the cursor on the left gray end of the CLW.
- Press and hold down the left button of the mouse.
- Keep pressing the left button, move the cursor.

- The CLW will appear as light gray box as shown in Figure 2-15b.

Figure 2-15b

- Keep holding down the left button and move the cursor above the ribbon (collection of the icon).
- Release the left button of the mouse and the gray box will be replaced by the CLW, Figure 2-15c.

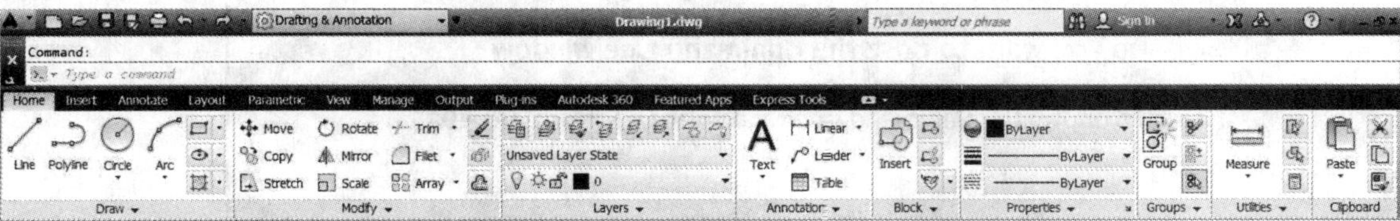

Figure 2-15c

2.10.2. Display/hide the CLW

The user can display the command line window on the interface or hide from the interface.

- Display CLW: To display the CLW, either hold the *Ctrl* key on the keyboard and press 9; or click the *View* tab and on the Palette panel click on *Command line* ( ) icon, Figure 2-16a. If the CLW is *On* then the *Command line* tool is highlighted.

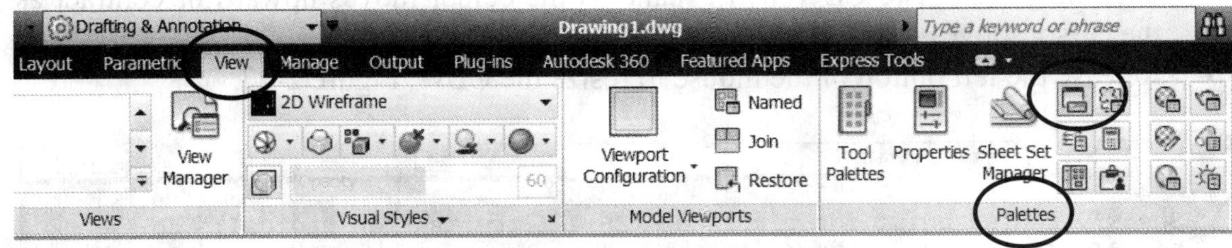

Figure 2-16a

- Hide CLW:
  a) To hide the CLW, either click on the small cross (Figure 2-16b); or click the *View* tab, on the Palette panel, and click on *Command line* ( ) icon, Figure 2-15. If the CLW is *Off* then the *Command line* tool is not highlighted.
  b) The dialog box shown in Figure 2-16c will appear. (ii) Click the *Yes* button. This will close the dialog box and hide the CLW.

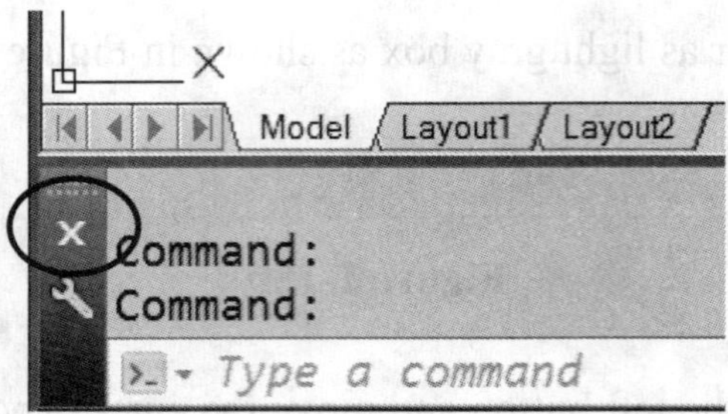

Figure 2-16b

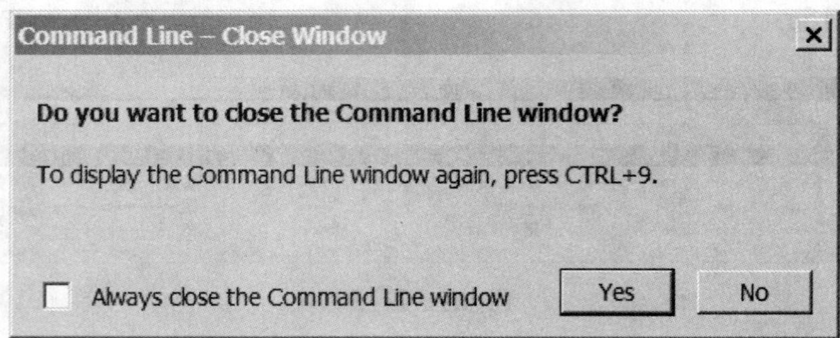

Figure 2-16c

2.10.3. Resize the CLW

In the CLW, at least two commands should be visible. The CLW can be resized as follow.

- Bring the cursor on the top edge of the CLW and a double arrow ($\updownarrow$) will appear.
- Hold the left button of the mouse, and move the cursor to the new location on the drawing screen. The CLW will expand as the cursor moves upward or contract as the cursor moves downward.
- Release the left button of the mouse to resize the CLW, Figure 2-17.

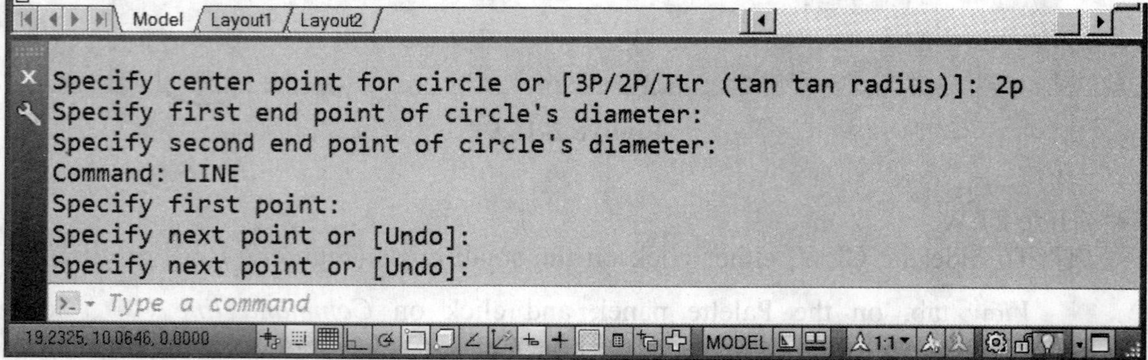

Figure 2-17

2.10.4. Change the color of the CLW

A user can change the background and the text color of the command line window as follow.

- Click with the right button of the mouse in the *Drawing area* and select the *Options* option or type *Options* on the command line and press the *Enter* key.
- The *Options* dialog box will appear on the screen, Figure 2-18a.
- Select the *Display* tab of the *Options* dialog box by clicking it.
- Press the *Color* button in the *Window Elements* panel to open the *Drawing Window Colors* dialog box.

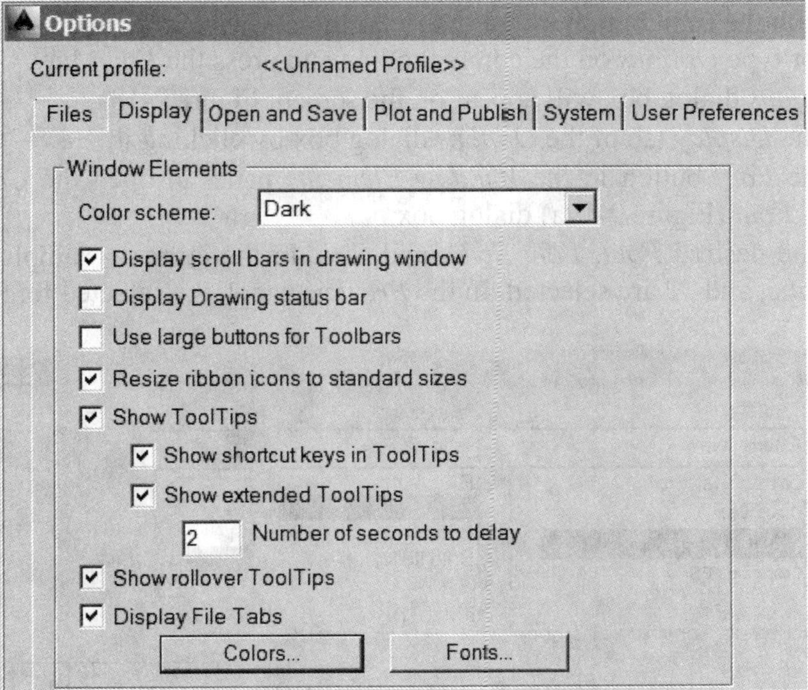

Figure 2-18a

- In the *Drawing Window Colors* dialog box, Figure 2-18b, under the *Context* choose the *Command line*, under the *Interface elements* choose the *Command history background* to change the color of the background, and under the *Color* option choose the desired color. The selection will be highlighted. In the current example, the *Yellow* color is selected. In the *Preview* window, the color of the CLW will change to the selected color.

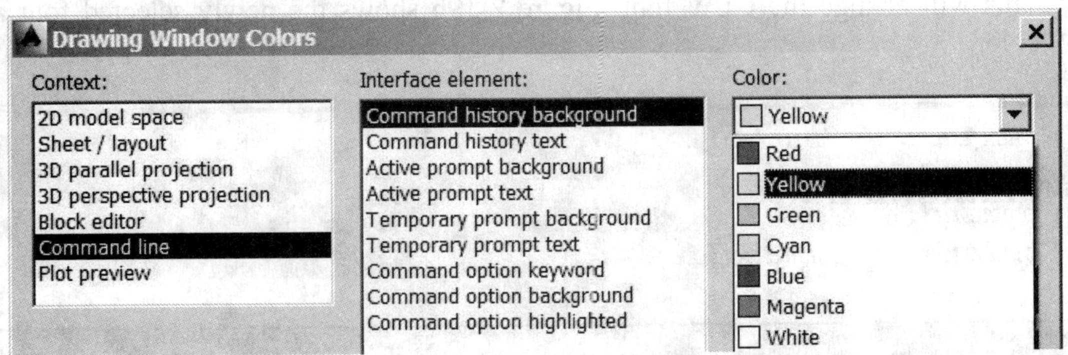

Figure 2-18b

- Finally, click on the *Apply & Close* button to close the dialog box.
- The color of the CLW will change to the selected color.
- Similarly, change the color of the text of the CLW.

2.10.5. Change the font of the CLW
A user can change the font, font style, and font size of the command line text as follow.

- Click with the right button of the mouse in the *Drawing area* and select the *Options* option or type *Options* on the command line and press the *Enter* key.
- The *Options* dialog box will appear on the screen, Figure 2-18a.
- Select the *Display* tab of the *Options* dialog box by clicking it.
- Press the *Font* button in the *Window Elements* panel to open the *Command Line Window Font* (Figure 2-19a) dialog box.
- Select the desired *Font*, *Font Style*, and *Size*. In the current example, the *Courier New*, *Italic*, and *12* are selected. In the *Preview* panel, the selected font will appear.

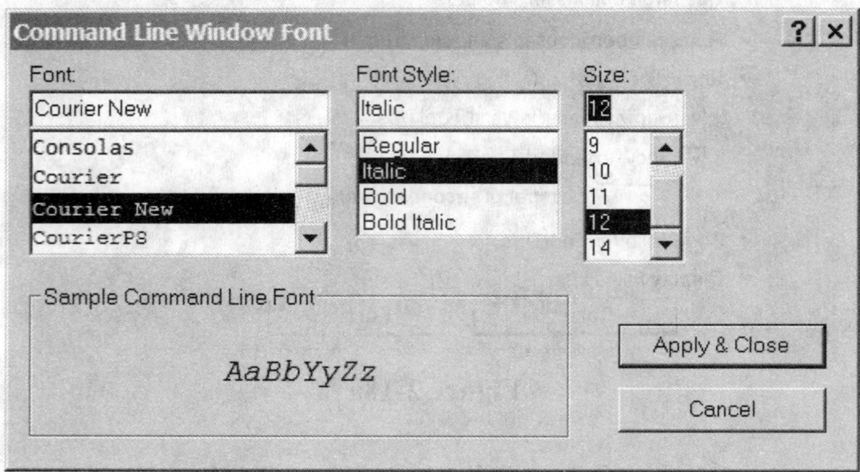

Figure 2-19a

- Click on the *Apply & Close* button. This will update the font of the CLW and will close the *Command Line Window Font* dialog box.
- Finally, click on the *OK* button on the *Options* dialog box to close it.
- This will change the CLW font. Figure 2-19b shows the newly selected font and color.

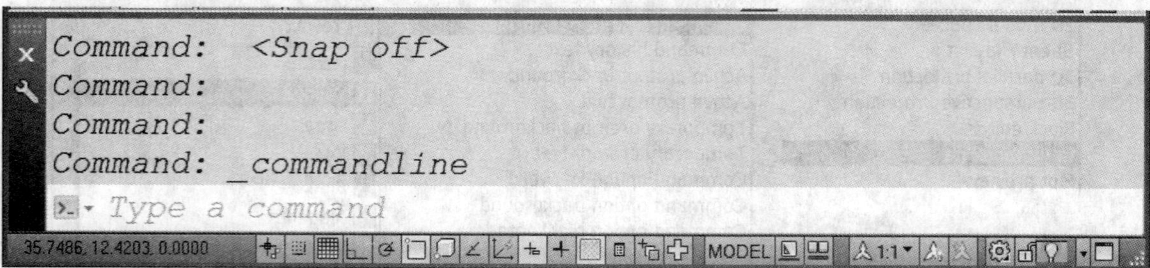

Figure 2-19b

2.11. Status bar

The set of commands below the command line are collectively known as a status bar, Figure 2-20. The commands on the status bar are available during the execution of the other commands. The first group on the left side of the status bar includes the most widely used commands. These commands are discussed in details in their respective sections.

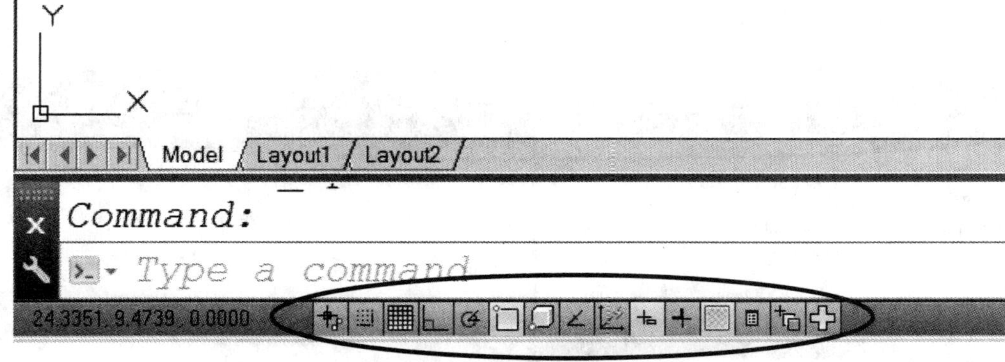

Figure 2-20

2.12. Ribbon

The ribbon is an important part of the AutoCAD's interface. By default, the ribbon is docked above the drawing area, Figure 2-21. The ribbon is a collection of tabs; a tab is collection of panels; and a panel is collection of tools. A tool is a pictured icon that represents an AutoCAD command or it is a graphical representation of a command.

In this text "Tab → Panel → Tool" means first select the "Tab" then on the "Panel" click the "Tool" icon. Figure 2-21 shows selection of the *Home* tab, *Modify* panel, and the *Fillet* command.

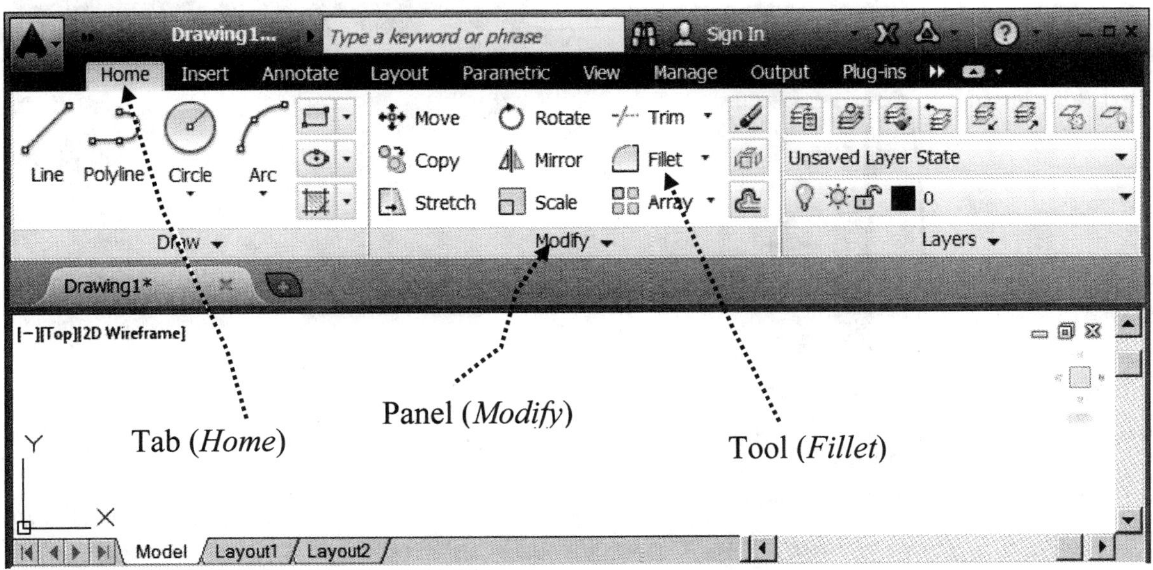

Figure 2-21

2.12.1. Move the ribbon

By default, the ribbon is docked above the drawing area, Figure 2-21. However, the user can move the ribbon to the left or right side of the interface.

- Undock the ribbon: (i) Bring the cursor in the tabs area and click with the right button of the mouse, Figure 2-22a. (ii) The selection list shown in Figure 2-22a will appear. Select the *Undock* option. (iii) This will close the option list and undock the ribbon, Figure 2-22b.

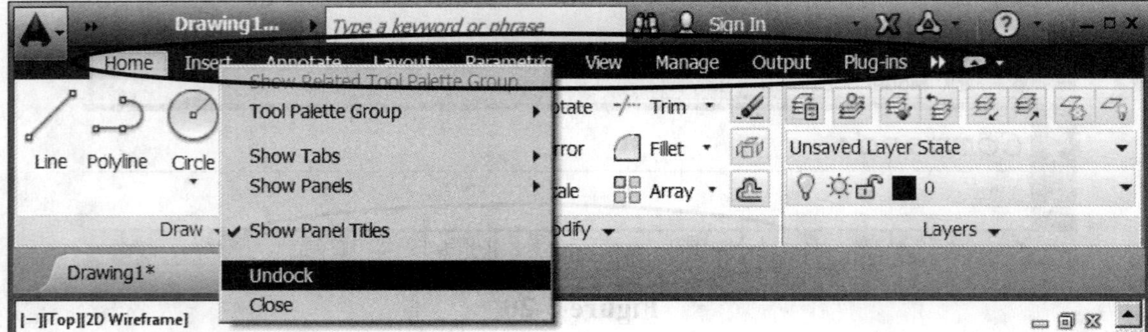

Figure 2-22a

- Select the ribbon by placing the cursor on the left gray end of the ribbon, Figure 2-22b.
- Press and hold down the left button of the mouse.
- Keep pressing the left button, move the cursor to the left or right side of the interface. In the current example, the ribbon will be moved to the left.
- Move the cursor to the left of the AutoCAD window, the ribbon will appear as light gray box.

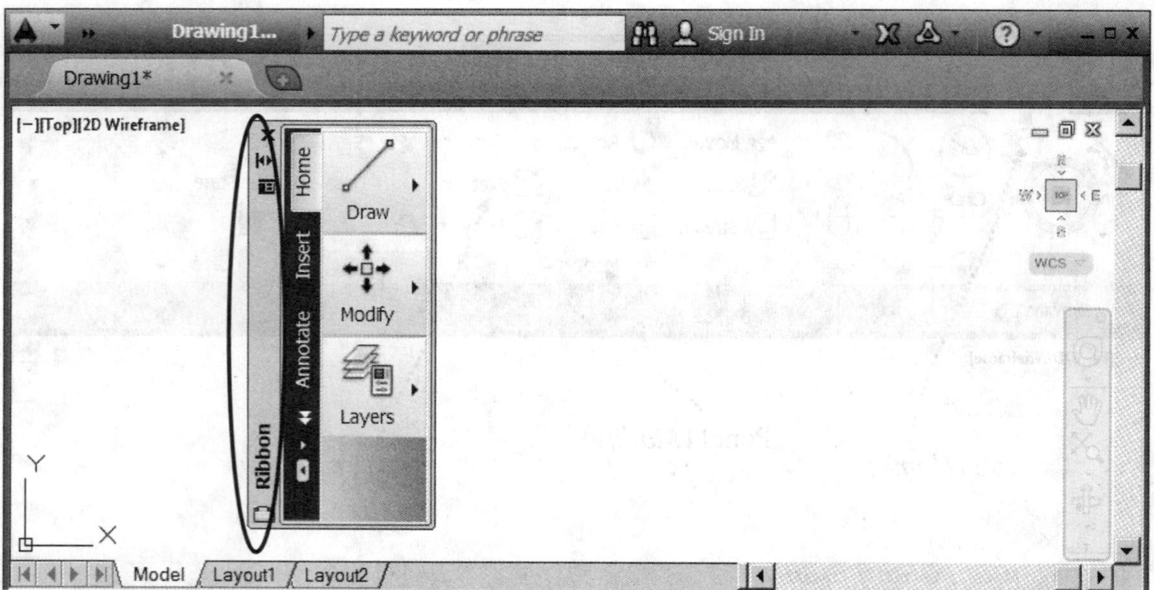

Figure 2-22b

- Release the left button of the mouse and the gray box will be replaced by the ribbon, Figure 2-22c. The ribbon is docked on the left side of the interface.

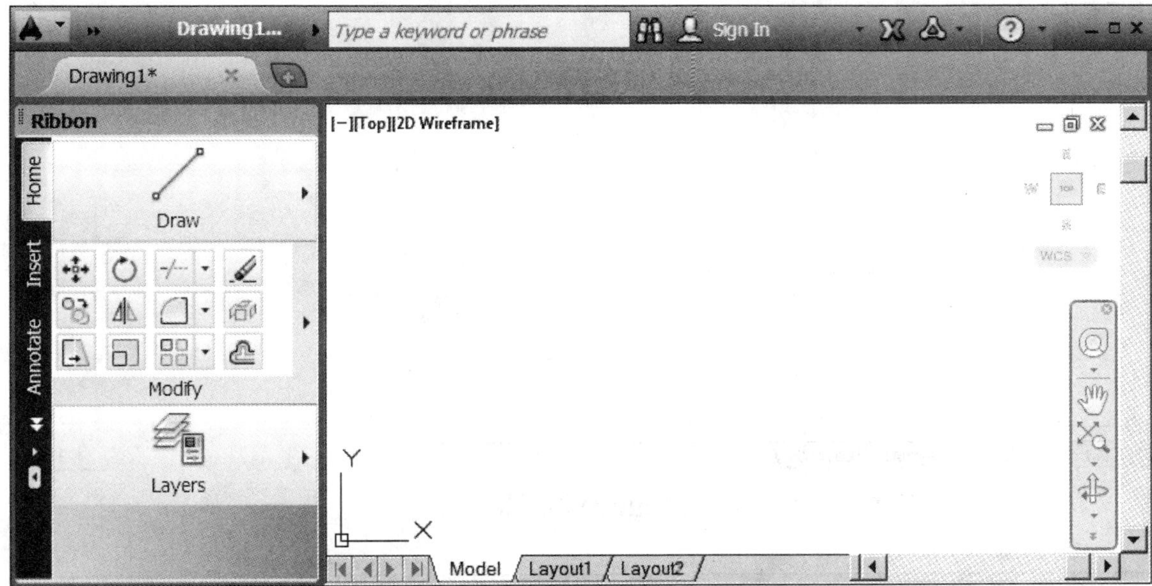

Figure 2-22c

2.12.2. Hide/Display the ribbon

By default the ribbon is *On*. However, the user can hide (turn *off*) the ribbon from the interface or display (turn *on*) on the interface.

- Hide ribbon: (i) Bring the cursor in the tabs area and click with the right button of the mouse, Figure 2-23a. (ii) The selection list shown in Figure 2-23a will appear. Select the *Close* option. (iii) This will close the option list and hide the ribbon from the interface, Figure 2-23b.

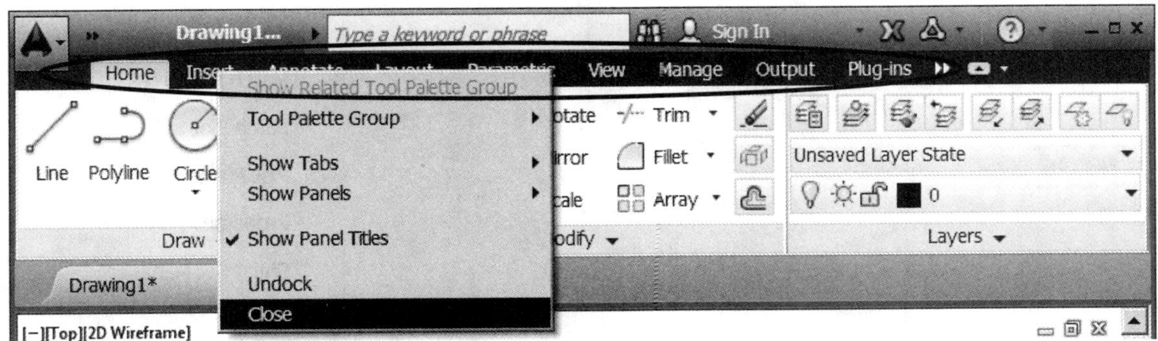

Figure 2-23a

- Display ribbon: The ribbon display is three steps process.
  a) <u>Display the menu bar:</u> Click on the small triangular arrow on the right side of the *Drafting and Annotation*, Figure 2-24a. (ii) The selection list shown in Figure 2-24a will appear. (ii) Select the *Show Menu Bar* option. (iii) This will close the option list and display the menu bar, Figure 2-24b.

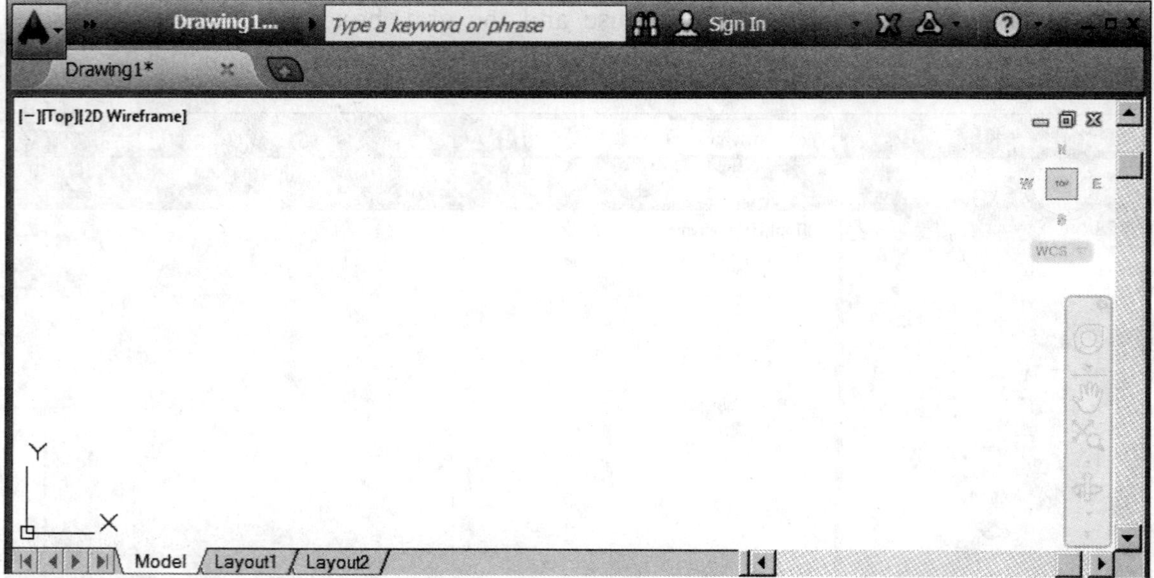

Figure 2-23b

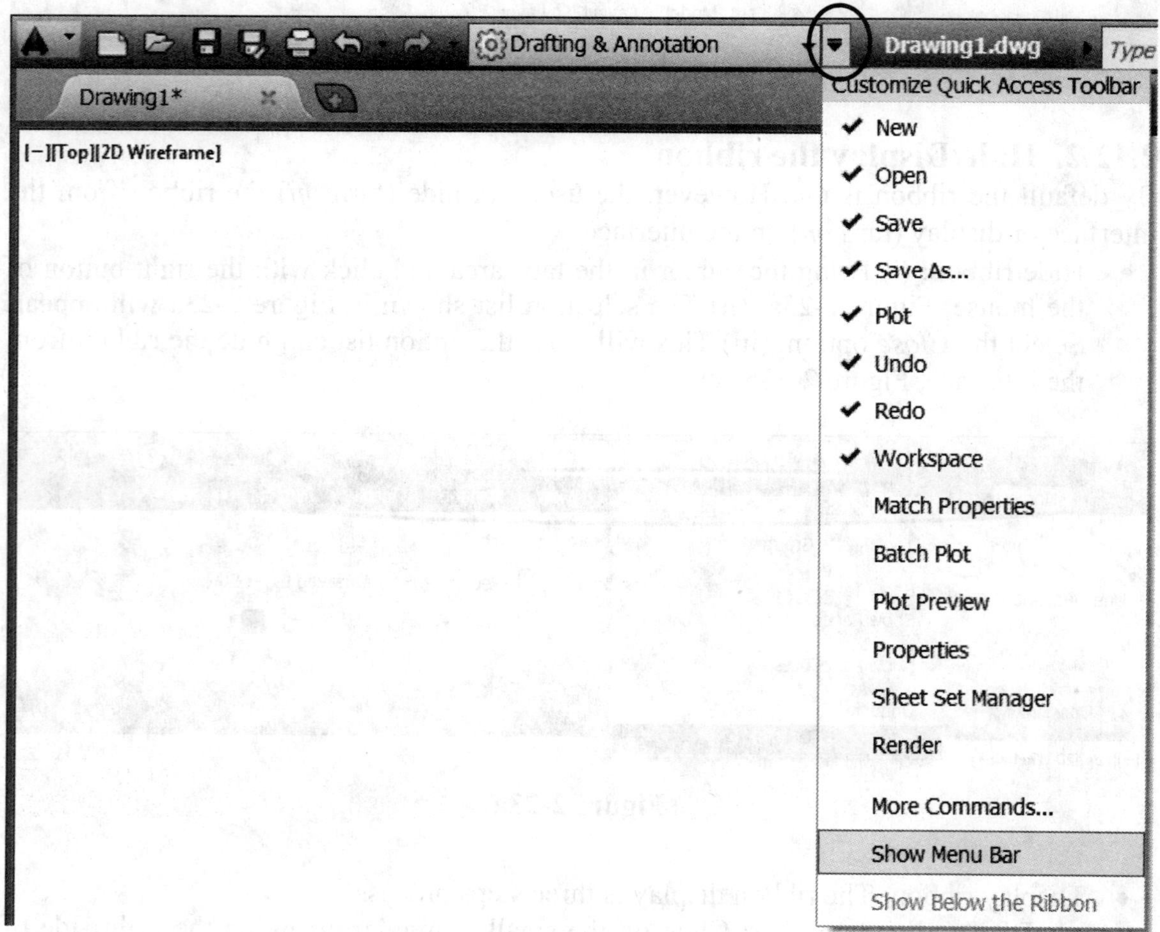

Figure 2-24a

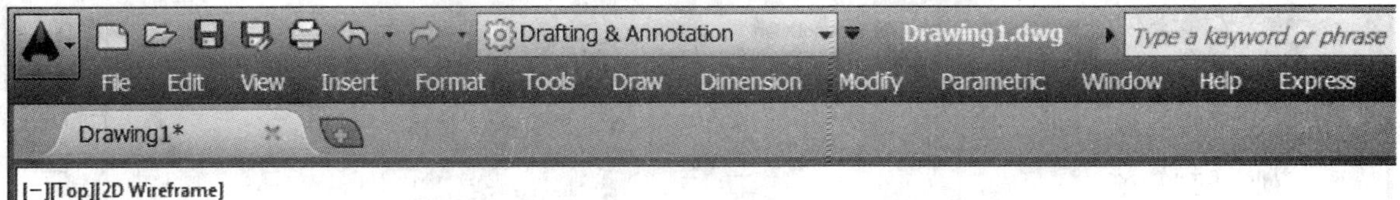

Figure 2-24b

b) <u>Display the ribbon:</u> (i) On the menu bar, select the *Tool* menu, Figure 2-24c and a selection list will appear. (ii) Select the *Palettes* option, Figure 2-24c and another selection list will appear. (iii) Finally, select the *Ribbon* option, Figure 2-24c. (iv) This will close the two selection lists and display the ribbon on the interface, Figure 2-24d.

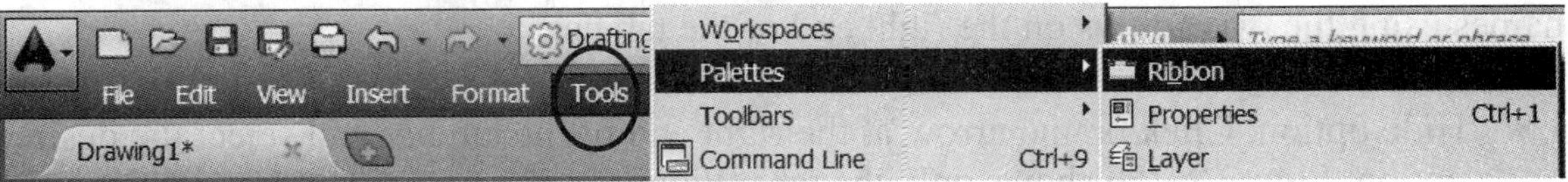

Figure 2-24c

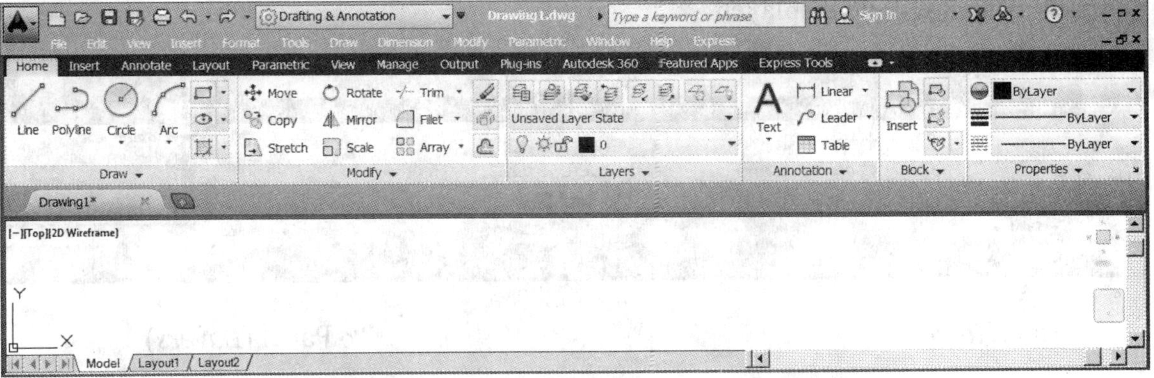

Figure 2-24d

c) <u>Hide the menu bar:</u> (i) Bring the cursor on the menu bar and click with the right button of the mouse. The *Show Menu Bar* option will appear on the screen, Figure 2-24e. (ii) Click the option, this will close the option and hide the menu bar, Figure 2-24f.

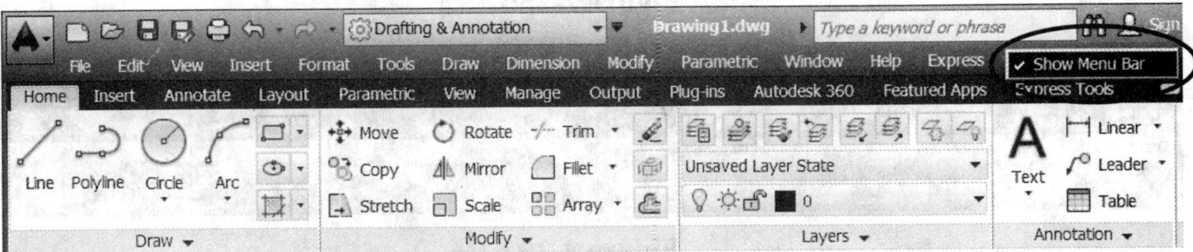

Figure 2-24e

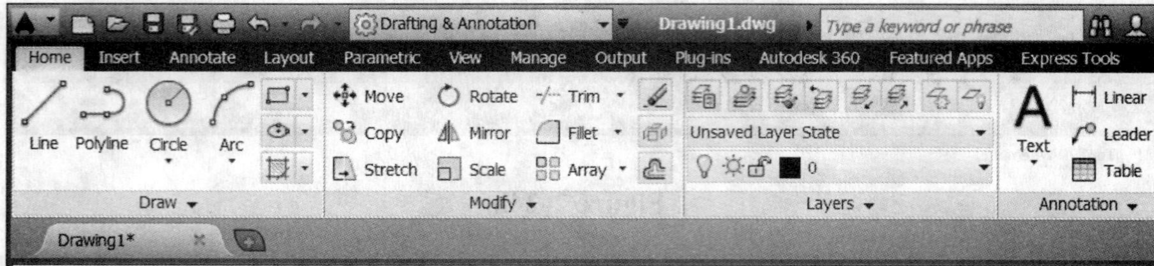

Figure 2-24f

2.12.3. Ribbon states

By default the ribbon is *On* and the tabs, the panels, and panel names are displayed, Figure 2-25a. However, the user can display/hide any of the tabs, panels, and/or panel names using the two arrows on the right end of the tab bar.

- Hide option: Click on the arrow at the right end of the tab bar and select the desired option. Figure 2-25b shows only the tabs; Figure 2-25c shows the tabs and the panel names; and Figure 2-25d shows the tabs and panel buttons.
- Display option: Click on the second arrow from the right end of the tab bar and the full ribbon will be displayed.

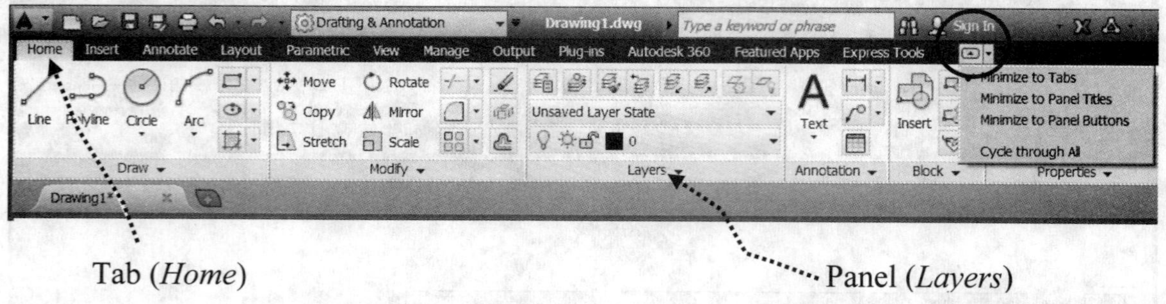

Figure 2-25a

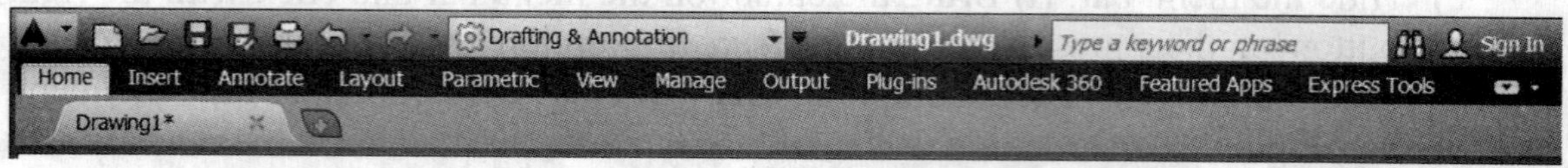

Figure 2-25b

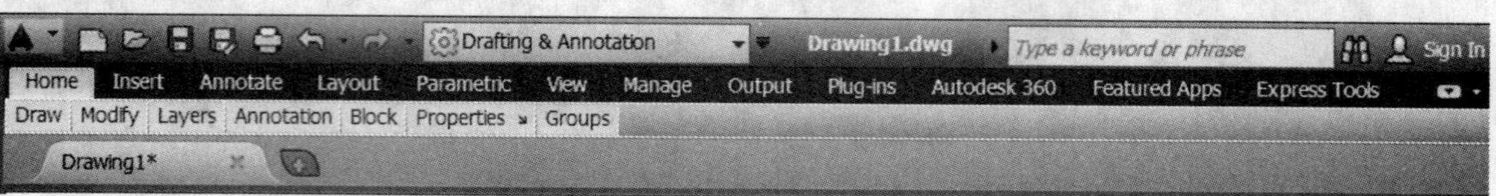

Figure 2-25c

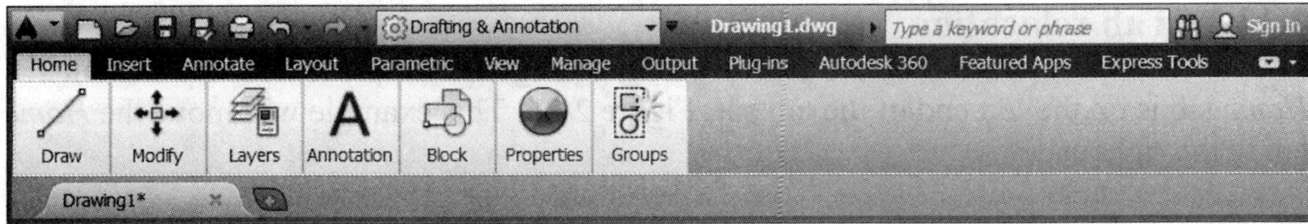

Figure 2-25d

2.13. Ribbon's Tab

The ribbon tabs are used to display the ribbon panel. The tabs are not used for command execution. A user can display or hide and relocate the default tabs, and can create new tabs.

2.13.1. Display/Hide Tabs

By default the tabs of the ribbon are *On*. However, the user can hide (turn *off*) the tabs from the ribbon or display (turn *on*) on the ribbon.

- Display a tab: (i) Bring the cursor in the tab area and click with the right button of the mouse, Figure 2-26. (ii) The selection list shown in Figure 2-26 will appear. Select the *Show Tabs* option. (iii) This will open a tab's list. If a tab is displayed on the ribbon then it will have a check mark beside its name, Figure 2-26. (iv) To display a tab, click on a tab without a check mark, *3D Tools* in the current example. (iv) This will close both the option lists and display the selected tab and associated panels on the ribbon.

- Hide a tab: (i) Bring the cursor in the tab area and click with the right button of the mouse, Figure 2-26. (ii) The selection list shown in Figure 2-26 will appear. Select the *Show Tabs* option. (iii) This will open a tab's list. If a tab is displayed on the ribbon then it will have a check mark beside its name, Figure 2-26. (iv) To hide a tab, click on a tab with a check mark, *Express Tools* in the current example. (iv) This will close both the option lists and hide the selected tab and associated panels from the ribbon.

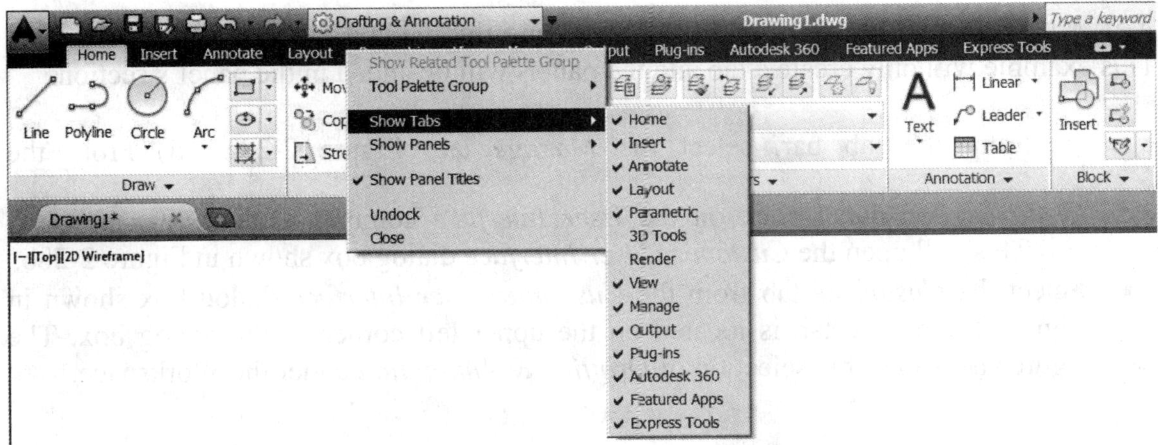

Figure 2-26

2.13.2. Tab relocation

A user can relocate a tab of the ribbon using a drag and drop method. By default the *Home* tab is on the left end of the tab bar, Figure 2-26. This example will move the *Home* tab to the right end.

- (i) Click on the *Home* tab with the left button of the mouse, (ii) keep pressing the left button, and (iii) move the cursor to the desired location. A grayed tab will appear at the new location, Figure 2-27a, the right end of the tab bar in the current example.
- Release the left button of the mouse and the tab will be moved to the new location. Figure 2-27b shows the new location of *Home* tab, the right end of the tab bar in the current example.

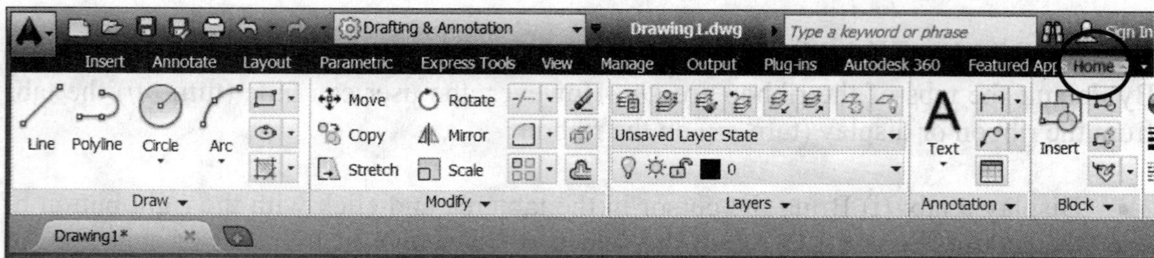

Figure 2-27a

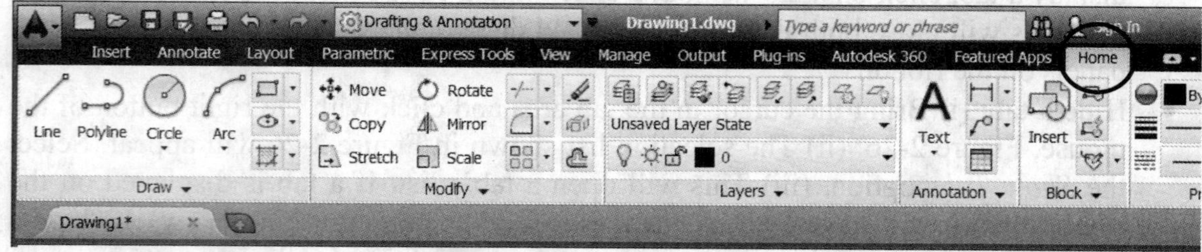

Figure 2-27b

2.13.3. New tab

A user can create a new tab for the ribbon using the method discussed in this section. This example will only create a tab and the panels will be added in the panel's section.

- (i) From the tab bar, select the *Manage* tab, Figure 2-28a. (ii) From the *Customization* panel click on the *User Interface* command, the *CUI* icon. (iii) This will open the *Customize User Interface* dialog box shown in Figure 2-28b.
- Select the *Customize* tab from the *Customize User Interface* dialog box shown in Figure 2-28b. The tab is located on the upper left corner of the dialog box. The figure also shows the selection of *Drafting & Annotation* under the Workspace.

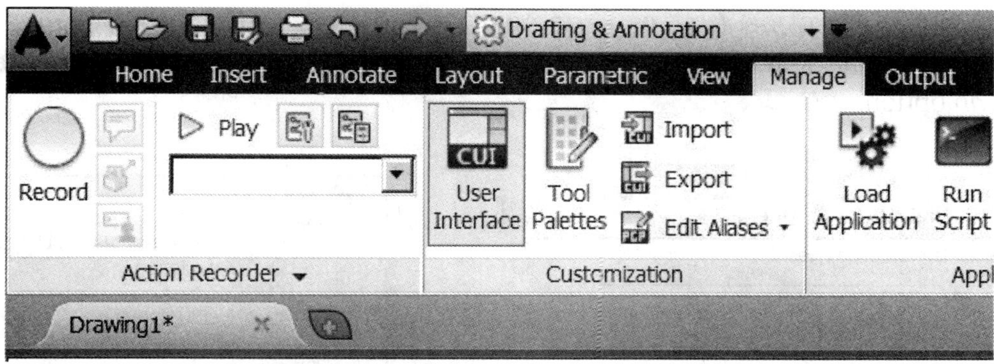

Figure 2-28a

- In the upper left quadrant, Figure 2-28b, click on the '+' adjacent to the *Ribbon* label. This will display an option list, Figure 2-29a.

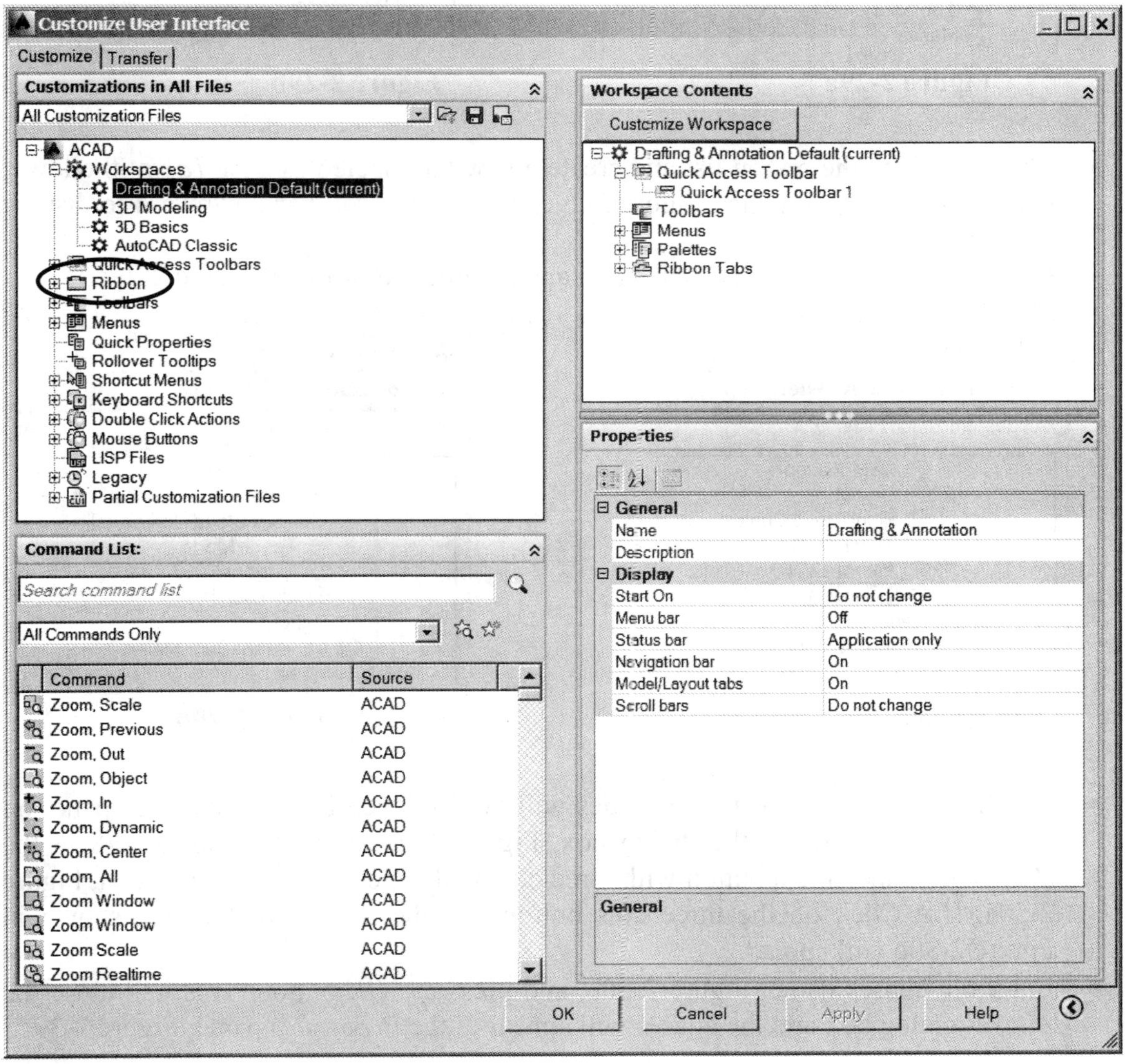

Figure 2-28b

- (i) Select the *Tab* option, Figure 2-29b, (ii) and click with the right button of the mouse on the *Tab* option. (iii) This will display an option list. (iv) Select the *New Tab* option.

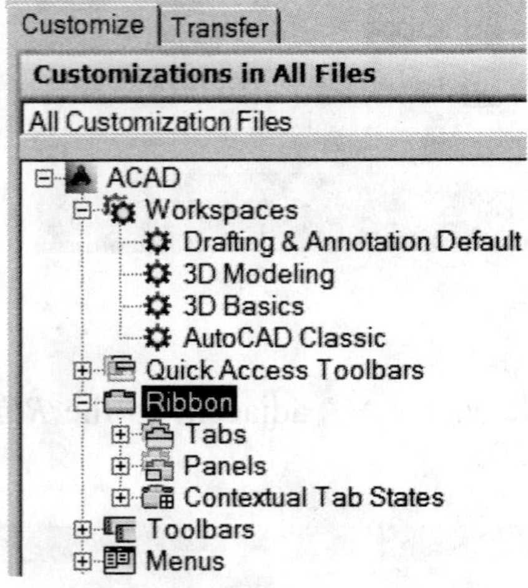

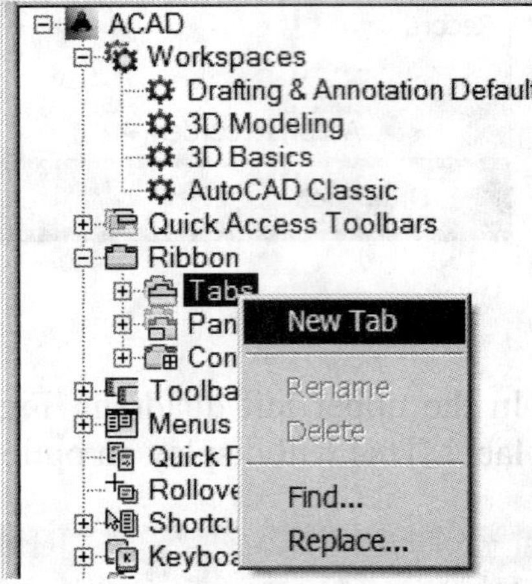

Figure 2-29a   **Figure 2-29b**

- This will close the option list and create a new tab labeled as *New Tab* at the lower end of the *Tab* options list, Figure 2-29c. Move the scroll bar downward to display the *New Tab*.
- (i) Select the *New Tab*, (ii) click again and rename it to *MyTab*, Figure 2-29d.

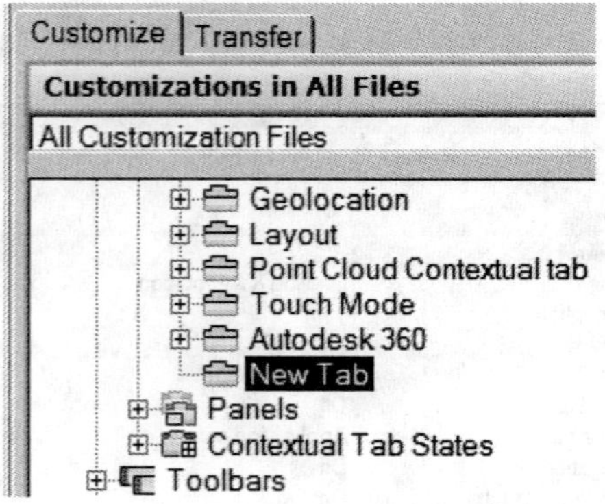

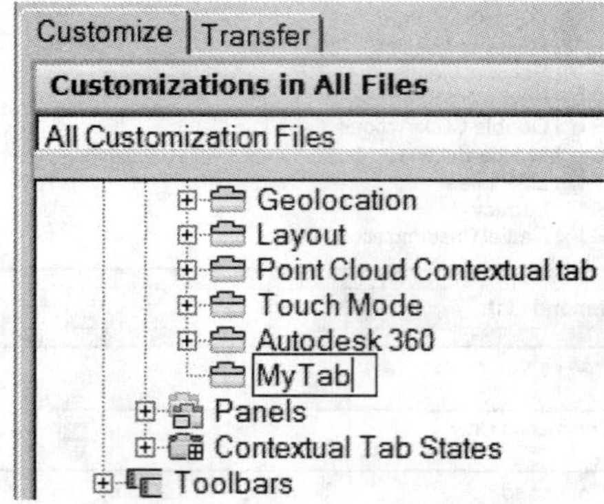

Figure 2-29c   **Figure 2-29d**

- (i) Click on *MyTab* and its properties will be displayed in the *Properties* panel on the upper right side of the dialog box, Figure 2-30a. (ii) Click on *Aliases* in the *Properties* panel and a button with three dots will appear in the adjacent cell, Figure 2-30a. (iii) Click on the three dots button and the *Aliases* dialog box shown in Figure 2-30b will appear.
- Enter the aliases name, Figure 2-30b, and press the *OK* button. This will close the *Aliases* dialog box and the aliases will appear in the *Properties* panel, Figure 2-30c.

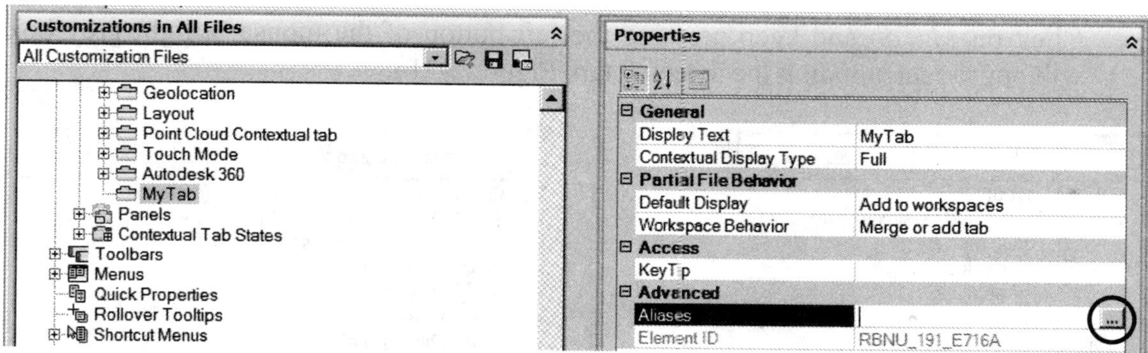

Figure 2-30a

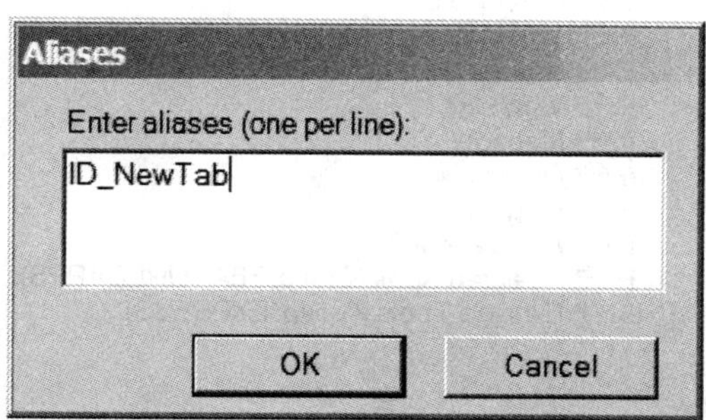

Figure 2-30b

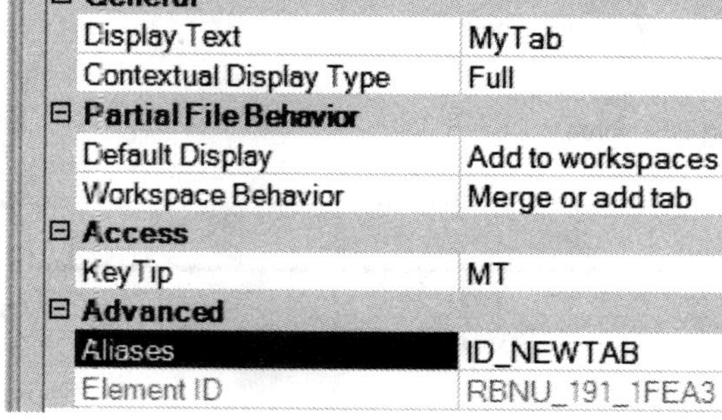

Figure 2-30c

- Double click on *Drafting & Annotation* under the *Workspaces*, Figure 2-30d, and the list of workspace content will appear on the right side of the dialog box.
- On the right side of the dialog box, click on the '+' adjacent to the *Ribbon Tabs* label. This will display an option list, Figure 2-30d.

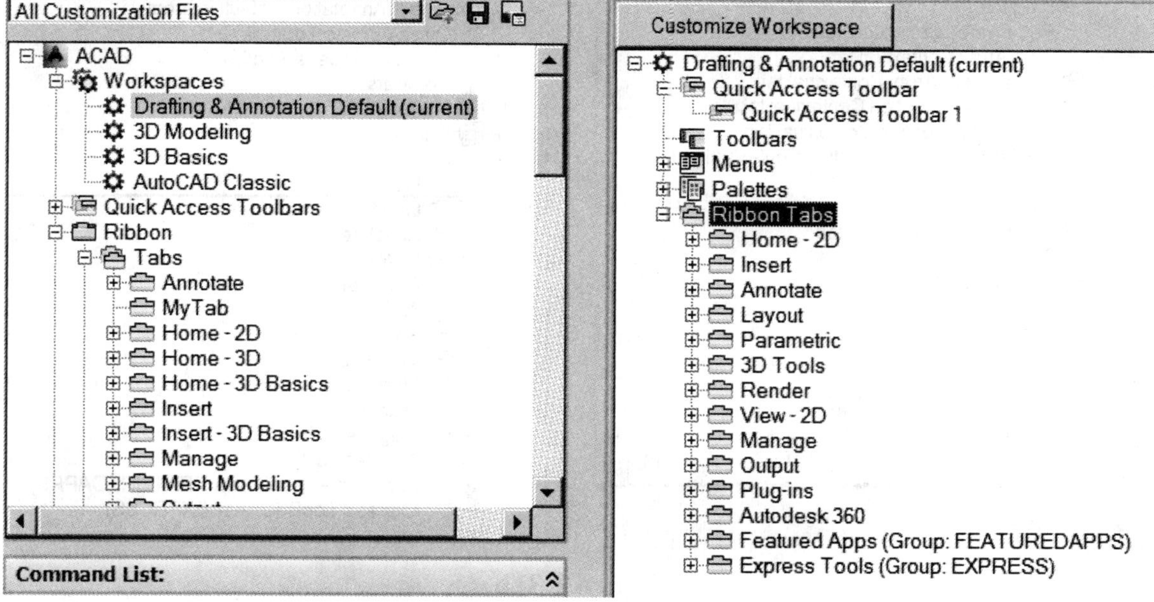

Figure 2-30d

- Click on *MyTab* and keep pressing the left button of the mouse; a light grey box will appear surrounding the selected tab, Figure 2-31a.

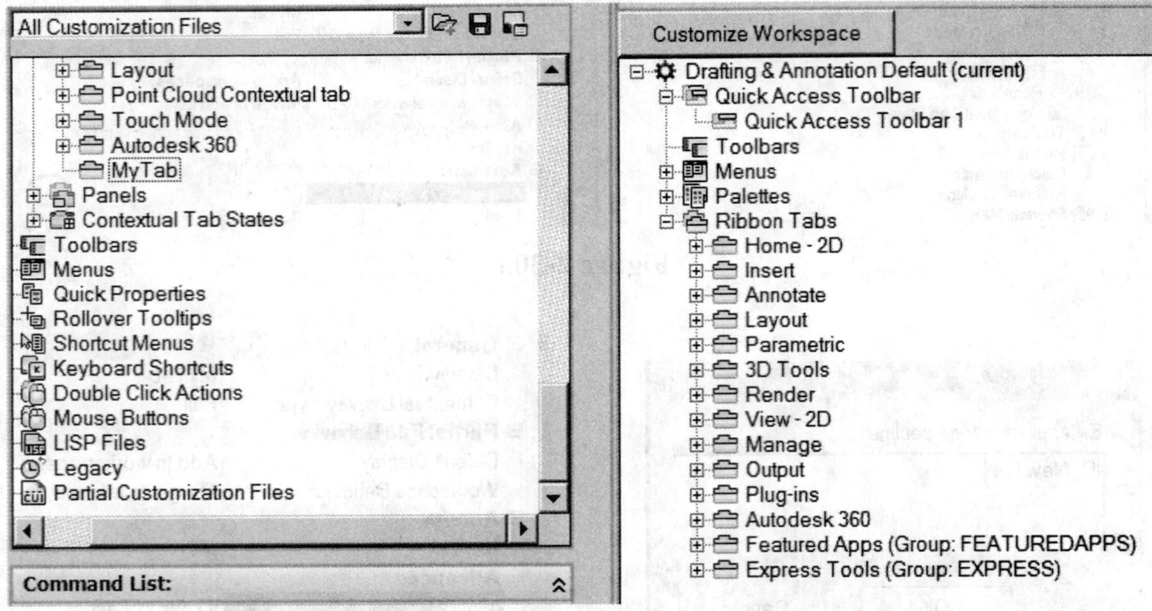

Figure 2-31a

- (i) Keep pressing the left button of the mouse, (ii) move the cursor to the right side of the dialog box under the *Ribbon Tabs*, Figure 2-31b. (iii) Click anywhere below the *Ribbon Tabs* and above *Express Tools* (the last tab) and release the left button of the mouse. The figure shows the cursor below the *Home* tab.

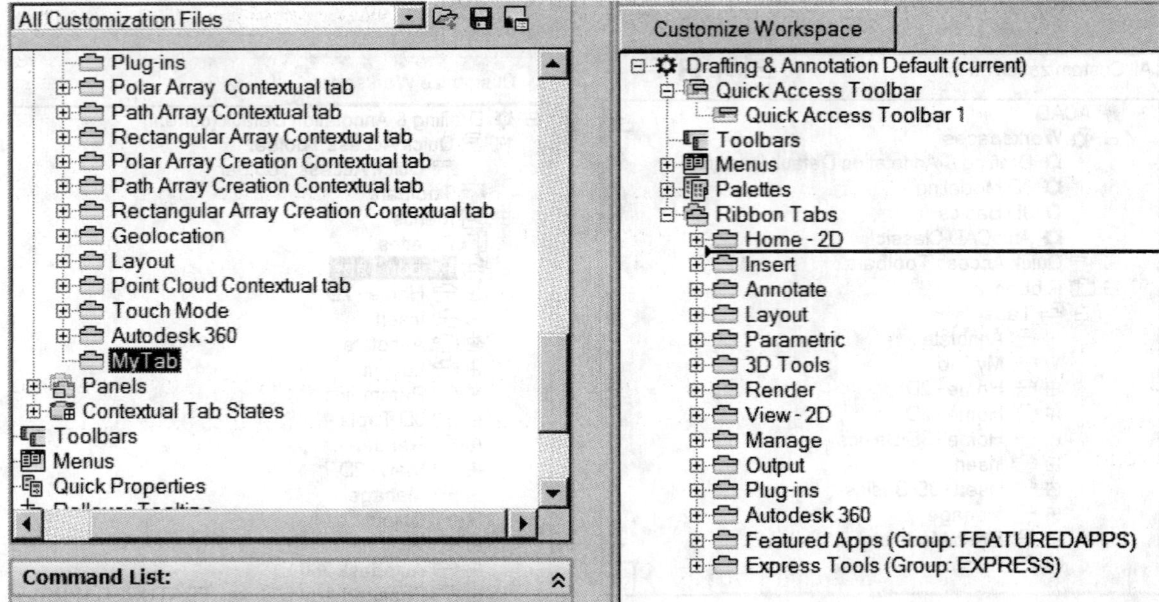

Figure 2-31b

- The new tab is added to the *Ribbon Tabs* list, Figure 2-31c. By default, the tab is always added at the end of the list (independent of the location selected). If necessary, move the new tab at the desired location.

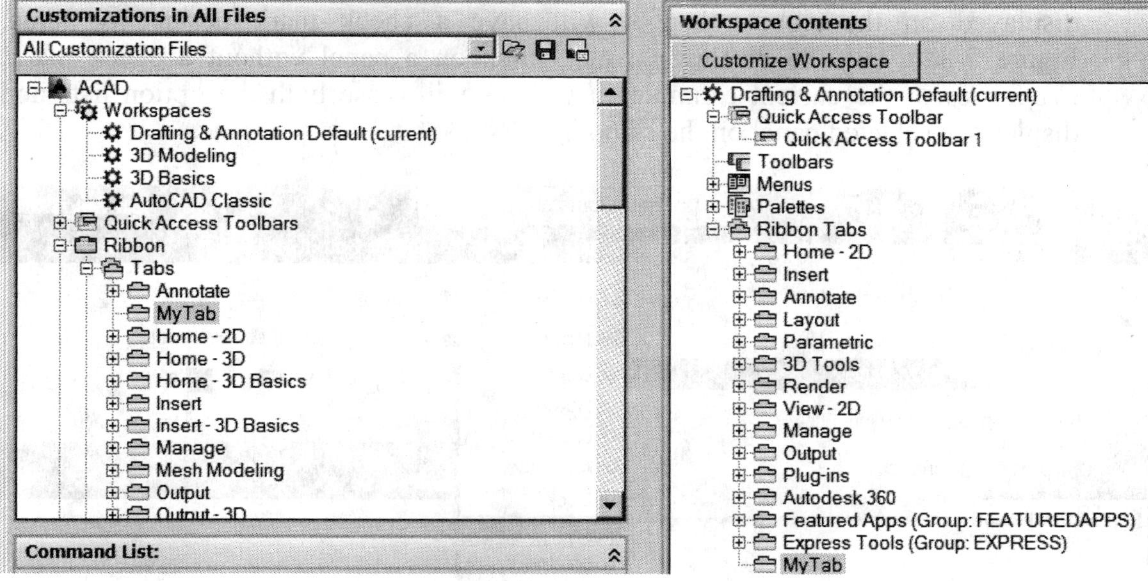

Figure 2-31c

- Click the *OK* button of the dialog box. This will close the dialog box and create the new tab (*MyTab*) in the tab bar of the workspace, Figure 2-31d. The new tab is at the end of the tab bar.

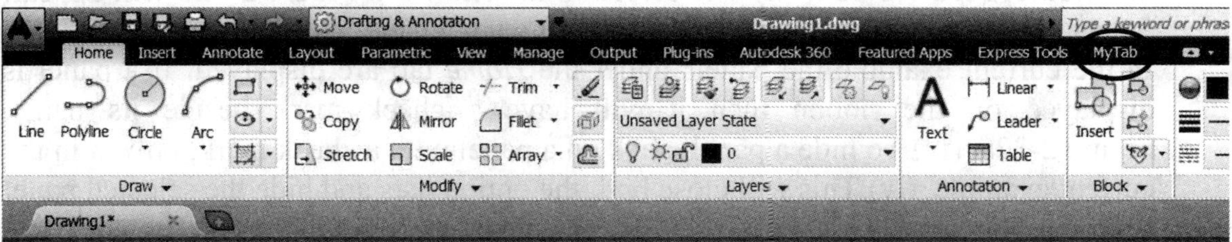

Figure 2-31d

2.14.   Ribbon's panel

The ribbon panels are used to display the commands. Some of the panels also provide access to dialog boxes. A user can display or hide and relocate the default panel, and can create new panels.

2.14.1. Display/Hide panel

By default the panels of the ribbon are *On*. However, the user can hide (turn *off*) the panel from the ribbon or display (turn *on*) on the ribbon.

- Display a panel: (i) Bring the cursor in the tab area and click with the right button of the mouse, Figure 2-32a. (ii) The selection list shown in Figure 2-32a will appear. Select the *Show Panels* option. (iii) This will open a panel's list for the selected tab. In the current example the panels under the *Home* tab are displayed. If a panel is displayed on the ribbon then it will have a check mark beside its name, Figure 2-32a. (iv) To display a panel, click on a panel without a check mark, *Properties* in the current example. (iv) This will close both the option lists and display the selected panel on the ribbon.

Figure 2-32a

- Hide a panel: (i) Bring the cursor in the tab area and click with the right button of the mouse, Figure 2-32b. (ii) The selection list shown in Figure 2-32b will appear. Select the *Show Panels* option. (iii) This will open a panel's list for the selected tab. In the current example the panels under the *Home* tab are displayed. If a panel is displayed on the ribbon then it will have a check mark beside its name, Figure 2-32a. (iv) To hide a panel, click on a panel with a check mark, *Layers* in the current example. (iv) This will close both the option lists and hide the selected panel from the ribbon.

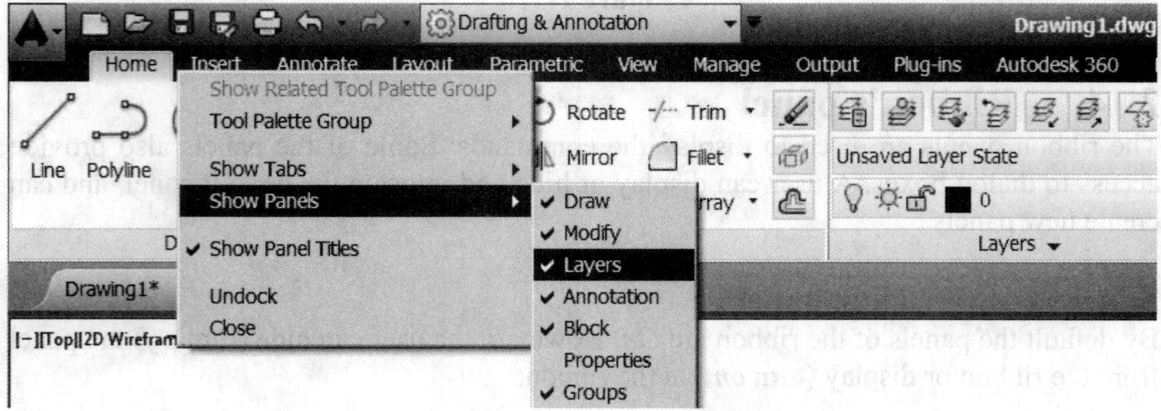

Figure 2-32b

2.14.2. Panel components

Every panel shows three rows of commands icons, Figure 2-33a. If a panel commands cannot be accommodated in three rows than those commands can be access through the panel expander, Figure 2-33a. If a command has several options then those options can be access through the command expander; and the command icon will display the most recently used option.

- Panel expender: (i) Bring the cursor on the tiny arrow near the panel label, Figure 2-33a and (ii) click with the left button of the mouse and the panel will expand, Figure 2-33b. However, if the user moves the cursor, then the panel will collapse to the original size.

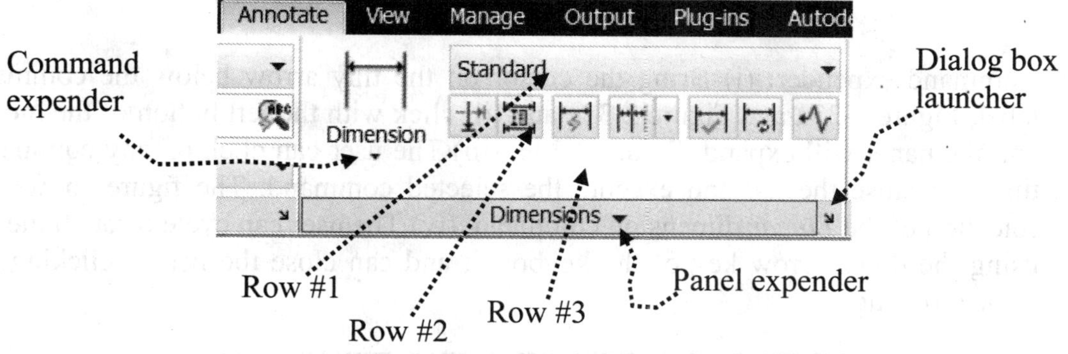

Figure 2-33a

- The user can pin the panel expansion using the *Pin* command. (i) The pin command is executed by clicking on the pin icon shown in the lower left corner of the expanded panel, Figure 2-33b. (ii) Figure 2-33b shows that the panel is pinned. Note carefully the appearance of the pin in the two figures.

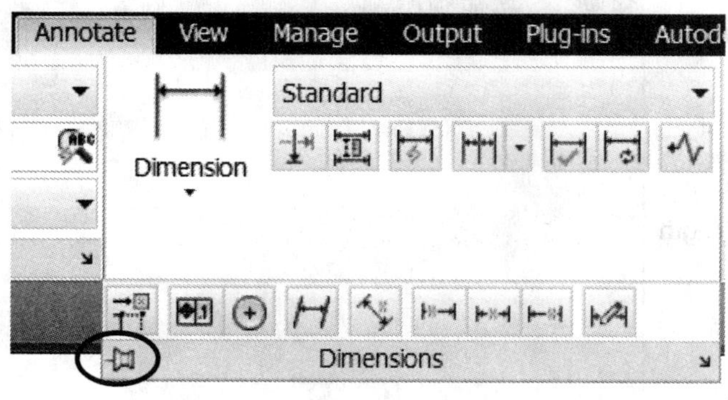

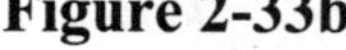

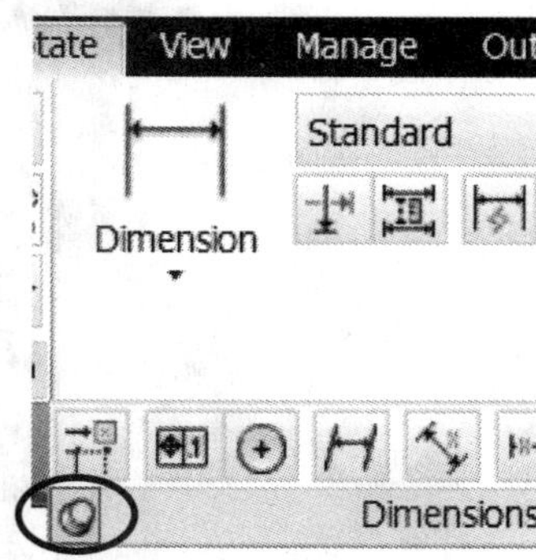

<table>
<tr><td>**Figure 2-33b**</td><td>**Figure 2-33c**</td></tr>
</table>

- Dialog box launcher: (i) Bring the cursor on the tiny arrow near the lower right corner of the panel, Figure 2-33a and (ii) click the arrow and the *Dimension Style Manager* dialog box will appear, Figure 2-33d. This dialog box will be discussed in detail in *Dimensions* chapter. Click the *Close* button to close the dialog box.

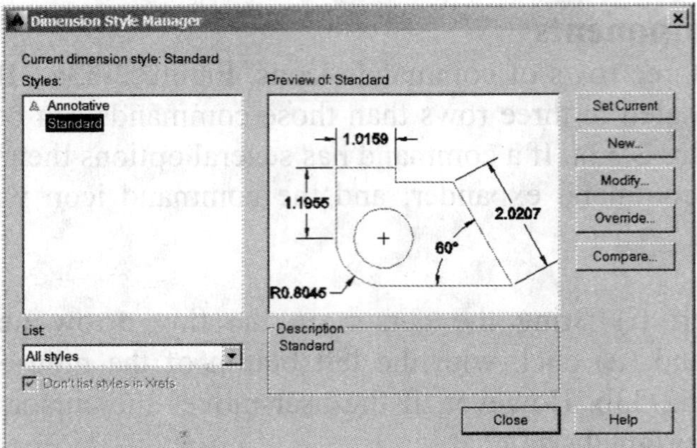

Figure 2-33d

- Command expender: (i) Bring the cursor on the tiny arrow below the command label, Figure 2-33a and Figure 2-33e and (ii) click with the left button of the mouse and the panel will expand, Figure 2-33e. (iii) The user can click on any command; this will close the list and execute the selected command. The figure shows the selection of the *Linear* dimension command. (iv) The user can cycle through the list using the down arrow key of the keyboard; and can close the list by clicking the same arrow again.

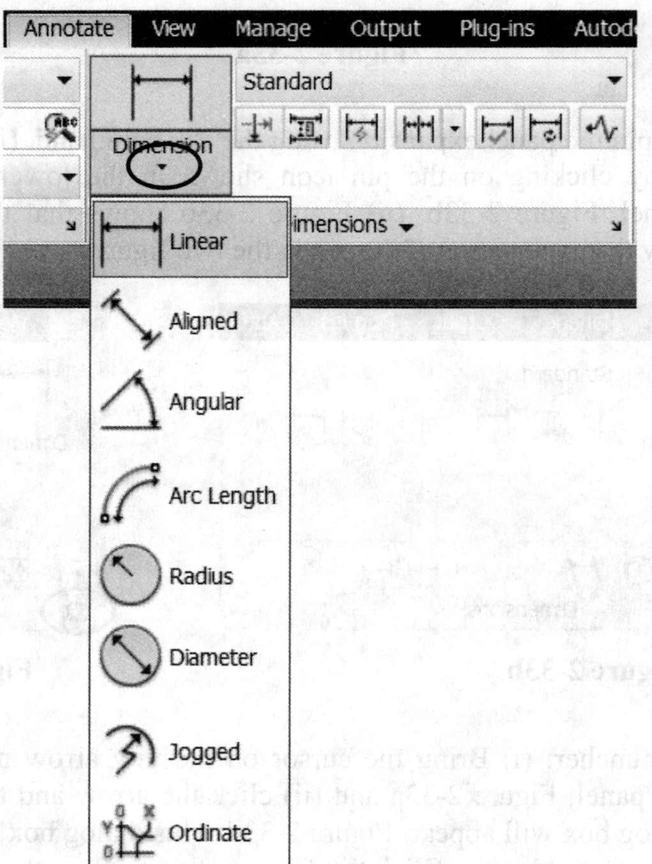

Figure 2-33e

2.14.3. Panel relocation

A user can relocate a panel of the ribbon using a drag and drop method. By default the *Home* tab is selected and the *Draw* panel is on the left end of the ribbon, Figure 2-25a. This example will move the *Draw* panel on the right side of the *Modify* panel.

- (i) Select the *Home* tab.
- (i) Click on the *Draw* panel with the left button of the mouse, (ii) keep pressing the left button, and (iii) move the cursor to the desired location. A grayed panel will appear at the new location, Figure 2-34a, the right end of the *Modify* panel in the current example.
- Release the left button of the mouse and the panel will be moved to the new location. Figure 2-34b shows the new location of the *Draw* panel, the right side of the *Modify* panel in the current example.

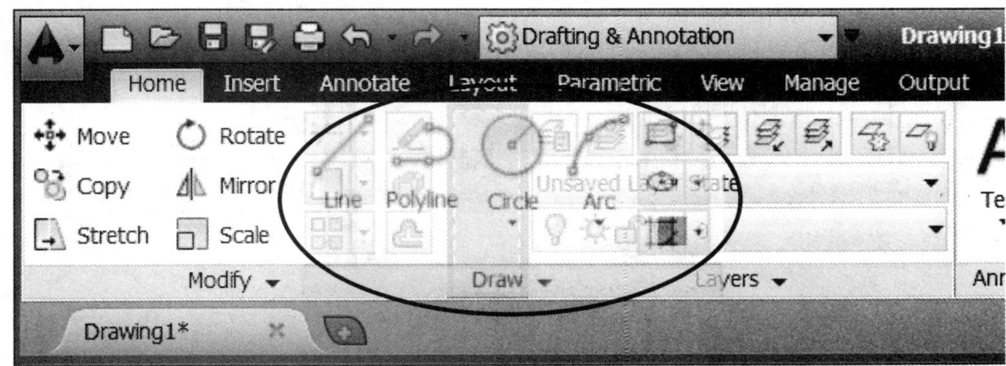

Figure 2-34a

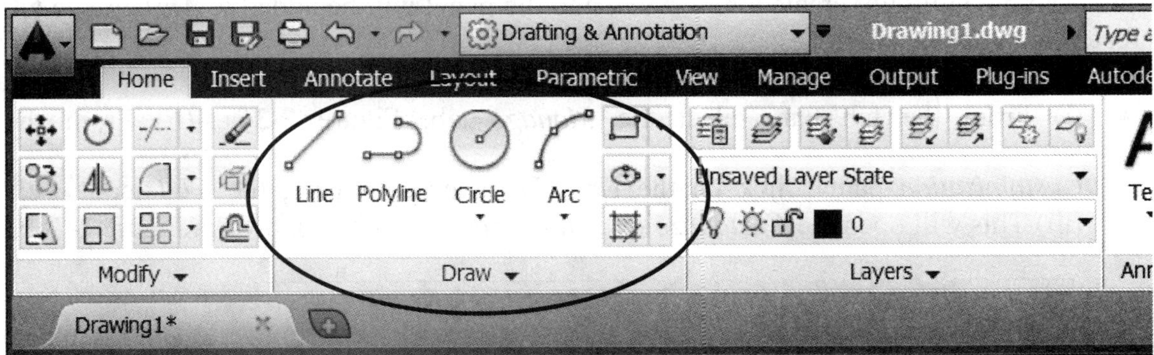

Figure 2-34b

2.14.4. Floating panel

If a user drags and drops the panel in the drawing area then it is called a floating panel. A panel can be converted to a floating panel using the following steps.

- (i) Bring the cursor on the panel's name, Figure 2-35a. (ii) Select the panel's label bar by pressing the left button. (iii) Keep pressing the left button and move the cursor to the drawing area.

- Release the left button of the mouse and the panel becomes the floating panel. The panel will stay in the drawing area till it is returned to the ribbon even if a different *Tab* is selected.

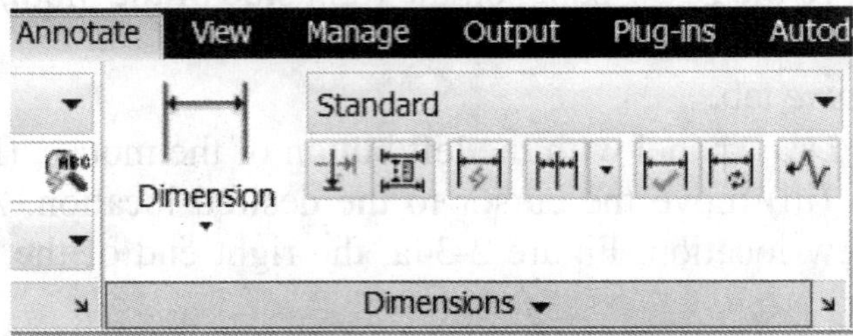

Figure 2-35a

- To return the panel back to its tab, click at *Return Panels to Ribbon button*, Figure 2-35b.

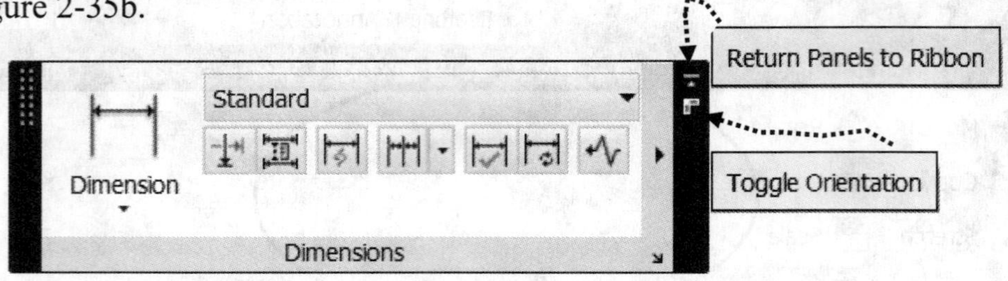

Figure 2-35b

2.14.5. New panel

A user can create a new panel for the ribbon using the method discussed in this section. This example will only create a new panel and the panel will be added to *MyTab*, the tab created in the tab section.

- (i) From the tab bar, select the *Manage* tab, Figure 2-36a. (ii) From the

  Customization panel click on the *User Interface* command, the *CUI* icon [CUI].
  (iii) This will open the *Customize User Interface* dialog box shown in Figure 2-36b.

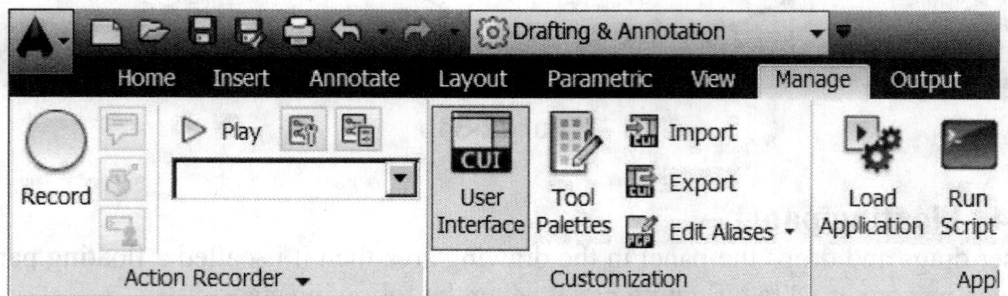

Figure 2-36a

- Select the *Customize* tab from the *Customize User Interface* dialog box shown in Figure 2-36b. The tab is located on the upper left corner of the dialog box. The figure also shows the selection of *Drafting & Annotation* under the Workspace.

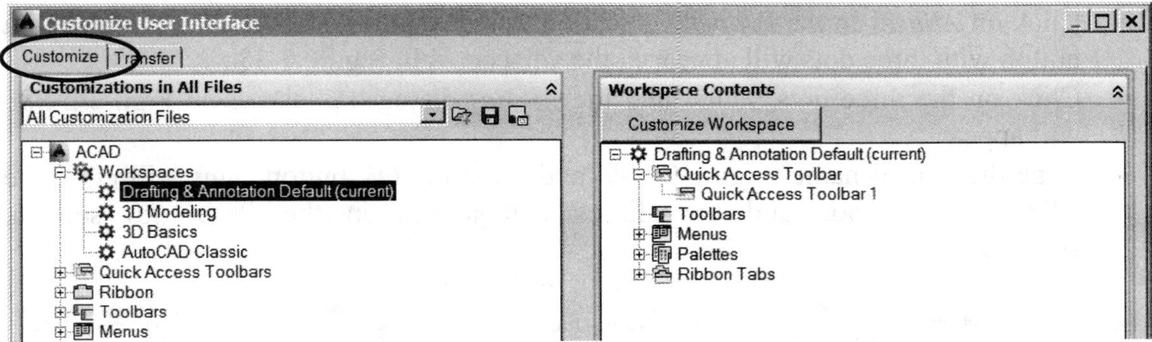

Figure 2-36b

- In the upper left quadrant, Figure 2-36b, click on the '+' adjacent to the *Ribbon* label. This will display an option list, Figure 2-37a.
- (i) Select the *Panel* option, Figure 2-37a. (ii) Click with the right button of the mouse on the *Panel* option, this will display an option list, Figure 2-37b. (iv) Select the *New Panel* option.

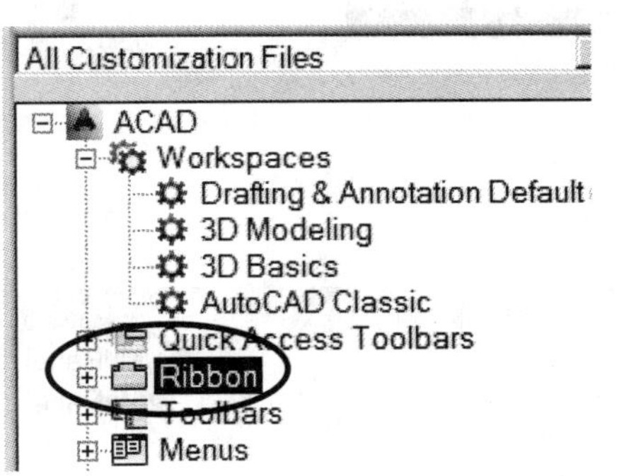

Figure 2-37a

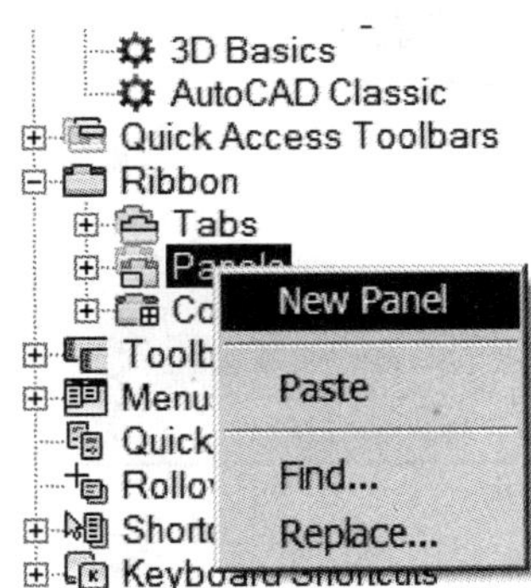

Figure 2-37b

- This will close the option list and create a new panel labeled as *Panel1* at the lower end of the *Panel* options list, Figure 2-37c. Move the scroll bar downward to display the *Panel1*.
- (i) Select the *Panel1*, (ii) click again and rename it to *MyPanel1*, Figure 2-37d.

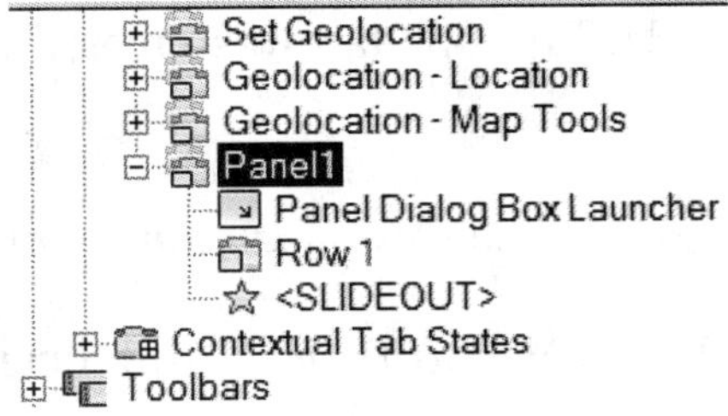

Figure 2-37c

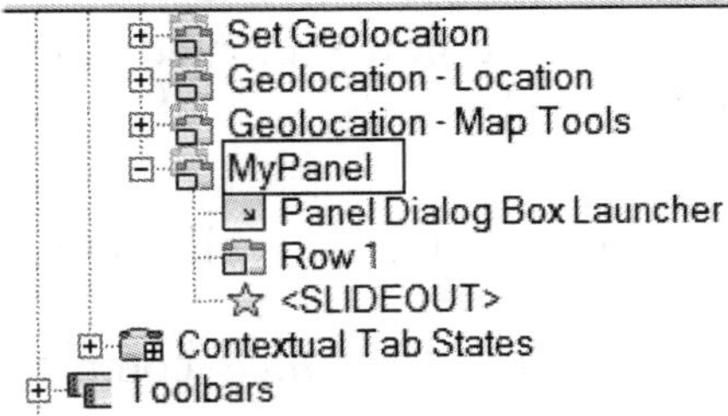

Figure 2-37d

- Click on *MyPanel* and its appearance is displayed in the *Panel Preview* and its properties will be displayed in the *Properties* panel on the upper right side of the dialog box, Figure 2-38a. Nothing is displayed in the *Panel Preview* because the commands are not added to the panel.
- Click on *Aliases* in the *Properties* section (lower right end of the dialog box) and a button with three dots will appear in the adjacent cell, Figure 2-38a.
- Click on the three dots button and the *Aliases* dialog box shown in Figure 2-38b will appear.
- Type the aliases name, Figure 2-38b, and press the *OK* button. This will close the *Aliases* dialog box and the aliases will appear in the *Properties* section, Figure 2-38c.

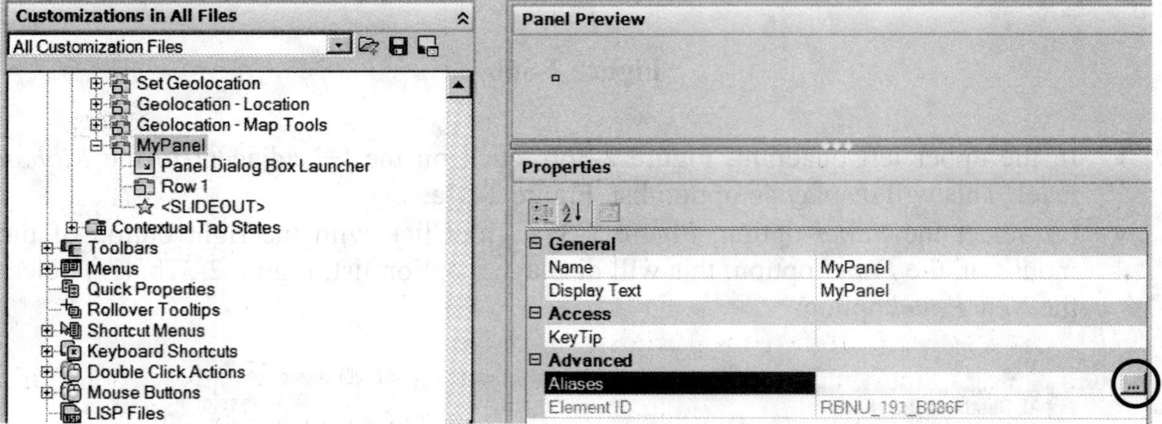

Figure 2-38a

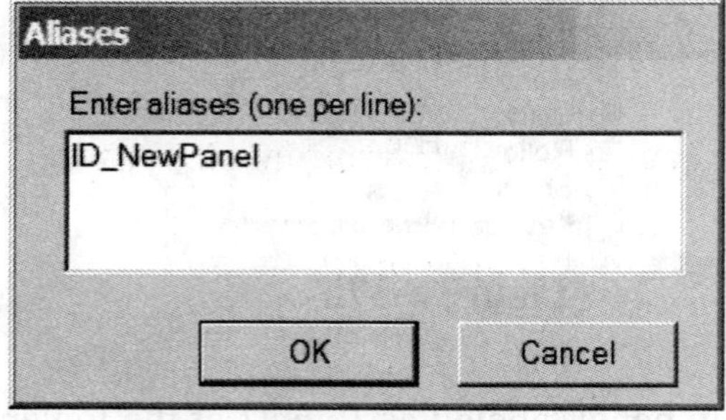

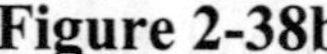

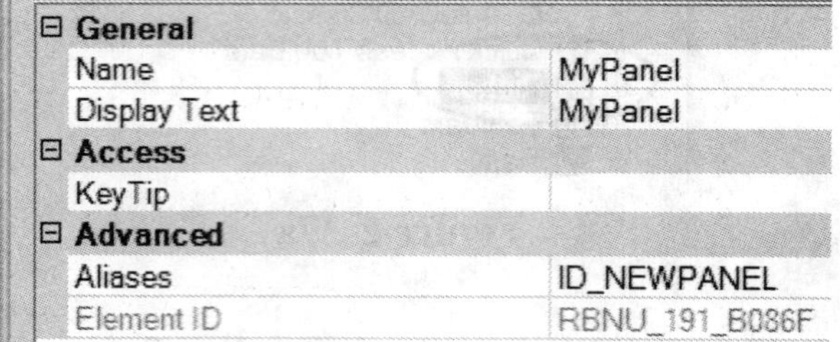

Figure 2-38b   **Figure 2-38c**

2.14.6. Add the panel to a tab

A user can add a panel to a tab using the method discussed in this section. This example will only add the newly created panel, *MyPanel*, to *MyTab*, this tab was created in the section New Tab.

- (i) From the tab bar, select the *Manage* tab. (ii) From the *Customization* panel click on the *User Interface* command, the *CUI* icon [CUI]. (iii) This will open the *Customize User Interface* dialog box.

- In the upper left quadrant, click on the '+' adjacent to the *Ribbon* label. This will display an option list.
- The move process described in this bullet is not necessary; however, it will make the process discussed in the next bullet easy to understand. (i) Select on the newly created panel, *MyPanel*. It is at the bottom of the panel list. (ii) Press the left button of the mouse and keep pressing. (iii) Move the cursor upward. (iv) Release the cursor when it is on the top of the panel list, Figure 2-39a.
- (i) Select the *MyPanel*. (ii) Press the left button of the mouse and keep pressing. (iii) Move the cursor upward to *MyTab*. A light grey rectangle will appear at the tail of the pointer and is not shown in the figure. (iv) Release the cursor when it is on *MyTab*. A small arrow head will appear beside *MyTab*, Figure 2-39b.
- The newly created panel is added to the previously created tab, Figure 2-39c.

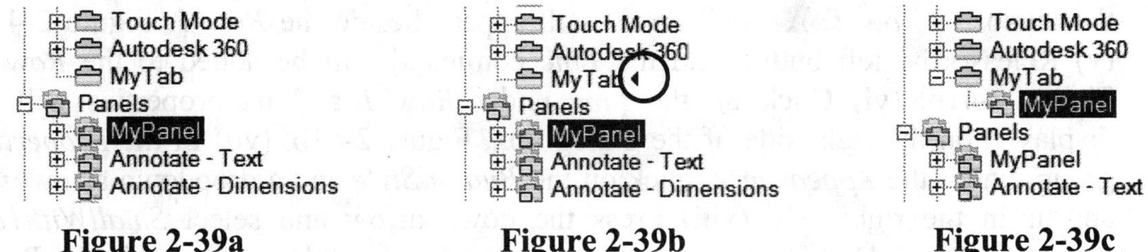

Figure 2-39a   **Figure 2-39b**   **Figure 2-39c**

2.14.7. Add commands to a panel

A user can add commands to a panel using the method discussed in this section. This example will use the user created panel and tab, *MyPanel* and *MyTab*, respectively.

- (i) From the tab bar, select the *Manage* tab. (ii) From the *Customization* panel click on the *User Interface* command, the *CUI* icon . (iii) This will open the *Customize User Interface* dialog box.
- In the upper left quadrant, click on the '+' adjacent to the *Ribbon* label. This will display an option list.
- The newly created panel has three components as shown in Figure 2-40a.

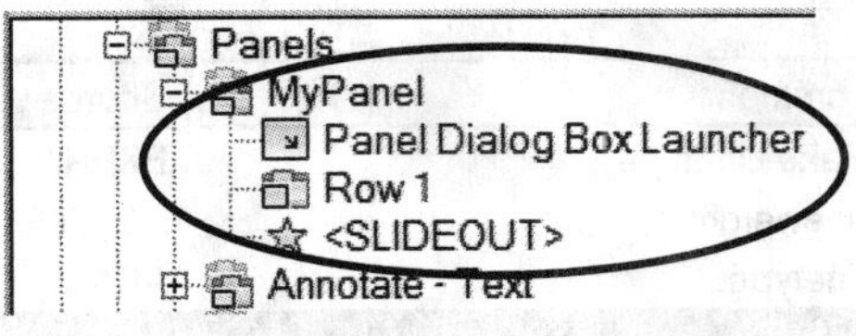

Figure 2-40a

- **Add a row:** (i) Select *Row 1*, Figure 2-40b, and (ii) click with the right button of the mouse. A selection list shown in Figure 2-40b will appear. (iii) Click on the *New Row* option. This will close the option list and a new row, *Row 2*, will be created, Figure 2-40c.

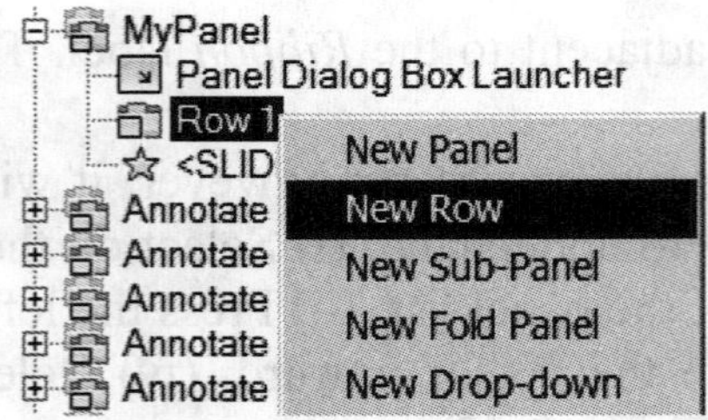

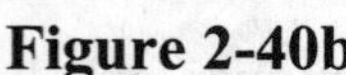

Figure 2-40b

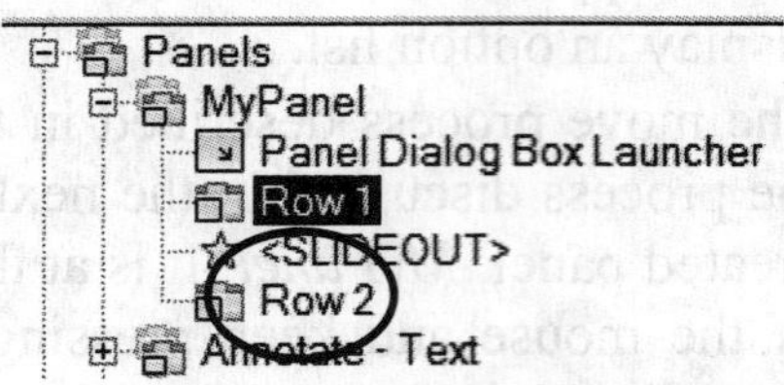

Figure 2-40c

- **Add a command:** Now add the *Line* command to *Row 1*. (i) Type *Line* in the search command list, Figure 2-41. The command list box will display all the commands containing the word "Line". (ii) Locate the *Line* command and select it, Figure 2-41a. (iii) Press the left button of the mouse and keep pressing. (iv) Move the cursor to *Row 1*. A small arrow will appear beside the *Row 1*, Figure 2-41a. (v) Release the left button and the *Line* command will be added to the *Row 1*, Figure 2-41b. (vi) Click on the *Line* under *Row 1* and its properties will be displayed on the right side of the dialog box, Figure 2-41b. (vii) In the *Properties* group, under the *Appearance*, click on the *Button Style* and a dropdown arrow will appear in the right cell. (viii) Press the down arrow and select *SmallWithText* option, Figure 2-41b. The command picture and label will be displayed in the *Panel Preview* window; it is on the upper right corner of the dialog box, Figure 2-41c.

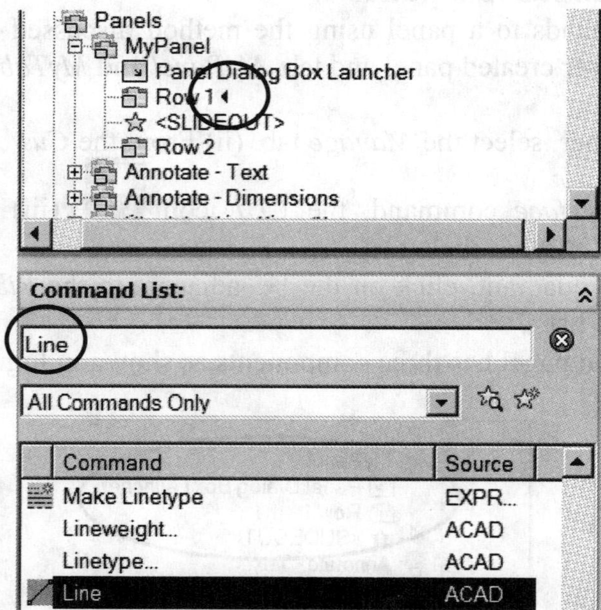

Figure 2-41a

- Similarly, add the circle command, Figure 2-41c.

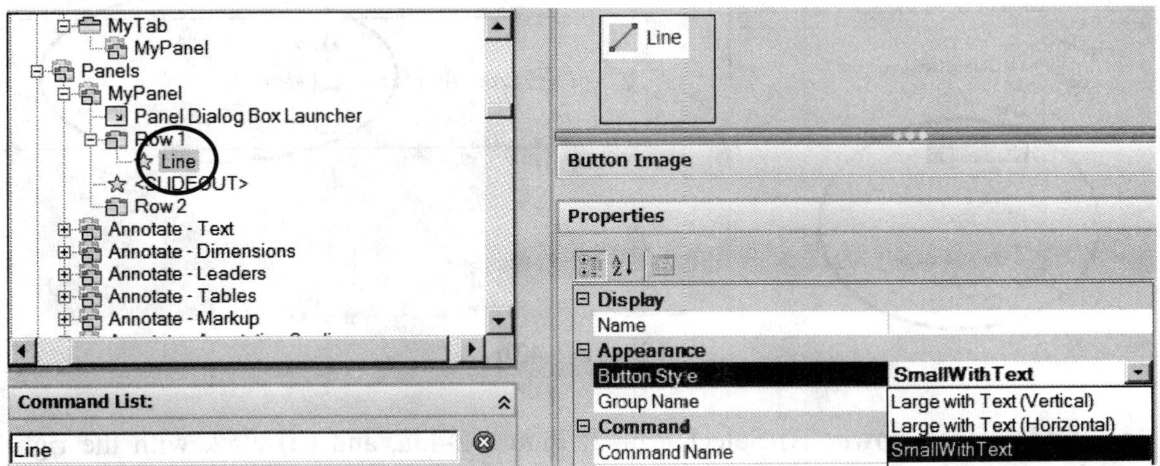

Figure 2-41b

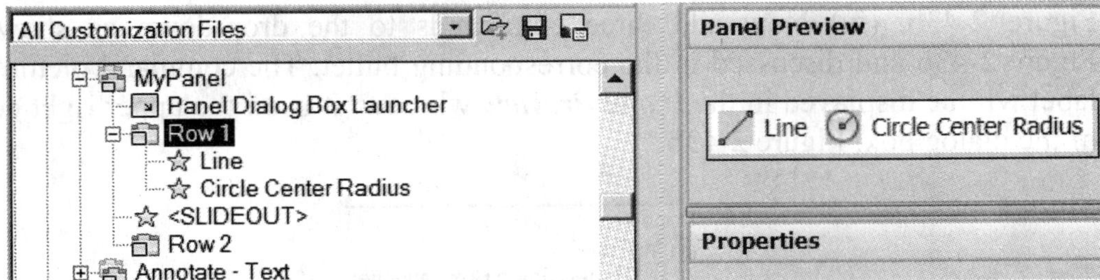

Figure 2-41c

- **Add a sub-panel:** (i) Select *Row 1*, Figure 2-42a, and (ii) click with the right button of the mouse. A selection list shown in Figure 2-42a will appear. (iii) Click on the *New Sub-Panel* option. This will close the option list and a new sub-panel, *Sub-Panel 1*, will be created, Figure 2-42b. (iv) Now add three rows and commands to the rows as shown in Figure 2-42b and discussed in the corresponding bullet. The command picture and label will be displayed in the *Panel Preview* window; it is on the upper right corner of the dialog box, Figure 2-42b.

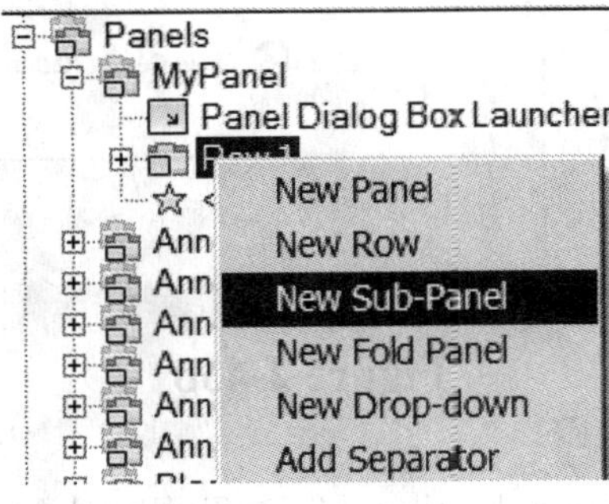

Figure 2-42a

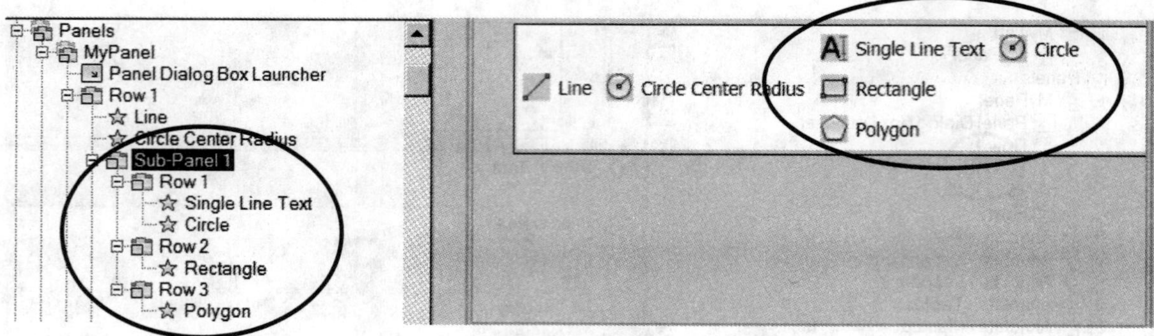

Figure 2-42b

- **Add a drop-down:** (i) Select *Row 1*, Figure 2-43a, and (ii) click with the right button of the mouse. A selection list shown in Figure 2-43a will appear. (iii) Click on the *New Drop-Down* option. This will close the option list and a new drop-down menu, *Drop-Down 1*, will be created. (iv) Rename the drop-down to Array, Figure 2-43b. (iv) Now add three commands to the drop-down as shown in Figure 2-43b and discussed in the corresponding bullet. The command picture and label will be displayed in the *Panel Preview* window; it is on the upper right corner of the dialog box, Figure 2-43b.

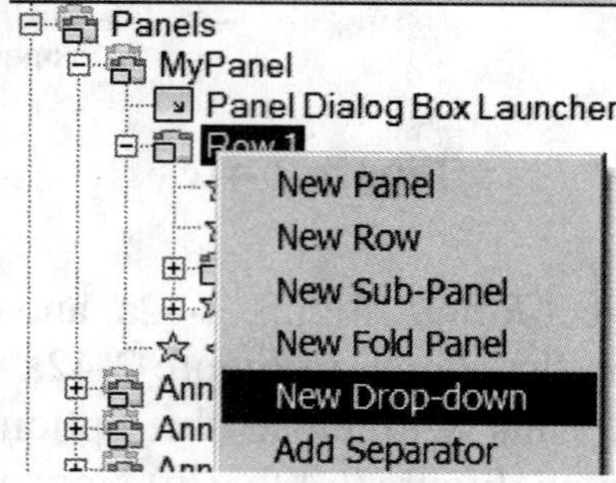

Figure 2-43a

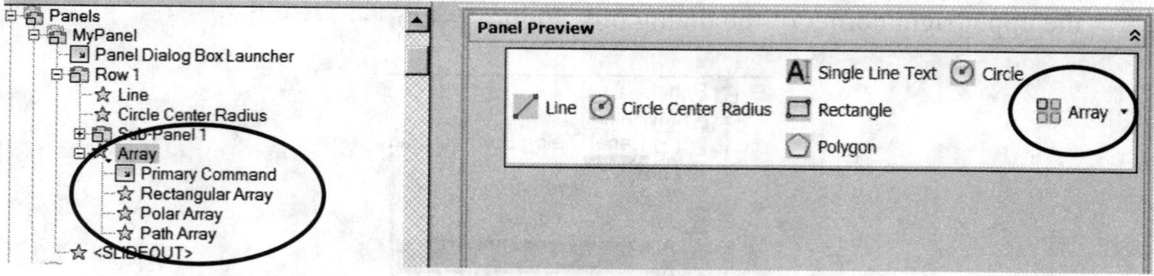

Figure 2-43b

- The Figure 2-44 shows the selection of *MyTab* and *MyPanel*. The figure also shows the Array drop-down menu expanded.

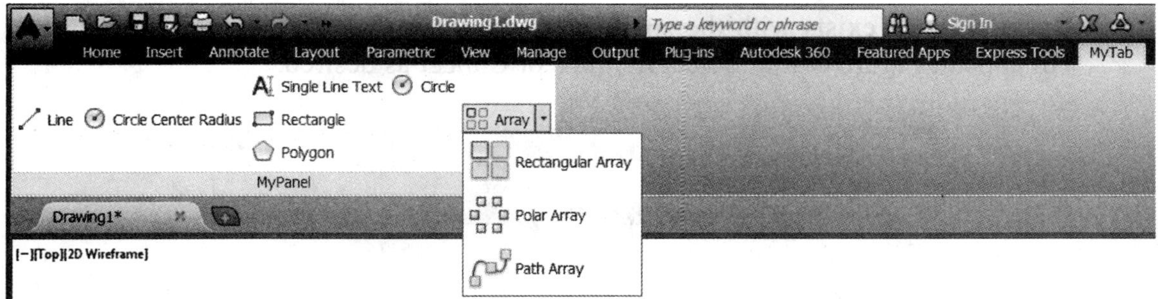

Figure 2-44

2.15. Workspace

The collection of the drawing area, cursor, World coordinate system, viewcube, drawing display format, scroll bars, ribbon, pull down menus, command line, status bar, toolbars, and dockable windows is known as workspace. The ribbon panels, set of toolbars and menus used in 2D and 3D drawings are different. Hence, to increase the efficiency and productivity, a user can customize the workspace according to the project at hand.

2.15.1. Save a workspace

A workspace can be saved as follow.

- Press the down arrow (⯆) on *Workspace Switching* icon, Figure 2-45a, it is located on the lower right side of the workspace and click on the *Save Current As* option, Figure 2-45b, to open the *Save Workspace* dialog box, Figure 2-45c.

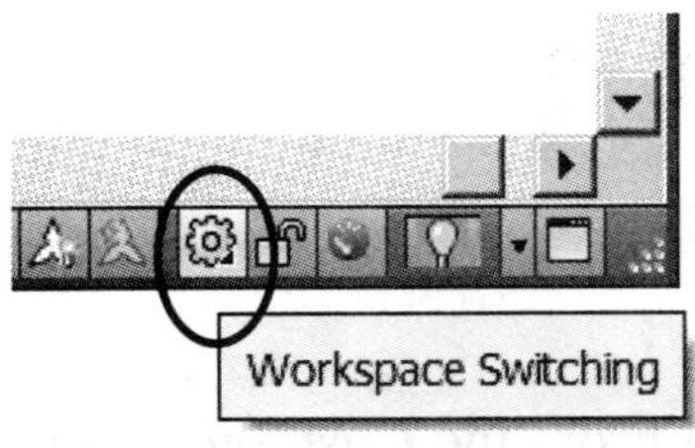

Figure 2-45a

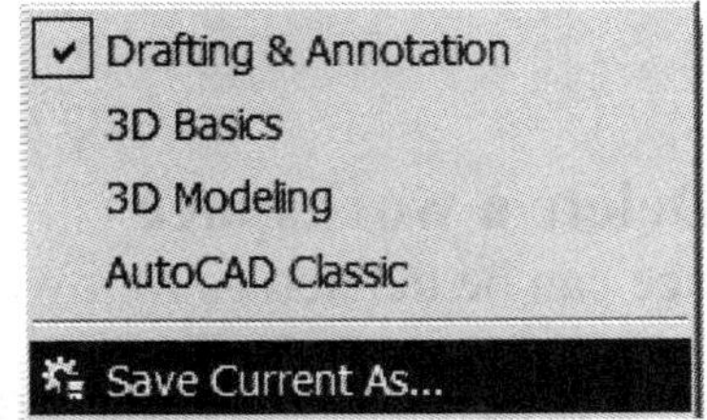

Figure 2-45b

- Specify the name for the workspace and press the *Save* button. The example workspace will be saved as *Sample*.

Figure 2-45c

- If a workspace exists with the specified name, then *AutoCAD* warning dialog box will appear, Figure 2-45d. Select *Replace* or *Cancel* as desired.

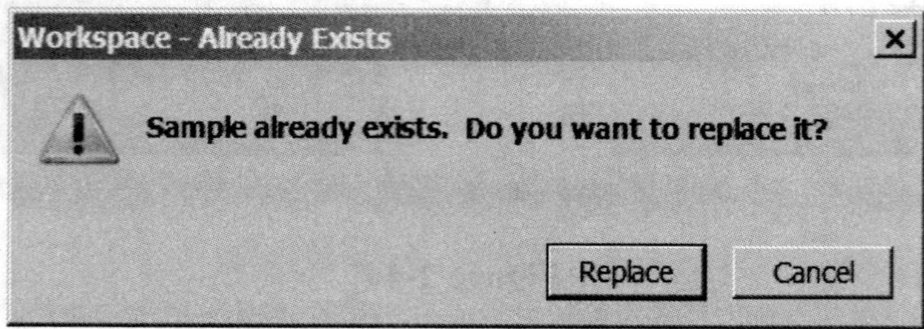

Figure 2-45d

- The new workspace will appear in the listing of the workspaces, Figure 2-45e.

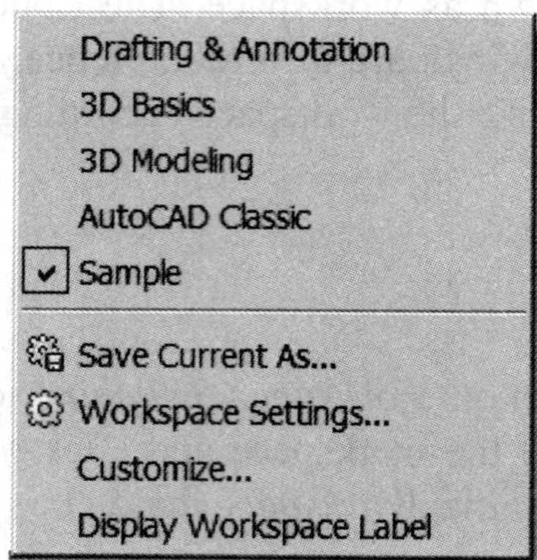

Figure 2-45e

2.15.2. Delete a workspace
A workspace can be deleted as follows.

- (i) From the tab bar, select the *Manage* tab. (ii) From the *Customization* panel click on the *User Interface* command, the *CUI* icon **CUI**. (iii) This will open the *Customize User Interface* dialog box.
- Click on the *Customize* tab of the *Customize User Interface* dialog box.
- Click on the workspace to be deleted, 'Sample' in our example, Figure 2-46a.
- Press the right button of the mouse, the option box shown in Figure 2-46a will appear on the screen.
- Select the *Delete* option.
- Press the *Enter* key or left or right button of the mouse.
- This will close the option box and open the *AutoCAD* error message box, Figure 2-46b.
- Click the *Yes* button, Figure 2-46b. This will close the *AutoCAD* error message box and activate the *Apply* button of the *Customize User Interface* dialog box.
- Click the *Apply* or *OK* button of the *Customize User Interface* dialog box.

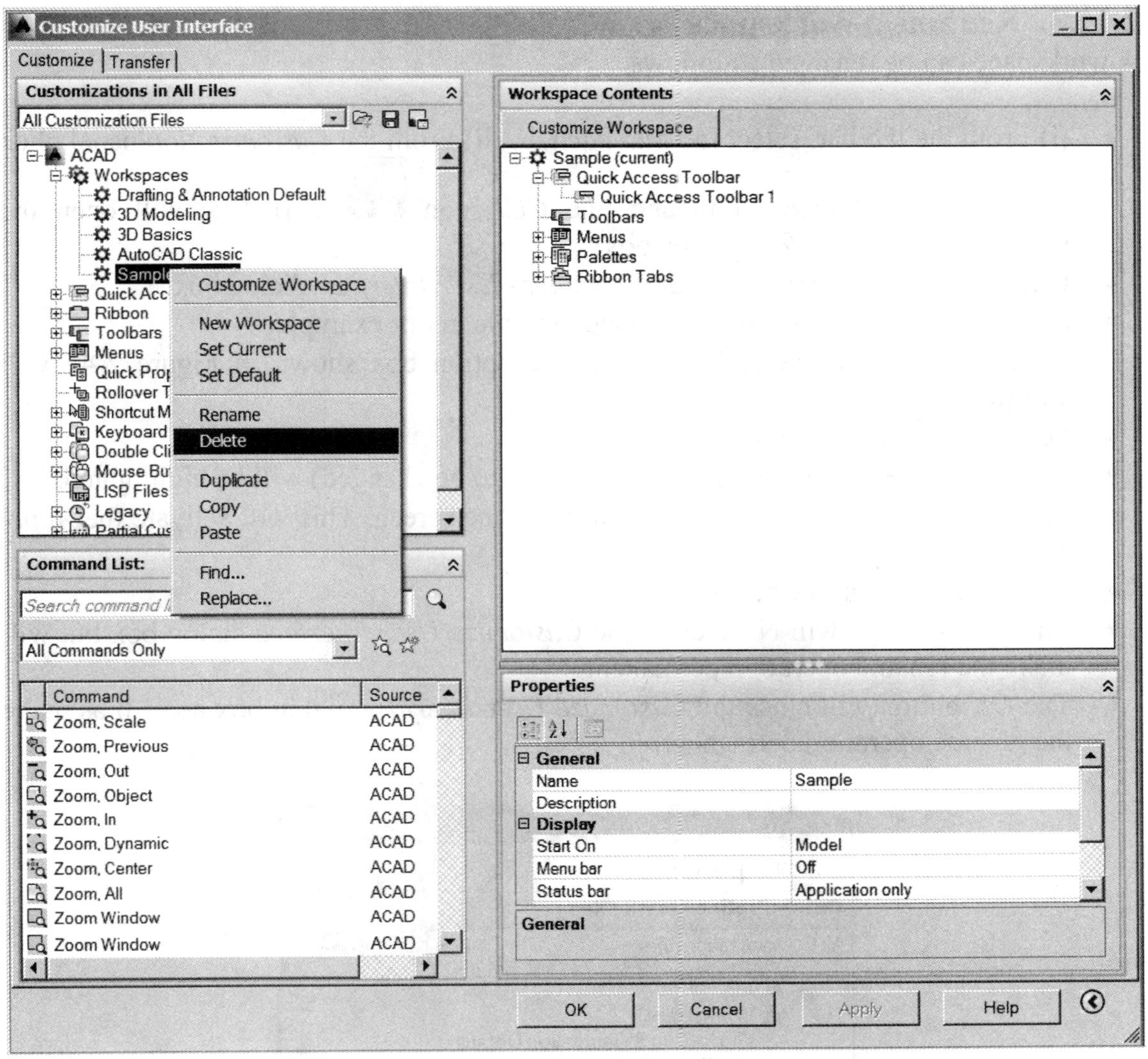

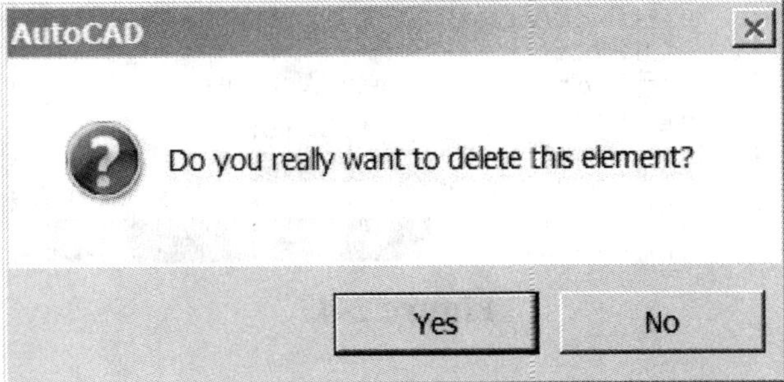

Figure 2-46a

Figure 2-46b

- The *Apply* button will NOT close the *Customize User Interface* dialog box but will make the delete operation permanent.
- The *OK* button will close the *Customize User Interface* dialog box as well as make the delete operation permanent.

2.15.3. Rename a workspace

A workspace can be renamed as follows.

- (i) From the tab bar, select the *Manage* tab. (ii) From the *Customization* panel click on the *User Interface* command, the *CUI* icon 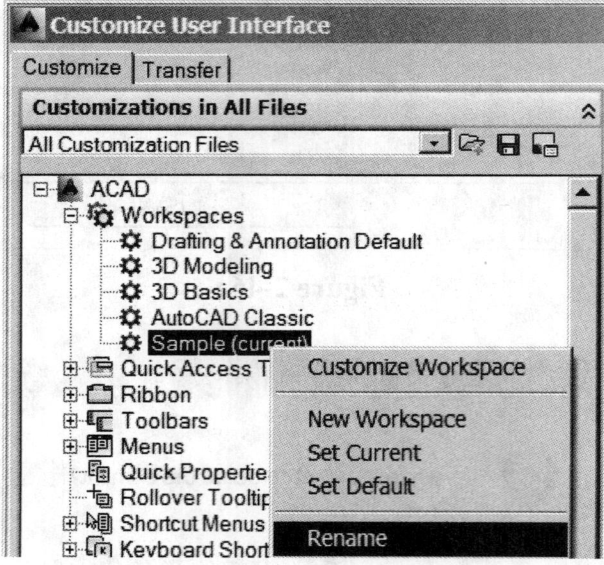. (iii) This will open the *Customize User Interface* dialog box.
- Click on the *Customize* tab of the *Customize User Interface* dialog box.
- Click on the workspace to be renamed, Sample in our example.
- Press the right button of the mouse, the option box shown in Figure 2-47 will appear on the screen.
- Select the *rename* option.
- This will close the option box and the name (to be changed) will be highlighted.
- Enter the new name and click anywhere on the screen. This will activate the *Apply* button.
- Click the *Apply* or *OK* button.
- The *Apply* button will NOT close the *Customize User Interface* dialog box but will make the rename operation permanent.
- The *OK* button will close the *Customize User Interface* dialog box as well as make the rename operation permanent.

Figure 2-47

2.15.4. Switch a workspace

A workspace can be switched as follows. In this example, the current workspace, *Drafting & Annotation*, will be switched to the '*Sample*' workspace.

- Press the down arrow (▾) on *Workspace Switching* icon, Figure 2-48a, it is located on the lower right side of the workspace and click on the desired workspace, '*Sample*', Figure 2-48b.

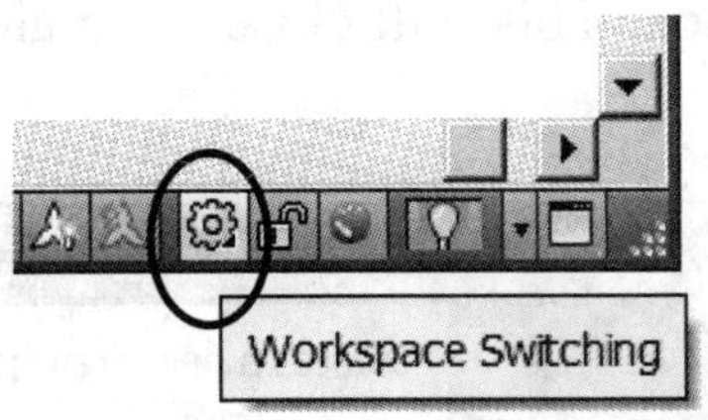

Figure 2-48a

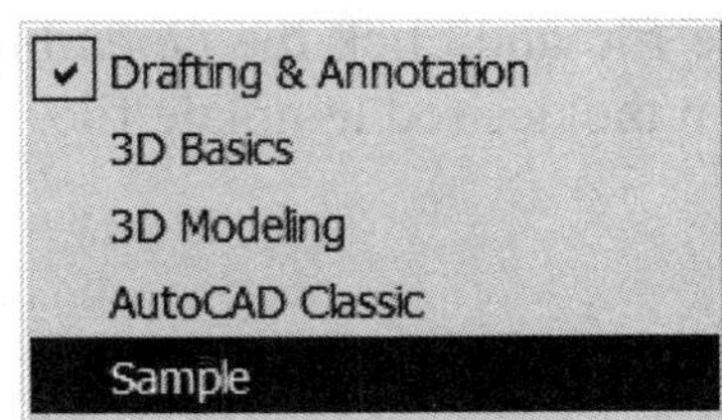

Figure 2-48b

2.16.   Basics of a drawing file

The basic features of any drawing are its name, input units format, drawing limits and grid and snap spacing. The user can select the default values when a new file is opened or reset as needed.

2.17.   New drawing

In AutoCAD, a new drawing can be opened using one of the following methods.

1. Menu method: Select the *Application* pull-down menu, Figure 2-49a, and select the *New* option, and finally select *Create a new drawing* option.

2. Toolbar method: Select the new drawing tool ( ), Figure 2-49b, in the quick access toolbar. It is located on the upper left corner of the dialog box.

3. Command line method: Type "new", "New", or "NEW" in the command line, Figure 2-49c, and press the *Enter* key.

4. From the interface: If at least one drawing open, then click on the "+" sign as shown in Figure 2-49d.

5. Key board method: Hold down the control "Ctrl" key and type "N".

Figure 2-49a

The various methods discussed above will open the *Select templat*e dialog box shown in Figure 2-50a and Figure 2-50b. Figure 2-50a shows the selection of "acad" template, giving the drawing imperial (inch) units and ANSI style dimensions. Figure 2-50b shows the "acadiso" template, giving the drawing metric (millimeters) units and ISO style dimensions. To open a particular template file based on the dimensions style, select the template file and click the *Open* button of the dialog box. This will close the dialog box and open the desired template file.

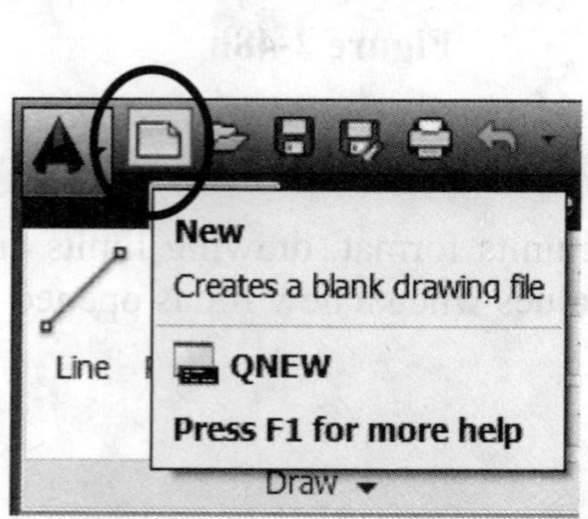

Figure 2-49b

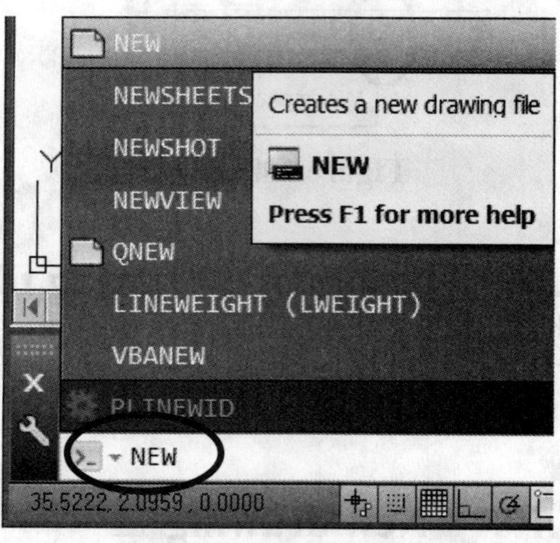

Figure 2-49c

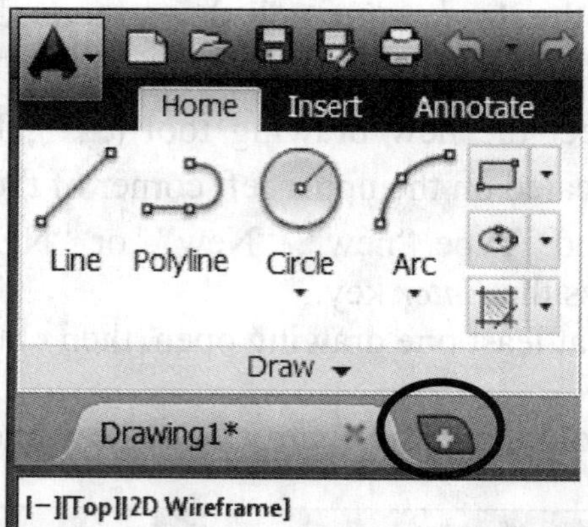

Figure 2-49d

The basic features of a drawing are its name, drawing units, drawing limits, and grid and snap size. The *name* represents the unique identification of the file. As the name suggests, *drawing units* is used to set the format of the sizes of the objects to create the drawing. The *drawing limit* is the metaphor for the size of the paper on which the drawing will be printed. The grid (a visible dotted or lined grid background) and snap (an invisible grid background) are used to improve the drawing process. These features are discussed in next few sections of this chapter.

Figure 2-50a shows the selection of "acad" template, giving the drawing imperial (inch) units and ANSI style dimensions. The drawing uses internal default values. In AutoCAD, a new drawing file is opened with the default values. For example, its name is Drawing1, Drawing2, etc.; its units are decimal; the drawing limits are 12 x 9 inches; and the default values for both the grid and snap are 0.5 inches.

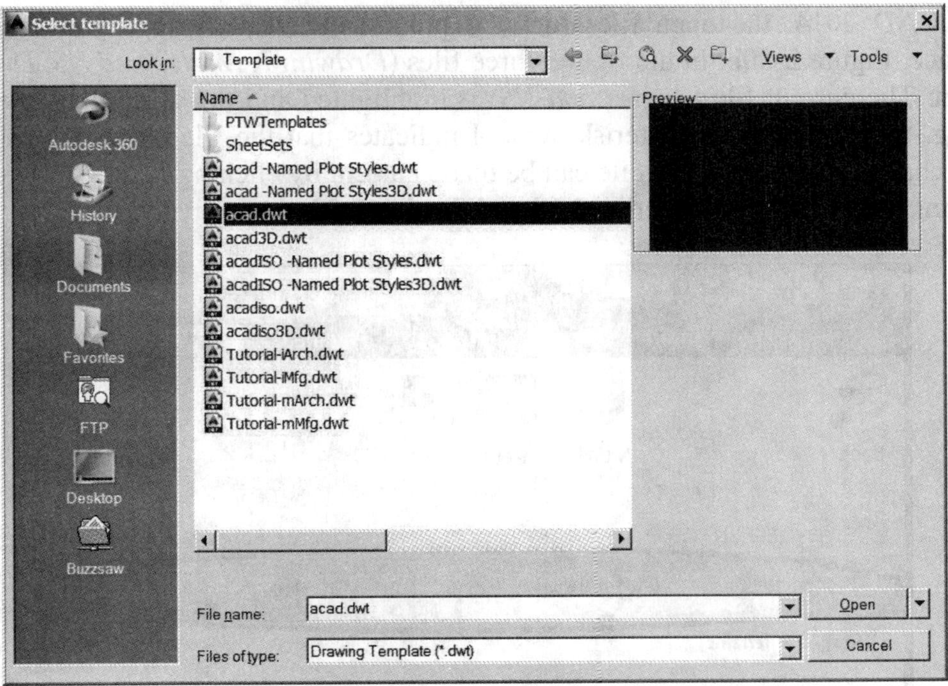

Figure 2-50a

Figure 2-50b shows the "acadiso" template, giving the drawing metric (millimeters) units and ISO style dimensions. The drawing uses internal default values. In AutoCAD, a new drawing file is opened with the default values. For example, its name is Drawing1, Drawing2, etc.; its units are decimal; the drawing limits are 420 x 290 millimeters; and the default values for both the grid and snap are 10 millimeters.

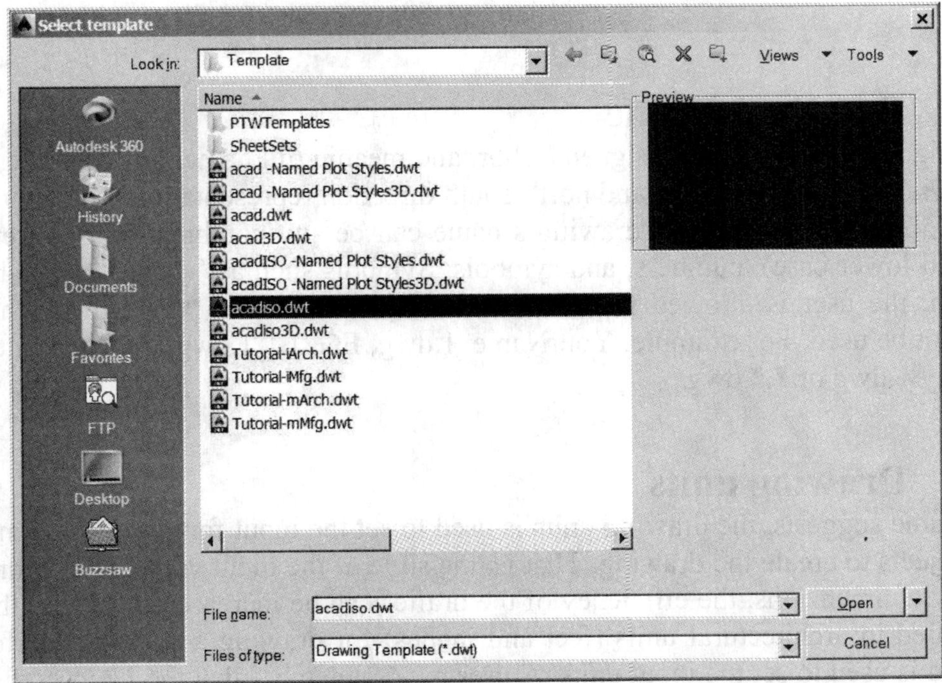

Figure 2-50b

In AutoCAD 2014, the open files (new or previously created) appear as tabs in the workspace, Figure 2-50b. In the figure, three files (*Drawing1, Angles and NS, Drawing2*) are open. The current file (*Angles and NS*) is highlighted and the other files (*Drawing1, Drawing2*) are grayed. The asterisk symbol indicates that the file contents are changes and the changes are not saved. File can be made current by clicking its tab. File renaming and saving are discussed in Section 2.18 and Section 2.22, respectively.

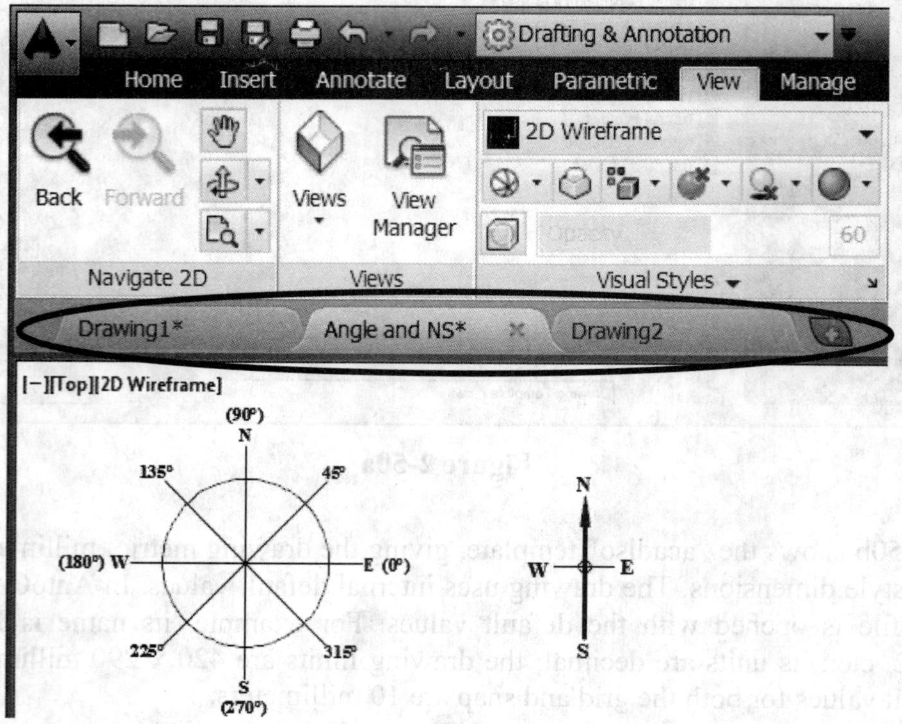

Figure 2-50c

2.18.   Drawing's name

A drawing should always be assigned a short and meaningful name. For example, the file *Angles and NS* contains angles and north-south direction representation. A drawing name can be 256 characters long. A drawing's name can be any combination of letters (both upper and lower case), numbers, and symbols. Symbols such as '-' and '_' can be used. Although, the user is allowed to use the characters $, %, and *, yet these characters should not be used. For example, YourName_1.dwg, EG210_1.dwg are legitimate names but not 1_%.dwg or *.*.dwg.

2.19.   Drawing units

As the name suggests, the drawing units is used to set the input format of the dimensions of the objects to create the drawing. That is, the style of the input values. For example, in ANSI style dimensions, the efficiency of the drafter can be increased if the lengths could be specified in architectural units (feet and inches) for drawing a floor plan. The *Units* command is used to set the input units. A user must remember that the *Units* command is used to set the input units; the type of the units ANSI or ISO is set when a new file was open as "acad" or "acadiso" template file, respectively.

1. Activate the *Units* command using command line method.
   a. Command line method: Type "units", "Units", or "UNITS" on the command line and press the *Enter* key.

The *Units* command will open the *Drawing Units* dialog box, shown in Figure 2-51. The dialog box allows for setting the type and precision of the linear and angular measurements through the *Length* and *Angle* panels.

By default, AutoCAD sets the length in decimal format with precision to four decimal places; so length appears in the form 0.0000. The angular unit precision is set to whole degrees, so an angle appears in the form 0. The dialog box also provides the capability to change the units of measurement for blocks and drawings that are inserted into the current drawing under *Insertion scale* panel.

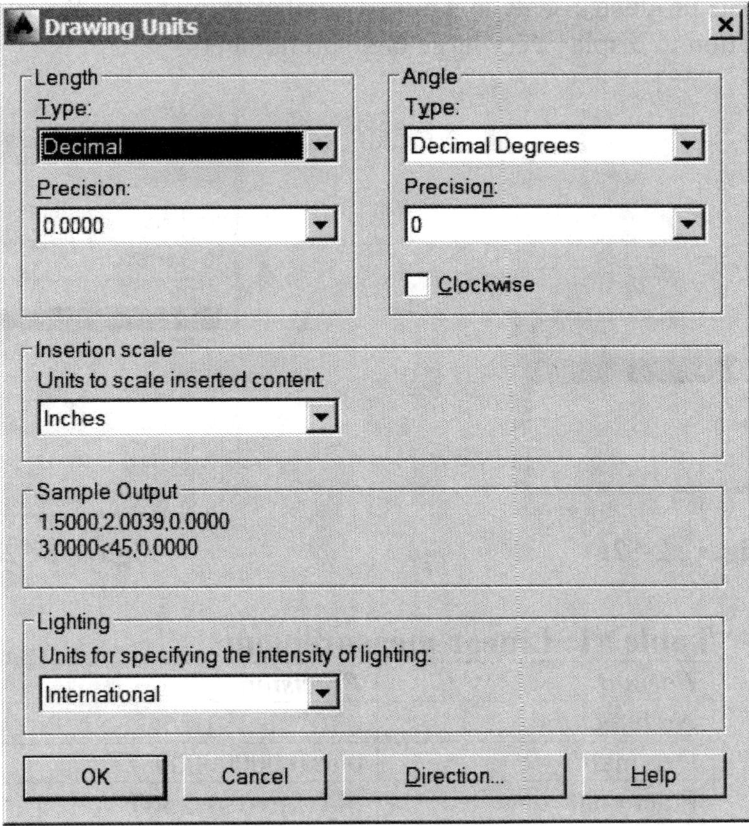

Figure 2-51

2.19.1. Length

The *Length* panel specifies the format and the precision for the linear measurement of the current drawing. The linear measurements can be in five different formats, Figure 2-52a. The various options for length units shown in Figures 2-52a can be visualized by clicking on the down arrow head (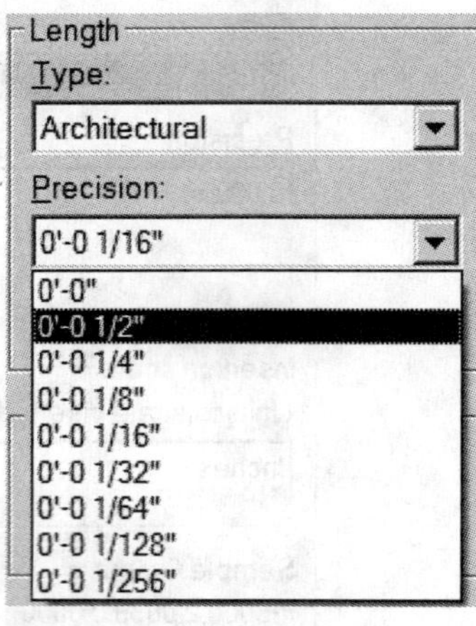) for *Type* window in the *Length* panel of the *Drawing Units* dialog box, Figures 2-51.

- To change the format, click on the desired format. This will update the format and close the dropdown list. The example figure shows the selection of *Architectural* units.
- To close the dropdown list without changing the format, either press the *Esc* key or click outside the length panel.
- Similarly, the precision can be modified, Figures 2-52b. The example figure shows the precision for the *Architectural* units.

Each of the linear measurement's formats can be specified to nine degrees of precision, Table #1. The *Engineering* and *Architectural* formats produce feet-and-inches displays, and assume that each drawing unit represents one inch. The other three can be used for both the SI and ANSI systems to represent any real-world units. The *Decimal* formats produce a scale broken down into 10's. This is the default unit system in AutoCAD. The *Fractional* formats produce a scale in a mixed number format. The *Scientific* formats uses exponential notation to display very large or small numbers.

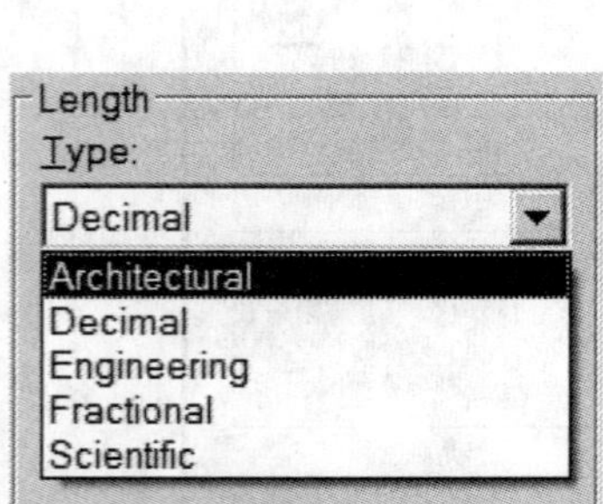

Figure 2-52a

Figure 2-52b

Table #1: Linear measurements

Format	Precision
Architectural	$0'-0''$ to $0'-1/256''$
Decimal	0 to 0.00000000
Fractional	$0'-0''$ to $0'-1/256''$
Engineering	$0'-0''$ to $0'-0.00000000''$
Scientific	0E+01 to 0.00000000E+01

2.19.2. Angle

The *Angle* panel specifies the format and the precision for the current angular measurement of the current drawing. The angular measurement can be in five different formats, Figure 2-53a. The various options for an angle shown in Figure 2-53a, can be visualized by clicking on the down arrow head (⏷) for *Type* window in the *Angle* panel of the *Drawing Units* dialog box, Figures 2-51.

- To change the angle format, click on the desired format. This will update the format and close the dropdown list. Figure 2-53a shows the selection of the *Decimal Degree*.
- To close the dropdown list without changing the format, either press the *Esc* key or click outside the *Angle* panel.
- Similarly, the precision can be modified, Figures 2-53b. The figure shows the shows the precision for the *Decimal Degree*.

Each of the angular measurement can be specified to seven degrees of precision, Table #2. **Remember** the conversion! 400 grads are equal to 360 degrees and 2 Pi radians are equal to 360 degrees (2 π = 360° = 400 grad).

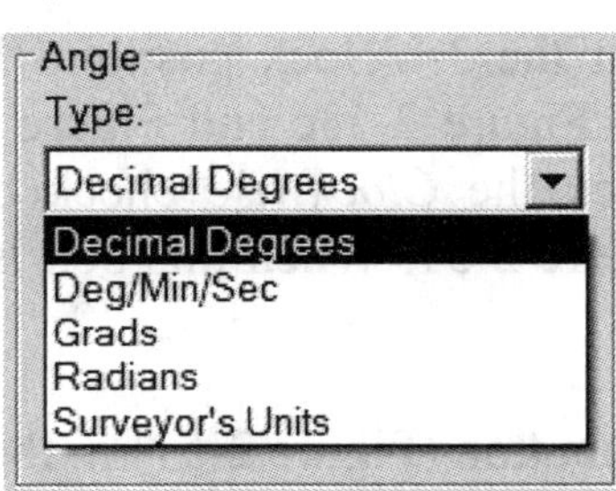
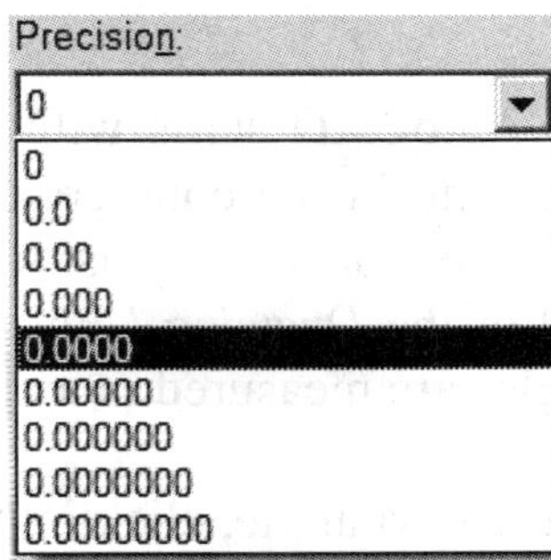

Figure 2-53a   **Figure 2-53b**

Each of the angular measurement can be specified to seven degrees of precision, Table #2. **Remember** the conversion! 400 grads are equal to 360 degrees and 2 Pi radians are equal to 360 degrees (2 π = 360° = 400 grad).

Table #2: Angular measurements

Format	*Precision*
Decimal degree	0 to 0.00000000
Deg/Min/Sec	0d to 0d00′00.0000″
Grads	0g to 0.00000000g
Radian	0r to 0.00000000r
Surveyor's Units	N 0d E to N 0d00′00.0000″ E

- An angle appears as a decimal number in the *Decimal* format.
- The *Deg/Min/Sec* format is represented with suffixes "d", "'", and "''" for degrees, minutes, and seconds, respectively.
- A lowercase "g" suffix is used for the *Grads* formats.
- A lowercase "r" suffix is used for the *Radians* formats.

- The *Surveyor's Units* show angles as bearings (angle always less than 90 degrees) measured from north or south towards east or west, Figures 2-53c. This representation has three parts: (i) N or S for north or south, (ii) angle's numerical value in degrees/minutes/seconds for how far from east or west, and (iii) E or W for east or west, for example N 35° 24′ 19″ W. If the angle is precisely north, south, east, or west, then only the single letter representing the compass point is displayed.

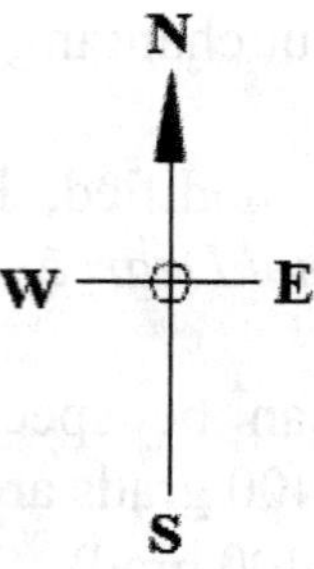

Figure 2-53c

By default, AutoCAD starts with the zero angles at the 3 o'clock position (East) with angles increasing in the counterclockwise direction, Figure 2-53c and Figure 2-53d. To change the direction of angular measurement, check the *Clockwise* check box in the *Angle* panel of the *Drawing Units* dialogue box, Figure 2-51. When this box is checked, positive angles are measured in a clockwise direction.

To change the start angle, click on the "Direction…" button (Figure 2-51) in the *Drawing Units* dialogue box. The *Direction Control* dialogue box appears. The user can set the *Base Angle* to any one of the four major directions by clicking on the appropriate radio button or can set it to a specific angle with the "Other" option, Figures 2-53e. The user can enter a specific angle into the edit box. To change the directions of angular measurement (to E, N, S, or W) simply click on the appropriate radio button.

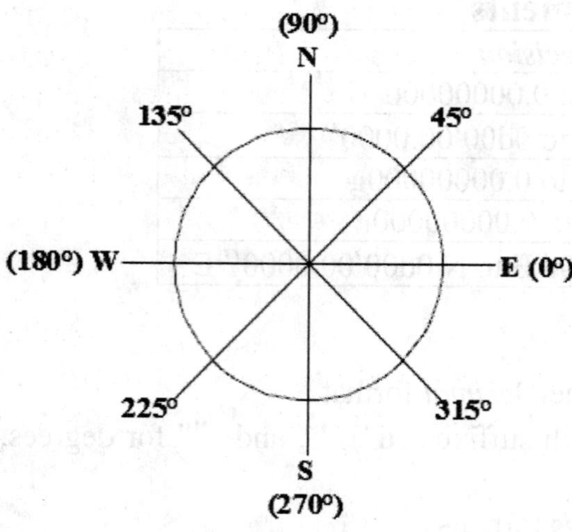

Figure 2-53d

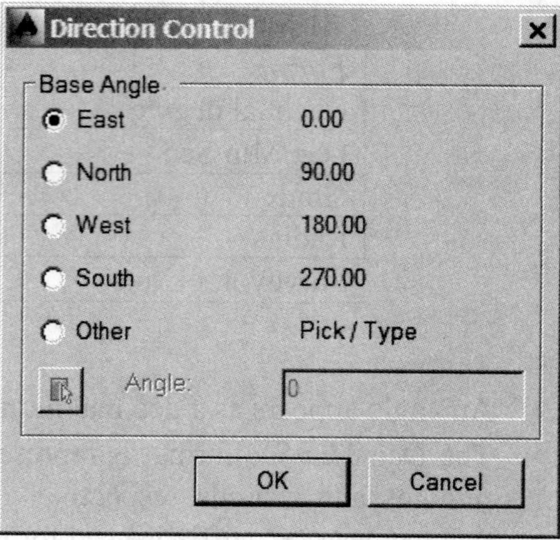

Figure 2-53e

2.19.3. Insertion scale

The insertion scale is the ratio of the units used in the source drawing and the units used in the target drawing. That is, it controls the units of measurement for a drawing (source) that is inserted into the current drawing (target). If no scaling is desired then choose the *Unitless* option, Figure 2-54. The various options for insertion scale shown in Figure 2-54 can be visualized by clicking on the down arrow head ( ) in the *Insertion scale* panel of the *Drawing Units* dialog box, Figures 2-51.

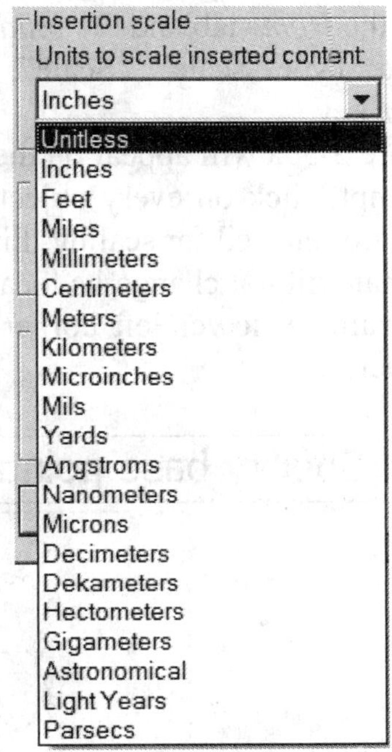

Figure 2-54

2.19.4. Convert measurements from ISO to ANSI (and vice versa)

Every object in AutoCAD is measured in the drawing units. Before starting the drawing, the user must decide on the type and format of the input unit. The input type can be ANSI (inches, feet, miles, etc.) or ISO (milli-, centi-, kilo-, meters, etc.); and the input format can be decimal, architectural, engineering, fractional, and scientific. Based on the type, a user should open the correct type of template file (acad for ANSI or acadiso for ISO). However, if a user opens an incorrect file type and realizes the mistake after drawing a part (or complete) drawing, then the user can fix the mistake using *Copy* and *Scale* command. The *Copy* and *Scale* commands are discussed in Chapter #4.

If a drawing is started in one system of measurement (ANSI or ISO), then it can be switched to the other system by scaling the model geometry with the appropriate scaling factor. For example, if a drawing is created in centimeters and needs to be converted to inches, then scale the model geometry by a factor of 0.3937 (1 cm = 1/2.54 inch). To convert from inches to centimeters, the scale factor of 1/0.3937 or 2.54 must be used (1 inch = 2.54 cm).

Convert a drawing from centimeters to inches
1. Select every object from the source file (hold the *Ctrl* key and press the '*A*' key).
2. Copy the content of the source drawing, (hold the *Ctrl* key and press the '*C*' key).
3. Open a new acad file (target file).
4. Click in the drawing area of the target file.
5. Paste the contents in the target drawing, (hold the *Ctrl* key and press the '*V*' key).
6. Now, scale the target drawing.
7. Activate the *Scale* (⬚) command using one of the following techniques
    a. Ribbon method: From the *Home* tab and the *Modify* panel select the *Scale* tool.
    b. Command line method: Type "scale", "Scale", or "SCALE" in the command line and press the *Enter* key.
8. The prompt shown in Figure 2-55a will appear on the screen.
9. At the *Select Objects* prompt, click on every object and then press the *Enter* key. All objects in the drawing are selected for scaling, Figure 2-55b.
10. A base point is the point that will not change its location after the completion of the scaling process. In this example, lower left corner is selected as the base point. Click at the lower left corner.

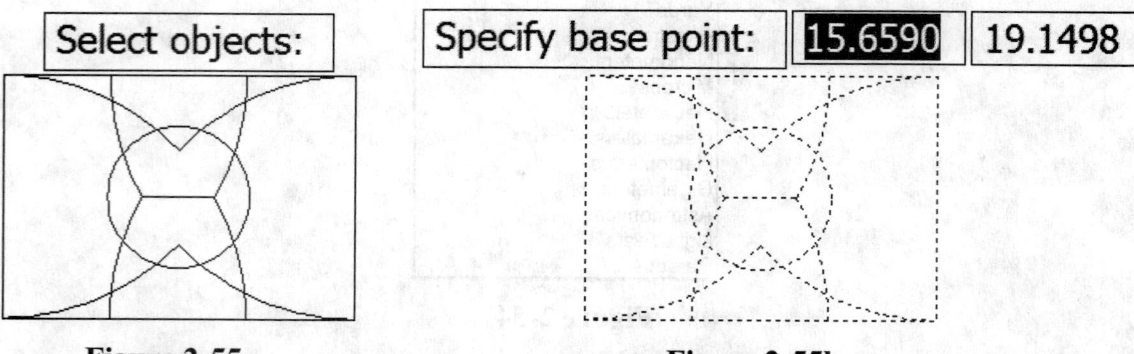

Figure 2-55a   Figure 2-55b

11. Enter a scale factor of 0.3937, Figure 2-55c, (1 inch = 2.54 cm or 1/2.54 = 0.3937).
12. All the objects in the drawing are now 2.54 times smaller, corresponding to the equivalent distance in inches, Figure 2-55d.
13. Scaling will be relative to the world coordinate system origin and the location of the drawing origin will remain at the WCS origin.

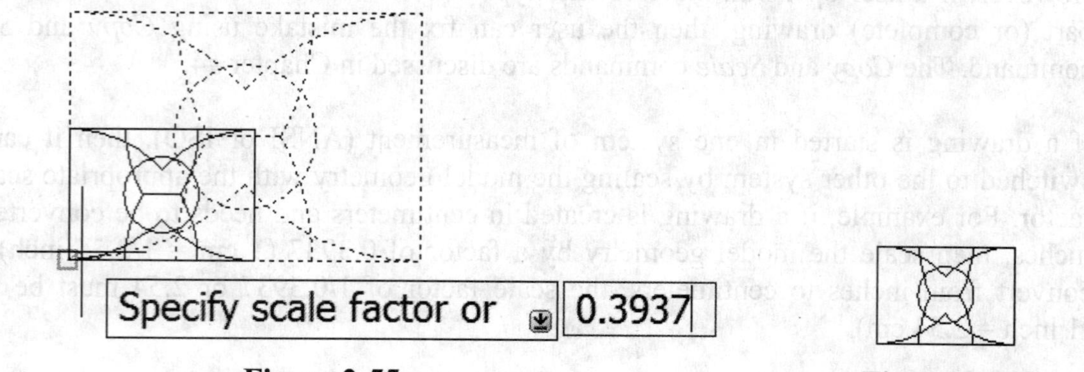

Figure 2-55c   Figure 2-55d

2.20.   Drawing limits

Generally, the *drawing limits* is the metaphor for the size of the paper on which the drawing will be printed. It is used to set the boundaries of the drawing or grid display in the current *Model* or *Layout* tab. Generally, limits are set to match the size of the paper (on which the drawing will be printed). Figure 2-56a shows the standard size drawing papers for the engineering and architectural applications. The default drawing limits are 12 x 9 inches in ANSI system and 420 x 290 millimeters in the ISO system.

Standard Drawing Sheet Sizes – Millimeters
A4 = 210 * 297
A3 = 297 * 420
A2 = 420 * 594
A1 = 594 * 841
A0 = 841 * 1189

Standard Drawing Sheet Sizes – Inches
A = 8.5 * 11.0
B = 11.0 * 17.0
C = 17.0 * 22.0
D = 22.0 * 34.0
E = 34.0 * 44.0

Figure 2-56a

The following section gives step by step instruction for setting the drawing limits.
1. Activate the *Drawing Limits* command using command line method.
   a. Command line method: Type "limits", "Limits", or "LIMITS" in the command line and press the *Enter* key.
2. This will display the prompt for the lower left corner shown in Figure 2-56b. The user can select any value for the lower limits. However, the *Limits* specification process can be simplified if the origin of the WCS is selected as the lower limits.
3. Press the down arrow on the keyboard to reveal the various options. The *ON* option will restrict entering points outside the drawing limits. However, portions of objects such as circles can extend outside the drawing limits because limits check only test points that are entered. The default is *Off* (no limits checking).
4. Press the up arrow on the keyboard to hide the various options.

5. Specify the coordinates of the lower left corner using one of the following methods. This example use (0, 0) for the lower left corner. (i) Type '0' at the prompt, press the 'TAB' key on the keyboard, the cursor will move to the second cell, type '0' and press the *Enter* key. Dynamic input is discussed in detail in Chapter #3. (ii) Specify the x,y (no space) coordinates in the command line and press the *Enter* key. (iii) Clicking with the left button of the mouse at the desired location.

6. The prompt for the upper right corner will appear, Figure 2-56c. Select the coordinates for this point in a manner similar to the lower left corner.
7. To choose the default values (for either of the lower left and upper right corners) just press the *Enter* key on the keyboard.

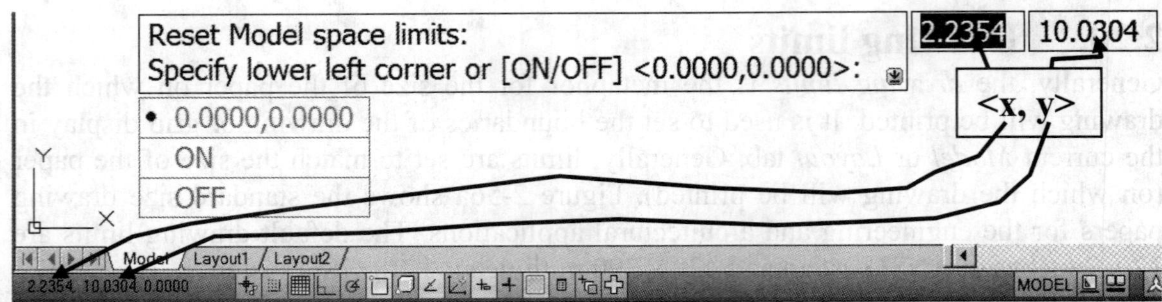

Figure 2-56b

Figure 2-56c

2.21.   Grid (▦) and Snap (▦) commands

The *Grid* command is used to display a visible grid (similar to graph or engineering paper) background on the drawing screen. The *Snap* command is used to set an invisible grid background on the drawing screen and to limit the movement of the cursor to the snap grid's points only. The *Grid* and *Snap* commands icons are located on the status bar in the lower left end of the interface, Figure 2-57. The snap grid is completely independent of the visible grid. However, the grid spacing and snap spacing are usually set to the same value to avoid confusion. The default *Grid* and *Snap* setting for an acad template is 0.50 inch and for an acadiso template is 10 millimeters.

By default the grid appear both in the drawing area of the model space and in the layouts. However, the user can set the grid and snap properties independently in the model space and layouts. Also, every layout can be set to its own style.

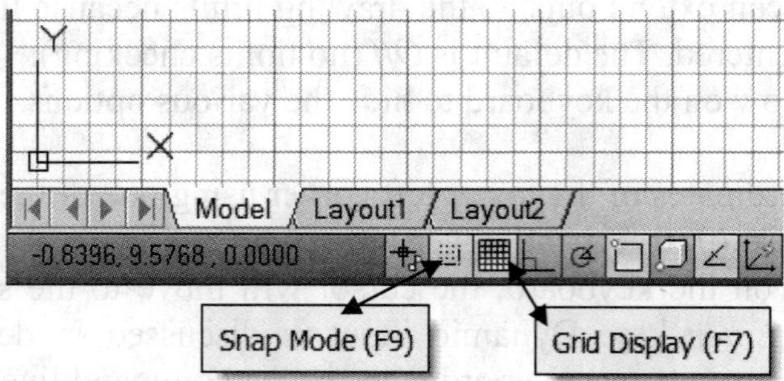

Figure 2-57

2.21.1. Toggle the Grid and Snap in the model space

A user can toggle the *Grid* and *Snap* options in the model space using one of the techniques listed below.

- Click the *Grid* and/or *Snap* buttons on the status bar (Figure 2-57), respectively.
- Press *F7* (for the *Grid*) and *F9* (for the *Snap*) keys of the keyboard, respectively.

- Bring the cursor on the *Grid* button on the status bar and click with the right button of the mouse, causing the option box shown in Figure 2-58a to appear; if the grid was in *Off* mode then the *Enabled* option will not be checked. To turn *On* the grid, bring the cursor on the *Enabled* option and press the left or right button of the mouse or the *Enter* key. The grid will appear in the model space.
- Bring the cursor on the *Snap* button on the status bar and click with the right button of the mouse, causing the option box shown in Figure 2-58b to appear; if the snap was *On* then the *Off* option will be available and vice versa. If the *PolarSnap* (or *GridSnap*) was *Off* then its option will be available. To turn *On* the desired snap, bring the cursor on the desired option and press the left or right button of the mouse or the *Enter* key. In the current example *Grid Snap On* option is selected.

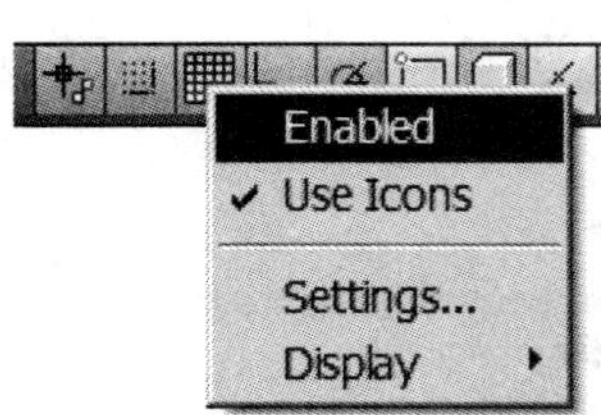

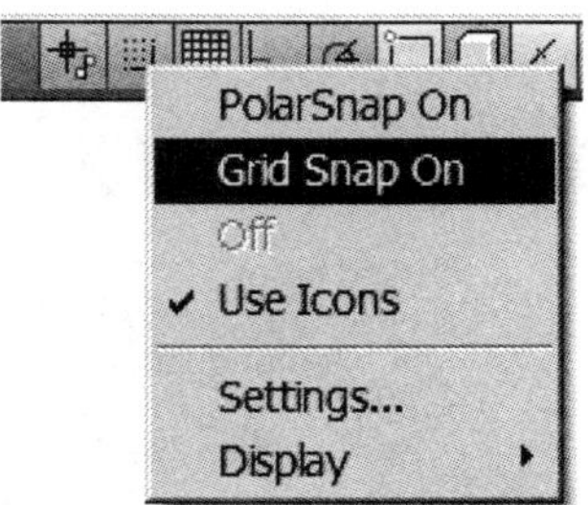

Figure 2-58a   **Figure 2-58b**

- A user can toggle the *Grid* and *Snap* options using the *Drafting Setting* dialog box, Figure 2-58c, using the following methods.

    o Bring the cursor on the *Grid* button on the status bar and click with the right button of the mouse, this will open the option box shown in Figure 2-58a. Click on the *Setting* option. This will open the *Drafting Setting* dialog box. Click the *Snap and Grid* tab. Check the boxes to the left of *Snap On and Grid On.*
    o Bring the cursor on the *Snap* button on the status bar and click with the right button of the mouse, this will open the option box shown in Figure 2-58b. Click on the *Setting* option. This will open the *Drafting Setting* dialog box. Click the *Snap and Grid* tab. Check the boxes to the left of *Snap On and Grid On.*

2.21.2. Toggle the Grid and Snap in the layout

In order to toggle the *Grid* and *Snap* in a layout, first double click in the viewport (the solid rectangle), this will make the solid rectangle bold and the WCS will appear in the viewport. Now toggle the grid and snap following the options discussed for the model space.

2.21.3. Grid properties

The grid properties can be set using the *Drafting Setting* dialog box, Figure 2-58c. Open the *Drafting Setting* dialog box as discussed in the last bullet of section 2.21.1 and click the *Snap and Grid* tab. If the *Grid On* box is checked, then the grid line covers the drawing area.

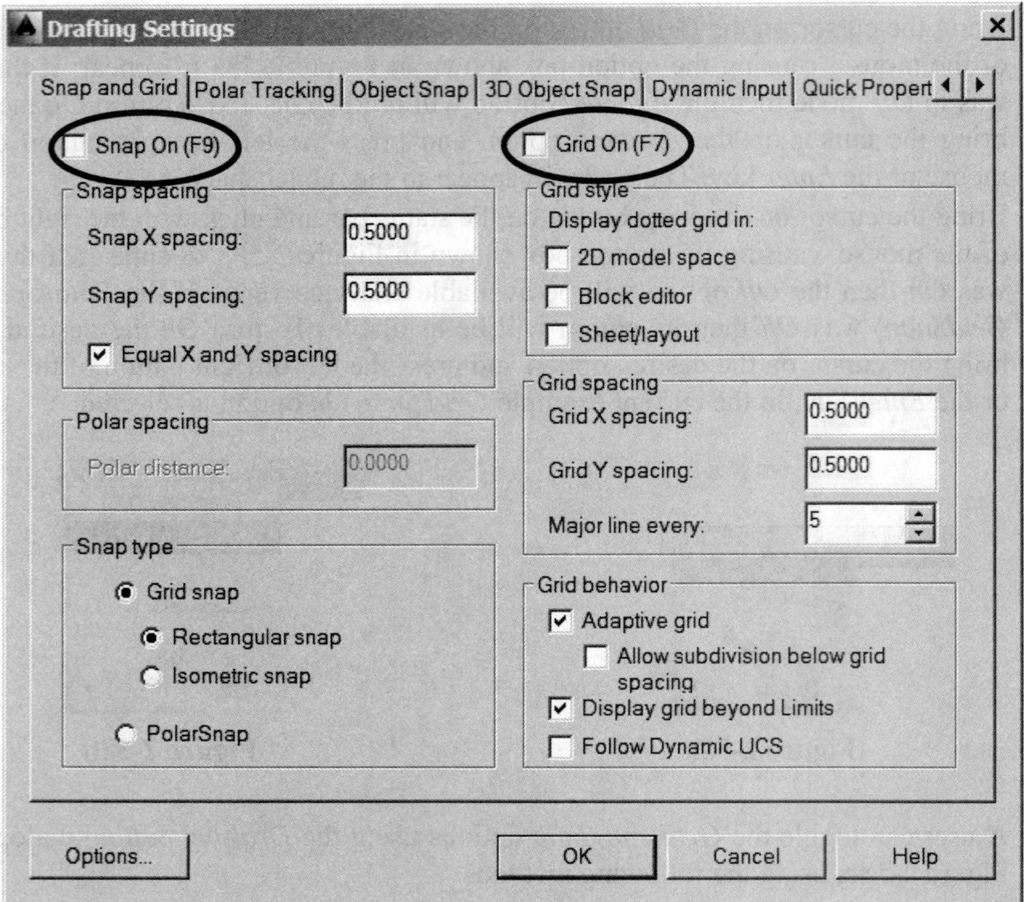

Figure 2-58c

2.21.3.1. Grid style

The user can convert the solid grid lines, Figure 2-59a, into the dotted line. In the *Drafting Setting* dialog box, Figure 2-58c, under the *Grid style* panel, the top panel on the left side of the dialog box; check the box beside the *2D model space*; then the grid in the model space will change its appearance as shown in Figure 2-59b. However, the grid in the layout will not be affected.

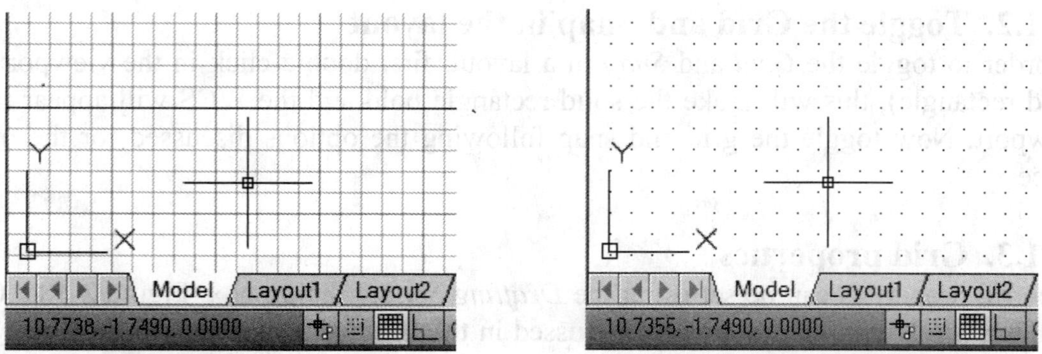

Figure 2-59a   **Figure 2-59b**

2.21.3.2.   Grid spacing

In the *Drafting Setting* dialog box, Figure 2-58c, the *Grid spacing* panel controls the spacing between the grid lines. It is the middle panel on the left side of the dialog box.

- *Grid X-* and *Grid Y-Spacing*: The *Grid X-* and *Grid Y-Spacing* specifies the grid spacing in the X- and Y-direction, respectively. If the value is 0, then the grid assumes the value set for the Snap X- and Snap Y-spacing, respectively. **Important point**: To enhance the drawing speed, choose the grid spacing such that it is multiple of the minimum dimension. For example in Figure 2-60a the X- and Y-spacing should be 0.5.

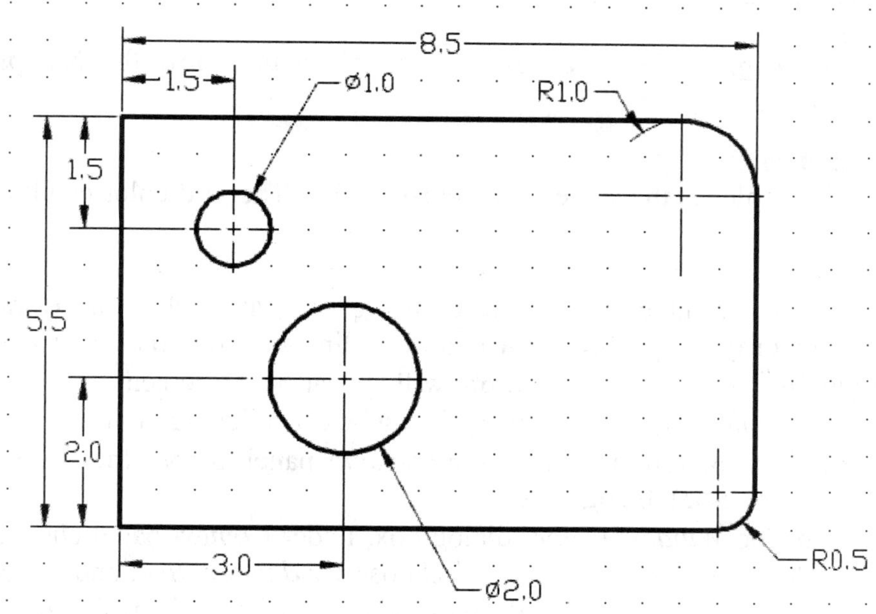

Figure 2-60a

- <u>Major Line Every</u>: This option is used to specify the frequency of major grid lines compared to minor grid lines. If the grid is displayed as lines then the bold lines are called major grid lines, and the lighter lines are called minor lines. In Figure 2-60b, the frequency is set to 5. When working in decimal units, major grid lines are especially useful for measuring distances quickly. In order to turn *Off* the display of major grid lines, set the frequency of the major grid lines to 1.

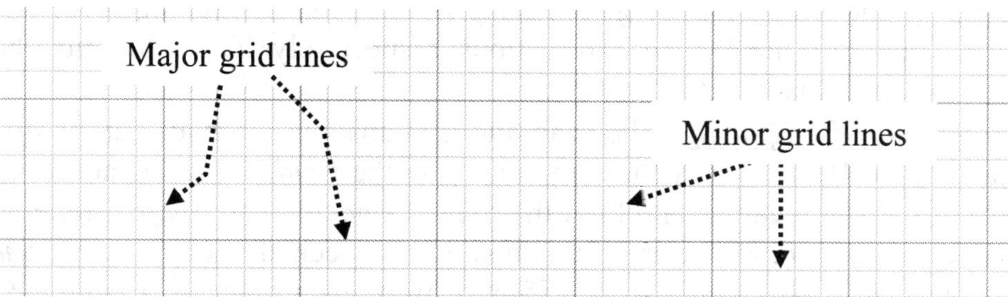

Figure 2-60b

2.21.3.3. Grid behavior

In the *Drafting Setting* dialog box, Figure 2-58c, the *Grid behavior* panel controls the appearance of the grid lines. It is the bottom panel on the left side of the dialog box. In case of the dotted grid, the grid dots are displayed only for the major grid lines.

- <u>Adaptive grid</u>: If the *Adaptive Grid* box is checked, then the density of the grid lines is updated when zooming options are used.
- *Allow subdivision below grid spacing*: This option generates additional, grid lines when zoomed in. The frequency of these additional lines is determined by the frequency of the major grid lines.
- <u>Display grid beyond limits</u>: Displays the grid beyond the area specified by the drawing limits.
- <u>Follow Dynamic UCS</u>: Changes the grid plane to follow the XY plane of the dynamic UCS.

2.21.3.4. Grid color

The dotted grid's color is the same as the cursor color. The grid color can be changed as follows:

- Click with the right button in the *Drawing area* and select the *Options* option, Figure 2-6a or type *Options* on the command line and press the *Enter* key.
- The *Options* dialog box (Figure 2-6b) will appear on the screen.
- Select the *Display* tab of the *Options* dialog box by clicking on it.
- Press the *Color* button in the *Window Elements* panel to open the *Drawing Window Colors* (Figure 2-6c) dialog box.
- In the *Drawing Window Colors* dialog box, under *Context* panel choose *2D model space*, under *Interface element* panel choose *Grid major line*, and under the *Color* options panel select the desired color. The selection will be highlighted. In the *Preview* window, the color of the grid will change to the selected color.
- Similarly, change the colors of the *Grid minor line* and *Grid axes line*.

2.21.4. Snap properties

2.21.4.1. Snap spacing

In the *Drafting Setting* dialog box, Figure 2-58c, the *Snap spacing* panel controls the spacing of the invisible, rectangular snap's grid.

- *Snap X-* and *Snap Y-Spacing*: The *Snap X-* and *Snap Y-Spacing* specify the invisible grid spacing in the X- and Y-directions, respectively. The value must be a positive real number (that is 0.5, 1.0, etc.).
- *Equal X-and Y-Spacing*: The snap and grid spacing intervals can be different from each other. If this box is checked, then both the *Grid X-spacing* and *Grid Y-spacing* are of the same values and both the *Snap X-spacing* and *Snap Y-spacing* are of the same values, too. However, if this box is not checked, then *Snap X-*, *Snap Y-*, *Grid X-*, and *Grid Y-spacing* can be different from each other. In Figure 2-61, the *Grid* and *Snap's X-* and *Y-spacing* are all different.

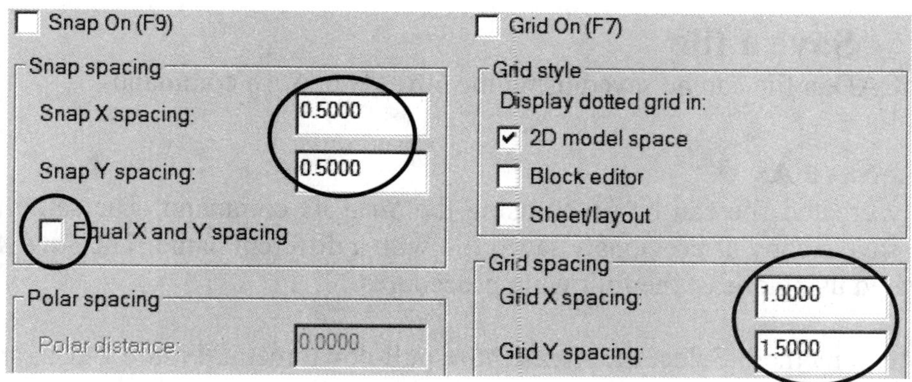

Figure 2-61

2.21.4.2.   Polar spacing

In the *Drafting Setting* dialog box, Figure 2-58c, the *Polar spacing* panel controls the polar snap's increment distance.

- *Polar Distance*: Sets the snap increment distance when *PolarSnap* is selected under the *Snap Type*. If this value is 0, then the *PolarSnap* distance assumes the value for the *Snap X spacing*.

2.21.4.3.   Snap type

In the *Drafting Setting* dialog box, Figure 2-58c, the *Snap type* panel controls the type of the snap.

- <u>Grid snap</u>: This option sets the snap type to the *Grid*. In this case, the cursor snaps along vertical or horizontal grid points. This type is further subdivided into two groups.
    - o <u>Rectangular snap</u>: This radio button sets the snap style to a rectangular snap mode. Now, the cursor will snap to the rectangular snap grid, Figure 2-62a.
    - o <u>Isometric snap</u>: This radio button sets the snap style to the isometric snap mode. Now, the cursor snaps to an isometric snap grid, Figure 2-62b.
- *PolarSnap*: Sets the snap type to *Polar*. When *Snap* mode is *On* and the user specify points with polar tracking turned *On*, the cursor snaps along polar alignment angles set on the *Polar Tracking* tab relative to the starting polar tracking point.

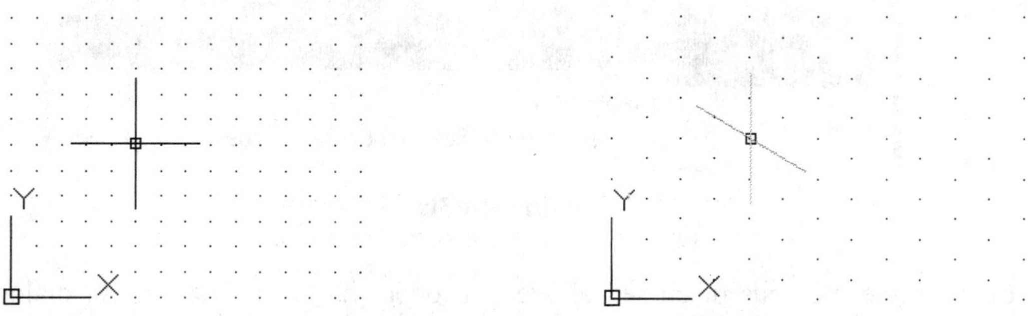

Figure 2-62a   **Figure 2-62b**

2.22.   Save a file

In AutoCAD, a file can be saved using the *Save As* or *Save* command.

2.22.1. Save As

A newly created file can be saved using the *Save As* command. The same technique is used to save a copy of previously saved file with a different name. The *Save As* command is activated using one of the following procedures.

1. Menu method: Select the *Application* pull-down menu, Figure 2-63a, and select the *Save As* option.

2. Toolbar method: Select the save as drawing tool ( ), Figure 2-63b, in the quick access toolbar. It is located on the upper left corner of the dialog box.

3. Command line method: Type "Saveas", "SaveAs", or "SAVEAS" in the command line and press the *Enter* key.

4. Key board method: Hold down the control "Ctrl" key and type "s".

Figure 2-63a

Figure 2-63b

Any of the three methods discussed above will open the *Save Drawing As* dialog box shown in Figure 2-63c. The dialog box shows the default name, *Drawing1*.

To save a file, specify the name in the *File Name* box using the naming convention discussed earlier and press the *Save* button. The AutoCAD files will automatically be saved with the extension 'dwg'. For example, if the user specifies the name Ex_2_1, it will be saved as Ex_2_1.dwg.

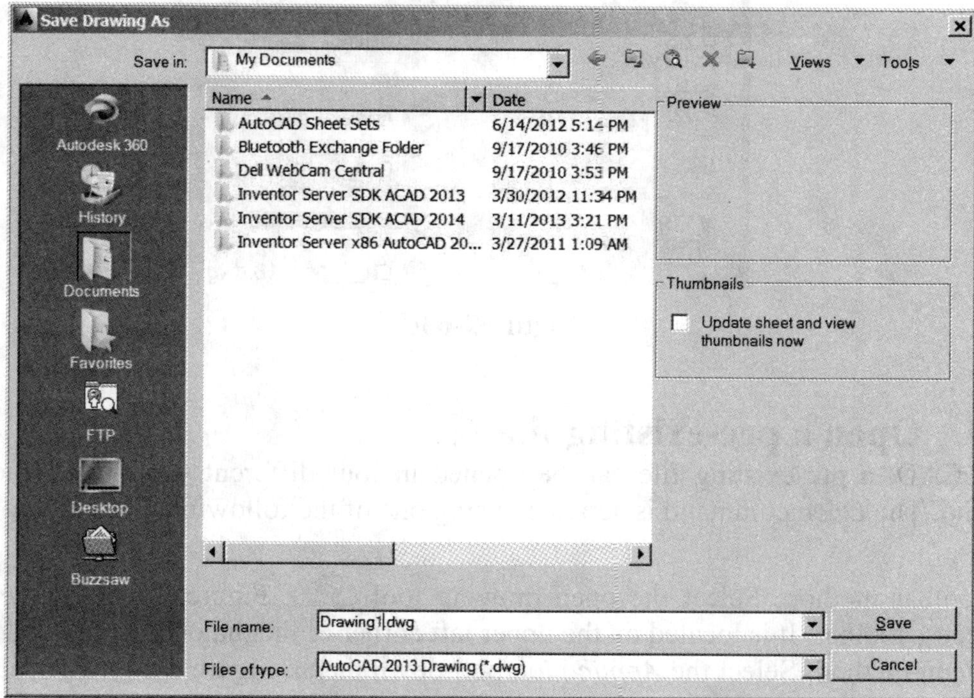

Figure 2-63c

2.22.2. Save 

The *Save* command is also called a quick save. It is mainly used to save previously saved files with the same name. The *Save* command is activated using one of the following procedures.

1. Toolbar method: Select the save as drawing tool ( ), Figure 2-63d, in the quick access toolbar. It is located on the upper left corner of the dialog box.
2. Menu method: Select the *Application* pull-down menu, Figure 2-63e, and select the *Save* option.
3. Command line method: Type "Save", "Save", or "SAVE" in the command line and press the *Enter* key.
4. Key board method: Hold down the control "Ctrl" key and type "s".

Figure 2-63d

Figure 2-63e

2.23.   Open a pre-existing file

In AutoCAD, a pre-existing file can be opened in four different ways using the open command. The *Open* command is activated using one of the following methods.

1. Toolbar method: Select the open drawing tool ( ), Figure 2-64a, in the quick access toolbar. It is located on the upper left corner of the dialog box.
2. Menu method: Select the *Application* pull-down menu, Figure 2-64b, and select the *Open* option.
3. Command line method: Type "open", "Open", or "OPEN" in the command line and press the *Enter* key.
4. Key board method: Hold down the control "Ctrl" key and type 'o' or 'O'

Any of the four methods discussed above will open the *Select File* dialog box shown in Figure 2-64c. The dialog box will list all of the drawing files in the folder. If the *Thumbnail* option under the *View* menu is selected, then thumbnails are displayed. If the *Preview* option under the *View* menu is selected then a bitmap of the selected file is displayed in the *Preview* window. The *Preview* window is blank if none of the files are selected. The preview option is the default method and is shown in Figure 2-64c.

To open a file, select the desired file and click the *Open* button. This will close the dialog box and open the selected file.

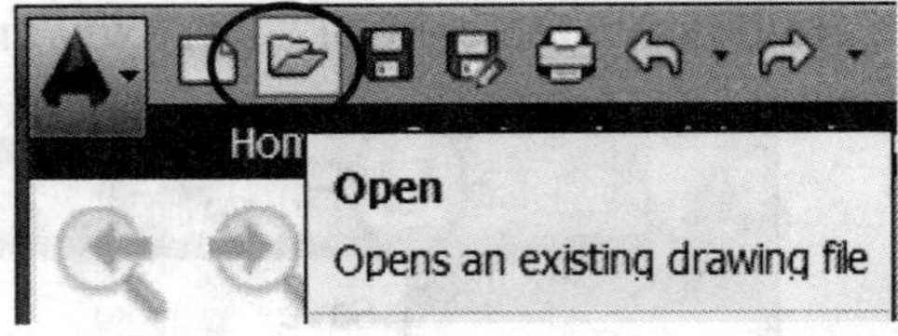

Figure 2-64a

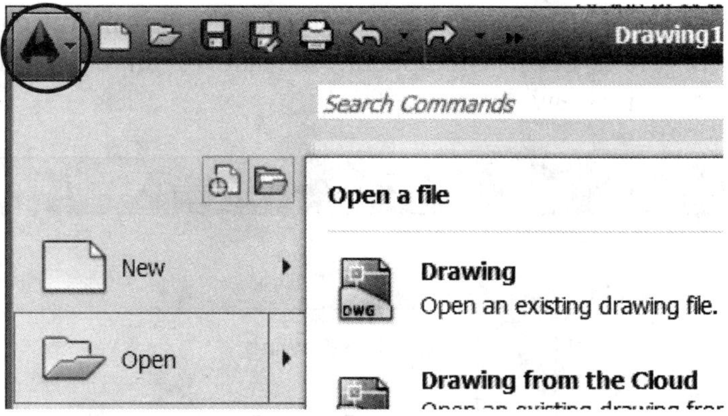

Figure 2-64b

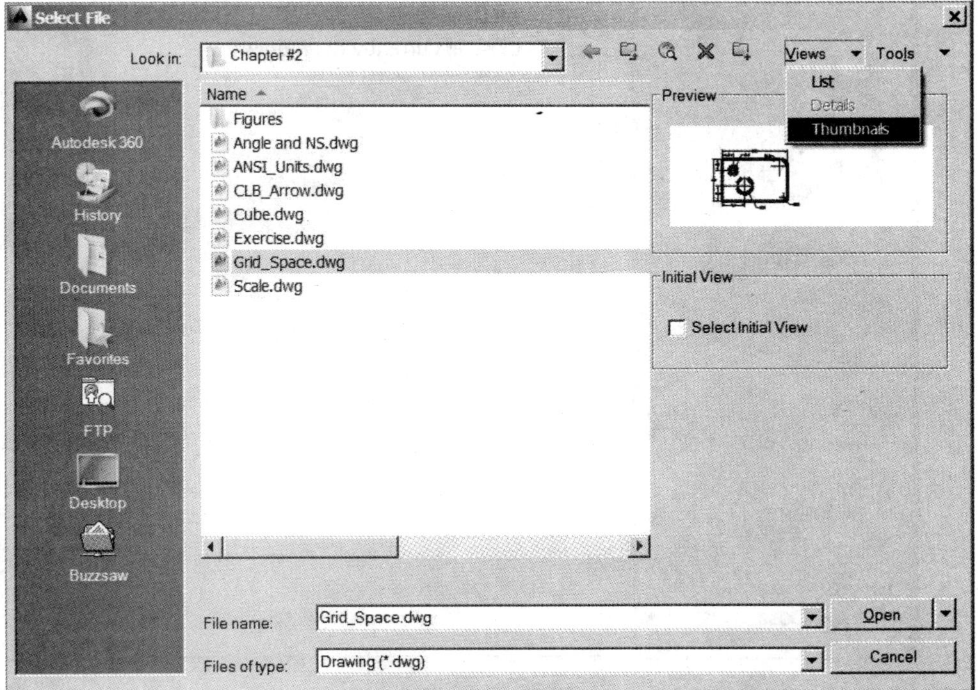

Figure 2-64c

2.24.   Close a file

In AutoCAD, an open file can be closed via *Close* command. The command is activated using one of the following procedures.

1. Menu method: Select the *Application* pull-down menu, Figure 2-65a, and select the *Close* option.
2. From the interface: Click on the "x" sign on the right side of the file name as shown in Figure 2-65b.
3. Command line method: Type "close", "Close", or "CLOSE" in the command line and press the *Enter* key.

This will either close the file (if it was saved after the last modification) or the file save error message (Figure 2-65c) will appear. In case of an error message, click on the appropriate button and follow the prompts.

Figure 2-64c

Figure 2-65b

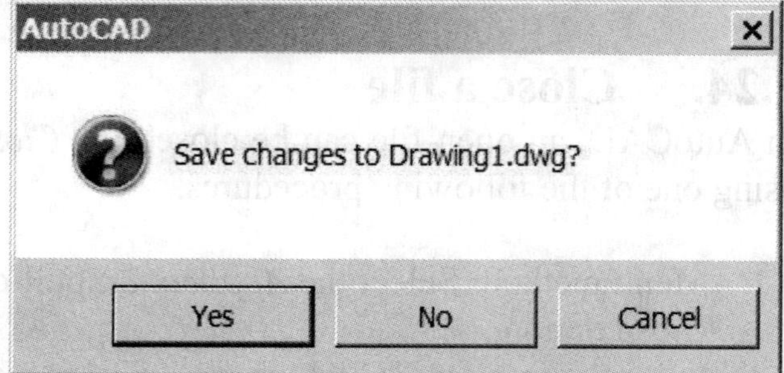

Figure 2-65c

2.25.   Plot

The *Plot* command is used to output a drawing file. The output can be sent to a printer/plotter or written to a file for use with another application. The *Plot* command is activated using one of the following procedures.

1. Menu method: Menu method: Select the *Application* pull-down menu, Figure 2-66a, and select the *Print* option.

2. Toolbar method: Toolbar method: Select the plot drawing tool (), Figure 2-66b, in the quick access toolbar. It is located on the upper left corner of the dialog box.

3. Panel method: Select the *Output* tab, from *Print* panel, select the *Plot* option to print tool (), Figure 2-66c.

4. Command line method: Type "plot", "Plot", or "PLOT" in the command line and press the *Enter* key.

5. Key board method: Hold down the control "Ctrl" key and type 'p' or 'P'.

Figure 2-66a

The activation of the command will open the *Plot* dialog box, Figure 2-67a. The plot *Preview* button is located in the lower right corner of the *Plot* dialog box. To activate the preview button, select a printer from the *Printer/plotter* panel. Now, click on the arrow, in the lower right corner of the *Plot* dialog box to display the hidden features of the dialog box, Figure 2-67b.

Figure 2-66b

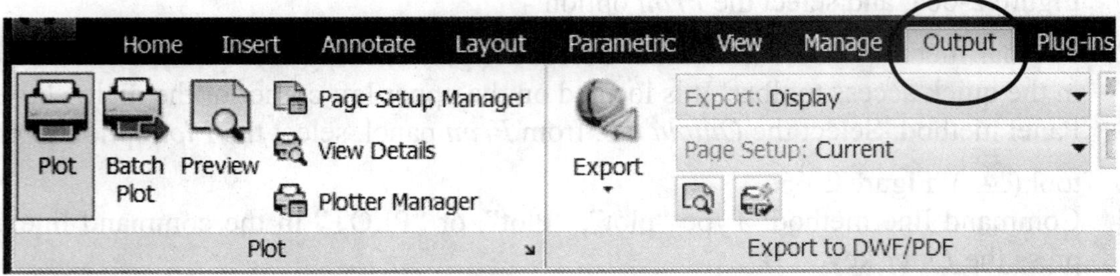

Figure 2-66c

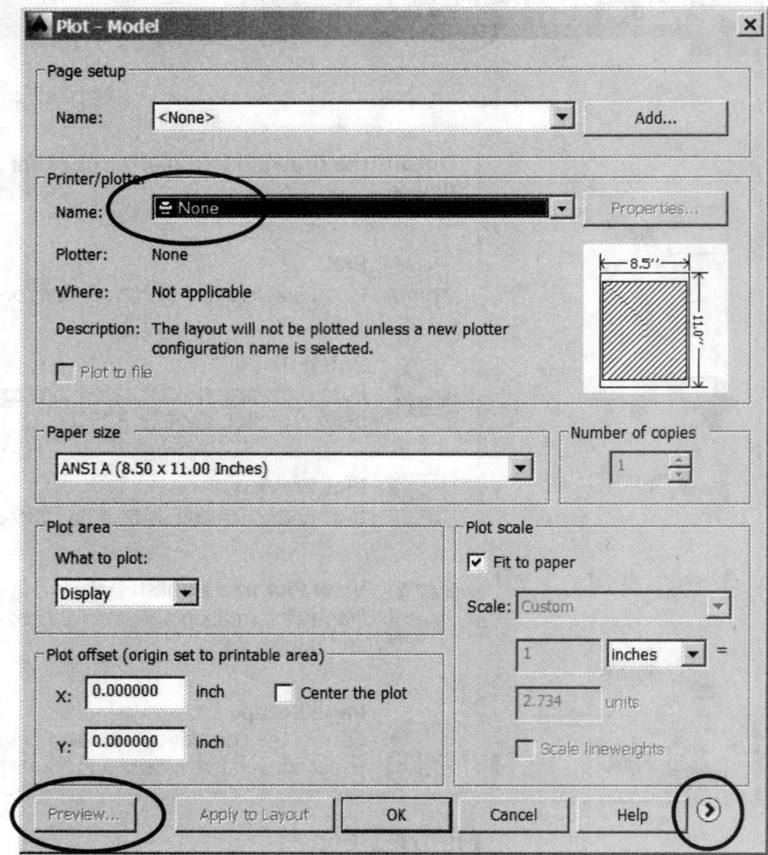

Figure 2-67a

The main features of the *Plot* dialog box are briefly discussed here. The greyed options of the *Plot* dialog box depends on the other options of the dialog box, and will be discussed in their respective sections.

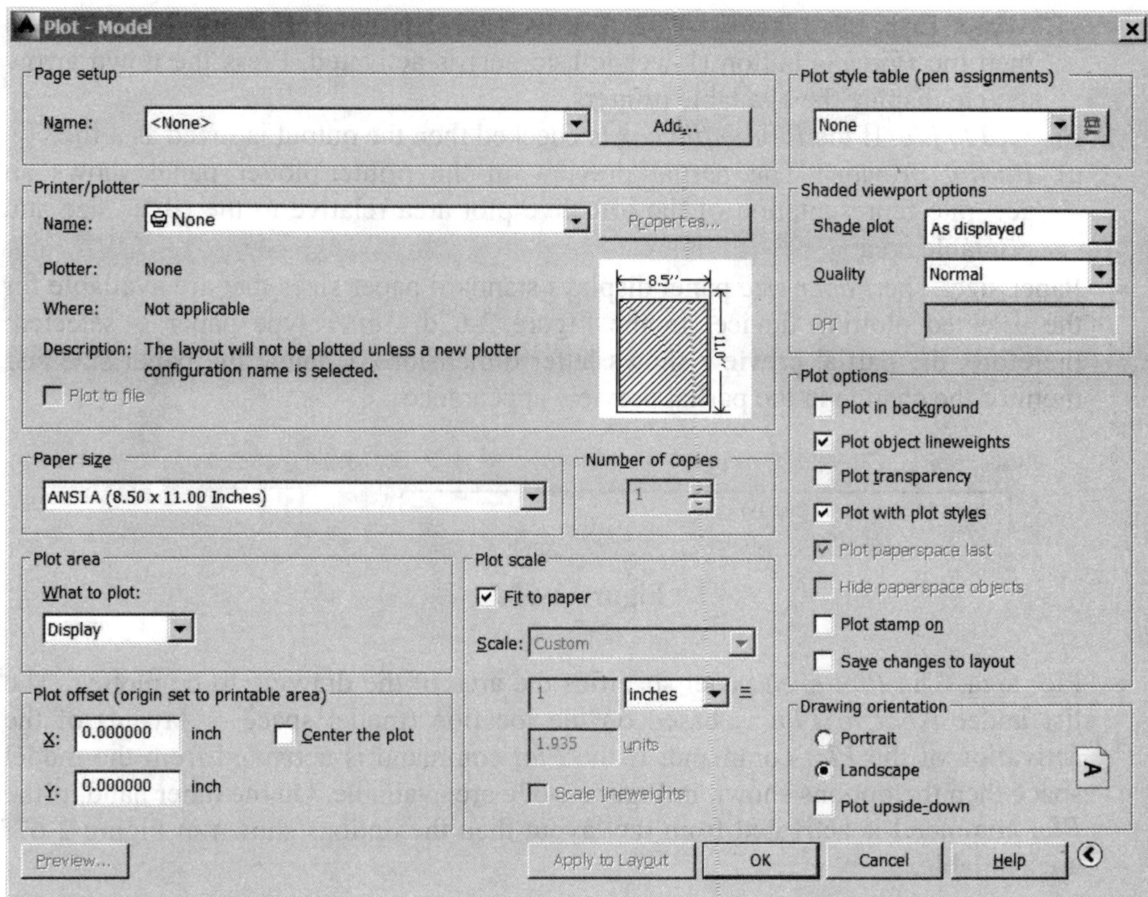

Figure 2-67b

- <u>Page setup</u>: The *Page setup* panel displays the name of the current page setup. If a user plots drawings in a specific style (certain combination of the options from the *Plot* dialog box) then the user can increase the productivity by saving and reusing those plot styles. Page setup or plot styles are attached to the layouts, therefor, creating and saving a page setup will be discussed in Chapter #7.
- <u>Printer/plotter</u>: The *Printer/plotter* panel provides the options for the selection of a configured plotting device to use when plotting or publishing from model space, layouts, or sheets, Figure 2-67c.

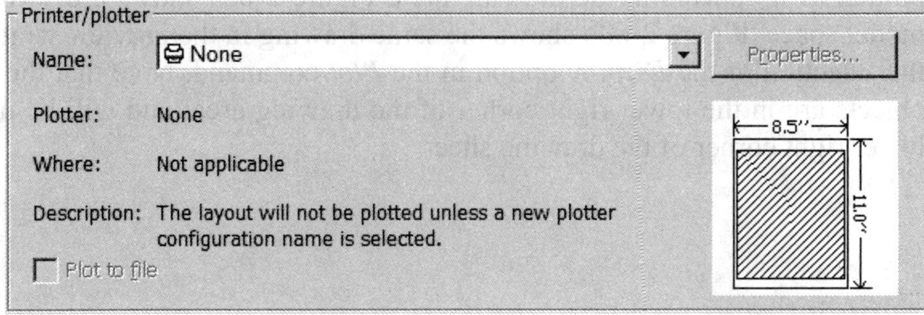

Figure 2-67c

a) *Name*: Lists the available PC3 files or system printers. If a printer is selected then the *Preview* button (lower left corner) is activated. Press the down arrow (▾) to display the available printers.

b) *Plot to file*: If the *Plot to file box* is checked then the output is saved as a file.

c) *Partial preview*: The partial preview in the printer/plotter panel shows an accurate representation of the effective plot area relative to the paper size and printable area.

- Paper size: The *Paper size* panel displays standard paper sizes that are available for the selected plotting device. In the Figure 2-67d, *Letter* type paper is selected; therefore, the partial preview shows letter dimensions. Change the paper size and monitor the change in the partial preview appearance.

Figure 2-67d

- Plot area: The *Plot area* panel specifies the area of the drawing to be plotted. The list under *What to Plot* is based on the location (model space or layout) of the activation of the *Plot* command. If the *Plot* command is activated from the model space then the options shown in Figure 2-67e are available. On the other hand, if the *Plot* command is activated from the layout then the options shown in Figure 2-67f are available.

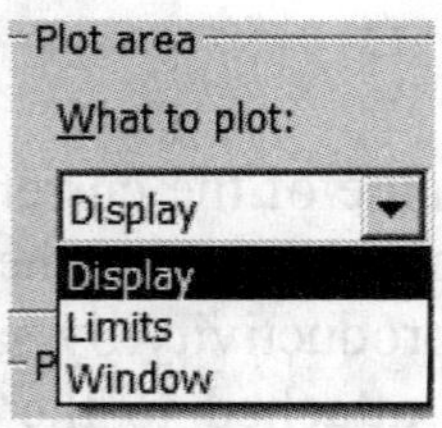

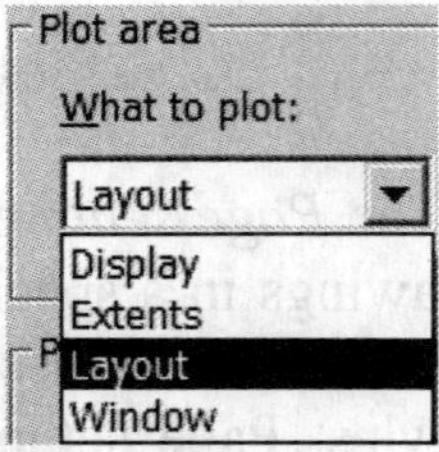

Figure 2-67e   **Figure 2-67f**

a) *Display*: This option plots the view in the current viewport in the *Model* tab or in the current paper space view in a layout tab. That is, the drawing will be plotted as it appears in the drawing area. Figure 2-68a shows a drawing in the model space. Figure 2-68b shows the same drawing in the preview window with the selection of the *Display* option in the *Plot* command. Note that the drawing objects are in the lower right corner of the drawing area; and will be printed in lower right corner of the drawing sheet.

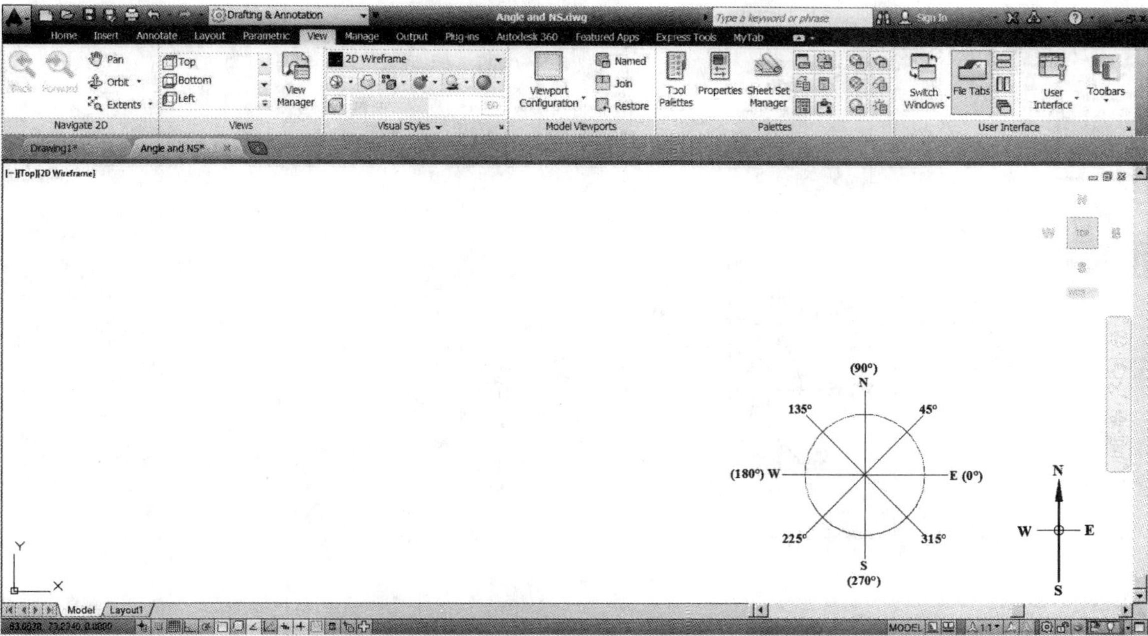

Figure 2-68a

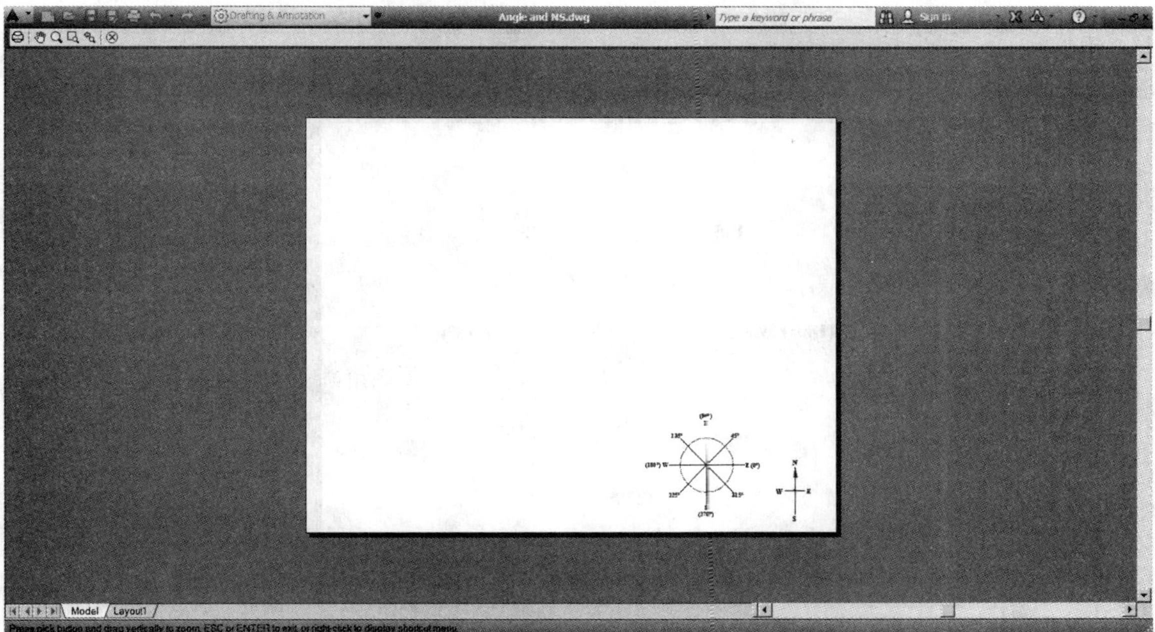

Figure 2-68b

b) *Limits*: This option plots the part of the drawing drawn in the drawing limits. Figure 2-69a shows that the left part of the drawing is in the drawing limits (grid shows the drawing limits). Figure 2-69b shows the same drawing in the preview window with the selection of the *Limits* option in the *Plot* command. Note that only the left part of the drawing appears in the preview window and only that part will be printed. Note that the grid is not appearing in the preview window because it will not be printed.

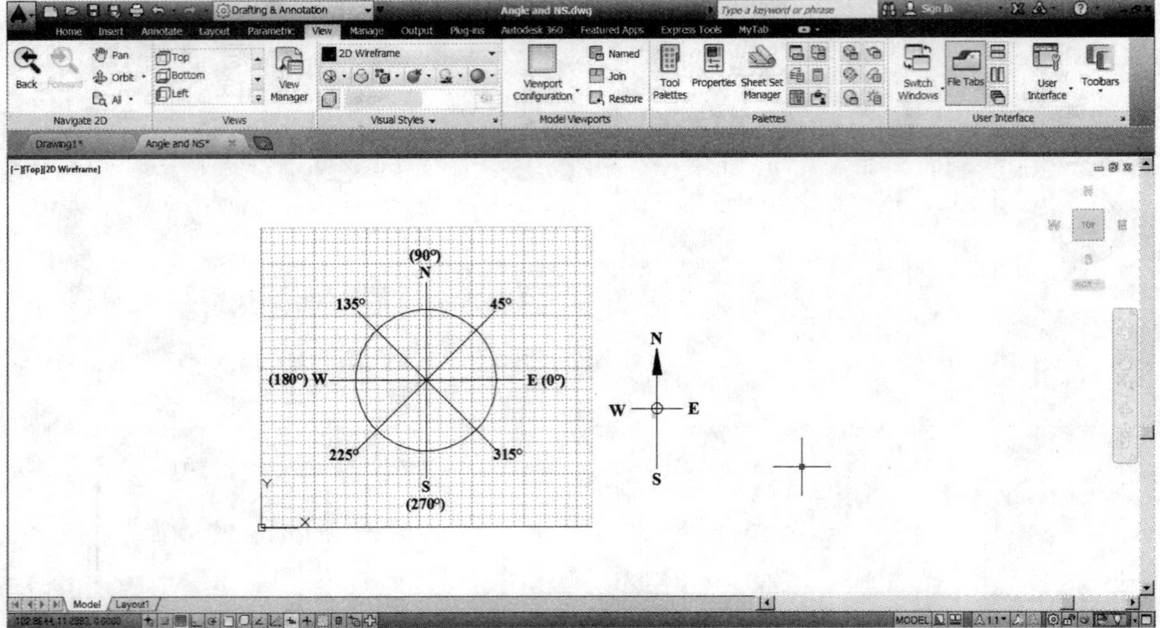

Figure 2-69a

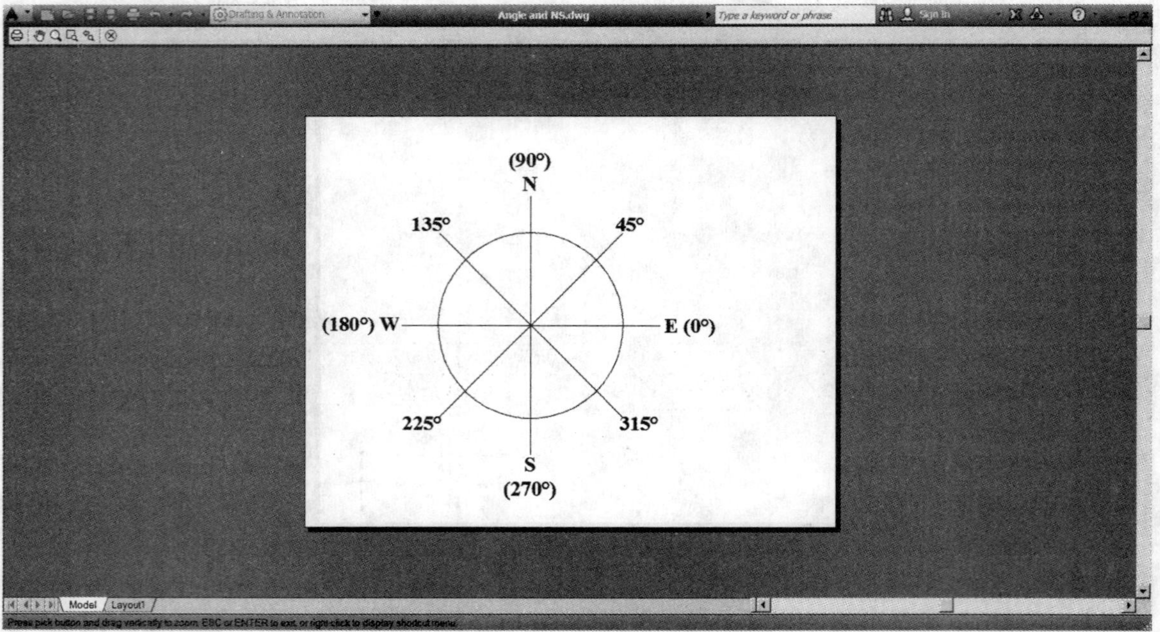

Figure 2-69b

c) *Window*: This option allows the user to plots any portion of the drawing that the user specifies. (i) When this option is selected, then the *Plot* dialog box closes temporarily and the prompt shown in Figure 2-70a will appear on the screen. (ii) Click at slightly above and to the left of the upper left corner of the drawing. (iii) This will create a rectangle starting at the point clicked in the previous step, Figure 2-70b. Also, the prompt shown in Figure 2-70b will appear on the screen. (iv) Click at slightly below and to the right of the lower right corner of the drawing. (v) Try to keep the border above and below same and the left and right border should be same, too. As soon as the second corner is selected, the *Plot* dialog box reappears. Also, *Window* button will appear in the plot area, Figure 2-70c. (vi) If necessary to change the window then click on the *Window* button and repeat the process. Figure 2-70d shows the same drawing in the preview window with the selection of the *Window* option in the *Plot* command.

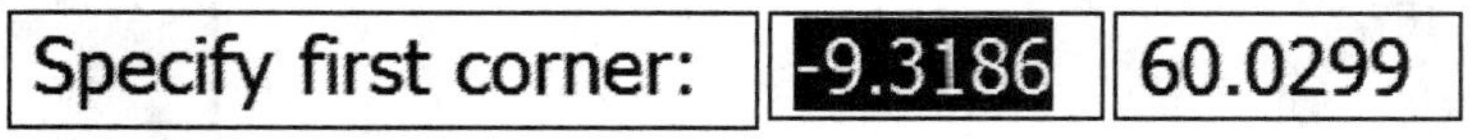

Specify first corner:
-9.3186
60.0299

Figure 2-70a

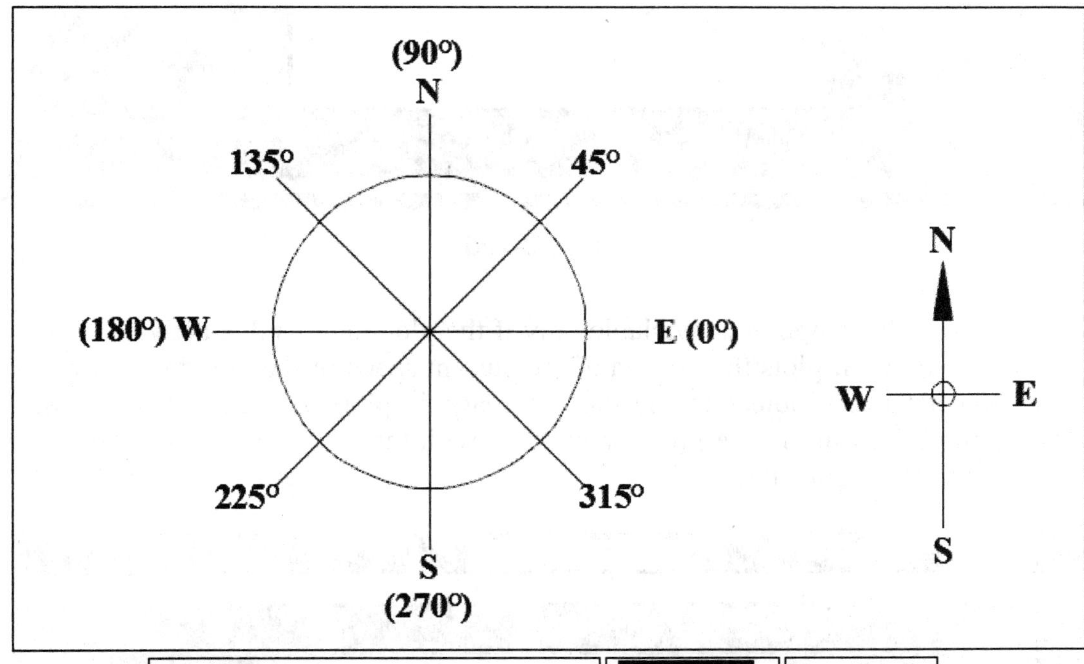

(90°)
N
135°
45°
(180°) W
E (0°)
225°
315°
S
(270°)
N
W
E
S
Specify opposite corner:
87.4386
0.6364

Figure 2-70b

Plot area
What to plot:
Window
Window<

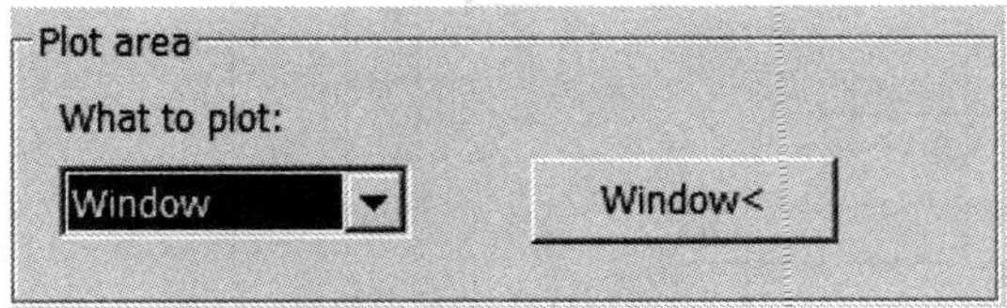

Figure 2-70c

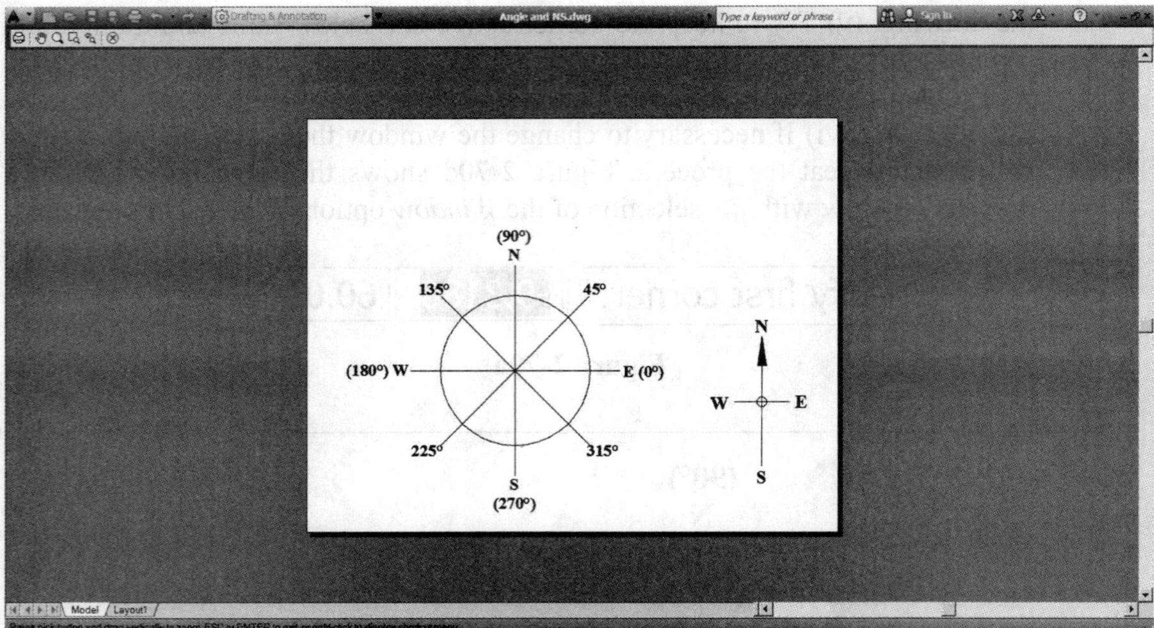

Figure 2-70d

d) *Extents*: This option is available only if the plot command is activated from the *Layout* tab. It plots the portion of the current space of the drawing that contains objects; every object in the current space is plotted. Figure 2-71 shows the sample drawing in the preview window with the selection of the *Extent* option in the *Plot* command.

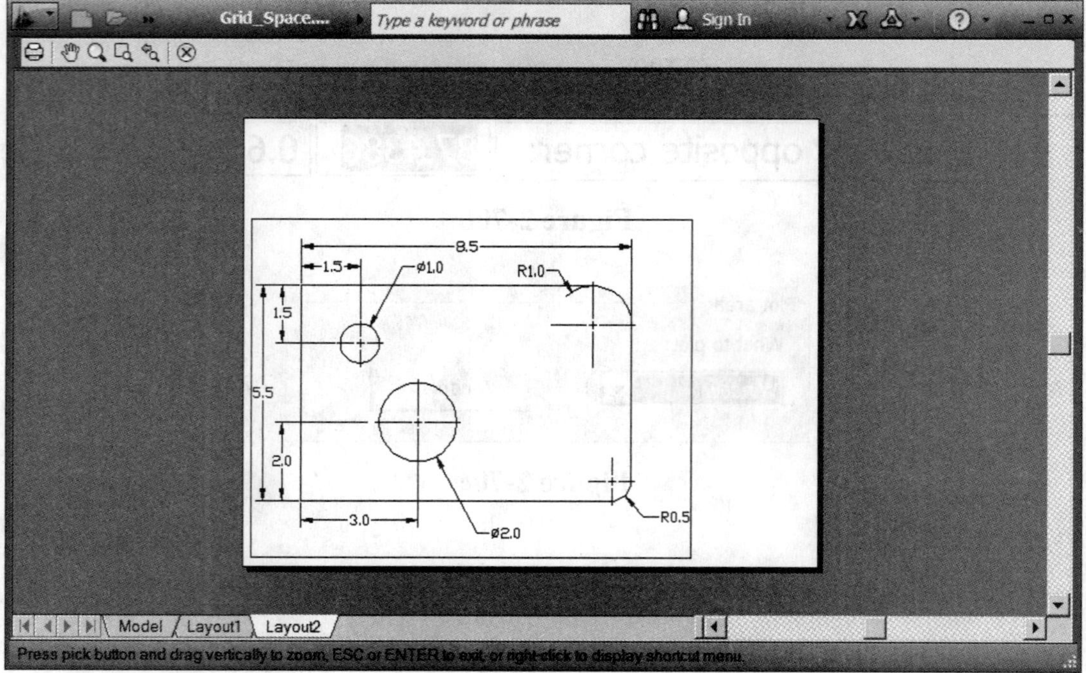

Figure 2-71

e) *Layout*: This option is available only if the plot command is activated from the *Layout* tab. When plotting a *Layout*, everything within the printable area of the specified paper size is plotted, with the origin calculated from (0, 0) in the layout.

- Plot offset: This option specifies an offset of the plot area relative to the lower-left corner of the printable area or from the edge of the paper. The printable area of a drawing sheet is defined by the selected output device and is represented by a dashed line in a layout.

a) *X and Y*: The X and Y values offset the geometry on the paper by entering a positive or negative value in the respective boxes, Figure 2-72a. The partial preview shows the accurate representation of the effective plot area relative to the paper size, printable area and plot offsets, Figure 2-72b

b) *Center the plot*: Automatically calculates the X and Y offset values to center the plot on the paper. This option is available only if the *Plot* command is activated from the model space, Figure 2-72a.

c) Repeat the previous examples with *Center the plot* option and observe the difference in the plot preview.

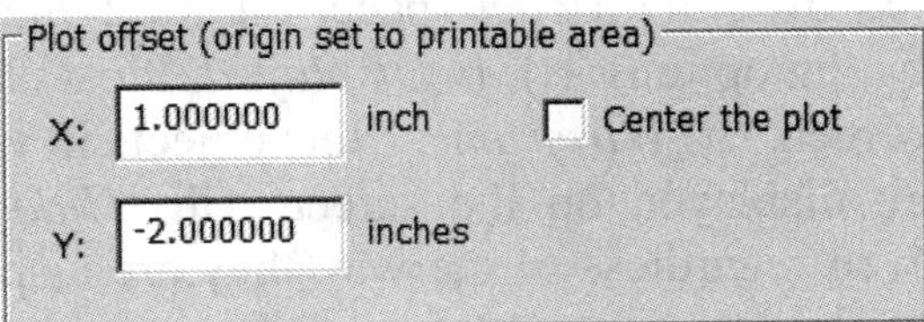

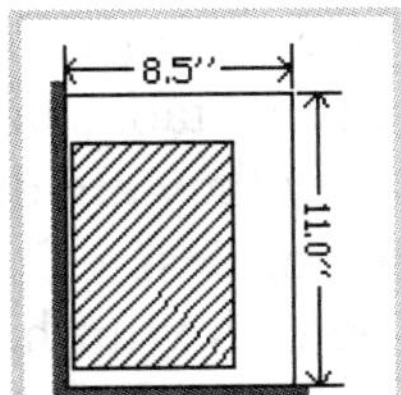

Figure 2-72a **Figure 2-72b**

- Plot scale: This panel controls the relative size of the drawing units to the plotted units. The default setting is *Fit to paper* when the *Plot* command is activated from the *Model* tab, Figure 2-73a. The default scale setting is 1:1 when the *Plot* command is activated from the *Layout* tab, Figure 2-73b.

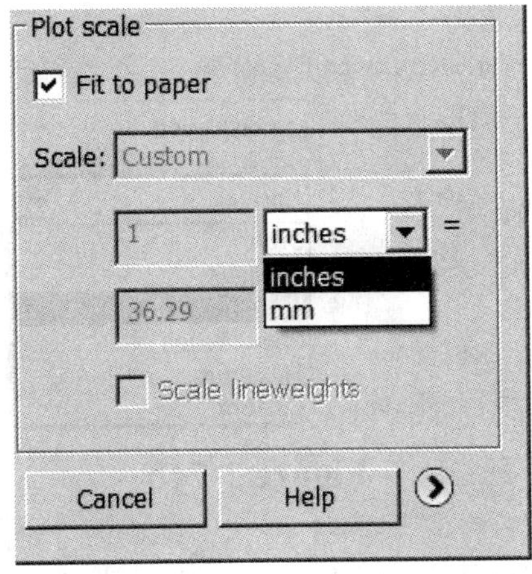

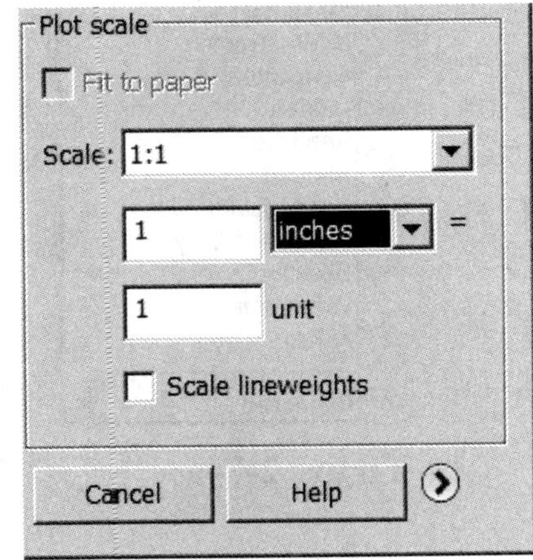

Figure 2-73a **Figure 2-73b**

a) *Fit to paper*: If this box is checked, then the plot is scaled to fit within the selected paper size and the rest of the options in the plot scale window are inactive.

b) *Scale*: The scale list defines the exact scale for the plot. A custom scale can be created by entering the number of inches (or millimeters) equal to the number of drawing units.

c) *inches = mm =* Specifies the number of inches or millimeters equal to the specified number of units. Pixel is available only when a raster output is selected.

d) *Units*: Specifies the number of units equal to the specified number of inches, millimeters, or pixels, Figure 2-73b.

e) *Scale lineweights*: This option is available only if the plot command is activated from the *Layout* tab. It scales the lineweights in proportion to the plot scale. Lineweights normally specify the line width of the plotted objects and are plotted with the line width size, regardless of the plot scale.

- Shaded viewport options: This panel specifies how shaded and rendered viewports are plotted and determines their resolution levels and dots per inch (dpi).

a) *Shade plot*: These options specify how views are plotted and are available only if the *Plot* command is activated from the *Model* space, Figure 2-74a. For the *Model* tab, select from the following options: (i) *As Displayed*: Plots objects the way they are displayed on the screen. (ii) *Wireframe*: Plots objects in wireframe regardless of the way they are displayed on the screen. (iii) *Hidden*: Plots objects with hidden lines removed regardless of the way they are displayed on the screen. (iv) *Rendered*: Plots objects as rendered regardless of the way they are displayed on the screen.

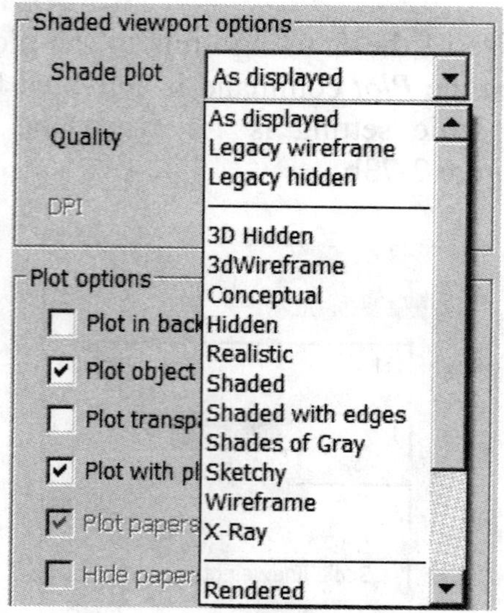

Figure 2-74a

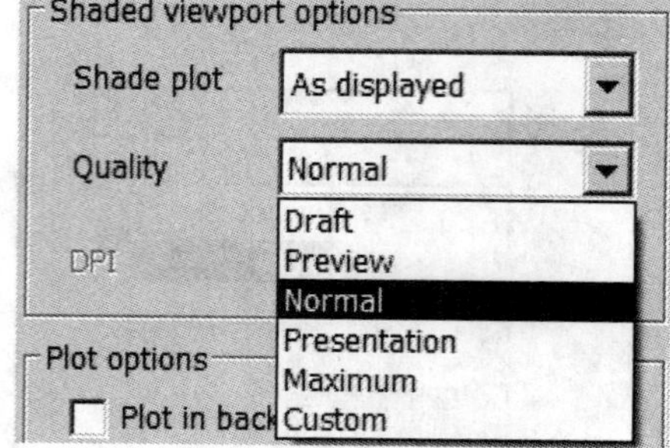

Figure 2-74b

b) *Quality*: These options specify the resolution at which shaded and rendered viewports are plotted, Figure 2-74b. Select one of the following options. (i) *Draft*: Sets rendered and shaded model space views to be plotted as wireframe. (ii) *Preview*: Sets rendered and shaded model space views to be plotted at one quarter of the current device resolution, to a maximum of 150 dpi. (iii) *Normal*: Sets rendered and shaded model space views to be plotted at one half of the current device resolution, to a maximum of 300 dpi. (iv) *Presentation*: Sets rendered and shaded model space views to be plotted at the current device resolution, to a maximum of 600 dpi. (v) *Maximum*: Sets rendered and shaded model space views to be plotted at the current device resolution with no maximum. (vi) *Custom*: Sets rendered and shaded model space views to be plotted at the resolution setting that user specify in the DPI box, up to the current device resolution.

c) *DPI*: Specifies the dots per inch for shaded and rendered views, up to the maximum resolution of the current plotting device. This option is available if the *Custom* option is selected in the *Quality* box.

- *Plot options*: Specifies options for lineweights, plot styles, shaded plots, and the order in which objects are plotted, Figure 2-75.

    a) *Plot object lineweights*: Specifies whether lineweights assigned to objects and layers are plotted.

    b) *Plot with plot styles*: Specifies whether plot styles applied to objects and layers are plotted. When the user selects this option, *Plot Object Lineweights* is selected automatically.

    c) *Plot paperspace Last*: Plots model space geometry first. Paper space geometry is usually plotted before model space geometry.

    d) *Hide paperspace Objects*: Specifies whether the HIDE operation applies to objects in the paper space viewport. This option is available only from a layout tab. The effect of this setting is reflected in the plot preview, but not in the layout.

    e) *Plot stamp on*:

    f) *Save changes to layout*:

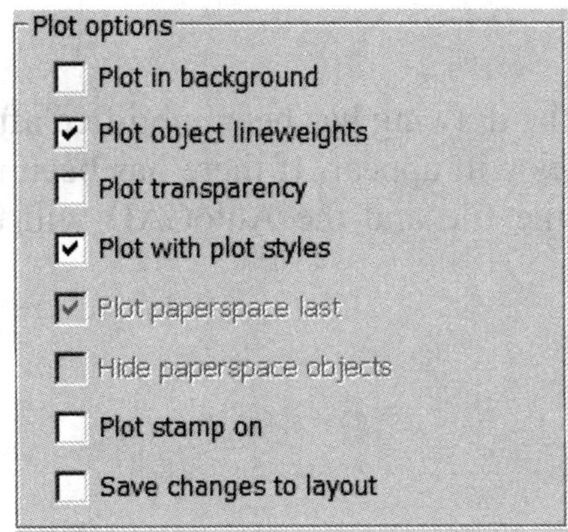

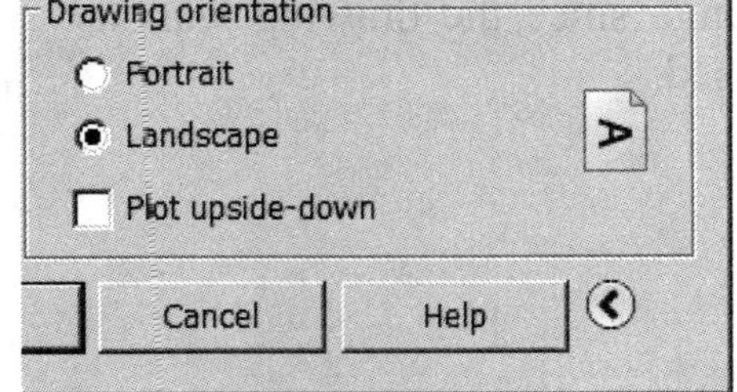

Figure 2-75   **Figure 2-76**

- *Drawing orientation*: Specifies the orientation of the drawing on the paper for plotters that support landscape or portrait orientation, Figure 2-76.

    a) *Portrait*: Orients and plots the drawing so that the short edge of the paper represents the top of the page.

b) *Landscape*: Orients and plots the drawing so that the long edge of the paper represents the top of the page.

c) *Plot upside-down*: Orients and plots the drawing upside-down.

- Preview: Displays the drawing as it will appear when plotted on paper. This option is available only if a *Name* is selected in the *Printer/plotter* option.

- To exit the print preview and return to the *Plot* dialog box, press the *Esc* or the *Enter* key.

2.26.   Exit AutoCAD

The *Exit* command is used to close AutoCAD; it can be activated using one of the following techniques.

1. Command line method: Type "exit", "Exit", "EXIT", "quit", "Quit", or "QUIT" on the command line and press the *Enter* key.
2. Keyboard method: Hold the *Ctrl* key and press the 'q' or 'Q' key.
3. From the interface: Click on the "X" at the upper right corner of the AutoCAD window, Figure 2-77.

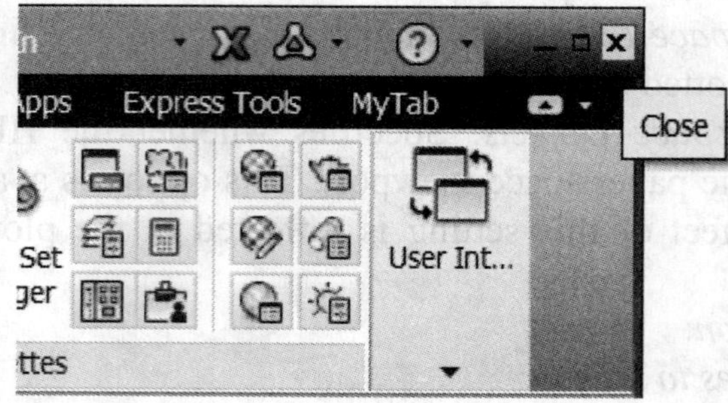

Figure 2-77

The activation of this command quits the program! If the drawing has been modified after the last save, the prompt to save or discard the changes will appear. If there has been no change since the drawing was last saved then both the file and the AutoCAD will be closed.

3.   Basics of 2-Dimensional Drawings

3.1.   Objectives

- Learn to use dynamic input capabilities
- Learn to draw 2D objects such as lines, circles, rectangles, polygons, polylines, arcs, ellipses, etc.
- Learn to change the appearance of an object by changing its color, line thickness, and pattern (dotted, dashed, phantom, etc.)
- Learn to hatch close object
- Learn to create tables and multiline text objects

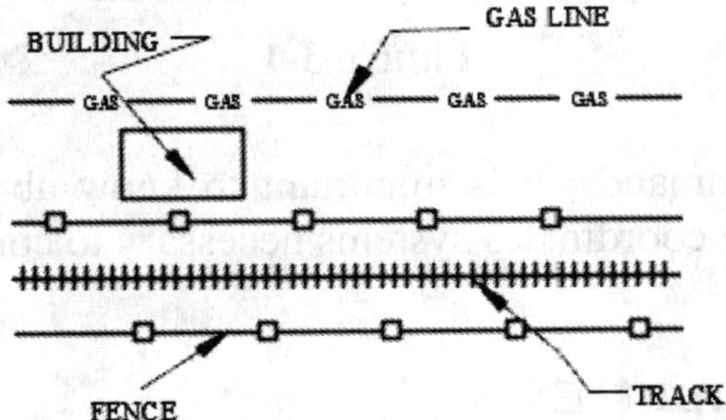

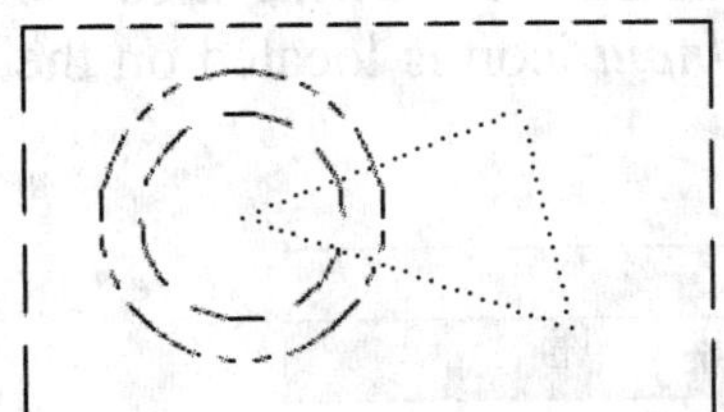

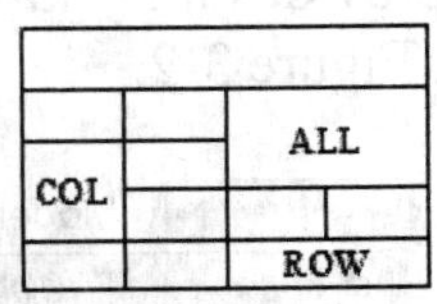

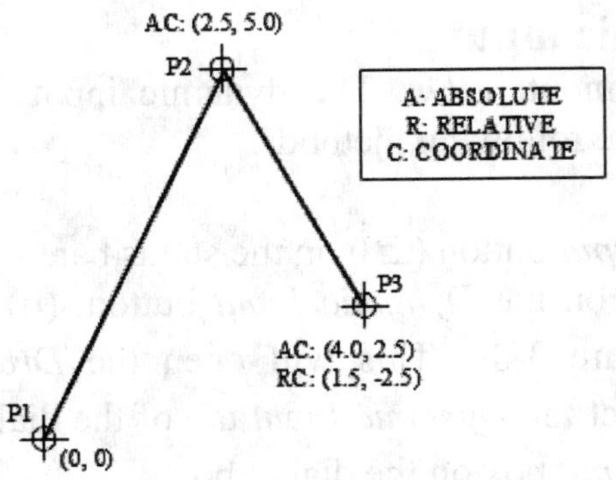

3.2.   Introduction

A drafter can create unlimited designs by creating new drawings and editing previously drawn drawing. The focus of this chapter is the AutoCAD capabilities to draw basic 2D objects. To achieve these functionalities, AutoCAD uses the *Draw* panel. The *Draw* panel can be accessed from the *Home* tab, Figure 3-1. The figure shows the expanded panel.

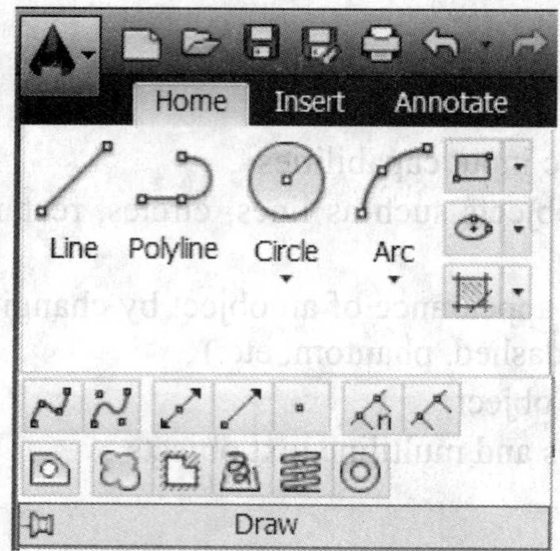

Figure 3-1

Before discussing the commands, it is important to know about the appearance of the prompt, data input, and the coordinates systems necessary to complete the command.

3.3.   Dynamic input

The dynamic input is the command interface near the cursor. A prompt to a command appears in the command line box. However, to keep the focus on the drawing area the software provides a *Dynamic Input* capability. The *Dynamic Input* icon is located on the status bar, Figure 3-2.

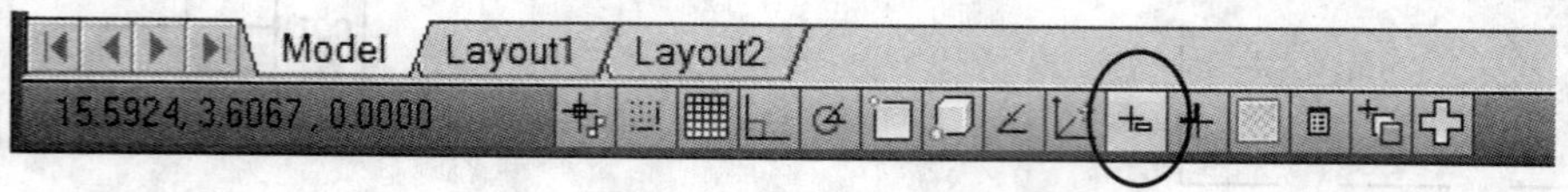

Figure 3-2

3.3.1.   Toggle dynamic input

By default, the dynamic input is *On*. The dynamic input option can be activated or deactivated using any of the following methods.

1. Click the *Dynamic Input* button ( ) on the status bar.
2. (i) Bring the cursor on the *Dynamic Input* button. (ii) Right click and select the *Settings* option, Figure 3-3b. This will open the *Drafting Settings* dialog box, Figure 3-3b. (ii) Select the *Dynamic Input* tab of the dialog box. (iii) Finally, check the *Enable Pointer Input* box on the dialog box.

3. The option can be activated by pressing the *F12* key.

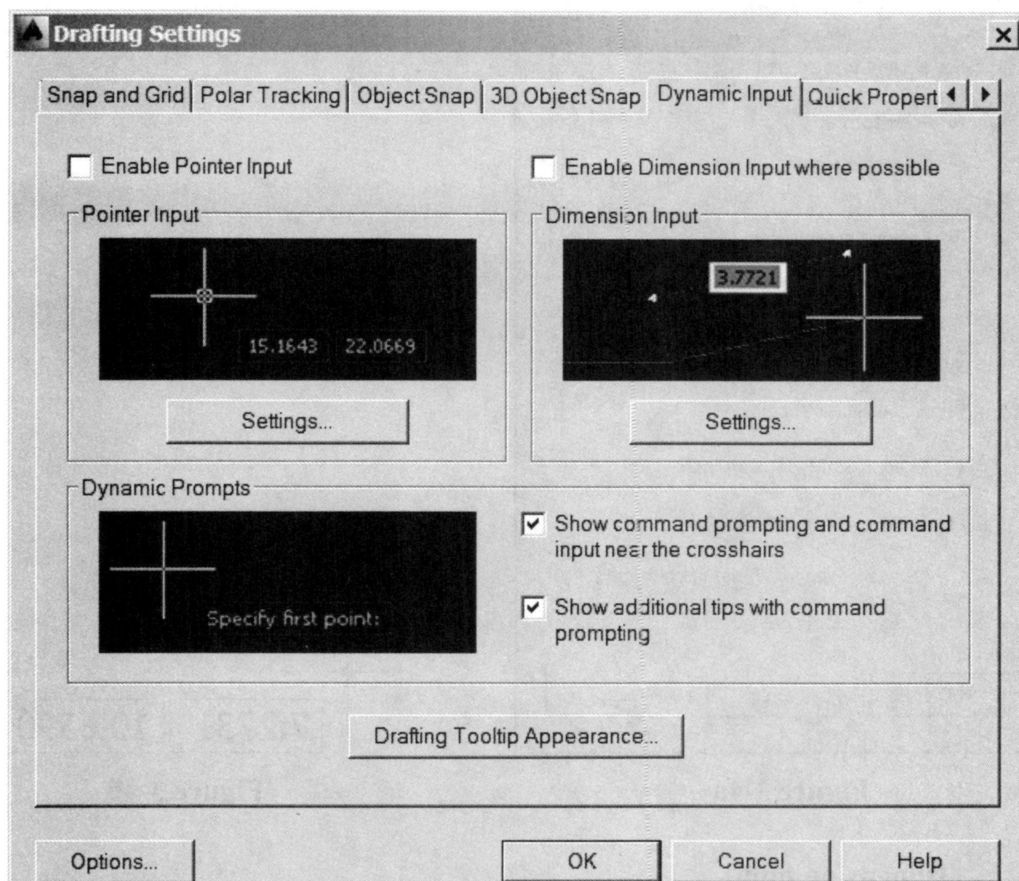

Figure 3-3b

3.3.2. Components of a dynamic input

A dynamic input has three major components, Figure 3-3b: the *Pointer Input*, *Dimensional Input*, and the *Dynamic Prompts*.

3.3.2.1. Pointer input

To check the capabilities of the pointer input, click the *Settings* button in the *Pointer Input* panel (Figure 3-3b) to open the *Pointer Input Settings* dialog box (Figure 3-4a). This dialog box is used to change the format for coordinates: polar or Cartesian and relative or absolute. The dialog box also controls the pointer input tooltips display. The coordinates are discussed in the next section.

When the *Enable Pointer Input* box is checked (Figure 3-3b) and on the *Pointer Input Settings* dialog box, the last option (*Always*) in the *Visibility* panel is selected then the location of the crosshairs is displayed as coordinates in the tooltip near the cursor, Figure 3-4b. To avoid confusion, it is a good drawing practice to use the *When a command asks for a point* option in the *Visibility* panel. The coordinate values can be entered in the tooltip, too.

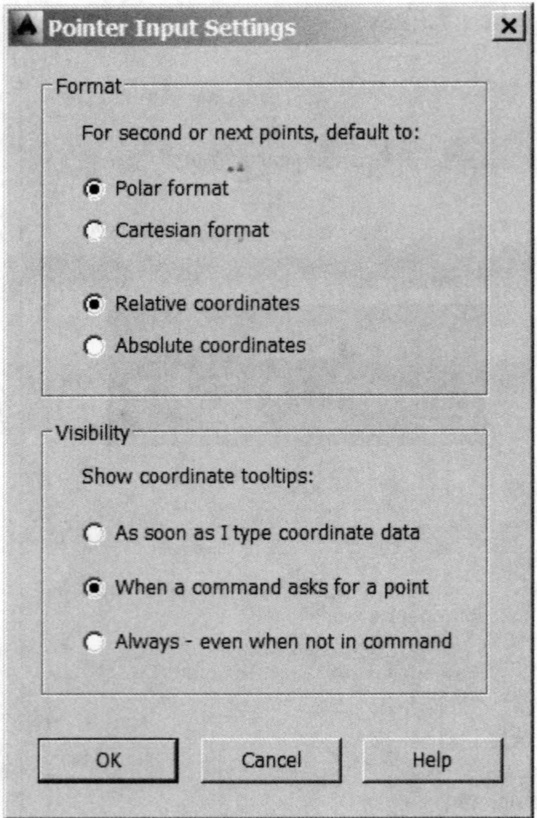

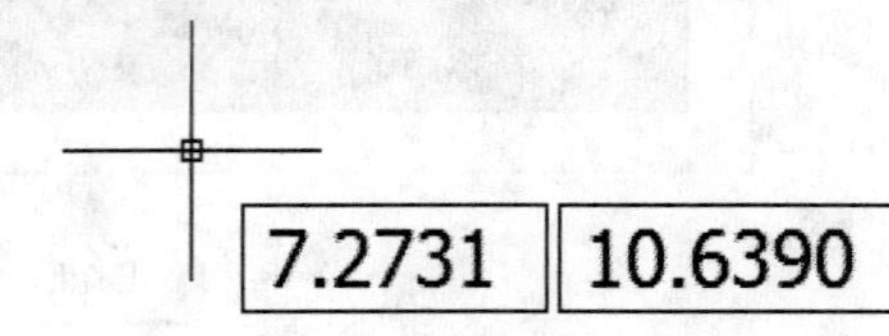

Figure 3-4a   **Figure 3-4b**

3.3.2.2.   Dimension input

To check the capabilities of the dimension input, click the *Enable Dimensional Input where possible* box (Figure 3-3b) to display the dimensions' values when a command demands for a second point. The value in the dimensional tooltip changes as the cursor moves.

Click the *Settings* button in the *Dimension Input* panel (Figure 3-3b) to open the *Dimension Input Settings* dialog box, Figure 3-5a.

- The *Show the following dimension input fields simultaneously* option displays a combination of the dimensions by checking the appropriate boxes. Figure 3-5b shows a line P1-P2 of length 4.3851 at an angle of 64° with the x-axis and point P3. When point P2 of the line P1-P2 is stretched to point P3, Figure 3-5c, the *Resulting Dimension* is 3.0596, *Angle Change* is 66°, *Length Change* is 1.3255, *Arc Radius* is 3.0596, and the *Absolute Angle* is 130°.
- If the *Show 2 dimension input fields at a time* option is selected then the distance and the angle are displayed when point P2 of the line P1-P2 is stretched to point P3.
- If the *Show only 1 dimension input field at a time* option is selected then only the distance is displayed when point P2 of the line P1-P2 is stretched to point P3.

The best option is the *Show 2 dimension input fields at a time* option.

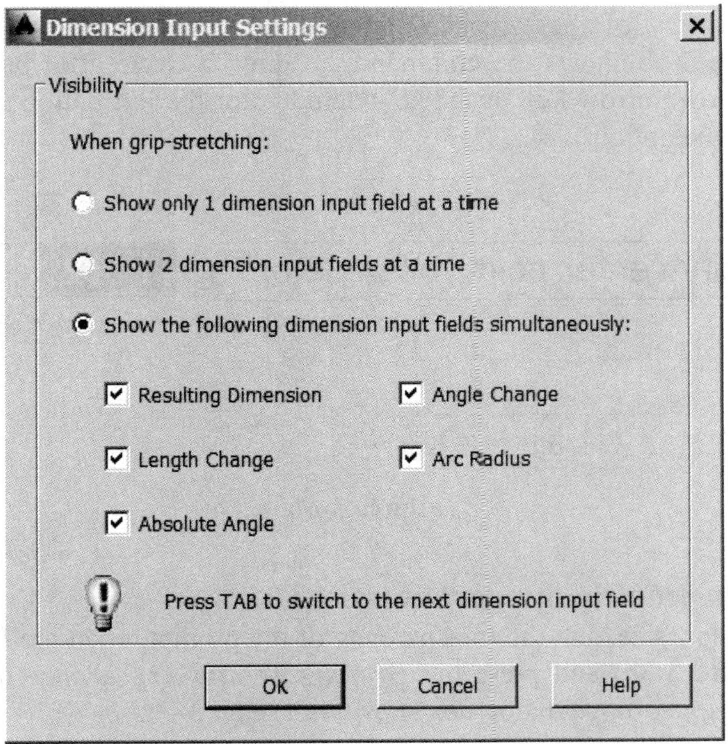

Figure 3-5a

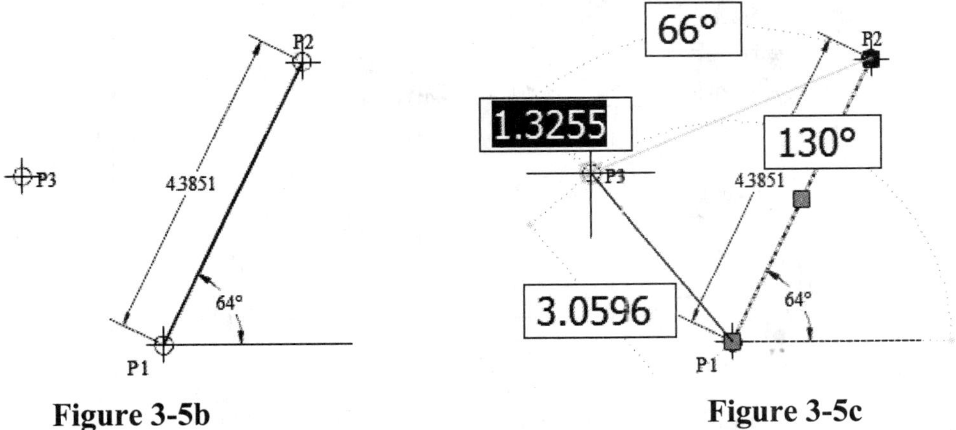

Figure 3-5b   **Figure 3-5c**

3.3.2.3. Dynamic prompts

To check the capabilities of the dynamic prompt, click the check box in the *Dynamic Prompts* panel (Figure 3-3b). If the box is checked then the prompts are displayed in a tooltip near the cursor. Figure 3-6a shows a command's prompt near the cursor.

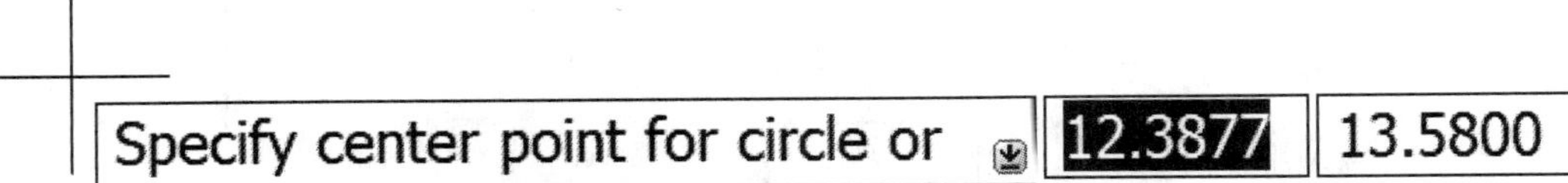

Figure 3-6a

The down arrow key of the keyboard is used to view the multiple options of the command. Figure 3-6b shows the commands to draw a circle after pressing the down arrow key. The down arrow key of the keyboard and/or the left button of the mouse can be used to select the options.

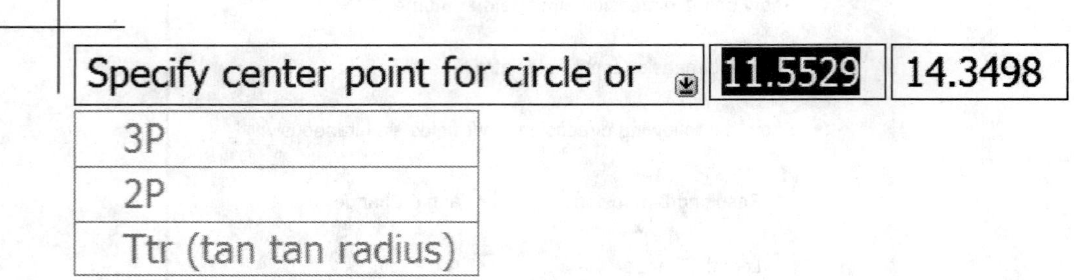

Figure 3-6b

3.3.3.   Drafting tooltip appearance

To change the color, size, and the transparency of the prompt, open the *Drafting Settings* dialog box (Figure 3-3b) and press the *Drafting Tooltip Appearance* button. This will open the *Tooltip Appearance* dialog box shown in Figure 3-7a.

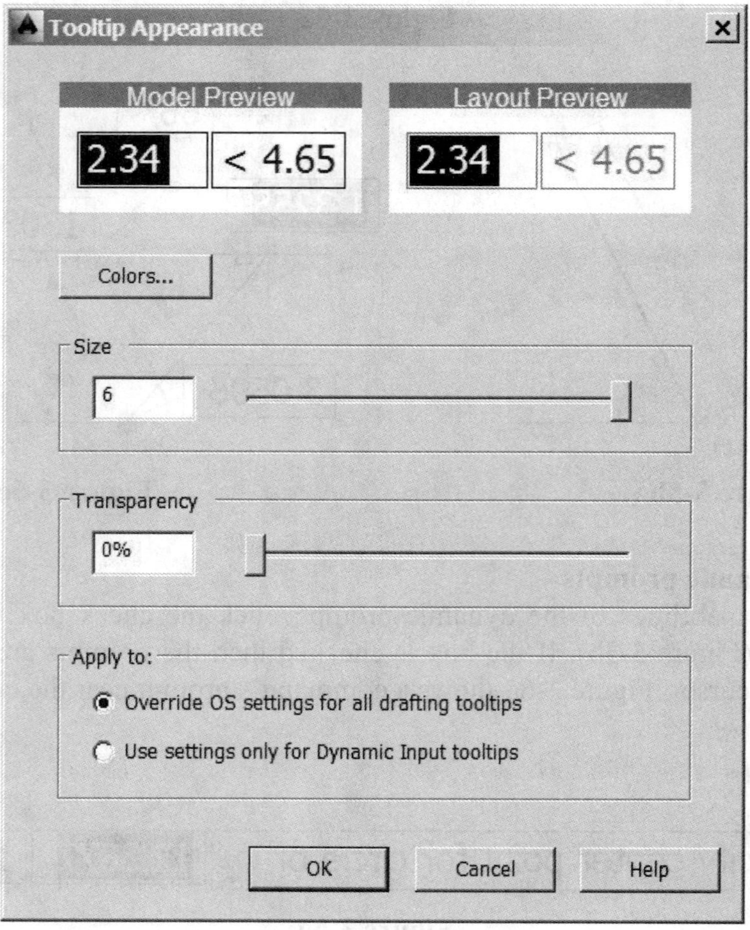

Figure 3-7a

- Size: The slider in the *Size* panel is used to change the size of the text in the tool tip. To increase the tooltip's font size move the slider to the right. To decrease the tooltip's font size move the slider to the left.
- Transparency: To change the transparency of the tooltip background, move the slider in the *Transparency* panel to the left or right.
- Color: To change the color of the tooltip and/or its background, press the *Colors* button to open the *Drawing Window Colors* dialog box.
    - Figure 3-7b shows the color of the *Drafting tool tip* that is, the text of the prompt.
    - Figure 3-7c shows the color of the *Drafting tool tip contour* that is, the rectangular outline of the prompt.
    - Figure 3-7d shows the color of the *Drafting tool tip background* used in the text. The *Drawing Window Color* dialog box is discussed in details in Chapter 2.

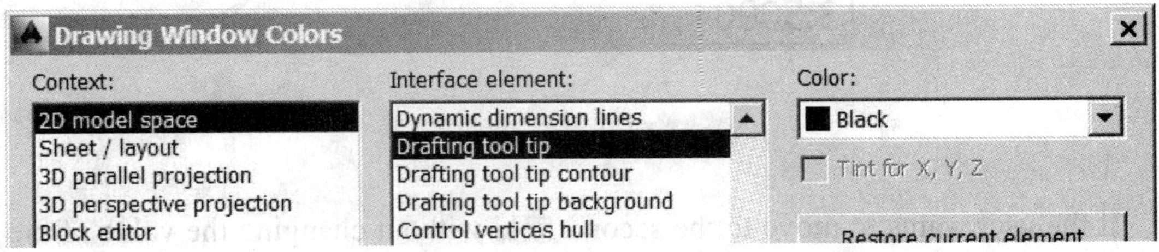

Figure 3-7b

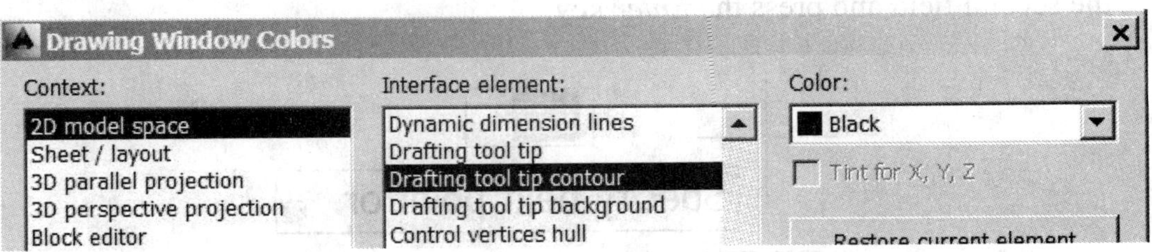

Figure 3-7c

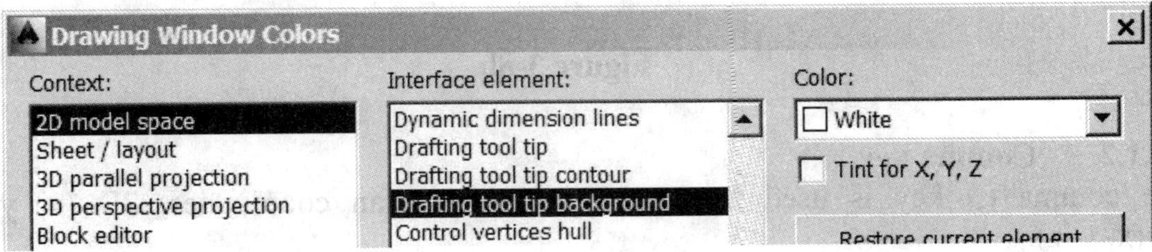

Figure 3-7d

3.4. Input data

The input prompt of the Figure 3.6a contains 2 input fields. The cursor can be moved from one input field to the other using the *Tab*, ",", or "<" keys of the keyboards. Type a value in an input field and press one of the three keys. However, if a value is typed followed by pressing the *Enter* key, then the second and subsequent input fields will be ignored.

3.4.1.1.   Tab key
The tab key is used for entering the polar (length, angle) coordinates.

1. Type a value in an input field and press the tab key; the field will display a lock icon (Figure 3-8a) and the cursor is constrained by the value just entered. The cursor will also move to the second input field. Finally, type in the value in the second field and press the *Enter* key.

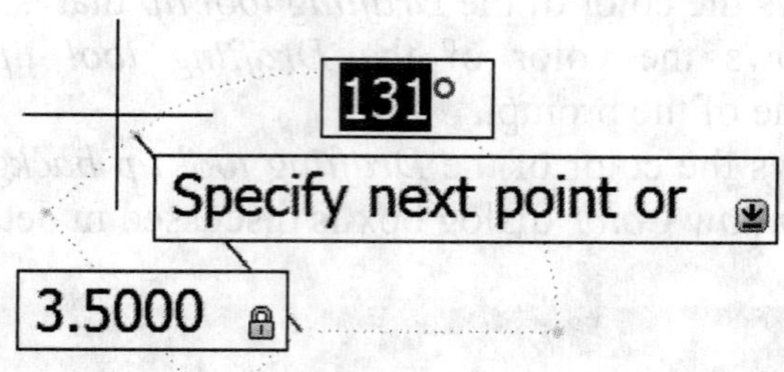

Figure 3-8a

2. If the user wants to move to the second field without changing the value of the first field then just press the tab key and the cursor will move to the second input field, Figure 3-8b. Note that the lock did not appear in the first field. Type in the value in the second field and press the *Enter* key.

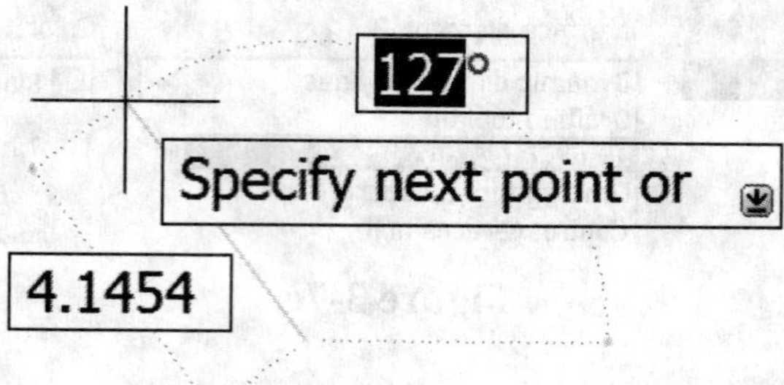

Figure 3-8b

3.4.1.2.   Comma key
The comma (,) key is used for entering the Cartesian coordinates, 2D (x, y) or 3D (x, y, z).

1. Type a value in an input field and press the "," key; the field will display a lock icon (Figure 3-8c) and the cursor is constrained by the value just entered. The cursor will, also, move to the second input field. Finally, type in the value in the second field and press the *Enter* key. For the 3-dimensional values, repeat the process of second input field with the third input field.
2. If the user wants to move to the second field without changing the value of the first field then first move the cursor to the right end of the input field and then just press the "," key and the cursor will move to the second input field, Figure 3-8c. Type in the value in the second field and press the *Enter* key.

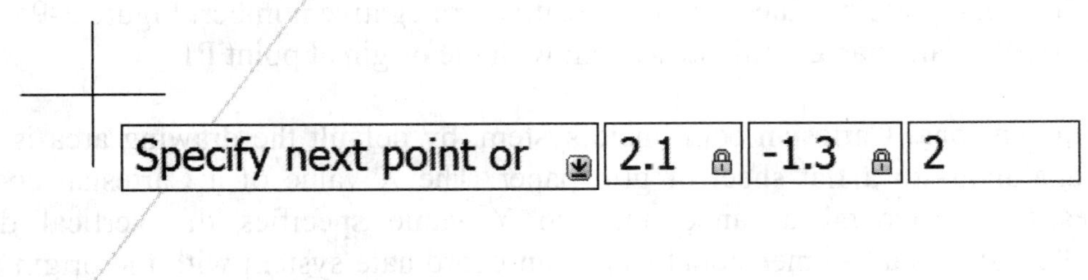

Figure 3-8c

3.4.1.3.   Less than key

The less than (<) key is used for entering the polar (length, angle) coordinates.

1. Type a value in an input field and press the "<" key; the field will display a lock icon (Figure 3-8d) and the cursor is constrained by the value just entered. The cursor will, also, move to the second input field. Finally, type in the value in the second field and press the *Enter* key.
2. If the user wants to move to the second field without changing the value of the first field then just press the "<" key and the cursor will move to the second input field, Figure 3-8d. Type in the value in the second field and press the *Enter* key.

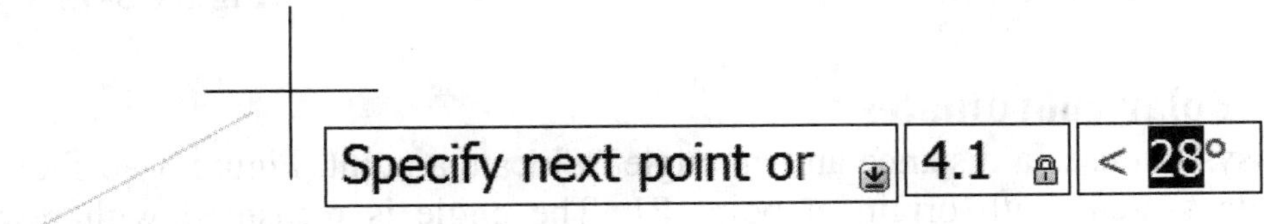

Figure 3-8d

3.4.1.4.   Remove typing errors from the dynamic input tooltips

If there is an error in the dynamic input then the tooltip displays the red error outline. To remove the error, just type over the selected text to replace it and continue the command.

3.5.   Reference system

For the 2-dimensional drawing, AutoCAD provides two reference systems: Cartesian coordinates and polar coordinates systems.

3.5.1.   Cartesian coordinates

A Cartesian (also known as a rectangular) coordinate system has three mutually perpendicular and intersecting axes, X, Y, and Z. The origin (0, 0, 0) is the location where the three axes intersect. The x-coordinate value indicates a point's distance in units and its direction, positive or negative, along the X-axis with respect to the origin. This principle also applies to the Y- and Z-axes.

In AutoCAD, the 3-dimensional Cartesian coordinates values are specified as a (x, y, z) tuple. The coordinate values are specified as a comma separated tuple (x,y,z) without any space. The coordinate's values can be a positive or negative number. Figure 3-9a shows a 3-dimensional Cartesian coordinate system with the origin at point P1.

In a 2-dimensional Cartesian coordinate system, by default the drawing area is the XY plane, analogous to a flat sheet of grid paper. The X value of a Cartesian coordinate specifies the horizontal distance and the Y value specifies the vertical distance. Figure 3-9b shows a 2-dimensional Cartesian coordinate system with the origin at point P1.

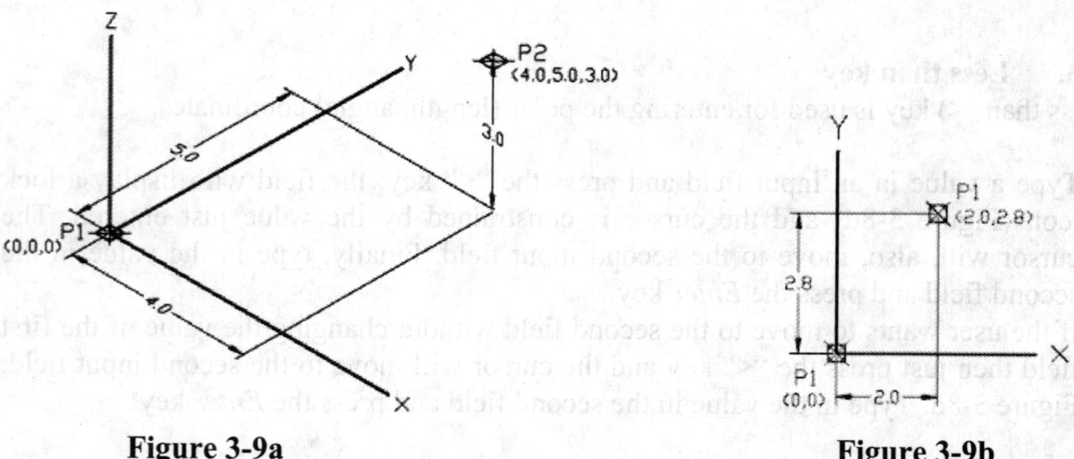

Figure 3-9a   **Figure 3-9b**

3.5.2.   Polar coordinates

A polar system uses a distance and an angle to locate a point. Figure 3-9c shows a polar coordinate system with origin at point P1. The angle is measured with respect to a reference axis. For polar coordinates, the coordinate values are specified as an ordered pair (distance, angle).

In AutoCAD, the coordinate values are specified as an ordered pair separated by an angle bracket, (distance<angle). By default, an angle increases in the counterclockwise direction and decrease in the clockwise direction. To specify a clockwise direction, enter a negative value for the angle. For example, (5<300) and (5<-60) locates the same point.

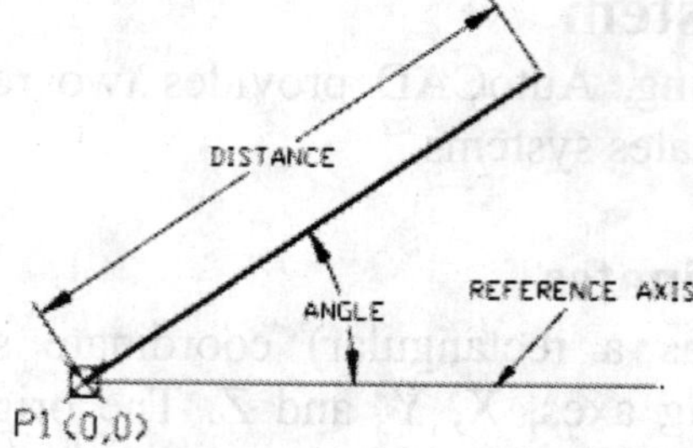

Figure 3-9c

3.5.3.   AutoCAD and the coordinate systems

Distance is always measured from a benchmark or a reference point. Based on the benchmark, there are two types of coordinate system, absolute and relative. The absolute coordinates are always measured from the benchmark. Whereas, the relative coordinates are measured with respect to the previous point. Both the Cartesian and polar coordinates can be measured either as absolute coordinates or relative coordinates.

In Figure 3-10, point P1 (0, 0) is the benchmark. The figure shows the absolute coordinates of the points P2 (2.5, 5.0) and P3 (4.0, 2.5). The figure also shows the relative coordinates of point P3 (1.5, -2.5) with respect to point P2.

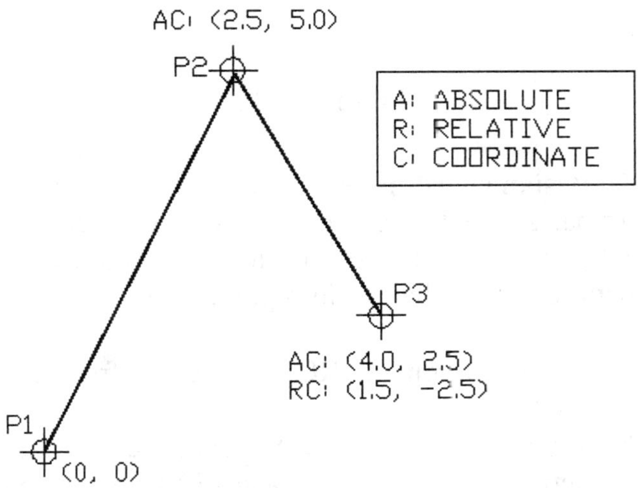

Figure 3-10

In AutoCAD, both the absolute and relative coordinates can be specified on the command line or on the tooltip of the dynamic input.

3.5.3.1.   Absolute Cartesian coordinates

In AutoCAD, the origin of the WCS is used as the benchmark for the absolute coordinates. The absolute Cartesian coordinates are used when the precise location of x- and y-coordinates of a point are known. In the dynamic input, the absolute coordinates are specified using the # prefix. However, for the command line the prefix is not used.

- ***Example:*** Using absolute coordinate (AC) draw a line from point P2 to point P3 of Figure 3-10.
- In the case of the dynamic input, specify the absolute coordinates with the # prefix, Figure 3-11a. (i) Activate the *Line* command. (ii) Click at point P2. (iii) Type the # sign (hold the *Shift* key and press # key). The # sign will appear in the dynamic input and cursor will move to the first input field. (iv) Type in the x-coordinate (that is 4). (v) Press the comma (,) key. The cursor will move to the second input field. (vi) Now, type the y-coordinate (that is 2.5). (vii) For a 2-dimensional drawing, press the *Enter* key. For the 3-diensional drawing, repeat the step (v) for the z-coordinate and then press the *Enter* key.

- For the command line the # is not used. Just type 4,2.5 (no space) and press the *Enter* key.

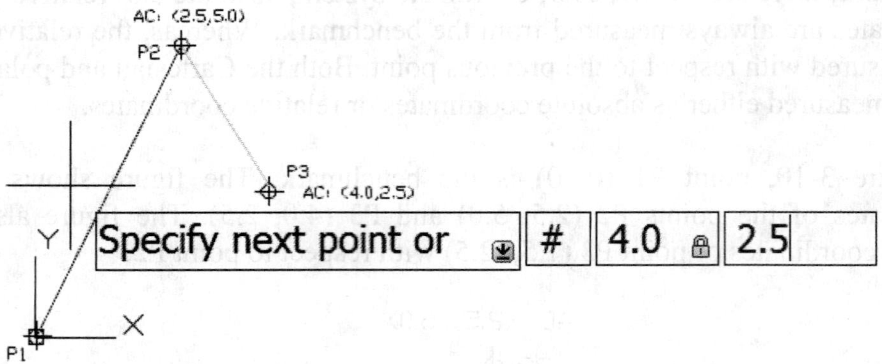

Figure 3-11a

3.5.3.2.   Relative Cartesian coordinates

For the relative coordinates, the last point is used as the benchmark for the relative coordinates of the next point. The relative coordinates are used when the location of the next point is known with respect to the previous point.

- ***Example:*** Using relative coordinate (RC) draw a line from point P2 to point P3 of Figure 3-10.
- In the case of the dynamic input, specify the relative coordinates with the @ prefix, Figure 3-11b. (i) Activate the *Line* command. (ii) Click at point P2. (iii) Type the @ sign (hold the *Shift* key and press @ key). The @ sign will appear in the dynamic input and cursor will move to the first input field. (iv) Type in the x-coordinate (that is 1.5). (v) Press the comma (,) key. The cursor will move to the second input field. (vi) Now, type the y-coordinate (that is -2.5). (vii) For 2-dimensional drawing, press the *Enter* key. For the 3-diensional drawing, repeat the step (viii) for the z-coordinate and then press the *Enter* key.
- For the command line the @ is used. Just type @1.5,-2.5 (no space) and press the *Enter* key.

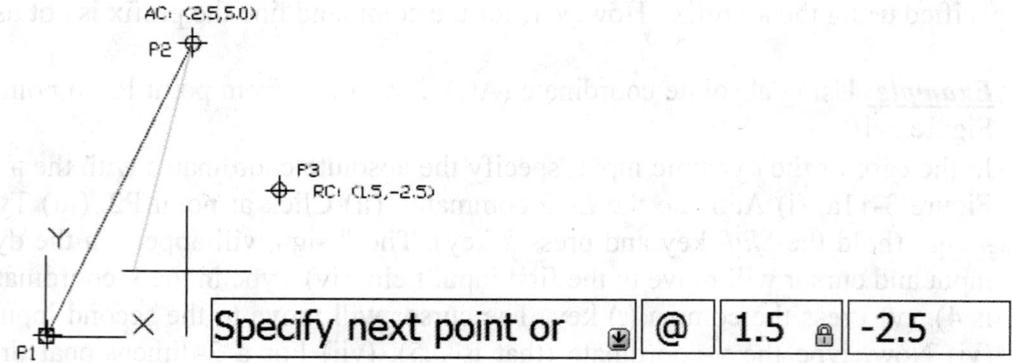

Figure 3-11b

3.5.3.3.   Absolute Polar coordinates

In AutoCAD, the origin of the WCS is used as the benchmark for the absolute coordinates. The absolute polar coordinates are used when the precise distance and angle coordinates of a point are known.

- ***Example:*** Draw a line from point P2 to point P3. The absolute polar coordinates of point P3 are (3, 0°).
- In case of the dynamic input, specify the absolute coordinates with the # prefix, Figure 3-12a. (i) Activate the line command. (ii) Click at point P2. (iii) Type the # sign (hold the *Shift* key and press # key). The # sign will appear in the dynamic input and cursor will move to the first input field. (iv) Type in the distance (that is 3). (v) Press the Less then (<) key. The cursor will move to the second input field. (vi) Now, type the angle (that is 0). (vii) Finally, press the *Enter* key.
- For the command line the # is not used. Just type 3<0 (no space) and press the *Enter* key.

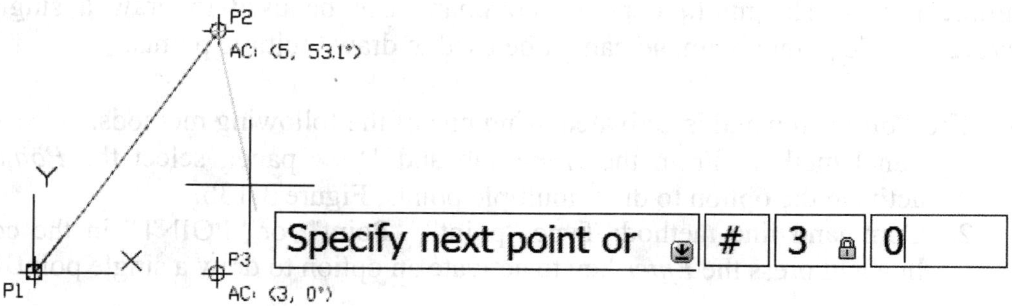

Figure 3-12a

3.5.3.4.   Relative Polar coordinates

For the relative coordinates, the last point is used as the benchmark for the relative coordinates of the next point. The relative coordinates are used when the location of the next point is known with respect to the previous point.

- ***Example:*** Draw a line from point P2 to point P3. The relative polar coordinates of point P3 with respect to P2 are (4, -90°).
- In the case of the dynamic input, specify the relative coordinates with the @ prefix, Figure 3-12a. (i) Click at point P2. (ii) Type the @ sign (hold the *Shift* key and press @ key). The @ sign will appear in the dynamic input and cursor will move to the first input field. (iii) Type in the distance (that is 4). (iv) Press the Less then (<) key. The cursor will move to the second input field. (v) Now, type the angle (that is 90). (vi) Finally, press the *Enter* key.
- For the command line the @ is used. Just type @4<-90 (no space) and press the *Enter* key.

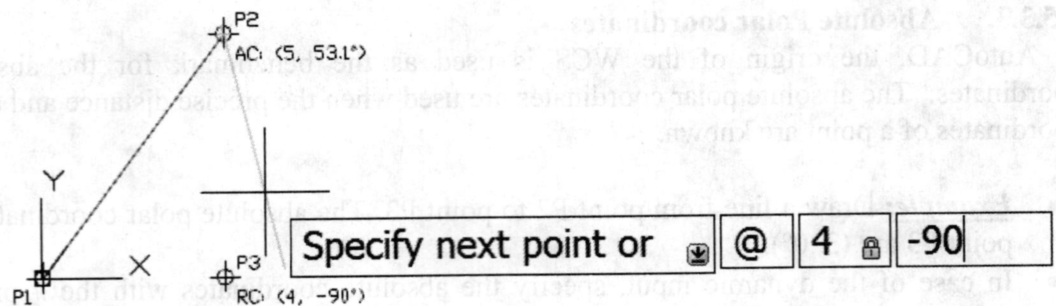

Figure 3-12b

3.6.   Point

Generally, a node in a drawing (Figure 3-13a) is shown as a point, and points are drawn using the *Point* command. Points are also used as reference geometry for object snaps. AutoCAD's *Point* command makes a distinction between drawing a single point and multiple points. The multiple points command can be used to draw a single point; however, single point command cannot be used to draw multiple points.

- The *Point* command is activated using one of the following methods.
  1. Panel method: From the *Home* tab and *Draw* panel, select the *Point* tool to activate the option to draw multiple points, Figure 3-13b.
  2. Command line method: Type "point", "Point", or "POINT" in the command line and press the *Enter* key to activate an option to draw a single point.

- The activation of the command will result in the prompt to specify a point as shown in Figure 3-13c. A point can be drawn using one of the following procedures.

  1. Click at a random point on the screen.
  2. Specify the coordinates on the command line: (i) type in the values of the point as x,y (no space); and (ii) press the *Enter* key.

  3. Specify the coordinates as a dynamic input.
     a. To specify the (x, y) coordinates (i) type the value of the x-coordinate in the first field; (ii) press the "," key; (iii) type the y-coordinate; and (iv) finally press the *Enter* key.
     b. To specify the (x, y, z) coordinates (i) type the value of the x-coordinate in the first field; (ii) press the "," key; (iii) type the y-coordinate; (iv) press the "," key; (v) type the z-coordinate; (vi) and finally press the *Enter* key.
     c. To specify the polar coordinates (length and angle), (i) type the value of length in the first field; (ii) press "<" or "tab" key; (iii) type the angle in the second field; and (iv) finally press the *Enter* key.

- **Note**: To change a locked value, keep pressing the *Tab* key to reach the desired field, and then follow the procedure discussed above.
- To **Exit** the command, press the *Esc* key on the keyboard. Do **NOT** press the *Enter* key on the keyboard.

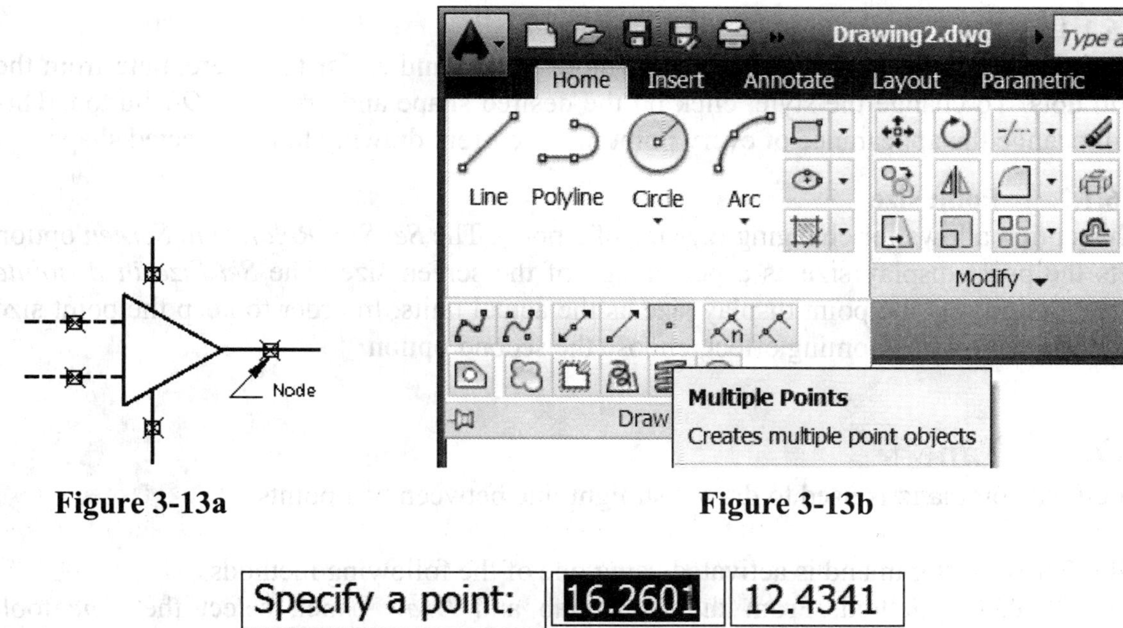

Figure 3-13a

Figure 3-13b

Figure 3-13c

3.6.1. Change style and size of a point

To change the appearance and size of a point, from the *Home* tab and *Utilities* panel select the *Point Style* option, Figure 3-13d. This will open the *Point Style* dialog box, Figure 3-13e. This dialog box is used to change the style and size of a point.

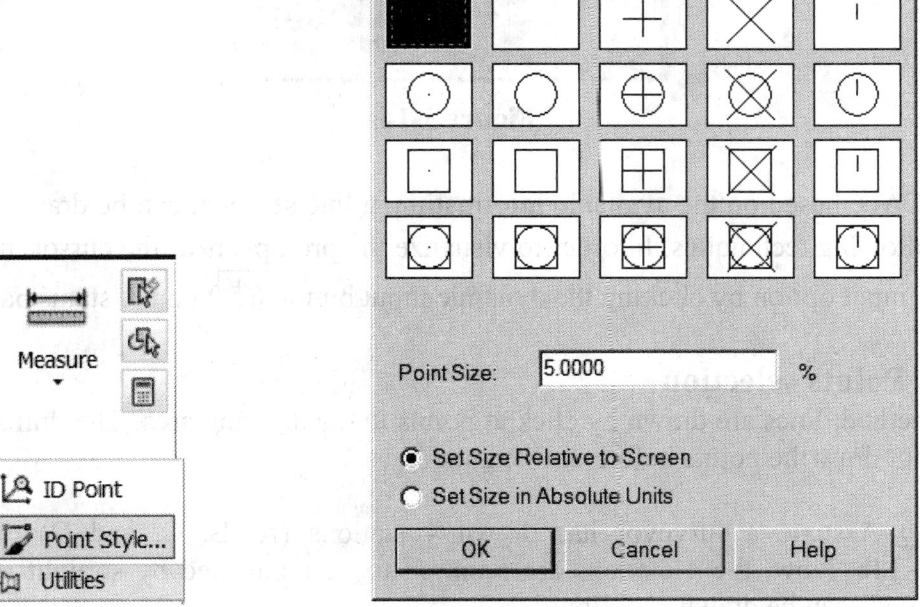

Figure 3-13c

Figure 3-13d

3.6.1.1.   Style

Changing the style will make the points more visible and easier to differentiate from the grid dots. To change the style, click on the desired shape and press the *OK* button. This will change the appearance of every point in the current drawing to the selected shape.

3.6.1.2.   Point size

This option allows for changing the size of a point. The *Set Size Relative to Screen* option sets the point display size as a percentage of the screen size. The *Set Size in Absolute Units* option sets the point display size as the actual units. In order to keep the point size independent of the zooming effect, choose the second option.

3.7.   Line

The *Line* command is used to draw a straight line between two points.

- The *Line* command is activated using one of the following methods.
    1. Panel method: From the *Home* tab and *Draw* panel, select the *Line* tool, Figure 3-14a.
    2. Command line method: Type "line", "Line", or "LINE" on the command line and press the *Enter* key.

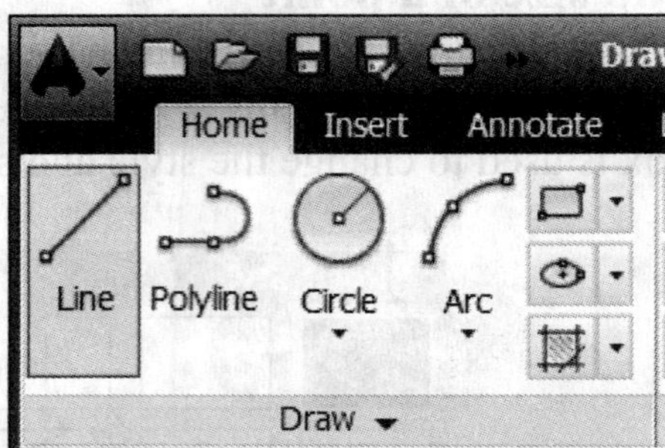

Figure 3-14a

In AutoCAD, based on the available information, a line segment can be drawn using one of the following techniques. In order to visualize the prompts near the cursor, turn on the dynamic input option by clicking the dynamic input button ( ) on the status bar.

3.7.1. Points selection

In this method, lines are drawn by click at points in the drawing area. The draftsman may or may not draw the points before drawing the lines.

Example: Assume a surveyor has drawn 4 stations (A, B, C, and D) on a map, Figure 3-14b. Now, the 4 stations are required to be connected by straight roads. The desired roads can be drawn as follow.

1. Activate the *Line* command.
2. Click at station A and then click at station B. A line segment will be drawn from station A to station B, Figure 3-14b. Press the down arrow key of the keyboard to check the available options. Only the *Undo* option is available.

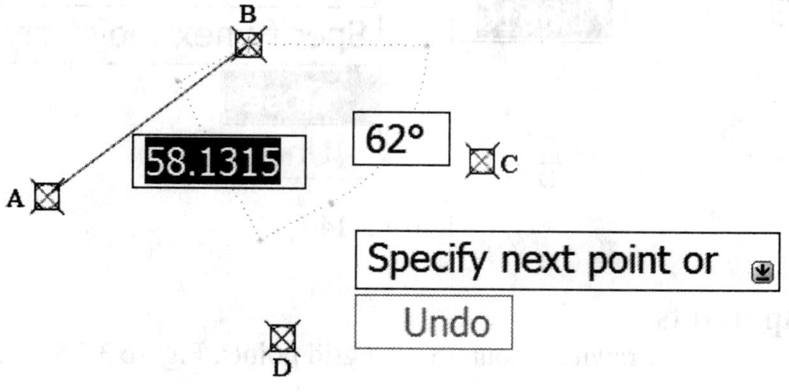

Figure 3-14b

3. Now, click at station C, a line segments will be drawn from station B to station C, Figure 3-14c. Press the down arrow key to check the available options. Now, the *Close* option is available, too. The close option is available only after the user has clicked at least three points (that is, have drawn two line segments).

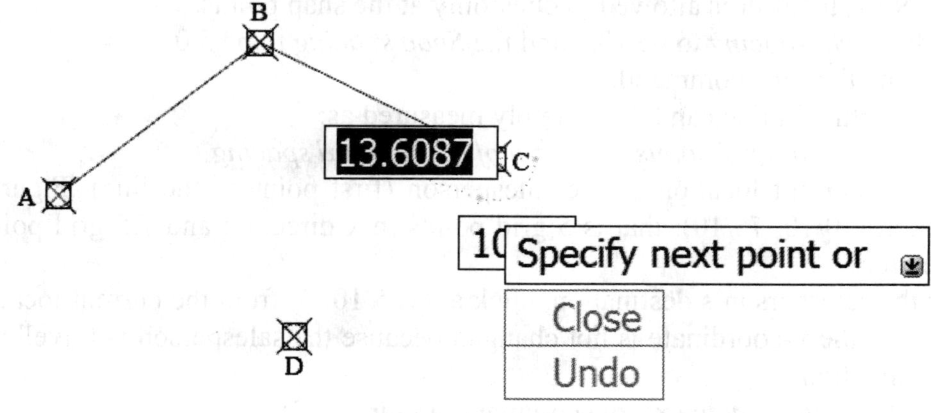

Figure 3-14c

4. Repeat step (3) to draw a line from station C to station D.
5. Press the down arrow key and click on the *Close* option, Figure 3-14d. The selection of the *Close* option will automatically draw a line from D to A and terminate the *Line* command.
6. To exit the command without creating a closed area, press the *Esc* or the *Enter* key.

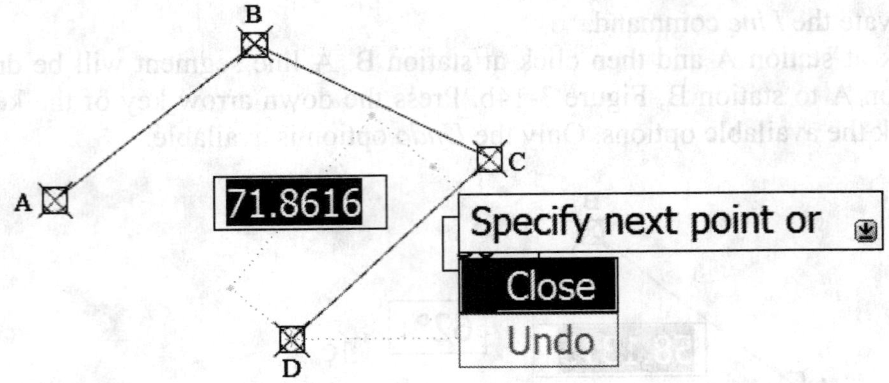

Figure 3-14d

3.7.2. Snap points

In the method, lines are drawn by counting the grid points, Figure 3-15b.

Example: A travelling salesperson wants to travel 125 meters to the east from the station at (50, 75) meters. That is, for the station x = 50m and y = 75m from the origin.

1. Turn on the dynamic input option by clicking the dynamic input button (⌞⌐) on the status bar.
2. Turn on the *Grid* and *Snap* options by clicking the respective buttons on the status bar. Now, the user is allowed to click only at the snap points.
3. Set the *Grid spacing* to be 10.0 and the *Snap spacing* to be 5.0
4. Activate the *Line* command.
5. The length of a line can be accurately measured as:
     No. of grid points = Length of a line /Grid spacing
6. For the current location of the salesperson (first point of the line), Figure 3-15a, click at (50/10, 75/10); that is 5 grid points in x-direction and 7.5 grid points in y-direction.
7. For the salesperson's destination, click at (125/10, 0) from the current location. The value of the y-coordinate is not changed because the salesperson is travelling to the east direction.
8. Press the *Enter* key to exit the command, Figure 3-15b.

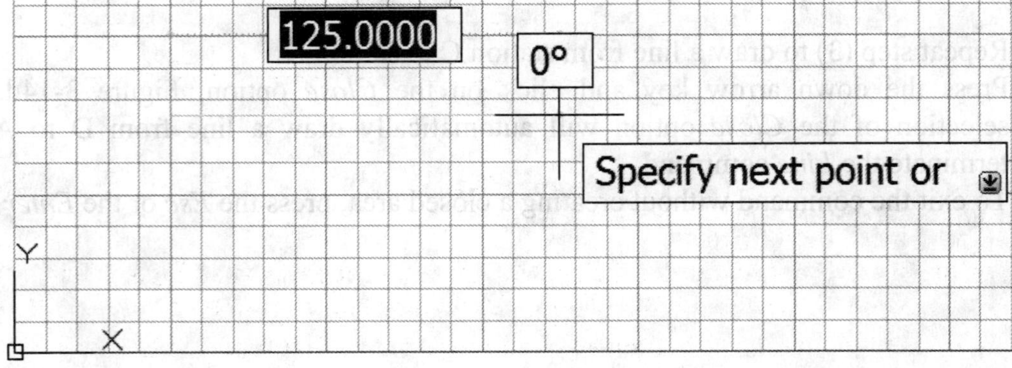

Figure 3-15a

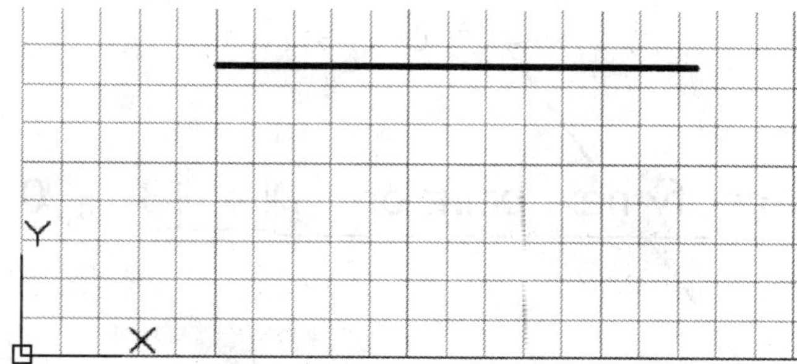

Figure 3-15b

3.7.3.   Cartesian coordinates

In the method, lines are drawn by specifying the coordinate of their end points.

Example: Draw a line from P2 to P3 using absolute and relative Cartesian coordinate.

1. Turn on the dynamic input option by clicking the dynamic input button ( ) on the status bar.
2. Activate the *Line* command.
3. Now, a user can draw lines using Cartesian (relative or absolute) coordinates.
4. Specify the first point.
5. For the <u>absolute coordinate</u> of the second and subsequent points, Figure 3-16a:
   - o   Type the # sign (hold the *Shift* key and press # key). The # sign will appear in the dynamic input and cursor will move to the first input field.
   - o   Type in the x-coordinate (that is 4).
   - o   Press the comma (,) key. The cursor will move to the second input field.
   - o   Now, type the y-coordinate (that is 2.5).
   - o   For 2-diensional drawing, press the *Enter* key. For the 3-diensional drawing, repeat the above step for the z-coordinate and then press the *Enter* key.

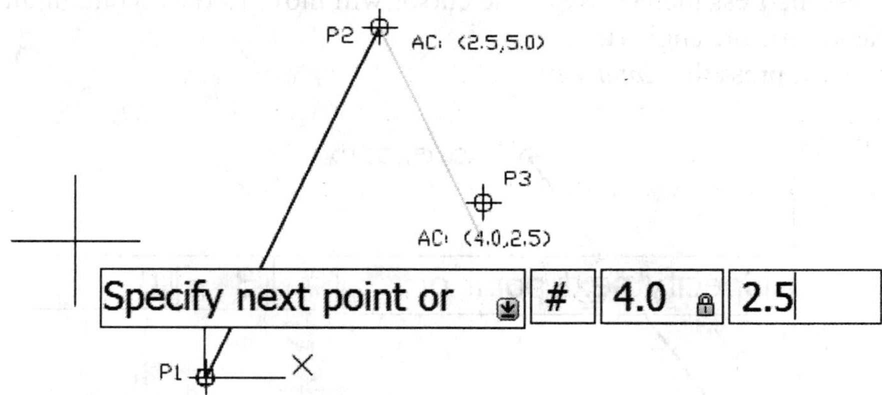

Figure 3-16a

6. For the <u>relative coordinate</u> of the second and subsequent points, Figure 3-16b:
   - o   Type the @ sign (hold the *Shift* key and press @ key). The @ sign will appear in the dynamic input and cursor will move to the first input field.

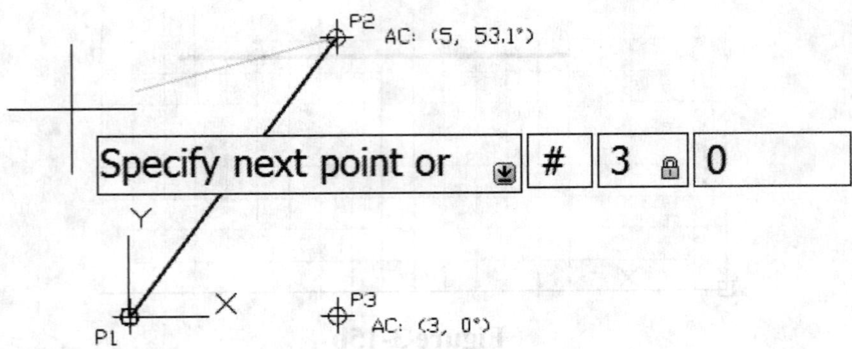

Figure 3-16b

- o   Type in the x-coordinate (that is 1.5).
- o   Press the comma (,) key. The cursor will move to the second input field.
- o   Now, type the y-coordinate (that is -2.5).
- o   For 2-diensional drawing, press the *Enter* key. For the 3-diensional drawing, repeat the above step for the z-coordinate and then press the *Enter* key.

3.7.4.   Polar coordinates

Example: Draw a line from P2 to P3 using absolute and relative polar coordinate system.

1. Turn on the dynamic input option by clicking the dynamic input button (⬚) on the status bar.
2. The angular values assume that 0° is horizontal line (east direction).
3. Activate the *Line* command. Specify the first point.
4. For the <u>absolute coordinate</u> of the second and subsequent points, Figure 3-17a:
   - o   Type the # sign (hold the *Shift* key and press # key). The # sign will appear in the dynamic input and cursor will move to the first input field.
   - o   Type in the distance (that is 3).
   - o   Press the Less then (<) key. The cursor will move to the second input field.
   - o   Now, type the angle (that is 0).
   - o   Finally, press the *Enter* key.

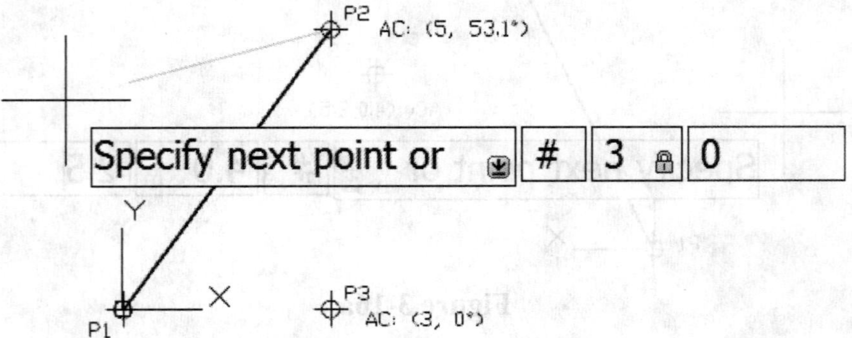

Figure 3-17a

5. For the <u>relative coordinate</u> of the second and subsequent points, Figure 3-17b:
   - o Type the @ sign (hold the *Shift* key and press @ key). The @ sign will appear in the dynamic input and cursor will move to the first input field.
   - o Type in the distance (that is 4).
   - o Press the Less then (<) key. The cursor will move to the second input field.
   - o Now, type the angle (that is -90).
   - o Finally, press the *Enter* key

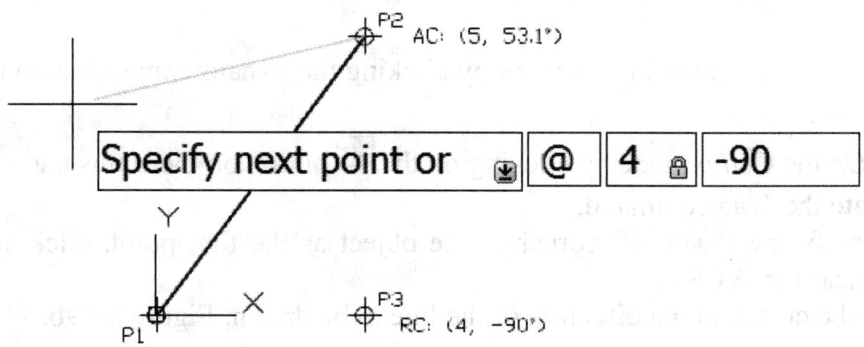

Figure 3-17b

3.7.5. Orthogonal lines

Figure 3-18a shows two pairs of perpendicular or orthogonal lines. In AutoCAD terminology, orthogonal lines mean that the horizontal and vertical lines, that is, the lines are parallel to X- and Y-axis.

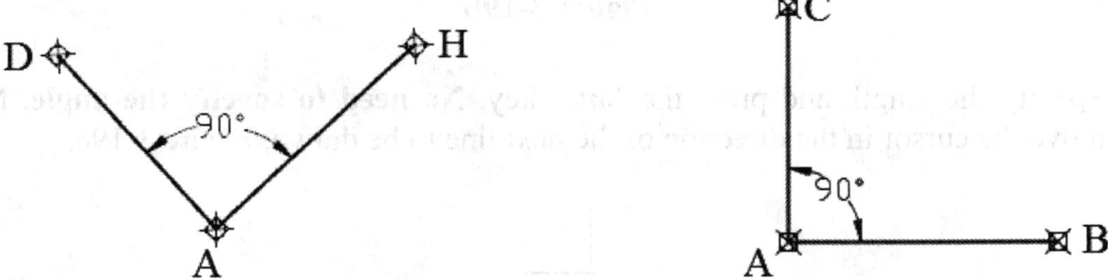

Figure 3-18a

Figure 3-18b shows the angles between two orthogonal lines. The angle can be 0°, 90°, 180°, or 270°.

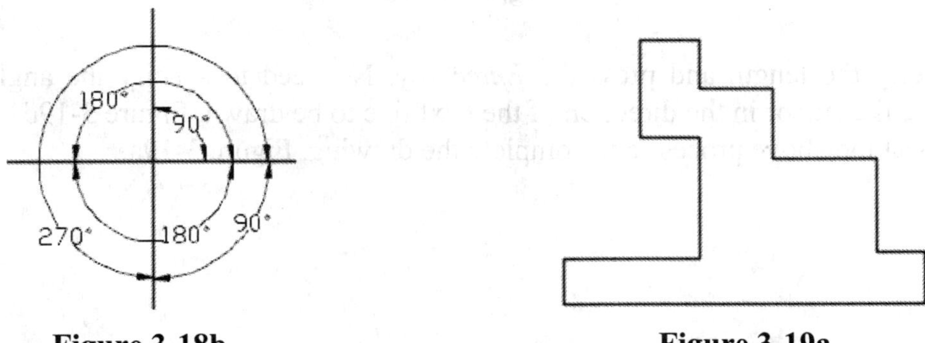

Figure 3-18b   **Figure 3-19a**

Example: Draw the object shown in Figure 3-19a using polar coordinates. Recall that the polar coordinate needs length and angle. In the current example, there are 14 line segments. Hence, the user needs to specify 14 lengths and 14 angles. Since the lines are horizontal and vertical; the AutoCAD user can increase the productivity by using the *Ortho* command. This command will allow the user to draw the orthogonal lines by specifying the lengths only. Thus, saving about 50% of the time require to draw the drawing using the following step. The example does not show the dimensions. For the practice, use some reasonable values for the lengths.

1. Turn *On* the dynamic input option by clicking the dynamic input button (⊞) on the status bar.
2. Turn *On* the *Ortho* mode by clicking on the ⊡ button on the status bar.
3. Activate the *Line* command.
4. To specify the lower left corner of the object as the first point, click at a random point near the WCS.
5. Move the cursor in the direction of the line to be drawn, Figure 3-19b.

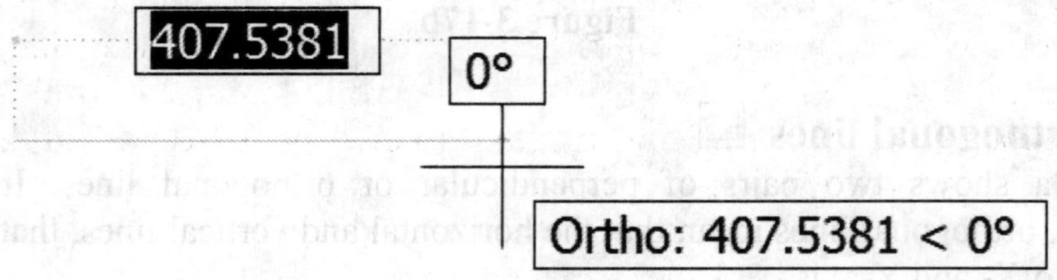

Figure 3-19b

6. Specify the length and press the *Enter* key. **No need to specify the angle**. Now, move the cursor in the direction of the next line to be drawn, Figure 3-19c.

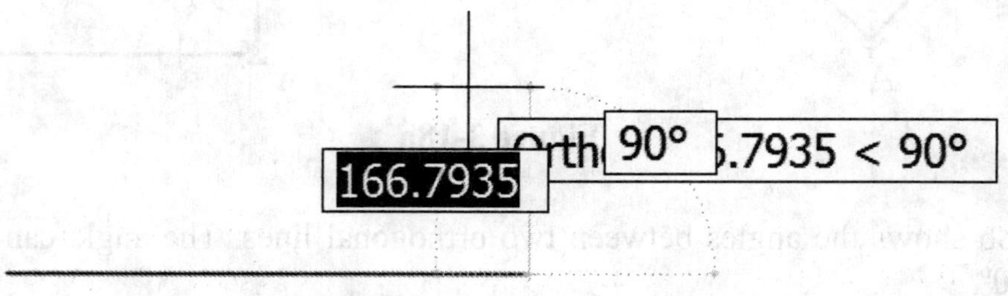

Figure 3-19c

7. Specify the length and press the *Enter* key. No need to specify the angle. Now, move the cursor in the direction of the next line to be drawn, Figure 3-19d.
8. Repeat the above process and complete the drawing, Figure 3-19a.

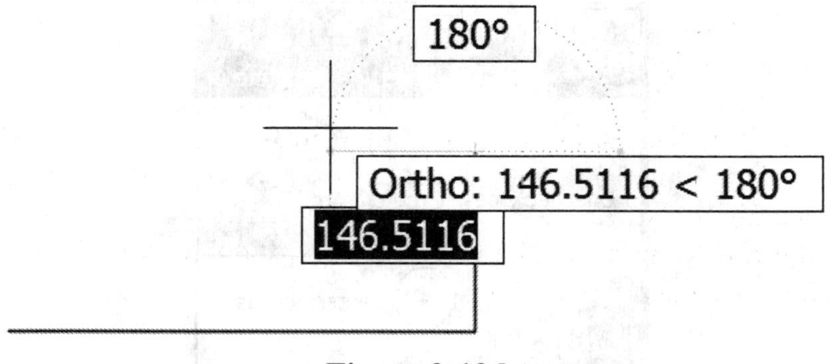

Figure 3-19d

3.8.   Circle

The *Circle* command is used to draw a circle by specifying the center of a circle and its radius or diameter. A circle can also be drawn with two or three points on its circumference. A circle of a known radius and tangent to two objects can be drawn, too.

- The *Circle* command is activated using one of the following procedures.
  1. Panel method: From the *Home* tab and *Draw* panel, select the *Circle* tool, Figure 3-20a.
  2. Command line method: Type "circle", "Circle", or "CIRCLE" in the command line and press the *Enter* key.

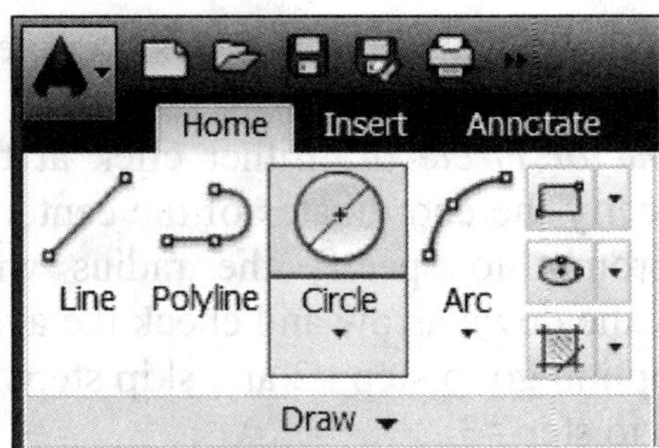

Figure 3-20a

- The activation of the command will result in the prompt shown in Figure 3-20b. Use the down arrow key to display the various options. However, if the user expands the *Circle*'s drop down menu, Figure 3-20c, then the user can select the desired option and the prompt will be for the selected option.

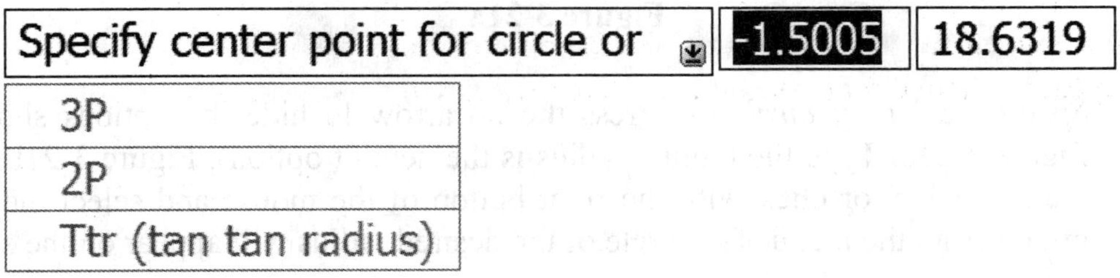

Figure 3-20b

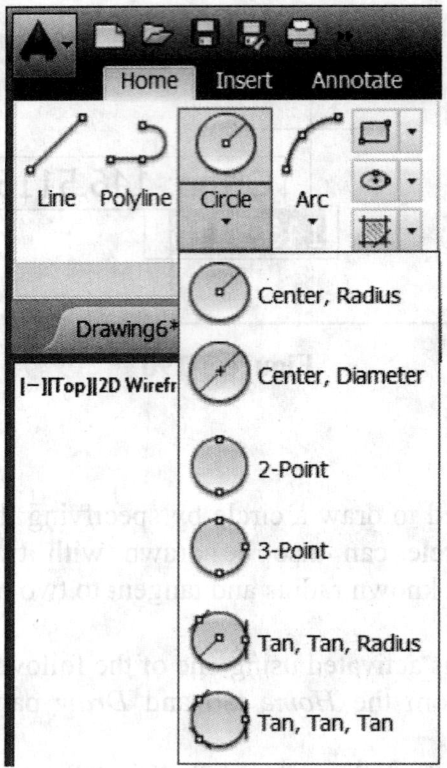

Figure 3-20c

- <u>Center point (default) option</u>: This option draws a circle based on the center point and the radius or the diameter of the circle.
  1. *Specify center point for circle or*: Either click at the desired location in the drawing area or specify the coordinates of the center of the circle and press the *Enter* key. The prompt to specify the radius will appear on the screen, Figure 3-21a. Click the down arrow and check the available option. To draw the circle with radius option go to step #2 and skip step #3; and for diameter option skip step #2 and go to step #3.

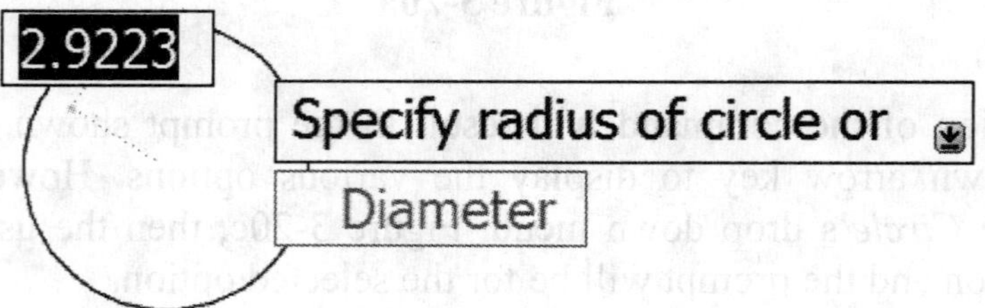

Figure 3-21a

  2. *Specify radius of circle or*: Press the up arrow to hide the options shown in Figure 3-21a. Type the radius (radius is the default option), Figure 3-21b. Press the *Enter* key or click with the right button of the mouse and select the *Enter* option from the menu. The circle of the desired radius will appear on the screen.

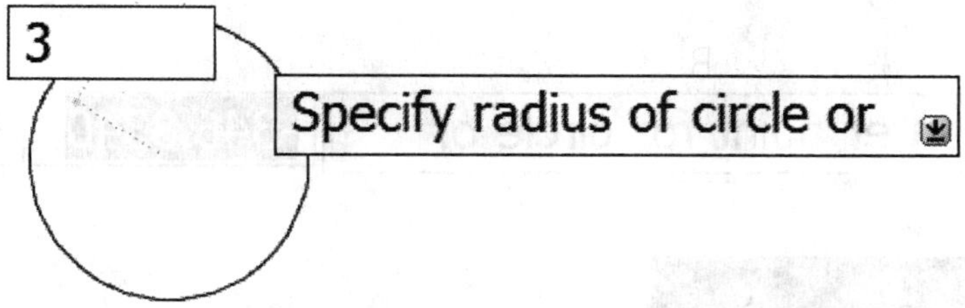

Figure 3-21b

3. *Diameter option*: In Figure 3-21a, click the *Diameter* option, Figure 3-21c. The prompt shown in Figure 3-21d will appear. Type the diameter and press the *Enter* key. The circle of the desired diameter will appear on the screen.

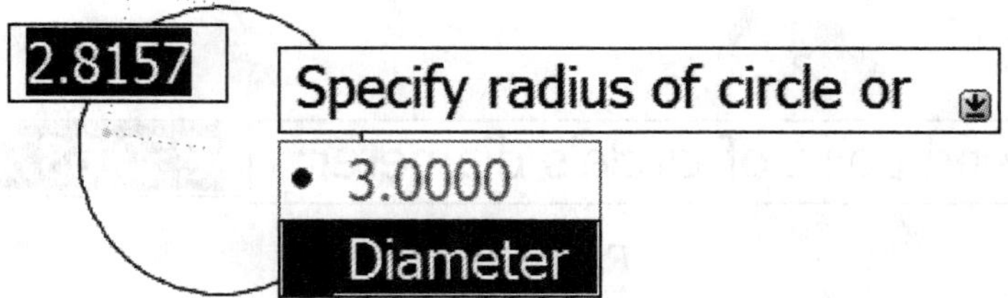

Figure 3-21c

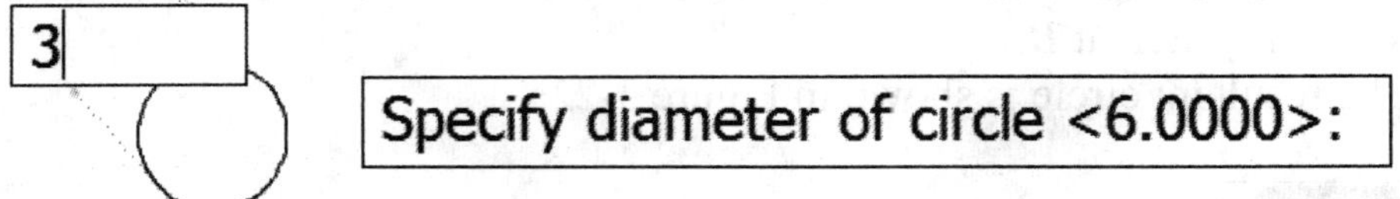

Figure 3-21d

- <u>Two points' option</u>: This option draws a circle based on the two endpoints of a diameter. The advantage of this command is that the user is not required to know the location of the center of the circle and its radius or diameter. This demonstration will use points *A* and *B* to draw the circle with *2P* option, Figure 3-22a.

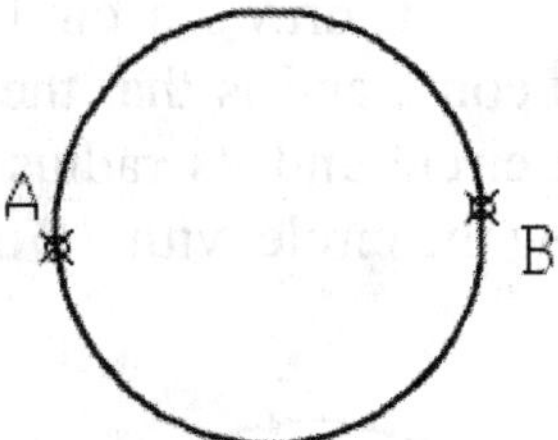

Figure 3-22a

1. Draw two points, *A* and *B*. Do not label them.
2. Activate the circle command. Press the down arrow and click on "*2P*" option, Figure 3-22b.

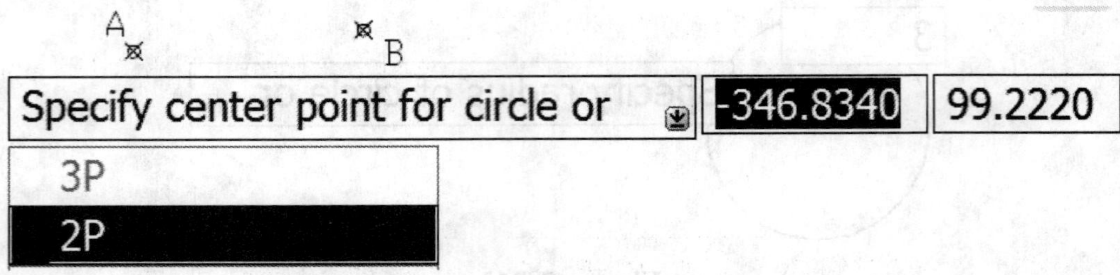

Figure 3-22b

3. *Specify the first end point of circle's diameter* (Figure 3-22c): Either type the comma separated coordinates of the first point or click at the desired location. Click at *A*.

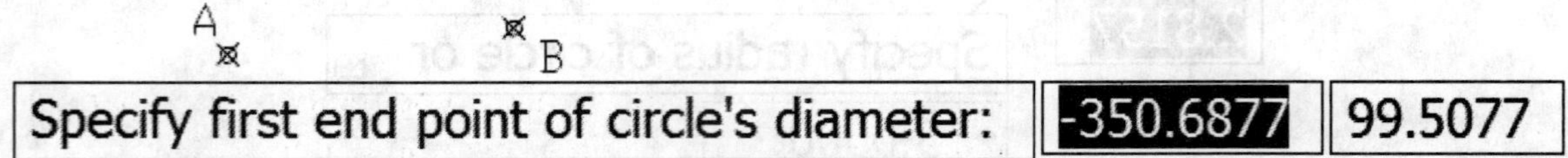

Figure 3-22c

4. *Specify the second end point of the circle's diameter* (Figure 3-22d): Either type the polar or Cartesian coordinates of the second point or click at the desired location. Click at *B*.
5. The resultant circle is shown in Figure 3-22a.

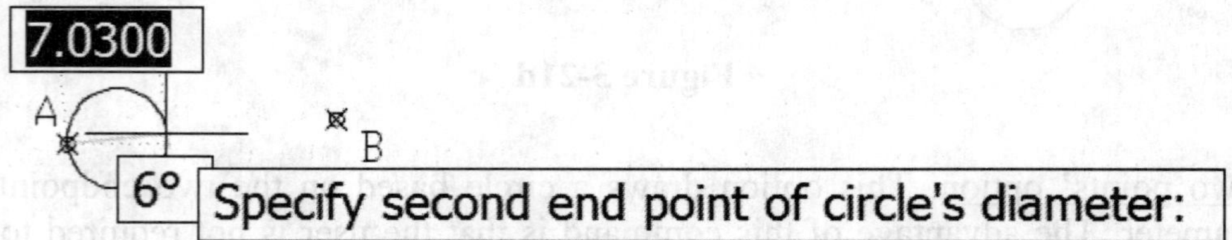

Figure 3-22d

- <u>Three points' option</u> : This option draws a circle based on the three points of a circle. The advantage of this command is that the user is not required to know the location of the center of the circle and its radius or diameter. This demonstration will use points *A*, *B*, *C* to draw the circle with *3P* option, Figure 3-23a.

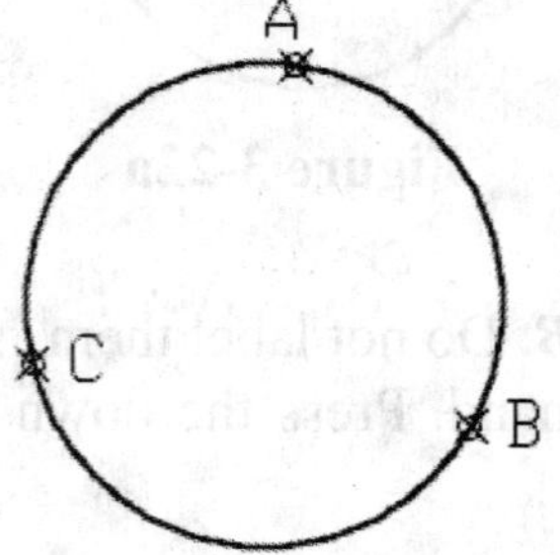

Figure 3-23a

1. Draw three points, *A*, *B* and *C*. Do not label them.
2. Activate the circle command. Press the down arrow and click on "*3P*" option, Figure 3-23b.

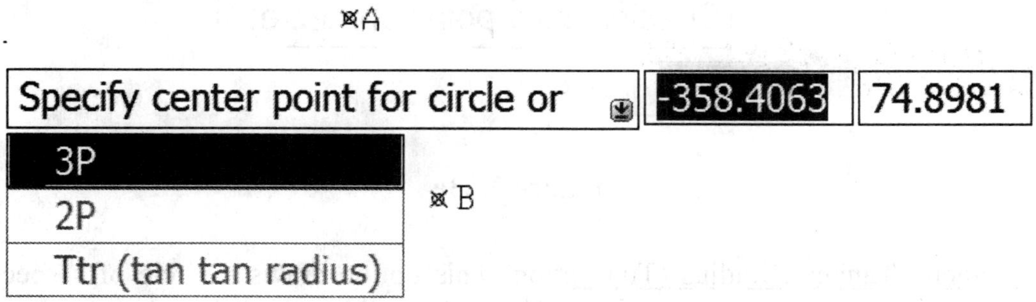

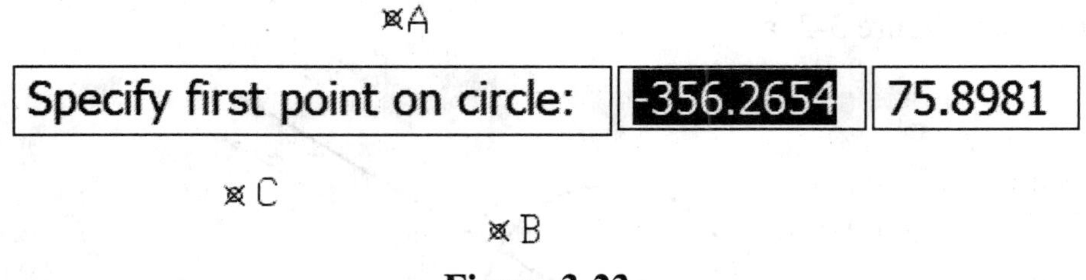

Figure 3-23b

3. *Specify the first point on circle* (Figure 3-23c): Either type the comma separated coordinates of the first point or click at the desired location. Click at *A*.

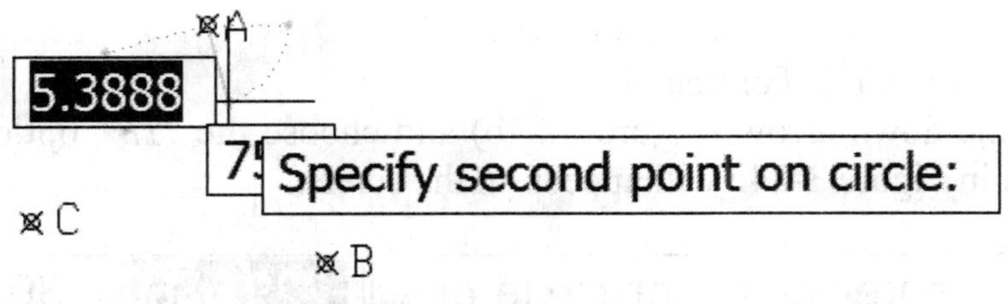

Figure 3-23c

4. *Specify the second point on circle* (Figure 3-23d): Either type the polar or Cartesian coordinates of the second point or click at the desired location. Click at *B*.

Figure 3-23d

5. *Specify third point on circle* (Figure 3-23e): Either type the polar or Cartesian coordinates of the third point or click at the desired location. Click at *C*.
6. The resultant circle is shown in Figure 3-23a.

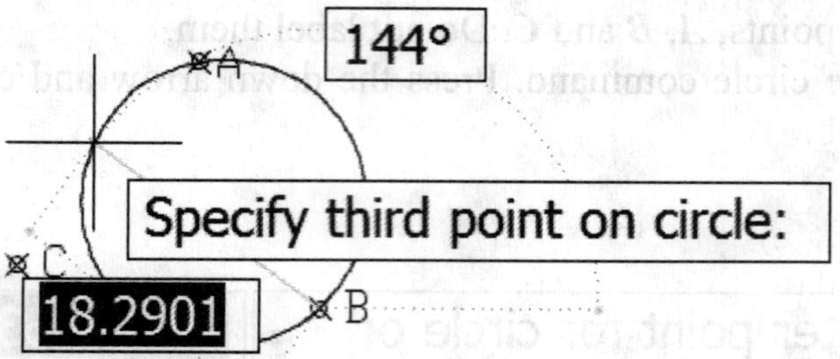

Figure 3-23e

- <u>Tangent, Tangent, Radius (Ttr) option</u>: This option draws a circle of a specified radius that is tangent to two objects. This command can draw a circle tangent to two circles, two arcs, two lines, or combination of two objects. The current example draws a circle tangent to a circle and a line.

1. Open an "acad" file and draw a 16 inches long line. Choose any value for the angle. Now draw a circle of diameter 6 inches with its center at the lower end of the line, Figure 3-24a.

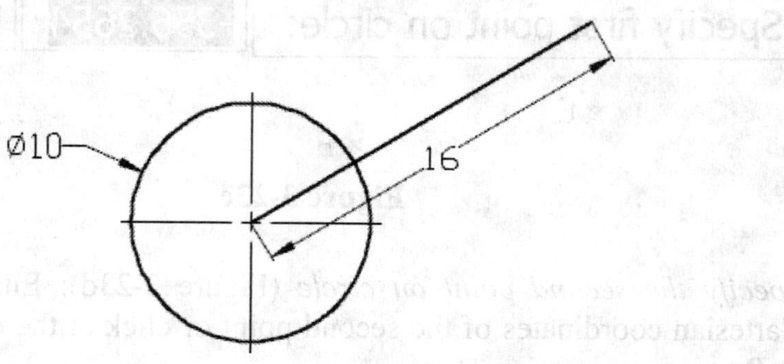

Figure 3-24a

2. Activate the circle command.
3. Press the down arrow (Figure 3-24b) and choose the "*Ttr*" option. The prompt shown in Figure 3-24c will appear on the screen.

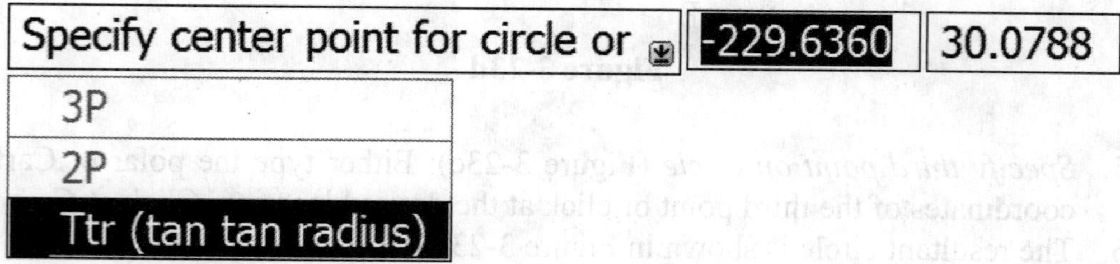

Figure 3-24b

4. *Specify point on the object for first tangent of circle* (Figure 3-24c). Either enter the comma separated coordinates of the tangent on the first object, or click

roughly in the vicinity of the tangent. In this example click near point *A* on the circle. Do not draw points A, B, C. These points will be used only for referencing.

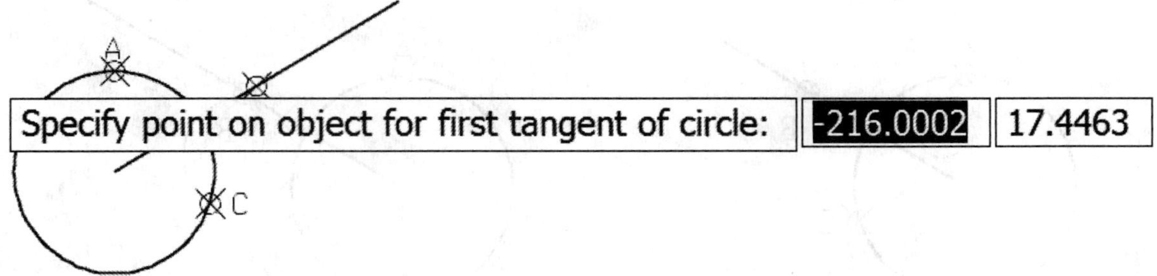

Figure 3-24c

5. *Specify point on object for second tangent of circle* (Figure 3-23d). Either enter the coordinates (Cartesian or polar) of the tangent on the second object, or click roughly in the vicinity of the tangent. In this example click near *B* on the line.

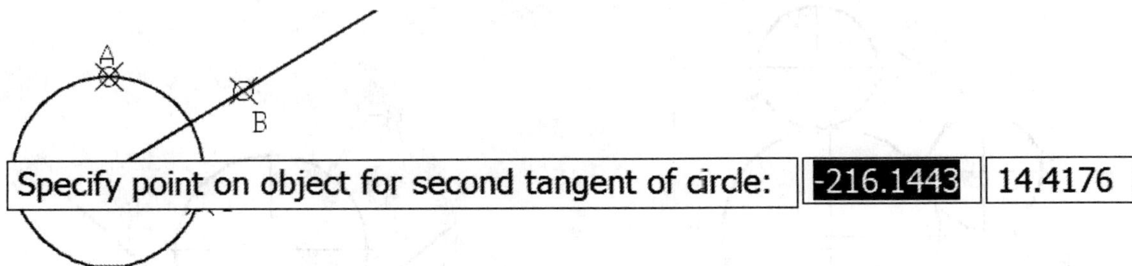

Figure 3-24d

6. *Specify radius of circle* (Figure 3-24e). Specify the radius to be 2.5 and press the *Enter* key.

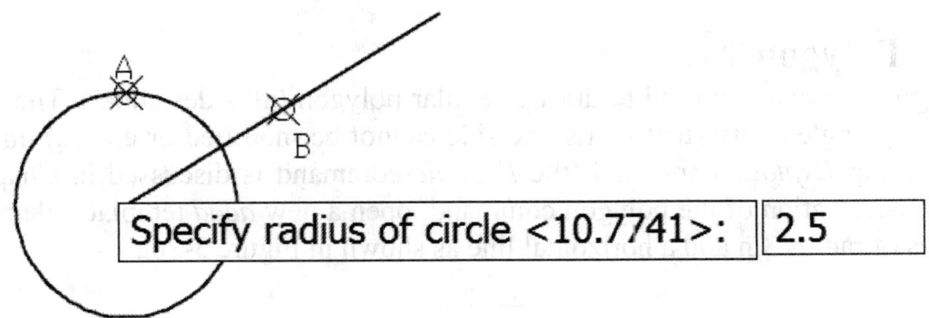

Figure 3-24e

7. This will exit the command and draws the circle, Figure 3-24f. The line thickness of the circle has been increased after it was drawn.
8. Repeat the process from step #2 - #6; click near point C in step #5. The resulting circle is shown in Figure 3-25a.

9. If the specified radius is smaller than the smallest possible circle tangent to the selected objects, then the program will not draw a circle. In Figure 3-25b, a circle tangent to the smaller circles and of radius less than 3" cannot be drawn.

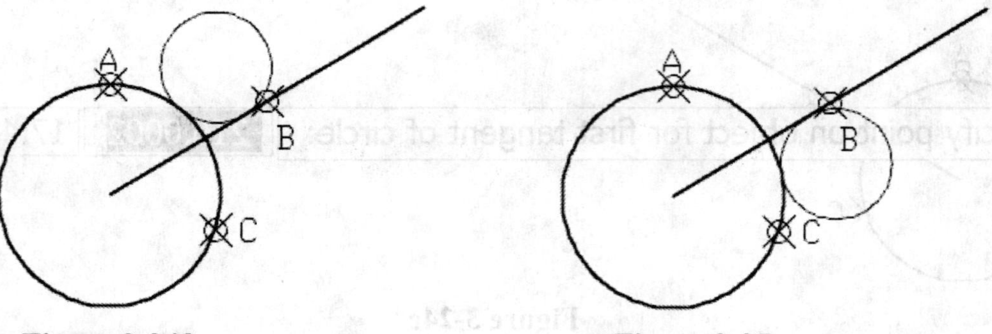

Figure 3-24f   **Figure 3-25a**

10. In Figure 3-25b and Figure 3-25c, a circle is drawn tangent to two circles and tangent to two lines, respectively.

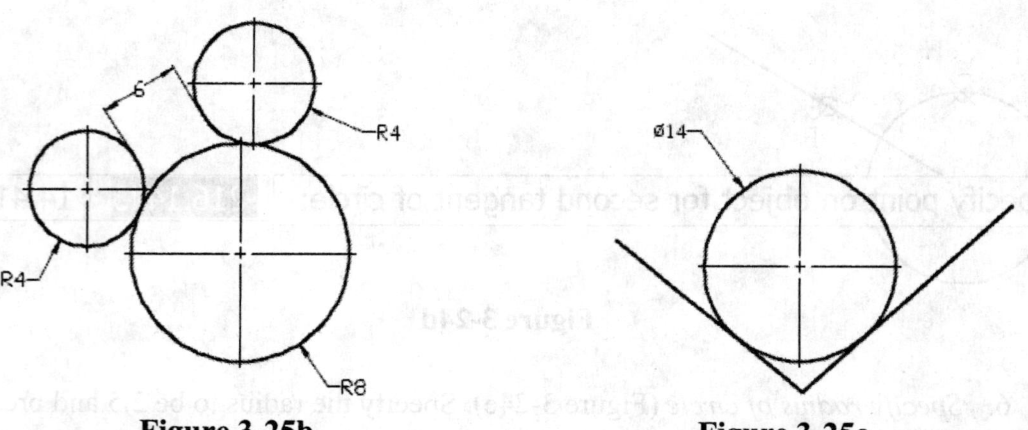

Figure 3-25b   **Figure 3-25c**

3.9.   Polygon

The *Polygon* command is used to draw a regular polygon (all sides equal). The resultant polygon is a single entity (that is, its one side cannot be modified or erased) unless it is exploded using *Explode* command (the *Explode* command is discussed in Chapter #4). For the demonstration of the polygon command, open a new *acad* template file and draw two circles of radius 3in and a horizontal line as shown in Figure 3-26a.

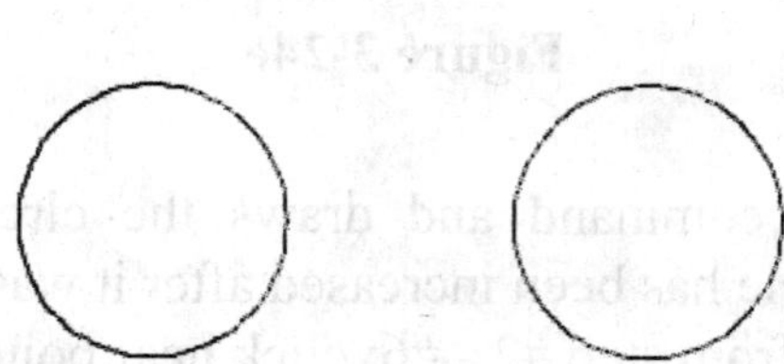

Figure 3-26a

- The *Polygon* command is activated using one of the following procedures.
  1. Panel method: From the *Home* tab and *Draw* panel, press the down arrow beside the rectangle and select the *Polygon* tool, Figure 3-26b.
  2. Command line method: Type "polygon", "Polygon", or "POLYGON" in the command line and press the *Enter* key.

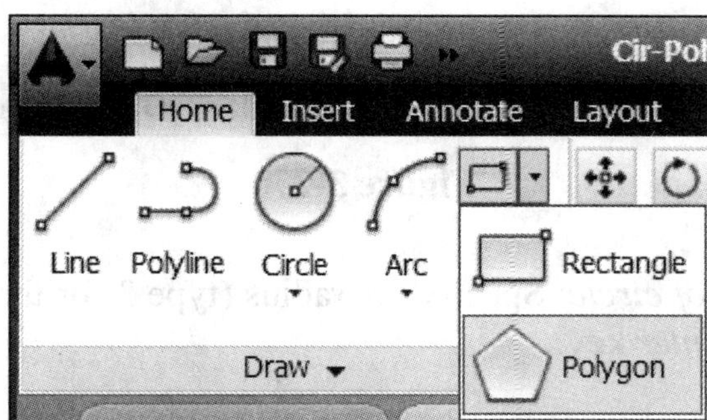

Figure 3-26a

- The activation of the command will result in the prompt to enter the number of sides of the polygon, Figure 3-27a

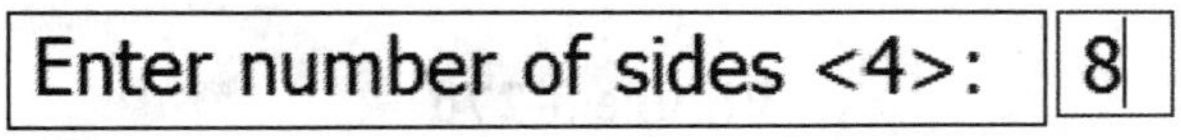

Enter number of sides <4>: 8

Figure 3-27a

- *Enter number of sides*: Specify a number between 3 and 1024 and press the *Enter* key. This example will create an octagon (8 sided polygon). Press the down arrow key to display the various options, Figure 3-27b.
- The user either specifies the center of the polygon or chooses the edge option.

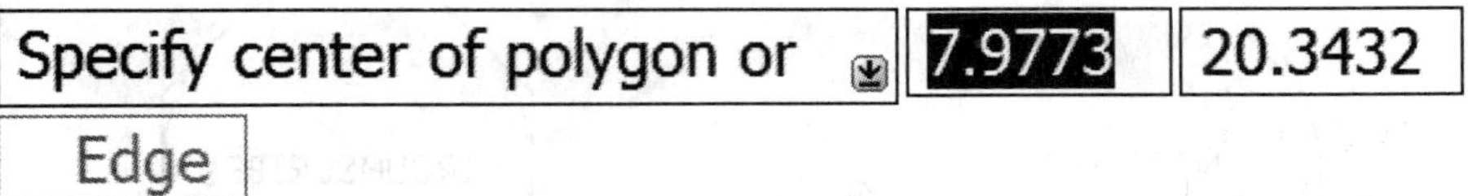

Figure 3-27b

- <u>Center option</u>: This option creates a polygon by specifying its center (the user had already specified the number of edges), Figure 3-27b.
  1. *Specify center of polygon*: Either specify the coordinates of the center point and press the *Enter* key; or click in the drawing area at the desired location. For this example, click at the center point of one of the circles drawn earlier. The next prompt is shown in Figure 3-27c.
  2. *Enter an option [Inscribed in circle/Circumscribed about circle]* Figure 3-27c. Click on the *Inscribed in Circle* option. The prompt shown in Figure 3-27d will appear on the screen.

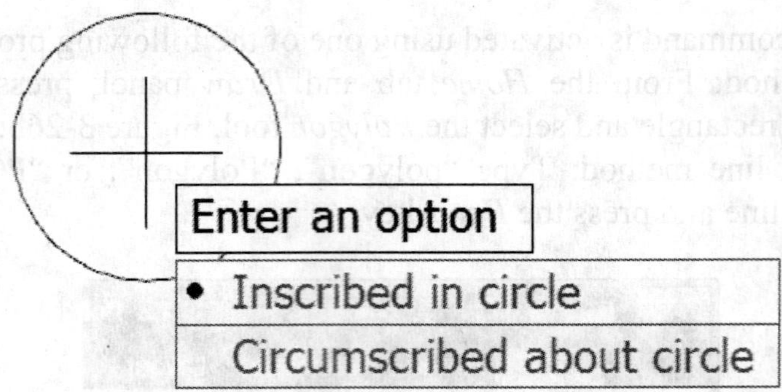

Figure 3-27c

3. *Specify radius of circle*: Specify the radius (type 3 for the radius), Figure 3-27d, and press the *Enter* key.

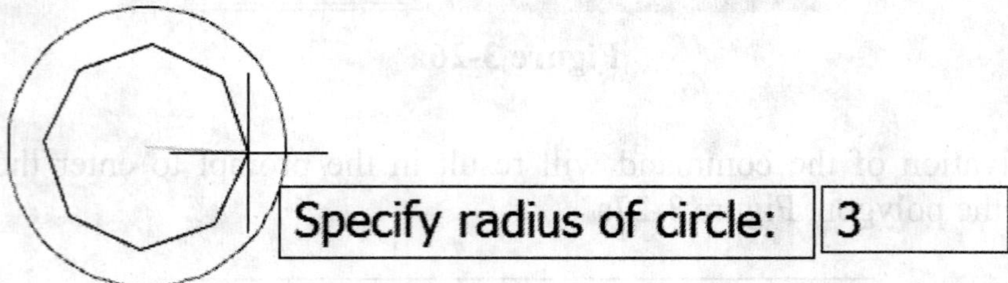

Figure 3-27d

4. The *Inscribed in Circle* option specifies the radius of a circle on which all the vertices of the polygon lie (that is, the polygon will be drawn inside the circle), Figure 3-27e. *Circumscribed about Circle* option specifies the distance from the center of the polygon to the midpoints of the edges of the polygon (that is, the polygon will be drawn outside the circle), Figure 3-27f.

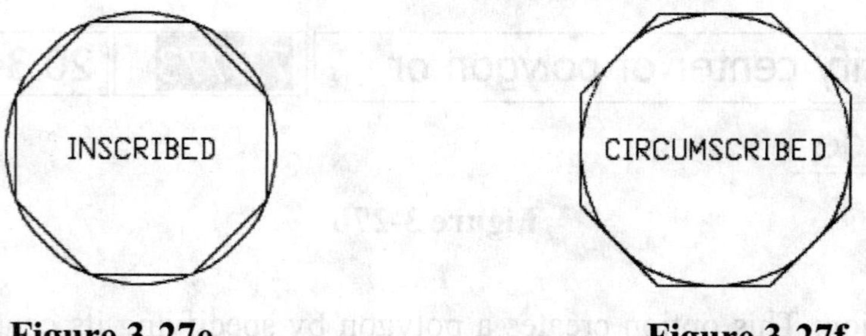

Figure 3-27e   **Figure 3-27f**

- <u>Edge option</u>: This option creates a polygon by specifying the endpoints of one of the edges (the user had already specified the number of edges). This example also creates an 8 sided polygon.

1. Click on the edge option as shown in Figure 3-28a. The prompt shown in Figure 3-28b will appear.

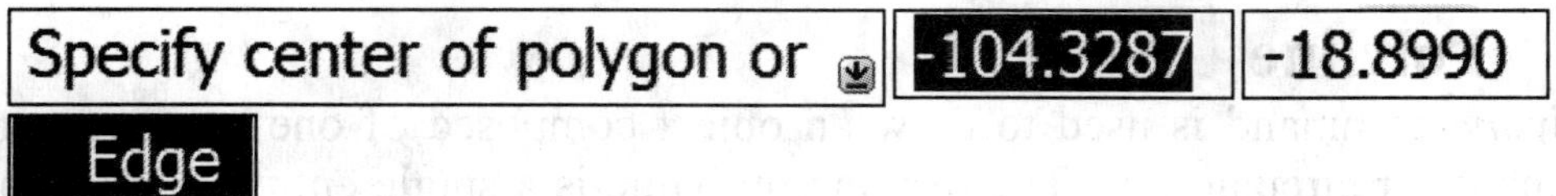

Figure 3-28a

2. *Specify first endpoint of the edge*: Figure 3-28b, either specify the coordinates and press the *Enter* key; or click in the drawing area. Click on one of the two ends of the line drawn earlier Figure 3-26a. The prompt shown in Figure 3-28c will appear.

Figure 3-28b

3. *Specify the second endpoint of the edge*: Figure 3-28c, either specify the coordinates and press the *Enter* key or click in the drawing area. The size of the polygon will change as the cursor is moved. Click on the other end of the line.
4. The resultant polygon is shown in Figure 3-28d. The lineweight of the reference edge is increased.

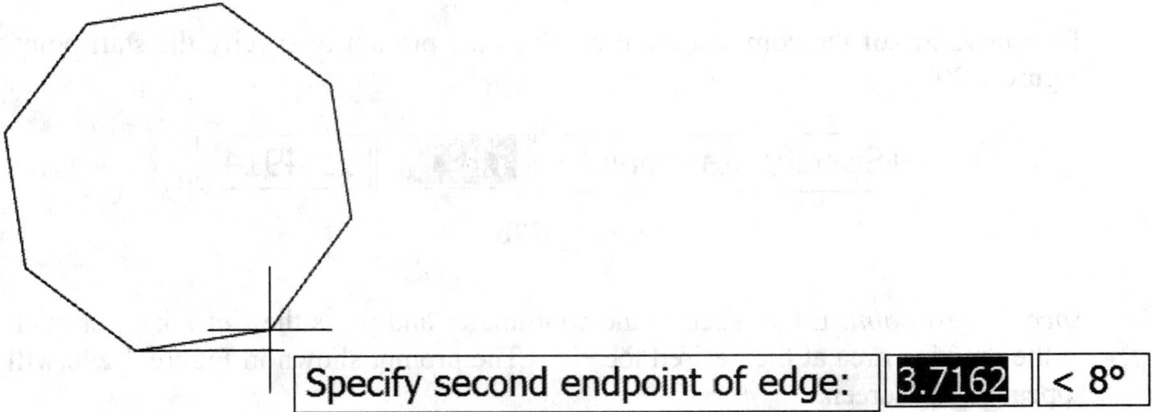

Figure 3-28c

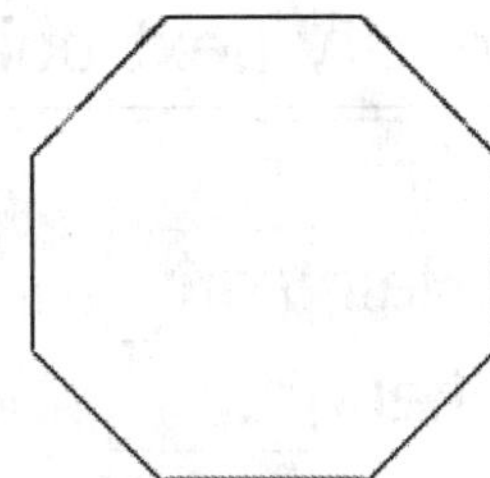

Figure 3-28d

3.10.   Polyline

The *Polyline* command is used to draw an object composed of one or more connected line segments or circular arcs. The resultant polyline is a single entity; that is, one of its segments cannot be modified independently. A polyline can be converted to multiple entities using *Explode* command (the *Explode* command is discussed in Chapter #4).

- The *Polyline* command is activated using one of the following procedures.
  1. Panel method: From the *Home* tab and *Draw* panel, select the *Polyline* tool, Figure 3-26b.
  2. Command line method: Type "pline", "Pline", or "PLINE" in the command line and press the *Enter* key.

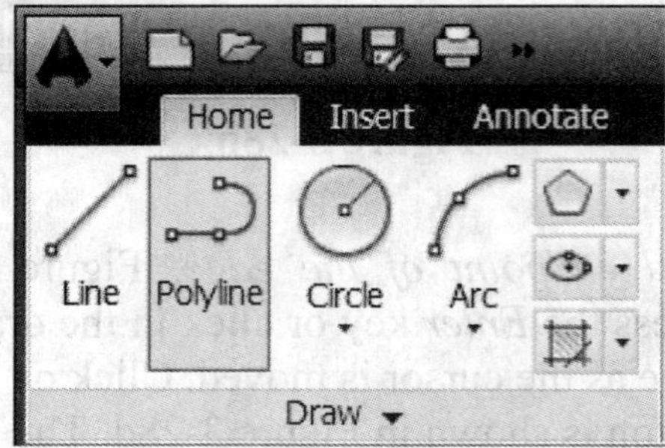

Figure 3-29a

- The activation of the command will result in the prompt to specify the start point, Figure 3-29b.

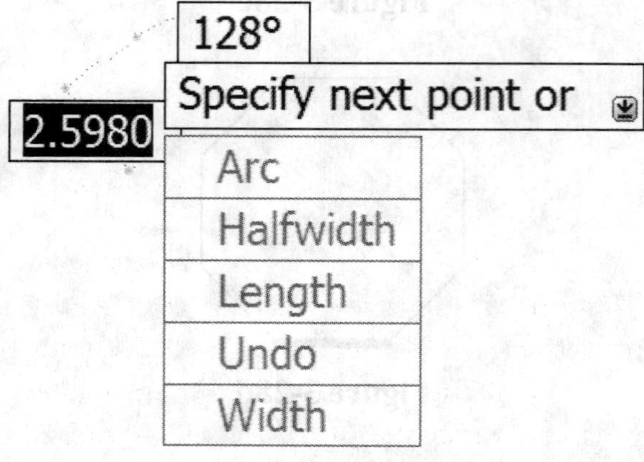

Figure 3-29b

- *Specify start point*: Either specify the coordinates and press the *Enter* key; or click in the drawing area at the desired location. The prompt shown in Figure 3-29c will appear on the screen.

Figure 3-29c

- Arc option: This option creates arc segments in a polyline. Click on the *Arc* option in Figure 3-29c. The prompt shown in Figure 3-30a will appear on the screen.

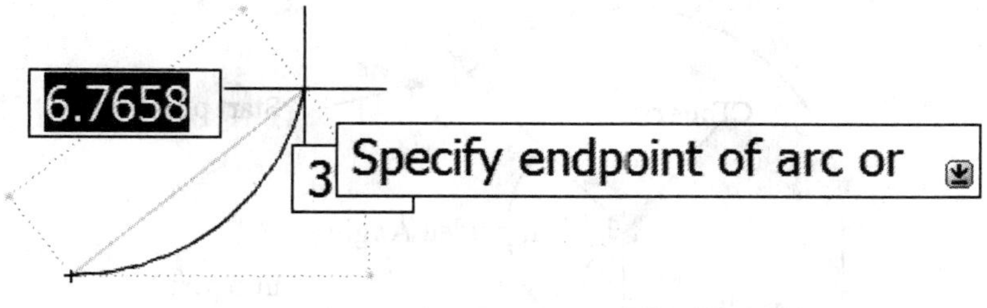

Figure 3-30a

- Either specify the endpoint of the arc or press the down arrow key to visualize the list of options, Figure 3-30b.

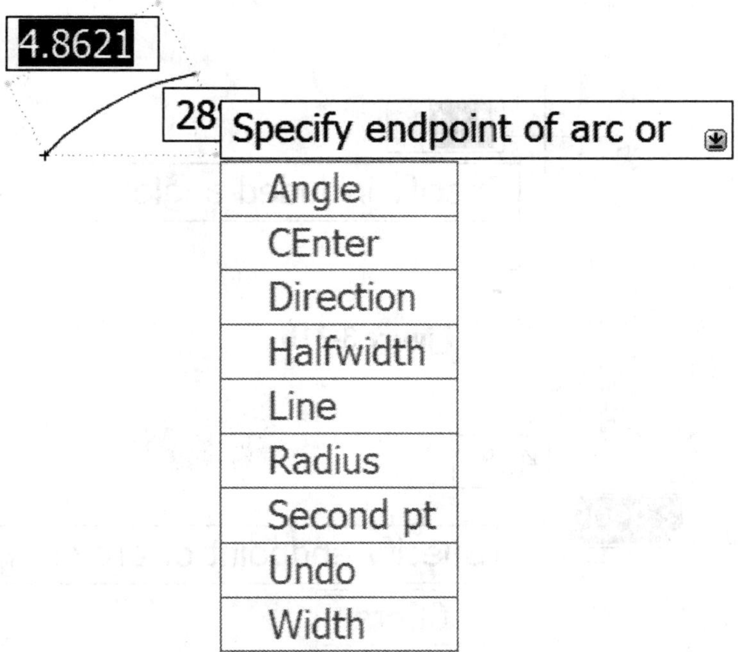

Figure 3-30b

1. Angle: The *Angle* option of Figure 3-30b allows for the specification of the included angle of an arc segment from the start point. A positive angle creates a counterclockwise arc segment and a negative angle creates a clockwise arc segment, Figure 3-31a. (i) Activate the polyline command. (ii) Click at the start point of Figure 3-31a. (iii) Press the down arrow on the keyboard and select the *Arc* option in Figure 3.29b. (iv) Press the down arrow on the keyboard and select the *Angle* option in Figure 3.30b. The prompt shown in Figure 3-31b will appear on the screen. (v) Specify the angle and press the *Enter* key, Figure 3-31c. (vi) For the *endpoint* option click at the END POINT of Figure 3-31a. For the *CEnter* option click at the CEnter of Figure 3-31a. For the

Radius option specify its value. (vii) Press the *Enter* key. The resultant arc is shown in Figure 3-31a. The user is ready to draw the next command.

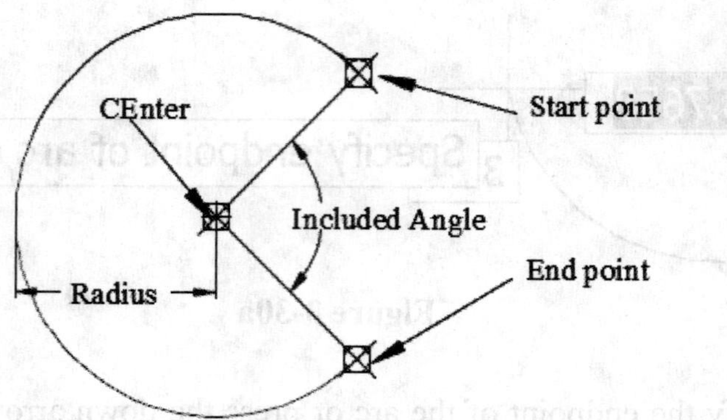

Figure 3-31a

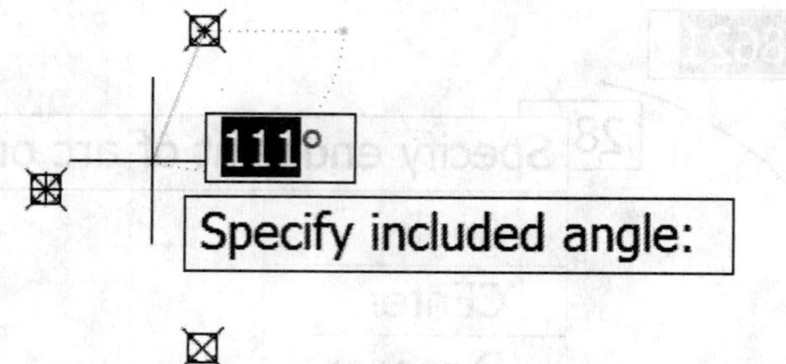

Figure 3-31b

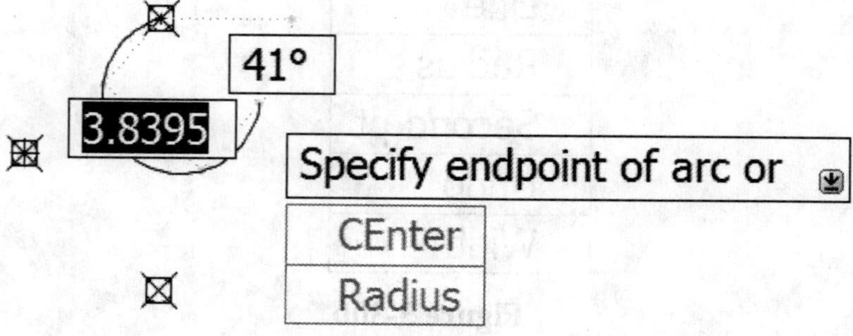

Figure 3-31c

2. <u>CEnter</u>: The *CEnter* option of Figure 3-30b allows for the specification of the center of the arc segment. (i) Activate the polyline command. (ii) Click at the start point of   Figure 3-29a. (iii) Press the down arrow on the keyboard and select the *Arc* option in Figure 3.29b. (iv) Press the down arrow on the keyboard and select the *CEnter* option in Figure 3.30b. (v) Specify the center of the arc segment, either through the coordinates or by clicking in the drawing area, Figure 3-32a. (vi) Choose endpoint, angle, or length option, specify the value, and press the *Enter* key, Figure 3-32b. For the current example, select the angle option, Figure 3-32c. (vii) Specify the included angle, Figure 3-32c. (viii) Press the *Enter* key. The resulting arc is shown in Figure 3-32d. Note that the positive

angle resulted in counterclockwise arc. The user is ready to draw the next command.

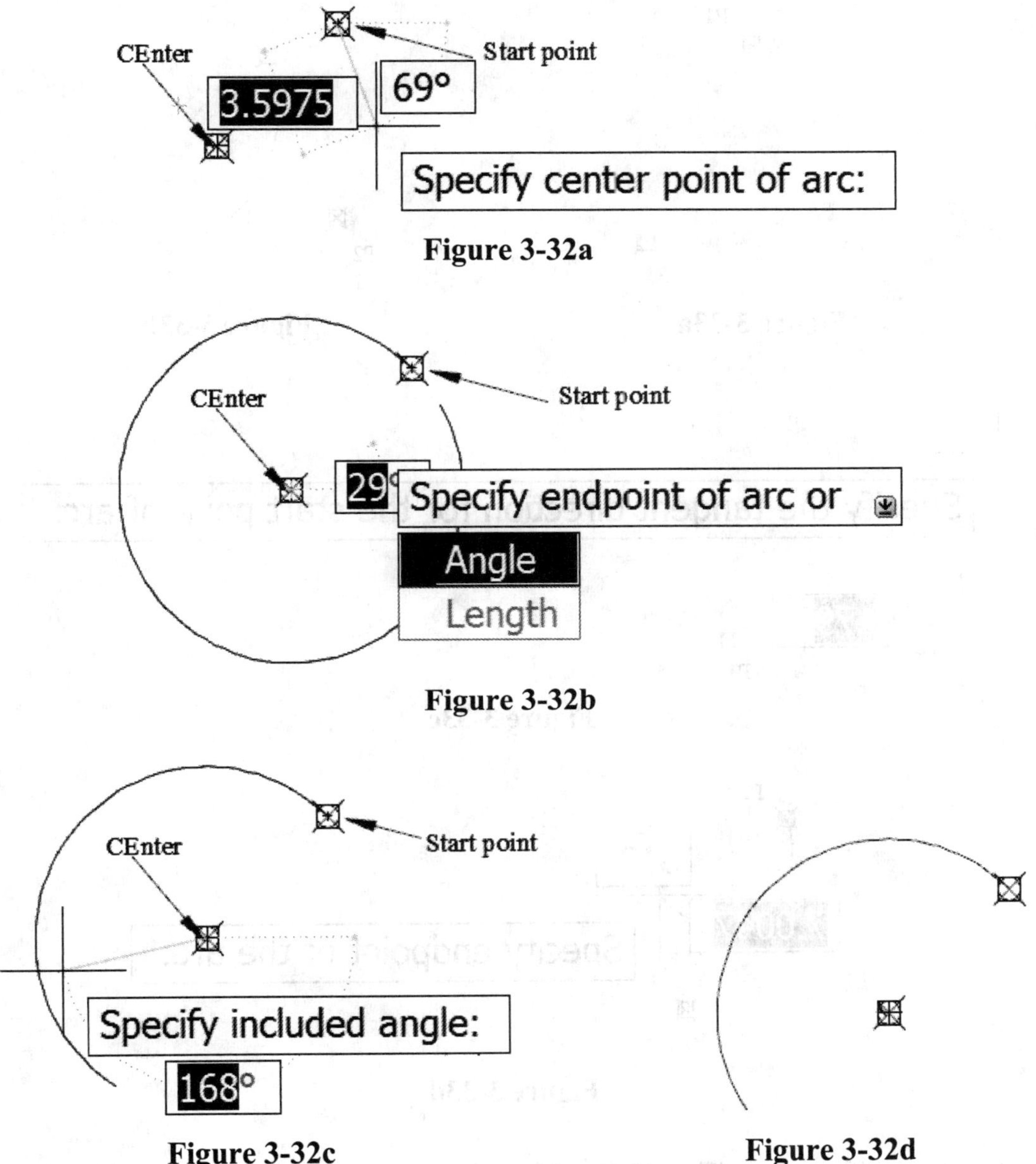

Figure 3-32a

Figure 3-32b

Figure 3-32c   **Figure 3-32d**

3. <u>Direction</u>: The *Direction* option of Figure 3-30b allows for the specification of the direction of the arc segment. (i) Draw three points as shown in Figure 3-33a. (ii) Activate the polyline command. (iii) Click at the point P1 for the start point. (iv) Press the down arrow on the keyboard and select the *Arc* option in Figure 3.29b. (v) Press the down arrow key on the keyboard and select the *Direction* option in Figure 3.30b. (vi) Specify the starting direction for the arc segment. In order to draw an arc from point P1 to P3 as shown in Figure 3-33b, point P2 should be clicked for the tangent direction, Figure 3-33c. (vii) Finally, for the endpoint, click at P3, Figure 3-33d. (viii) Press the *Enter* key. The

resulting arc is shown in Figure 3-32b. The user is ready to draw the next command.

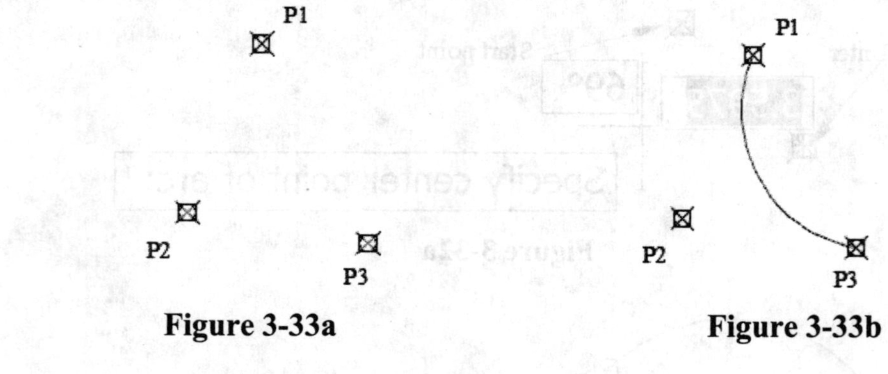

Figure 3-33a   **Figure 3-33b**

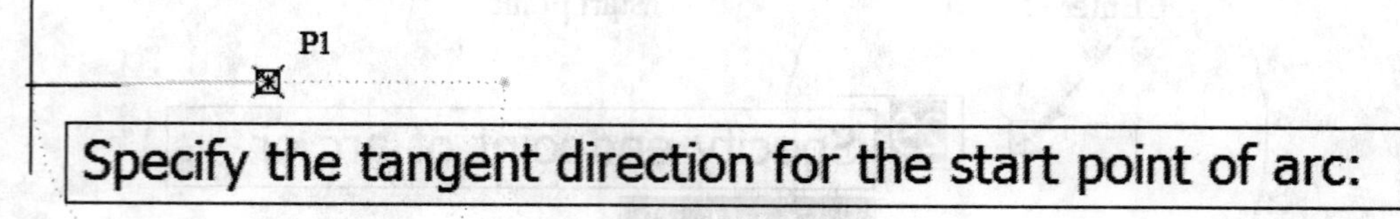

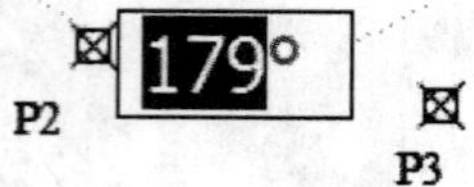

Figure 3-33c

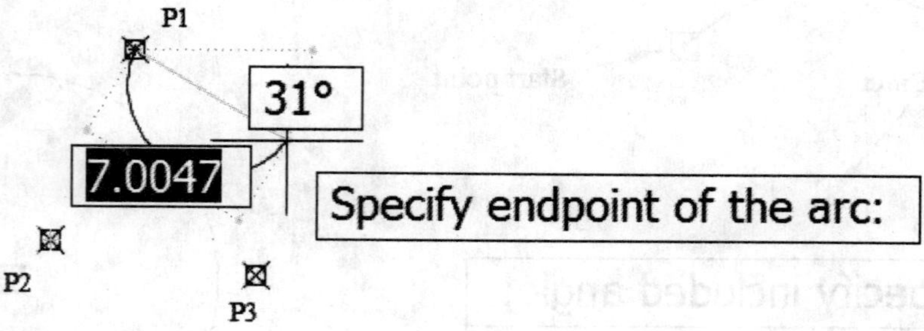

Figure 3-33d

4. <u>Halfwidth option</u>: This *Halfwidth* option is used to specify the width from the center of a wide polyline line segment to one of its edges. The process is similar to the *Width* option.
5. <u>Line</u>: This option allows the user to exit the *Arc* option and returns to the initial polyline command prompts.
6. <u>Radius option</u>: The *radius* option requires to specify the radius of the arc after the specification of its start point.
7. <u>Second pt</u>: Specifies the second point and endpoint of a three-point arc.
8. <u>Undo option</u>: The *Undo* option deletes the most recent line segment added to the polyline.

9. <u>Width option</u>: The *Width* option specifies the width of the next line segment.
- *Specify starting width*: Enter a value and press the *Enter* key, Figure 3-34a.
- *Specify ending width*: Enter a value and press the *Enter* key, Figure 3-34b.
- The ending width is the uniform width for all the subsequent segments until the width is changed again, Figure 3-34c.

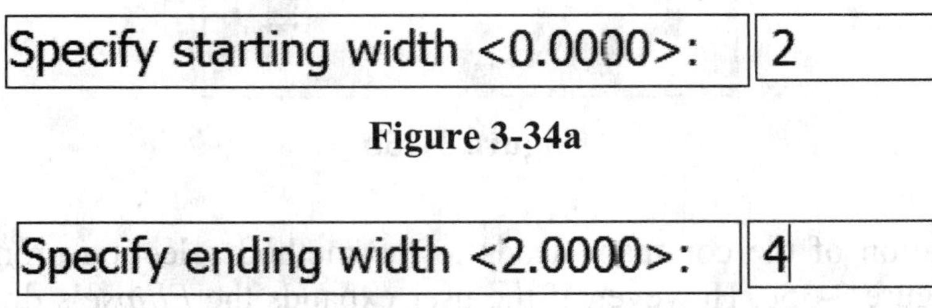

Figure 3-34a

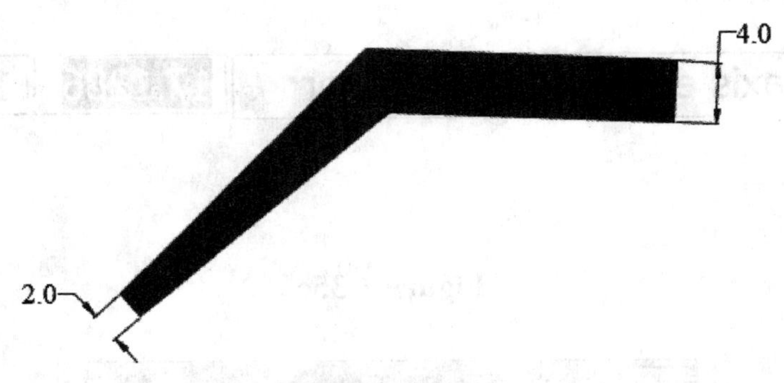

Figure 3-34b

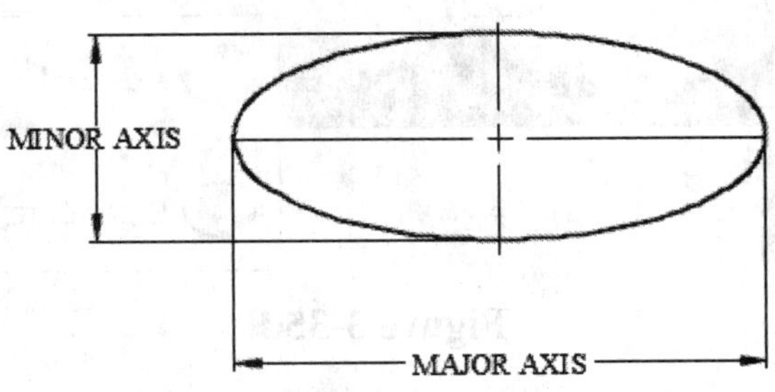

Figure 3-34c

3.11. Ellipse

The *Ellipse* command is used to draw elliptical shapes. An ellipse is determined by it two axes: the major (longer) and the minor (shorter) axis, Figure 3-35a.

Figure 3-35a

- The *Ellipse* command is activated using one of the following procedures.
  1. Panel method: From the *Home* tab and *Draw* panel, select the *Ellipse* tool, Figure 3-35b.
  2. Command line method: Type "ellipse", "Ellipse", or "ELLIPSE" in the command line and press the *Enter* key.

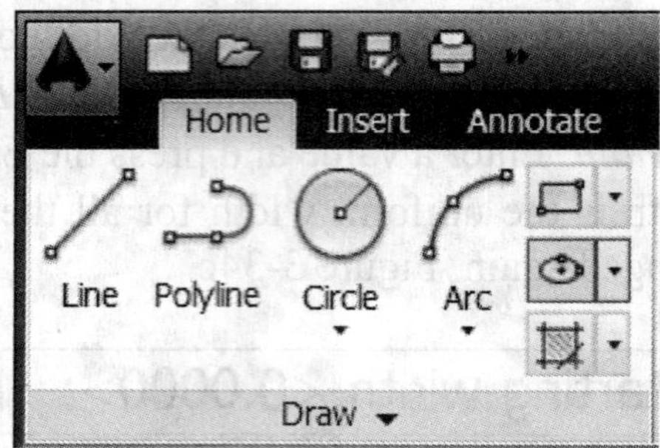

Figure 3-35b

- The activation of the command leads to the method selection prompt to draw an ellipse, Figure 3-35c. However, if the user expands the *Ellipse*'s drop down menu, Figure 3-36c, then the user can select the desired option and the prompt will be for the selected option.

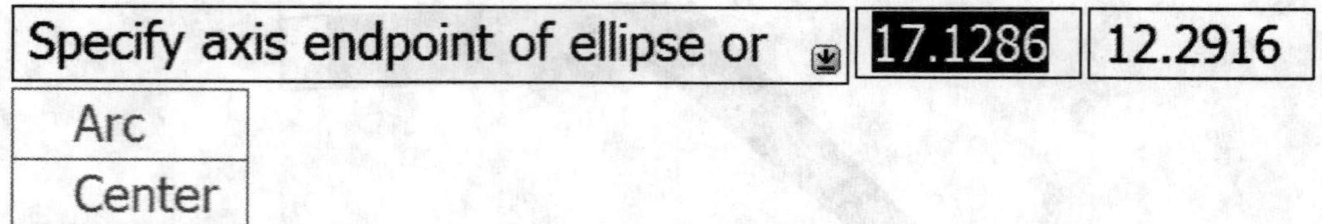

Figure 3-35c

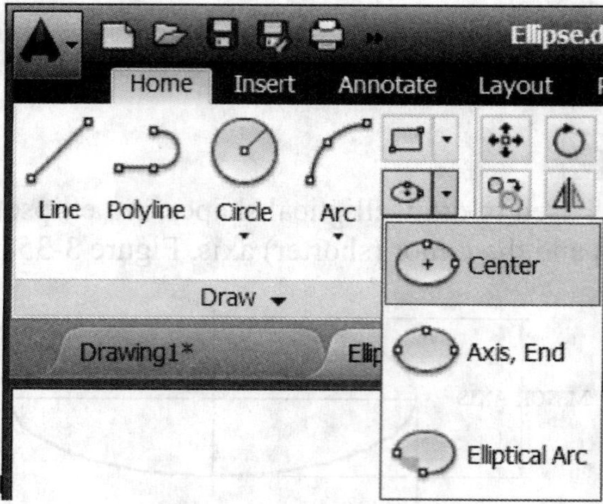

Figure 3-35d

- <u>Axis endpoint option</u>: This option draws an ellipse by specifying the end points of the two axes. **Note**: The order of the points' selection is important.

    1. The user can draw the four end points or draw two perpendicular straight lines, Figure 3-36a, representing the major and minor axes before the activation of the *Ellipse* command.

2. For the execution of the *Ellipse* command, either click at the points or specify their coordinates and press the *Enter* key.

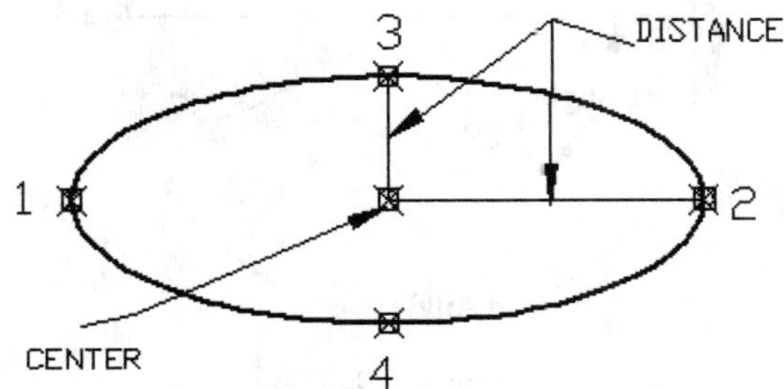

Figure 3-36a

3. Activate the *Ellipse* command and select the *Axis endpoint* option. The default option of Figure 3-35c. The resulting prompt is shown in Figure 3-36b.

Specify axis endpoint of ellipse or -32.5014 -249.6821

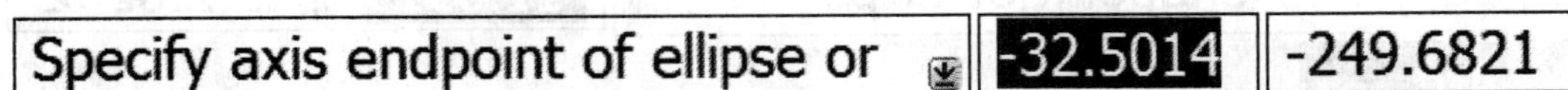

Figure 3-36b

4. Click at points 1 of Figure 3-36a and the prompt shown in Figure 3-36c will appear.

Specify other endpoint of axis:

Figure 3-36c

5. Click at points 2 of Figure 3-36a and the prompt shown in Figure 3-36d will appear.
6. Click at points 3 of Figure 3-36a and the ellipse is created as shown in Figure 3-36a.

Specify distance to other axis or

Figure 3-36d

- Arc option: This option draws an elliptical arc. The order of the points' selection is important.

- ***Example:*** Draw an elliptical arc between points 6 and 7.
  1. The user can draw the points as shown in Figure 3-37a before the activation of the *Ellipse* command.
  2. For the execution of the *Ellipse* command, either click at points or specify their coordinates and press the *Enter* key.

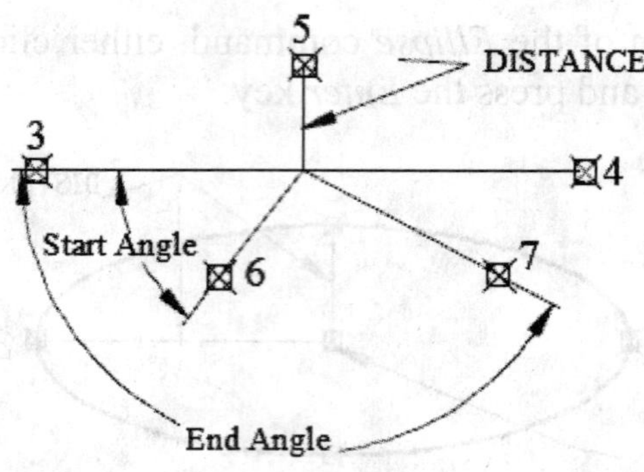

Figure 3-37a

3. Activate the *Ellipse* command and select the *Arc* option, 3-37b. The resulting prompt is shown in Figure 3-37c.

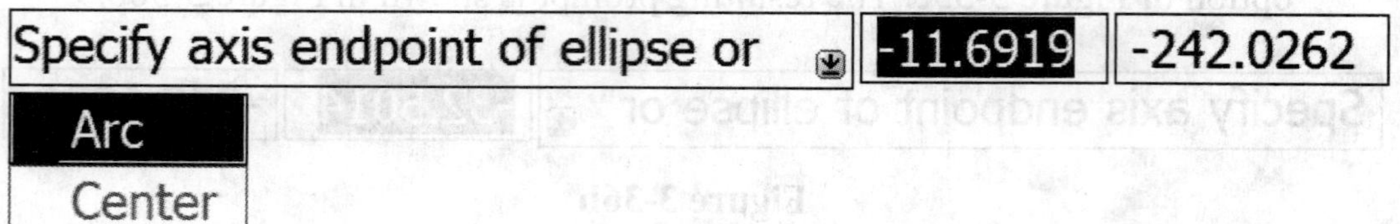

Figure 3-37b

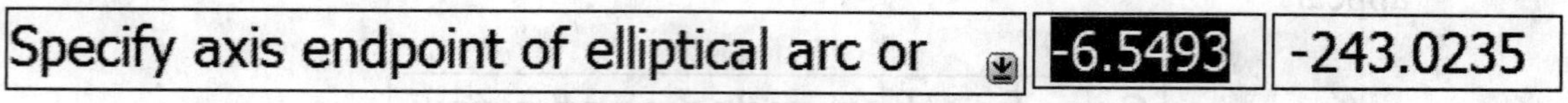

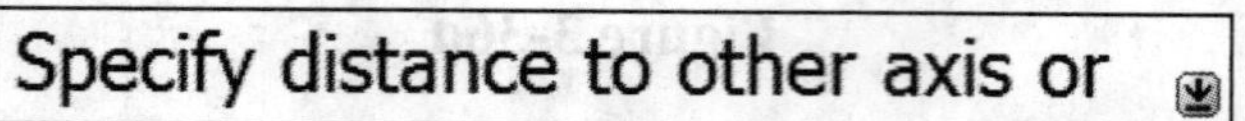

Figure 3-37c

4. Specify point 3, Figure 3-37a. The resulting prompt is shown in Figure 3-37d.

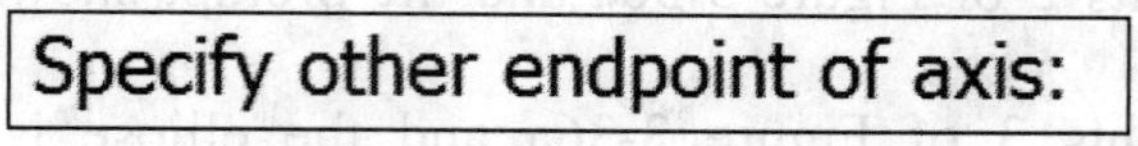

Figure 3-37d

5. Specify point 4, Figure 3-37a. The resulting prompt is shown in Figure 3-37e.

Figure 3-37e

6. Specify the distance to the other axis by clicking at point 5, Figure 3-37a. The resulting prompt is shown in Figure 3-37f.

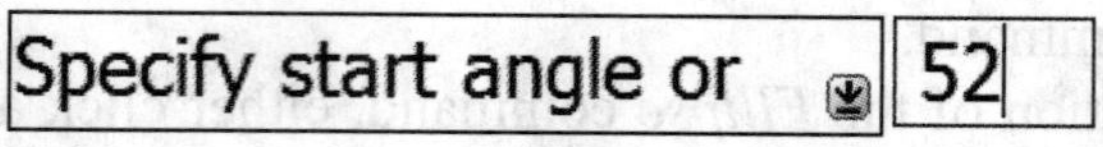

Figure 3-37f

7. Specify the start angle by clicking at point 6; either click on the point or specify the angle (52°) and press the *Enter* key, Figure 3-37c. The resulting prompt is shown in Figure 3-37g.

Figure 3-37g

8. Specify the end angle by clicking at point 7; either click on the point or specify the end angle (127°) and press the *Enter* key. The resultant arc is shown in Figure 3-37h.

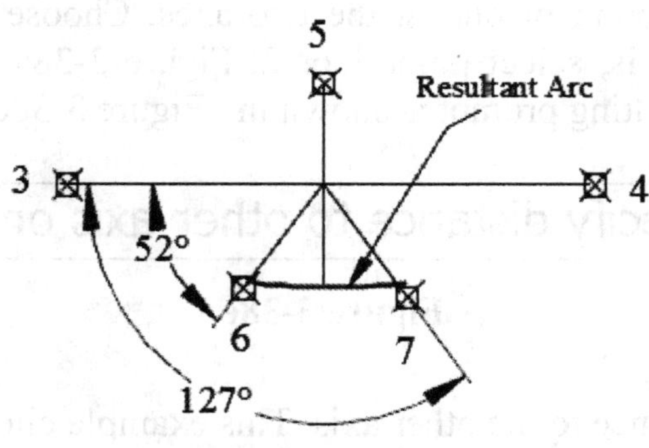

Figure 3-37h

- Center option: This option creates an ellipse by specifying its center.

1. The user can draw the points as shown in Figure 3-38a before the activation of the *Ellipse* command.

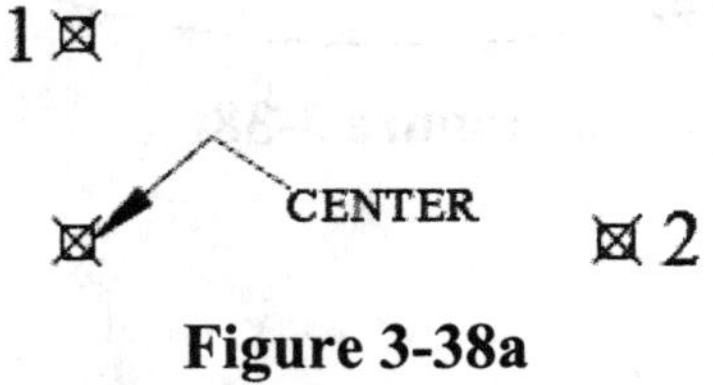

Figure 3-38a

2. For the execution of the *Ellipse* command, either click at points or specify their coordinates and press the *Enter* key
3. Activate the *Ellipse* command and select the *Center* option, Figure 3-38a. The resulting prompt is shown in Figure 3-38c.

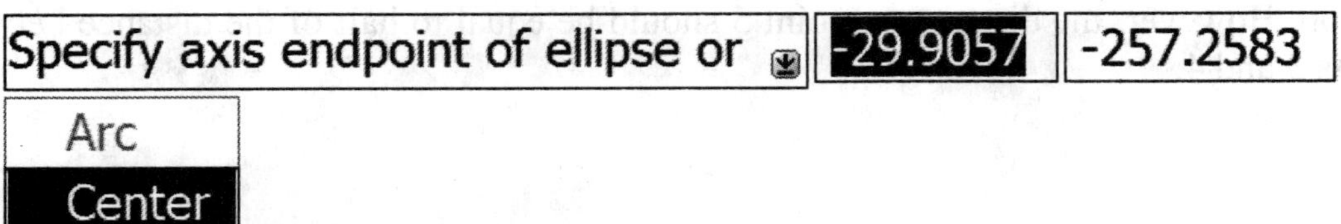

Figure 3-38b

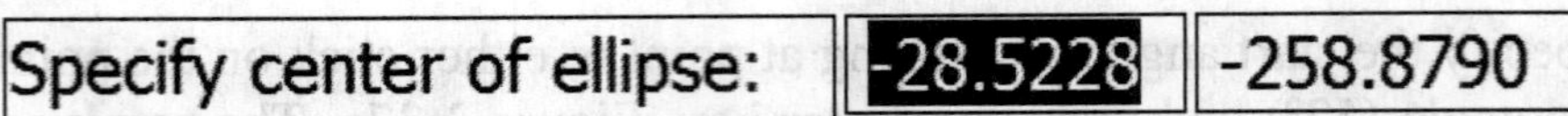

Figure 3-38c

4. Specify the center point, Figure 3-38a. The resulting prompt is shown in Figure 3-38d.

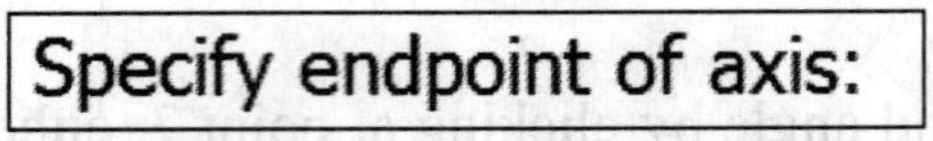

Figure 3-38d

5. Specify the endpoint of one of the two axes. Choose the end of the major or minor axis; that is, select point 1 or 2, Figure 3-38a. This example clicks on point 1. The resulting prompt is shown in   Figure 3-38e.

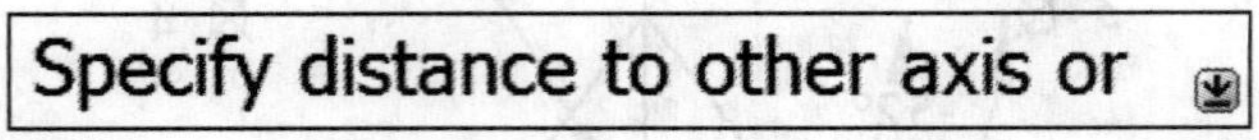

Figure 3-38e

6. Specify the distance to the other axis. This example clicks on point 2.
7. The resulting ellipse is shown in Figure 3-38f.

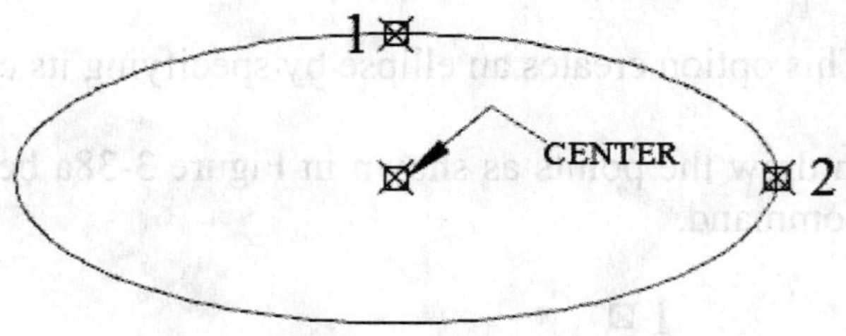

Figure 3-38f

3.12.   Elliptical Arc

To create an elliptical arc, follow the procedure of the *Arc option* explained in the Ellipse's section.

3.13.   Circular Arc

To create a circular arc, follow the procedure of the *Arc option* explained in the Ellipse's section. However, the distance to point 5 should be equal to half of the distance between points 3 and 4.

3.14.   Rectangle

The *Rectangle* command is used to draw a rectangular shape. Under this command a rectangle is created by specifying the distance between points diagonally apart. The resultant rectangle is a single entity; that is, one of its sides cannot be erased. A rectangle can be converted to multiple entities using *Explode* command (the *Explode* command is discussed in Chapter #4).

- The *Rectangle* command is activated using one of the following procedures.
  1. Panel method: From the *Home* tab and *Draw* panel, select the *Rectangle* tool, Figure 3-39a.
  2. Command line method: Type "rectangle", "Rectangle", or "RECTANGLE" in the command line and press the *Enter* key.

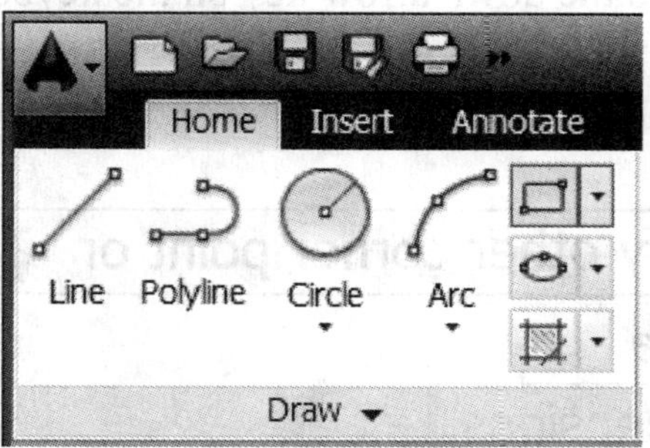

Figure 3-39a

- The activation of the command will result in the prompt shown in Figure 3-39b. Use the down arrow key to display the various options. The *Elevation* and *Thickness* options are useful for the 3D modeling. The *width* option specifies the width of the polyline used to draw a rectangle and is discussed in the polyline section. The *Chamfer* and *Fillet* options control the type of corners for the rectangle and will be discussed in Chapter #4.
- Use the up arrow to hide the options list.

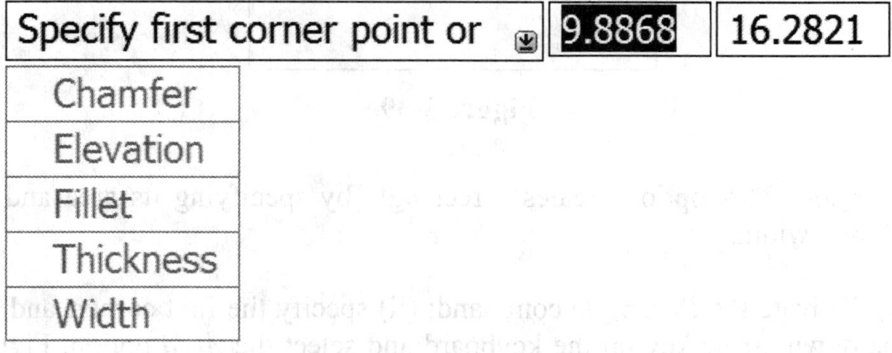

Figure 3-39b

- <u>Corner option</u>: This option creates a rectangle by specifying its diagonally opposite corners.

    1. Activate the *Rectangle* command, the resulting command is shown in Figure 3-39c.

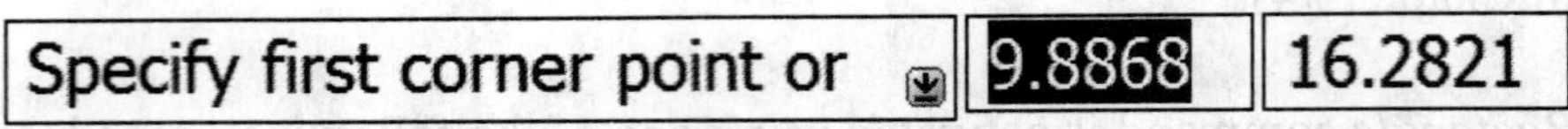

Figure 3-39c

    2. *Specify the first corner point*: Either enter the coordinate's values and press the *Enter* key or click at the desired location. The next prompt is shown in Figure 3-39d. Press the down arrow key on the keyboard to check the option.

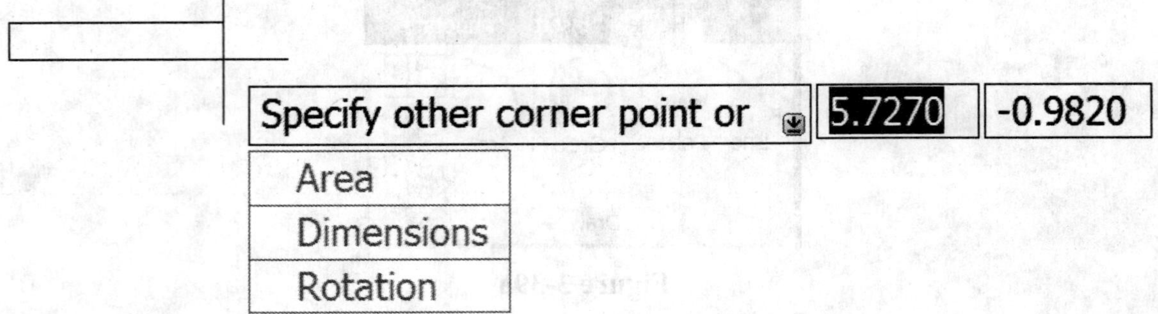

Figure 3-39d

    3. *Specify the other corner point*: Press the up arrow on the keyboard to hide the option in Figure 3-39d. Either specify the coordinates of the diagonally opposite corner. The resulting Rectangle is shown in Figure 3-39e.

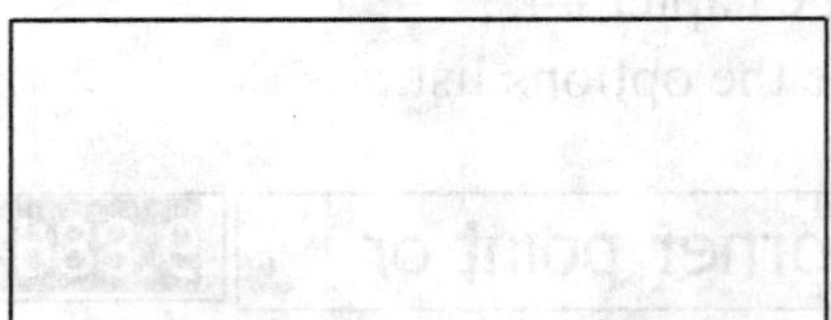

Figure 3-39e

- <u>Area option</u>: This option creates a rectangle by specifying its area and either its length or a width.

    1. (i) Activate the *Rectangle* command; (ii) specify the first corner; and (iii) press the down arrow key on the keyboard and select the *Area* option, Figure 3-40a. The resulting command is shown in Figure 3-40b.
    2. *Enter area of a rectangle*: Specify area as a positive number (300 in this example) and press the *Enter* key, Figure 3-40c.

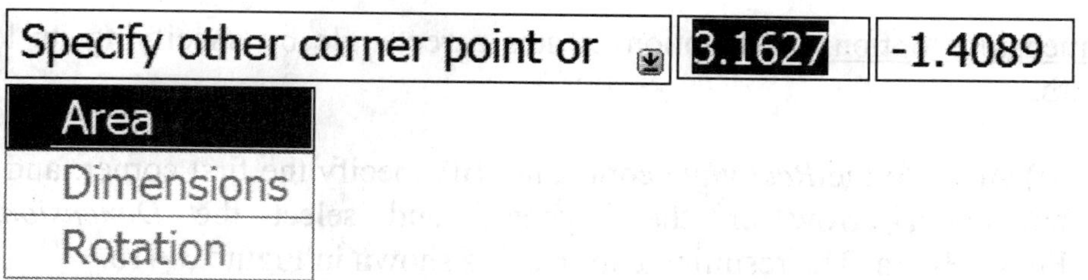

Figure 3-40a

Enter area of rectangle in current units <100.0000>:   300

Figure 3-40b

3. *Calculate rectangle dimensions based on [Length/Width]*: Press the down arrow key on the keyboard. Select the *Length* or *Width* option (the default is Length), Figure 3-40c; specify its value as a positive number; and press the *Enter* key. This example chooses the *Length* option; and it is 25 units, Figure 3-40d.

Calculate rectangle dimensions based on [Length/Width] <Length>:
Length
Width

Figure 3-40c

Enter rectangle length <10.0000>:   25

Figure 3-40d

4. The resultant rectangle of area 300 and length 25 is created, Figure 3-40e.

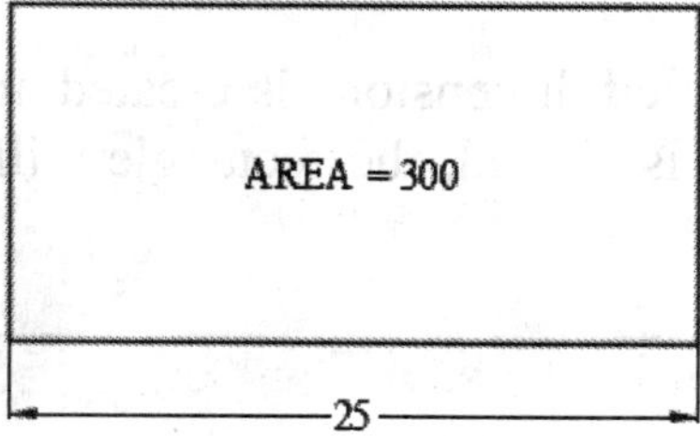

Figure 3-40e

- <u>Dimensions option</u>: This option creates a rectangle by specifying its length and width.

1. (i) Activate the *Rectangle* command; (ii) specify the first corner; and (iii) press the down arrow on the keyboard and select the *Dimensions* option, Figure 3-41a. The resulting command is shown in Figure 3-41b.

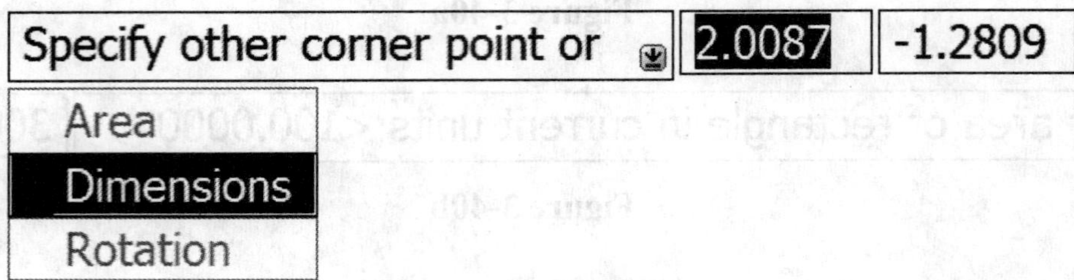

Figure 3-41a

2. *Specify length of the rectangle*: Specify length as a positive number (30 in this example) and press the *Enter* key, Figure 3-41b.

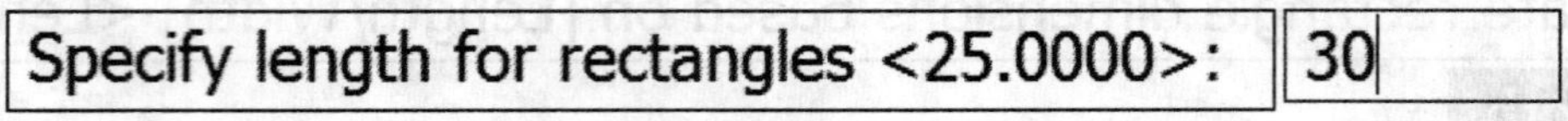

Figure 3-41b

3. *Specify width of the rectangle*: Specify width as a positive number (10 in this example) and press the *Enter* key, Figure 3-41c. A rectangle of specified dimensions is created and is pinned at the first corner point. As the cursor is moved, the rectangle will rotate around the first corner point, Figure 3-41d.

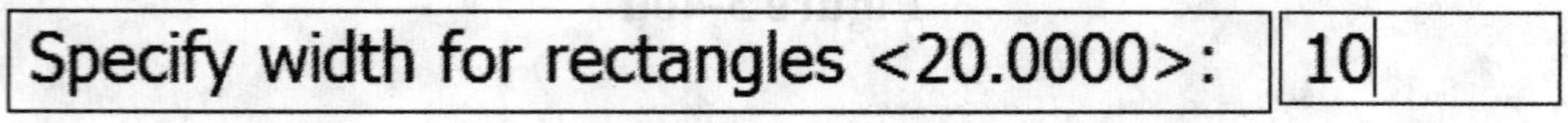

Figure 3-41c

4. A rectangle of specified dimensions is created and is pinned at the first corner point. As the cursor is moved, the rectangle will rotate around the first corner point, Figure 3-41d.

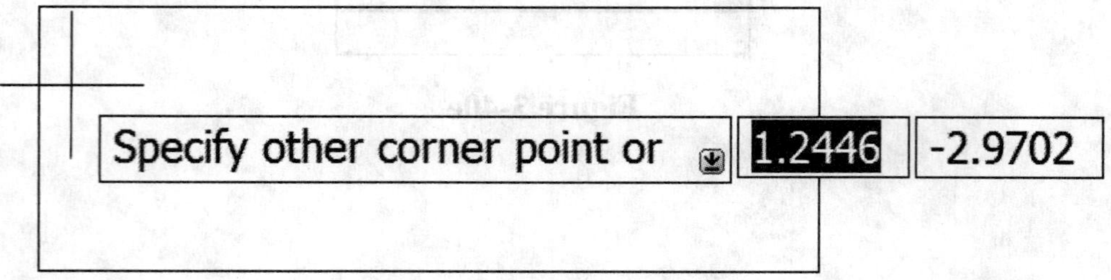

Figure 3-41d

5. Press the *Enter* key. The resultant rectangle of length 30 units and width 10 units is created, Figure 3-41d.

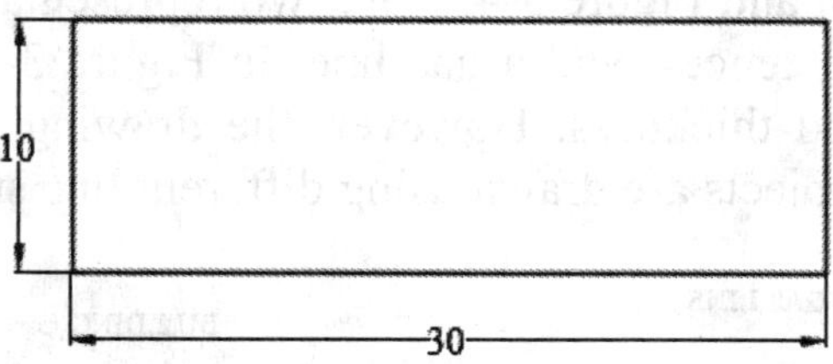

Figure 3-41d

- <u>Rotation option</u>: This option creates a rectangle at a specified rotation angle.

1. (i) Activate the *Rectangle* command; (ii) specify the first corner; and (iii) press the down arrow on the keyboard and select the *Rotation* option, Figure 3-42a. The resulting command is shown in Figure 3-42b.

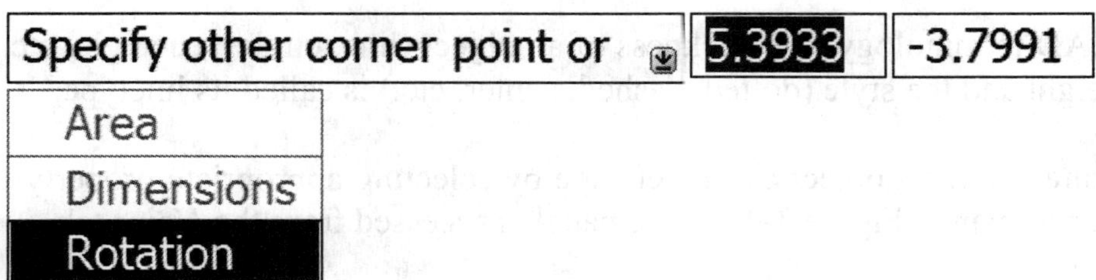

Figure 3-42b

2. Specify rotation angle: Specify the rotation angle (135 degrees in this example) and press the *Enter* key, Figure 3-42b.

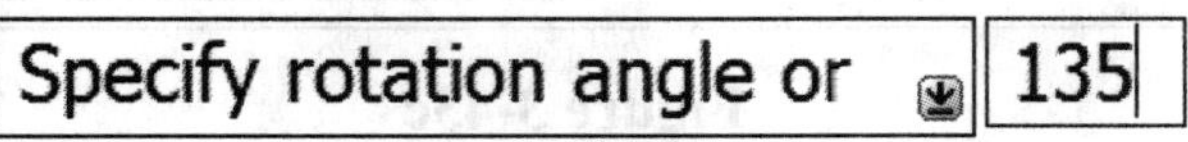

Figure 3-42b

3. Create a rectangle using one of the techniques discussed (area or dimensions), Figure 3-42c. Note that the positive angle will create a rectangle rotated counterclockwise. For the clockwise rotation, specify the negative angle, Figure 3-42d.

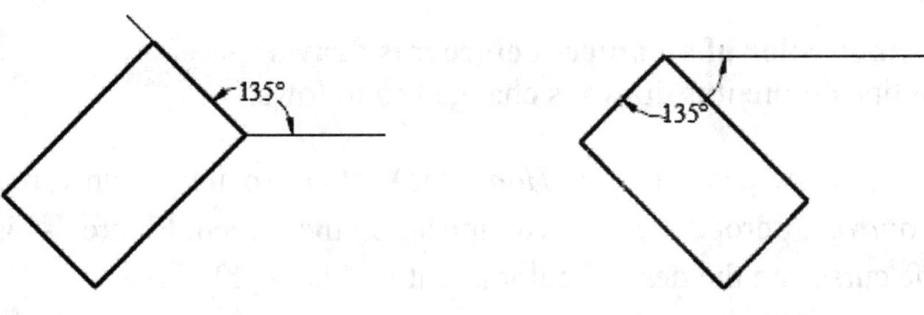

Figure 3-42c   **Figure 3-42d**

3.15.   Object Appearance

The usage of different line style and/or line thickness visually distinguishes objects from one another. Figure 3-43a and Figure 3-43b are two representations of the same drawing, a building, railway track, fences, and a gas line. In Figure 3-43a every object is drawn using same line style and thickness. However, the drawing shown in Figure 3-43b is easily readable because objects are drawn using different line style and thickness.

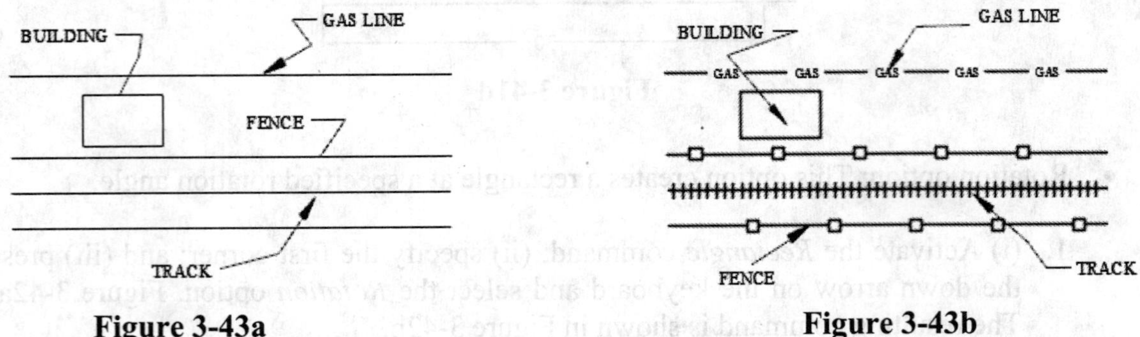

Figure 3-43a

Figure 3-43b

In AutoCAD terminology, the thickness of an object (line, circle, rectangle, etc.) is called its lineweight and the style (dotted, dashed, center, etc.) is called its linetype.

The appearance of an object can be change by selecting appropriate property tools from the *Properties* panel, Figure 3-43c. The panel is accessed from the *Home* tab.

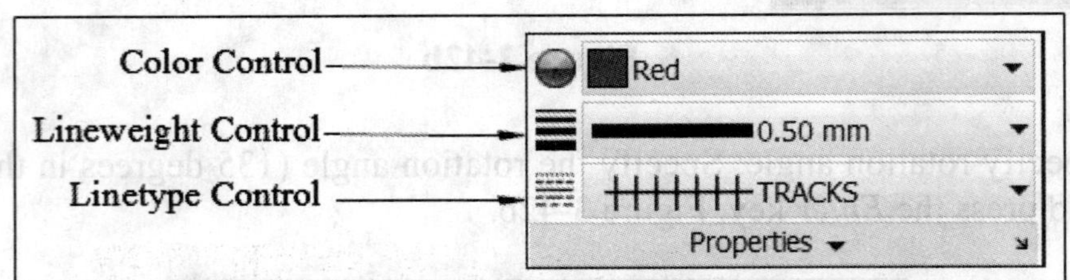

Figure 3-43c

3.15.1. Color Control

The Figure 3-44a shows the available options under the *Color Control*. The figure shows only some of the colors available in AutoCAD. However, the user can select the colors not shown in the list, too. The color of most of two-dimensional objects can be changed in two ways, (i) set the color before drawing the object and (ii) change the color after the object is drawn. This section will use a line to demonstrate the *Color Control*.

3.15.1.1.   Change color of an object before it is drawn

The color of a line before it is drawn is changed as follows.

1. In the *Properties* panel (under *Home* tab), click on the down arrow (⊡) of the *Color Control*. A dropdown list will appear on the screen, Figure 3-44a.
2. Bring the cursor on the desired color and it will be highlighted.

3. Click on the highlighted color; this will close the list and the selected color will appear in the *Color Control*, Figure 3-44b.
4. Now draw a line, the line will be drawn with the selected color.
5. If the desired color is not listed in the color list, then click on *Select Color* option of Figure 3-44a. The *Select Color* dialog box shown in Figure 3-44c will appear on the screen. Click on the desired color and press the *OK* button and proceed with the drawing. In the example, color 240 is selected.

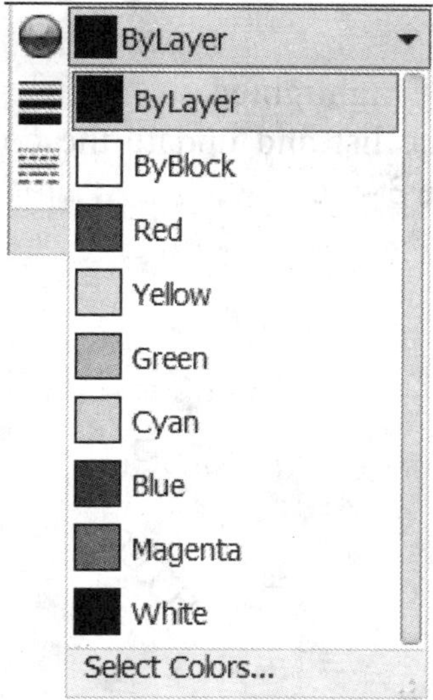

Figure 3-44a

Figure 3-44b

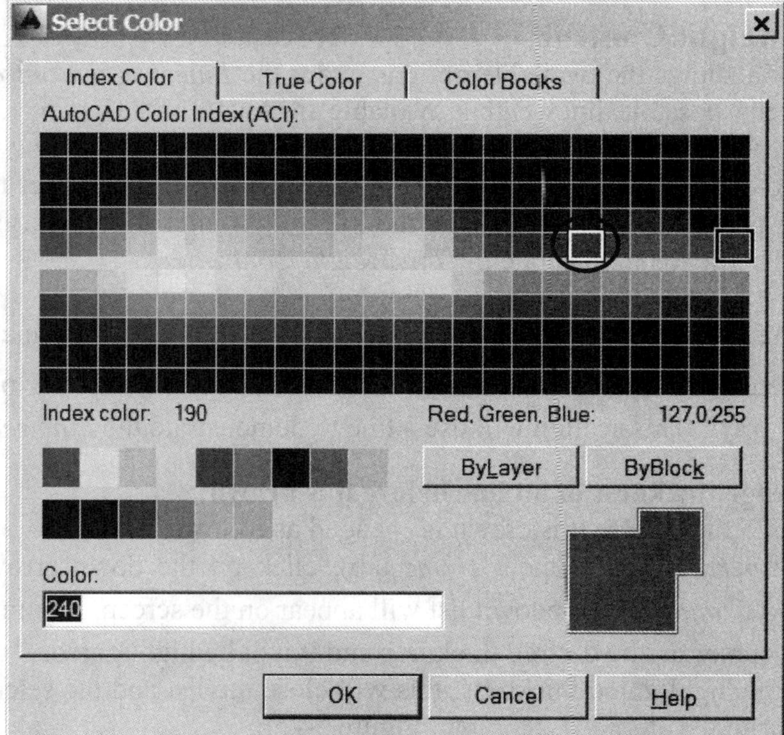

Figure 3-44c

3.15.1.2.   Change color of an object after it is drawn

The step-by-step process to change the color of an object after it is drawn is shown in Figure 3-44d.

1. Draw a line, (the line labeled as *Before* in Figure 3-44e).
2. Select the line by clicking with the left button of the mouse, (the line with three square boxes in Figure 3-44e). The three blue squares are called grip points.
3. Click on the arrow (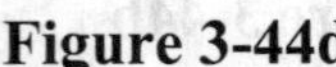) of the *Color Control* dropdown list of the *Properties* panel; the color list will appear on the screen, Figure 3-44d.
4. Bring the cursor on the desired color and it will be highlighted.
5. Click on the highlighted color; this will close the list and update the color of the selected object, (the line labeled as *After* in Figure 3-44e).

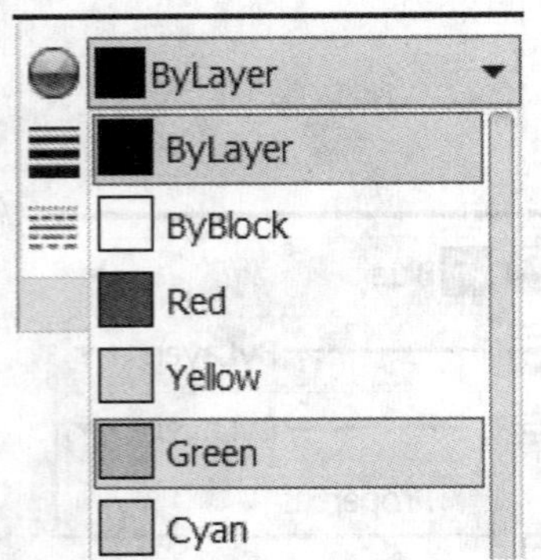

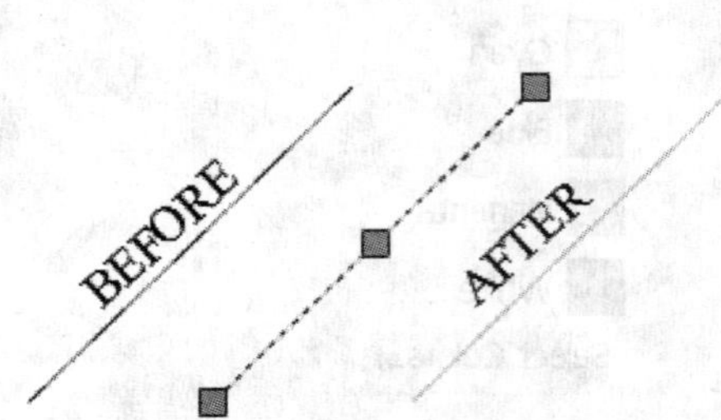

Figure 3-44d   **Figure 3-44e**

3.15.2. Lineweight Control

The Figure 3-45a shows the available options under the *Lineweight Control*. The figure shows that all the possible lineweights available in AutoCAD. However, the user can select the linetypes not shown in the list, too. The lineweight (that is, line thickness) for most of the two-dimensional objects can be changed in two ways; (i) set the lineweight before drawing the object and (ii) change the lineweight after the object is drawn. This section will use a line to demonstrate the *Lineweight Control*.

In order to display thickness of an object in the drawing area, click the lineweight button ( ) on the status bar. The thickness of most of the two-dimensional objects can be changed in two ways. This section will use a line to demonstrate the *Lineweight Control*.

3.15.2.1.   Change thickness of an line before it is drawn

The thickness of a line before it is drawn is changed as follows.
1. In the *Properties* panel (under *Home* tab), click on the down arrow ( ) of the *Lineweight Control*. A dropdown list will appear on the screen, Figure 3-45a.
2. Bring the cursor on the desired thickness and it will be highlighted.
3. Click on the highlighted thickness; this will close the list and the selected thickness will appear in the *Properties* toolbar, Figure 3-45b.
4. Now draw a line, the lines will be drawn with the desired thickness.

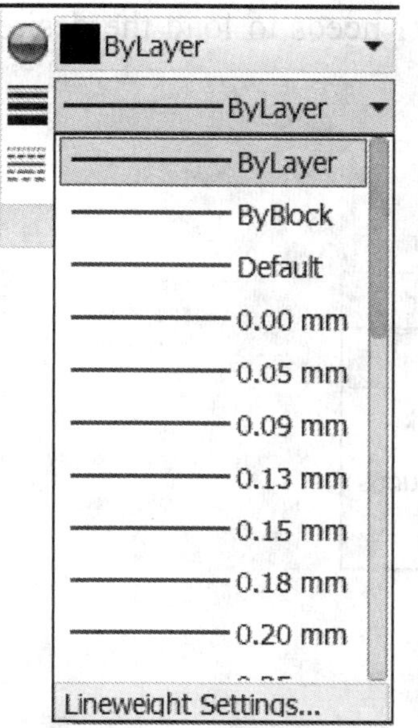

Figure 3-45a

Figure 3-45b

3.15.2.2. Change thickness of a line after it is drawn

The step-by-step process to change the thickness of a line after it is drawn is shown in Figure 3-45c.

1. Draw a line, (the line labeled as *Before* in Figure 3-45c).
2. Select the line by clicking with the left button of the mouse, (the line with three square boxes in Figure 3-45c). The three blue squares are called grip points.
3. Click on the arrow (⬛) of the *Lineweight Control* dropdown list in the *Properties* panel; the thickness list will appear on the screen, Figure 3-45a.
4. Bring the cursor on the desired thickness and it will be highlighted.
5. Click on the highlighted thickness; this will close the list and update the thickness of the selected object, (the line labeled as *After* in Figure 3-45c).

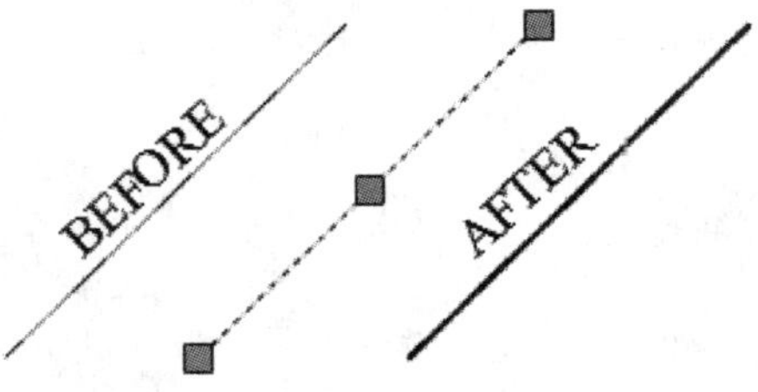

Figure 3-45c

3.15.3. Linetype Control

The Figure 3-46a shows the available options under the *Linetype Control*. The figure shows that only one linetype is available in AutoCAD. However, the user can select the linetypes not shown in the list, too. A line style (that is, linetype) for most of the two-dimensional objects can be changed in two ways; (i) set the linetype before drawing the object and (ii) change the linetype after the object is drawn. This section will use a line to demonstrate the *Linetype Control*. However, the user needs to load the desired line type before using it.

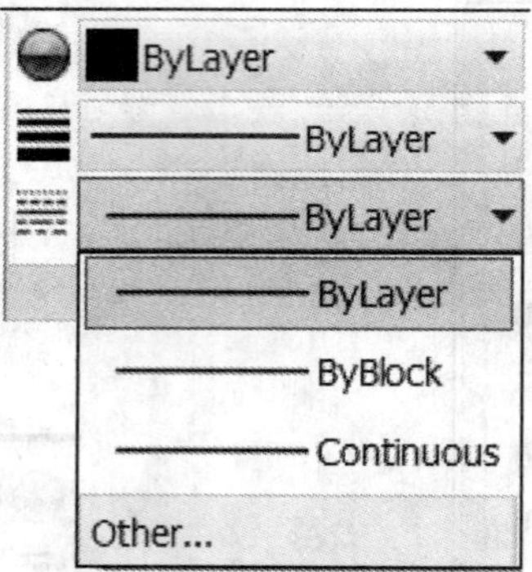

Figure 3-46a

3.15.3.1.   Load a linetype

- (i) Expand the *Linetype control*'s drop down list. (ii) Select the *Other* option; this will open a *Linetype Manager* (Figure 3-46b) dialog box.
- In the *Linetype Manager* dialog box, click the *Load* button; this will open a *Load or Reload Linetypes* (Figure 3-46c) dialog box.

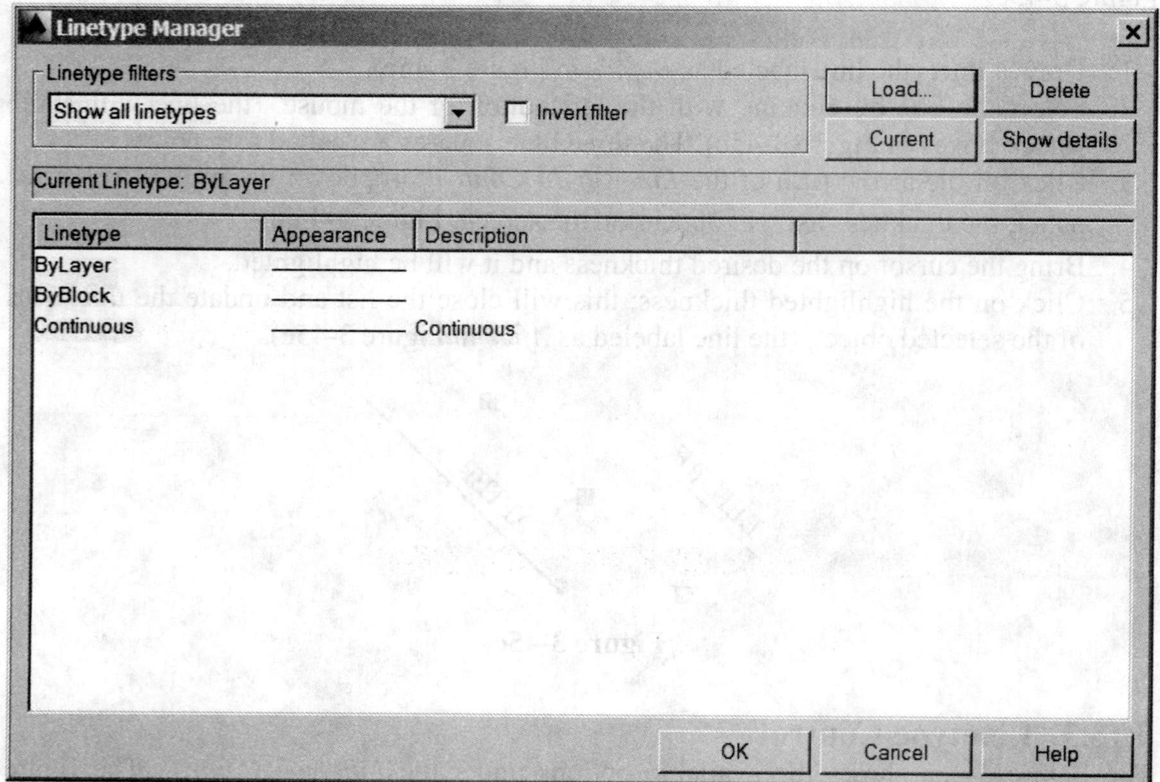

Figure 3-46b

- In the *Load or Reload Linetypes* dialog box, select a linetype and click the *OK* button. This will close the *Load or Reload Linetypes* dialog box and the selected line type will appear in the *Linetype Manager* Dialog box. This example selects a *Phantom* pattern, which is a combination of long and short dashes, Figure 3-46d.
- In the *Linetypes Manager* dialog box, click the *OK* button. This will close dialog box.

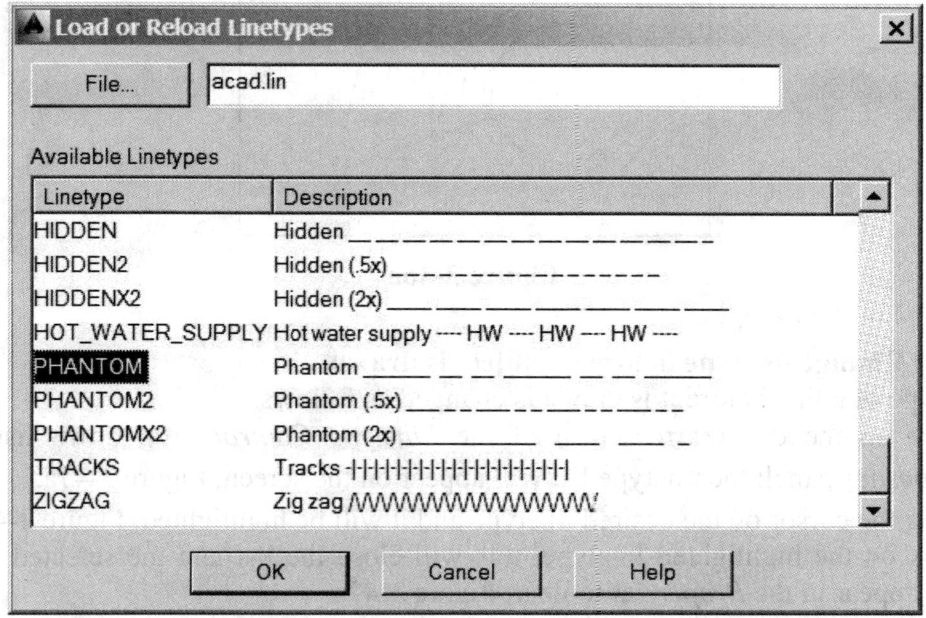

Figure 3-46c

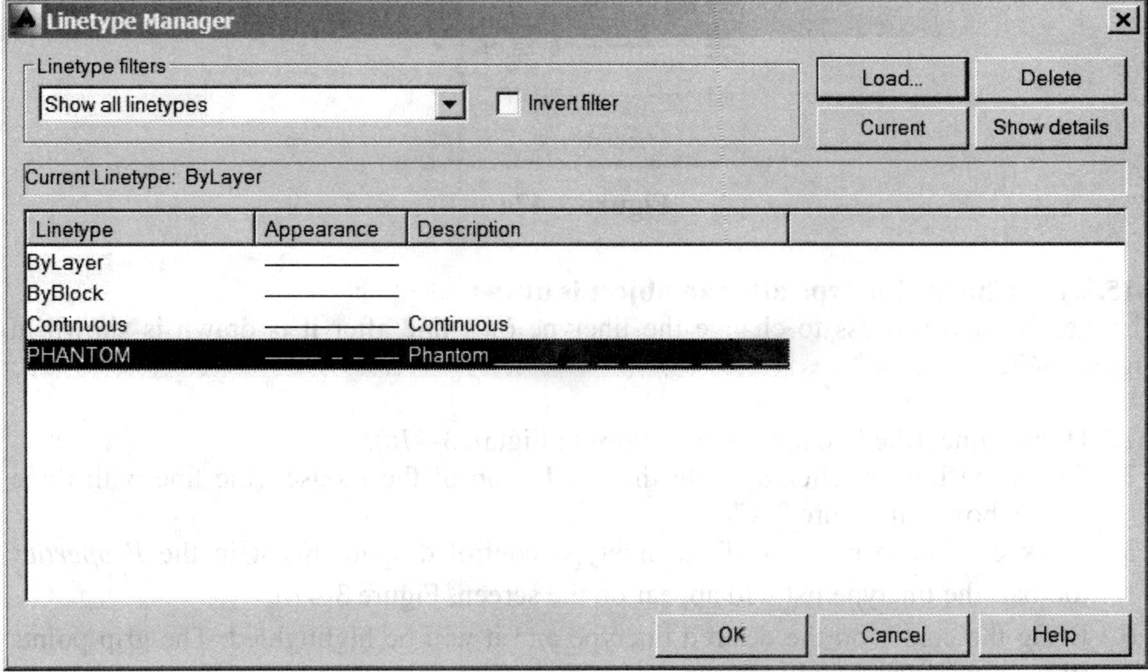

Figure 3-46d

3.15.3.2.   Current linetype

- Click on the down arrow (▾) of the *Linetype Control* dropdown list in the *Properties* panel; the linetype list will appear on the screen, Figure 3-46d. The figure shows only the *Linetype Control*. This example selects a *Phantom* line.
- Now, the 2-dimensional object will be drawn in the selected format, Figure 3-46e.

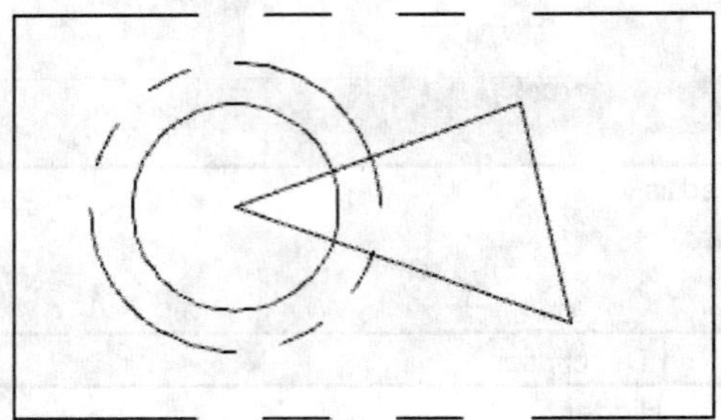

Figure 3-46e

3.15.3.3.   Change linetype before an object is drawn

The linetype of a line before it is drawn is changed as follows.

1. Click on the down arrow (▾) of the *Linetype Control* drop down list in the *Properties* panel; the linetype list will appear on the screen, Figure 3-47a.
2. Bring the cursor on the desired linetype and it will be highlighted, Figure 3-47a.
3. Click on the highlighted linetype; this will close the list and the selected linetype will appear in the *Properties* toolbar, Figure 3-47a.
4. Now draw a line, the lines will be drawn with the selected linetype.

Figure 3-47a

3.15.3.4.   Change linetype after an object is drawn

The step-by-step process to change the linetype of a line after it is drawn is shown in Figure 3-47c.

1. Draw a line, (the line labeled as *Before* in Figure 3-47c).
2. Select the line by clicking with the left button of the mouse, (the line with three square boxes in Figure 3-47c).
3. Click on the arrow (▾) of the linetype control dropdown list in the *Properties* toolbar; the linetype list will appear on the screen, Figure 3-47b.
6. Bring the cursor on the desired linetype and it will be highlighted. The grip points (three blue squares) will appear.

4. Click on the highlighted linetype; this will close the list and update the linetype of the selected object (the line labeled as *After* in Figure 3-47c).

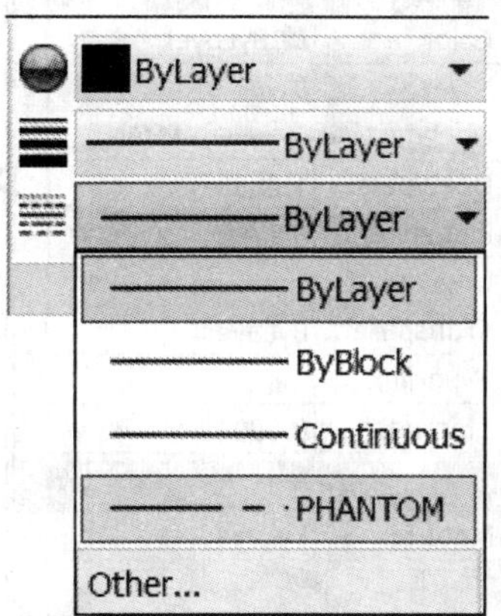

Figure 3-47b

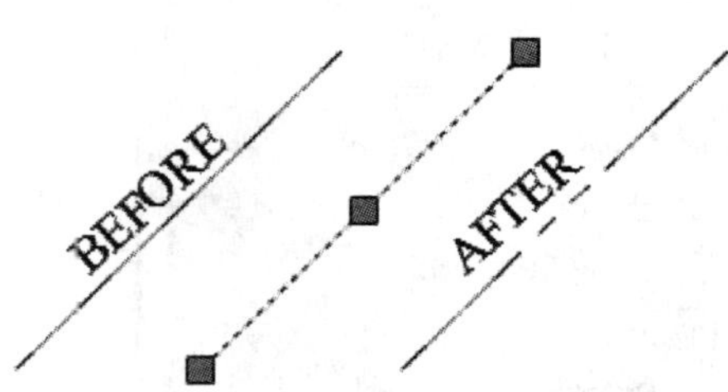

Figure 3-47c

3.15.3.5. Linetype scale

The *Linetype scale* capability is used to change the appearance of a pattern. In Figure 3-46e every object is drawn using *Phantom* linetype; however, the pattern is not visible for some of the segment. A user can change the linetype scale to make the pattern visible as follows:

- Select a line, by clicking with the left button of the mouse.
- Open the *Properties* sheet (Figure 3-48b) using one of the techniques listed below.
    1. Panel method: Open the *Properties* sheet using one of the two panel methods.
        a. From the *Home* tab and *Properties* panel, click on the dialog box launcher (a small arrow on the lower right corner of the panel), Figure 3-48a.
        b. (i) From the *View* tab and *Palette* panel, click on *Properties* icon, Figure 3-48b.
    2. Object method: (i) Click on the object. (ii) Press the right button of the mouse and choose the *Properties* option, Figure 3-48c.

Figure 3-48a

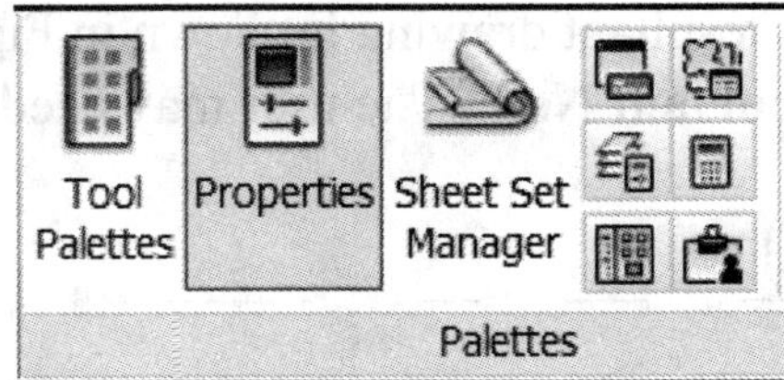

Figure 3-48b

- Any of the above three methods, will open the *Properties* sheet of the selected object, Figure 3-48d. On the upper left corner of the *Properties* sheet, the type of the object (Line in our example) is displayed. On the *Properties* sheet, some of the properties are greyed indicating that those properties could not be changed.

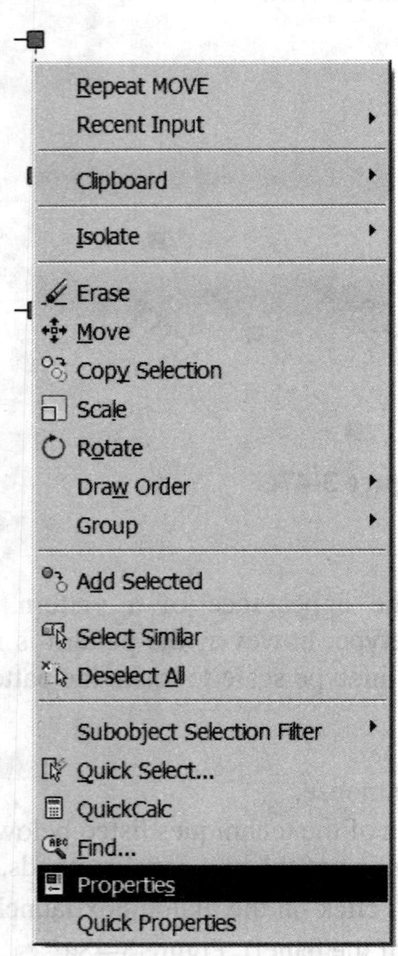

Figure 3-48c

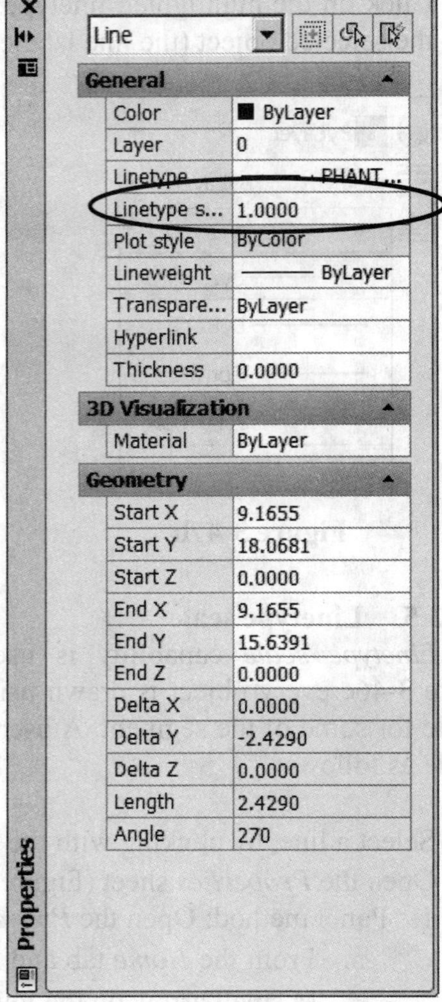

Figure 3-48d

- Select the lines as shown in Figure 3-48d; and open the *Properties* sheet Figure 3-48e. Choose *Linetype scale* (Figure 3-48f) and change the value to 0.2. If necessary change the scale of other lines.
- The resultant drawing is shown in Figure 3-48g.
- **Important Note**: The user may need to reset the linetype scale in the layout.

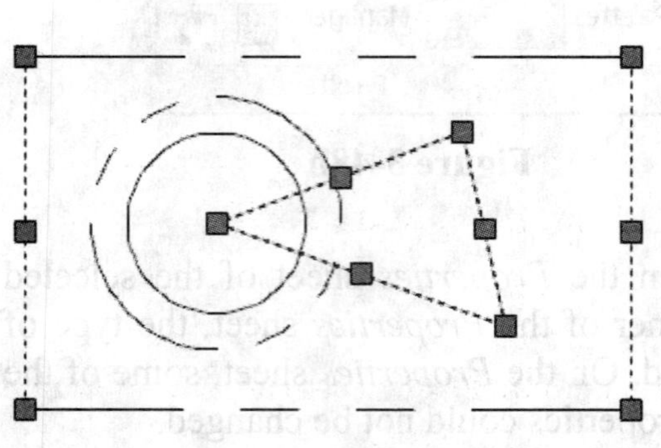

Figure 3-48e

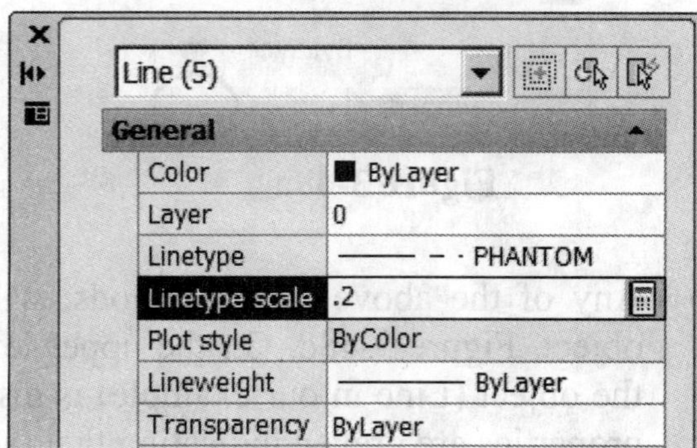

Figure 3-48f

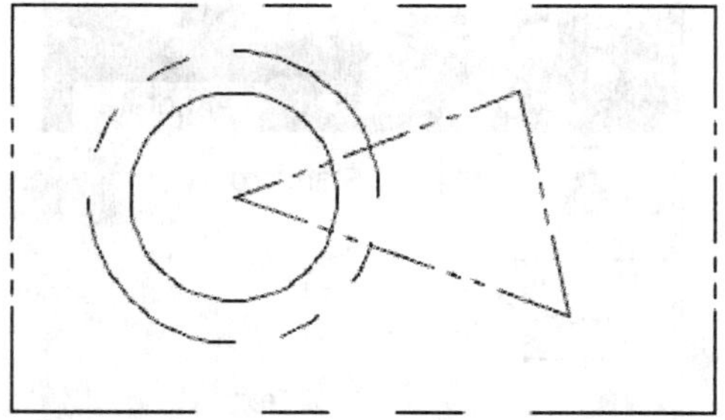

Figure 3-48g

3.16.   Text 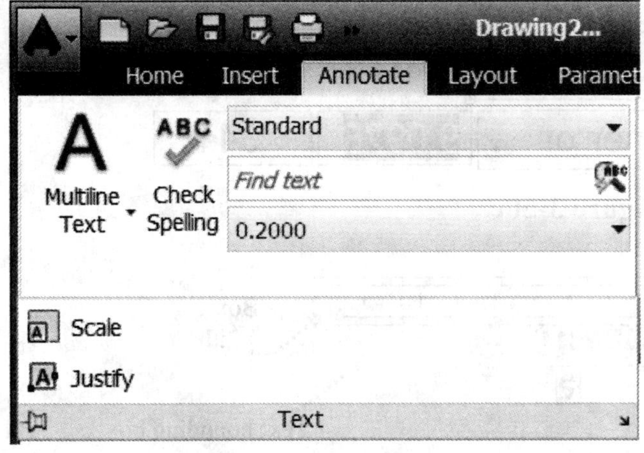

AutoCAD's *Text* command makes a distinction between a single line and multiline text. A multiline text object includes one or more paragraphs of text that can be manipulated as a single object. Since the multiline text command can be used to create a single line text object, this section will discuss the creation of a multiline text object. To modify previously created text, just double click on the text and the text formatting dialog box will appear. To create a new text, follow the method discussed below.

- The *Text* command is activated using one of the following procedures.
  1. Panel method: Text related commands can be activated using one of the two panel methods
     a. From the *Annotate* tab and *Text* panel, click on the *Text* tool, Figure 3-49a.
     b. From the *Express Tools* tab and *Text* panel, click on the *Text* tool, Figure 3-49b.
  2. Command line method: Type "mtext", "MText", or "MTEXT" in the command line and press the *Enter* key will activate an option to create a multiline text.

Figure 3-49a

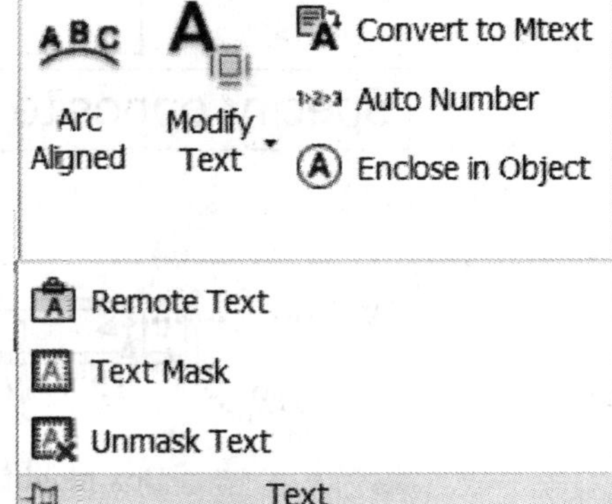

Figure 3-49b

3.16.1. Create multiline text
- Activate the multiline text command from the command line; or from the *Annotate* tab and *Text* panel, select the *Multiline text* tool, Figure 3-50a.

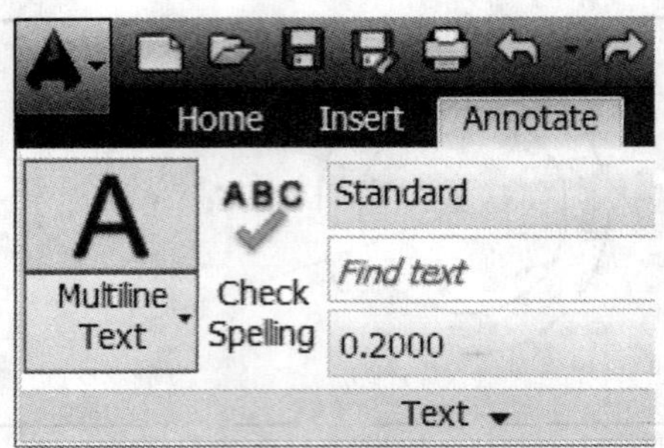

Figure 3-50a

- The activation of the command leads to the specification of the diagonally opposite corner of the text bounding box, Figure 3-50b. Note the appearance of *abc* at the cursor.
- For the first corner, click at the desired location in the drawing area or specify the coordinate of the point and press the *Enter* key, Figure 3-50c.

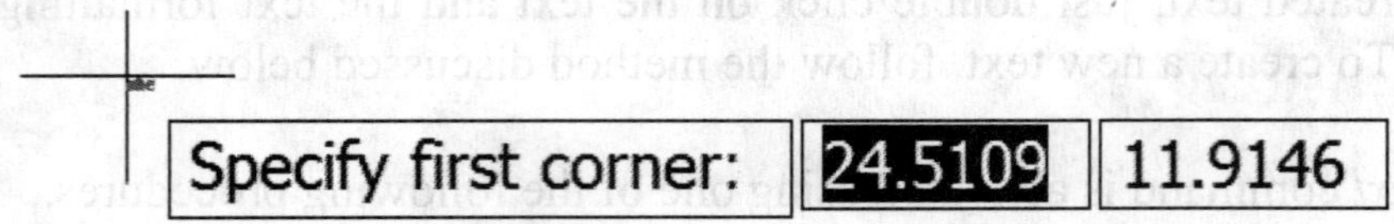

Figure 3-50b

- The specification of the second point will create the bounding box, Figure 3-50c, and open the text insertion box, Figure 3-50d. Also, the *Text Editor* tab becomes the current tab. The details of the *Text Editor* are discussed in next section.
- Type in the text and click in the drawing area. The box will disappear and the text will appear in the drawing area.

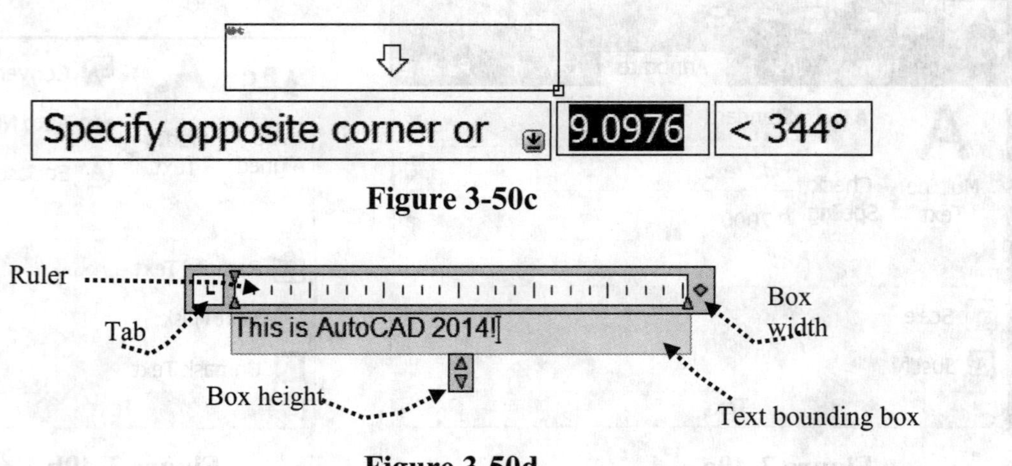

Figure 3-50d

3.16.2. Text Editor

The *Text Editor* tab, Figure 3-51, provides the options to modify the style, format, paragraph properties, etc. of the selected multiline text object. These capabilities are available through the *Style, Formatting, Paragraph, Insert, Spell Check, Tools, Options,* and *Close* panels. The editor is available only if the text is open as shown in Figure 3-51 (double click on the text and it will be open to make changes). When the text editor is open, AutoCAD will not allow the user to access any other functionality. Exit the editor mode by clicking outside the text's bounding box or by pressing the *Esc* key on the keyboard.

The changes will affect only the selected text and the current text style will not be changed. That is, the user must select the text to be changed and then select the facilities provided by the various panels. For example, in Figure 3-51 to underline the word "Water", the user should first select the text and then apply the underline option to the selected text. Most of the characteristics discussed in the remaining of this section, can be updated using properties sheet, too.

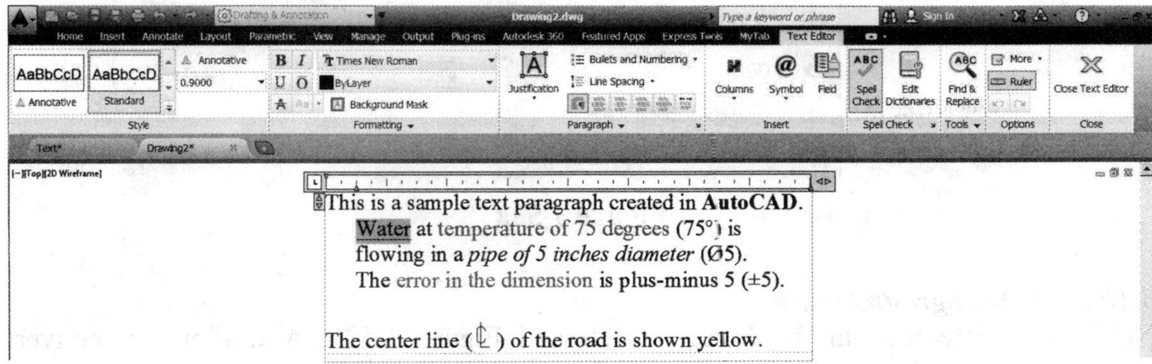

Figure 3-51

3.16.2.1. Style

The *Style* panel is shown in Figure 3-52. This panel provides the options to turns *on* or *off* the *Annotative* and *Standard* for the selected multiline text object; and change the font height. The font height setting specifies the height of the capitalized text.

Figure 3-52

3.16.2.2. Formatting

The expanded *Formatting* panel is shown in Figure 3-53a. This panel provides the options to change the font type and color of the selected text. To change the color and font, just click the down arrow and select the desire option. The boldface and italics options are available for some of the fonts. The selected text can also be underlined, over lined, and/or strike through. The case change option will allow the user to convert the lowercase to uppercase and vice versa by pressing the down arrow key and choosing the appropriate option. The background mask and stack options are discussed in detail.

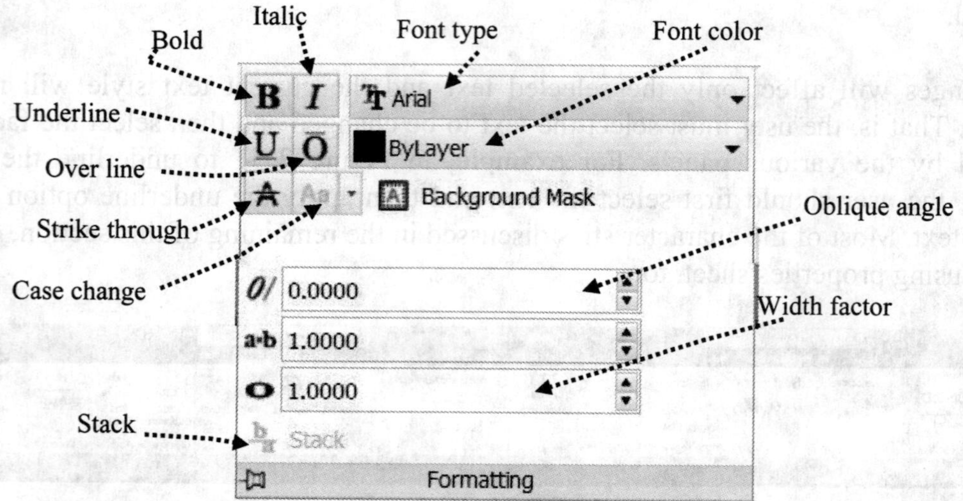

Figure 3-53a

3.16.2.2.1. *Background mask*

Notice the difference in the Figure 3-53b and Figure 3-53c. A drafter can convert Figure 3-53b into Figure 3-53c using the *Trim* command (discussed in Chapter 4) or by masking the background discussed in this section.

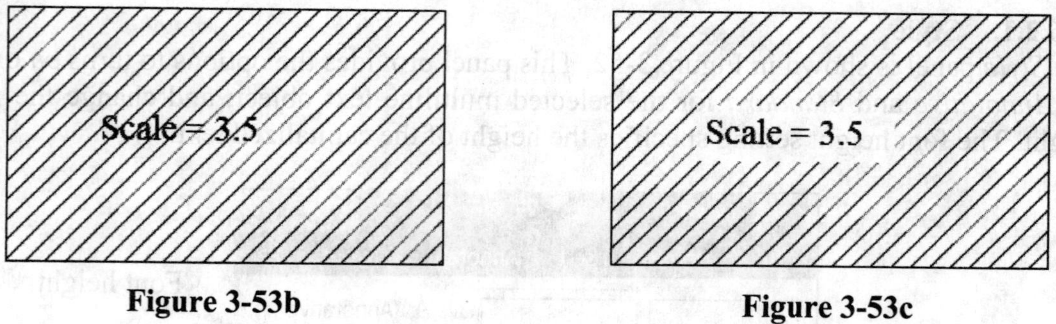

Figure 3-53b   **Figure 3-53c**

To mask the background, (i) double click the multiline text of Figure 3-53b and the Text Editor will appear on the screen; (ii) from the *Formatting* panel, click the *Background mask* option and the *Background Mask* dialog box will appear on the screen, Figure 3-53d; (iii) check both boxes on the *Background Mask* dialog box, and (iv) finally, click the *OK* button. The resultant masked text is shown in Figure 3-53c.

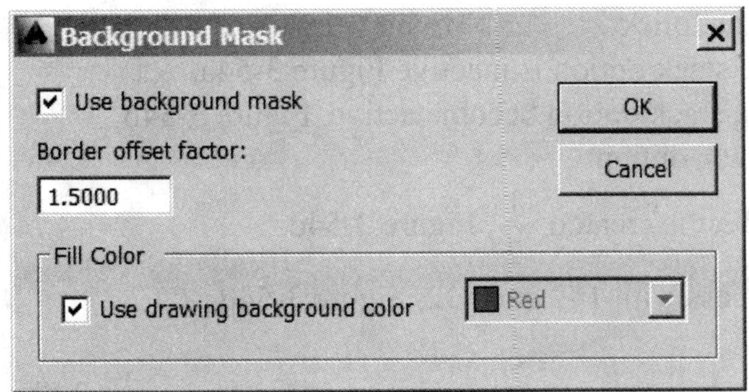

Figure 3-53d

The background can be masked from the property sheet as follow. (i) Select the multiline text; (ii) press the right button; (iii) choose the *Properties* option (the last option) to open the properties sheet; (iv) in the *Text* panel of the property sheet, select the *Background mask* option (Figure 3-53e) and [...] will appear in the left column; (v) click on the [...] button and the *Background Mask* dialog box will appear on the screen, Figure 3-53d; (vi) check both boxes on the *Background Mask* dialog box; and (v) finally, click the *OK* button. The resultant masked text is shown in Figure 3-53c.

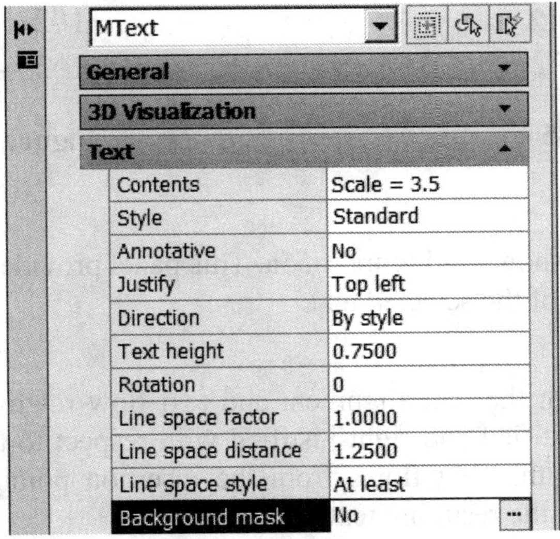

Figure 3-53e

3.16.2.2.2. Stacked characters

AutoCAD provides the capability to create stacked characters within multiline text. It uses special characters to indicate how the selected text should be stacked. Figure 3-54a and Figure 3-54d.

- Slash (/) stacks text vertically, separated by a horizontal line.
- Pound sign (#) stacks text diagonally, separated by a diagonal line.
- Carat (^) creates a tolerance stack, which is not separated by a line.

Text can be stacked as follow.

- Write 1/2, note stack option is inactive Figure 3-54a.
- Select 1/2, note stack option become active, Figure 3-54b.
- Click on the stack option.
- The desired effect is created, $\frac{1}{2}$, Figure 3-54c.
- Repeat the process with 1#2 and 1^2, Figure 3-54d.

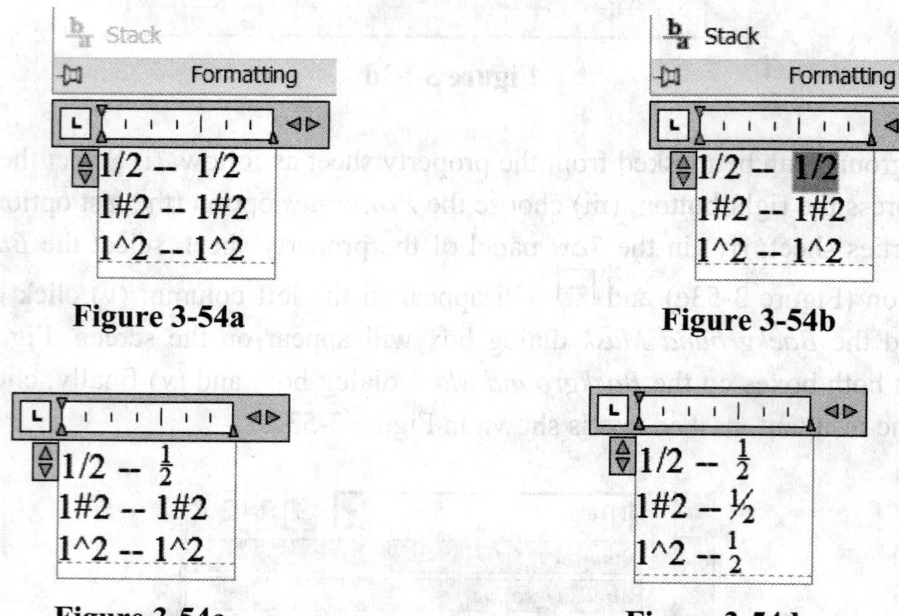

Figure 3-54a   Figure 3-54b

Figure 3-54c   Figure 3-54d

3.16.2.3.   Paragraph

The *Paragraph* panel is shown in Figure 3-55a. This panel provides the options to change the paragraph properties of the selected text.

3.16.2.3.1. Justification

Justification controls both the text alignment and text flow relative to the text insertion point. The text is left-justified and right-justified with respect to the boundary rectangle that defines the text width. Text flows from the insertion point, which can be at the middle, top, or bottom of the resulting text object.

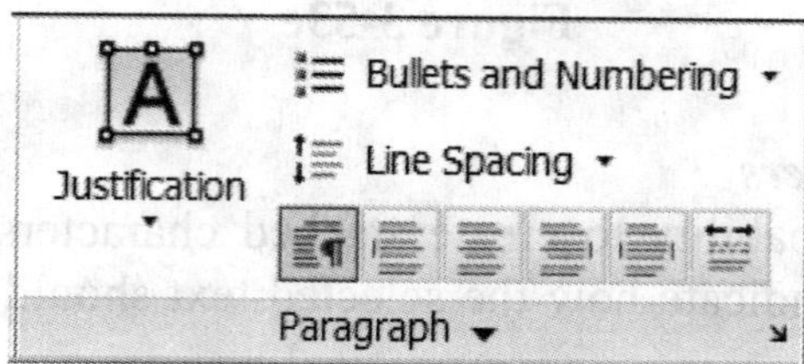

Figure 3-55a

Press the down arrow under the *Justification* on the *Paragraph* panel and check the various options, Figure 3-55b.

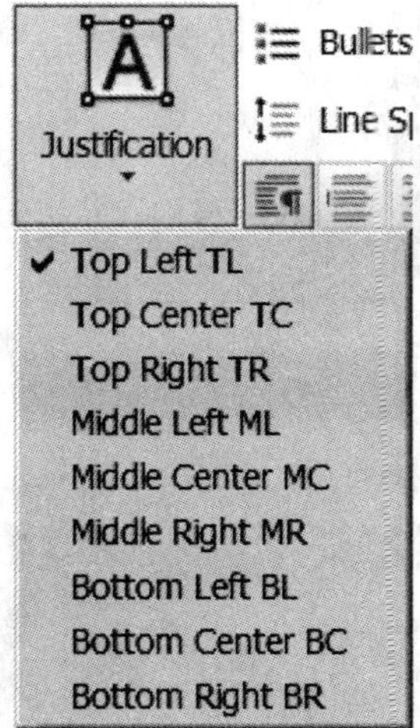

Figure 3-55b

Suppose a dafter has created the text shown in Figure 3-55c and desired to place the text in the center of the solid rectangle as shown in Figure 3-55d.

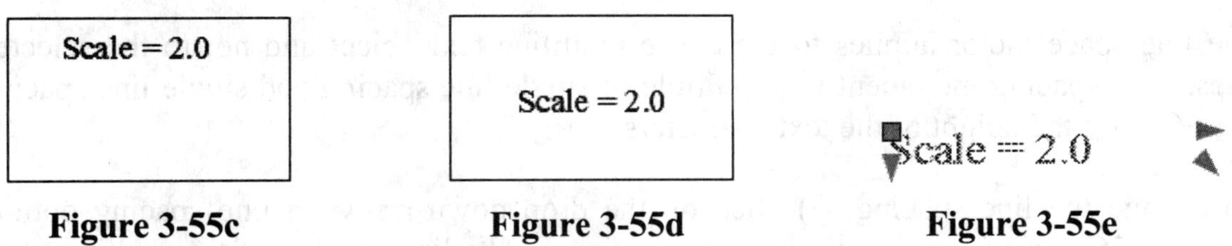

Figure 3-55c   **Figure 3-55d**   **Figure 3-55e**

The user can achieve the goal by performing the following steps. (i) Select the text and check the location of the grip points (the small blue square and blue triangle), Figure 3-55e. (ii) Double click the text and the *Text Editor* will appear on the screen. (iii) Expand the *Justification* option, Figure 3-55b, and select the *Middle Center* option. (iv) Select the text and check the location of the grip points (the small blue square and blue triangle),   Figure 3-55f. (v) Match the four arrows with the corresponding corner of the square, Figure 3-55g. Click on one of the triangular grip point; keep pressing the left button; move the cursor to the nearest corner; repeat the process with the diagonally opposite grip pint. The resultant text is shown in Figure 3-55g.

Figure 3-55f   **Figure 3-55g**

3.16.2.3.2. List
The list can be created using bullets, uppercase or lowercase letters, or numbers. Press the down arrow under the *Bullets and Numbering* on the *Paragraph* panel and check the various options, Figure 3-56a.

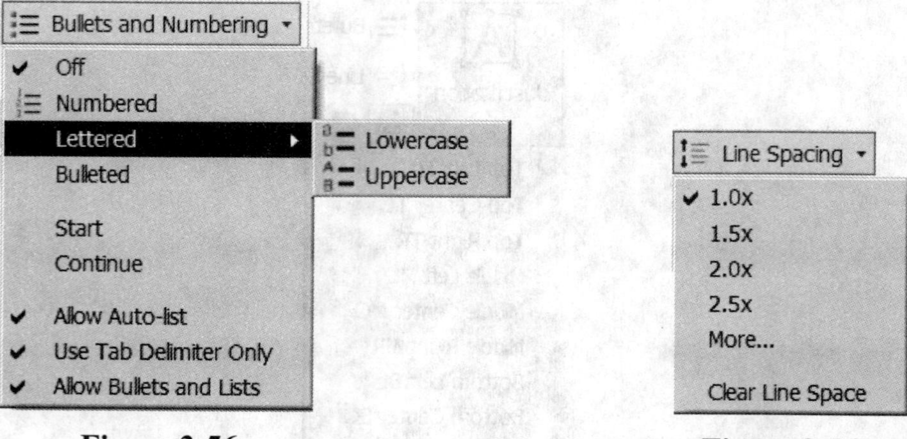

Figure 3-56a   Figure 3-56b

3.16.2.3.3. Line spacing
The line spacing is the clear distance between the two consecutive lines in a multiple line paragraph. Press the down arrow under the *Line Spacing* on the *Paragraph* panel and check the various options, Figure 3-56b.

The line space factor applies to the entire multiline text object and not to the selected lines. Line spacing increment to a multiple of single line spacing and single line spacing is 1.66 times the height of the text characters.

To change the line spacing, (i) click on the drop down arrow in line spacing option, Figure 3-56b, and (ii) select the *Line space factor*. The line spacing of the multiline text will be updated.

The line spacing can also be changed as follow, (i) select the multiline text, (ii) press the right button, (iii) choose the *Properties* option (the last option) to open the properties sheet, (iv) set the *Line space factor* field (for the example, to 1.5), and (v) press the *Enter* key.

3.16.2.3.4. Paragraph dialog box
The *Paragraph* dialog box, Figure 3-56c, can be open by clicking the dialog box launcher (a small arrow on the lower right corner of the panel) in the *Paragraph* panel. The dialog box is used to set the tabs, indentations, and paragraphs spacing and alignment.

- Multiline text can be indented using tabs. The ruler in the in-place text editor shows the settings for the current paragraph.
- Sliders on the ruler show indentation relative to the left side of the bounding box. The top slider indents the first line of the paragraph, and the bottom slider indents the other lines of the paragraph.
- Tabs and indents which are set before the entering the text applies to the whole multiline text object. To apply different tabs and indents to individual paragraphs, click in a single paragraph or select multiple paragraphs and then change the settings.

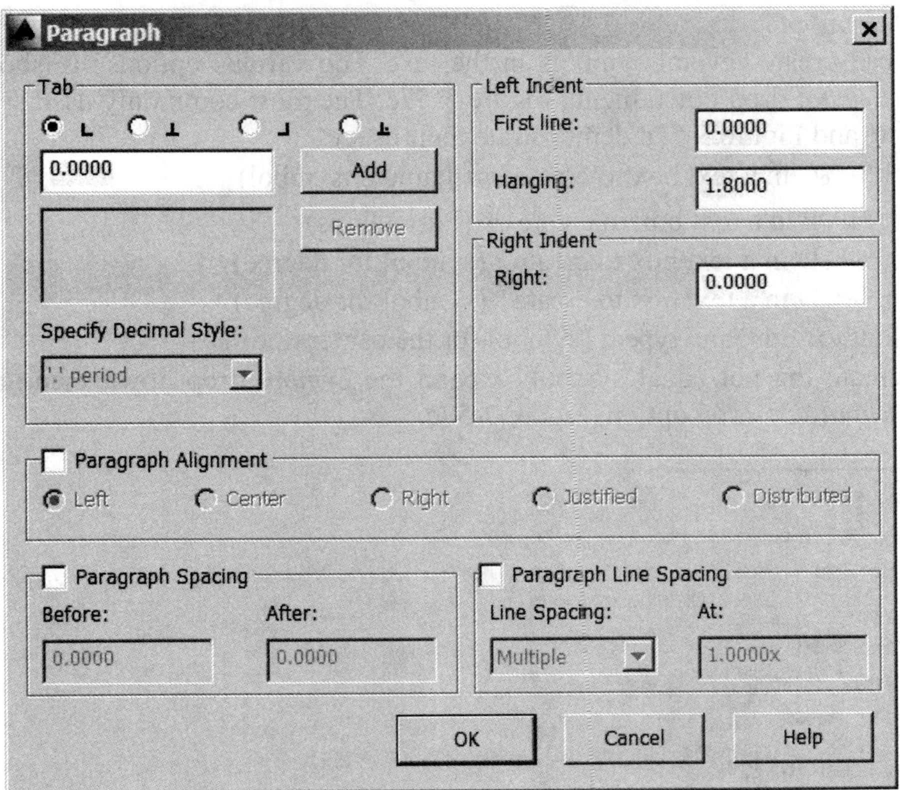

Figure 3-56c

3.16.2.4. Insert

The *Insert* panel is shown in Figure 3-57a. This panel provides the options to insert columns and symbols in the multiline text.

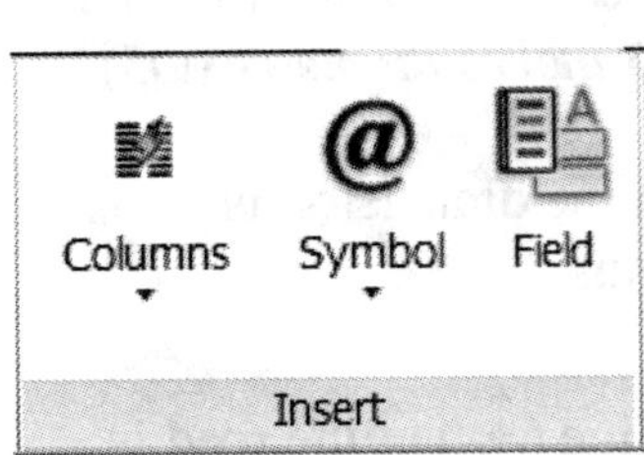

Figure 3-57a

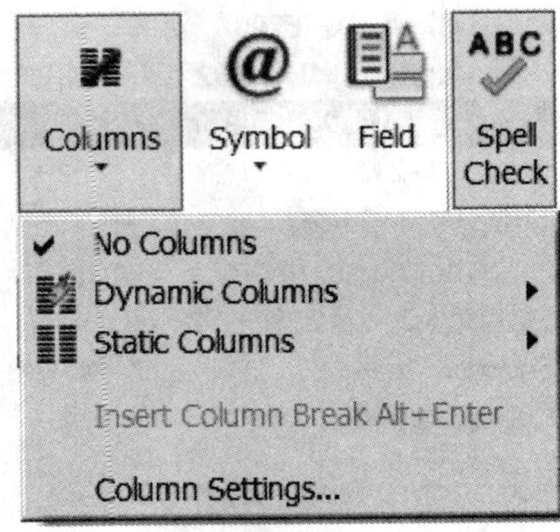

Figure 3-57b

3.16.2.4.1. Column

The user can create and edit multiple columns. The various options are shown in the expanded *Columns* drop down menu, Figure 3-57b.

3.16.2.4.2. Symbol

The user can create several symbols in the text. The various options are shown in the expanded *Symbol* drop down menu, Figure 3-57c. The most commonly used symbols are listed below and Figure 3-57d demonstrate their usage.

- Enter %%C in a text box to create ϕ (diameter symbol)
- Enter %%P in a text box to create $\pm$ (Plus Minus)
- Enter %%D in a text box to create $^\circ$ (symbol for degree)
- Enter %%D in a text box to create $^\circ$ (symbol for degree)
- Set font to "gdt" and type q (symbol for the center line)
- To create the not equal symbol, expand the *Symbol* drop down menu and select *Not Equal \U+2260* option, Figure 3-57c.

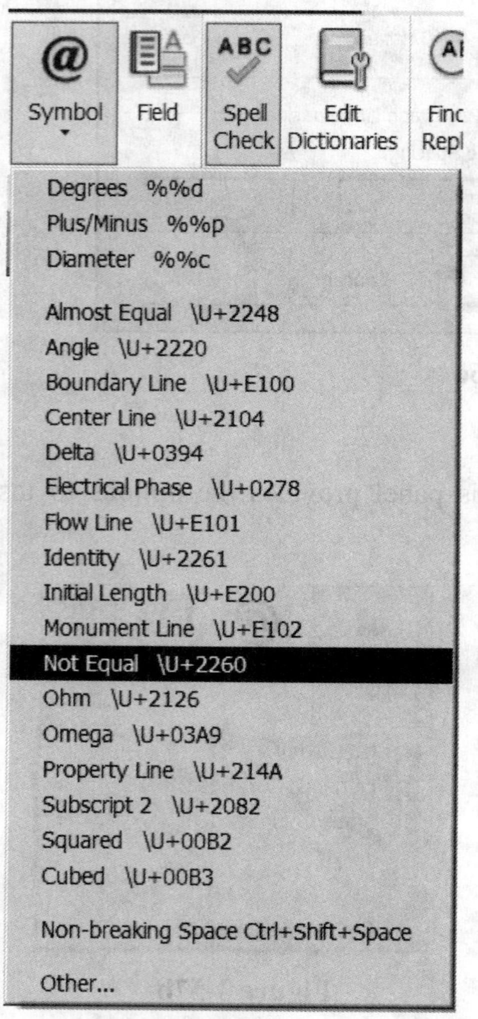

Figure 3-57c

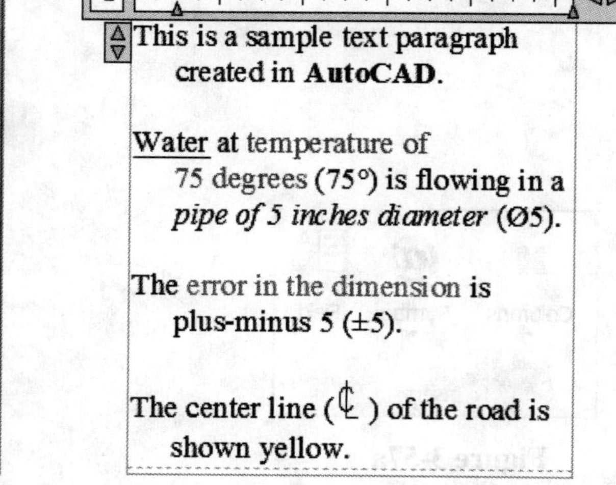

Figure 3-57d

3.16.2.5.   Spell check

The *Spell Check* panel is shown in Figure 3-58a. By default the spell check is *on*. A user can turn *off* or *on* by clicking the *Spell Check* icon. This panel provides the options to spell check any text (single, multiline, dimension, qleader, etc.).

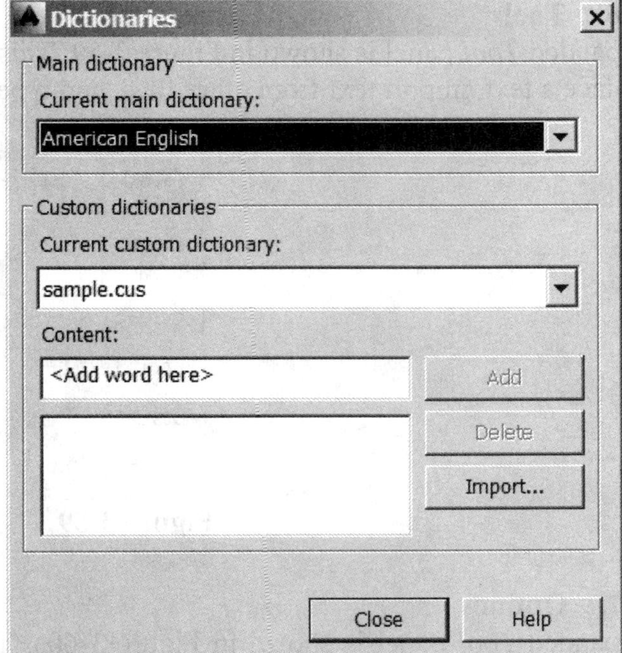

Figure 3-58a   **Figure 3-58b**

- A user can open the *Dictionaries* dialog box, Figure 3-58b, by clicking *Edit Dictionaries* icon in the panel. A user can select a dictionary by pressing the down arrow in the *Main dictionary* group.
- A user can open the *Check Spelling Setting* dialog box, Figure 3-58c, by clicking the dialog box launcher (a small arrow on the lower right corner of the panel). This dialog box allows to set options for the spell checking.

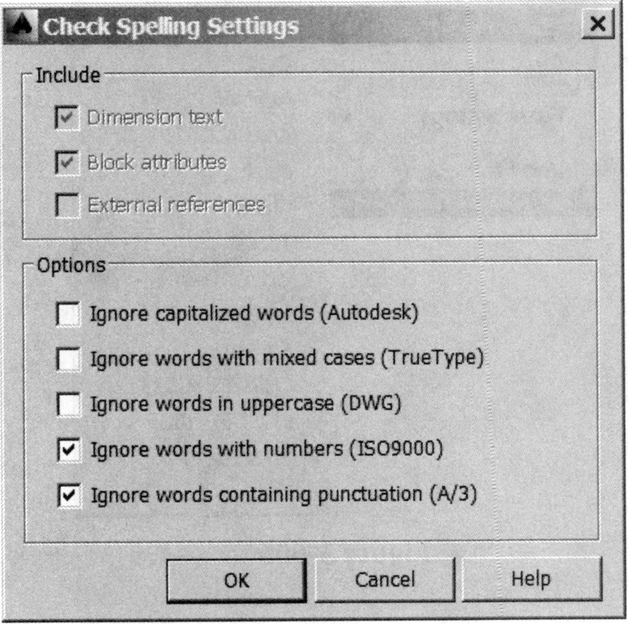

Figure 3-58c

3.16.2.6. Tools

The expanded *Tool* panel is shown in Figure 3-59. This panel provides the options to find and replace a text, import text from other files, and type the uppercase text.

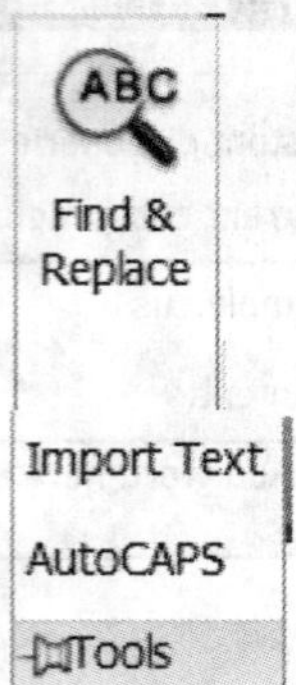

Figure 3-59

3.16.2.7. Options

The expanded *Tool* panel is shown in Figure 3-60a. This panel provides the options to find and replace a text, import text from other files, and type the uppercase text. Click on the down arrow, Figure 3-60b, beside *More* and expand the *Character Set* to display the available character sets.

3.16.2.8. Close

The *Close* panel, Figure 3-61, is used to close the *Text Editor*. Click on the *Close Text Editor*, and the editor will be closed. The user can also exit the editor mode by clicking outside the text's bounding box or by pressing the *Esc* key on the keyboard.

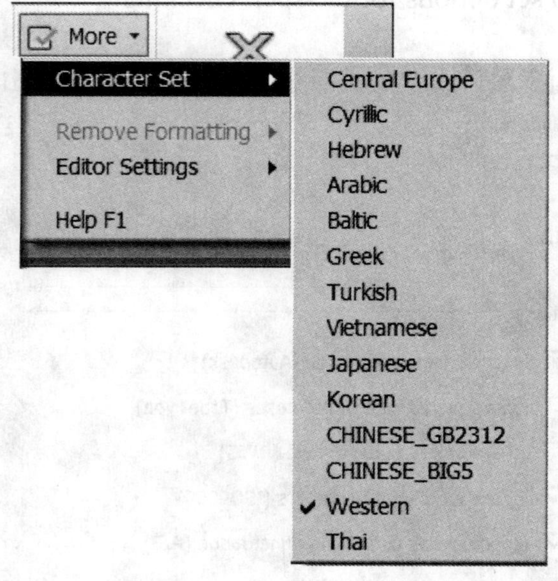

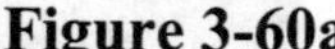

Figure 3-60a   Figure 3-60b   Figure 3-61

3.16.3. Annotate tab and Text panel

The expanded *Text* panel from the *Annotate* tab is shown in Figure 3-62a. This panel provides the options to create single and multiline text, spell checker, font height, text scaling, and justification.

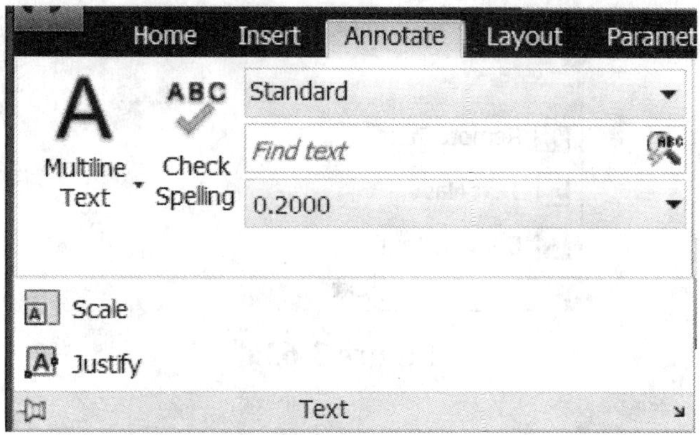

Figure 3-62a

The user can open *Text Style* dialog box from the dialog box launcher, Figure 3-62b.

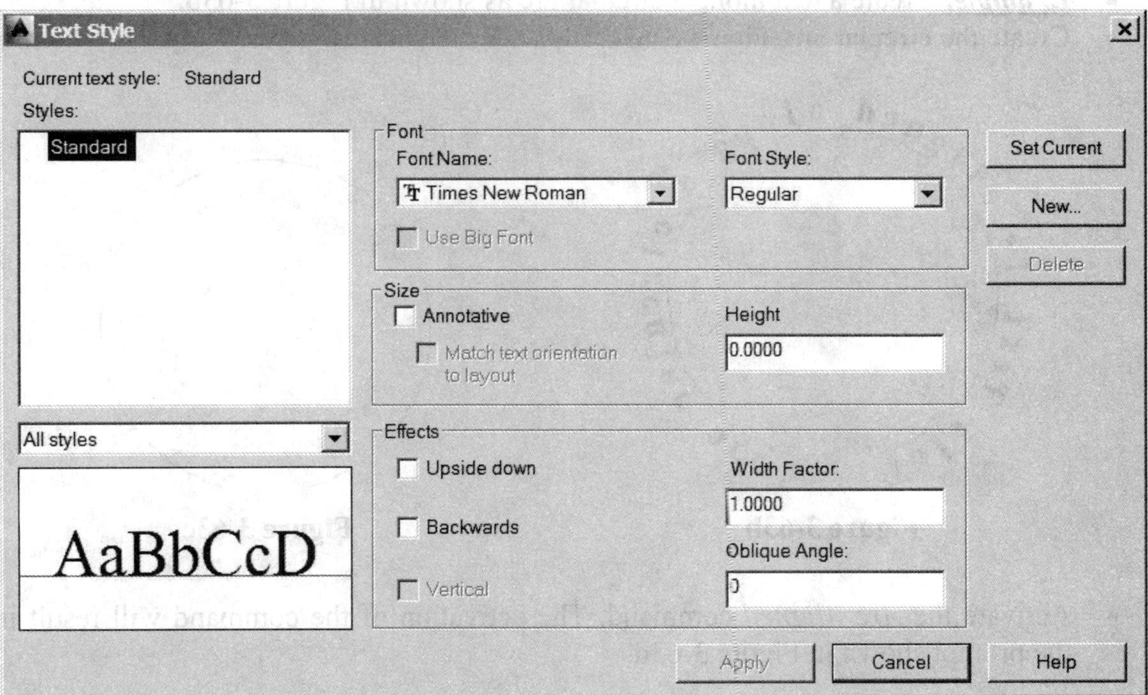

Figure 3-62b

3.16.4. Express Tools tab and Text panel

The expanded *Text* panel from the *Express Tools* tab is shown in Figure 3-63a. This panel provides the options to mask and unmask, modify (press the down arrow and check the options) the text. These options are discusses earlier. This panel also provides the options to create text along an arc and to enclose a text object in a circle. These two options are discussed in details.

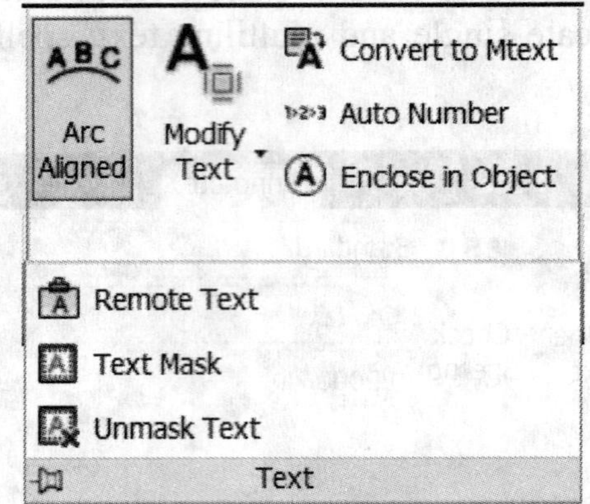

Figure 3-63a

3.16.4.1.1. *Arc Aligned*

As the name suggest, the *Arc Aligned* command allows to create text only along a circular arc.

- **_Example:_** Create a text along a circular arc as shown in Figure 3-63b.
- Create the circular arc, Figure 3-63c.

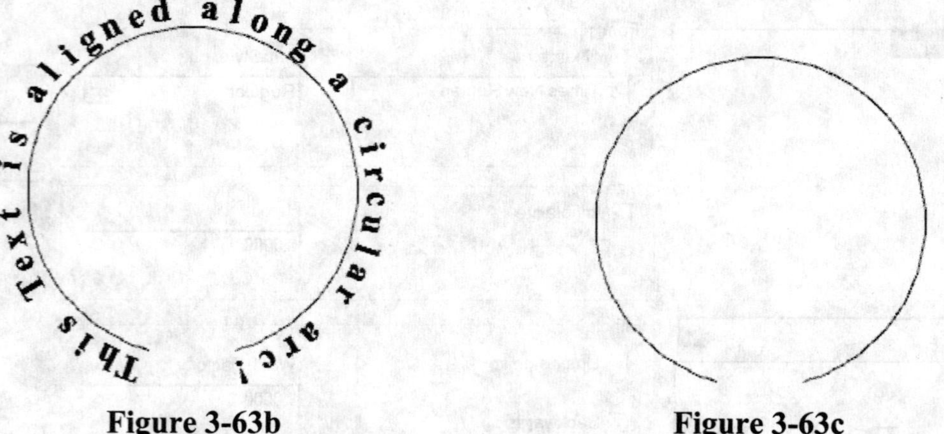

Figure 3-63b   **Figure 3-63c**

- Activate the *Arc Aligned* command. The activation of the command will result in the prompt shown in Figure 3-63d.

Select an Arc or an ArcAlignedText:

Figure 3-63d

- Click at the arc and *ArcAlignedText Workshop – Create* dialog box will appear, Figure 3-63e.
- Type the desired text; and change the properties (if necessary).

- Click the *OK* button. This will close the dialog box and the text will appear along the arc, Figure 3-63b.

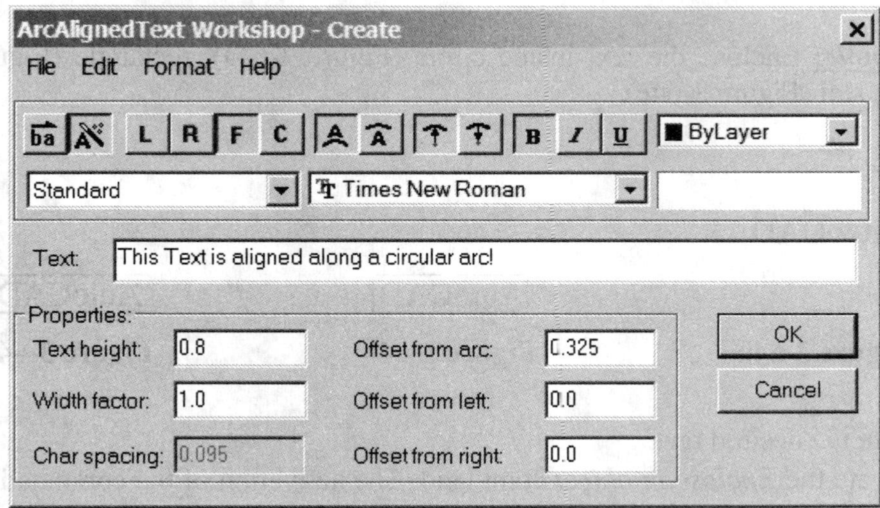

Figure 3-63e

- To edit the arc aligned text, just double click at the text and the property sheet will appear on the screen, Figure 3-63f. Now the user can make the desired changes.
- The user should try to create the second text, Figure 3-63g.

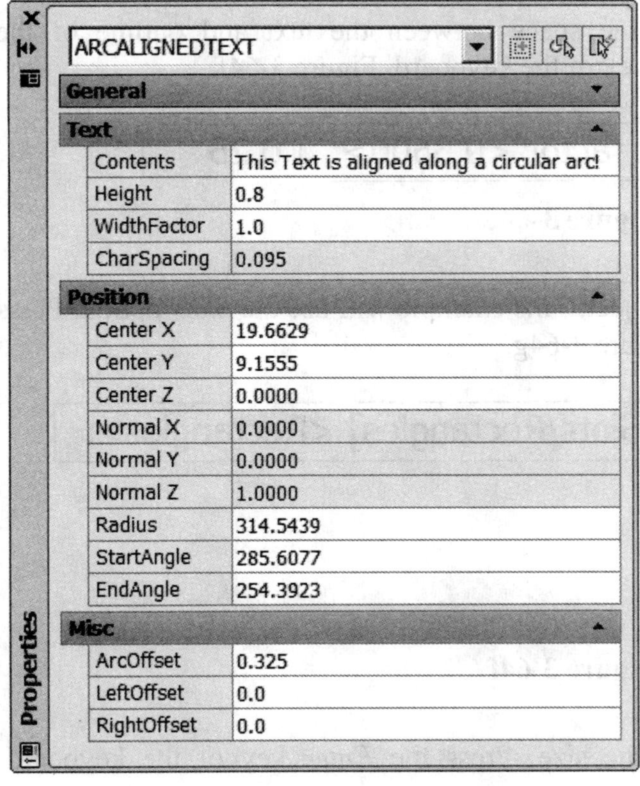

Figure 3-63f

Figure 3-63g

3.16.4.1.2. Enclose in object

The *Enclose in Object* command can be used to enclose single or multiline text object in a circle, rectangle, and a slot.

- *Example:* Enclose the text inside circle (Figure 3-64a), rectangle (Figure 3-64b), and a slot (Figure 3-64c).

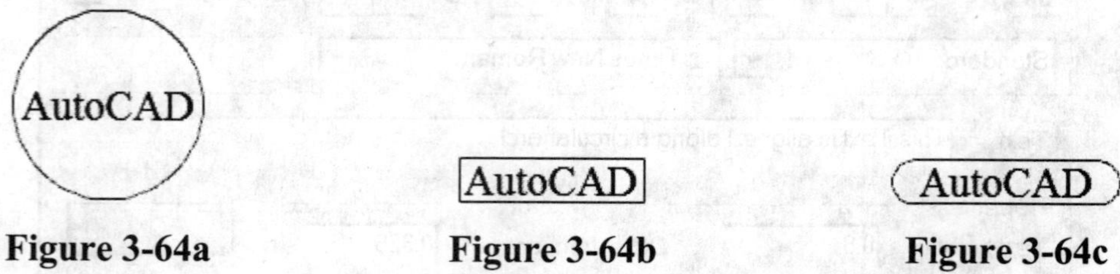

Figure 3-64a   Figure 3-64b   Figure 3-64c

- Create the desired text.
- Activate the *Enclose in object* command. The activation of the command will result in the prompt shown in Figure 3-64d.

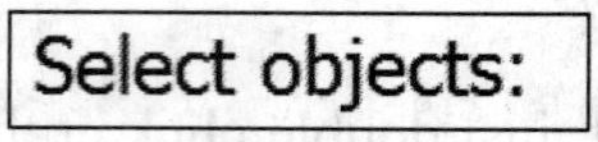

Select objects:

Figure 3-64d

- Click at the text and press the *Enter* key of the keyboard, Figure 3-64e.
- Specify the offset factor. It is the space between the text and outline of the enclosing object. Press the *Enter* key of the keyboard, Figure 3-64f.

Enter distance offset factor <0.3500>: 0.25

Figure 3-64e

- Select the type of the enclosing object. This example will use the *Slots* option. Press the *Enter* key of the keyboard, Figure 3-64g.

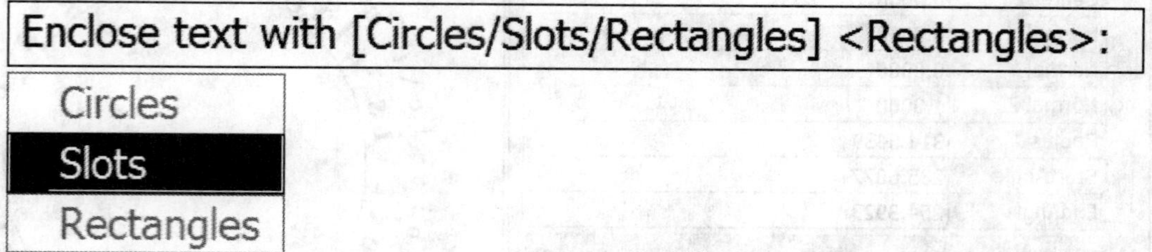

Figure 3-64f

- Select the *Constant* option for the size. Press the *Enter* key of the keyboard, Figure 3-64h.

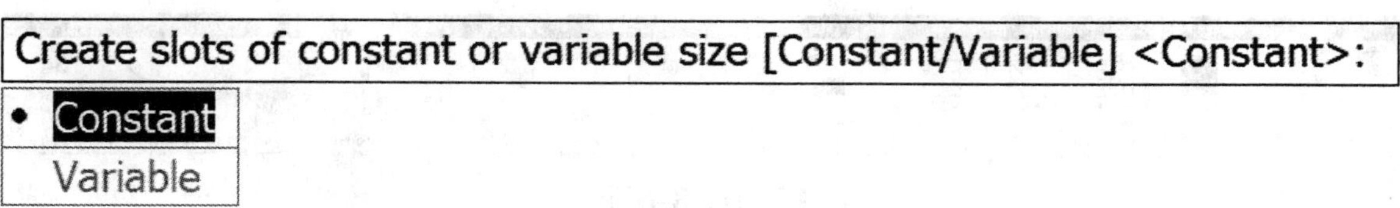

Figure 3-64g

- Select the *Both* option for maintain the object. Press the *Enter* key of the keyboard. The text is enclosed in a slot, Figure 3-64c.

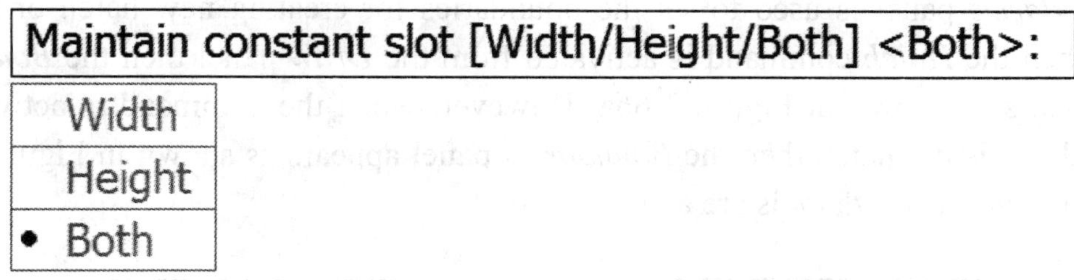

Figure 3-64h

- Repeat the process for the circle (Figure 3-64a) and rectangle (Figure 3-64b).

3.17.   Hatch

The *Hatch* command allows the user to create a hatch, that is, fill a space enclosed by closed boundary with a specified pattern.

- The *Hatch* command can be activated using one of the following procedures.
  1. Panel method: From the *Home* tab and *Draw* panel, select the *Hatch* tool, Figure 3-65a.
  2. Command line method: Type "hatch", "Hatch", or "HATCH" in the command line and press the *Enter* key.

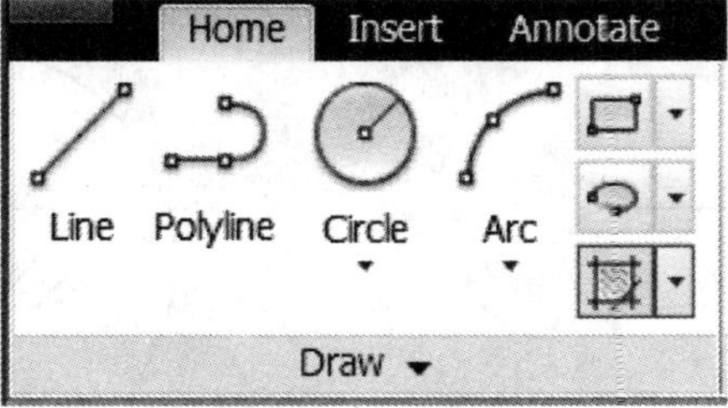

Figure 3-65a

- The activation of the command will open the *Hatch Creation* tab (or *Hatch Editor*) with the *Boundaries, Pattern, Properties, Origin, Options, Close* panels, Figure 3-65b. Also, the *Hatch Creation* tab will become the current tab.

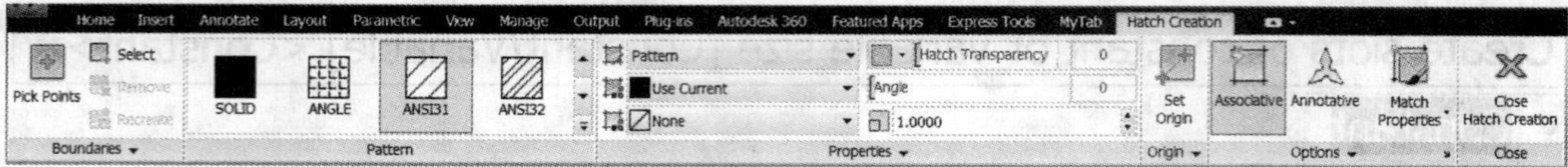

Figure 3-65b

3.17.1. Hatch editor
This section will first describe most of the command on the panels.

3.17.1.1.1. Boundaries
The *Boundaries* panel is used to set the boundaries for creating new hatch or existing hatch. When the *Hatch* command is activated from the *Draw* panel then the *Boundaries* panel appears as shown in Figure 3-66a. However, when the command is activated by clicking the existing hatch then the *Boundaries* panel appears as shown in Figure 3-66b, the *Remove* and *Recreate* tools are active.

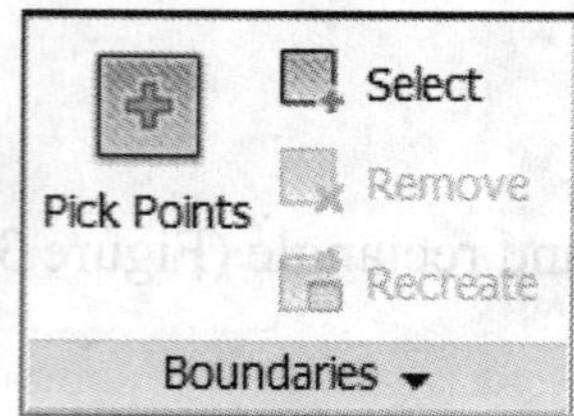

Figure 3-66a

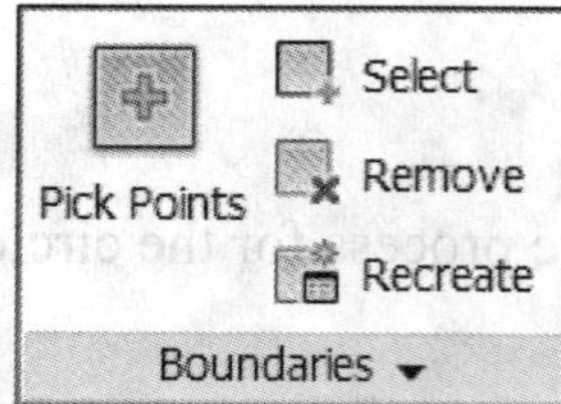

Figure 3-66b

- **Pick Points:** The *Pick Points* option allows the user to select an area enclosed by one or more objects, Figure 3-66c. In the figure, the user has clicked inside the part of the slot inside the circle. The hatch boundary is highlighted.
- **Select:** The *Select* option allows the user to select closed object. For example, close shape created using polyline, circle, polygon, etc., Figure 3-66d. In the figure, the user has clicked at the slot. Therefore, the part of the circle inside the slot is ignored. The hatch boundary is highlighted.

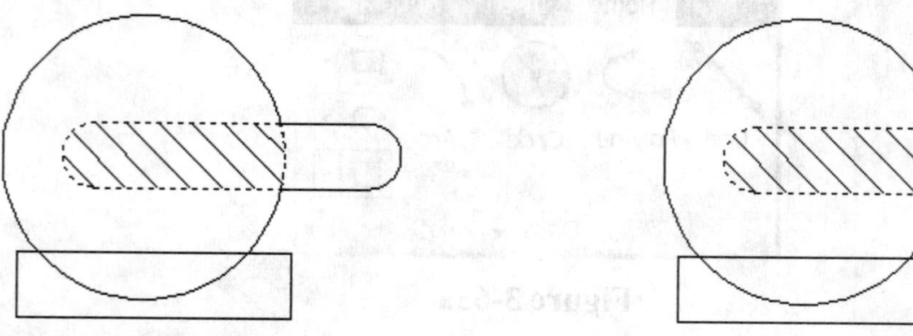

Figure 3-66c   **Figure 3-66d**

3.17.1.1.2. Pattern
The *Pattern* panel is used to set the hatch pattern, Figure 3-67a. The user can click up or down arrow to check the other patterns.

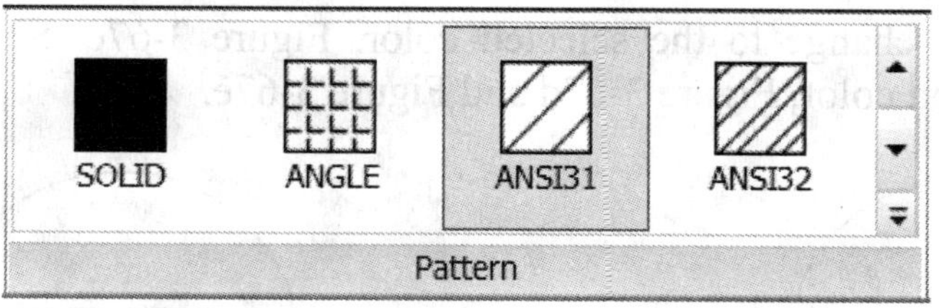

Figure 3-67a

- The user can change the pattern before the hatch command by click on the desired pattern.
- The user can change the pattern after the hatch command using the following steps: (i) Click on the hatch and a circular grip point will appear, Figure 3-67b. (ii) Select the desired pattern. (iii) Press the *Esc* key on the keyboard. DO NOT PRESS THE *ENTER* KEY. The hatch appearance will change to the selected pattern, Figure 3-67c.

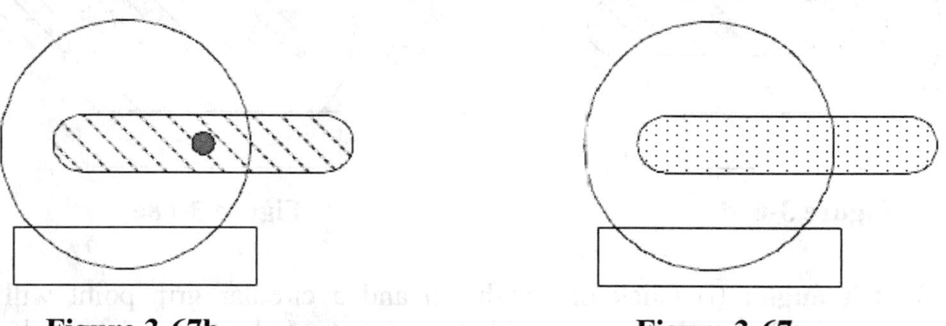

Figure 3-67b   **Figure 3-67c**

3.17.1.1.3. *Properties*
The *Properties* panel is used to set hatch color, angle and scale, Figure 3-68a.

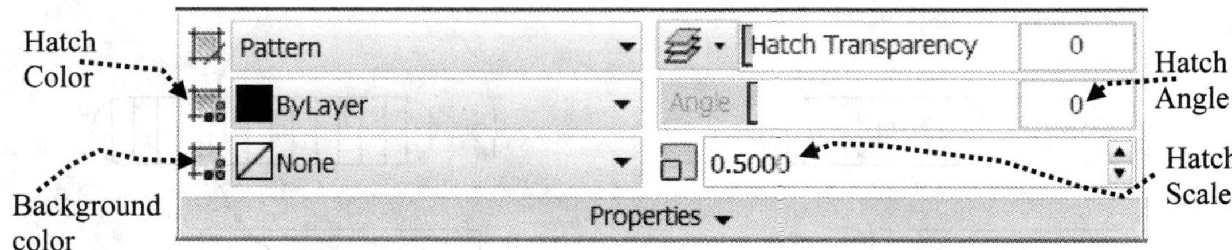

Figure 3-68a

- The user can change the pattern properties before the hatch command by selecting the desired properties.
- The user can change the pattern properties after the hatch command using the following steps.

  o **Hatch color:** (i) Click on the hatch and a circular grip point will appear, Figure 3-68b. (ii) Press the down arrow and select the desired color. (iii) Press the *Esc* key on the keyboard. DO NOT PRESS THE *ENTER* KEY. The hatch color will change to the selected color, Figure 3-67c. Similarly, change the background color, Figure 3-67d and Figure 3-67e.

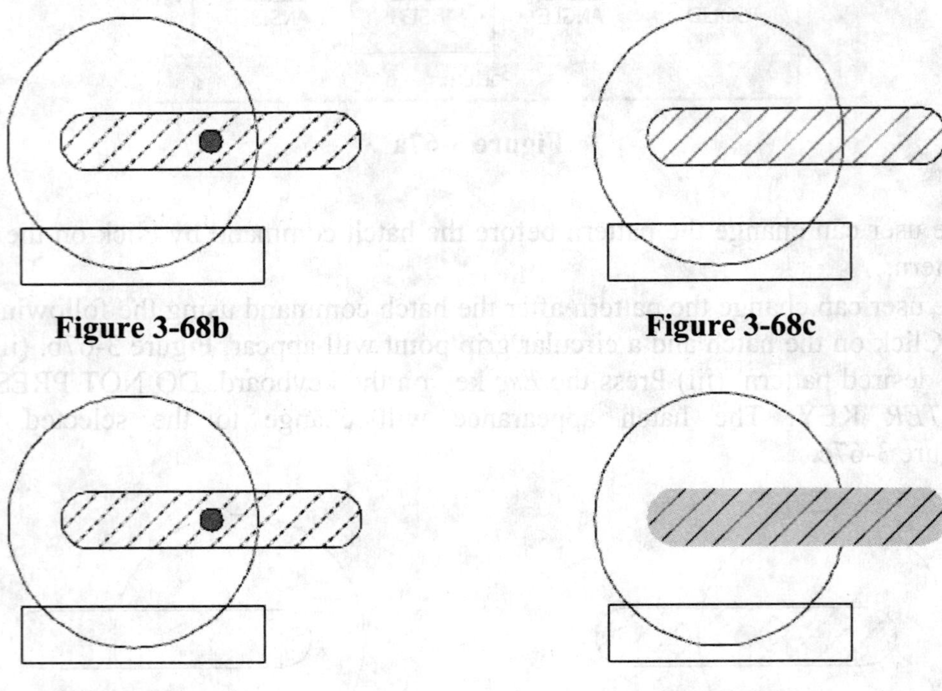

Figure 3-68b   **Figure 3-68c**

Figure 3-68d   **Figure 3-68e**

o **Hatch angle:** (i) Click on the hatch and a circular grip point will appear, Figure 3-69a (angle = 0). (ii) Click at the *Angle* button and type the desired angle. (iii) Press the *Esc* key on the keyboard. DO NOT PRESS THE *ENTER* KEY. The hatch angle will change to the selected angle, Figure 3-69b (angle = 45).

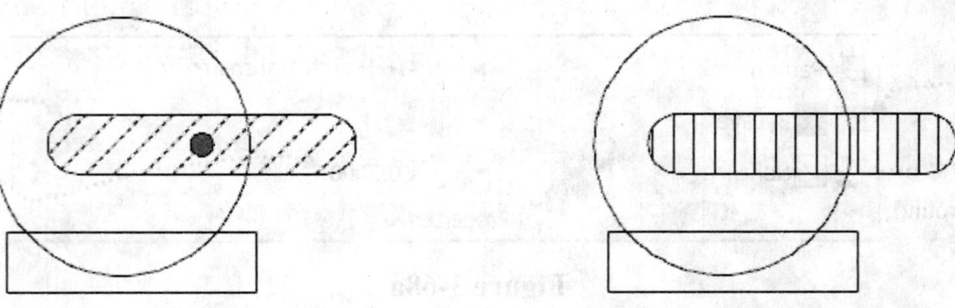

Figure 3-69a   **Figure 3-69b**

o **Hatch scale:** (i) Click on the hatch and a circular grip point will appear, Figure 3-69c (scale factor = 0.5). (ii) Press the down arrow and select the desired scale factor. (iii) Press the *Esc* key on the keyboard. DO NOT PRESS THE *ENTER* KEY. The hatch scale will change to the selected scale, Figure 3-69d (scale factor = 1.0). The scale factor should be selected such that the pattern is clearly visible.

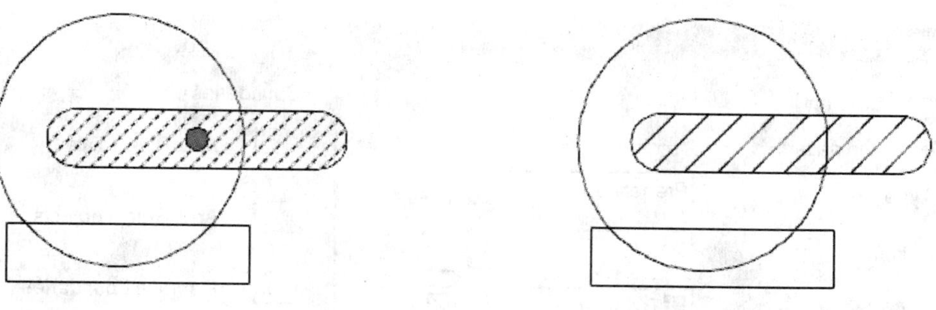

Figure 3-69c   **Figure 3-69d**

3.17.1.1.4. Options

The *Options* panel, Figure 3-70a, is used to set various hatch properties.

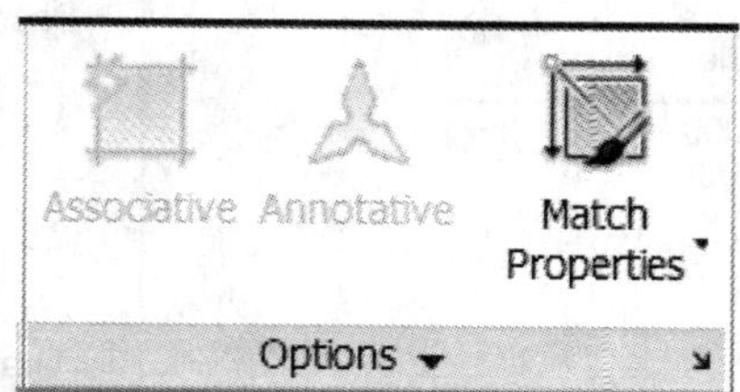

Figure 3-70a

- The user can open the *Hatch Editor* dialog box from dialog box launcher (a small arrow on the lower right corner of the panel). The dialog box is shown in Figure 3-70b on the next page. The panels in the dialog box are similar the panels in the *Hatch Creation* tab or *Hatch Editor*.

3.17.1.1.5. Close

The *Close* panel, Figure 3-71, is used to close the *Hatch Creation* tab or *Hatch Editor*. Click on the *Close Hatch Editor*, and the editor will be closed. The user can also exit the editor mode by pressing the *Esc* key on the keyboard.

Figure 3-71

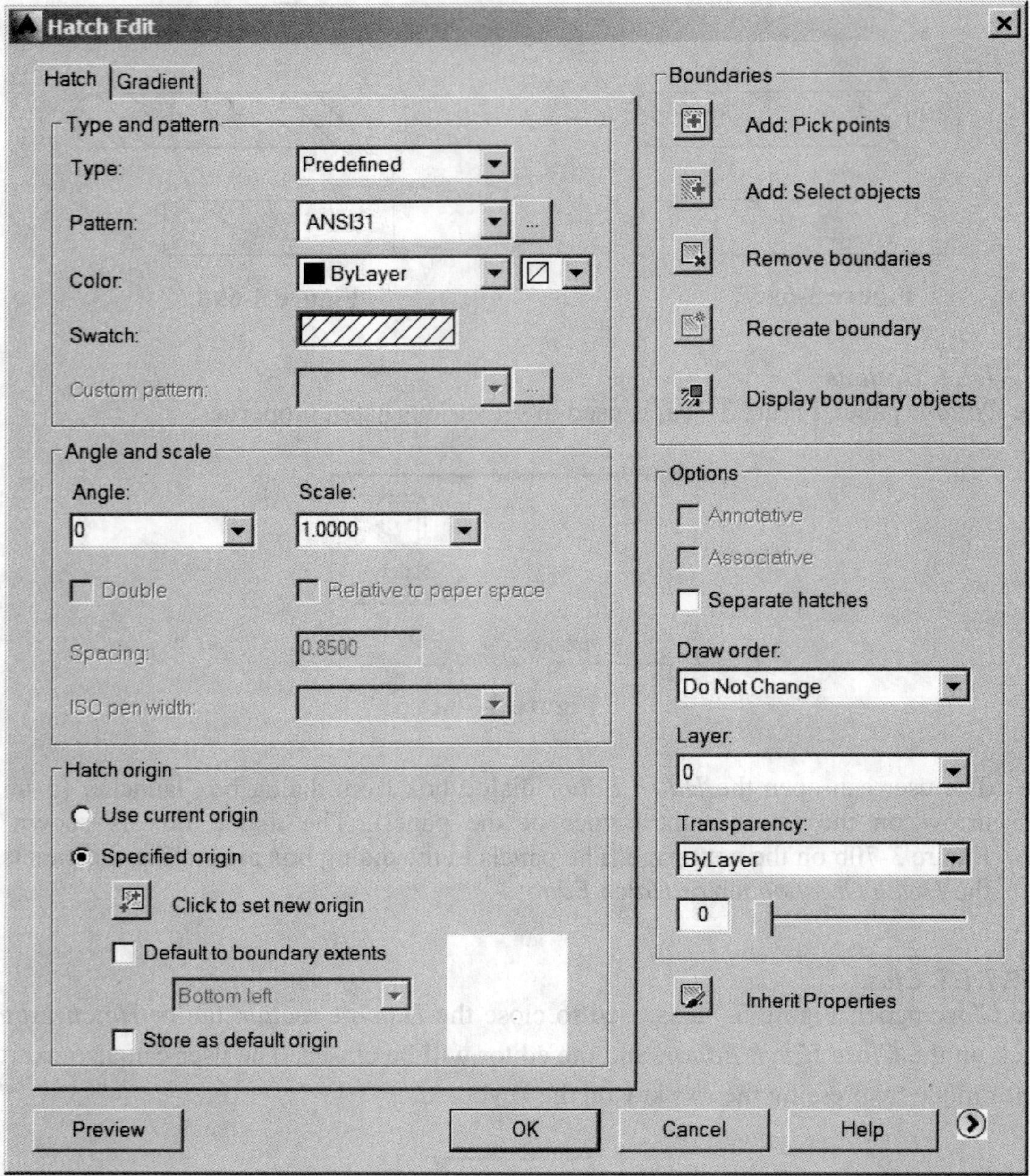

Figure 3-70b

3.17.2. Hatch an area
This section explains the hatch process.

- Draw the objects to be hatched. For the current example, create the building as shown in Figure 3-72a.
- Activate the *Hatch* command.
- The activation of the command will open the *Hatch Editor* and the prompt shown in Figure 3-72b will appear on screen. Press the down arrow and check the various

options. This example will use the *internal point* option; press the up arrow and close the option list.

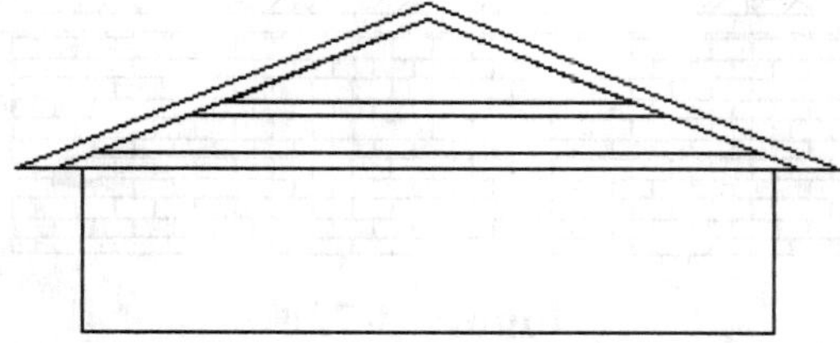

Figure 3-72a

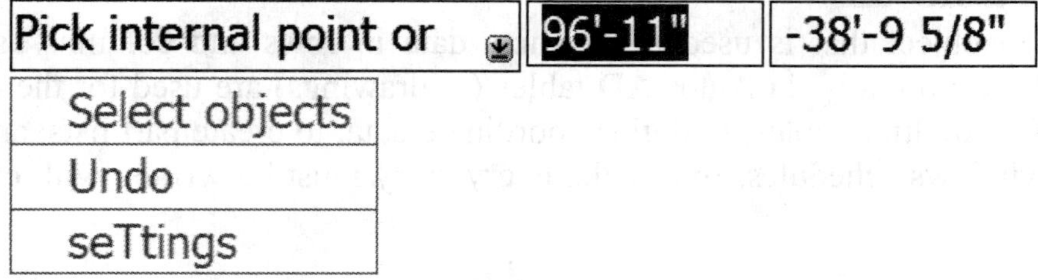

Figure 3-72b

- Click inside the large rectangle and its boundary will be highlighted and the area will be hatched with the current pattern, Figure 3-72c.
- Press the *Enter* key and the hatch command is complete.

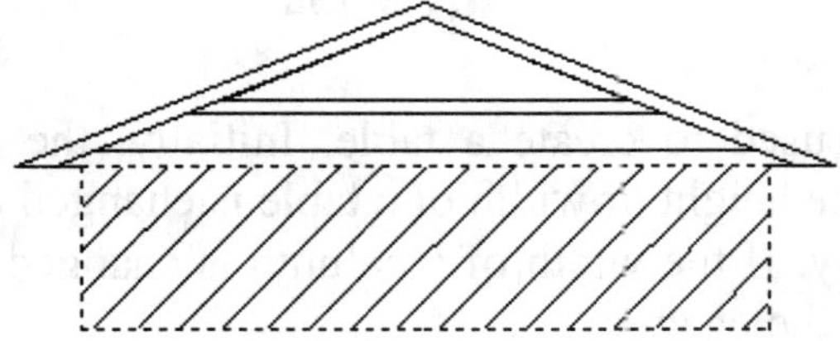

Figure 3-72c

- Now, change the pattern and its scale. The scale is change to *AR-B816* (a brick pattern) and the scale to 1.5, Figure 3-72d.
- Similarly, hatch the smaller triangle, Figure 3-72e. Similarly, hatch the middle part using *AR-RSHKE* pattern, Figure 3-72e.

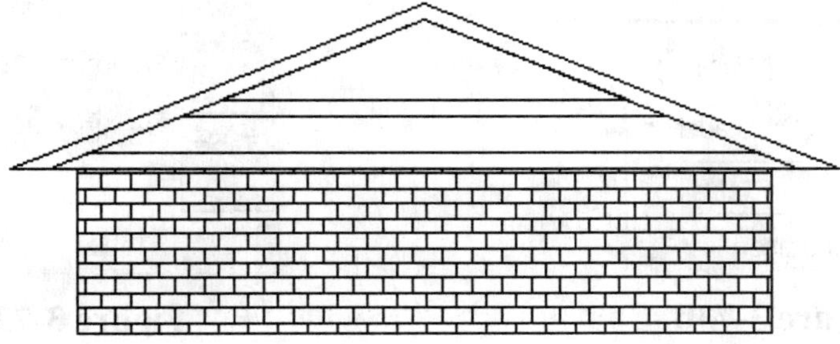

Figure 3-72d

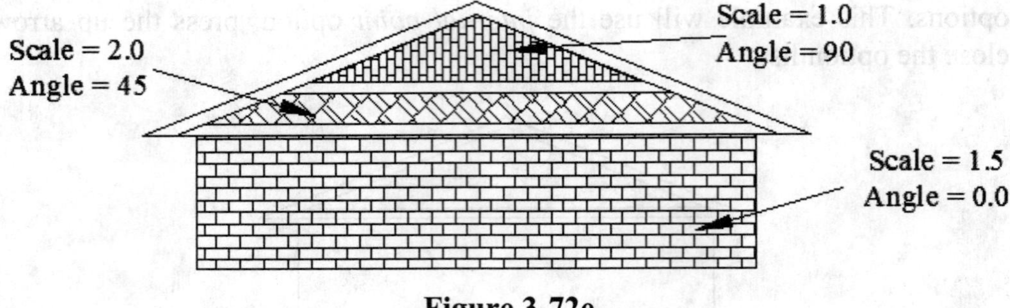

Figure 3-72e

3.18.   Table

A table is an object that is used to organize data in rows and columns as shown in Figure 3-73a. Commonly, in AutoCAD tables (in drawings) are used for the dimensions of objects with multiple holes, to define coordinate data, to create part lists, and to create doors and windows schedules. In a table, every entry must be written with caps lock or upper case.

DIMENSION			
NAME	X-COORD	Y-COORD	Ø
A1	2.34	45.00	13.00
B1	-1.80	23.45	11.50
C1	4.98	35.12	9.00

Figure 3-73a

The *Table* command is used to create a table. Initially, the table is empty but it is populated as needed. If the height or width of a table is changed then the rows or columns will change proportionally. If the width of a column is changed then the table widens or narrows to accommodate the change.

- The *Table* command is activated using one of the following procedures.
  1. Panel method: (i) From the *Home* tab and *Annotation* panel, select the *Table* tool, Figure 3-73b. (ii) From the *Annotate* tab and *Table* panel, select the *Table* tool, Figure 3-73c.
  2. Command line method: Type "table", "Table", or "TABLE" in the command line and press the *Enter* key.

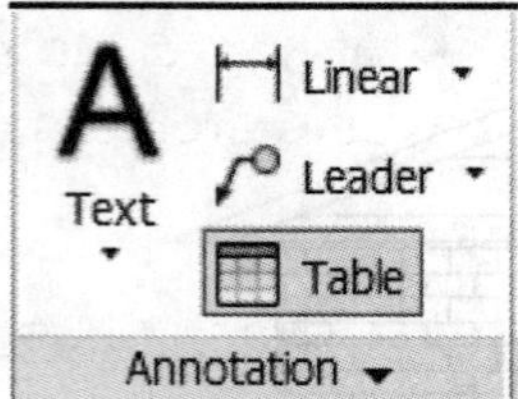

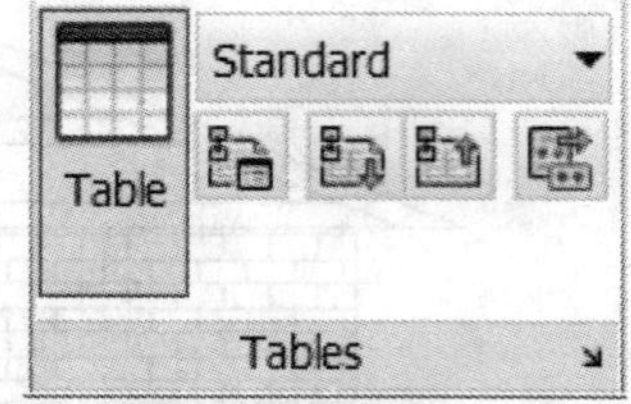

Figure 3-73b   **Figure 3-73c**

- The activation of the command will open the *Insert Table* dialog box shown in Figure 3-73d.

- ***Example:*** Create the table shown in Figure 3-73a.

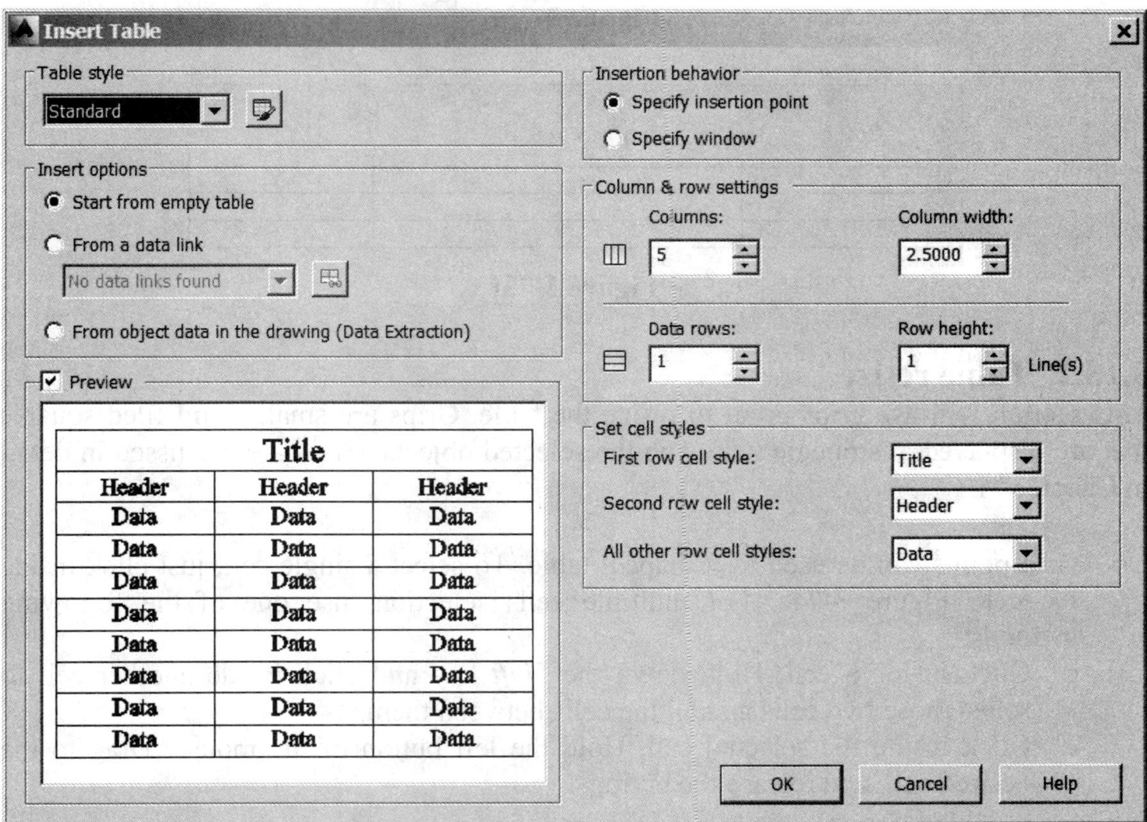

Figure 3-73d

3.18.1. Insert Table dialog box

In the *Insert Table* dialog box, from the *Table style* panel select a style from the list or click the button to create a new table style. In the *Insertion option* panel, select *Start from empty table* option to create a table without any entries. In the *Insertion behavior* panel, select *Specify insertion point* option to insert the table in the drawing area. In the *Column & row settings* panel, set the number of columns and rows. For the example, set the number of columns to 4 and number of data rows 3. Assume the default values for the column width and row height. For the *Specify window* insertion method in *Insertion behavior* panel, the user can enter only the number of columns and the rows height. Finally, click the *OK* button. This will close the dialog box and prompt to specify the insertion point will appear, Figure 3-73e.

Specify the insertion point in the drawing area by clicking at the desired location. The resulting table is shown Figure 3-73f.

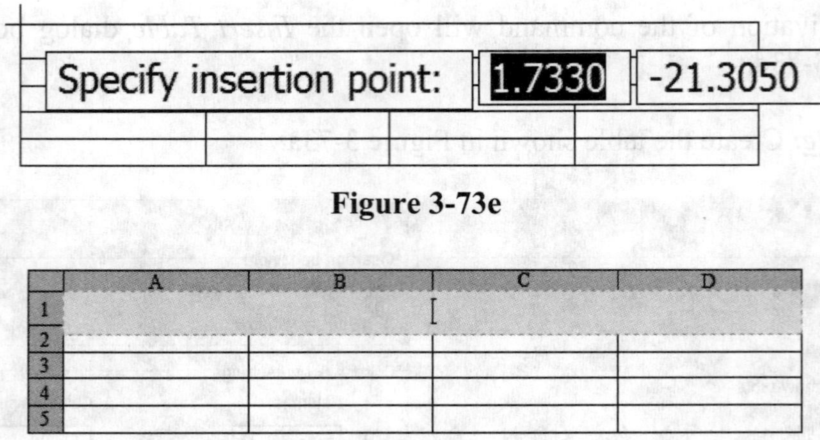

Figure 3-73e

Figure 3-73f

3.18.2. Table resize

This section will use grips point to resize the table. Grips are small, solid filed squares that are displayed at strategic points on the selected objects. Grips are discussed in detail in Chapter #4.

- Grip points can be used to reshape a table. To select a single cell, just click inside the cell, Figure 3-74a. For multiple cells selection, use one of the following methods:
  - o Click inside a cell. Hold down the *Shift* key and click inside another cell to select those two cells and all the cells between them.
  - o Click inside the selected cell. Hold the left button of the mouse. Drag to the desired cell, and release the button.

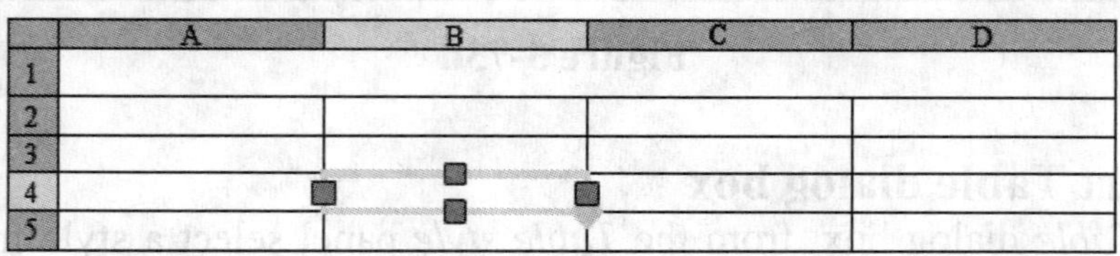

Figure 3-74a

- <u>Change the row height</u>: To change the row height of the selected cell, drag the top or bottom grips point upward or downward, respectively. The resized table is shown in Figure 3-74b. If more than one cell is selected, then the row height changes equally for each row.
- <u>Change the column width</u>: To change the column width of the selected cell, drag the left or right grips point to the left or right, respectively. The resized table is shown in Figure 3-74b. If more than one cell is selected, then the column width changes equally for each column.
- <u>Resize table</u>: Select the table. To stretch uniformly: use the grips point at upper right corner to stretch the width, lower left corner to stretch the height, and lower right corner to stretch both the width and height of the table, Figure 3-74c. That is,

all the rows and/or columns will be stretched by the same amount. Although the Figure 3-74c shows multiple options simultaneously, the software does not allow for multiple options display.

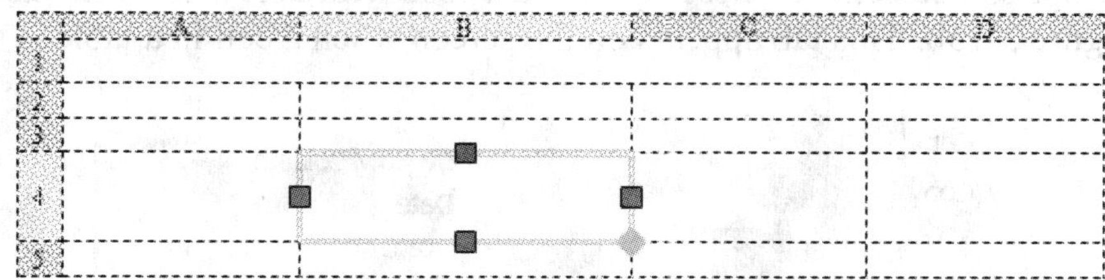

Figure 3-74b

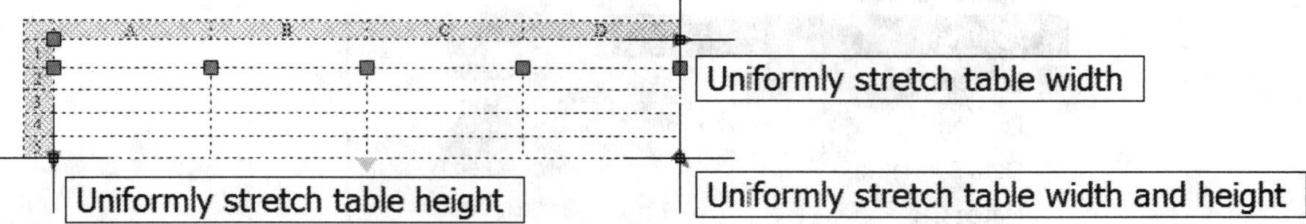

Figure 3-74c

- Press the *Esc* key to remove the selection.
- <u>Move the table</u>: Select the table; use the grips point at the upper left corner to move the table, Figure 3-74d.

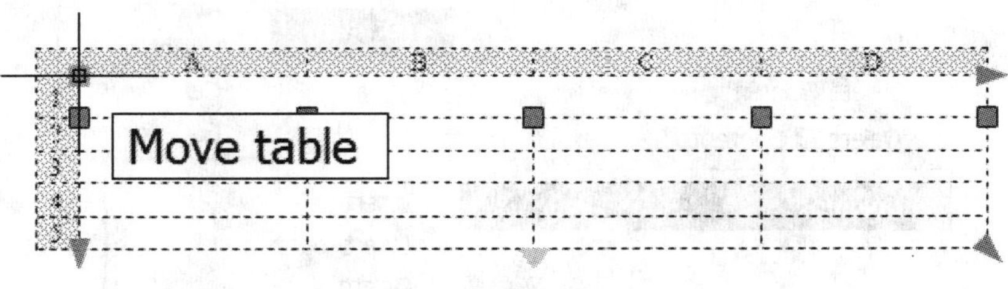

Figure 3-74d

- <u>Break the table</u>: Select the table; use the lower middle (light blue) grips point to break the table, Figure 3-74e. The user should avoid to use this option.

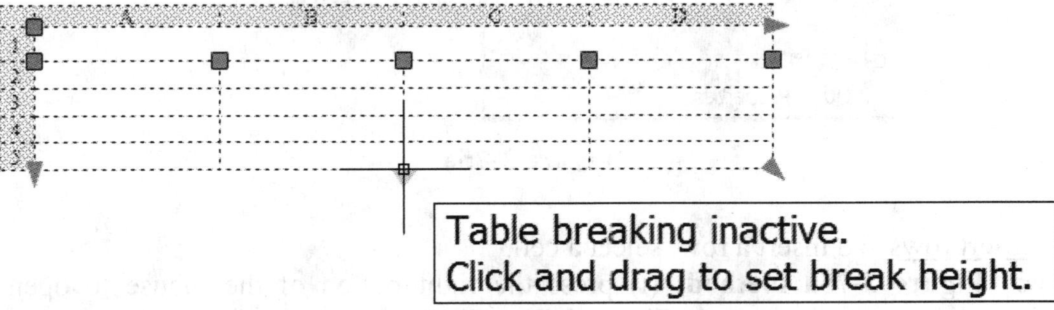

Figure 3-74e

3.18.3. Modify table's shape

Figure 3-75a shows the various options available to reshape the table. The figure shows the selection of multiple options simultaneously. However, the software does not allow for multiple options selection. These options are also available from the *Table Cell* tab shown in Figure 3-75b. This tab appears on the screen when a cell in a table is selected.

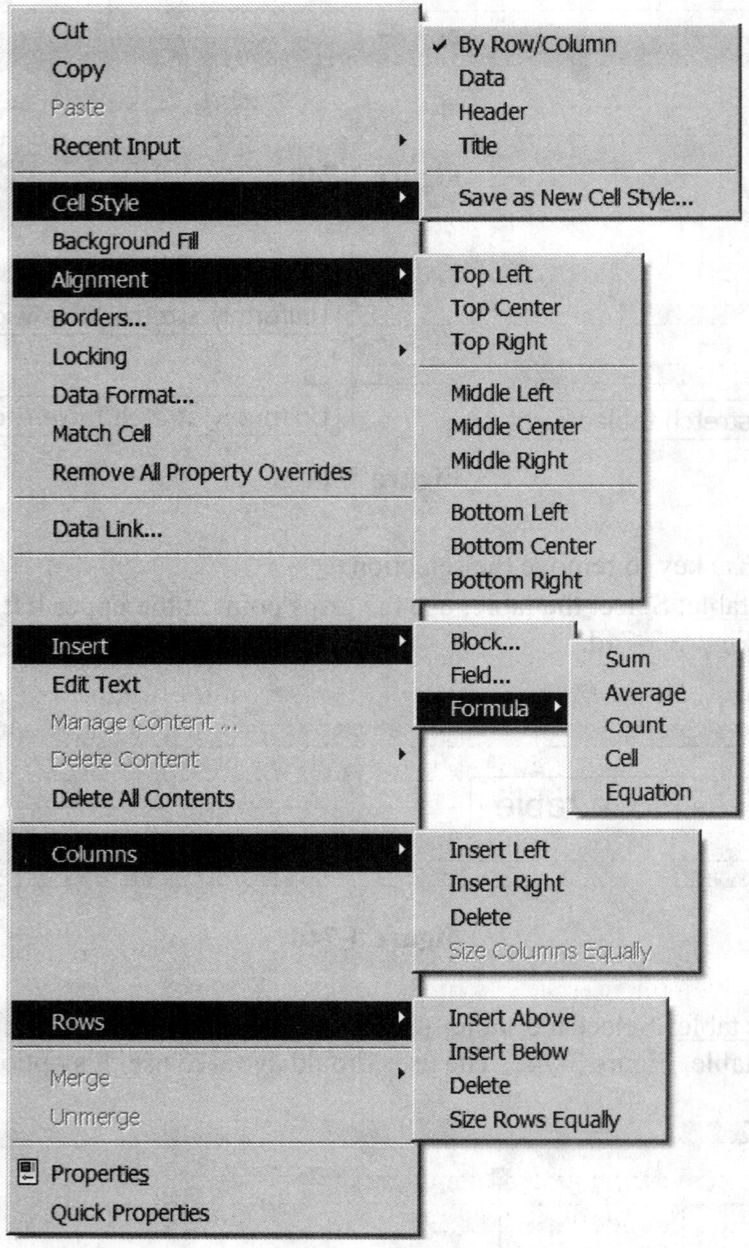

Figure 3-75a

- <u>Insert rows</u>: To insert a row, select a cell.
  - o **Figure 3-75a method:** (i) press the right button of the mouse to open the options panel shown in Figure 3-75a. (ii) Click on the *Rows* option. (iii) Select the *Insert Above* or *Insert Below*. A row will be added above or below the

selected cell, respectively. In the current example, a row is added above the selected cell, Figure 3-75c. If '*n*' cells are selected than '*n*' rows will be inserted, where n >1.

- o **Figure 3-75b method:** Press the desired tool from the *Row* panel. In the current example, a row is added above the selected cell, Figure 3-75c. If '*n*' cells are selected than '*n*' rows will be inserted, where n >1.

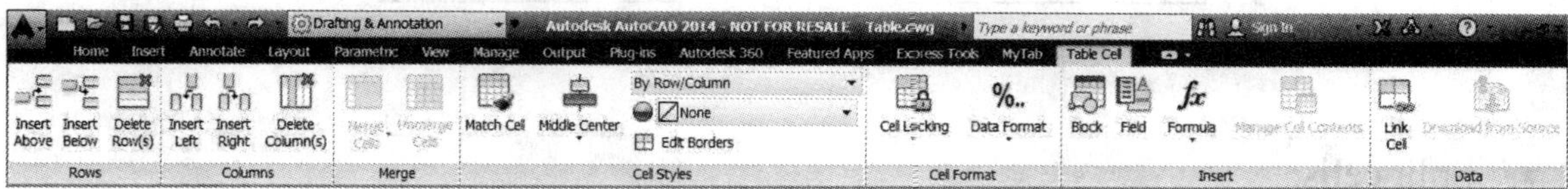

Figure 3-75b

- Insert Columns: Same as insert a row.

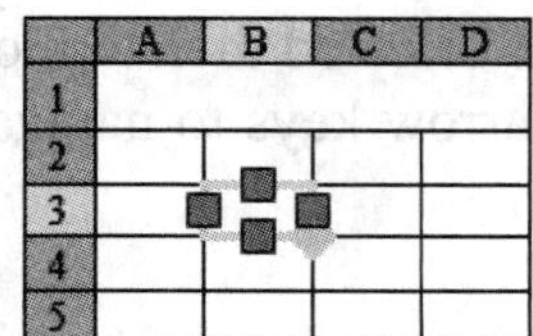 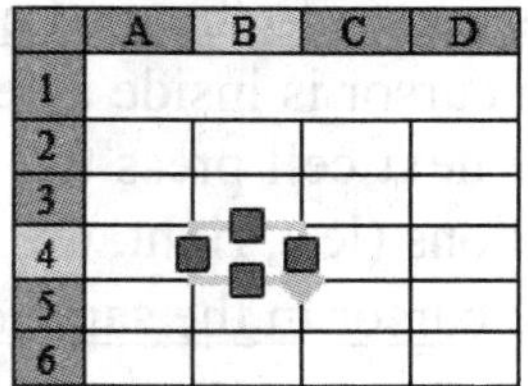

Figure 3-75c

- Delete rows: To delete a row, select a cell in the row to be deleted.
  - o **Figure 3-75a method:** (i) Press the right button of the mouse to open the options panel shown in Figure 3-75a. (ii) Click on the *Rows* option. (iv) Select the *Delete* option. A row will be deleted containing the selected cell. If '*n*' cells are selected than '*n*' rows will be deleted, where '*n*' >1.
  - o **Figure 3-75b method:** Press the desired tool from the *Row* panel. A row will be deleted containing the selected cell. If '*n*' cells are selected than '*n*' rows will be deleted, where '*n*' >1.
- Delete columns: To delete a column, select a cell in the column to be deleted.
  - o Same as deleting a row.
- Merge cells: To merge multiple cells, select the cells to be merged.
  - o *By Row* merges the cells horizontally by removing the vertical gridlines and leaving the horizontal gridlines intact.
  - o *By Column* merges the cells vertically by removing the horizontal gridlines and leaving the vertical gridlines intact, Figure 3-75d.
  - o **Figure 3-75a method:** (i) Press the right button of the mouse to open the options panel shown in Figure 3-75a. (iii) Click on the *Merge* option and click on *By Row*. The selected cells will be merged into one cell. Similarly merge cells in a *Column*, or *All* (both direction, that is, row and column). Figure 3-75d shows the merge of cell using different options.
  - o **Figure 3-75b method:** Press the desired tool from the *Merge* panel. The selected cells will be merged into one cell. Similarly merge cells in a *Column*,

or *All* (both direction, that is, row and column). Figure 3-75d shows the merge of cell using different options.

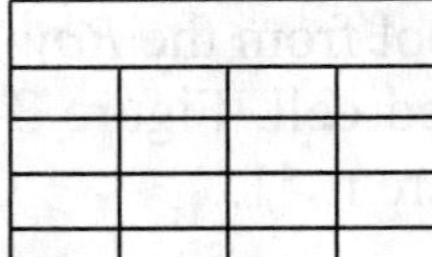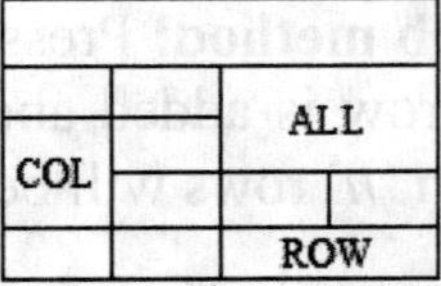

Figure 3-75d

- Split cells:
  o Cells cannot be split EXCEPT the cells that were merged previously.
- Press the *Esc* key to remove the selection.

3.18.4. The cursor movement
- Move the cursor to the next cell:
  o If the cursor is inside a cell and the text is NOT selected then to move the cursor to the next cell press the *TAB* key; or use the arrow keys to navigate in all four directions (left, right, up, and down).
- Move the cursor in the same cell:
  o *Left or right arrow keys:* If the cursor is inside a cell and the text is highlighted (that is, selected) then the left (or right) arrow key moves the cursor one character in the left (or right) direction. However, if the cursor is in the beginning (or end) of the text, then pressing the arrow key will move the cursor to the previous (or next) cell.
  o *Up or down arrow keys* If the cursor is inside a cell and the text is highlighted (that is, selected) then the up (or down) arrow key moves the cursor to the beginning (or end) of the text.

3.18.5. Insert a multiline text in a cell
The row height of the cell increases to accommodate the number of lines of the text. If the length of the single line text is longer than the width of a cell, then the text will wrap automatically to the next line. If the user presses the *Enter* key on the keyboard, the cursor will move to the next cell, Figure 3-76.

This is a sample text. Its length is longer than the cell width. Therefore, the text is wrapped automatically to multiple lines. Press the *Enter* key and the cursor will move to the next cell.	This is a sample text. To format the text, hold the Alt key on the keyboard and press the *Enter* key twice. The cursor is still in the same cell.

Figure 3-76

If a user desired to create multiline line text object in a cell then hold the *Alt* key and press the *Enter* key to move to the cursor to the next line. To format the text as shown in the right column of the table in Figure 3-76 the *Alt- Enter* keys are used twice to create a blank line between the two paragraphs.

3.18.6. The data type

The data in a table cell can be a text, a block, or a field. Select three cells of a column in the table and press the right button of the mouse, an options list will appear on the screen, Figure 3-77a. Click on the *Data Format*, and the *Table Cell Format* dialog box will appear on the screen, Figure 3-77b. In the current example, for the angle *Data type*, thr Surveyor's units are used. The content of the *Preview* panel represent the selection of the *Data type*.

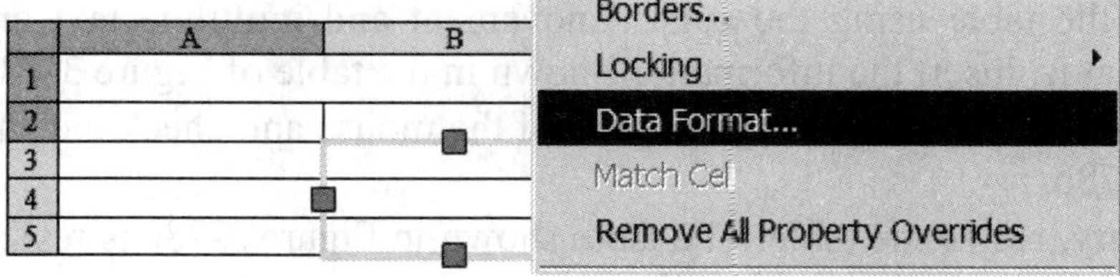

Figure 3-77a

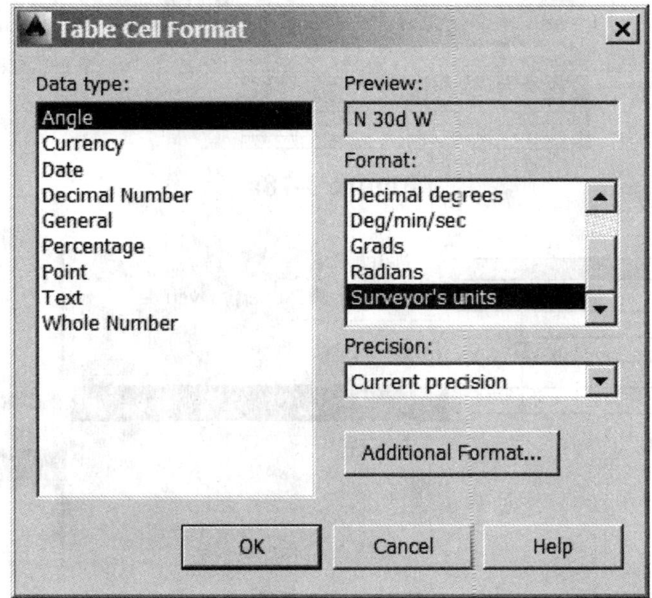

Figure 3-77b

The Figure 3-77c shows the entries in the table. The left column data is in the Surveyor's units; whereas, the right column represent the same angle in the decimal degree format. Remember that the angles are measured counterclockwise from the east. To enter the data (i) type the data as decimal number; (ii) press the *Enter* key from the keyboard; and the data will appear selected data format (the Surveyor's units).

	N 51d0' E	39.0	
	N 85d0' W	175.0	
	S 34d6' W	239.5	

Figure 3-77c

3.18.7. Populate the table

When a new table is inserted, then its first cell is highlighted, cursor is in the first cell, and the *Text Editor* tab becomes the current tab, Figure 3-78a. The table is ready to be populated (that is, to insert data).

- If necessary, set the data type for the cell.
- Populate the table using the cursor movement and multiline text entry discussed earlier, that is, insert the information shown in the table of Figure 3-78c.
- If necessary, click with the right button of the mouse and check the various options, Figure 3-78b.
- If necessary, resize the table. The table shown in Figure 3-78c is resized using table resizing techniques discussed earlier.

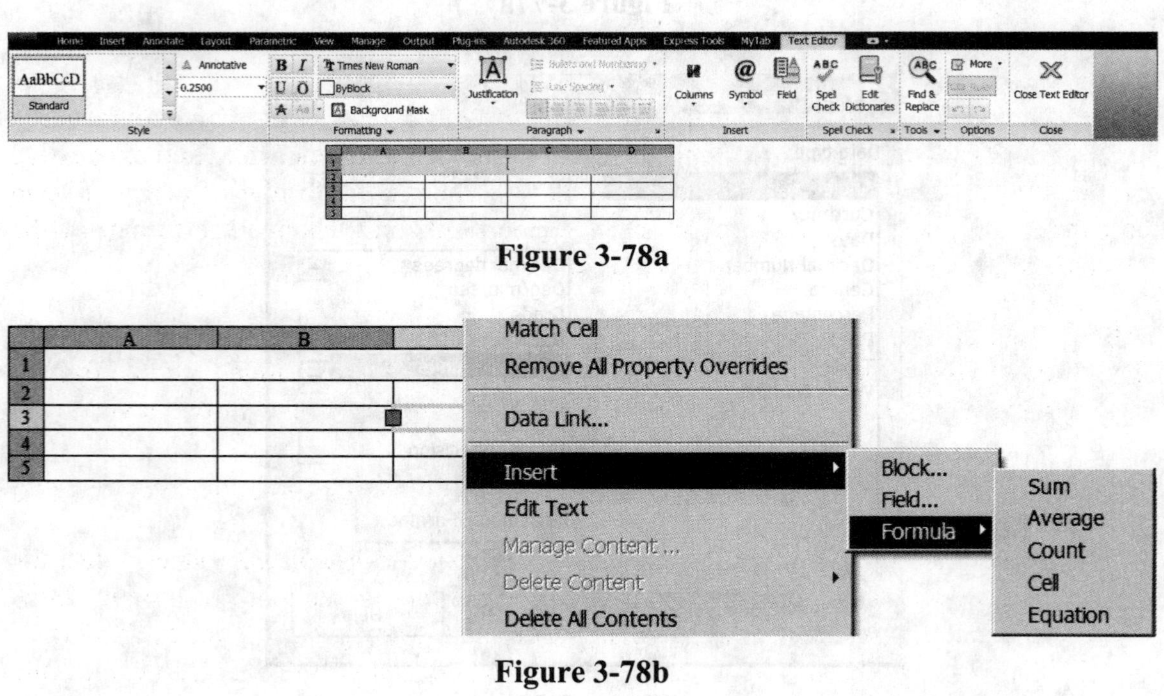

Figure 3-78a

Figure 3-78b

DIMENSION			
NAME	X-COORD	Y-COORD	Ø
A1	2.3400	45.0000	13
B1	-1.8000	23.4500	11.5000
C1	4.9800	35.1200	9

Figure 3-78c

3.18.8. Modify the contents of a table

Suppose a user has created the table shown in Figure 3-78c and wants to modify to the format shown in Figure 3-79.

The *Title* cell is shaded blue, the *Header* cells are shaded pink, and the *Data* cells are shaded yellow. The *Title* cell is shaded blue, the *Header* cells are shaded pink, and the *Data* cells are shaded yellow. The line weight of the border is set to 0.3. The content of the table are aligned in the middle center. The font is set to Times New Roman. The text height is 0.25 for the *Title* cell and 0.18 for the *Header* and the *Data* cells. The contents of the *Title* and the *Header* cells are set to *Bold* style whereas the contents of the *Data* cells are kept plain.

DIMENSION			
NAME	X-COORD	Y-COORD	Ø
A1	2.34	45.00	13.00
B1	-1.80	23.45	11.50
C1	4.98	35.12	9.00

Figure 3-79

There are multiple techniques to change the table format: (i) Use of the *Table Style* dialog box, (ii) use of the property sheet, and (iii) update one cell at a time (long and exhaustive approach). The *Table Style* dialog box method will change the format of every table in the current drawing; and the property sheet method will only change the format of the selected table. This section will discuss only the first two techniques.

3.18.8.1. Table Style dialog box

This section will use the *Table Style* dialog box, Figure 3-79b, to change the table format. However, every table in the current drawing will be reformatted to the current style.

- Open the *Table Style* dialog box, Figure 3-79b, using one of the following procedures.
  1. Panel method: (i) From the *Home* tab and expanded *Annotation* panel, select the *Table Style* tool, Figure 3-79a. (ii) From the *Annotate* tab and *Table* panel, click the dialog box launcher (a small arrow on the lower right corner of the panel).
  2. Dialog box method: (i) From the *Home* tab and *Annotation* panel, and select the *Table* tool. (ii) In the *Insert Table* dialog box Figure 3-73c, from the *Table style* panel click on the button to open the *Table Style* dialog box.
  3. Command line method: Type "tablestyle", "Tablestyle", or "TABLESTYLE" in the command line and press the *Enter* key.

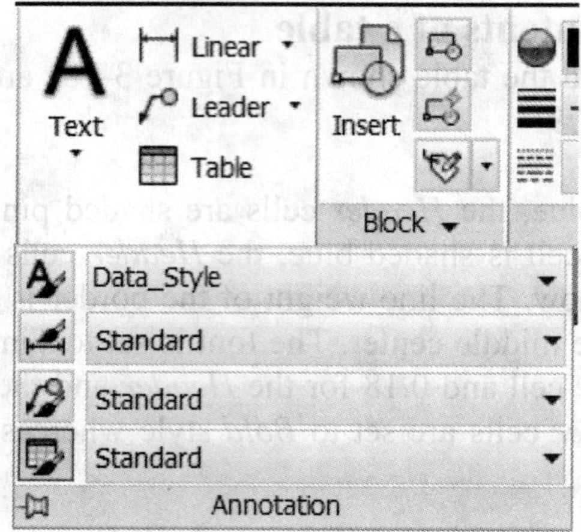

Figure 3-79a

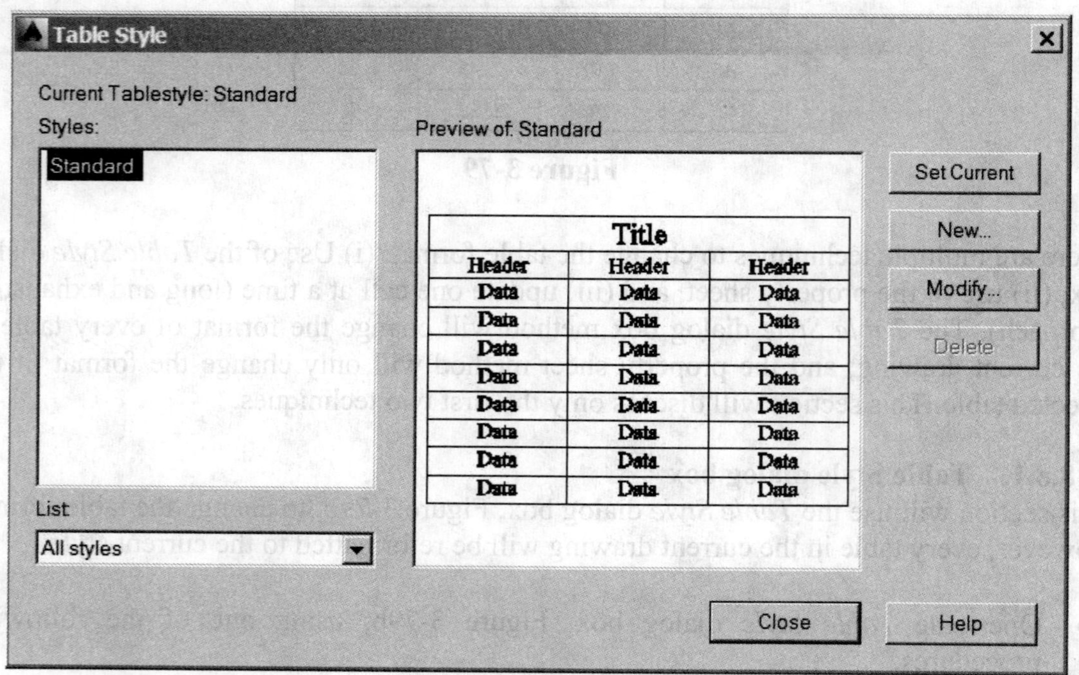

Figure 3-79b

- Click on the *Modify* button of the *Table Style* dialog box to open the *Modify Table Style: Standard* dialog box, Figure 3-79c.

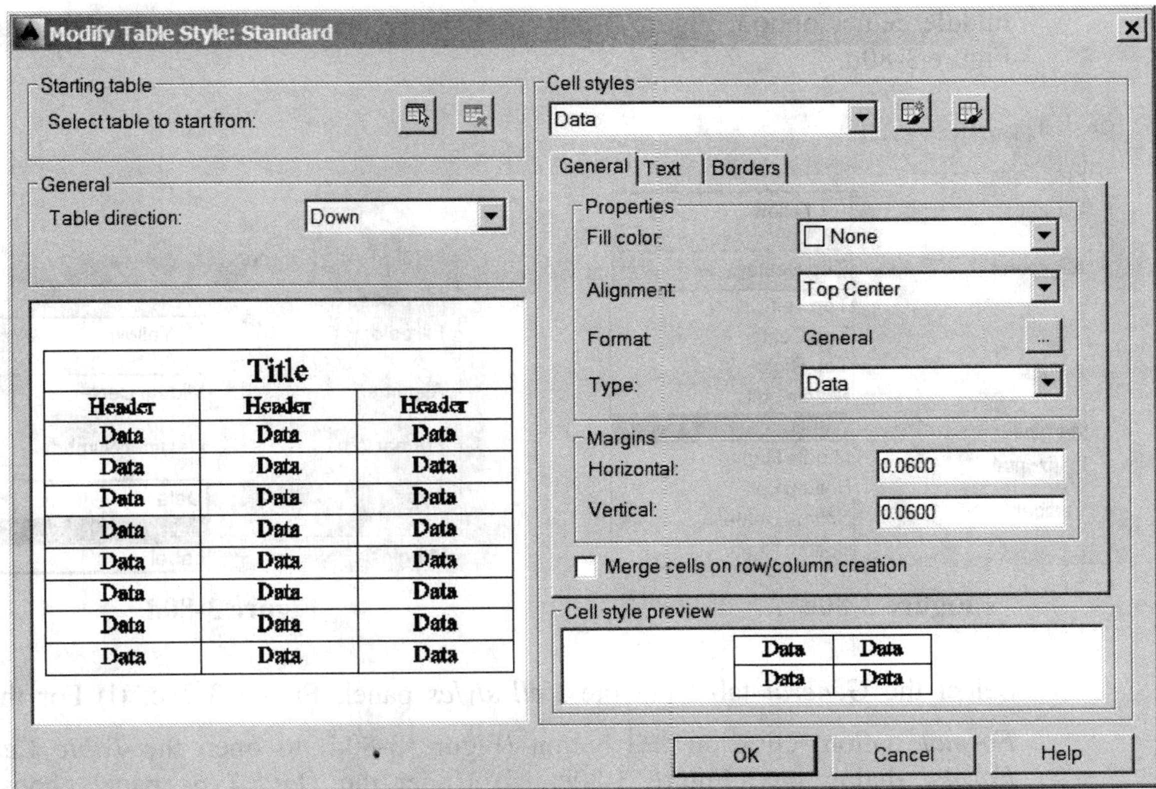

Figure 3-79c

- On the *Modify Table Style: Standard* dialog box, perform the following actions.

   1. From the *Cell styles* panel select the *Data*, Figure 3-79c and Figure 3-80a.

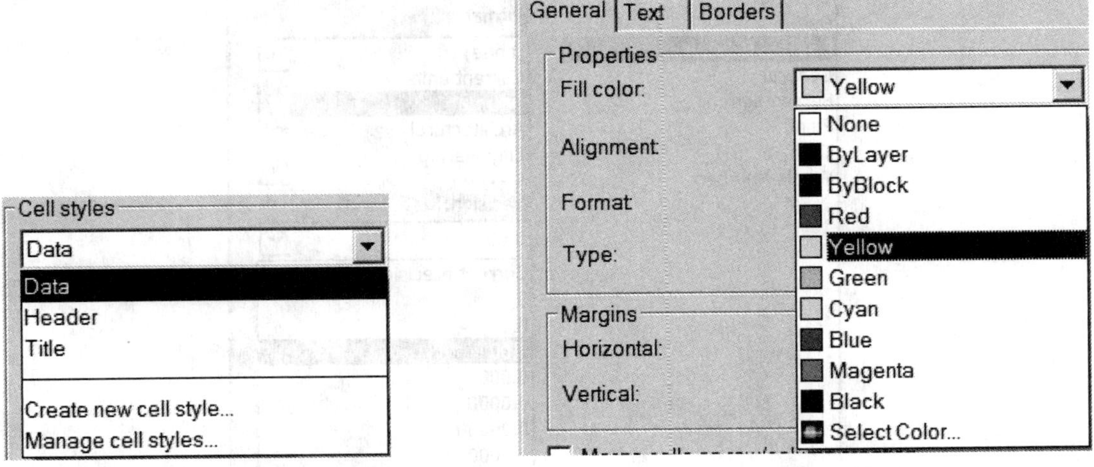

Figure 3-80a   **Figure 3-80b**

   2. Select the *General* tab from the *Cell styles* panel, Figure 3-79c. (i) Under the *Fill color* option, choose the desired color, Figure 3-80b. In the current example, the yellow color is chosen. (ii) Under the *Alignment* option, choose

middle center option, Figure 3-80c. (iii) Under the *Type* option, choose data, Figure 3-80d.

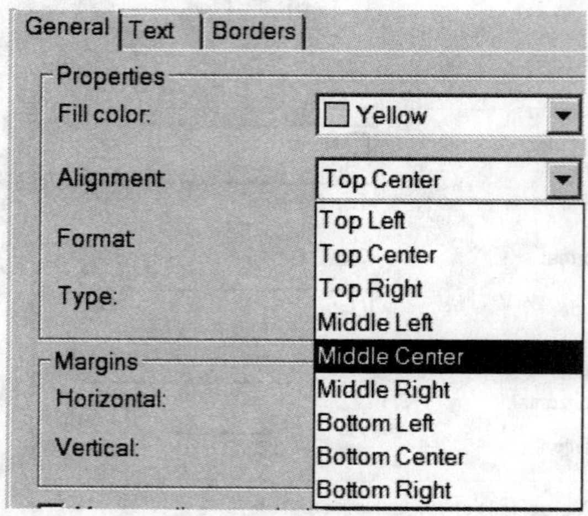

Figure 3-80c

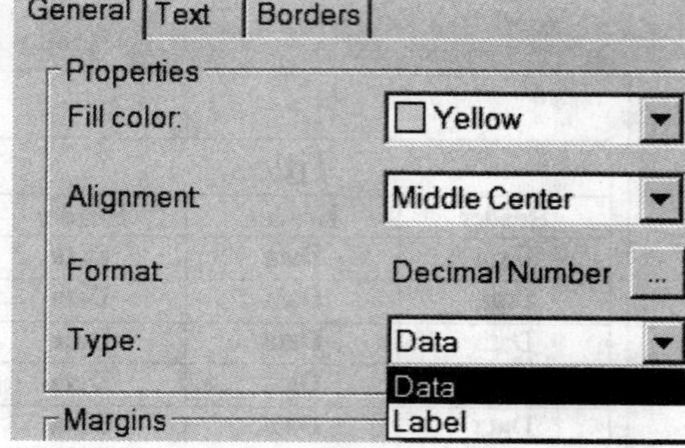

Figure 3-80d

1. Select the *General* tab from the *Cell styles* panel, Figure 3-79c. (i) For the *Format* option, click on ⬛ button (Figure 3-80d) to open the *Table Cell Format* dialog box, Figure 3-80e. (ii) Under the *Data Type* panel choose *Decimal Number*. (iii) Under the *Format* panel choose *Decimal*. (iv) Under the *Precision* panel choose two decimal places. (v) Press *OK* button to close this dialog box.

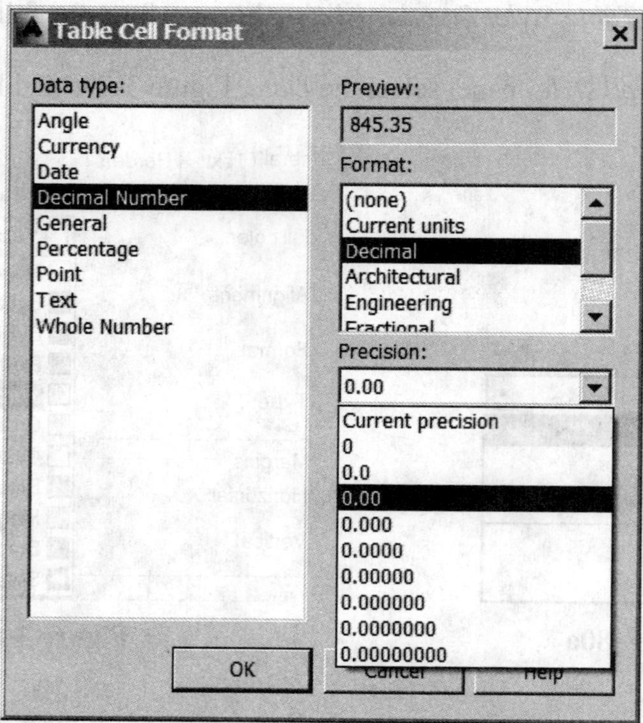

Figure 3-80e

2. Select the *Text* tab from the *Cell styles* panel, Figure 3-79c and Figure 3-81a. Choose the options shown in Figure 3-81a. To set the font information, in Figure 3-80a, click on the [...] button to open the *Text Style* dialog box, Figure 3-81b.

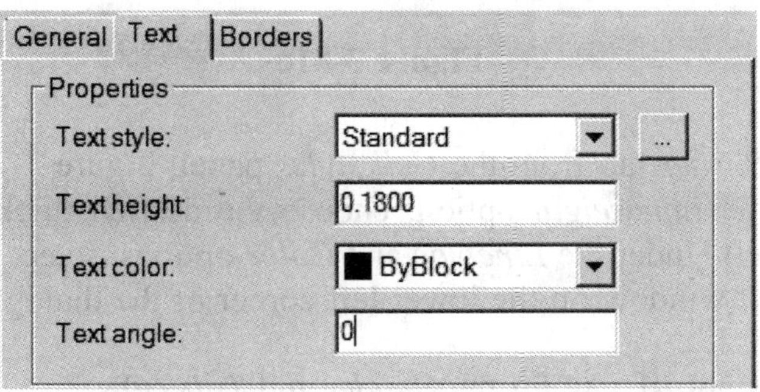

Figure 3-81a

The software does not allow to display the multiple options simultaneously, although, the dialog box shows multiple selection, Figure 3-81b. (i) In the dialog box, choose the *Times New Roman* font under the *Font Name*. (ii) To create a new style click on the *New* button and this will open the *New Text Style* box, Figure 3-81c. (iii) Name and save the style with an easily recognizable name (Data_Style) and press the *OK* button. (iv) This will close the *New Text Style* box and activate the *Apply* button on the *Text Style* dialog box and convert the *Cancel* button to the *Close* button. (v) Press the *Apply* button and then the *Close* button.

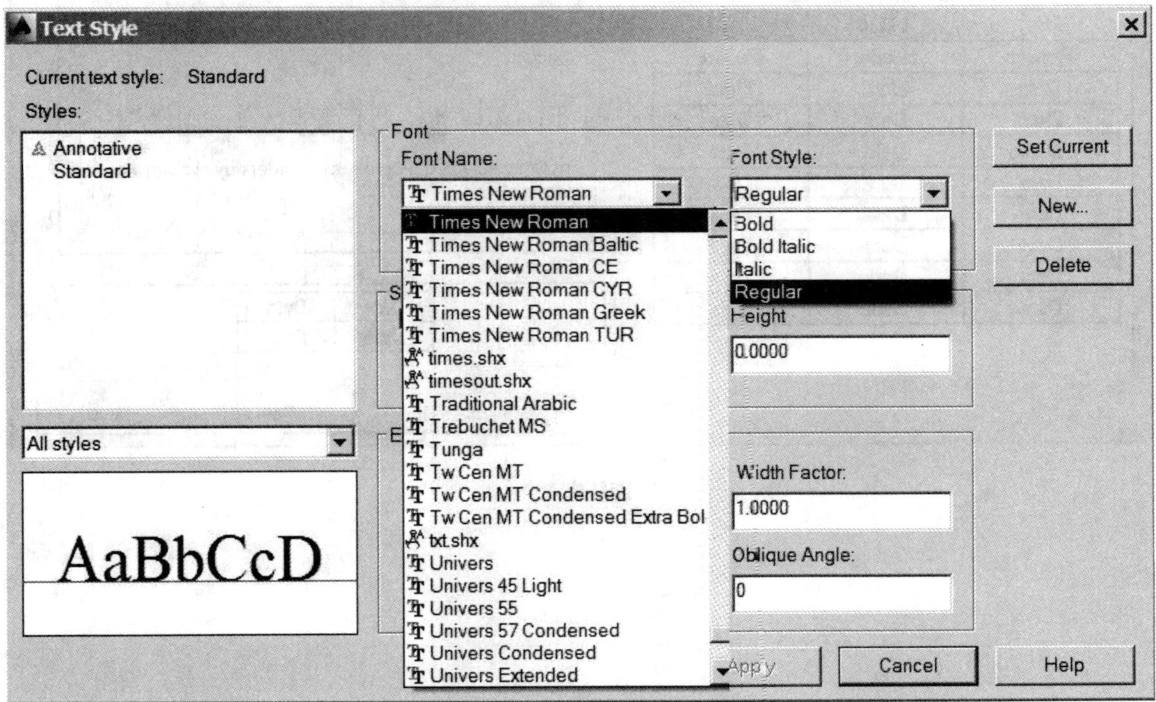

Figure 3-81b

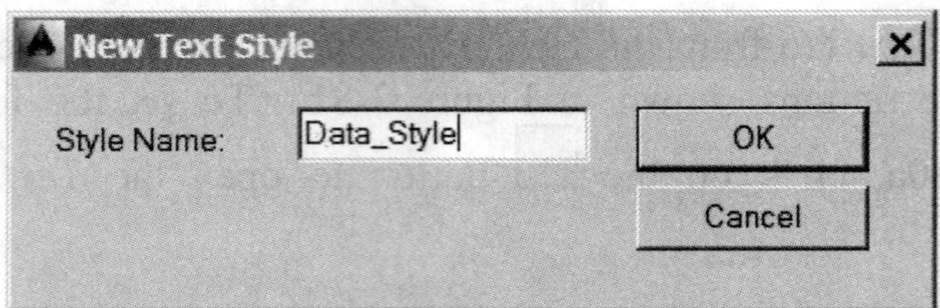

Figure 3-81c

3. Select the *Border* tab from the *Cell styles* panel, Figure 3-79c and Figure 3-82. (i) Under the *Lineweight* option, choose the desired thickness (0.3mm in the example). (ii) Under the *Linetype* and *Color* options, select the *By Layer* option. The preview window on the lower left corner of the dialog box will display the changes.
4. Repeat the steps #1 - #4 for the *Header* and *Title* cells.
5. The resultant table is shown in Figure 3-79. For the reader's convenience, the figure is shown on the next page, too.

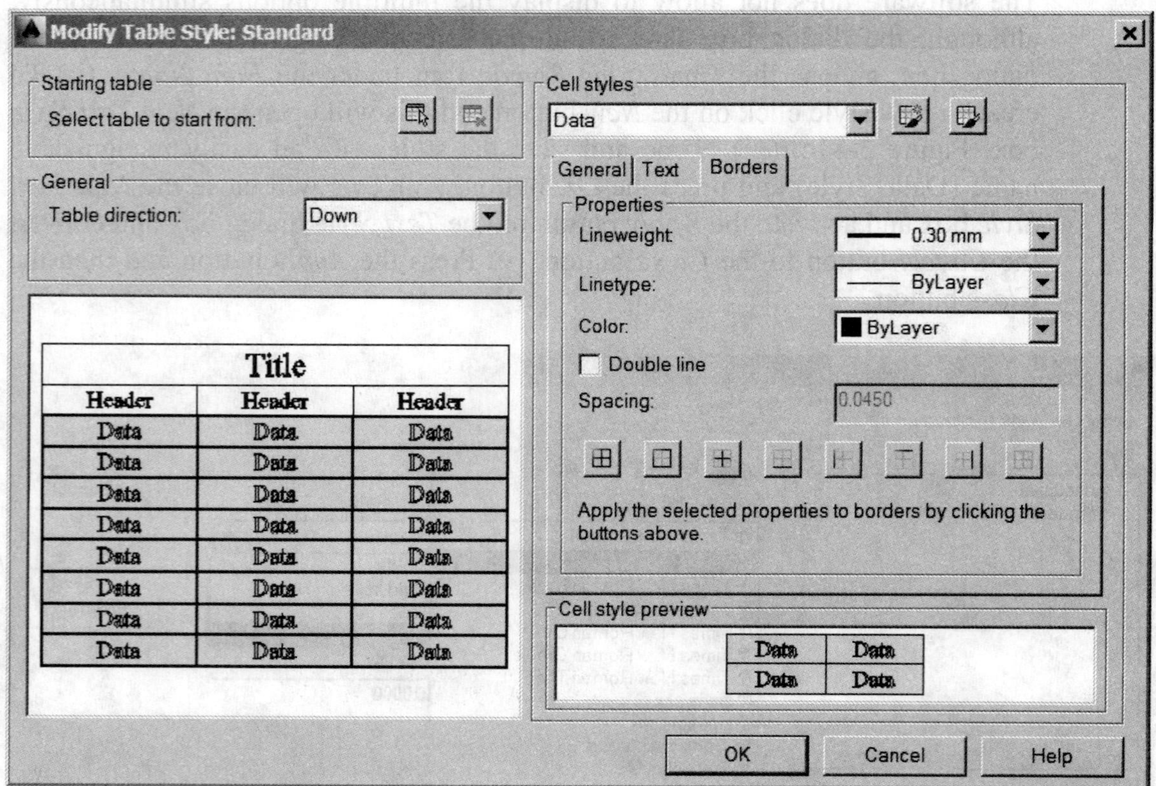

Figure 3-82

DIMENSION			
NAME	**X-COORD**	**Y-COORD**	**Ø**
A1	2.34	45.00	13.00
B1	-1.80	23.45	11.50
C1	4.98	35.12	9.00

Figure 3-79

3.18.8.2. Table update using the property sheet

A table can also be updated using the *Properties* sheet. The advantage of this technique is that only the selected table's format will change. This section will show the process to modify the contents of the *Data cells*. The user can use the same process to modify the contents of the *Title cell* and the *Header cells*.

- To open the *Properties* sheet use one of the following methods.
    1. Select all of the data cells, Figure 3-83a, press the right button of the mouse, and select the *Properties* option from the list of options.
    2. From the View tab and Palettes pane, select the *Properties* tool (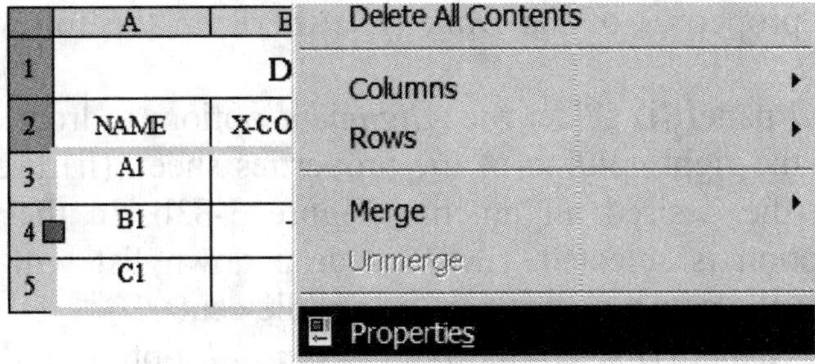). The *Properties* sheet is shown in Figure 3-83b.
- The upper left corner of the *Properties* sheet displays the name of the selected object.
- To expand the *General* panel (or contract the *Cell* panel) in Figure 3-83b, click the down or up arrow in front of the panel name.
- A user cannot change the grayed option in the *Properties* sheet. For example, the user cannot change the *Cell type* under the *Content* panel.

Figure 3-83a

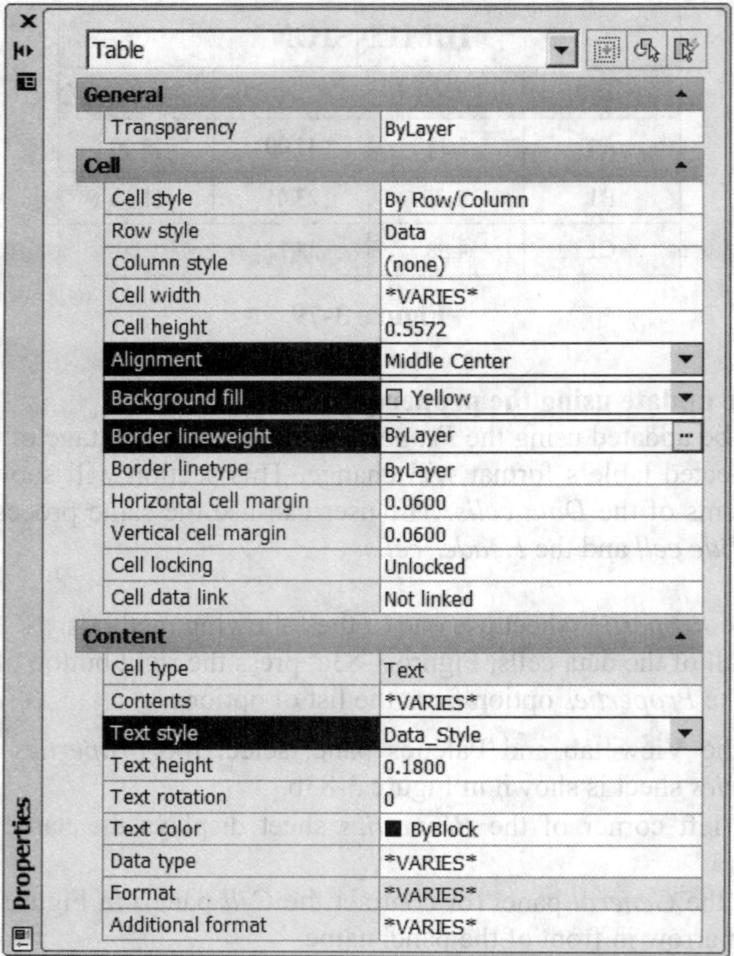

Figure 3-83b

- To change the properties of the *Data cells*, perform the following actions in the *Properties* sheet.
  1. In the *Cell* panel (i) select the *Alignment* option; a dropdown list arrow will appear in the right column of the properties sheet. (ii) Press the down arrow and click the desired alignments, Figure 3-83b. In the figure, the *Middle Center* option is selected. (iii) The drop down list will be closed and the contents of the data cell move in the middle center.
  2. In the *Cell* panel (i) select the *Background fill* option; a dropdown list arrow will appear in the right column of the properties sheet. (ii) Press the down arrow and click the desired color, Figure 3-83b. In the figure, the *Yellow* is selected. (iii) The drop down list will be closed and the background color of the data cell will change to the selected color.
  3. In the *Cell* panel (i) select the *Border Lineweight* option; the *Choose* button ( ) will appear in the right column of the properties sheet. (ii) Click the button and the *Cell Border Properties* dialog box will appear, Figure 3-83c. (iii) For the border, select *All Border* option. (iv) Under the *Lineweight* option, choose the desired thickness (0.3mm in the example). (v) Under the *Linetype*

and *Color* options, select the *By Layer* option. (vi) Click the OK button of the dialog box. This will close the dialog box; the *Choose* button will disappear from the *Properties sheet* and the border of the *Data cell* will change to the selected options.

4. In the *Content* panel (i) select the *Text style* option; a dropdown list arrow will appear in the right column of the properties sheet. (ii) Press the down arrow and select the desired style. The *Data_Style* is a user defined style and the previous section describes the creation process. In this example, the *Data_Style* is selected. (iii) The drop down list will be closed and the background color of the data cell will change to the selected style.

5. In the *Content* panel (i) select the *Text height* option, Figure 3-67b. (ii) Type the desired height in the right column. (iii) Press the *Enter* key on the keyboard. (iv) The selection will be cleared and size of the content of the data cell will change to the selected height.

6. Repeat the steps #1 - #5 for the *Header* and *Title* cells.

7. The resultant table is shown in Figure 3-84. For the reader's convenience, the figure is shown on the next page.

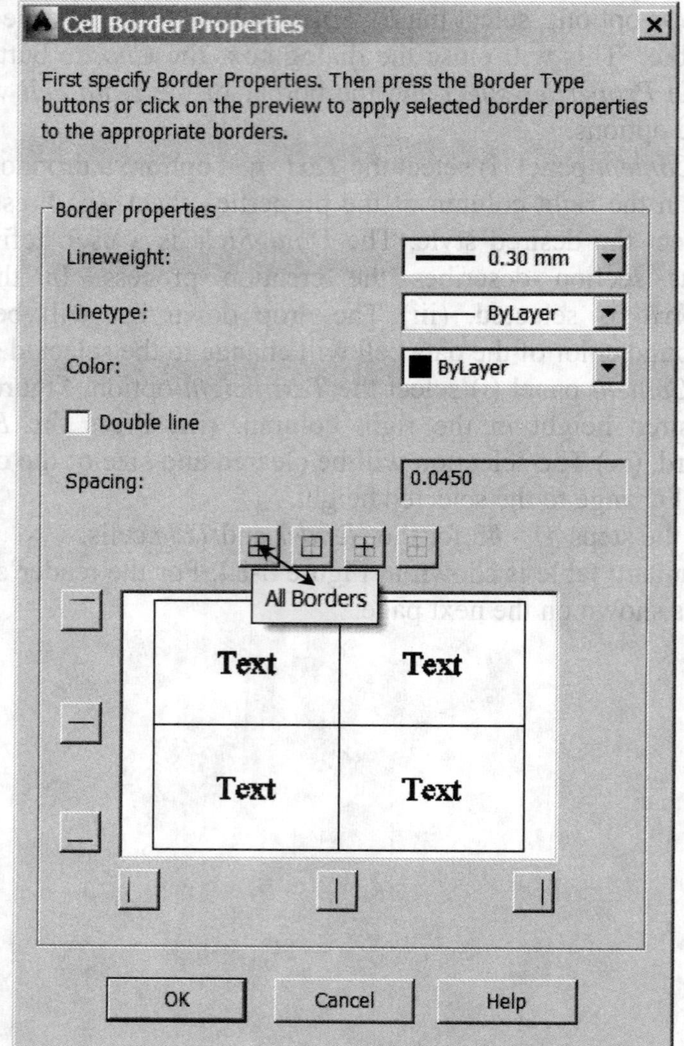

Figure 3-83c

DIMENSION			
NAME	**X-COORD**	**Y-COORD**	**Ø**
A1	2.34	45.00	13.00
B1	-1.80	23.45	11.50
C1	4.98	35.12	9.00

Figure 3-84

4.   Basics of 2-Dimensional Editing

4.1.   Objectives

- Learn to use grips points to modify objects
- Learn to use one or more object selection methods
- Learn to use zoom capabilities
- Learn to use draw order to move object in front or behind other objects
- Learn to use the object snap facility to locate strategic points on a 2D objects
- Learn to use *Erase, Undo, Redo, Oops, Copy, Array, Mirror, Offset, Move, Rotate, Scale, Stretch, Break, Explode, Join, Fillet, Chamfer, Trim, Extend, Cancel*, and *Polyline Edit* commands use to modify 2D objects

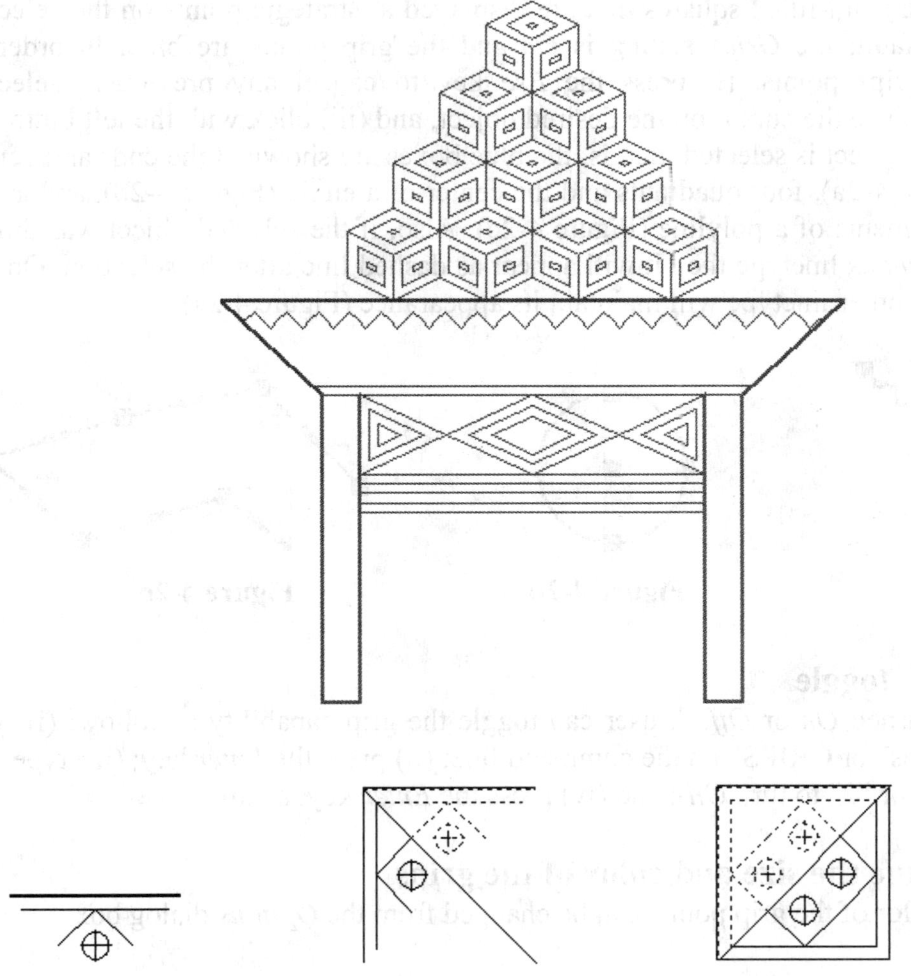

4.2.   Introduction

A drafter can create unlimited design by creating new drawings and editing previously drawn drawings. The focus of this chapter is the AutoCAD capabilities to edit basic 2D objects. To achieve these capabilities, AutoCAD uses the *Modify* panel from the *Home* tab, Figure 4-1a. The figure shows the expanded panel.

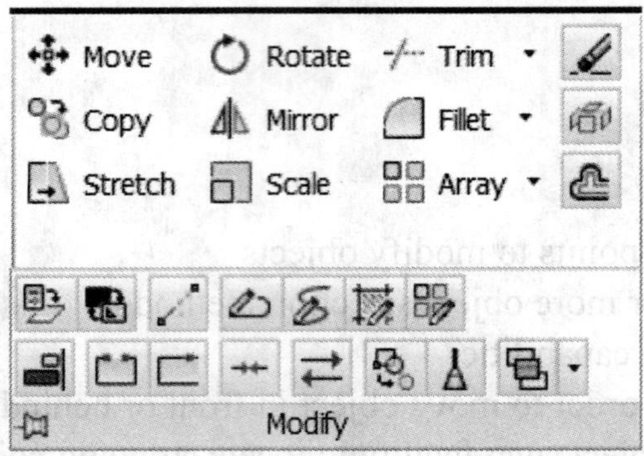

Figure 4-1a

4.3.   Grips

Grips are small, solid-filled squares that are displayed at strategic points on the selected objects. By default, the *Grips* setting is *On* and the grip points are blue. In order to visualize the grips points, (i) press the *Esc* key to cancel any previously selected command, (ii) place the cursor on the desired object, and (iii) click with the left button of the mouse. The object is selected, that is, the blue boxes are shown at the ends and center of a line (Figure 4-2a), four quadrants and the center of a circle (Figure 4-2b), and at the ends of the segments of a polyline (Figure 4-2c). Also, if the selected object was drawn with the *Continuous* linetype then it will appear as dashed line after the selection. On the other hand, any other linetype will maintain its appearance (Figure 4-2a).

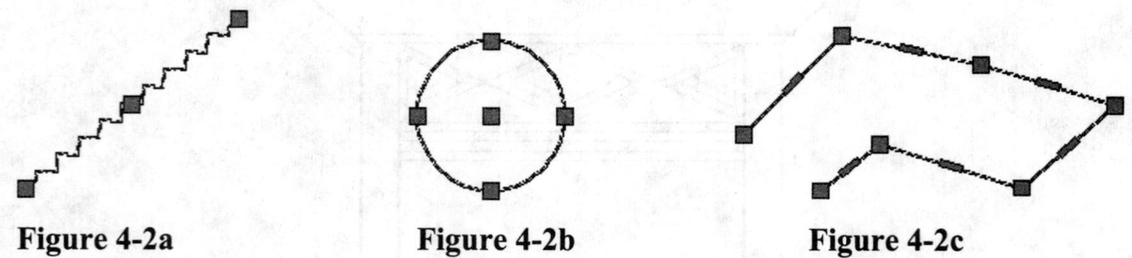

Figure 4-2a   **Figure 4-2b**   **Figure 4-2c**

4.3.1.   Grips toggle

Grips can be turned *On* or *Off*. A user can toggle the grip capability as follow: (i) type "Grips" or "grips" or GRIPS" on the command line; (ii) press the *Enter* key; (iii) type "0" to turn *Off* ("1" or "2" to turn *On*); and (iv) press the *Enter* key, again.

4.3.2.   Change the size and color of the grips

The size and color of the grip points can be changed from the *Options* dialog box.

- Open the *Options* dialog box using one of the two methods
  1. Click with the right button in the *Drawing area* and select the *Options* option. The *Options* dialog box (Figure 4-3a) will appear on the screen.
  2. Command line method: Type "options", "Options", or "OPTIONS" in the command line and press the *Enter* key.
- Select the *Selection* tab of the *Options* dialog box by clicking on it.
- The slider in the *Grip size* panel, Figure 4-3a, is used to change the size of the grip points. Move the slider to the right to increase the size and to the left to reduce the size.
- Click on the *Grip Colors*, Figure 4-3a button in the *Grip* panel to open *Grip Colors* dialog box, Figure 4-3b. Make the desired changes and click *OK* button on both dialog boxes.

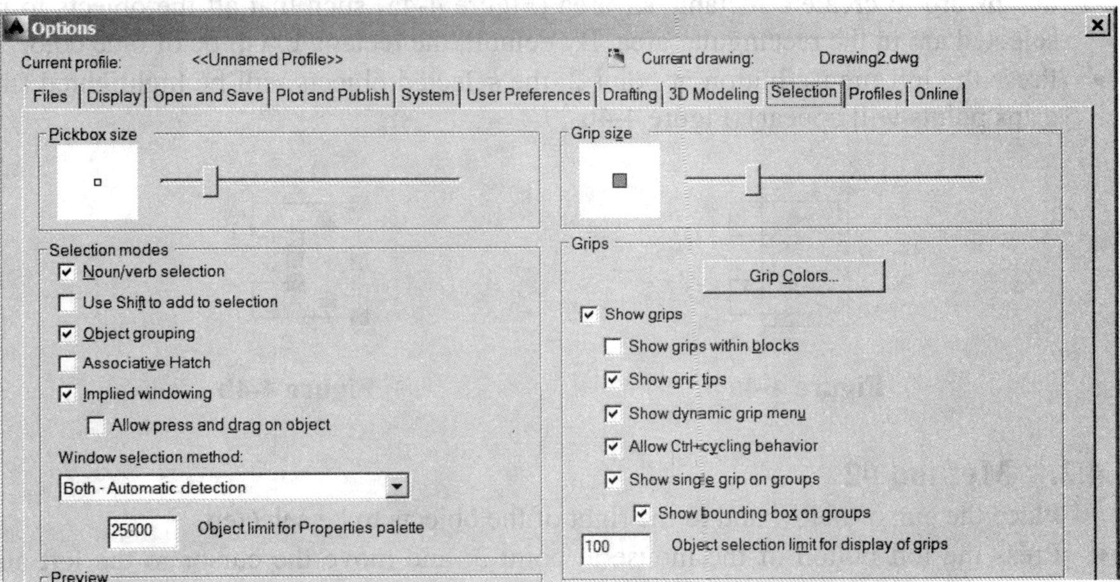

Figure 4-3a

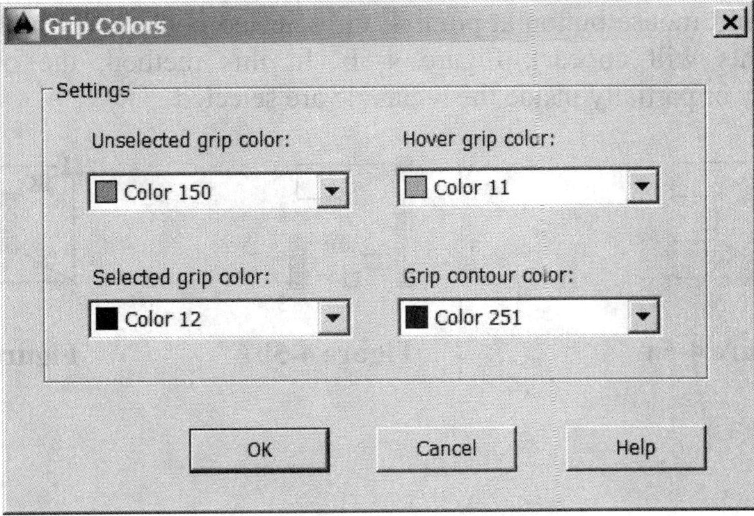

Figure 4-3b

4.4.   Object selection

Object selection is the prerequisite for the functionality of the editing commands is the focus of this chapter. One or more graphical elements such as text, dimension, line, circle, polyline, are treated as a single element for creation, manipulation, and modification is called an object or entity. If one object needs to be modified then object selection process is very simple. Just click on the object and it will be highlighted (the grips points appear and will be discussed in details in section 4.6). However, if a user need to select more than one object, then one of the following methods must be used.

4.4.1.   Method #1
- Place the cursor above and to the left of the objects to be selected.
- Press the left button of the mouse at point 1; and move the cursor to the right and downward to create a rectangular area (Figure 4-4a) such that all the objects to be selected are in the rectangular area. By default, the rectangle will be of blue color.
- Press the left mouse button at point 2, the selected objects will be highlighted (the grips points will appear), Figure 4-4b.

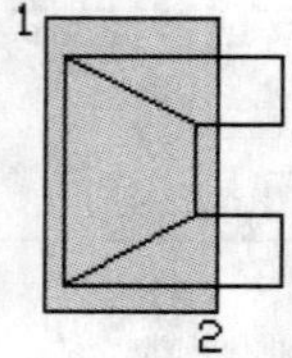   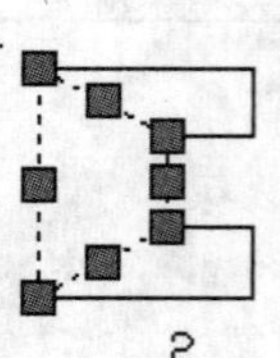

Figure 4-4a   **Figure 4-4b**

4.4.2.   Method #2
- Place the cursor below and to the right of the objects to be selected.
- Press the left button of the mouse at point 3; and move the cursor to the left and upward to create a rectangular area (Figure 4-5a) such that all the objects to be selected are completely or partially in the rectangular area. By default, the rectangle will be of green color.
- Press the left mouse button at point 4, the selected objects will be highlighted (the grips points will appear), Figure 4-5b. In this method, the objects that are completely or partially inside the rectangle are selected.

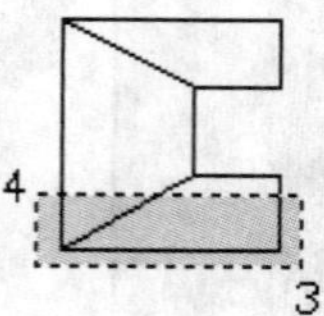   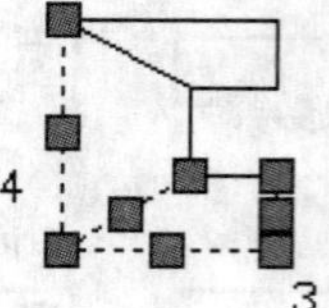   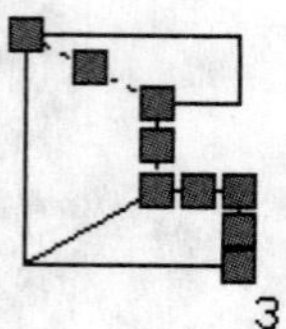

Figure 4-5a   **Figure 4-5b**   **Figure 4-5c**

4.4.3.   Method #3

- If the objects to be selected cannot be enclosed in a rectangle because other objects will be part of the rectangle then select the objects individually by clicking it, Figure 4-5c.

4.5.   Object de-selection

Object selection is the prerequisite for the functionality of the editing commands. However, object de-selection is equally important, too. Figure 4-6a shows the selection of four objects. The user can de-select the entire selection by just pressing the *Esc* key on the keyboard. Figure 4-6b shows the effect of pressing the *Esc* key. However, if the user wants to de-select few objects from the set (for example wants to deselect the square), then hold the Shift key and click with the left button of the mouse on the desired object (the square in the example). The result is shown in Figure 4-4c.

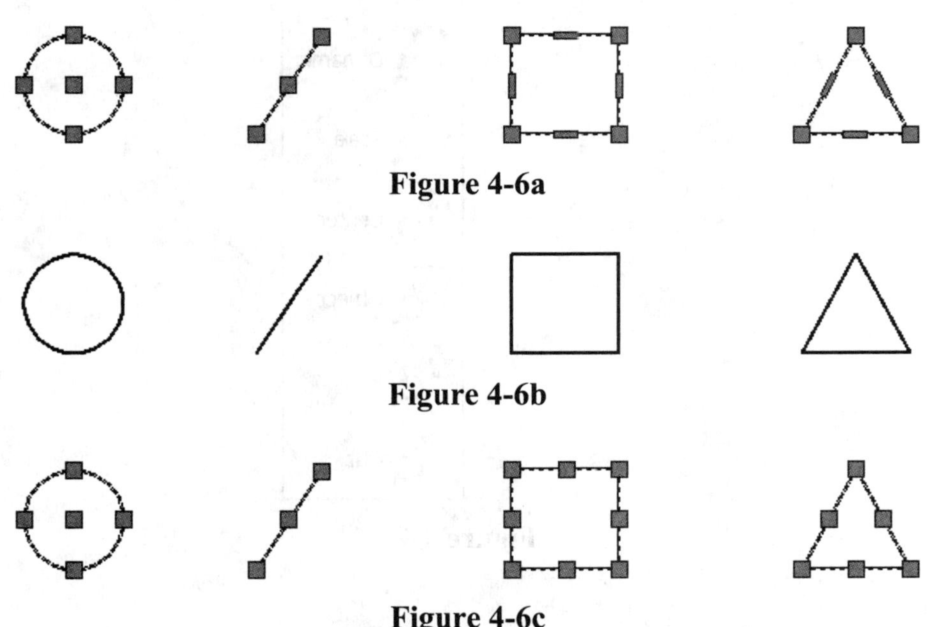

Figure 4-6a

Figure 4-6b

Figure 4-6c

4.6.   Zoom capabilities

The zoom capabilities are used to change the magnification of the objects in the drawing. The user access the zoom commands from the *View* tab and *Navigate 2D* panel and clicking on the desired tool, Figure 4-7. In the figure, the down arrow key is pressed to display the various options. The details of the zoom capabilities are discussed in the remaining of this section.

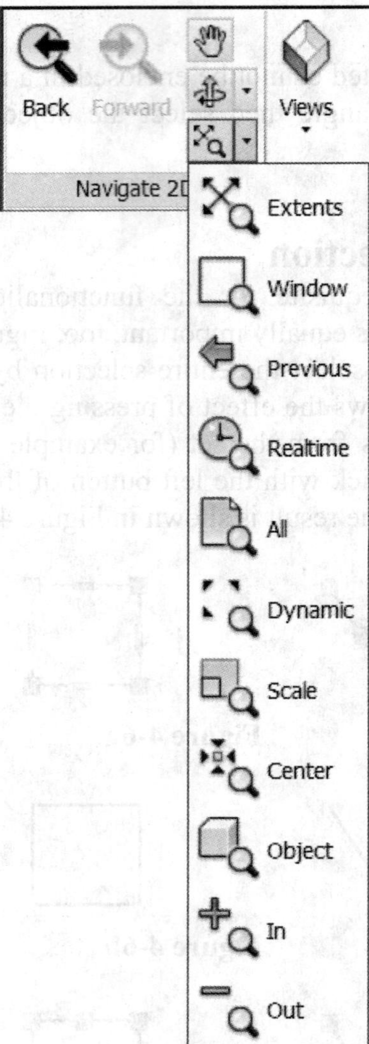

Figure 4-7

4.6.1. Zoom window

The *Zoom window* command is used to display the part of the drawing enclosed in a rectangular window. (i) Activate the *Zoom window* command by clicking the button. The prompt shown in Figure 4-8a will appear. (ii) Click above and to the left of the drawing as shown in Figure 4-8a. The prompt shown in Figure 4-8b will appear. (iii) Click below and to the right of the drawing. This will exit the command and the object will be zoomed in. The first point can be any of the four corners of the rectangular window; however, the second point must be the diagonally opposite corner. The zoomed object is shown in Figure 4-8c.

Figure 4-8a

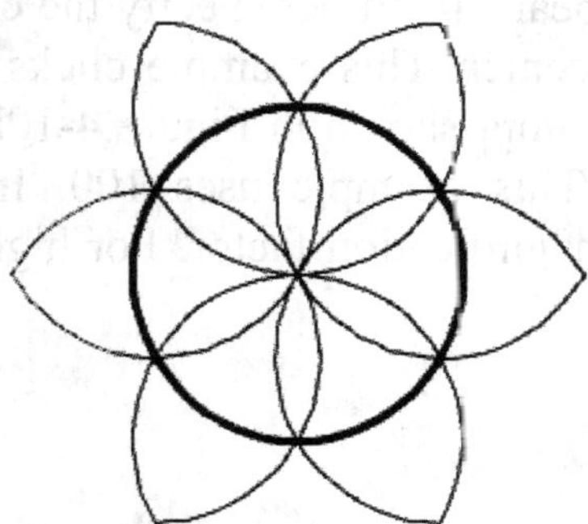

Figure 4-8b

Figure 4-8c

4.6.2. Zoom scale

The *Zoom scale* command is used to zoom (in or out) using the scale factor. (i) Activate the *Zoom scale* command by clicking the button. The prompt shown in Figure 4-9a will appear. (ii) Specify the desired value. The value in Figure 4-9b make every object in the drawing to appear one and half time as big as the original size. In Figure 4-9b the 'X' implies that the scaling will be relative to the current view. (iii) The Figure 4-9c shows the original object whereas Figure 4-9d shows the scaled object.

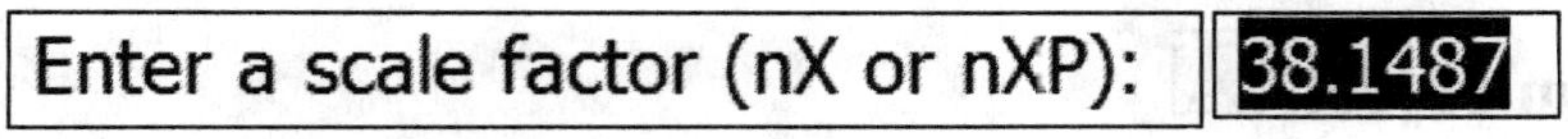

Figure 4-9a

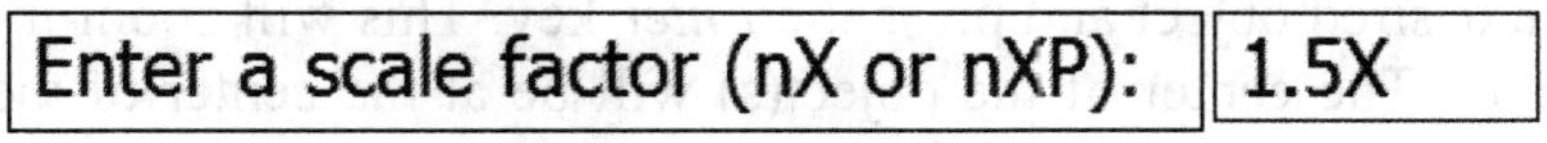

Figure 4-9b

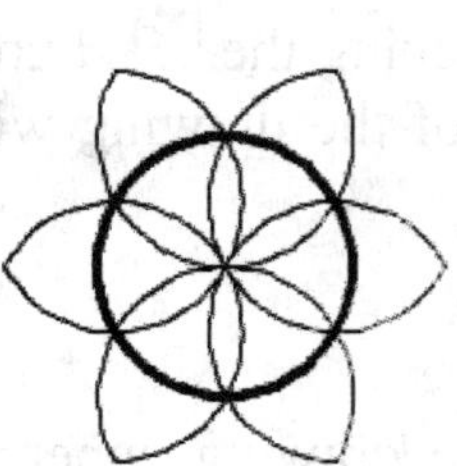

Figure 4-9c

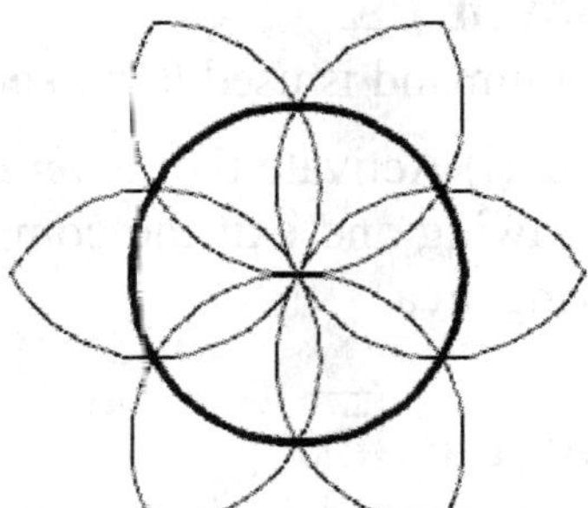

Figure 4-9d

4.6.3. Zoom center

The *Zoom center* command is used to zoom the center of the drawing using the scale factor. (i) Activate the *Zoom center* command by clicking the button. The prompt shown in Figure 4-10a will appear. (ii) Either specify the coordinated of the center of the desired object or click in the center. This example clicks at the center of the rectangle shown in Figure 4-10a. The prompt shown in Figure 4-10b will appear. (iii) Specify the desired magnification value. This example uses 100. In this command, zooming is inversely proportional to the magnification factor. For higher magnification number, the zooming will be smaller.

Figure 4-10a

Enter magnification or height <83.2100>:   100

Figure 4-10b

4.6.4. Zoom object

The *Zoom object* command is used to zoom the selected object(s). (i) Activate the *Zoom object* command by clicking the button. The prompt to select object will appear. (ii) Click on the desired object and press the *Enter* key. This will zoom-in the object and exit the command. The center of the object(s) will be at the center of the drawing area and object will appear as big as possible.

4.6.5. Zoom in

The *Zoom in* command is used to make the size of the drawing appears twice as big as of the current size. (i) Activate the *Zoom in* command by clicking the button. This will zoom-in the drawing and exit the command. The center of the drawing will stay in the center of drawing area.

4.6.6. Zoom out

The *Zoom out* command is used to make the size of the drawing appears half of the current size. (i) Activate the *Zoom out* command by clicking the button. This will zoom-out the drawing and exit the command. The center of the drawing will stay in the center of drawing area.

4.6.7.   Zoom all

The *Zoom all* command is used to make every object in the drawing to appear in the viewing area of the drawing. (i) Activate the *Zoom all* command by clicking the button. This will make every object in the drawing to appear in the viewing area of the drawing and exit the command. The center of the drawing will stay in the center of drawing area.

4.6.8.   Zoom-wheel

The *Zoom wheel* command is NOT available through the panel. This command is available through the command line ONLY. The command is used to relate the magnification with the wheel of the mouse. (i) Type *Zoomwheel* on the command line and press the *Enter* key.

> *0:* Move wheel forward for zoom-in and backward for zoom-out.
> *1:* Move wheel backward for zoom-in and forward for zoom-out

4.7.   Draw order

The draw order capabilities are used to change the relative positions of overlapping objects. The user can access the commands through the *Draw Order* drop down menu (Figure 4-11) or from a selection list as shown in, Figure 4-12.

To understand the associated command, draw two overlapping objects and change their color. This example uses green and red overlapping lines. The details of the draw-order capabilities are discussed in the remaining of this section.

4.7.1.   Bring to front

The *Bring to Front* command is used to bring the selected object in front of every other object. The command can be activated using one of the following methods.

- The *Bring to Front* command is executed using one of the following procedures.
    1. Panel method: (i) From the *Home* tab and *Modify* panel, expand the *Draw order* drop down menu, and select the *Bring to Front* tool. (ii) Click on the desired object. (iii) Press the *Enter* key.
    2. Selection list method: (i) Click on the desired object. (ii) Press the right button of the mouse. A selection list, Figure 4-12, will appear. (iii) Click on the desired option.

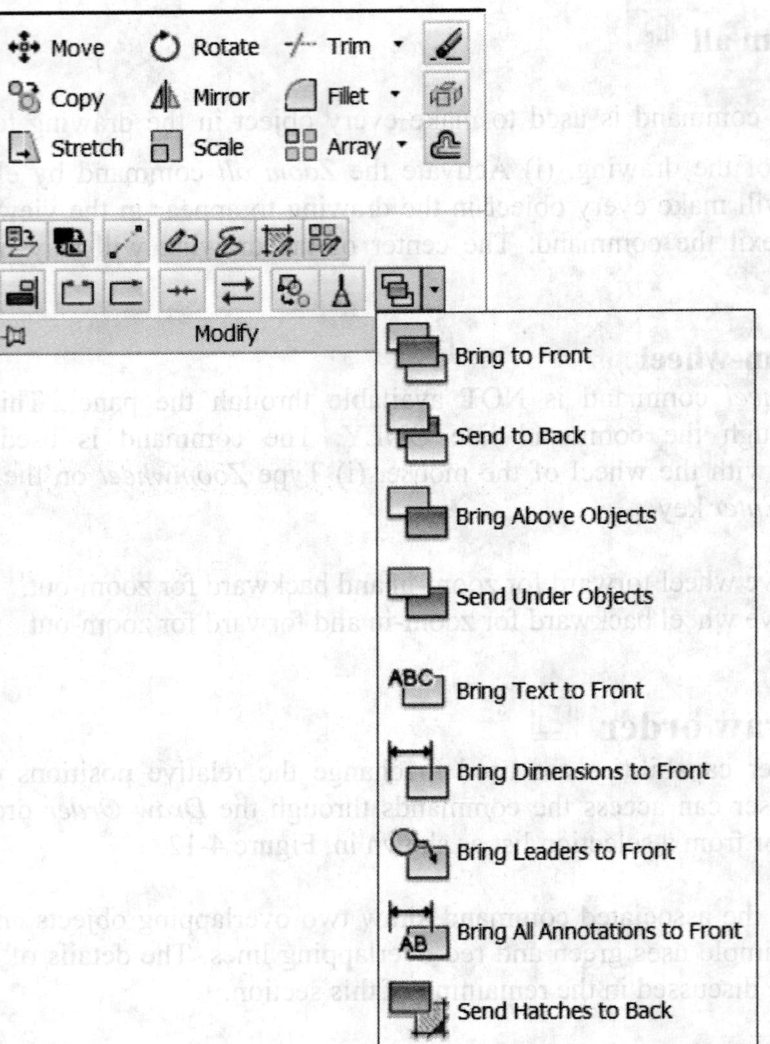

Figure 4-11

4.7.2. Send to back

The *Send to Back* command is used to send the selected object back of every other object.
The command can be activated using one of the following methods.

- The *Send to Back* command is executed using one of the following procedures.
  1. Panel method: (i) From the *Home* tab and *Modify* panel, expand the *Draw order* drop down menu, and select the *Send to Back* tool. (ii) Click on the desired object. (iii) Press the *Enter* key.
  2. Selection list method: (i) Click on the desired object. (ii) Press the right button of the mouse. A selection list, Figure 4-12, will appear. (iii) Click on the desired option.

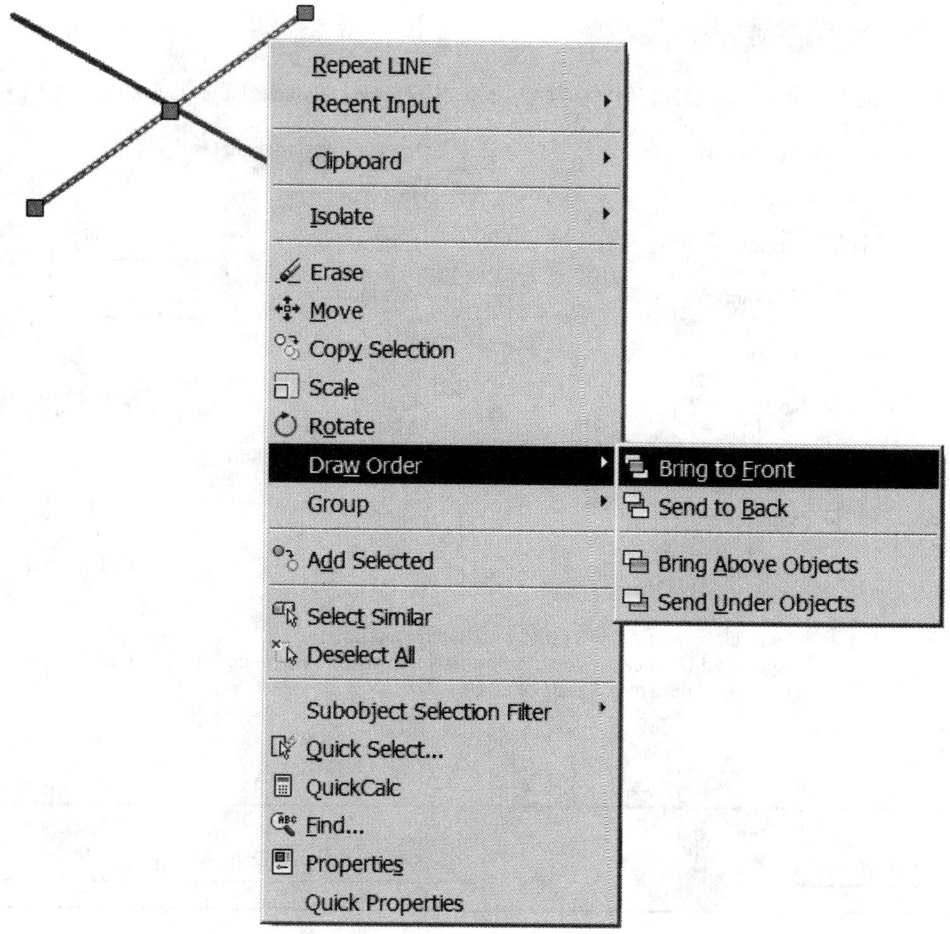

Figure 4-12

4.8.   Object Snap

The *Object Snap* command allows snapping at strategic points on the selected objects in the drawing area. Recall that the *Snap* option allows snapping to the snap points.

4.8.1. Toggle Object Snap

Toggle the *Object snap* option using one of the explained below.

- Click the *Object Snap* button ( ) on the status bar.
- Press the *F3* key on the keyboard.
- Bring the cursor on the *Object Snap* button of the status bar; click with the right button of the mouse and click on the *Setting* option. This will open the *Drafting Settings* dialog box with the *Object Snap* tab selected, Figure 4-13a. Finally, check the *Object Snap On* box on the dialog box.
- Type "dsettings" or "osnap" on the command line and press the *Enter* key. This will open the *Drafting Setting* dialog box with the *Object Snap* tab selected. Finally, check the *Object Snap On* box, Figure 4-13a.

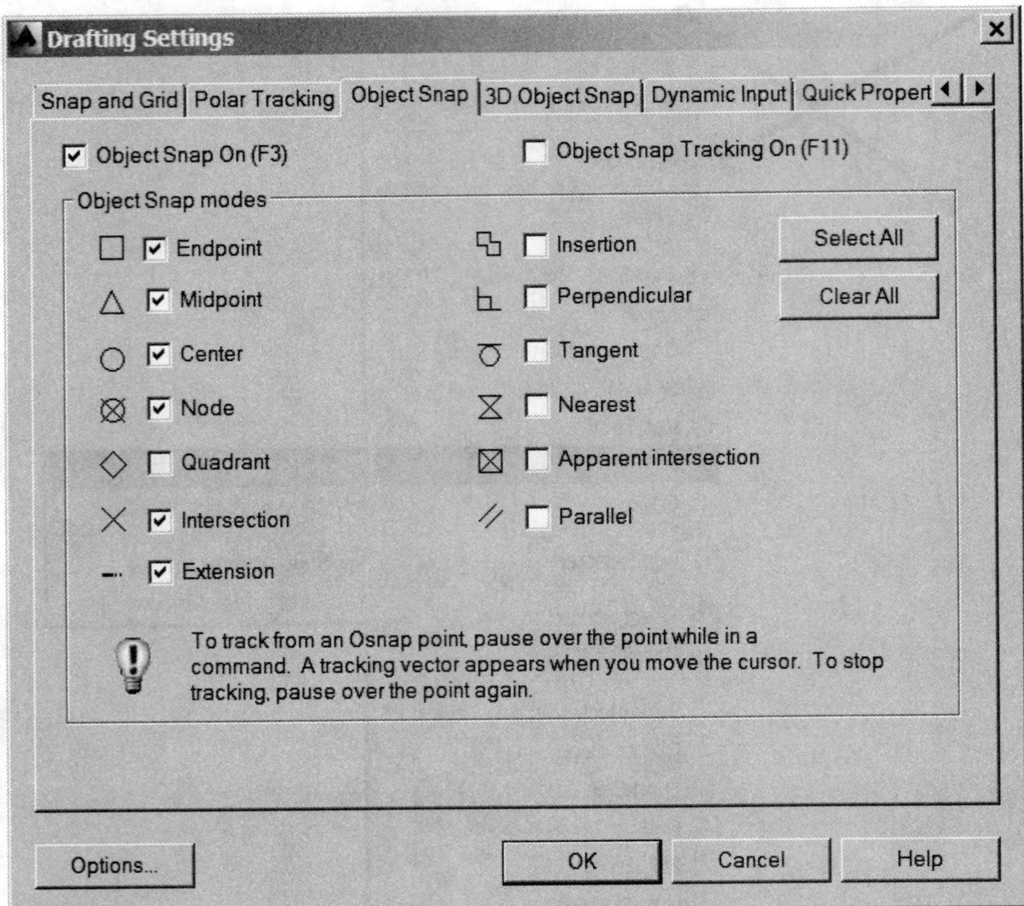

Figure 4-13a

The *Drafting Setting* dialog box (Figure 4-13a), provides several modes; however, normally only very few modes are selected at a time. This dialog box can be open during the execution of a command from the status bar, too; (bring the cursor on the *Object Snap* button on the status bar; click with the right button of the mouse; bring the cursor on the *Setting* option; press the left button of the mouse). In order to distinguish various object snap points, AutoCAD provides different pattern for each mode, Figure 4-13a.

4.8.2.   Change the size and color of the object snap cursor box

To change the size and color of the cursor box (for the object snap), click on the *Options* (lower left corner) button in the *Drafting Setting* dialog box (Figure 4-13b) and this will open the *Options* dialog box. In the *Options* dialog box, select the *Drafting* tab, Figure 4-13b, and make the desired changes.

4.8.3.   Object Snap commands

Most of the *Object Snap* commands do not work independently but work in conjunction with other commands. For example, to draw a line starting at a quadrant point of a circle, (i) activate the *Line* command; (ii) click on the quadrant tool in the *Drafting setting* dialog box (in the object snap tab); (iii) bring the cursor on the circle and the nearest quadrant will be highlighted; and (iv) now proceed with the line construction process.

Important points: It is good drawing practice to check two or three modes of *Object Snap* if those modes are used most of the time.

The *Object Snap* commands are activated by checking the corresponding box in the *Drafting setting* dialog box (first select *Object Snap* tab). *If the object snap command is activated by checking the box in the dialog box, then it will be effective as long as the box is checked.* ***Therefore, for the multiple uses, always activate the object snap commands from the dialog box.***

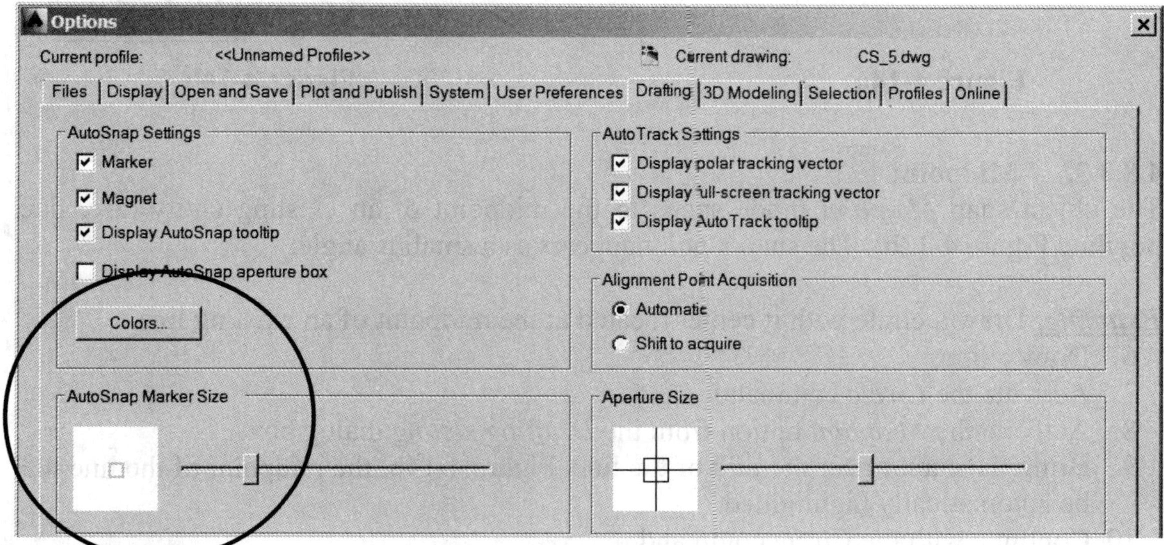

Figure 4-13b

4.8.3.1.   Endpoint

The object snap *Endpoint* mode snaps to the closet endpoint of an existing entity (arc, line, polyline), Figure 4-14a. The snap's point appears as a small square.

Example: Draw a circle with it center located at the end point of an existing line.
1. Draw a line.
2. Activate the *Circle* command.
3. Activate the *Endpoint* option from the *Drafting setting* dialog box.
4. Bring the cursor near the end of the line, Figure 4-14a; the end of the line will be automatically highlighted.
5. Continue with the *Circle* command.

4.8.3.2.   Midpoint

The object snap *Midpoint* mode snaps to the midpoint of an existing entity (arc, line, polyline Figure 4-13b). The snap's point appears as a small triangle.

Example: Draw a circle with it center located at the midpoint of an existing line
1. Draw a line.
2. Activate the *Circle* command.
3. Activate the *Midpoint* option from the *Drafting setting* dialog box.

4. Bring the cursor near the mid of the line, Figure 4-14b; the midpoint of the line will be automatically highlighted.
5. Continue with the *Circle* command.

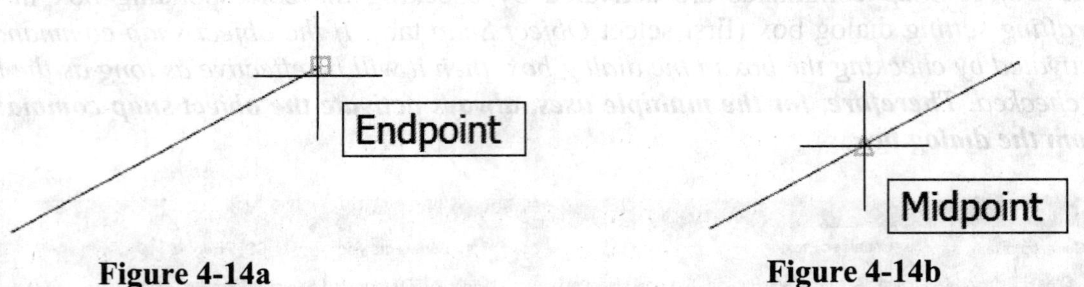

Figure 4-14a   **Figure 4-14b**

4.8.3.3.   Midpoint

The object snap *Midpoint* mode snaps to the midpoint of an existing entity (arc, line, polyline Figure 4-13b). The snap's point appears as a small triangle.

Example: Draw a circle with it center located at the midpoint of an existing line
6. Draw a line.
7. Activate the *Circle* command.
8. Activate the *Midpoint* option from the *Drafting setting* dialog box.
9. Bring the cursor near the mid of the line, Figure 4-14b; the midpoint of the line will be automatically highlighted.
10. Continue with the *Circle* command.

4.8.3.4.   Intersection

The object snap *Intersection* mode snaps to the intersection of two or more existing entities (arc, circle, line, polyline combination) Figure 4-15. The figure shows the intersection of a circle and a line segment. The snap's point appears as a small x mark.

Example: Draw a circle with it center located at the intersection of a circle and a line.
1. Draw a circle and a line.
2. Activate the *Circle* command.
3. Activate the *Intersection* option from the *Drafting setting* dialog box.
4. Bring the cursor near the intersection of the circle and the line, Figure 4-15; the intersection point will be automatically highlighted.
5. Continue with the *Circle* command.

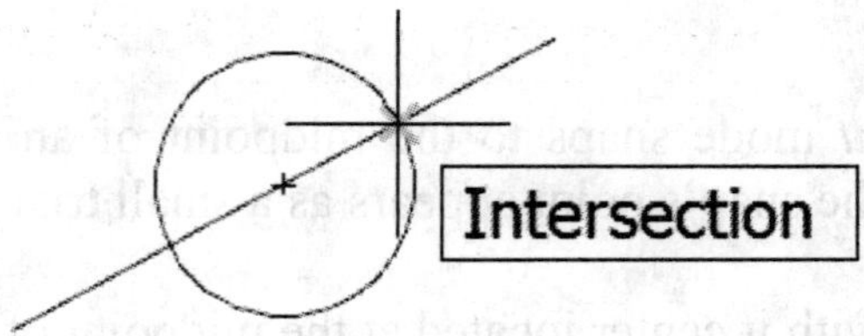

Figure 4-15

4.8.3.5.   Extension 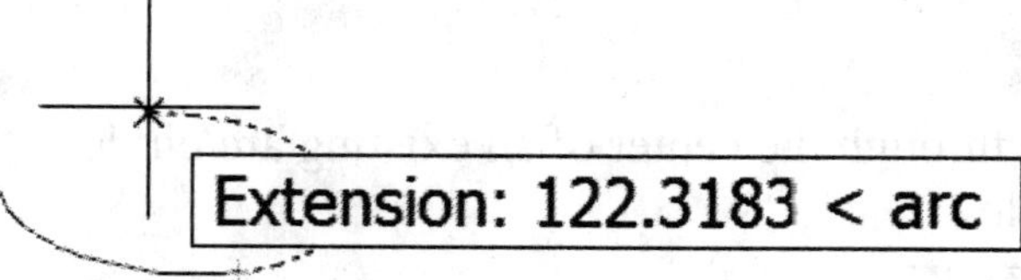

The object snap *Extension* mode creates a temporary extension of the object on its natural path. Figure 4-16a, Figure 4-16b, and Figure 4-16c shows the extension of a straight line, a circular arc, and an elliptical arc, respectively. The snap's point appears as a small x mark.

Example: Draw a circle with it center located at the extension point of an object.
1.   Draw the object (circular arc, elliptical arc, or a straight line).
2.   Activate the *Circle* command.
3.   Activate the *Extension* option from the *Drafting setting* dialog box.
4.   Bring the cursor near the end of the object and move the cursor on the natural path of the object, Figure 4-16a, Figure 4-16b, or Figure 4-16c.
5.   The extension point will be automatically highlighted.
6.   Extend the object to the desired point.
7.   Continue with *Circle* command.

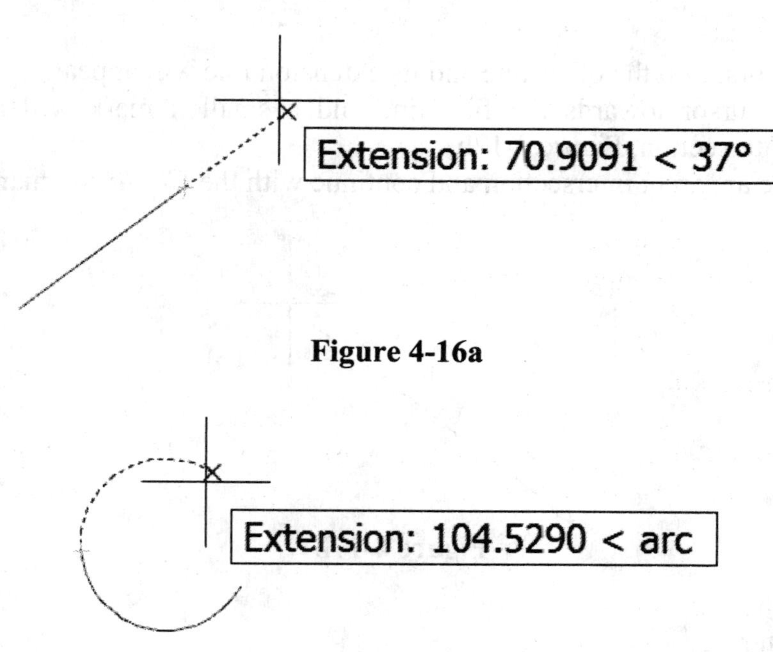

Figure 4-16a

Figure 4-16b

Figure 4-16c

4.8.3.6.   Apparent Intersection

The object snap *Apparent Intersection* mode snaps to the imaginary intersection of the two existing entities that would intersect if they were extended along their natural paths, Figure 4-17b. The snap's point appears as a small x mark.

Example: Draw a circle at the apparent intersection of two lines.
1. Draw two lines as shown in Figure 4-17a.
2. Activate the *Apparent Intersection* and *Extension* commands from the *Drafting setting* dialog box.
3. Activate the *Circle* command.
4. Bring the cursor on one of the lines and its extension line will appear, Figure 4-17a.

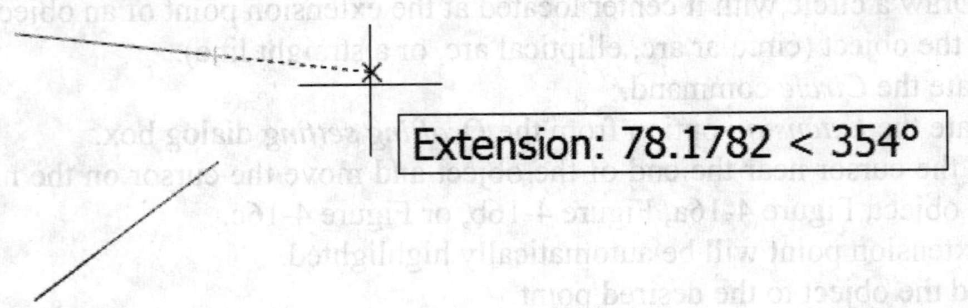

Figure 4-17a

5. Bring the cursor on the other line and its extension line will appear.
6. Move the cursor towards the first line and a small x mark will appear at the apparent intersection, Figure 4-17b.
7. Click at the apparent intersection and continue with the *Circle* command.

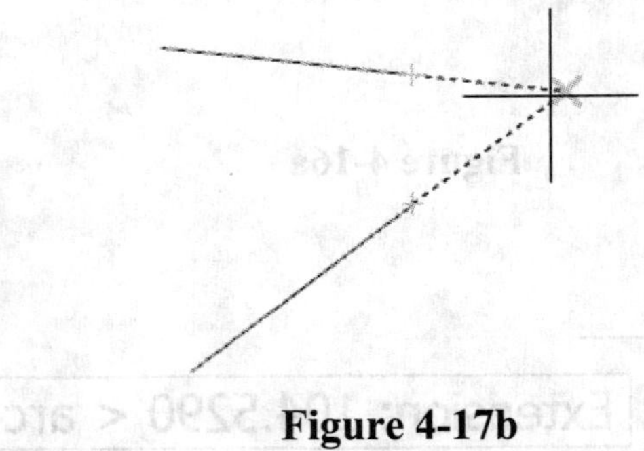

Figure 4-17b

4.8.3.7.   Center

The object snap *Center* mode highlights the center of a circle to draws a line, arc, circle, and ellipse from or to the center of an arc/circle. The snap's point appears as a small plus sign.

Example: Draw a line through the center of an existing arc/circle.
1. Draw an arc/circle.
2. Activate the *Line* command.
3. Activate the *Center* command from the *Drafting setting* dialog box.
4. Bring the cursor on the circumference of the circle, Figure 4-18a; the center of the circle will be automatically selected.
5. Continue with *Line* command.

4.8.3.8.   Quadrant

The object snap *Quadrant* mode is used to snap directly to one of the quadrant of an existing arc/circle. The snap's point appears as a small diamond mark.

Example: Draw a line between two quadrants of a circle as follow.
1. Draw a circle.
2. Activate the *Line* command.
3. Activate the *Quadrant* command from the *Drafting setting* dialog box.
4. Bring the cursor on the circumference of the circle (Figure 4-18b) the closest quadrant will be highlighted.
5. Continue with *Line* command.
6. If in the dialog box both the *Center* and *Quadrant* boxes are checked, then the center and the closet quadrant will be highlighted as the cursor is moved on the circumference, Figure 4-18c.

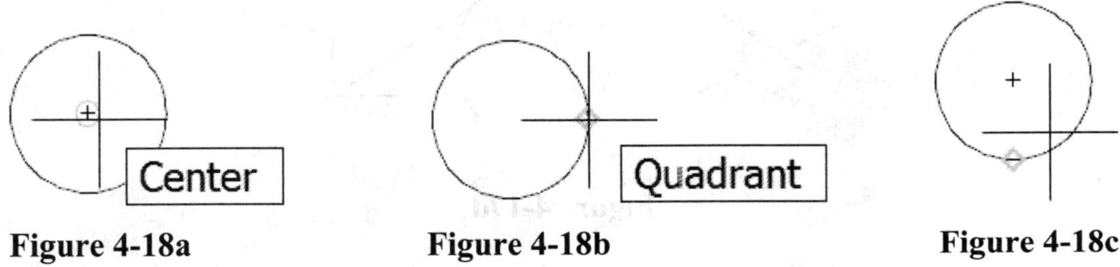

Figure 4-18a   **Figure 4-18b**   **Figure 4-18c**

4.8.3.9.   Tangent

The object snap *Tangent* mode is used to draw a tangent to an existing arc/circle. The snap's point appears as a small circle with a horizontal line on top.

Example: Draw a line (the line is highlighted in Figure 4-19c) with the starting point tangent to a circle and ending point is the intersection of two lines.
1. Draw two lines, Figure 4-19b.
2. Draw a circle, Figure 4-19b.
3. Activate the *Line* command.
4. Activate the *Tangent* command from the *Drafting setting* dialog box.
5. Bring the cursor on the circumference of the circle, Figure 4-19c and Figure 4-19d. The point at the cursor location is highlighted.
6. Click for the start of the line.
7. The start point or tangent is called deferred, Figure 4-19c, because this is not the actual start of the line. If the cursor is moved around the circumference then the start point will also move (Figure 4-19c and Figure 4-19d).
8. The location of the start point of the tangent will be determined by the location of the end point.
9. Click at the intersection of the two lines for the end point of the line under construction. Notice that how the start point has moved, Figure 4-19a.

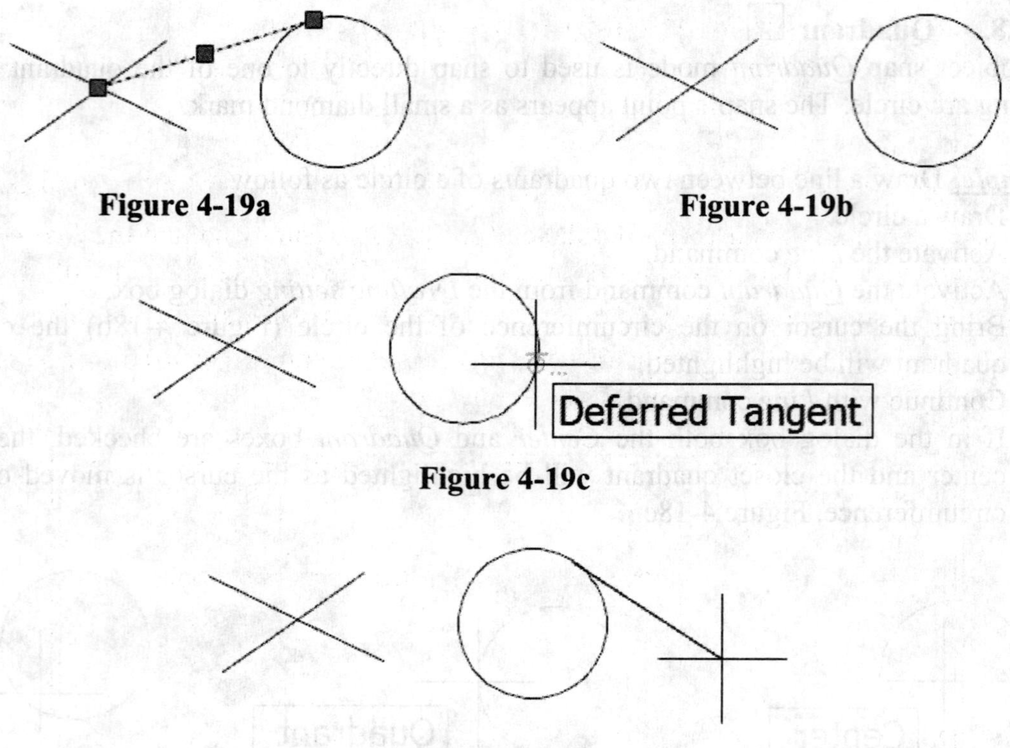

Figure 4-19a   **Figure 4-19b**

Figure 4-19c

Figure 4-19d

4.8.3.10.   Perpendicular

The object snap *Perpendicular* mode is used to draw a line perpendicular to an existing object. The snap's point appears as a two small lines intersecting at 90°.

Example: Draw a line perpendicular to another line.
1. Draw a line.
2. Activate the *Line* command.
3. Activate the *Perpendicular* command from the *Drafting setting* dialog box.
4. Bring the cursor on the line. The point at the cursor location is highlighted.
5. Click for the start of the line.
6. The start point is called deferred, Figure 4-20a, because this is not the actual start of the line. The location of the starting point of the perpendicular will depend on the location of the ending point of the perpendicular. If the cursor is moved on the line then the start point will also move, Figure 4-20b.

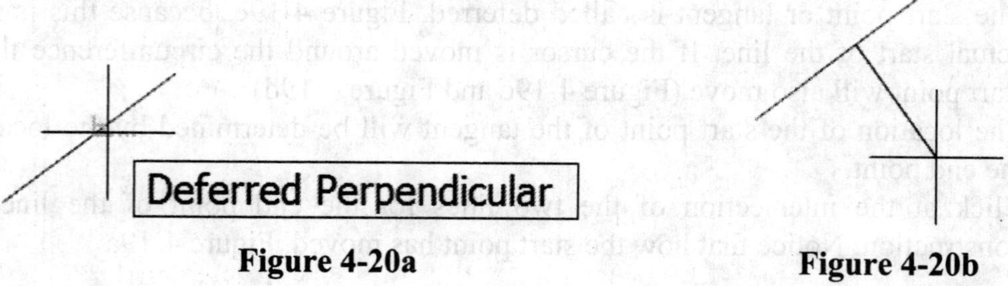

Figure 4-20a   **Figure 4-20b**

4.9.   Introduction of the editing commands

This section introduces the editing command discussed in the remaining of this chapter. Figure 4-21 shows the classification of the editing command.

- <u>Mistake correction</u>: Most of the commands are obvious from their names. The *Cancel* command is used to exit the currently active command and the *Erase* (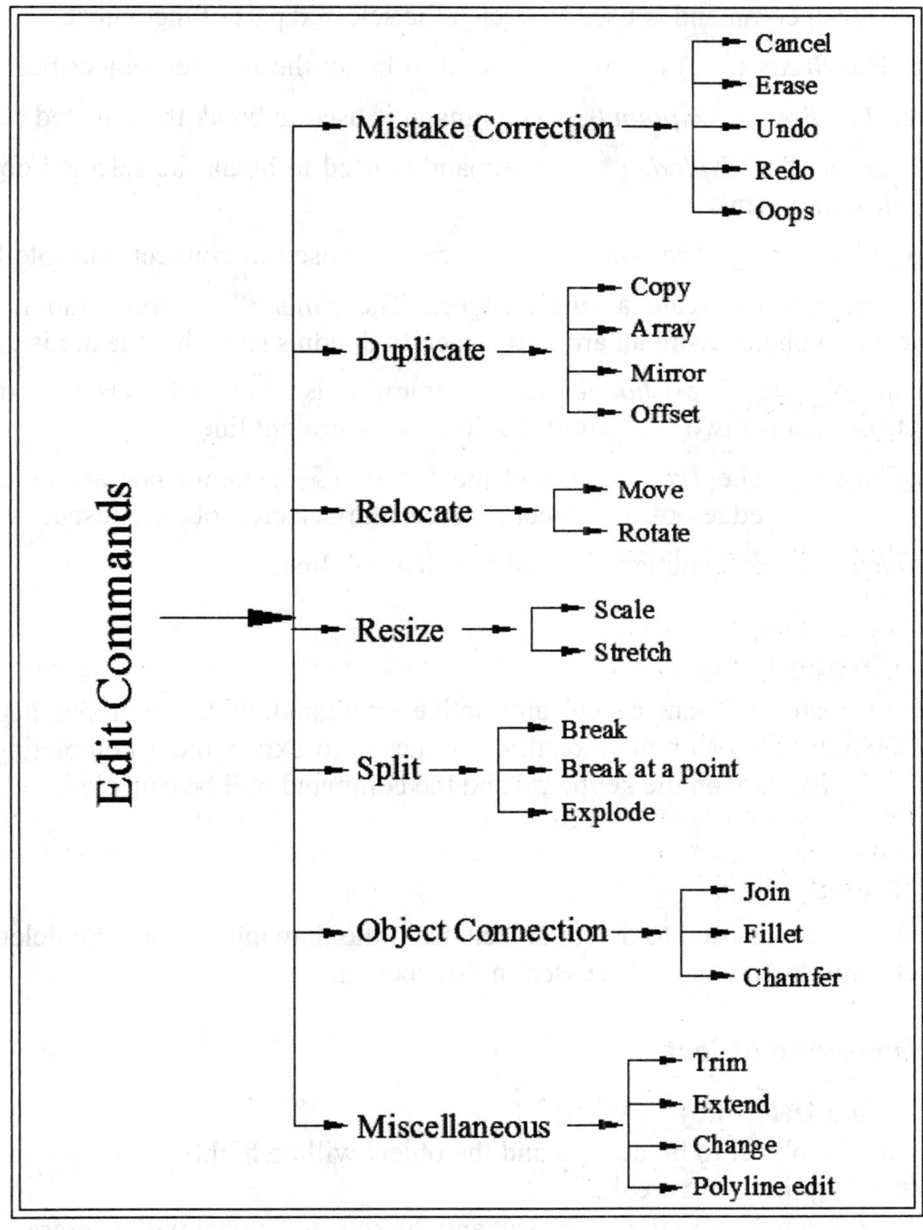) command is used to erase the selected object(s). The *Oops* command will undo the last erase command. The *Undo* ( ) command is used to reverse the effect of the one or more previous commands. The *Redo* ( ) command is used to reverse the effect of one or more previous *Undo* commands.

Figure 4-21

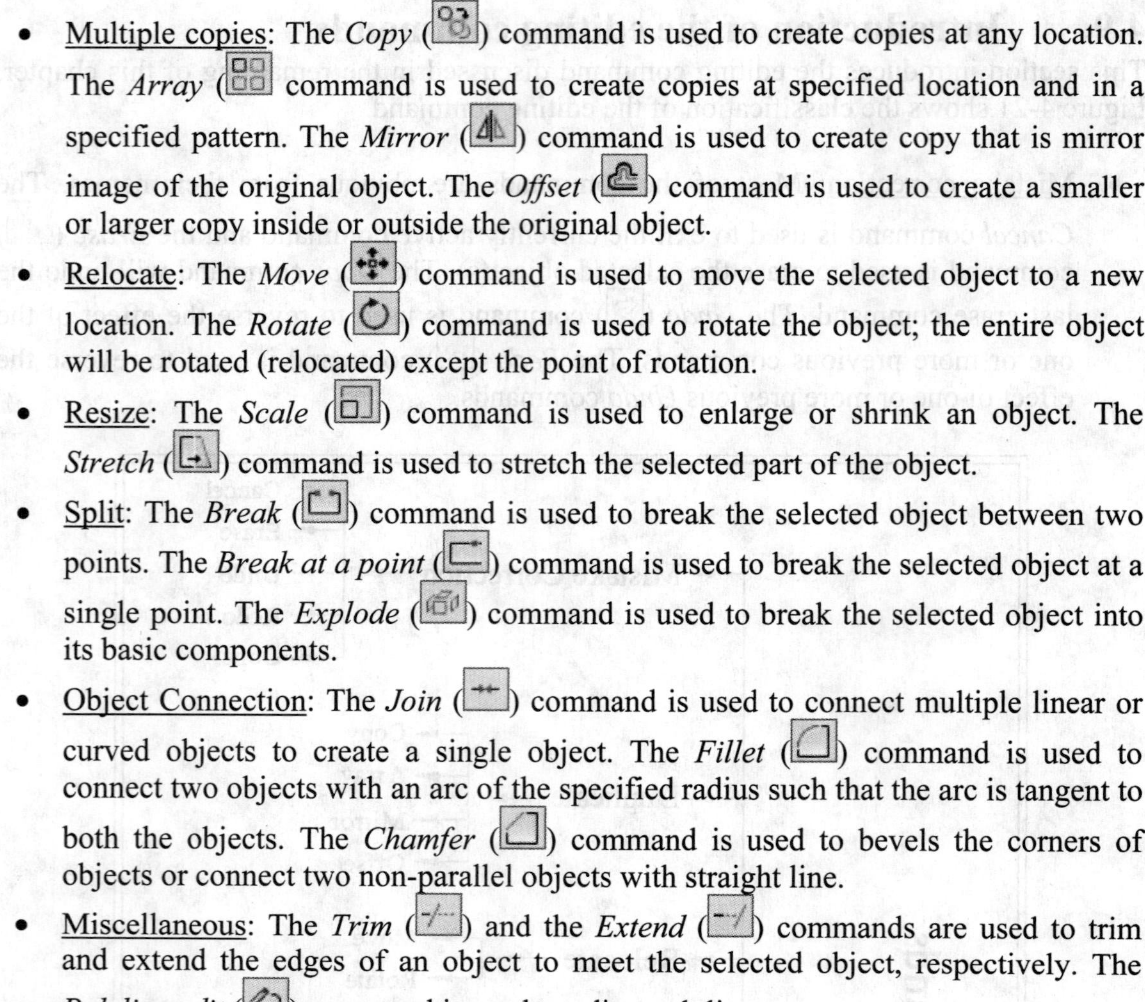

- <u>Multiple copies</u>: The *Copy* (⬚) command is used to create copies at any location. The *Array* (⬚) command is used to create copies at specified location and in a specified pattern. The *Mirror* (⬚) command is used to create copy that is mirror image of the original object. The *Offset* (⬚) command is used to create a smaller or larger copy inside or outside the original object.
- <u>Relocate</u>: The *Move* (⬚) command is used to move the selected object to a new location. The *Rotate* (⬚) command is used to rotate the object; the entire object will be rotated (relocated) except the point of rotation.
- <u>Resize</u>: The *Scale* (⬚) command is used to enlarge or shrink an object. The *Stretch* (⬚) command is used to stretch the selected part of the object.
- <u>Split</u>: The *Break* (⬚) command is used to break the selected object between two points. The *Break at a point* (⬚) command is used to break the selected object at a single point. The *Explode* (⬚) command is used to break the selected object into its basic components.
- <u>Object Connection</u>: The *Join* (⬚) command is used to connect multiple linear or curved objects to create a single object. The *Fillet* (⬚) command is used to connect two objects with an arc of the specified radius such that the arc is tangent to both the objects. The *Chamfer* (⬚) command is used to bevels the corners of objects or connect two non-parallel objects with straight line.
- <u>Miscellaneous</u>: The *Trim* (⬚) and the *Extend* (⬚) commands are used to trim and extend the edges of an object to meet the selected object, respectively. The *Polyline edit* (⬚) command is used to edit a polyline.

4.10.   Cancel

A user of the AutoCAD can cancel any active command. If the user has activated a command intentionally or unintentionally; and needs to exit without completing it then simply press the *Esc* key on the keyboard and the command will be canceled.

4.11.   Erase ⬚

The *Erase* command is used to delete objects from the drawing. A user can delete one or more object using the methods discussed in this section.

4.11.1. Erase one object

4.11.1.1.   Using Delete key

- Click on the object to be deleted and the object will be highlighted (that is, its grips points will appear), Figure 4-22a.
- Press the *Delete* key on the keyboard, and the selected object will be erased.

4.11.1.2. Using Erase tool

- The *Erase* command is activated using one of the following procedures.
    1. Panel method: From the *Home* tab and *Modify* panel select the *Erase* tool.
    2. Command line method: Type "erase", "Erase", or "ERASE" in the command line and press the *Enter* key.

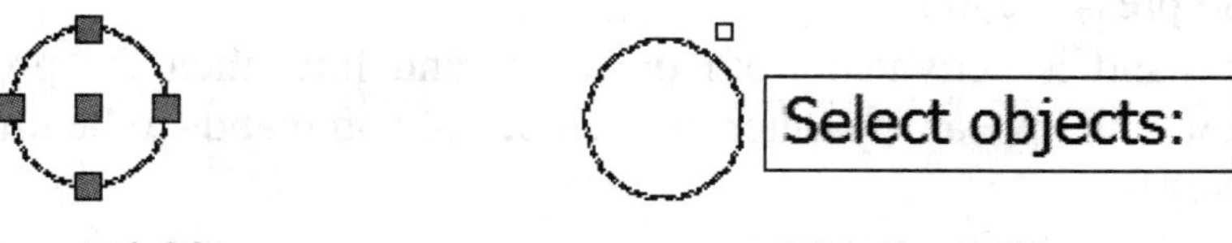

Figure 4-22a   **Figure 4-22b**

- The *Erase* command is used in two ways.

Method #1:
- o   First click on the object to be deleted, Figure 4-22a.
- o   Activate the *Erase* tool.
- o   The activation of the command will erase the selected object.

Method #2
- o   Activate the *Erase* tool.
- o   The *Select objects* prompt will appear, Figure 4-22b.
- o   Click on the object to be deleted, Figure 4-22b.
- o   Press the *Enter* key or press the right button of the mouse to complete the erase process.

4.11.2. Erase multiple object simultaneously

Multiple objects can be erased using the same procedure used for erasing one object. The main difference is instead of selecting one object at a time select multiple objects simultaneously using selection methods discussed earlier.

4.12. Undo

The *Undo* command is used to reverse the effect of one or more of the previous commands. However, the commands such as *Plot*, *Save*, *Open*, *Export* cannot be undone.

4.12.1. Undo one command

The following methods of undo will be available during the activation of another command. For example, if a user is drawing a polyline, then the previous segment can be deleted using any one of these two methods.

- Hold the *Ctrl* key and press the 'z' key on the keyboard. The most recent command will be undone.
- Press the '*u*' or '*U*' key on the keyboard and press the *Enter* key. The most recent command will be undone.

4.12.2. Undo several commands

The following method of undo is available only if none of the other commands are active.

- The *Undo* command is activated from the command line.
  1. Command line method: Type "undo", "Undo", or "UNDO" in the command line and press the *Enter* key.
- If the command is activated from the command line, then the prompt shown in Figure 4-23a will appear. (i) Enter the number of commands to be undone. (ii) Press the *Enter* key.

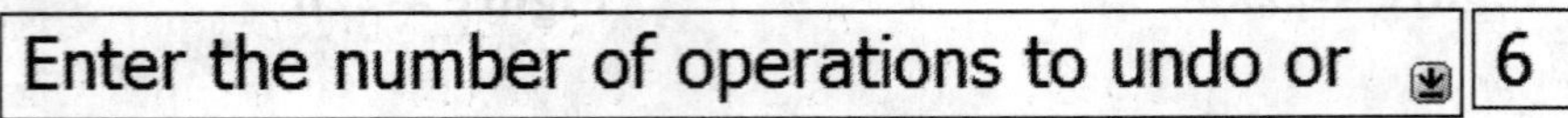

Figure 4-23a

4.13.   Redo

The *Redo* command is used to reverse the effect of the one or more previous *Undo* commands. However, the commands must be activated immediately after the *Undo* command.

4.13.1. Redo one command

Hold the *Ctrl* key and press the '*y*' key on the keyboard. The most recent *Undo* command will be redone.

4.13.2. Redo several commands

This following method of redo is available only if none of the other commands are

- The *Redo* command is activated from the command line.
  1. Command line method: Type "redo", "Redo", or "REDO" in the command line and press the *Enter* key.

4.14.   Oops

The *Oops* command is used to restore the objects deleted from the previous *Erase* command. The drawing of Figure 4-24 shows a bold triangle. The triangle is erased from the drawing of Figure 4-25a. In the drawing of Figure 4-25b, the user has added few more objects and realized that the bold triangle was deleted before and want to restore the triangle without deleting the newly created objects. The user can restore the previously deleted object using the restore command.

- The *Oops* command can be activated only from the command line.
  1. Command line method: Type "oops", "Oops", or "OOPS" in the command line and press the *Enter* key.
- The object deleted in the previous *Erase* command will appear on the screen. In the example, the triangle will appear on the screen, Figure 4-25c.

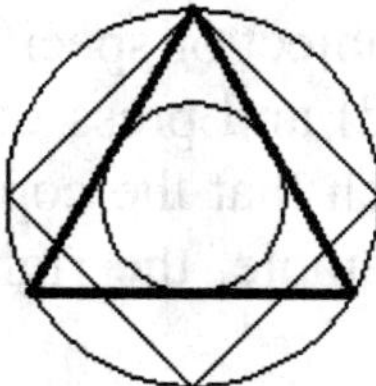

Figure 4-24 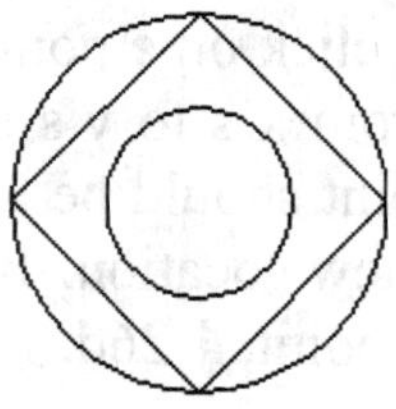   Figure 4-25a 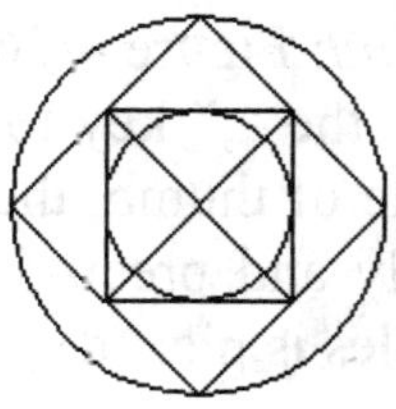   Figure 4-25b 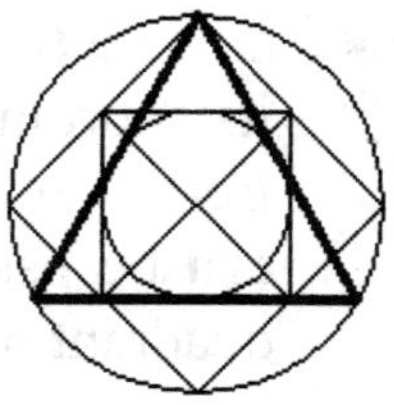   Figure 4-25c

4.15.   Copy 

The *Copy* command is used to create duplicates of drawing objects and place the duplicates in a specified direction and at a specified distance from the original object. This technique is useful for creating multiple copies at a non-uniform spacing. For uniform spacing generally the *Array* command is faster than the *Copy* command. The Figure 4-26a shows six objects: the original object is labeled and is created using the commands from the *Draw* and *Modify* panels, however, the other five objects are created using the Copy commands. The most efficient technique to complete the drawing is to use the *Copy* command with the *Object snaps* mode *On* (to copy objects with precision).

Example: Create five copies of the original object.

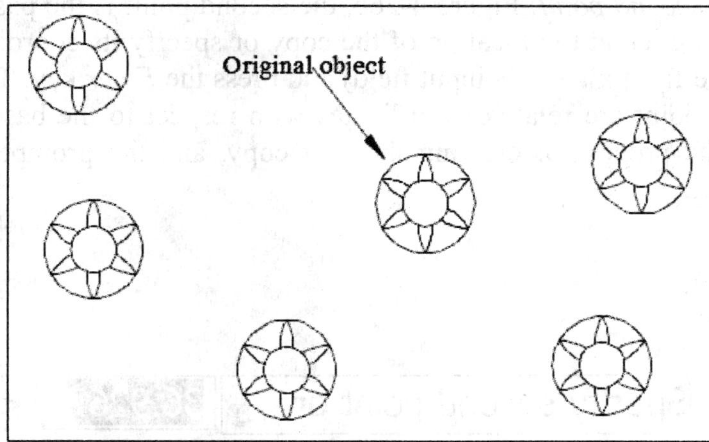

Figure 4-26a

- The *Copy* command is activated using one of the following procedures.
    1. Panel method: From the *Home* tab and *Modify* panel select the *Copy* tool.
    2. Command line method: Type "copy", "Copy", or "COPY" in the command line and press the *Enter* key
- The activation of the command leads to the object selection prompt, Figure 4-26b. Use one of the object selection methods discussed earlier. Finally, press the *Enter* key to complete the object selection.

Select objects:

Figure 4-26b

- *Specify the base point*: Figure 4-26c, either click on a point on the object or specify its coordinates (use the "," key to move from x's to y's input field) and press the *Enter* key. As a rule of thumb, the base point should be a point such that the copy can be pasted easily and precisely at its new location. In this example, the right quadrant of the circles is picked as the base point, 4-26d.

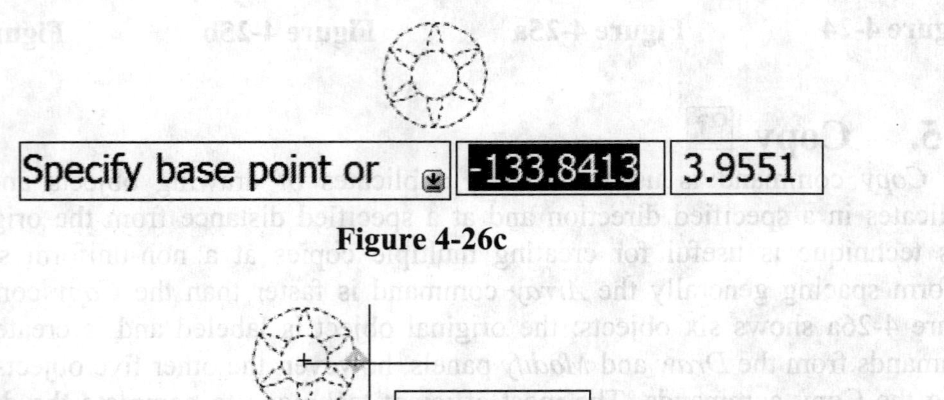

Figure 4-26c

Figure 4-26d

- *Specify the second point*: Figure 4-26e, the second point is the paste location of the copy. Either click at the location of the copy or specify its coordinates (use the "," key to move from x's to y's input field) and press the *Enter* key. The coordinates of the second point are relative coordinates with respect to the base point. This will complete the process of creating the first copy, and the prompt will not change, Figure 4-26f.

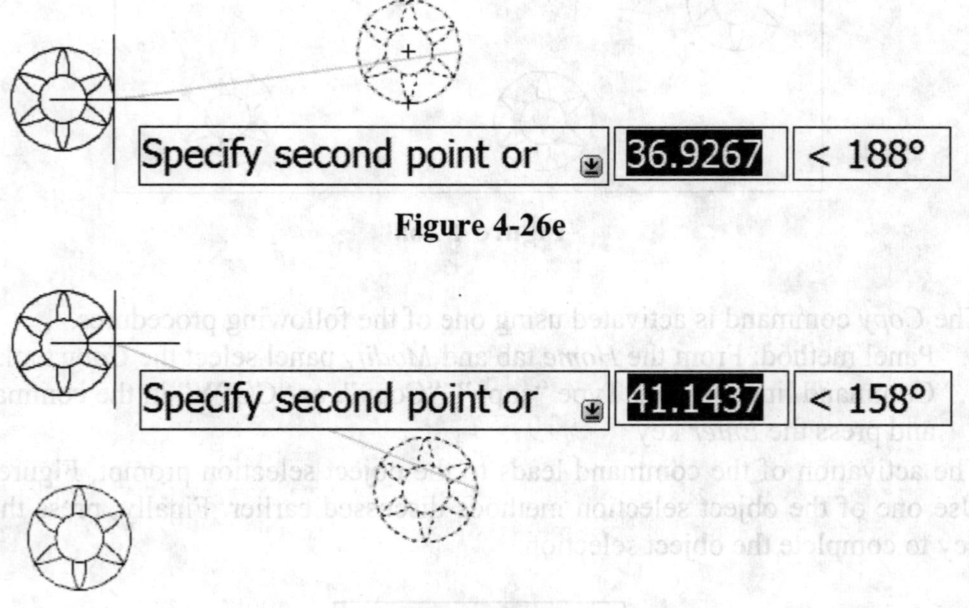

Figure 4-26e

Figure 4-26f

- Make another copy: To create another copy, repeat the process of the specification of the second point. To exit the command, press the *Esc* or *Enter* key.
- The distance between the original to a copy location is determined by the distance and direction between the base and the second points.

4.16.   Array

The *Array* command creates multiple copies of an object and arranges the copies in a specific pattern. Objects can be copied and arranged in a pattern using the *Copy*, *Rotate*, and *Move* commands, too. However, the drawing accuracy is increased and its creation duration is greatly reduced if the *Array* command is used to create the multiple copies in a pattern. AutoCAD allows to create rectangular, circular, and path arrays.

The rectangle array command will place the copies in rows and column, Figure 4-27a; the polar array command will place the copies in a circular arrangement at a specific center, Figure 4-27b; and the path array command will make the copies along the specified path, Figure 4-27c.

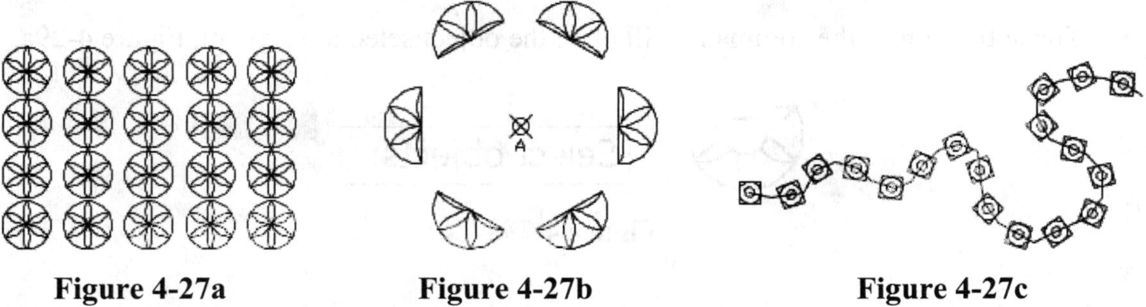

| Figure 4-27a | Figure 4-27b | Figure 4-27c |

4.16.1. Rectangular Array

The *Rectangular Array* command creates a rectangular array of the selected object. In a rectangular array, rows and columns are used to arrange objects in the array. If an array contains one row then it must have more than one column and vice versa. By default, the maximum number of array elements generated in one command is 100000. The default number of elements in an array is 12 (3 rows and 4 columns). However, for large arrays it will take longer time to create the array.

- The ***ArrayRectangular*** command is activated using one of the following procedures.
  1. Panel method: From the *Home* tab and *Modify* panel, expand the *Array* drop down menu and select the *Rectangular Array* tool, Figure 4-28a.
  2. Command line method: Either type "array", "Array", or "ARRAY" and select the *ARRAYRECT* option, Figure 4-28b; or type "arrayrect", "Arrayrect", or "ARRAYRECT" in the command line and press the *Enter* key.

Example: Create a drawing for a class room seating with 5 columns and 4 rows as shown in Figure 4-29m. The figure also shows the rows and column spacing.

- Create the basic element of the array.
- Activate the *Array Rectangular* command.

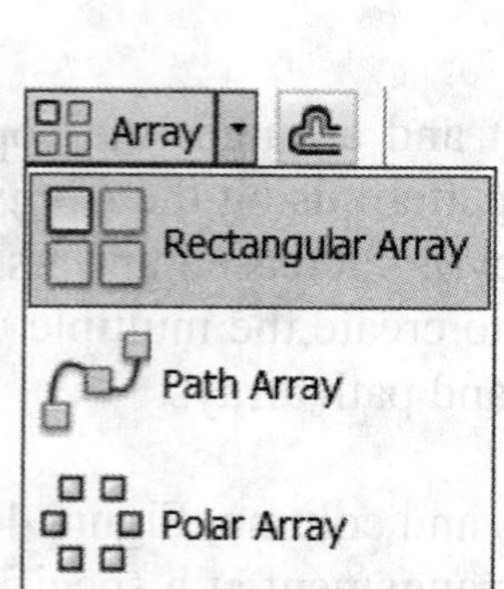
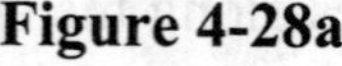

Figure 4-28a

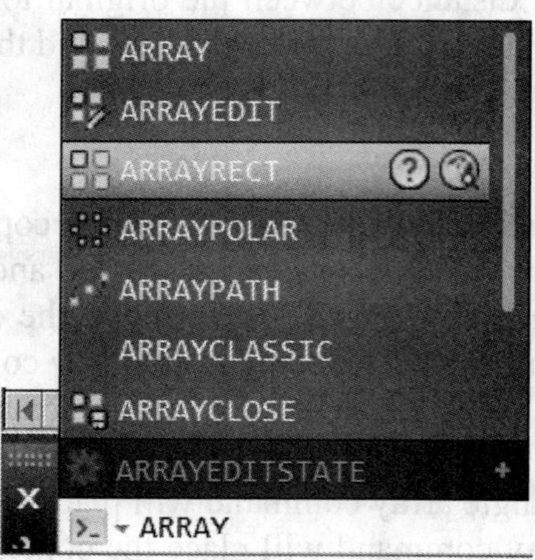

Figure 4-28b

- The activation of the command will open the object selection prompt, Figure 4-29a.

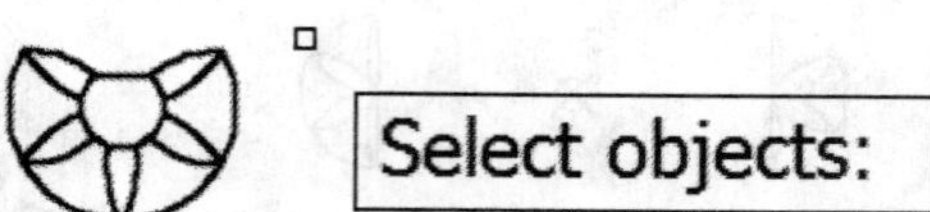

Figure 4-29a

- Select the desired objects and press the *Enter* key. The prompt shown in Figure 4-29b will appear on the screen.

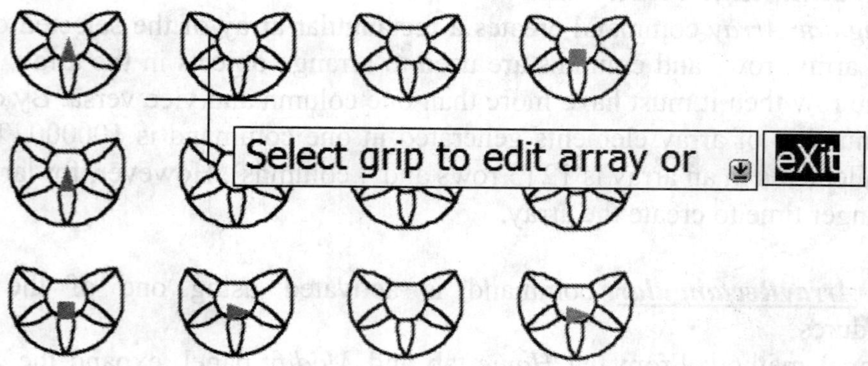

Figure 4-29b

- *Select grip to edit array or*: If the user press the *Enter* key then the array shown in Figure 4-29b will appear on the screen; and will neglect the remaining bullets in this section. The array will be a single entity, that is, the elements of the array could not be manipulated independently. However, the user can edit the array using panels from the *Edit* tab. Array editing is discussed later.

- However, in this example, press the down arrow key of the keyboard to check the various options, Figure 4-29c. Click on the *ASsociative* option.

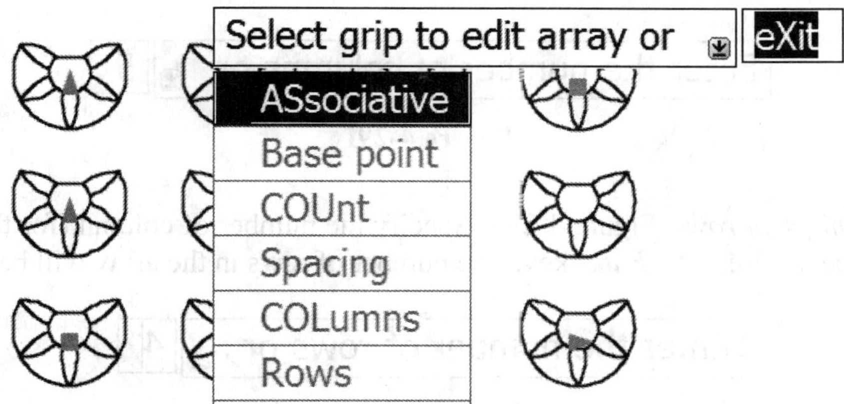

Figure 4-29c

- *Create associative array*, Figure 4-29d: The *Yes* option will create the array as a single entity. The user may need to change one or more elements. However, for the current example, click on the *Yes* option.

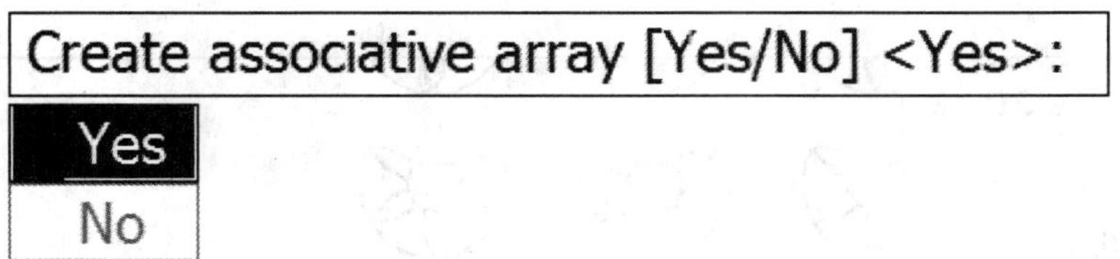

Figure 4-29d

- *Select grip to edit array or*, Figure 4-29e: Press the down arrow key of the keyboard and click on the *COUnt* option.

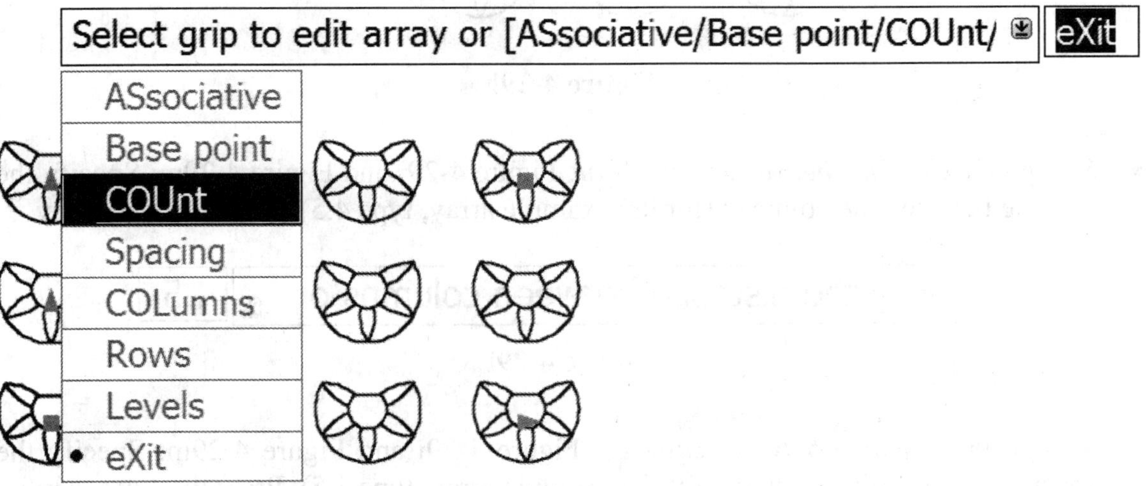

Figure 4-29e

- *Enter number of Column*, Figure 4-29f: Specify the number of column (for the example array, type 5). Press the *Enter* key. The number of columns in the array will be set to 5.

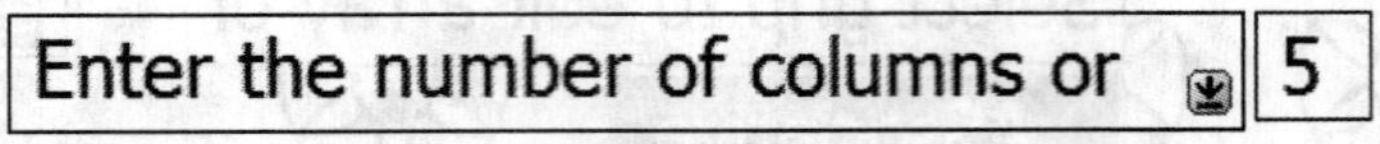

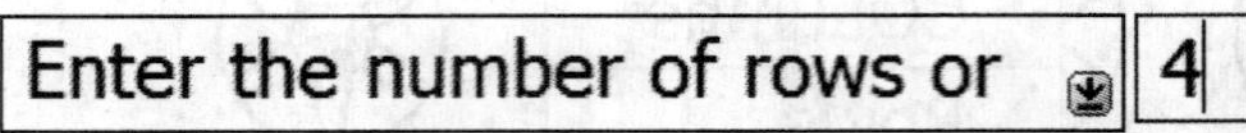

Figure 4-29f

- *Enter number of rows*, Figure 4-29g: Specify the number of column (for the example array, type 4). Press the *Enter* key. The number of rows in the array will be set to 4.

Figure 4-29g

- *Select grip to edit array or*, Figure 4-29h: Press the down arrow key of the keyboard and click on the *Spacing* option.

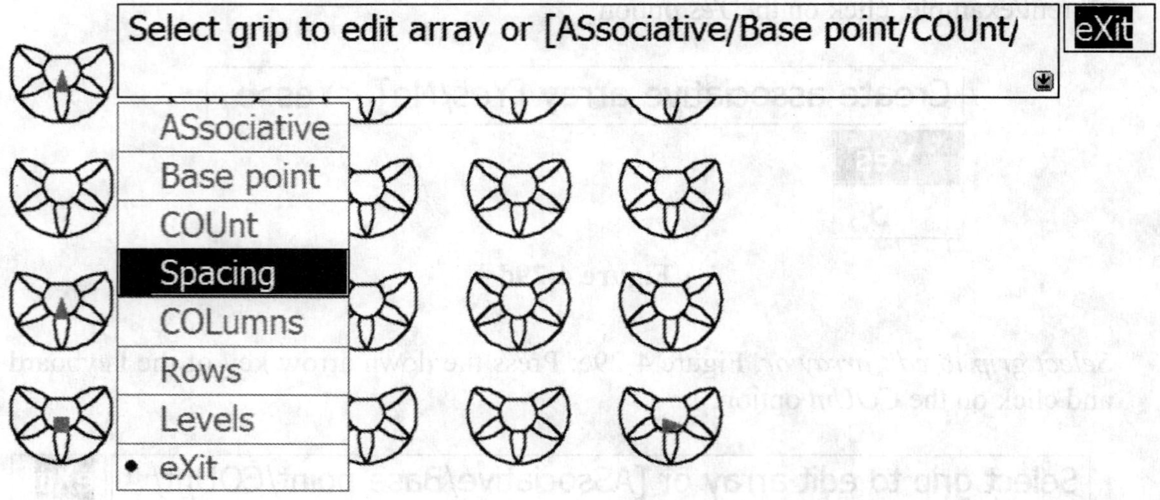

Figure 4-29h

- *Specify the distance between columns or*, Figure 4-29i and Figure 4-29m: Specify the spacing between the columns (for the example array, type 4.5). Press the *Enter* key.

Figure 4-29i

- *Specify the distance between rows or*, Figure 4-29j and Figure 4-29m: Specify the spacing between the columns (for the example array, type 3.5). Press the *Enter* key.

Specify the distance between rows <3.9734>: 3.5

Figure 4-29j

- *Select grip to edit array or*, Figure 4-29k: Press the *Enter* key to complete the array command. The resulting array is shown in Figure 4-29m.

Select grip to edit array or eXit

Figure 4-29k

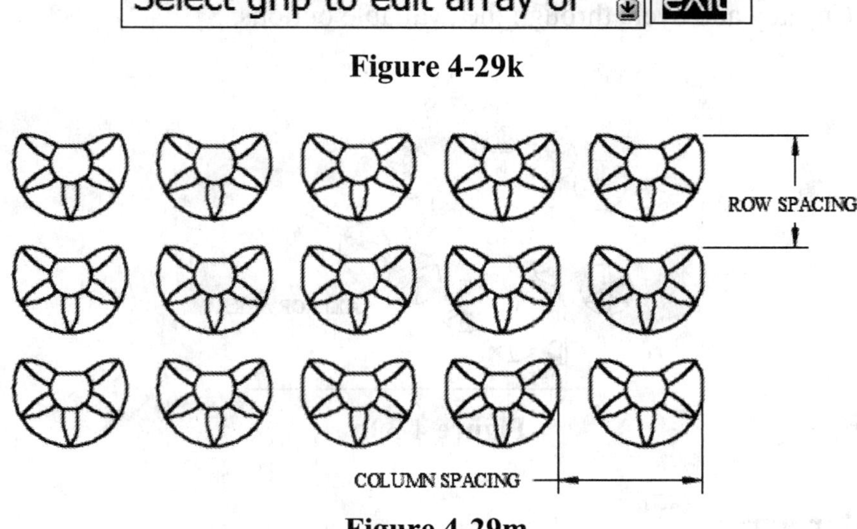

Figure 4-29m

4.16.1.1. Rectangular array's grip points

- To use the options shown in Figure 4-30a (i) bring the cursor on the desired grip point and it will be highlighted (its color will change) and its options will appear; (ii) move the cursor to the desired option; (iii) finally, either press the *Enter* key or click with the left button of the mouse and follow the prompts. The figure shows the selection of four different options simultaneously; however, the user can select only one option at a time.

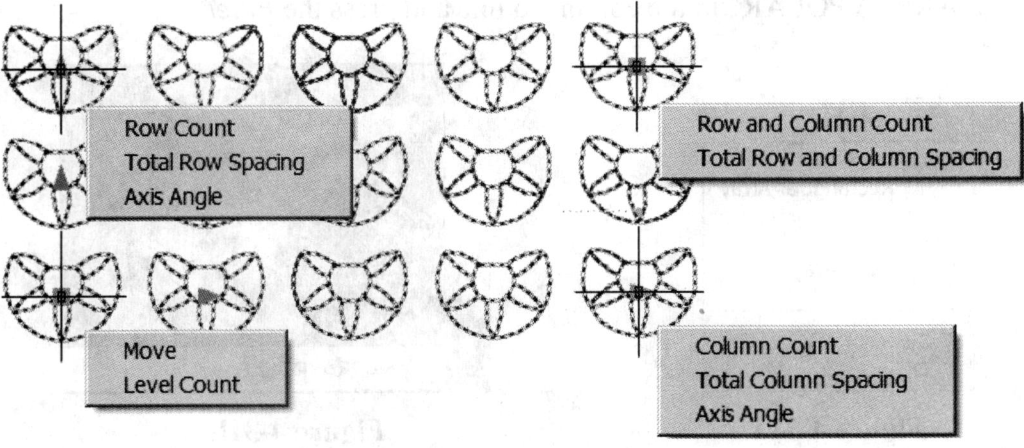

Figure 4-30a

- The grip point at the lower right corner of the array can be used to change the number of column, the column spacing, and the axis angle of the array, Figure 4-30b. The user can hold the Ctrl key and cycle through the available options.
- The grip point at the lower left corner of the array can be used to move the array.
- The grip point at the upper right corner of the array can be used to change the number of rows and columns, and the row and column spacing the array.
- The grip point at the upper left corner of the array can be used to change the number of rows, the row spacing, and the axis angle of the array, Figure 4-30b. The user can hold the *Ctrl* key and cycle through the available options.

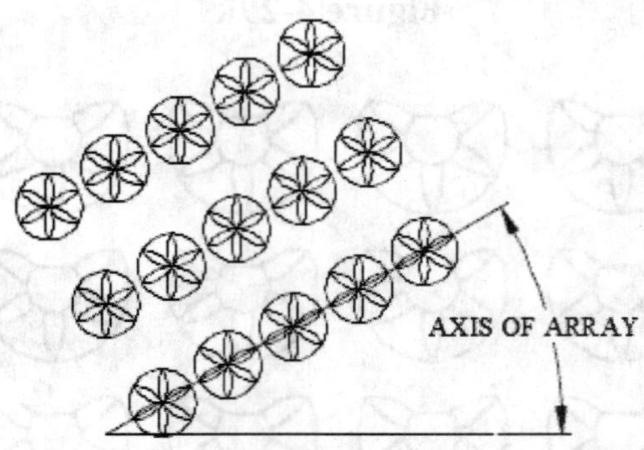

Figure 4-30b

4.16.2. Polar array

The *Polar Array* command creates a circular array of the selected objects around a specified center point. Also, the objects will be rotated to face the center point. This section explains the options available to create a polar array.

- The ***ArrayPolar*** command is activated using one of the following procedures.
    1. Panel method: From the *Home* tab and *Modify* panel, expand the *Array* drop down menu and select the *Polar Array* tool, Figure 4-31a.
    2. Command line method: Either type "array", "Array", or "ARRAY" and select the *ARRAYPOLAR* option, Figure 4-31b; or type "arraypolar", "Arraypolar", or "ARRAYPOLAR" in the command line and press the *Enter* key.

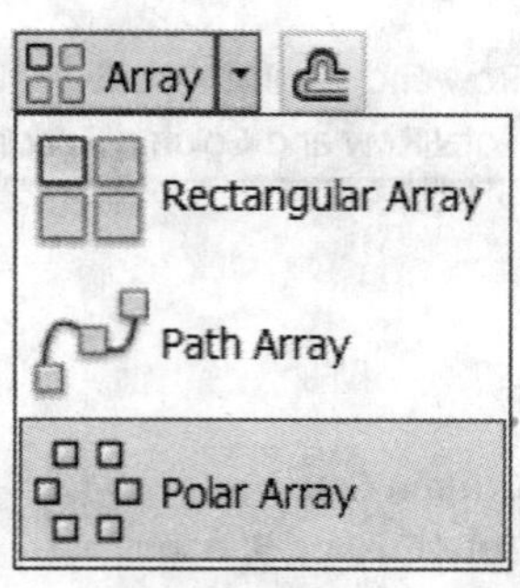

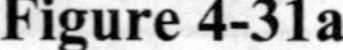

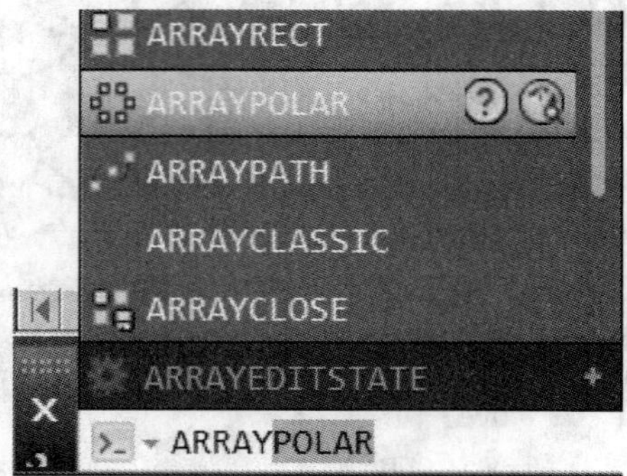

Figure 4-31a   **Figure 4-31b**

- The Figure 4-31c shows basic terminology of a polar array.

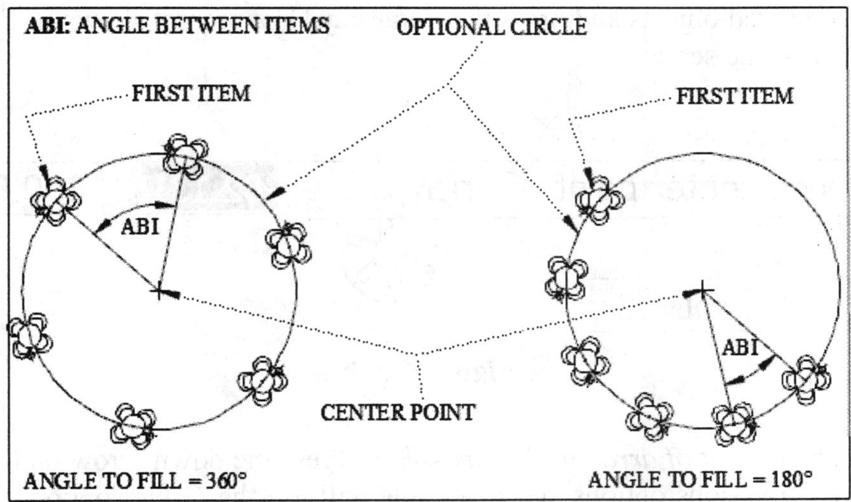

Figure 4-31c

Example: Create a circular arrangement of seven chairs occupying three quarter of a circle and facing towards the center as shown in Figure 4-32a or Figure 4-32b. The two figures represent the same array. The Figure 4-32a is created using the fill angle of 270°; and the Figure 4-32b is created using the angle between items of 45°.

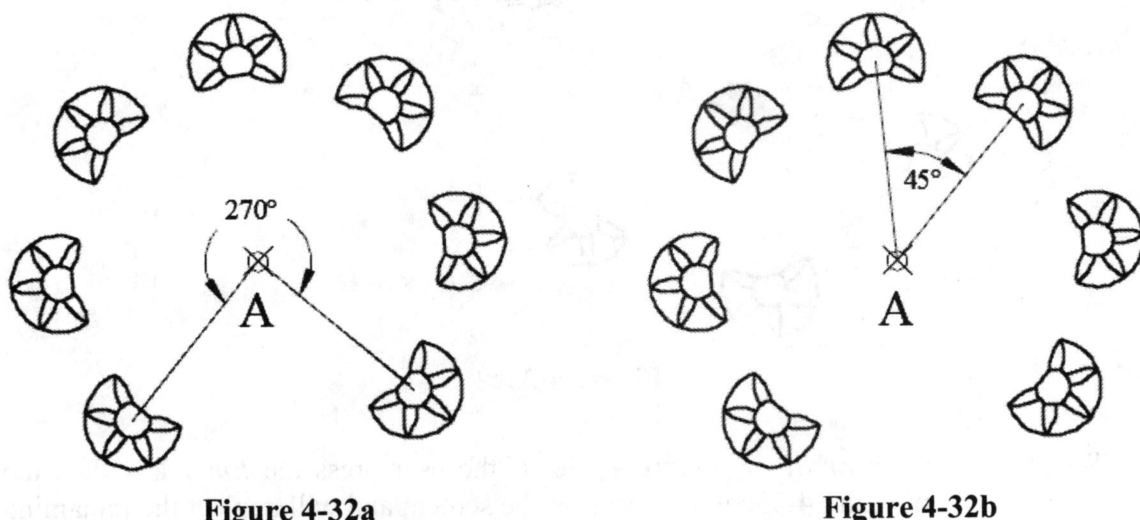

| **Figure 4-32a** | **Figure 4-32b** |

- Create the basic element of the array. In this example the point A (Figure 4-33a) is marked as the center point of the array; it is not necessary to draw the point A.
- Activate the *Array Polar* command.
- The activation of the command will open the object selection prompt, Figure 4-33a.

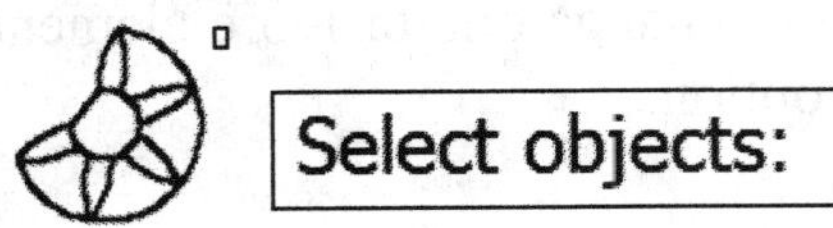

Figure 4-33a

- Select the desired objects and press the *Enter* key. The prompt shown in Figure 4-33b will appear on the screen.

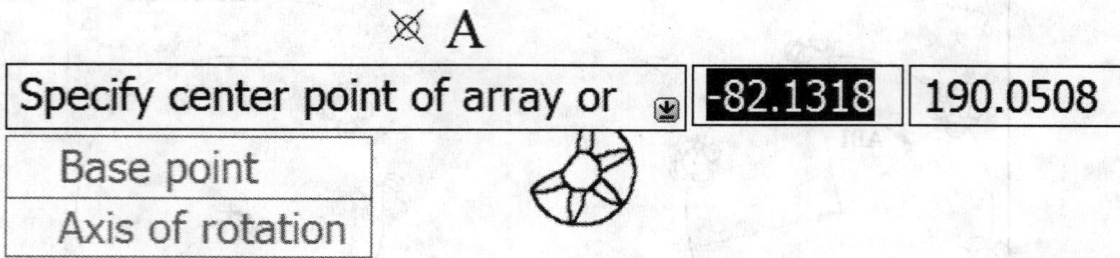

Figure 4-33b

- *Specify center point of array or*, Figure 4-33b: Press the down arrow on the keyboard to display the various options. This example will use the *Center* option. Press the up arrow of the keyboard to hide the option list. Turn *On* the *Node* option in the *Object snap*. Click at point A. The prompt shown in Figure 4-33c will appear on the screen.

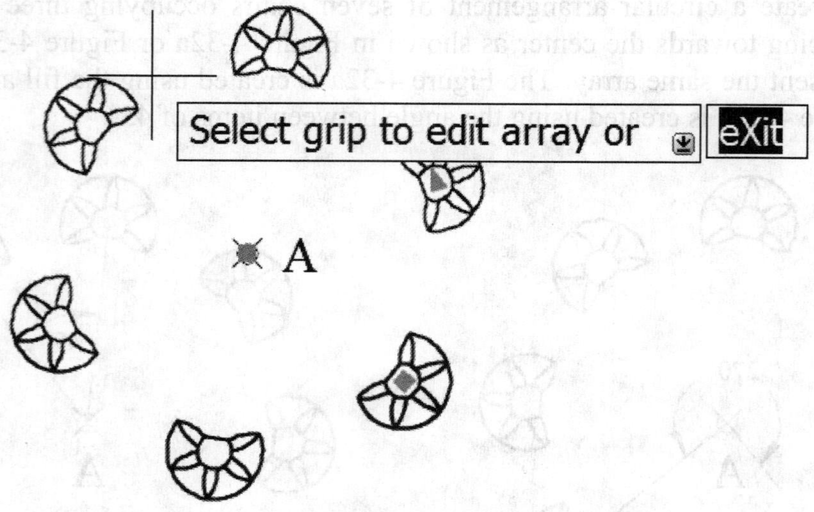

Figure 4-33c

- *Select grip to edit array or*, Figure 4-33c: If the user press the *Enter* key then the array shown in Figure 4-33c will appear on the screen; and will neglect the remaining bullets in this section. The array will be a single entity, that is, the elements of the array could not be manipulated independently. However, the user can edit the array using panels from the *Edit* tab. Array editing is discussed later.
- However, in this example, press the down arrow key of the keyboard to check the various options, Figure 4-33d. Click on the *ASsociative* option.
- *Create associative array* Figure 4-33e: The *Yes* option will create the array as a single entity. The user may need to change one or more elements. However, for the current example, click on the *Yes* option.

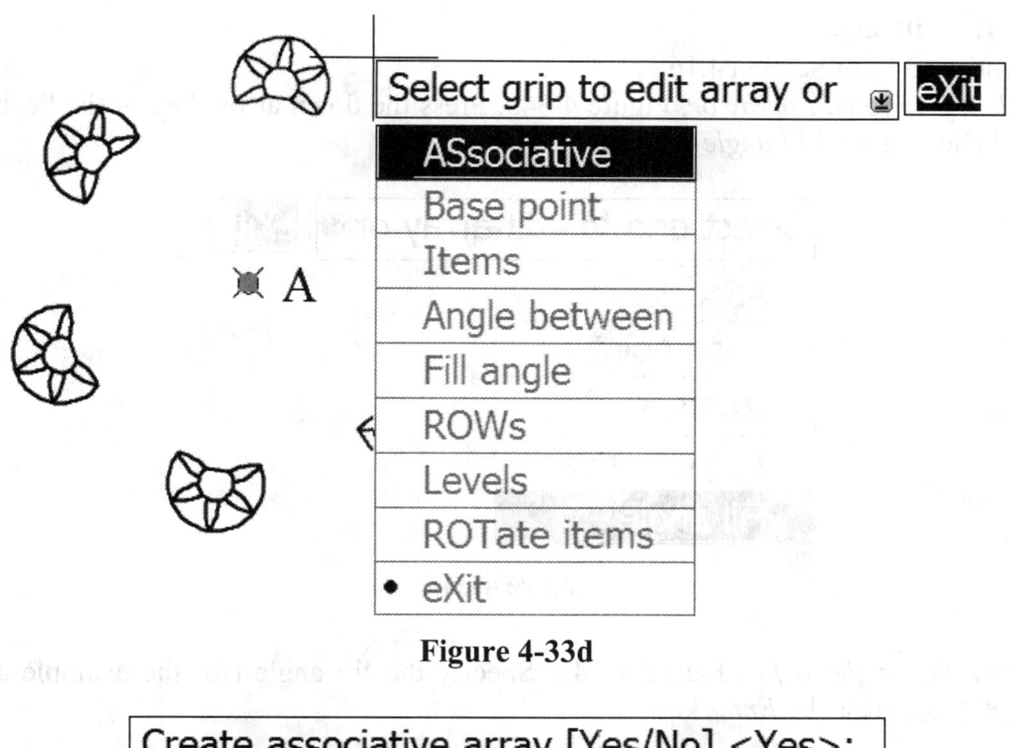

Figure 4-33d

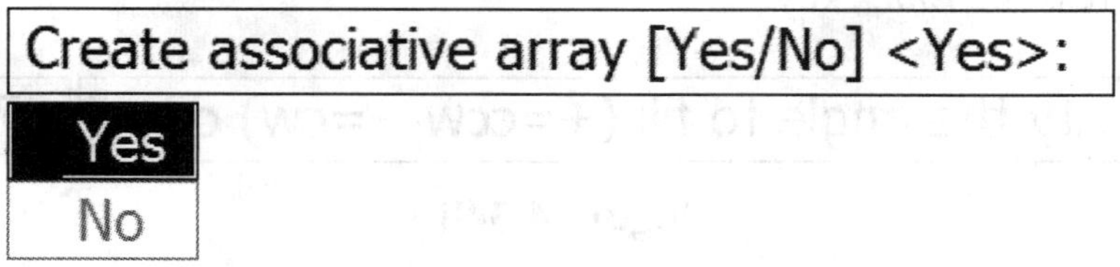

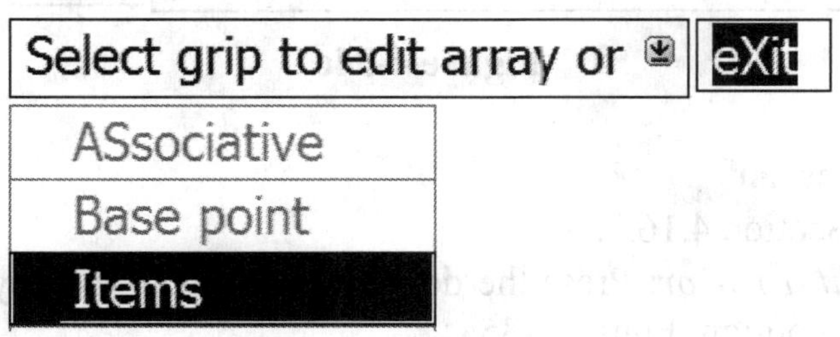

Figure 4-33e

- *Select grip to edit array or*, Figure 4-33f: Press the down arrow key of the keyboard and click on the *Items* option.

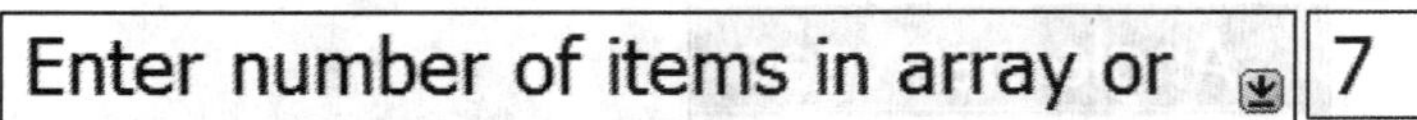

Figure 4-33f

- *Enter number of items in array or*, Figure 4-33g: Specify the number of items (for the example array, type 7). Press the *Enter* key.
- The next two subsections describe the *Fill angle* and the *Angle between* options; and the user should follow the desired option.

Figure 4-33g

4.16.2.1.   Fill angle

- Continued from Section 4.16.2.
- *Select grip to edit array or*, Figure 4-34a: Press the down arrow key of the keyboard and click on the *Fill angle* option.

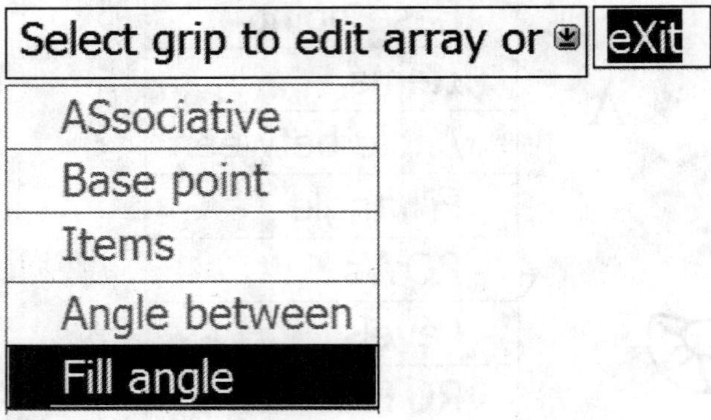

Figure 4-34a

- *Enter the angle to fill*, Figure 4-34b: Specify the fill angle (for the example array, type 270). Press the *Enter* key.

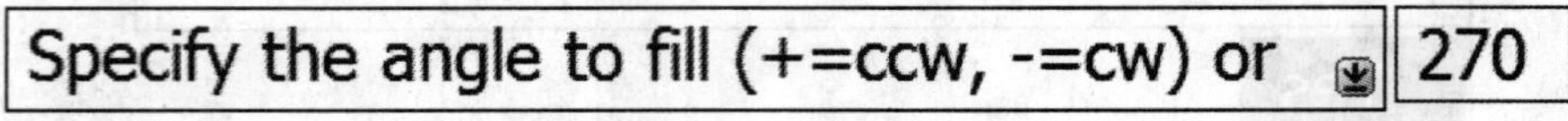

Figure 4-34b

- *Select grip to edit array or*, Figure 4-34c: Press the *Enter* key to complete the array command. The resulting array is shown in Figure 4-32a.

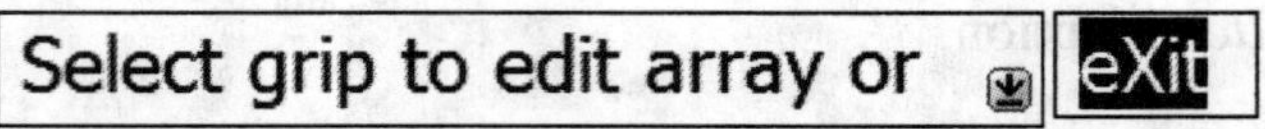

Figure 4-34c

4.16.2.2.   Angle between

- Continued from Section 4.16.2.
- *Select grip to edit array or*: Press the down arrow key of the keyboard and click on the *Angle between* option, Figure 4-35a.

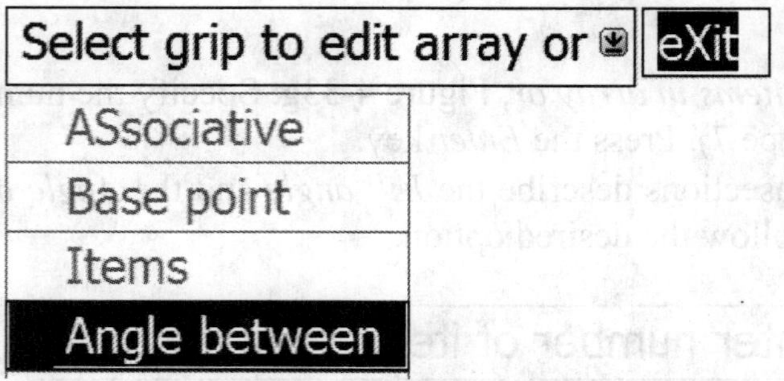

Figure 4-35a

- *Specify angle between items or*: Figure 4-35b, Specify the angle between two consecutive elements. For the example array, type 45. The positive angle will create counterclockwise array. Press the *Enter* key.
- *Select grip to edit array or*, Figure 4-35c: Press the *Enter* key to complete the array command. The resulting array is shown in Figure 4-32b.

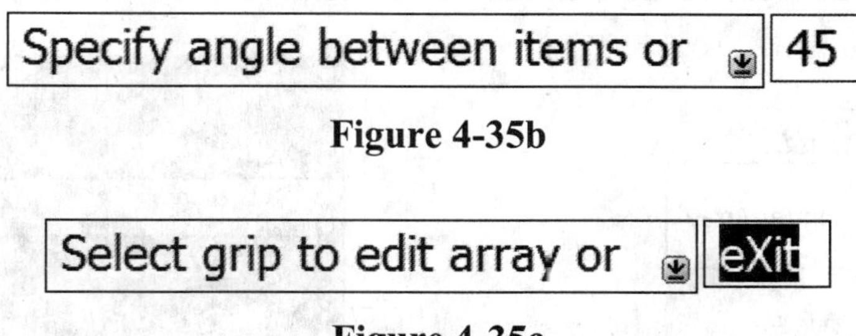

Figure 4-35b

Figure 4-35c

4.16.2.3.   Polar array and grip points

- Figure 4-36 shows the behavior of the grip point at the basic element of the array. These grip points can be used to change the number of items (*Item Count*) and the fill angle (*Fill Angle*) of the polar array. It is also used to change the radius (*Stretch Radius*) and the number of circles in the polar array using *Row Count* option.
- To use the options shown in Figure 4-37 (i) bring the cursor on the desired grip point and it will be highlighted (its color will change) and its options will appear; (ii) move the cursor to the desired option; (iii) finally, either press the *Enter* key or click with the left button of the mouse and follow the prompts.

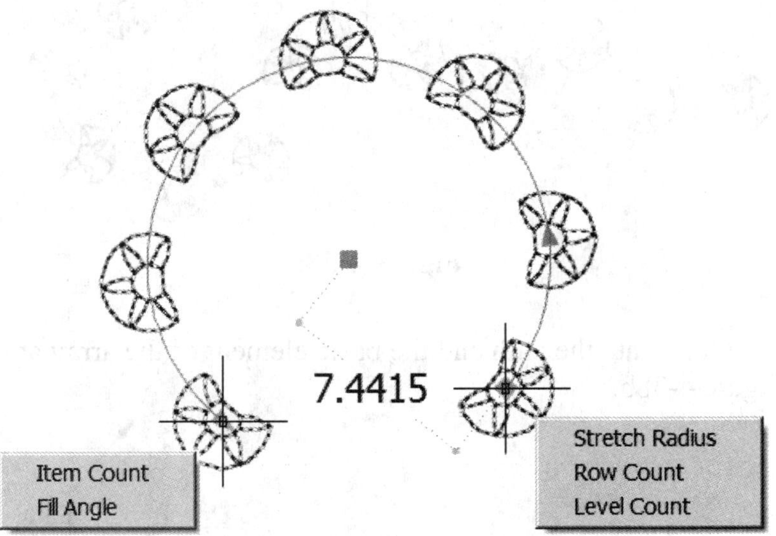

Figure 4-36

4.16.3. Path array

The *Array Path* command distributes the desired number of the object (to be arrayed) evenly on a path. The path can be a line, polyline, spline, helix, arc, circle, or ellipse. In the example the path is created using a polyline.

- The ***ArrayPath*** command is activated using one of the following procedures.
  1. Panel method: From the *Home* tab and *Modify* panel, expand the *Array* drop down menu and select the *Path Array* tool, Figure 4-37a.
  2. Command line method: Either type "array", "Array", or "ARRAY" and select the *ARRAYPATH* option, Figure 4-37b; or type "arraypath", "Arraypath", or "ARRAYPATH" in the command line and press the *Enter* key.

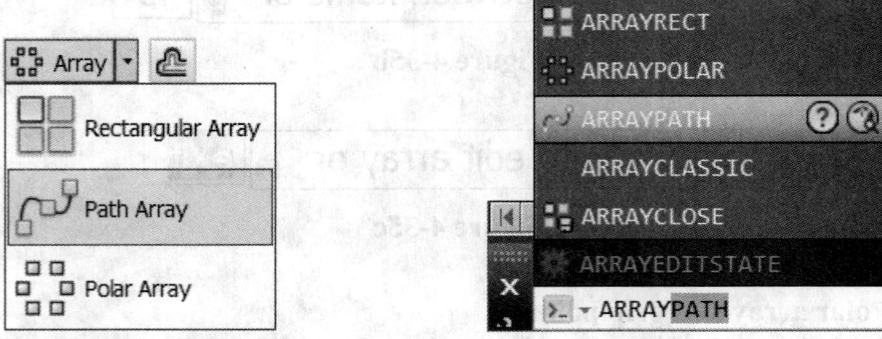

Figure 4-37a   **Figure 4-37b**

Example: Mark the survey station for a road survey as shown in Figure 4-38a.

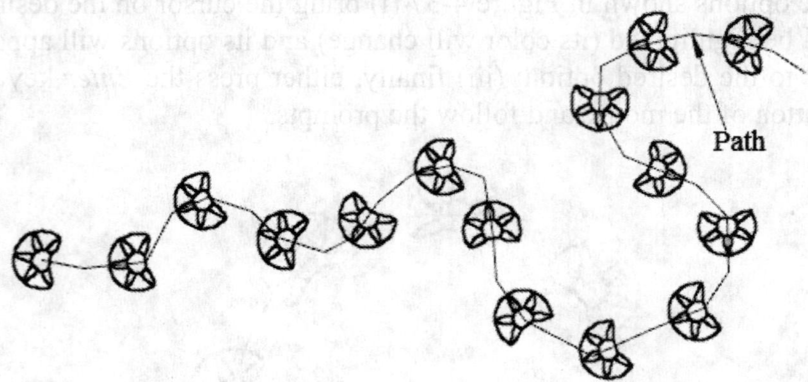

Figure 4-38a

- For the example, create the path and the basic element of the array at the beginning of the path, Figure 4-38b.

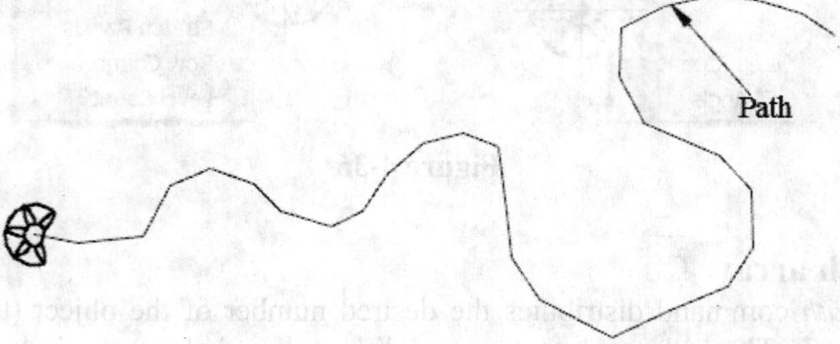

Figure 4-38b

- Activate the *Array Path* command.
- The activation of the command will open the object selection prompt, 4-38c.

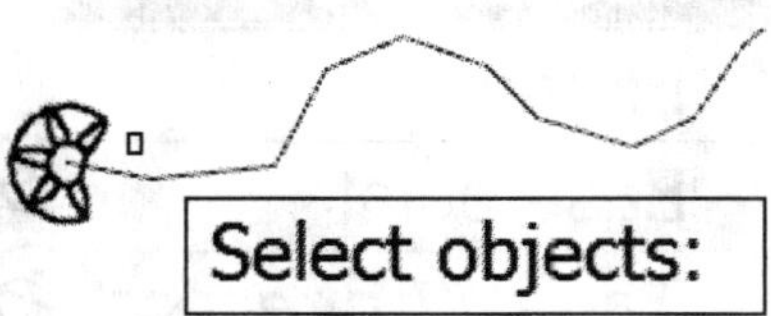

Figure 4-38c

- Select the desired objects and press the *Enter* key. The prompt shown in Figure 4-38d will appear on the screen.
- *Select path curve*, Figure 4-38d: Bring the cursor on the path and press the left button of the mouse. In the example, click the ployline labeled as Path.

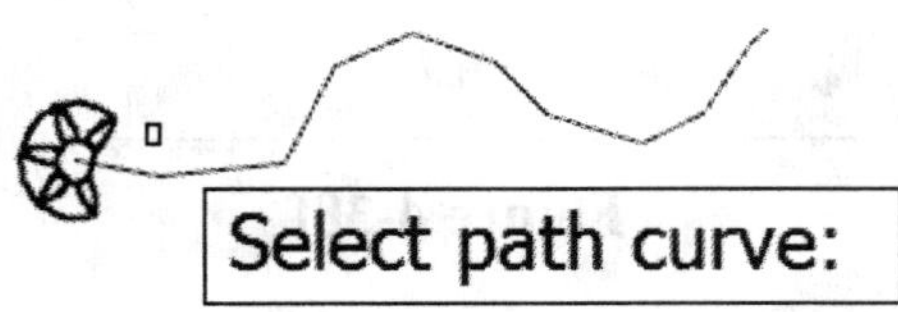

Figure 4-38d

- *Select grip to edit array or*, Figure 4-38e: If the user press the *Enter* key then the array shown in Figure 4-38e will appear on the screen; and will neglect the remaining bullets in this section. The array will be a single entity, that is, the elements of the array could not be manipulated independently. However, the user can edit the array using panels from the *Edit* tab. Array editing is discussed later.

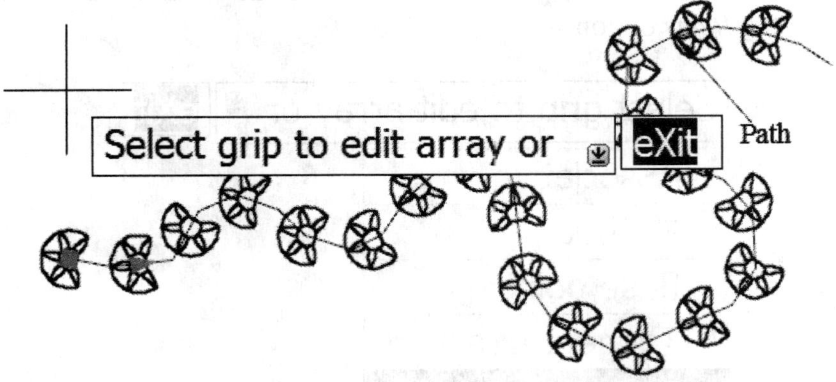

Figure 4-38e

- However, in this example, press the down arrow key of the keyboard to check the various options, Figure 4-38f. Click on the *ASsociative* option.
- *Create associative array*, Figure 4-39a: The *Yes* option will create the array as a single entity. The user may need to change one or more elements. However, for the current example, click on the *Yes* option.

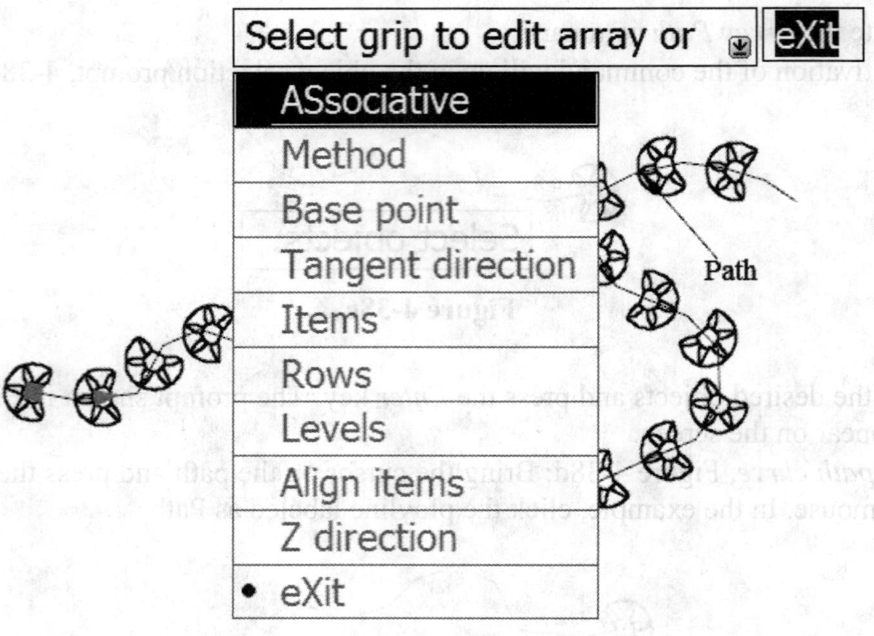

Figure 4-38f

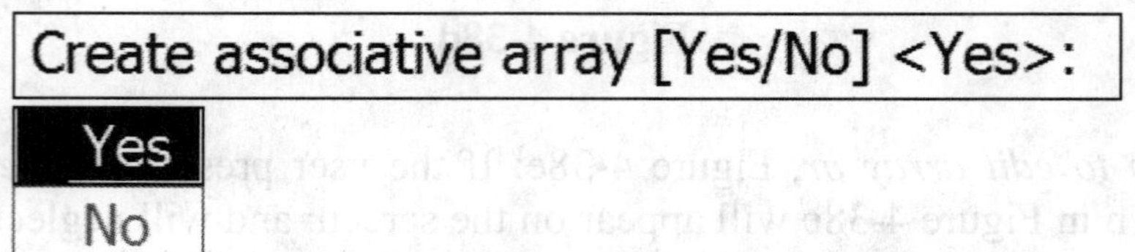

Figure 4-39a

- *Select grip to edit array or*, Figure 4-39b: Press the down arrow key of the keyboard and click on the *Items* option.

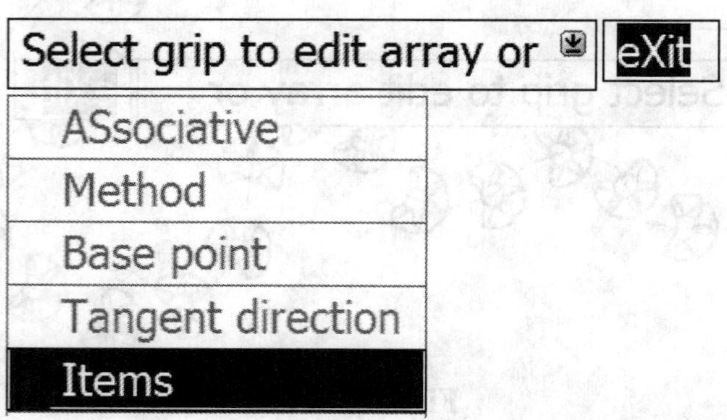

Figure 4-39b

- *Specify the distance between items along path or*, Figure 4-39c: Press the down arrow key of the keyboard and check the various options. However, in this example specify the distance to be 6. Press the *Enter* key.

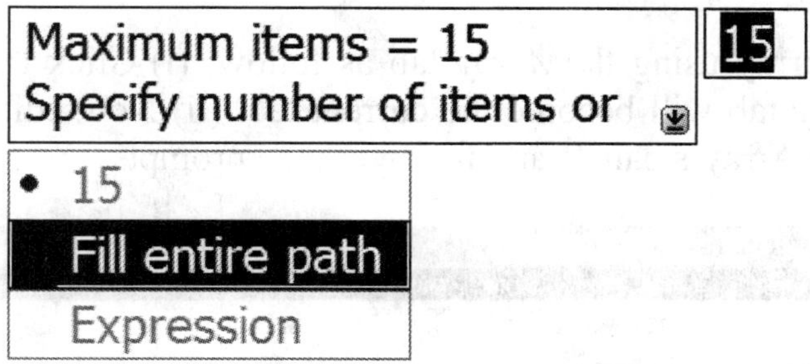

Figure 4-39c

- *Specify number of items or*, Figure 4-39d: The prompt will display the maximum number of items Figure 4-39d, calculated as the length of the path divided by distance between the two items.
- Press the down arrow key of the keyboard and check the various options. However, in this press the *Enter* key to accept the *Maximum number of items*.

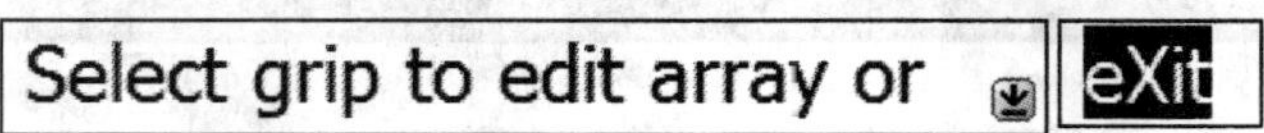

Figure 4-39d

- Press the *Enter* key again to complete the command. The resulting array is shown in Figure 4-38a.

Figure 4-39e

4.16.4. Path array and grip points

- Figure 4-39f shows the behavior of the grip point at the basic element of the array. These grip points can be used to move the array to a different location (*Move*) and the number of paths in the path array using *Row Count* option.

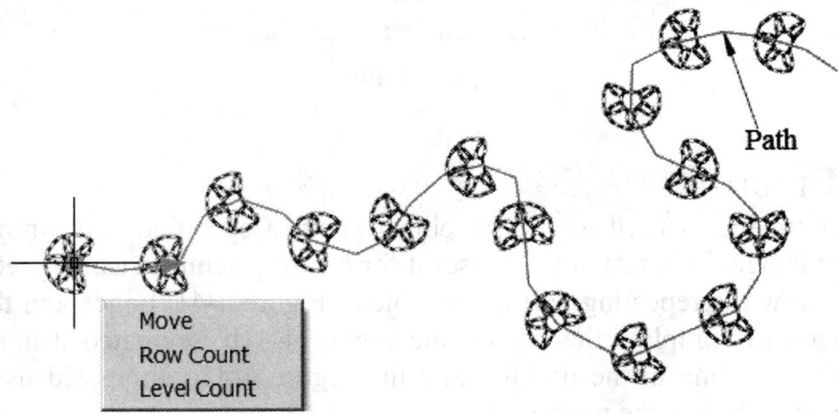

Figure 4-39f

- To use the options shown in Figure 4-40e (i) bring the cursor on the desired grip point and it will be highlighted (its color will change) and its options will appear; (ii) move the cursor to the desired option; (iii) finally, either press the *Enter* key or click with the left button of the mouse and follow the prompts.

4.16.5. Edit array

The arrays can be edited using the grip points as discussed earlier. However, a user can also edit an array using the *Array* tab. The Figure 4-40a shows the *Array* tab for the rectangular array; the Figure 4-40b shows the *Array* tab for the polar array; and the Figure 4-40c shows the *Array* tab for the path array.

A user can edit an array using the *Array* tab as follow: (i) Click the array needs to be edited then the *Array* tab will become the current tab. (ii) Now edit the array using the desired tool from the Array's panels and following the prompts.

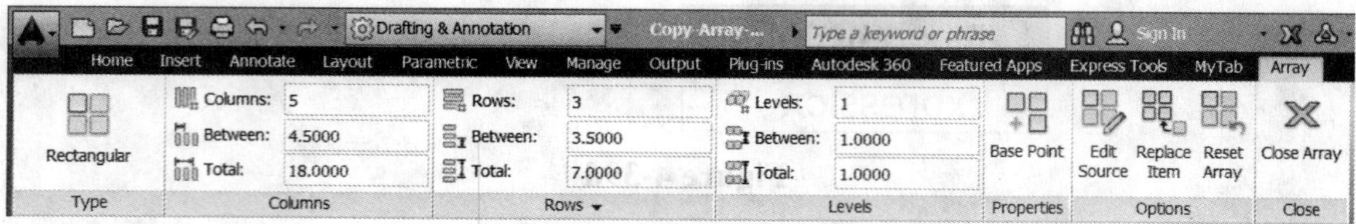

Figure 4-40a

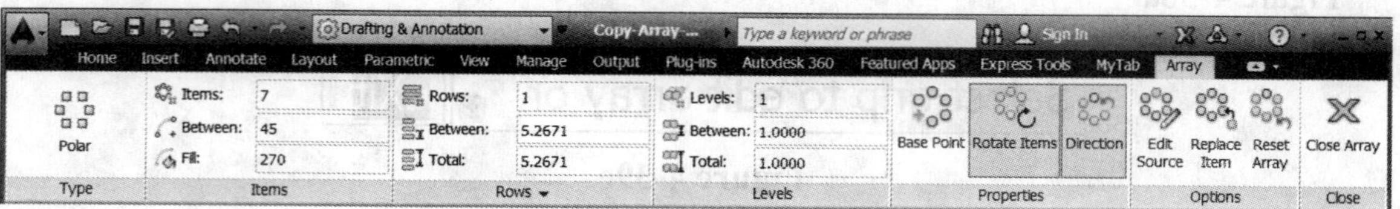

Figure 4-40b

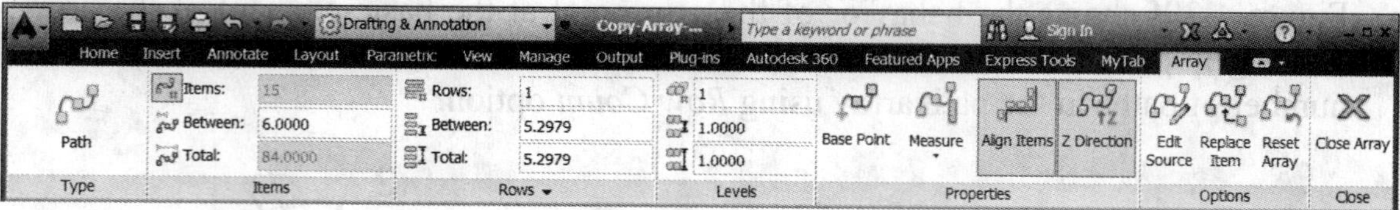

Figure 4-40c

4.17. Mirror

The *Mirror* command is used to flip an object about a specified axis (mirror line) to create a mirror image. This technique is useful for creating symmetrical objects. The user is required to draw the repeating part of the object (Figure 4-41a) once and then use the mirror command to complete the object; the Figure 4-41b is created using horizontal mirror line (the thin line in the middle) and the Figure 4-41c is created using vertical mirror line (the thin line in the middle).

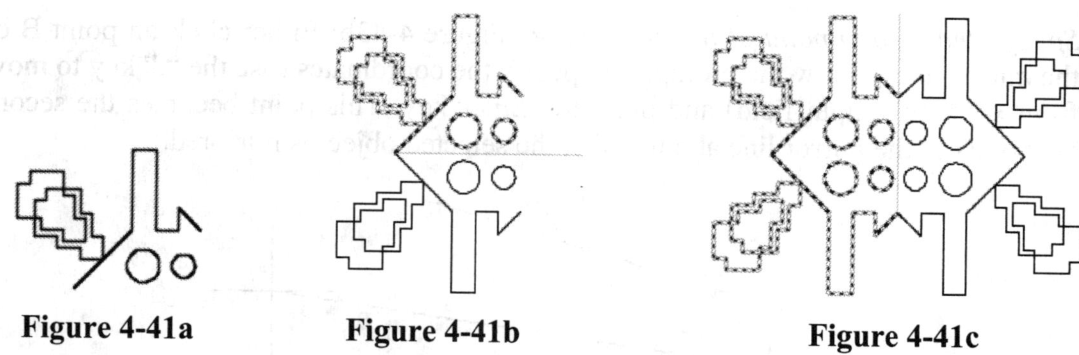

| Figure 4-41a | Figure 4-41b | Figure 4-41c |

Example: Create the mirror image of the object shown in Figure 4-42a as follow.

- The *Mirror* command is activated using one of the following procedures.
    1. Panel method: From the *Home* tab and *Modify* panel select the *Mirror* tool.
    2. Command line method: Type "mirror", "Mirror", or "MIRROR" in the command line and press the *Enter* key.

- The activation of the command leads to the object selection prompt, Figure 4-42b.

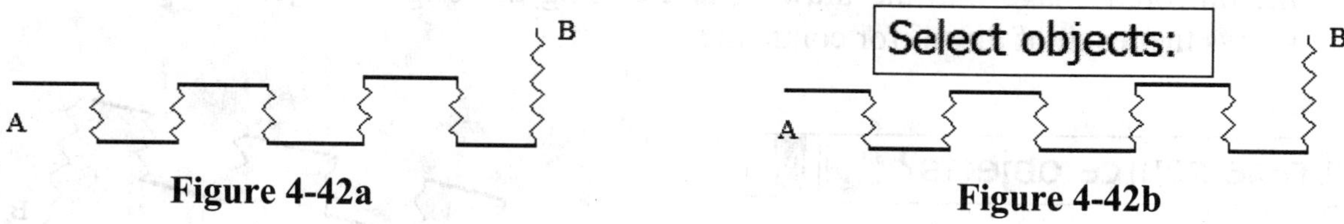

| Figure 4-42a | Figure 4-42b |

- *Select objects*: Object selection process is shown in Figure 4-42c and Figure 4-42d. Make the selection rectangle and press the *Enter* key to complete the object selection.

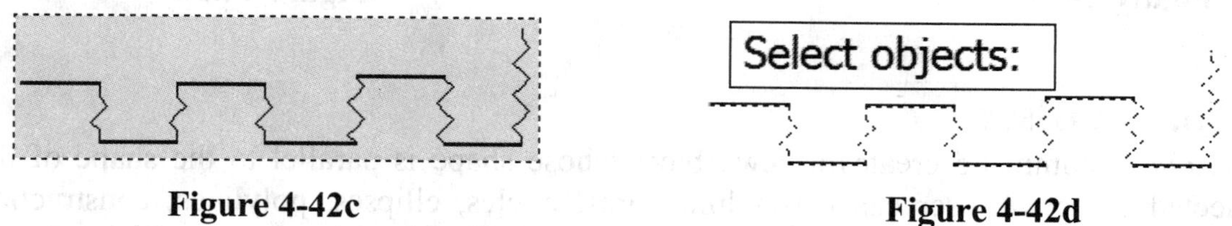

| Figure 4-42c | Figure 4-42d |

- *Specify the first point of the mirror line*, Figure 4-43a: Either click on point A on the mirror line (follow the prompt) or specify the coordinates (use the "," key to move from x's to y's input field) and press the *Enter* key. This point becomes the first endpoints of the mirror line about which the selected object is mirrored.

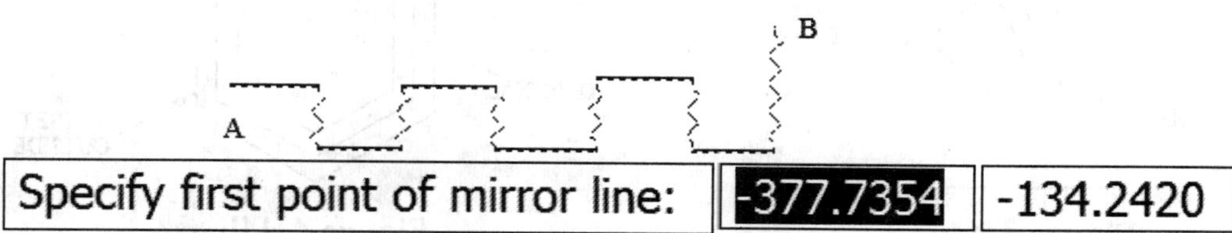

Figure 4-43a

- *Specify the second point of the mirror line*, Figure 4-43b: Either click on point B on the mirror line (follow the prompt) or specify the coordinates (use the "," key to move from x's to y's input field) and press the *Enter* key. This point becomes the second endpoints of the mirror line about which the selected object is mirrored.

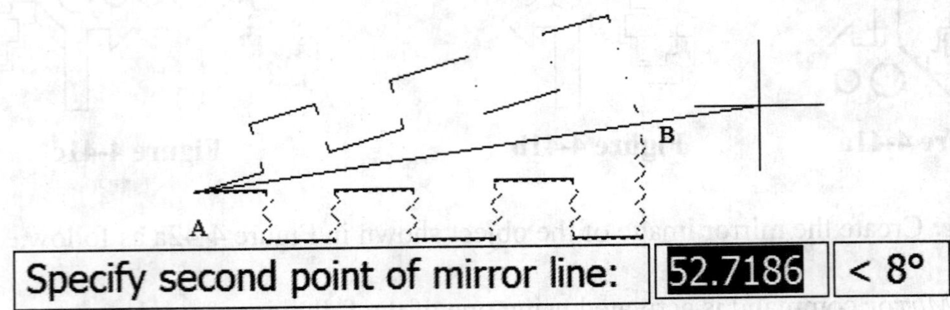

Figure 4-43b

- *Erase source objects? [Yes or No]*, Figure 4-43c: Type *n* and press the *Enter* key. The *No* option is used to flip the image by placing the mirrored image into the drawing and retaining the original objects. The *Yes* option is used to flip the image by placing the mirrored image into the drawing and erasing the original objects. Figure 4-31d shows the result of the mirror command.

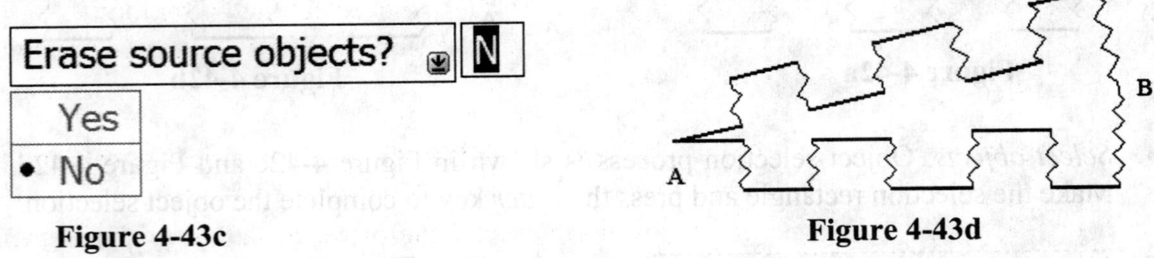

Figure 4-43c

Figure 4-43d

4.18.   Offset

The *Offset* command creates a new object whose shape is parallel to the shape of the selected object. A user can offset lines, arcs, circles, ellipses, polylines, construction lines, splines, and rays. Offsetting closed shapes and arcs will create smaller or larger shapes or arcs if offset is inside or outside, respectively (Figure 4-44a and Figure 4-44b).

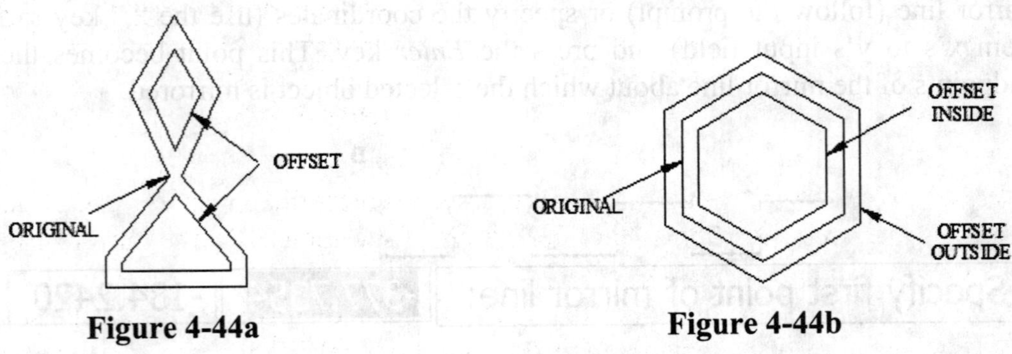

Figure 4-44a   **Figure 4-44b**

An efficient and precise drawing technique is to offset objects and then trim or extend their ends, Figure 4-44c. 2D polylines and splines are trimmed automatically when the offset shape is larger than that can be accommodated inside the polyline or spline, Figure 4-44a.

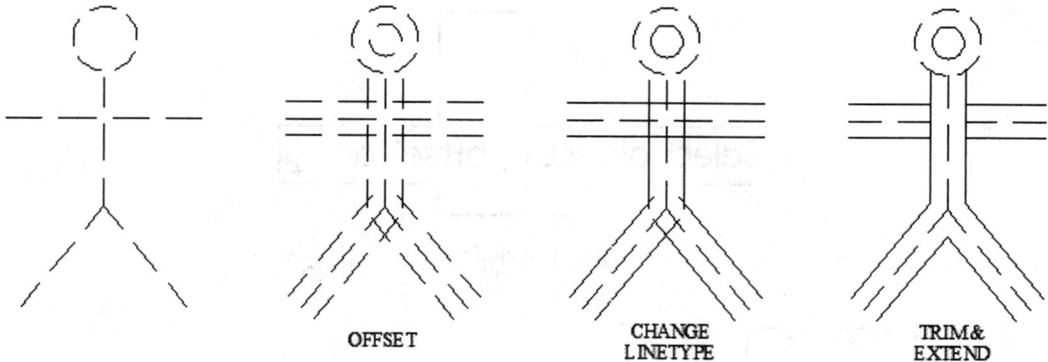

Figure 4-44c

Example: Create the door panel shown in Figure 4-45g, using the offset command.
- Open a new "acad" file.
- Draw a rectangle as shown in Figure 4-45a.
- The *Offset* command is activated using one of the following procedures.
    1. Panel method: From the *Home* tab and *Modify* panel select the *Offset* tool.
    2. Command line method: Type "offset", "Offset", or "OFFSET" in the command line and press the *Enter* key.

- The activation of the command leads to the offset distance specification prompt, Figure 4-45b.
- *Specify the offset distance or,* Figure 4-45b: Enter the offset distance and press the *Enter* key. In this example, the offset distance is 3.5. The prompt to select the object to offset (Figure 4-45c) appears.

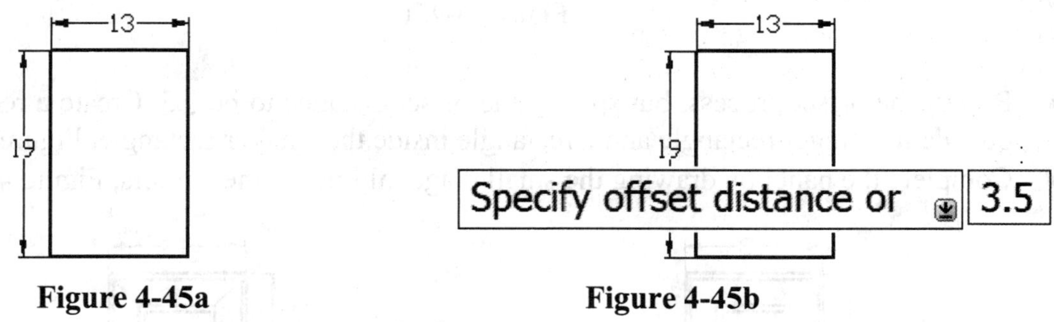

Figure 4-45a   **Figure 4-45b**

- *Select object to offset or,* Figure 4-45c: In order to select the object to offset, bring the cursor on the object and press the left button of the mouse. In the current example click on the rectangle, Figure 4-45d.
- *Specify point on side to offset or:* In Figure 4-45d, the cursor is outside the selected rectangle and the offset rectangle (shown as solid line) is shown, too. However, for

the example, click inside the original rectangle and a smaller rectangle will be created inside; and the prompt will go back to creating an offset, Figure 4-45e.

- Exit the command by pressing the *Esc* key.

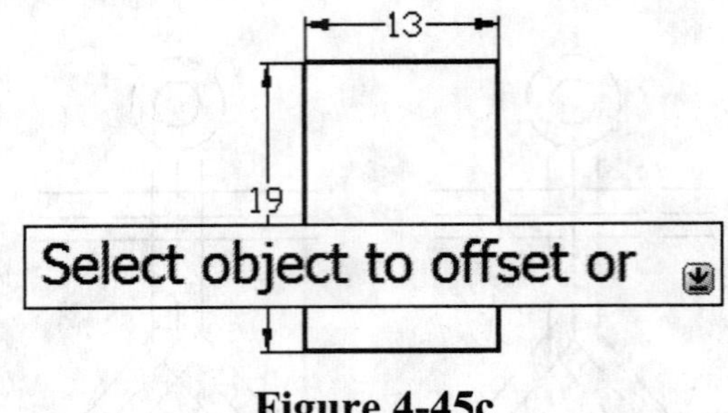

Figure 4-45c

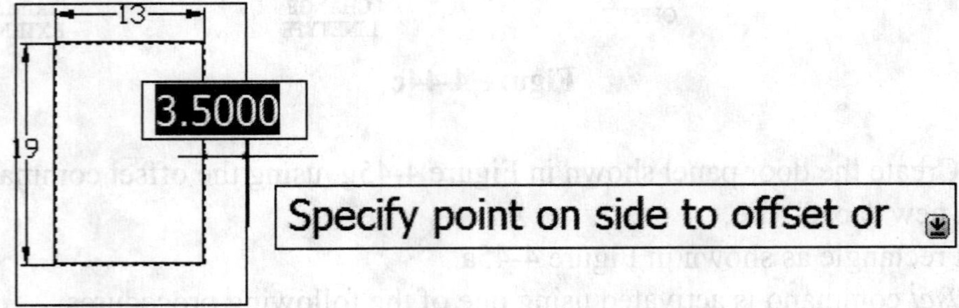

Figure 4-45d

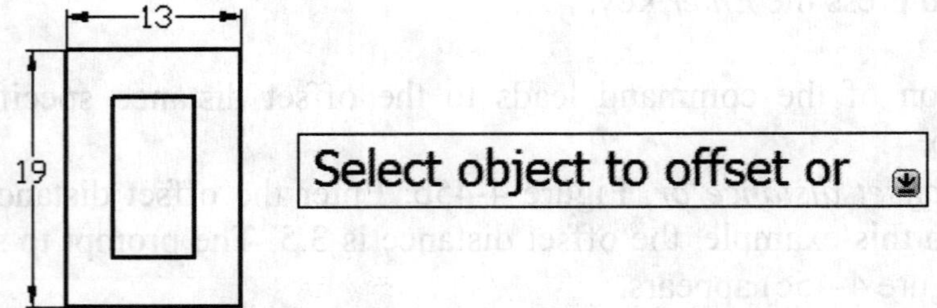

Figure 4-45e

- Repeat the offset process, but specify the offset distance to be 0.5. Create a rectangle outside the bigger rectangle and a rectangle inside the smaller rectangle, Figure 4-45f.
- Complete the panel by drawing the small diagonal lines at the corners, Figure 4-45g.

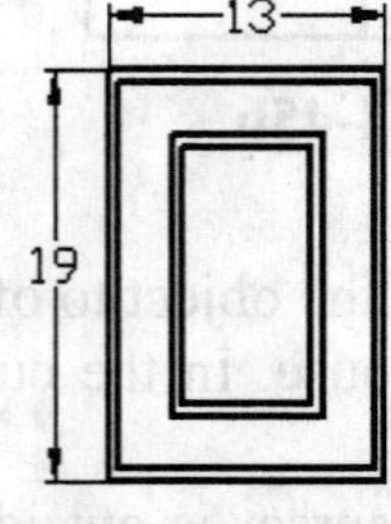

Figure 4-45f

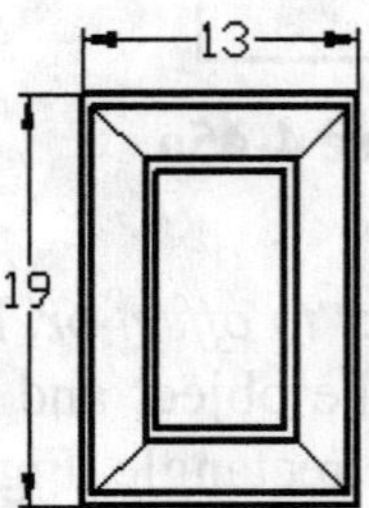

Figure 4-45g

4.19.   Move

The *Move* command is used to relocate an object in a specified direction and at a specified distance from the original position. The user must activate the object snap command to move the objects with precision.

Example: Move the object shown in Figure 4-46a to its new location using the *Move* command.
- Open a new "acad" file.
- Draw the objects shown in Figure 4-46a.
- The *Move* command is activated using one of the following procedures.
    1. Panel method: From the *Home* tab and *Modify* panel select the *Move* tool.
    2. Command line method: Type "move", "Move", or "MOVE" in the command line and press the *Enter* key.

- The activation of the command leads to the object selection prompt. Use one of the object selection methods discussed earlier. Finally, press the *Enter* key to complete the object selection. The prompt shown in Figure 4-46b will appear.

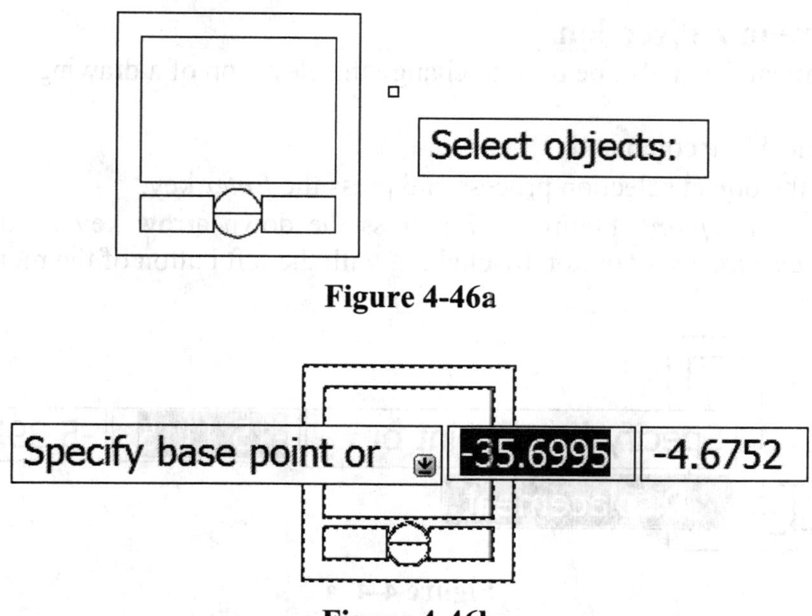

Figure 4-46a

Figure 4-46b

4.19.1. Move in xy-plane
- *Specify the base point*, Figure 4-46b: As a rule of thumb, the base point should be a point such that the object can be relocated easily and precisely at its new location. Either click on a point in the object or specify the coordinates (use the "," key to move from x's to y's input field) and press the *Enter* key. In the example, the lower left corner of the object is selected as the base point, Figure 4-46c.
- *Specify the second point*, Figure 4-46c: The second point is the new location of the object. Either click at the new location or specify its coordinates (use the "," key to move from x's to y's input field) and press the *Enter* key. The coordinates of the

second point are relative coordinates with respect to the base point. This will complete the process of moving the object from the original location to the new location and will exit the command, too.

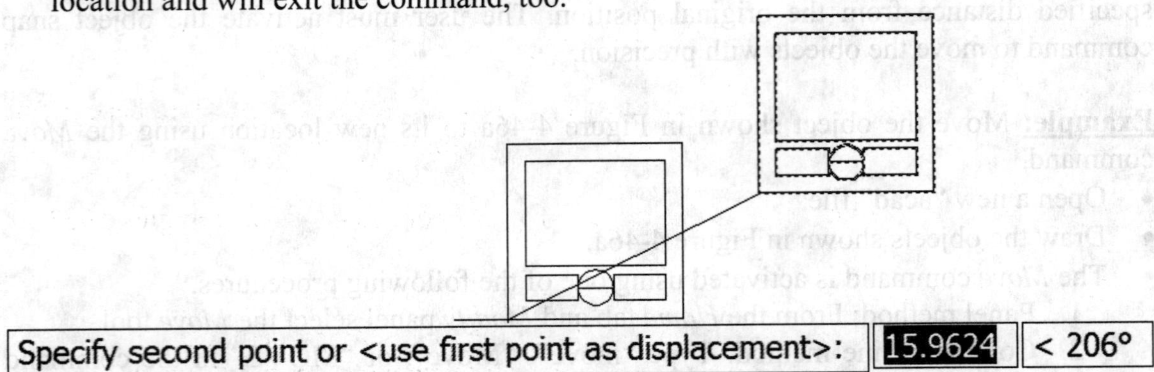

Figure 4-46c

- The distance from the original to the new location is determined by the distance and direction between the base and second points.

4.19.2. Move in z-direction
The *Move* command can also be used to change the elevation of a drawing.

- Activate the *Move* command.
- Complete the object selection process and press the *Enter* key.
- *Specify the base point*, Figure 4-47a: Press the down arrow key on the keyboard. Select the *Displacement* option by clicking with the left button of the mouse.

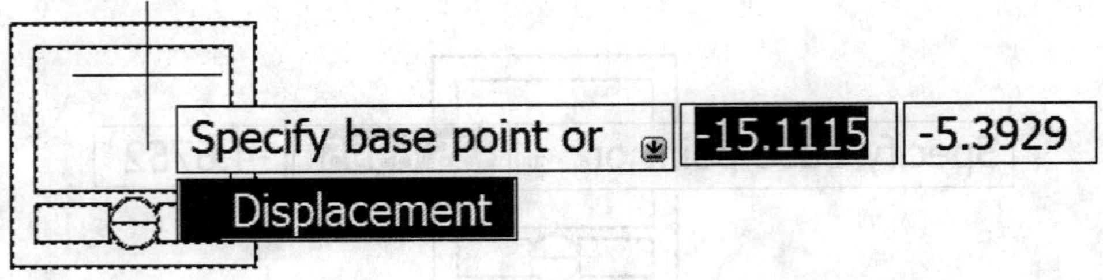

Figure 4-47a

- *Specify displacement*, Figure 4-47b: Specify the coordinates, use the "," key to move from one input field to the next, and press the *Enter* key. In the example, for the vertical displacement x and y are set to "0" and 75 is entered for the z coordinate.

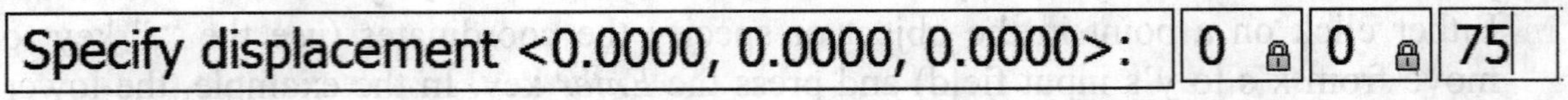

Figure 4-47b

- The base point's elevation (and of every point's elevation) is incremented by 75. Initially, the elevation was zero. To check the elevation (or Z value) of the base point.

(i) Activate the *Line* command, (ii) bring the cursor on the base point, and (iii) check the coordinate in the lower left corner of the workspace.

4.20.   Rotate

The *Rotate* command is used to rotate objects in a drawing around a specified base point. The user must activate object snaps to rotate objects with precision.

Example: Rotate the object shown in Figure 4-48a at a counter-clockwise angle of 75°.
- Open a new "acad" file.
- Draw the basic objects shown in Figure 4-48a.
- The *Rotate* command is activated using one of the following procedures.
    1. Panel method: From the *Home* tab and *Modify* panel select the *Rotate* tool.
    2. Command line method: Type "rotate", "Rotate", or "ROTATE" in the command line and press the *Enter* key.

- The activation of the command leads to the object selection prompt, Figure 4-48a. Select the object and press the *Enter* key to complete the object selection.

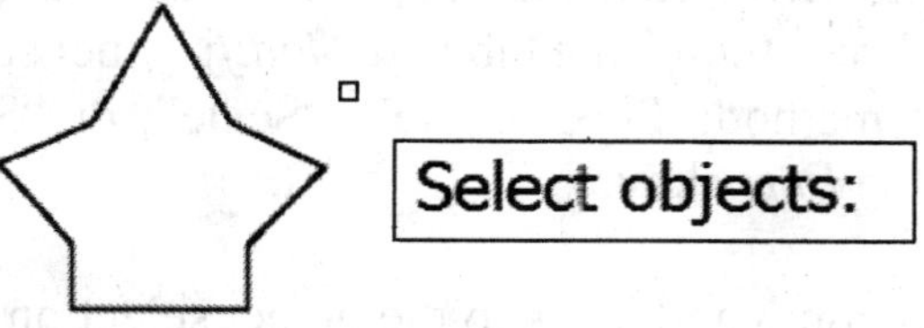

Figure 4-48a

- *Specify the base point*, Figure 4-48b: In *Rotate* command, the base point is the pivot to rotate the object. Either click on a point in the object or specify the coordinates (use the "," key to move from x's to y's input field) and press the *Enter* key. In this example, the upper point of the object is chosen as a base point, Figure 4-48b.

Figure 4-48a

- *Specify rotation angle*, Figure 4-48c: Either click at the desired orientation or specify its value and press the *Enter* key. Positive angles will rotate the object counterclockwise and the negative angles will rotate the object clockwise. In this example, the rotation angle is set to 75, Figure 4-48c.
- Figure 4.48d shows the rotated object.

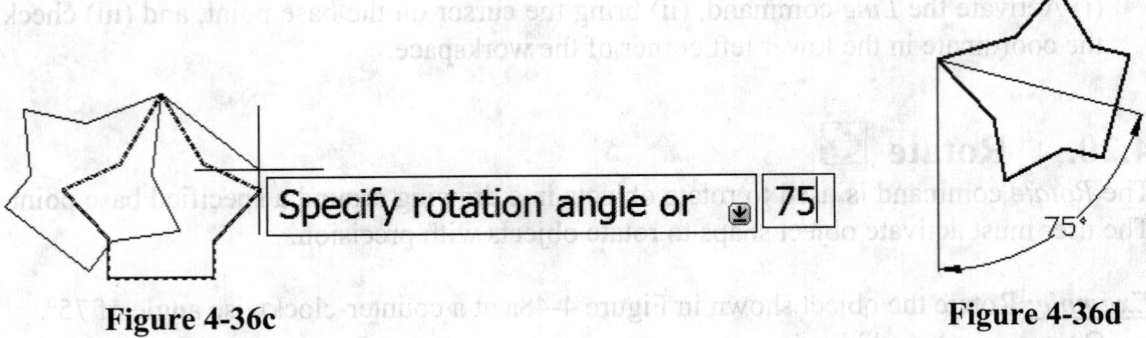

<table>
<tr><td align="center">Figure 4-36c</td><td align="center">Figure 4-36d</td></tr>
</table>

4.21.   Scale

The *Scale* command is used to enlarge or shrink the object.

Example: Reduce the object shown in Figure 4-49a by 50%.

- Open a new "acad" file.
- Draw the objects shown in Figure 4-49a.
- The *Scale* command is activated using one of the following procedures.
    1. Panel method: From the *Home* tab and *Modify* panel select the *Scale* tool.
    2. Command line method: Type "scale", "Scale", or "SCALE" in the command line and press the *Enter* key.

- The activation of this command leads to the object selection prompt, Figure 4-49a.

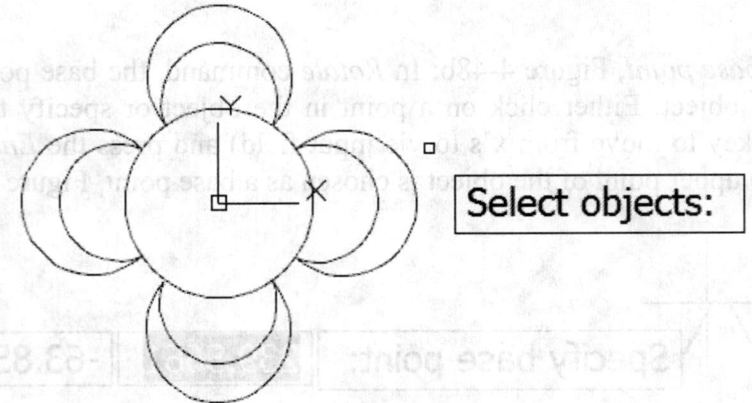

Figure 4-49a

- Select the object to scale and press the *Enter* key to complete the object selection, Figure 4-39b.
- *Specify the base point*, Figure 4-49b: When an object is scaled up/down; every point in the object will move from its current location except on point. For the *Scale* command, the base point should be the point that stays at its current location. Either, click on a point in the object or specify the coordinates and press the *Enter* key. In

this example, the center of the full circle is chosen as the base point, Therefore, just click at the center point. The base point can be outside the object, too.

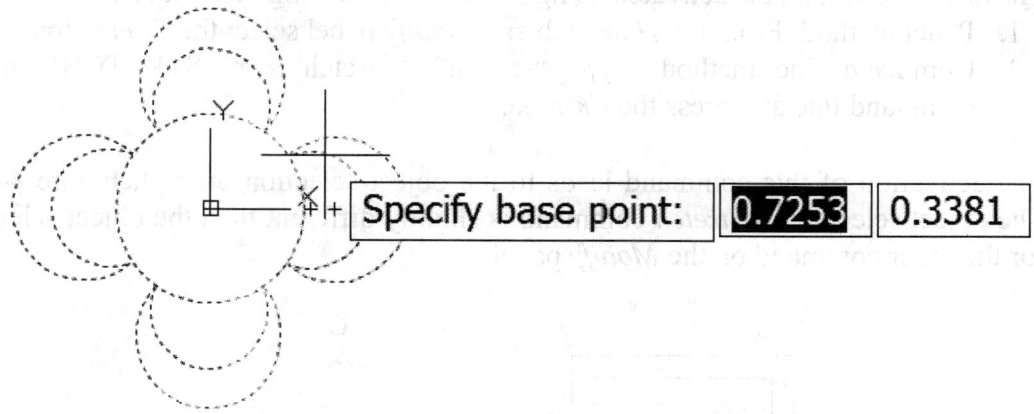

Figure 4-49b

- *Specify scale factor*, Figure 4-49c: Enter the desired value and press the *Enter* key. In this example, the goal is to shrink the content of the drawing. Therefore, the scale factor of 0.5 (less than 1) is used.

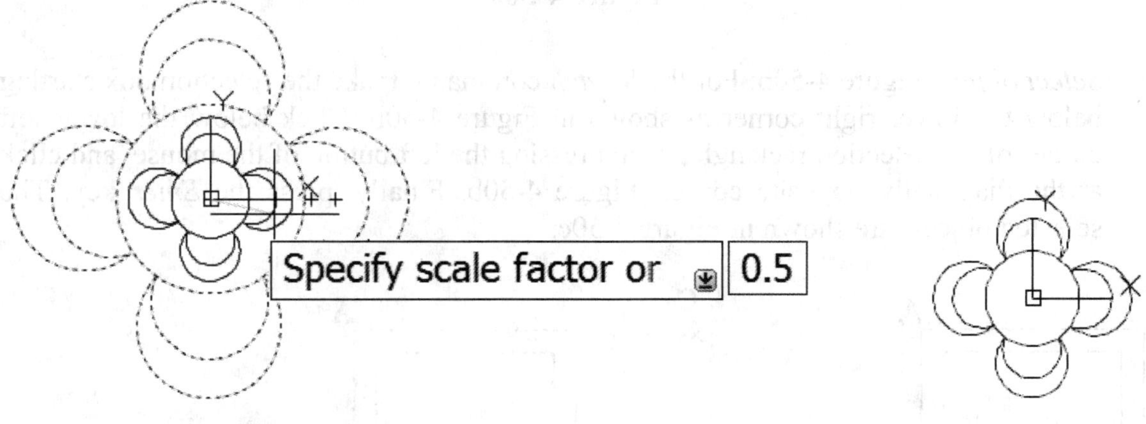

Figure 4-49c   **Figure 4-49d**

- Every object in the drawing is now 50% smaller, Figure 4-49d.
- Scaling is relative to the world coordinate system's origin and the location of the drawing origin will remain at the WCS origin.
- Repeat the process with the scale factor of 1.5. The size of every object in the drawing will increase by 50%.

4.22.   Stretch

The *Stretch* command is used to lengthen or shorten an object.

Example: Stretch the side AB to the line created by joining points C and D for the objects shown in Figure 4-50a.

- Open a new "acad" file.
- Draw the objects shown in Figure 4-50a.
- The *Stretch* command is activated using one of the following procedures.
  1. Panel method: From the *Home* tab and *Modify* panel select the *Stretch* tool.
  2. Command line method: Type "stretch", "Stretch", or "STRETCH" in the command line and press the *Enter* key.

- The activation of this command leads to the object selection prompt, Figure 4-50a. The object selection in *Stretch* command is slightly different then the object selection for the other command on the *Modify* panel.

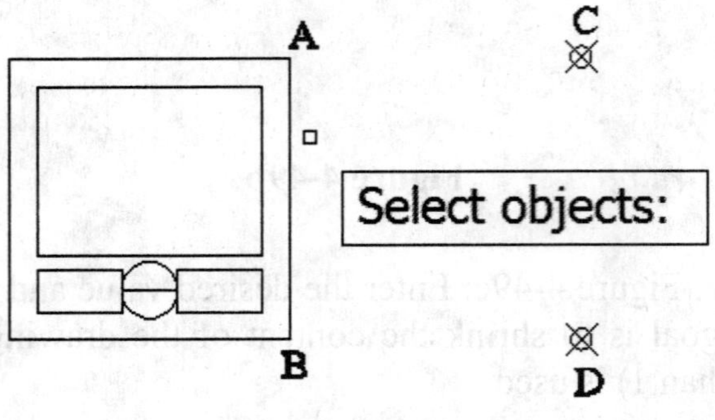

Figure 4-50a

- *Select object*, Figure 4-50b: For the *Stretch* command, make the selection box starting below the lower right corner as shown in Figure 4-50b. Click below the lower left corner of the selection rectangle, keep pressing the left button of the mouse, and click at the diagonally opposite corner, Figure 4-50b. Finally, press the *Enter* key. The selected objects are shown in Figure 4-50c.

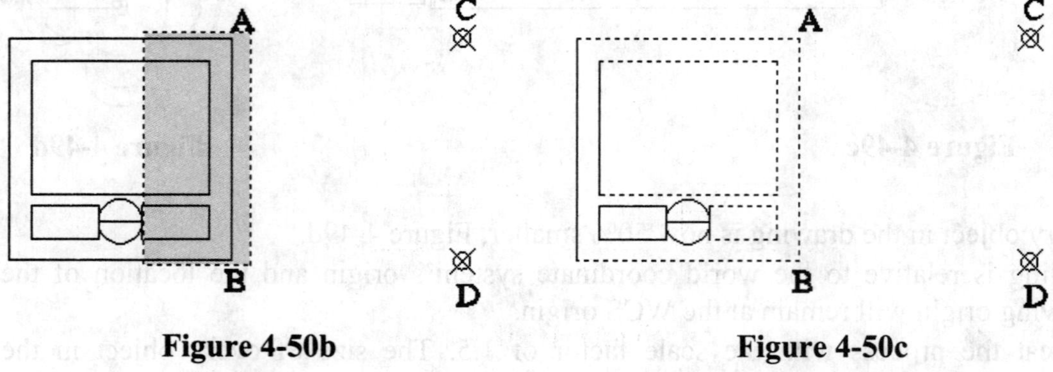

Figure 4-50b   **Figure 4-50c**

- *Specify the base point*, Figure 4-50d: For the *Stretch* command, the base point should be the point that needs to be stretched to the new location. Either click on the point or specify its coordinates and press the *Enter* key. In this example, click at point B.

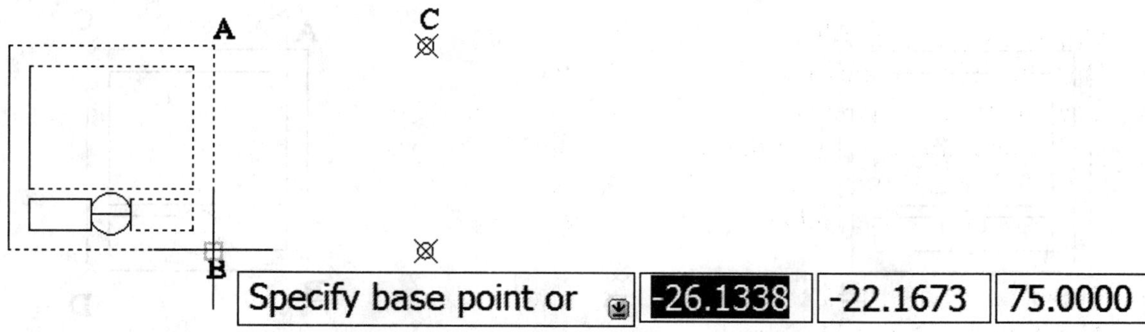

Figure 4-50d

- *Specify second point*, Figure 4-50e: For the *Stretch* command, the second point is the new location of the base point. Either click on the point or specify its coordinates and press the *Enter* key. In this example, click at point D.

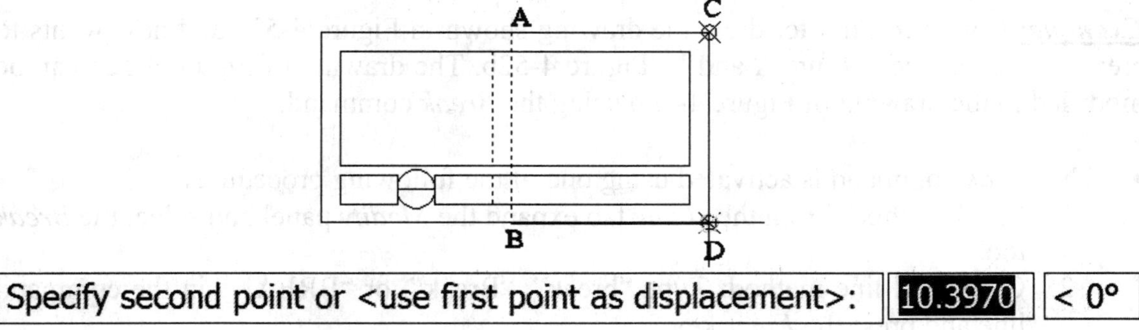

Figure 4-50e

- The side AB is stretched to the line created by joining points C and D, Figure 4-50f.

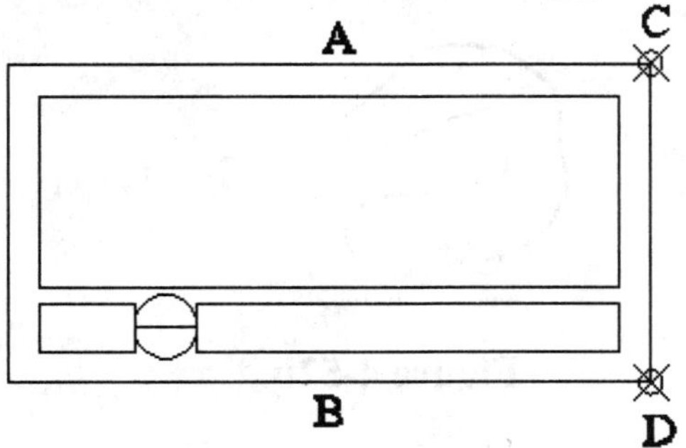

Figure 4-50f

- For the *Stretch* command, if the object is completely inside the selection rectangle, Figure 4-51a, then the object will simply move from the initial location B (clicked as base point) to new location D clicked as second point, Figure 4-51b.

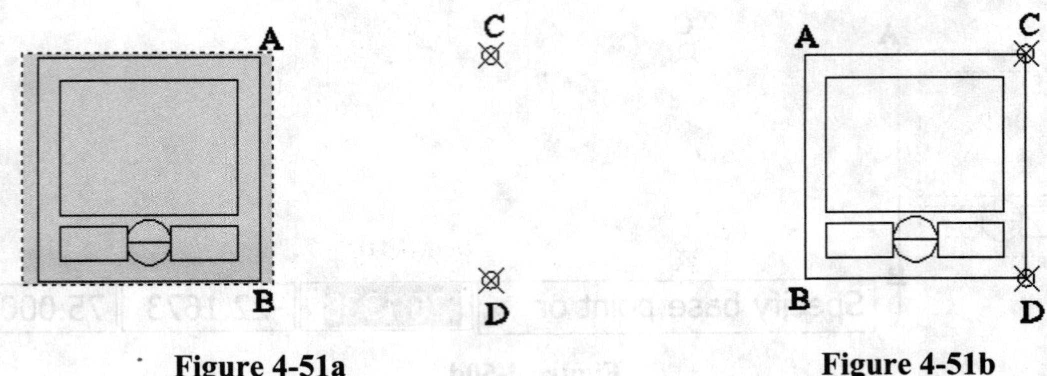

Figure 4-51a   Figure 4-51b

4.23.   Break

The *Break* command is used to create a gap or open space in the given object by specifying two points on the object.

Example: Consider a drafter drew the drawing shown in Figure 4-52a and now wants to create a gap between points A and B, Figure 4-52b. The drawing of Figure 4-52a can be modified to the drawing of Figure 4-52b using the *Break* command.

- The *Break* command is activated using one of the following procedures.
  1. Panel method: From the *Home* tab expand the *Modify* panel and select the *Break* tool.
  2. Command line method: Type "break", "Break", or "BREAK" in the command line and press the *Enter* key.

- The activation of the command will display the prompt to select the object, Figure 4-53a.

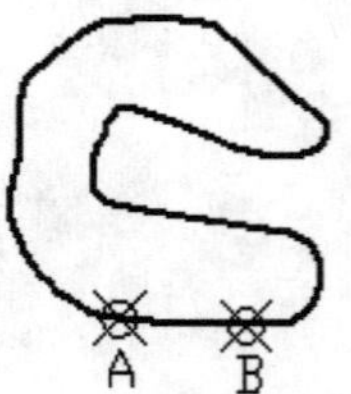

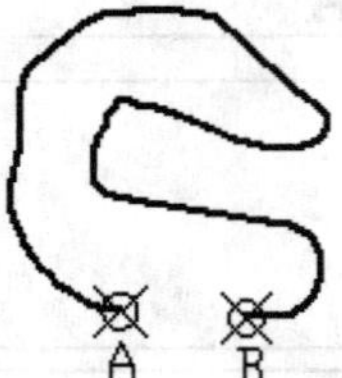

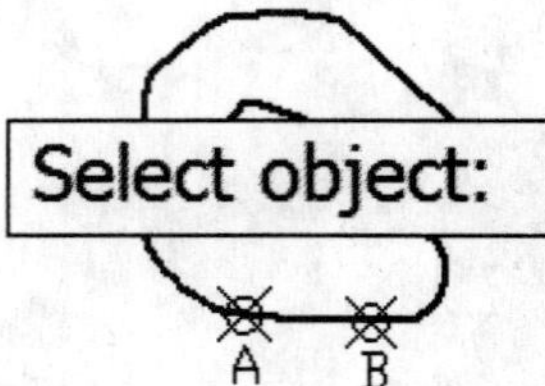

Figure 4-52a   Figure 4-52b   Figure 4-53a

- *Select object*, Figure 4-53a: Bring the cursor on the object and click with the left button of the mouse. The prompt shown in Figure 4-53b will appear.
- *Specify second break point or*, Figure 4-53b: Press the down arrow key on the keyboard to display the available options. Select the First point option. The prompt shown in Figure 4-53c will appear.
- *Specify first break point or*, Figure 4-53c: Either click at the desired point or specify its coordinate and press the *Enter* key. In the example, click at point A.

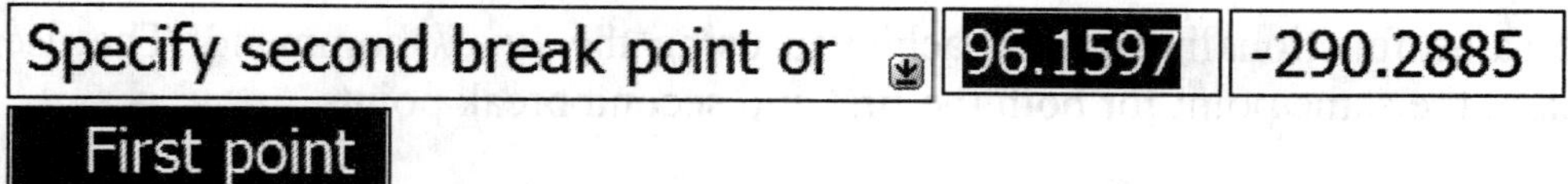

Figure 4-53b

Specify first break point: 96.0916   -290.9006

Figure 4-53c

- *Specify second break point or*, Figure 4-53d: Either click at the desired point or specify its coordinate and press the *Enter* key. In the example, click at point B.
- The gap between point A and B is created as shown in Figure 4-52b.

Specify second break point: 101.8776   -291.0366

Figure 4-53d

- The same effect can also be created by (i) drawing two temporary lines, Figure 4-54a; (ii) using the *Trim* command trim the object between the two lines, Figure 4-54b; (iii) delete the lines using *Erase* command, Figure 4-54c.

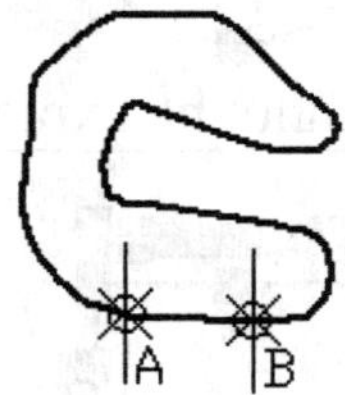

Figure 4-54a

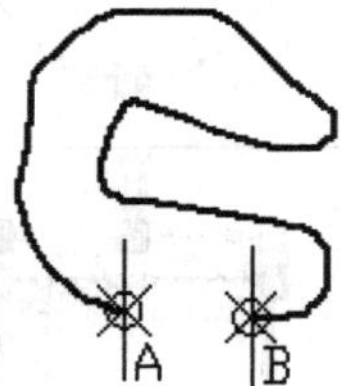

Figure 4-54b

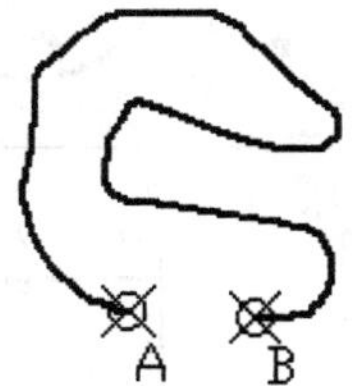

Figure 4-54c

4.24.   Break at a point

The *Break at a point* command is used to break objects (line, polyline, and arcs) without creating a gap or open space in the object.

- The *Break at a point* command is activated using one of the following procedures.
  1. Panel method: From the *Home* tab expand the *Modify* panel and select the *Break at a point* tool.
  2. Command line method: Type "break", "Break", or "BREAK" in the command line and press the *Enter* key.

- The activation of the command will display the prompt to select the object.
- After the object selection, click at the desired point. The objet will be broken without creating a gap.

- The same functionality can be achieved using the *Break* command. The user must click at the same point for both the first and second break points.

4.25.   Explode

The *Explode* command is used to break a compound object into its basic component objects. To practice the command, create a rectangle, pentagon, circle, a closed polyline, and a dimension using the *Rectangle*, *Polygon*, *Circle*, *Polyline*, and *dimension* commands, respectively, as shown in the left column of Table #1. Only one side of the rectangle is dimensioned.

- The *Explode* command is activated using one of the following procedures.
    1. Panel method: From the *Home* tab and *Modify* panel select the *Explode* tool.
    2. Command line method: Type "explode", "Explode", or "EXPLODE" in the command line and press the *Enter* key.

Table #1: Explode command demonstration

Object	Original	Exploded
		Circle cannot be exploded

- The activation of the command leads to the object selection prompt. Select the object (bring the cursor on the rectangle) and press the *Enter* key. The object will be broken into its basic component.
- The *Explode* command will not change the appearance of the object, left column of the Table #1. However, if the original and the exploded object are selected, then their grip points will be different. The middle column of the Table #1 shows the original objects. Whereas, the right column of the Table #1 shows the exploded objects.
- A circle cannot be exploded.
- The rectangle, pentagon, and the closed polyline are broken into line segment.
- The dimension is exploded into extension and dimension lines, the text, and the arrows.

4.26.   Join

The *Join* command is used to connect multiple linear or curved objects to create a single object. The command can be used to connect lines, circular arcs, elliptical arcs, polylines, spline, and their combination. However, the command cannot be used to connect close objects. The order of the object selection will affect the resultant object.

- The *Join* command is activated using one of the following procedures.
    1. Panel method: From the *Home* tab expand the *Modify* panel and select the *Join* tool.
    2. Command line method: Type "join", "Join", or "JOIN" in the command line and press the *Enter* key.

- The activation of the command leads to the source object selection prompt.
- *Select source object*, Figure 4-55a: (i) Click the source object with the left button of the mouse. In this example, click on the line labeled as C. (ii) Press the *Enter* key.

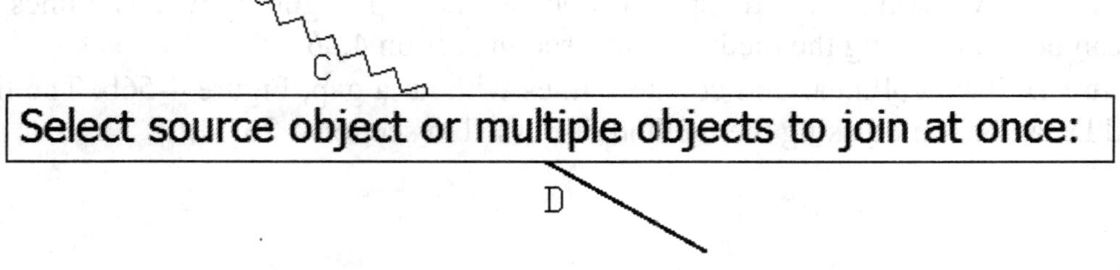

Figure 4-55a

- *Select object to join*, Figure 4-55b: (i) Click the object to be connected with the left button of the mouse. In this example, click on the line labeled as D. (ii) Press the *Enter* key.
- The joined object is shown in Figure 4-55c.

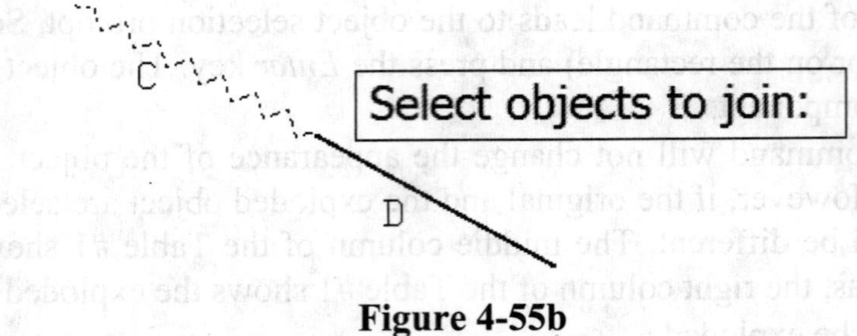

Figure 4-55b

- In the *Join* command the order of the object selection will affect the resultant object. In Figure 4-55c, the line labeled as C is selected as the source object. In Figure 4-55d, the line labeled as D is selected as the source object.

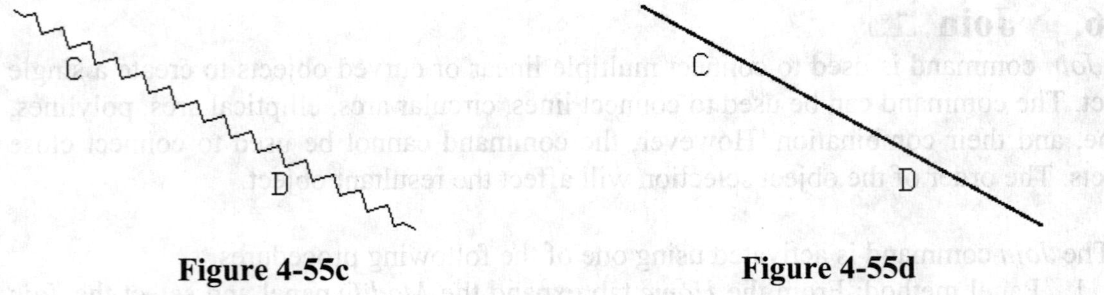

Figure 4-55c   **Figure 4-55d**

4.26.1.1.   Lines
The *Join* command can connect non-intersecting collinear and coplanar lines with or without gaps. The collinear lines are in the same direction. The coplanar lines are in the same plane, that is, they have the same elevation. The resultant object will be a single line.

Example: Connect A to B, C to D, and E to F.
- **A and B**: Two collinear and coplanar lines with a gap, Figure 4-56a. The lines A and B can be joined using the method discussed in section 4.26.
- **C and D**: Two collinear and coplanar lines without a gap, Figure 4-56b. The lines C and D can be joined using the method discussed in section 4.26.

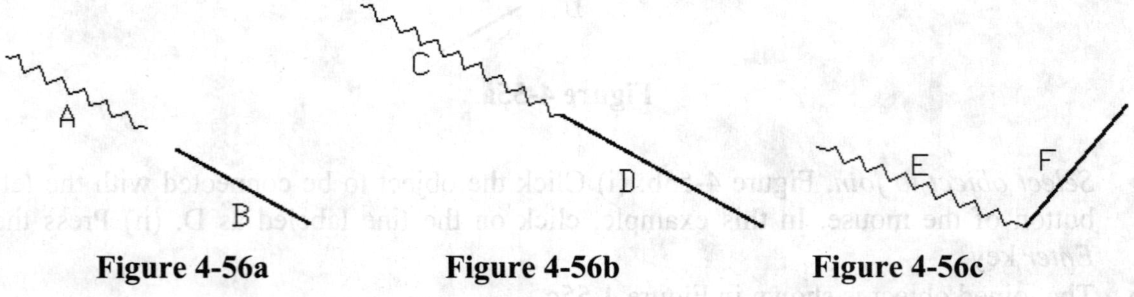

Figure 4-56a   **Figure 4-56b**   **Figure 4-56c**

- **E and F**: Two coplanar lines without a gap, Figure 4-56c. The lines E and F can be joined as follow: (i) activate the *Join* command; (ii) click on E; (iii) click on F; and (iv) finally, press the *Enter* key.

4.26.1.2.   Circular arc

The *Join* command can connect circular arcs with the same radius and same center point. The resultant object will be an arc or a circle. The arcs will be connected in counterclockwise direction starting from the source arc.

Example: Connect the arcs A to B and C to D, Figure 4-57a. The figure shows four arcs. Arcs labeled as A, B, and C has the same radius. Although, the arc D has the same center but its radius is different. Therefore, it cannot be joined to any arc of the figure.

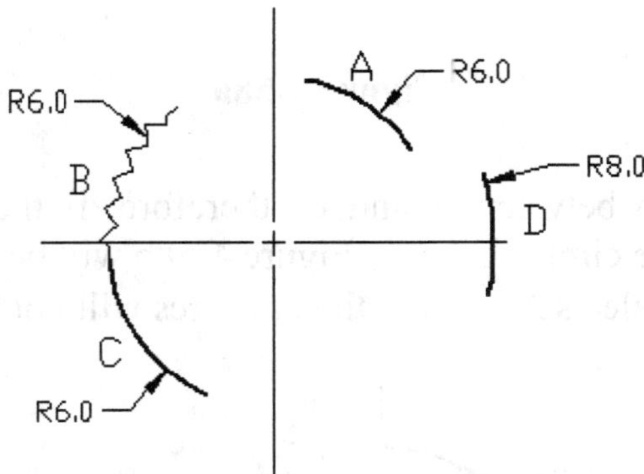

Figure 4-57a

- **A and B**: Figure 4-57a, the arcs A and B can be joined using the method discussed in section 4.26. In this figure, A is the source arc. Arcs are connected in the counterclockwise direction starting from the source arc, Figure 4-57b.
- **B and A**: Figure 4-57a, the arcs B and A can be joined using the method discussed in section 4.26. In this figure, B is the source arc. Arcs are connected in the counterclockwise direction starting from the source arc, Figure 4-57c.

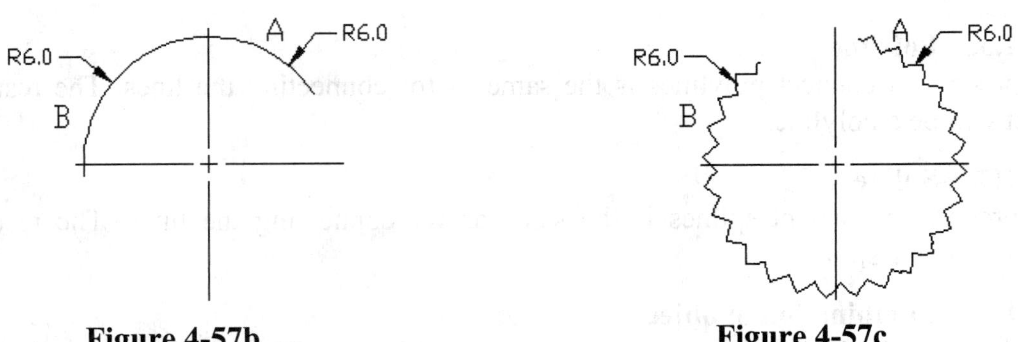

Figure 4-57b   **Figure 4-57c**

- In Figure 4-57a, arcs A, B, and C have the same radius and same center. The three arcs can be connected as follow: (i) activate the *Join* command; (ii) click on A (source arc); (iii) click on B; (iv) click on C; and (v) finally, press the *Enter* key.
- In Figure 4-57a, the user can also connect the arcs by setting B as the source arc.
- However, in Figure 4-57a, if the user desire to connect the arcs by setting C as the source arc then after selecting C, A, and B and pressing the *Enter* key, the prompt shown in Figure 4-58a will appear.

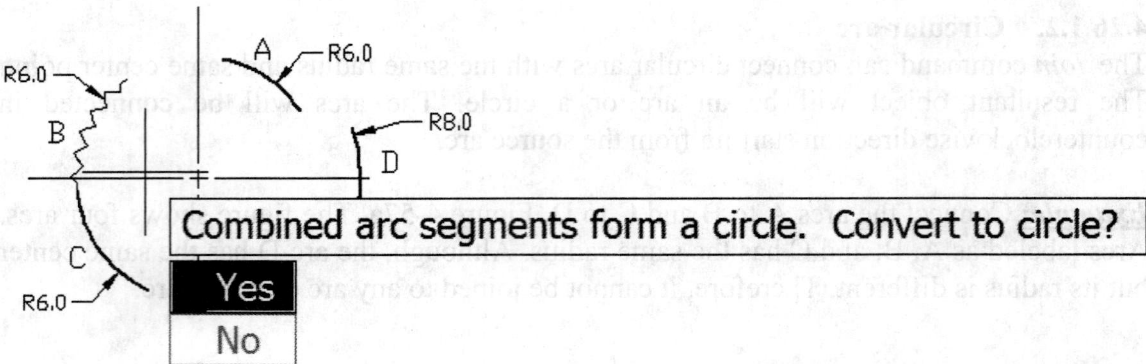

Figure 4-58a

- Since there is no gap between B and C, therefore, if the user selects *Yes* option (Figure 4-58a) then the circle shown in Figure 4-58b will be created.
- However, if the user selects *No* option then the arcs will not be connected.

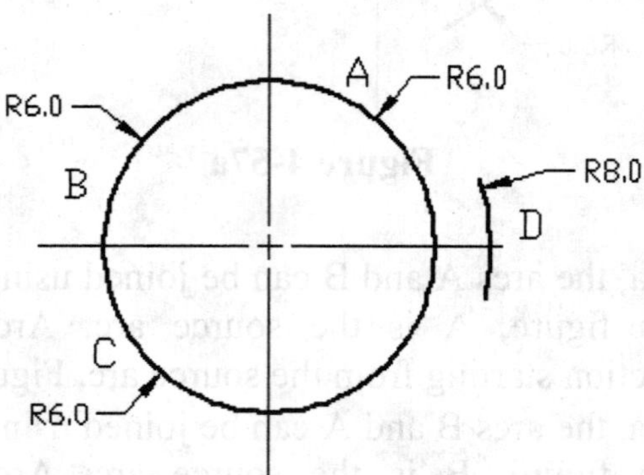

Figure 4-58b

4.26.1.3. Polyline
The process to connect polylines is the same as for connecting the lines. The resultant object will be a polyline.

4.26.1.4. Spline
The process to connect splines is the same as for connecting the lines. The resultant object will be a spline.

4.26.1.5. Combination of objects
The *Join* command can be used to connect combination of arcs, lines, polyline, and spline, too. However, the various objects should be contiguous, that is, one object will end at a point where the next object will start. The Figure 4-59 shows a drawing composed of combination of objects.

- Join line and arc: The resultant object will be a polyline.
- Join polyline and arc: The resultant object will be a polyline.
- Join line, polyline, and arc: Resultant object will be a polyline.
- Join spline and arc: The resultant object will be a spline.

- Join line, spline, and arc: The resultant object will be a spline.
- Join line, polyline, spline, and arc: The resultant object will be a spline.

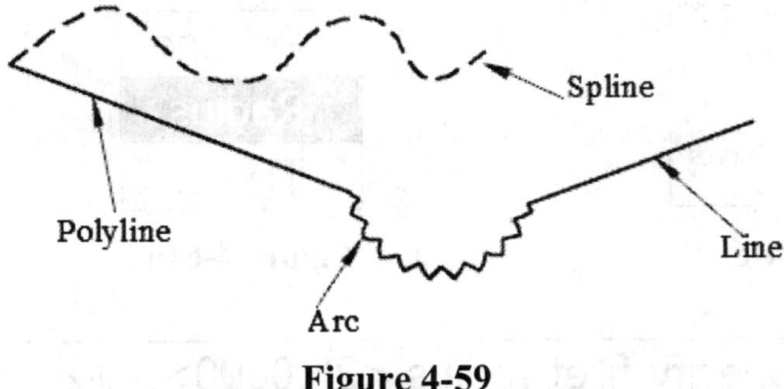

Figure 4-59

4.27.   Fillet

The *Fillet* command is used to connect two objects with an arc of the specified radius such that the arc is tangent to both objects. The connecting objects can be arcs, circles, ellipses, elliptical arcs, lines, polylines, rays, splines, or the combination of any two.

Example: In order to follow the *Fillet* command, draw the lines and circles as shown in Figure 4-60a and Figure 4-60b. In the figure, the symbol ϕ represents the diameter..

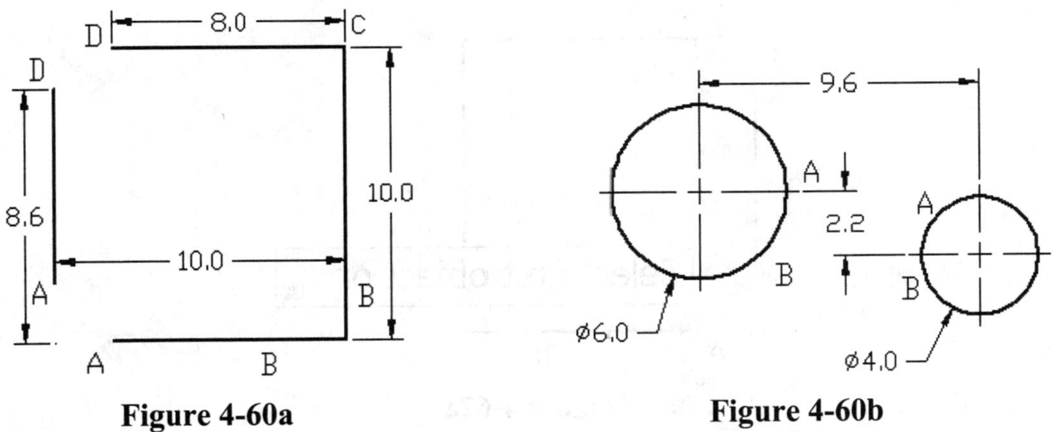

Figure 4-60a   **Figure 4-60b**

- The *Fillet* command is activated using one of the following procedures.
    1. Panel method: From the *Home* tab and *Modify* panel expand the *Fillet* drop down menu and select the *Fillet* tool, Figure 4-60c.
    2. Command line method: Type "fillet", "Fillet", or "FILLET" in the command line and press the *Enter* key.

- The activation of the command leads to the first object selection prompt, Figure 4-61a. (i) Press the down arrow key, (ii) select the radius option, and (iii) press the *Enter* key.
- Specify the radius and press the *Enter* key, Figure 4-61b.
- This section describes to fillet lines and circles.

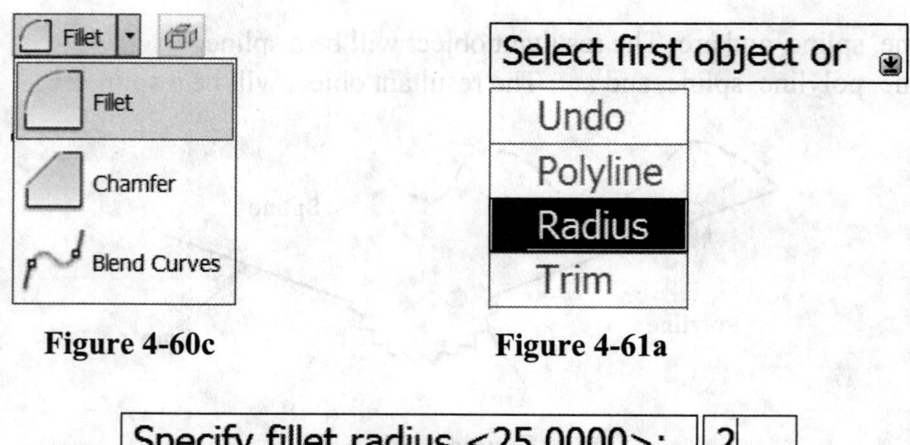

Figure 4-60c   Figure 4-61a

Specify fillet radius <25.0000>: 2

Figure 4-61b

- Fillet lines: The *Fillet* command trims the lines and draws the arc that meets the lines smoothly.
    1. Activate the *Fillet* command, if it is not active.
    2. Specify the radius (in this example, the radius is 2).
    3. For the first object, click in the vicinity of point A on line AB, Figure 4-62a.
    4. For the second object, click in the vicinity of point A on line AD, Figure 4-62b.

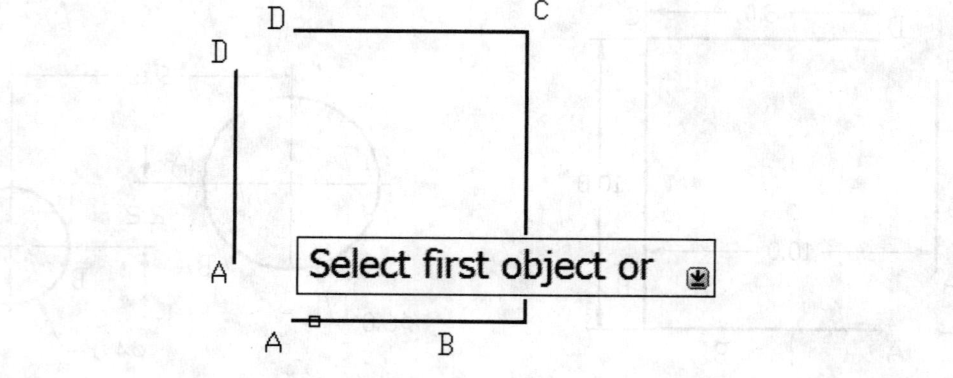

Figure 4-62a

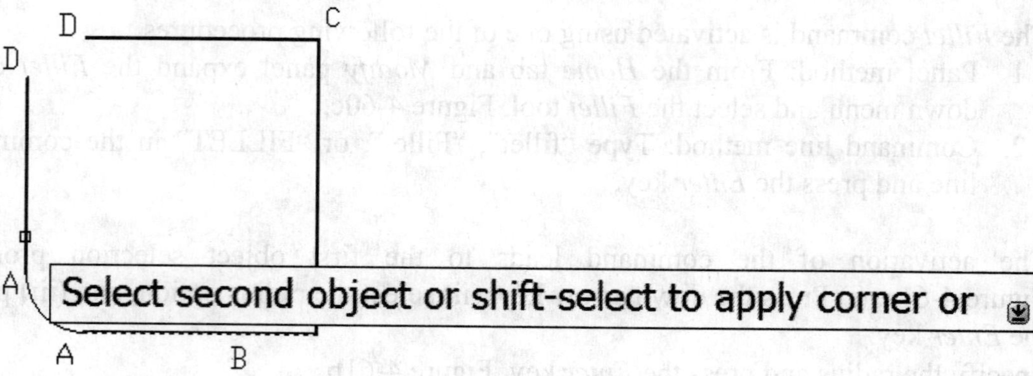

Figure 4-62b

5. An arc (of radius 2) is created from A to A which is tangent to lines AB and AD, Figure 4-62c.
6. Repeat the process from step #1 - #4 in the vicinity of points B. An arc (of radius 2) is created from B to B which is tangent to lines BA and BC. The corners of the lines are also trimmed, Figure 4-62d.

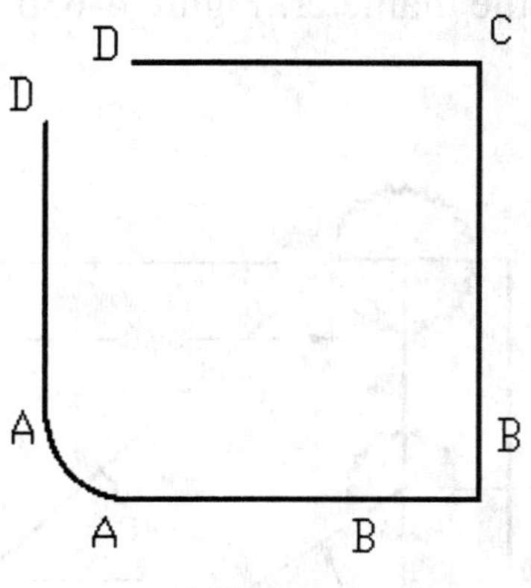

Figure 4-62c

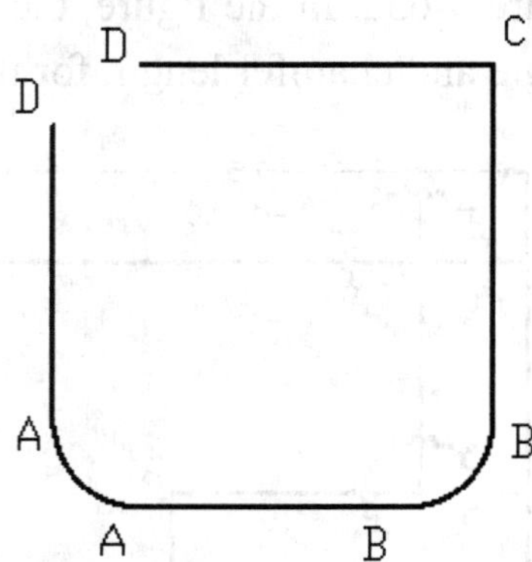

Figure 4-62d

7. Repeat the process from step #1 - #4 in the vicinity of points D. At step #2, specify a radius of 0.0. An arc (of radius 0) is created from D to D tangent to lines DA and DC, Figure 4-62e. Notice the difference of an arc for *radius > 0* and *radius = 0*.

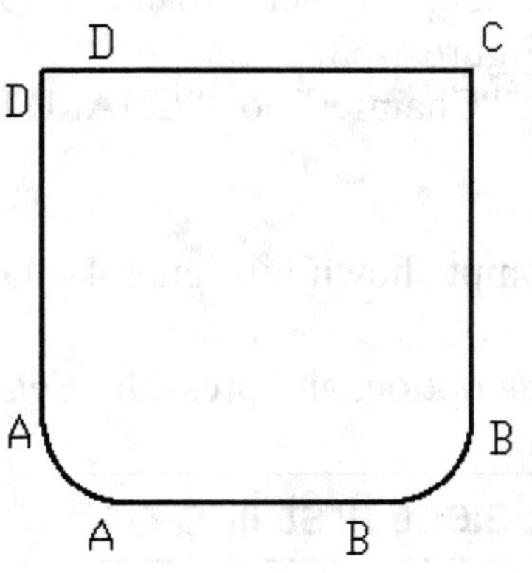

Figure 4-62e

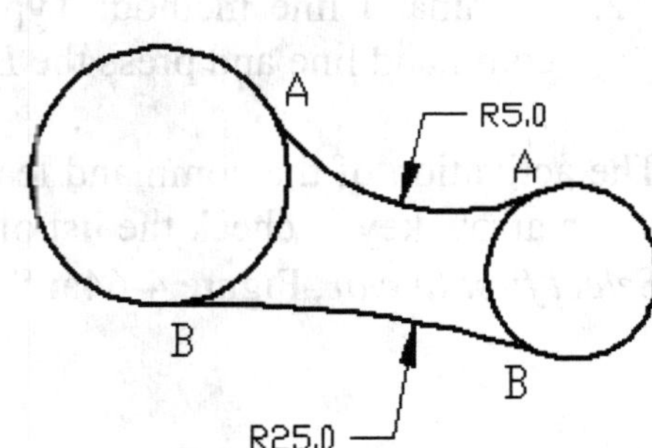

Figure 4-62f

- Fillet Circles: The *Fillet* command does not trim the circles. However, the command draws an arc that meets the circles smoothly.

  1. Activate the *Fillet* command, if it is not active.
  2. Create a fillet with a specific radius (5 in the example) Figure 4-62f, by clicking in the vicinity of points labeled as A on both circles.
  3. Create a fillet with a specific radius (25 in the example) Figure 4-62f, by clicking in the vicinity of points labeled as B on both circles.

4.28.   Chamfer

The *Chamfer* command is used to connect two objects with a straight line. The connecting objects can be lines and polylines or combination of any two.

Example: In order to follow the *Chamfer* command, draw the lines and circles as shown in Figure 4-63a. In the figure, the symbol ϕ represents the diameter. Figure 4-63b shows the angle and chamfer length for the corners A and B.

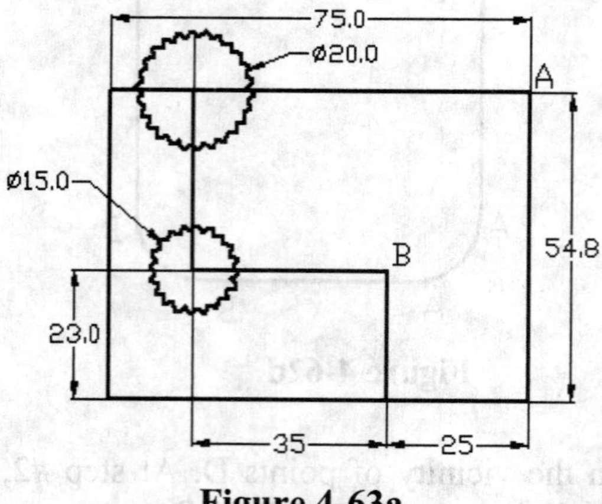

Figure 4-63a

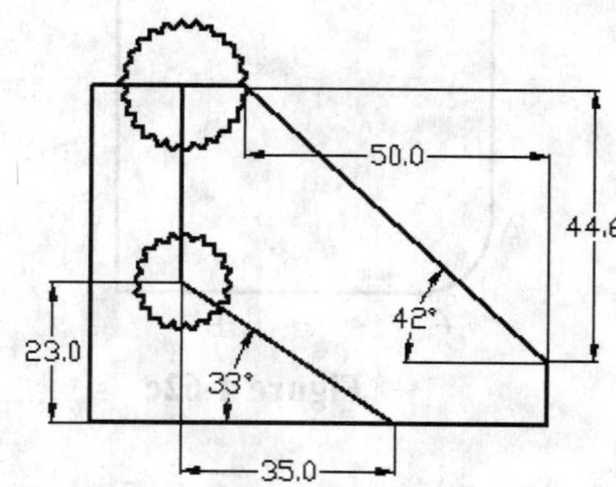

Figure 4-63b

- The *Chamfer* command is activated using one of the following procedures.
  1. Panel method: From the *Home* tab and *Modify* panel expand the *Fillet* drop down menu and select the *Chamfer* tool, Figure 4-63c.
  2. Command line method: Type "chamfer", "Chamfer", or "CHAMFER" in the command line and press the *Enter* key.

- The activation of the command leads to the prompt shown in Figure 4-64a. Press the down arrow key to check the list of options.
- *Select first line or*, Figure 4-64a: Select the *Angle* option, and press the *Enter* key.

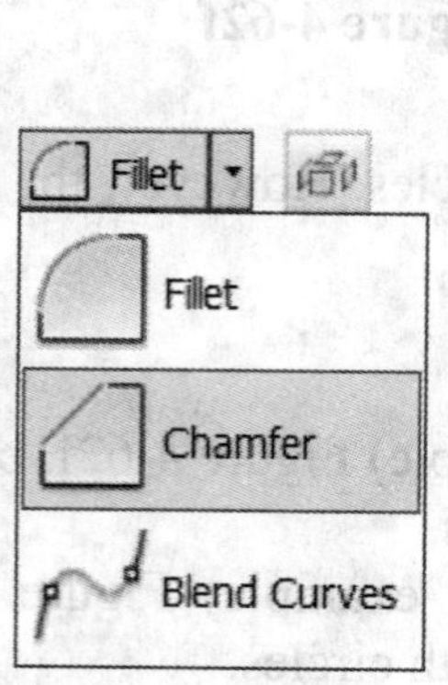

Figure 4-63c

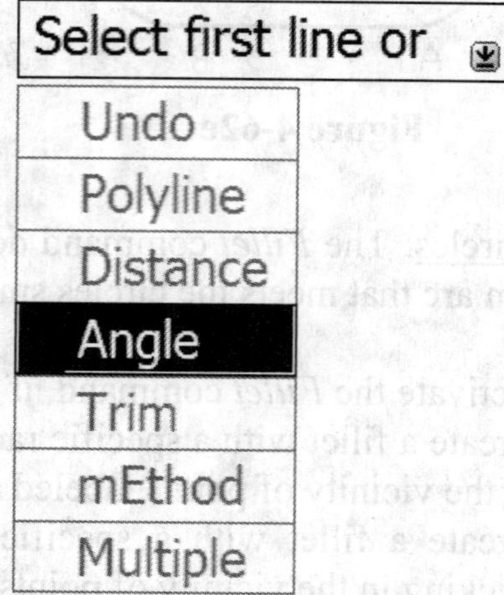

Figure 4-64a

- *Specify chamfer length on the first line*, Figure 4-64b: Specify the length and press the *Enter* key. In the example, for corner A the length is 50.
- *Specify chamfer angle from the first line*, Figure 4-64c: Specify the angle and press the *Enter* key. In the example, for corner A the angle is 42.

Specify chamfer length on the first line <35.0000>:   50

Figure 4-64b

Specify chamfer angle from the first line <33>:   42

Figure 4-64c

- *Select the first line or*, Figure 4-64d: Click on the horizontal line at corner A. The line will change its appearance, Figure 4-64e.

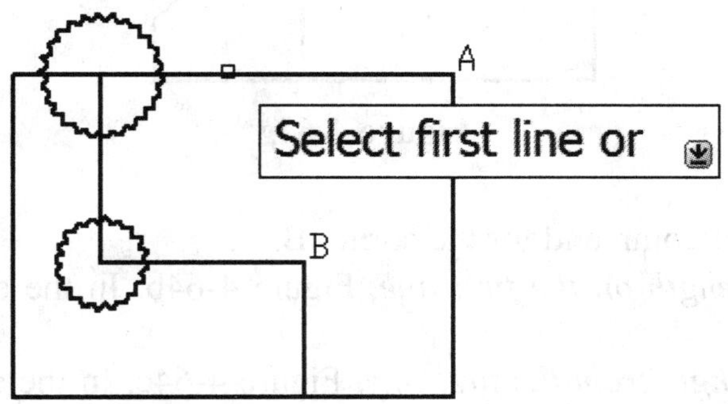

Figure 4-64d

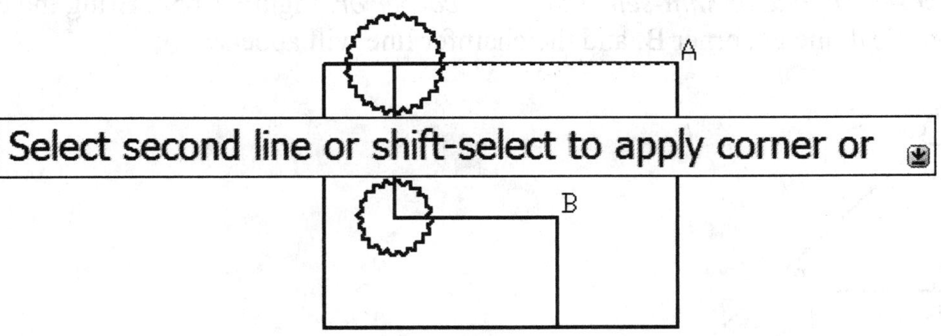

Figure 4-64e

- *Select second line or shift-select to apply corner or*, Figure 4-64f: Bring the cursor on the vertical line at corner A and the chamfer line will appear.
- *Select second line or shift-select to apply corner or*, Figure 4-64g: Click on the vertical line at corner A. The chamfer line will replace the corner at A.

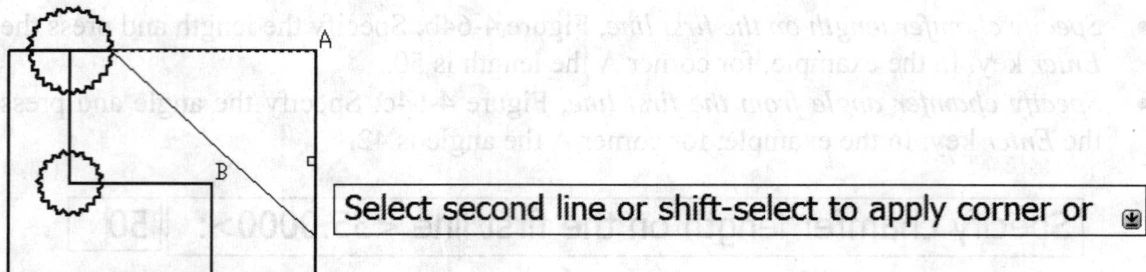

Figure 4-64f

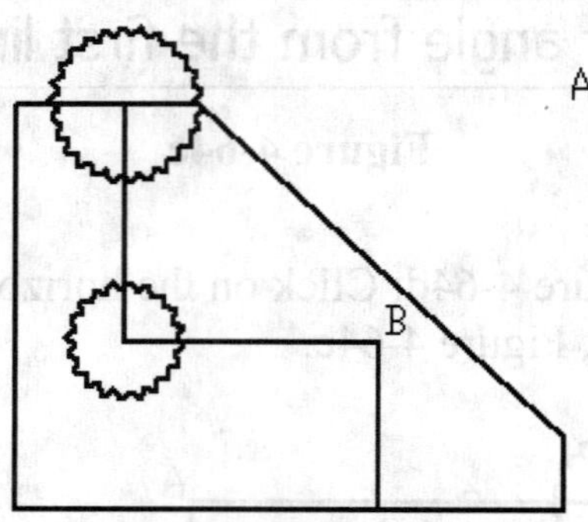

Figure 4-64g

- Repeat the chamfer command for the corner B.
- *Specify chamfer length on the first line*, Figure 4-64b: In the example, for corner B the length is 35.
- *Specify chamfer angle from the first line*, Figure 4-64c: In the example, for corner B the angle is 33.
- *Select the first line or*: Click on the horizontal line at corner B.
- *Select second line or shift-select to apply corner or*, Figure 4-65a: Bring the cursor on the vertical line at corner B, and the chamfer line will appear.

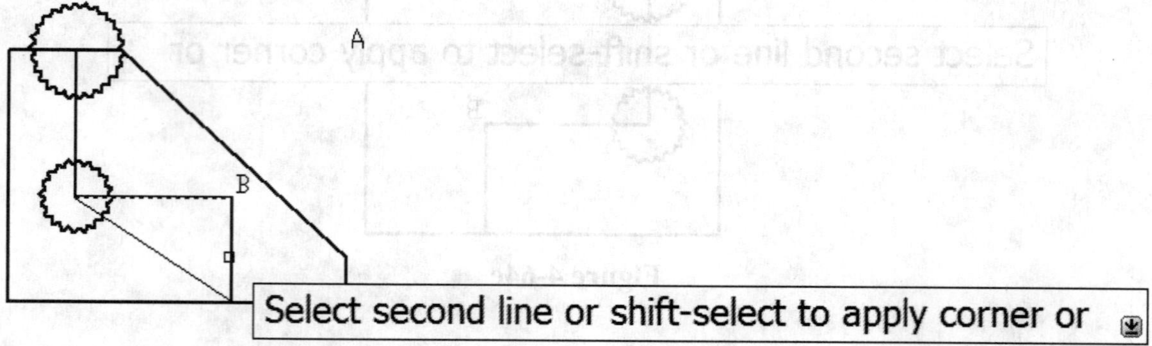

Figure 4-65a

- Click on the vertical line at corner B. The chamfer line will disappear and the error message shown in Figure 4-65b will appear.

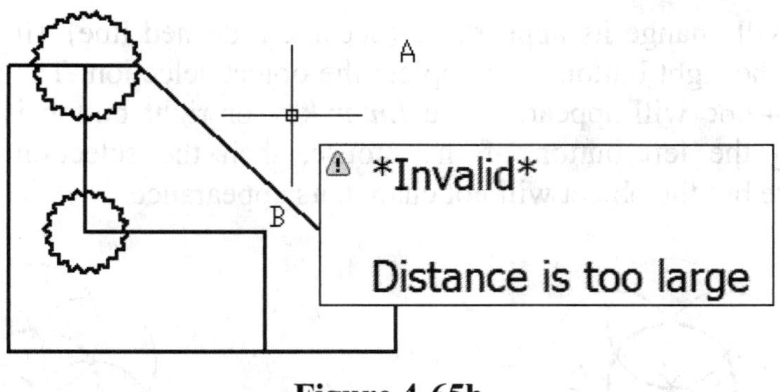

Figure 4-65b

4.29. Trim 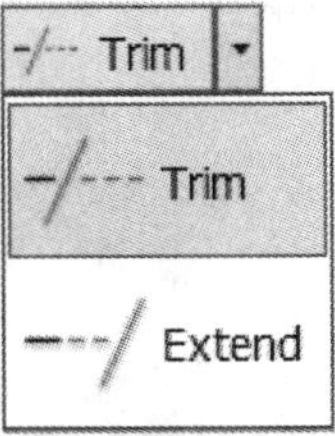

The *Trim* command is used to trim objects at a cutting edge. The cutting edge is defined by other objects. The concept of trim command can be better understood by comparing it to hair trimming at a barber shop. The barber holds the customer's hairs in her hands and then trims the hairs (above the fingers) with reference to her fingers. In this example, the barber fingers are the cutting edge, "above the fingers" is the desired side for trimming. The difference in the trim command and hair trimming is that the barber can cuts hairs only above her fingers. However, AutoCAD allows trimming on either side of the cutting edge.

Example: Create the top of a patio umbrella (Figure 4-67a) using circle and trim commands.
- Draw the circles shown in Figure 4-66a.
- The *Trim* command is activated using one of the following procedures.
    1. Panel method: From the *Home* tab and *Modify* panel expand the *Trim* drop down menu and select the *Trim* tool, Figure 4-66a.
    2. Command line method: Type "trim", "Trim", or "TRIM" in the command line and press the *Enter* key.

Figure 4-66a

- The activation of this command leads to the object selection prompt to choose which object will serve as the cutting edge.
    1. *Select all the objects*, Figure 4-66a: To select all displayed objects as potential cutting edges, press the *Enter* key without selecting any of the objects.
    2. *Select one object*, Figure 4-66b: In the figure the circle #1 is selected as the cutting edge. (i) Bring the cursor on top of the object, the object will be highlighted. (ii) Click the object with the left button of the mouse, and the

object will change its appearance (became a dashed line). (iii) Press the *Enter* key, or the right button, to complete the object selection. The prompt shown in Figure 4-66c will appear. If the *Enter* key or right button is pressed without pressing the left button of the mouse, then the selection process will be complete but the object will not change its appearance.

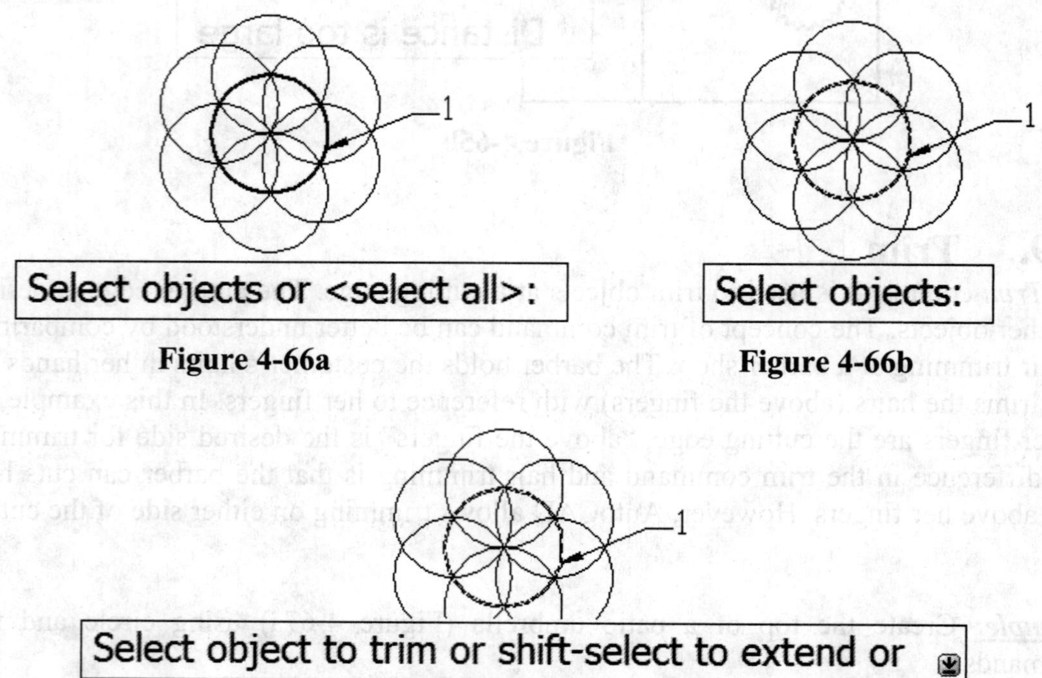

Figure 4-66a   **Figure 4-66b**

Figure 4-66c

- *Select the objects to trim*, Figure 4-66d: Bring the cursor on the top of the object to be trimmed. Since, to create the object shown in Figure 4-67a, the part of the selected circle outside the circle #1 needs to be removed. Therefore, click on outside part of circle #2, Figure 4-66e.

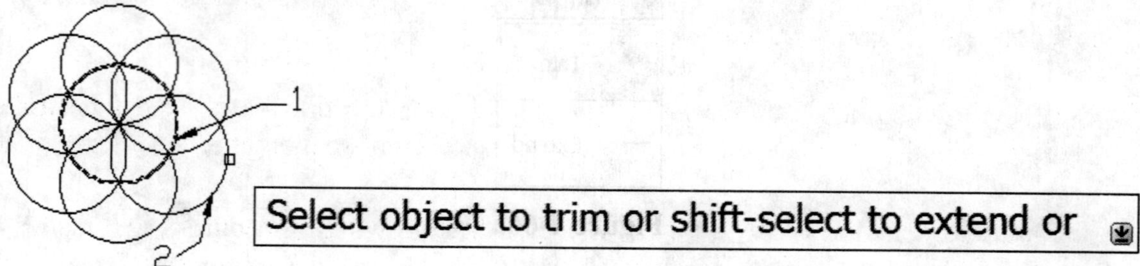

Figure 4-66d

- Repeat the process with other circles to create the object shown in Figure 4-67a.
- Press the *Esc* or the *Enter* key to exit the command.
- Figure 4-67b and Figure 4-67c are created from the circles of Figure 4-66a. In these examples, every circle represents the cutting edge for one or more circles,

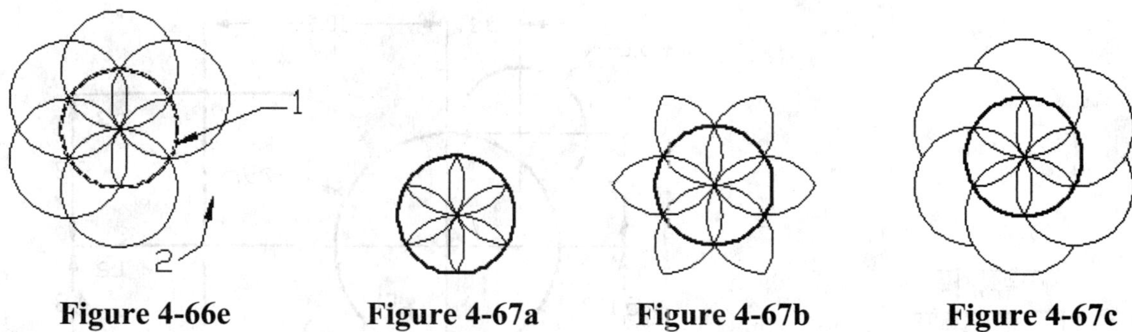

| Figure 4-66e | Figure 4-67a | Figure 4-67b | Figure 4-67c |

4.29.1. What to do if an object cannot be trimmed

If the trim command is not trimming then do one or more of the following procedures.

1. If the object exists after the *Trim* command is executed once:
    a. Check if there are multiple objects lying on top of each other.
    b. If the answer to the above bullet is yes, then delete the object in question if there is another object under it; repeat the process until only one object is left.
2. One of the objects (reference and to be trimmed) may have a clear space invisible to the human eye:
    a. Activate the *Extend* command.
    b. Extend the object to be trimmed to the reference object.
    c. Now, perform the *Trim* command.
3. The trim command cannot be continued:
    a. Check if the layer containing the objects (reference and/or to be trimmed) is locked.
    b. If the answer to the above bullet is yes, then unlock the layers. Layers are discussed in next chapter.

4.30.   Extend

The *Extend* command is used to extend an object to reach another object. The *Extend* command extends the object on its natural path. For example, a circular arc will change to a circle, a horizontal line will stay horizontal, etc. The extend command is executed in a manner similar to the *Trim* command.

Example: In order to follow the extend capability; draw the lines, arcs, and the circle shown in Figure 4-69. In the figure, the symbol ϕ represents the diameter.

- The *Extend* command is activated using one of the following procedures.
    1. Panel method: From the *Home* tab and *Modify* panel expand the *Trim* drop down menu and select the *Extend* tool, Figure 4-68.
    2. Command line method: Type "extend", "Extend", or "EXTEND" in the command line and press the *Enter* key.

- The activation of the command leads to choosing the object that will serve as the extension edges to which the other objects will be extended, Figure 4-70a.

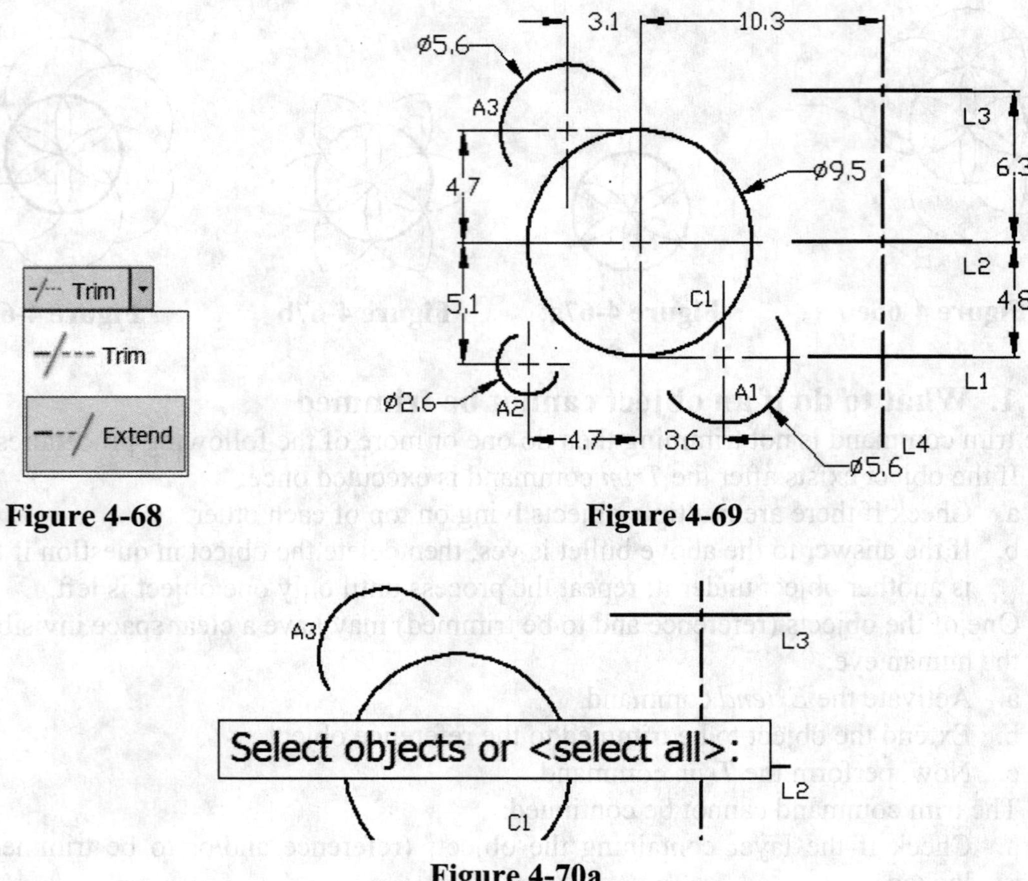

Figure 4-68   **Figure 4-69**

Figure 4-70a

- *Select objects*, Figure 4-70b: In the figure, the circle C1 is selected as the extension edge. In this example, every line and arc will be extended to the circle. (i) Bring the cursor on top of the reference object (circle in the example) and it will be highlighted. (ii) Click the circle with the left button of the mouse, and it will change its appearance (became a dashed line). (iii) Press the *Enter* key or right button to complete the reference object selection. If the *Enter* key or right button is pressed without pressing the left button of the mouse, the selection process will be complete but the object will not change its appearance.

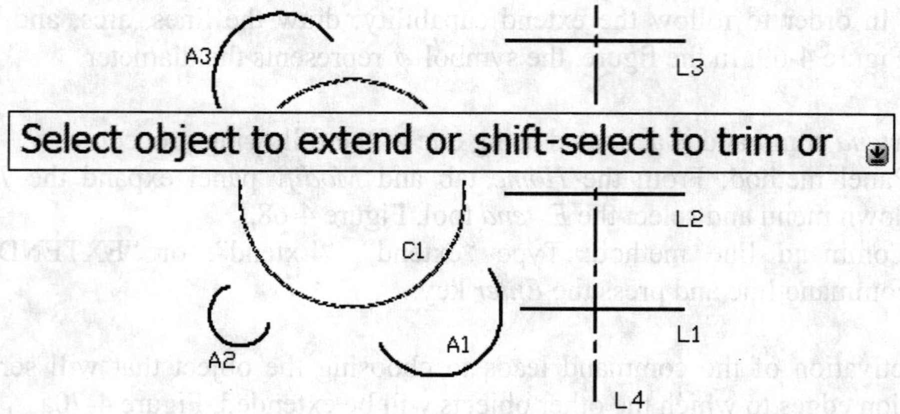

Figure 4-70b

- *Select the objects to extend*, Figure 4-70c: Bring the cursor on top of the object to be extended. In the example, the circular arc A1 is selected; for arcs, click near the ends of the arcs. Finally, press the left button of the mouse. The circular arc A1 will be extended to the circle C1, Figure 4-70d.

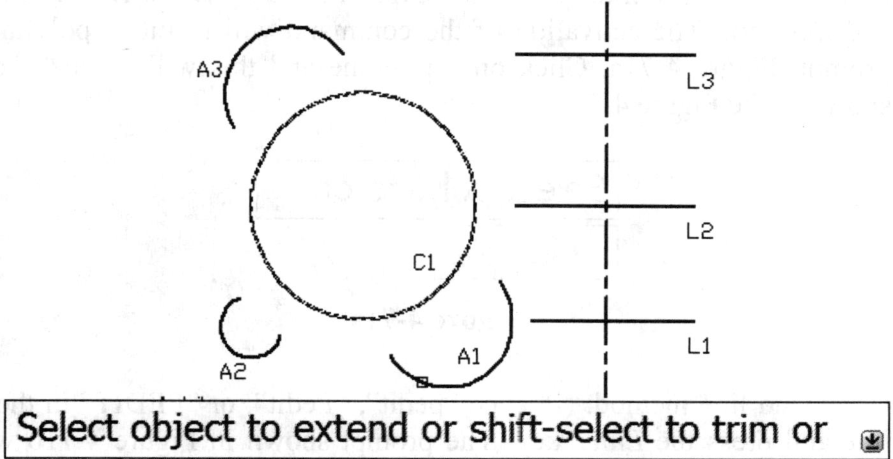

Figure 4-70c

- *Select the objects to extend*: Now, extend the line L2. Bring the cursor on top of the line to be extended and it will be highlighted. If the selection is made to the right of midpoint (in this example), that is, to the right of L4, then L1 will not be extended. Finally, press the left button of the mouse. The line will be extended to the circle selected in the previous step, Figure 4-70d.
- Repeat the process with the L1, L3, A2, and A3, Figure 4-70d.
  - o If L1 and L3 are extended on their natural paths, then these lines will not cross the circle C1. Hence, the *Extend* command will not extend L1 and L3.
  - o Similarly, if A2 is completed to be a circle it will not touch the circle C1. Hence, the *Extend* command will not extend A2.
- Press the *Esc* or the *Enter* key to exit the command.

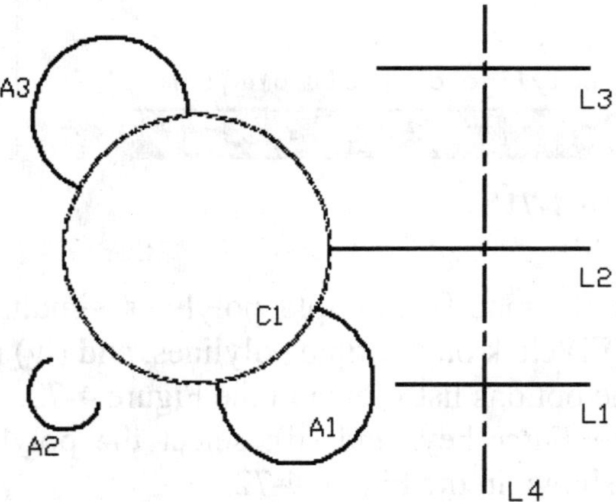

Figure 4-70d

4.31.   Polyline edit 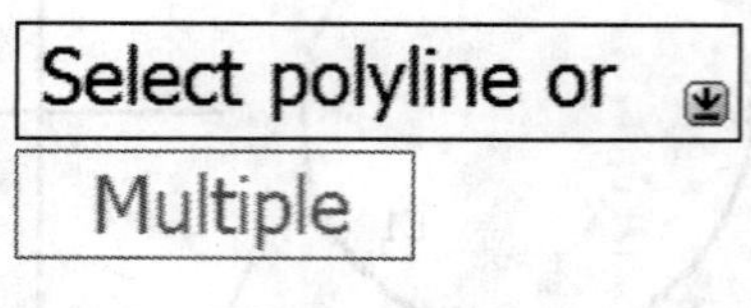

The polyline edit capabilities allow the drafter to modify the existing polylines.

- The *Edit Polyline* command is activated using one of the following procedures.
  1. *Panel method:* From the *Home* tab expand the *Modify* panel and select the *Edit Polyline* tool. The activation of the command will result in polyline selection prompt, Figure 4-71a. Click on a polyline and this will open the options list shown in the Figure 4-72.

Figure 4-71a

  2. Command line method: (i) Type "pedit", "Pedit", or "PEDIT" in the command line and press the *Enter* key. The prompt shown in Figure 4-71b will appear; follow one of the following two methods.

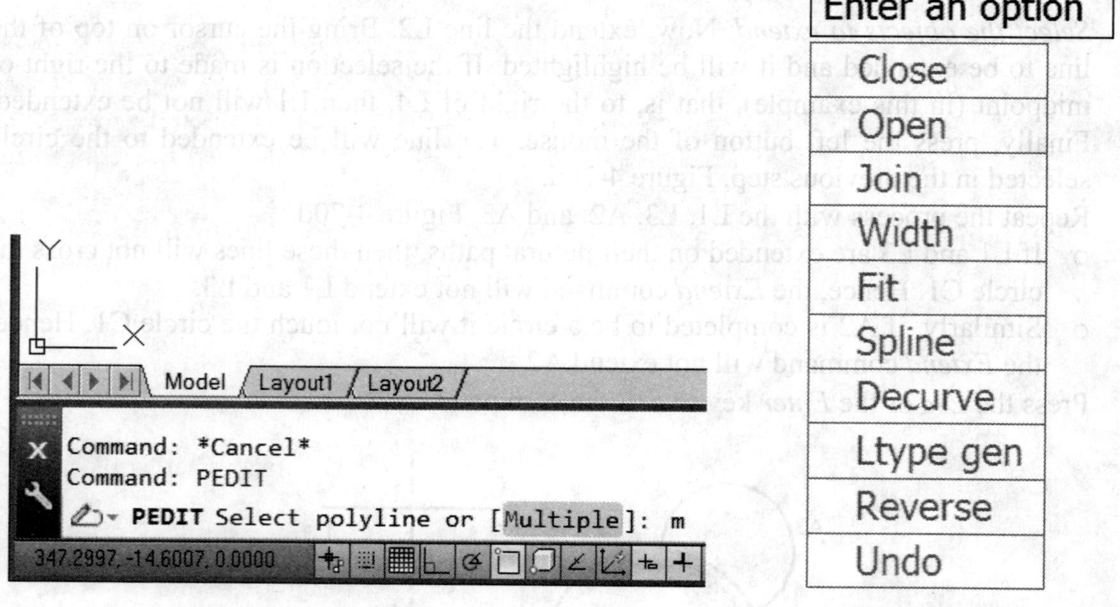

Figure 4-71b   **Figure 4-72**

  - o (i) Type *m* (to modify multiple polylines simultaneously), (ii) press the *Enter* key, (iii) click on multiple polylines, and (iv) press the *Enter* key. This will open the options list shown in the Figure 4-72.
  - o (i) Press the *Enter* key, and (ii), select the polyline. This will open the options list shown in the Figure 4-72.

- The remaining of this section will discuss the option from Figure 4-72.

- Close: The *Close* option is used to connect the starting point of a polyline with its ending point by drawing a segment between the two points. The selected polyline must contain at least two segments. Assume the drafter wants to close multiple segments polyline. (i) Draw two polylines as shown in Figure 4-73a. (ii) Activate the *PEdit* command. (ii) Choose the *Multiple* option. (iii) Select multiple polylines, Figure 4-73a. (iv) Press the *Enter* key. (v) Choose the *Close* option from the list of options. (vi) Press the *Enter* key, Figure 4-73b. To close a single polyline, activate the *PEdit* command and follow the above steps. Note, the closed polylines will maintain their linetypes.

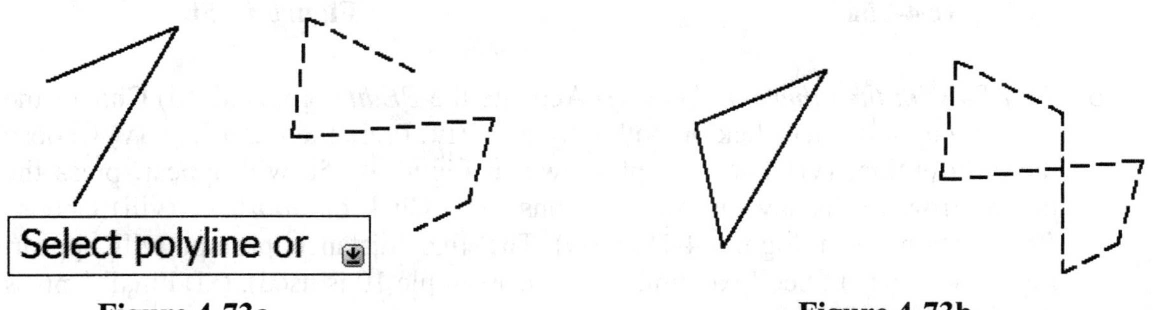

Figure 4-73a   **Figure 4-73b**

- Open: The *Open* option is used to remove the segment connecting the starting point of a polyline with its ending point. The selected polyline must be closed and contain at least three segments. Assume the drafter wants to open multiple polylines. (i) Draw two polylines as shown in Figure 4-74a. (ii) Activate the *PEdit* command. (ii) Choose the *Multiple* option. (iii) Select multiple polylines, Figure 4-74a. (iv) Press the *Enter* key. (v) Choose the *Open* option from the list of options. (vi) Press the *Enter* key, Figure 4-74b. To open a single polyline, activate the *PEdit* command and follow the above steps. Note, the open polylines will maintain their linetypes.

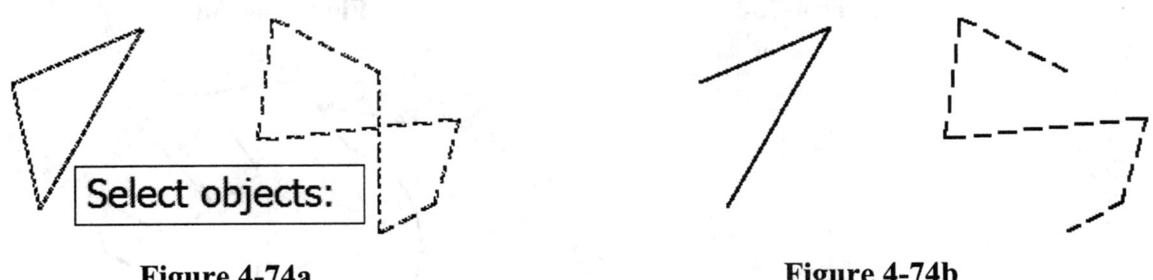

Figure 4-74a   **Figure 4-74b**

- Join: The *Join* option is used to connect multiple polylines, or a polyline with an arc and/or line segments. A drafter wants to join the polylines P1, P2, P3, and P4, Figure 4-75a. (i) Activate the *PEdit* command and select the single polyline option and select the polyline P1. (ii) Choose the *Join* option. (iii) Click on P2, P3, and P4. (iv) Press the *Enter* key twice.
    - *Important point to notice*: (i) Since the command was activated from P1, the new polyline follows the style of P1, Figure 4-57b. (ii) P4 is not joined to the other polylines because it did not share a vertex with the other polylines, Figure 4-75b.

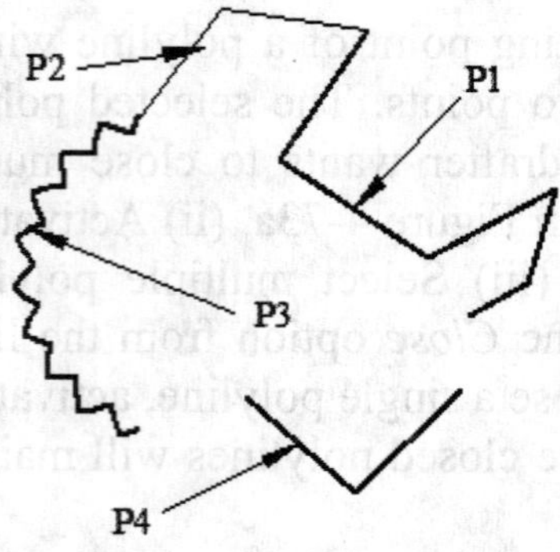

Figure 4-75a

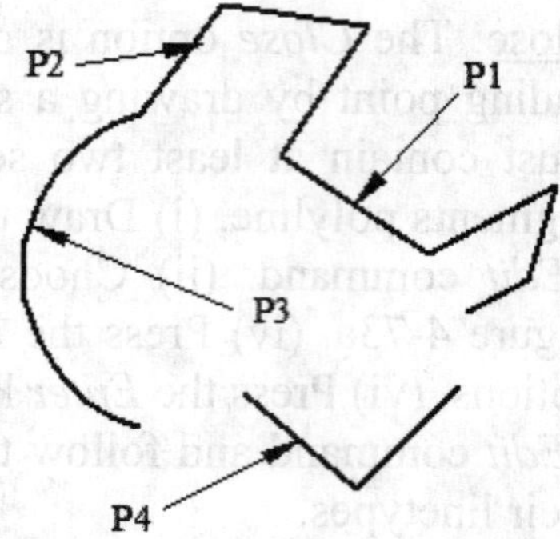

Figure 4-75b

o *Join P4 with the other polylines*: (i) Activate the *PEdit* command. (ii) Choose the *Multiple* option. (iii) Click on both polylines. (iv) Press the *Enter* key. (v) Choose the *Join* option. (vi) The prompt shown in Figure 4-75c will appear, press the down arrow to display the other options. (vii) Click on *Jointype*. (viii) Choose *Both* option from Figure 4-75d. (ix) The fuzz distance prompt will appear, Figure 4-75e. (x) Specify a number (in the example 10 is used). (xi) Finally, press the *Enter* key.

o The new polyline is shown in Figure 4-75f. Since the polyline P1-P2-P3 was selected first in step (ii) above, the new polyline follows its style.

Figure 4-75c

Figure 4-75d

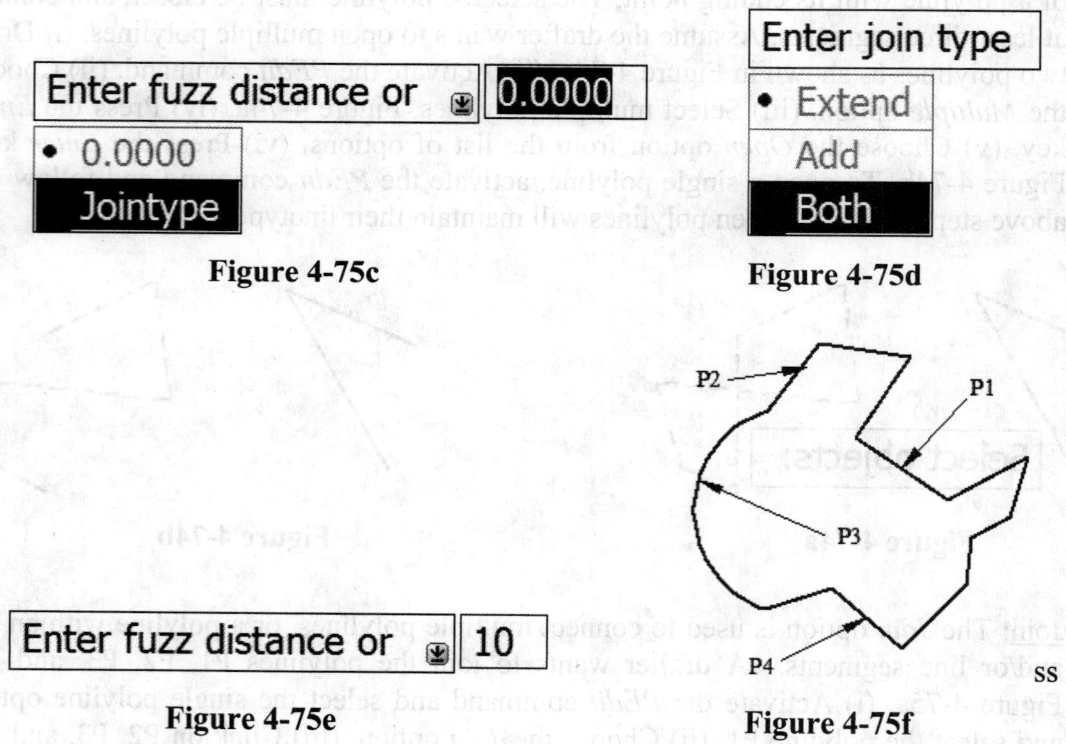

Figure 4-75e

Figure 4-75f

- <u>Width</u>: The *Width* option is used to change the width of a polyline. (i) Select a polyline. (ii) Activate the command. (iii) Specify the new width, Figure 4-76a. (iv) Press the *Enter* key, twice. The width of the polyline will be changed. The width of the polyline shown in Figure 4-76a is increased to '2' and is shown in Figure 4-76b.

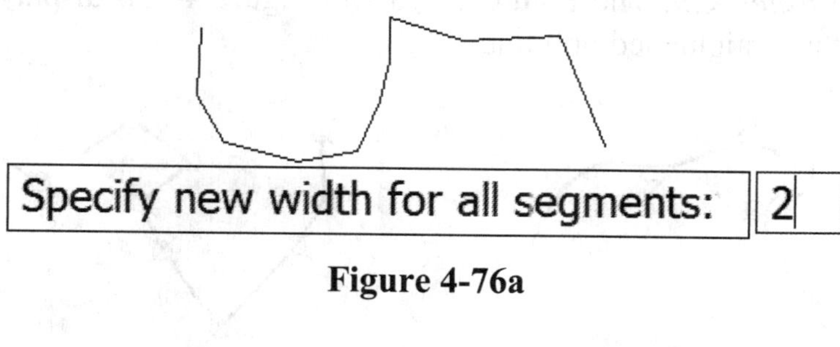

Figure 4-76a

Figure 4-76b

- Fit: The *Fit* option is used to replace a selected polyline with a smooth curve. The fitted curve passes through each vertex of the polyline. (i) Select the polyline. (ii) Activate the command. (iii) Press the *Enter* key. The Figure 4-77a displays an original polyline and the Figure 4-77b displays the polyline transformed into a fitted curve.

Figure 4-77a   **Figure 4-77b**

- Spline: The *Spline* option is used to replace the selected polyline with a quadratic spline curve. The curve passes through the starting and ending points of the polyline, other vertices may or may not be on the spline. (i) Select the polyline. (ii) Activate the command. (iii) Press the *Enter* key. The Figure 4-77a and Figure 4-78 displays a polyline and the corresponding splined curve.

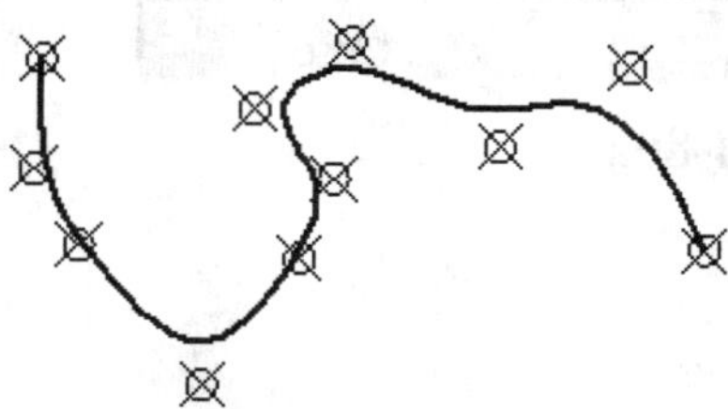

Figure 4-78

- <u>Decurve</u>: The *Decurve* option is used to replace a curve fitted or splined polyline with a polyline of straight segments. (i) Select a polyline. (ii) Activate the command. (iii) Press the *Enter* key. The Figure 4-79a and Figure 4-79b displays a curve fitted polyline and the straightened polyline.

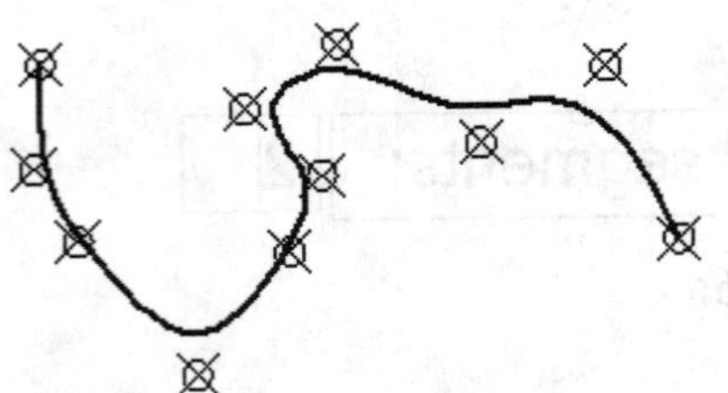

Figure 4-79a

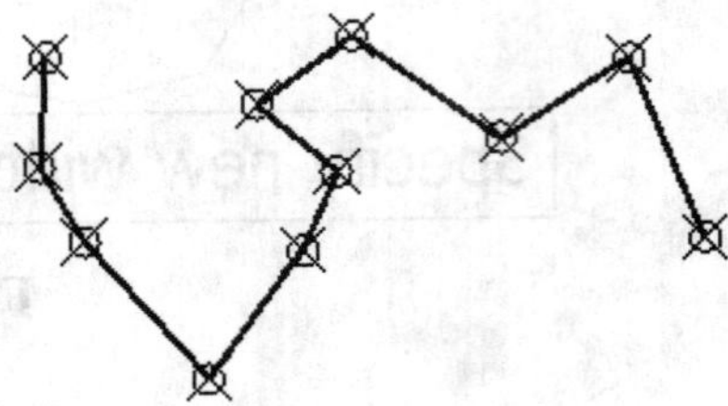

Figure 4-79b

- <u>Edit vertex</u>: The *Edit vertex* option is available only if the *Edit polyline* command is activated using a single polyline. This option is used to edit a selected vertex. (i) Select the polyline, Figure 4-80a. (ii) Press the right button and select the *Polyline* option. (iii) Select the *Polyline Edit* option (iv) Select the *Edit vertex* command, Figure 4-80b. (v) Vertex editing option list will appear and the first vertex will be selected, Figure 4-80c. (iv) Choose the desired option and follow the prompt.
- <u>Undo</u>: As the name suggest, the *Undo* option cancels out the previous step.

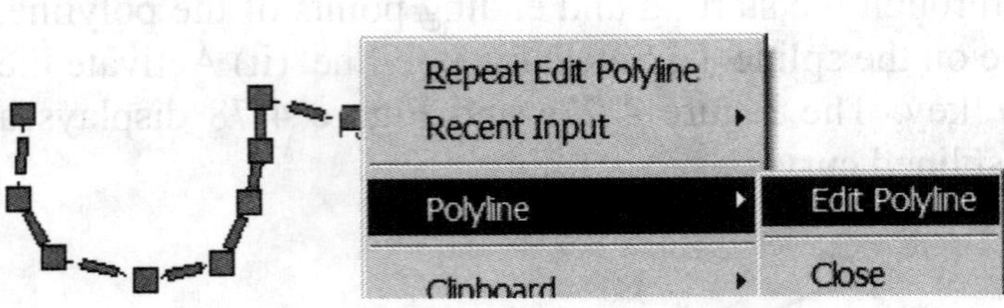

Enter an option
Close
Join
Width
Edit vertex
Fit
Spline
Decurve
Ltype gen
Reverse
Undo

Figure 4-80a   **Figure 4-80b**

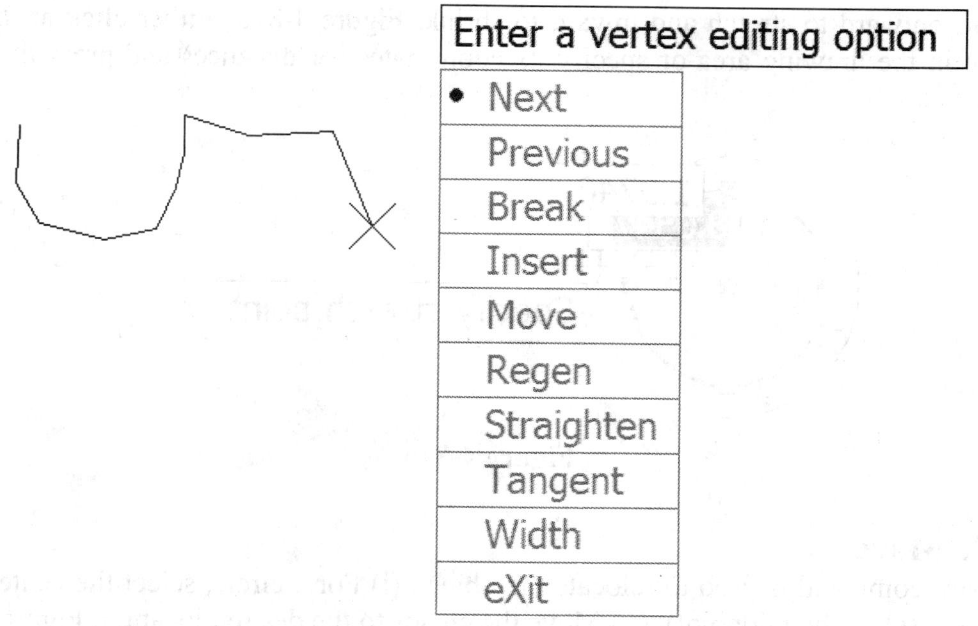

Figure 4-80c

4.32.   Grips and object editing

After selecting an object the grip points are shown on the object. These grip points can be used to edit the object using the pointing device instead of entering the respective commands. Some of the editing capabilities activated when grips are displayed on an object are: stretch, move, rotate, copy, erase, and scale.

4.32.1. Select a point

(i) Select the object. (ii) Place the cursor on any of the grip points it will become RED, Figure 4-81a. (iii) Click with the right button of the mouse and list of commands will appear. The commands are object and grip point dependent. (iii) Click with the left button of the mouse on the desired command and follow the prompts.

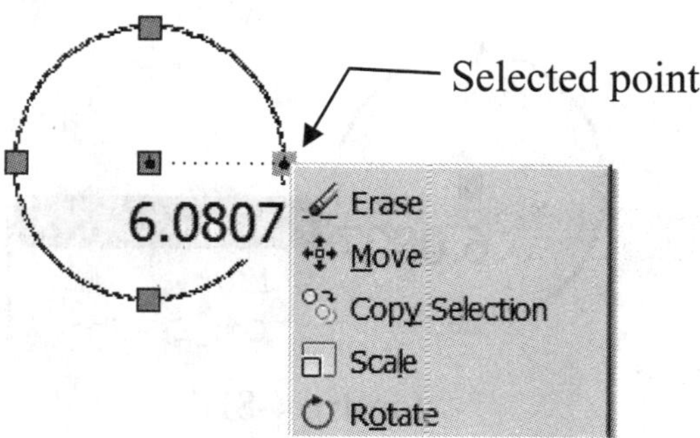

Figure 4-81a

4.32.2. Stretch/shrink

The *Stretch/shrink* command is used to resize the object. (i) For a circle, select one of the quadrant points (for a line, select one of the endpoint). (ii) Move the cursor to the desired location; outward to stretch and inward to shrink, Figure 4-81b. Either click at the new location in the drawing area or specify its coordinates (or distance) and press the *Enter* key.

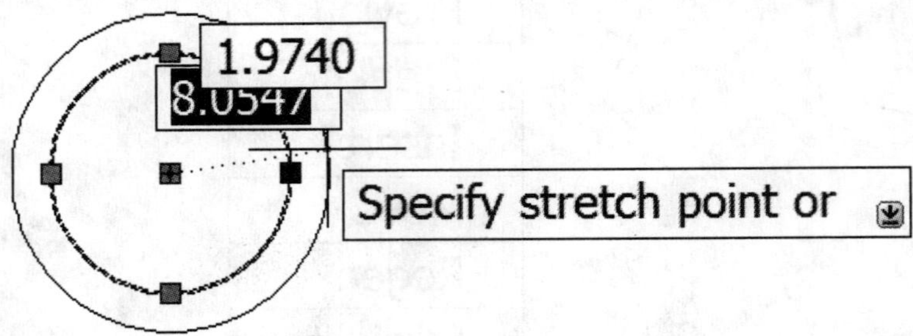

Figure 4-81b

4.32.3. Move

The *Move* command is used to relocate the object. (i) For a circle, select the center point (for a line, select the midpoint). (ii) Move the cursor to the desired location, Figure 4-81c. Either click at the new location in the drawing area or specify its coordinates (or distance) and press the *Enter* key.

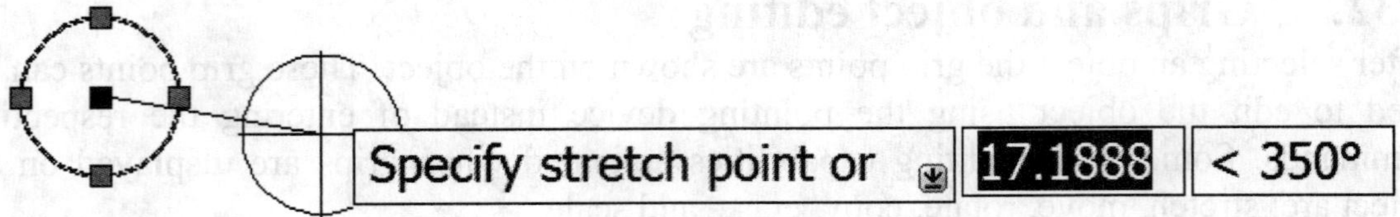

Figure 4-81c

4.32.4. Erase

The *Erase* command is used to delete the object from the drawing. (i) Select a grip point. (ii) Click with the right button of the mouse and the option panel will appear. (iii) Select the *Erase* option, Figure 4-81d. The object will be deleted.

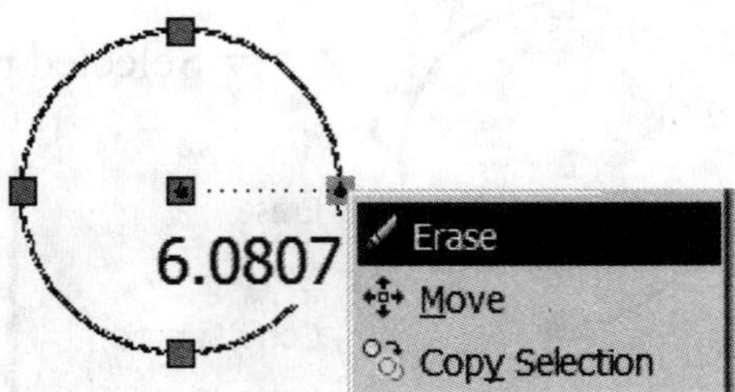

Figure 4-81d

4.32.5. Rotate

As the name suggests, the *Rotate* command is used to rotate the object about a point. (i) Select a grip point. (ii) Click with the right button of the mouse and the options panel will appear, Figure 4-81e. (iii) Select the *Rotate* option. (iv) The prompt to select the base point (point of rotation) will appear. (v) Click at the desired location. (vi) The prompt to specify the angle of rotation will appear, Figure 4-81f. (vii) Rotate the selected object around the base point by moving the cursor. Alternatively, specify the angle value (Figure 4-81f) and press the *Enter* key. This is an excellent method for rotating block references.

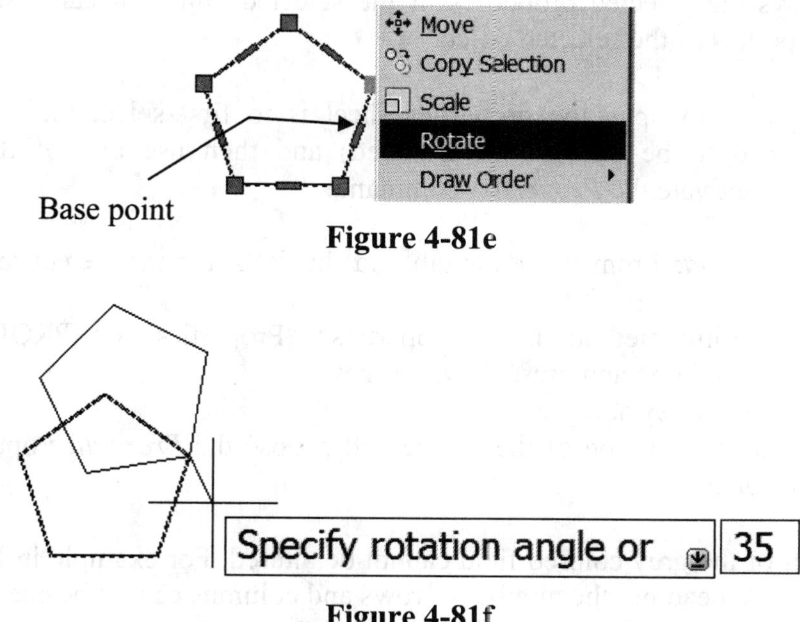

Figure 4-81e

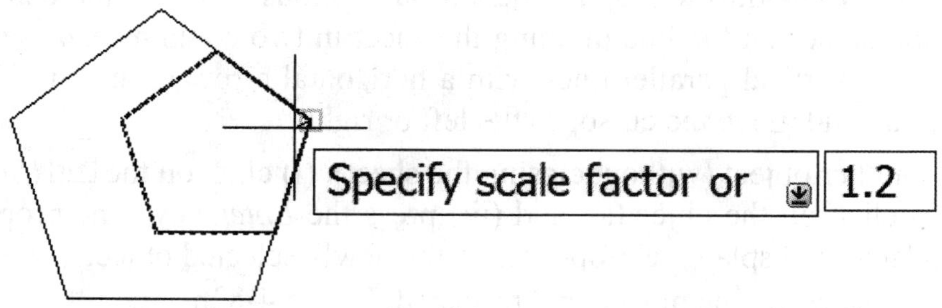

Figure 4-81f

4.32.6. Scale

The *Scale* command is used to resize the object. (i) Select a grip point. (ii) Click with the right button of the mouse and the option panel will appear, Figure 4-81e. (iii) Select the *Scale* option. (iv) The prompt to select the base point (the point that will not change its location) will appear. (v) Click at the desired location. The command will scale the selected object relative to the base point. (vi) The prompt to specify the scale factor will appear. (vii) Increase the size of an object by dragging the cursor outward or decrease the size by dragging inward. Alternatively, specify the scale factor for the relative scaling (Figure 4-81g) and press the *Enter* key.

Figure 4-81g

4.33.   The Properties sheet and object editing 🔲

The *Properties* sheet displays the properties of the selected object(s). The content of the sheet are object dependent. Figure 4-82a shows the properties for a table created in the previous chapter and Figure 4-82b shows the properties of a polyline. The type of the object is displayed in the upper right corner of the property sheet. The *Properties* sheet not only displays the selected properties of the selected object, it can also be used to modify the properties of the selected object.

- The prerequisite to open the properties sheet is to first select the object (whose properties need to be checked or changed) and then use one of the following procedures to activate the *Properties* command.

  1. *Panel method:* From the *View* tab and the *Palette* panel select the *Properties* tool.
  2. Command line method: Type "properties", "Properties", or "PROPERTIES" in the command line and press the *Enter* key.
  3. Hold the *Ctrl* key and press 1.
  4. Press the right button of the mouse and choose the *Properties* option from the option panel.

- The content of the grey colored field cannot be altered. For example in Figure 4-82a, under the *Table* heading, the number of rows and columns cannot be changed.
- If desired, the content of the other fields can be altered. Type or choose the new value and press the *Enter* key.
- The up and down arrows (▾ ▴) are used to hide or display the option under a particular heading.
- The properties sheet can be elongated or widened to see the various options. To elongate the sheet, (i) move the cursor on the top or bottom edge (the cursor will change to a double headed arrow); (ii) hold the left button and move the cursor up or down. To widen the sheet (i) move the cursor to the edge opposite to the sheet heading (in Figure 4-82a move the cursor on the left edge); (ii) hold the left button and move the cursor horizontally.
- The columns width of the properties sheet can be altered (without changing the properties sheet's width) to display the various options. To alter the columns width, (i) move the cursor on the line dividing the sheet in two columns and the cursor will change to two vertical parallel lines with a horizontal arrow on either side; (ii) hold the left button and move the cursor to the left or right.

- To select another object (without closing the sheet), (i) click on the 🔲 (*Select object*) button, (ii) click on the object(s), and (iii) press the *Enter* key. The properties sheet will be updated to display the properties of the newly selected object.
- The property sheet can be moved and reshaped, Figure 4-82b.

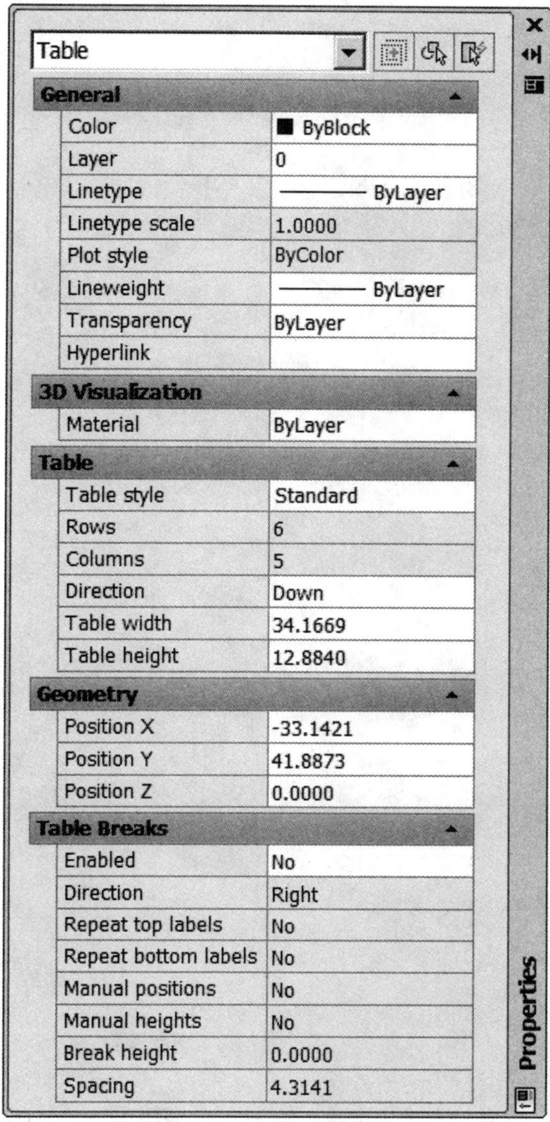

Figure 4-82a   **Figure 4-82b**

<u>Notes:</u>

5.   Layers

5.1.   Objectives

- Learn to create new layers
- Learn to change objects appearance, color, and thickness by changing the properties of the existing layers
- Learn to move objects from one layer to the other
- Learn to control the visibility of layers

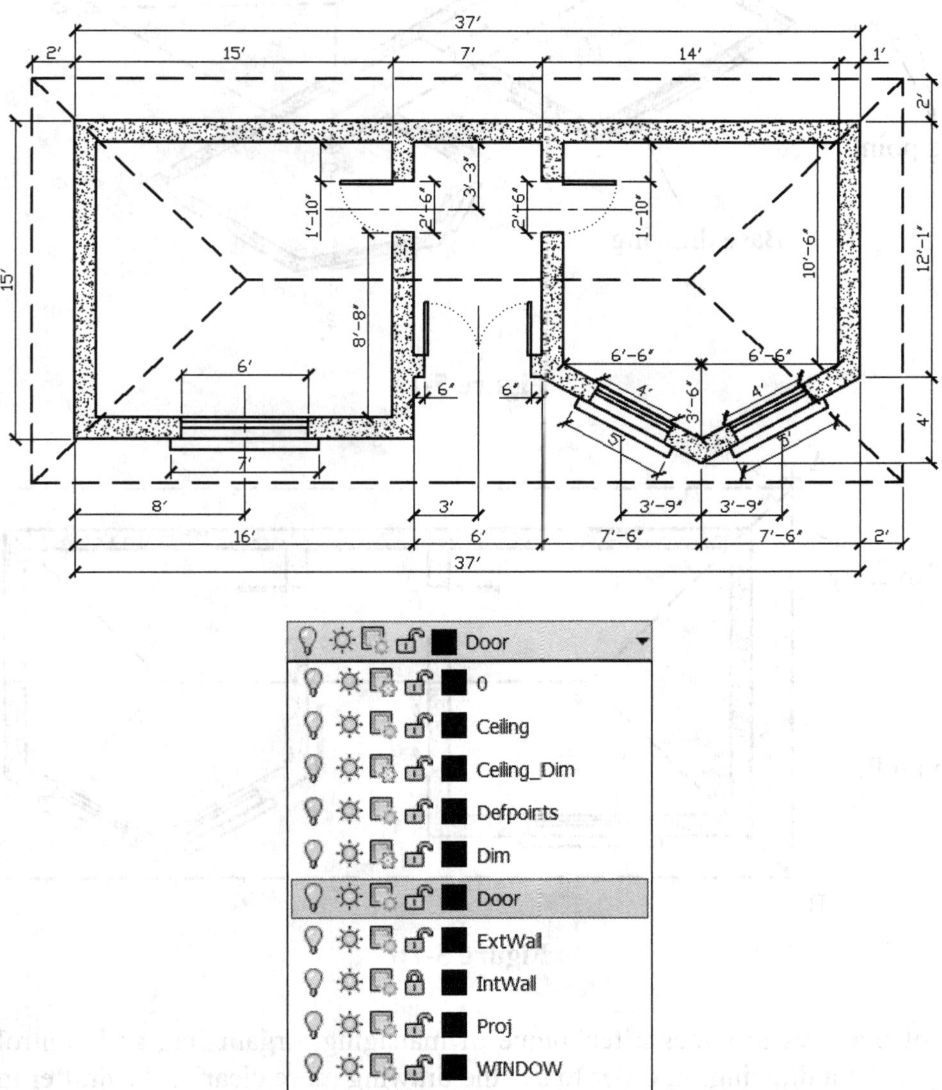

5.2.   Introduction

Prior to the computer use in drafting, architects drew different parts of the drawing on transparent overlays. The base drawing and the overlays maintained matching points for the alignment. Figure 5-1a demonstrates the base drawing (floor plan) and the roof overlay and both the base drawing and the roof overlay has four matching points (A, B, C, and D). Figure 5-1b shows the roof overlay placed on the base drawing by aligning the matching points.

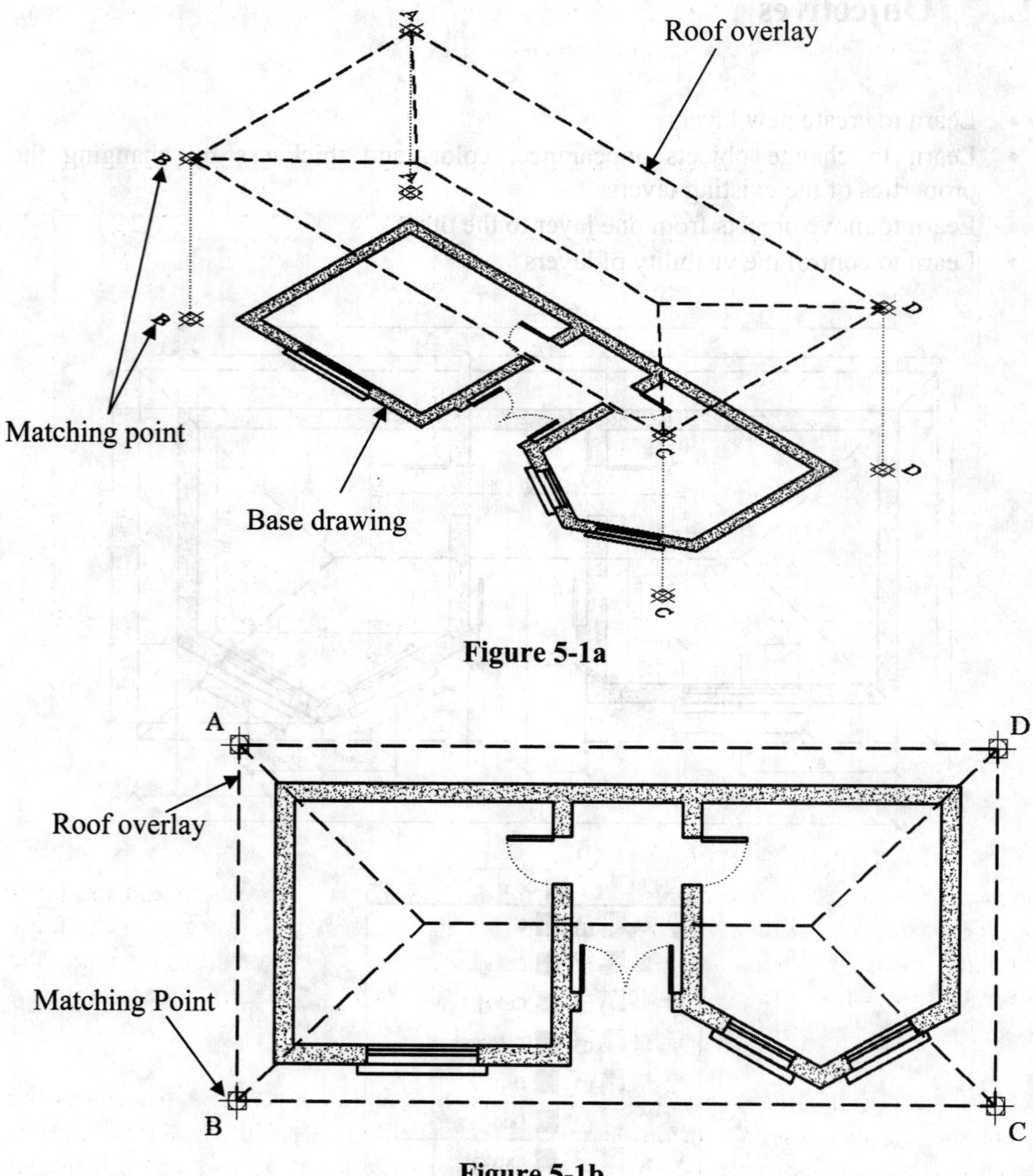

Figure 5-1a

Figure 5-1b

The use of overlays provides a technique of managing, organizing, and controlling the visual layout of a drawing. In order to see the drawing more clearly, the drafter may want to remove all the text and dimensions from the drawing. **The drafter wants to keep the information, but just wants to hide them from the view**. Deleting the information would not be appropriate as the drafter would lose all the work. Hence, just hiding the selected overlays will solve the problem.

In AutoCAD, an overlay is replaced by a layer. Layers can be thought of as large piece of clear plastic of the size of the drawing area. In other words, the layer is invisible and the objects drawn on the layer are visible. An entire drawing (or part of a drawing) can be made visible or hidden. Figure 5-1c shows a drawing with three layers, the floor plan, roof plan (shown as dashed lines), and the dimension.

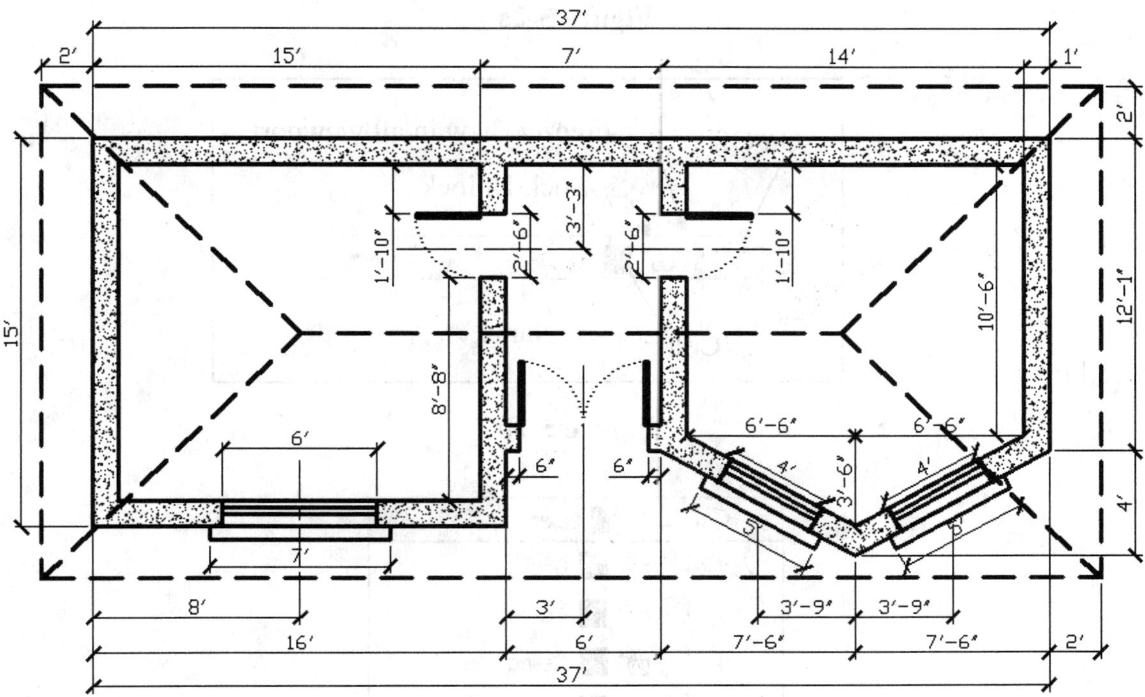

Figure 5-1c

5.3.   Layer in AutoCAD

Layers are controlled by the *Home* tab and the *Layers* panel, Figure 5-2a and the layer properties manager button which is located on the *Layers* panel, Figure 5-2b. The tools on the toolbar are not the command tool, but the indicator of the status. For example, the light bulb shows that the selected layer is *On* (visible) or *Off* (hidden). The yellow and grey colors of the bulb represent that the layer is *On* or *Off*, respectively.

In AutoCAD, by default, everything is drawn on the default layer which is set as the current layer. *Layer 0* is the current layer when a new file is created. Each new layer is created by the user. Normally, it is recommended to create a different layer for different parts of a drawing. Each layer could be assigned its own color, linetype, and line thickness so that every object drawn on that layer appears in the same color, linetype, and line thickness. Figure 5-2c shows the layer created for the drawing shown in Figure 5-1c.

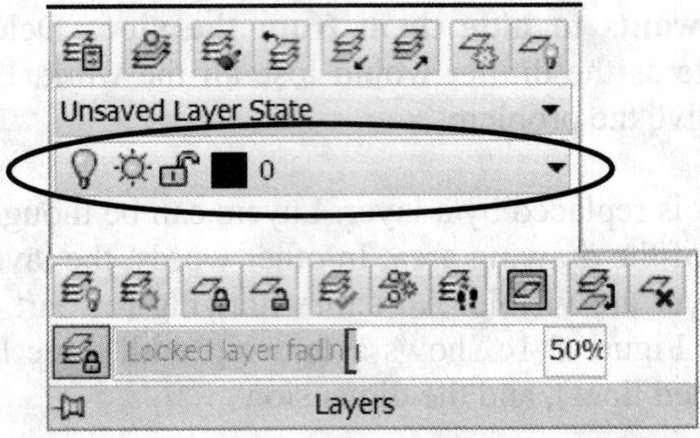

Figure 5-2a

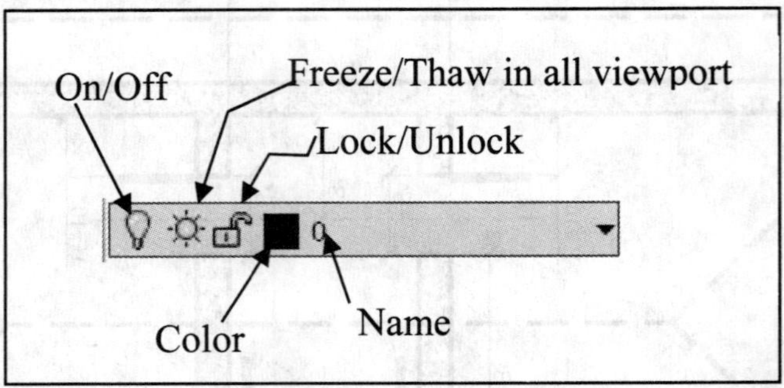

Figure 5-2b

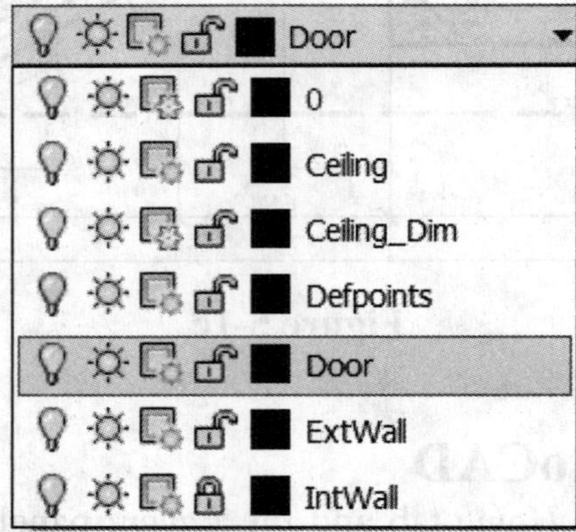

Figure 5-2c

5.4.   Layer command

The *Layer* command is used to create new layers and modify the existing layers.

- The *Layer* command is activated using one of the following procedures.
  1. Panel method: From the *Home* tab and the *Layers* panel click on the *Layer Properties* tool (⊟).
  2. Command line method: Type "layer", "Layer", or "LAYER" on the command line and press the *Enter* key.

- The activation of the command will open the *Layer Properties Manager* palettes shown in Figure 5-3.

5.5.   Layer Properties Manager

The *Layer Properties Manager* palette is shown in Figure 5-3. It is used to create a new layer, delete an empty layer, and change the characteristics of the existing layers.

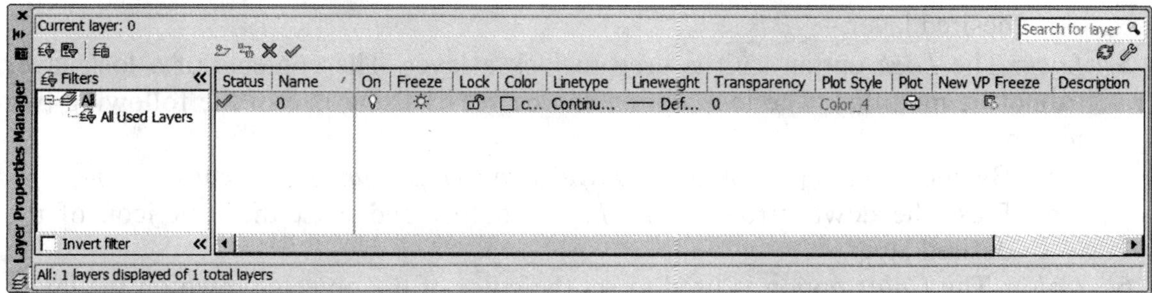

Figure 5-3

5.5.1.   Characteristics of a layer

The *Layer Properties Manager* dialog box, as shown in Figure 5-3, is used to change the characteristics of the layers. Each layer has the following characteristics.

1. *Status*: The *Status* field shows if a layer is the current layer. The current layer will have a green check mark (✓). Others layers (not shown in the figure) will have small parallelogram ( ) in this field.
2. *Name*: The *Name* field displays the layer's name. The Layer *0* cannot be renamed; however, the user created layers can be renamed. The layers names should be based on their functionality (this will help if there are several layers). For example a layer for the dimension should be named DIM or Dimension. To rename a layer, (i) press the *F2* key or click inside the name field (ii) type the new name, and (iii) press the *Enter* key.
3. *On*: The *On* option controls the visibility of a layer. Select the light bulb ( ) to turn the layer *Off* on the drawing. The drawing of an *On* layer is visible and available for plotting. The drawing of an *Off* layer is invisible and is unavailable for drawing and plotting. The visibility can be switched by using one of the following two methods.
   a. By clicking the bulb button in *Layer Properties Manager* palettes.
   b. Press the down arrow of the *Layer* toolbar and click the bulb icon of the desired layer, Figure 5-2c.
4. *Freeze*: This option is available for layouts. The layouts are discussed in Chapter #7. The *Freeze or thaw in current view port* option ( ) is used to hide a layer for a longer period of time. If a layer is turned *Off* in the *Model* space then it will disappear from the *Model* space and fro all the viewports, too. However, freezing a layer in a particular viewport will only hide the contents of the layer in question in the selected viewport. Freezing of layers improves the performance and reduces the object regeneration time. The freeze option should be used only for those layers that

need to be invisible for long periods. Otherwise, the *On/Off* option should be used. **Before freezing the layer, the viewport must be selected. The viewport is selected by double clicking inside the viewport. For the selected viewport, its boundary will change the lineweight and the coordinate system will appear in the viewport.** The freeze option can be set by using one of the following two methods.

   a. By clicking the *Freeze* button in *Layer Properties Manager* palettes.

   b. Press the down arrow of the *Layer* toolbar and click the *Freeze* icon of the desired layer.

5. *Lock*: The *Lock* option (⬚) is used to lock a layer. The contents of a lock layer cannot be modified. The lock option can be set by using one of the following two methods.

   a. By clicking the lock button in *Layer Properties Manager* palettes.

   b. Press the down arrow of the *Layer* toolbar and click the lock icon of the desired layer.

6. *Color*: The *Color* option is used to set the color of the objects drawn on the layer. To change the color (i) open the *Layer Properties Manager* palettes, (ii) click on the small colored box (⬛) under the *Color* column to open the *Select Color* dialog box, Figure 5-4a, (iii) select the desired color from the *Select Color* dialog box, and (iv) press the *OK* button of the *Select Color* dialog box. This will close the *Select Color* dialog box and change the color of the small box to the selected color. All the objects drawn on the layer will be displayed in the chosen color, provided that the *Color Control*'s setting in the *Properties* panel of *Home* tab is set to *By Layer*, Figure 5-4b.

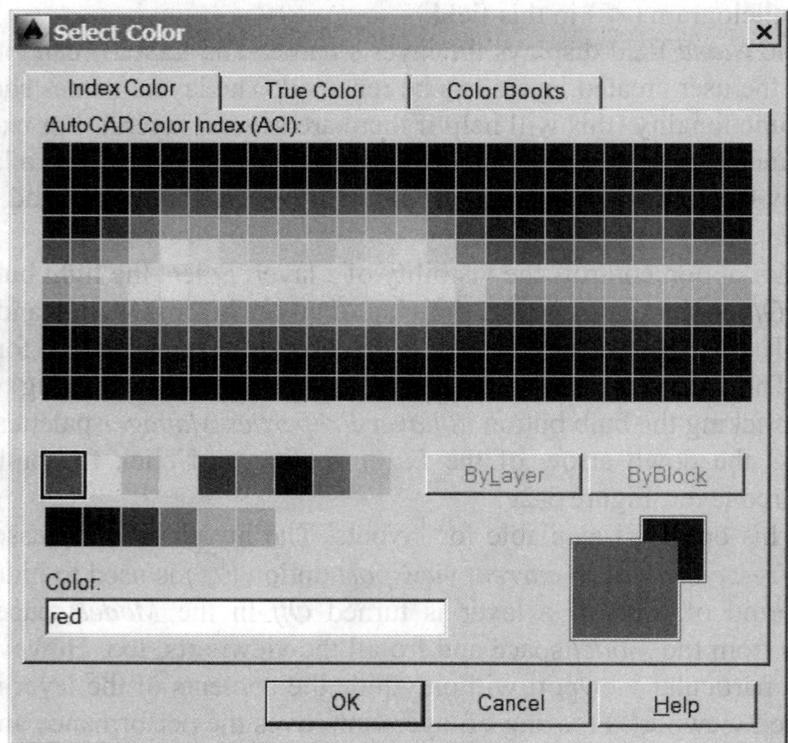

Figure 5-4a

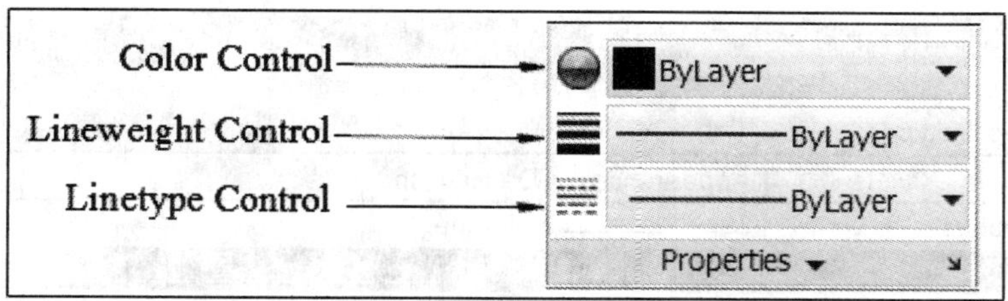

Figure 5-4b

7. <u>Linetype</u>: The *Linetype* option sets the default linetype for all objects drawn on the layer. The linetype of a layer can be changed as follow. (i) Open the *Layer Properties Manager* palettes, (ii) Click on the *Continuous* under the *Linetype* column to open the *Select Linetype* dialog box, Figure 5-5a. (iii) Click on the *Load* button to open the *Load or Reload Linetype* dialog box, Figure 5-5b. (iv) Select the desired linetype (Figure 5-5b shows the selection of *Hidden*) and press the *OK* button. The *Hidden* linetype will appear in the *Select Linetype* dialog box, Figure 5-5c. (v) Select the *Hidden* linetype and press the *OK* button. This will close the *Load or Reload Linetype* dialog box and changes the linetype to the selected style. All objects drawn on the layer will be displayed in the chosen linetype style, provided that the *Line Type Control*'s setting in the *Properties* panel of *Home* tab is set to *By Layer*, Figure 5-4b. Linetype is discussed in detail in Chapter 3.

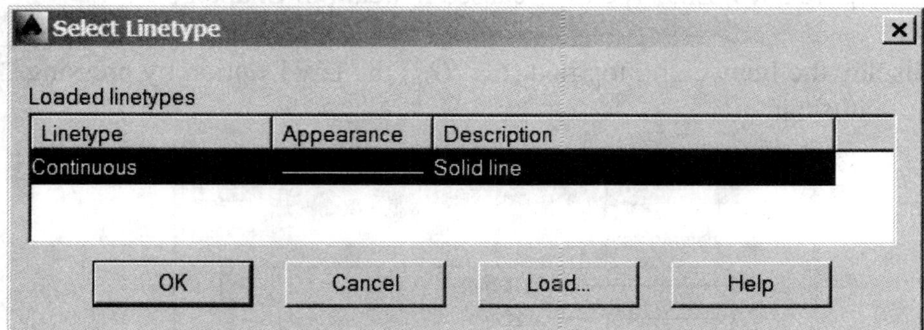

Figure 5-5a

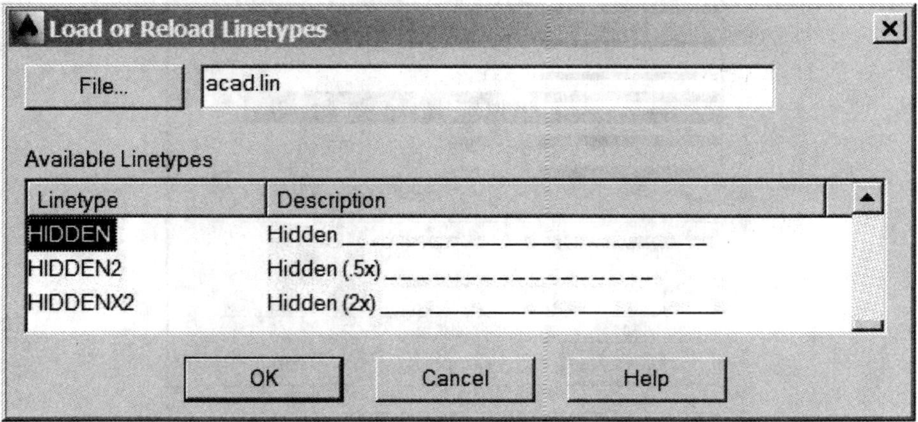

Figure 5-5b

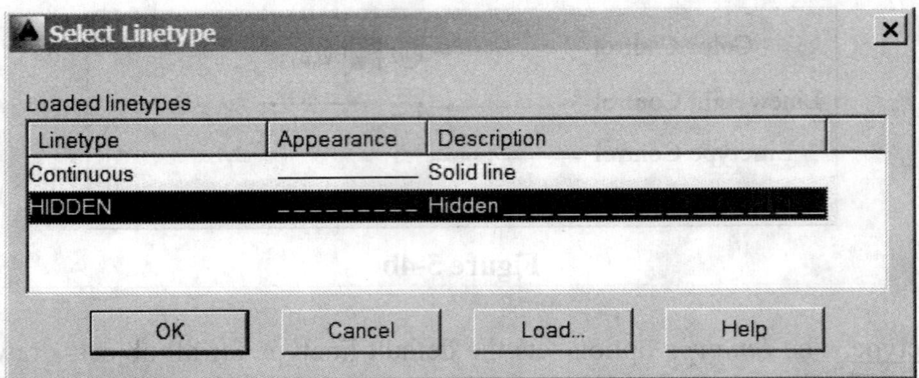

Figure 5-5c

8. <u>Lineweight</u>: The *Lineweight* option sets the thickness of the lines drawn on the layer. The lineweight of a layer can be changed as follow. (i) Open the *Layer Properties Manager* palettes (ii) Click on the *Default* under the *Lineweight* column to open the *Lineweight* dialog box, Figure 5-6, (iii) select the desired lineweight (Figure 5-6 shows the selection of *0.60mm*) and press the *OK* button. This will close the *Lineweight* dialog box and change the lineweight to the selected lineweight. All objects drawn on the layer will be displayed in the chosen lineweight, provided that the *Line Weight Control*'s setting in the *Properties* panel of *Home* tab is set to *By Layer*, Figure 5-4b. Linetype is discussed in detail in Chapter 3.

To display the lineweight, toggled (*On /Off*) the LWT option by pressing ⊞ button in the status bar.

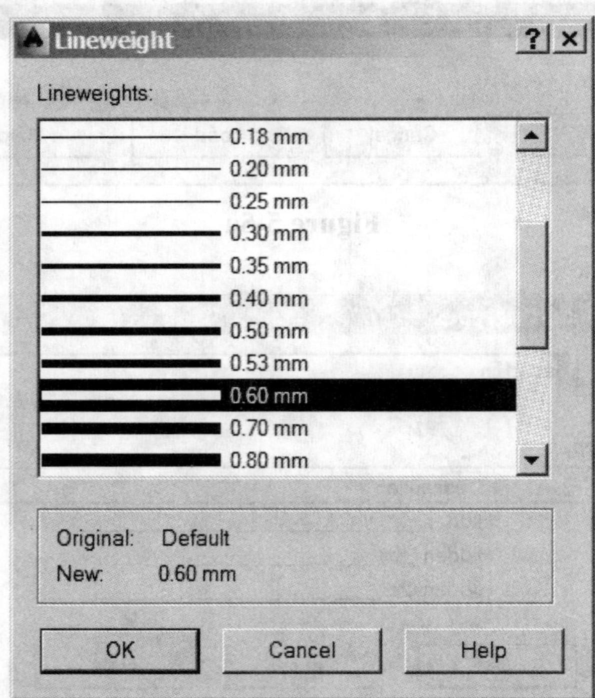

Figure 5-6

9. <u>Plot</u>: The *Plot* option (🖶) is used to allow the objects on the layer to be printed if the drawing is plotted (printed). If the content of a particular layer need not to be printed, then turn *Off* the plot option by clicking on the printer icon (a no entry sign will appear on the printer, and it will look like 🖶).

5.5.2.   Create a new layer

To create a new layer, click on the *New Layer* button (in the *Layer Properties Manager* toolbar. The new layer inherits the properties of the current layer, Figure 5-7. If necessary, change the properties of the new layer. By default, the new layers are named as *Layer1*, *Layer2*, etc. To rename a layer, (i) press the *F2* key or click inside the name field (ii) type the new name, and (iii) press the *Enter* key, Figure 5-7. Close the *Layer Properties Manager* dialog box to make the change permanent by clicking the cross on the upper left corner of the toolbar.

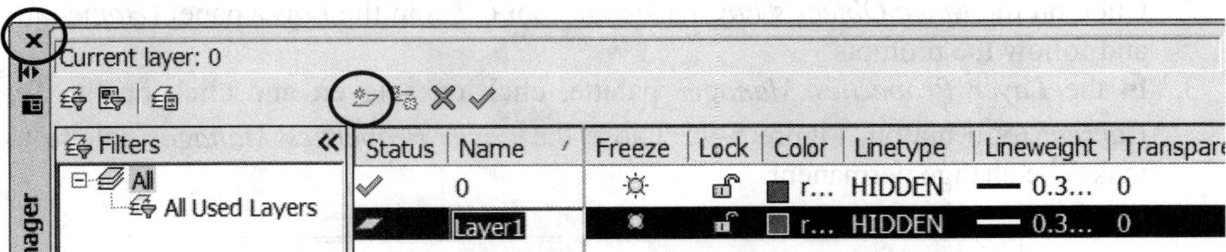

Figure 5-7

5.5.3.   Delete an existing layer

To delete an existing layer (i) select the layer by clicking on it; (ii) click on the *Delete Layer* button (in the *Layer Properties Manager* dialog box, Figure 5-8a. The selected layer will be deleted only if it is not one of the layers shown in Figure 5-8b. Close the *Layer Properties Manager* toolbar to make the change permanent.

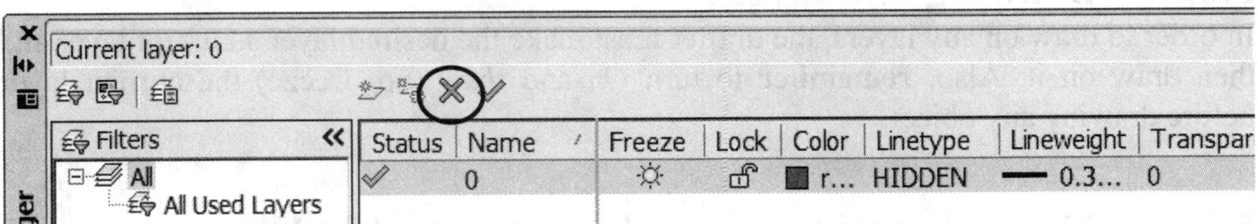

Figure 5-8a

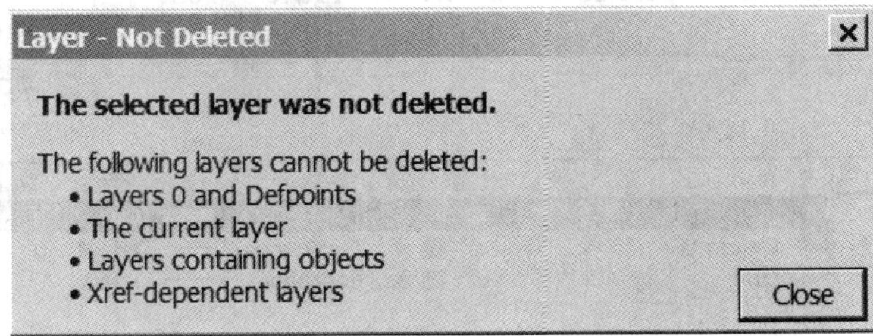

Figure 5-8b

5.5.4. Make a layer a current layer 

AutoCAD provides three ways to make a layer the current layer.

1. Use the down arrow in *Layer* toolbar (*Home* tab and *Layer* panel) and choose the desired layer, Figure 5-9a.

Figure 5-9a

2. Click on the *Make Object's Layer Current* tool ( ) in the *Layer* panel (*Home* tab) and follow the prompts.
3. In the *Layer Properties Manager* palette, click on a layer, and click on the *Set Current* ( ) button, Figure 5-9b. Close the *Layer Properties Manager* palette to make the change permanent.

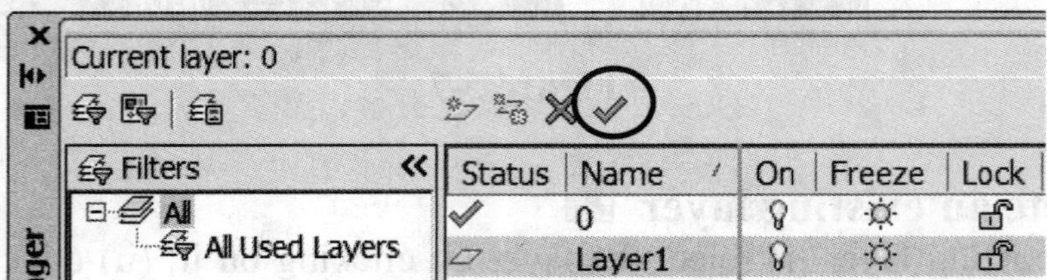

Figure 5-9b

5.6.   Drawing and layers

In order to draw on any layers, the drafter must make the desired layer a current layer and then draw on it. Also, **remember** to turn *On* and *thaw* (not freeze) the current layer before drawing any object.

5.7.   Move objects from one layer to another layer

The drafter desired to place the dimensions on the dimension layer. The *DIM* layer was previously created and its properties are shown in Figure 5-10a.

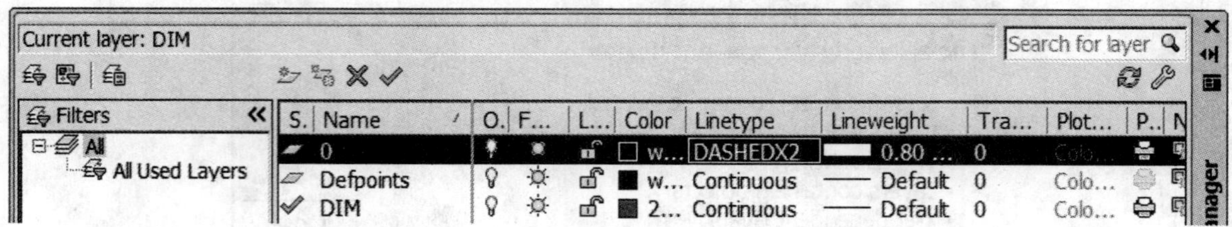

Figure 5-10a

After drawing the objects and adding the dimension, Figure 5-10b, the drafter realized that the dimensions are not on the DIM layer. The drafter can correct the mistake by moving the dimensions to the DIM layer, Figure 5-10c.

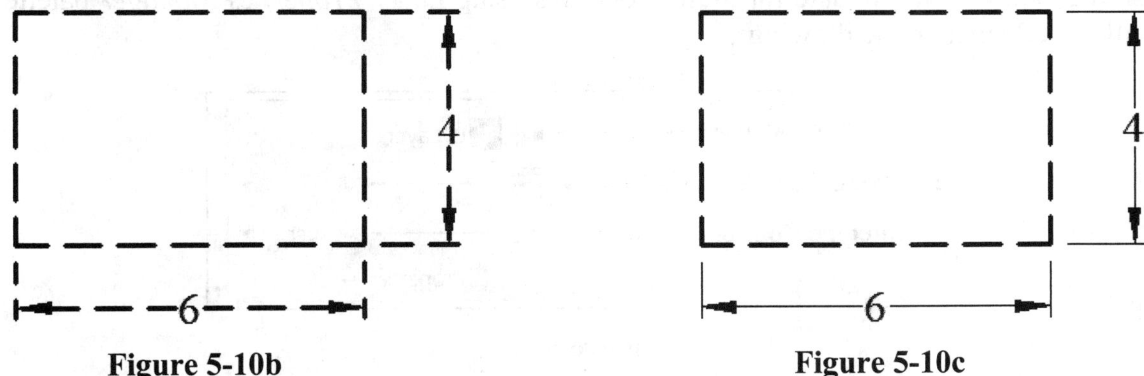

Figure 5-10b   **Figure 5-10c**

If objects are created on one layer, and later it is necessary to move them to another layer then use the following step to move the objects.

1. Select the objects to be moved, Figure 5-10d, dimensions in the example.
2. Select the layer as shown in Figure 5-10e, that is, press the down arrow in the *Layers* toolbar and click on the desired layer.
3. The selected objects (dimensions in the example) will move to the selected layer (DIM layer in the example). The dimensions were created on *Layer 0* but are now moved to the *DIM* layer.
4. <u>***Check***</u>: To make sure that the objects have moved to the selected layer, turn *Off* the selected layer and if the objects disappear then it means that the objects have moved. If the objects do no disappear then repeat steps #1 - #3.
5. The objects (dimensions) are moved to the desired layer (DIM), Figure 5-10e, however, the current layer is still the *Layer 0*.

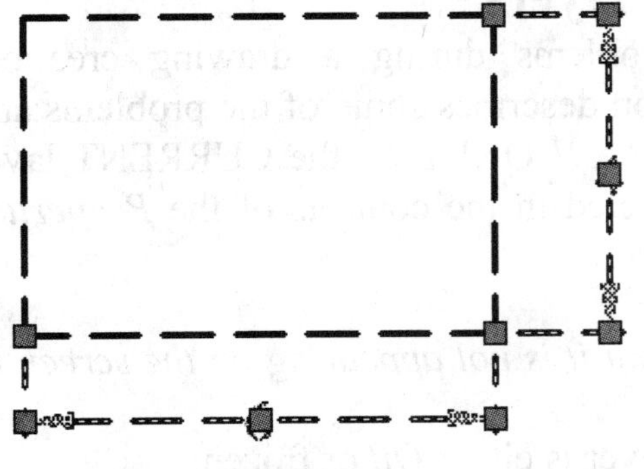
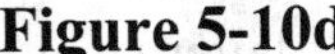
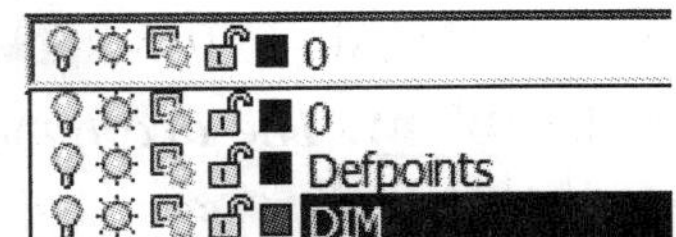

Figure 5-10d   **Figure 5-10e**

5.8. The *Defpoints* layer

Both the Figure 5-10c and Figure 5-10e shows a layer named as "*Defpoint*". The *Defpoint* layer is created by the system during the dimensioning process. The user has no control over this layer. That is, the layer cannot be renamed or deleted and its contents cannot be printed.

5.9.   Update layer properties

In order to draw on specific layers with the layer properties, it is important that on the *Properties* panel, the color, linetype, and lineweight are set to *By Layer*, Figure 5-4b (shown below). Any update for these properties using *Layer Properties Manager* palette will be reflected on the drawing.

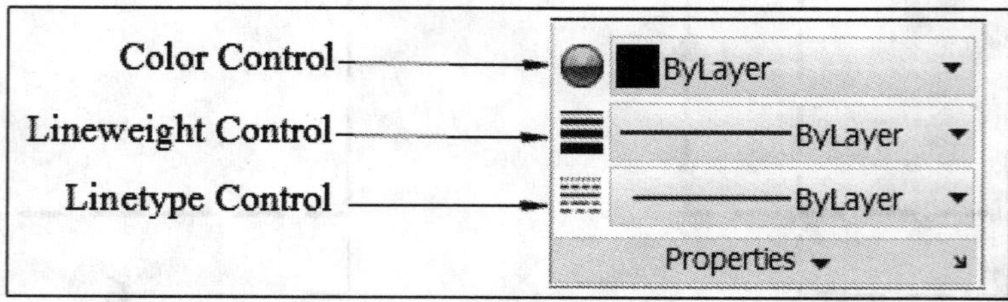

Figure 5-4b

1. <u>Color</u>: All objects drawn on the layer will be displayed in the chosen color provided that the objects' color setting in the *Properties* toolbar is set to *By Layer*, Figure 5-4b.
2. <u>Lineweight</u>: All objects drawn on the layer will be displayed in the chosen lineweight, provided that the objects' lineweight setting in the *Properties* toolbar is set to *By Layer*, Figure 5-4b. Lineweight is discussed in detail in Chapter #3.
3. <u>Linetype</u>: All objects drawn on the layer will be displayed in the chosen linetype, provided that the objects' linetype setting in the *Properties* toolbar is set to *By Layer*, Figure 5-4. Linetype is discussed in detail in Chapter #3.

If the properties of the object drawn are not set *By Layer*, then any update for the layer properties will **NOT** be reflected on the drawing.

5.10.   Frequent problems with the layers

The user may come across one or more problems during a drawing creation, modification, and plotting using layers. This section describes some of the problems and their solution. **Remember** that, the drafter can DRAW ONLY on the CURRENT layer and objects will appear based on the options selected in the controls of the *Properties* toolbar.

1. **<u>Problem</u>:** *The drafter is creating an object but it is not appearing on the screen in the drawing area.*
   <u>Reason</u>: This problem occurs if the current layer is either *Off* or frozen.
   <u>Solution</u>: This problem can be solved by turning *On* the current layer (if it was *Off*) or thawing the current layer (if it was frozen).

2. **Problem:** *The drafter has created an object but its color/lineweight/linetype is different for the object's layer color.*
   Reason: This problem occurs if the current layer is not the object's layer or the layer toolbar is not set correctly.
   Solution: This problem can be solved as follow.
   1. If the current layer is not the object's layer then move the object to its layer. Also, make sure that the current layer is the object's layer.
   2. If the layer toolbar is not set correctly then select the object and set the *color/lineweight/linetype* controls to *By Layer*. Also, make sure that the three controls are set to *By Layer* before drawing the objects.

3. **Problem:** *The drafter is changing the layers color/lineweight/linetype in Layer Properties Manager palette but the objects are not changing their color/lineweight/linetype in the drawing area.*
   Reason: This problem occurs if the *Color color/lineweight/linetype* of the *Properties* toolbar is not set to *By Layer* option.
   Solution: This problem can be solved by as follow: (i) Select the objects; (ii) press the down arrow of the *color/lineweight/linetype Control* in the *Properties* toolbar; and (iii) select the *By Layer* option.

4. **Problem:** *The drafter can see the objects but cannot plot them.*
   Reason: This problem occurs if the objects in question are drawn in the *defpoints* layer or the layer's plot option is *off* (⊟).
   Solution: This problem can be solved as follow.
   1. If the objects are drawn on the *defpoints* layer, then move them to their respective layers and the drafter will be able to plot the objects.
   2. If the objects are not drawn on the *defpoints* layer then open the *Layer Properties Manager* palette. If the layer's (containing the objects in question) plot option is *off*, that is, the layer's printer icon shows the no entry sign (⊟) then just click on the printer icon. The no entry sign will disappear (🖨) and the drafter will be able to plot the drawing.

5.11.   Illustrative example

Example: Draw the objects shown in Figure 5-11 using layers. The drafter can use the following commands to create the drawing.

- Open a new acad template file.
- Create three layers and name them as *Circle, Rectangle,* and DIM. Set the properties (color, linetype, and lineweight) of the layers as shown in Figure 5-12.

- In order to draw on different layers with the layer properties, it is important that on the *Properties* toolbar, the *Color, Linetype,* and *Lineweight* controls must be set to *By Layer*, Figure 5-11.

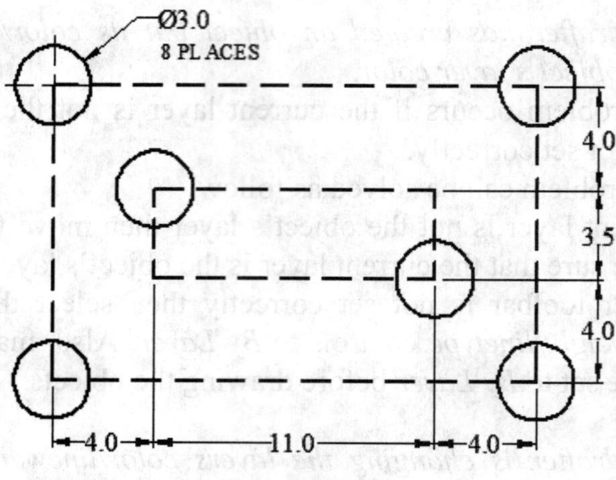

Figure 5-11

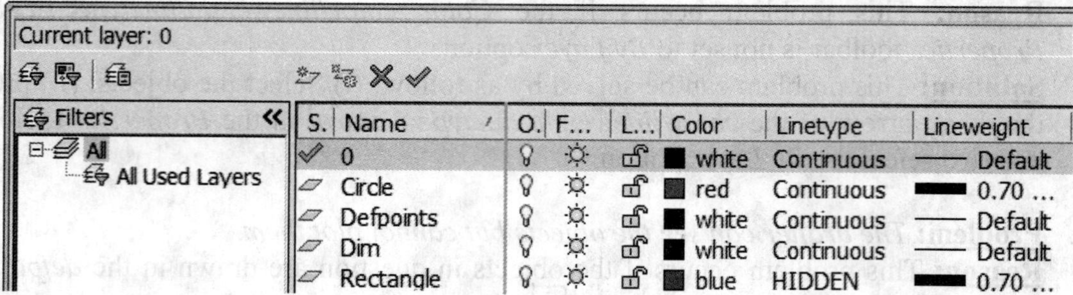

Figure 5-12

- Make the *Rectangle* layer as the current layer and draw the rectangles.
- Make the *Circle* layer as the current layer and draw the circles.
- The resulting drawing is shown in Figure 5-13.
- Make the *Dim* layer as the current layer and add the dimensions. If the user has not learnt the dimensioning techniques, then skip this step.

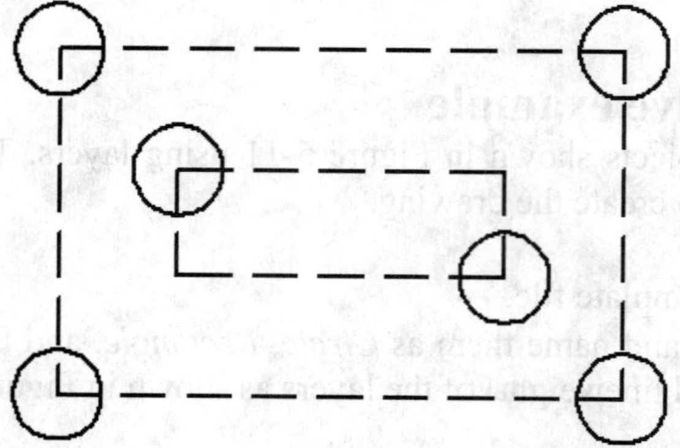

Figure 5-13

- Although, the linetype of the rectangles shown in Figure 5-13 and Figure 5-14c is the same, yet, the line appearance is different because the linetype scale is different.

- To change the linetype scale, select the rectangles, Figure 5-14a.

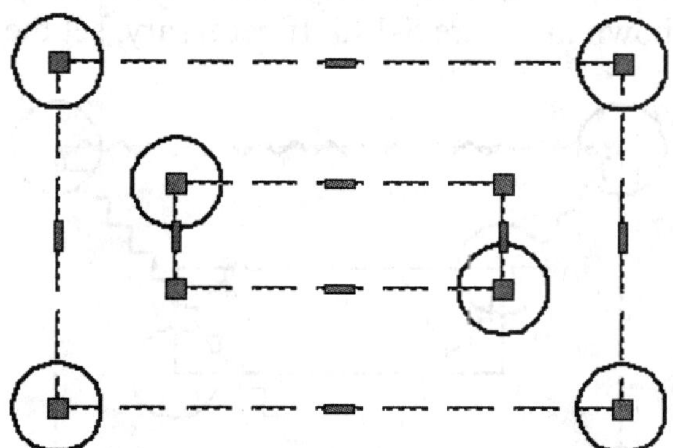

Figure 5-14a

- Press the right button of the mouse and choose the *Properties* option.
- This will open the *Properties* palette, Figure 5-14b.
- Select the *Linetype scale* and type 0.5 in the corresponding right column.
- Press the *Enter* key on the keyboard.
- The resulting drawing is shown in Figure 5-14c.

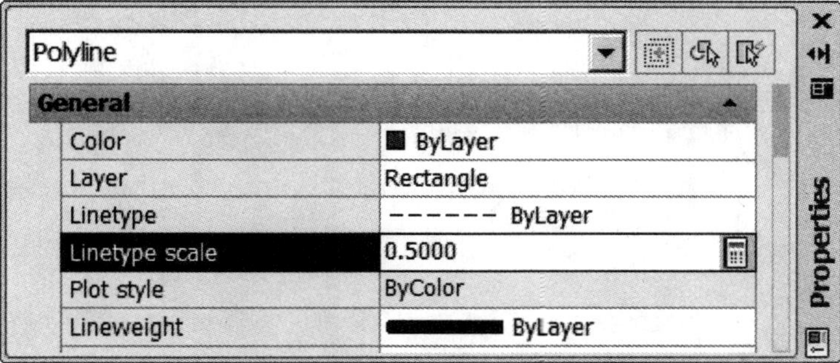

Figure 5-14b

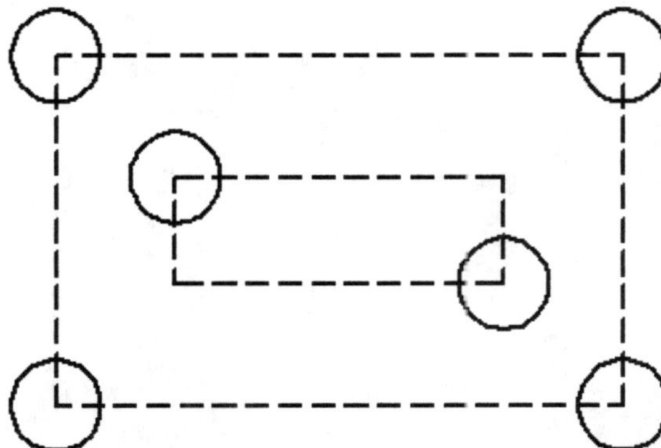

Figure 5-14c

Now, create a layer and rename it to be *Triangle*. Set its color, linetype, and lineweight to be *magenta*, *ZIGZAG*, and *default*, respectively. Make the *Triangle* to be the current layer and draw the triangles shown in Figure 5-14d. If necessary, set the linetype scale.

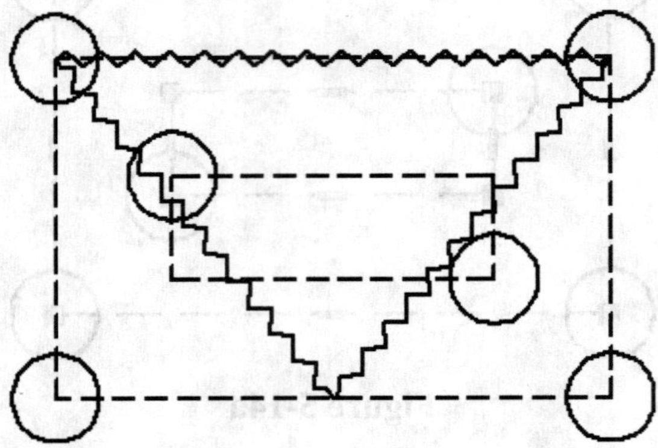

Figure 5-14d

6.   Blocks

6.1.   Objectives

- Learn about different types of block
- Learn to create and insert blocks
- Learn to combine blocks
- Learn to use blocks from the *Design Center*

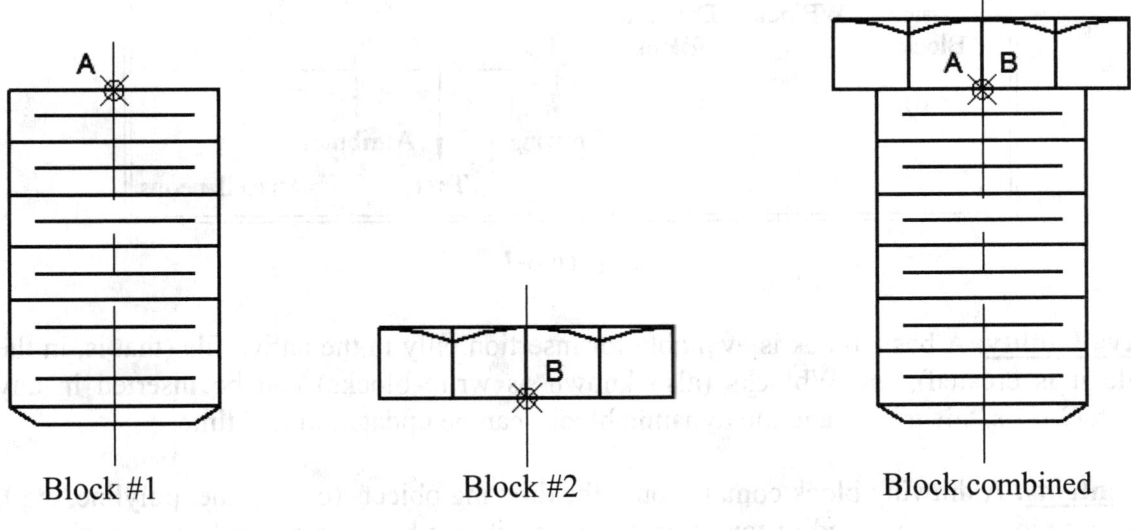

Block #1   Block #2   Block combined

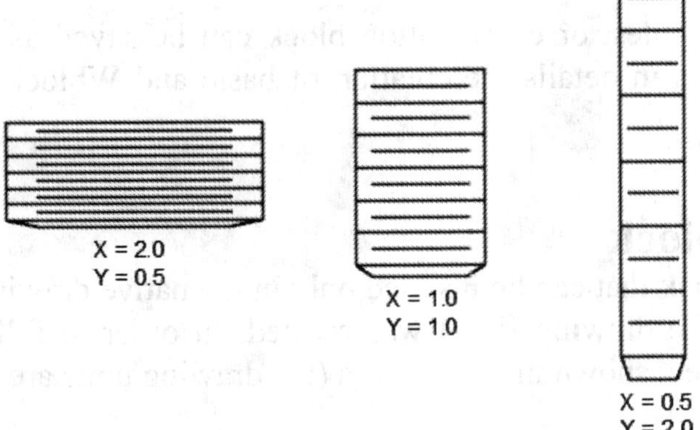

6.2.　　Introduction

In AutoCAD, block is a general term for one or more objects that are combined to create a single entity. That is, a block is a group of entities saved as a single unit. If an object (or group of objects) is used frequently, then time can be saved if the object is created once and inserted as many time as needed in the same or a different drawing.

A Block can be classified, Figure 6-1, on the basis of its availability or its contents.

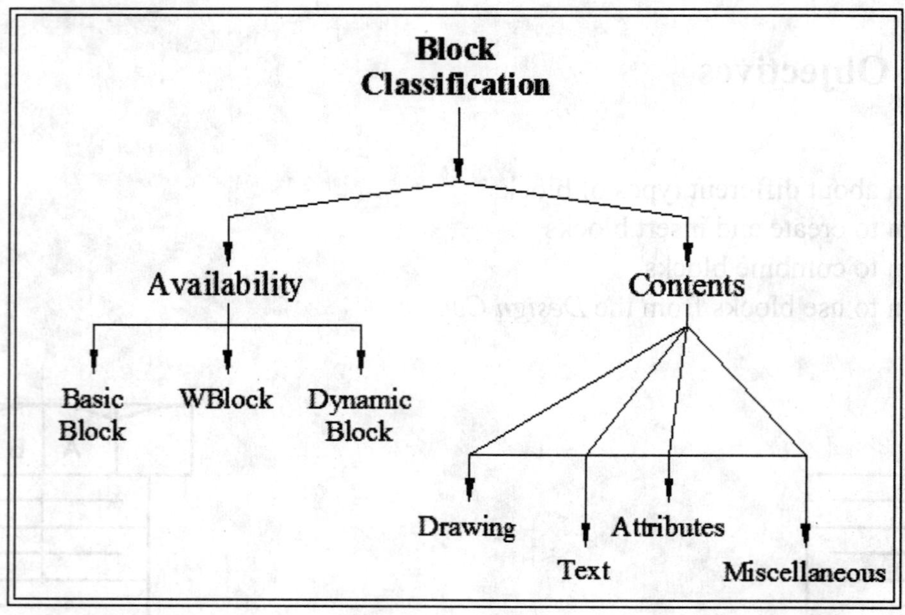

Figure 6-1

<u>Availability</u>: A basic block is available for insertion only in the native file (that is, in the file it is created), the Wblocks (also known as write blocks) can be inserted in any AutoCAD's ".dwg" file and the dynamic blocks can be updated in real time.

<u>Contents</u>: A drawing block contains only the drawing objects (circle, line, polyline, etc.). A text block is composed of text objects. An attributes block is created using attributes, (attributes are the sections of text added to a block that prompts the user to add information to the drawing). A miscellaneous block can contain any combination.

A drawing, text, attributes, or combination block can be saved as a basic or Wblocks. This chapter discusses in details the creation of basic and Wblock using drawing, text, and attributes.

6.3.　　Basic block

A basic block is a block that can be inserted only in the native drawing file. That is, it can be inserted only in the drawing file it was created. In order to follow a block creation process, draw the object shown in Figure 6-2a (the drawing units are in inches).

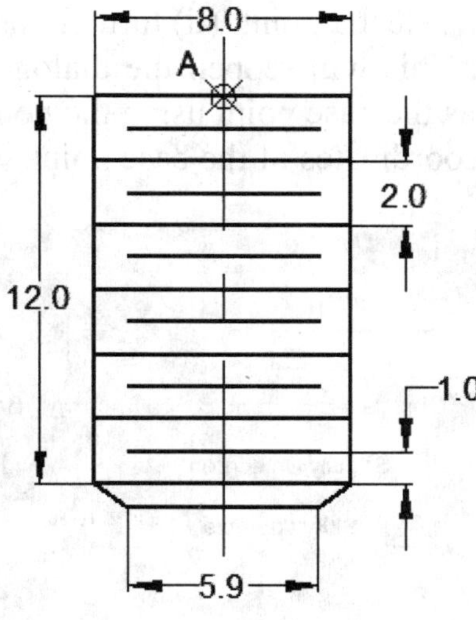

Figure 6-2a

6.3.1. Create a basic block

- The *Make Block* command is activated using one of the following procedures.
  1. Panel method: Either from the *Home* tab and *Block* panel select the *Make Block* ( ) tool; or from the *Insert* tab and *Block Definition* panel select the *Make Block* tool.
  2. Command line method: Type "block", "Block", or "BLOCK" on the command line and press the *Enter* key.

- The activation of the command will open the *Block Definition* dialog box as shown in Figure 6-2b.

6.3.2. Block definition dialog box

The main features of the *Block Definition* dialog box (Figure 6-2b) are briefly discussed here.

- *Name*: The *Name* field is used to name the block. The name can be 255 characters long and can include letters, numbers, and blank spaces. However, blocks should be given meaningful names. In the current example, the block is named "Thread".
- *Base point*: The *Base point* panel is used to choose an insertion base point (or a reference point) for the block. The selection of a proper base point is an important factor in the block creation process. Its default value is (0,0,0). However, to make the insertion process efficient, select the base point on the object itself. In the current example, point 'A' will be selected to be the base point. The base point is selected using one of the following techniques.
  - ○ *Specify On-screen*: The selection of this box will make the other two options inactive. The prompts to specify the base point will appear when the *Block Definition* dialog box is closed. In the current example, check this box.
  - ○ *Pick point*: In order to choose the base point using the pointing device: (i) click on the pointing device button ( ), this will temporarily close the dialog box

and allows the user to select a point; (ii) turn on the *object snap* option and click on the desired point. This will reopen the dialog box. In the current example, point 'A' is selected as the base point using the pointing device.

- o *X, Y, Z*: Specify the coordinates of the base point.

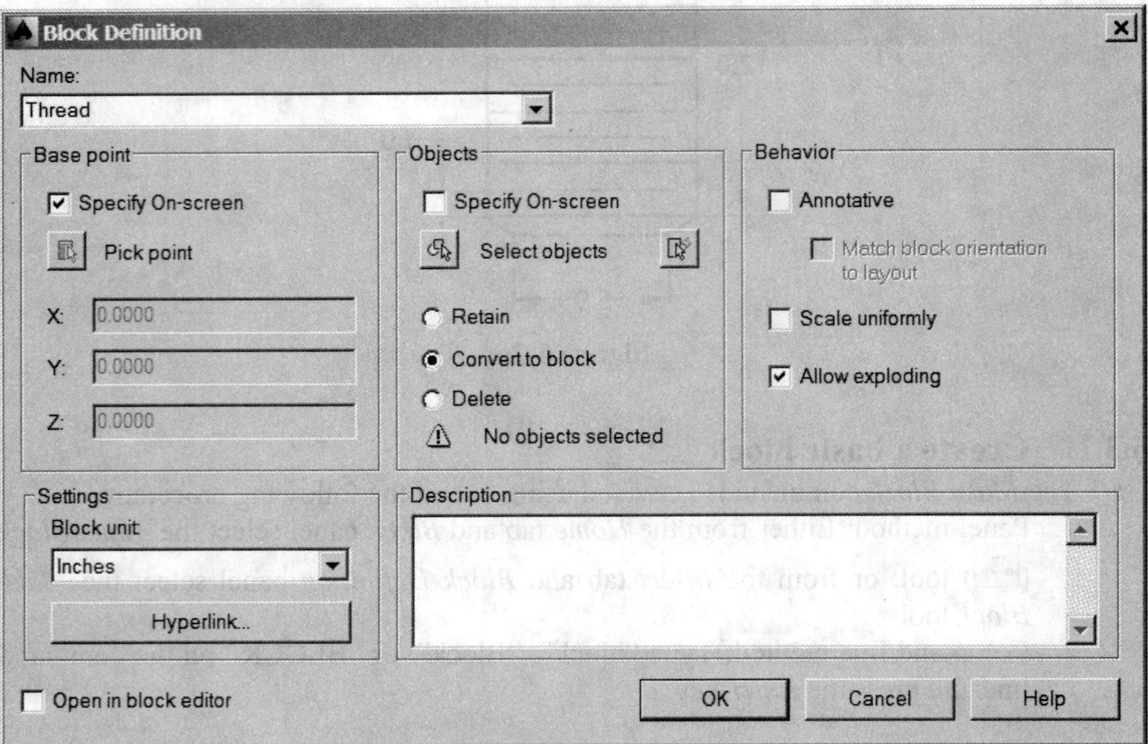

Figure 6-2b

- *Object*: The *Object* panel is used to select the objects to be included in the block.
  - o *Specify On-screen*: The selection of this box will make the other two options inactive. The prompts to select the object will appear when the *Block Definition* dialog box is closed.
  - o *Select objects*: In the current example, this option will be used. (i) Click on the object selection pointing device button (⬚). This will temporarily close the dialog box and allows the user to select the objects. (ii) Select the objects using one of the object selection methods; this will reopen the dialog box. In this example, the dimensions are excluded from the block.
  - o *Retain*: This option retains the selected objects as distinct objects in the drawing after the block is created.
  - o *Convert to block*: This option converts the selected objects to a block in the drawing after the block is created. In the current example, this option is used.
  - o *Delete*: This option deletes the selected objects from the drawing after the block is created.
- *Behavior*: The behavior panel is used to specify the behavior for a block.
  - o *Scale uniformly*: During the insertion process the user may want to (i) scale the object uniformly (same scale factors in *X*, *Y*, and *Z* direction) or (ii) use different

scale factors in *X*, *Y*, and *Z* direction. Since a block can only be scaled uniformly from the second option, therefore, do not check this box. In the current example, this box is not checked.

- o ***Allow exploding***: This box specifies whether or not a block can be decomposed to the basic object (exploded). Checking of this box will allow the user to modify the block. In the current example, check this box.
- *Setting*: The setting panel is used to specify the settings for a block.
  - o ***Block units***: This option specifies the insertion units for the block reference.
- *Open in block editor*: This option will insert the block in the block editing mode. In the current example, this box is not checked.
- *OK*: Click the *OK* button to save the changes and to close the dialog box.
- When the user clicked the *OK* button, the prompt shown in Figure 6-2c will appear.

Specify insertion base point:	20.0411	-32.6788

Figure 6-2c

- Turn on the object snap and click at point *A*.
- The object selection prompt will appear, Figure 6-2d.
- In this example, the dimensions and the label *A* are excluded from the block. Select the objects as shown in Figure 6-2d.
- Either press the right button of the mouse or press the *Enter* key.
- This will complete the basic block creation process.
- Click on the block, the block will have only one grip point. The base point is the only grip point, Figure 6-2e.

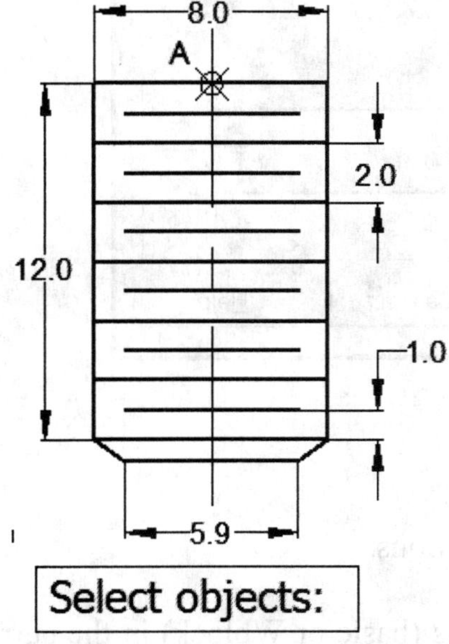

Figure 6-2d

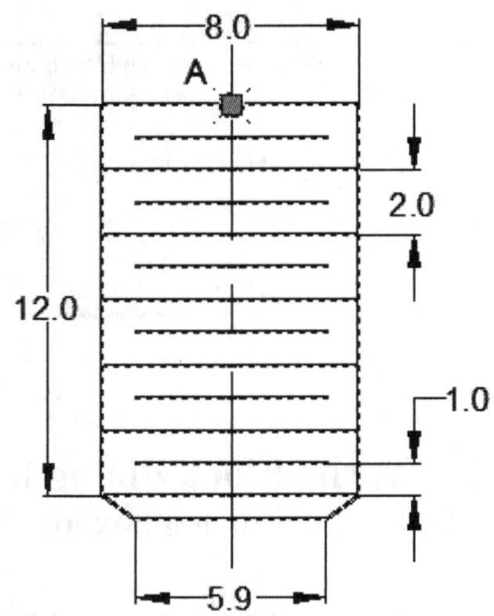

Figure 6-2e

6.4.   Wblock

Wblocks (write blocks) are the blocks that can be inserted into any drawing. These blocks are saved as independent drawing files.

6.4.1.   Create a Wblock

- Create a basic block. This example will use the 'Thread' block created in the basic block section.
- Activate the *Wblock* command.
  - o The *WBlock* command is activated using the command line method. At the command prompt, type *Wblock* and press the *Enter*. The *Write Block* dialog box will appear, Figure 6-3a.

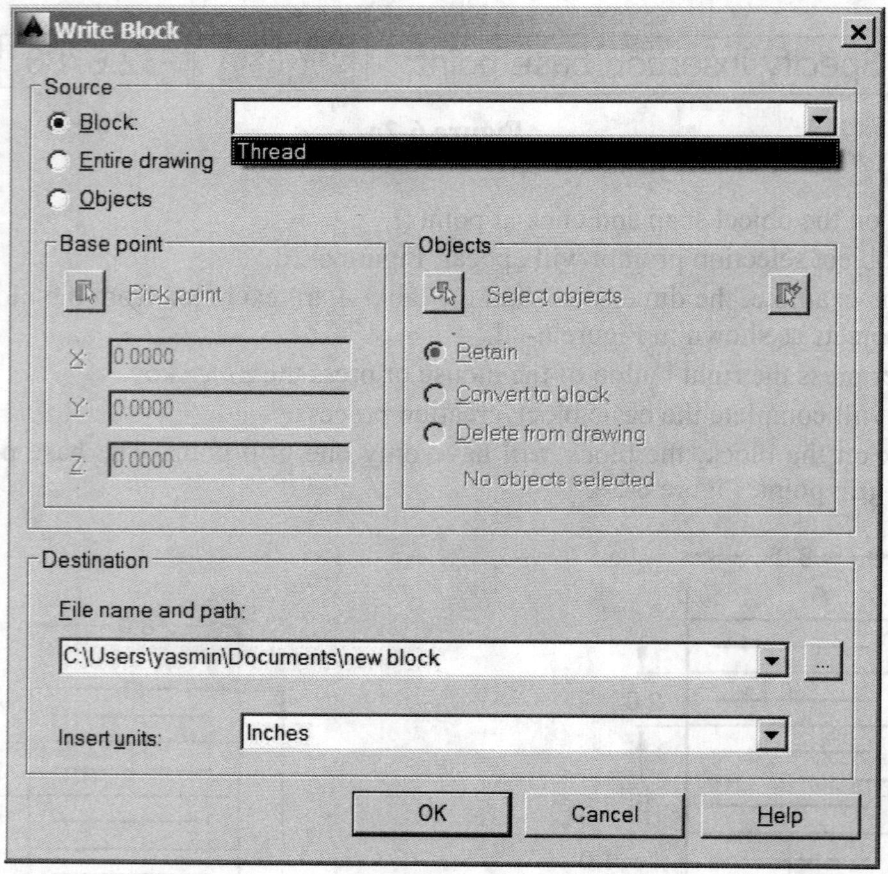

Figure 6-3a

6.4.2.   Write block dialog box

In the *Write Block* dialog box, perform the following actions.

- *Source*: Select the *Block* option. The list of blocks (basic or Wblock) in the current file will be available. Press the down arrow to choose the block. Select the "Thread" block created in the basic block section.

- *Base point*: This option is deactivated if the *Block* option is selected in the *Source* panel.
- *Object*: This option is deactivated if the *Block* option is selected in the *Source* panel.
- *Destination*: Select the location to store the Wblock file by clicking (⬚) destination button. This will open *Browse for Drawing File* dialog box, Figure 6-3b. Specify the location and click the *Save* button.

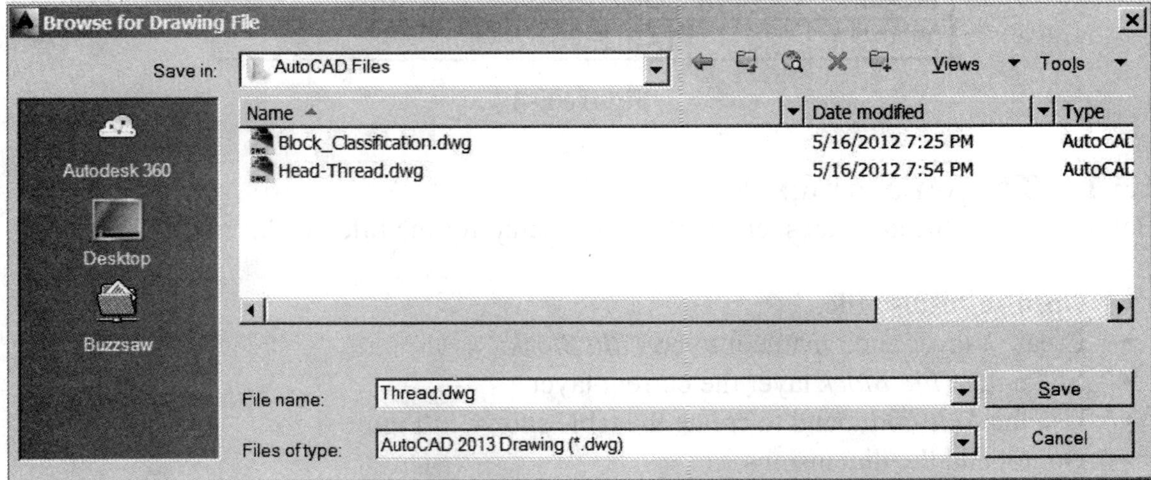

Figure 6-3b

- *OK*: Now, click the *OK* button in the *Write Block* dialog box to save the changes.
- This will close the *Write Block* dialog box, and the *Wblock Preview* window shown in Figure 6-3c will pop up for a very short time. This is the indication that the *Wblock* is created properly.

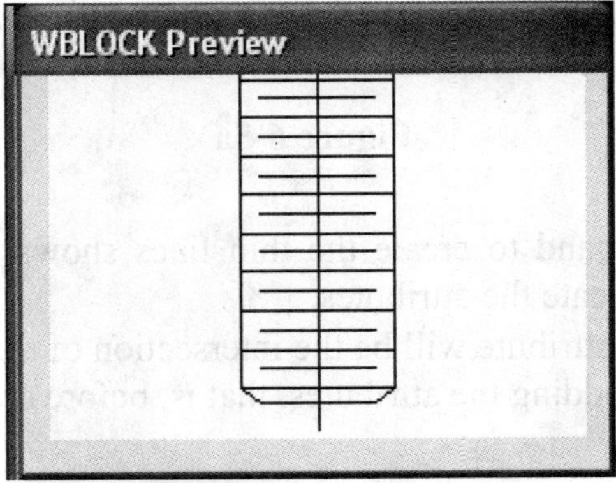

Figure 6-3c

6.5.   Block with attributes

Attributes are the sections of text added to a block that prompts the user to add information to the drawing. This section will create a title block with attributes shown in Figure 6-4. The title block includes the information to uniquely identify the drawing. The title block is generally located on the lower right corner of a drawing. A title block entries depend on a company. The block created in this section is typically used in academic institutions.

CLEMSON UNIVERSITY		
SECTION #1	NIGHAT YASMIN	
EX 3-4	LAB #8	SHT 1 OF 2
SCALE: 1:1	MILLIMETERS	LETTER
05/16/2013	TABLE #0	

Figure 6-4

6.5.1.   The initial setup

Before creating the attributes, create the initial setup for the title block.

- Open an acadiso file.
- Create a layer and rename it to be *Title Block*.
- Make the *Title Block* layer the current layer.
- Use the *Line* command to create the table shown in Figure 6-5a.
- Do not add the dimensions.

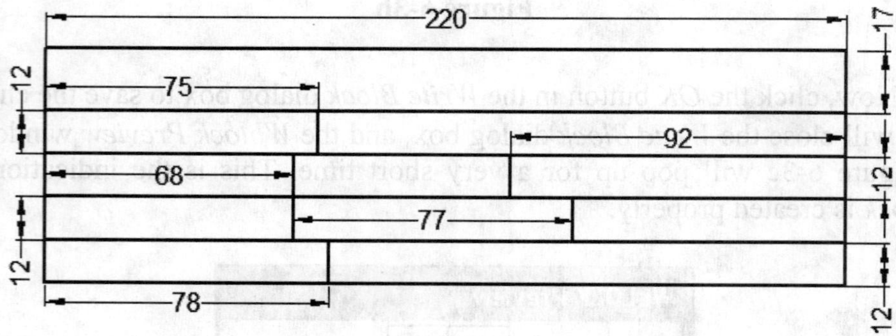

Figure 6-5a

- Use the *Offset* command to create the thin lines shown in Figure 6-5b. The thin lines are created to locate the attributes.
- The start point of an attribute will be the intersection of the thin lines. The thin lines will be deleted after adding the attributes, that is, before creating the block.

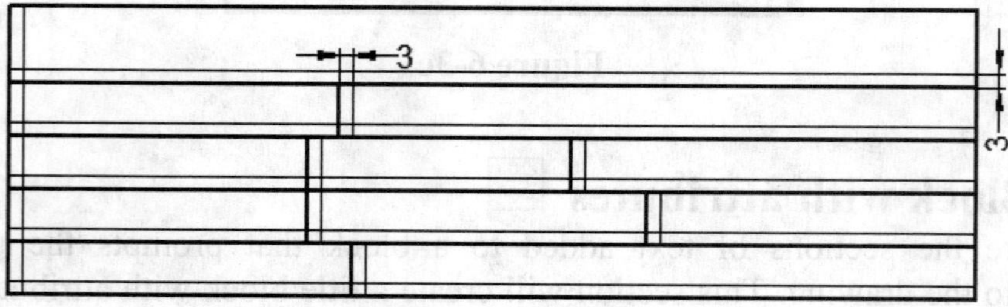

Figure 6-5b

An attribute is defined through the *Attribute Definition* dialog box, Figure 6-5c, and the dialog box is open using one of the following procedures.

1. Panel method: Either from the *Home* tab and expanded *Block* panel select the *Define Attributes* tool; or from the *Insert* tab and *Block Definition* panel select the *Define Attributes* tool.
2. Command line method: Type "attdef", "Attdef", or "ATTDEF" on the command line and press the *Enter* key.

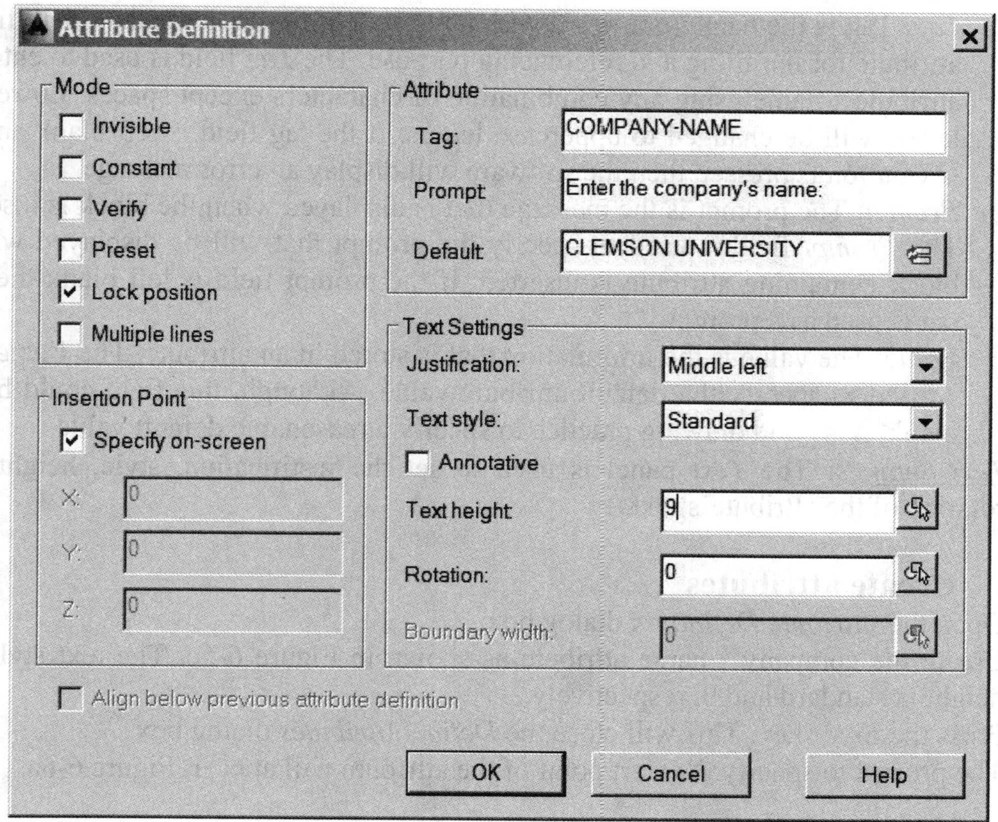

Figure 6-5c

6.5.2. Attribute definition dialog box

The main features of the *Attribute Definition* dialog box (Figure 6-5c) are briefly discussed here.

- *Mode*: The *Mode* panel is used to set the options of attribute for inserting the attributes in the drawing.
  - o *Lock position*: This option allows for the locking of the position of the attribute within the block reference. In the current example, this box is checked.
- *Insertion Point*: The *Insertion Point* panel is used to set the location of an attribute in the drawing. The user can specify either the coordinates or pick the location in the drawing area. In the current example, the *Specify on-screen* box is checked,

because the drafter has defined the location of the attributes, the intersection of the thin lines.

- *Align below previous attribute definition*: If this box is checked then the second and subsequent attribute tags are placed directly below the previously defined attribute. This option is not available for the first attribute. In the current example, this option is not checked, because the drafter has defined the location of the attributes, the intersection of the thin lines.
- *Attribute*: The *Attribute* panel is used to set attribute data. An attribute has three characteristics.
  - *Tag*: Tag is the name (one word with no space) of the attribute that identifies an attribute for the filing and referencing purpose. The *Tag* field is used to enter the attribute's name using any combination of characters except spaces. Lowercase letters will be changed to uppercase letters. If the tag field is left blank and the *OK* button is pressed then the software will display an error message.
  - *Prompt*: The prompt is the message that is displayed when the block is inserted. The *Prompt* field is used to specify the prompt that will be displayed when a block containing attribute is inserted. If the prompt field is left blank then the tag is used as a prompt.
  - *Value*: The value is the information that is stored in an attribute. The *Value* field is used to specify the default attribute value. Although, this field could be left blank, it is good drawing practice to specify a reasonable default value.
- *Text Settings*: The *Text* panel is used to set the justification, style, height, and rotation of the attribute's text.

6.5.3. Create attributes
1. Open the *Attribute Definition* dialog box.
2. Create the company's name attribute as shown in Figure 6-5c. The text style and height is standard and 9, respectively.
3. Press the *Enter* key. This will close the *Define Attributes* dialog box.
4. The prompt to specify the start point of the attribute will appear, Figure 6-6a.

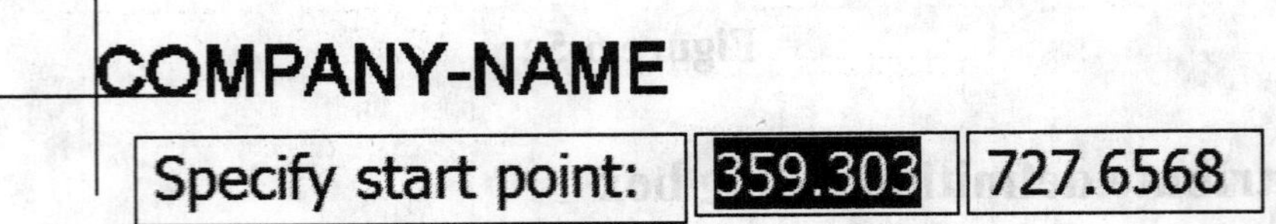

Figure 6-6a

5. Click at the lower left corner of the thin lines intersection in the topmost cell, Figure 6-6b.
6. Repeat steps #2 to #5 to create the remaining attributes. Set the text height to 6, Figure 6-6b.
7. The tag, prompt, and values of the attributes used in the title block are shown in Table #1. The first entry in each cell is the tag, the second entry is the prompt, and the third entry is the default value of the attribute.

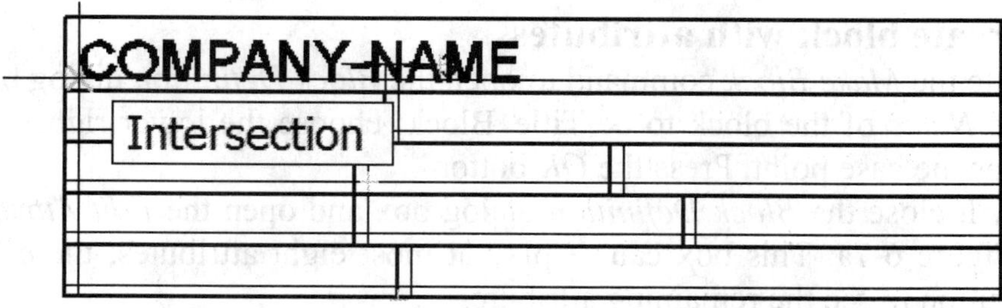

Figure 6-6b

8. The resulting title block is shown in Figure 6-6c.
9. Delete the thin lines, and the final version of the title block is shown in Figure 6-6d.

Table #1: Tag, prompt, and default values for attributes

COMPANY-NAME Enter the company's name: CLEMSON UNIVERSITY		
SECTION_NO Enter section #: EG210 - 024	NAME Enter your name: NIGHAT YASMIN	
EX-NO Enter the exercise #: EX 6_4	HW-LAB-# Enter HW # or LAB #: LAB #8	SHEET-NO Enter sheet #: SHT 1 OF 2
SCALE Scale of the drawing: SCALE: 1:1	UNITS Enter the units of the drawing: MILLIMETERS	PAPER Enter the paper type: LETTER
DATE Enter today's date: 05/16/2013	TABLE-NO Your table #: TABLE #0	

COMPANY-NAME		
SECTION_NO	NAME	
EX-NO	HW-LAB-#	SHEET-NO
SCALE	UNITS	PAPER
DATE	TABLE-NO	

Figure 6-6c

COMPANY-NAME		
SECTION_NO	NAME	
EX-NO	HW-LAB-#	SHEET-NO
SCALE	UNITS	PAPER
DATE	TABLE-NO	

Figure 6-6d

6.5.4. Create block with attributes

1. Activate the *Make Block* command to open the *Block Definition* dialog box.
2. Set the *Name* of the block to be Title_Block; choose the lower right corner of the block as the base point. Press the *OK* button.
3. This will close the *Block Definition* dialog box and open the *Edit Attributes* dialog box, Figure 6-7a. This box can display at most eight attributes; therefore, use the *Next* button to see the remaining attributes.
4. Make any changes (if necessary) and press the *OK* button.
5. This will close the *Edit Attributes* dialog box. The block will display the default values of the various attributes, Figure 6-7b.

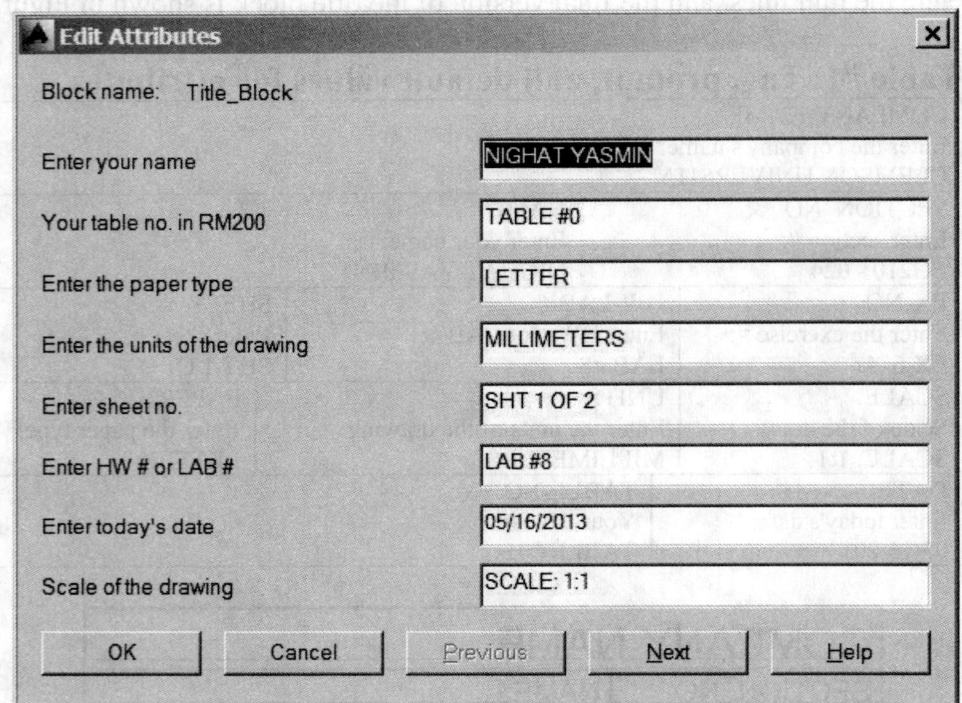

Figure 6-7a

CLEMSON UNIVERSITY		
SECTION #1	NIGHAT YASMIN	
EX 3-4	LAB #8	SHT 1 OF 2
SCALE: 1:1	MILLIMETERS	LETTER
05/16/2013	TABLE #0	

Figure 6-7b

6.5.5. Convert to Wblock

The process to convert a block with attributes into a Wblock is identical to converting a basic block into a Wblock.

6.6.   Block with text boxes

This section will create a block that contains several text boxes. This example will create a release block. A release block contains a list of approval signatures or initials required before the drawing is released for the production. Create a release block as follow.

- Open an acadiso file.
- Create a layer and rename it to be *Release Block*.
- Make the *Release Block* layer the current layer.
- Use the *Line* command to create a table shown in Figure 6-8a.
- Do not add the dimensions.
- Use the *Offset* command to create the thin lines shown in Figure 6-8a.

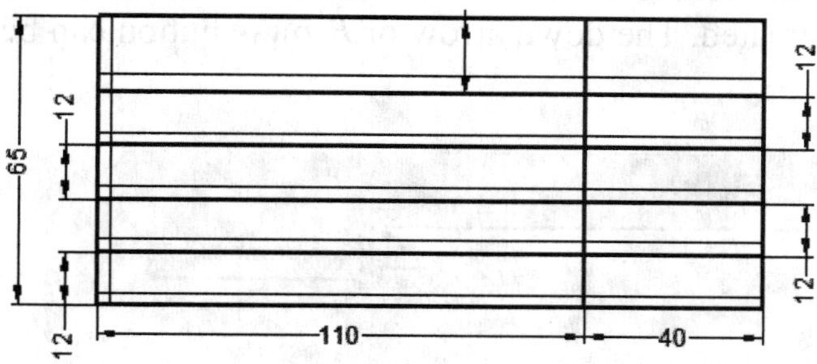

Figure 6-8a

- Use the *Text* command to create the text shown in Figure 6-8b. Select the font type as Arial and the text height as 9 for the team manager and 6 for the others.
- Remove the thin lines, Figure 6-8c.
- Create a basic block, set the *Name* of the block to be Release_Block, and choose the lower right corner of the block as the base point.
- Convert it to a Wblock.

TEAM MANAGER	
DRAWN BY	
DESIGNED BY	
CHECKED BY	
CUSTOMER	

Figure 6-8b

TEAM MANAGER	
DRAWN BY	
DESIGNED BY	
CHECKED BY	
CUSTOMER	

Figure 6-8c

6.7.   Basic Block Insertion

The basic block, *Thread*, created earlier will be used to demonstrate the block insertion process.

- The *Insert Block* command is activated using one of the following procedures.
  1. Panel method: Either from the *Home* tab and *Block* panel select the *Insert Block* ( ) tool; or from the *Insert* tab and *Block* panel select the *Insert Block* tool.
  2. Command line method: Type "insert", "Insert", or "INSERT" on the command line and press the *Enter* key.

- The activation of the command will open the *Insert* dialog box, Figure 6-9.

6.7.1. Insert dialog box
The main features of the *Insert* dialog box (Figure 6-9) are briefly discussed here.

- *Name*: The *Name* field is used to choose a named block. By default, it will display the block just created. The down arrow or *Browse* button can be used to choose any other block.

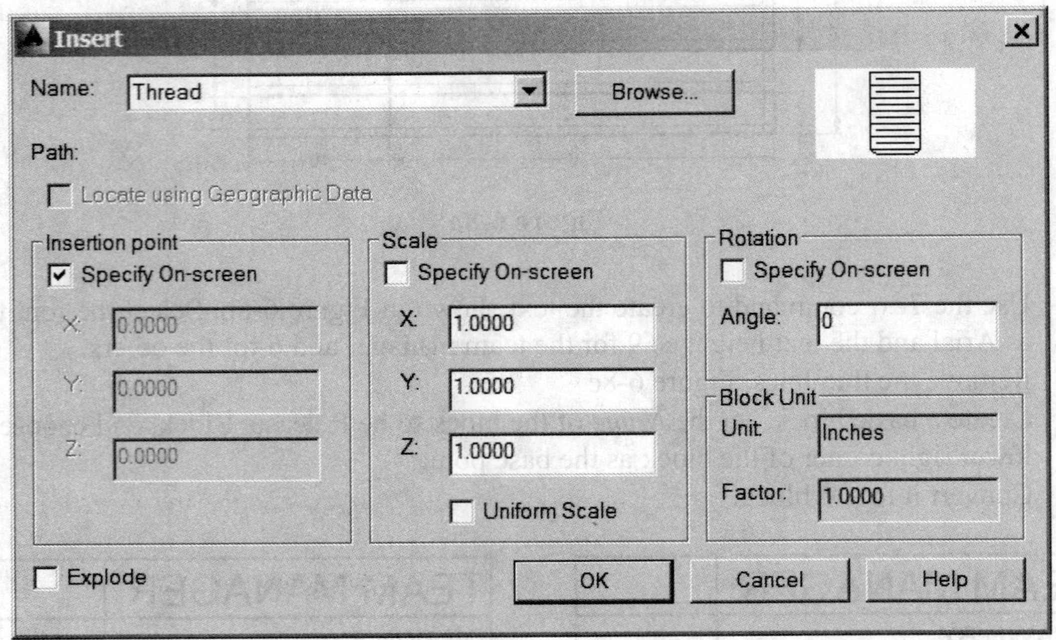

Figure 6-9

- *Path*: The *Path* option displays the location of the block. If the selected block is a basic block then *Path* will be empty and the block preview is shown in upper right corner of the block. However, if the block is saved as a wblock then the *Path* will display the location of the selected block and the preview area will be blank.
- *Insertion point*: This panel is used to specify the insertion point for the block.
  - o *Specify On-screen*: Check this box to choose the insertion point using the pointing device.
  - o *X, Y, Z*: These boxes are used to set the coordinate values. If the *Specify On-screen* option is selected, then these boxes are not available.
- *Scale*: This panel is used to specify the scale for the inserted block. The negative value for the X, Y, and Z scale factors inserts a mirror image of the block.

o *Specify On-screen*: Check this box to specify scale factors during the insertion process using the pointing device.
o *X, Y, Z*: These boxes are used to set the scale factors in the respective directions. If the *Specify On-screen* option is selected then these boxes are not available.
o *Uniform Scale*: This box is checked to specify a single scale value for the *X, Y,* and *Z* coordinates. In this case, the *Y* and *Z* fields are deactivated by the software and the value specified for X is displayed in the *Y* and *Z* fields, too.
- *Rotation*: This panel is used to specify the rotation angle for the inserted block.
  o *Specify On-screen*: Check this box to specify the angle during the insertion process using the pointing device.
  o *Angle*: Specify the value of the rotation in the dialog box. In the current example the rotation angle is set to zero.
- *Block Unit*: This panel is used to display the information regarding the inserted block. The user cannot control the content of this panel.
  o *Unit*: Displays the unit's value for the inserted block.
  o *Factors*: Displays the unit scale factor, which is calculated based on the units used in the block creation and the drawing units.
- *Explode*: If this box is checked, then the block is exploded and its parts are inserted as the individual objects. Generally, this box is not checked.
- *OK*: Click the *OK* button to insert the block and to close the dialog box.

6.7.2.   Insert a block with default values

The default scale factor is 1.00 in X, Y, and Z direction and the angle of rotation is zero. In order to insert a block with default values perform the following operation. The default options are shown in Figure 6-9.

- *Name*: Select the name of the block to be inserted. In the current example, the "Thread" block is selected.
- *Insertion point*: Check on the *Specify On-screen* box to choose the insertion point using the pointing device.
- *Scale*: Keep the *Specify On-Screen* box unchecked, and make sure that the *X, Y,* and *Z* values are 1.
- *Rotation*: Keep the *Specify On-Screen* box unchecked, and make sure that the angle of rotation values is 0.
- *Explode*: Do not check this box.
- *OK*: Click the *OK* button to insert the block. The dialog box will be closed and the block insertion process will start.
  o The prompt shown in Figure 6-10a will appear on the screen. The block will appear on the screen with its insertion (base point in the block creation process) point aligned with the cursor. The block will move with the cursor.
  o Specify the insertion point using one of the two methods. (i) Move the cursor to the desired location and press the left button of the mouse. (ii) Type the values of the x and y coordinated of the insertion point and press the *Enter* key.
  o The block shown in Figure 6-10b will appear on the screen. Recall that the dimensions were not selected as a part of the block.

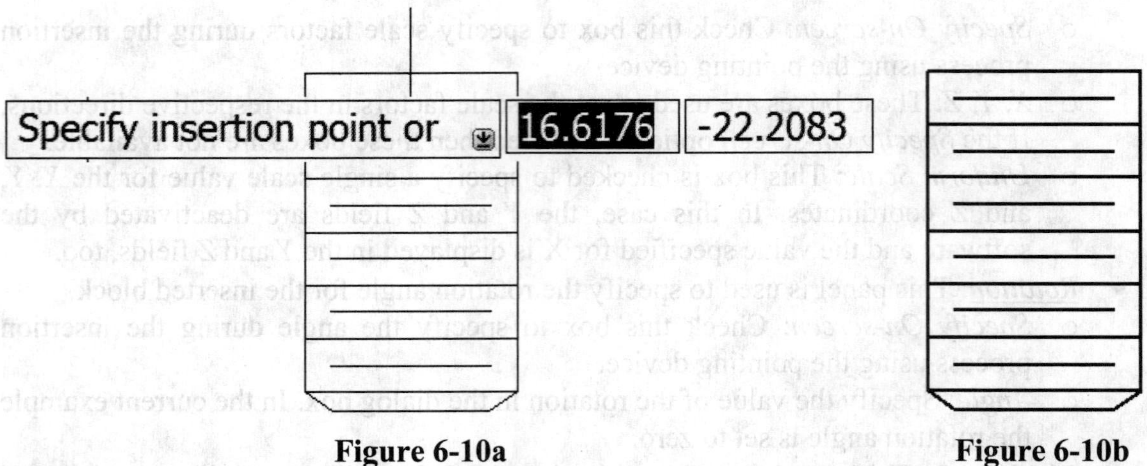

Figure 6-10a   Figure 6-10b

6.7.3. Change the scale of the block at the insertion

Figure 6-11c shows the effect of changes in the scale factors.

- *Name*: Select the name of the block to be inserted. In the current example, the "Thread" block is selected.
- *Insertion point*: Check the *Specify On-screen* box to choose the insertion point using the pointing device.
- *Scale*: Check the *Specify On-Screen* box.
- *Rotation*: Keep the *Specify On-Screen* box unchecked, and make sure that the angle of rotation values is 0.
- *Explode*: Do not check this box.
- *OK*: Click the *OK* button to insert the block. The dialog box will be closed and the block insertion process will start.
  - o The prompt to specify the insertion point will appear on the screen.
  - o Specify the insertion point.
  - o The prompt to specify the scale factor will appear on the screen, Figure 6-11a. Specify the *X* scale factor and press the *Enter* key.
  - o The prompt to specify the *Y* scale factor will appear on the screen, Figure 6-11b. Specify the Y scale factor and press the *Enter* key.
  - o The block will be inserted at the specified insertion point and at the specified scale factor, Figure 6-11c.

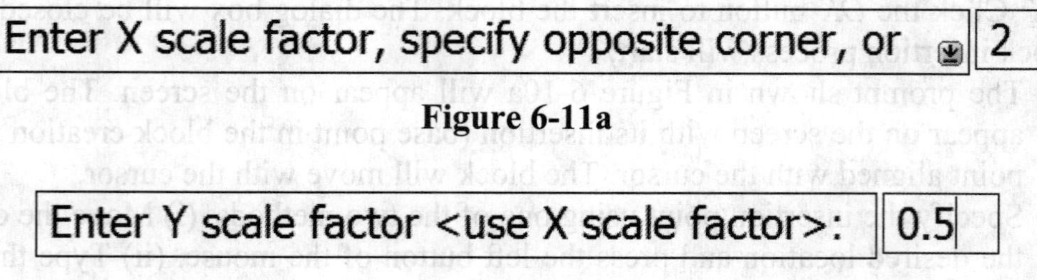

Figure 6-11a

Figure 6-11b

- Repeat the process with the following changes: (i) in the *Scale* panel, do not check the *Specify On-Screen* box (ii) type the following three set of values for the (x, y, z) fields (0.5, 2.0, 1.0), (1,0, 1.0,1.0), and (0.5, 2.0,1.0), respectively, for the three representations shown in Figure 6-11c.

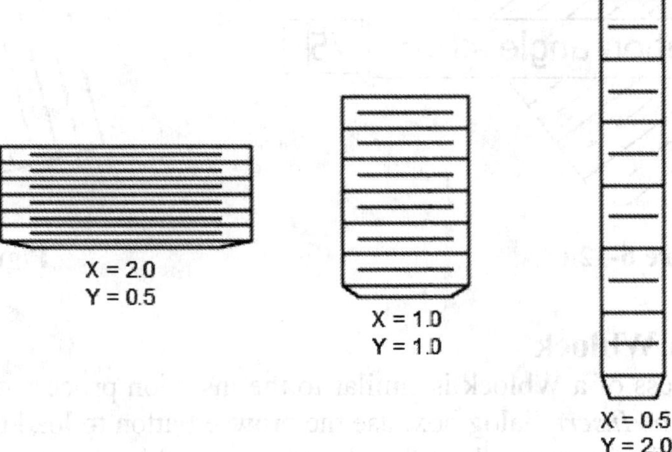

Figure 6-11c

6.7.4.   Rotate the block at the insertion

Figure 6-12a shows the effect of changes in the rotation angle.

- *Name*: Select the name of the block to be inserted. In the current example, the "Thread" block is selected.
- *Insertion point*: Check the *Specify On-screen* box to choose the insertion point using the pointing device.
- *Scale*: Keep the *Specify On-Screen* box unchecked, and make sure that the scale factors value is 1.
- *Rotation*: Do not check the *Specify On-Screen* box.
- *Explode*: Do not check this box.
- *OK*: Click the *OK* button to insert the block. The dialog box will be closed and the block insertion process will start.
  - The prompt to specify the insertion point will appear on the screen and specify the insertion point.
  - The prompt to specify the rotation angle will appear on the screen and specify the angle and press the *Enter* key Figure 6-12a.
  - The block will be inserted at the specified insertion point and rotated at the specified angle, Figure 6-12b.

- Repeat the process with the following changes: (i) in the *Scale* panel, do not check the *Specify On-Screen* box and keep the default scale; (ii) in the *Rotation* panel, do not check the *Specify On-Screen* box and type 75 in the *Angle* field, Figure 6-12b.

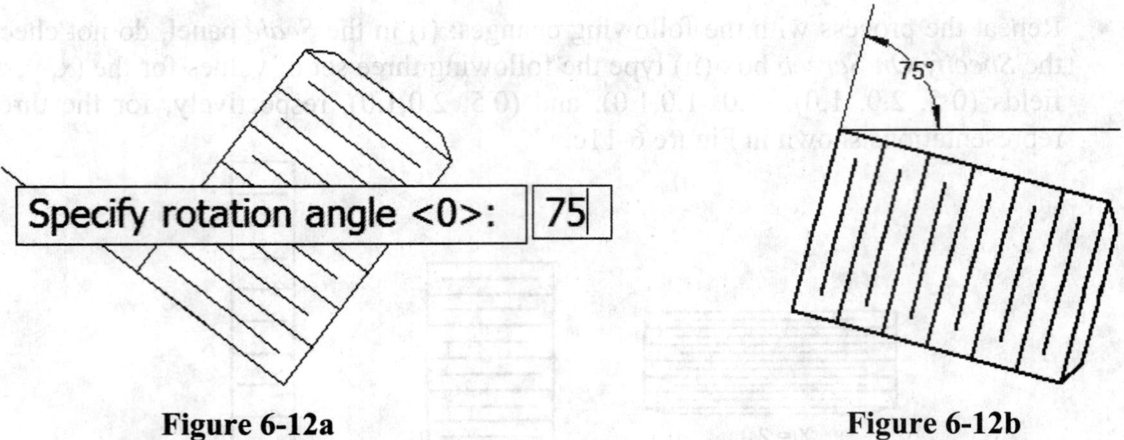

Figure 6-12a

Figure 6-12b

6.7.5. Insert a Wblock

The insertion process of a Wblock is similar to the insertion process of a basic block. In the *Name* field of the *Insert* dialog box, use the browse button to load the Wblock created and saved earlier. Furthermore, the Wblocks can be combined or exploded in a manner similar to a basic block.

6.7.6. Insert a block with attributes

1. Activate the *Insert* command to open the *Insert* dialog box.
2. Choose the Title_Block, Set various options as discussed earlier. Press the *OK* button.
3. Specify the insertion point.
4. The prompt to set the user name, Figure 6-13a will appear. If the name is correct then press the *Enter* key; otherwise, change the name and then press the *Enter* key.

Enter your name <NIGHAT YASMIN>: NIGHAT YASMIN

Figure 6-13a

5. If necessary, change the value of the data field; and press the *Enter* key to move to the next prompt. At the prompt to enter the units of the drawing, Figure 6-13b, the user decided to change the units, change the units to INCHES and press the *Enter* key.
6. Repeat step #4 until the block is inserted.

Enter the units of the drawing <MILLIMETERS>: INCHES

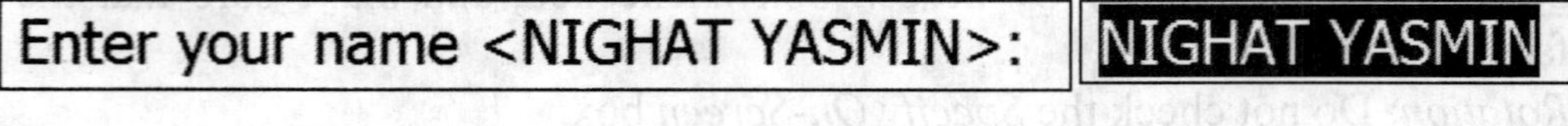

Figure 6-13b

6.7.7. Insert a block with text boxes

The insertion process of a block with the text boxes is similar to the insertion process of a basic block. In the *Name* field of the *Insert* dialog box, use the browse button to load the respective block created and saved earlier. Furthermore, block with the text boxes can be combined or exploded in a manner similar to a basic block.

6.8.   Combine blocks

Complicated shape objects can be created by inserting different blocks at the desired locations. Figure 6-14c shows a bolt created by combining a thread and a head block. Simply, insert a thread block follow by inserting a head block.

Blocks can be combined as follow.
- Do not include the dimensions in the basic block.
- Create the thread block with point A selected as the base point, Figure 6-14a.
- Create the head block with point B selected as the base point, Figure 6-14b.
- Insert the thread block.
- Insert the head block on top of the thread block, Figure 6-14c. The points A and B will overlap.
- Repeat the process with different scale factors to create different size bolts.

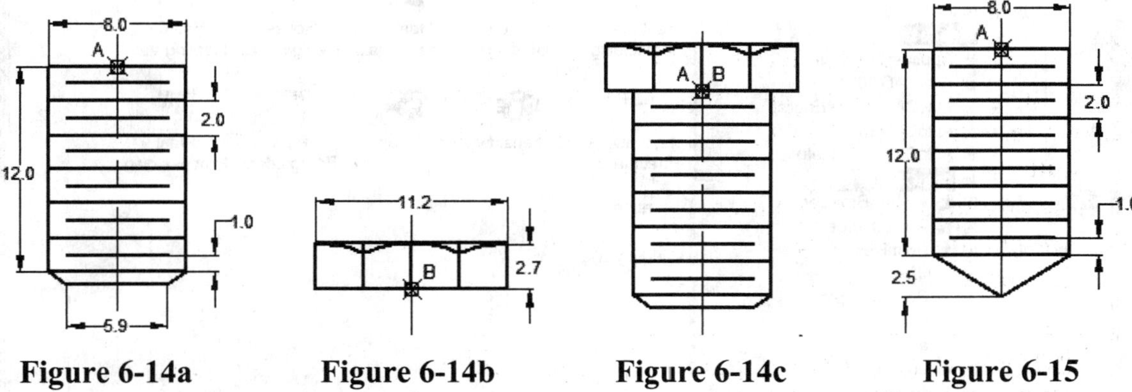

Figure 6-14a   Figure 6-14b   Figure 6-14c   Figure 6-15

6.9.   Modify block

In some situations, a user of the block is required to modify the block. Figure 6-15 shows the modification of bolt threads into screw thread. The process is given as:

- Insert the bolt threads block and the block will become part of the drawing.
- From the *Modify* toolbar use the *Explode* command to explode the block.
- Edit the block as desired; that is, create the pointed tip for the screw thread.
- If the new shape will be used frequently then save it as *Screw Thread* (a new block).

6.10.   Design center

AutoCAD provides a *Design Center*. The *Design Center* is the collection of blocks. The block can be inserted in both ANSI and ISO file.

- The *Design Center* can be opened using one of the following procedures.

  1. Panel method: Either from the *Vew* tab and *Palettes* panel select the *Design Center* (▦) tool.
  2. Command line method: Type "adcenter", "Adcenter", or "ADCENTER" on the command line and press the *Enter* key.
  3. Hold the *Ctrl* key and press the '*2*' key.

- The activation of the command will open the *Design Center* palette, Figure 6-16a.
- Expand the *Design Center* option by expanding *Program File*, *Autodesk*, *AutoCAD 2014 – English*, *Sample*, *en-us*, and finally, the *Design Center*, Figure 6-16a.

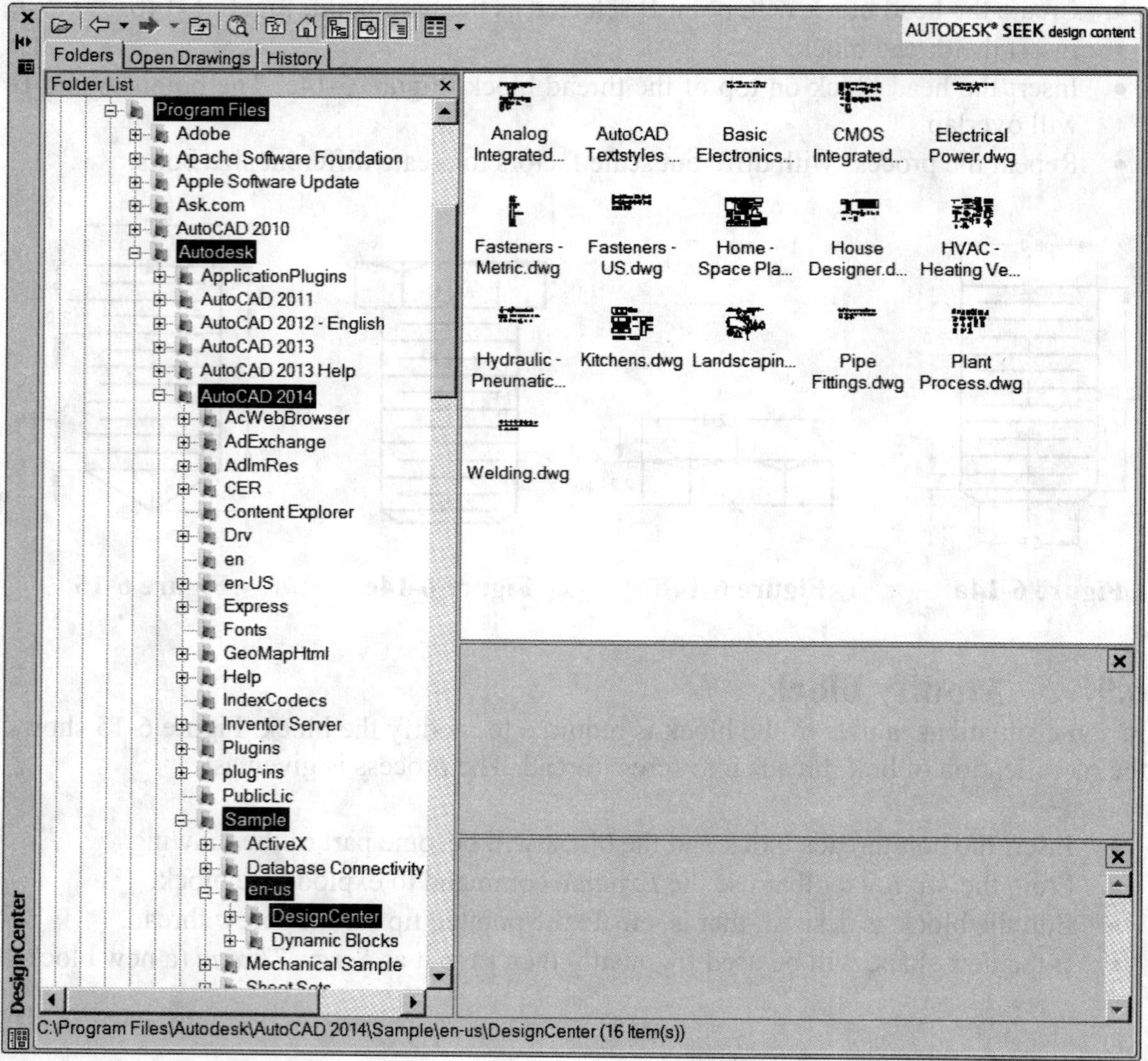

Figure 6-16a

The remaining of this section will explain how to insert a block from the *Kitchens.dwg* of the *Design Center*.

- Expand the *Design Center* and select the *Kitchens.dwg*, Figure 6-16b.

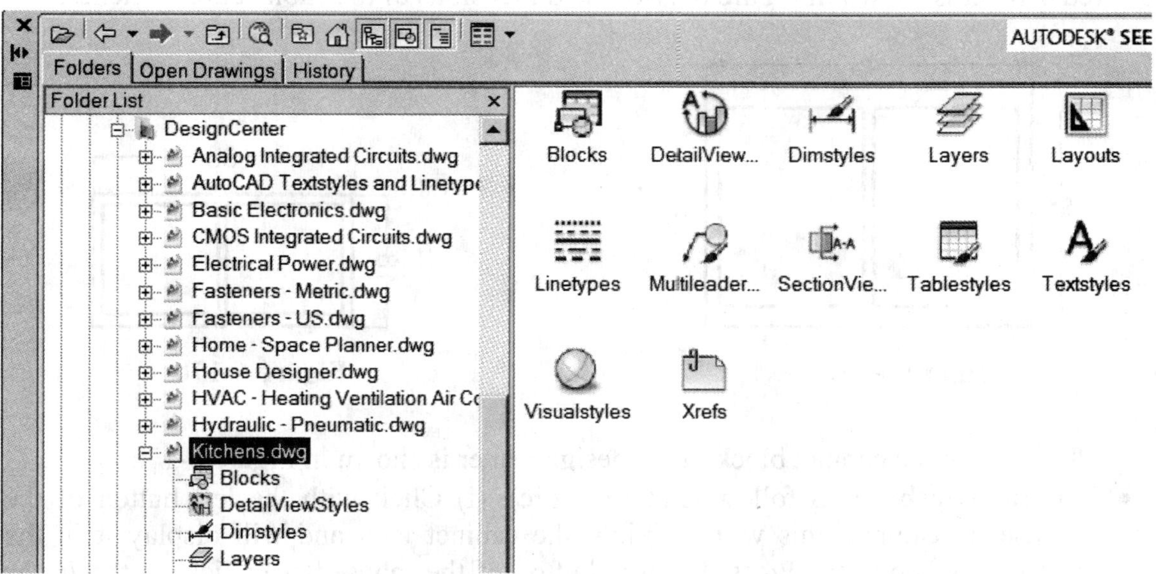

Figure 6-16b

- Either click on the *Blocks* in the left column or double click on the *Blocks* in the preview window; the content of the drawing will appear in the preview window, Figure 6-16c; the figure displays the available blocks under the *Kitchen.dwg* file.

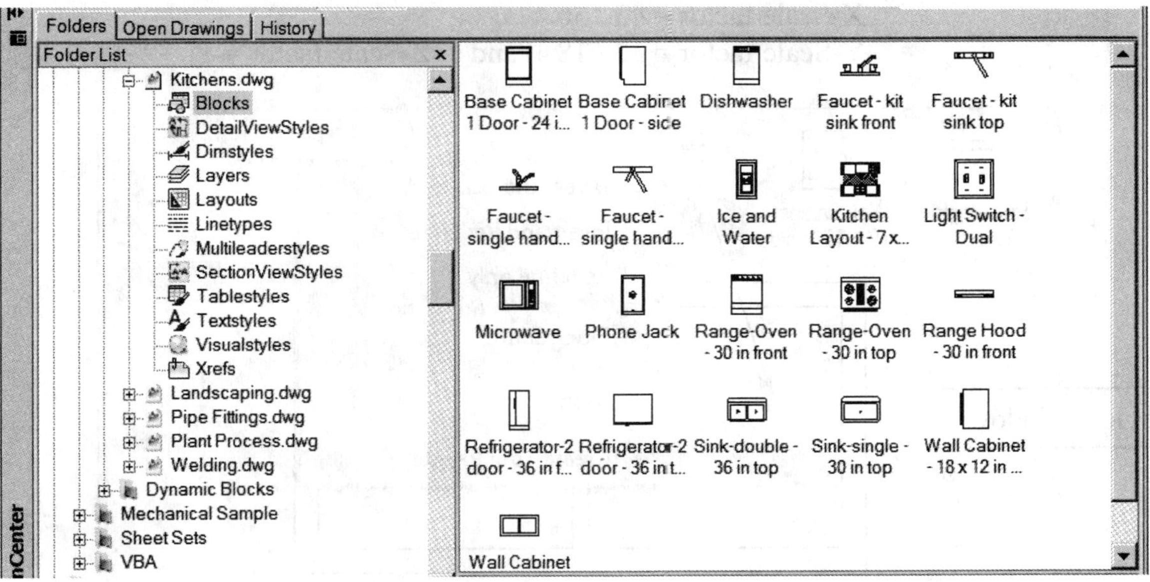

Figure 6-16b

6.10.1. Insert a block (known dimension)

This section will explain how to insert a block from the *Design Center* whose dimension are known by explaining the insertion process of the *"Wall Cabinet 18 X 36 in front"* block.

Example: The drafter wants to draw a cabinet in the floor plan (top view). The size of the desired cabinet is shown in Figure 6-17a. The dimensions of the cabinet are in inches.

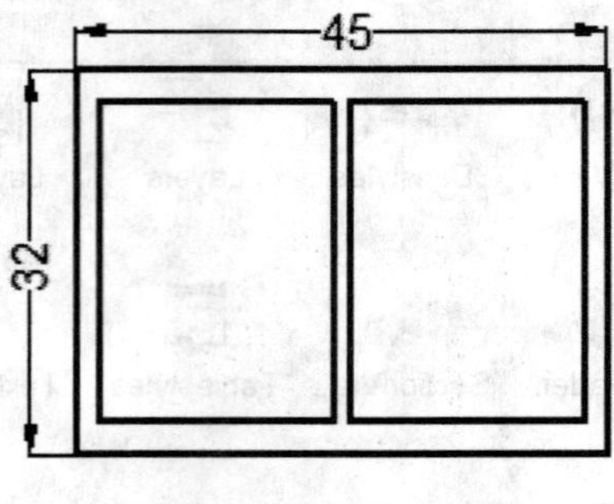

Figure 6-17a

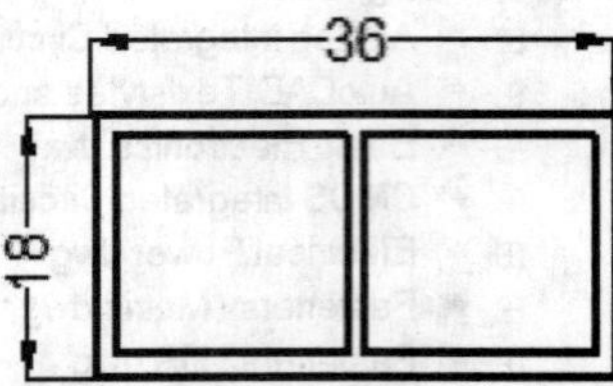

Figure 6-17b

- The size of the cabinet block in the design center is shown in Figure 6-17b.
- Insert the cabinet as follow (Figure 6-17c). (i) Click with the left button of the mouse on cabinet; this will highlight the cabinet icon and will display it in the preview window. (ii) Press the right button of the mouse. (iii) Click on the *Insert Block* option. The Insert block dialog box will appear on the screen. (iv) Follow the procedure to insert a block.
- In this example, the desired size is different than the actual size. Hence, the cabinet must be scaled before the insertion. The scale factor is calculated as:

  Scale factor = Desired size / Actual size

  Therefore,

  X-Scale factor = 45 / 36

  Y-Scale factor = 32 / 18   and   Z-Scale factor = 1

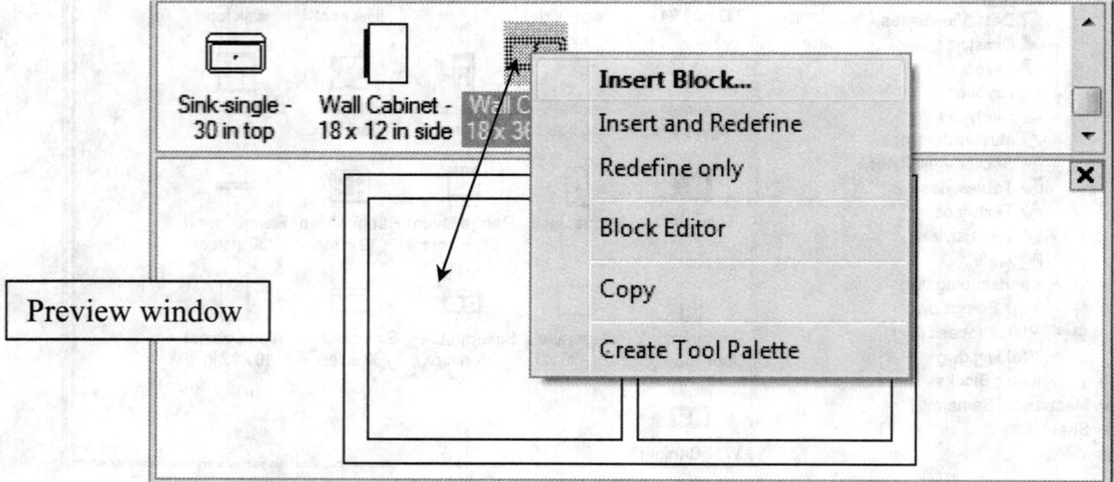

Figure 6-17c

6.10.2. Insert a block (unknown dimension)

This section will explain how to insert a block from the *Design Center* whose dimension are not known by explaining the insertion process of the "*Microwave*" block.

Example: The drafter wants to draw a microwave in the elevation (front view). The size of the desired microwave is shown in Figure 6-18a. The dimensions of the microwave are in inches.

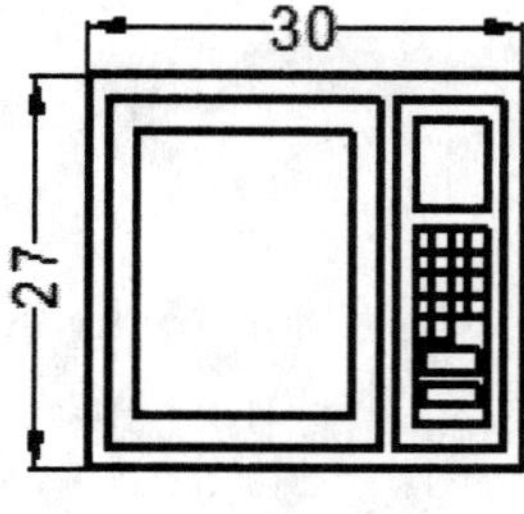

Figure 6-18a

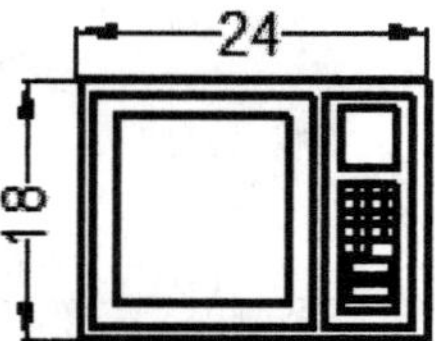

Figure 6-18b

- The microwave's block of Figure 6-16b does not contain any dimension. Therefore, the first step is to find out the block dimension.
- To find the dimension of a block, (i) insert the block in question at the scale factor of 1.0 in X, Y, and Z-direction and Angle = 0. (ii) Add the dimensions to the block. Figure 6-18b show the trial block.
- Now insert the microwave block at the desired location and the desired scale factor.

  Scale factor = Desired size / Actual size

  Therefore,

  X-Scale factor = 30 / 24

  Y-Scale factor = 27 / 18   and

  Z-Scale factor = 1

- Finally, delete the trial block and its dimensions.

Notes:

7. Layouts and Template Files

7.1. Objectives

- Learn to manipulate (add, delete, rename, move) layouts
- Learn to make entries in the scale list
- Learn to create a template file
- Learn to plot from a layout

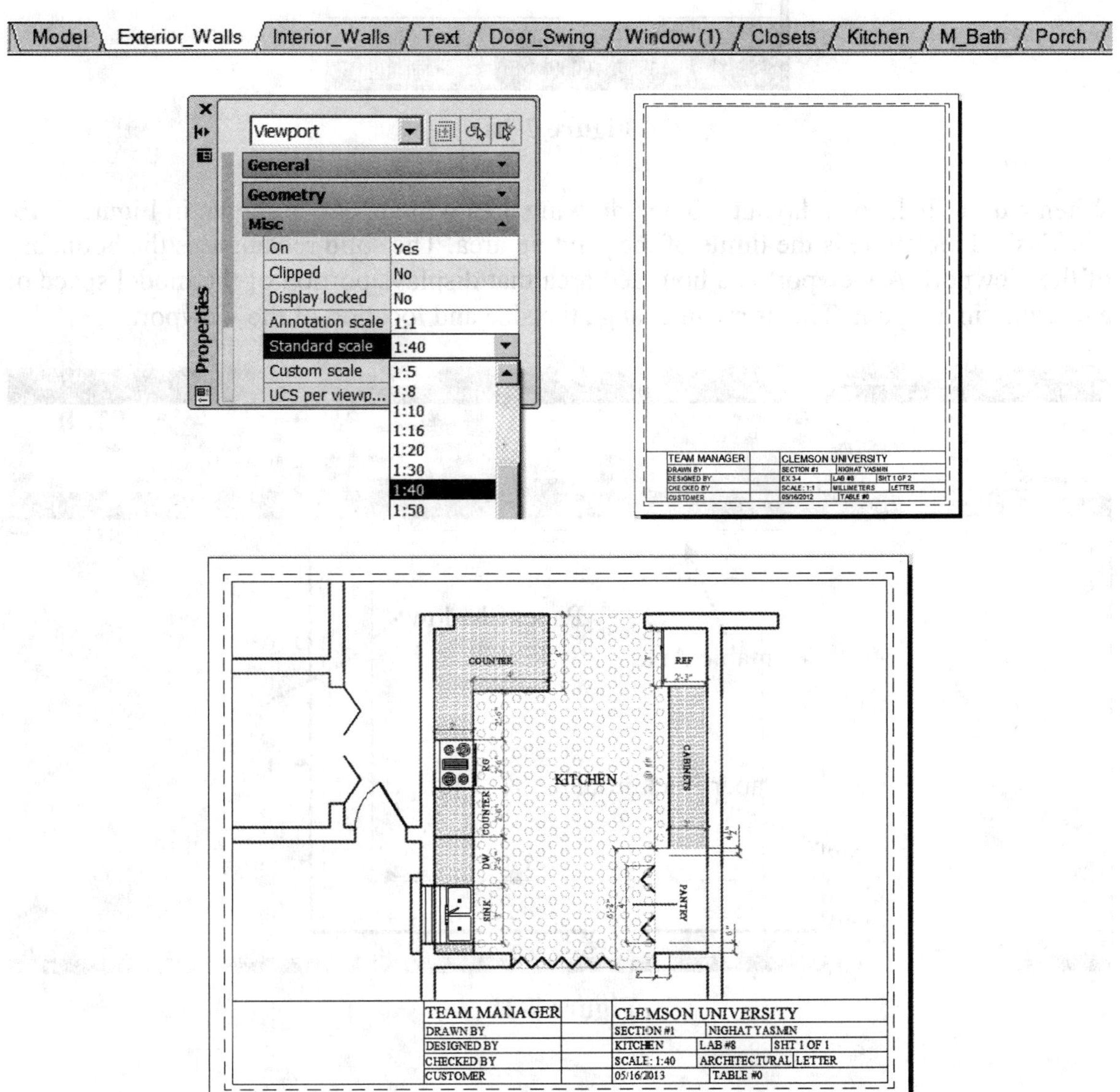

7.2.   Introduction

In AutoCAD, a layout is a drawing environment mainly used for printing or plotting the drawing. New layouts can be created and existing layouts can be modified. This chapter explains the usage and advantages of layouts. Furthermore, this chapter creates template files using layouts and title and release blocks created in the previous chapter.

7.3.   Layout

Generally, layouts are used for printing or plotting the drawing. By default, AutoCAD creates two layouts. The user can switch to a layout by selecting the *Layout1* or *Layout2* tab, respectively, from the lower left corner of the AutoCAD's interface, Figure 7-1a.

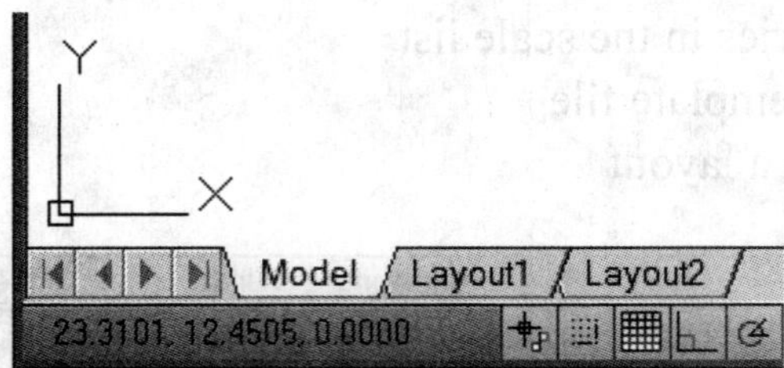

Figure 7-1a

When a user clicks on a layout tab, the drawing area will appear as shown in Figure 7-1b. The dashed rectangle is the limits of the printing area. The solid rectangle is the boundary of the viewport. A viewport is a bounded area that displays portion of the model space of a drawing in a layout. The user can change the size and location of the viewport.

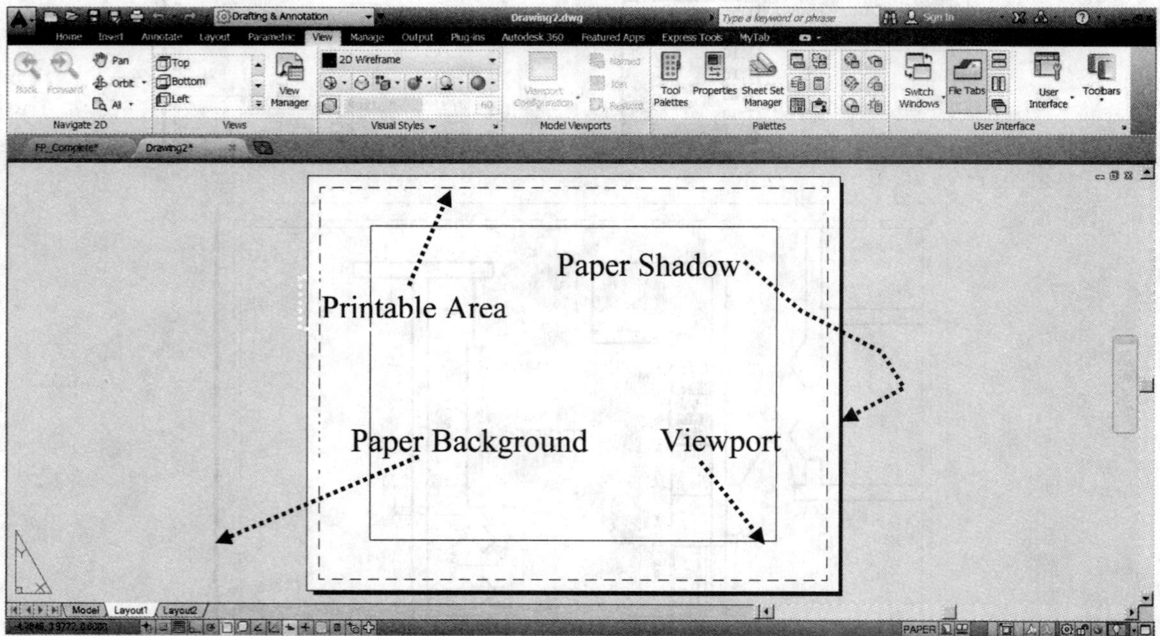

Figure 7-1b

7.3.1. Paper background and shadow

The paper background and shadow does not affect the quality or efficiency of a drawing. However, it is good drawing practice to keep the two options *On*. The user can hide or display the paper background and/or shadow of the layouts as follow. (i) Type the *Options* in the command line. This will open the *Options* dialog box. (ii) Select the *Display* tab. The lower left corner, Figure 7-2, contains the layout controls. (iii) Clear or check the appropriate boxes. (iv) Finally, click the *OK* button to make the changes effective and close the dialog box. The changes will be applied to each layout in the drawing file.

7.3.2. Printable area

The printable area does not affect the quality of a drawing. However, it may affect the productivity of the draftsmen. If the printable area limits are not displayed, then the draftsmen may draw outside the printable area; and will be required to adjust the drawing before the printing. Hence, it is good drawing practice to display the printable area in layouts.

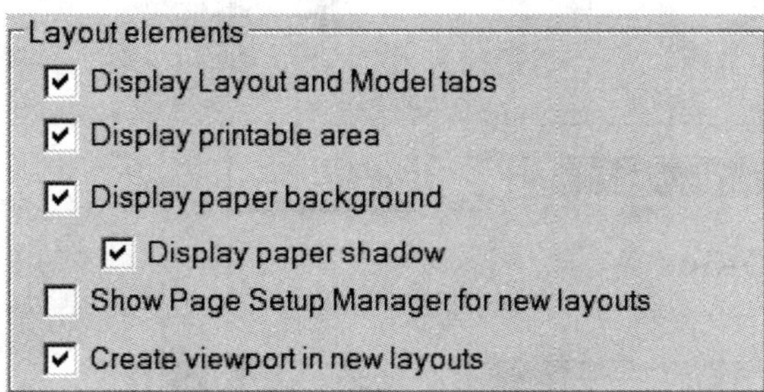

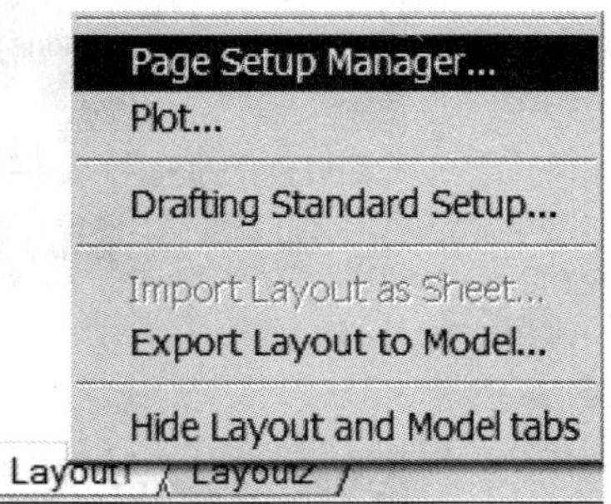

Figure 7-2   **Figure 7-3a**

The user can hide or display the printable area of the layouts as follow. (i) Type the *Options* in the command line. This will open the *Options* dialog box. (ii) Select the *Display* tab. The lower left corner, Figure 7-2, contains the layout controls. (iii) Clear or check the *Display printable area* box. (iv) Finally, click the *OK* button to make the changes effective and close the dialog box. The changes will be applied to each layout in the drawing file.

The user can adjust the printable area of the layouts as follow, Figure 7-3b.

- (i) Click the *Layout1* tab. (ii) Bring the cursor on the *Layout1* tab. (iii) Press the right button of the mouse and the option selection panel, Figure 7-3a, will appear. (iv) Move the cursor to the *Page Setup Manager* option and press the left button of the mouse. This will open the *Page Setup Manager* dialog box, Figure 7-3b.
- Click the *Modify* button of the *Page Setup Manager* dialog box. This will open *Page Setup – Layout1* dialog box, Figure 7-3c.
- Select the printer from the *Page Setup – Layout1* dialog box in the *Printer/plotter* panel and click the *Properties* button. This will open *Plotter Configuration Editor* dialog box, Figure 7-3d.

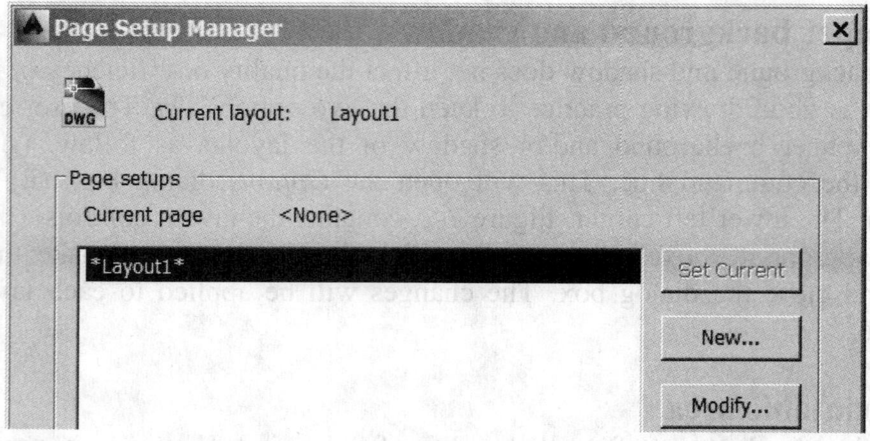

Figure 7-3b

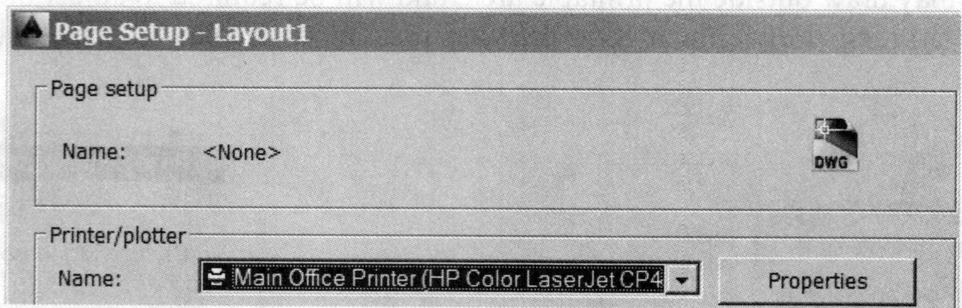

Figure 7-3c

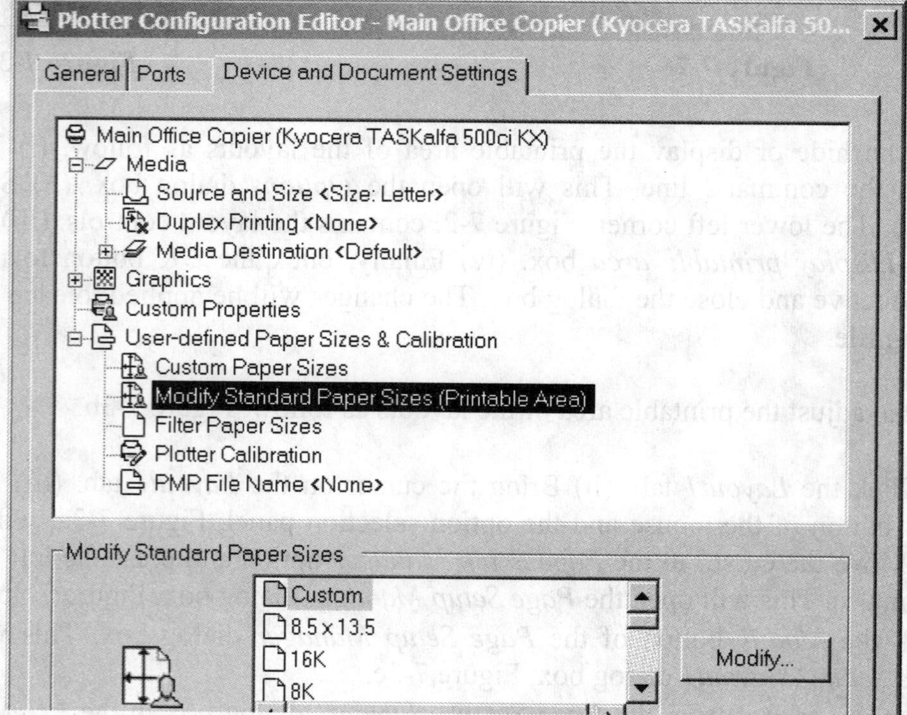

Figure 7-3d

- Select the *Modify Standard Paper Sizes (Printable Area)* from the *Plotter Configuration Editor* dialog box, Figure 7-3d, and click the *Modify* button. This will open *Custom Paper Sizes - Printable Area* dialog box, Figure 7-3e.

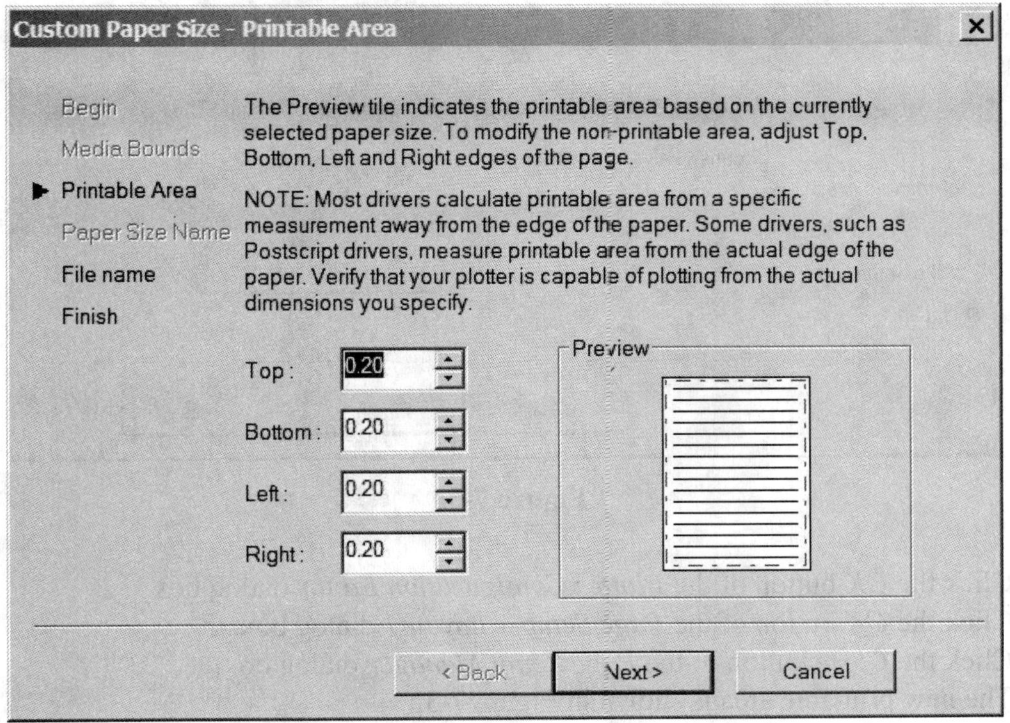

Figure 7-3e

- In the *Custom Paper Sizes - Printable Area* dialog box, Figure 7-3e, set the value for the *Top*, *Bottom*, *Left*, and *Right* limits and click the *Next* button. This will open *Custom Paper Sizes – File name* dialog box, Figure 7-3f.
- In the *Custom Paper Sizes – File name* dialog box, Figure 7-3f, specify the file name and click the *Next* button. This will open *Custom Paper Sizes - Finish* dialog box, Figure 7-3g.

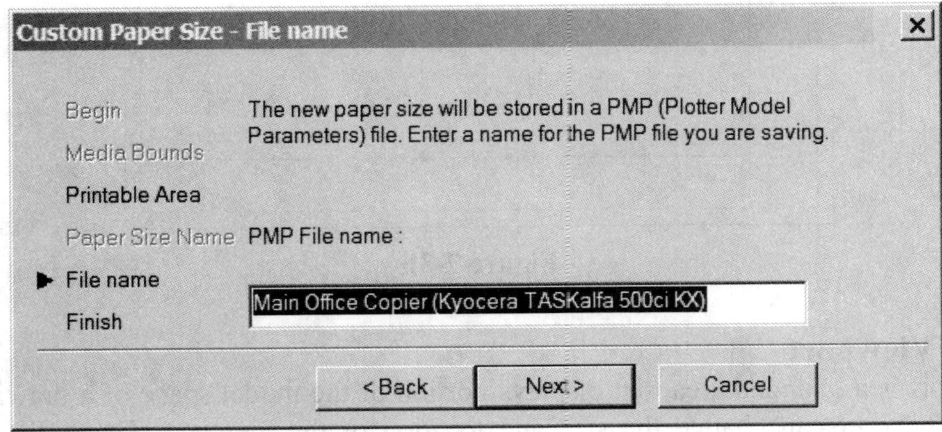

Figure 7-3f

- In the *Custom Paper Sizes - Finish* dialog box, Figure 7-3g, click the *Finish* button. This will close the *Custom Paper Sizes – Finish* and *Custom Paper Sizes – File name* dialog boxes.

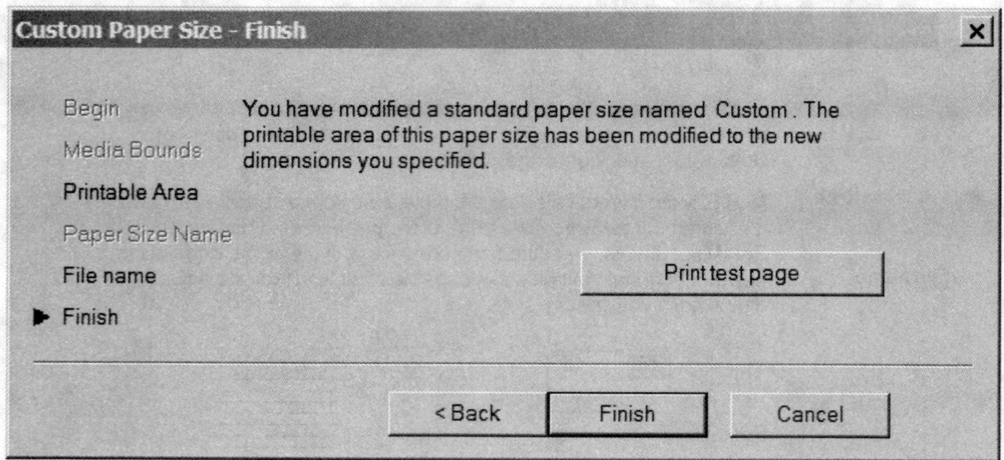

Figure 7-3g

- Click the *OK* button of the *Plotter Configuration Editor* dialog box.
- Click the *OK* button of the *Page Setup – Layout1* dialog box.
- Click the *Close* button of the *Page Setup Manager* dialog box.
- The new printable area is shown in Figure 7-3h.

Figure 7-3h

7.3.3. Viewport

A viewport is a bounded area that displays portion of the model space of a drawing in a layout. The user can change the size and location of the viewport. Generally, drafter needs to scale the viewport before the plotting.

7.3.3.1.   Viewport scaling

Consider the floor plan of three bedrooms house shown in Figure 7-4a. The architect wants to show the client the entire floor plan and the details of the kitchen as shown in Figure 7-4a and Figure 7-4b, respectively. The architect can achieve the desired goal by creating two layouts at two different scale factors. In the figures, the floor plan is at the scale of 1:100 and the kitchen plan is at the scale of 1:30.

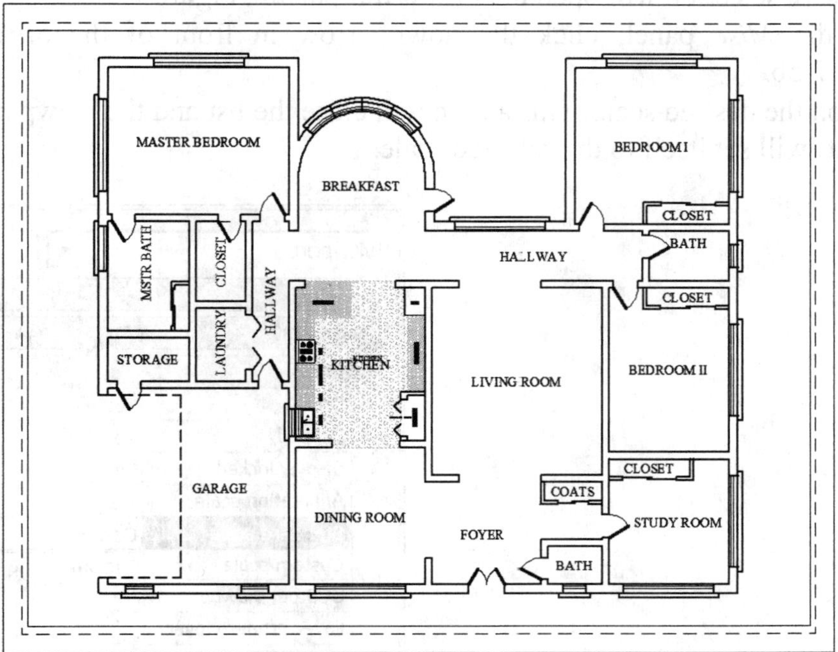

Figure 7-4a

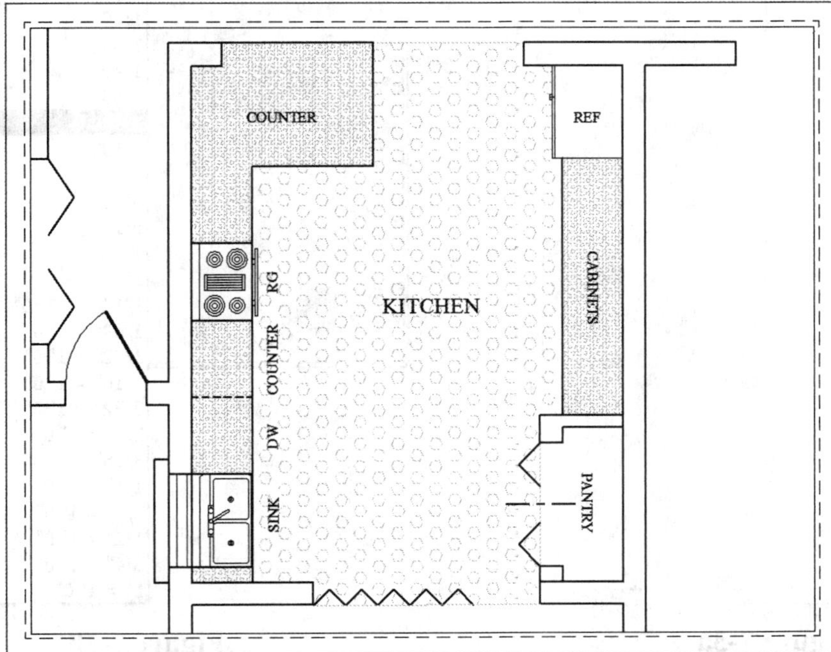

Figure 7-4b

7.3.3.2.   Rescale a viewport

A viewport can be rescaled using the *Properties* palette as follow.

- Select the viewport, Figure 7-5a. The corner grips point will appear.
- Press the right button of the mouse and select the *Properties* command from the commands panel.
- The above selection will open the *Properties* palette, Figure 7-5b.
- From the *Misc* panel, click the down arrow in front of the *Standard scale*, Figure 7-5b.
- Click on the desired scale. This action will close the list and the viewport (that is, its content) will set itself to the selected scale.

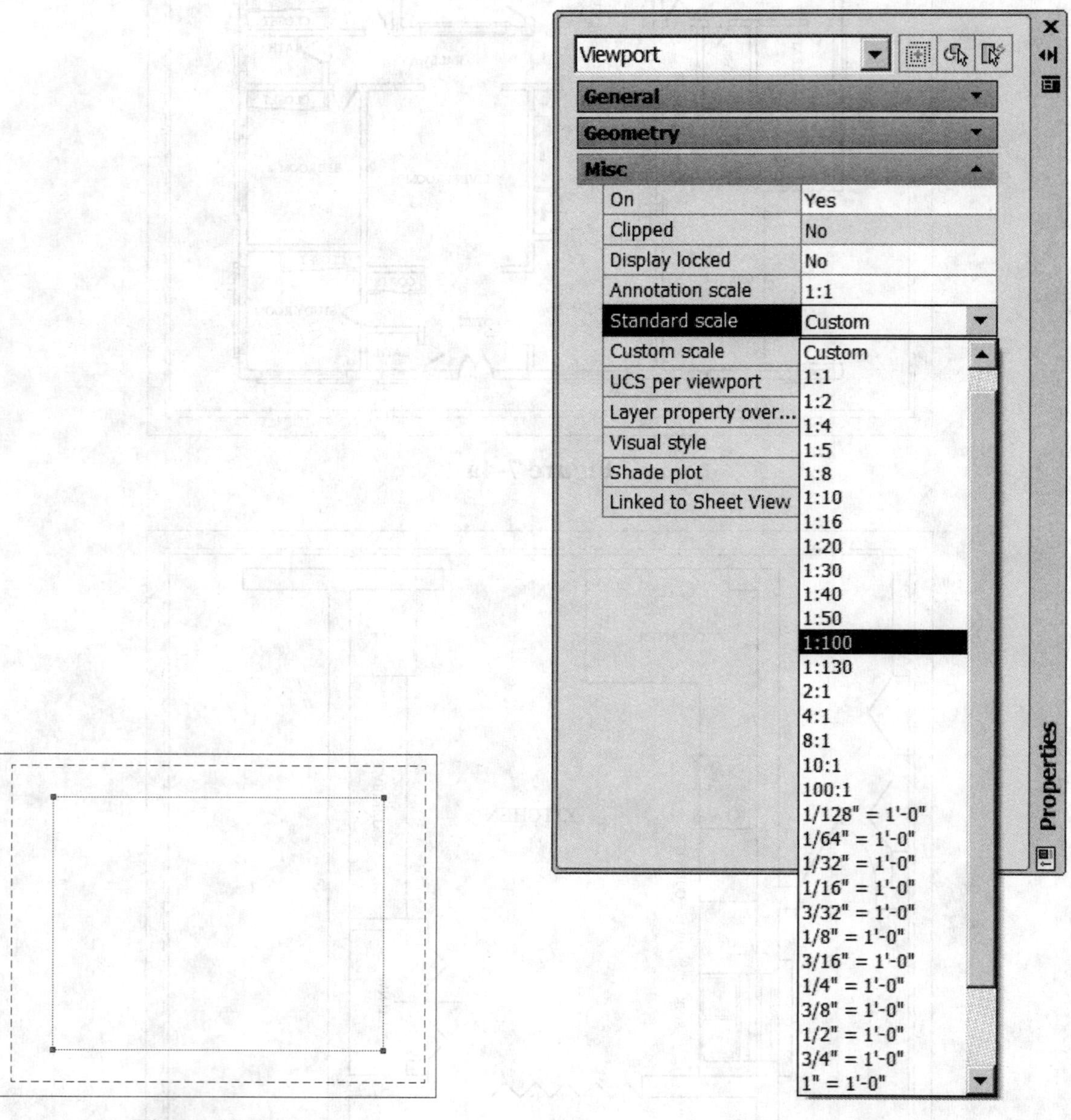

Figure 7-5a   **Figure 7-5b**

7.3.3.3.   Lock the scale of a viewport

The draftsman should lock the viewport scale to avoid rescaling of the viewport accidentally using zoom/unzoom commands. By locking the viewport scale, the drawing can be zoomed and unzoomed without changing the viewport scale. A viewport's scale can be locked using the *Properties* palette as follow.

- Select the viewport, the corner grips point will appear, Figure 7-5a.
- Press the right button of the mouse and select the *Properties* command from the commands panel.
- The above selection will open the *Properties* palette, Figure 7-6a.
- From the *Misc* panel, click in the cell on the right side of the *Display locked*, Figure 7-6b.
- A down arrow will appear in the cell labeled as *No*.

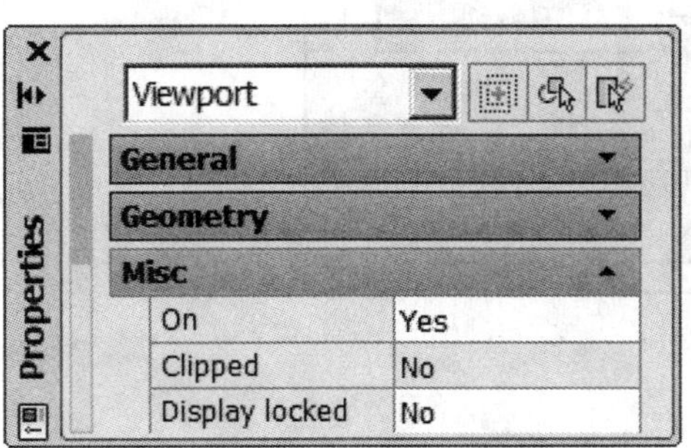

Figure 7-6a

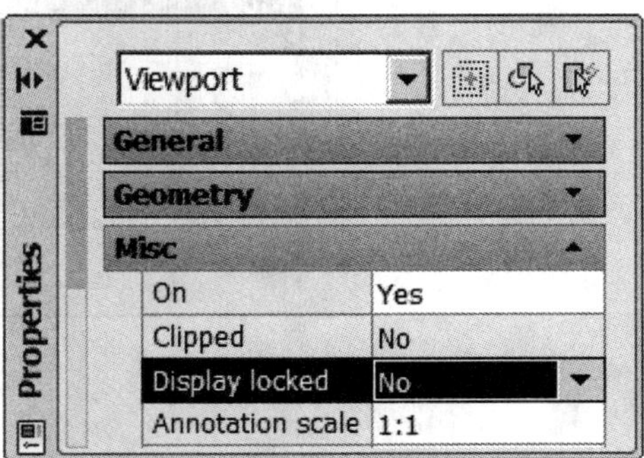

Figure 7-6b

- Press the down arrow and select the *Yes* option, Figure 7-6c.
- By locking the viewport scale, the user can zoom into the viewport at different levels of detail without altering the viewport (or drawing) scale.

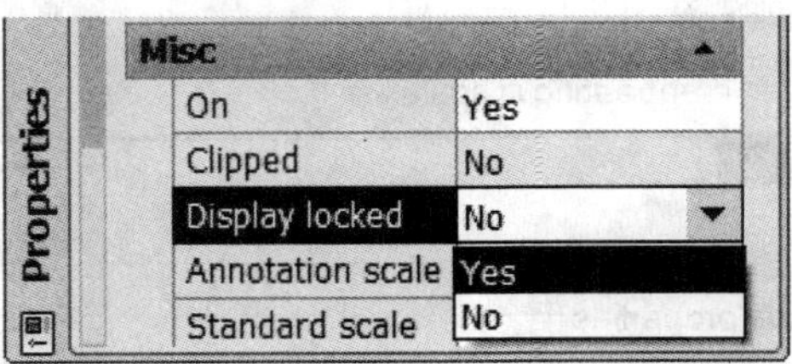

Figure 7-6c

7.4.   Add an entry in the scale list

A situation may arise when the user need to use a scale factor not available in the default scale list of AutoCAD.

Example: Add *1:120* entry in the scale list. The user can add a new scale factor in the edit scale list as follow.

- From the *Annotate* tab and *Annotation Scaling* panel, select the *Scale List*. This will open the *Edit Drawing Scales* dialog box, Figure 7-7a.

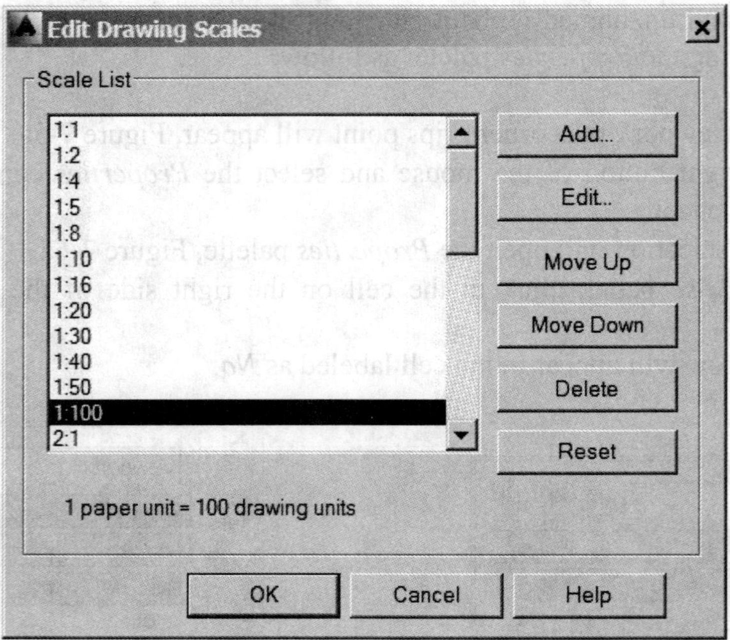

Figure 7-7a

- Select the entry labeled as 1:100. This will help in the addition of the new entry at its correct location. (1:120 should be after 1:100.)
- Click the *Add* button of the *Default Scale List* dialog box. This will open the *Add Scale* dialog box, Figure 7-7b.

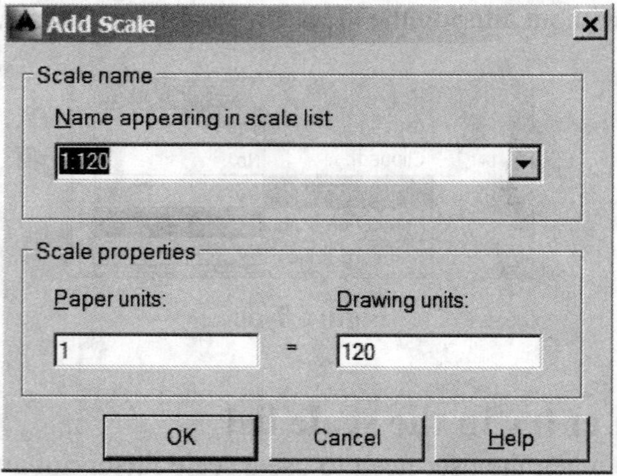

Figure 7-7b

- Enter the desired values. Press the *OK* button on the *Add Scale* dialog box. This action will accept the new scale factor and close the dialog box.
- The new scale will appear in the *Edit Scale List* dialog box, Figure 7-7c.

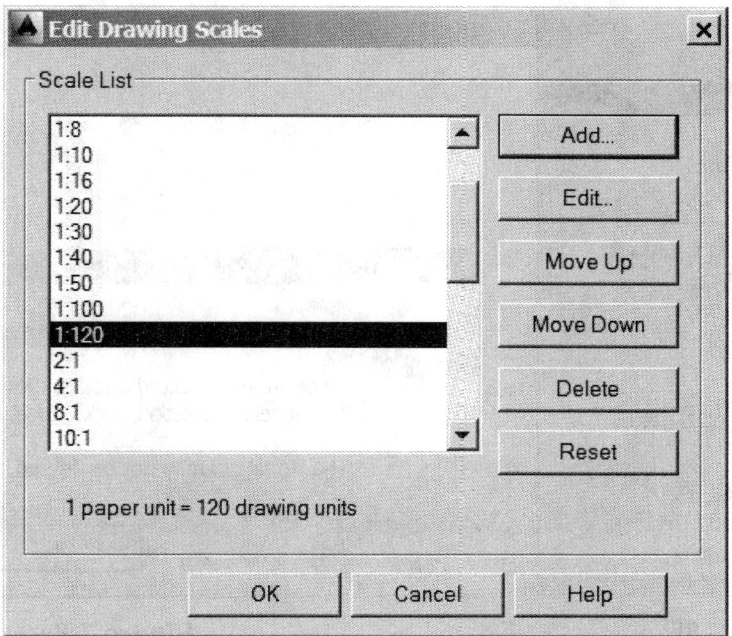

Figure 7-7c

- If the new scale is not created at its correct location, then use the *Move Up* or *Move Down* button to move the newly created scale to move to the appropriate location.
- Click the *OK* button to close the *Edit Drawing Scale* dialog box.

7.5.   Layout manipulation

By default, AutoCAD creates two layouts *Layout1* and *Layout2*. However, existing layouts can be deleted, moved, copied, renamed, and more layouts can be inserted. Figure 7-8a shows the layouts created for a floor plan drawing and renamed based on their functionality.

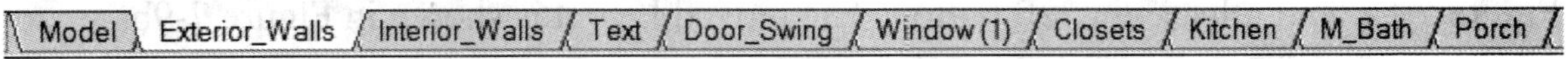

Figure 7-8a

7.5.1.   Delete a layout

This section will describe the process of deleting layouts.

Example: Delete the layout labeled as *Window(1)* in Figure 7-8a.
(i) Bring the cursor on the *Window(1)* tab. (ii) Click the *Window(1)* tab. (iii) Press the right button of the mouse and the option selection panel shown in Figure 7-8b will appear. (iv) Move the cursor to the *Delete* option (Figure 7-8b), and press the left button of the mouse. (v) The AutoCAD warning shown in Figure 7-8c will appear. (vi) Finally, click the *OK* button to complete the deletion process. Figure 7-8d shows that the *Window(1)* layout is deleted.

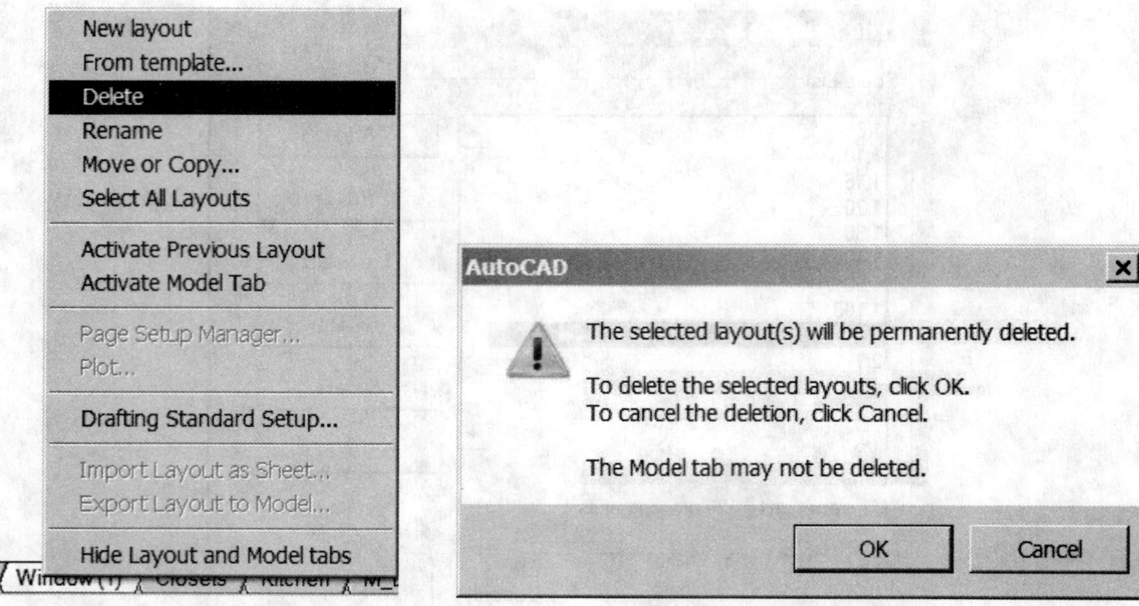

Figure 7-8b   Figure 7-8c

Figure 7-8d

7.5.2.   Move a layout

This section will describe the process of moving a layout.

Example: In Figure 7-8a, move the *Closets* layout in front of *Text* layout.

Method #1:
(i) Bring the cursor on the *Closets* tab. (ii) Click the *Closets* tab. (iii) Press the left button of the mouse and keep pressing it. (iv) Move the cursor to the desired location, Figure 7-8a, and release the left button. The moved layout is shown in Figure 7-9b.

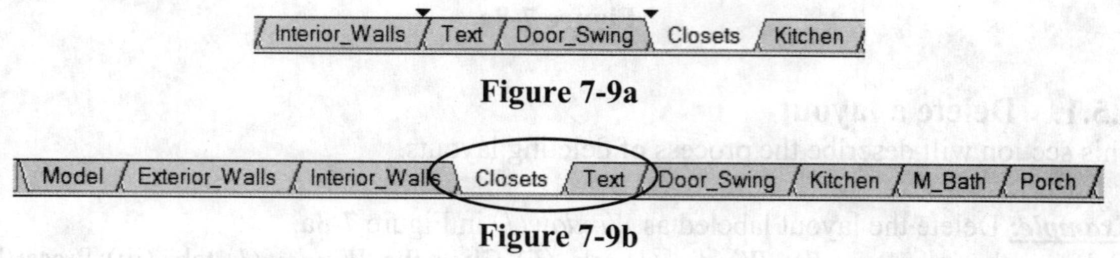

Figure 7-9a

Figure 7-9b

Method #2:
(i) Bring the cursor on the *Closets* tab. (ii) Click the *Closets* tab. (iii) Press the right button of the mouse and the option selection panel shown in Figure 7-8b will appear. (iv) Move the cursor to the *Move or Copy* option (Figure 7-9c), and press the left button of the mouse. This will open the *Move or Copy* dialog box, Figure 7-9d. (v) Select the

new location. Since, the *Closets* is required to move in front of *Text*, therefore, *Text* is selected. (vi) Click the *OK* button to complete the move command. The moved layout is shown in Figure 7-9b.

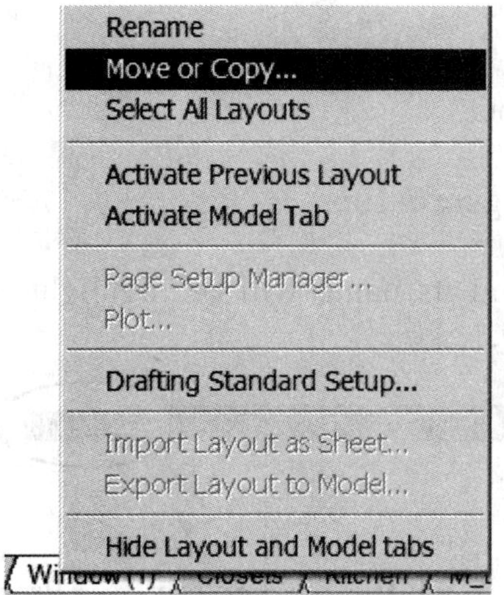

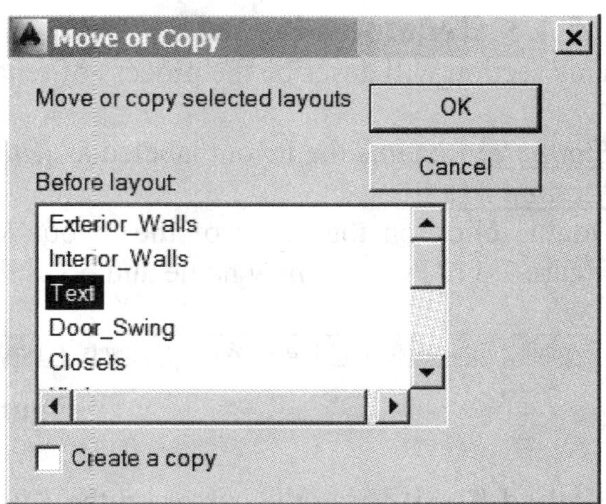

Figure 7-9c	**Figure 7-9d**

7.5.3. Copy a layout
This section will describe the process of copying a layout.

Example: Make a copy of the *Kitchen* layout.
(i) Bring the cursor on the *Kitchen* tab. (ii) Click the *Kitchen* tab. (iii) Press the right button of the mouse and the option selection panel shown in Figure 7-9c will appear. (iv) Move the cursor to the *Move or Copy* option (Figure 7-9c), and press the left button of the mouse. This will open the *Move or Copy* dialog box, Figure 7-10a. (v) Check the *Create a copy* box. (vi) Select the location of the copy. Since, the *copy* is required to be last layout, therefore, *move to end* is selected. (vii) Click the *OK* button to complete the copy command. The copied layout is shown in Figure 7-10b.

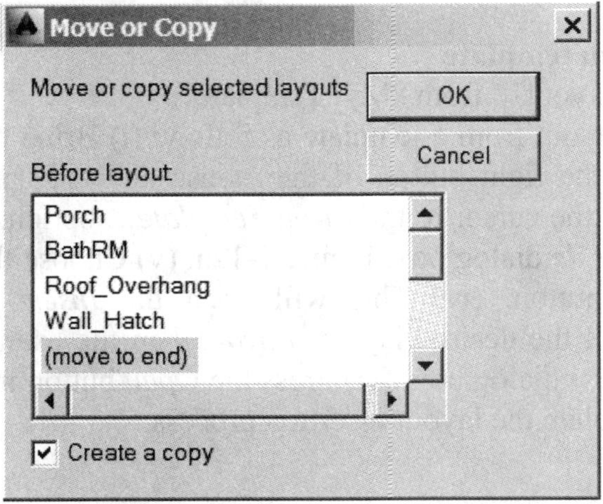

Figure 7-10a

Figure 7-10b

7.5.4. Rename a layout
This section will describe the process of renaming a layout.

Example: Rename the layout labeled as *Kitchen(2)* in Figure 7-10b.
Method #1:
Double click on the name of the layout *Kitchen(2)* and its name will be highlighted, Figure 7-11. Type the new name and press the *Enter* key.

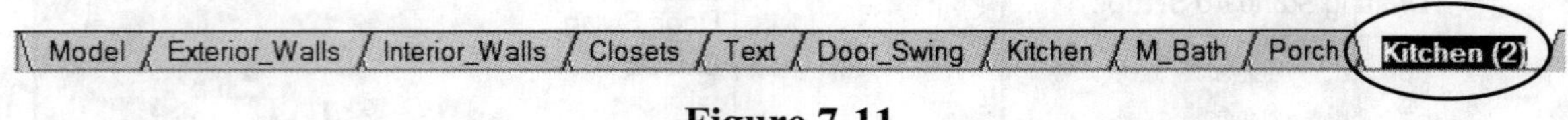

Figure 7-11

Method #2: (i) Bring the cursor on the *Kitchen* tab. (ii) Click the *Kitchen* tab. (iii) Press the right button of the mouse and the option selection panel shown in Figure 7-9c will appear. (iv) Move the cursor to the *Rename* option. The selected layout will be highlighted, Figure 7-11. Type the new name and press the *Enter* key.

7.5.5. Insert a layout
AutoCAD allows its user to insert two types of layouts: a default layout or a layout from a specific template file. Template files are discussed in the later sections of this chapter.

7.5.5.1. Default layout
Example: Insert a default layout.
The user can insert a default layout as follow: (i) Bring the cursor on any of the layouts tab. (ii) Press the right button of the mouse and the option panel will appear, Figure 7-9c. (iii) Move the cursor to the *New layout* option. (iv) Finally, press the left or right button of the mouse. (v) The option panel will be closed and new layout will be added to the drawing.

7.5.5.2. Layout from template
Example: Insert the "Layout1" from "My_Template".
The user can insert a layout from a template as follow: (i) Bring the cursor on any of the layouts tab. (ii) Press the right button of the mouse and the option panel will appear, Figure 7-9c. (iii) Move the cursor to the *From Template...* option. (iv) This will open the *Select Template From File* dialog box, Figure 7-12a. (v) Choose the appropriate template and press the *Open* button. (iv) This will open the *Insert Layout(s)* dialog box, Figure 7-12b. (v) Select the desired layout, *Layout 1* in the example. (vi) Press the *OK* button in *Insert Layout(s)* dialog box. (vi) Press the *Open* button in *Select Template From File* dialog box to complete the layout insertion process.

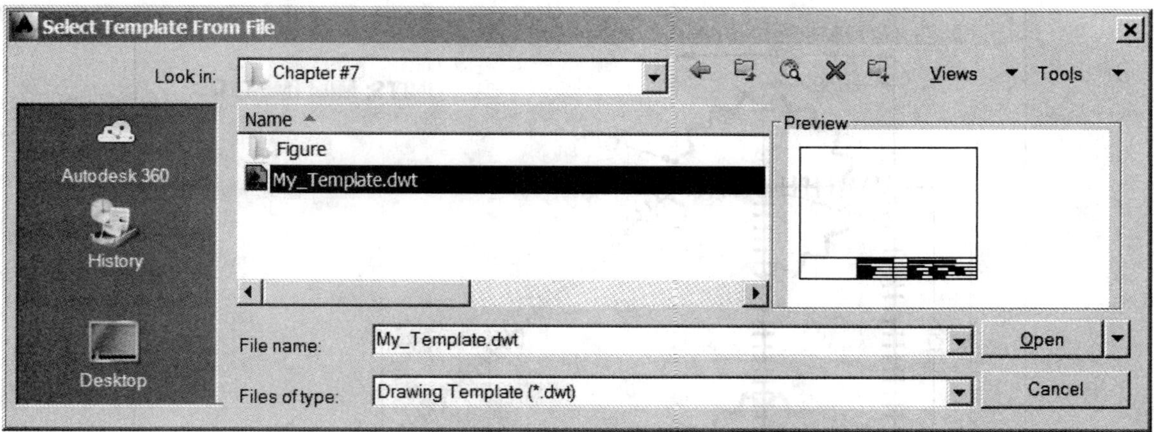

Figure 7-12a

Figure 7-12b

7.5.6.   Grid and Snap commands

The *Grid* command is used to display a visible grid (similar to graph or engineering paper) background on the drawing screen. The *Snap* command is used to set an invisible grid background on the drawing screen and to limit the movement of the cursor to the snap grid's points only. The snap grid is completely independent of the visible grid. The process of grid and snap manipulation in layout is same as in the model space and is discussed in detail in Chapter #2.

7.6.   Layers freezing and layouts

Consider a draftsman need to create a drawing of the model shown in Figure 7-13a. However, the draftsman needs to display different parts of the drawing to different clients. The drafter has two choices: (i) create multiple drawings specific to each client (wastage of resource and time) or (ii) create one drawing with multiple layers and multiple layouts and display the desired views to the clients. The drafter has decided to follow the second choice. This section will explain the process to create the desired views.

- <u>File</u>: Open a new acadiso file.
- <u>Layouts</u>: Create the layouts and labeled them as shown in Figure 7-13b.

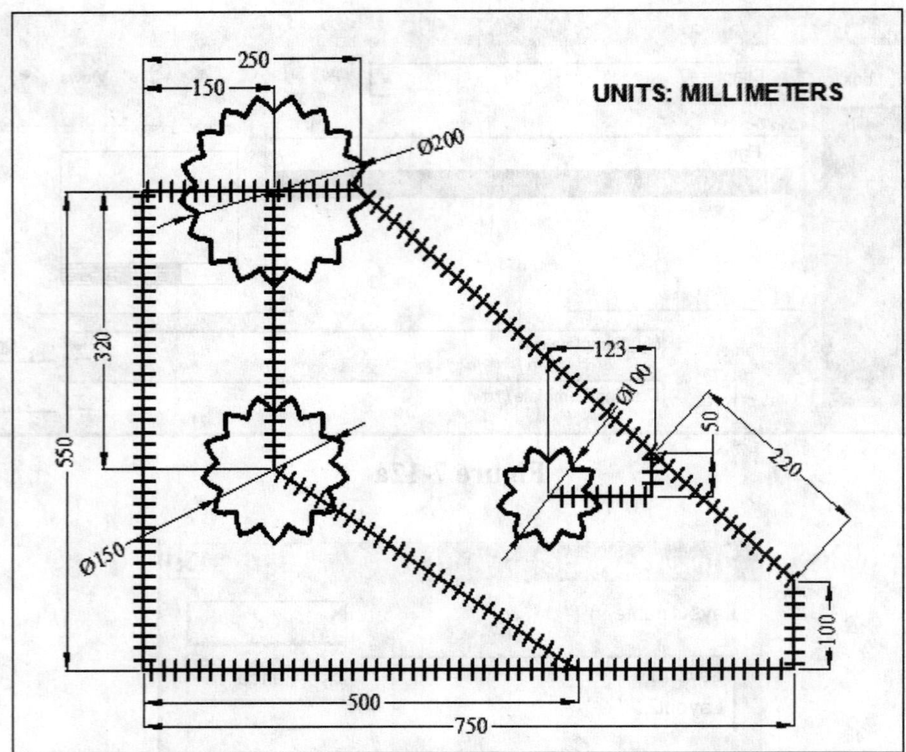

Figure 7-13a

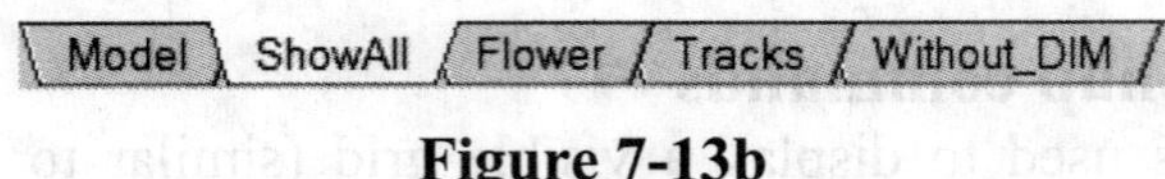

Figure 7-13b

- <u>Layers</u>: Create the layers and labeled them as shown in Figure 7-13c.
- <u>Important point</u>: The names of the layers and layouts should be small and descriptive. The naming of a layer and layouts are independent processes. The names can be the same or different; note the names of layout in Figure 7-13b and layers in Figure 7-13c. In the example, only two layers and two layouts have the same name.

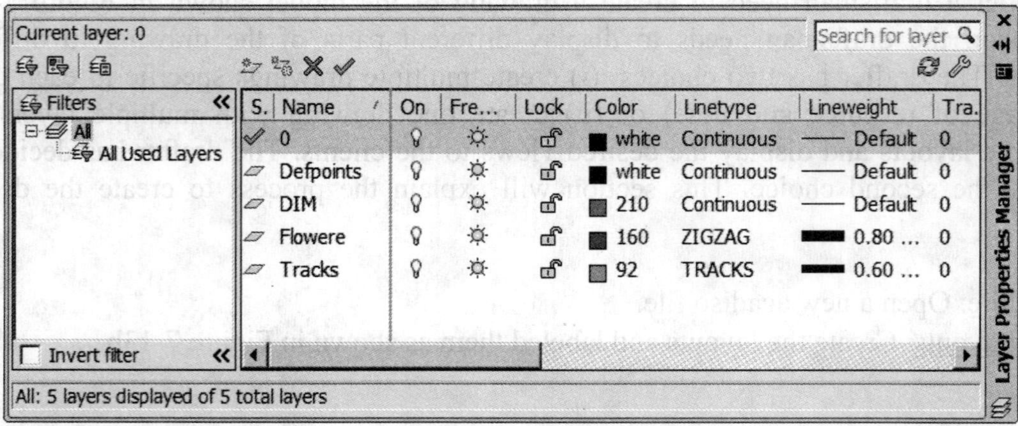

Figure 7-13c

- <u>Create the drawing</u>: (i) Make the *Lines* layer the current layer and draw the lines. (ii) Make the *Circles* layer the current layer and draw the circles. (iii) Make the *DIM* layer the current layer and add the dimensions to the drawing. However, the user can skip the dimensioning step.

- <u>Create the views</u>: (i) Select the layout tab labeled as *Without_DIM*. (ii) Either double click inside the viewport or click on PAPER button on the status bar (lower right corner of the interface). The layout appears as shown in Figure 7-14a. **Note that, the viewport boundary is bold and the coordinate and the viewcube appear inside the viewport**. (iii) Press the down arrow on the layer toolbar and freeze the '*0*' and *DIM* layers by clicking its *Freeze or thaw in current viewport* button as shown in Figure 7-14b. (iv) The resulting layout is shown Figure 7-14c.

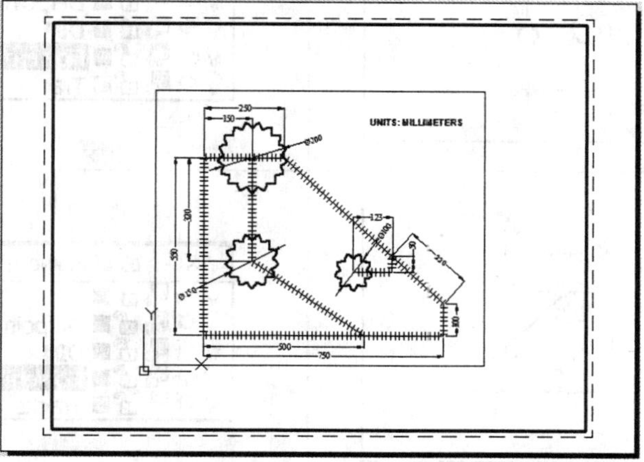

Figure 7-14a

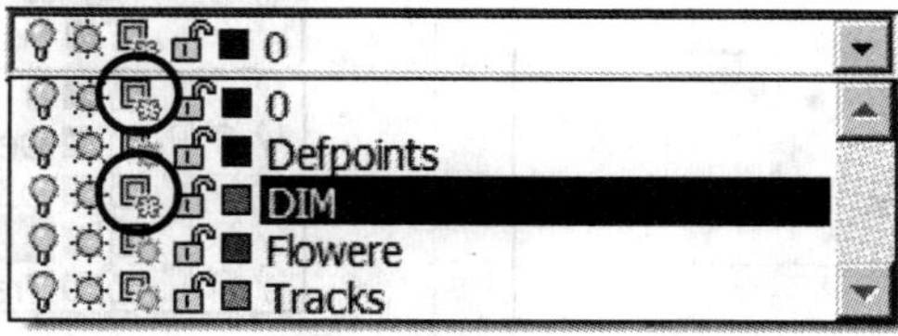

Figure 7-14b

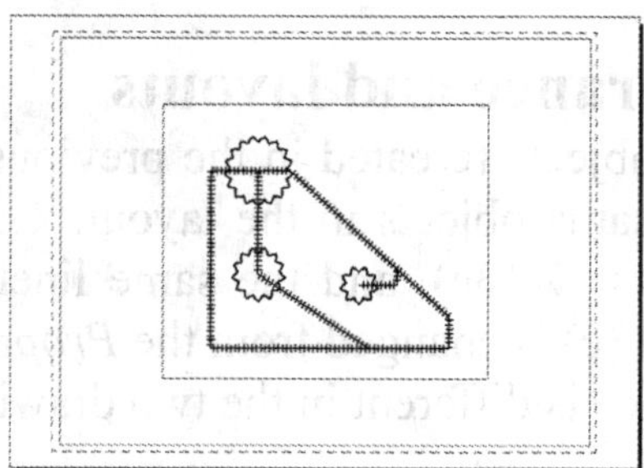

Figure 7-14c

- <u>Repeat the process</u>: Repeat the above process with each layout. The layouts and corresponding layers manipulation are shown in Table #1. For the *Circle* and *Lines* layouts, everything is frozen except the *Circles* and *Lines* layers, respectively. On the other hand, for the *ShowAll* layout nothing is frozen.

- <u>Important point</u>: Freezing a layer is an independent process then the current layer. Note that, in the layers of the Table #1, *Flower* is the current layer in all three cases.

Table #1: Layouts and their layers

Layouts	Layers
	Flowere 0 Defpoints DIM Flowere Tracks
	Flowere 0 Defpoints DIM Flowere Tracks
	Flowere 0 Defpoints DIM Flowere Tracks

7.7. Object appearance and layouts

The Figure 7-15a shows the objects (created in the previous section) in the model space and Figure 7-15c shows the same objects in the layout. The two figures have the same lineweight and linetype (Figure 7-13c), and the same linetype scale (0.4); the linetype scale (not shown in Figure 7-13c) is changed from the *Properties* sheet. Every property is same, yet, the object appearance is different in the two drawing environment.

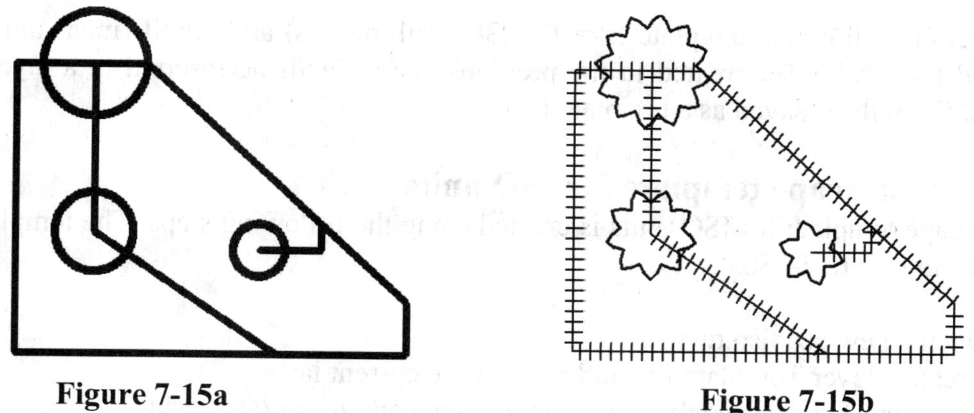

Figure 7-15a   Figure 7-15b

The user must decide about the drawing environment for the demonstration of the drawing and activation of the plotting command before setting the lineweight and the linetype scale. **If the user is planning to plot or demonstrate the drawing from the layout then set the lineweight and the linetype scale for the layout and ignore the appearance in the model space and vice versa.** Generally, the lineweight is a higher number in the layout; however, the linetype scale is a pattern and lineweight dependent number.

Lineweight can be changed for a layer from the layer manager. On the other hand, the linetype scale is changed from the *Properties* sheet. A property of an object can be changed using the *Properties* sheet as follow.

- Select the object and its grip points will appear.
- Press the right button of the mouse and select the *Properties* option from the list of options.
- On the *Properties* sheet, under the *General* panel, change the *Linetype scale* to 0.4, Figure 7-15c.

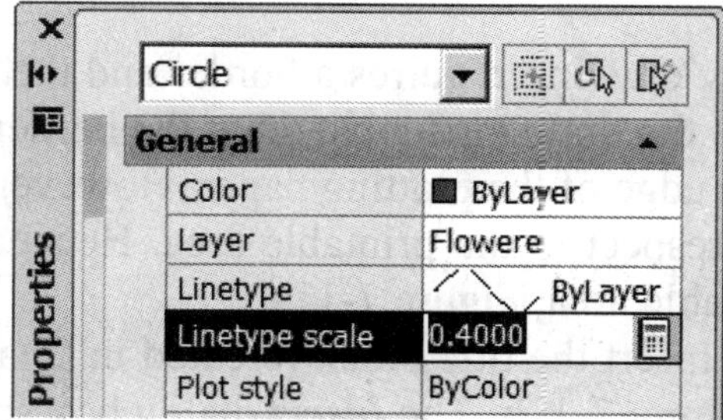

Figure 7-15c

7.8.   Template file

A template file is a mold or a pattern file that gives consistency to every drawing file in the company. AutoCAD provides few template file. However, this section will create, a typical template file used in the academia.

This section will create template files for ISO (millimeters) and ANSI (inch) units. The title and release blocks created in the previous chapter will be inserted in a layout and then the file will be saved as a template file.

7.8.1.   Landscape template for ISO units

A landscape template for ISO units is created using the following steps. The template file is shown in Figure 7-18b.

1. Open a new acadiso.dwt file.
2. Create a layer Template file and make it the current layer.
3. Select the *Layout1*; double click in the layout and turn *off* the grid.
4. Delete the *Layout2*.
5. Click on the *Layout1* tab and rename it to ISO-Landscape. The Figure 7-16a shows the viewport and the printable area of the layout.
6. Click on the viewport and (its grip points will appear) delete it using the *Erase* command, Figure 7-16b.

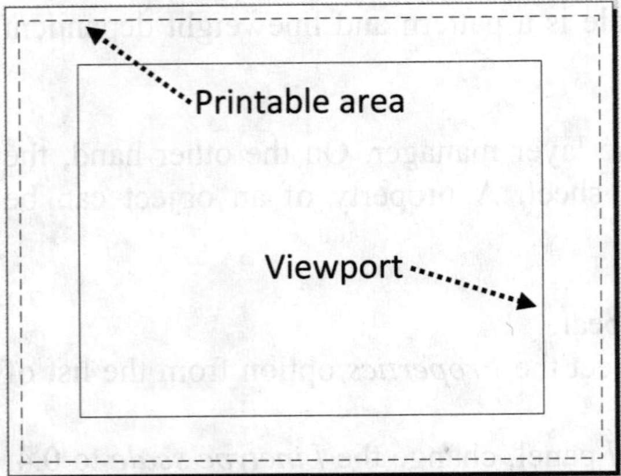

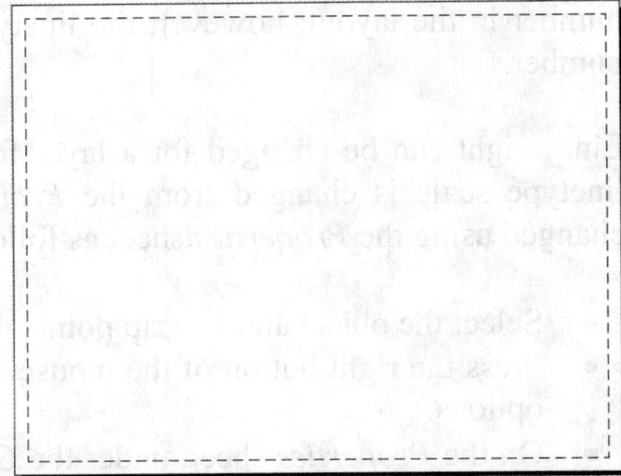

Figure 7-16a   **Figure 7-16b**

7. *Add the border*: Every drawing requires a border and the viewport's boundaries are not printed; therefore, the draftsman must draw the border. The border of a drawing is 1/2 inches from the edge of the plotting paper. However, in this section the border will be created with respect to the printable area. Hence, draw a rectangle slightly smaller than the printable area, Figure 7-17a.
8. *Insert the title block*: Insert the title block (created in Chapter #6) in the lower right corner as shown in Figure 7-17b. The *Insert* dialog box settings are shown in 7-17c. Press the *Enter* key for the prompts. If the title block is overpowering the drawing, then scale it down; if it is too small then scale it up. As a rule of thumb, the height of the title block should be about 1/6 of the height of the printable area.

Figure 7-17a   Figure 7-17b

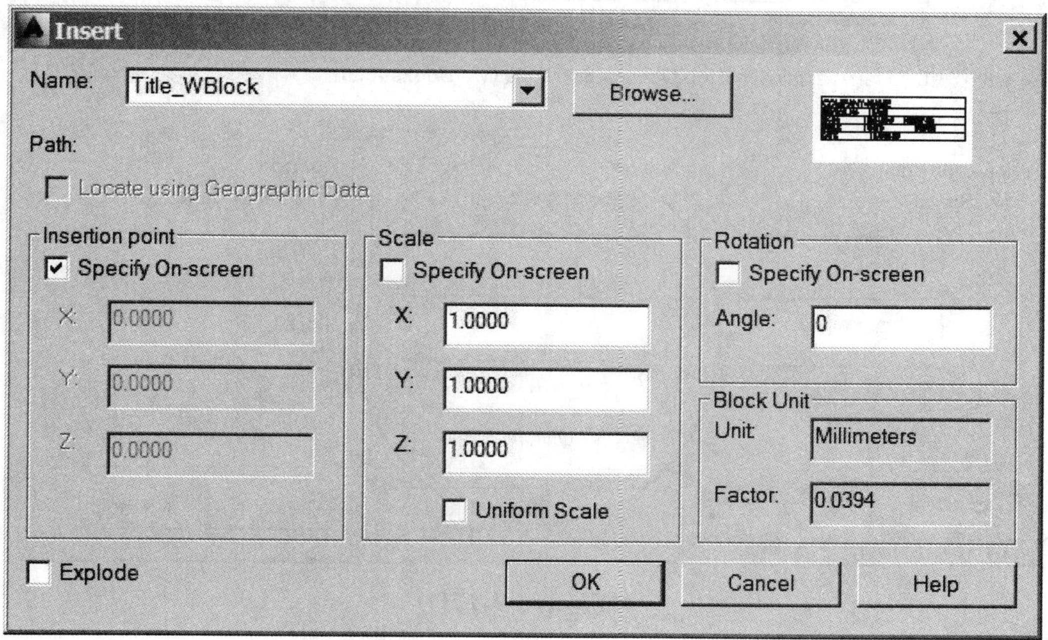

Figure 7-17c

9. _Scale down the title block_: (i) Activate the _Scale_ command. (ii) In response to the prompt _Select objects_, click on the title block and press the _Enter_ key. (iii) In response to the prompt _Specify the base point_, click on the lower right corner of the title block and press the _Enter_ key. (iv) In response to the prompt _Specify scale factor_, type 0.5 and press the _Enter_ key. (v) The title block is reduced by 50% as shown in Figure 7-17d.

10. _Insert the release block_: Insert the release block in the lower left corner of the title block, Figure 7-17e. The _Insert_ block dialog box shows the entries for the release block insertion. Notice that the release block is scale down during the block insertion process, Figure 7-17f.

Figure 7-17d

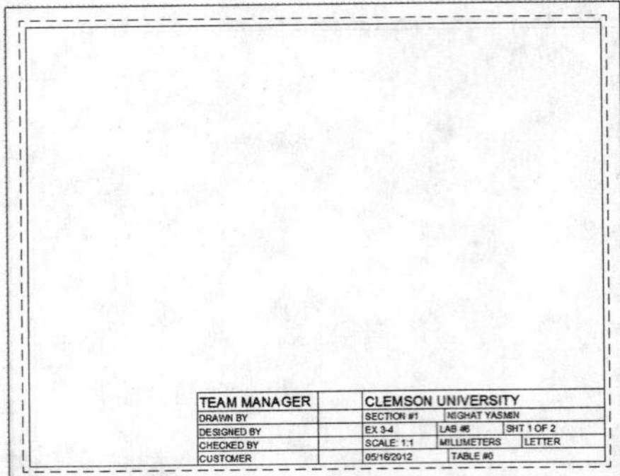

Figure 7-17e

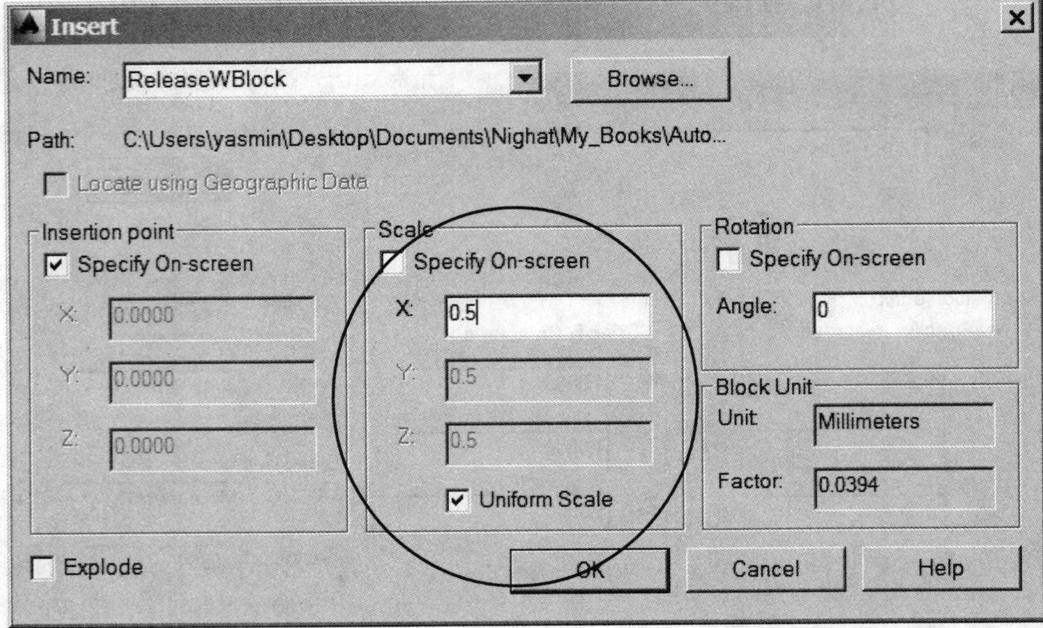

Figure 7-17f

11. *Create a new viewport*: (i) Select the *Layout* tab, Figure 7-18a. (ii) Select the *Layout Viewports* panel. (iii) Expand the *Rectangular* dropdown menu and select the *Rectangular* option, Figure 7-18a.

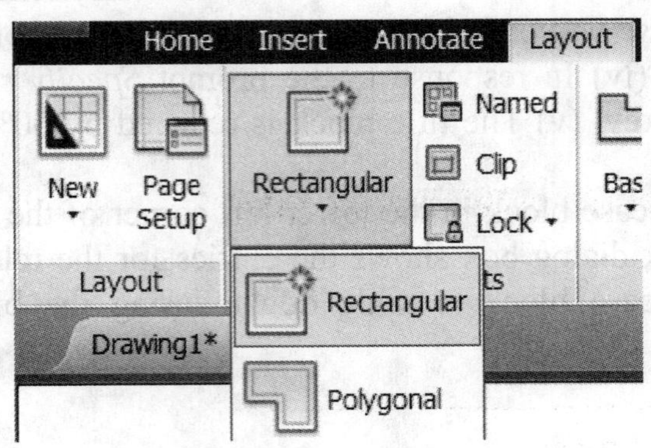

Figure 7-18a

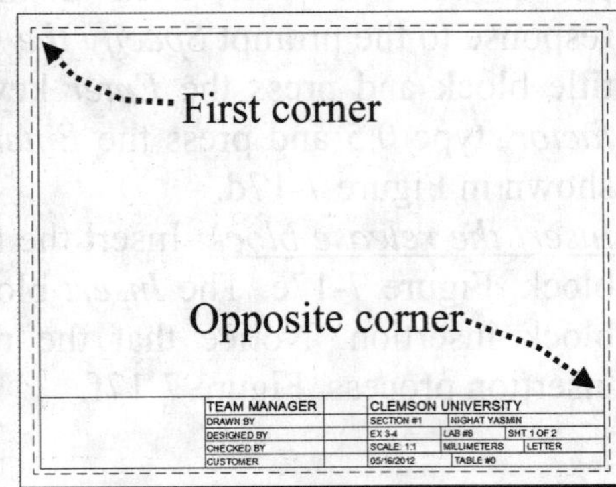

Figure 7-18b

(iv) The prompt to specify the first corner of the viewport will appear, Figure 7-18c. Click at the upper left corner of the border rectangle for the first point, Figure 7-18b and Figure 7-18c. (v) The prompt to specify the opposite corners of the viewport will appear. For the opposite corner point, click at the upper right corner of the Title block, Figures 6-18b and Figure 7-18d.

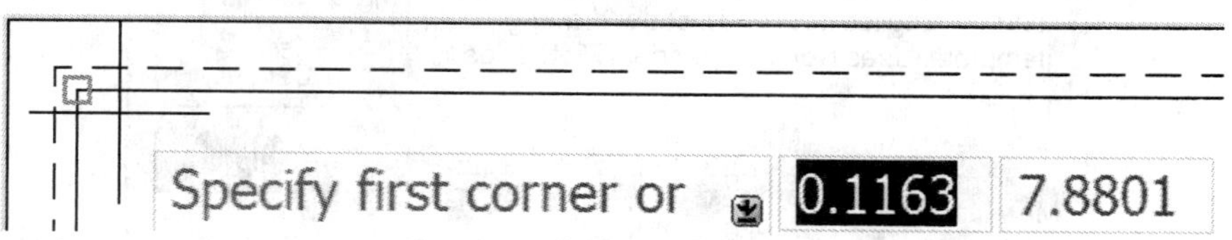

Figure 7-18c

Figure 7-18d

12. _Save the template file_: (i) From the _Quick Access_ toolbar, click the _Save As_ ( ) icon and this will open the _Save Drawing As_ dialog box. (ii) In the dialog box, for the _Files of type_ field press the down arrow to display the option list, Figure 7-19a. (iii) Click with the left mouse button on _dwt_ type, Figure 7-19a; and this will open the template folder. (iii) Specify the template file name, for the example, My_acadiso_Landscape_tmplt. (v) Press the _Save_ button and this will open _Template Options_ dialog box, Figure 7-19b. (vi) Press the _OK_ button to complete the template creation process.

13. By default the template file is saved in _Template_ folder. However, if the software is reloaded frequently then save the template file in different folder (for example, in the user folder).

14. The template file is shown in Figure 7-18b.

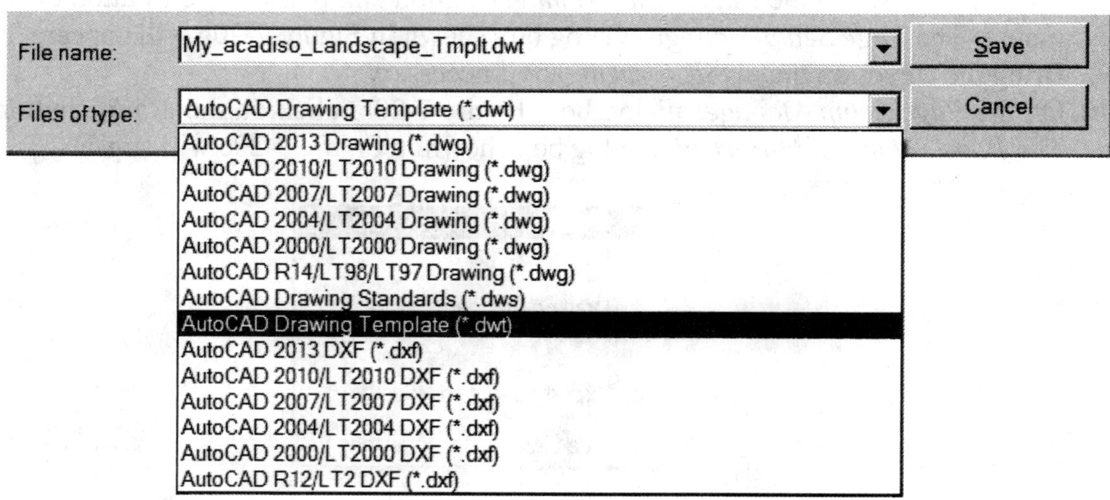

Figure 7-19a

15. User created template files can also be saved as *dwg* file in manner similar to the software created files are saved as *dwg* files.

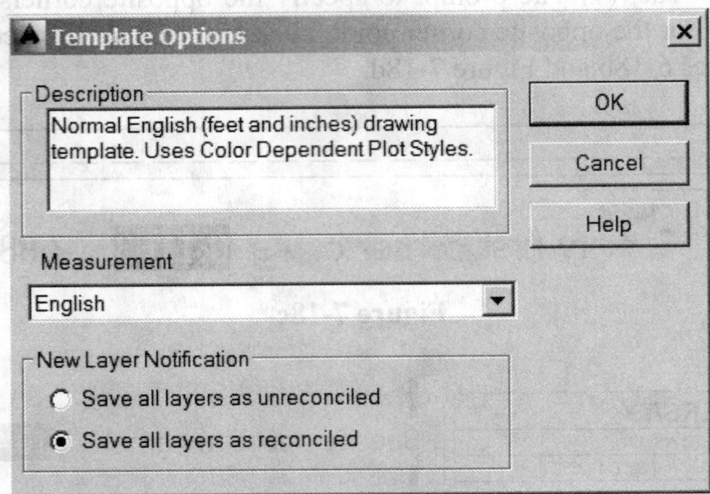

Figure 7-19b

7.8.2.   Portrait template for ISO units

A portrait template for ISO units is created using the following steps.

1.   Open a new acadiso.dwt file.
2.   Create a layer Template file and make it the current layer.
3.   Select the *Layout1*; double click in the layout and turn *off* the grid.
4.   Delete the *Layout2*.
5.   Click on the *Layout1* tab and rename it to ISO-Portrait.
6.   Click on the viewport (its grip points will appear) and delete it using the *Erase* command.
7.   Click on the ISO-Portrait layout and press the right button of the mouse. The option panel will appear, Figure 7-20a.
8.   Move the cursor to the *Page Setup Manager* option and press the left button of the mouse. The *Page Setup Manager* dialog box shown in Figure 7-20b will appear.
9.   Bring the cursor on the *ANSI-Portrait* tab, if necessary.
10. On the *Page Setup Manager* dialog box, Figure 7-20b, click on the *Modify* button. The *Page Setup – ISO-Portrait* Dialog box shown in Figure 7-20c will appear.

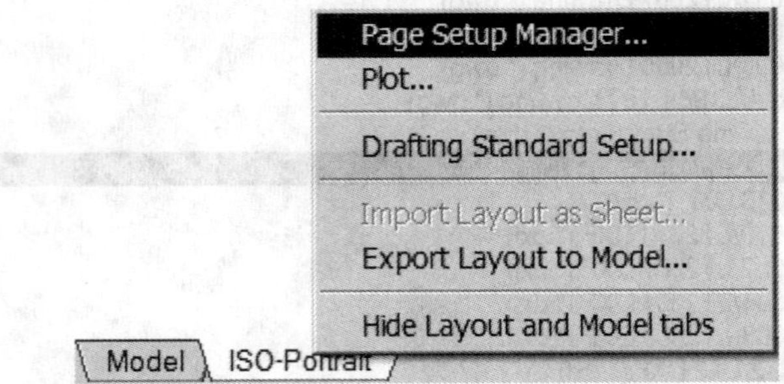

Figure 7-20a

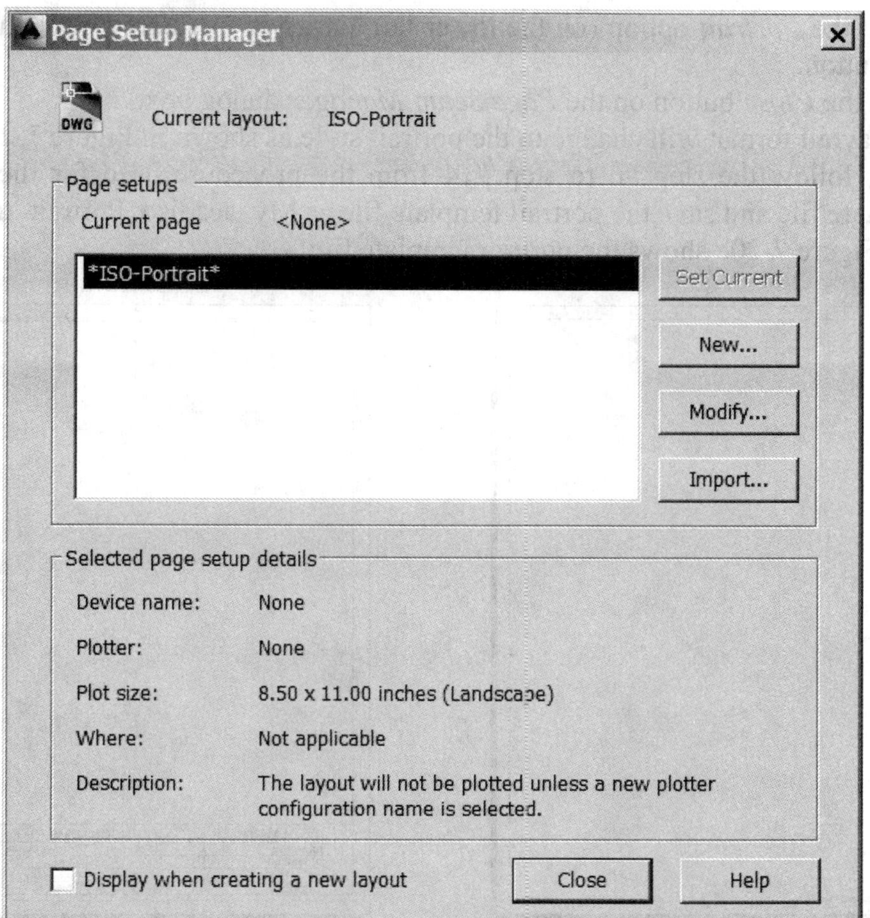

Figure 7-20b

Figure 7-20c

11. Select the *Portrait* option (on the lower left corner of the dialog box) and press the *OK* button.
12. Press the *Close* button on the *Page Setup Manager* dialog box.
13. The layout format will change to the portrait style as shown in Figure 7-20d.
14. Now, follow the step #6 to step #14 from the procedure used for the landscape template file and save the portrait template file as My_acadiso_Portrait_tmplt.
15. The Figure 7-20e shows the portrait template file.

Figure 7-20d

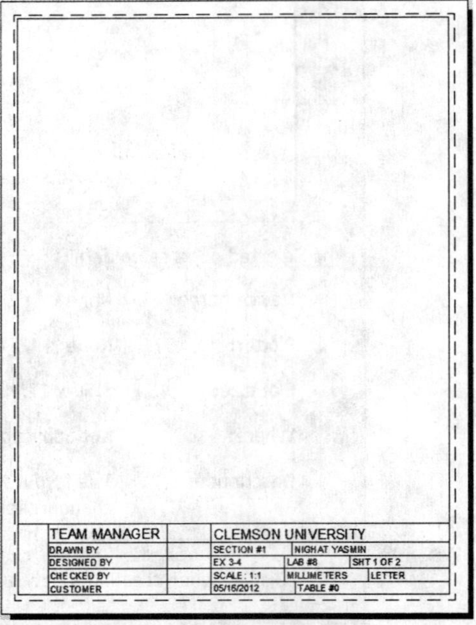

Figure 7-20e

7.8.3.   Template for ANSI units

Open a new acad.dwt file and repeat the process of creating acad templates (landscape and portrait) to create the ANSI template files.

7.9.   Modify attribute of a block in a template file

1. Open a new *My_acdiso_Portrait _tmlt* file.
2. This example will change the *Date* field in the title block.
   a. Bring the cursor on top of the *Date* field in the title block and double click with the left button of the mouse; this will open the *Enhanced Attribute Editor* dialog box, Figure 7-21.
   b. Select the *Attribute* tab.
   c. If necessary click the desired attribute and change its value in the *Value* field. This will activate the *Apply* button.
   d. If necessary, change the value of the other attributes, too.
   e. Press the *Apply* or the *OK* button. The *Apply* button will not close the dialog box, but the *OK* button will close the dialog box, too.

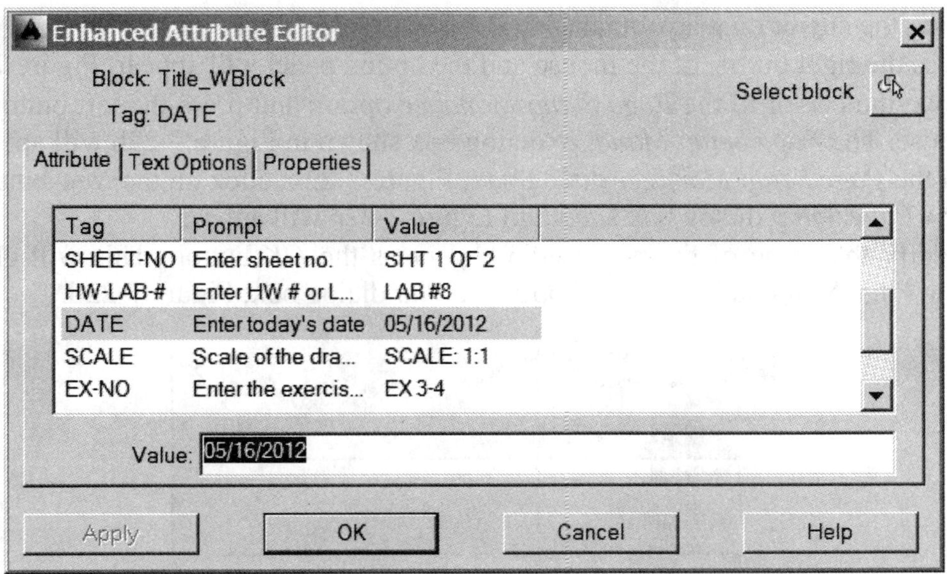

Figure 7-21

7.10. Page setup from layouts

If a user plots drawings in a specific style (certain combination of the options from the *Plot* dialog box) then the user can increase the productivity by saving and reusing those plot styles. Page setup or plot styles are attached to the layouts, therefor, creating and saving a page setup will be discussed here.

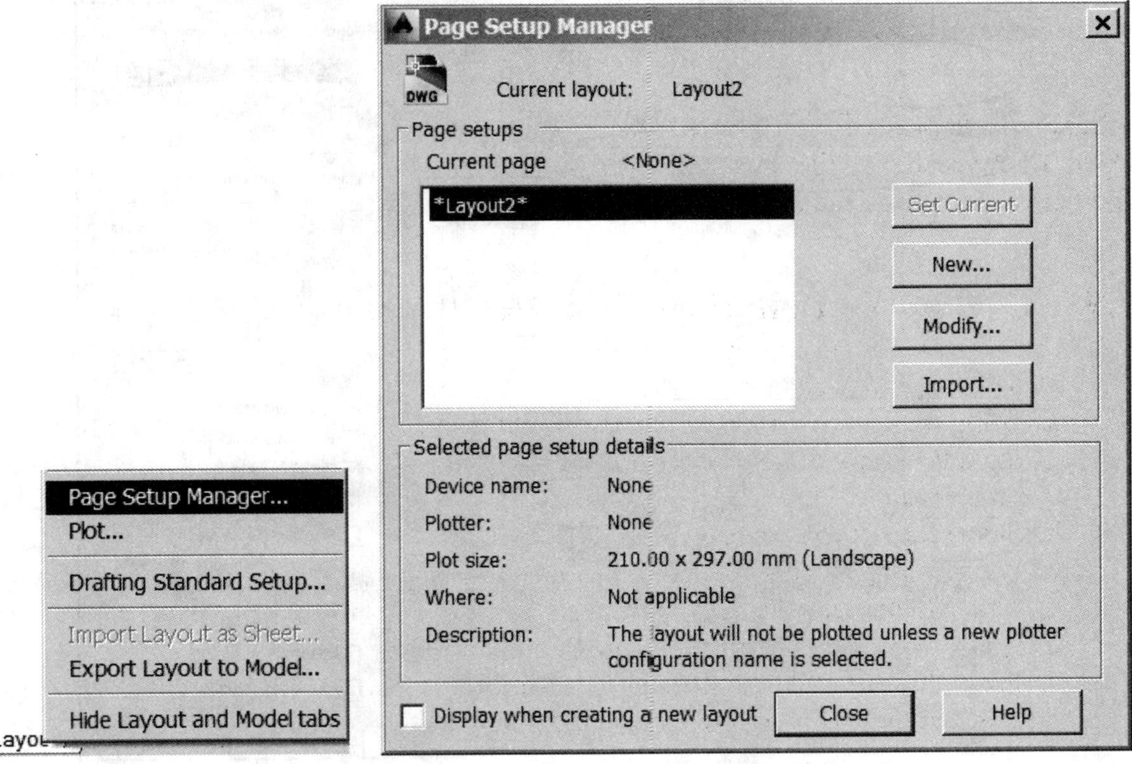

Figure 7-22a   **Figure 7-22b**

- Bring the cursor on a layout tab.
- Press the right button of the mouse and the option panel will appear, Figure 7-22a.
- Move the cursor to the *Page Setup Manager* option and press the left button of the mouse. The *Page Setup Manager* dialog box shown in Figure 7-22b will appear.
- On the *Page Setup Manager* dialog box, Figure 7-22b, click on the *New* button. The *New Page Setup* dialog box shown in Figure 7-22c will appear.
- Specify the name of the page setup and press the *OK* button. This will close the *New Page Setup* dialog box and open the *Plot* dialog box, Figure 7-22d.

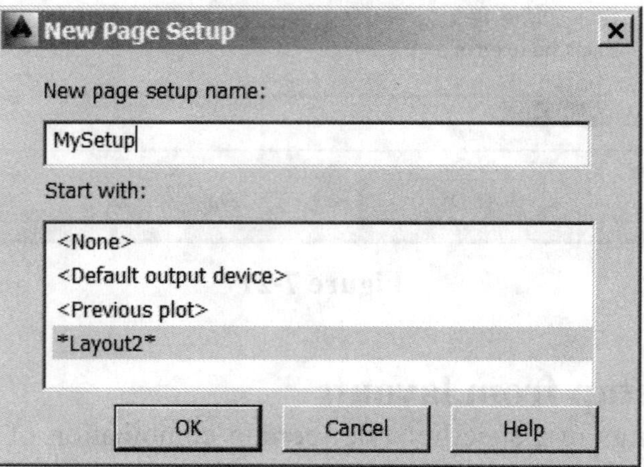

Figure 7-22c

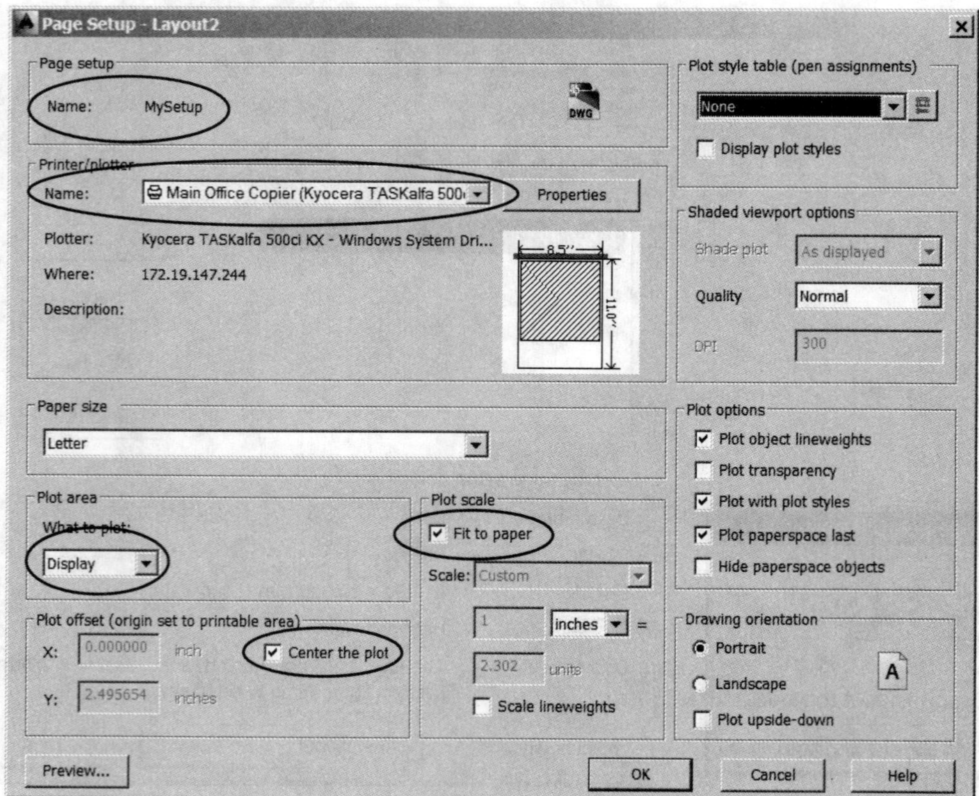

Figure 7-22d

- Figure 7-22d shows the settings of the *Plot* dialog box for the new page setup.
    - Note that, in the *Page setup* panel the name is *MySetup*, the newly created page setup's name.
    - In the *Plotter/printer* panel under *Name*, the default printer's name is selected.
    - In the *Plot area* panel under *What to Plot*, the *Display* is the default option.
    - In the *Plot offset* panel, the *Center the plot* option is selected.
    - In the *Plot Scale* panel, the *Fit to paper* option is selected.
    - In the *Plot options* panel, three options are selected.
    - In the *Drawing orientation* panel, the *Portrait* option is selected.
    - Click *OK* button of the dialog box. This will close the dialog box and create the new page setup.
- Activate the Plot command and check the available options under the *Page Setup* options.

Figure 7-22e

7.11.   Plot from layouts

The *Plot* command is used to plot a drawing file. The *Plot* command is discussed in detail in Chapter #2. When plotting a *Layout*, everything within the printable area of the specified paper size is plotted.

The process of plotting from a layout is summarized in the following steps.
1. Click on the desired layout.
2. Double click INSIDE the viewport (WCS will appear) and center the drawing using the scroll bars.
3. Freeze the un-necessary layers.
4. If necessary, set the linetype scale.
5. Double click OUTSIDE the viewport (WCS will disappear).
6. From the *Properties* sheet, set the viewport scale and lock the scale.
7. Update the *Title* block by modifying the block attributes to the desired value.
8. Activate and complete the *Plot* command.
9. On the printout, hand initials the *Release* block entries.

Figure 7-23 shows the settings of the *Plot* dialog box when the *Plot* command is activated for a layout.

- In the *Plot area* panel under *What to Plot*, the *Layout* is the default option.
- In the *Plot offset* panel, the *Center the plot* option is inactive.
- In the *Plot Scale* panel, the *Fit to paper* option is inactive.
- In the *Shaded viewport options* panel, the *Shade plot* option is inactive.

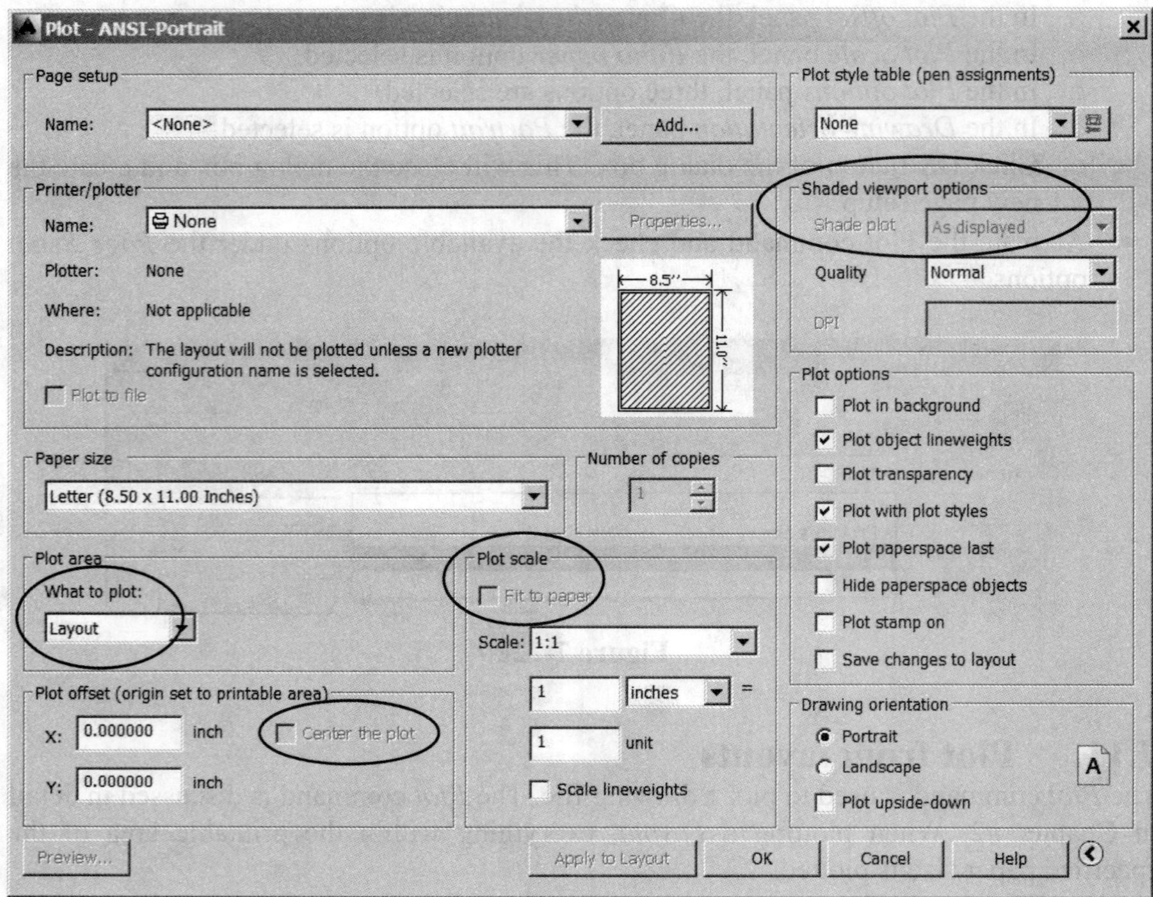

Figure 7-23

7.12. Layout plotting problems

Sometime the user relates the problem associated with layers with plotting from layouts. The most commonly occurred problem is that the user *can see the objects but cannot plot them*. Generally, there are two reasons for this situation: either the objects in question are drawn in the *defpoints* layer or the layer's plot option is *off* (⊘). This problem can be solved as follow.

1. If the objects are drawn on the *defpoints* layer, then move them to their respective layers and the drafter will be able to plot the objects.
2. If the objects are not drawn on the *defpoints* layer then perform the following steps. (i) Open the *Layer Properties Manager* palette. (ii) If the layer's (containing the objects in question) plot option is *off*, that is, the layer's printer icon shows the no entry sign (⊘) then just click on the printer icon. The no entry

sign will disappear (▣) and the drafter will be able to plot the objects on the layer in question.

<u>Notes:</u>

8.   Dimensioning Techniques

8.1.   Objectives

- Learn the art of creating and reading a dimensional drawing
- Learn the basics of dimensioning techniques
- Learn the characteristics of the dimension and extension lines, spacing of the dimensions, making of arrow heads, etc.
- Learn about the placement of the dimensions.
- Learn standard practice to dimension circles, arcs, and inclined surfaces

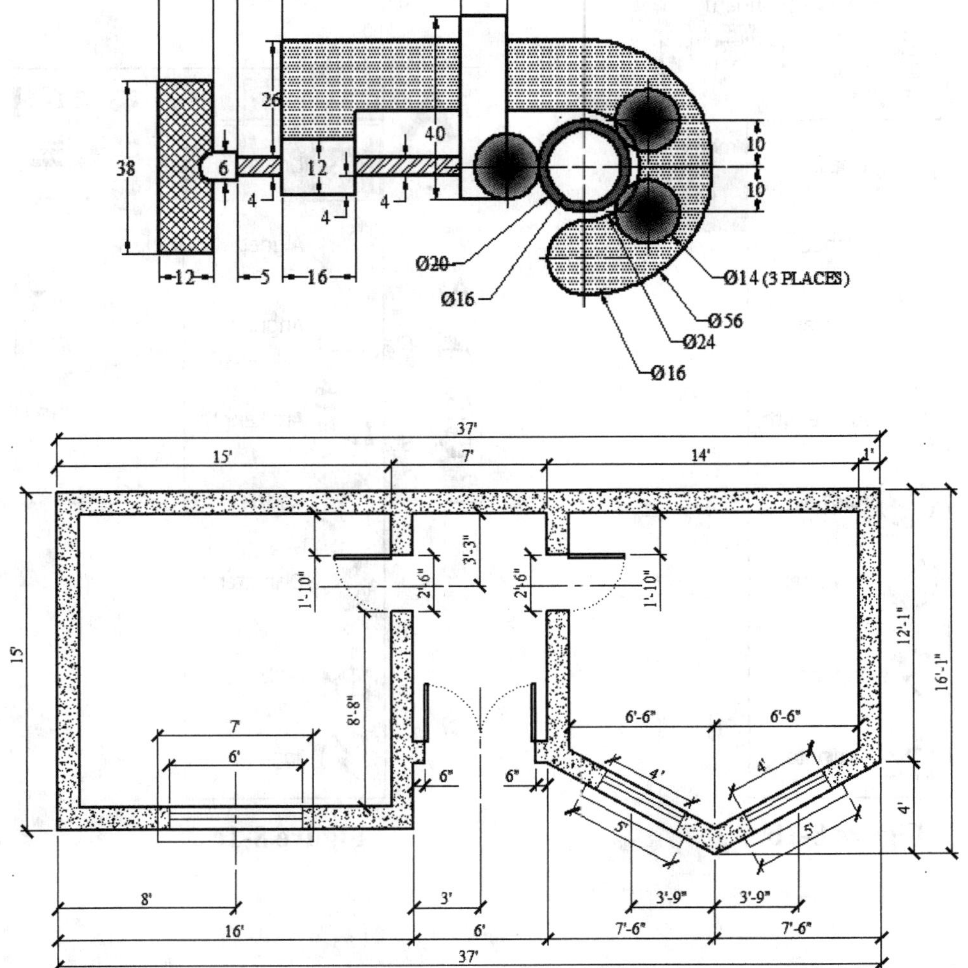

8.2.   Introduction

A dimension describes the size and location of the feature of an object. Hence, it is given in the form of a distance, an angle, or a note, irrespective of the type of the drawing and units used in the drawing. To achieve these functionalities AutoCAD uses from the *Annotate* tab the *Dimension* panel (Figure 8-1a and Figure 8-1b) and from the *Home* tab the *Annotation* panel (Figures 8-1c). This chapter explains the concepts and techniques used to add dimensions to a drawing.

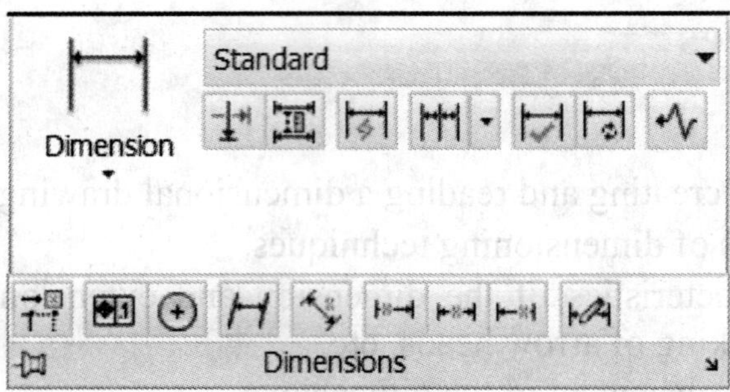

Figure 8-1a

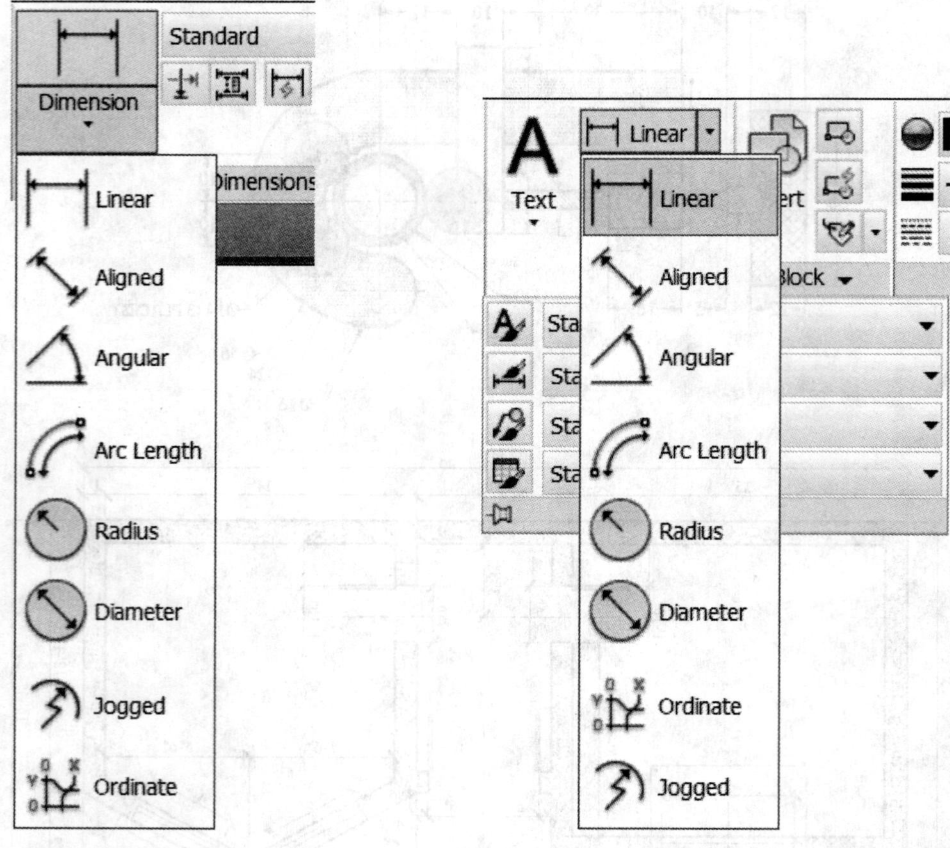

Figure 8-1b   **Figure 8-1c**

8.3.   Dimensioning in general

In addition to describing the shape of objects, generally, a drawing must show the sizes of the objects, so that the workers can build the structure or fabricate the parts that will fit together. This is accomplished by placing the required values (measurements) along the dimension lines usually located outside the outlines of the object; and by giving additional information in the form of notes which are referenced to the parts in question by angled lines called leaders.

A dimensioned drawing should provide all the information necessary for a finished product or part to be manufactured. Dimensions are always drawn using continuous thin lines. Two projection lines indicate where the dimension starts and ends. Projection lines do not touch the object and are drawn perpendicular to the element being dimensioned. In general, units can be omitted from the dimensions if a statement of the units is included on the drawing. All notes and dimensions should be clear and easy to read. In general, all notes should be written in capital letters to aid legibility and all lettering should be of the same size.

8.4.   Terminology

- *Dimension*: A dimension is the numerical value that defines the size, shape, location, or geometrical characteristics of a feature Figure 8-2a. Normally, dimension text is 3mm (or 0.125") high and the space between lines of text is 1.5mm (or 0.0625").
- *Dimension lines*: A dimension line is a thin continuous line that shows the extent and direction of the dimension, Figure 8-2a and Figure 8-2b.
- *Extension lines*: An extension line is a thin, solid line positioned perpendicular to the dimension line that extends from the object. It allows the dimension to be located off the object, Figure 8-2a and Figure 8-2b.

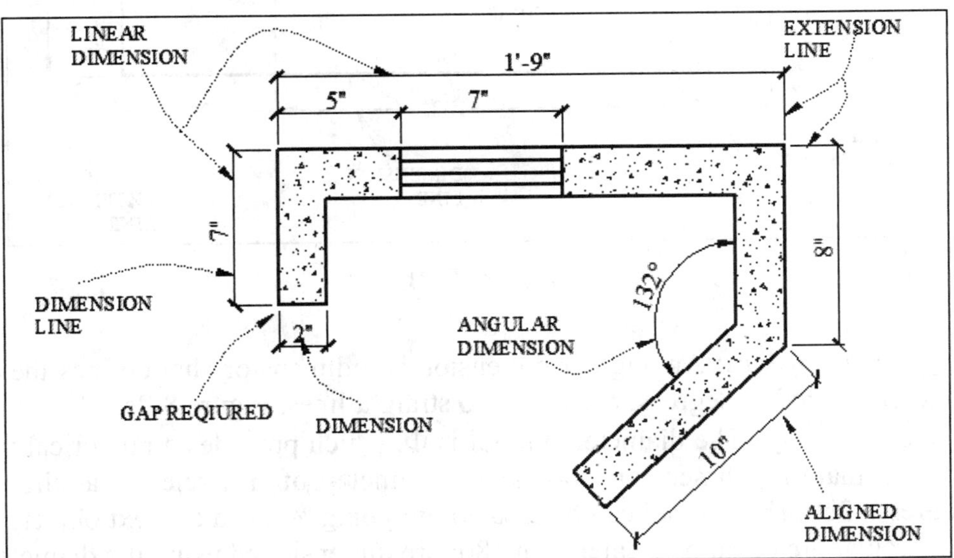

Figure 8-2a

- *Leader lines*: A leader line is a thin, solid line used to indicate the feature with which a dimension, note, or symbol is attached, Figure 8-2a and Figure 8-2b. Leader lines begin with an arrowhead or dot.
  - *For the best appearance make leader lines*
    - near each other and parallel, and
    - across as few lines as possible.
  - *Do not make leader lines*
    - parallel to the nearby line,
    - through the corner of the view,
    - longer than needed, and
    - horizontal or vertical.
- *Center lines*: A center line is a thin line with alternate long and short dashes, Figure 8-2b.
- *Linear dimensions*: A linear dimension is a straight line distance between two points; it can only be horizontal and/or vertical, Figure 8-2a and Figure 8-2b.
- *Align dimensions*: An align dimension a straight line distance between two points and can be horizontal, vertical, or inclined (that is, it is always parallel to the line), Figure 8-2a and Figure 8-2b.

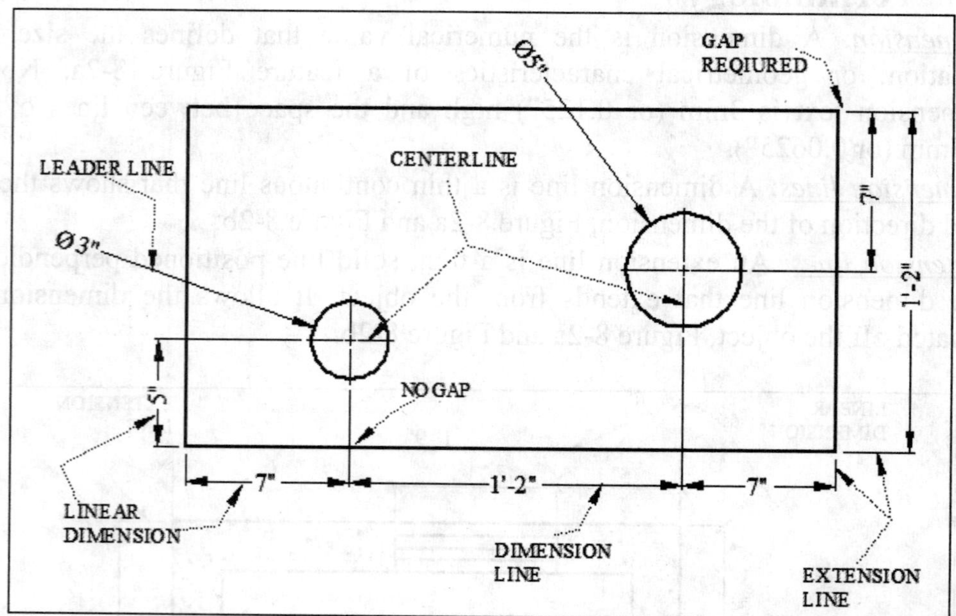

Figure 8-2b

- *Angular dimensions*: An angular dimension is a dimension that defines the angular value, measured in degrees, between two straight lines, Figure 8-2a.
- *Diameter symbol*: The diameter symbol is Φ, which precedes a numerical value, to indicate that the dimension shows the diameter of a circle or a circular arc, Figures 7-2b. (The symbol can be created by typing %%c in the text object). Circles and circular arc equal or greater than 180° are dimensioned using the diameter.
- *Radius symbol*: The radius symbol is *R*, which precedes a numerical value, to indicate that the dimension shows the radius of a circular arc less than 180 degrees.

- *Architectural drawing*: In an architectural drawing:
  - o The dimension lines ends with tick marks, and the dimension value is located above the dimension line, Figure 8-2a.
  - o The leader lines can end with a dot or an arrow.

8.5.   Important points to remember

Figure 8-2a, Figure 8-2b, and Figure 8-3 shows rules for placing dimensions. If possible, turn on the *Grid* so dimension placement becomes faster.

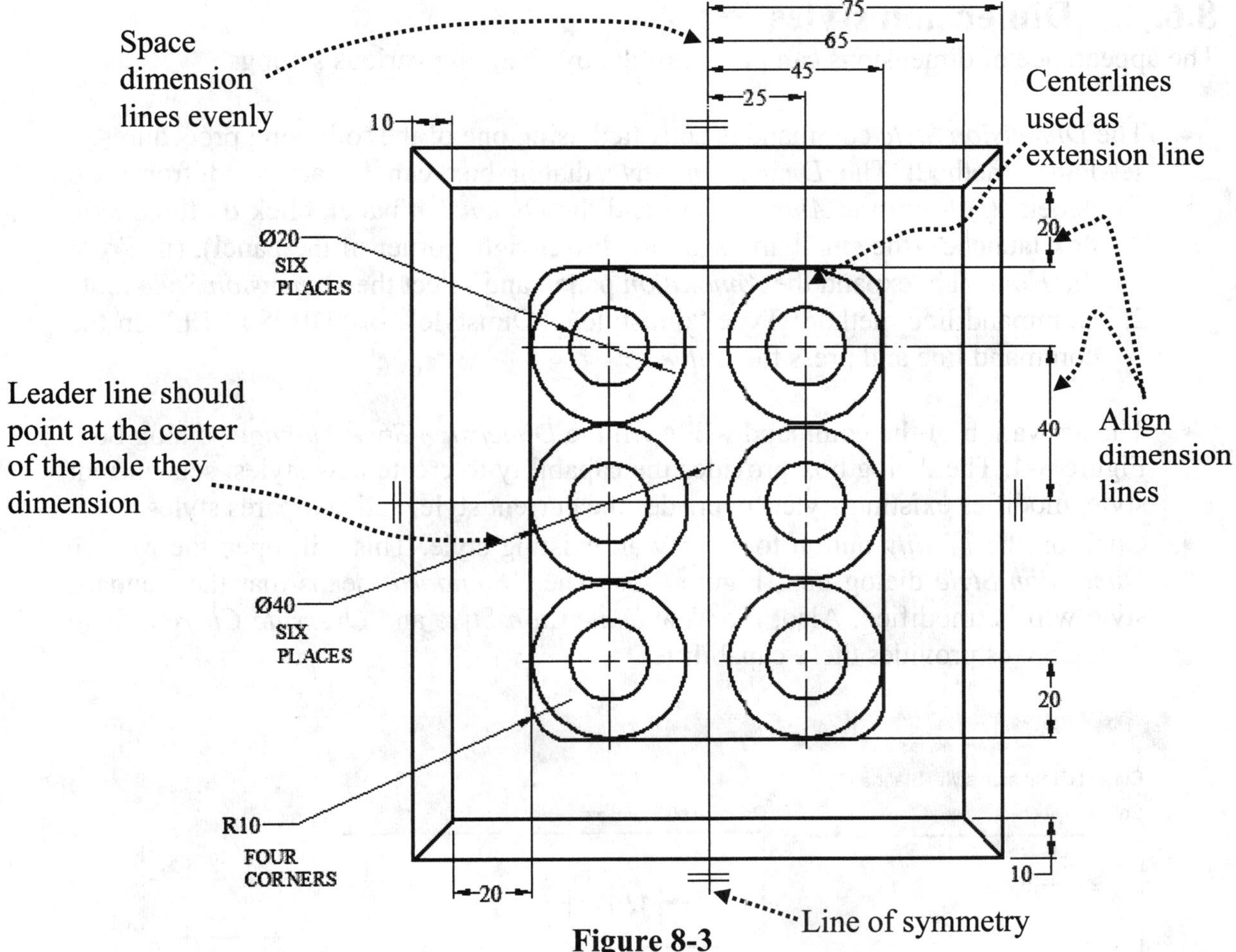

Figure 8-3

- Space between dimension lines: Dimension lines should be uniformly spaced.
- Dimension placement:
  - o Place dimensions near the features they are dimensioning.
  - o Do not place dimensions on the surface of the object.
  - o Align and group dimensions for neatness and easy understanding.
  - o Avoid crossing extension lines.
  - o Place smaller dimension closer to the object than the longer ones.
  - o Always place overall dimensions the farthest away from the object.
- Alignment of the dimensions: Align and group dimensions.

- Gap between the object and the extension line: There should be a noticeable gap between the object and the extension line to create a visual break. The visual effects can also be enhanced by using different color lines.
- Center line used as an extension line: For the circled and circular arcs, use the end of the centerline as the beginning of the extension lines.
- Line of symmetry: If a drawing is symmetrical at a certain axis (two sides are mirror images) then show the line of symmetry. It is enough to show the dimension for one side.

8.6.   Dimension styles

The appearance of dimensions can be controlled by changing various settings.

- The *Dimension Style* command is activated using one of the following procedures.
  1. Panel method: The *Dimension Style* dialog box can be activated from two panels. (i) From the *Annotate* tab and the *Dimension* panel, click on the dialog box launcher (the small arrow on the lower right corner of the panel). (ii) From the *Home* tab, expand the *Annotation* panel, and select the *Dimension Style* tool.
  2. Command line method: Type "dimstyle", "Dimstyle", or "DIMSTYLE" on the command line and press the *Enter* key.

- The activation of the command will open the *Dimension Style Manager* dialog box, Figure 8-4. The dialog box provides the capability to create new styles, sets current style, modifies existing styles, overrides the current style, and compares styles.
- Click on the *Modify* button to modify an existing style. This will open the *Modify Dimension Style* dialog box, Figure 8-5a. The *: Standard* means that the standard style will be modified. Also, the *New Dimension Style* and *Override Current Style* dialog boxes provides these capabilities.

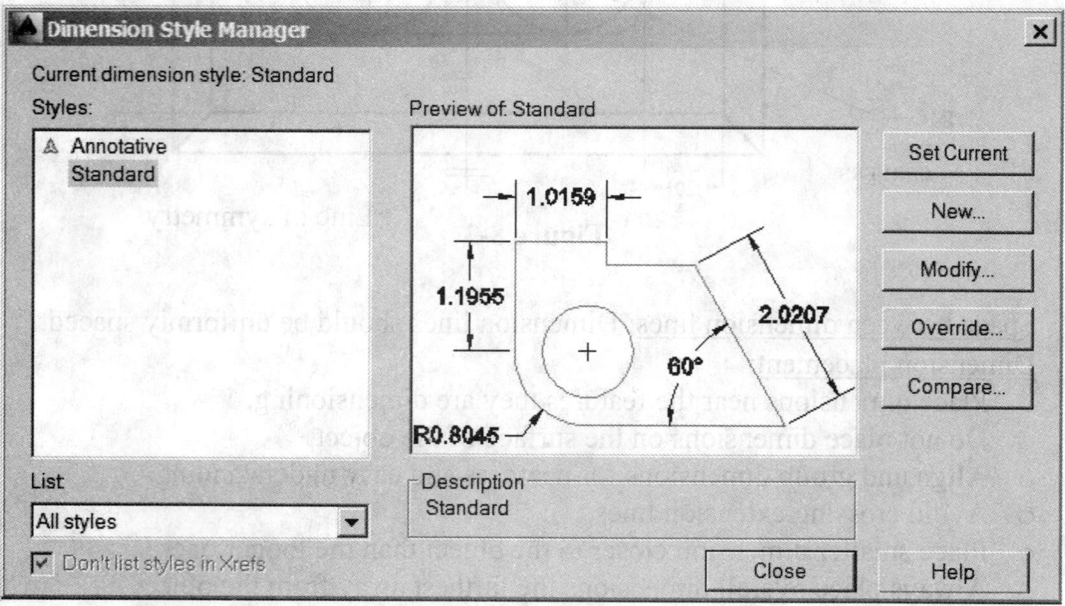

Figure 8-4

8.7.   Modify dimension style

The *Modify Dimension Style* dialog box, allows for changes in lines (dimension and extension), symbol and arrows (arrow heads, center mark, etc.), text (appearance, placement, and alignment), primary units (linear and angular), and tolerance.

8.7.1. Lines

The selection of the *Lines* tab (shown in Figure 8-5a) sets the format and properties for the dimension and extension lines. The most commonly used features are shown in Figure 8-5b.

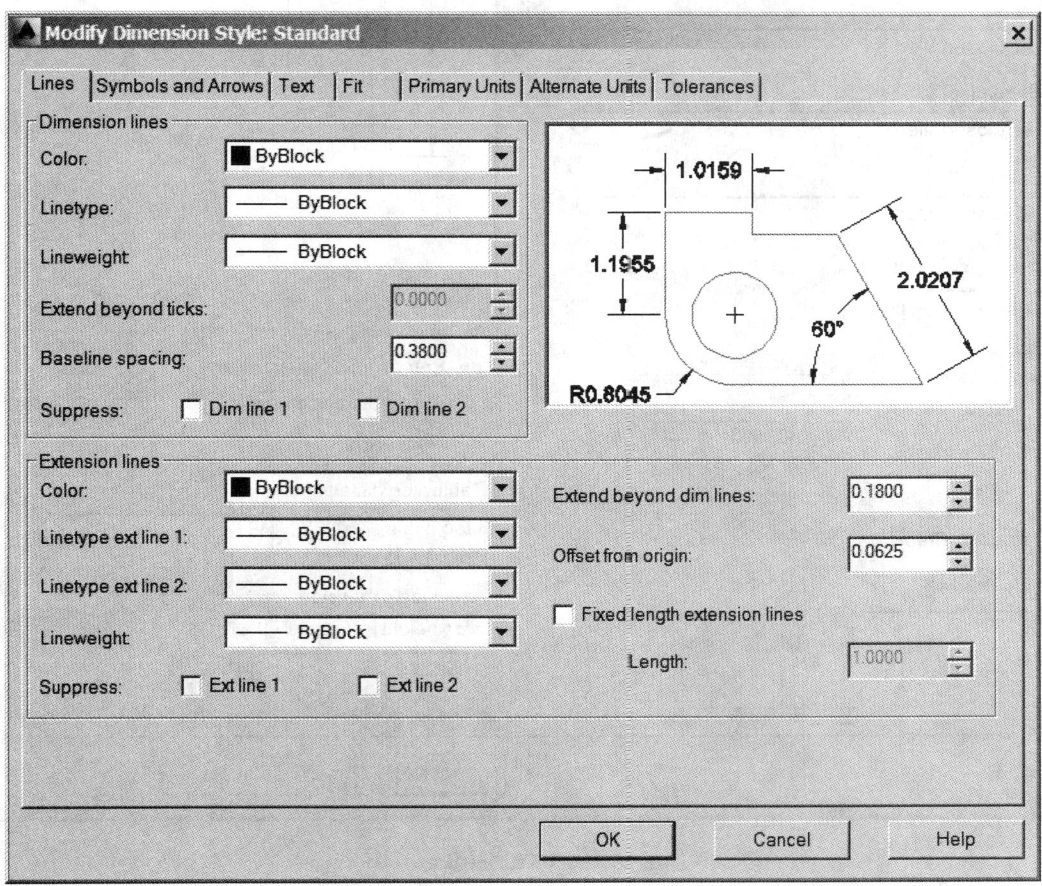

Figure 8-5a

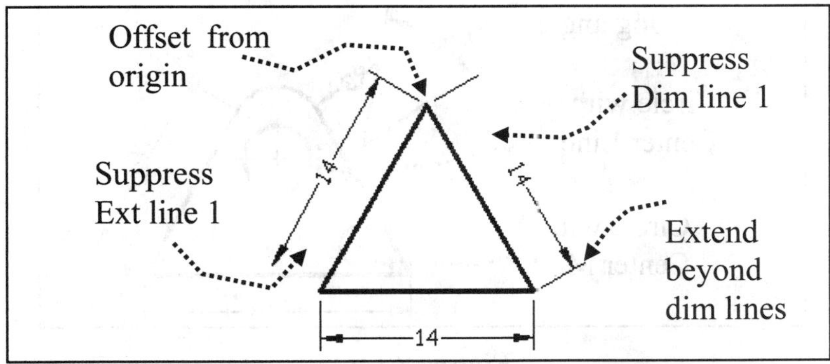

Figure 8-5b

8.7.2. Symbols and Arrows

The selection of the *Symbols and Arrows* tab, Figure 8-6a, sets the format and size of the arrowhead, center marks, arc length symbols, and radius dimension jog. The effect of some of the commonly used features are shown in Figure 8-6b; the figure also shows the use of different types of arrowheads.

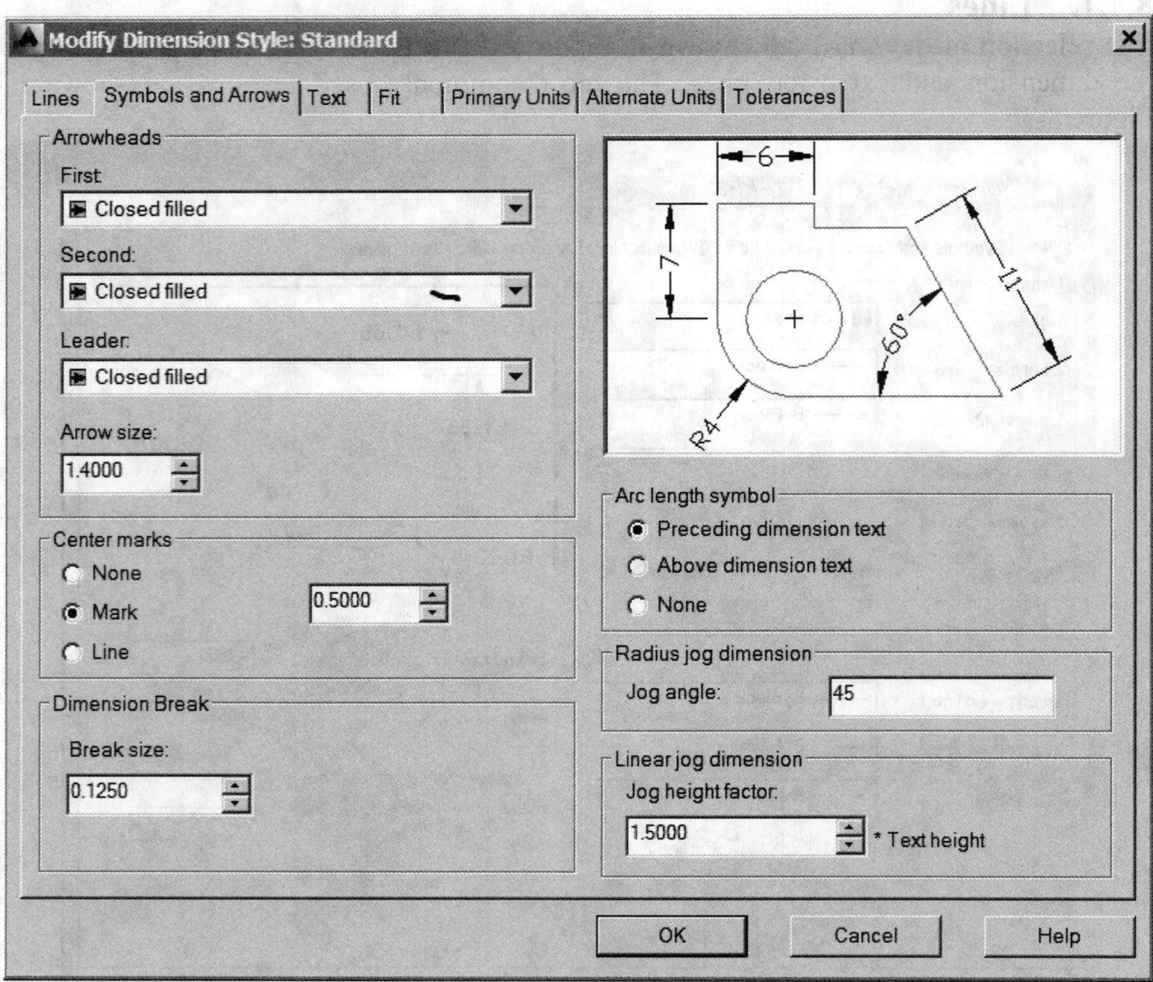

Figure 8-6a

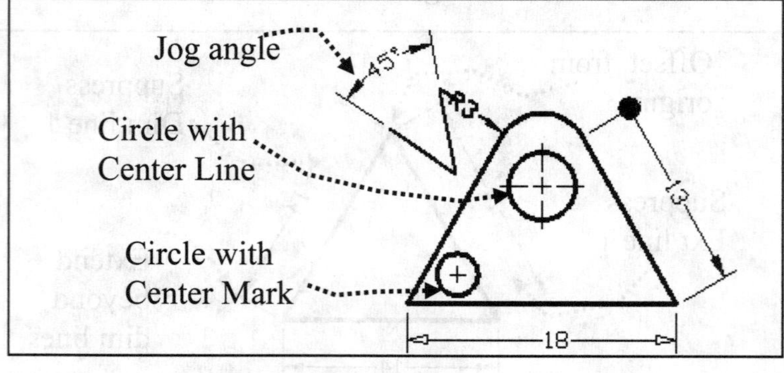

Figure 8-6b

8.7.3. Text

The selection of the *Text* tab (shown in Figure 8-7a) sets the format, placement, alignment, and size of the dimension text. The effect of some of the commonly used features are shown in Figure 8-7b.

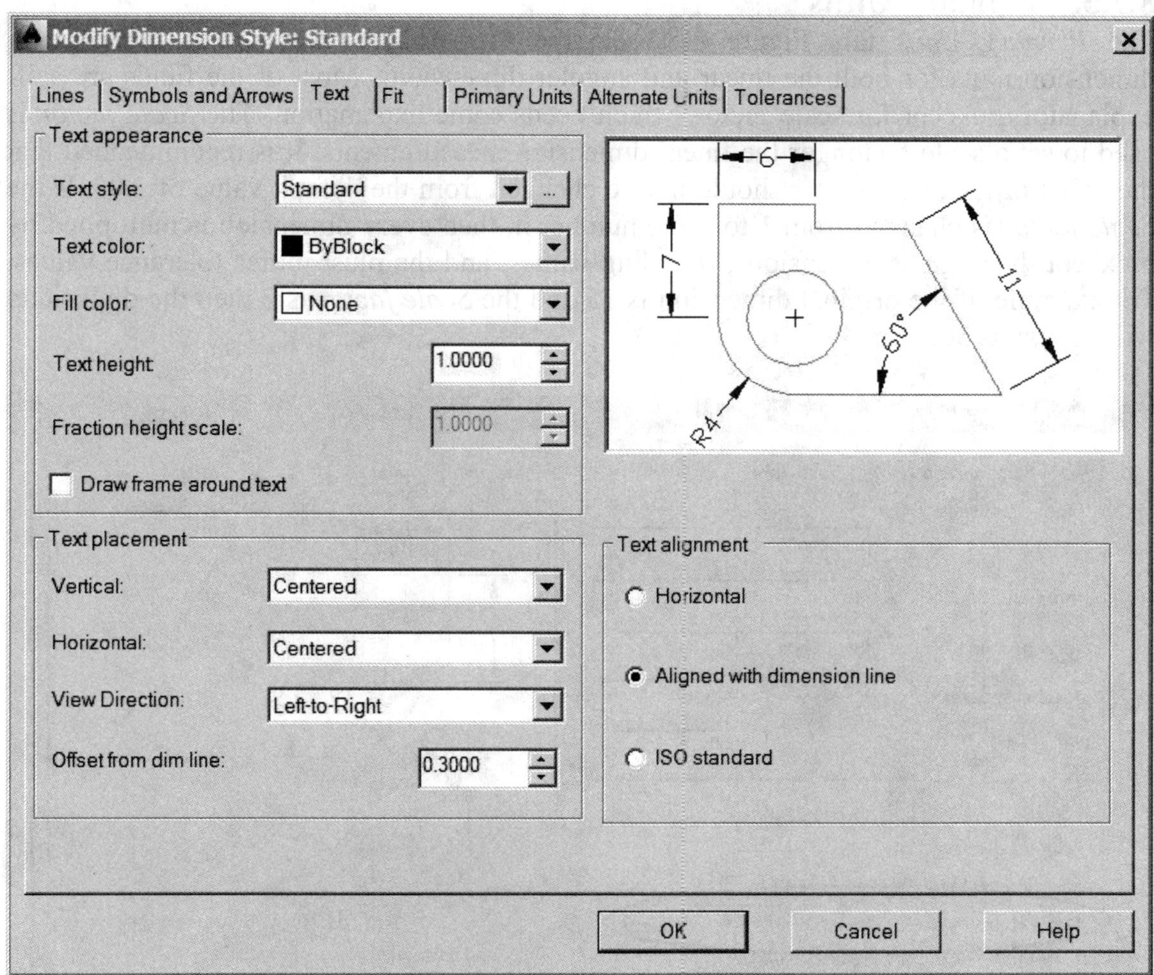

Figure 8-7a

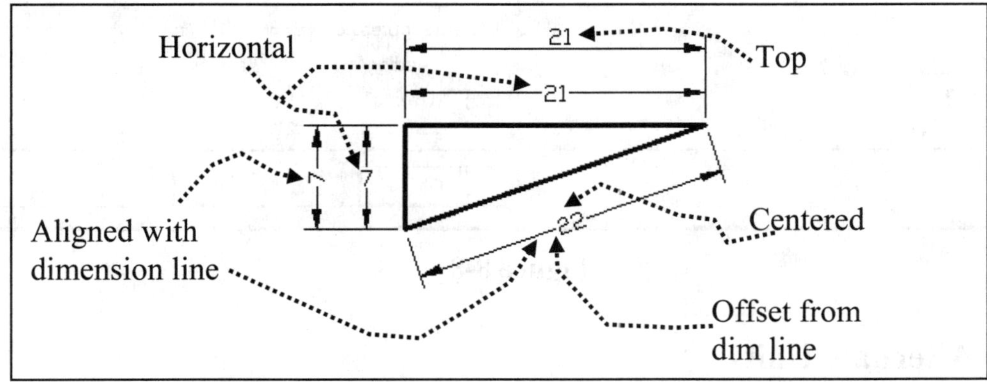

Figure 8-7b

8.7.4. Fit

The *Fit* tab controls the placement of the dimension text and arrowheads based on the space available between the extension lines, leader lines, and dimension lines.

8.7.5. Primary Units

The *Primary Units* tab, Figure 8-8, sets the format and precision of the primary dimension units for both the linear and angular dimensions. Most of the fields are self-explanatory, except for scale factor, which needs some explanation. The *Scale factor* is used to set a scale factor for the linear dimension measurements. It is recommended that the value of the *Scale factor* should not be changed from the default value of 1.00. If the *Scale factor* is changed from 1 to some number n, then every dimension is multiplied by n except the angular dimensions, rounding values, and the plus/ minus tolerance values. For example, if the original dimension is 15 and the *Scale factor* is 2 then the dimension will appear as 30.

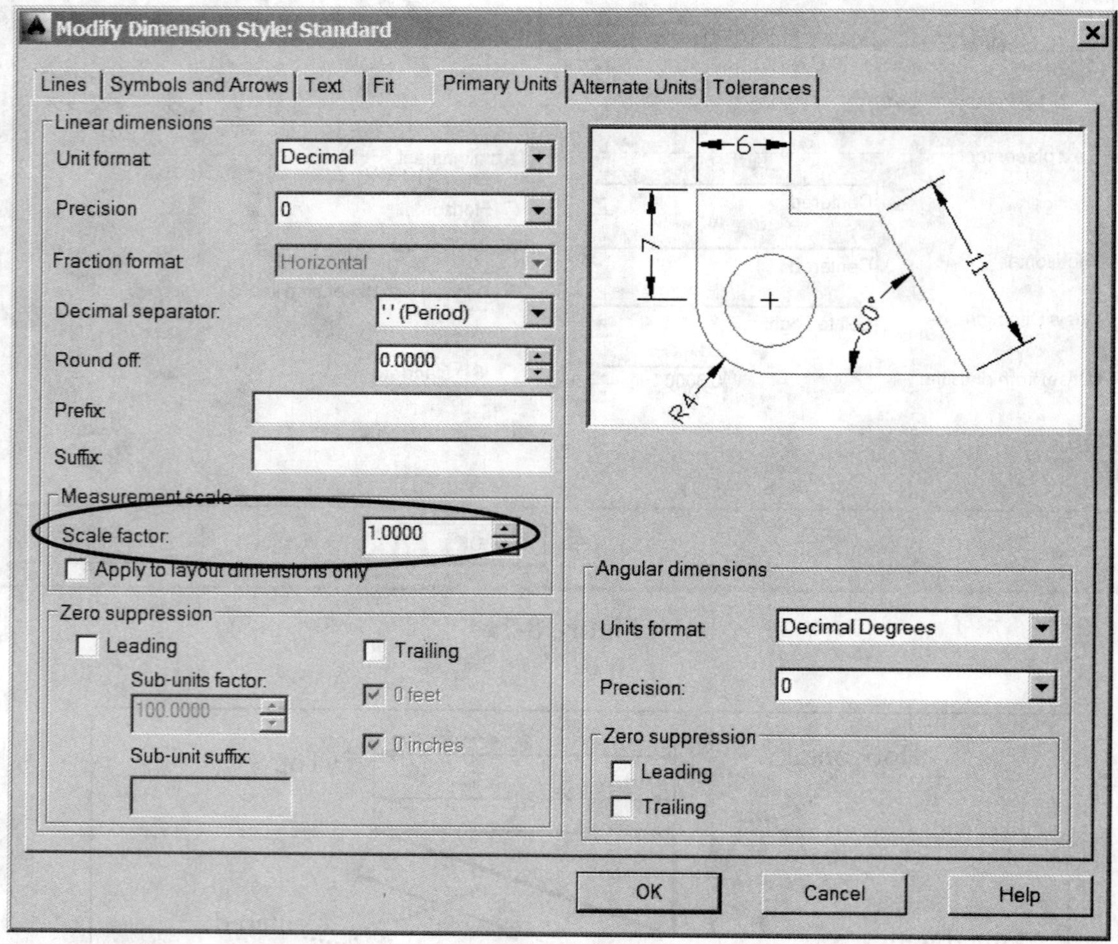

Figure 8-8

8.7.6. Alternate Units

The selection of the *Alternate Units* tab specifies display of alternate units in dimension measurements and sets their format and precision.

8.7.7. Tolerance

The selection of the *Tolerances* tab controls the display and format of dimension text tolerances. Although, theoretically possible, it is economically unfeasible to manufacture products to the exact figures displayed on an engineering drawing. The cost of a part rapidly increases as an absolute correct size is approached. Hence, accuracy depends largely on the manufacturing process used and the care taken to manufacture a product. Since different companies make different parts of a system, it is very important that these parts should be interchangeable. A tolerance value shows the manufacturing department the maximum permissible variation from the basic dimension.

8.8.   Modify dimension style

A user can modify the dimension style using the dialog box or the property sheet.

8.8.1. Modify dimension style using the dialog box

If the user desired to change the settings for all the dimensions then open the *Modify Dimension Style* dialog box. Using *Modify Dimension Style* dialog box to change the dimension setting will change all the dimensions in the drawing. For example, if *Suppress Dim line 1* option under the *Lines* tab is selected, then the first dimension line will be suppressed from every dimension (both linear and angular dimensions).

8.8.2. Modify dimension style using the property sheet

If the user desired to change the settings for one (or more but not all) dimension then using the *Properties* sheet, Figure 8-9, perform the following steps.

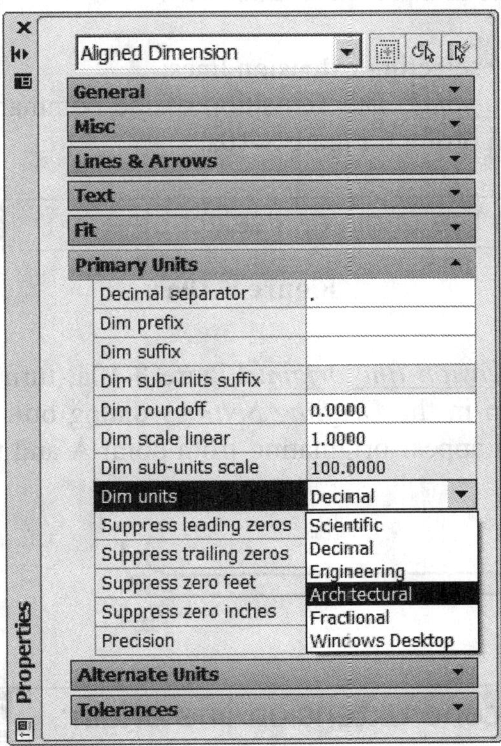

Figure 8-9

- Select the desired dimension(s) by clicking with the left mouse button.
- Open the option panel by pressing the right button of the mouse.
- Click on the last option; this will open the *Properties* sheet, Figure 8-9.
- On the *Properties* sheet select the desired option.
- In Figure 8-9 under the *Primary Units* panel the *Architectural* option for *Dim units* is selected. Modifying the desired option will affect only the selected dimension(s).
- The *Properties* sheet has a panel for the corresponding tab in the *Modify Dimension Style* dialog box.

8.9.   Linear dimensions

The *Linear* dimension command is used to create only horizontal and vertical dimensions. In Figure 8-10f, the dimension for the sides labeled as ED and AB are the linear dimensions.

Example: Add the dimension for the side AB and ED, Figure 8-10f.

- The *Linear* dimension is activated using one of the following methods.
    1. Panel method: The *Linear* dimension command can be activated from two panels. (i) From the *Annotate* tab and the *Dimension* panel, expand the *Dimension* dropdown menu and click the *Linear* tool. (ii) From the *Home* tab, expand the *Annotation* panel, expand the *Linear* dropdown menu and click the *Linear* tool.
    2. Command line method: Type "dimlinear", "Dimlinear", or "DIMLINEAR" on the command line and press the *Enter* key.

- Linear dimension by selecting extension lines:
    o *Activate the command*: The activation of the command leads to the extension line specification prompt, Figure 8-10a.

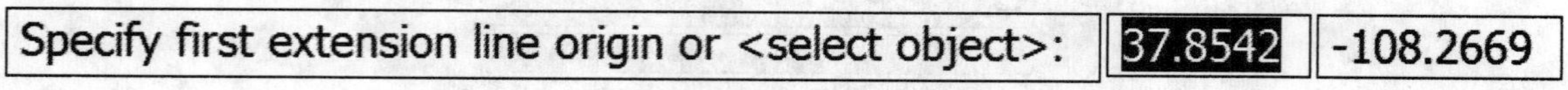

Specify first extension line origin or <select object>:   37.8542   -108.2669

Figure 8-10a

    o *Specify first extension line origin*: Figure 8-10a, turn on the object snap with *Endpoints* option in the *Drafting Settings* dialog box. Click on point A and a rubber band will appear originating from point A and terminating at the cursor, Figure 8-10b.

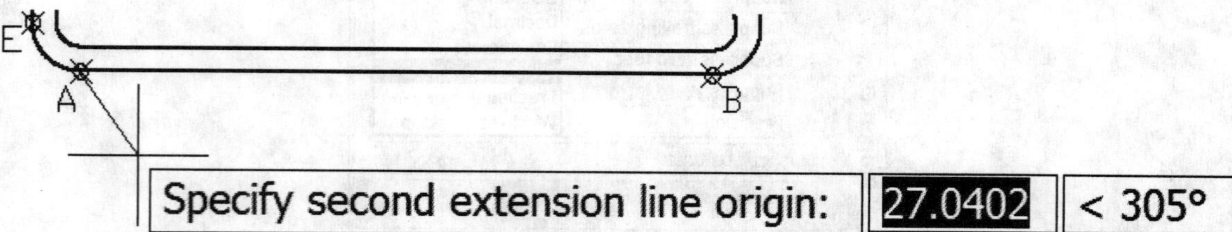

Figure 8-10b

o   *Specify second extension line origin*: Figure 8-10b, click on point B, the resulting prompt is shown Figure 8-10c.

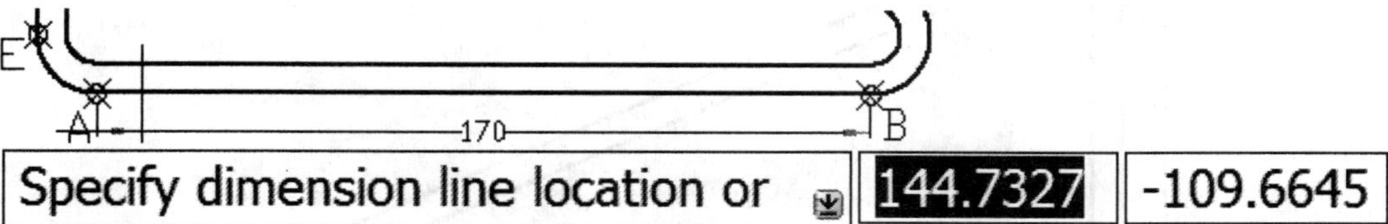

Figure 8-10c

o   *Specify the dimension line location*: Figure 8-10c, locate the dimension line by moving the crosshairs, following the dimension placement rules. Press the left mouse button at the desired location, Figure 8-10d.

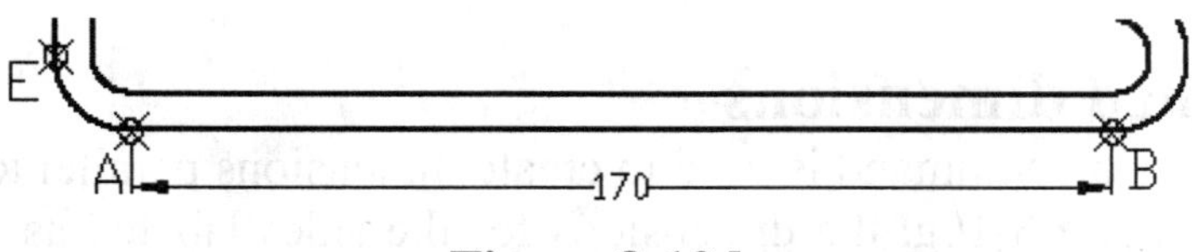

Figure 8-10d

- Linear dimension by selecting the object to be dimensioned:
  o   *Activate the command*: The activation of the command leads to the extension line specification prompt, Figure 8-10a.
  o   Press the *Enter* key.
  o   *Select object to dimension*: Bring the cursor on the side ED and press the left mouse button, Figure 8-10e.
  o   *Specify dimension line location*: Locate the dimension line by moving the crosshairs, following the dimension placement rules. Press the left mouse button at the desired location.
- Figure 8-10f shows the linear dimension for the sides labeled as ED and AB.

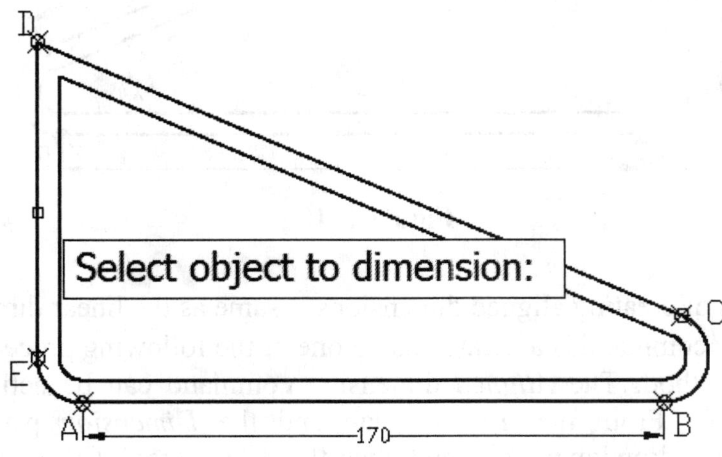

Figure 8-10e

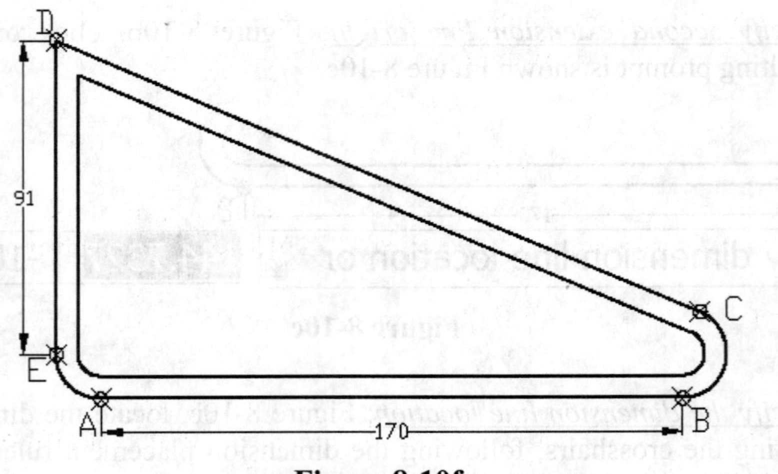

Figure 8-10f

8.10.   Aligned dimensions

The *Aligned* dimension command is used to create dimensions parallel to the object being dimensioned. In Figure 8-10g, the dimensions for the sides labeled as AB, CD, and DE are aligned dimension. Every linear dimension (dimensions for AB and DE) is aligned dimension but every aligned dimension (dimensions for the side labeled as CD) is NOT a linear dimension.

Example: Add the dimension for the side CD, Figure 8-10g.

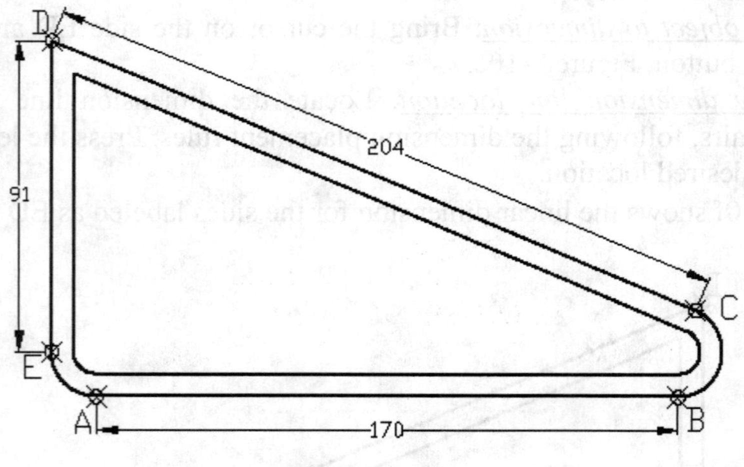

Figure 8-10g

- The process of creating aligned dimensions is same as the linear dimensions.
- The *Aligned* command is activated using one of the following procedures.
  1. Panel method: The *Aligned* dimension command can be activated from two panels. (i) From the *Annotate* tab and the *Dimension* panel, expand the *Dimension* dropdown menu and click the *Aligned* tool. (ii) From the *Home* tab, expand the *Annotation* panel, expand the *Linear* dropdown menu and click the *Aligned* tool.

2. Command line method: Type "dimaligned", "Dimaligned", or "DIMALIGNED" on the command line and press the *Enter* key.

8.11. Angular dimensions

The *Angular* dimension command is used to create angular dimensions. In Figure 8-11c, the dimension for the path labeled as ABCD and CDE are the angular dimensions.

Example: Add the dimension for the angle formed by AB & CD and DE & DC, Figure 8-11d.

- The *Angular* command is activated using one of the following procedures.
  1. Panel method: The *Angular* dimension command can be activated from two panels. (i) From the *Annotate* tab and the *Dimension* panel, expand the *Dimension* dropdown menu and click the *Angular* tool. (ii) From the *Home* tab, expand the *Annotation* panel, expand the *Linear* dropdown menu and click the *Angular* tool.
  2. Command line method: Type "dimangular", "Dimangular", or "DIMANGULAR" on the command line and press the *Enter* key.

- The activation of the command leads to the line selection prompt, Figure 8-11a.

Select arc, circle, line, or <specify vertex>:

Figure 8-11a

- *Select arc, circle, line*: Click on the line AB, Figure 8-11b.

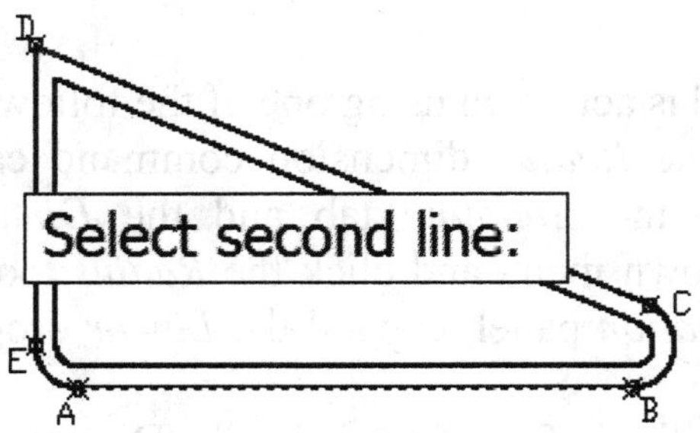

Figure 8-11b

- *Select second line*: Click on the line CD, Figure 8-11c.
- *Specify dimension line location*: Locate the dimension line by moving the crosshairs, following the dimension placement rules. Press the left mouse button at the desired location, Figure 8-11d.
- Similarly add the dimension to the angle formed by DE and DC.
- Figure 8-11d shows the two angled dimensions added to the drawing.

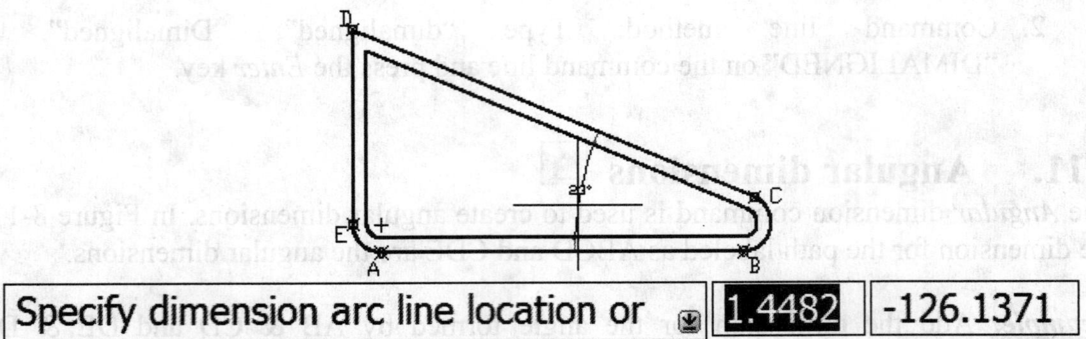

Figure 8-11c

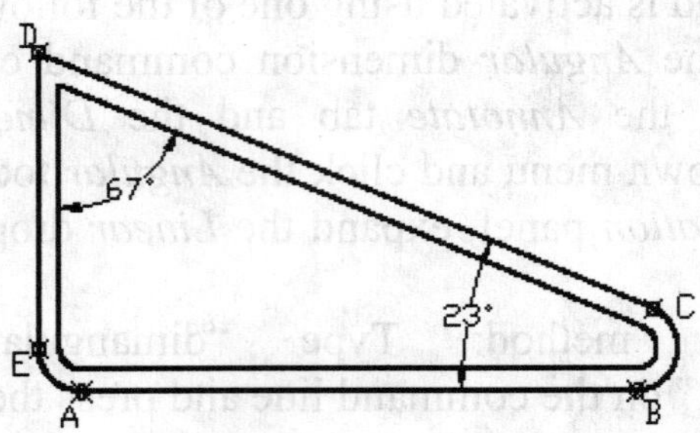

Figure 8-11d

8.12. Dimensioning radii

The *Radius* dimension command is used to create radius dimensions. Arcs less than 180 degrees are dimensioned using the radius. All radial dimensions are preceded by the uppercase *R*.

Example: Add the dimension for the arc AE, Figure 8-12a.

- The *Radius* command is activated using one of the following procedures.
  1. Panel method: The *Radius* dimension command can be activated from two panels. (i) From the *Annotate* tab and the *Dimension* panel, expand the *Dimension* dropdown menu and click the *Radius* tool. (ii) From the *Home* tab, expand the *Annotation* panel, expand the *Linear* dropdown menu and click the *Radius* tool.
  2. Command line method: Type "dimradius", "Dimradius", or "DIMRADIUS" on the command line and press the *Enter* key.

- The activation of the command leads to the arc/circle selection prompt, Figure 8-12b.
- *Select arc or circle*: Click on the arc AE.
- *Specify dimension line location*, Figure 8-12c: Locate the dimension line by moving the crosshairs, following the dimension placement rules. Press the left mouse button at the desired location.

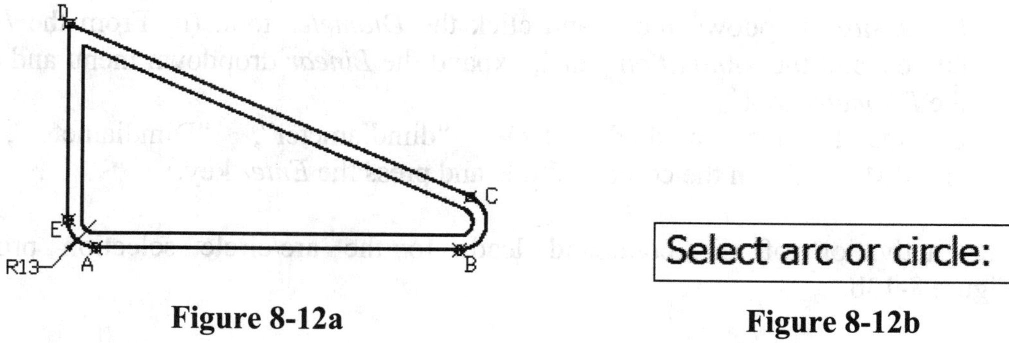

Figure 8-12a   **Figure 8-12b**

- *Select arc or circle*: Click on the arc AE.
- *Specify dimension line location*, Figure 8-12c: Locate the dimension line by moving the crosshairs, following the dimension placement rules. Press the left mouse button at the desired location.

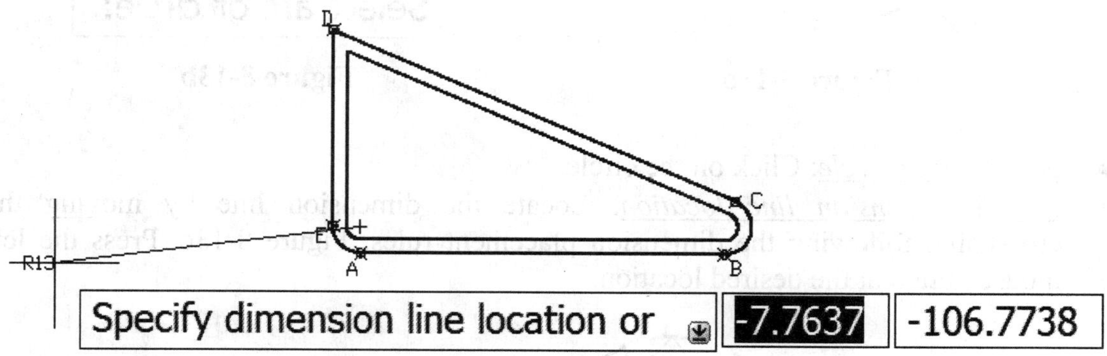

Figure 8-12c

- Position the radius dimension so that the leader line is neither horizontal nor vertical, Figure 8-12a.
- The radius tool will automatically include the center point. However, the center point can be replaced by the center line (or no center mark) by selecting the *Format* dropdown menu → *Dimension Style Manager* dialog box → *Modify* button → *Symbols and Arrows* tab: *Center mark* or *Line* or *None*.

8.13. Dimensioning circles

The *Diameter* dimension command is used to create diameter dimensions. Circles, semicircles, or arcs greater than 180 degrees are dimensioned using the diameter, Figure 8-13c. All of the diameter dimensions are preceded by the symbol Φ. The symbol Φ can be created by typing %%c in a text box.

Example: Add the dimension to a circles and circular arc shown in Figure 8-13a.

- The *Diameter* command is activated using one of the following procedures.
  1. Panel method: The *Linear* dimension command can be activated from two panels. (i) From the *Annotate* tab and the *Dimension* panel, expand the

Dimension dropdown menu and click the *Diameter* tool. (ii) From the *Home* tab, expand the *Annotation* panel, expand the *Linear* dropdown menu and click the *Diameter* tool.

2. Command line method: Type "dimdiameter", "Dimdiameter", or "DIMMETER" on the command line and press the *Enter* key.

- The activation of the command leads to the arc/circle selection prompt, Figure 8-13b.

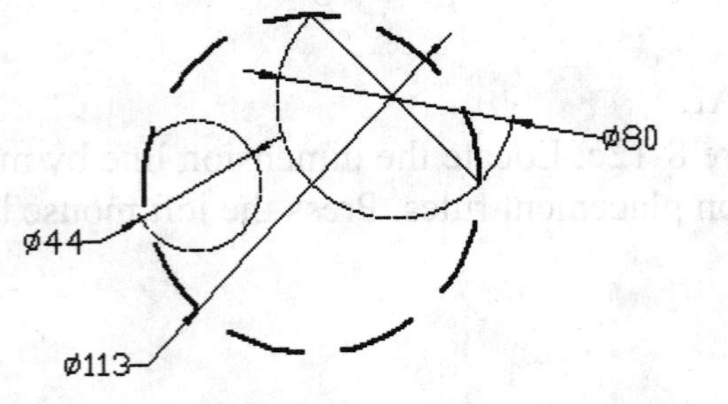

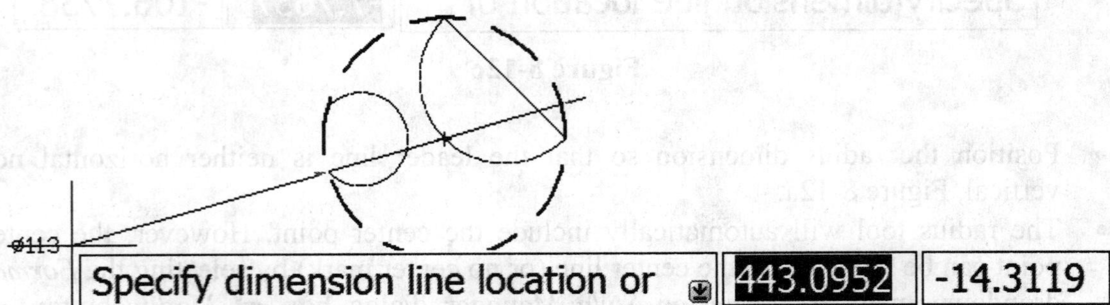

Figure 8-13a   **Figure 8-13b**

- *Select arc or circle*: Click on the circle.
- *Specify dimension line location*: Locate the dimension line by moving the crosshairs, following the dimension placement rules, Figure 8-13c. Press the left mouse button at the desired location.

Figure 8-13c

- Position the diameter dimension so that the leader line is neither horizontal nor vertical.
- Similarly add dimensions to the arcs, Figure 8-13a.
- The diameter tool will automatically include the center mark. However, the user can replace the center mark with the center line.

8.14.   Center mark

The *Center mark* dimension command is used to draw a center mark or center line at the center of a circle or circular arc.

- The *Center Mark* command is activated using one of the following procedures:
    1. Panel method: From the *Annotate* tab and the expanded *Dimension* panel click the *Center Mark* tool.
    2. Command line method: Type "dimcenter", "Dimcenter", or "DIMCENTER" on the command line and press the *Enter* key.

- The activation of the command leads to the prompt for the arc or circle selection, Figure 8-14a.
- Click at the circumference of the circle and the center mark is drawn at the center of the circle, Figure 8-14b.

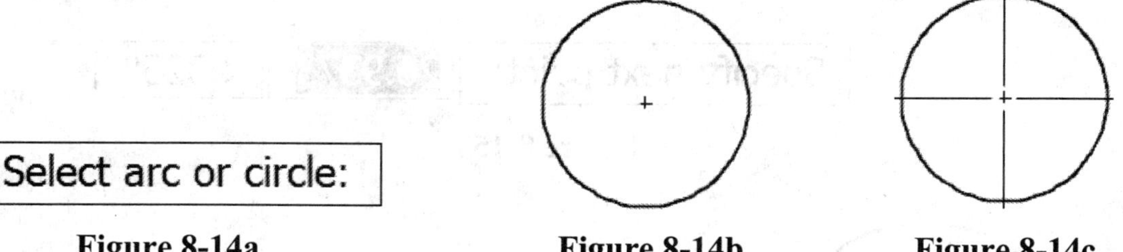

| Figure 8-14a | Figure 8-14b | Figure 8-14c |

- However, if the user wants to display the center line, Figure 8-14c, then perform the following steps. (i) Delete the center mark from a circle. (ii) In Figure 8-6a, under the *Center marks* window, switch to *Line* option. (iii) Activate the *Center marks* command and click at the circumference of the circle. The center line is drawn at the center of the circle, Figure 8-14c. (iv) If the center line does not appears as shown in Figure 8-14c, then increase/decrease the number field in the *Center marks* window.
- If the user desire to display the center line of a circle, then switch to *Line* option in Figure 8-6a before marking the circles.

For further details, check the Section 8.7.2 (Symbols and Arrow) and Figure 8-6a and Figure 8-6b.

8.15. Leader lines

The *Quick Leader* dimension command is used to create a line that connects an annotation to a feature. A leader object is a line with an arrowhead at one end (the starting end) and a multiline text object at the other end.

- The *Quick Leader* command is activated using command line as follow:
    1. Command line method: Type "qleader", "Qleader", or "QLEADER" on the command line and press the *Enter* key.

- The activation of the command leads to the prompt for the specification of the first leader point, Figure 8-15a. The arrowhead will be created at the first point. Click on the desired location (click at point A). This example will create a leader to point A.

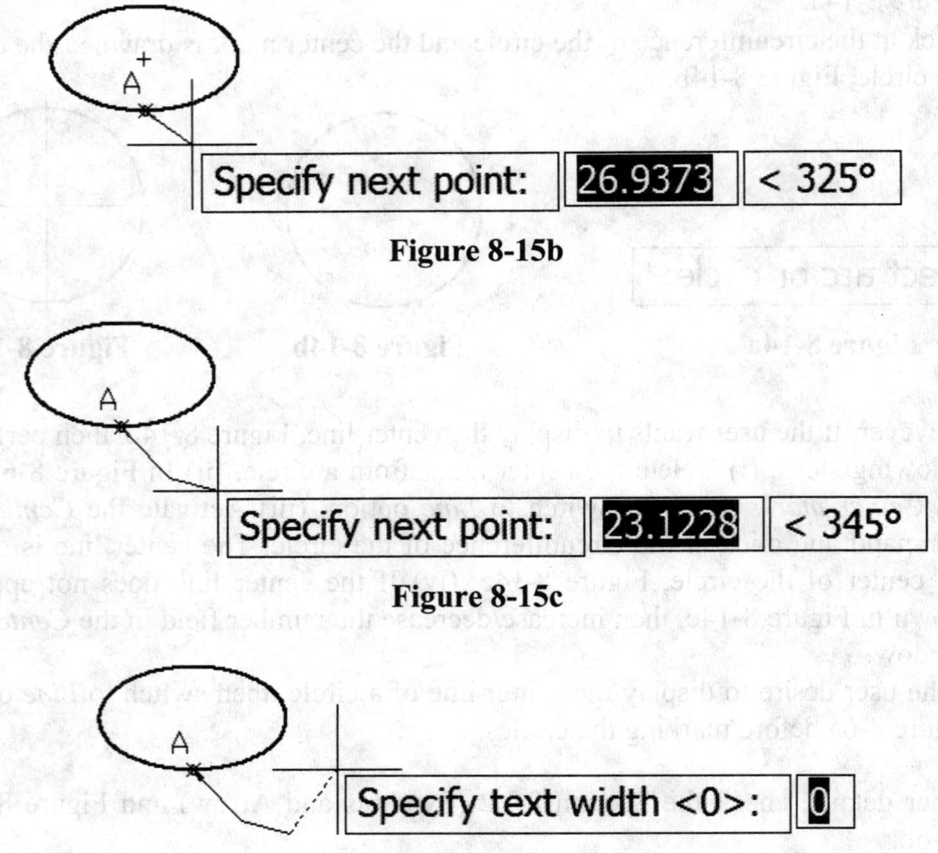

Figure 8-15a

- The next three prompts are for the specification of the three points on the leader line as shown in Figure 8-15b, Figure 8-15c, and Figure 8-15d.

Figure 8-15b

Figure 8-15c

Figure 8-15d

- For the text width take the default value and press the *Enter* key, Figure 8-15d.
- The next prompt is to enter the text for the annotation, Figure 8-15e. The user can enter multiline text, when the text is completed, press the *Enter* key TWICE.

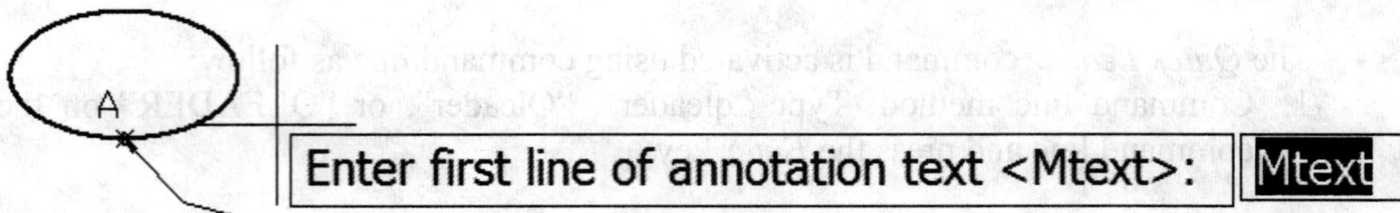

Figure 8-15e

- The leader shown in Figure 8-15f will be created.
- The text can be edited just like multiline text.

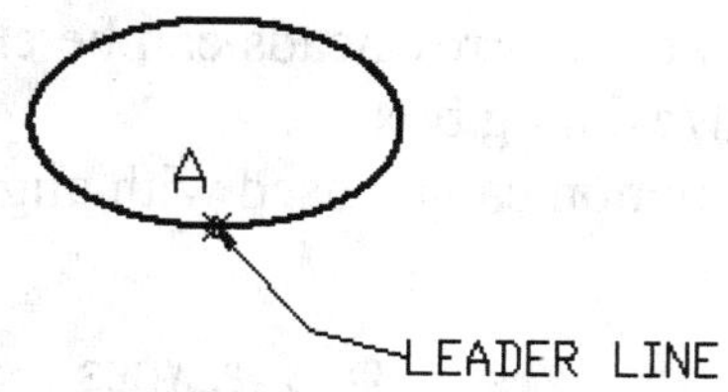

Figure 8-15f

8.16.   Types of dimensions

8.16.1. Continue dimension

The *Continue* dimension is a type of linear dimension that uses the second extension line's origin of a selected dimension as the first extension line's origin for the next feature. This technique breaks one long dimension into shorter segments that add up to the total measurement, Figure 8-16b. However, the continue dimension should only be used if the function of the object won't be affected by the accumulation of the error. This dimensioning technique is also known as the *Chains of dimension*.

- The *Continue* dimensions command is activated using one of the following procedures.
  1. Panel method: From the *Annotate* tab and the *Dimension* panel, expand the *Continue* dropdown menu and click the *Continue* tool.
  2. Command line method: Type "dimcontinue", "Dimcontinue", or "DIMCONTINUE" on the command line and press the *Enter* key.

- In Figure 8-15b, the object is dimensioned using the continue dimensioning technique. The *Continue* dimensions can be added as follows.
  1. Create a linear dimension for the first feature. In Figure 8-16a, the dimension between the circles labeled as A and B is a linear dimension.
  2. Activate the *Continue* command.
  3. Now click on the second extension for the next feature as shown in Figure 8-16a. That is, for the second extension line, click at the center of the circle C.

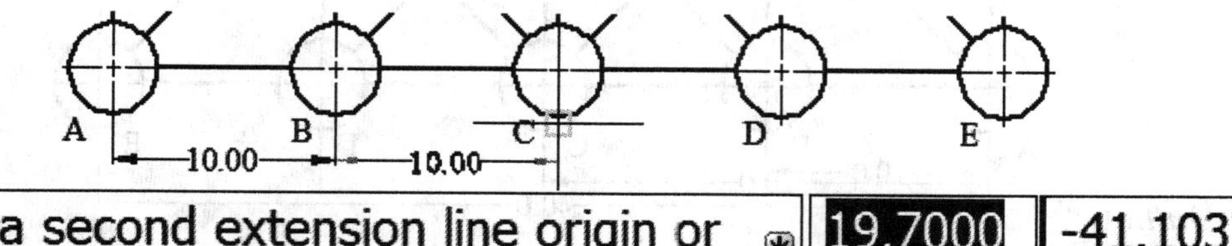

Figure 8-16a

  4. Since circles D and E can be dimensioned with respect to the dimension of circles A and B, repeat step #3 for the circles D and E, Figure 8-16b.
  5. Press the *Esc* key to exit the command.

6. The location of the text and arrowheads can be changed using the *Fit* tab of the *Modify Dimension Style* dialog box.
7. Continue dimensions option can be used with aligned dimensions, too.

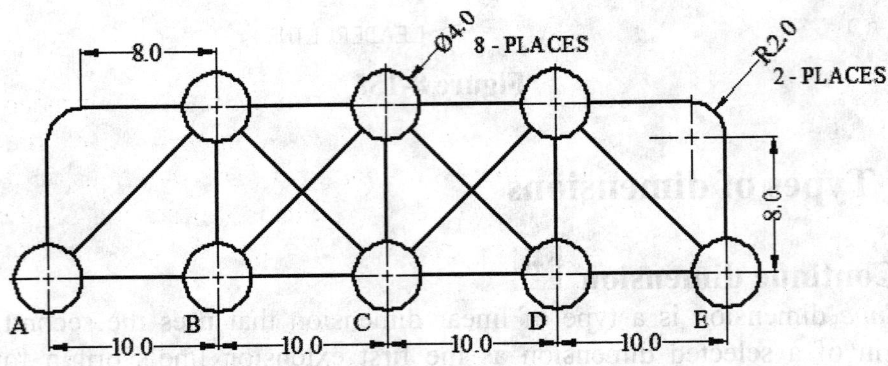

Figure 8-16b

8.16.2. Baseline dimensions

The *Baseline* dimension is a dimensioning technique in which multiple dimensions are measured from the same baseline or datum; that is, several dimensions originate from one extension line as shown in Figure 8-17a and Figures 8-17b. The baseline dimensions are useful because they help eliminate error build up associated with the each dimension. However, it requires a large area on the drawing. This dimensioning technique is also called *parallel dimensions* and *datum dimensioning*.

- The *Baseline* dimensions command is activated using one of the following procedures.
  1. Panel method: From the *Annotate* tab and the *Dimension* panel, expand the *Continue* dropdown menu and click the *Baseline* tool.
  2. Command line method: Type "dimbaseline", "Dimbaseline", or "DIMBASELINE" on the command line and press the *Enter* key.

- In Figure 8-17a and Figure 8-17b, the object is dimensioned using the baseline dimensioning technique. The *Baseline* dimensions can be added as follow.

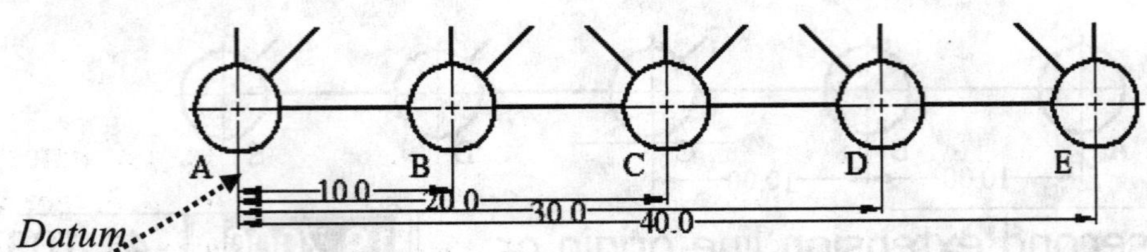

Figure 8-17a

- Create a linear dimension for the first feature. In Figure 8-17a, the dimension between circles labeled as A and B is a linear dimension.

1. Activate the *Baseline* command.
2. Now click at the center of the circle C; this will cause the dimension from the datum line to be created.
3. Repeat step #2 for circles D and E, Figure 8-17a.
4. Press the *Esc* key to exit the command.

- To enhance the appearance of Figure 8-17a, perform the following procedure:
  1. Open the *Dimension Style Manager* and *Modify Dimension Style* dialog boxes. (i) Select the *Text* tab under the *Text Alignment* panel and choose the *Aligned with dimension line* option. (ii) Select the *Lines* tab under the *Dimension lines* panel and increase the *Baselines spacing*. (iii) Click the *OK* and *Close* buttons to close the two dialog boxes, respectively.
  2. This will change the alignment of every dimension in the drawing. However, it will not update the baseline spacing. To reflect the change in the baseline spacing, delete the baseline dimensions and re-dimension the object.
  3. To reset the dimensions created using the *Radius* and *Diameter* tool, delete those dimensions and recreate using the *Leader* line option.
  4. Figure 8-16b shows the updated version. To emphasize the effect, the radius dimension is not updated.
  5. Also, the vertical baseline dimensions are add, Figure 8-17b

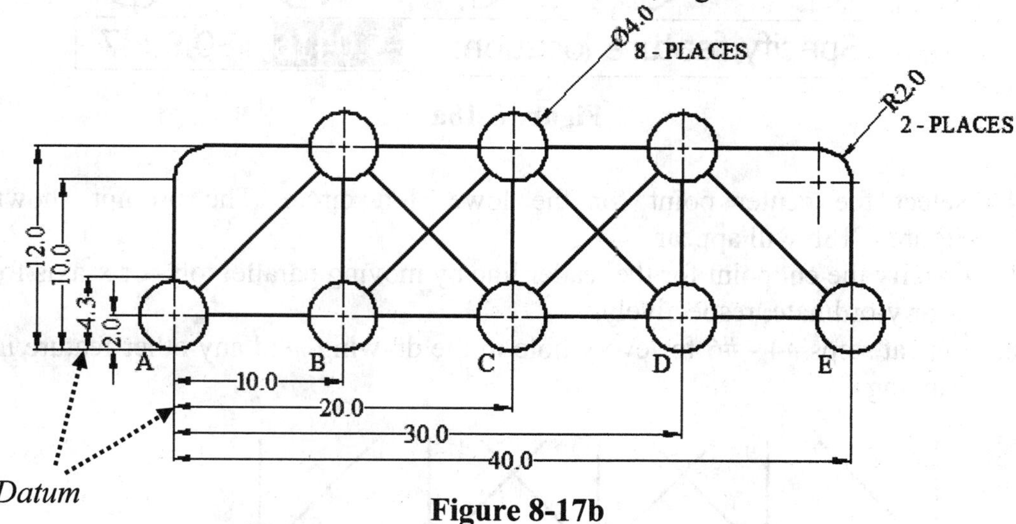

Figure 8-17b

8.16.3. Ordinate dimensions

The *Ordinate* dimensions are based on the X, Y coordinates and the ordinates are calculated from the origin. The technique is useful when dimensioning an object with many holes. Instead of using extension and dimension lines and arrowhead, the ordinate dimensioning includes horizontal and vertical leader lines originating directly from the features of the object.

Since, the ordinates are based on the origin; therefore, it is important that the origin of the coordinate system is located on the object, as shown in Figure 8-18c. This can be achieved in two ways: (i) either start the drawing from the origin (the center of lower left circle at the origin) or (ii) move the drawing to origin (the center of lower left circle at the origin).

- The *Ordinate* dimensions command is activated using one of the following procedures.
  1. Panel method: (ii) From the *Home* tab, expand the *Annotation* panel and click the *Ordinate* tool.
  2. Command line method: Type "dimordinate", "Dimordinate", or "DIMORDINATE" on the command line and press the *Enter* key.

- In Figure 8-18c, the object is dimensioned using the ordinate dimensioning technique. The *Ordinate* dimensions can be added as follow.
  1. Relocate the origin (if necessary).
  2. Turn the ORTHO command *On* by clicking the ⌞ button on the status bar.
  3. Activate the *Ordinate* command. The prompt is shown in Figure 8-18a.

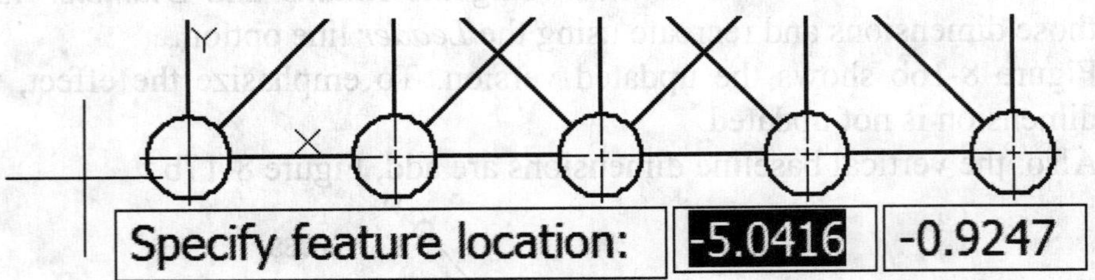

Figure 8-18a

4. Select the center point for the lower left circle. The prompt shown in Figure 8-18b will appear.
5. Specify the endpoint for the leader line by moving parallel to y- or x-axis for the x- or y-ordinate, respectively.
6. Repeat steps #4 - #6 for every hole in the drawing, and any other feature in the drawing.

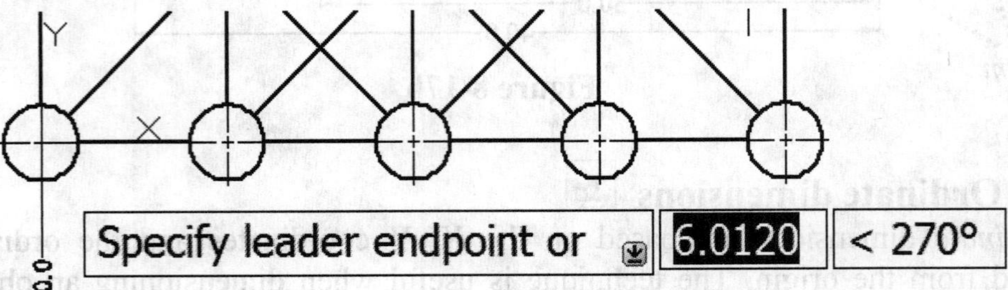

Figure 8-18b

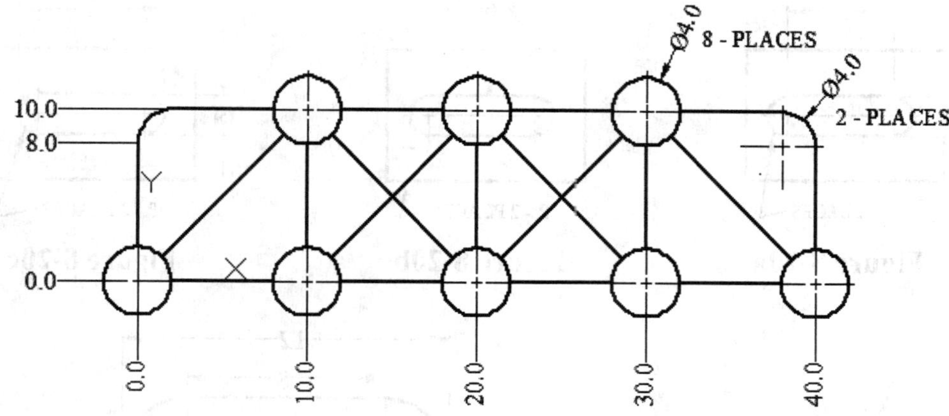

Figure 8-18c

8.16.4. Coordinate dimensions

The *coordinate* dimensions are useful when dimensioning an object that has many holes. Coordinate dimension uses a chart (or a table), Figure 8-19. Holes are labeled by letters and number; holes of the same diameters are labeled with the same letters.

The coordinate dimension can be added as follow:
- Define X and Y-axis as baselines.
- Labeled the circles (or holes).
- Create a table.
- Populate the table using the coordinates for the centerlines of the circles.
- The diameter symbol is created by typing %%c in the text box.

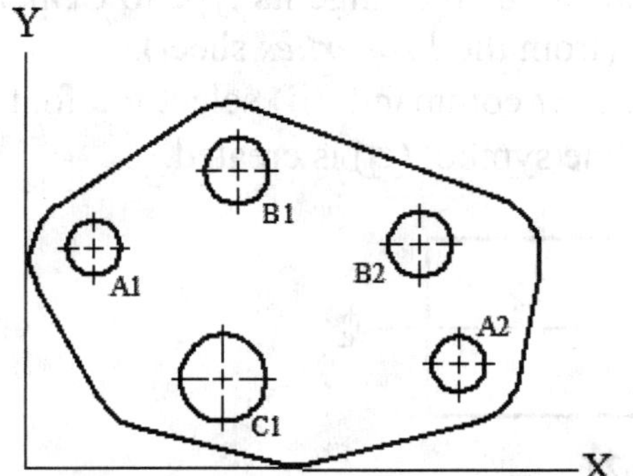

COORDINATE TABLE FOR HOLES			
HOLE	X-COORD	Y-COORD	Ø
A1	3.2100	10.2100	2
A2	21.1200	4.8000	2
B1	9.9400	13.7600	3
B2	18.5300	10.3700	3
C1	9.2800	4.1400	4

Figure 8-19

8.16.5. Combined dimensions

A combined dimension uses the combination of the dimensioning techniques discussed in the previous sections.

8.16.6. Dimensioning fillets and rounds

Fillets and rounds may be dimensioned individually or by a note. Figure 8-20 shows different methods of dimensioning fillets and rounds.

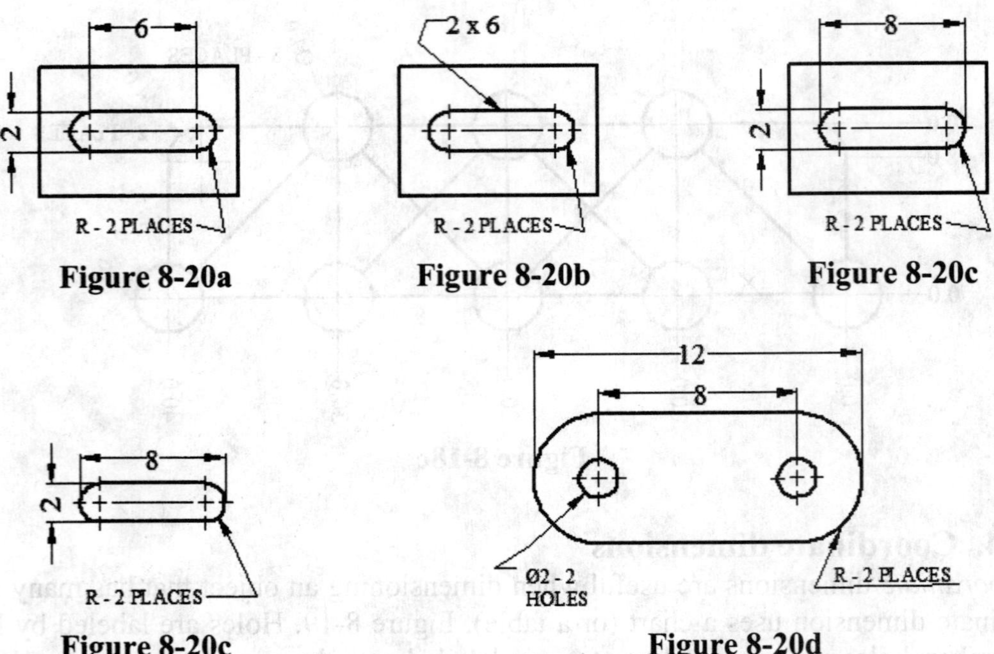

Figure 8-20a   Figure 8-20b   Figure 8-20c

Figure 8-20c   Figure 8-20d

8.17.   Centerline and line of symmetry

The centerlines are used to indicate the center of an individual component or the object as a whole. A centerline has two parts: the centerline and its label, Figures 8-21. A centerline can be drawn as follow.

- *For the centerline*: (i) Load linetype *Center*, (ii) either select linetype *Center* and then draw a line in the center or draw a line and then change its type to *Center*. The user may need to change the linetype scale (from the *Properties* sheet).
- *For the centerline symbol*: (i) Activate the *Text* command, (ii) select the font 'gdt', and (iii) type lower case q. (iv) The center line symbol (℄) is created.

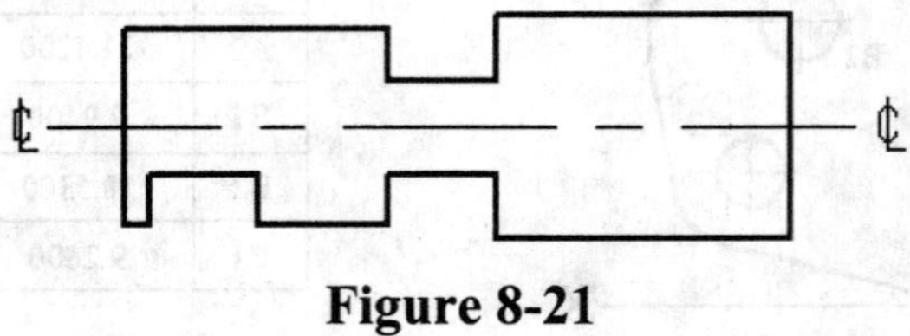

Figure 8-21

The line of symmetry indicates that the object is a mirror image on either side of the line of symmetry. The advantage of the line of symmetry is that it reduces the time to draw the object; just draw the repeating part of the object and then use the mirror command to complete the object, Figure 8-22a, Figure 8-22b, Figure 8-22c, and Figure 8-22d.

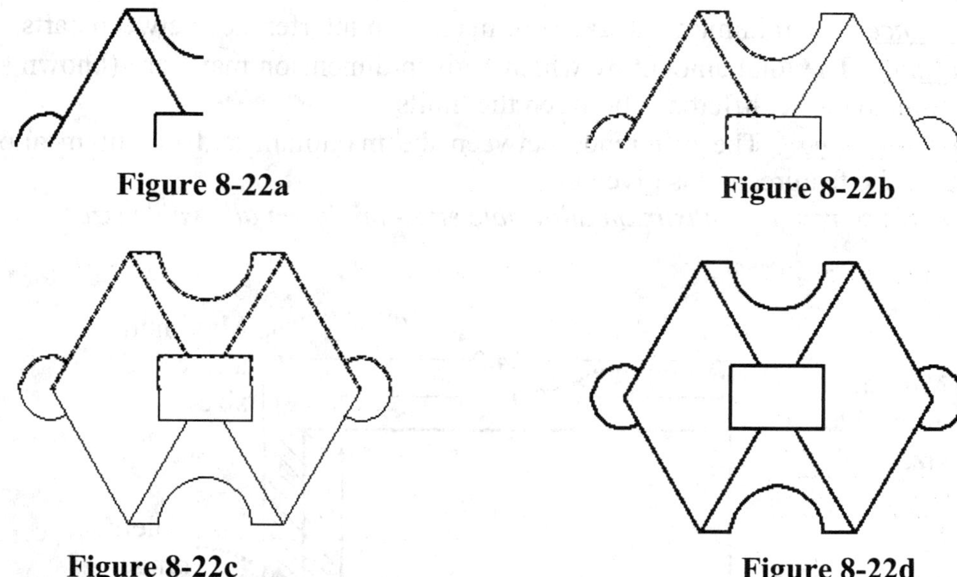

Figure 8-22a

Figure 8-22b

Figure 8-22c

Figure 8-22d

The line of symmetry can be shown in two ways.
* _Method #1_: Draw two parallel lines perpendicular to the line passing through the axis of symmetry, Figures 8-23a.
* _Method #2_: Write a note OBJECT IS SYMMETRICAL ABOUT THIS AXIS pointing to the line passing through the axis of symmetry, Figures 8-23b.

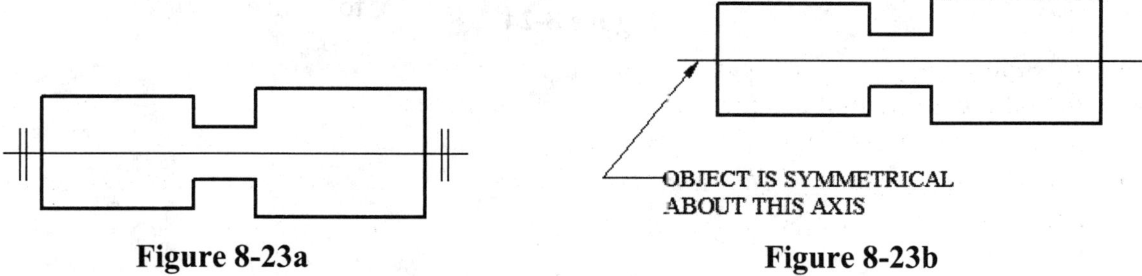

Figure 8-23a

Figure 8-23b

8.18.   Tolerance

Dimensions describe the size and location of features of an object; therefore, dimensions are given in the form of distance, angle, or notes irrespective of the units used in the drawing. Although, theoretically possible, it is economically unfeasible to manufacture products to the exact figures displayed on an engineering drawing. The cost of a part rapidly increases as an absolute correct size is approached. Hence, accuracy depends largely on the manufacturing process used and the care taken to manufacture a product. Since, different companies make different parts of an object; therefore, it is very important that these parts should be interchangeable. A tolerance value shows the manufacturing department the maximum permissible variation from the basic dimension. Refer to Figures 8-24 for the following definition.

* _Basic dimension_: Theoretical dimension.
* _Actual dimension_: The measured size of the finished product.

- *Allowance*: The minimum clearance or maximum interference between parts.
- *Tolerance*: The total amount by which a given dimension may vary (known as plus and minus) or the difference between the limits.
- *Tolerance range*: The difference between the maximum and minimum allowable sizes of the feature, and is given as

  Tolerance range = maximum allowable size - minimum allowable size

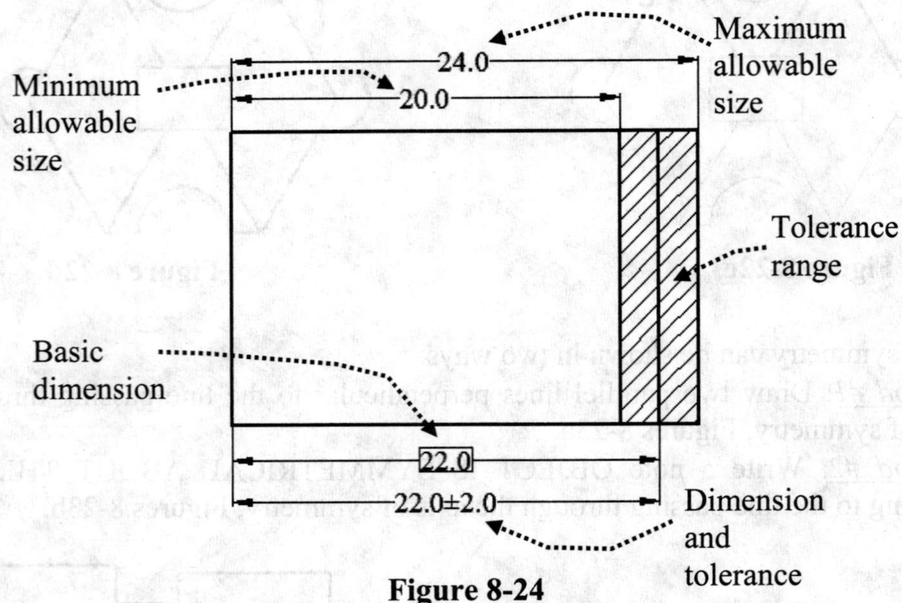

Figure 8-24

9.   Land Survey

9.1.   Objectives

- Learn about deed and parcel of land
- Learn to find/calculate area of a parcel
- Learn about different type of survey systems

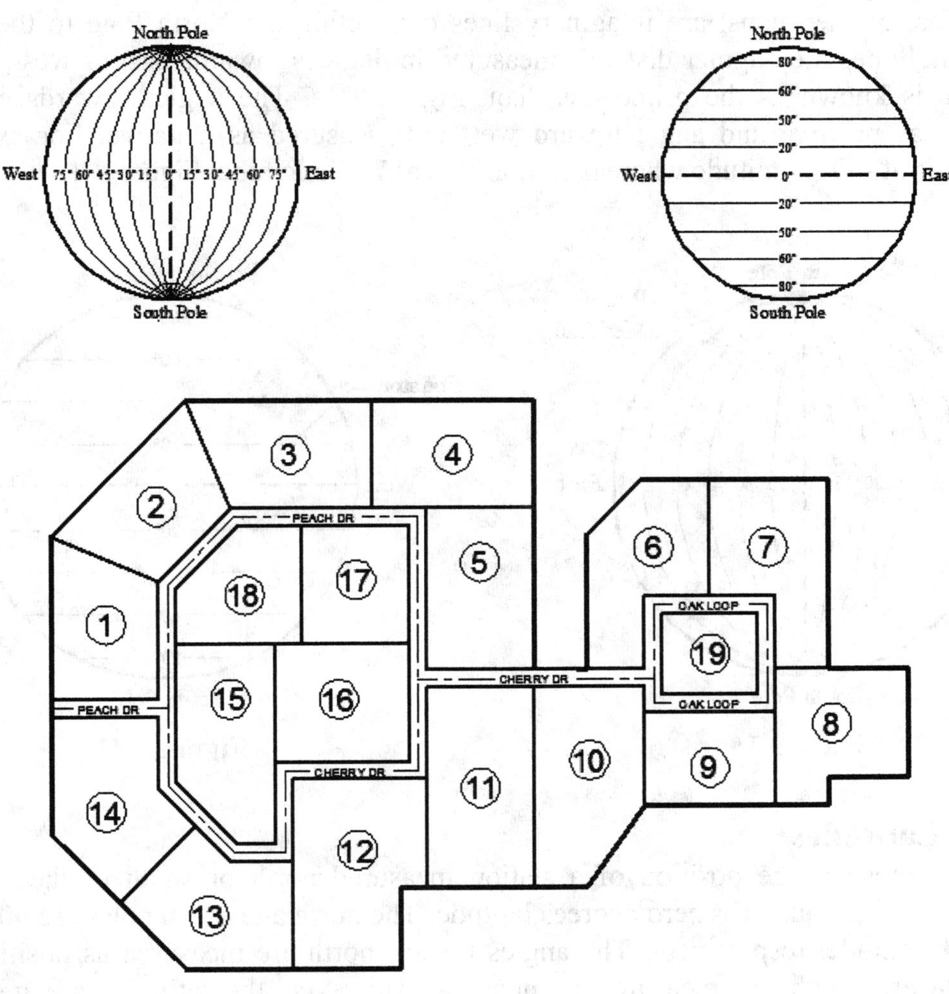

THE WHITE OAK SUBDIVISION

9.2. Introduction

According to Webster New Collegiate Dictionary, survey is defined as "To determine and delineate the forms, extent, position, etc., of, as a tract of land, by taking linear and angular measurement, and by applying the principles of geometry and trigonometry". Thus, surveying is an art of measuring (angles, distances, etc.), calculating quantities (area, volume, etc.), and plotting of the measurements (profile, contour maps, etc.). Generally, in surveying the point of measurement is known as a station and stations are identified using their position and direction with respect to a reference location.

9.3. Location

The position of a station on the surface of the earth can be specified by its longitude and latitude.

9.3.1. Longitudes

Longitudes, or meridians, are imaginary lines connecting the North Pole to the South Pole. Longitudes are angular distance measured in degrees towards east or west. The 0° longitude is known as the prime meridian, Figure 9-1a. The angles towards east are measured as positive and angle toward west are measured as negative. For example, station A is at -60° longitude whereas station B is at 75° longitude, Figure 9-1a.

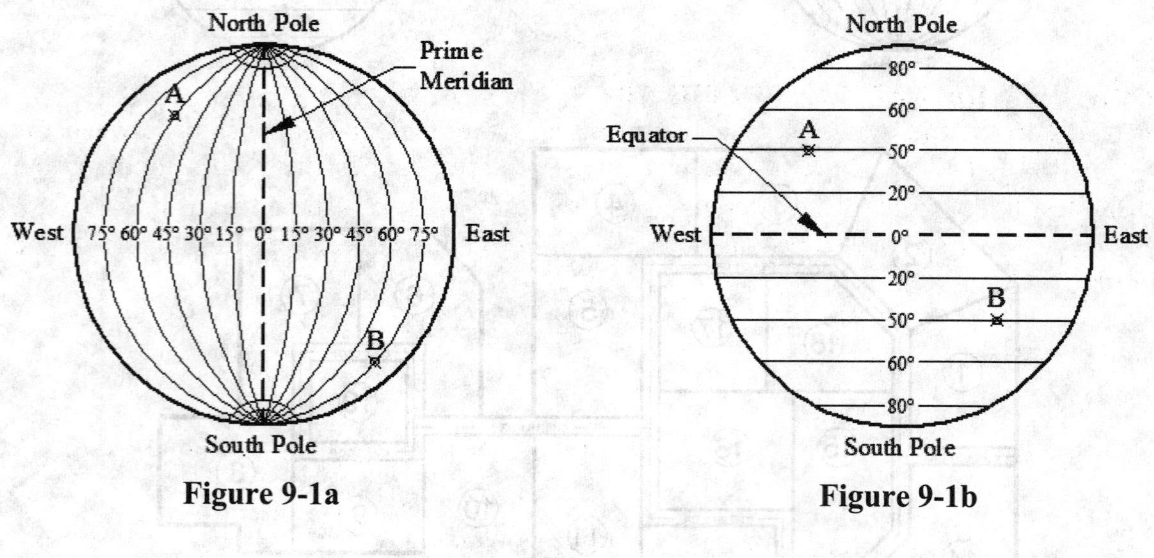

Figure 9-1a   Figure 9-1b

9.3.2. Latitudes

Latitude represents the position of a station measured north or south of the equator, Figure 9-1b. The equator is zero degrees latitude. The north and south poles are 90° north and south latitude, respectively. The angles toward north are measured as positive and angles toward south are measured as negative. However, the latitudes are generally written with N or S. For example, the latitude of station A is 50° N whereas the latitude of station B is 50° S, Figure 9-1b.

9.3.3.   Location on a map

Together, the latitudes and longitudes can be used as a coordinate system to find the location of a station on a map. Figure 9-1c shows a map with two longitude (85° and 75°), two latitudes (27° and 23°), and 4 stations (R, H, T, and C). For example, C is located east of 85° longitude and to the south of 27° latitude. Also, latitudes and longitudes can be used to find the location of places with respect to each other. For example, Figure 9-1c shows that R is to the north of every other station and C is to the east of every other station (on the map). It is clear from the Figure 9-1c, that both H and T are to the north of 23° latitude and south of 27° latitude; on the other hand, H is to the west of T.

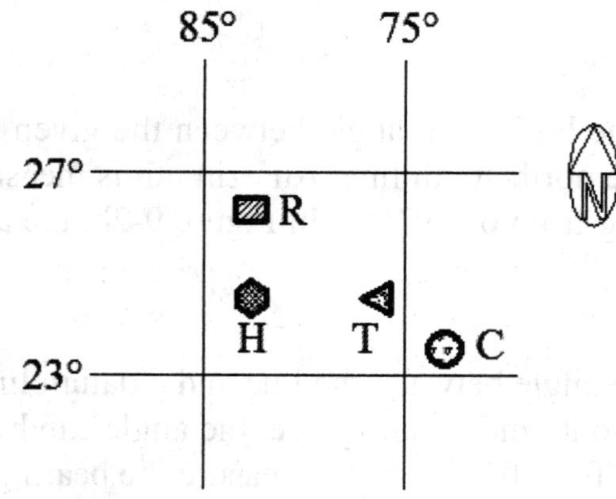

Figure 9-1c

9.4.   Angular measurement

In land survey, the direction of a line represents the angular relationship between the given line and a reference (or datum) line. Generally, either the North-South or the East-West line is used as the reference line. In Figure 9-2a, α is the angle of line $L1$ with respect to the East-West line, and β is the angle of the same line with respect to the North-South line.

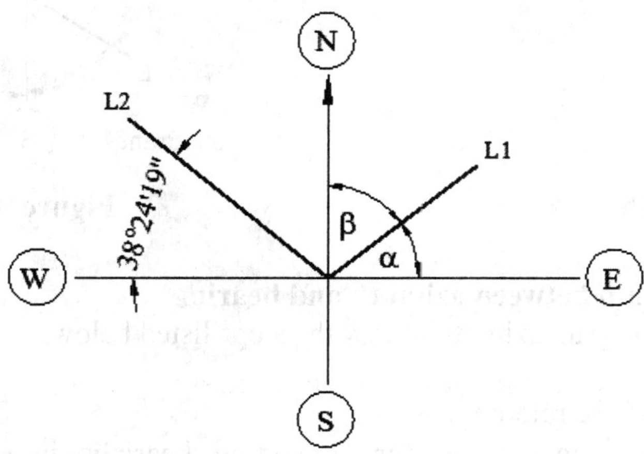

Figure 9-2a

9.4.1.   Units of measurement

Angles are measured in degrees, radians, etc. The degrees are denoted by the symbol °. Each degree is divided into 60 minutes (denoted by the symbol ′) and each minute is subdivided into 60 seconds (denoted by the symbol ″). In Figure 9-2a, the angle of line *L2* with respect to the East-West datum line is 38 degrees, 24 minutes, and 19 seconds (or 38° 24′ 19″).

9.4.2.   Direction

The direction of the angular measurement is either represented as the azimuth or the bearing.

9.4.2.1.   Azimuth

The azimuth of a line is the horizontal angle between the given line and the datum line. Generally, the datum is the north-south line. An azimuth is measured clockwise from the north with its value ranging from 0° to 360°. In Figure 9-2b, the azimuth of L1 is 53° and that of L2 is 308°.

9.4.2.2.   Bearing

The bearing of a line is the angle between the line and a datum line. Generally, the datum can be either the north or south meridian. Hence, the angle can be measured clockwise or counter-clockwise ranging from 0° to 90°. To measure the bearing of a line, the angle of a circle (360°) is divided into four quadrants: NE, SE, SW, and NW, Figure 9-2c. Therefore, the value of the bearing angle is preceded by *N* or *S* and followed by *E* or *W*. For example, the bearing of the line L1 in Figure 9-2c is N39°E and for *L2* is S71°E.

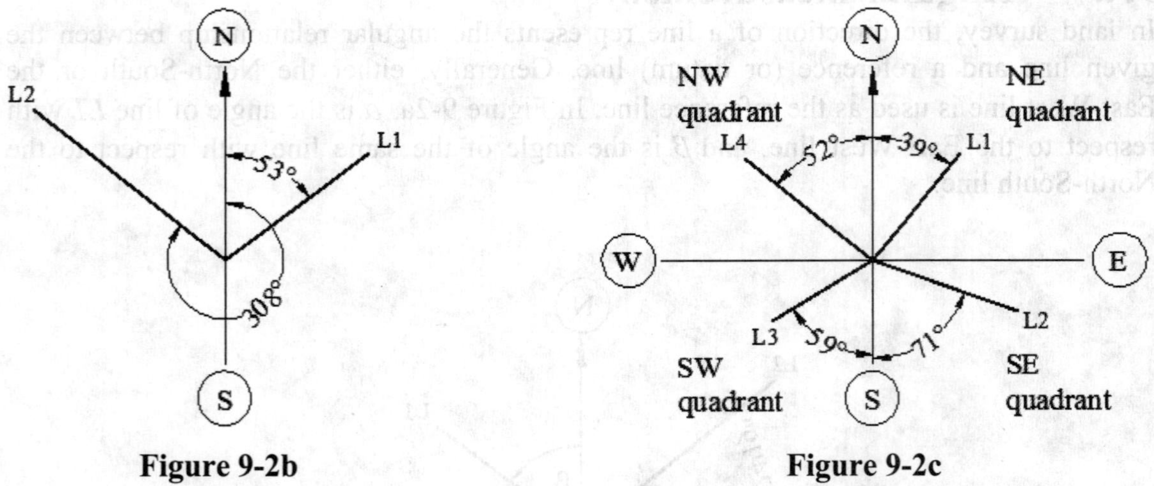

Figure 9-2b   Figure 9-2c

9.4.2.3.   Relationship between azimuth and bearing

To convert a bearing into an azimuth follow the steps listed below.

- Sketch a line and the reference line.
- Table #1 shows the process for converting bearings into the corresponding azimuths. In the figures of the Table #1, the angles with the dimension lines ending

with dots are the azimuths and the angles with the dimension lines ending with arrowheads are the corresponding bearings.

Table #1: Conversion of bearing to azimuth

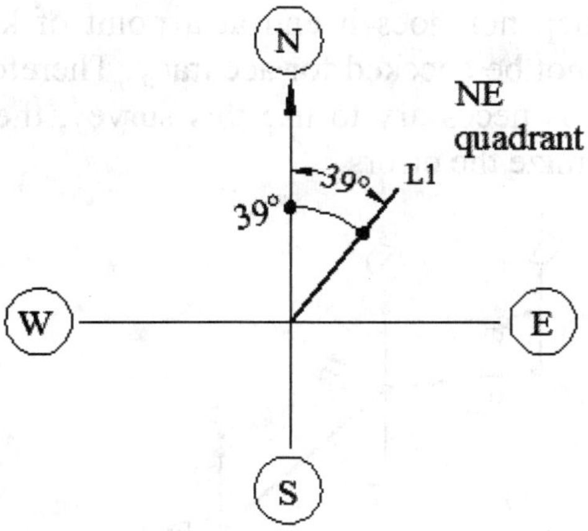

<table>
<tr><td>

Bearing: N39°E
Azimuth : 39°
Azimuth = Bearing
39° = 39°

</td><td>

Bearing: S71°E
Azimuth : 109°
Azimuth = 180° − Bearing
109° = 180° − 71°

</td></tr>
<tr><td>

Bearing: N52°W
Azimuth : 308°
Azimuth = 360° − Bearing
308° = 360° − 52°

</td><td>

Bearing: S59°W
Azimuth : 239°
Azimuth = 180° + Bearing
239° = 180° + 59°

</td></tr>
</table>

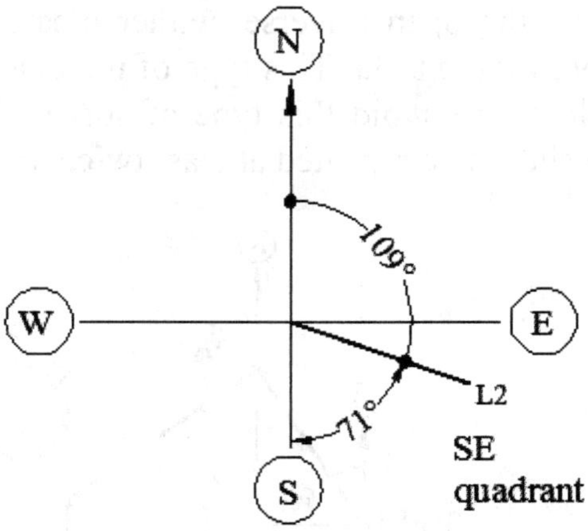

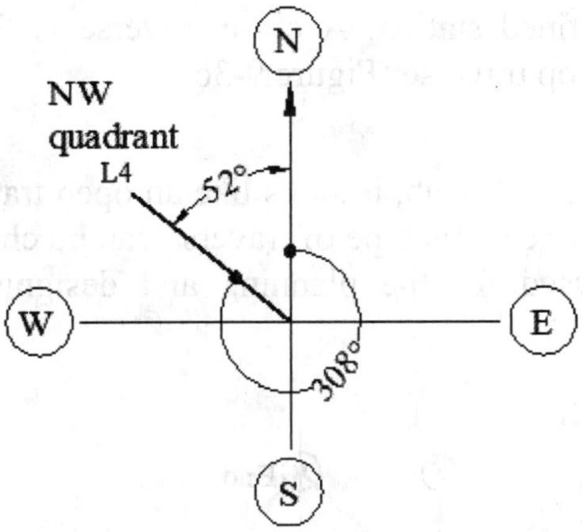

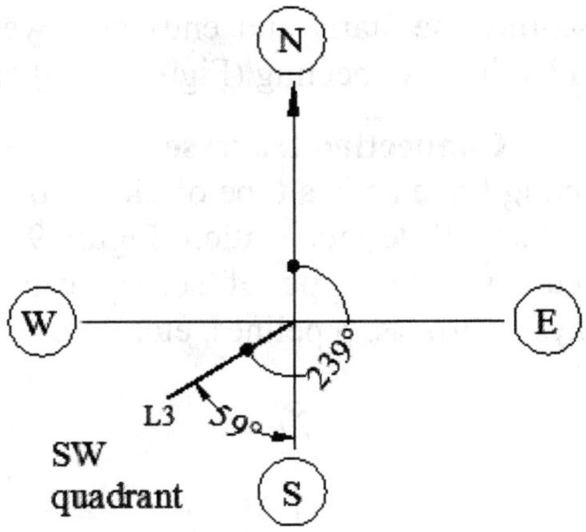

9.5.   Traverse

Traverse is a series of interconnected lines between a series of points. The connecting lines are called courses, and the points are called traverse stations. The main purpose of a traverse survey is to find out the distance between the traverse stations and angle of the courses. A traverse can be classified as an open or a closed traverse. A closed traverse is further subdivided into loop or connecting traverse.

9.5.1. Open traverse

This type of survey is commonly used for the exploratory purposes. As the name suggests, the open traverse neither create a loop nor does it end at a point of known position, Figure 9-3a. This type of traverse cannot be checked for accuracy. Therefore, if possible try to avoid this type of survey. If it is necessary to use this survey, then the survey should be repeated at least twice to minimize the errors.

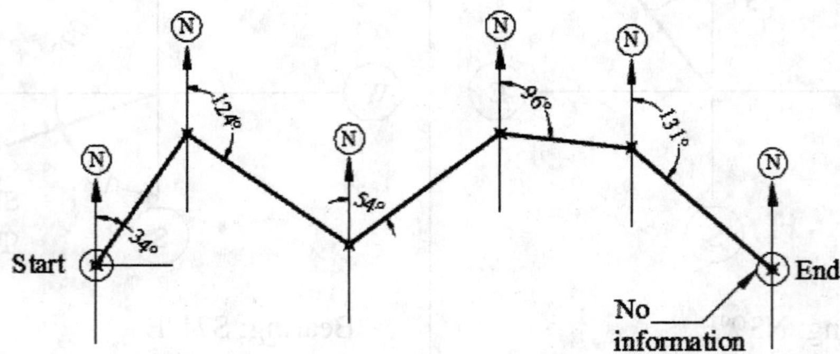

Figure 9-3a

9.5.2. Closed traverse

A close traverse starts and ends at a well-defined station. A close traverse is further subdivided into connecting (Figure 9-3b) and loop traverse (Figure 9-3c).

9.5.2.1. Connecting traverse

Connecting traverse is a type of closed traverse. Although, it looks like an open traverse, it ends at a well-defined station, Figure 9-3b. Hence, this type of traverse can be checked for accuracy. This type of survey can be used for the planning and designing of highways, railroads, pipelines, etc.

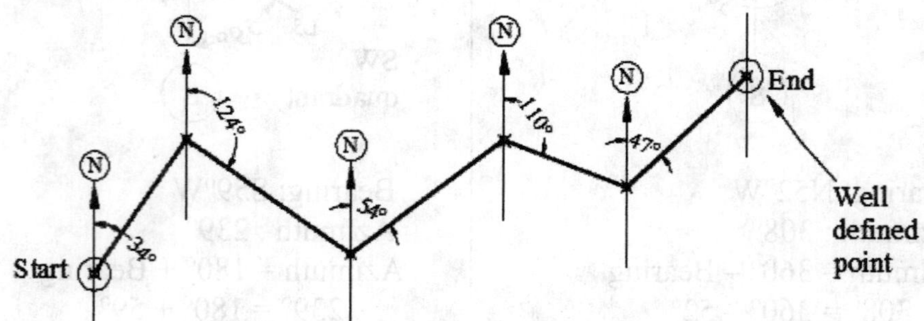

Figure 9-3b

9.5.2.2. Loop traverse

Loop traverse is a type of a closed traverse that starts and ends at the same station, thus creating a polygon, Figure 9-3c. This type of traverse can also be checked for its accuracy. This type of survey is used for the boundary line of a piece of land.

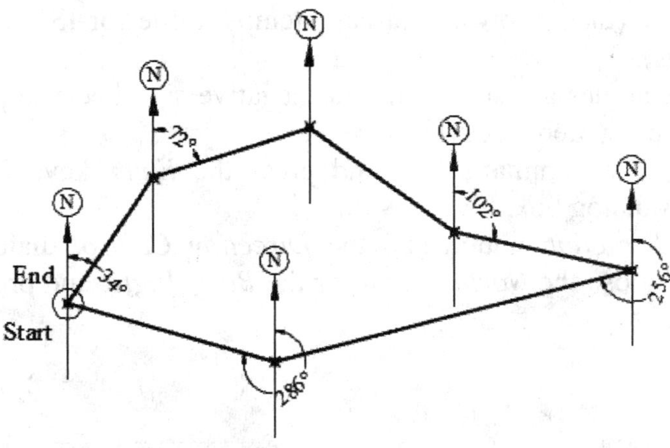

Figure 9-3c

9.6.   Drawing a traverse using AutoCAD

This section explains how to draw traverses using azimuth and bearings. Although the examples create loop traverses, the process is similar for any other traverse.

9.6.1.   Traverse for the given azimuths

In the current section, using length of the courses and their azimuth a closed traverse will be drawn, Figure 9-4a. The drawing units are millimeters, and the angles are the azimuths from the North (that is, the angles are measured in the clockwise direction from North). Create the drawing as follows.

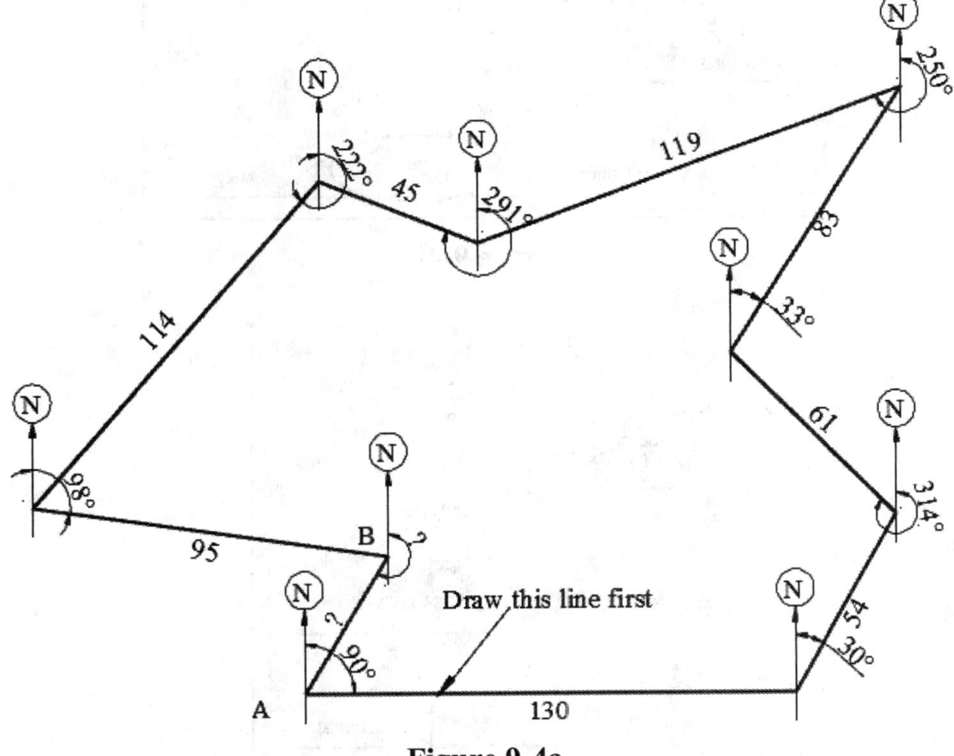

Figure 9-4a

1. Open a new file (that is, open landscape template file for ISO units created in the earlier chapters).
2. The clockwise angles are specified with negative sign because positive angles are measured in the counter-clockwise direction.
3. Type *Units* in the command line and press the *Enter* key. This will open the *Drawing Units* dialog box, Figure 9-4b.
4. Click on the *Direction* button and the *Direction Control* dialog box will open, Figure 9-4c. Choose the *North* option for the *Base Angle*; and press the *OK* buttons on both dialog boxes.

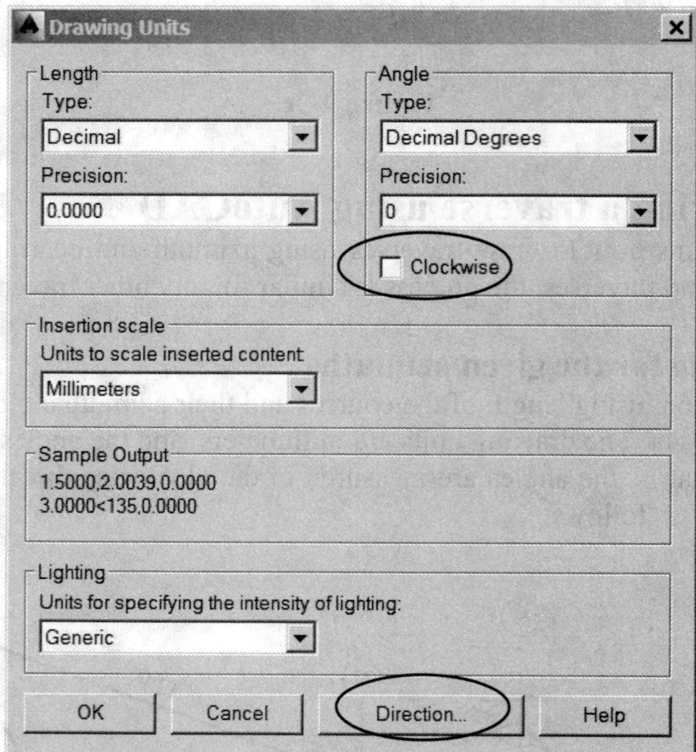

Figure 9-4b

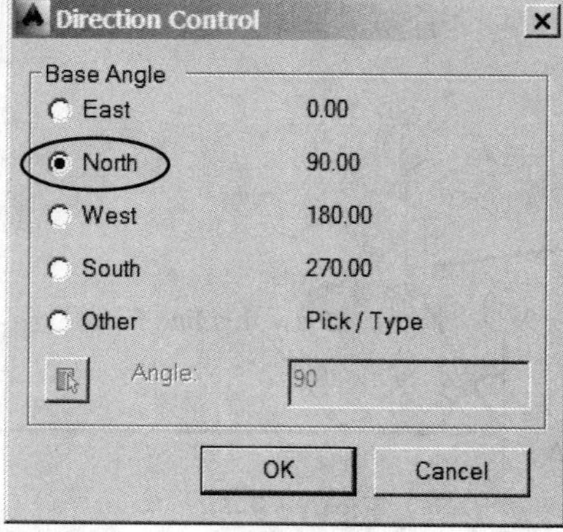

Figure 9-4c

5. Start the *Line* command and click at point *A* (a random point in the drawing area) to start the traverse.
6. Press the @ key to specify the relative coordinates; the prompt is shown in Figure 9-4d.

Figure 9-4d

7. First draw the 130mm long line with the azimuth of 90 degrees from the North. (i) Specify the length (130); (ii) press the *Tab* key; (iii) specify the angle (-90); and (iv) press the *Enter* key. The first line segment is drawn.
8. Similarly, draw the line of length 54mm at 30 degrees azimuth.
9. Now, draw the line of length 61mm at 314 degrees azimuth, Figure 9-4e.

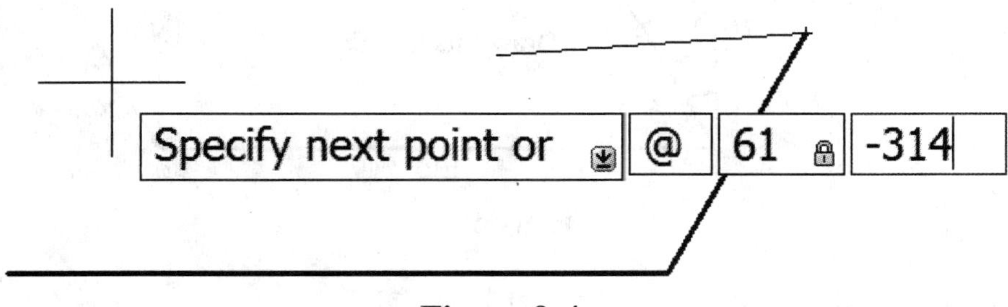

Figure 9-4e

1. Repeat the process with the remaining traverse.
2. Find the length and azimuth for the last course, *BA*.
3. The resulting traverse is shown in Figure 9-4a.
4. Find the length and azimuth for the last course, *BA*.
5. The resulting traverse is shown in Figure 9-4a.

9.6.2. Traverse for the given bearings

In the current section, a closed traverse shown in Figure 9-5 will be drawn. The drawing units are millimeters, and the angles are the bearing from the North or South (that is, the angles are measured in the clockwise or counter clockwise direction). Create the drawing as follow.

1. Open a new file (that is, open landscape template file for ISO units created in the earlier chapters).
2. The clockwise angles are specified with negative sign because the positive angles are measured counter-clockwise.
3. Type *Units* in the command line and press the *Enter* key. This will open the *Drawing Units* dialog box, Figure 9-4b.
4. Click on the *Direction* button and the *Direction Control* dialog box will open, Figure 9-4c. Choose the *North* option for the *Base Angle*; and press the *OK* buttons on both dialog boxes.

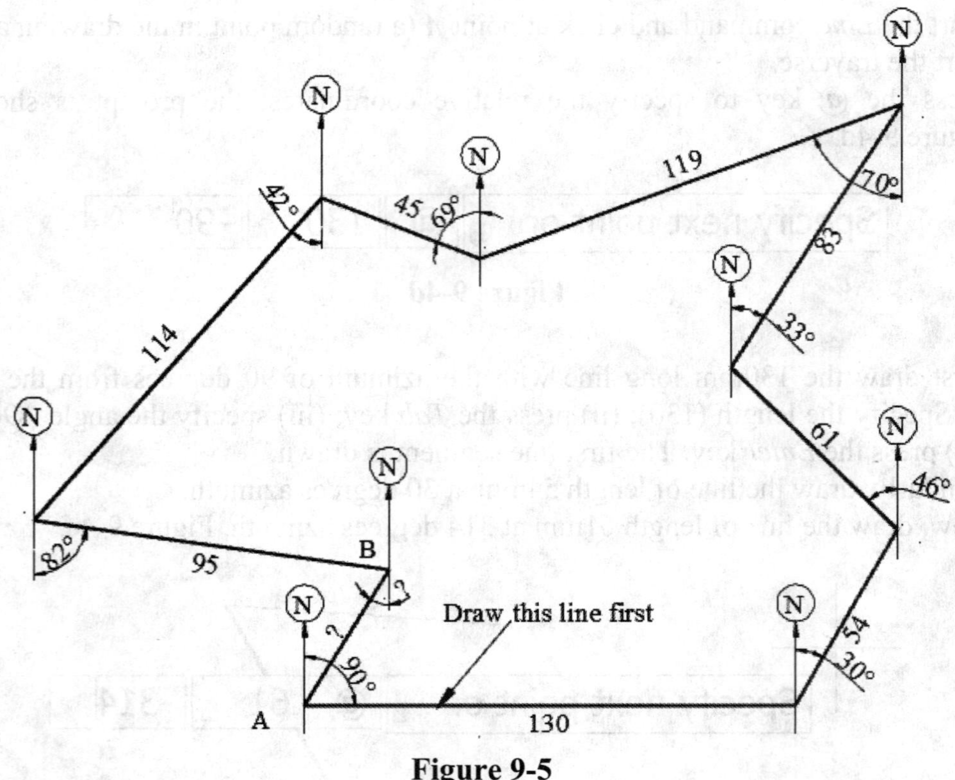

Figure 9-5

5. Start the *Line* command and click at point *A* to start the traverse.
6. Press the @ key to specify the relative coordinates; the prompt is shown in Figure 9-4d.
7. First draw the 130mm long line with the azimuth of 90 degrees from the North. (i) Specify the length (130), (ii) press the *Tab* key, (iii) specify the angle (-90), and (iv) press the *Enter* key.
8. Similarly draw lines of lengths and angles (54, -30), (61, 46), and (83, -33).
9. For the next line (length 119mm) the bearing is in the SW quadrant; therefore the base angle needs to be changed.
10. The *Direction* control box can be activated even if the line command is active. (i) Type *Units* in the command line and press the *Enter* key. This will open the *Drawing Units* dialog box, Figure 9-4b. (ii) Click on the *Direction* button and the *Direction Control* dialog box will open. (iii) Choose the *South* option for the *Base Angle*. (iv) Press the *OK* button on both of the dialog boxes.
11. Now draw the line of length 119mm. (i) Press the @ key to specify the relative coordinates. (ii) Specify the length (119), (iii) press the *Tab* key, (iv) specify the angle (-70), and (v) press the *Enter* key.
12. Repeat the process with the remaining courses. Change the base angle as needed.
13. Find the length and bearing for the last course, *BA*.

9.7.   Add dimensions to a traverse

Every course will need both the linear and angular dimensions. The linear dimension will be the length of the course and the angular dimension will be its azimuth or bearing.

9.7.1. Length

Add the length to a course as follow.

1. (i) Create a layer for linear dimension and name it as Linear_Dim. (ii) Make the Linear_Dim layer to be the current layer.
2. Display the *Aligned* dimension, Figure 9-6a.
3. Click with the left button of the mouse on the align dimensions, and the grip points will appear, Figure 9-6b.
4. Press the right button of the mouse, and options list will appear.
5. Select the *Properties* option with the left button of the mouse.
6. Under the *Lines & Arrows* panel, turn *Off* the *Dim line 1*, *Dim line 2*, *Ext line 1*, and *Ext line 2*. Press the down arrow in the right column and then choose the *Off* option, Figure 9-6d.
7. The resultant dimensions are shown in Figure 9-6c.

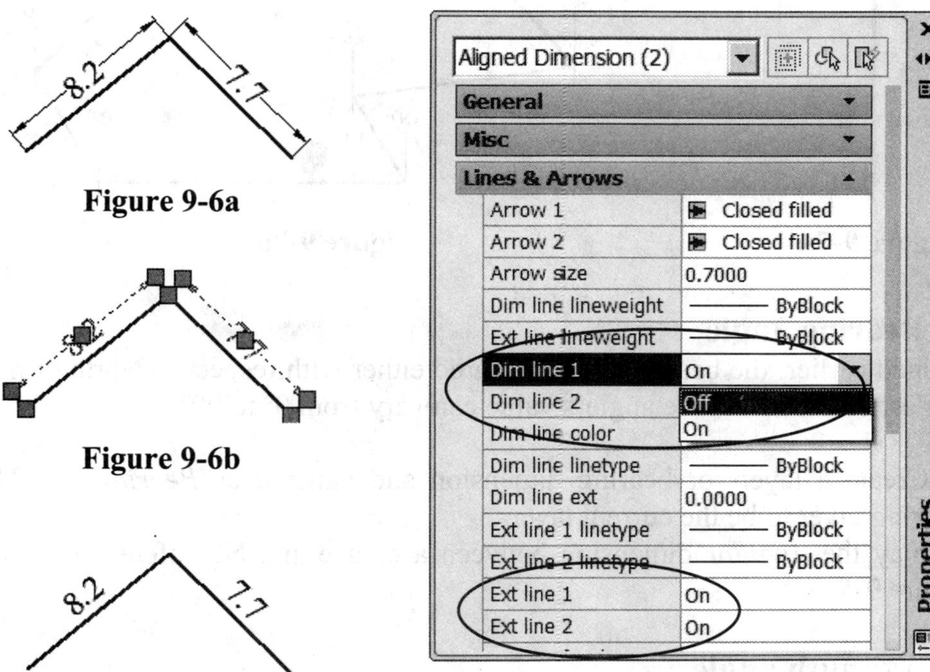

Figure 9-6a

Figure 9-6b

Figure 9-6c

Figure 9-6d

9.7.2. Add reference line to a traverse

To make the dimensioning process faster and accurate draw an arrow, north label, and reference line at every traverse station. The reference line is necessary because leader (arrow) cannot be used for angular dimensions.

1. (i) Create a layer for NS reference lines and name it as *NS_Reference*. (ii) Make the *NS_Reference* layer to be the current layer.
2. The North direction is created by drawing a quick leader. (i) Turn on the ORTHO option by clicking the ⌞⌟ icon on the status bar. (ii) Activate the *QLEADER*

command; and draw a vertical arrow with arrow head pointing upward. (iii) Press the Esc key from the keyboard to exit the *QLEADER* command without completing it, Figure 9-7a.

3. Write N using a text command. Encircle the N using *Enclose in Object* command; use circle option, Figure 9-7a.
4. Activate the *Line* command and draw a line on top of the arrow.
5. Activate the *Copy* command and paste the north at each station, Figure 9-7b.

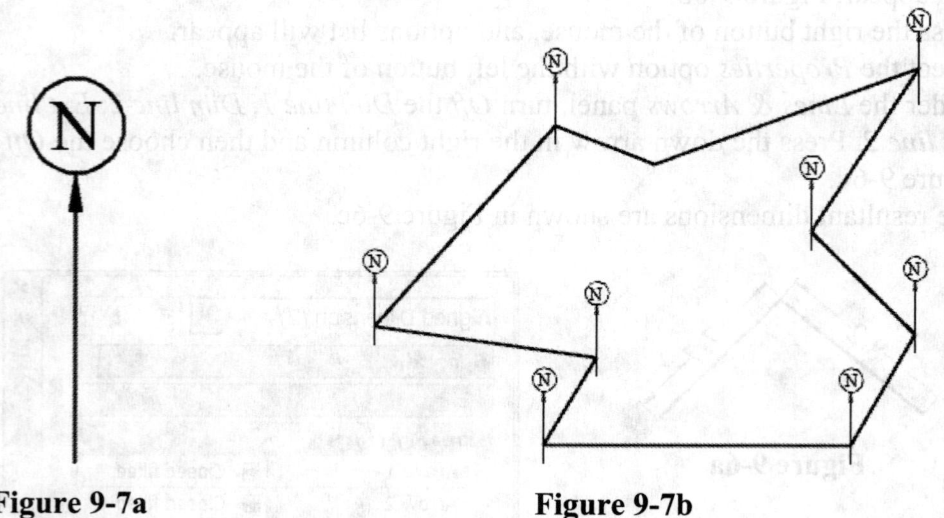

Figure 9-7a   **Figure 9-7b**

9.7.3. Bearing angle

As explained earlier, the bearings are measured either with respect to North or South and towards East or West; and the angle's value can vary from 0° to 90°.

1. (i) Create a layer for bearing dimension and name it as *Bearing*. (ii) Make the *Bearing* layer to be the current layer.
2. Display the *Angular* dimension between a course and NS reference, as shown in Figure 9-5.

9.7.4. Azimuth angle

As explained earlier, the azimuths are measured with respect to North in the clockwise direction, and the angle's value can range from 0° to 360°.

1. Activate the *Angular* dimension command, and the prompt shown in Figure 9-8a will appear.

Select arc, circle, line, or <specify vertex>:

Figure 9-8a

2. Press the *Enter* key and the prompt shown in Figure 9-8b will appear. This option allows the specification of three points for an angular dimension.

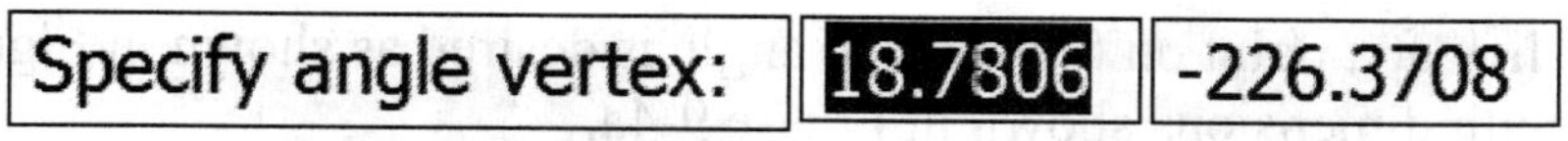

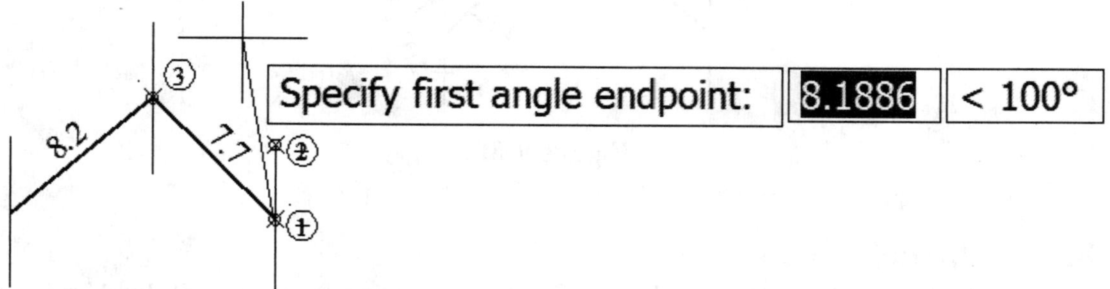

Figure 9-8b

3. Click at point #1 (the intersection of the reference line and 7.7mm course), Figure 9-8c.

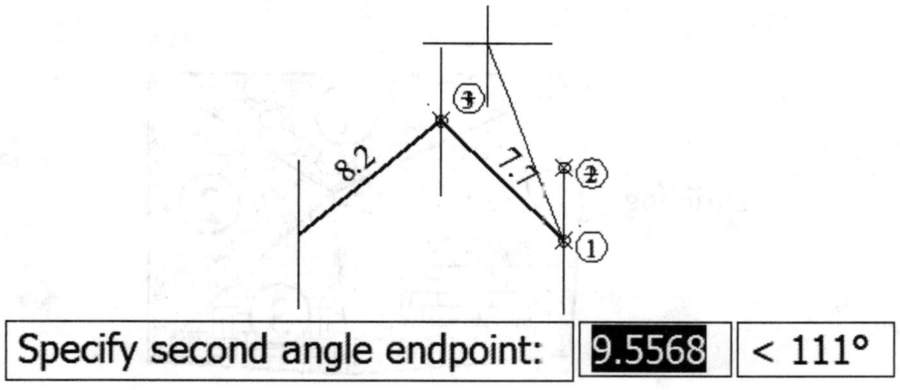

Figure 9-8c

4. Click at point #2 (the upper end of the reference line), Figure 9-8d.

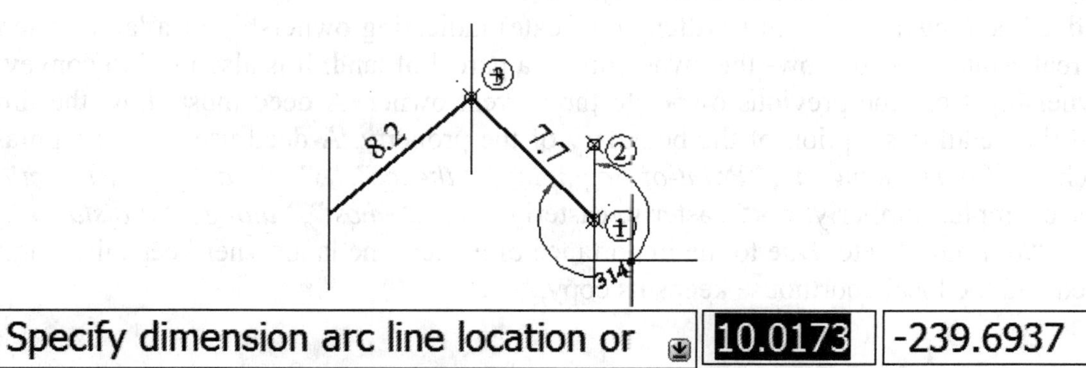

Figure 9-8d

5. Click at point #3 (the far end of the 7.7mm course), Figure 9-8e.

Figure 9-8e

6.   Finally click at a point on the side the angle is desired as shown in Figure 9-8f.
7.   The azimuth dimensions shown in Figure 9-4a.

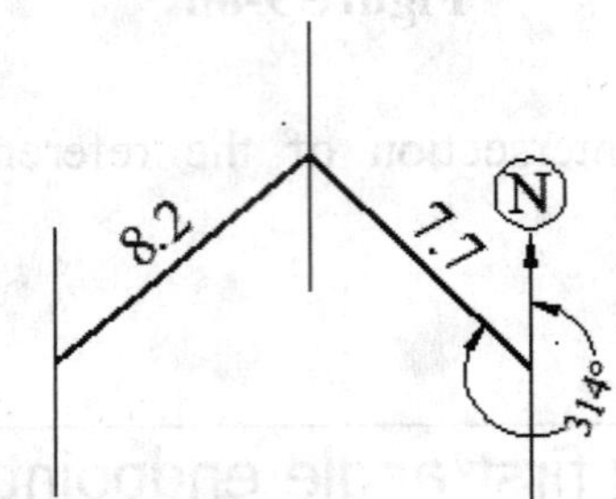

Figure 9-8f

9.8.   Parcel

In real estate terminology, a parcel is defined as a contiguous area of land, with or without buildings, owned by one or multiple owners and described by a single deed. For example, a residential area plot owned by a single owner and a form land owned by multiple owners (may be one family) is a parcel. In Figure 9-9, person X is the owner of lot #3 and person Y is the owner of lot #4, whereas lot #1 and #2 are owned by multiple (A, B, and C) owners.

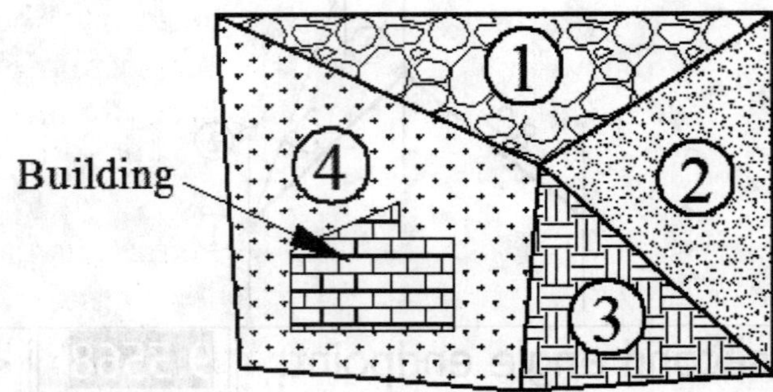

Figure 9-9

9.9.   Deed or legal description

A deed is a legal document (written certificate) indicating ownership of a land. In terms of real estate, a deed shows the ownership of a parcel of land. It is also used to convey an ownership from the previous owner to the current owner. A deed must show the limits and the detail description of the boundary of the property. A deed uses specific phrases such as "*Commencing at*", "*Point-of-Beginning*", "*thence*", "*;*", "*in a _____ly direction*" (for example, northerly, northeasterly, easterly, etc.), "*–most*", "*along*", "*a distance of*", "*to*", "*to a point*", etc. Due to the importance of a deed, the landowner keeps the original deed and the local courthouse keeps its copy.

9.10. Land survey

The basic purpose of the land survey is to measure existing boundaries and layout new boundaries. Based on the size of the area to be surveyed, the survey is carried out by government agencies or private surveyors. In the United States, a parcel of land is usually described using *rectangular* system, *metes and bound*, and *lots and blocks* methods.

9.11. Rectangular system

The rectangular system is used by the Public Land Survey System (PLSS) of the United States. The system was created by the *Land Ordinance of 1785*. It has been expanded and slightly modified but is still in use in the states of Alabama, Alaska, Arizona, Arkansas, California, Colorado, Florida, Idaho, Illinois, Indiana, Iowa, Kansas, Louisiana, Michigan, Minnesota, Mississippi, Missouri, Montana, Nebraska, Nevada, New Mexico, North Dakota, Ohio, Oklahoma, Oregon, South Dakota, Utah, Washington, Wisconsin, and Wyoming. In the rectangular system, the basic units of the land are the township and range. The townships and ranges are formed by the intersection of the reference lines (baseline and meridians).

9.11.1. Reference lines

The two reference lines are the baseline and meridians. The baseline (or latitude) runs east-west, and the principle meridian (or longitude) runs north-south; and lines parallel to the principle meridian and the baseline are created. The interval between these parallel lines is 6 miles, Figure 9-10a and Figure 9-10b. The intersection of these lines forms a grid of 6 miles by 6 miles which is used as the base for the rectangular survey, Figure 9-10c.

The initial point of PLSS survey is the intersection of the meridian and baselines or lines running parallel to the baseline and meridian. The parallel lines to the principle meridian are named. The first surveys in the rectangular system were carried out in eastern Ohio; hence, its west boundary is the first principal meridian. The first six principal meridians are labeled as first, second, third, fourth, fifth, and sixth principal meridians. The rest of the meridians are named using local names. For example, in Louisiana the PLSS uses *Louisiana meridian*.

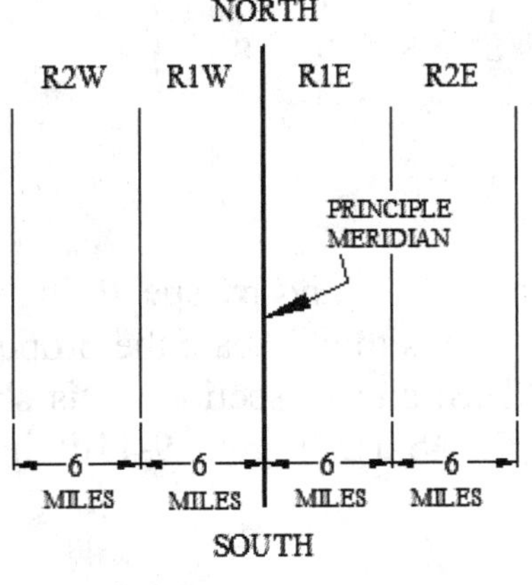

Figure 9-10a

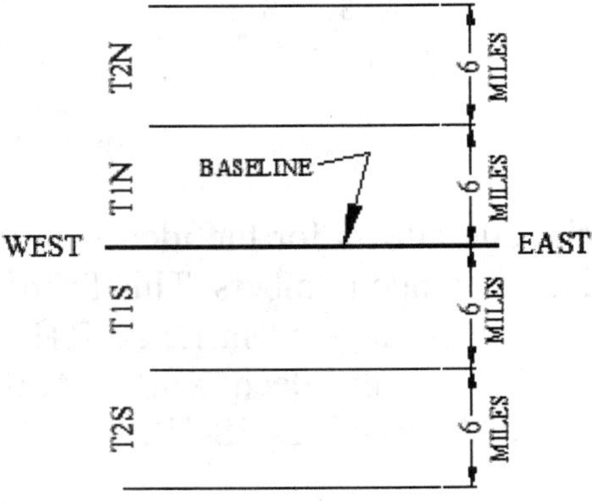

Figure 9-10b

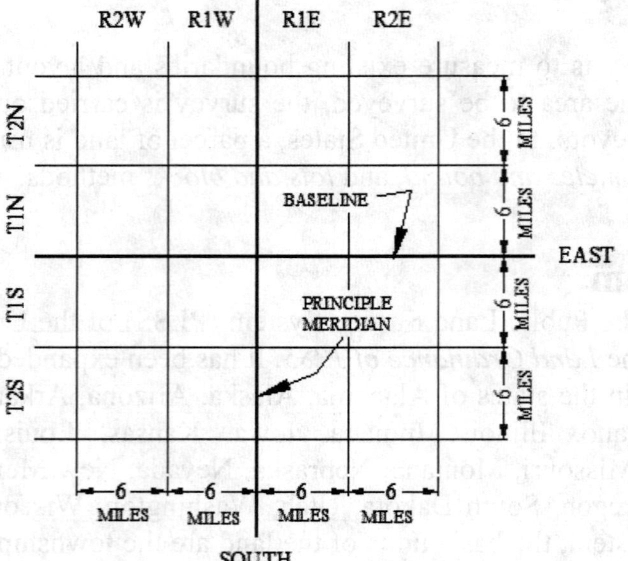

Figure 9-10c

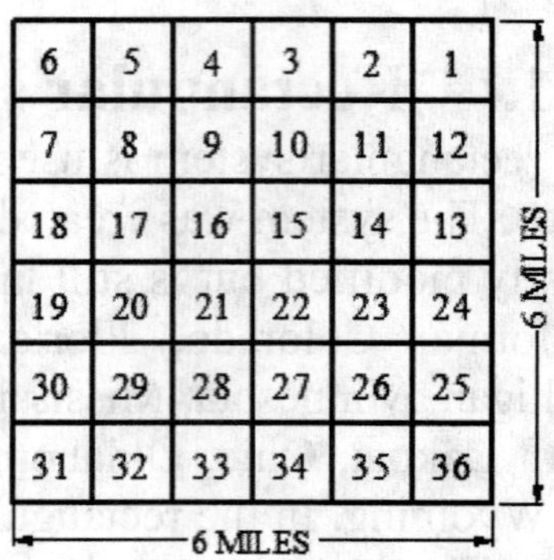

Figure 9-11a

9.11.2. Township and range

The columns of the grid shown in Figure 9-10c are called range, and rows are called township. Each cell of the grid is called a township. Each township is further subdivided into 36 sections of one square mile (640 acres), Figure 9-11a. The numbering of the sections (of a township) starts from the upper right corner and follows the zigzag pattern as shown in Figure 9-11a. Each section can be further subdivided into two half-sections of 0.5 square mile (320 acres) each. Each section can also be further subdivided into four quarter-sections of 0.25 square mile (160 acres) each. The federal government typically surveys only to the quarter-section level. Smaller parcels are usually surveyed later by private surveyors if necessary. In governmental surveys, the township corner is established every six miles and followed by the marking of the section, half-section and the quarter- section corners, denoted as T, S, $\frac{1}{2}$, and $\frac{1}{4}$ as shown in Figure 9-11b.

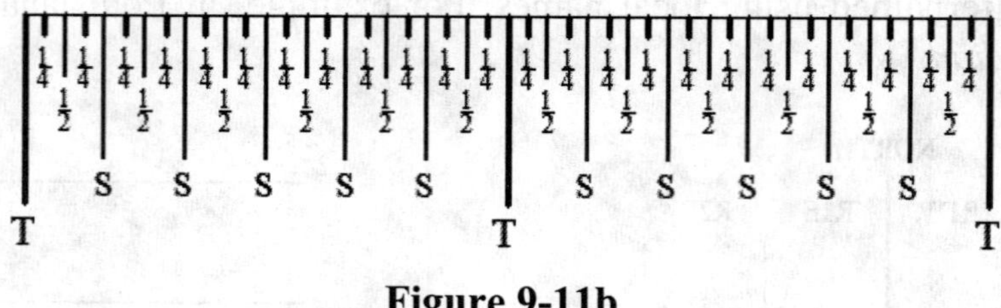

Figure 9-11b

This technique allows for the identification of any parcel of land by specifying section, township, and range numbers. This format is used in deeds to delineate the property. For example, a parcel located in range R1E, township T4S, and in section 15 is shown in Figure 9-11c, and the deed will contain the entry 15-4S-1E. Figure 9-11d shows the further subdivisions of 15- 4S-1E.

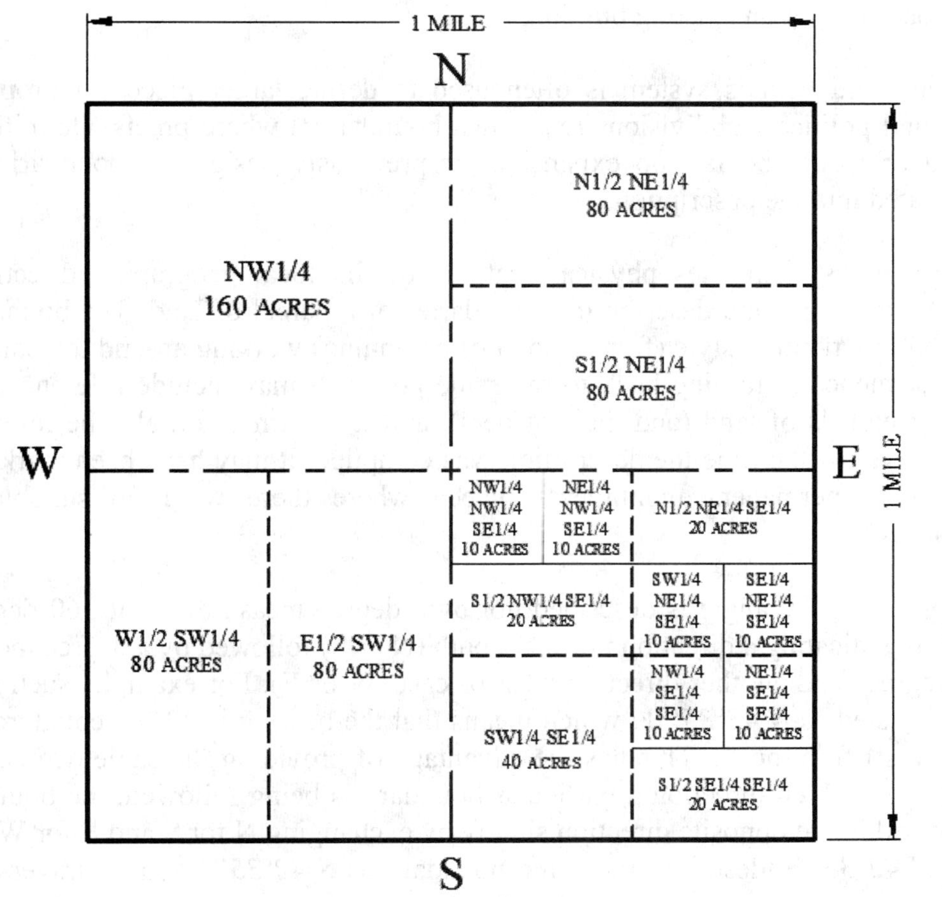

Figure 9-11c

Figure 9-11d

The area of the subdivisions shown in the Figure 9-11d can be obtained by multiplying "the product of the factors" with "640 ACRES". The area calculations for four of the subsections shown in the Figure 9-11d are shown in Table #2.

Table #2: Area calculation

Subdivision	Product of Factor	Area (Acres)
SW1/4 NE1/4 SE1/4	1/4 * 1/4 * 1/4 = 1/64	1/64 * 640 = 10
S1/2 SE1/4 SE1/4	1/2 * 1/4 * 1/4 = 1/32	1/32 * 640 = 20
N1/2 NE1/4	1/2 * 1/4 = 1/8	1/8 * 640 = 80
NW1/4	1/4	1/4 * 640 = 160

9.12.   Metes and bounds

The term *metes* refers to a boundary defined by the measurement of each straight run. A run is specified by a distance between the terminal points and an orientation (or direction). A direction may be a simple compass bearing or a precise orientation determined by accurate survey methods. The term *bounds* refer to a more general boundary description, such as along a certain watercourse, a stone wall, an adjoining public road way, or an existing building.

The metes and bounds system is often used to define larger pieces of property (e.g. farms), and political subdivisions (e.g. town boundaries) where precise definition is not required or would be far too expensive, or previously designated boundaries can be incorporated into the description.

Typically the system uses physical features of the local geography, directions, and distances, to define and describe the boundaries of a parcel of land. The boundaries are described in a running style (from a point of beginning) working around the parcel of the land in sequence (returning back to the same point). It may include references to other adjoining parcels of land (and their owners), and it in turn could also be referred to in later surveys. At the time the description was compiled, it may have been marked on the ground with permanent monuments placed where there were no suitable natural monuments.

In many deeds, the angle is described not by a degree measure out of 360 degrees, but instead by indicating a direction north or south (N or S) followed by a degree measure out of 90 degrees and another direction west or east (W or E). For example, such a bearing might be listed as *N 42°35' W*, which means that the bearing is 42°35' counterclockwise (to the west) from north. This has the advantage of providing the same degree measure regardless of which direction a particular boundary is being followed; the boundary can be traversed in the opposite direction simply by exchanging N for S and E for W. In other words, *N 42°35' W* describes the same boundary as *S 42°35' E*, but is traversed in the opposite direction.

Once such a survey is in place, tradition and long use establishes the boundaries. The description might refer to *landmarks* such as the *large oak tree* which could die, rot, and disappear. Streams might dry up or change course. Man-made features such as roads, walls, markers, or stakes may also have been used to determine the real boundaries. But these features move, change, and disappear over time. When it comes time to re-establish these boundaries (for sale, subdivision, or building construction) it can become difficult, even impossible, to determine the original location of the boundary. Court cases are sometimes required to settle the matter.

9.12.1. Land description using meets and bounds

A typical description for a small parcel of land using meets and bounds is illustrated below and the corresponding parcel of land is shown in Figure 9-12a. In the description below, POB is the abbreviation for the Point Of Beginning.

Beginning at a point 212' 7.1" south of the NW corner NW/4 NE/4 of section13-T8N-R1E,

Thence S0° 15' 0" E a distance of 74' 6.7", Thence S89° 55' 0" W a distance of 151' 2.4",

Thence N0° 15' 0" W a distance of 74' 6.7", Thence N89° 55' 0" E a distance of 151' 2.4" to POB.

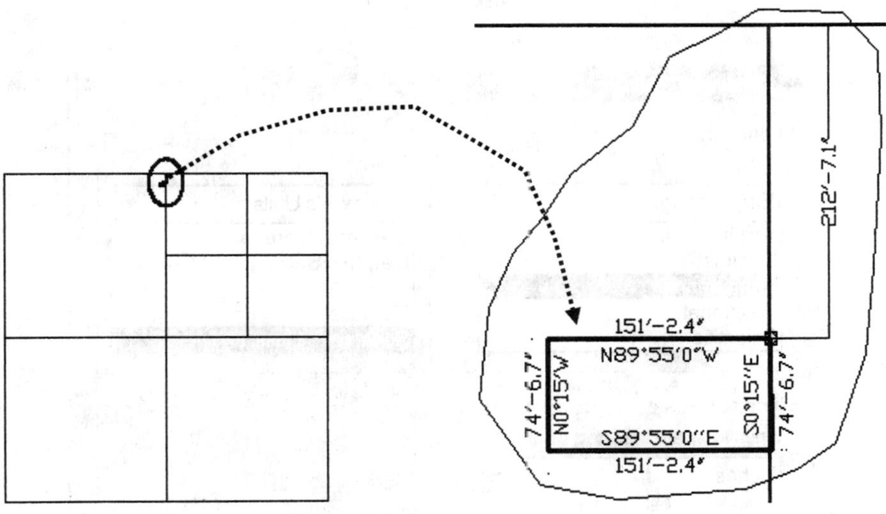

Figure 9-12a

9.12.2. AutoCAD and meets and bounds

If the surveyor's angles are used when specifying the polar coordinates, indicate whether the surveyor's angles are in the north or south direction and towards east or west direction.

Example: Draw the boundary of the parcel described using meets and bounds as follow.

1. Open a new file (that is, open landscape template file for ANSI units created in the earlier chapters).
2. Type *Units* in the command line and press the *Enter* key. This will open the *Drawing Units* dialog box, Figure 9-12c.

3. In the *length*'s panel, choose the *Engineering*'s option, Figure 9-12c.
4. In the *Angle*'s panel, choose the *Surveyor's Units* option, Figure 9-12c. The figure shows multiple selections, however, the AutoCAD provides only one selection at a given time.
5. Click on the *Direction* button, Figure 9-12c, and the *Direction Control* dialog box will open, choose the *North* option for the *Base Angle*, and press the *OK* buttons on both dialog boxes.
6. Start the *Line* command.
7. Click for the first point at the *NW* of *NW/4 NE/4* corner.
8. Draw the 212 ft 7.1 inches long line with *ORTHO* mode *On*.
9. Press the @ key to specify the relative coordinates; the prompt is shown in Figure 9-12b.
10. (i) Specify the length (151'2.4), (ii) press the *Tab* key, (iii) specify the angle (N89d55'0W) without any space, and press the *Enter* key.
11. Repeat the process to complete the course.

Figure 9-12b

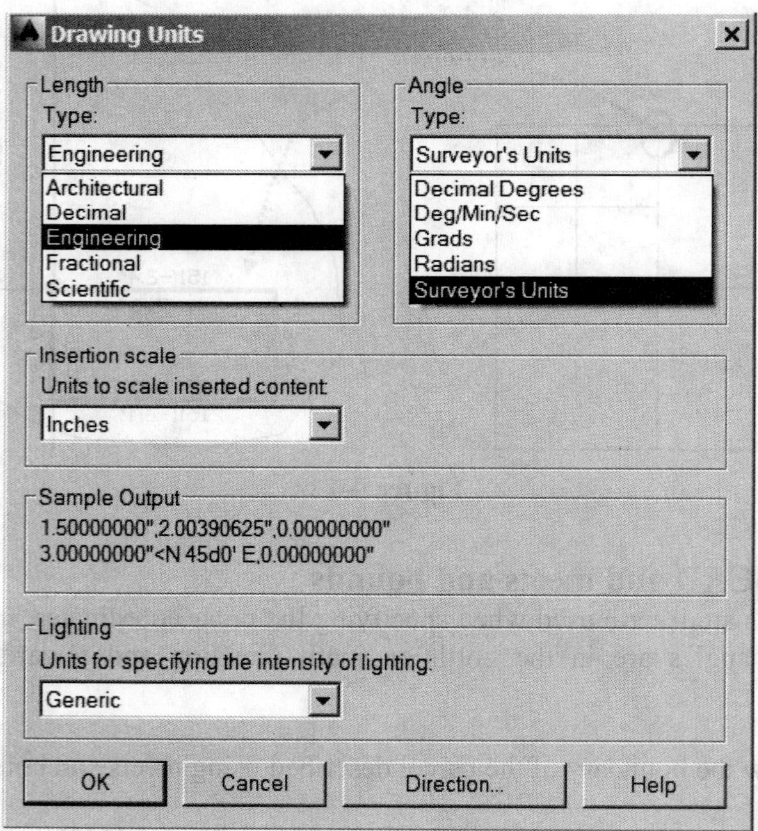

Figure 9-12c

9.13.   Lots and blocks

9.13.1. Terminology
- Suburb: A suburb is defined as a residential area on the outskirts of a city or a large town adjacent to the main employment centers. Most of the time it has a lower population density than the inner city neighborhoods.
- Exurb: An exurb, also known as a bedroom community or dormitory town, is defined as a residential area where residents sleep in, but mostly work elsewhere because there are very few local businesses.
- Subdivision: Subdivision is the act of dividing land into pieces that are easier to sell or otherwise develop. If it is used for housing it is typically known as a housing subdivision or housing development, although some developers tend to call these areas communities.

9.13.2. Lots and blocks
The Lot and Block Survey System is used in the United States and Canada to locate and identify land, particularly for lots in densely populated metropolitan areas, suburban areas, and exurbs. It is sometimes referred to as the Recorded Plat Survey System or the Recorded Map Survey System.

The system is the most recent and may be the simplest of the three main survey systems. In this system, a large parcel is defined by metes and bounds or the PLSS. The owners of the parcel would divide the land into smaller parcels known as block. Blocks are further subdivided into even smaller parcels known as lots. Blocks and lots can be of any size. However, usually the municipality restricts their sizes. Each block and lot is given identification (a number or a letter). In some cases, blocks may be part of a subdivision. All surveys and identification are recorded with an official government record keeper. The officially recorded map then became the legal description of all of the lots in the subdivision.

A legal description of a lot in a lot and block system must identify the following:
  i.   an individual lot number,
  ii.   the block in which the lot is located, if applicable,
  iii. a reference to a platted subdivision or a phase thereof,
  iv.   a reference to find the cited plat map (i.e., a page and/or volume number), and
  v.   a description of the map's place of official recording (e.g., recorded in the files of the County Engineer).

The legal description of a 0.3542 acre property under the Lot and Block system may be something like; (i) Lot 11 of (ii) Block 8 of the (iii) White Oak Subdivision (iv) as recorded in Map Book 35, Page 64 (v) at the Recorder of Deeds office, Figure 9-13. Some simple maps may only contain a lot and map number, such as Lot C of the Riverside Subdivision map as recorded in Map Book 12, Page 8 in the office of the City Engineer. The more technical details of the legal description are contained in the recorded plat map and there is no need to reiterate them in a deed or other legal description.

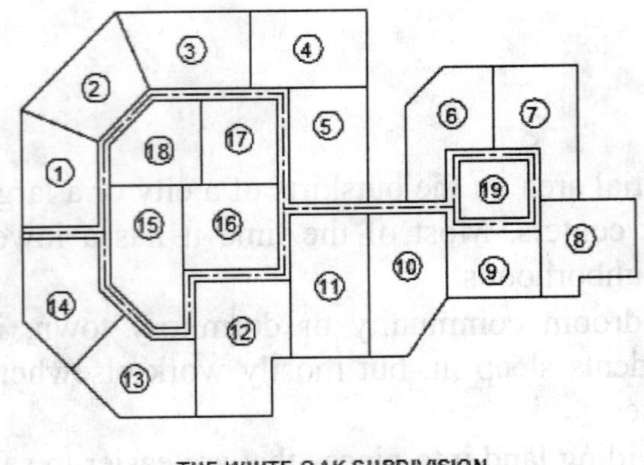

THE WHITE OAK SUBDIVISION

Figure 9-13

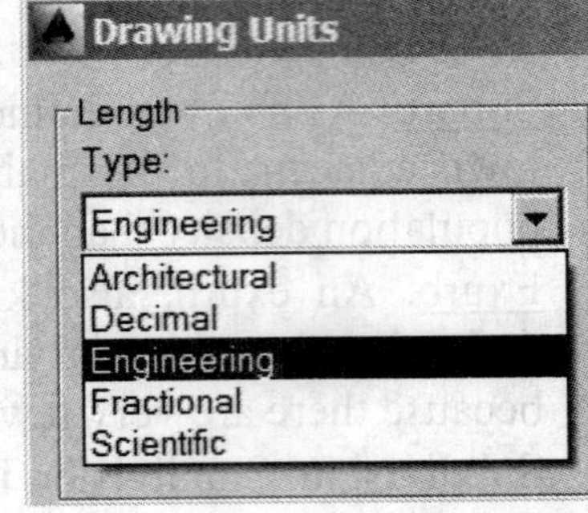

Figure 9-14a

9.13.3. AutoCAD and lot and block

In AutoCAD, a lot and block system can be created by following a step-by-step given below.

1. Open a new acad landscape template file created in the earlier chapters.
2. Change units to *Engineering* units as follow: (i) Type *Units* on the command line to open the *Drawing Units* dialog box; (ii) expand the *Length* panel; and (iii) select the *Engineering* option, Figure 9.14a.
3. Create the layers as shown in Figure 9.14b.

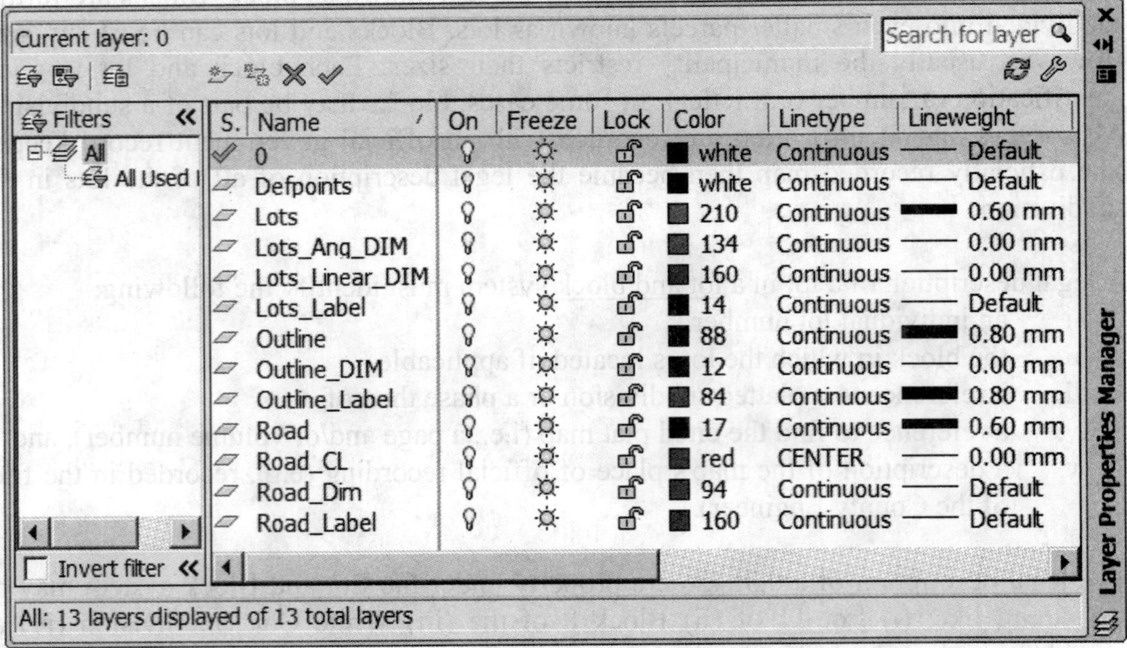

Figure 9-14b

4. Draw the outline of the subdivision: Figure 9-15.
    3. Make the *Outline* to be the current layer and draw the outline of the subdivision using the *Polyline* command.

4. Make the *Outlin_DIM* to be the current layer and add the dimensions to the outline of the subdivision.

5. Make the *Outline_Label* to be the current layer and add the label to outline of the subdivision using the *Text* command.

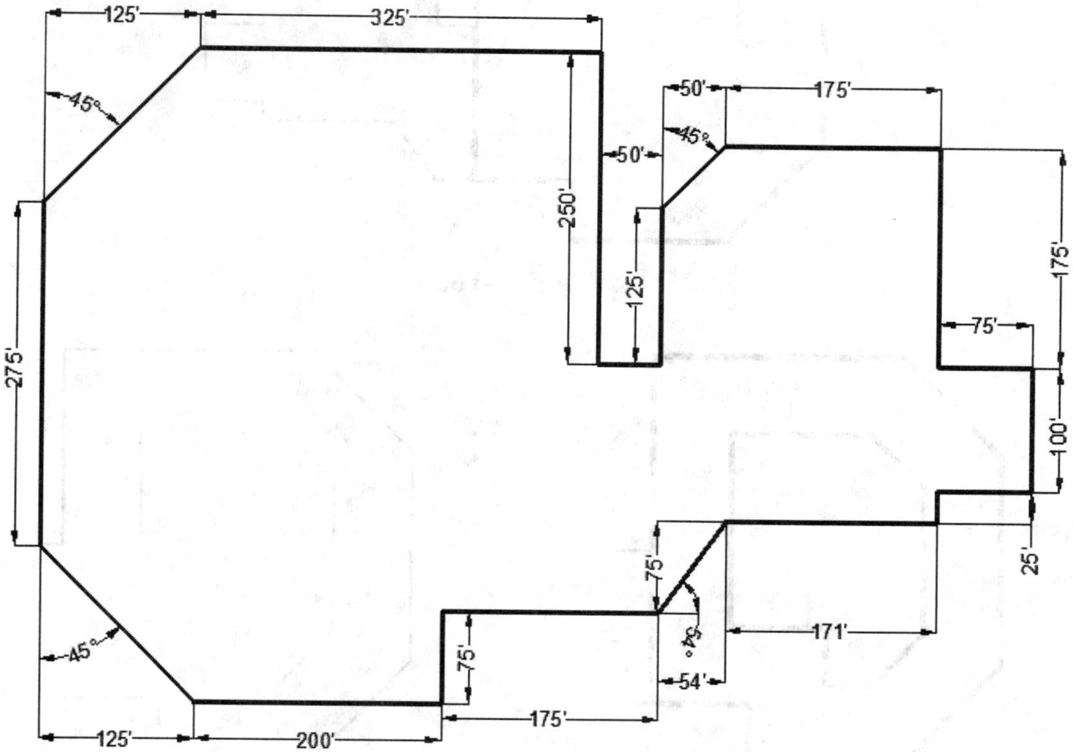

THE WHITE OAK SUBDIVISION

Figure 9-15

5. Draw the left loop of the road of the subdivision: Figure 9-16f and Figure 9-16g.

a. Make the *Road* be the current layer and draw a polyline over the left part of the subdivision, Figure 9-16a. In the figure, the line weight is changed for the demonstration purpose.

b. Using the *Offset* command with the offset distance of 100ft create an offset inside the polyline created in the previous step, Figure 9-16b. This is outer edge of the road.

c. Delete the polyline created in the step #a. Move the line created by the *Offset* command in the step #b line to the *Road* layer; and set the line weight of the road *By layer* in the *Lineweight control* of the *Property* toolbar, Figure 9-16c.

d. The road is 16 feet wide. Hence, create the inner edge of the road using the *Offset* command with the offset distance of 16ft, Figure 9-16d.

e. Create the centerline of the road using the *Offset* command with the offset distance of 8ft. Move the center line to the *Road_CL* layer; set the linetype *By layer* in the *Linetype control* of the *Property* toolbar. Set the Linetype scale (from the *Property* sheet) to 0.3, Figure 9-16e.

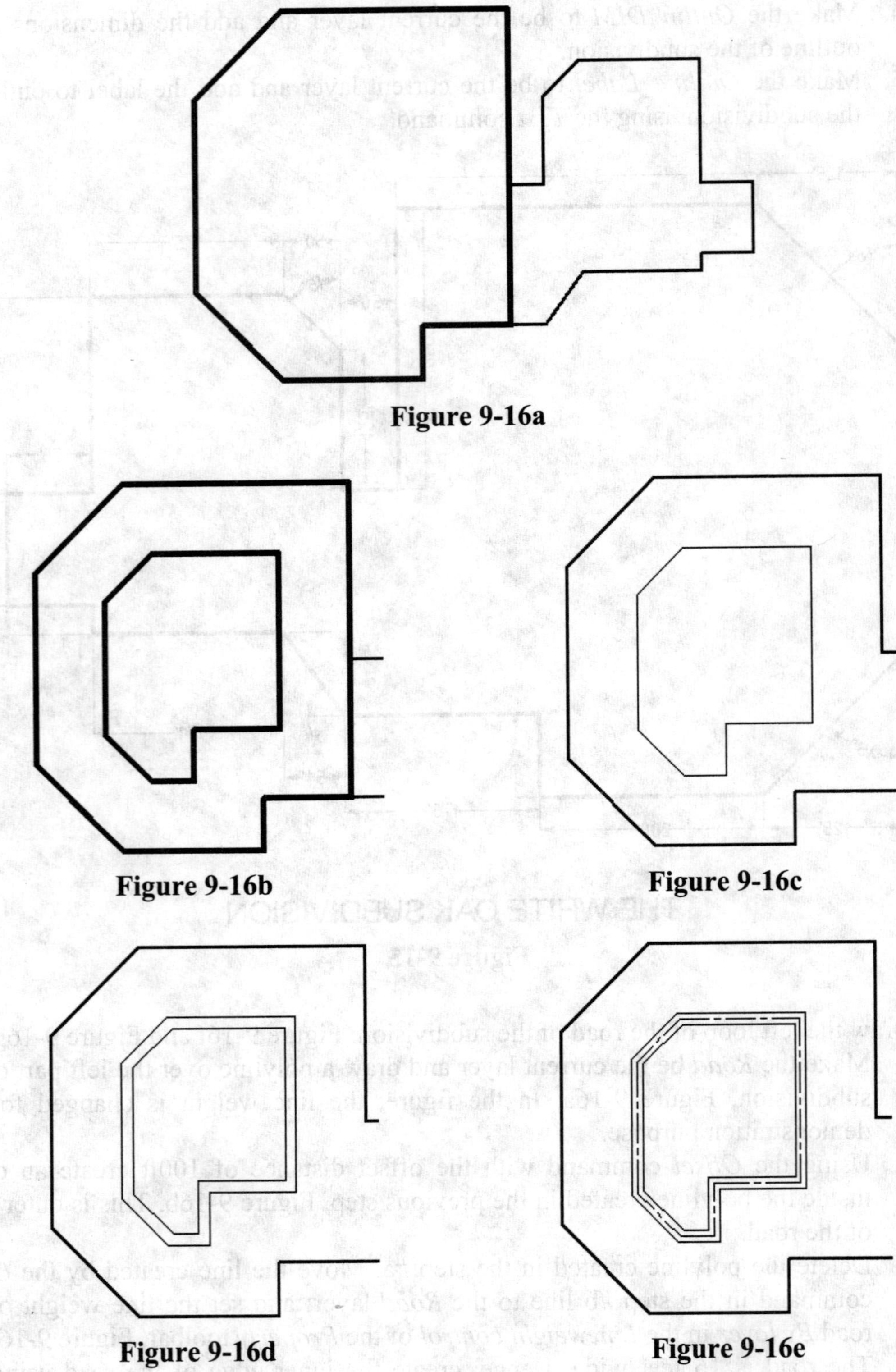

Figure 9-16a

Figure 9-16b

Figure 9-16c

Figure 9-16d

Figure 9-16e

6. Draw the right loop of the road of the subdivision, Figure 9-16f and Figure 9-16g.
   a. Make the *Road* to be the current layer and draw a polyline for the outer edge of
      the road.

b. Using the *Offset* command with the offset distance of 16ft to create the inner edge of the road.

c. Create the centerline of the road using the *Offset* command with the offset distance of 8ft. Move the center line to the *Road_CL* layer; set the linetype *By layer* in the *Linetype control* of the *Property* toolbar. Set the Linetype scale (from the *Property* sheet) to 0.3.

7. Draw the remaining roads of the subdivision, Figure 9-16f and Figure 9-16g.

8. Using the trim command, trim the unnecessary parts of the roads, Figure 9-16f.

9. Make the *Road_DIM* be the current layer and add the dimensions of the roads, Figure 9-16f.

10. Make the *Road_Label* to be the current layer and add the labels of the roads, Figure 9-16g.

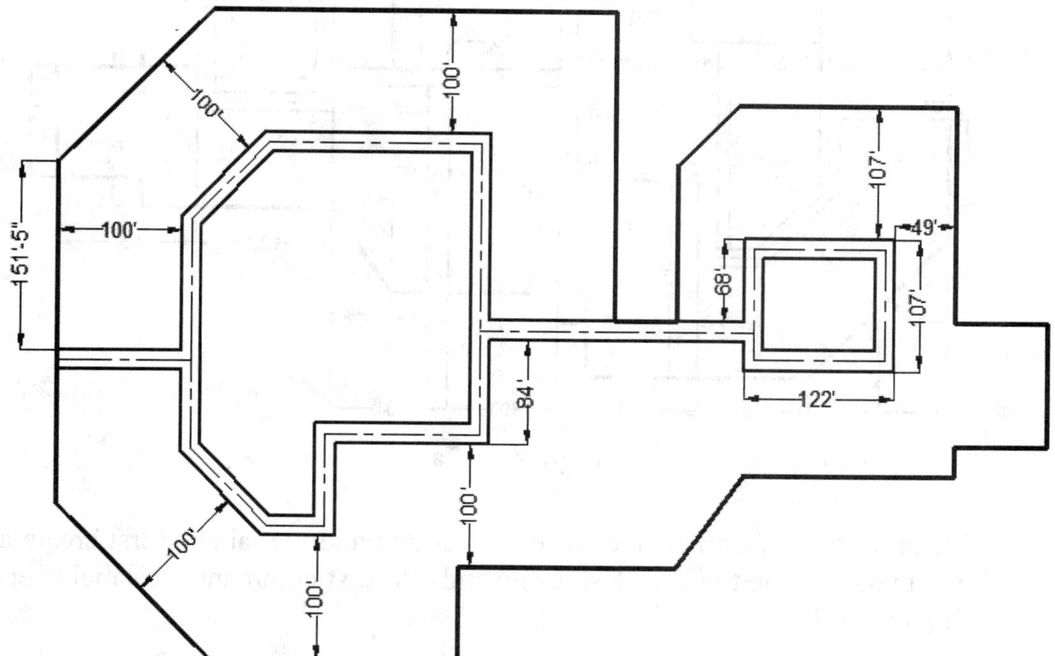

Figure 9-16f

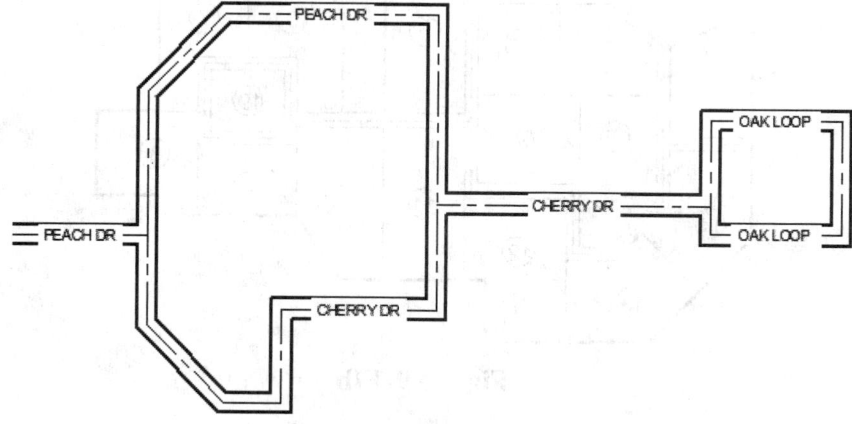

Figure 9-16g

11. Draw the lots of the subdivision: Figure 9-17a and Figure 9-17b.
   a. Make the *Lots* be the current layer and draw the boundaries of the lots, Figure 9-17a.
   b. Make the *Lots_DIM* be the current layer and add the dimensions to the lots, Figure 9-17a.

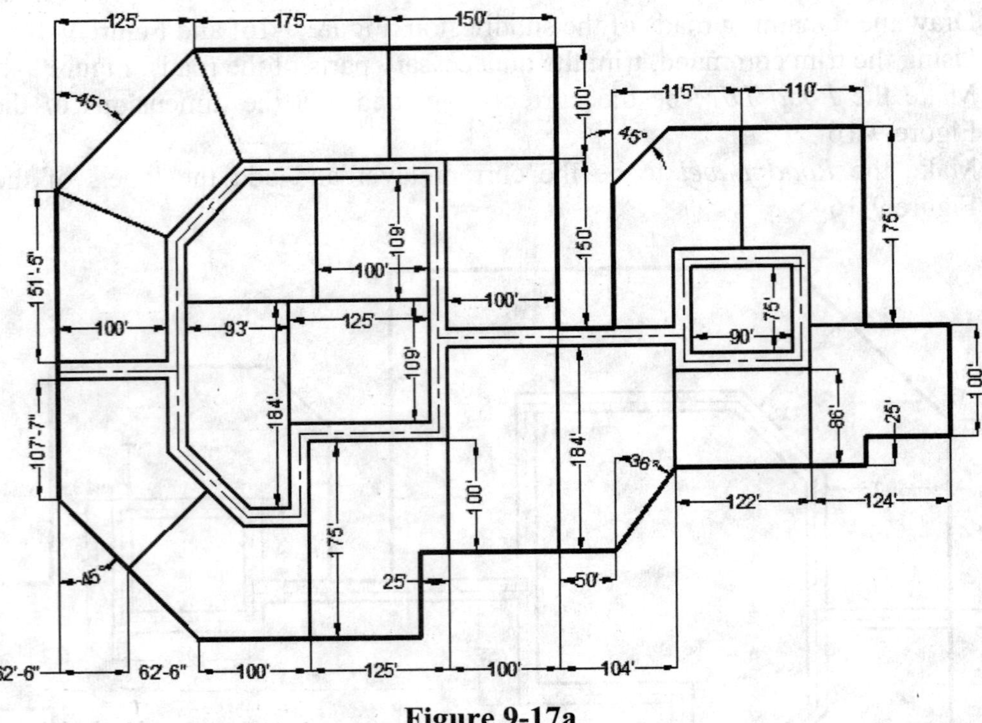

Figure 9-17a

   a. Make the *Lots_Label* be the current layer and add the labels. First create a text and then encircle the text. Use *Copy* and edit text commands to label every lot, Figure 9-17b.

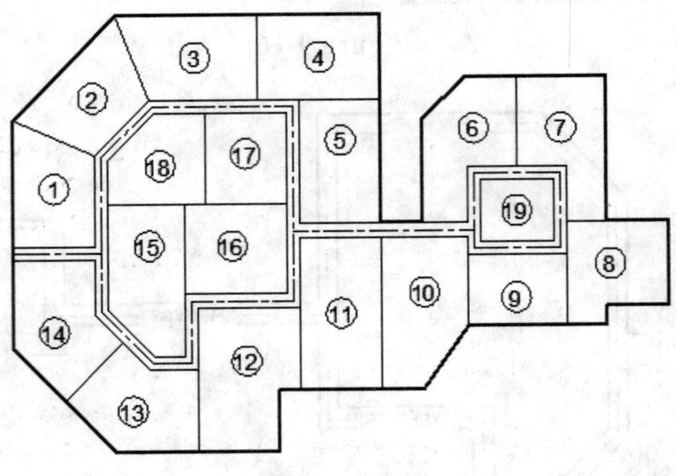

Figure 9-17b

12. Finally, display the drawing in a layout and update the Title block: Figure 9-17c.

   a. Set the scale of the drawing's viewport to be 1:1320, Figure 9-17c.
   b. Lock the viewport.
   c. Update the Title block.
   d. The resultant drawing in the layout is shown in Figure 9-17c.

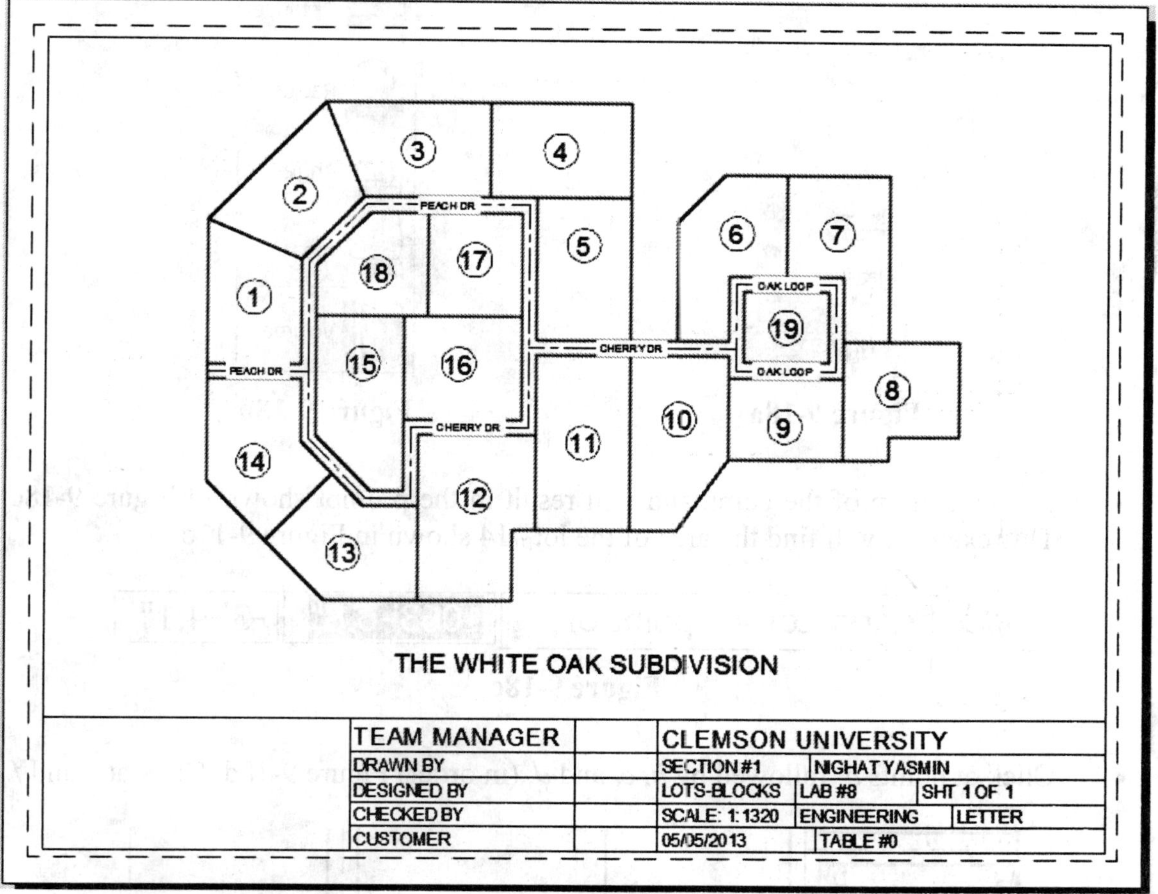

TEAM MANAGER		CLEMSON UNIVERSITY		
DRAWN BY		SECTION #1	NIGHAT YASMIN	
DESIGNED BY		LOTS-BLOCKS	LAB #8	SHT 1 OF 1
CHECKED BY		SCALE: 1:1320	ENGINEERING	LETTER
CUSTOMER		05/05/2013	TABLE #0	

Figure 9-17c

9.13.4. Area of a lot

In the lot and block system shown in Figure 9-15c and Figure 9-16a, the area of the lot #4, #5, #9, #11, #16, and #19 can be calculated by multiplying the width and length of the rectangle. However, the area of the remaining lots can be found using AutoCAD. In AutoCAD, the area and perimeter of a lot can be found using the *Area* command by specifying the points on the boundary. All points must lie in a plane parallel to the XY plane of the UCS.

- The *Area* command is activated using one of the following procedures.
  1. Panel method: from the *Home* tab and the *Utilities* panel, expand the *Measure* dropdown menu and click *Area* option, Figure 9-18a and Figure 9-18b.
  2. Command line method: Type "area", "Area", or "AREA" in the command line and press the *Enter* key.

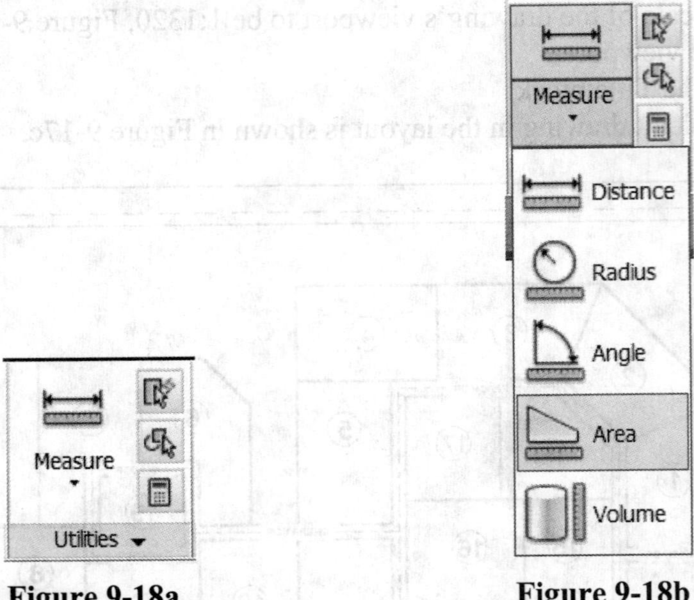

Figure 9-18a   **Figure 9-18b**

- The activation of the command will result in the prompt shown in Figure 9-18c. This example will find the area of the lot #14 shown in Figure 9-17c.

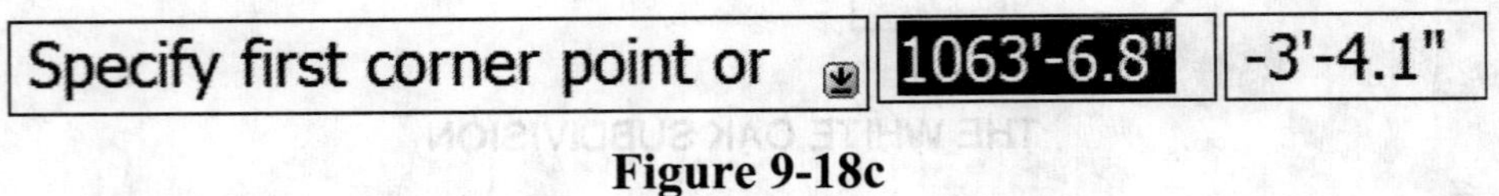

Figure 9-18c

- Click at points *a*, followed by *b*, *c,* and *d*, (in order) Figure 9-18d. Click at *e* and *f*.

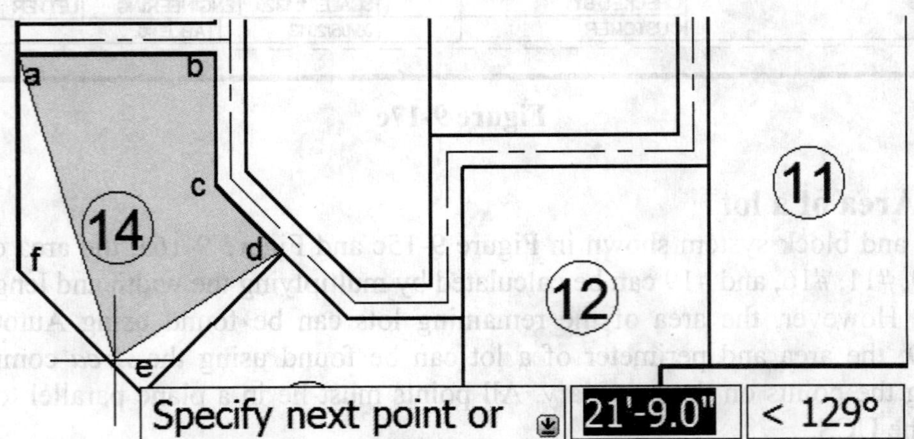

Figure 9-18d

- Press the *Enter* key. The area and perimeter information shown in Figure 9-18e will appear on the screen.
- Either choose *eXit* option in Figure 9-18e or press the *Esc* key to exit the command.
- The area and perimeter will also be available on the command line.

- If the polygon is not closed then the area is calculated as if a line was drawn from the last point to the first. For the perimeter calculation the length of that line is added to the existing lines.
- Convert the area into acres using the relationship: 1 acre = 43560 sq. ft.

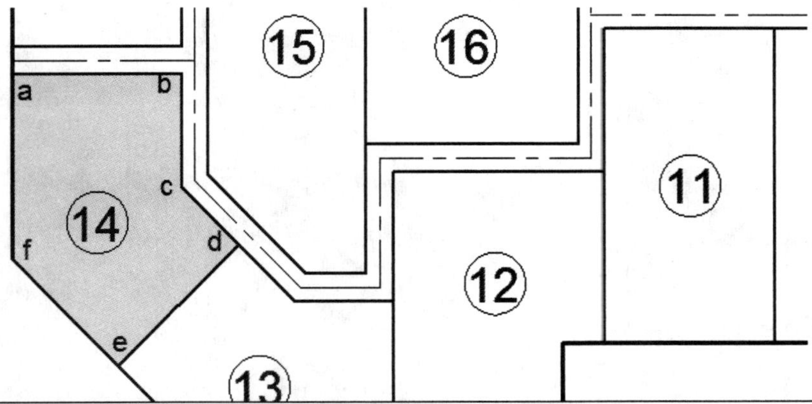

Figure 9-18e

1	13070.082111	4	18397.961970
2	13537.225810	12	19998.895531
3	15429.756381	13	14697.090349
4	14977.711905	14	15455.190007
5	14966.759298	15	15456.164658
6	14679.192041	16	13424.974138
7	15636.767147	17	10900.523991
8	13593.674104	18	11233.448797
9	10493.592195	19	6750
10	17102.095637		

<u>Notes:</u>

10. Contours

10.1.   Objectives

- Learn to identify different types of contour lines
- Learn to identify stream, ridges, peak, depression, and saddle on a contour map
- Learn to identify steep and mild slopes on a contour map
- Learn to create a contour map
- Learn to mark and label the index contours

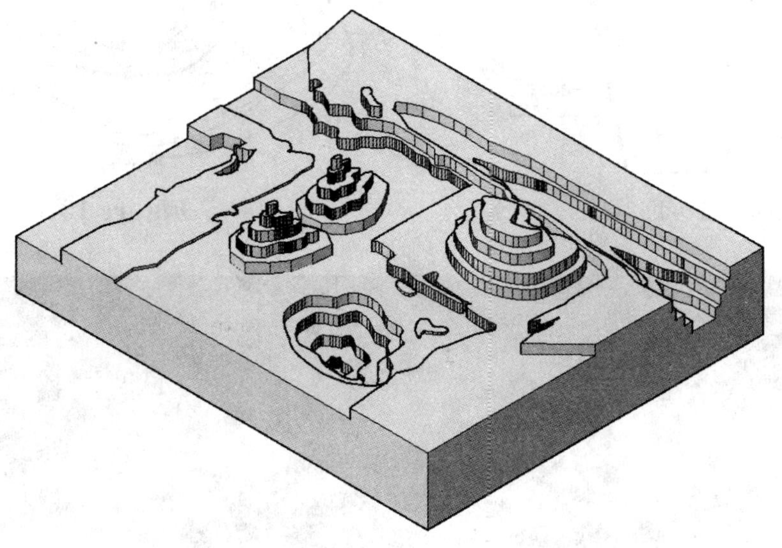

10.2.   Introduction

Consider a cup of coffee and assume that the coffee has evaporated. Figure 10-1a shows the coffee marks as circular rings in the top view and straight lines in the front view. In the coffee marks plotting the parameter is the time when the coffee was evaporated. Similarly, isobars and isotherms are wavy or closed looped lines representing constant pressure and constant temperature, respectively. These wavy or looped lines, representing a constant value of a parameter, are called contour. In a land survey, a contour line is an imaginary horizontal line passing through the points of same elevation drawn on a topographic map, Figure 10-1b. Shorelines are also good example of contour lines, since the water receding marks create non-intersecting loops, Figure 10-1c.

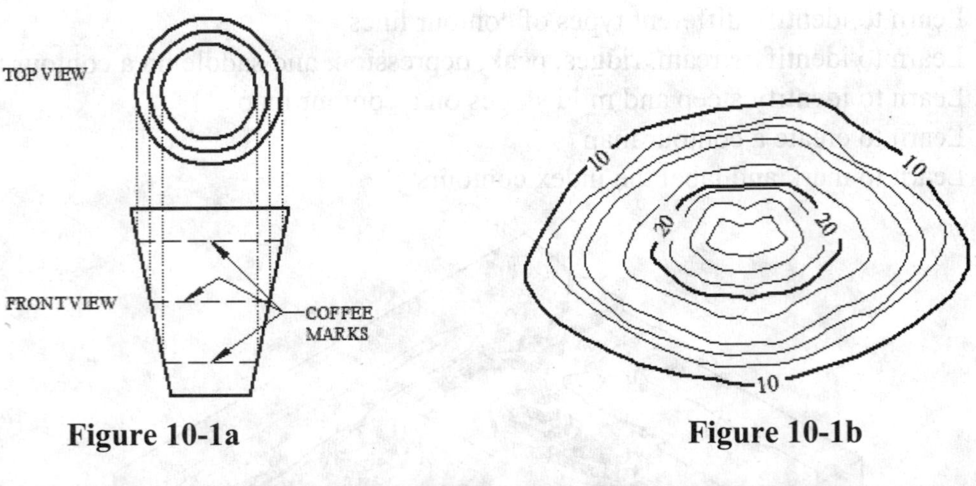

Figure 10-1a

Figure 10-1b

Figure 10-1c

10.3.   Characteristics of a contour line

A contour line is an imaginary line representing a constant value of a parameter.

- A counter line represents a constant parameter. For example, Figure 10-1b represents elevation contours. The elevation is 10 units for every point on the loop labeled as 10 in the figure.
- Contour lines never end.
- If a large enough area is available then the contour lines will loop around and will join themselves.
- Contour lines neither join with other contour lines nor bifurcate.
- Contour lines never cross each other.

10.4.   Terminology

- *Bench Mark*: A bench mark is a point of reference for the measurement. In land survey, a bench mark is the point of known elevation.
- *Mean sea level*: The average elevation between the low and high tide of a sea is called the mean sea level.
- *Elevation*: The elevation of a point is the vertical distance from a bench mark, a datum line, or a reference plane. In the Figure 10-2a, the vertical distance of the point A is 5ft from the datum line aa. Generally, the elevation of a geographic location is its height above (or depth below) the mean sea level. The mean sea level is the datum line. Figure 10-2b shows the elevation of one of the trees on the shore with respect to the mean sea level (datum).

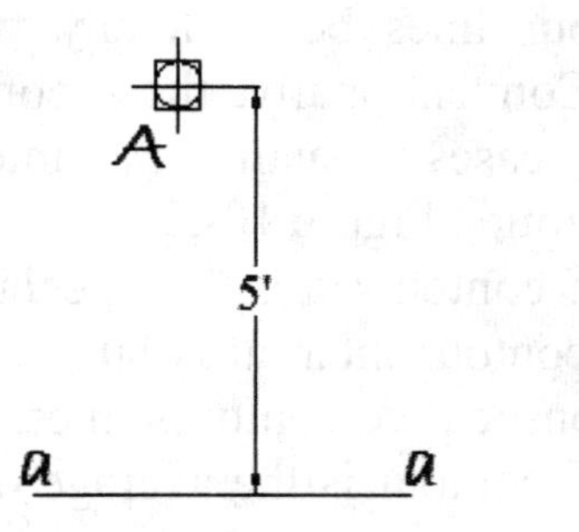

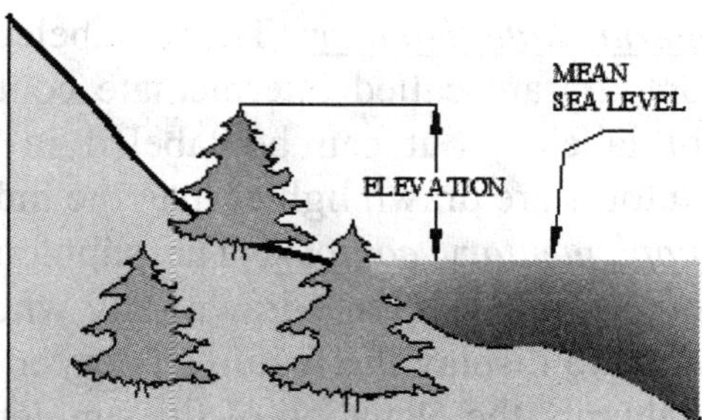

Figure 10-2a	Figure 10-2b

- *Contour interval*: The contour interval of a map is the vertical distance. It is the difference in elevation between two consecutive contour lines. The contour intervals are closely related to the terrain, purpose of the map, and scale of the drawing. On a given map, the contour interval should be constant. Assuming the units of measurement is feet, the contour interval is 2ft in Figure 10-1b.
- *Types of contour lines*: Contour lines can be classified into three groups.
  - *Index contour*: To make the reading of contour maps easy, every fifth contour is labeled. The labeled contour lines are called index contour, Figure 10-3. The index contour line is broken at certain places and text labels are added. The labels represent the elevations with respect to the mean sea level. Usually, the index contours are drawn thicker than the other contour lines. Index contours

can be marked as: (i) Identify the elevation of the first index contour (FIC). (ii) Specify the contour interval (CI). (iii) The elevation of the second index contour (SIC) is calculated as: *Elevation of SIC = FIC + 5*CI*. If the elevation is decreasing then the second index contour (SIC) is calculated as: *Elevation of SIC = FIC - 5*CI*. Similarly, calculate the reaming index contours. In Figure 10-3, the contour interval is 10 feet.

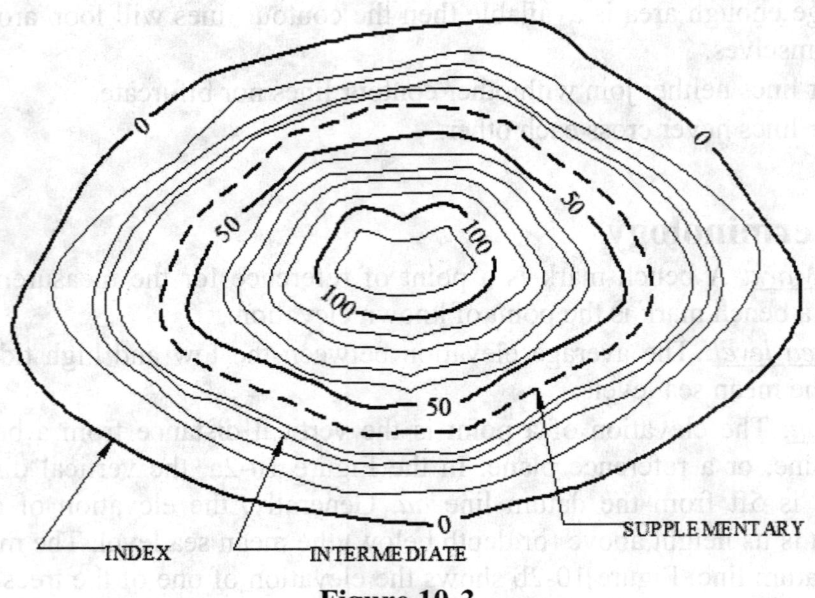

Figure 10-3

- o *Intermediate contour*: The unlabeled contour lines between any two index contours are called intermediate contours. Conventionally, these contours are not labeled, but can be labeled in special cases. Usually, the intermediate contours are drawn lighter than the index contours, Figure 10-3.
- o *Supplementary contour*: The supplementary contours are the special type of contour lines and are drawn only when the contour interval is large and a user wants to display the features between two consecutive contours lines. As a rule of thumb, the elevation of the supplementary contour is the average of the two contours on its either side, Figure 10-3.
- *Peak*: The peak of a hill or mountain is shown by the closed looped contour lines of decreasing diameters and increasing elevation. Figure 10-4a shows the contour map of a peak and Figure 10-4b shows the corresponding peak in 3D contour map.

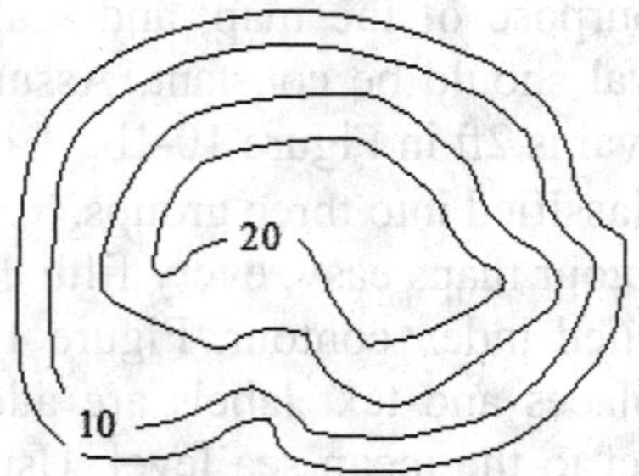

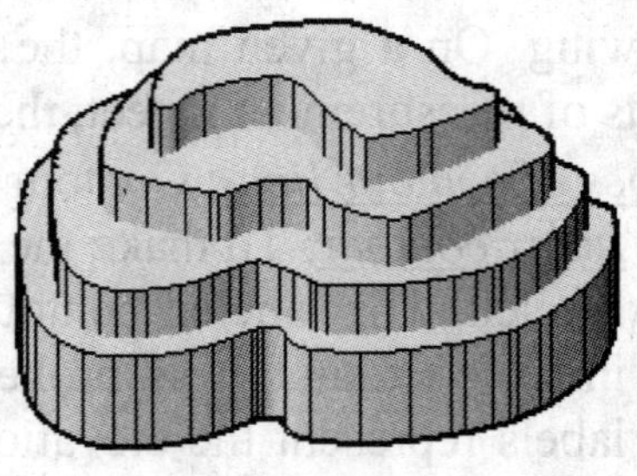

Figure 10-4a   **Figure 10-4b**

- *Depression*: A depression (hole or excavation pit without any drainage outlets) is shown by the closed looped contour lines of decreasing diameters and decreasing elevation. Figure 10-5a shows the contour map of a depression and Figure 10-5b shows the corresponding depression in 3D contour map. The innermost circle is marked with small lines on the inside, Figure 10-5a. These small lines are called hachures.

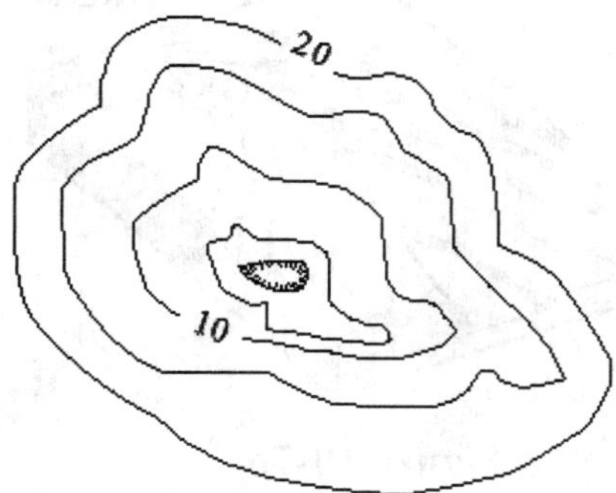

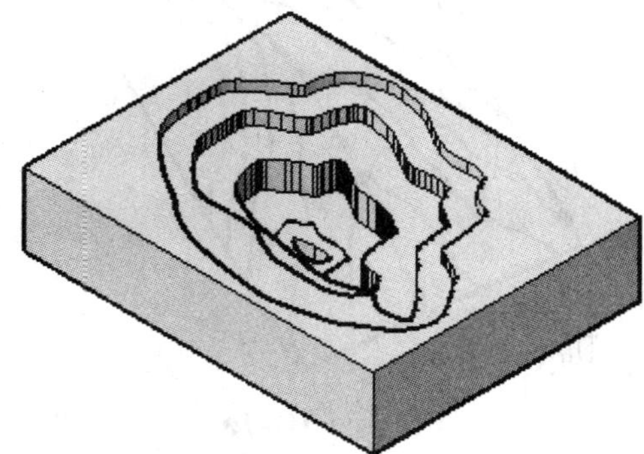

Figure 10-5a   **Figure 10-5b**

- *Saddle*: Two peaks side by side form a saddle. Figure 10-6a shows the contour map of a saddle and Figure 10-6b shows the corresponding peaks in 3D contour map. In the Figure 10-6a, the arrow shows the downward slope.

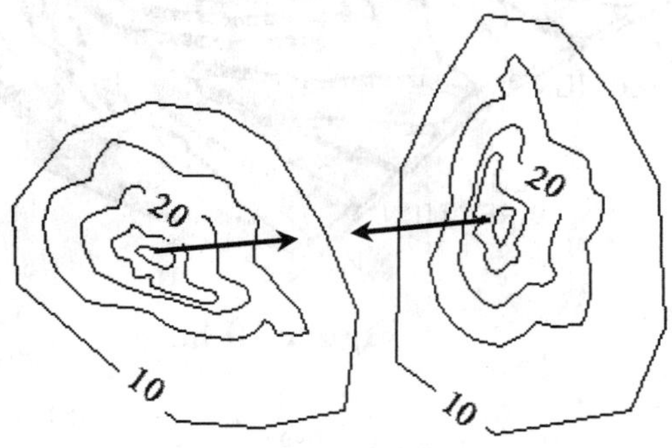

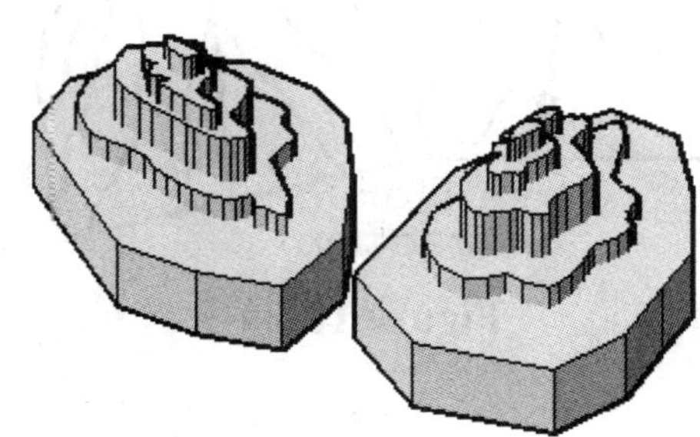

Figure 10-6a   **Figure 10-6b**

- *Streams*: Contour lines are roughly parallel to stream. The contour lines cross the streambed upstream by creating V with the closed end of the V's pointing upstream and the open end of the V's pointing downstream. Figure 10-7a shows contour map of a stream and Figure 10-7b shows the corresponding stream in 3D contour map.
- *Ridge or hill or mountain*: Contour lines are roughly parallel to ridge, and the contour lines cross the ridge downstream by creating V's or U's. The closed end of the V's or U's points downstream and the open end of the V's or U's points upstream. Figure 10-8a shows contour map of a stream and ridge line and Figure 10-8b shows the corresponding stream and ridge in 3D contour map.
- *Slope verses space*: Closely spaced contour lines represent steep slope and widely spaced contour lines represent mild slope. The top portion of Figure 10-9a shows the contour map of closely spaced (left side → steep slope) and widely spaced (right side → mild slope) contour lines; and its lower parts show the profile indicating the

steep and mild slope. Figure 10-9b shows the corresponding 3D contour map. Notice carefully that the slope is perpendicular to the contour lines.

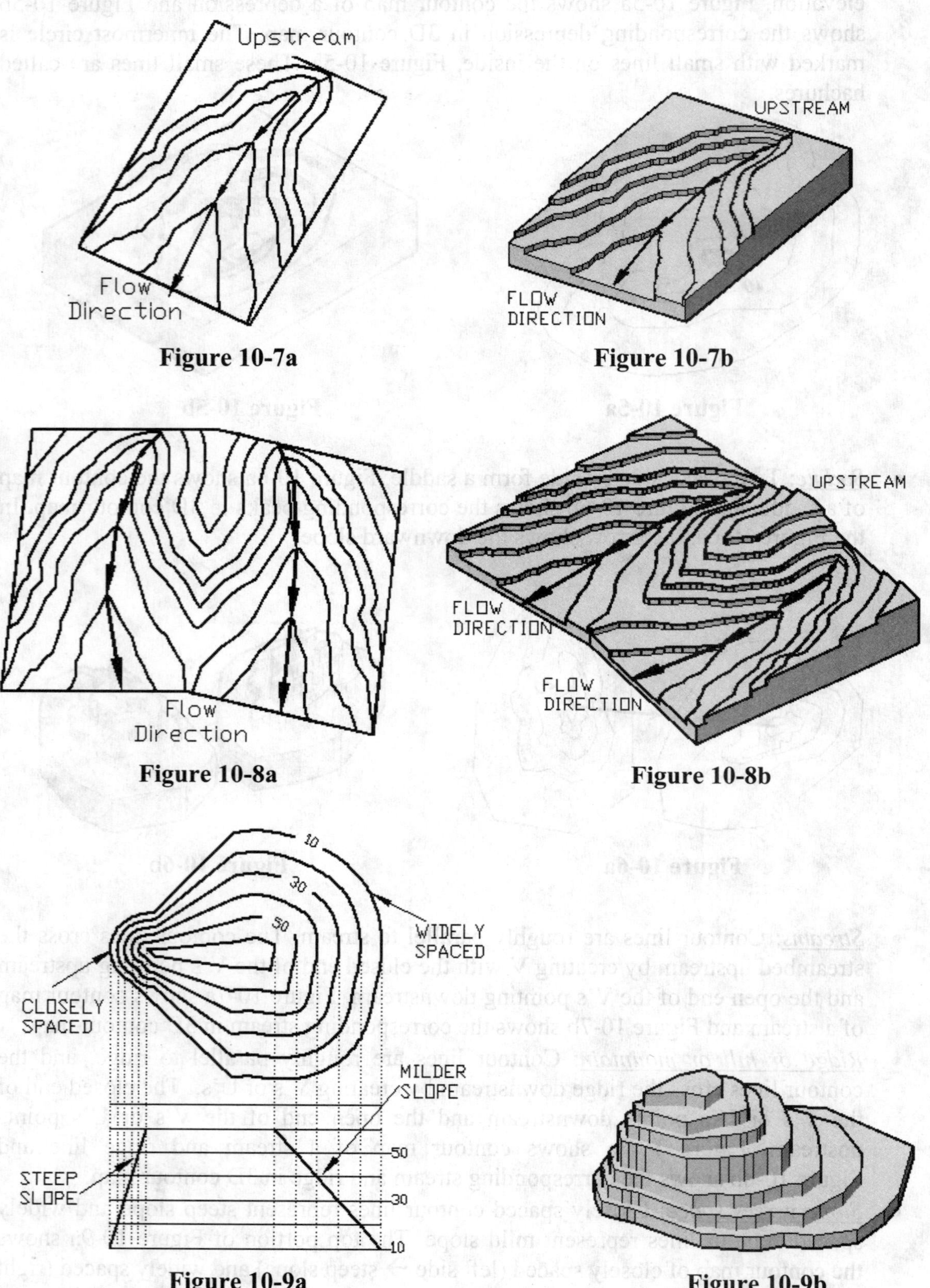

Figure 10-7a

Figure 10-7b

Figure 10-8a

Figure 10-8b

Figure 10-9a

Figure 10-9b

- *Topographic map*: A topographic (contour) map is a two dimensional representation of the three dimensional earth. The three dimensions are the longitude, latitude, and the elevation. A topographic map is used to represent the shape of the earth using contour lines. On these maps, the contour interval depends upon the gradient of the land; and it is represented on the map. A typical map is shown in Figure 10-10. In these maps the contour line are shown in brown color, water bodies (lakes, rivers, streams, etc.) in blue color, man-made structures (buildings, roads, etc.) in black color, and woodlands in the green color.

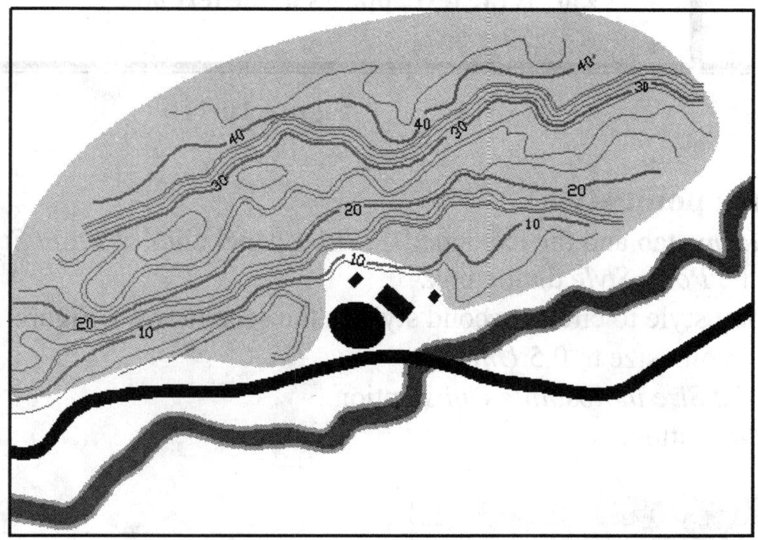

Figure 10-10

10.5.   AutoCAD and Contour map

In AutoCAD contour maps can be created by drawing polylines through the elevation data. This section assumes that the user has interpolated the field data. This section also assumes that the user has created a script file. To draw a contour map, the color of the point is not important. However, for better understanding, every elevation is assigned its distinct color. The remaining of this section provides step-by-step instructions to create a contour map.

10.5.1. Create Script file

- Create a script file or download the script files. The script file is saved with "*.scr*" extension and can be created in *Notepad*. The Figure 10-11a shows a part of a script (Script.scr) file and the Figure 10-11b explains the contents of the script file.

10.5.2. Create layers

- Launch AutoCAD 2014.
- Open a new portrait file (your template file for the ANSI units).
- (i) Create '*Data*' layer for the elevation data pint. (ii) Create '*Contour*' layer for the contour lines. (iii) Create '*Label*' layer for the contours' labels.

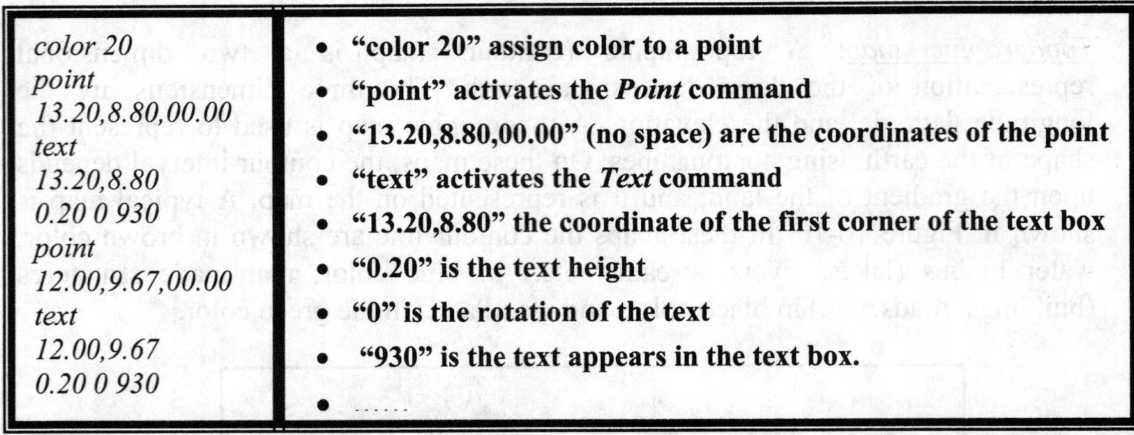

Figure 10-11a   **Figure 10-11b**

10.5.3. Change point style

- From the *Home* tab and the expanded *Utilities* panel click at *Point Style...* tool. This will open the *Point Style* dialog box.
- Change point style to circle (second style in the second row), Figure 10-12.
- Change the point size to 0.5 *Units*.
- Select the *Set Size in Absolute Units* option.
- Press the *OK* button.

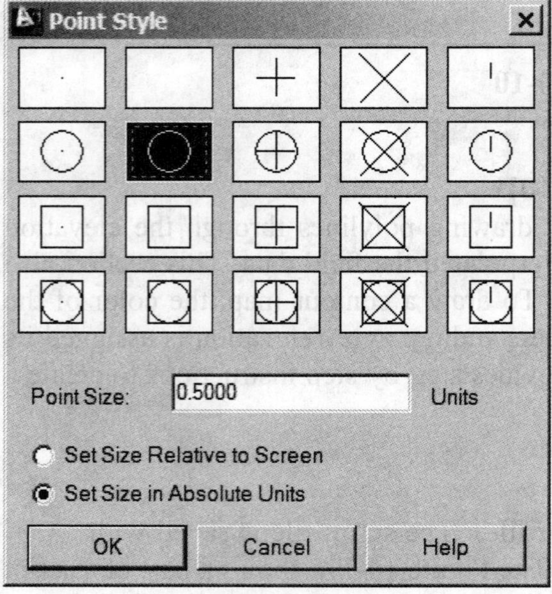

Figure 10-12

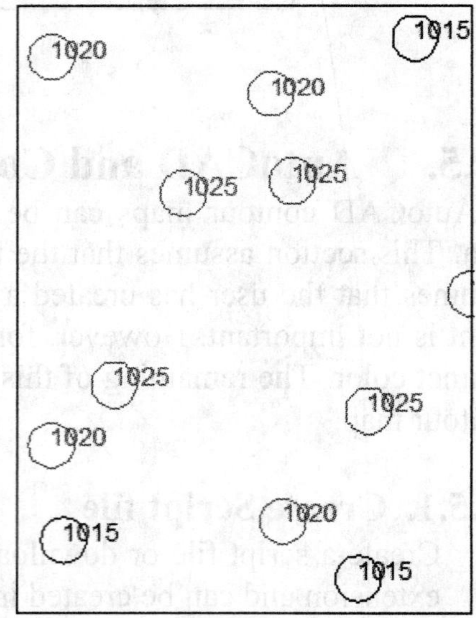

Figure 10-13a

10.5.4. Read the script files

- Make the *Data* layer as the current layer.
- Read the script file by activating the script command.
  - Command line method: Type "script", "Script", or "SCRIPT" on the command line and press the *Enter* key.

- Figure 10-13a shows the close-up of the selected elevation data points.
- The complete elevation data is shown in Figure 10-13b.

Figure 10-13b

10.5.5. Create the contour map

- Select the 'Contour' layer.
- Activate the *Polyline* command and draw a polyline through the points of elevation 930, Figure 10-14a.

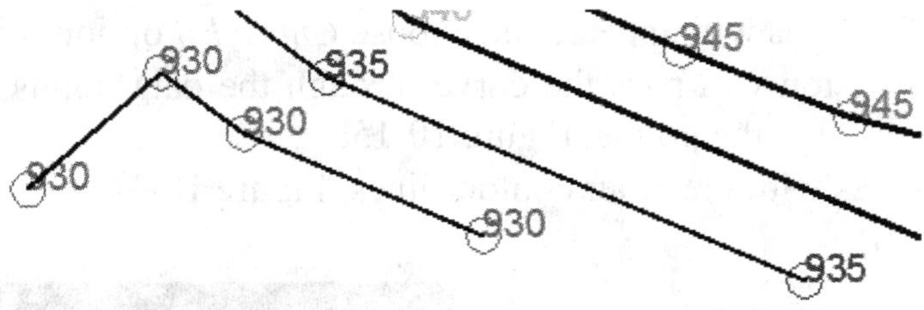

Figure 10-14a

- Repeat the process with the elevation 935, 940, ..., 1025, Figure 10-14b.
- Fit a curve through each polyline, Figure 10-14c. Curve fitting is discussed in the next section.
- If polylines are created in the multiple activations of the commands then first join the line and then perform the curve fitting operation. The *Join* operation is briefly

described at the end of this chapter. For the details of polyline editing refer to Chapter #4.

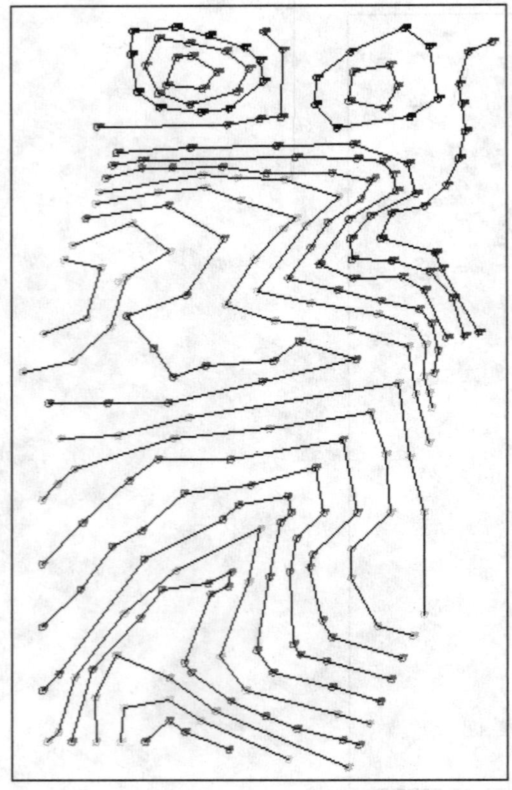

Figure 10-14b   **Figure 10-14c**

10.5.6. Curve fitting
Curve fitting is optional; however, this section explains the curve fitting technique.
- Select a polyline for the elevation 930 (the grips points will appear), Figure 10-15a.
- Press the right button of the mouse, and the options list will appear.
- Choose the *Polyline* from the list, Figure 10-15a.
- Another list of options will appear, and choose *Curve Fit* option, Figure 10-15a.
- The *Curve Fit* option will pass the curve through the data points. A smooth curve will be drawn through the points, Figure 10-15b.
- Repeat the process with the other contour lines, Figure 10-14c.

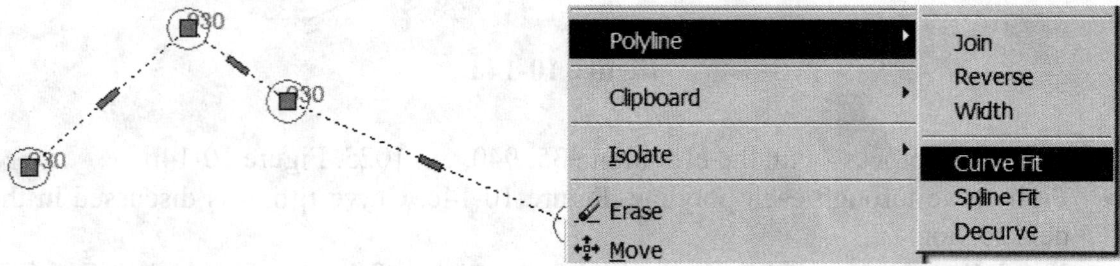

Figure 10-15

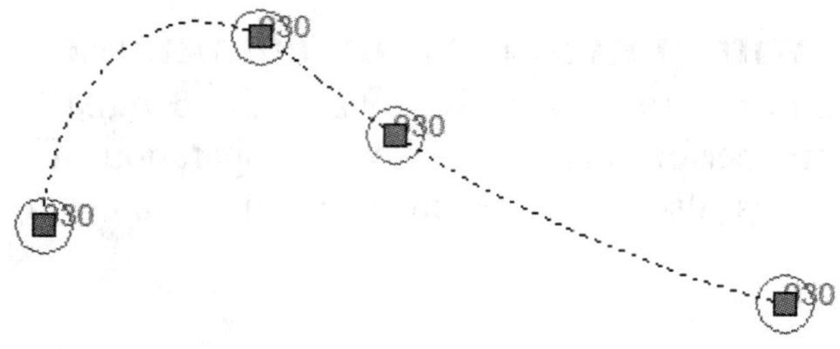

Figure 10-15b

10.5.7. Add the labels to the index contours

- If polylines are created in the multiple activations of the commands, then first join the line, and then perform the labeling and masking operation. The *Join* operation is briefly described at the end of this chapter and is also discussed in detail in Chapter #4.
- Mark the index contours (that is, increase the lineweight for the index contours).
- Use the *Text* command from the *Home* tab and *Annotate* panel to create the text of a label. The text should be parallel to the polyline. If necessary, use the *Rotate* command from the *Home* tab and *Modify* panel to rotate the text.
- The Figure 10-16 shows a contour map with only two labeled index contours.
- Similarly add labels to the other contours.
- Hide the contour line behind the label using the *Background mask* option from the *Properties* sheet. The *Background mask* command is discussed in Chapter 3.
- Finally, add the North direction block from the *Design Center* → *Landscaping.dwg* → *North Arrow*. Scale the north block appropriately, Figure 10-16.

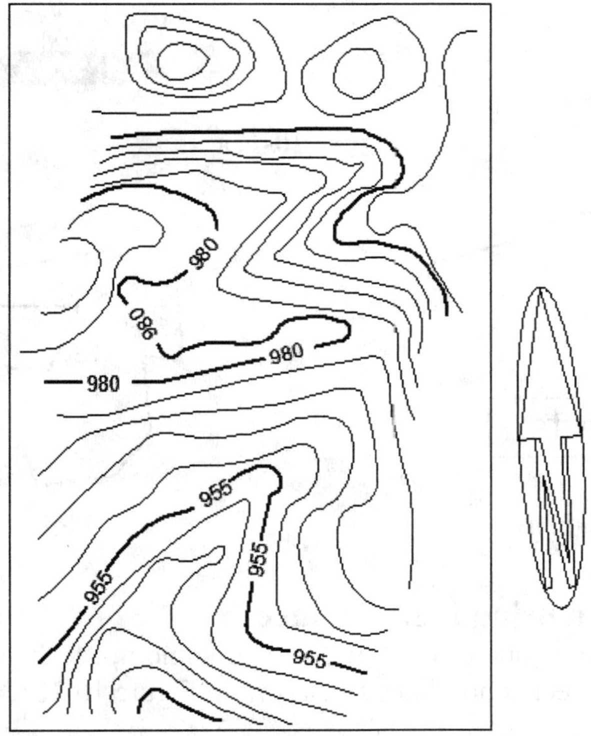

Figure 10-16

10.6.   Problem with polyline's *Join* command

If polylines are created in the multiple activations of the commands then, if necessary, join the polylines before performing any collective operation. The *Join* command is briefly described here. It is also discussed in detail in Chapter #4. A polyline can be joined in two ways.

10.6.1. Simple join

This method of polyline join is used if at least one end of the two polylines is common, Figure 10-17a.

- Select ONLY one polyline (the grip points will appear).
- Press the right button of the mouse and select the *Polyline* option, Figure 10-17a.
- This will open another option list shown in Figure 10-17a.
- Select the *Join* option by clicking the left button of the mouse. This will close the option selection lists and the user is required to select the polylines to be joined.
- Click the second polyline with the left button of the mouse Figure 10-17b and press the *Enter* key **TWICE**.
- The multiple polylines are converted to a single polyline.
- The result is shown in Figure 10-17c.

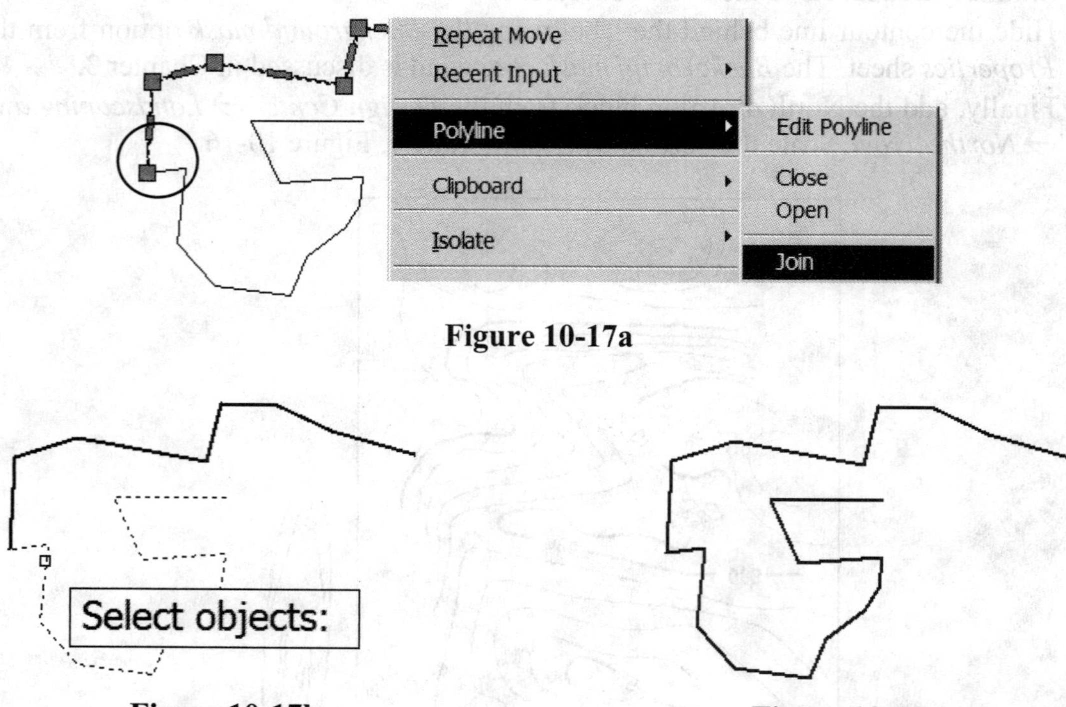

Figure 10-17a

Figure 10-17b   **Figure 10-17c**

10.6.2. Polyline join using fuzz distance

This method of polyline join is used if there is some space between two polylines, Figure 10-18a. The connected polylines are shown in Figure 10-18b.

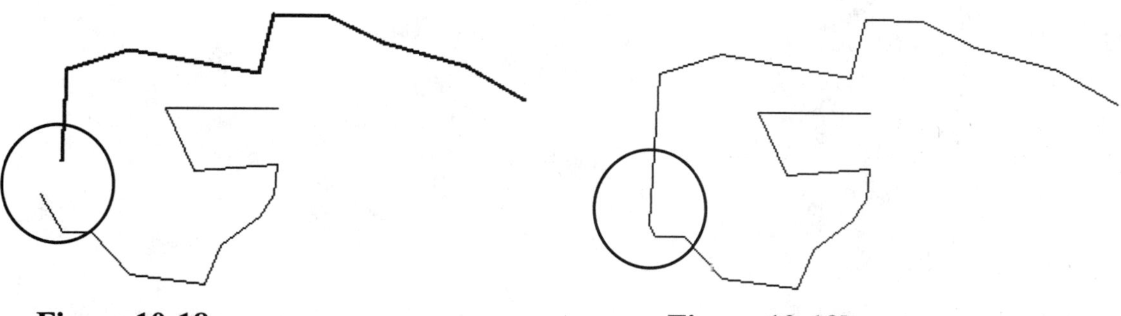

Figure 10-18a   **Figure 10-18b**

- From the *Home* tab and the expanded *Modify* panel, select the *Polyline Edit* tool,
  .
- The prompt shown in Figure 10-18c will appear.
- Press the down arrow and choose the *Multiple*'s option, Figure 10-18c.
- At the object selection prompt, select both the polylines and press the *Enter* key,
  Figure 10-18d.

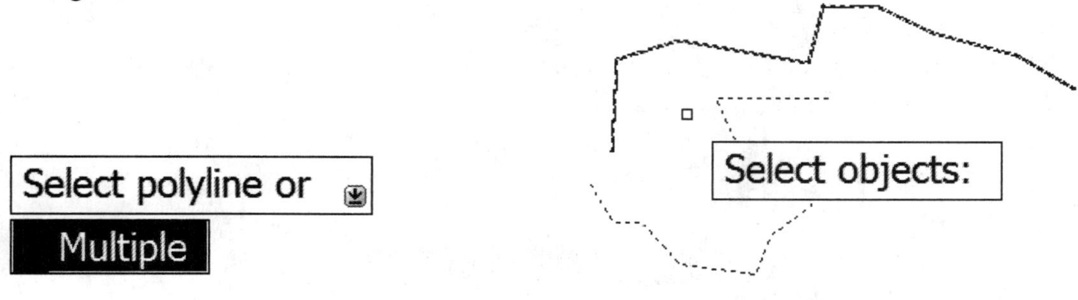

Figure 10-18c   **Figure 10-18d**

- The prompt shown in Figure 10-18e will appear.
- Specify the *Fuzz distance* to be 100 (that is, if the space between the two lines is
  less than or equal to this number, the lines will be connected).

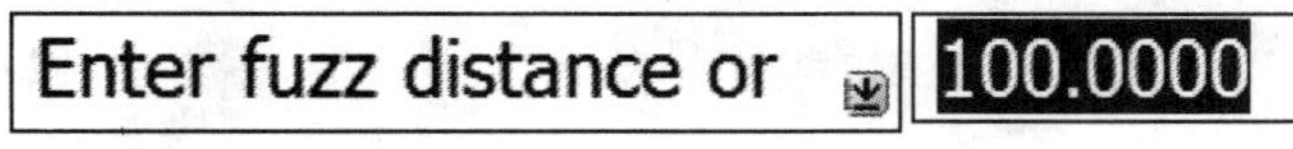

Figure 10-18e

- Press the *Enter* key twice.
- The multiple polylines (Figure 10-18a) are converted to a single polyline,
  Figure 10-18b.

Notes:

11. Drainage Basin

11.1.   Objectives

- Learn basics of a water cycle
- Learn basics of a drainage basin
- Learn to delineate a drainage basin of a channel using AutoCAD

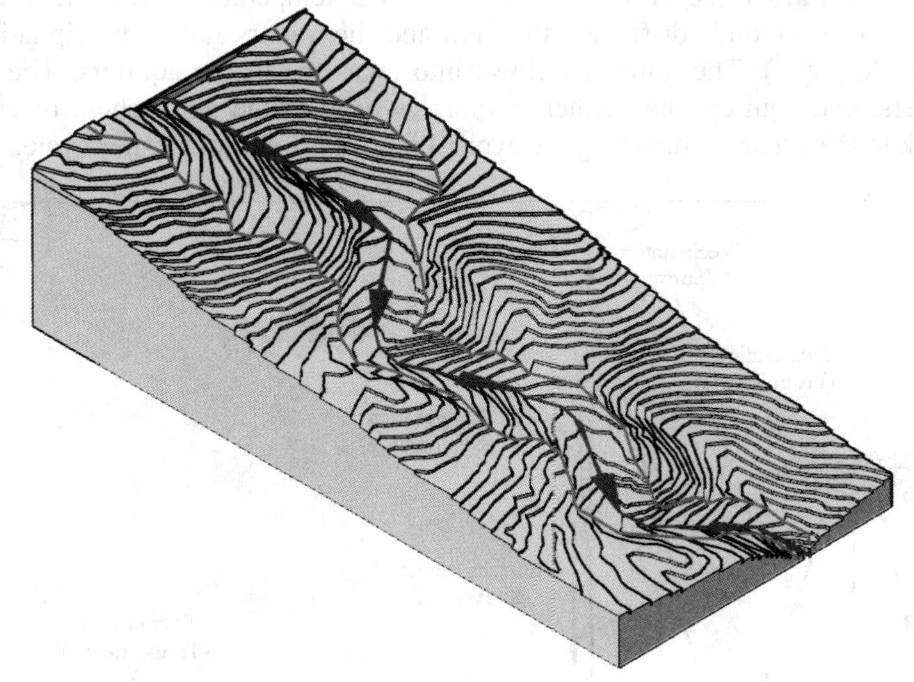

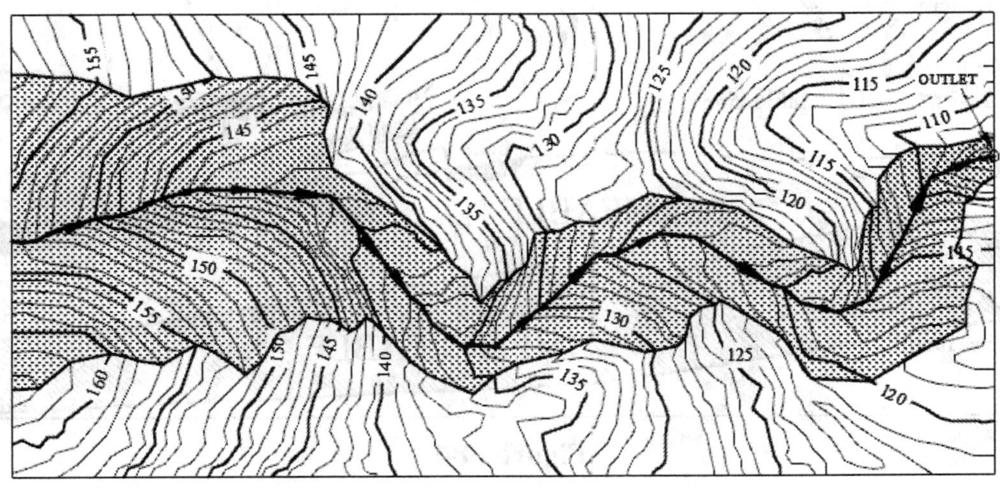

11.2.   Introduction

Hydrology is a Greek word, and it means the study of water. In the engineering community, hydrology is the scientific study of the movement, distribution, and quality of water throughout the earth. Hydrology addresses both the hydrologic cycle and water resources.

11.3.   Hydrologic cycle

The hydrologic cycle, also known as the water cycle, is the continuous movement of the water above, on, and below the surface of earth. Hence, there is no beginning or ending of this cycle. In the various stages of this cycle, water is available in one of the three different possible states: liquid, vapor, and ice. The most simplified representation of the hydrologic cycle is as follows. The major driving force of the hydrologic cycle is the sun. It heats the water in the oceans, lakes, rivers, streams, etc. and causes some of it to evaporate. The vapors rise into the air where cooler temperatures cause it to condense into clouds. These clouds drift over the land and the vapors fall as precipitation (rain, hail, snow, fog, etc.). The rainwater flows into lakes, rivers, or aquifers. The water in lakes, rivers, and aquifers then either evaporates back to the atmosphere or eventually flows back to the ocean, completing the cycle. Figure 11-1 shows a water cycle.

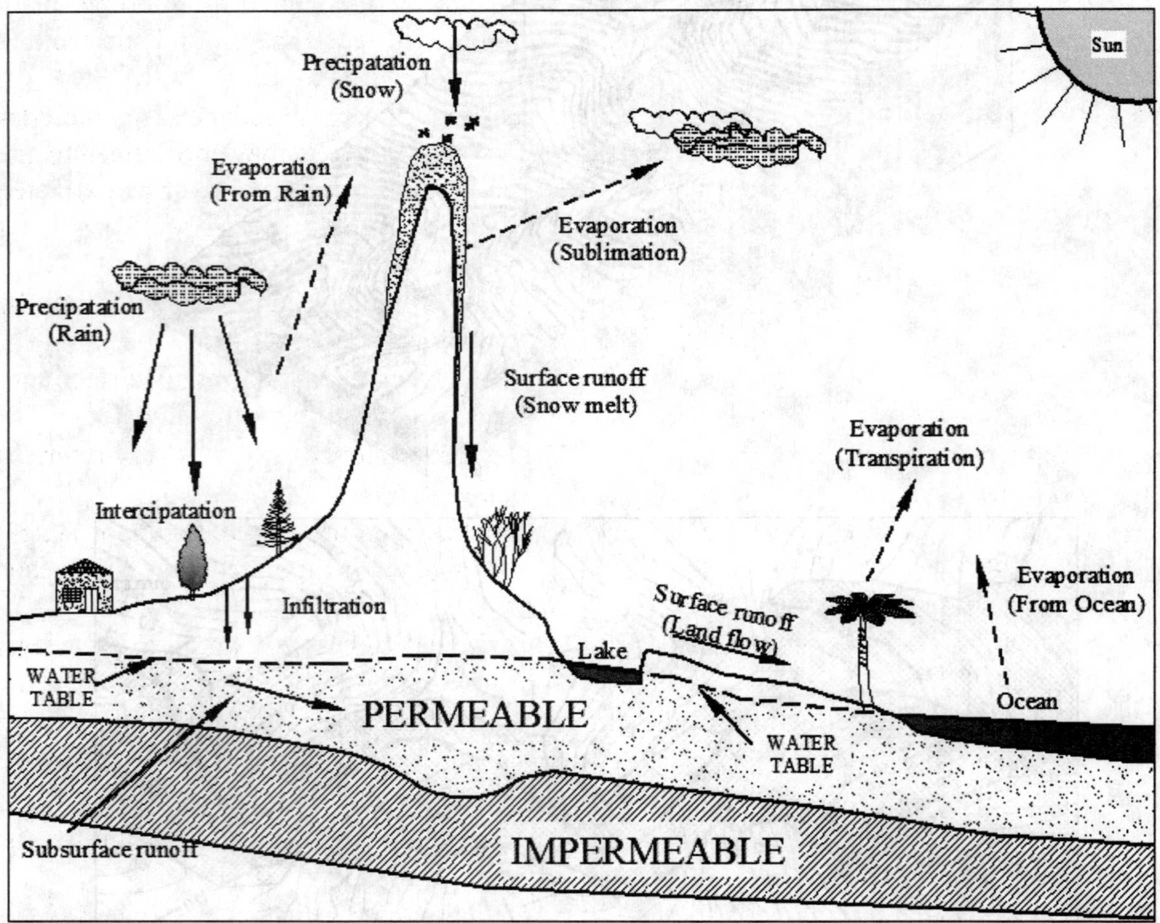

Figure 11-1

The hydrological cycle can be affected by the environmental effect and by humans. The following list shows some of the human factors affecting the water cycle.

- Agriculture
- Alteration of the chemical composition of the atmosphere
- Construction of dams
- Deforestation and afforestation
- Removal of groundwater from wells
- Water abstraction from rivers
- Urbanization

11.4.   Terminology

Refer to the Figure 11-1 for the terms discussed in this section.

- Condensation: Condensation is the transformation of water vapor to liquid water. For example, the droplets in the air that produce clouds and fog.
- Precipitation: Precipitation is the process of condense water vapor falling to the earth's surface. Generally, precipitation occurs as rain. It also occurs as snow, sleet, hail, and fog drip.
- Interception: Interception is the precipitation that is intercepted by building, plant foliage, etc. Part of the intercepted precipitation will reach the ground surface and the remaining part will evaporate back to the atmosphere.
- Runoff: Runoff is the method by which water moves across the land. This includes both surface runoff and channel runoff. As water flows, it may infiltrate into the ground, evaporate into the air, become stored in lakes or reservoirs, or be extracted for agricultural or other human uses.
- Snowmelt: Snowmelt is the runoff produced by the melting snow.
- Groundwater: Groundwater is the water found below the ground surface. It may be available as soil moisture, liquid form, or frozen form.
- Infiltration: Infiltration is the percolation of the water from the ground surface into the ground. Once infiltrated, the water becomes soil moisture or groundwater.
- Subsurface flow: Subsurface flow is the underground flow of water. It may return to the surface as a spring or by the extraction using pumps.
- Advection: Advection is the movement of water (in solid, liquid, or vapor states) through the atmosphere. Without advection, water that evaporated over the oceans could not precipitate over the land.
- Evaporation: Evaporation is the transformation of water from a liquid to a gaseous state.
- Sublimation: Sublimation is the transformation of water from a solid (ice) to gaseous (vapor) state.
- Transpiration: Transpiration is the evaporation of water from the plants.
- Evapotranspiration: Evaporation and transpiration are collectively known as evapotranspiration.
- Water table: Water table is the underground water level at which the ground water pressure is equal to the atmospheric pressure.

11.5.   Watershed or Drainage basin

A watershed is the area of land that drains into a stream at a given location; that is, it is an area of land bounded by a hydrologic system. Generally, a watershed is defined in terms of a point or outlet and all the land area that sheds (pours) water to the outlet during a rainstorm. Using the concept that "water runs downhill," a watershed is defined by all points enclosed within an area from which the rain falling at these points will contribute water to the outlet. Figure 11-2 represents the delineation of a watershed boundary. Watersheds come in all shapes and sizes and cross state and national boundaries. For example, the Mississippi river drainage basin covers more than 30 states and two Canadian provinces.

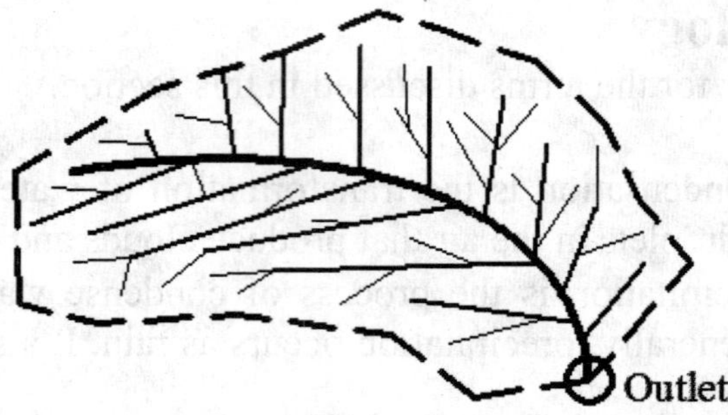

Figure 11-2

A drainage basin is a region of land where the precipitation's water flows downhill into a river, lake, dam, or ocean. The drainage basin includes both the channels and the land from which water drains into those channels. Each drainage basin is separated topographically from adjacent basins by a ridge, hill, or mountain, which is known as a water divide. In Figure 11-2, the dashed line is the main water divide of the hydrographic basin. In North America, watershed refers to the drainage basin itself. The terms catchments, catchment area, catchment basin, drainage area, river basin, and water basin are also used to represent the same concept.

The majority of water that discharges from the basin outlet originated as the precipitation falling on the basin. In hydrology, the drainage basin is a logical unit of focus for studying the movement of water within the hydrological cycle. A portion of the water that enters the groundwater system beneath the drainage basin may flow towards the outlet of another drainage basin because groundwater flow directions do not always match those of their overlying drainage network. Measurement of the discharge of water from a basin may be made by a stream gauge located at the basin's outlet.

11.6.   Watershed characteristics

11.6.1. Drainage area

The drainage area (A) is probably the single most important watershed characteristic for a hydrologic design. It reflects the volume of water that can be generated from rainfall. The drainage area is used to indicate the potential for rainfall to provide a volume of water. It is common in hydrologic design to assume a constant depth of rainfall occurring over the watershed. Under this assumption, the volume of the water available for the runoff would be the product of rainfall depth and the drainage area. Thus the drainage area is required as input to models ranging from simple linear prediction equations to complex computer models.

11.6.2. Watershed length

The length (L) of a watershed is the second greatest characteristic of interest. While the length increases as the drainage increases, the length of a watershed is important in hydrologic computations. Watershed length is usually defined as the distance measured along the main channel from the watershed outlet to the basin divide. Since the channel does not extend to the basin divide, it is necessary to extend a line from the end of the channel to the basin divide following a path where the greatest volume of water would travel. The straight-line distance from the outlet point on the watershed divide is not usually used to compute L because the travel distance of floodwaters is conceptually the length of interest. Thus, the length is measured along the principal flow path. Since it will be used for hydrologic calculations, this length is more appropriately labeled the hydrologic length. The length is usually used in computing as a time parameter, which is a measure of the travel time of water through the watershed.

11.6.3. Watershed slope

Flood magnitudes reflect the momentum of the runoff. Slope is an important factor in the momentum. Both watershed and channel slope may be of interest. Watershed slope reflects the rate of change of elevation with respect to distance along the principal flow path. Typically, the principal flow path is delineated, and the watershed slope (S) is computed as the difference in elevation (ΔE) between the end points of the principal flow path divided by the hydrologic length of the flow path (L).

The elevation difference, ΔE, may not necessarily be the maximum elevation difference within the watershed since the point of highest elevation may occur along a side boundary of the watershed rather than at the end of the principal flow path.

11.6.4. Miscellaneous

Some of the other important watershed factors are listed here.
- Land cover and use
- Surface roughness
- Soil characteristics
  - Texture
  - Soil structure
  - Soil moisture
  - Hydrologic soil groups

11.7.   Major steps in a watershed delineation

The major steps in watershed delineation process are listed below.

Step 1: Mark the centerline of the channel by joining the Vs. For a channel, the tip of the V is upstream.

Step 2: Show the direction of flow. A channel flows from a higher elevation (upstream) to the lower elevation (downstream).

Step 3: Delineate the watershed boundary by connecting the ridge lines in the elevation contour lines map. For a ridge, the tip of the V or U is downstream.

Step 4: Choose and label the point of the watershed outlet. The outlet is usually a monitoring location or hydraulic structure.

11.8.   Watershed delineation using AutoCAD

In AutoCAD the watershed delineation can be performed using the following steps.

1. Launch AutoCAD 2014.
2. <u>Contour map</u>
   - Open the contour map previously created or downloaded map.
   - Create the layers as shown in Figure 11-3.
   - Change the color, linetype, and lineweight of the layers.

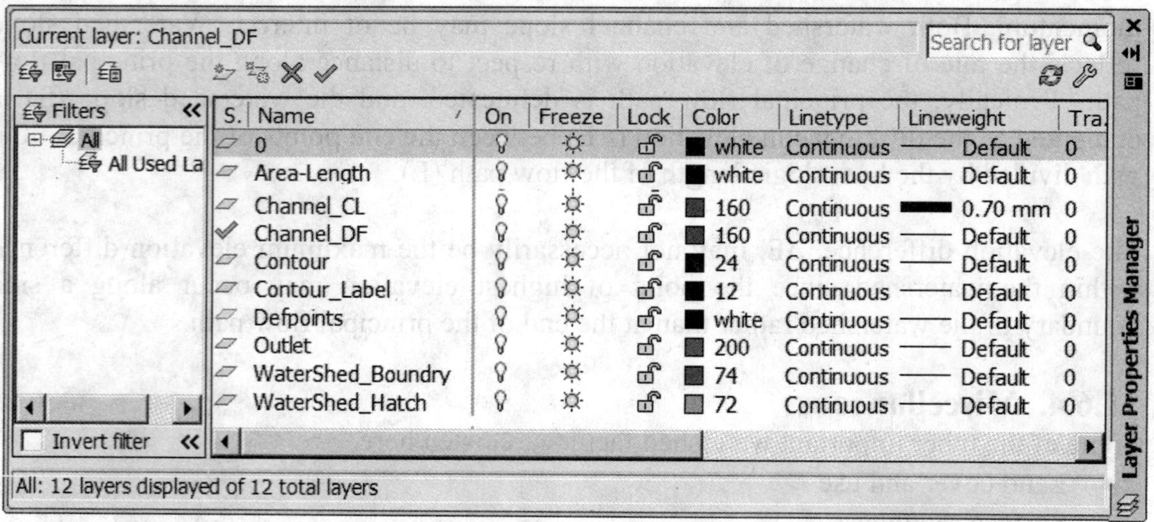

Figure 11-3

3. <u>Counter labels</u>
   - Make the *Contour_Labels* layer to be the current layer.
   - Label the index contour using the *Text*, *Background Mask*, and the *Rotate* commands, Figure 11-4. The text height is 12 feet in the sample watershed.

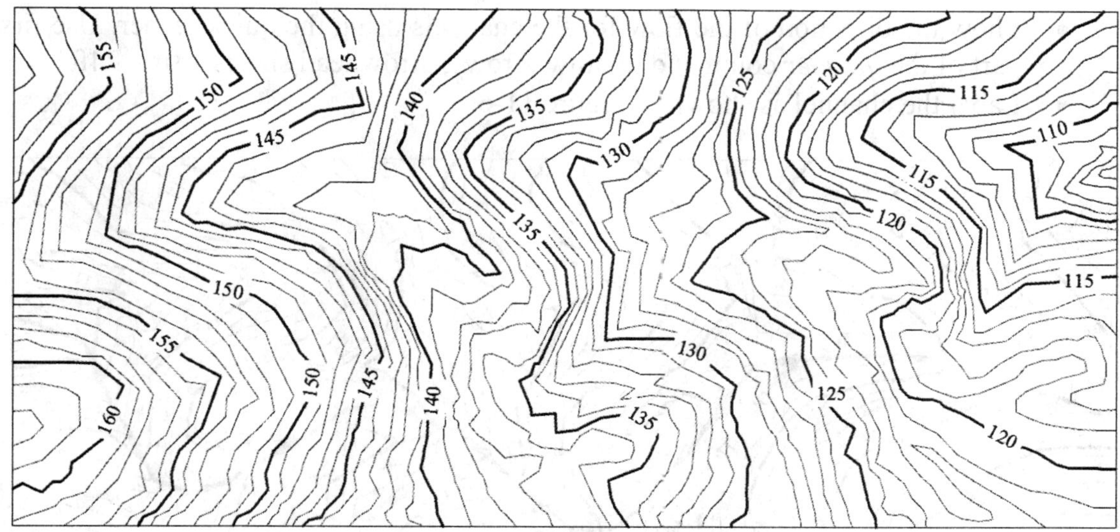

Figure 11-4

4. <u>Center line</u>
   - Make the *Channel_CL* to be the current layer.
   - A channel flows from the higher elevation to the lower elevation. As mention earlier, the contour lines cross the streambed upstream by creating V with the bottom of the V's pointing upstream.
   - Draw the centerlines for the channel, Figure 11-5.
     - o Activate the *Polyline* command.
     - o Draw a polyline through the bottom of Vs as shown in Figure 11-5.

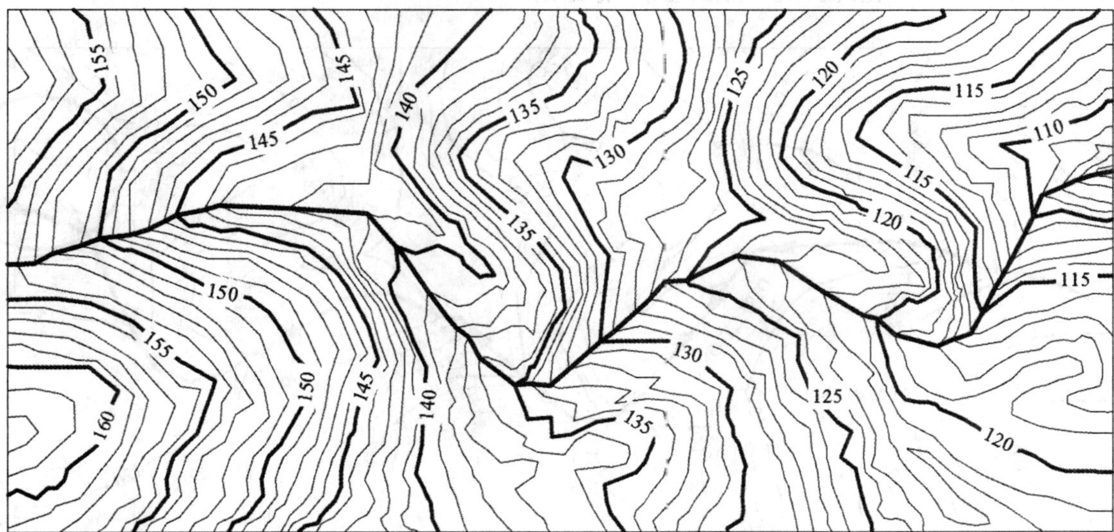

Figure 11-5

5. <u>Direction of the flow</u>
   - Make the *Channel_DF* to be the current layer.

- Show the direction of the flow for the channels using the quick leader. Use first part of the *qleader* command to draw arrows; arrowhead size is 18ft – 24ft.
- Label the channel as shown in Figure 11-6.

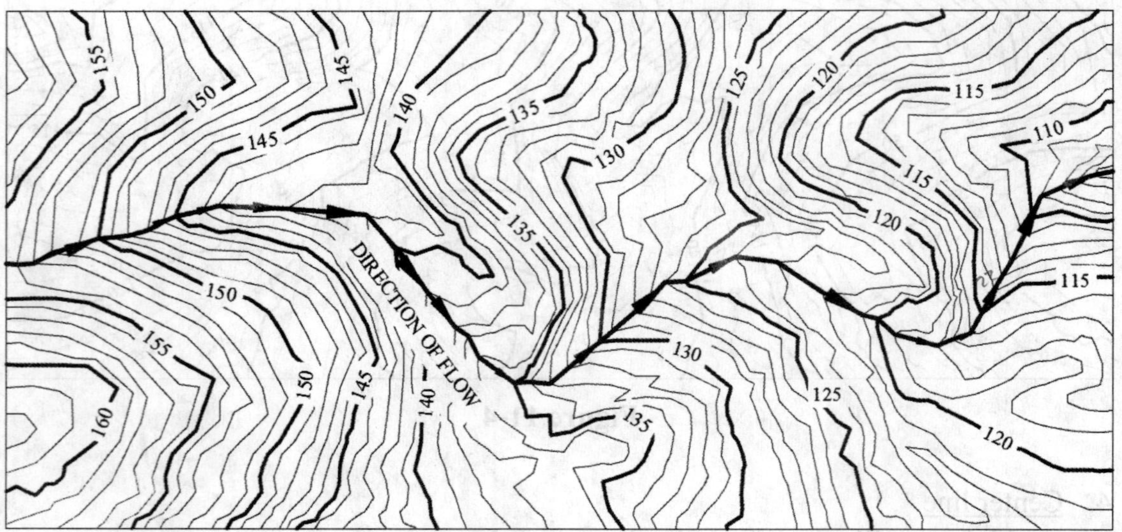

Figure 11-6

6. <u>Outlet point</u>
   - Make the *Outlet* layer to be the current layer.
   - In Figure 11-7, Outlet, the intersection of the channel and the edge of the contour map is selected as the outlet point for the watershed.
   - Draw a point at the outlet and label it.

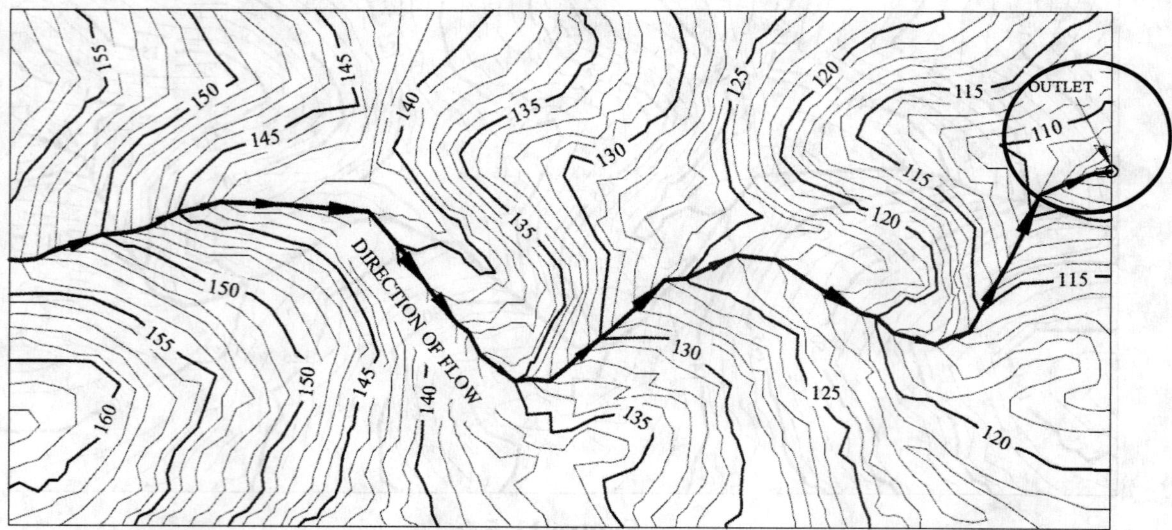

Figure 11-7

7. <u>Delineate the watershed</u>
   - Make the *Watershed_Boundary* layer to be the current layer.

- The contour lines cross the ridge downstream by creating V's or U's pointing downstream.
- Draw the boundary lines for the channel.
  - Activate the *Polyline* command.
  - Draw a polyline through the bottom of Us as shown in Figure 11-8.

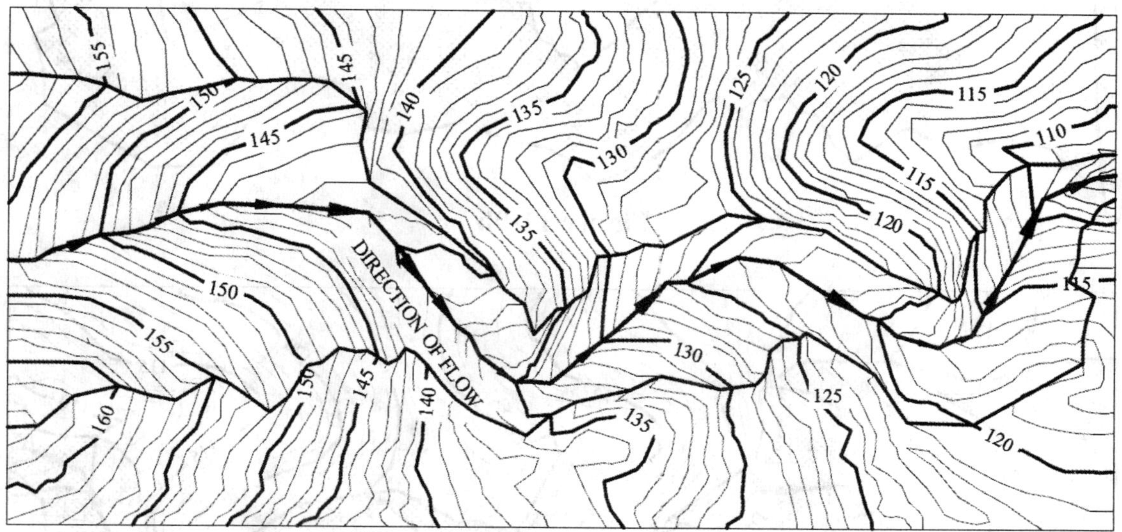

Figure 11-8

8. <u>Hatch the watershed</u>
   - Make the *Watershed_Hatch* layer to be the current layer.
     - Turnoff all the layers except the *Watershed_Boundary* and *Watershed_Hatch* layers, Figure 11-9a.

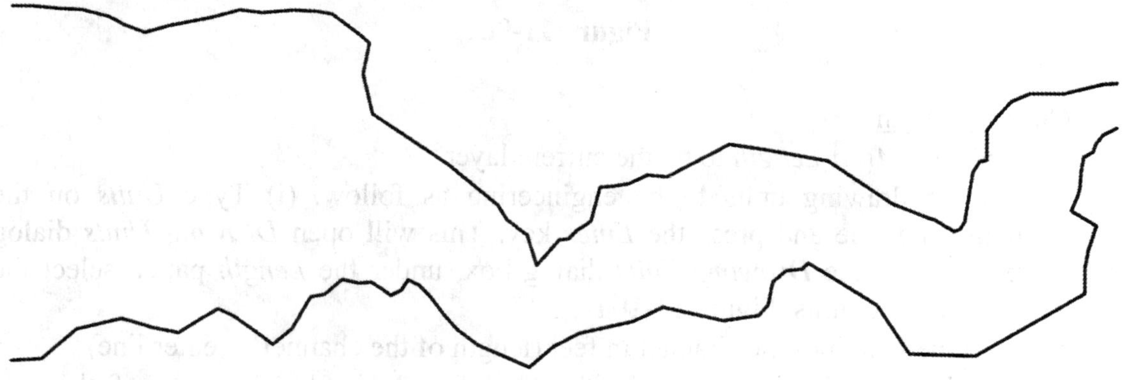

Figure 11-9a

   - Draw polylines to close the open ends of the water shed boundary.
   - Join the polylines (using polyline edit command) to form a single close polyline.
   - Activate the *Hatch* command.
   - Hatch the watershed, using the pattern *GRASS* and the scale of 70, Figure 11-9b and Figure 11-9c.

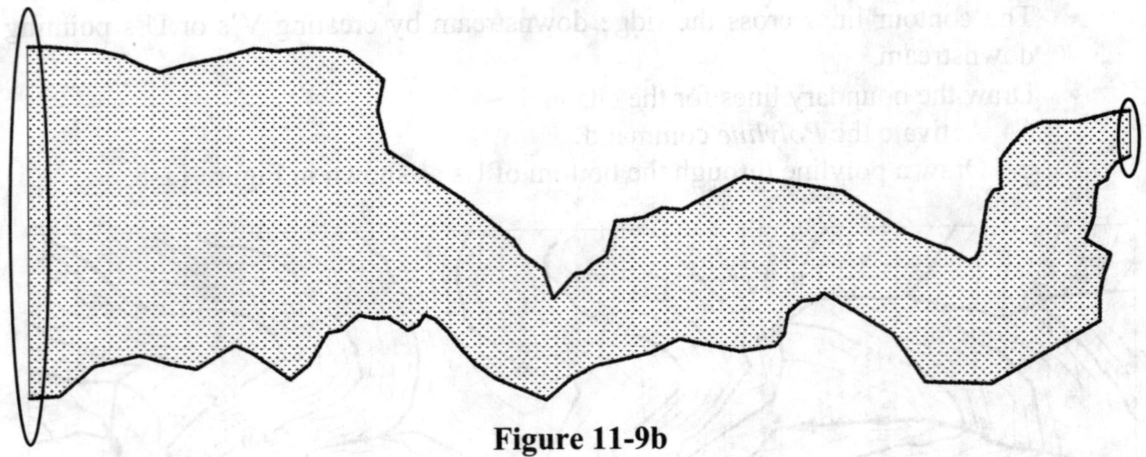

Figure 11-9b

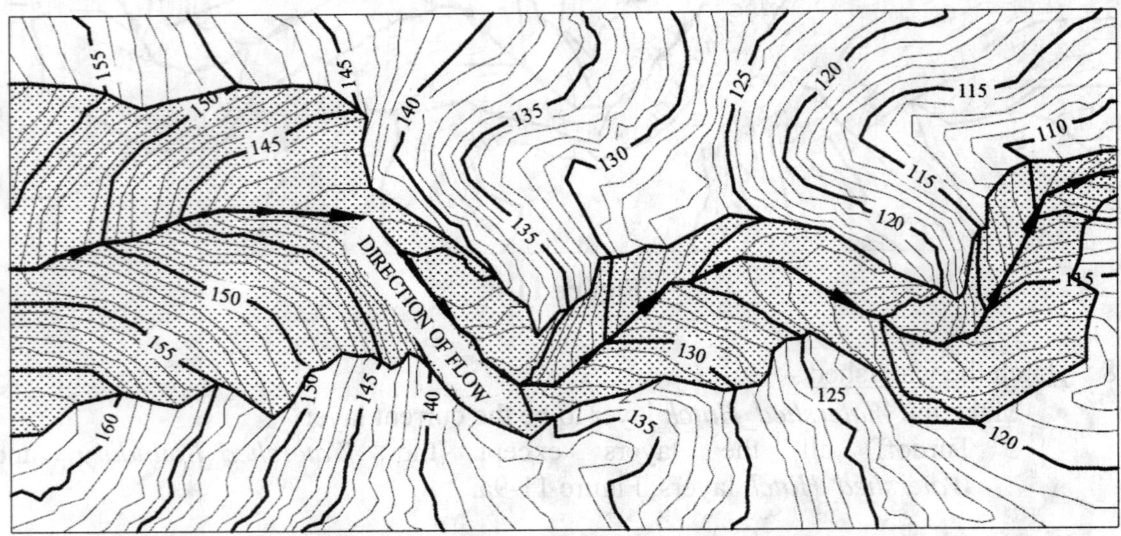

Figure 11-9c

9. <u>Channel length</u>
    - Make the *Area-Length* to be the current layer.
    - Set the drawing units to be engineering as follow. (i) Type *Units* on the command line and press the *Enter* key. This will open *Drawing Units* dialog box. (ii) In the *Drawing Units* dialog box, under the *Length* panel, select the *Engineering* units, Figure 11-10a.
    - Find the length of the channel in feet (length of the channel's center line).
    - The length of the channel in feet can be obtained using one of the two techniques.
        (a) Using the *Property* sheet
            o The easiest and the fastest method is the property sheet.
            o Select the centerline of the channel and open its property sheet, Figure 11-10b
            o The last entry in the *Geometry* panel is the length of the channel.
        (b) Using the *Distance* command
            o Lengthy method!

- o From the *Home* tab and *Utilities* panel, expand the *Measure* drop down menu and select the *Distance* (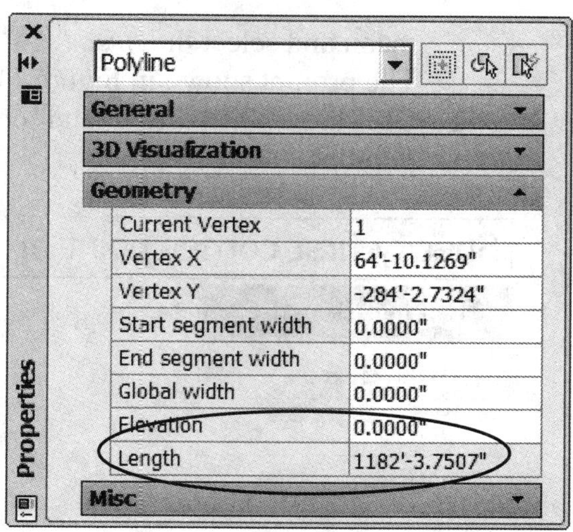) tool.
- o Follow the prompts.

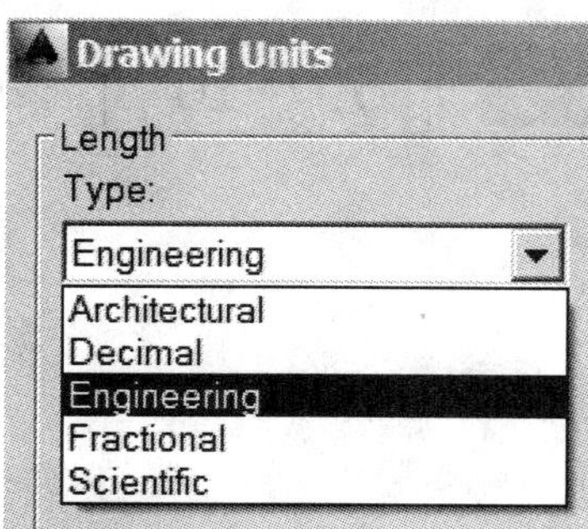

Figure 11-10a

Figure 11-10b

10. <u>Watershed area</u>
- Make the *Area-Length* to be the current layer.
- Find the area of the watershed in acres.
- The area of the watershed can be obtained using one of the two techniques.
- (a) Using the *Property* sheet
  - o Select the boundary of the watershed, connect and closed the polyline.
  - o Open its property sheet, Figure 11-11a.
  - o The second last entry in the *Geometry* panel is the area of the watershed.
  - o The area is in square feet.

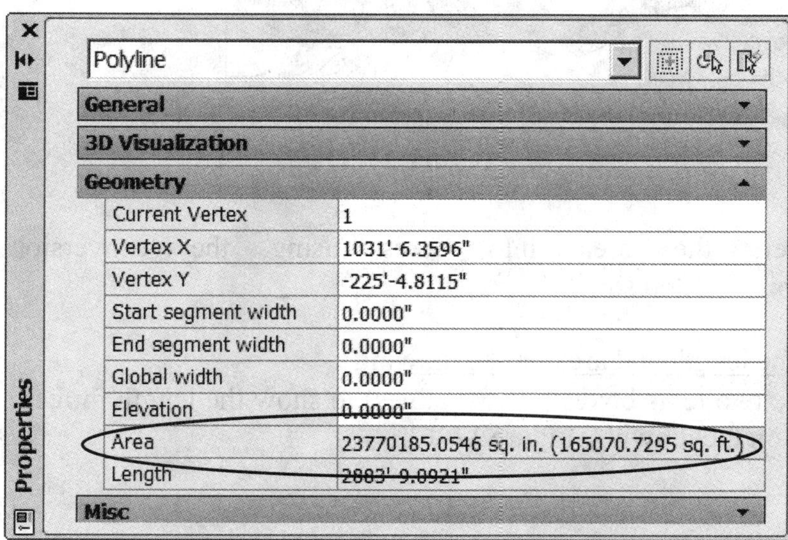

Figure 11-11a

(c) Using the *Distance* command
  o Lengthy method!
  o From the *Home* tab and *Utilities* panel, expand the *Measure* drop down
    menu and select the *Area* (⬜) tool.
  o The prompt shown in Figure 11-11b will appear.
  o Use the down arrow and choose the *Object* option for the closed
    polyline.

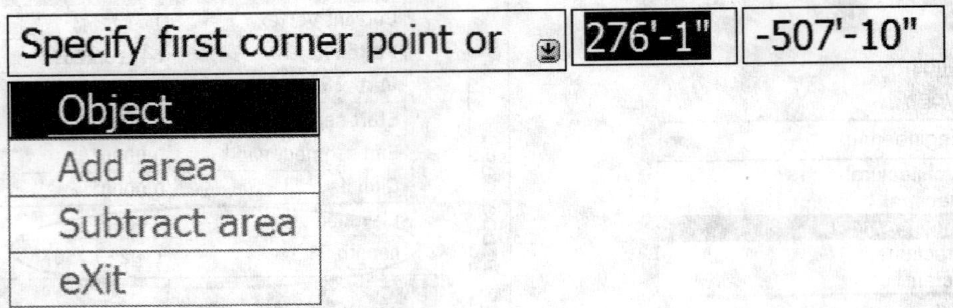

Figure 11-11b

  o Click on the watershed boundary (make sure the boundary is represented
    by a single closed polyline).
  o The area information will appear on the screen, Figure 11-11c.
  o Press the *Esc* key to exit the command.

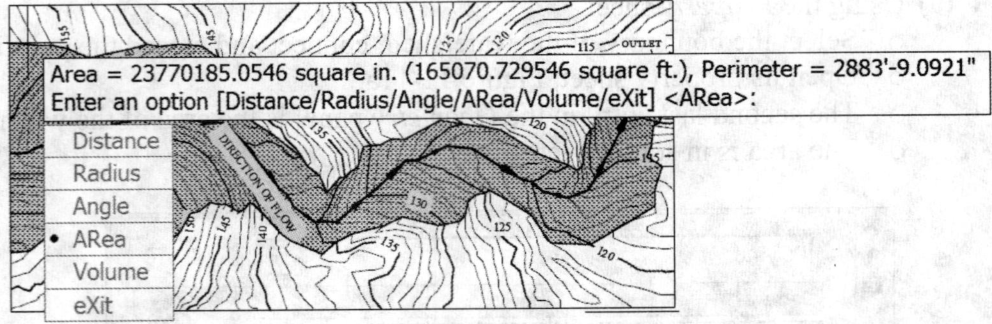

Figure 11-11c

• Convert the area into acres using the conversion factor of
  1 Acres = 43560 sq. ft.

11. <u>Display the length and area on the drawing</u>
  • Create two texts boxes (or two tables) to show the length in feet and the area in
    acres on the drawing, Figure 11-12.

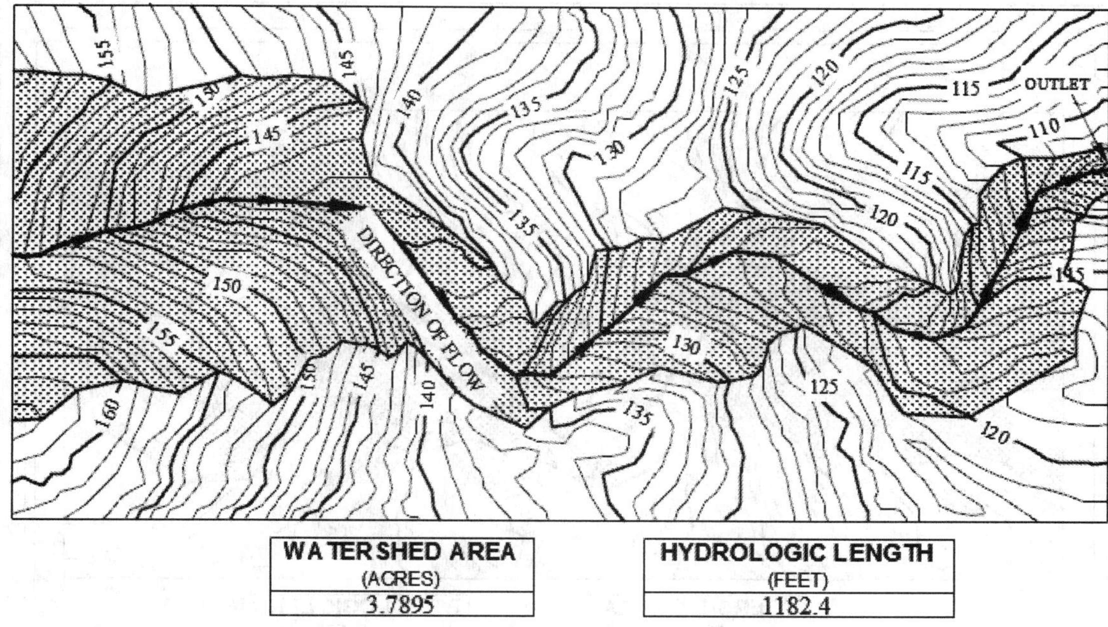

WATERSHED AREA	HYDROLOGIC LENGTH
(ACRES)	(FEET)
3.7895	1182.4

Figure 11-12

12. <u>Insert Template file</u>
   - Finally, insert a layout from the template file labeled as "My_acad_Landscape_tmplt.dwt".
   - Set the viewport scale to 1:1200.
   - Lock the viewport scale.
   - Update the Title block.
   - The resultant drawing in the layout is shown in Figure 11-13.

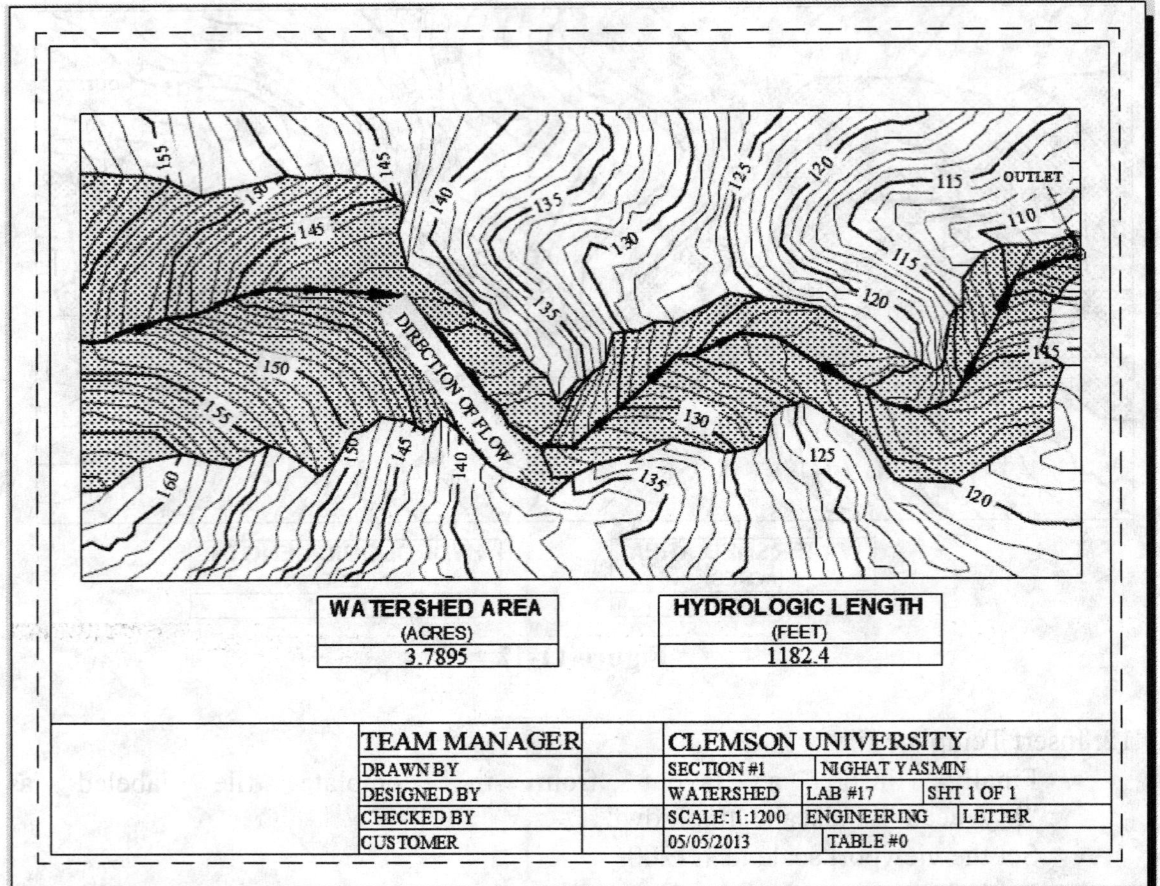

WATERSHED AREA	HYDROLOGIC LENGTH
(ACRES)	(FEET)
3.7895	1182.4

TEAM MANAGER	CLEMSON UNIVERSITY		
DRAWN BY	SECTION #1	NIGHAT YASMIN	
DESIGNED BY	WATERSHED	LAB #17	SHT 1 OF 1
CHECKED BY	SCALE: 1:1200	ENGINEERING	LETTER
CUSTOMER	05/05/2013	TABLE #0	

Figure 11-13

12. Floodplains

12.1. Objectives

- Learn the basics of floodplains
- Learn the basics of hydrographs
- Learn to delineate floodplains of a channel using AutoCAD

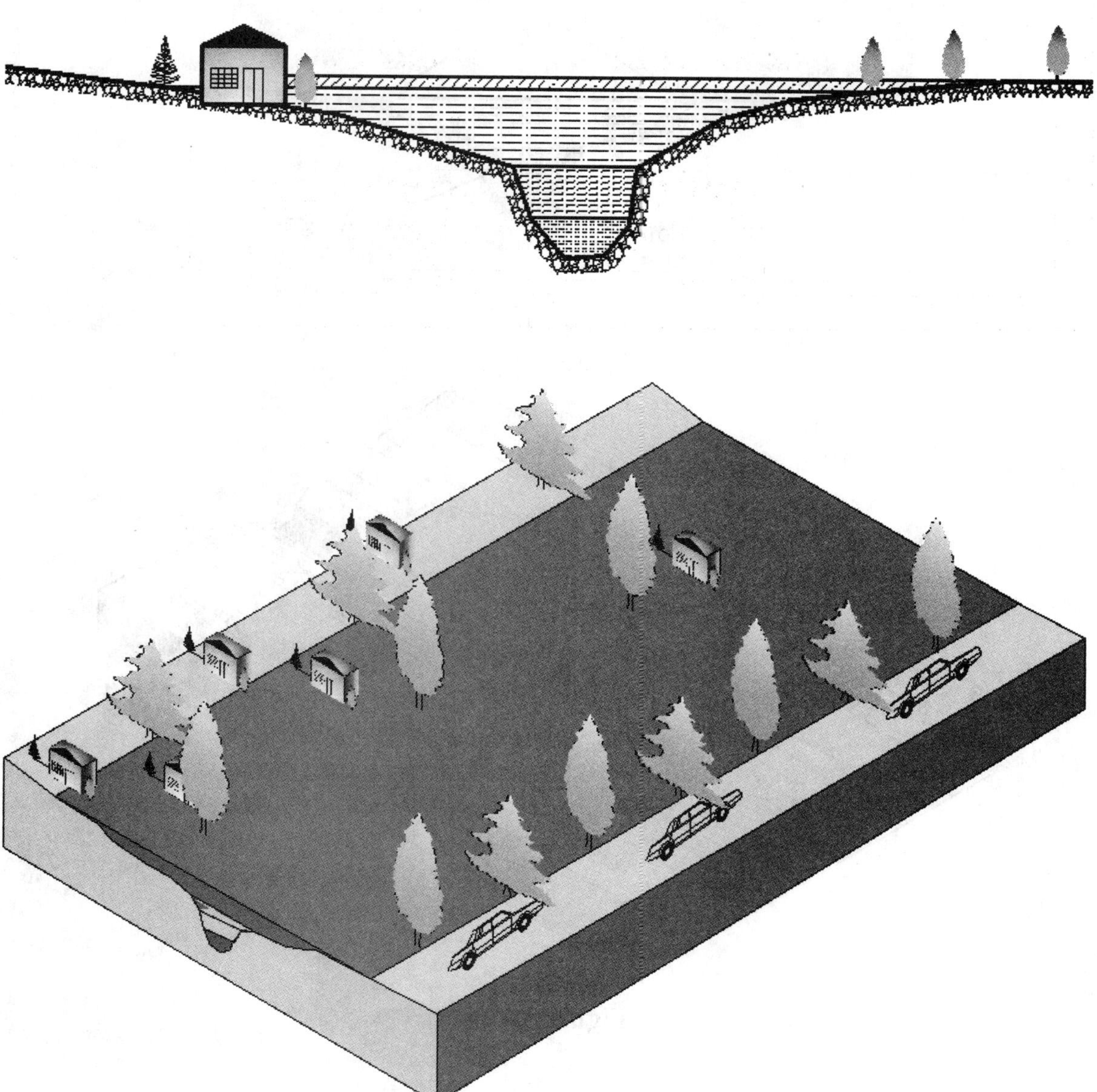

12.2.   Introduction

Generally, a floodplain is the dry and flat (or mild slope) land area adjacent to a river, stream, creek, or lake which is subject to inundation by floodwaters from the source. In order to save life and property on the floodplain, it is important to estimate their extent and geometry. The area of the floodplains can be determined by delineating the boundaries of the floodplain. The focus of this chapter is the floodplain delineation.

12.3.   Terminology

- <u>Open channel flow</u>: An open channel flow is a surface water flow with a free surface, e.g. flow in rivers, streams, or partially filled pipes.
- <u>Main channel</u>: The main channel is referred to as the normal capacity of a channel, Figure 12-1a and Figure 12-1b.

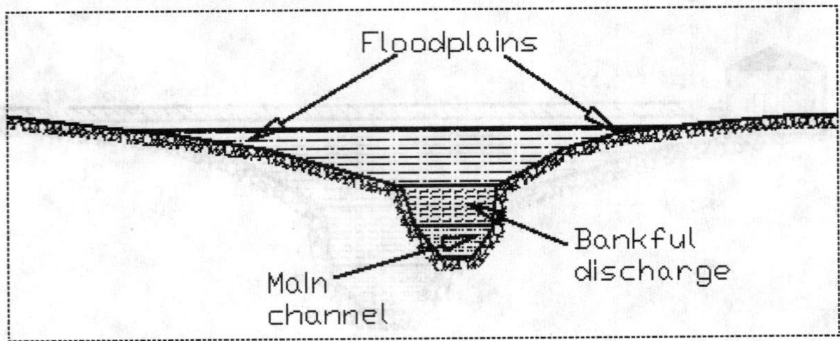

Figure 12-1a

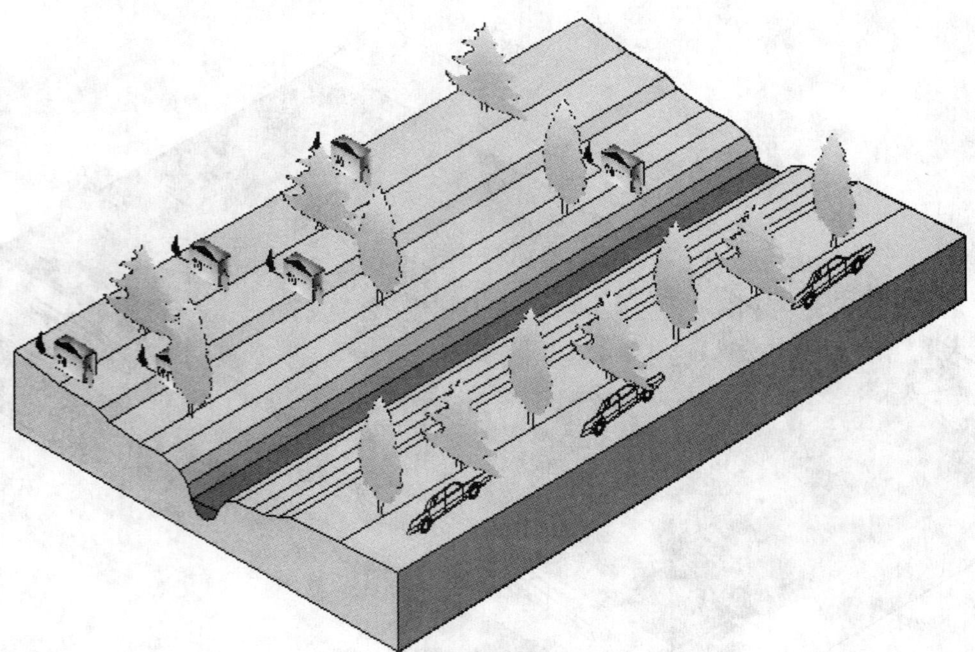

Figure 12-1b

- <u>Bankfull</u>: The bankfull capacity of a channel is referred to as the maximum capacity of a channel without overflowing, Figure 12-1a and Figure 12-1c.

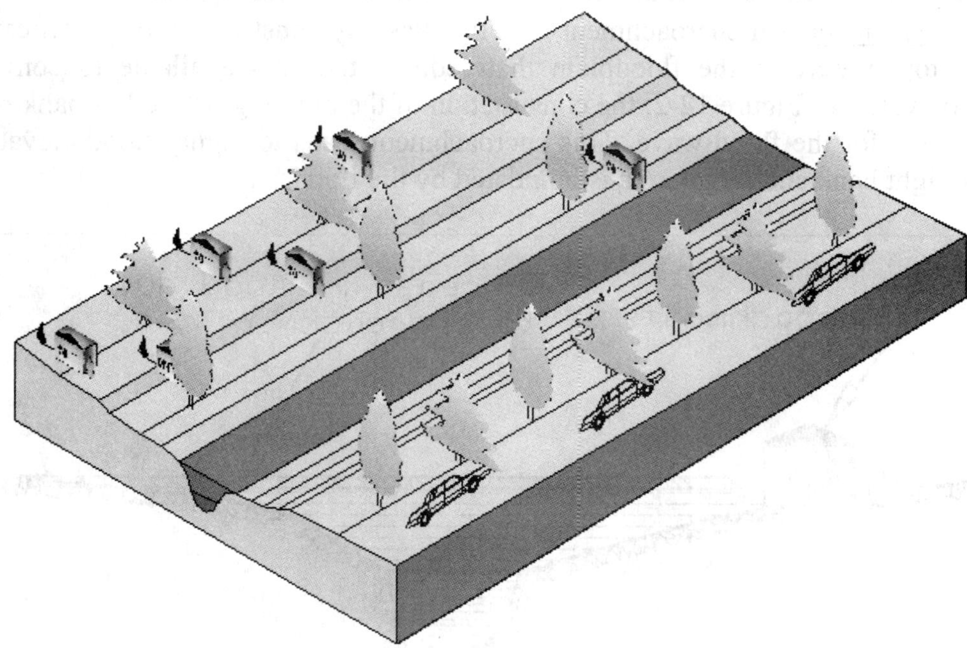

Figure 12-1c

- <u>Floodplain</u>: A floodplain is defined as the dry and flat (or mild slope) land area adjoining a river, stream, creek, or lake which is subject to inundation by floodwaters from the source, Figure 12-1a and Figure 12-1d.

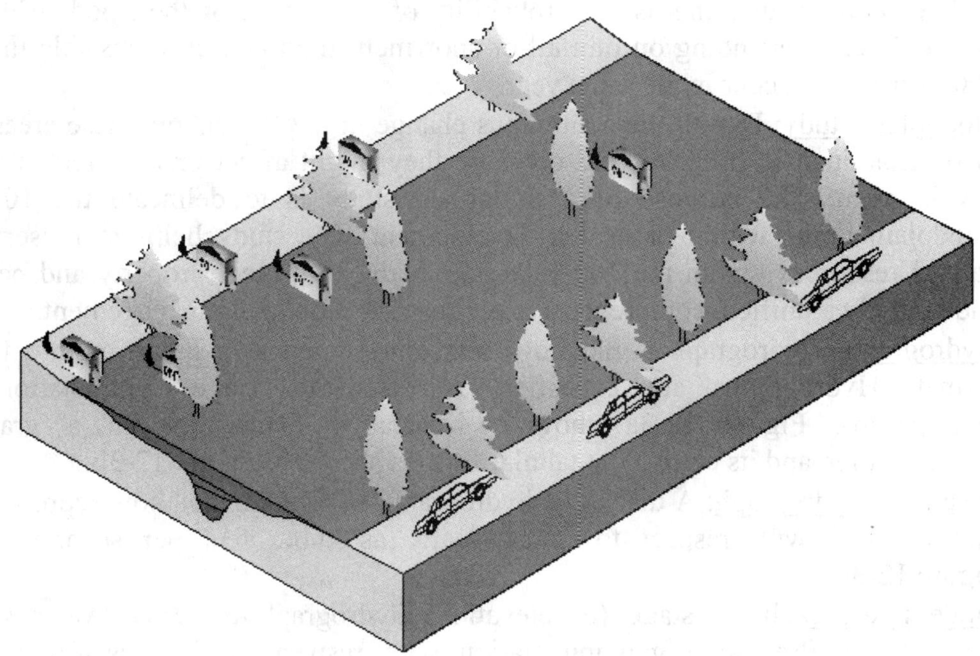

Figure 12-1d

- <u>Flooding/flood</u>: A flood, also known as flooding, is the phenomenon by which water level exceeds the capacity of a stream, river, or a drainage channel. Flooding occurs due to excessive rainfall, snowmelt, or a dam break upstream.
- <u>Encroachment</u>: An encroachment is defined as any construction or modification of the topography in the floodplain that reduces the area available to convey the floodwater. In Figure 12-2, the construction of the building on the left bank reduces the area for the flood wave. This encroachment leads to higher flood elevation on the right bank and larger area is inundated by the flood.

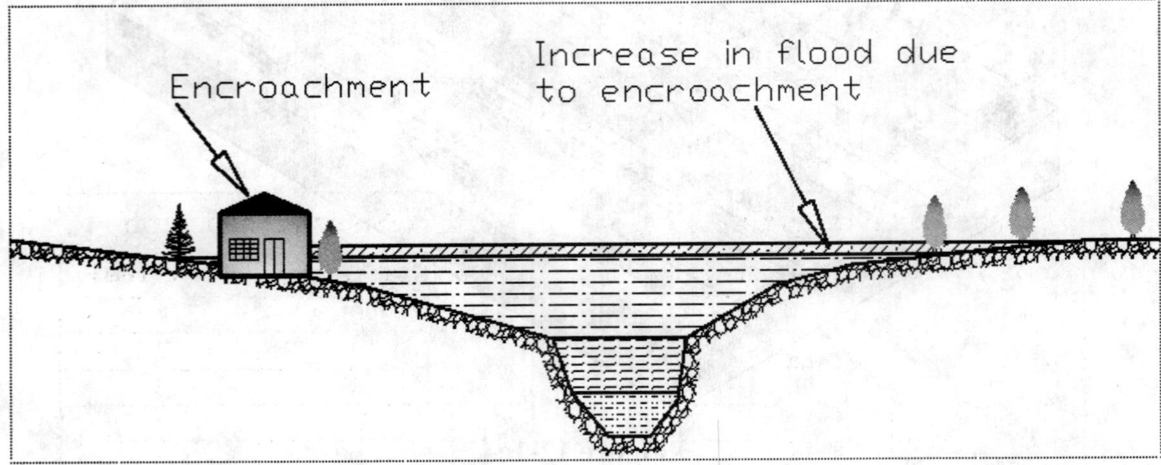

Figure 12-2

- <u>100 year flood</u>: A 100 year flood is defined as the flood water level expected to occur at least once in a 100-year period. More precisely the 100 year flood is known as 1% flood because this is the probability of occurrence of the flood. Although, very unlikely, depending on rainfall or snowmelt in an area it is possible that two 100 year floods occur in the same year.
- <u>Floodplain study</u>: Due to the continuous change in the floodplain, these areas need to be examined in order to find out how they might affect or be affected by the development. The purpose of a floodplain study is to delineate the 100-year floodplain limits within or near a development. The study helps to preserve the natural resources within the 100-year floodplain, to protect property and persons, and to apply a unified, comprehensive approach to floodplain management.
- <u>Hydrograph</u>: Hydrograph is the flow data represented as a graph or in a tabular format. Hydrographs are classified as discharge, stage, and station-stage hydrographs. Figure 12-3a shows a discharge hydrograph in a graphical representation and its equivalent tabular form is shown in Figure 12-3b.
- <u>Discharge hydrograph</u>: A discharge hydrograph, at a gauging station, represents the rate of flow with respect to time usually as cubic feet per second or cfs, Figure 12-3b.
- <u>Stage hydrograph</u>: A stage (or elevation) hydrograph represent water surface elevation of flow at a gauging station with respect to time usually as feet, Figure 12-3c.

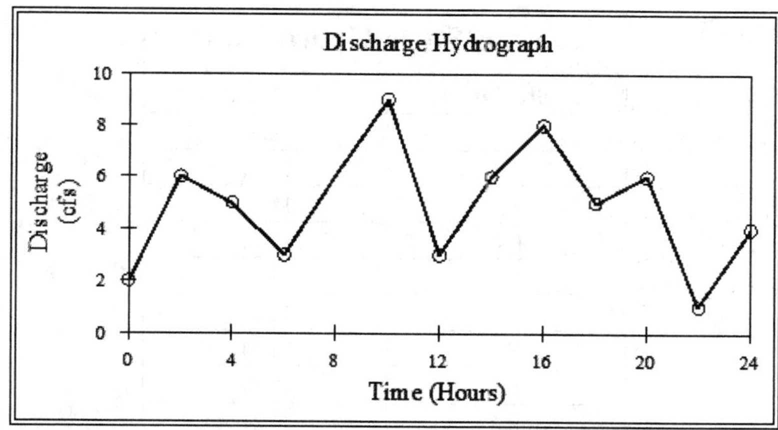

Figure 12-3a

Discharge Hydrograph	
Time (Hour)	Discharge (cfs)
0	2
2	6
4	5
6	3
8	6
10	9
12	3
14	6
16	8
18	5
20	6
22	1
24	4

Figure 12-3b

Stage Hydrograph	
Time (Hour)	Stage (Feet)
0	1
2	2
4	3
6	4
8	5
10	6
12	7
14	6
16	5
18	4
20	3
22	2
24	1

Figure 12-3c

- <u>Station-Stage hydrograph</u>: A station-stage hydrograph represent water surface elevation of flow at a given time for several gauging stations, Figure 12-3d.

12.4.   Major steps in a floodplain delineation

The major steps in watershed delineation process are listed below.

<u>**Step 1**</u>: Mark the centerline of the channel by joining the Vs. For a channel, the tip of the V is upstream.
<u>**Step 2**</u>: Show the direction of flow. A channel flows from a higher elevation (upstream) to the lower elevation (downstream).
<u>**Step 3**</u>: Draw the main channel.
<u>**Step 4**</u>: Draw the bankfull discharge.
<u>**Step 5**</u>: Draw the floodplain's boundary.

Station-Stage Hydrograph	
Station	**Stage (Feet)**
P1	1150
P2	1144
P3	1143
P4	1140
P5	1138
P6	1137
P7	1134
P8	1129
P9	1127
P10	1125
P11	1124
P12	1123
P13	1121

Figure 12-3d

12.5.   Floodplain delineation using AutoCAD

The term delineate is defined as outlining the boundary. The floodplain delineation is the technique to mark the floodplain for the given stage. This section provides step-by-step instruction to delineate a floodplain. The station-stage hydrograph for a 100-year flood shown in Table #1 will be used to delineate the floodplain.

Table #1: Station-Stage Hydrograph

Station	Stage (ft)	Station	Stage (ft)	Station	Stage (ft)
P1	155	P9	140	P17	124
P2	154	P10	139	P18	123
P3	152	P11	137	P19	122
P4	150	P12	136	P20	119
P5	148	P13	134	P21	118
P6	145	P14	130	P22	116
P7	144	P15	127	P23	113
P8	141	P16	125	P24	111

1. Launch AutoCAD 2014.

2. <u>Contour map</u>
    - Open the contour map previously created or downloaded map.
    - Create the layers as shown in Figure 12-4.
    - Change the color, linetype, and lineweight of the layers.

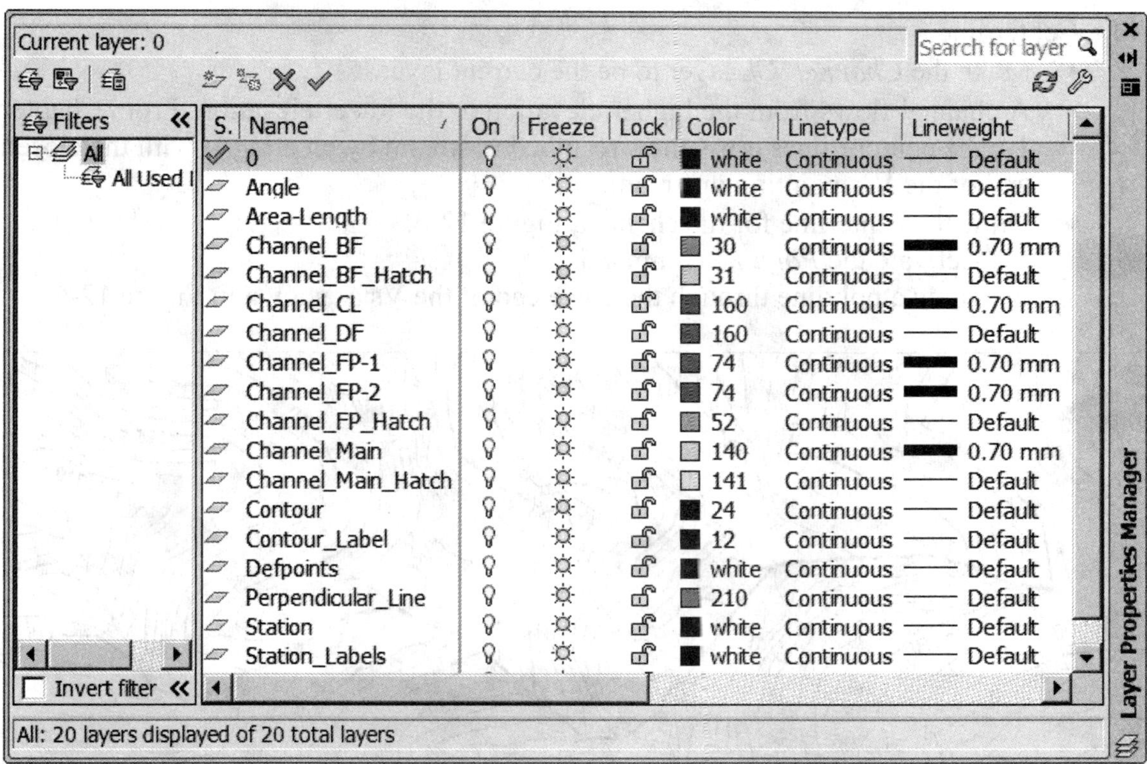

Figure 12-4

3. <u>Counter labels</u>
   - Make the *Contour_Labels* layer to be the current layer.
   - Label the index contour using the *Text*, *Background Mask*, and the *Rotate* commands, Figure 12-5. The text height is 12 feet in the sample contour map.

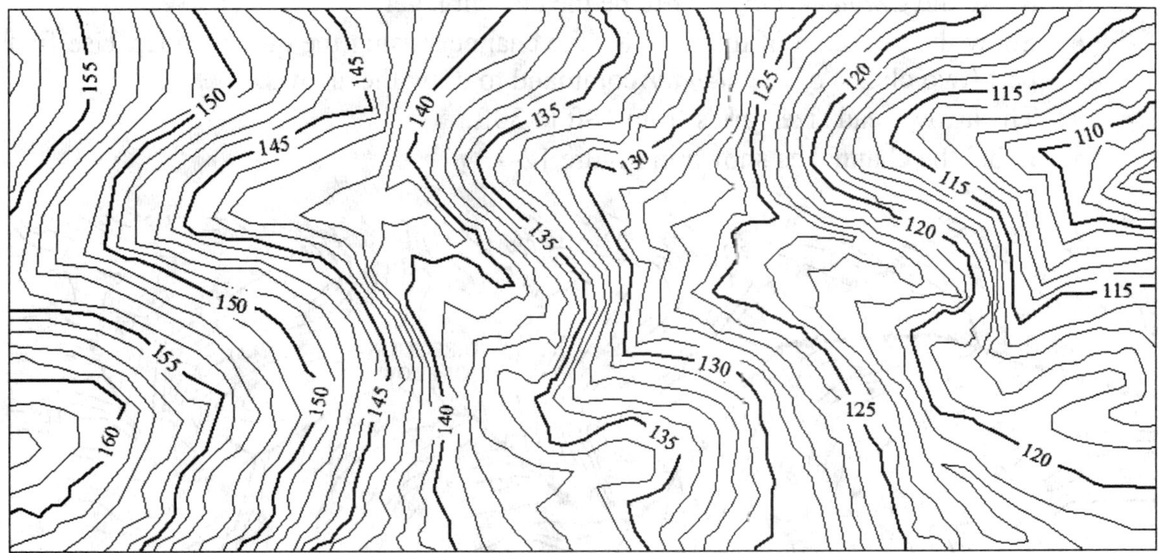

Figure 12-5

4. <u>Center line</u>
   - Make the *Channel_CL* layer to be the current layer.
   - A channel flows from the higher elevation to the lower elevation. From Chapter 10, the contour lines cross the streambed upstream by creating V with the closed end of the V's pointing upstream.
   - Draw the centerline for the channel, Figure 12-6.
     o Activate the *Polyline* command.
     o Draw a polyline through the close end of the Vs as shown in Figure 12-6.

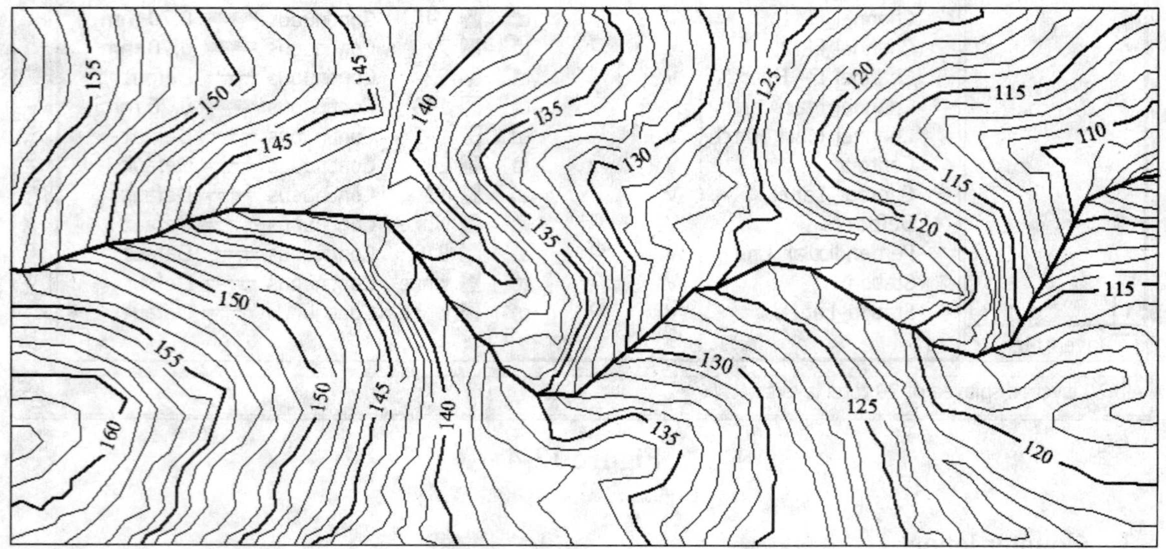

Figure 12-6

5. <u>Direction of the flow</u>
   - Make the *Channel_DF* layer to be the current layer.
   - Show the direction of the flow for the channels using the quick leader. Use first part (two click) of the *qleader* command to draw the arrows.
   - The arrow head size varies from 18ft to 30ft.
   - Label the channel as shown in Figure 12-7.

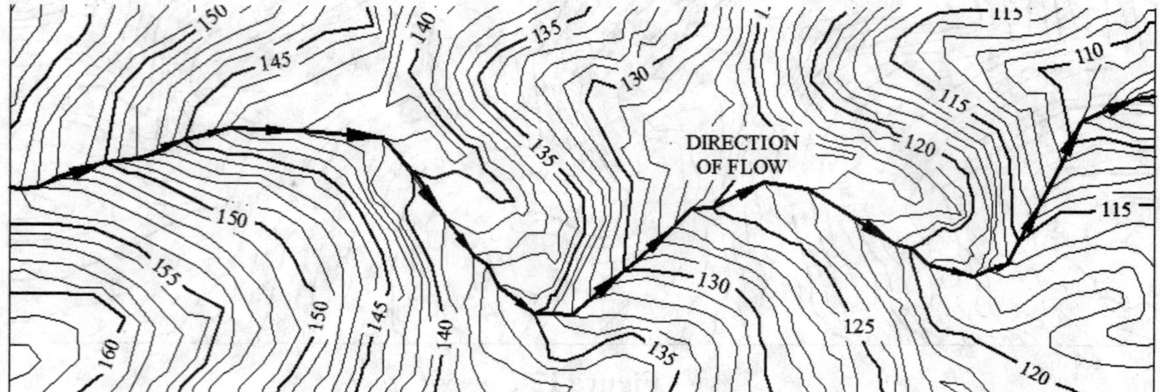

Figure 12-7

6. <u>Main channel</u>
    - Make the *Channel_Main* layer to be the current layer.
    - The main channel is 20', Figure 12-8.
        o Activate the *Offset* command.
        o Set the offset distance to be 10'.
        o Create an offset on the either side of the centerline.
        o Move the offsets to the *Channel_Main* layer.
        o If necessary, use *Trim* and *Extend* commands near the ends of the centerline.

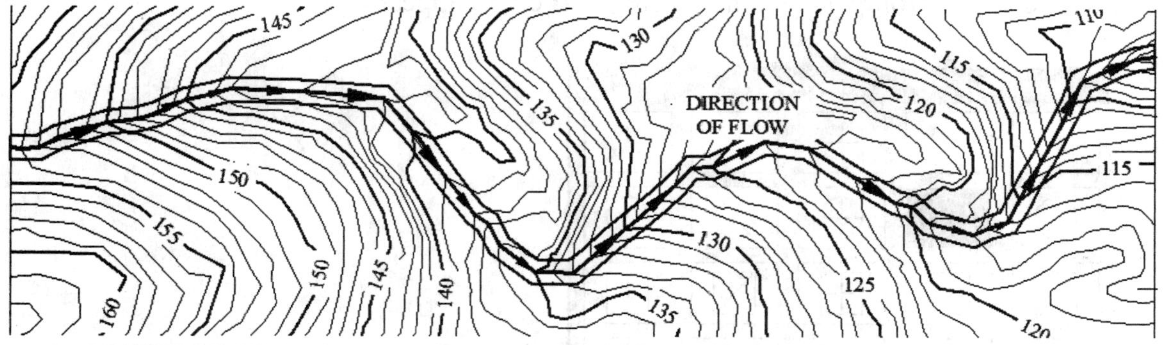

Figure 12-8

7. <u>Bankfull</u>
    - Make the *Channel_BF* layer to be the current layer.
    - The bankfull is 40', Figure 12-9.
        o Activate the *Offset* command.
        o Set the offset distance to be 20'.
        o Create an offset on the either side of the centerline of the main channel.
        o Move the offsets to the *Channel_BF* layer.
        o If necessary, use *Trim* and *Extend* commands near the ends of the centerline.

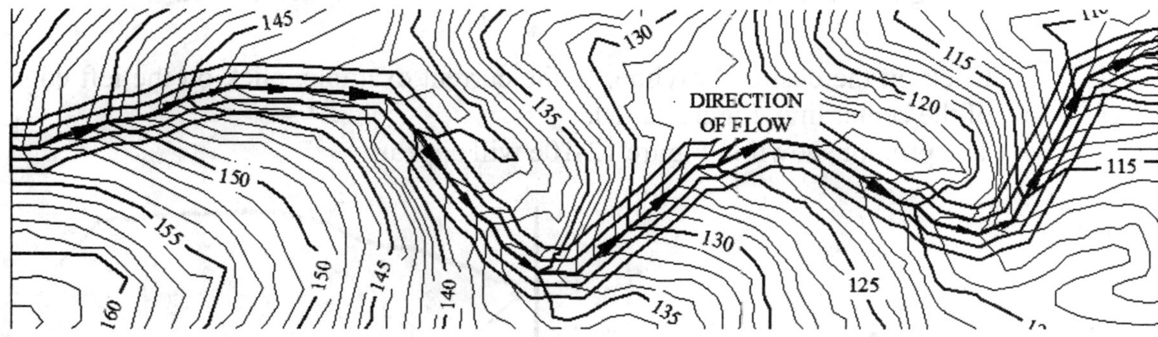

Figure 12-9

8. <u>Gauging station</u>
    - Turn *Off* the *Counter*, *Counter_Label*, *Channel_DF*, *Channel_Main*, and *Channel_BF* layers. Only the *Channel_CL* layer should be *On*.
    - Make the *Station* layer to be the current layer.
    - Add the stations' locations as shown in Figure 12-11.

- From the *Home* tab and the expanded *Utilities* panel, click on the *Point Style…* tool to open the *Point Style* dialog box, Figure 12-10a.
- Change the point style and size. In the figure, the point size is set to be 9'. The *Point Style* dialog box takes input ONLY in inches. So set the size to be 108.
- From the *Home* tab and the expanded *Draw* panel, click on the *Point Measure* ( ) tool, Figure 12-10b, to activate the point command to draw points at a regular interval.
- The prompt shown in Figure 12-10c will appear.

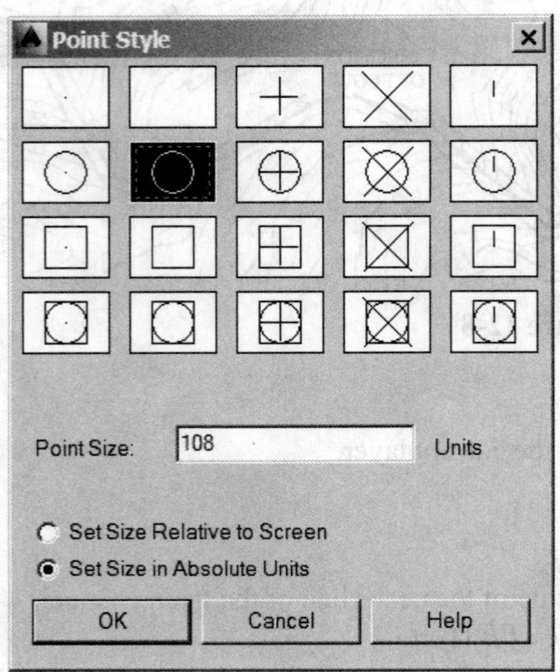

Figure 12-10a

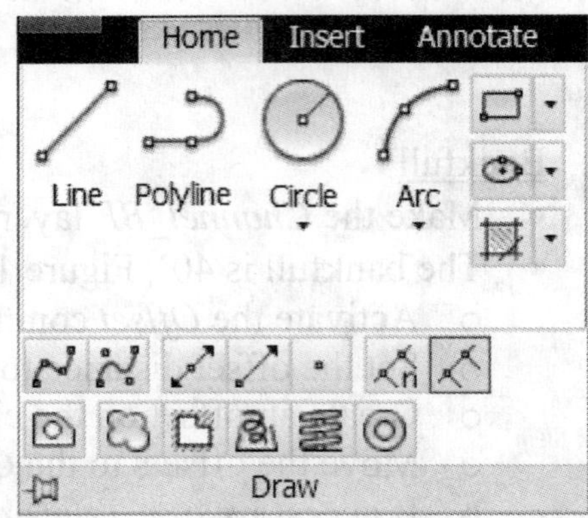

Figure 12-10b

- Click on the desired polyline. In the current example, click on the left edge of the center line, Figure 12-10d.
- The prompt shown in Figure 12-10e will appear.

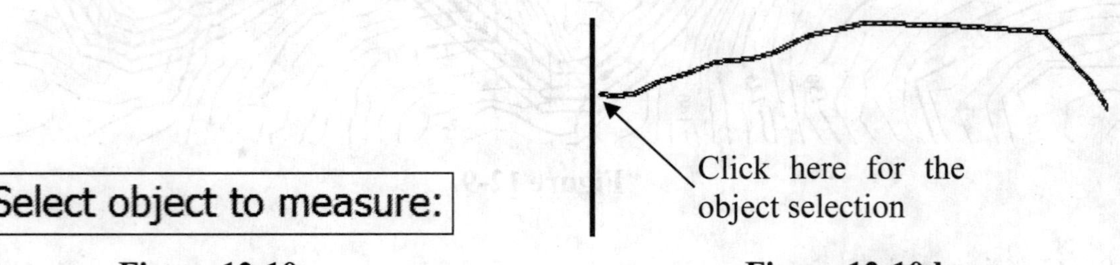

Select object to measure:

Figure 12-10c

Click here for the object selection

Figure 12-10d

Specify length of segment or 50'

Figure 12-10e

- o Specify the distance between the stations (in the current example the distance is 50'), and press the *Enter* key. The software assumes that the distance between the stations is constant, Figure 12-10e.
- o The points will appear on the centerline. The first point is 50' from the beginning of the polyline, Figure 12-10f.
- o Draw a point at the beginning of the center line, Figure 12-10f.
- Make the *Station_Label* layer to be the current layer.
- Label the stations using *Text* and *Background Mask* commands, Figure 12-10g and Figure 12-11.

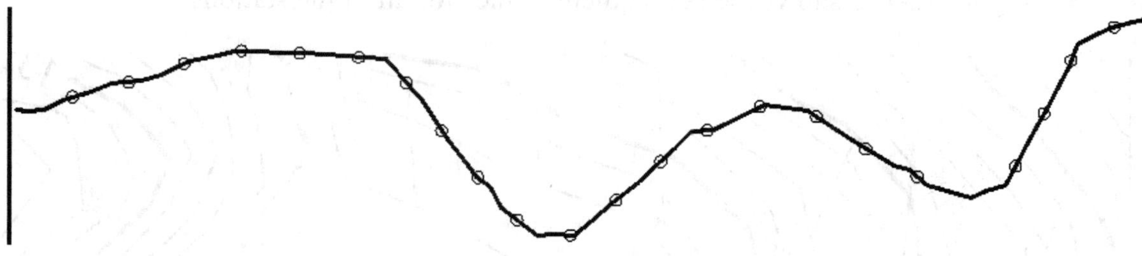

Figure 12-10f

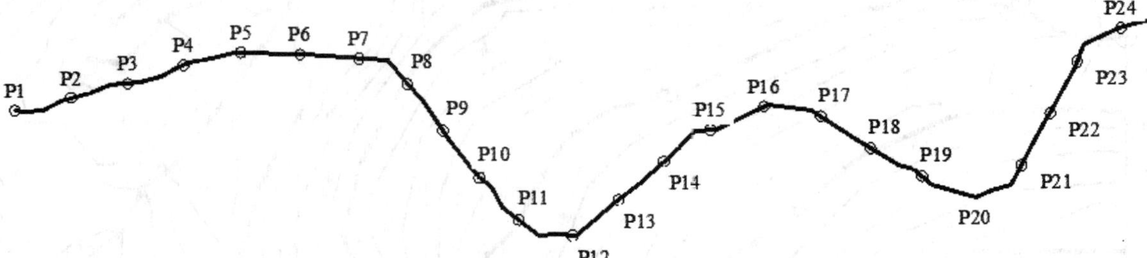

Figure 12-10g

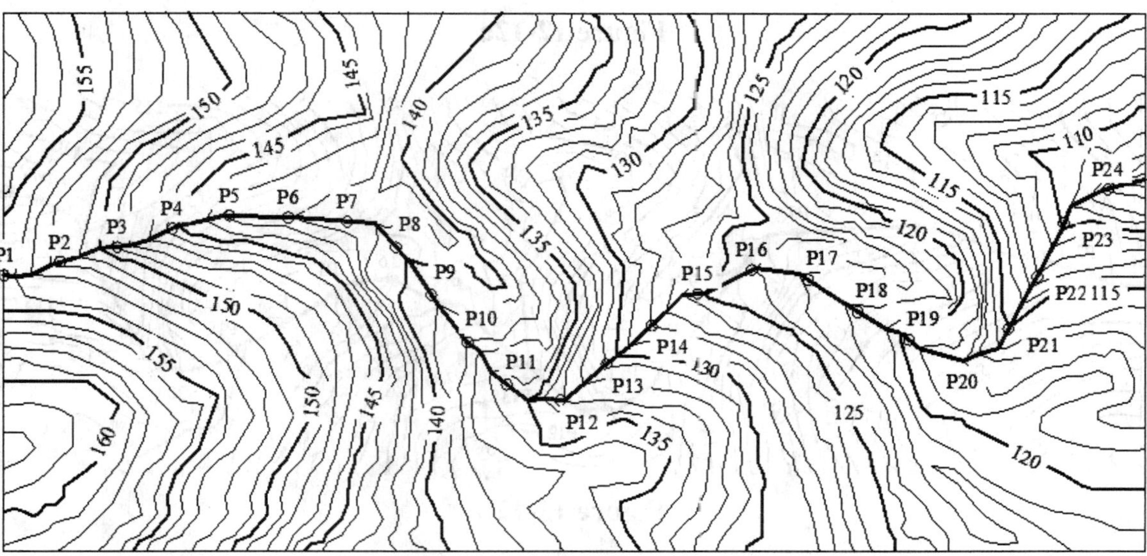

Figure 12-11

9. <u>Perpendicular lines</u>
   - Make the *Perpendicular_Line* layer to be the current layer.
   - Draw a line originating at station P2 and ending at the nearest contour (151').
   - Use the end of the line at P2 be the base point for the rotation. Rotate the line at 90 degrees. The line will be perpendicular to the center line, Figure 12-12a.
   - Refer to the Station-Stage hydrograph shown in Table #1. The stage at P2 is 154. Extend the perpendicular line at P2 to the 154' contour.
   - Repeat the process for the other stations.
   - Figure 12-12a shows the perpendicular lines for the first eleven stations.
   - Figure 12-12b shows the perpendicular lines for all of the stations.

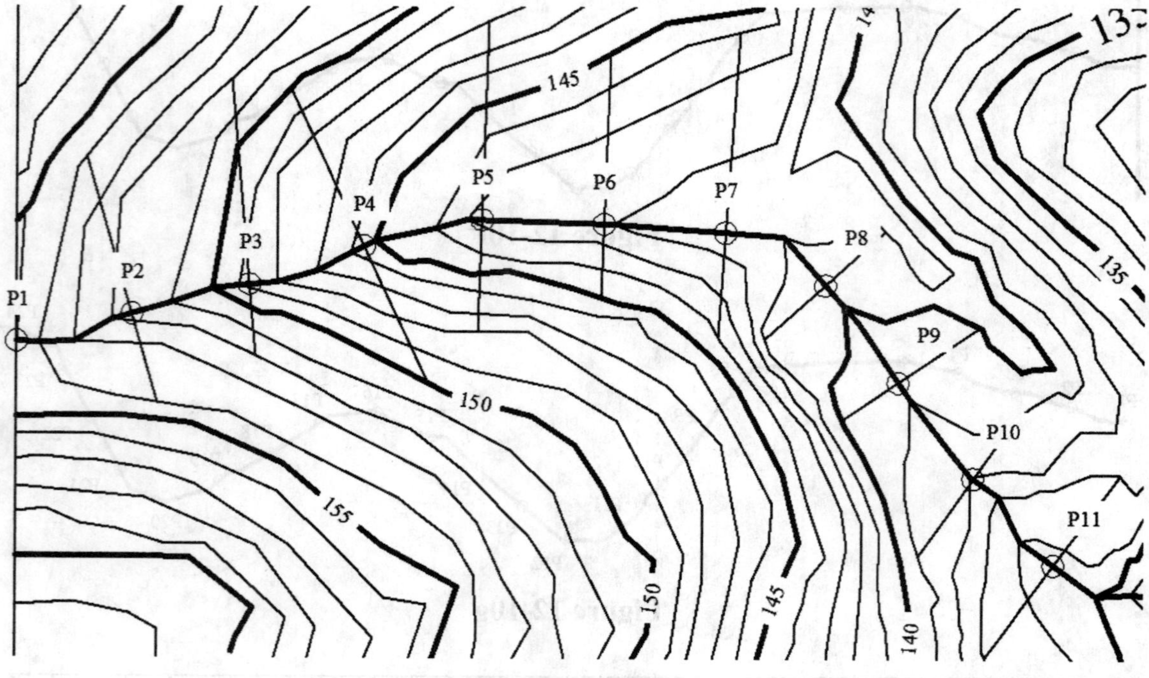

Figure 12-12a

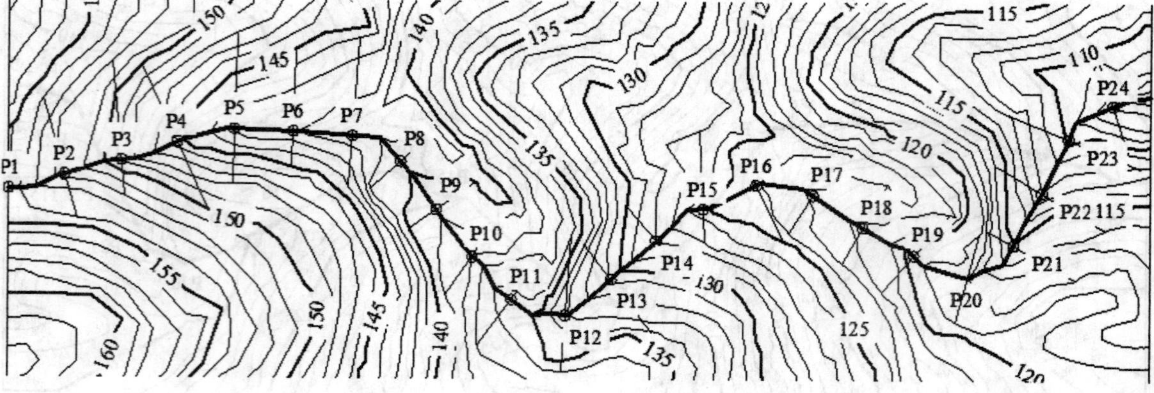

Figure 12-12b

   - Make the *Angle* layer to be the current layer.
   - Add the angle to the perpendicular lines, Figure 12-12c.

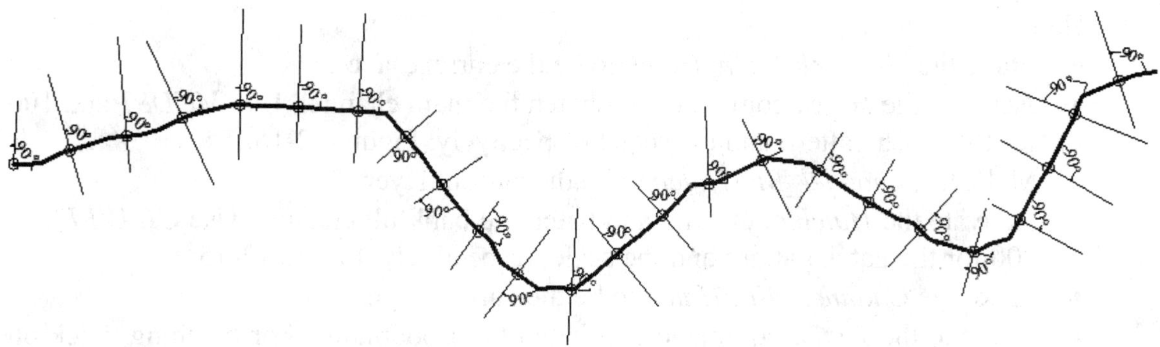

Figure 12-12c

10. <u>Delineate the floodplain</u>
    - Make the *Channel_FP-1* layer to be the current layer.
    - Draw a polyline passing through the upper end point of the perpendicular lines.
    - Make the *Channel_FP-2* layer to be the current layer.
    - Draw a polyline passing through the lower end point of the perpendicular lines.
    - These polylines represents the floodplain for the 100 year flood, Figure 12-13.

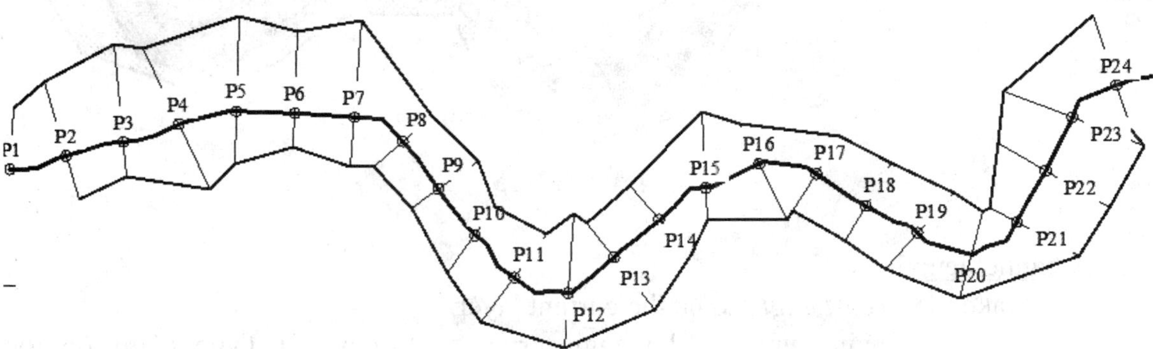

Figure 12-13

11. <u>Display the channel, bankfull, and floodplains</u>
    - Turn on the *Channel_Main*, *Channel_BF*, *Channel_FP-1*, and *Channel_FP-2* layers, Figure 12-14. Turn *Off* the other layers.

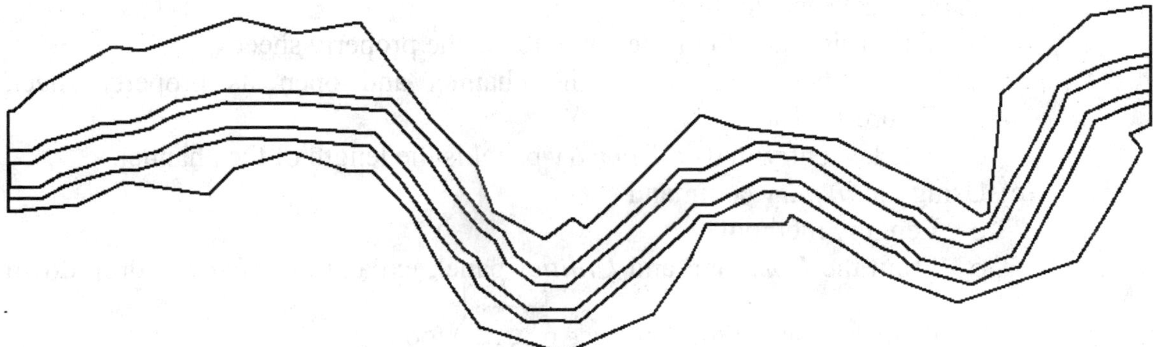

Figure 12-14

12. Hatch
   - Make the *Channel_Main_Hatch* to be the current layer.
   - Activate the *Hatch* command and hatch the main channel. Use *MUDST* and 100 for the hatch pattern and the scale, respectively, Figure 12-15.
   - Make the *Channel_BF_Hatch* to be the current layer.
   - Activate the *Hatch* command and hatch the bankfull channel. Use *GRAVEL* and 100 for the hatch pattern and the scale, respectively, Figure 12-15.
   - Make the *Channel_ FP_Hatch* to be the current layer.
   - Activate the *Hatch* command and hatch the floodplains. For hatching, click on one of the floodplains. Use *GRASS* and 50 for the hatch pattern and the scale, respectively, Figure 12-15. Repeat the process for the other floodplain. Hatching the floodplain independently, will help in finding the area of the floodplain.

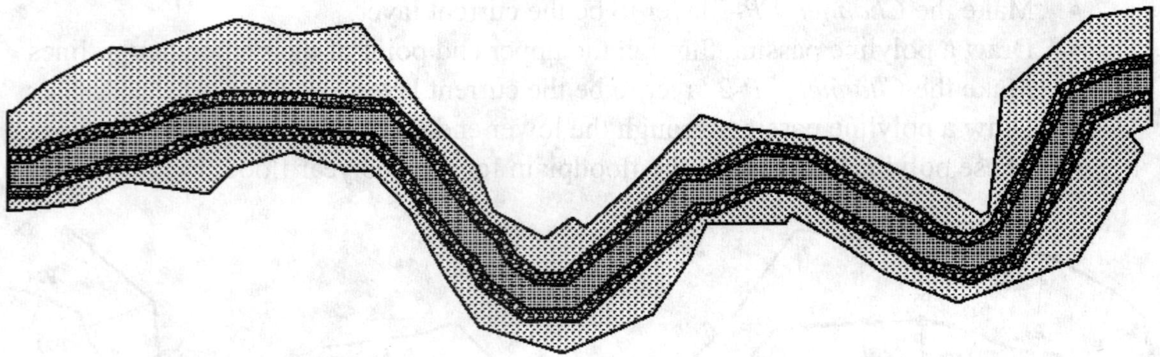

Figure 12-15

13. Channel length
   - Make the *Area-Length* to be the current layer.
   - Set the drawing units to be engineering as follow. (i) Type *Units* on the command line and press the *Enter* key. This will open *Drawing Units* dialog box. (ii) In the *Drawing Units* dialog box, under the *Length* panel, select the *Engineering* units, Figure 12-16a.
   - Find the length of the channel in feet (length of the channel's center line).
   - The length of the channel in feet can be obtained using one of the two techniques.
     (d) Using the *Property* sheet
        o The easiest and the fastest method is the property sheet.
        o Select the centerline of the channel and open its property sheet, Figure 12-16b
        o The last entry in the *Geometry* panel is the length of the channel.
     (e) Using the *Inquiry* command
        o Lengthy method!
        o From the *Home* tab and *Utilities* panel, expand the *Measure* drop down menu and select the *Distance* ( ) tool.
        o Follow the prompts.

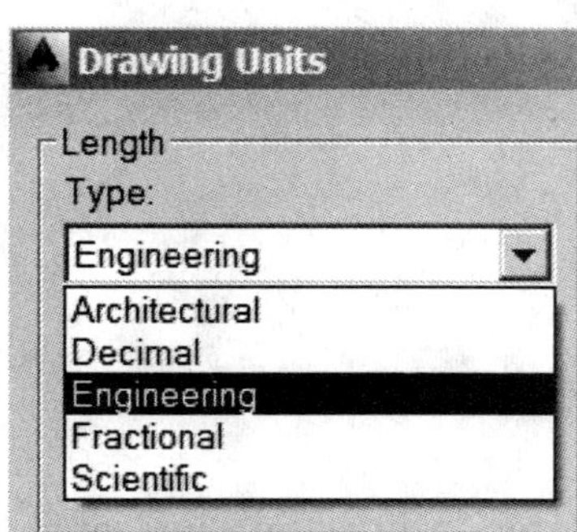

Figure 12-16a

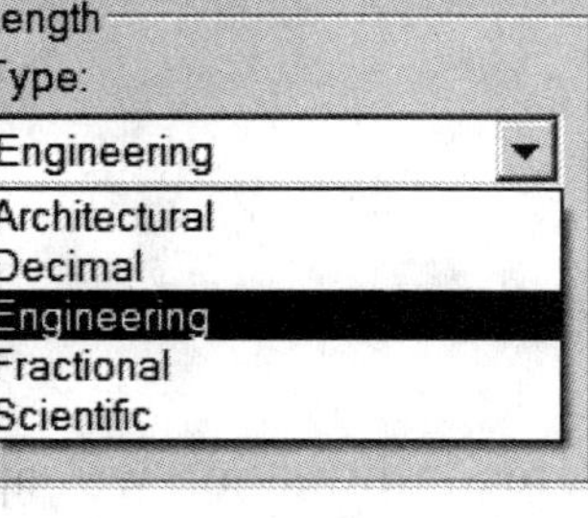

Figure 12-16b

14. <u>Floodplains area</u>
- Label the floodplains as shown in Figure 12-17d.
- Make the *Area-Length* to be the current layer.
- Find the area of the floodplains in acres.
- The area of the floodplains can be obtained using one of the two techniques.

(b) Using the *Property* sheet
  - o Select the hatch of the floodplain labeled as A and open its property sheet, Figure 12-17a.
  - o The second entry in the *Geometry* panel is the area of the floodplain A.
  - o Similarly, find the area of floodplain labeled as B.

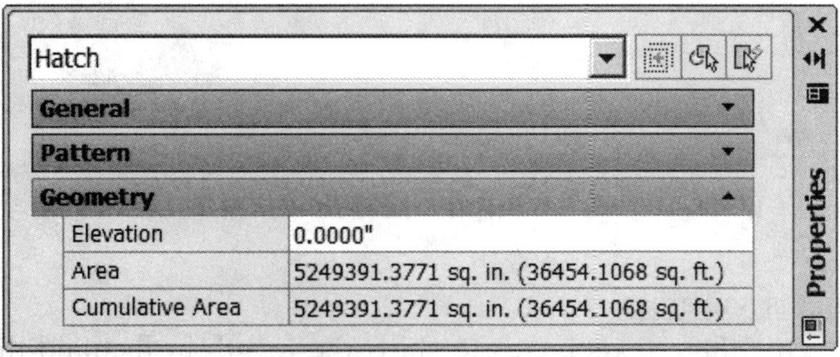

Figure 12-17a

(a) Use the *Inquiry* command.
  - o Lengthy method!
  - o From the *Home* tab and *Utilities* panel, expand the *Measure* drop down menu and select the *Area* ( ) tool.

o The prompt shown in Figure 11-17b will appear. Use the down arrow and choose the object option for a closed polyline.

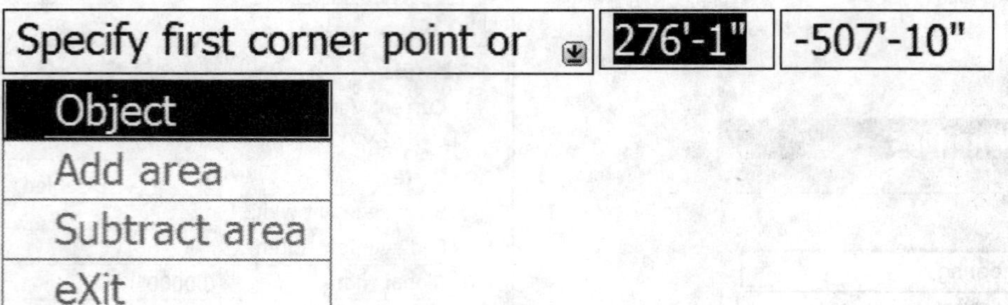

Figure 12-17b

o Click on the hatch of the floodplain A. The area information will appear on the screen, Figure 11-17c.
o Press the *Esc* key to exit the command.
o The information will be available in the command line.
o Repeat the process with the floodplain B.
- Convert the area into acres using the conversion factor of 1 Acres = 43560 sq. ft

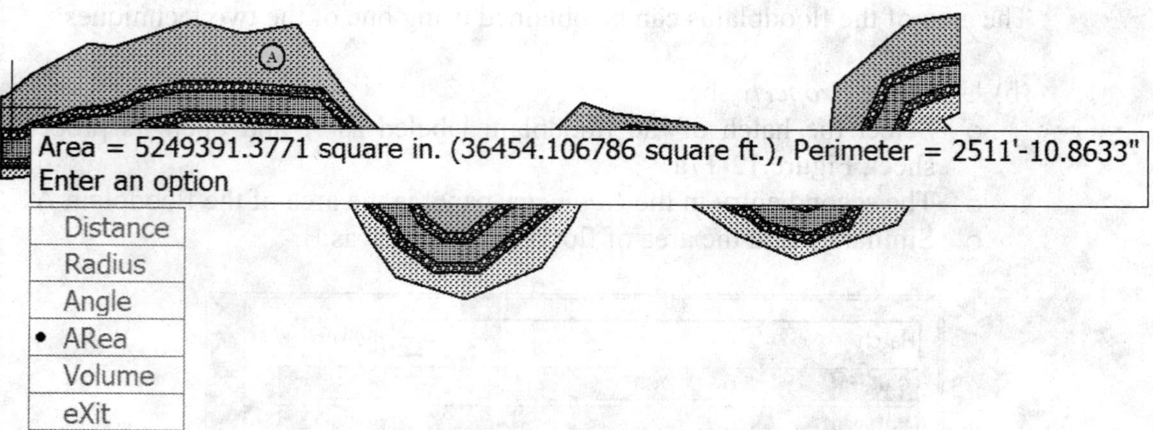

Figure 12-17c

15. <u>Display lengths and areas</u>
- Either create three texts boxes to show the length in feet and the areas in acres on the drawing; or create two tables to show the length in feet and the areas in acres on the drawing. The example creates two tables, Figure 12-17d.
- Show the length and the area as on the drawing.

16. <u>Insert Template file</u>
- Finally, insert a layout from the template file labeled as "My_acad_Landscape_tmplt.dwt".
- Set the viewport scale to be 1:1200.
- Lock the viewport

- Update the Title block.
- The resultant drawing in the layout is shown in Figure 12-18.

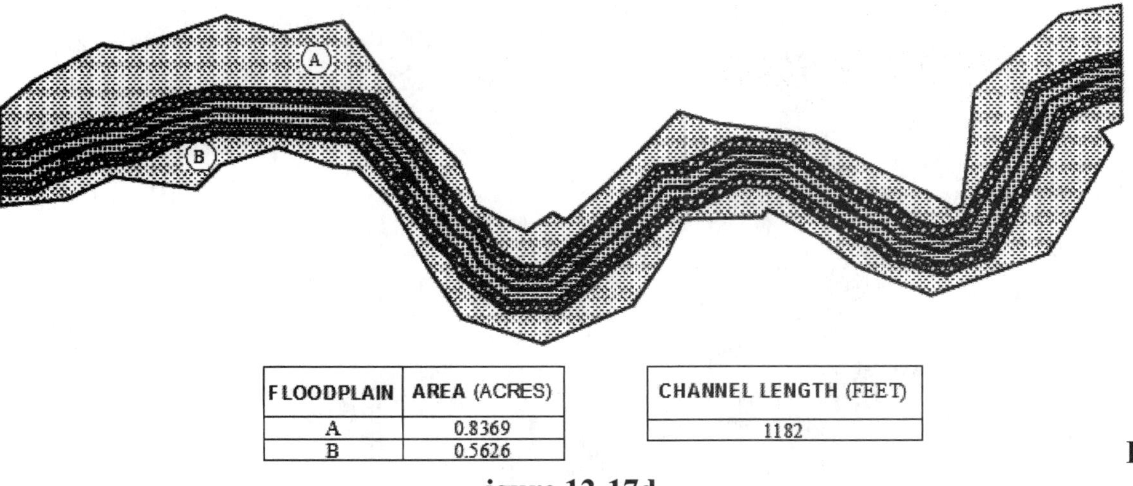

FLOODPLAIN	AREA (ACRES)
A	0.8369
B	0.5626

CHANNEL LENGTH (FEET)
1182

Figure 12-17d

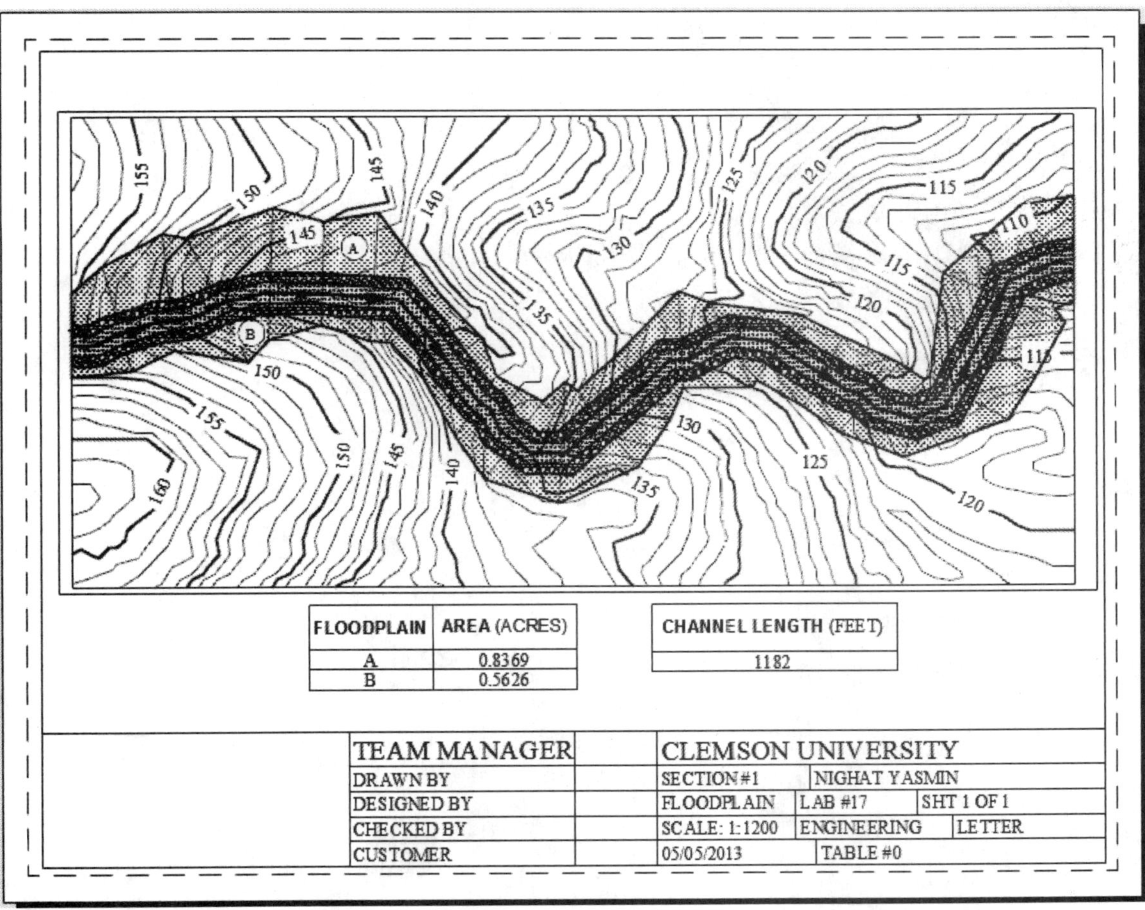

FLOODPLAIN	AREA (ACRES)
A	0.8369
B	0.5626

CHANNEL LENGTH (FEET)
1182

TEAM MANAGER		CLEMSON UNIVERSITY		
DRAWN BY		SECTION #1	NIGHAT YASMIN	
DESIGNED BY		FLOODPLAIN	LAB #17	SHT 1 OF 1
CHECKED BY		SCALE: 1:1200	ENGINEERING	LETTER
CUSTOMER		05/05/2013	TABLE #0	

Figure 12-18

Notes:

13. Road Design

13.1.   Objectives

- Learn the basics of plan, profile, and cross-section of a road
- Learn to draw plan, profile, and cross-sections using AutoCAD

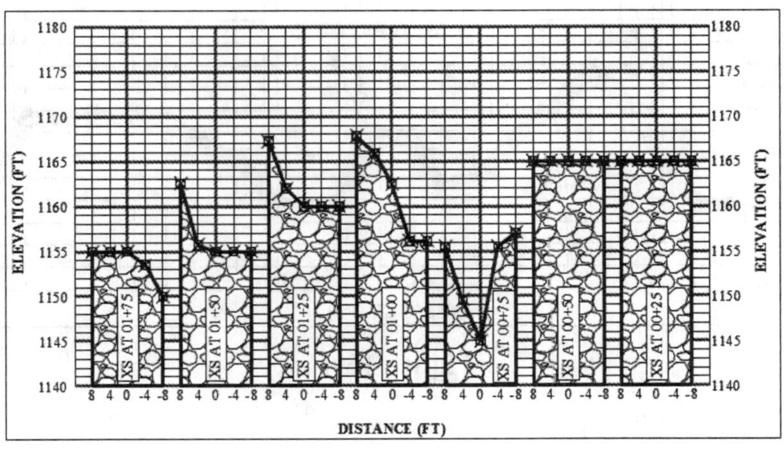

13.2. Introduction

Humans have been using many different modes of transportation on land, from horseback to automobiles (car, bus, truck, etc.). One common feature among these modes is the road. A road can be as simple as a walking trail to several lane paved road. A road design is a complicated process. It depends on several factors. Some of the factors are listed here: location of the road, types of the vehicles using the road, geometric design, drainage system, and parking facilities. The road location factor is further subdivided into the land topography, soil characteristics, and environmental effects. Once the decision for the road location is made, the area is surveyed and various drawings are prepared. The focus of this chapter is two of the major drawings: (i) the plan and profile and (ii) the cross-sections drawings.

13.3. Plan and Profile

The plan and profile drawing is commonly known as the PnP drawing. It is a two-view drawing. It is divided into two parts, Figure 13-1. The upper half always displays the plan view (and the contour map), and the lower half displays the profile. The PnP drawing is also an important drawing for most of the civil engineering projects, such as water and sewer pipelines, storm drainage system, curbs, and sidewalk construction.

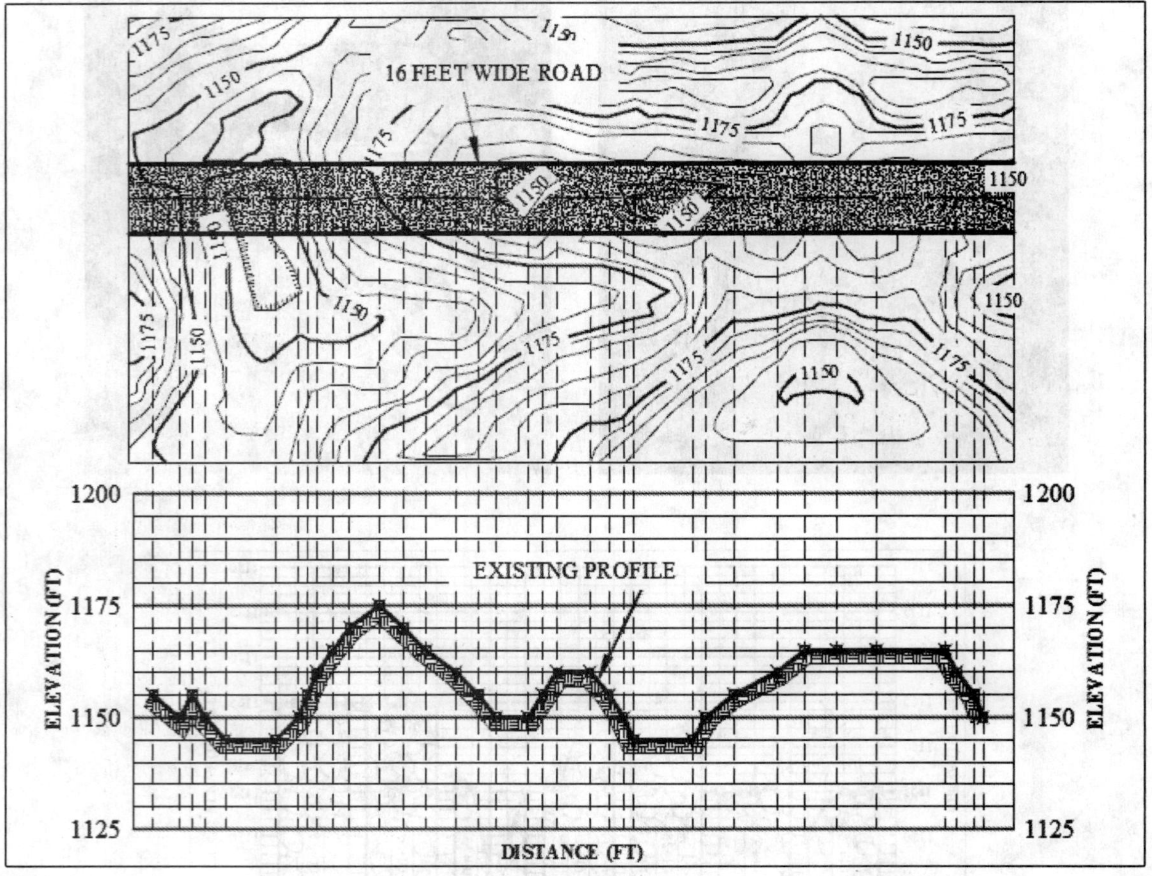

Figure 13-1

13.3.1. Plan

The plan view represents the area as seen from the top or a bird-eye-view. A plan view contains all the necessary information for the road construction. The upper half of the Figure 13-9 shows a plan of a road.

13.3.2. Profile

The profile is the representation of the natural ground. It is defined as a display of the elevation of a set of equidistant points along a continuous line, for example the centerline of a road. It is represented as a graph of elevation with respect to the distance along the centerline. The elevation is represented on the y-axis and the distance along the centerline is shown on x-axis. The lower half of the Figure 13-9 shows the profile of the centerline of the road.

13.4.   Draw road plan using AutoCAD

This section provides step-by-step instructions to create a plan of a proposed road.

1. Launch AutoCAD 2014.
2. Create the layers as needed. Assign color, linetype, and lineweight appropriately to each layer, Figure 13-2.

S.	Name	On	Freeze	Lock	Color	Linetype	Lineweight
✓	0				white	Continuous	Default
	Contours-Label				172	Continuous	Default
	Contours-Line				32	Continuous	Default
	Defpoints				white	Continuous	Default
	Grid-1				140	Continuous	Default
	Grid-2				140	Continuous	Default
	Profile-Hatch				43	Continuous	Default
	Profile-Points				red	Continuous	Default
	Profile_Existing				white	Continuous	1.00 mm
	Profile_Existing-Label				white	Continuous	Default
	Proj				210	HIDDEN	Default
	Road-CL				red	CENTER	0.80 mm
	Road-Dim				74	Continuous	Default
	Road-Label				200	Continuous	Default
	Road-plan				white	Continuous	1.00 mm
	Road_Hatch				62	Continuous	Default
	Stations				white	Continuous	Default
	Stations-Dim				74	Continuous	Default
	Stations-Label				white	Continuous	Default
	XS-Dist				74	Continuous	Default
	XS-Draw_Hatch				white	Continuous	Default
	XS-Draw_Label				white	Continuous	Default
	XS-Draw_LN				white	Continuous	1.00 mm
	XS-Draw_PT				white	Continuous	Default
	XS-PT				white	Continuous	Default
	XS_DS				white	Continuous	Default
	XS_LN				white	Continuous	Default

Figure 13-2

3. Turn *On/Off* and freeze the layers as needed.
4. <u>Contour map</u>
   - Open a previously created or downloaded contour map, Figure 13-3a.

Figure 13-3a

5. <u>Add label to the contour map</u>
   - Make the *Contour-Label* layer to be the current layer.
   - Label the index contour using the *Text* and the *Background Mask* commands, Figure 13-3b.
   - Set the height of the text to be 3'.

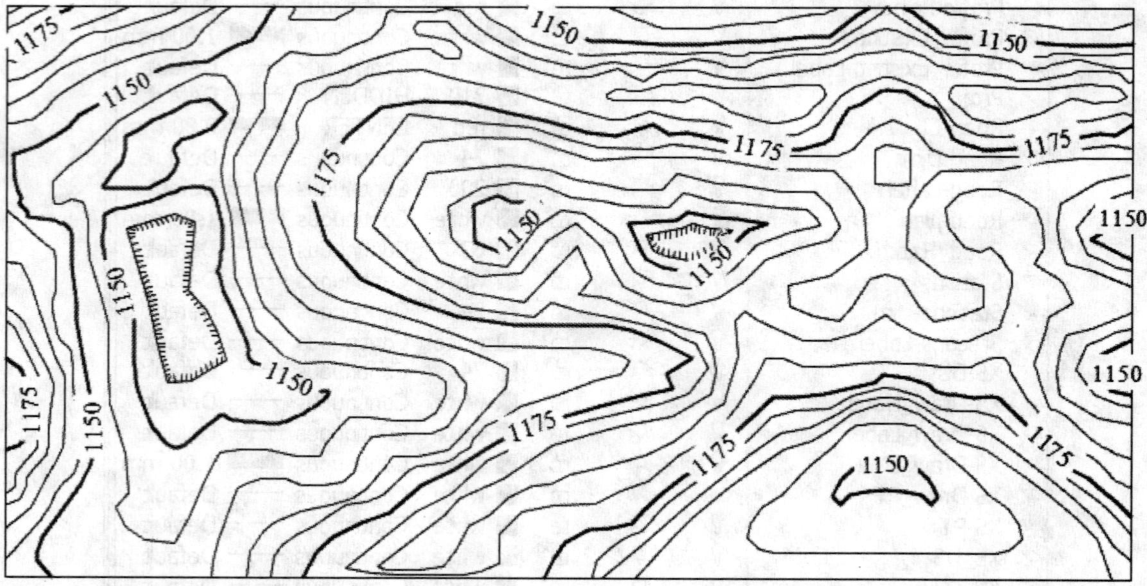

Figure 13-3b

6. Center line
    - Make the *Road-CL* layer to be the current layer.
    - Draw the center line of the road, Figure 13-4. The center line of the road is 59 feet and 10 inches above the lower edge of the counter map.
    - Make the *Road-Dim* layer to be the current layer.
    - Add the dimensions to the centerline of the road.

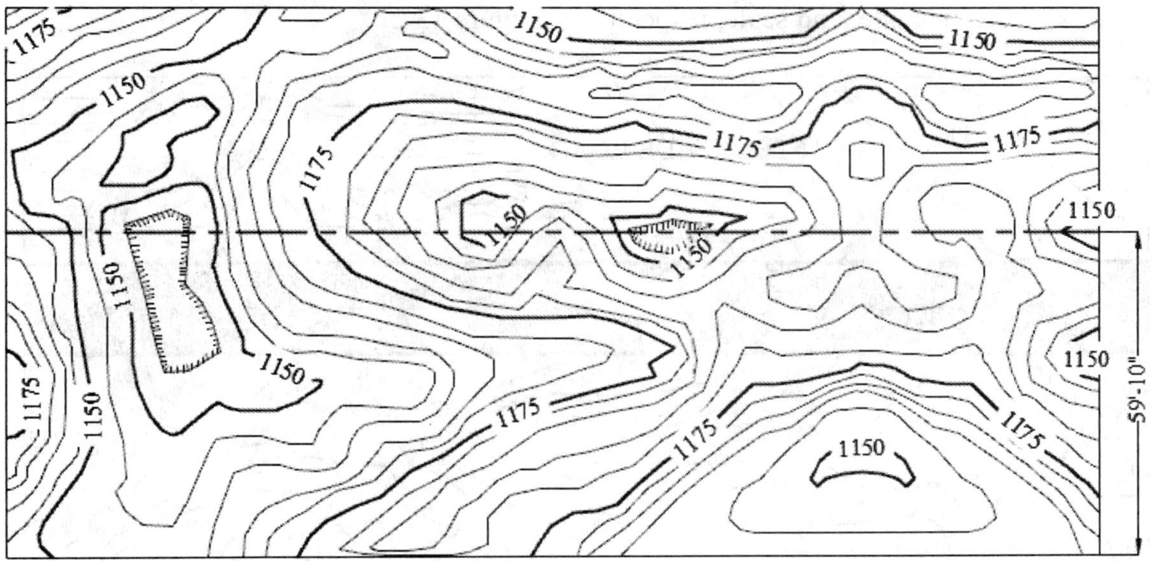

Figure 13-4

7. Road plan
    - Make the *Road-Plan* layer to be the current layer.
    - The road is 16' wide, Figure 13-5a.
        o Activate the *Offset* command. Set the offset distance to be 8'.

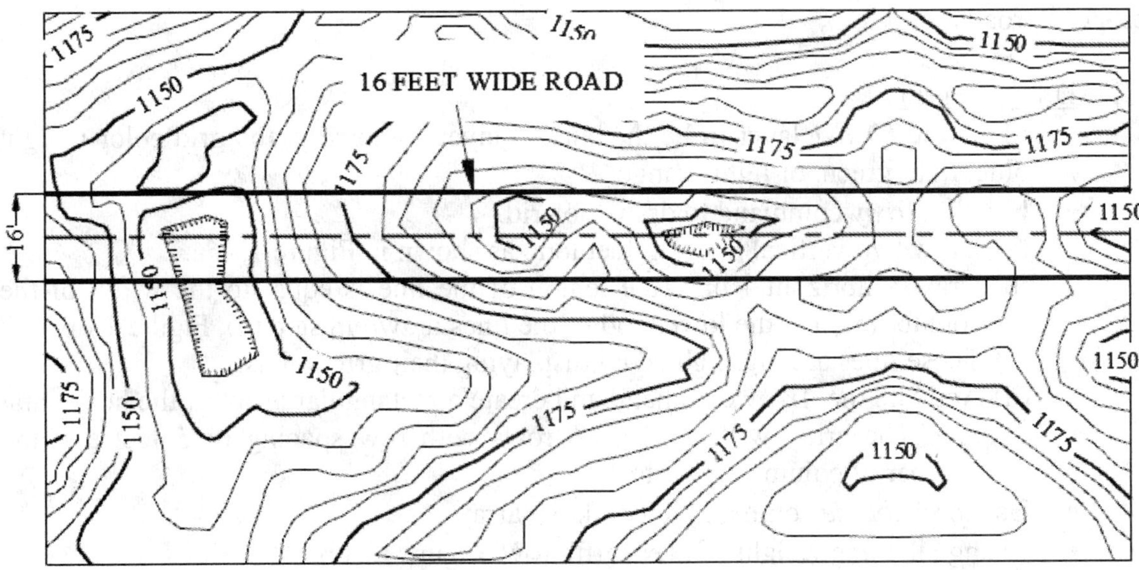

Figure 13-5a

- o Create an offset of the centerline on either side of the centerline.
- o Move the offsets to the road plan's road.
- o The road plan is shown in Figure 13-5a.
- Make the *Road-Dim* layer to be the current layer.
- Add the dimensions to the plan of the road; that is, display the road's width.
- Make the *Road-Hath* layer to be the current layer.
- Add the hatch to the plan of the road. Use AR-CONC, 0, and 3 for the hatch pattern, angle, and scale, respectively, Figure 13-5b.

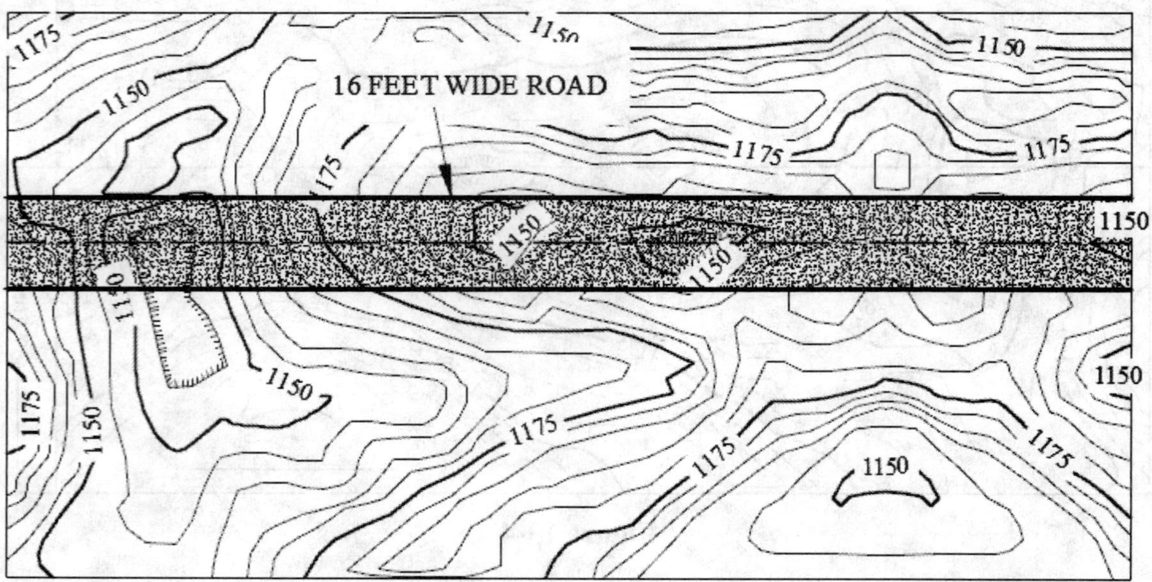

Figure 13-5b

13.5.   Plot the profile using AutoCAD

This section provides step-by-step instructions to create a profile of the centerline of the proposed road.

1. <u>Draw the grid</u>
   - Make the *Grid-1* layer to be the current layer. Generally, the grid color is light blue, light green, or light orange.
   - Use the *Array* command to draw the grid.
   (a) Draw two vertical lines 75 feet long as shown in Figure 13-6a.
   (b) Draw a horizontal line (the length of the line is equal to the width of the counter map) at the lower end of the lines drawn in step (a), Figure 13-6a.
   (c) These lines are highlighted by displaying their grip points.
   (d) Activate the *Array* command and create a rectangular array of the horizontal line. The array will contain 16 rows with row spacing of 5 feet and the number of columns is set to 1.
   - Use the *Explode* command to break the array.
   - Change the line weight of every fifth row, Figure 13-6b.
   - Add the labels as shown in Figure 13-6b.

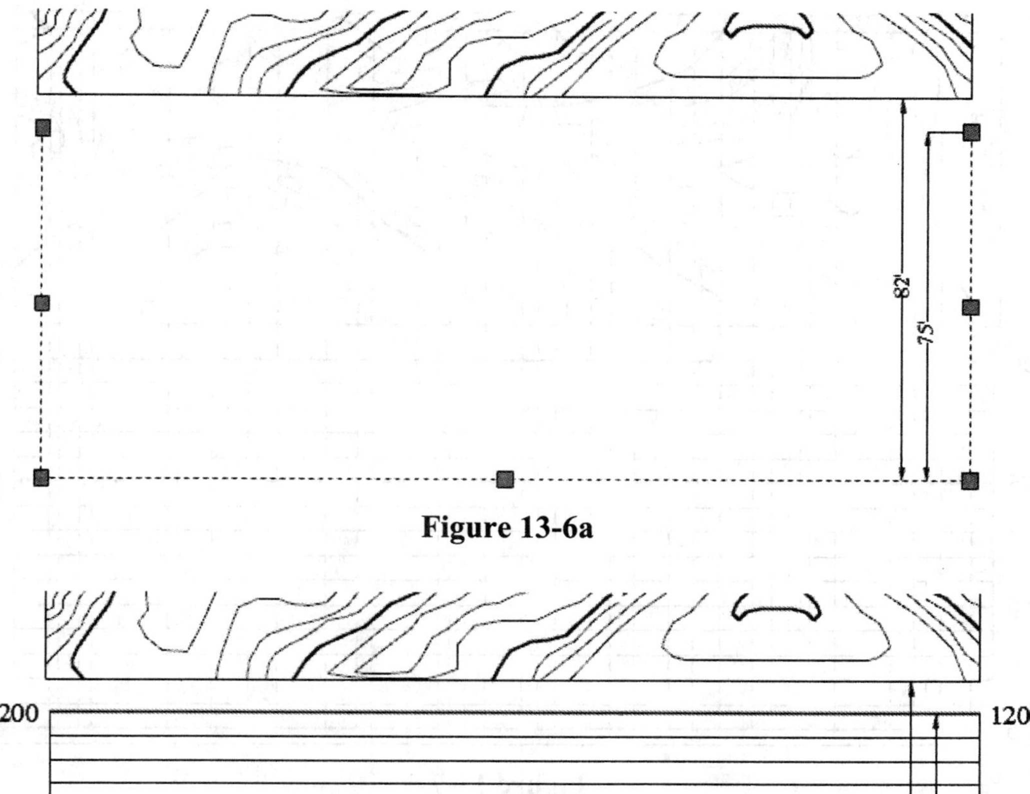

Figure 13-6a

Figure 13-6b

2. <u>Draw the projection line</u>
   - Make the *Proj* layer to be the current layer.
   - Draw straight lines originating at the intersection of the centerline and the contour lines and terminating at the x-axis of the grid, Figure 13-7.
   - Set the linetype scale of the projection line to 0.5.

3. <u>Plot the elevation on the grid</u>
   - From the *Home* tab and expanded *Utilities* tab select the *Point Style...* to open the *Point Style* dialog box, Figure 13-8a.
   - Change point style and size as shown in Figure 13-8a. Although, the dialog box shows the point size in feet, but the input is always in inches. The user must type 24.

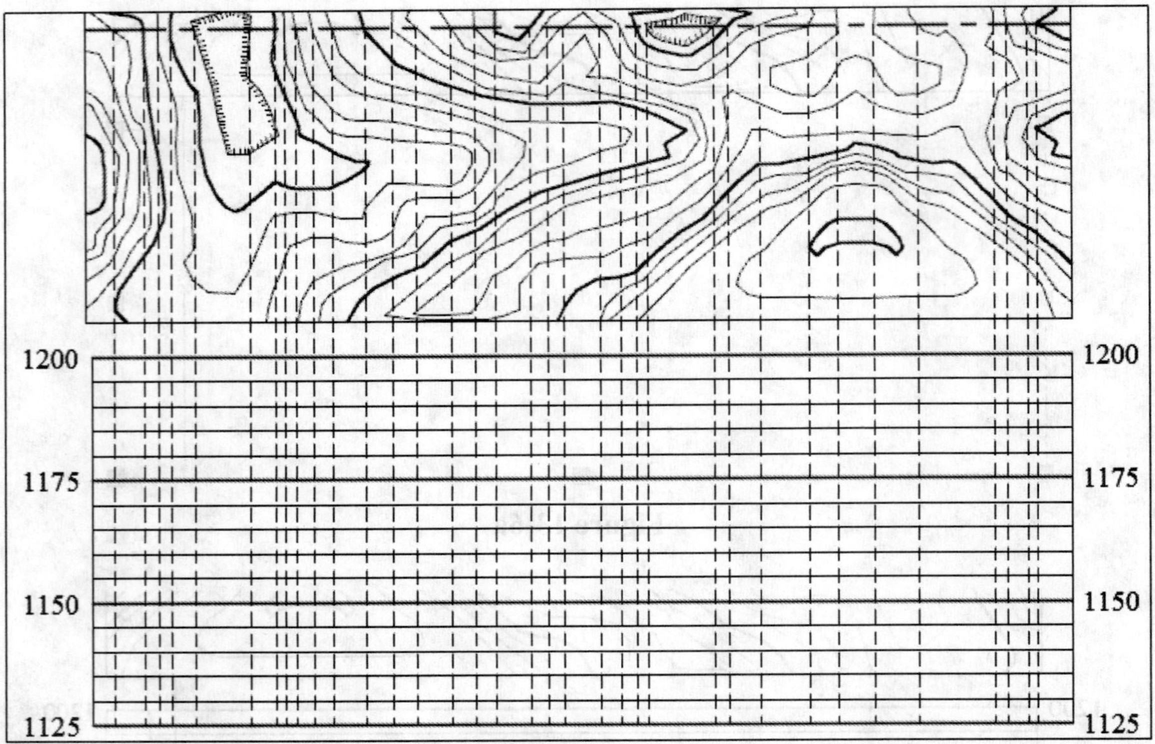

Figure 13-7

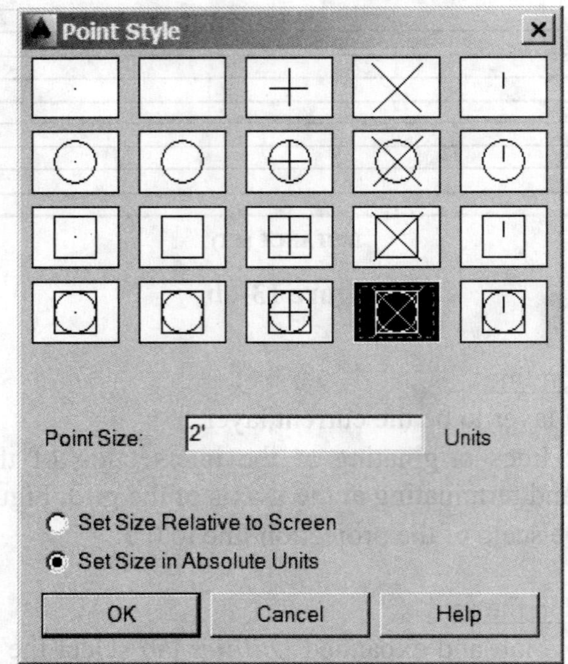

Figure 13-8a

- Make the *Profile-Point* layer to be the current layer.
- The first projection line originates at 1155' contour. On the profile's grid, draw a point on this projection line at an elevation of 1155 feet.

- Repeat the process for the other projection lines, Figure 13-8b.
- Make the *Profile-Existing* layer to be the current layer.
- To create the profile, activate the *Polyline* command and connect the profile points, Figure 13-8c. This profile is known as the existing profile or the ground line.

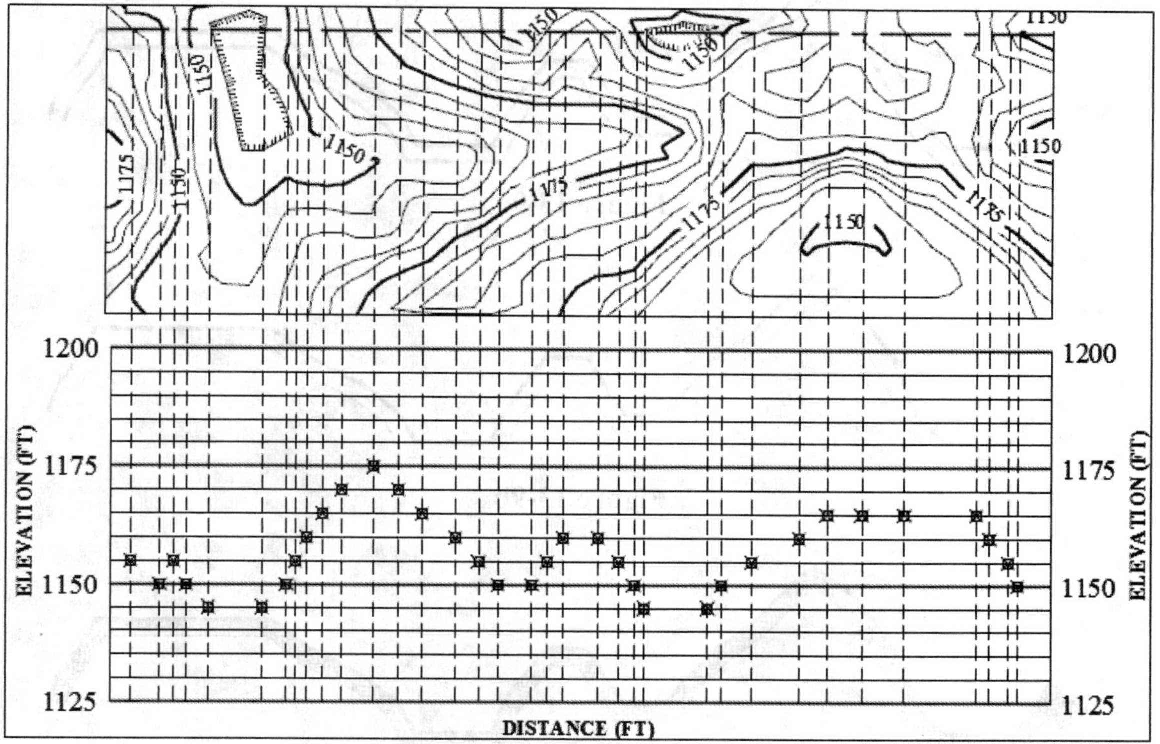

Figure 13-8b

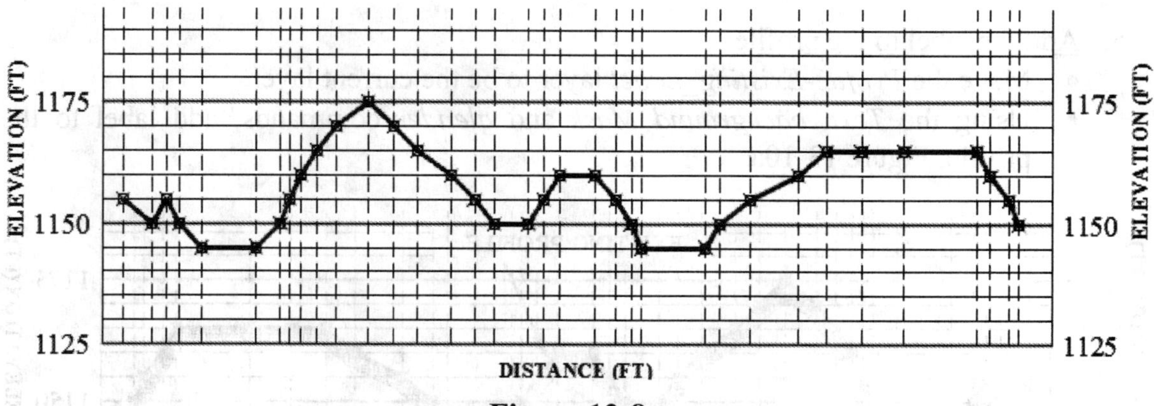

Figure 13-8c

4. <u>Hatch the profile</u>
   - Turn *Off* the grid and projection layers.
   - Make the *Profile-Hatch* layer to be the current layer.
   - Using an *Offset* command, create an offset of the profile with the offset distance of 3 feet, Figure 13-9a.

- Move the offset to the hatch layer.
- Connect the ends of the profile and using small lines, Figure 13-9b.
- Activate the *Hatch* command.
- Add the hatch. Set the pattern: *EARTH*, Angle: 0, and Scale: 120, Figure 13-9c.

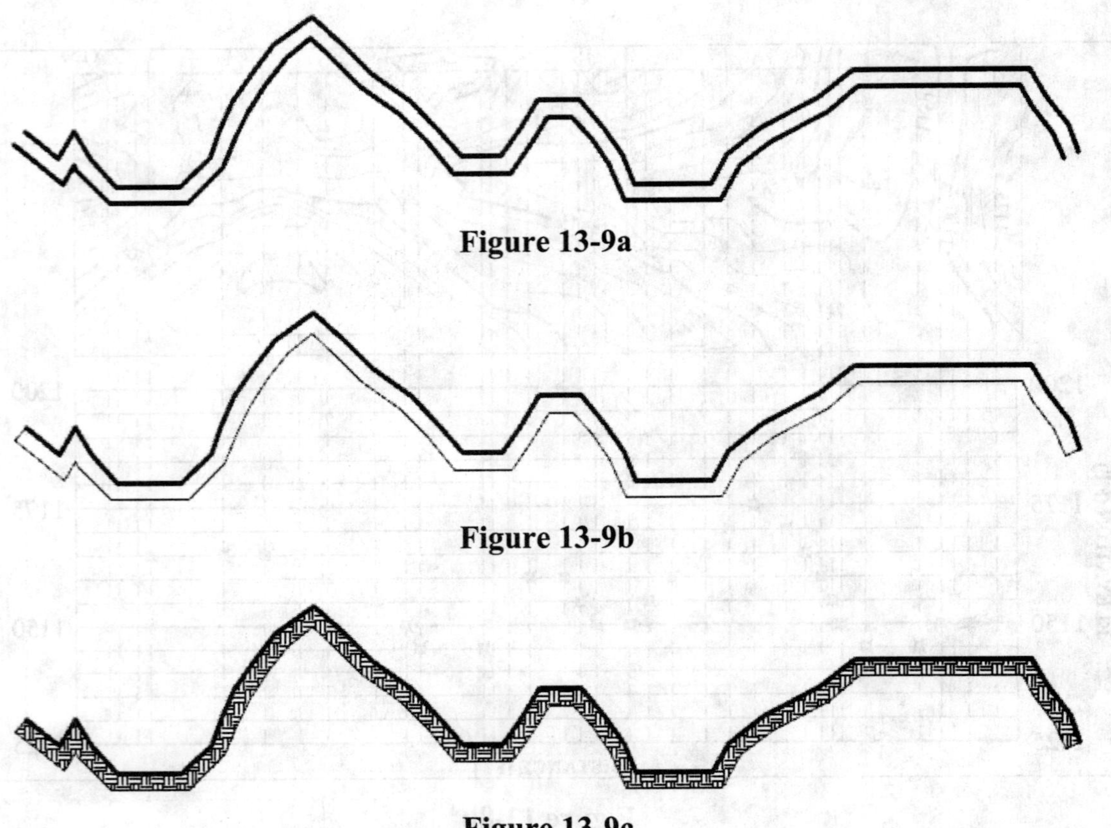

Figure 13-9a

Figure 13-9b

Figure 13-9c

5. <u>Add the label to the profile</u>
   - Make the *Profile-Existing_Label* layer to be the current layer.
   - Using the *Text*, *background Mask* and *qleader* commands, add label to the profile, Figure 13-10a.

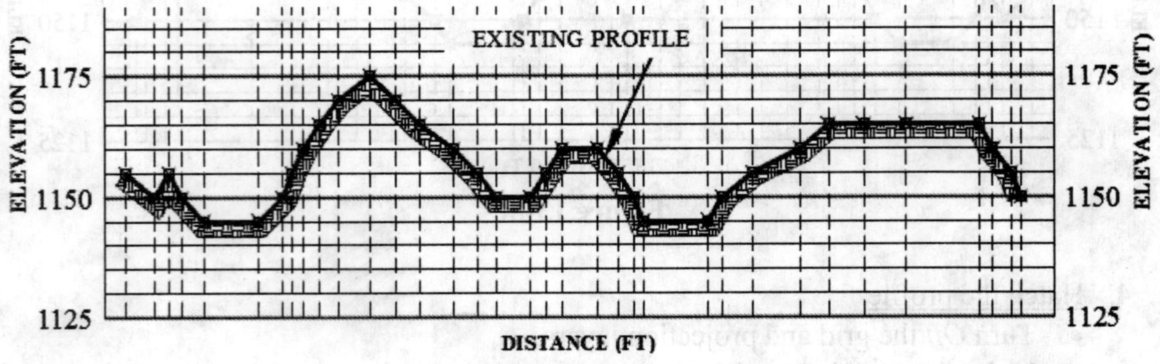

Figure 13-10a

6. PnP
   - Finally, insert a layout from the template file labeled as "My_acad_Landscape_tmplt.dwt", Figure 13-10b.
   - Set the scale of the drawing to 1:360, Figure 13-10b.
   - Update the blocks, Figure 13-10b.
   - The complete PnP drawing is shown in Figure 13-10b.

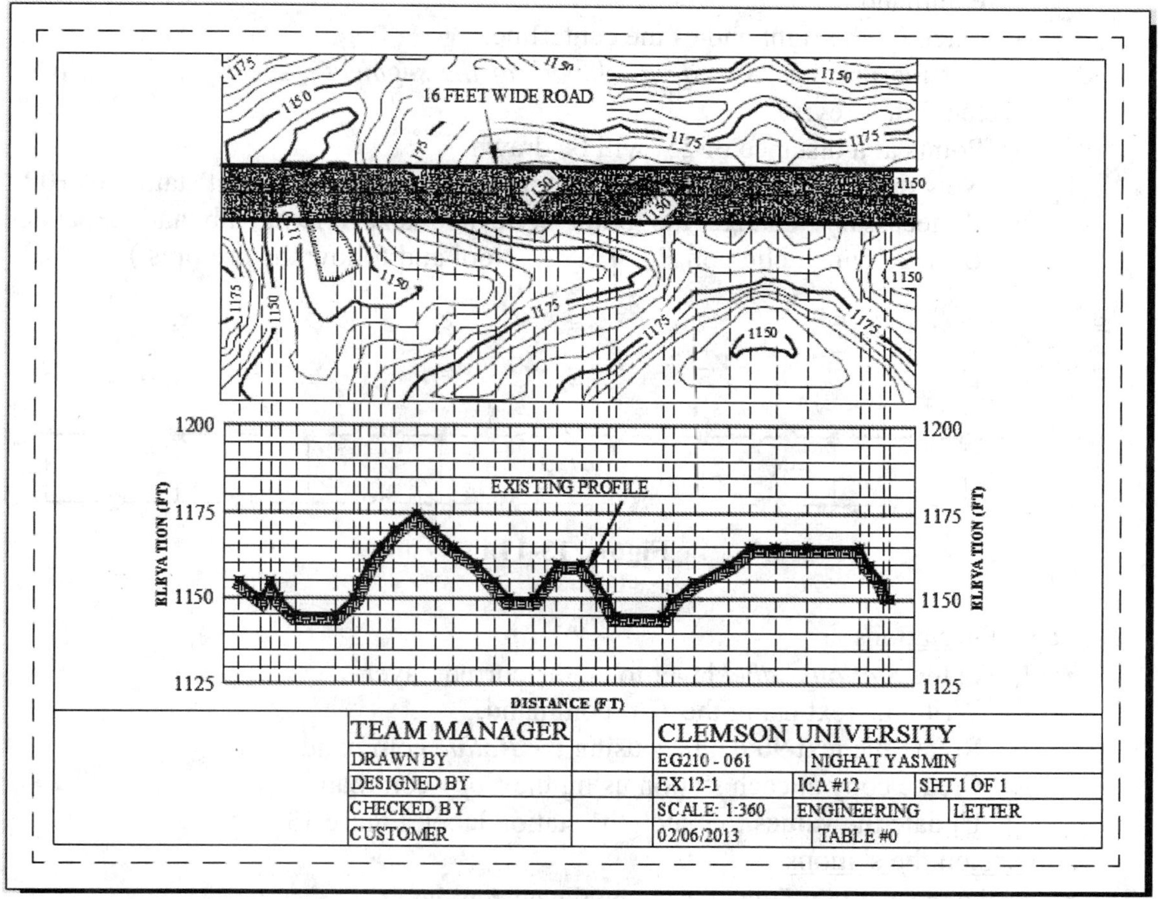

Figure 13-10b

13.6.   Cross-section

A cross-section is defined as a display of the elevation of a set of equidistant points along a continuous line that runs perpendicular to the centerline. Usually, the sections are drawn at a regular interval, for example, at every station (and stations are 25' apart). The process for creating cross-sections is the same as for a profile. However, cross-sections are smaller than profiles. Generally, for cross-sections, both the existing and proposed shapes are drawn. For discussion purposes, only the existing shape will be drawn. The proposed shape is left for the readers.

13.7.   Draw cross-section using AutoCAD

1. <u>Draw stations</u>
    - Make the *Station* layer to be the current layer.
    - Add the stations locations Figure 13-11a and Figure 13-11b using *Point* command. The command is performed as follow:
        o From the *Home* tab and expanded *Draw* panel, select the *Point Measure* command.
        o Click on the right end of the centerline.
        o For the prompt "*Specify the length of the segment*", specify 25', and press the *Enter* key.
        o Points at a distance of 25' will be drawn.
        o Now draw a point at the right end of the center line, that is at station 00+00.
        o If necessary, change the point style and size (*Home* tab and expanded *Utilities* panel, click on *Point Style...* tool and follow the prompts.)

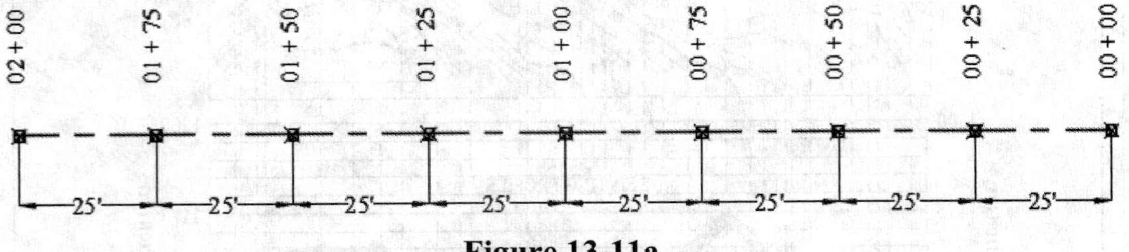

Figure 13-11a

2. <u>Label the stations</u>
    - Make the *Station_Label* layer to be the current layer.
        o Write the text using the *Text* command.
        o Rotate the text 90 degrees using the *Rotate* command.
        o Create copy at each station using the *Copy* command.
        o Update the values to match the station label, Figure 13-11a.
3. <u>Dimension the stations</u>
    - Make the *Station_Dim* layer to be the current layer.
        o Add the dimensions to the station, Figure 13-11a and Figure 13-11b.

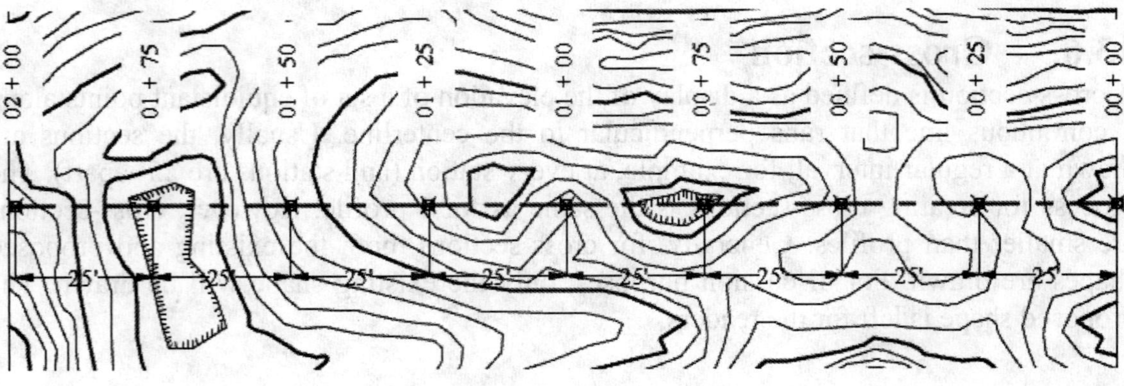

Figure 13-11b

4. <u>Draw the section line perpendicular to the centerline at a selected station.</u>
   - Make the *XS_LN* layer to be the current layer.
   - Turn *Off* the contour and contour labels layers.
   - In the example, the cross-section at station 00+25 will be created.
   - Turn on the *Perpendicular* option in object snap setting dialog box.
   - Start a line at the centerline of the station 00+25 and move to the outer edge of the road, Figure 13-12a.

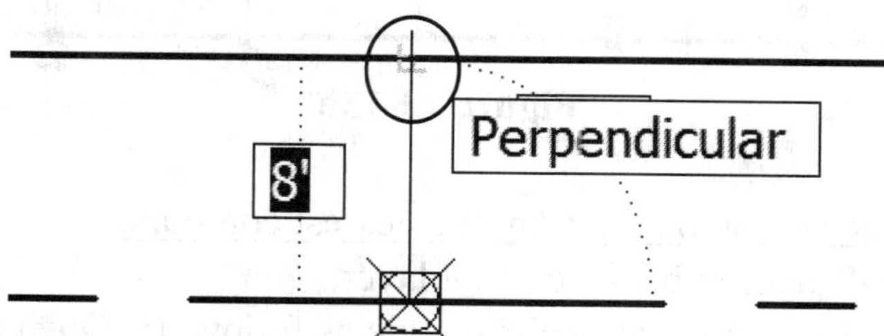

Figure 13-12a

   - Click at the perpendicular point, Figure 13-12b. A perpendicular line is created from the center line to the outer edge.
   - Repeat the process on the other side of the center line or use the *Mirror* command. Figure 13-12c shows the perpendicular lines.
   - Repeat the process at the other stations or use the *Copy* command.

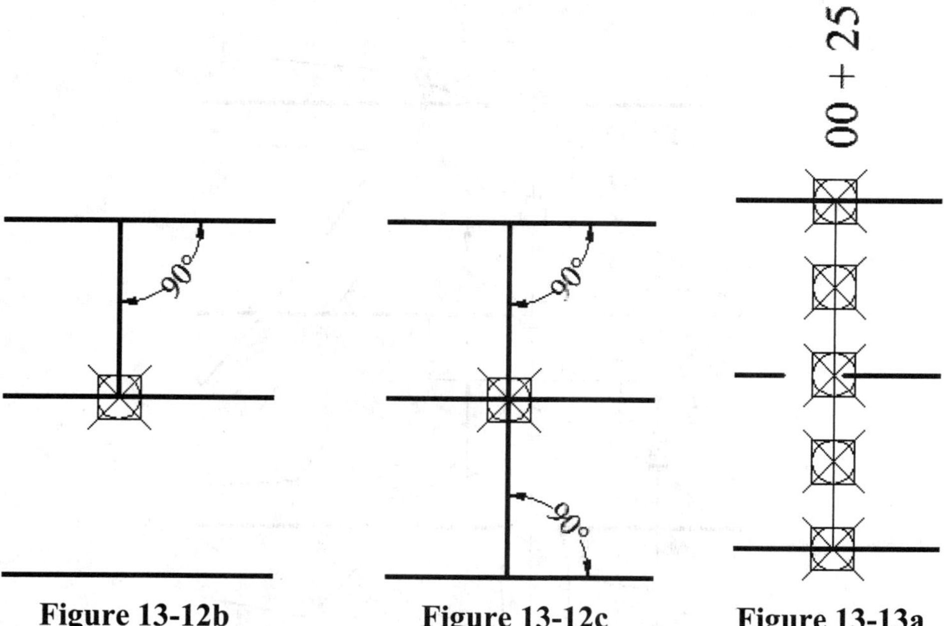

Figure 13-12b   **Figure 13-12c**   **Figure 13-13a**

5. <u>Draw points on the perpendicular lines.</u>
   - Make the *XS_PT* layer to be the current layer.
   - Draw four points, two on each line drawn in step #4 as shown in Figure 13-13a (two at the midpoints and two at the outer edges of the road).

- Repeat the process at the other stations or use the *Copy* command, Figure 13-13b.

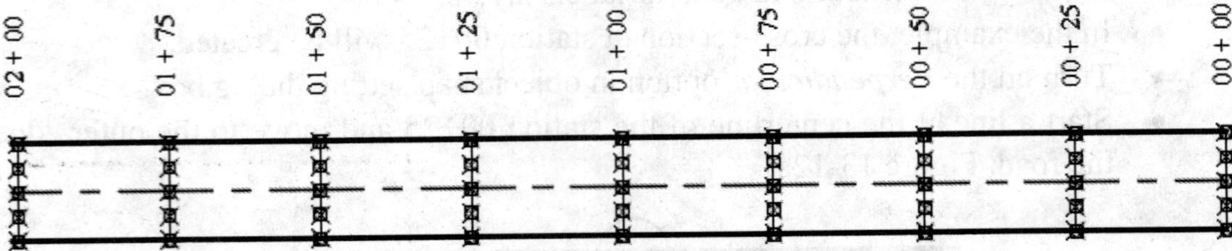

Figure 13-13b

6. <u>Show the distance to the points from the nearest contours.</u>
   - Make *XS_DS* layer to be the current layer.
   - Change the dimensions to decimal style as follow. (i) Open the *Dimension Style Manger* dialog box. (ii) Click the *Modify* button. (iii) Open the *Modify Dimension Style* dialog box, select the *Primary Units*. (iv) Finally, under the *Linear Dimension* panel and for *Unit Format* select *Decimal*.
   - Use the *Align* dimension command to add the distance to every point from the two contours (one on each side), Figure 13-14a.
   - If necessary, extend the perpendicular line (beyond the edge of the road) to the nearest contour line.

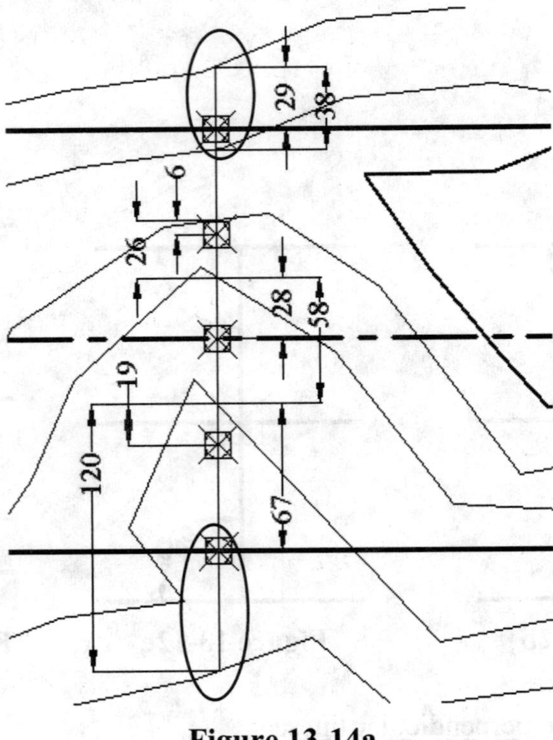

Figure 13-14a

- Repeat the process for the other stations, Figure 13-14b.

- Note that in Figure 13-14b; there are no dimensions for station 00+25 because all of the points are on the same contour line.

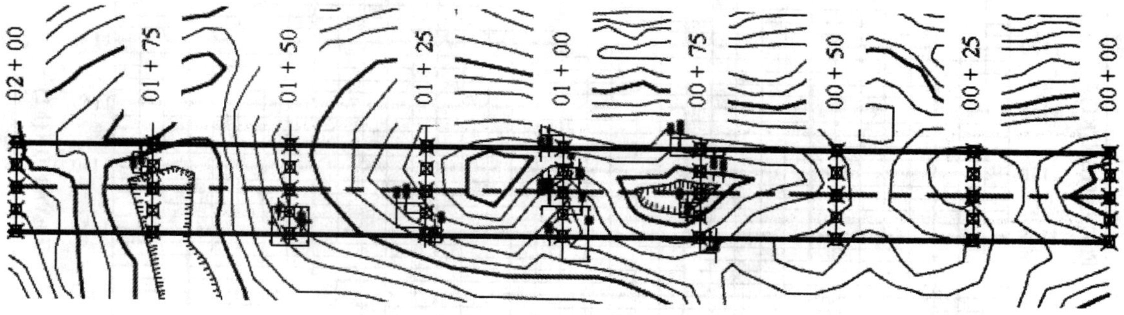

Figure 13-14b

7. <u>Find the elevation of the cross-section points using interpolation.</u>
   - Interpolation is not needed if a contour line is passing through a station or if a contour line above and below a station has the same value. Hence, skip this step.
   - If a contour line is not passing through a station and the station is not enclosed by the same contour then find the elevation of the station using linear interpolation
   - Let *es* be the elevation of the station in question (unknown); *e1* and *e2* are the elevations of the contours above and below the station, respectively; and *d1* and *d2* are the distance as shown Figure 13-15. Find the elevation of the station (*es*) using the formula: $d1/d2 = (e1 - es) / (e1 - e2)$.
   - Similarly, find the elevation of the other stations.

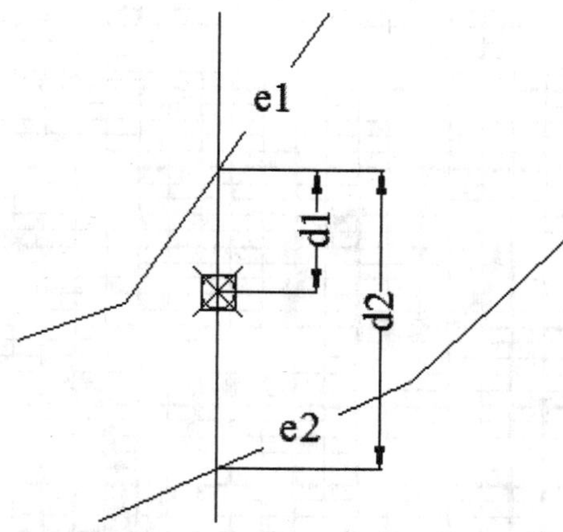

Figure 13-15

8. <u>Cross-section grid</u>
   - Draw the grid as shown in Figure 13-16. In the figure:
     - *-8* represents the upper edge of the road.
     - *-4* represents the midpoint of the upper lane of the road.
     - *0* represents the centerline of the road.
     - *4* represents the midpoint of the lower lane of the road.
     - *8* represents the lower edge of the road.

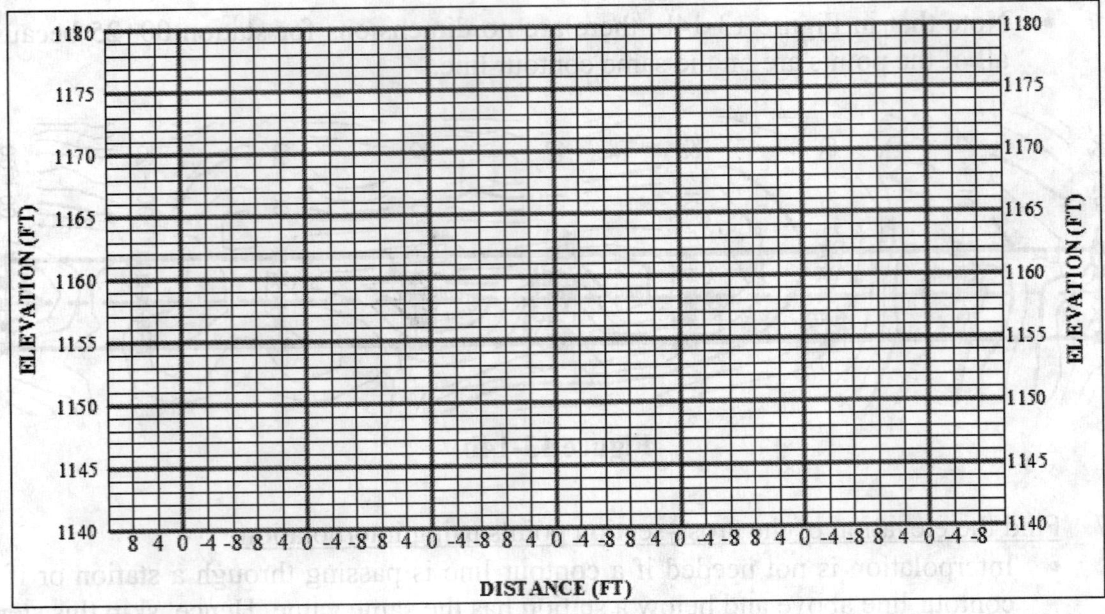

Figure 13-16

9. Cross-section drawing
- Make *XS_Draw_PT* layer to be the current layer.
- Draw points for the elevation of stations across the center line, Figure 13-17.
- Make *XS_Draw_LN* layer to be the current layer.
- Draw polylines through the points for the elevation of station, Figure 13-17.

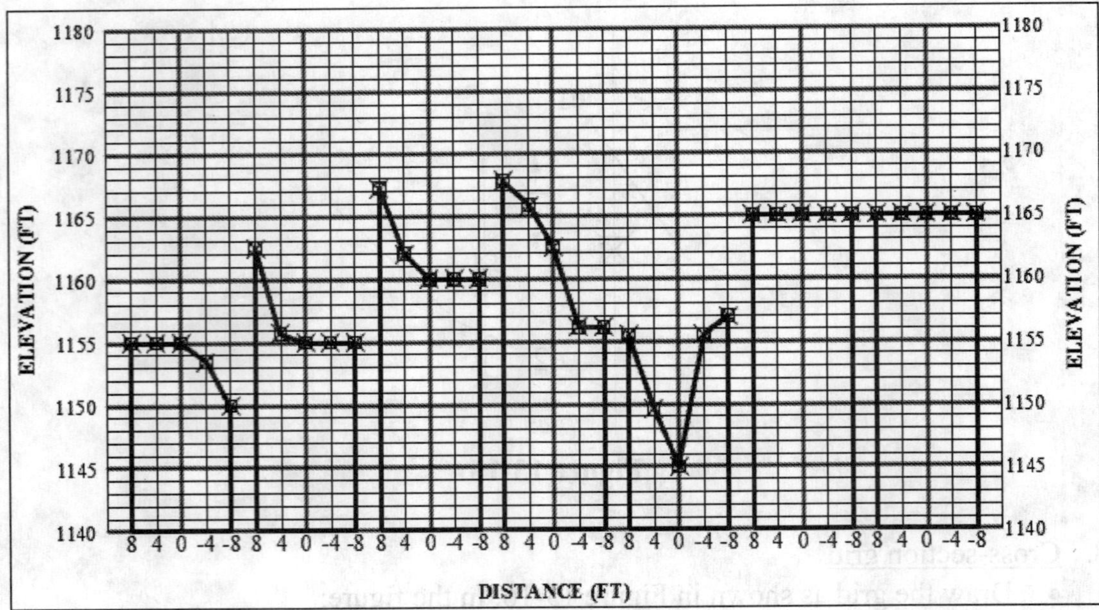

Figure 13-17

10. Cross-section labels
- Trim the grid from the cross-sections, Figure 13-18.

- Make *XS_Draw_Label* layer to be the current layer.
- Add the labels to the cross-sections; and the rectangles around the labels.

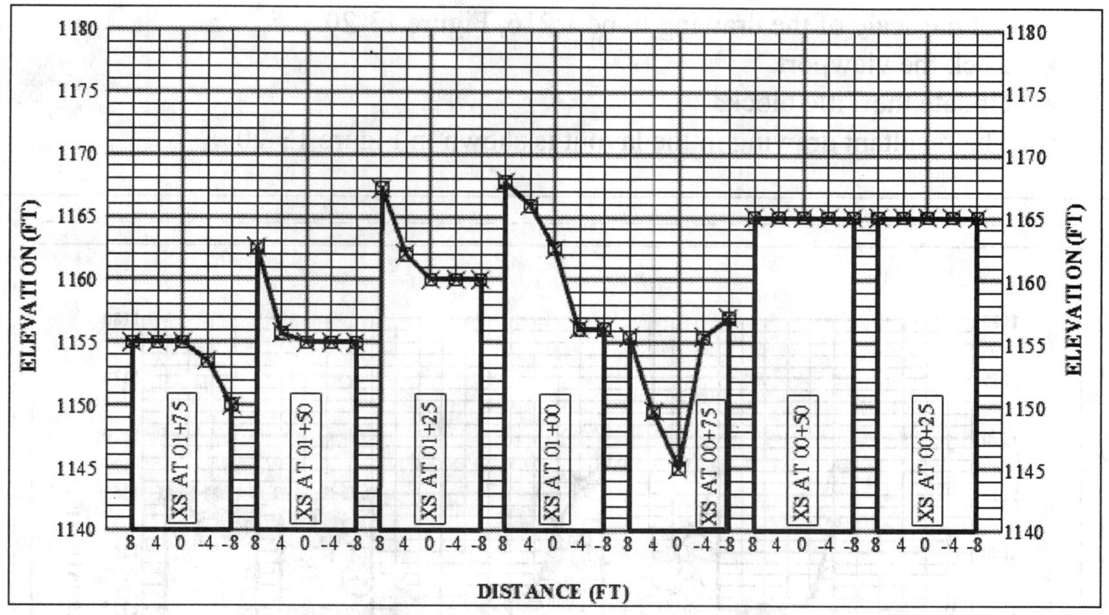

Figure 13-18

11. <u>Hatch</u>
- Make *XS_Draw_Hatch* layer to be the current layer.
- Activate the *Hatch* command and hatch the cross-sections.
- Use *GRAVEL* pattern and 75 for the scale, respectively, Figure 13-19.

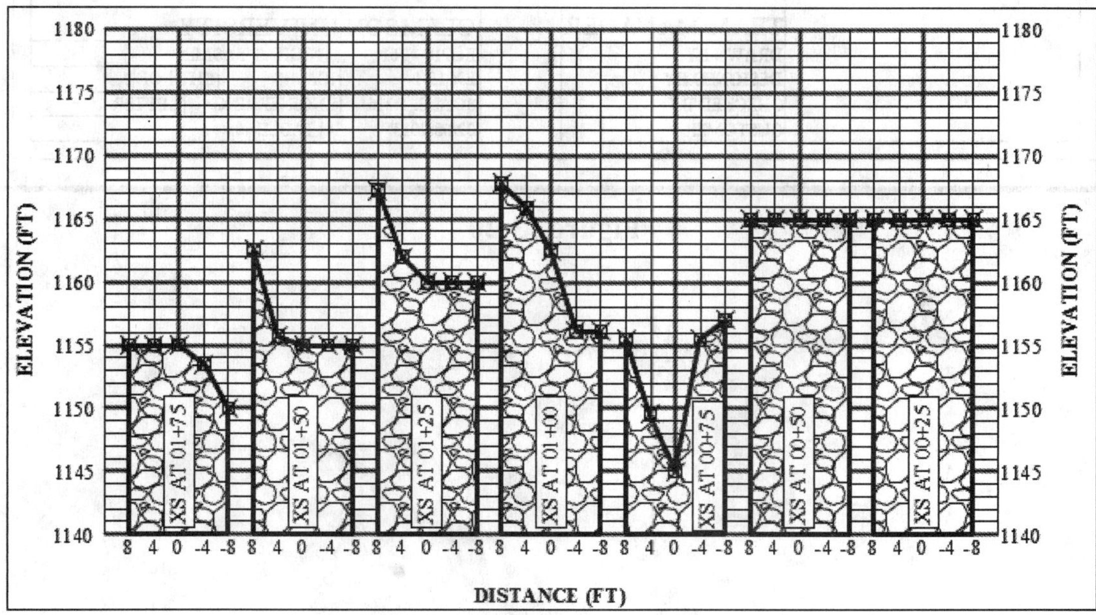

Figure 13-19

12. <u>Insert Template file</u>
   - Finally, insert a layout from the template file labeled as "My_acad_Landscape_tmplt.dwt".
   - Set the scale of the drawing to be 1:216, Figure 13-20.
   - Lock the viewport
   - Update the Title block.
   - The resultant drawing in the layout is shown in Figure 13-20.

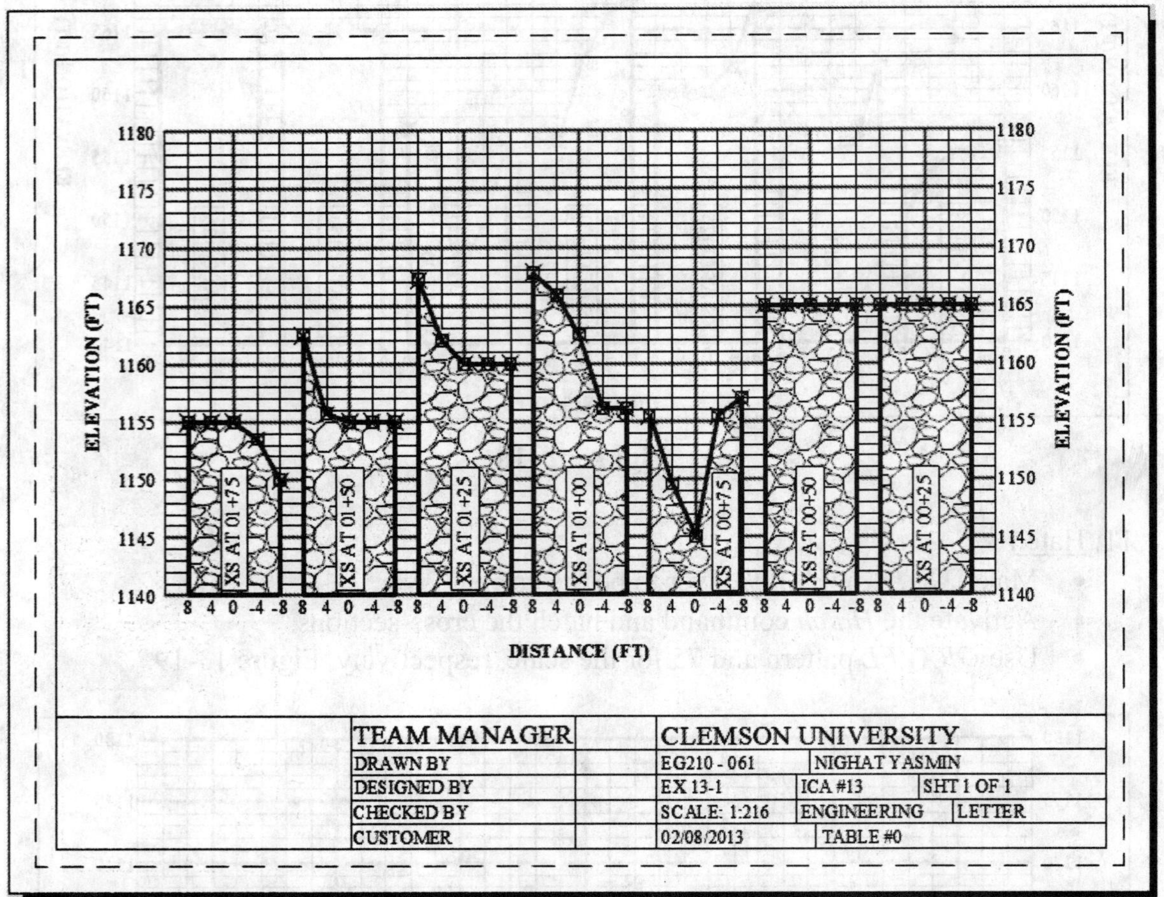

Figure 13-20

14. Earthwork

14.1.   Objectives

- Learn the basics of earthwork in a road design
- Learn to delineate earthwork using AutoCAD

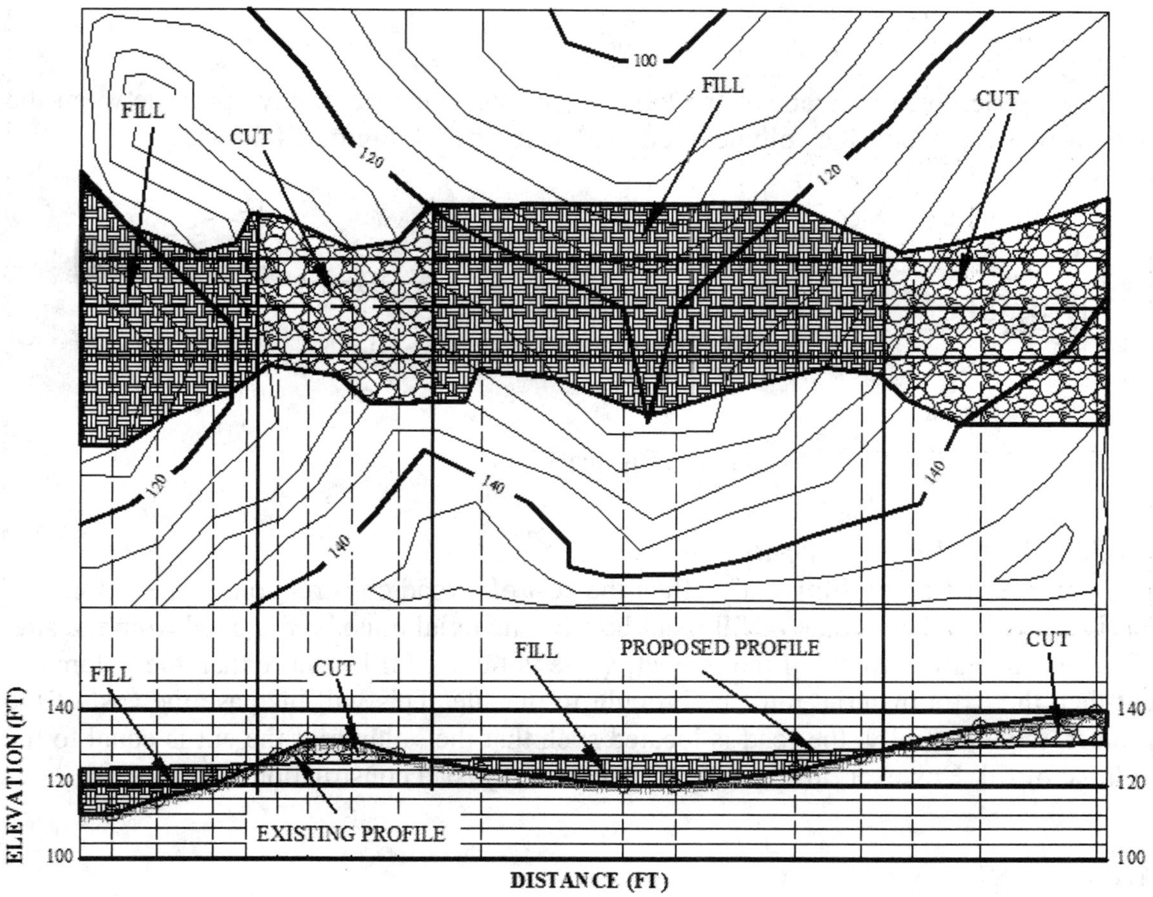

14.2.   Introduction

The earthwork, also known as the cut and fill, in road construction terminology refers to the excavation and embankment of the earth. The amount of earthwork plays an important role in the selection of a road location because the cost of the road construction is greatly influenced by the earthwork.

14.3.   Earthwork

In the plan and profile drawing, the profile represents the natural ground. After developing the PnP, the proposed profile is added to the drawing. The slope of the proposed profile represents the elevation of the centerline of the proposed road.

14.3.1. Cut

If the proposed profile is below the existing profile, then the extra material between the two profiles represents the volume of excavation or cut, Figure 14-1.

14.3.2. Fill

If the proposed profile is above the existing profile, then the empty space between the two profiles represents the volume of embankment or fills, Figure 14-1.

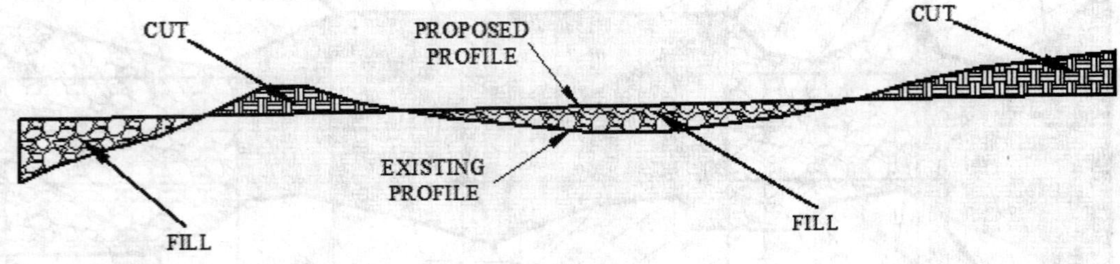

Figure 14-1

14.3.3. Location of a road

The volume of cut and fill greatly affect the cost of a road construction. If the volume of cut is more than the volume of fill then the extra material must be removed from the site. This will increase the cost of the project. If the volume of fill is more than the volume of cut then the extra material must be brought to the site. This will increase the cost of the project, too. Generally, the road is located such that the volume of the cut is equal to the volume of fill. However, this is not possible in every road construction.

14.4.   Slope

A slope of a line is defined as the ratio of change in altitude (ΔV_d) to the change in horizontal distance (ΔH_d). The slope is positive for an upward line (Figure 14-2a), whereas it is negative for a downward line (Figure 14-2b).

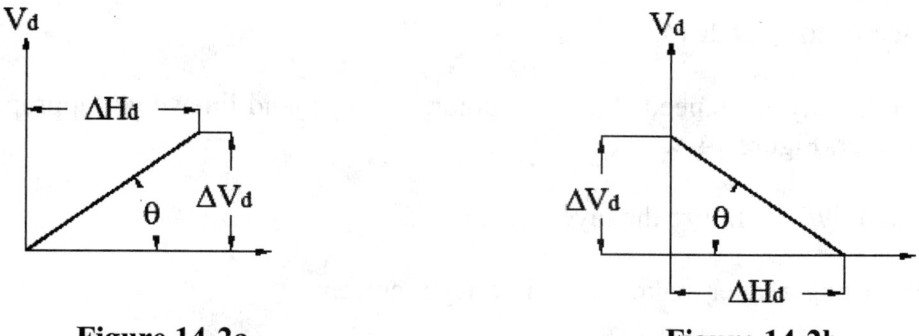

Figure 14-2a   **Figure 14-2b**

Slope can be specified as a percentage or an angle. It can be calculated using one of the following equations.

$$\text{Slope (ratio)} = (\Delta V_d / \Delta H_d) * 100$$
$$\text{Slope (angle)} = \tan^{-1}(\Delta V_d / \Delta H_d)$$

14.5.   Angle of repose

When a granular material is poured on a horizontal surface it will make a pile, Figure 14-3 shows a pile of sand. The height of the pile will increase as more material is poured. However, when the height of the pile reaches to V_d, pouring of any more material will collapse the pile. The angle of the incline surface (Φ), just before the collapse, is known as the angle of repose. Some of the factors affecting the angle of repose are density, surface area of the particle, and coefficient of friction of the material.

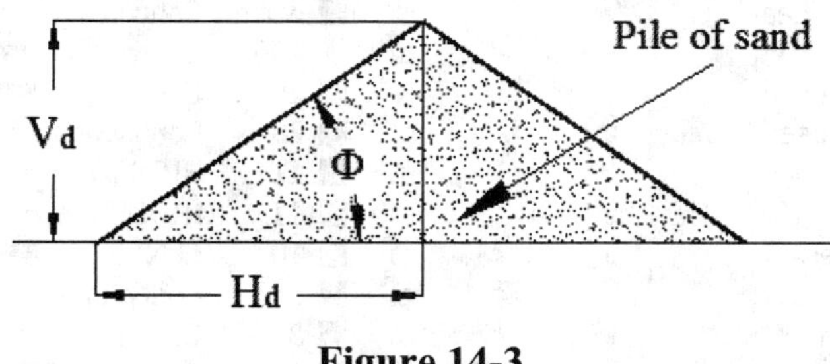

Figure 14-3

The angle of repose can be specified as a ratio or an angle. It can be calculated using one of the following equations.

$$\Phi \text{ (ratio)} = H_d : V_d$$
$$\Phi \text{ (angle)} = \tan^{-1}(\Delta V_d / \Delta H_d)$$

14.6.   Plan and existing profile of a road

This section will briefly describe the plan and profile drawing process. For more details refer to the Chapter #13, Road Design that discusses the *Plan, Profile, and Cross-sections* of a road.

1. Launch AutoCAD 2014.

2. Create the layers as needed. Assign color, linetype, and lineweight appropriately to each layer, Figure 14-4.

3. Turn *On/Off* and freeze the layers as needed.

4. Before using a layer make the desired layer current

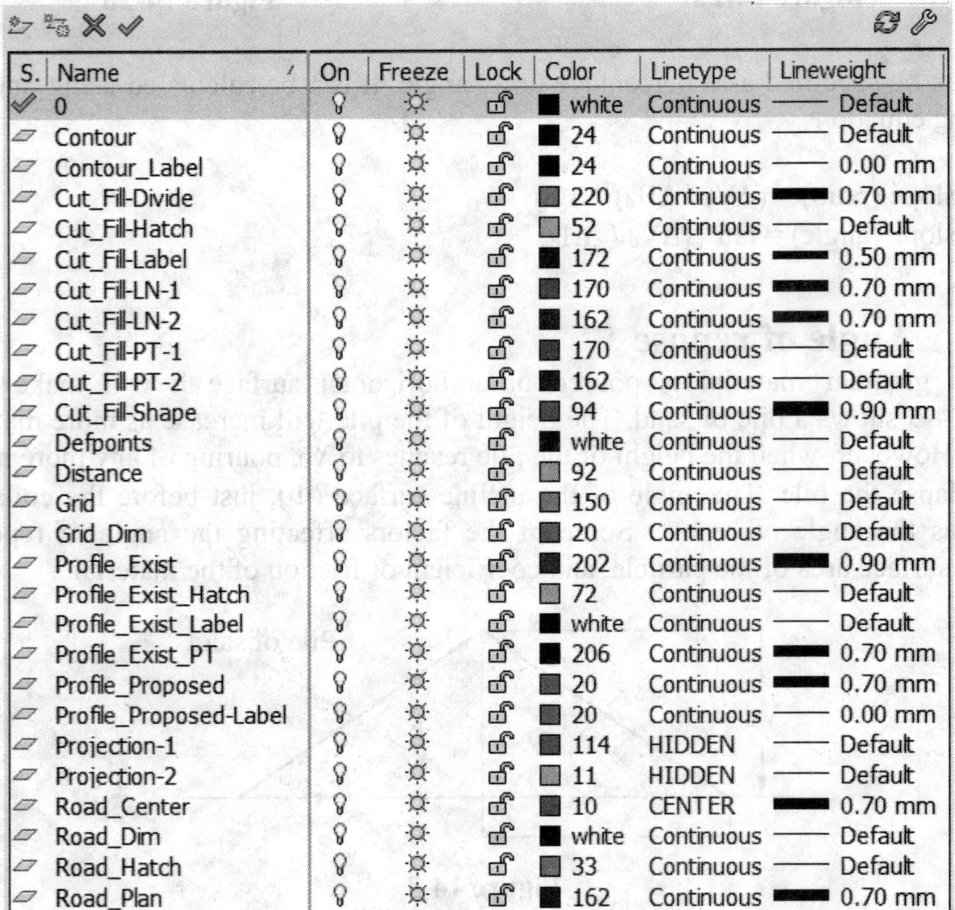

S.	Name		On	Freeze	Lock	Color	Linetype	Lineweight
✓	0	✓	♀	☼	🔓	■ white	Continuous	—— Default
▱	Contour		♀	☼	🔓	■ 24	Continuous	—— Default
▱	Contour_Label		♀	☼	🔓	■ 24	Continuous	—— 0.00 mm
▱	Cut_Fill-Divide		♀	☼	🔓	▨ 220	Continuous	▬▬ 0.70 mm
▱	Cut_Fill-Hatch		♀	☼	🔓	▨ 52	Continuous	—— Default
▱	Cut_Fill-Label		♀	☼	🔓	■ 172	Continuous	▬▬ 0.50 mm
▱	Cut_Fill-LN-1		♀	☼	🔓	■ 170	Continuous	▬▬ 0.70 mm
▱	Cut_Fill-LN-2		♀	☼	🔓	■ 162	Continuous	▬▬ 0.70 mm
▱	Cut_Fill-PT-1		♀	☼	🔓	■ 170	Continuous	—— Default
▱	Cut_Fill-PT-2		♀	☼	🔓	■ 162	Continuous	—— Default
▱	Cut_Fill-Shape		♀	☼	🔓	■ 94	Continuous	▬▬ 0.90 mm
▱	Defpoints		♀	☼	🔓	■ white	Continuous	—— Default
▱	Distance		♀	☼	🔓	▨ 92	Continuous	—— Default
▱	Grid		♀	☼	🔓	■ 150	Continuous	—— Default
▱	Grid_Dim		♀	☼	🔓	■ 20	Continuous	—— Default
▱	Profile_Exist		♀	☼	🔓	■ 202	Continuous	▬▬ 0.90 mm
▱	Profile_Exist_Hatch		♀	☼	🔓	▨ 72	Continuous	—— Default
▱	Profile_Exist_Label		♀	☼	🔓	■ white	Continuous	—— Default
▱	Profile_Exist_PT		♀	☼	🔓	■ 206	Continuous	▬▬ 0.70 mm
▱	Profile_Proposed		♀	☼	🔓	▨ 20	Continuous	▬▬ 0.70 mm
▱	Profile_Proposed-Label		♀	☼	🔓	▨ 20	Continuous	—— 0.00 mm
▱	Projection-1		♀	☼	🔓	▨ 114	HIDDEN	—— Default
▱	Projection-2		♀	☼	🔓	▨ 11	HIDDEN	—— Default
▱	Road_Center		♀	☼	🔓	■ 10	CENTER	▬▬ 0.70 mm
▱	Road_Dim		♀	☼	🔓	■ white	Continuous	—— Default
▱	Road_Hatch		♀	☼	🔓	▨ 33	Continuous	—— Default
▱	Road_Plan		♀	☼	🔓	■ 162	Continuous	▬▬ 0.70 mm

Figure 14-4

5. <u>Labels</u>: Open a previously created or downloaded contour map. Make the *Contour_Label* layer to be the current layer. Add the labels using *Text* and *Background Mask* commands. Set the height of the text to be 4 feet, Figure 14-5.

6. <u>Road Plan</u>: Using the *Road_Dim*, *Road_Center*, *Road_Plan*, and *Road_Hatch* layers, Draw the road plan. (i) Draw the center line of the road. It is 92'-6" above the lower edge of the contour map. (ii) Draw plan of the road. The road is 26'-8" wide. (iii) Add the dimensions to the centerline of the road. (iv) Hatch the road using AR-CONC, 0, and 5 for the hatch pattern, angle, and scale, respectively, Figure 14-6.

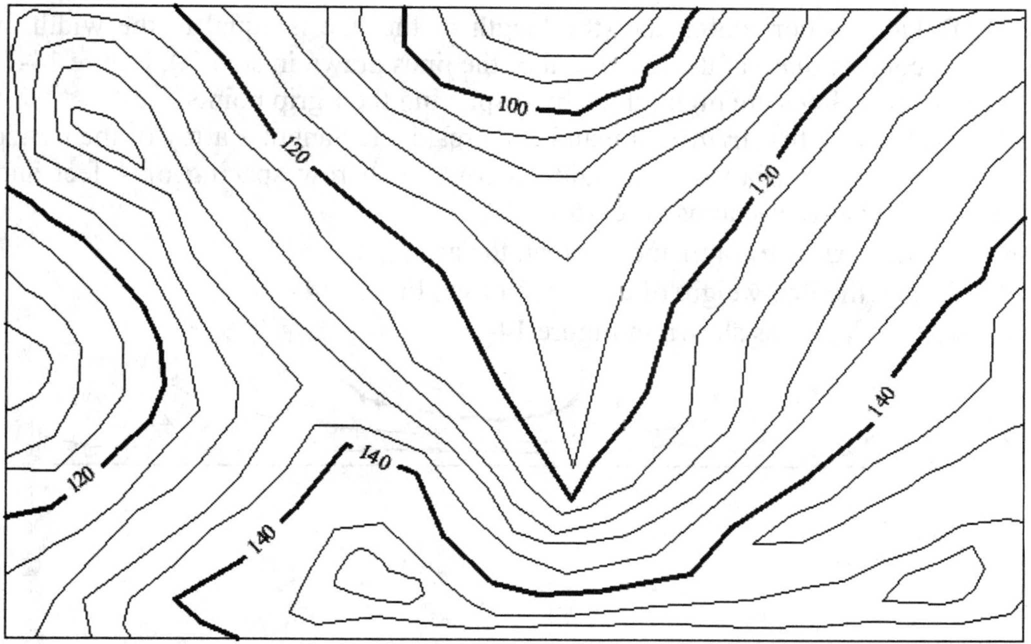

Figure 14-5

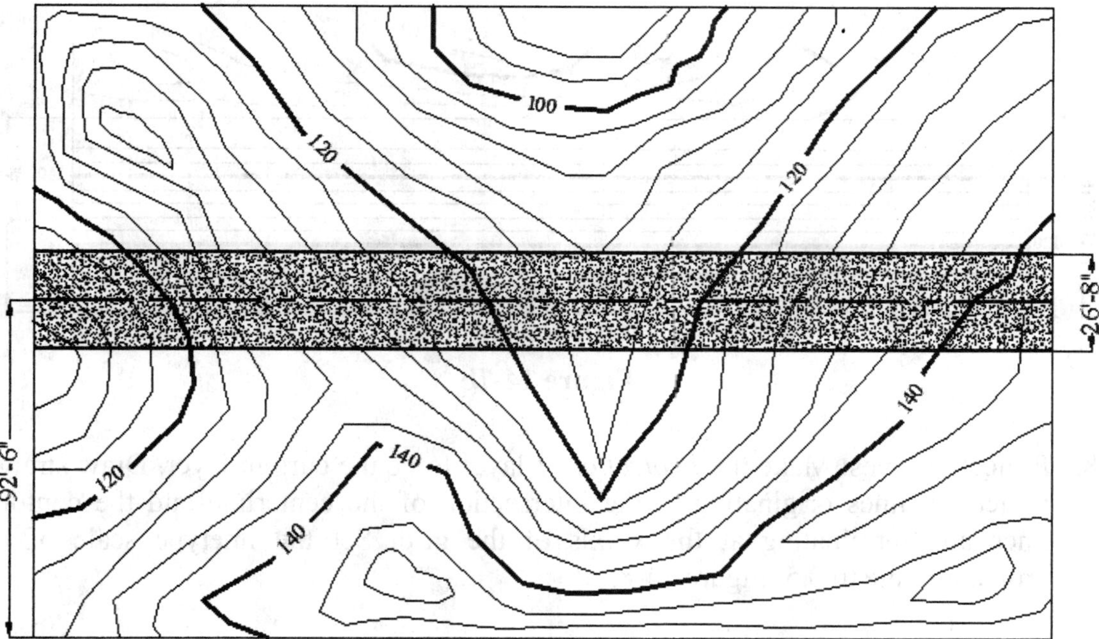

Figure 14-6

7. <u>Profile Grid</u>: Draw and label the grid for the profile.
   - Make the *Grid* layer to be the current layer. Generally, the grid color is light blue, light green, or light orange.
   - Use the *Array* command to draw the grid.
     (e) Draw two vertical lines 57'-7" long as shown in Figure 14-7a.

(f) Draw a horizontal line (the length of the line is equal to the width of the counter map) at the lower end of the lines drawn in step (a), Figure 14-7a.

(g) These lines are highlighted by displaying their grip points.

(h) Activate the *Array* command and create a rectangular array of the horizontal line. The array will contain 13 rows with row spacing of 4 feet and the number of columns is set to 1.

- Use the *Explode* command to break the array.
- Change the line weight of every fifth row, Figure 14-7b.
- Add the labels as shown in Figure 14-7b.

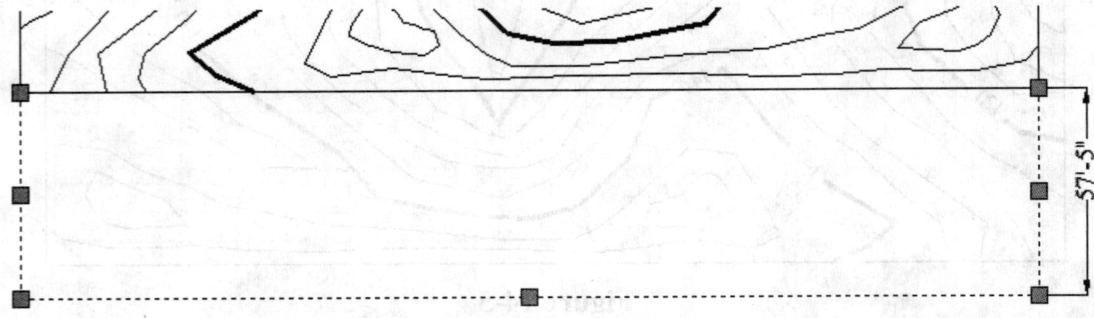

Figure 14-7a

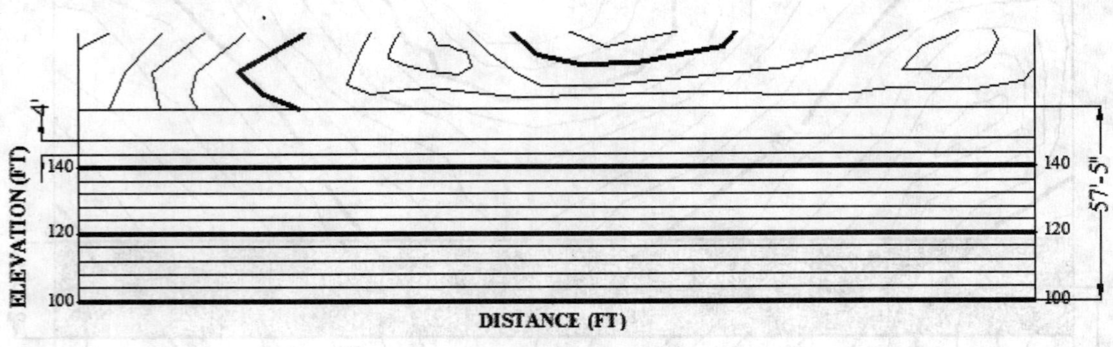

Figure 14-7b

8. <u>Projection lines</u>: Make the *Projection_1* layer to be the current layer. Draw straight projection lines originating at the intersection of the centerline and the contours lines and terminating at the x-axis of the grid. Set the linetype scale of the projection line to 0.5, Figure 14-8.

9. <u>Draw the existing profile</u>:
- Change point style and size using *Point Style* dialog box. Open the dialog box from the *Home* tab, expanded *Utilities* panel and clicking the *Point Style* tool.
- (i) Make the *Profile_Exist_Pt* layer to be the current layer. (ii) The first projection line originates at 112' contour. On the profile's grid, draw a point on this projection line at an elevation of 112'. (iii) Repeat the process for the other projection lines, Figure 13-9.

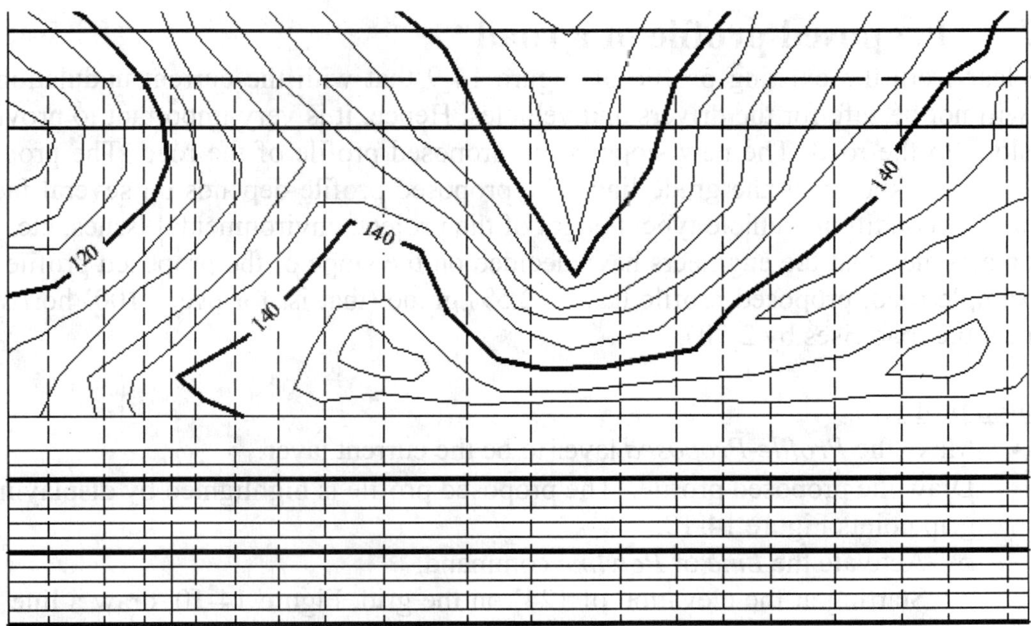

Figure 14-8

- (i) Make the *Profile-Exist* layer to be the current layer. (ii) To create the profile, activate the *Polyline* command and connect the profile points, Figure 13-9. This profile is known as the existing profile or the ground line.
- Turn *Off* the grid and projection layers.
- (i) Make the *Profile-Exist_Hatch* layer to be the current layer. (ii) Using an *Offset* command, create an offset of the profile with the offset distance of 3 feet. (iii) Move the offset to the hatch layer. (iv) Connect the ends of the profile using small lines. (v) Activate the *Hatch* command. (vi) Add the hatch. Set the pattern: *EARTH*, Angle: 0, and Scale: 100. (vii) Make the *Profile-Exist_Label* layer to be the current layer. Using the *Text, background Mask* and *qleader* commands, add label to the profile, Figure 13-9.

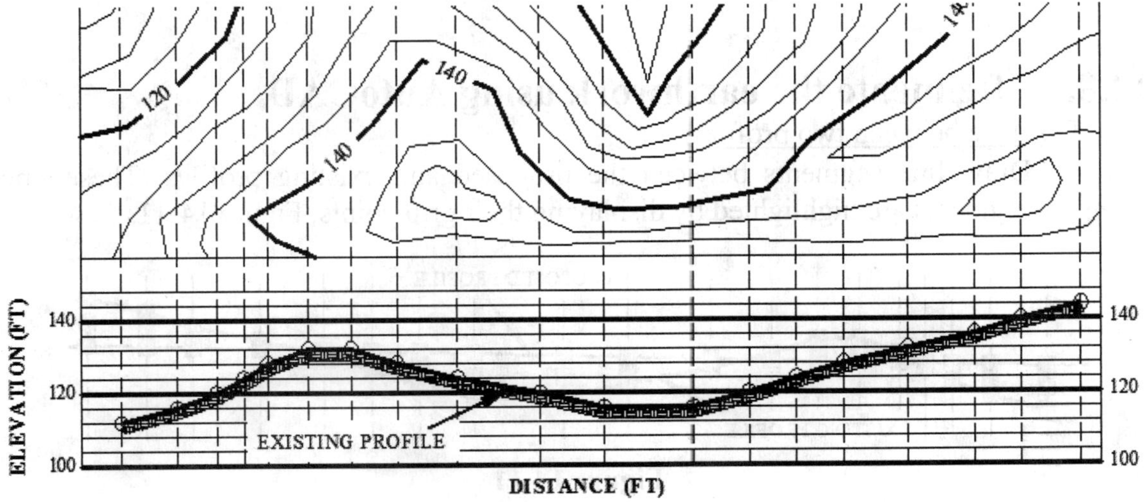

Figure 14-9

14.7.   Proposed profile of a road

It is clear from the existing profile of Figure 14-9 that with the current undulation the road will not be safe for the drivers and vehicles. Hence, it is very important to provide a safe slope to the road. The new slope is the proposed profile of the road. The proposed profile is also known as the grade line. The proposed profile depends on several factors such as soil condition, vehicle type, budget of the project, environmental issues, etc. This section assumed that the engineers have decided on the slope of the proposed profile. For the example road, proposed profile has a +2.5% grade (that is, for every 100' horizontal distance, the road rises by 2.5ft).

Proposed profile:
- Make the *Profile-Proposed* layer to be the current layer.
- Draw the proposed profile. The proposed profile is highlighted by displaying its grip points Figure 14-10.
  - o Activate the *Line* or *Polyline* command.
  - o Starting at the elevation of 124' on the grid, Figure 14-10, draw a line with +2.5% slope.
- Make the *Profile-Proposed-label* layer to be the current layer.
- Label the proposed profile as shown in Figure 14-10.

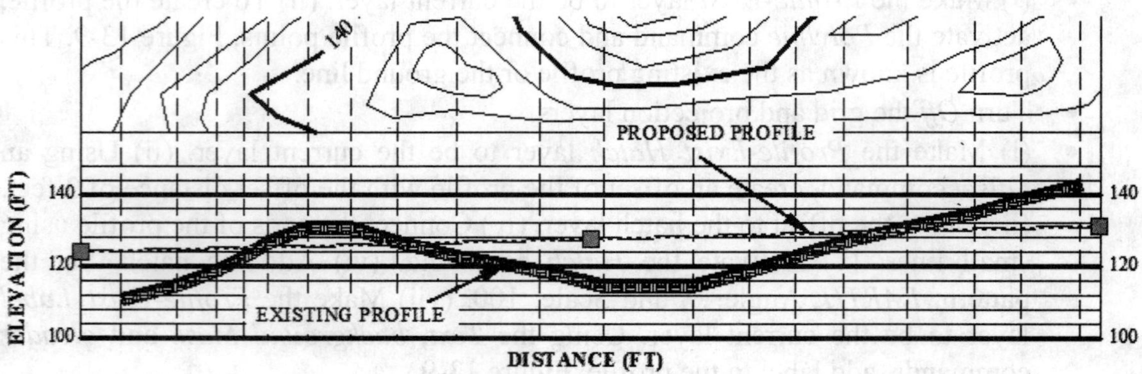

Figure 14-10

14.8.   Delineate the earthwork using AutoCAD

1. <u>Distance between two profiles</u>:
   - Draw line segments between the proposed and existing profiles. These line segments are highlighted by displaying their grip points, Figure 14-11.

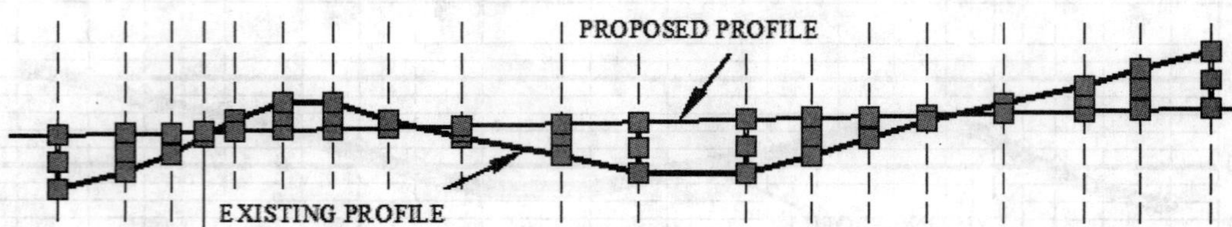

Figure 14-11

2. <u>Delineation of cut and fill</u>: The angle of repose for both the cut and fill is 2:1.
   - The example shows the delineation of the (cut or fill) boundary for the 112' and 120' contours.
   - If the projection line was originated at the intersection of the 120' contour and the centerline, then in the delineation process the segment between two profiles is referred as d120, Figure 14-12a. These line segments are highlighted by displaying their grip points.

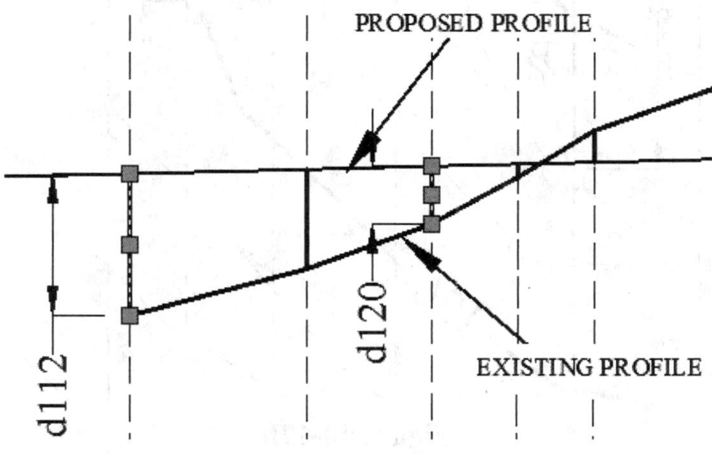

Figure 14-12a

   - Since the angle of repose is 2:1, multiply d120 by 2.
   - Make the *Cut_Fill_LN_1* layer to be the current layer.
   - Refer to Figure 14-12b.
   - Draw line segment A of length 2*d120 from the edge of the road. In AutoCAD, this can be achieved by creating two copies of d120 as follow, Figure 14-12b. (i) Turn *On* ORTHO mode from the status bar by clicking the [button] button. (ii) Activate the *Copy* command. (iii) Select d120 between the two profiles. (iv) Select the upper end as the base point for the *Copy* command. (v) Place one copy at the intersection of the lower edge of the road and the projection line originated at 120' contour. (vi) Place the second copy at the lower end of the first copy.
   - Draw line segment B starting at the lower end of the line A and terminating at the 120' contour (the length of B can be few inches to few feet).
   - Make the *Cut_Fill_PT_1* layer to be the current layer. Draw point C at the intersection of line B and the 120' contour.
   - Figure 14-12b shows lines A and B for the 112' and 120' contour lines.
   - These line segments are highlighted by displaying their grip points
   - Repeat the process for the remaining contours, Figure 14-12c. Draw points on *Cut_Fill_LN_1* layer.

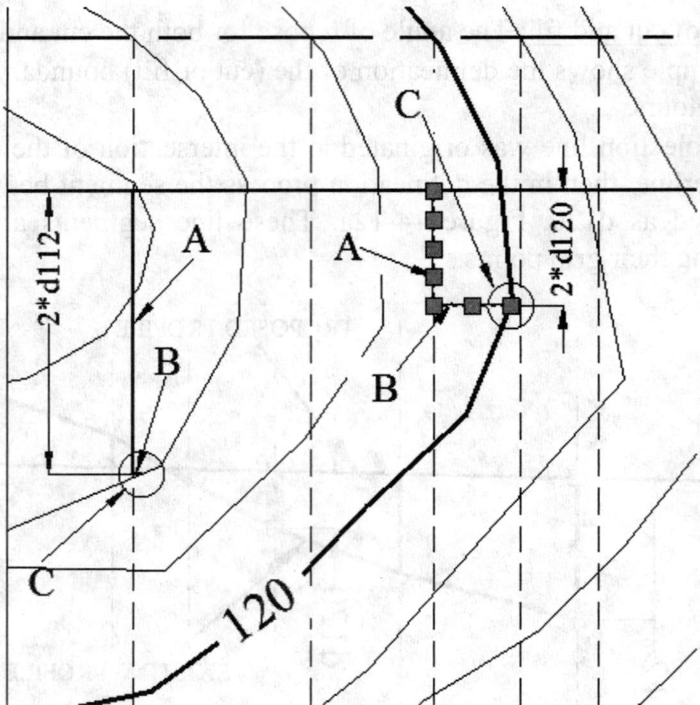

Figure 14-12b

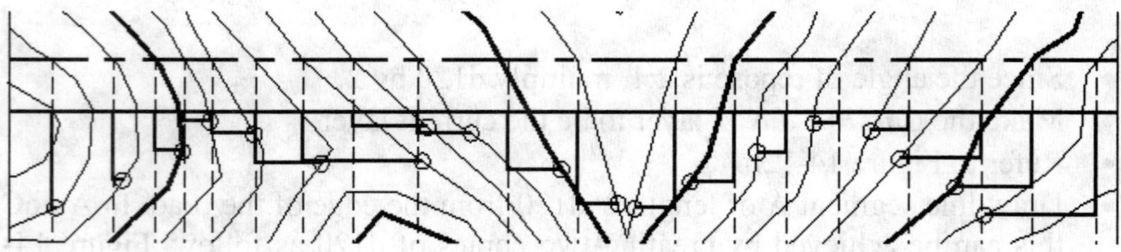

Figure 14-12c

- Extend the projection lines to the other edge of the road, Figure 14-13a.

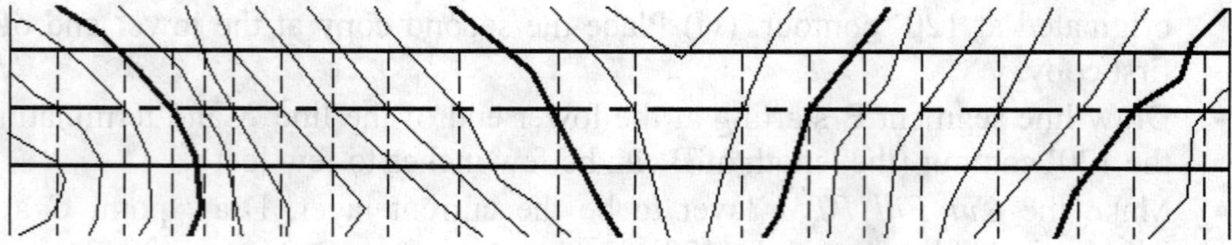

Figure 14-13a

- Repeat the delineation process for the other edge of the road using layers *Cut_Fill_LN_2* for lines and *Cut_Fill_PT_2* for points, Figure 14-13b.

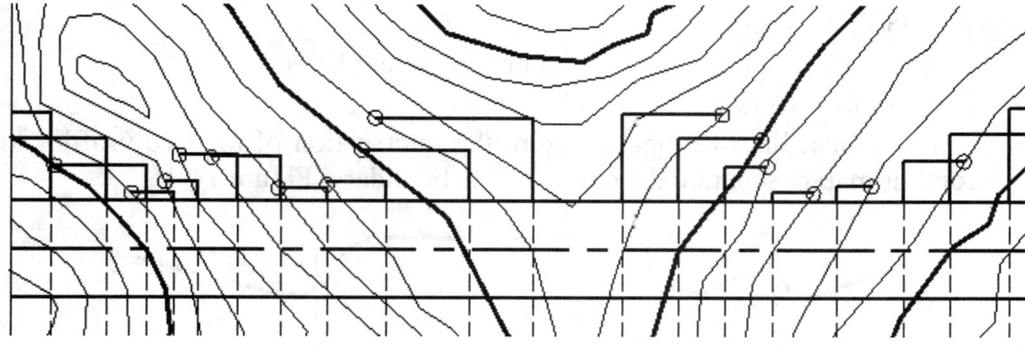

Figure 14-13b

3. <u>Draw boundary</u>:
    - Make the *Cut_Fill_Shape* layer to be the current layer.
    - Draw polylines through the points to delineate the boundary, Figure 14-14a.
    - Extend the polylines drawn in the above step to the end of the contour map using the *Extend* command, Figure 14-14b.

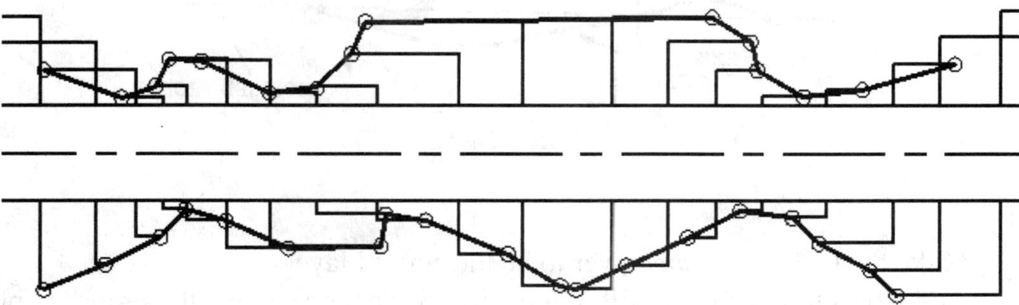

Figure 14-14a

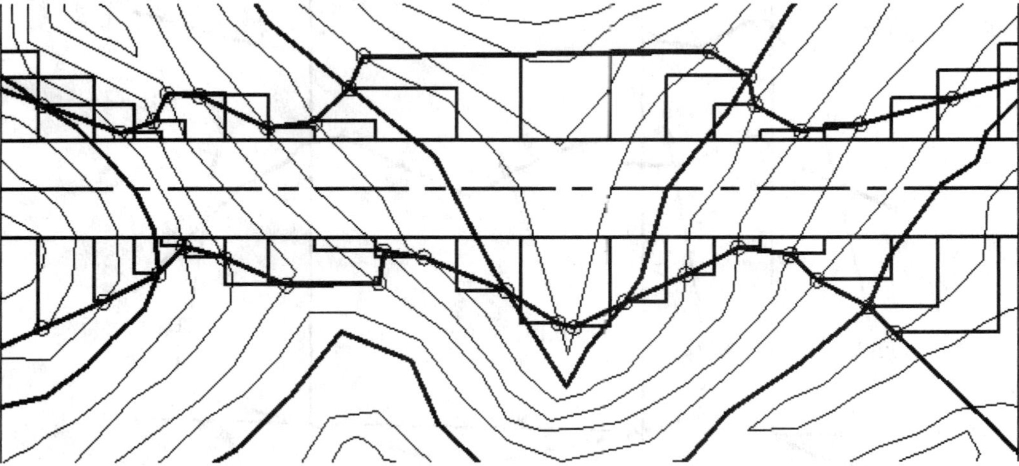

Figure 14-14a

4. <u>Separate the cut and fill</u>:
    - Make the *Cut_Fill_Divide* layer to be the current layer.
    - Turn *Off* the layers as shown in Figure 14-15.
    - Draw vertical lines originating from the intersection of the two profiles to the contour map to separate the cut and fill's boundary, Figure 14-15.

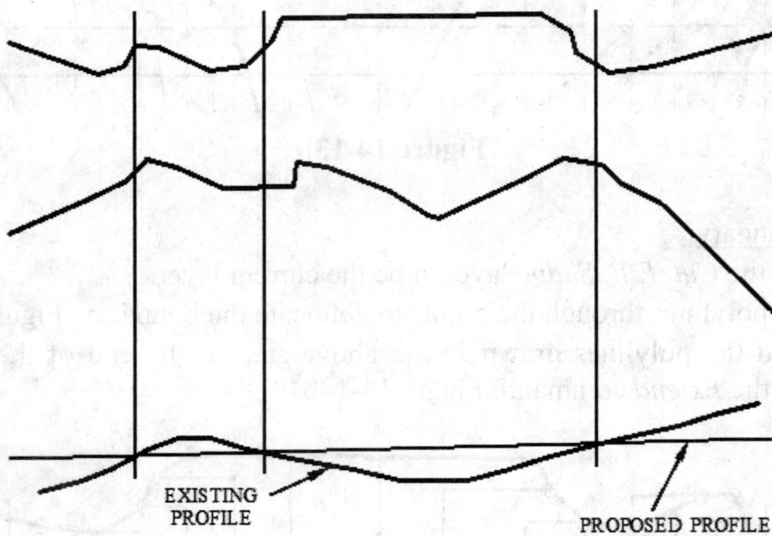

Figure 14-15

5. <u>Label</u>:
    - Make the *Cut_Fill_Label* layer to be the current layer
    - Add labels to the cut and fill, Figure 14-16. The area above the proposed profile represents the cut, and the area below the proposed profile represents the fill.

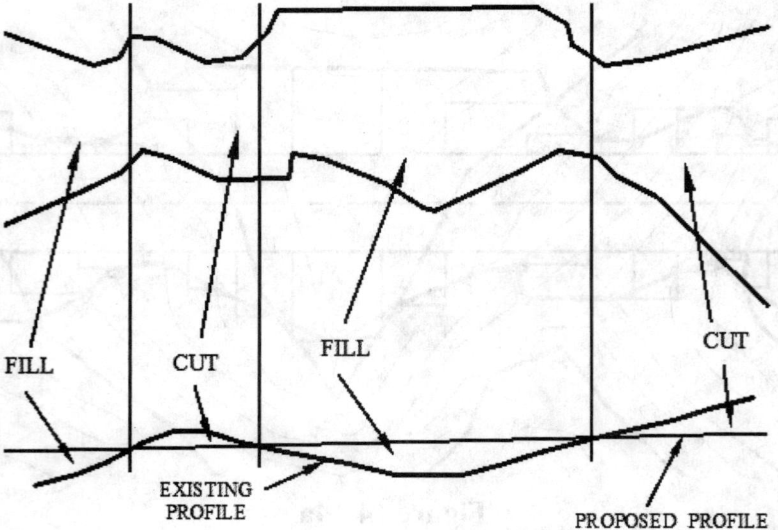

Figure 14-16

6. Hatch:
    - Make the *Cut_Fill_Hatch* layer to be the current layer
    - Draw vertical lines to close the open ends of the cut and fill, Figure 14-17. These line segments are highlighted by displaying their grip points.
    - Hatch the areas as shown in the Figure 14-17. The cut is hatched using GRAVEL pattern at the scale of 100 and the fill is hatched using EARTH pattern at the scale of 175.

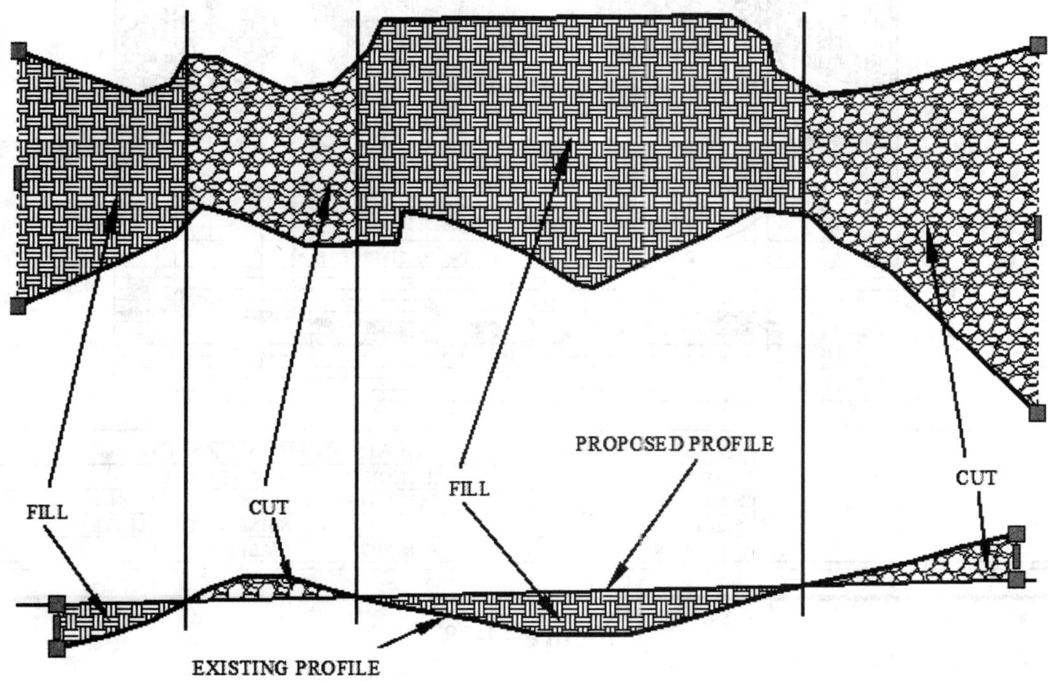

Figure 14-17

7. Insert Template file:
    - Finally, insert a layout from the template file labeled as "My_acad_Landscape_tmplt.dwt".
    - Set the scale of the drawing to be 1:450, Figure 16-18.
    - Lock the viewport
    - Update the Title block.
    - The resultant drawing in the layout is shown in Figure 16-18.

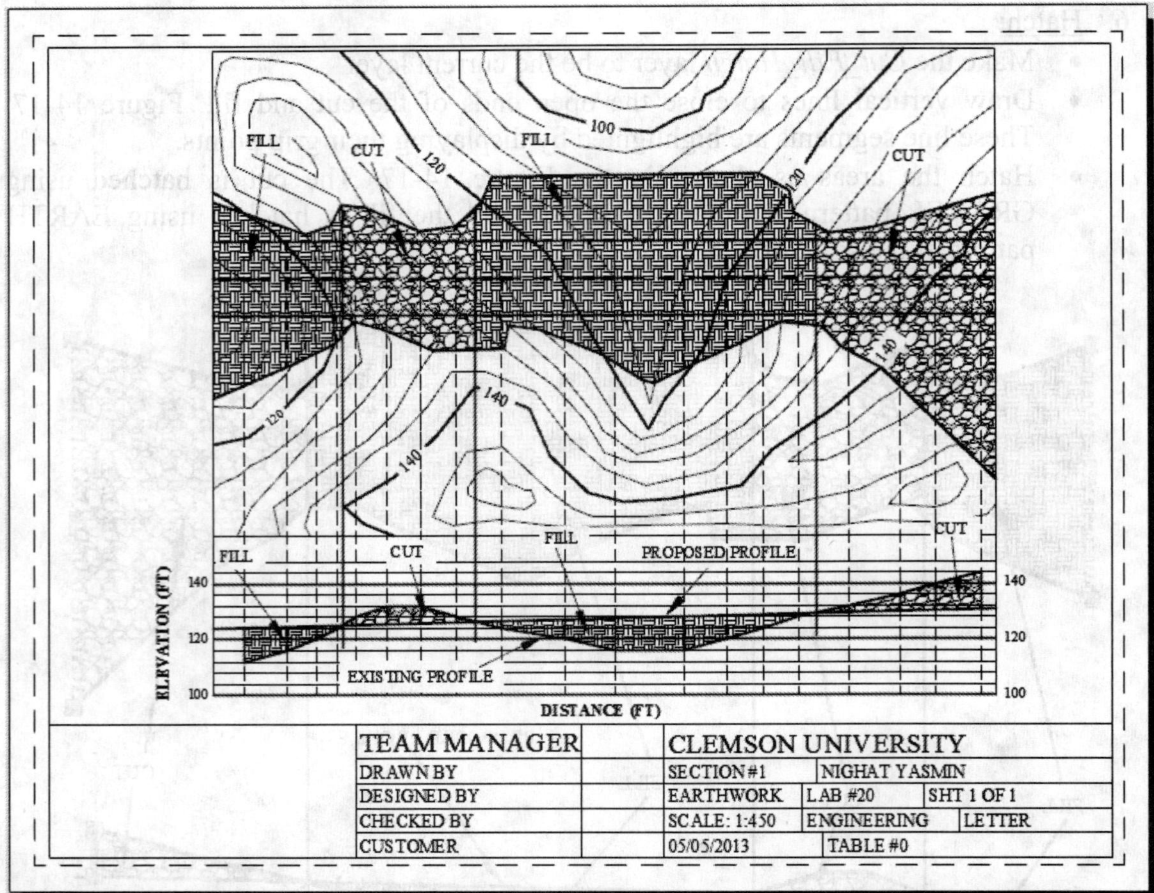

TEAM MANAGER	CLEMSON UNIVERSITY		
DRAWN BY	SECTION #1	NIGHAT YASMIN	
DESIGNED BY	EARTHWORK	LAB #20	SHT 1 OF 1
CHECKED BY	SCALE: 1:450	ENGINEERING	LETTER
CUSTOMER	05/05/2013	TABLE #0	

Figure 14-18

15. Floor Plan

15.1.   Objectives

- Learn to design and draw a floor plan
- Learn to create windows and doors openings
- Learn to insert user created and *Design Center*'s block in the floor plan
- Learn to add dimensions to the floor plan
- Learn to create doors and windows schedules for the floor plan

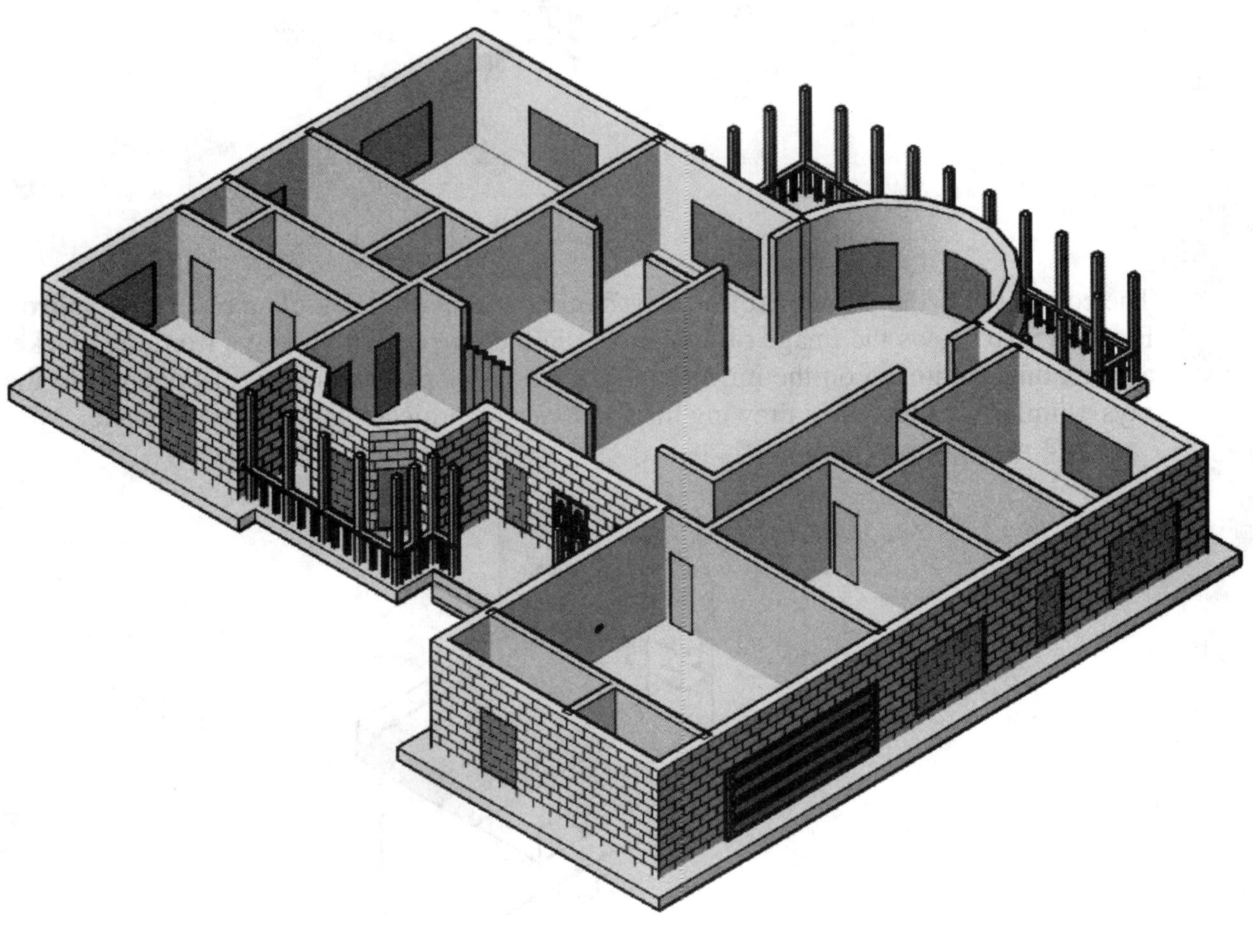

15.2.   Introduction

Consider a simple angle bracket shown in Figure 15-1a. The question is how it can be sketched to convey its shape correctly in 2D?

- The bracket is three dimensional and describing it in words is difficult.
- To make the drawing process of a 3D objects easier, engineers use a standard system called orthographic projection or orthographic views.
- The orthographic projection shows two dimensional views of three dimensional objects.

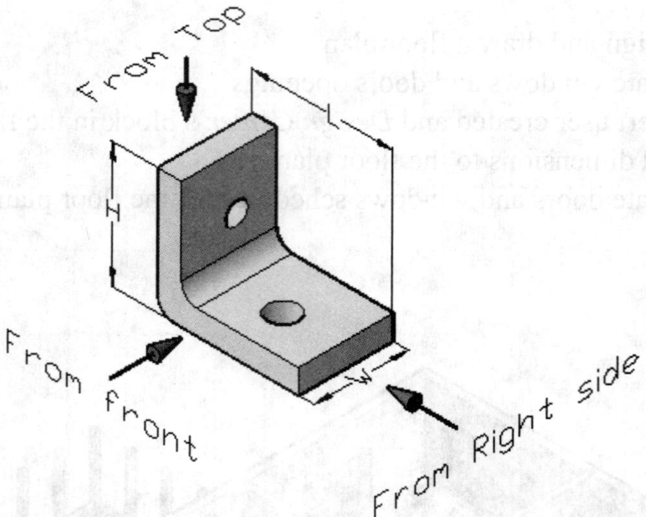

Figure 15-1a

The concept of orthographic projection is similar to the reflection of an object in a mirror. Figure 15-1b shows the image of the bracket in the mirror. Parallel rays from the bracket are creating the image on the mirror, and the mirror is perpendicular (orthogonal) to the rays. Similarly, in technical drawing the front view is projected on the frontal plane.

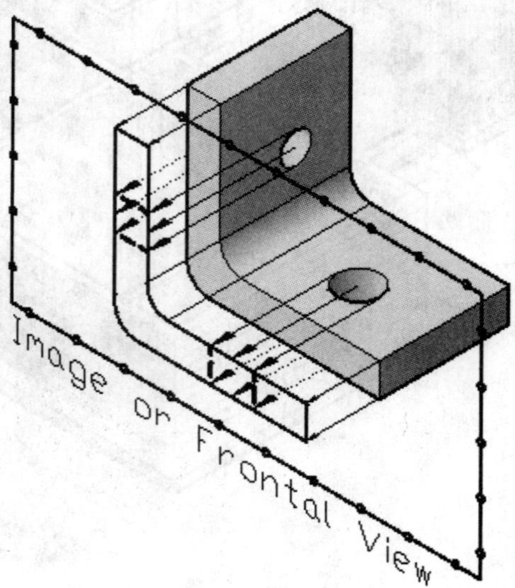

Figure 15-1b

If the bracket is looked at from the top, front, and right sides (Figure 15-1a), then its orthographic projections will be two dimensional views, Figure 15-1c. Vertical lines are used to project information between top and front views. Horizontal lines are used to project information between front and right-side views. Horizontal and vertical lines are used to project information between front and right-side views using 45 degree miter line, Figure 15-1c.

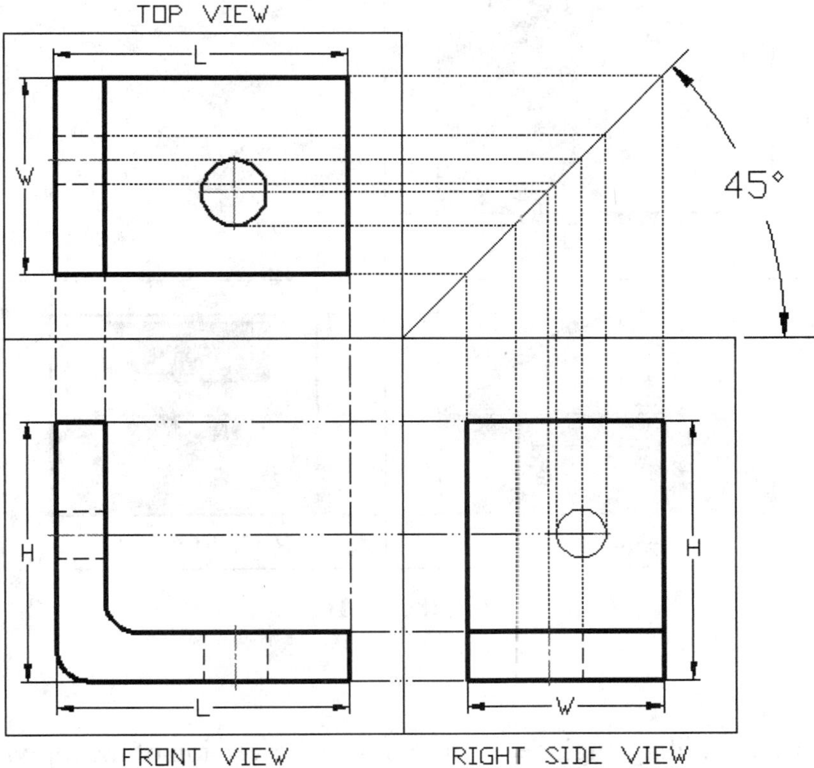

Figure 15-1c

The focus of this chapter is the top view of a building, also known as a floor plan. The next chapter emphasis is on the front view of the floor plan developed in this chapter. Consider a simple building shown in Figure 15-1d. The figure shows the south east isometric view of the building.

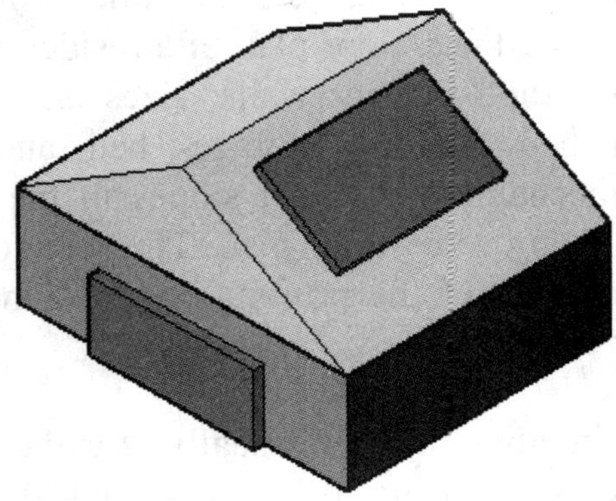

Figure 15-1d

The three orthographic views (top, front, and right side view) are shown in Figure 15-1e. Notice the projection of the skylight (the box in the roof), front door, and the gable roof (the triangular roof) in the three orthographic views.

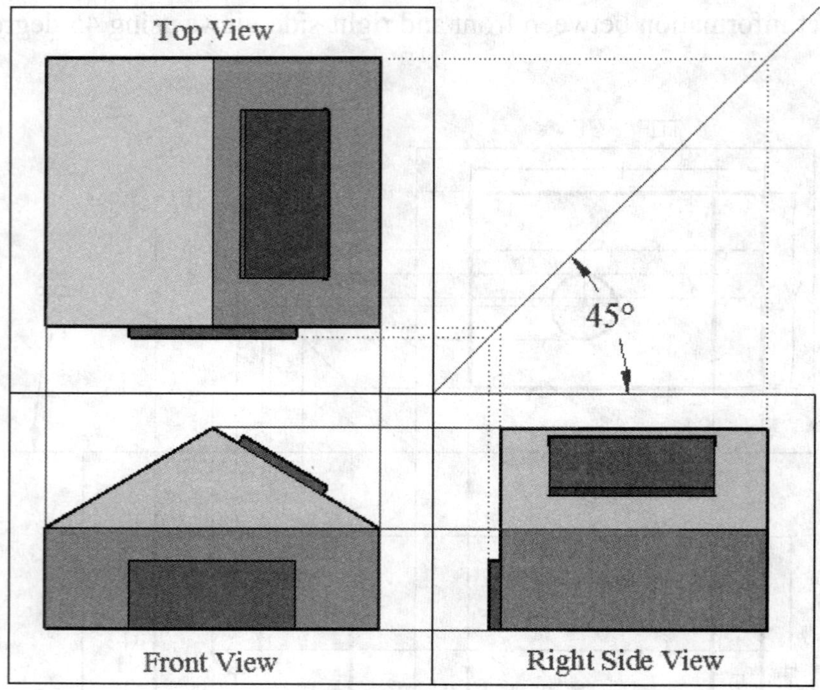

Figure 15-1e

15.3.   Floor plan

In architecture and building engineering terminology, a version of the top view is called a floor plan. A floor plan is a simple two-dimensional line drawing resulting from looking at a building from above (below the ceiling level). It displays the relationship between rooms, windows, doors, walls, stairs, fireplace, and other features at one level of a building as if it seen from the top. The focus of this chapter is designing and drawing a floor plan for a typical residential building with three bedrooms, three bathrooms, a study room, and a two cars garage.

The floor plan is the most important and detailed dimensioned drawing of a building. Some of the information included in a floor plan of a residential building is: the location and thickness of the exterior and interior walls; sizes and location of the doors and windows; details of the kitchen, laundry-, storage-, bed- and bath- rooms; ventilation, plumbing, electrical, and mechanical systems; slopes in the floor; etc. For multistory buildings, stairs are also shown on the floor plan. The scale of the drawing depends on the size of the building and size of the printing paper. Generally, the floor plans are printed at a scale of 1:48 or 1:96.

The floor plan design is an iterative process. Usually, it is the first drawing to be started. On the other hand, it is the last drawing to be completed. It is revised several times to accommodate the decision made in the elevations and sectional views' design.

15.4. Windows

The windows are important part of a building. Windows have evolved over time, from an opening in the wall for fresh air to enter and smoke to leave to the modern day sophisticated windows. Windows provide light and ventilation to the residents and architectural enhancement to the building; however, improperly placed windows will detract from the house's appearance. Generally, 12% of a wall should be windows and the total glass area of the window should be about 10% of the floor area.

15.4.1. Types of windows

Based on the method of opening a window, the commonly used windows are classified as fixed, casement, sliding, and double-hung.

- Fixed: The fixed windows are also known as picture windows. These windows do not have any moving parts. Although, these windows can provide 100% light, they provide 0% ventilation. These are the cheapest windows.
- Casement: The casement window provides 100% ventilation and 100% light. These windows are hinged.
  - **Side hinge:** These windows can be hinged at the side, Figure 15-2a. Usually side hinged windows are narrow but can be joined to one another, or to a fixed window, to fill wider openings.
  - **Awning or top hinge:** These windows can be hinged at the top, Figure 15-2b. Awning windows are wider and shorter. Generally, open awning windows swing outward.
  - **Hopper or bottom hinge:** These windows can be hinged at the bottom, Figure 15-2c. Hopper windows are commonly used in the commercial buildings. Open windows generally swing inward; otherwise, rain water will come inside if it opens outward.

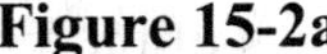
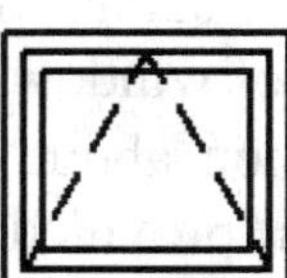
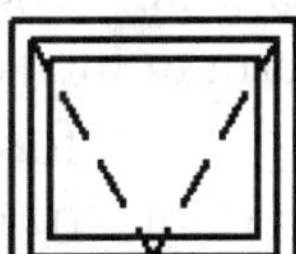

Figure 15-2a	**Figure 15-2b**	**Figure 15-2c**

- Sliding: The sliding windows are opened by gliding window panels on horizontal tracks in pairs, Figure 15-2d. These windows provide 50% ventilation and 100% light.
- Double-hung: The double-hung (also known as vertical-slide) windows are open by gliding window panels on vertical tracks, Figure 15-2e. These windows provide 50% ventilation and 100% light. These windows are commonly used in small residential buildings.

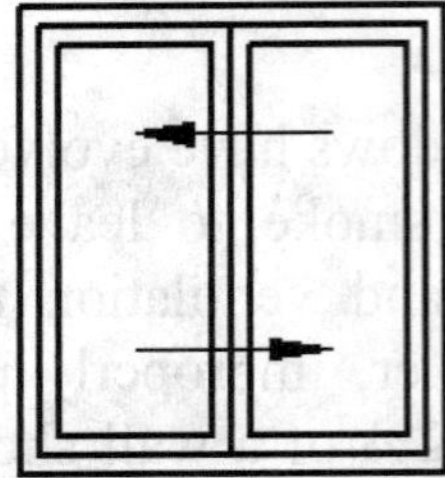

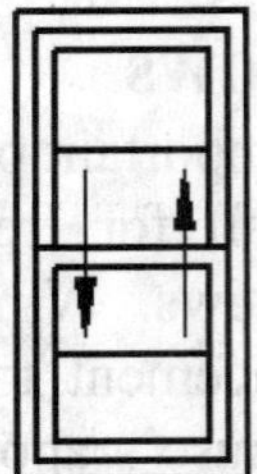

Figure 15-2d   **Figure 15-2e**

15.4.2. Window sizes

A window can be of any size. Companies manufacture windows in various shapes and sizes. Nonetheless, the type and size of the windows depends on the building style and the client's requirements. As a rule of thumb, the width of a window is about half of its height. Typically, the top of a window opening is 6'–8" from the floor. The bottom of the opening depends on the type of the room; for example, a bedroom, dining, and a living room window's openings are 3'–10", 2'–10", and 1'– 10", respectively, above the floor level.

15.4.3. Window selection

The selection of a window type and its location depends on several factors. Windows should be located to improve the cross ventilation. Also, the hinged window opening in the hallways or walkways should be high enough (per se 6 feet) to avoid injures.

- <u>Site orientation</u>: In the Northern Hemisphere, the windows should be located in the southern walls, thus allowing sunlight to enter the room during the winter months.
- <u>Insulation</u>: The information regarding thermal performance (how much energy is lost for heating or cooling the building) of a window is very important. Inadequately insulated windows will increase the air-conditioning cost, cause discomfort to the residents, and stain and decay the window material due to condensation.
- <u>Operation</u>: The ease of opening, closing, and cleaning a window are important criteria in the selection of the type of window.
- <u>Service</u>: Before making the decision about the style and size of a window, it is important to check the services provided by the manufacturer, such as the warranties, accessibility of spare parts, and availability of representative at the site.
- <u>Floor level</u>: In two stories residential buildings, generally, windows of the first floor are taller than the windows on the second floor.
- <u>Safety</u>: In the residential buildings, at least one window should have a clear space big enough for occupants to exit and firefighters to enter the room. The window opening space should be at least 1'–8" wide and 2' high; and its area should be at least six square-feet.
- <u>Security</u>: The windows should be built from the break-resistant material.
- <u>Window sill</u>: The window sills should be located below the eye level of the seated person. For example, it should be 1' above the floor level in the living room and 4' in the bedrooms.

15.5.   Doors

The doors are also important parts of a building. They provide access to a building from outside and to different parts of a building from inside and outside.

15.5.1. Types of Door

Doors are classified as exterior and interior based on their location; flush, panel, and louvered doors based on their appearance; hinged, folding, sliding, accordion, and overhead based on the method of door opening. French and Dutch doors are the special purpose doors.

- Exterior: As the name suggest, the exterior doors are used to enter a building from the outside. The front and rear entrance doors are the exterior doors.
- Interior: The interior doors are used to access different parts of a building. These doors include bedroom, bathroom, kitchen, and laundry room doors.
- Flush: The flush doors have smooth and easy-to-maintain surfaces, Figure 15-3a. These doors are the most commonly used door due to their low maintenance and construction cost. These doors may be solid- or hollow-core. The solid-core doors are heavier and denser than the hollow-core doors.

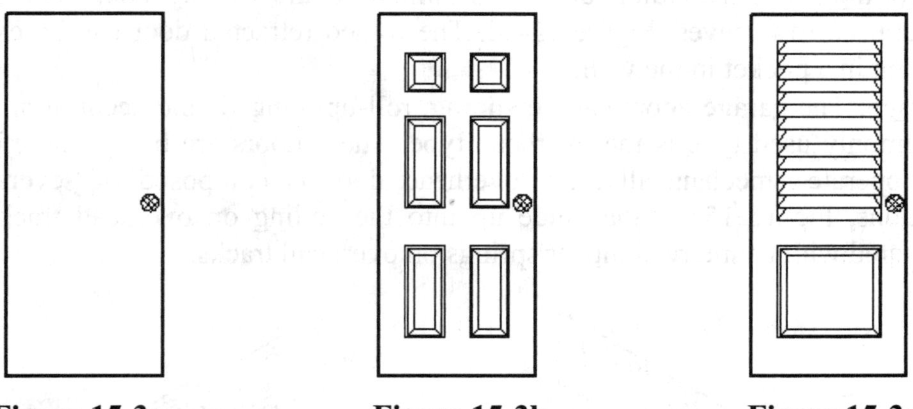

Figure 15-3a   **Figure 15-3b**   **Figure 15-3c**

- Panel: The panel doors were developed centuries ago to overcome the dimensional distortions caused by weathering effects. The changes in the moisture content would expand and contract wooden doors. These doors contain built-in panels which help maintain the door's shape. The panels can be of different shape and sizes. Figure 15-3b shows 6-paneled doors with two types of panel.
- Louvered: The louvered doors have horizontal stripes placed on the diagonal for the ventilation. These doors are attractive but difficult to maintain (dusting and painting will take very long time), Figure 15-3c.
- Hinged: Typically, these doors are hinged at the side. These doors may be flush, panel, or louvered. These doors can swing inward or outward and for 90 or 180 degrees (also known as swinging doors). These doors can be installed as a double unit or two-leaved, where one is hinged on the left side and the other is hinged on the right side, Figure 15-4a. The minimum space requirement for these doors is the width of one panel of the door.

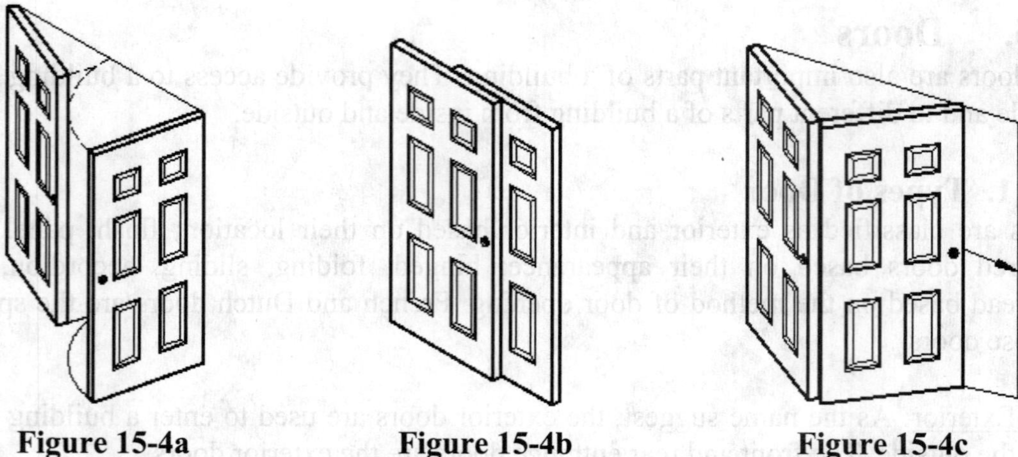

Figure 15-4a   **Figure 15-4b**   **Figure 15-4c**

- <u>Folding</u>: The folding doors are the combination of hinged and the sliding doors. The two leaves are hinged together and one of the leaves is also hinged at the side, Figure 15-4c. The advantage of the folding doors is that the door can be completely open and thus all of the doorway space is available. These doors can be single (two leaves as shown in Figure 15-4c) or double units (four leaves).
- <u>Accordion</u>: The accordion doors are similar to the folding doors but consist of several narrow leaves, Figure 15-4d. The folded retracted door can be exposed or hidden in a pocket in the wall.
- <u>Garage</u>: The garage doors can be sliding, roll-up, hinged, and accordion. The most commonly used type is the overhead type. These doors are bulky; therefore, most are operated mechanically. An overhead door is composed of several hinged sections, Figure 15-4e, that slide up into the ceiling on overhead tracks, and is operated with counterweights or springs on overhead tracks.

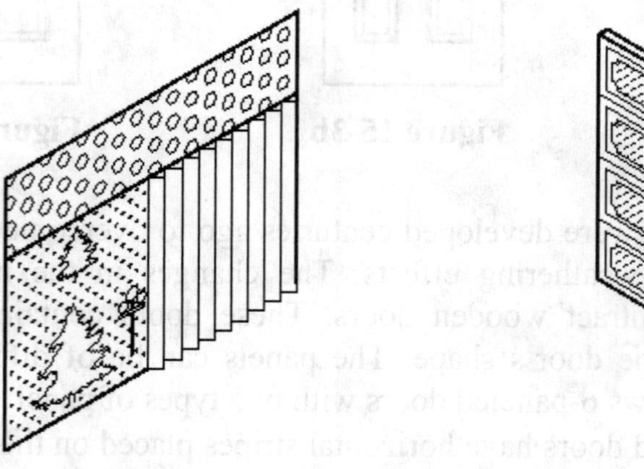

Figure 15-4d   **Figure 15-4e**

15.5.2. Door sizes

A door can be of any size. Companies manufacture doors in various sizes. Nonetheless, the type and size of the door depends on the building style, room type, and the client's requirements. Typically, a door opening is 3 inches wider and 3 inches longer than the size of the door. As a rule of thumb, the width of a door is about half of its height. The commonly used residential door sizes are listed below.

- Front entrance door 3'-0" X 6'-8" X 1 3/4"
- Bedroom doors 2'-6" or 2'-8" X 6'-8" X 1 3/8"
- Bathroom doors 2'- or 2'-6" X 6'-8" X 1 3/8"
- A garage door is 7 feet high and its width can be 8 feet or 9 feet for single-car garages and 16 feet for a double-car garage.

15.5.3. Door selection

The selection of a door depends on the location of the door. Other factors affecting the door selection process in a typical residential building are listed below.

- Weather- and break-resistances are the major factors in selecting the exterior doors.
- Fire- and noise-resistances are the major factors in selecting the interior doors.
- Solid-core flush doors are typically used for exterior entrances and hollow-core doors are suitable for the interior use.
- Louvered doors are the best candidate for the closet doors.
- Hinge doors are commonly used for main entrances, bedrooms, and bathrooms.
- Swinging doors are commonly used in kitchens and dining areas for easy operation in both directions.
- Sliding doors are selected for closets and exterior doors (opening in the porch or backyard) from the living area.
- Folding doors are used for the closets and laundry room.
- Accordion doors are used between dining and living areas.

15.5.4. Door appearance in floor plan

The following list is the plan view of the different types of doors discussed earlier.
- <u>Figure 15-5a</u>: Hinged, single panel, swing inward.
- <u>Figure 15-5b</u>: Hinged, single panel, swing outward.
- <u>Figure 15-5c</u>: Hinged, double panel, swing inward.
- <u>Figure 15-5d</u>: Accordion.
- <u>Figure7-5e</u>: Folding, double panel, 4 leaves.
- <u>Figure 15-5f</u>: Sliding, double panel.

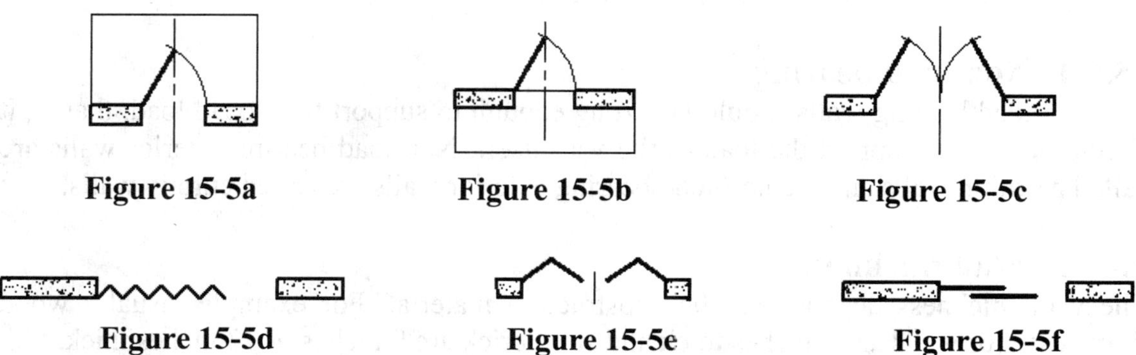

Figure 15-5a	Figure 15-5b	Figure 15-5c

Figure 15-5d	Figure 15-5e	Figure 15-5f

15.6.   Wall

The walls are the structures that demarcate a building from the surrounding buildings or open spaces. They support the load of the superstructure (roof, ceiling, and upper level floors) of the building and divide the building space into rooms or hallways. They provide security against intrusion and shelter from the weather. The walls in a building can be grouped as exterior and interior walls or load bearing and non-load bearing walls.

15.6.1. Exterior

The design of an exterior wall is a crucial part in the architectural design of a building. Some basic features of an exterior wall are listed here.

- Access to the building: The exterior wall should provide method of entry and exit to the occupants of the building yet keep intruders out. The access is achieved through the doors.
- Vision: The vision from the exterior walls should be unidirectional; that is, the resident could be able to look outside. On the other hand, outsiders should not be able to look inside.
- Surface finish: The exterior surface of an exterior wall is exposed to the weather; therefore, it should be heat, wind, and rain resistant.
- Climate control: The exterior wall should provide for the methods of ventilation, heat transfer, and noise control. These characteristics can be achieved by appropriate placement of windows and by properly insulating doors and windows.
- Fire control: The exterior wall should prevent the spreading of a fire from inside to outside and vice versa.
- Durability: The walls should be durable for the life of the building.
- Miscellaneous: Generally, power outlets, phone connections, lighting switches, thermostats, and plumbing ducts are placed inside the walls.

15.6.2. Interior

The interior walls should also satisfy the vision, fire control, durability, and miscellaneous characteristics as mentioned in the exterior walls.

15.6.3. Load bearing

The load bearing walls not only support the dead load of the structure, but also support the load of the roof, ceiling, and upper level floors.

15.6.4. Non-load bearing

The non-load bearing walls should be strong enough to support their dead load; that is, it should be able to support the load of the wall itself. Non-load bearing interior walls are called partition walls and the non-load bearing exterior walls are called curtain walls.

15.6.5. Wall thickness

The wall thickness depends on the construction material. For example, usually wood frame exterior walls are 6 inches thick and solid brick are 9 inches or 12 inches thick.

15.7. Stair

For multilevel buildings, the inter-level movement (also known as vertical movement) is made possible through the stairs, elevators, ramps, and escalators. This section will discuss stairs. The terms stairwell, stairway, staircase, and stairs are often used interchangeably. A stairwell is the space in the building where the stairs are constructed. A staircase is often used for the stairs (steps, railings, landings, etc.). The expression stairway is reserved for the entire stairwell and staircase in combination.

The location of stairs is very important. In case of emergency, the stairs are used to evacuate the building. In case of tornado, a stairwell can also be used as an area of refuge.

15.7.1. Terminology

Some of the commonly used terms are explained in this section and are illustrated in Figure 15-6.

- <u>Flight</u>: A flight is an uninterrupted series of steps.

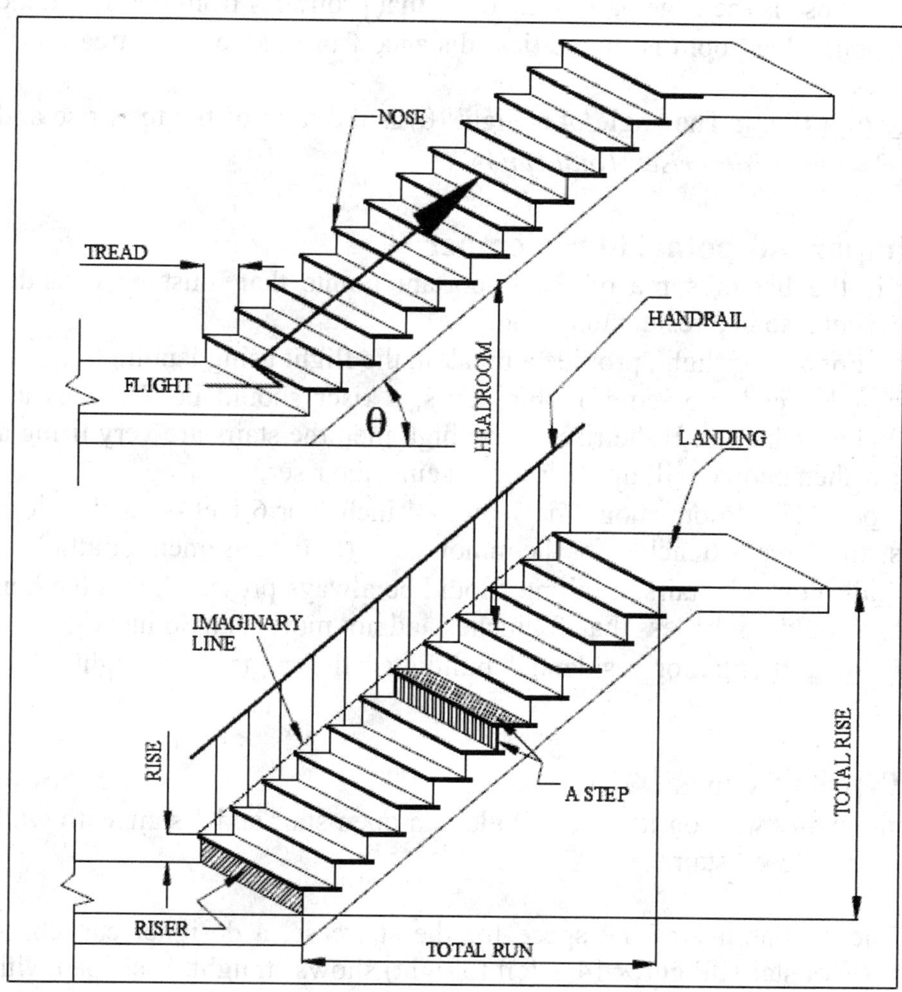

Figure 15-6

- Landing: A landing is the floor area near the top or bottom step of a stair, or a small platform built as part of the stair used to change flight's direction, or to provide the user a resting place.
- Tread (or going): A tread is the horizontal surface part of each step that is stepped on. The tread length is measured from the outer edge of the step to the riser between two adjacent steps.
- Riser: A riser is the vertical portion of the step between two adjacent steps.
- Rise: A rise is the vertical distance between two adjacent treads.
- Total rise: The total rise represents the total vertical distance traveled by a stair; that is, it is the floor-to-floor distance.
- Total run: Total run is the total horizontal length of the stair (from the first riser to the last riser).
- Handrail: Handrail is the round or decorative member of a railing used for hand holding during ascent or descent. It runs parallel to the imaginary line drawn from the top of the first tread to the top of the last tread.
- Step: A step is the combination of a riser and one of the adjacent treads.
- Nose: A nose is the edge part of the tread that protrudes from the riser underneath.
- Headroom: Headroom is the vertical distance from the top of a tread to the ceiling above it.
- Angle of a flight: The angle of a flight (θ) is the ratio of the total rise and the total run ($\theta = tan^{-1}(Total\ rise\,/\,Total\ run)$).

15.7.2. Important points to remember

Following is the list of some of the important points that must be considered when designing a staircase in a residential building.

- Flight: For a long flight, provide a break in the flight using landing(s).
- Riser and Tread: For comfortable stairs, a riser should be 7 inches and a tread should be 11 inches. If the riser is too high then the stairs are very tiring and if it is too low then people will hit their toes against the riser.
- Headroom: Headroom should be 7 feet - 4 inches or 6 feet - 8 inches for the major stairs, and 6 feet - 6 inches for the minor stairs (to the basement or attic).
- Handrail: For safe stairs, a railing should be always provided, and the height of the railing should not be less than 32 inches and not more than 36 inches.
- Angle of a flight: For residential buildings, the angle of a flight (θ) should be 30°-33°.

15.7.3. Types of stairs

A stair without any wall on its side is called an open stair and a stair with walls on both sides is called a closed stair.

Based on the availability of the space for the staircase, a designer can choose among different types of stairs. Figures 14-7(left to right) shows straight, L-shaped with winders, L-shaped with landing, narrow U, and spiral stairs, respectively.

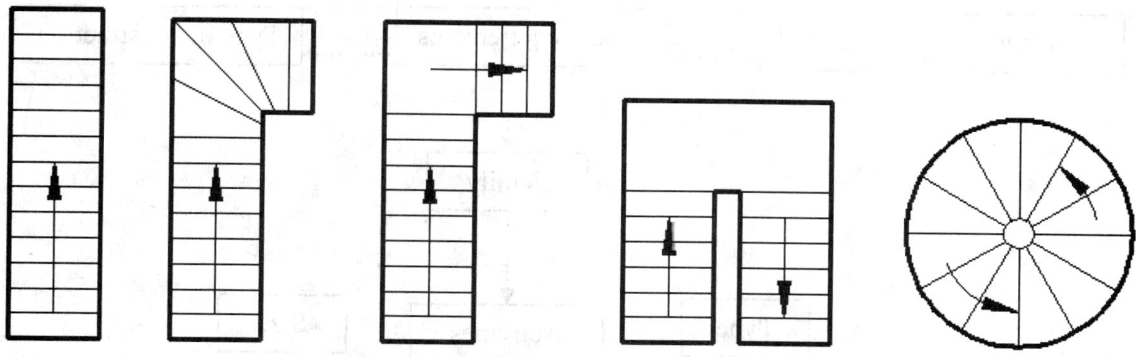

Figure 15-7

15.8.   Basics of floor plan design

A building's planning is one of the fundamental architectural and engineering design problems. A residential building is smaller in size as compared to a large commercial building, yet it involves various aspects of design and very intricate details. Hence, the focus of this section is a floor plan design for a small residential building. Figure 15-8a shows a simple flow chart of the major steps involved in the design.

- <u>Budget</u>: In designing a house, the monthly and yearly income of the family greatly influences the cost of the house. As a rule of thumb, the price of the house should not be more than three times the yearly income. Also, the cost of the house and the price of the lot should be proportional. On average, the price of the lot should be 15% to 20% of the house cost.

- <u>Site</u>: Some of the important features of the lot that must be considered before designing and creating architectural drawings are listed here.
  - *Size*: The number and size of the rooms is directly related with the lot size. For the same size and number of the rooms, a single story house on a larger lot and multistory house on a smaller plot may be the best options.
  - *Shape*: The shape of the house depends on the shape of the lot. A house design for a broader lot may not be feasible for a narrow lot.
  - *Contours*: Contour lines indicate the change in the elevation. Special design criteria must be considered for the steep lots. If the lot is sloped inward, based on the contours, a split-level house may be the only option.
  - *Utilities*: The cost of the house may increase if the basic utilities (water, electricity, gas, sewer, trash collection) are not available near the lot under consideration.
  - *Orientation*: If possible the living areas should have the southern exposure. Also, if a house is properly planned than the summer breeze can come in and the winter cold air can be kept out.
  - *Convenience to amenities*: The cost of daily commute to school, office, and shopping area may increase or decrease the cost of a lot which in turn will affect the cost of the house.
- <u>Type of construction</u>: Consider the type of the construction material (for example, wood, brick, steel, etc.).

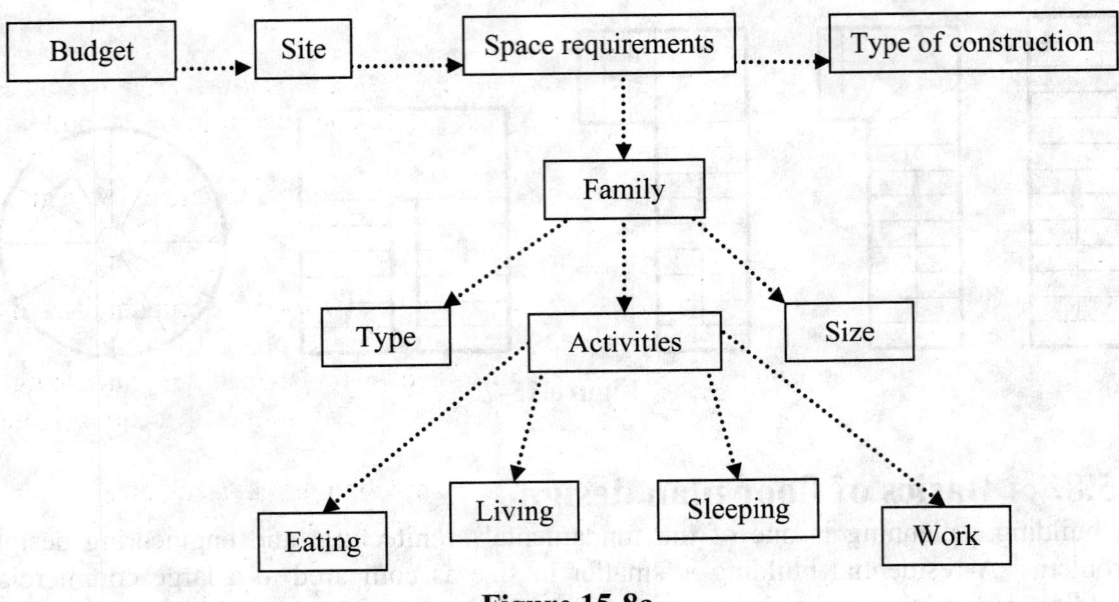

Figure 15-8a

- <u>Space requirements</u>: The space requirement depends on the following factors.
  - *Family type*: The space requirement depends on the building's occupants. For example, a single story house may the better option for a family with small children or senior citizen.
  - *Family size*: The number and size of the rooms depends on the number of occupants.
  - *Family's activities*: The main activities in a residential building can be grouped into eating, sleeping, living/entertainment, and work zones. Figure 15-8b shows the movement between various zones. The activities zones divide a house into the following rooms.
    - Eating: Kitchen, breakfast room, and dining room
    - Sleeping: Bedrooms and guest rooms
    - Living/entertainment: Living room, exercise room, library, entrance hall
    - Work: Kitchen, pantry, laundry, garage, and storage room

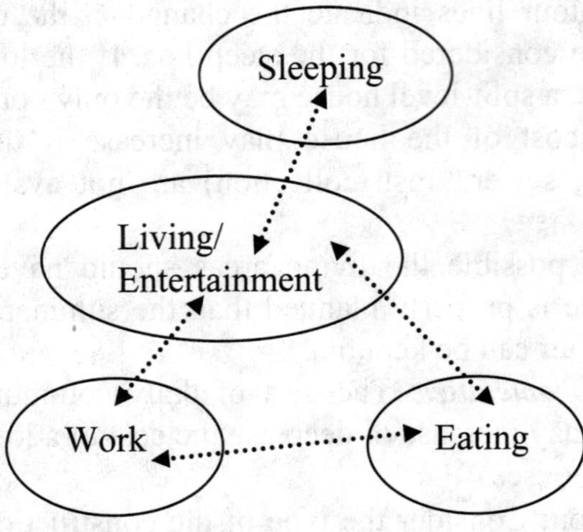

Figure 15-8b

15.9.   Design technique

The arrangement of the various rooms depends upon the residents. However, appearance, comfort, and convenience are the main factor that must be considered in every building without compromising the cost.

The best method of a floor plan design is called as *inside-out*. This technique can be divided into four major sections.

1. Space requirements: Find the space requirement of (i) every occupant, (ii) the family collectively, and (iii) special needs for the guests.
2. Setup: (i) Find the arrangement of the rooms, size of the rooms, and furnishings. (ii) Revise the plan (if necessary) for comfort, convenience, economy, and appearance.
3. Construction type: Find the method of construction: wood, brick, steel, etc.
4. Finance: Find the method to finance the construction project.

15.10.   AutoCAD and floor plan

This section will provide step-by-step instruction to create a floor plan using AutoCAD 2014.

15.10.1.   New file

New file: Open a new "My_acad-Landscape_tmplt" file. It is one of the template files created in Chapter #7.

15.10.2.   The drawing units

Before starting the floor plan, set the drawing units (the input units) to Architectural (the user inputs units in feet and inches) units as follows:

(i) Type *Units* in the command line and press the *Enter* key. This will open the *Drawing Units* dialog box. (ii) From the *Drawing Units* dialog box, select the *Architectural* from the *Length Type* panel, Figure 15-8c. (iii) Press the *OK* button.

Now the user can specify the information in architectural units (feet and inches). The length 5'-6" is entered as follow: (i) activate the *Line* or *Polyline* commands. (ii) Type 5. (iii) Type the apostrophe (') key. (iv) Type 6. (v) Press the *Enter* key. (vi) DO NOT TYPE hyphen (-) to separate feet from inches and double apostrophe to represent inches.

15.10.3.   Load linetypes

Load linetype: The floor plan will use solid or visible (known as continuous in AutoCAD), dashed (known as hidden in AutoCAD), and center lines. Therefore, load *Hidden* and *Center* linetype; *Continuous* is the default linetype. Figure 15-8e shows the loaded linetypes. Load different types of lines as follows:

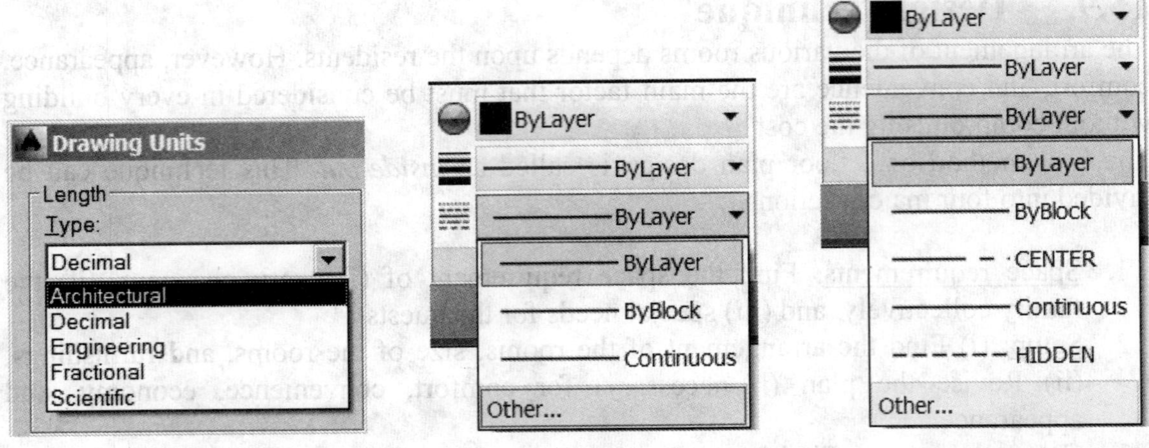

Figure 15-8c   Figure 15-8d   Figure 15-8e

(i) From the *Home* tab and *Properties* panel, click on the down arrow of the *Line Type Control* and select the *Other* option, Figure 15-8d. This will open the *Linetype Manager* dialog box. (ii) From the *Linetype Manager* dialog box, click on the *Load* button. This will open the *Load or Reload Linetypes* dialog box. (iii) From the *Load or Reload Linetypes* dialog box, click on the desired linetype. For multiple selections, hold the CTRL key and select the desired linetypes. (iv) Press the *OK* button on both dialog boxes. From the *Home* tab and *Properties* panel, click on the down arrow of the *Line Type Control* and the newly loaded line will be available to use, Figure 15-8e.

15.10.4.   Orthogonal lines

Orthogonal lines: Since most of the lines in a floor plan are either horizontal or vertical, turn *On* the *ORTHO* option by pressing the corresponding button (⌐) on the status bar.

15.10.5.   The floor plan

This section provides step-by-step instructions for drawing a floor plan of a typical single story residential building with three bedrooms, three bathrooms, a study room, and a two cars garage.

- Do not add any dimensions! Dimensions will be added later.
- The drawing will be printed from the layout! Keep checking the appearance of the linetypes and lineweights in the layouts.

1. Draw the exterior walls:
    a. Create a layer, **Main_Drawing** and set its lineweight to be 0.7mm. This layer will be used for the walls, doors, and windows.
    b. Make the **Main_Drawing** layer to be the current layer.
    c. Use a *Polyline* command to draw the exterior face of the exterior wall, Figure 15-9a.

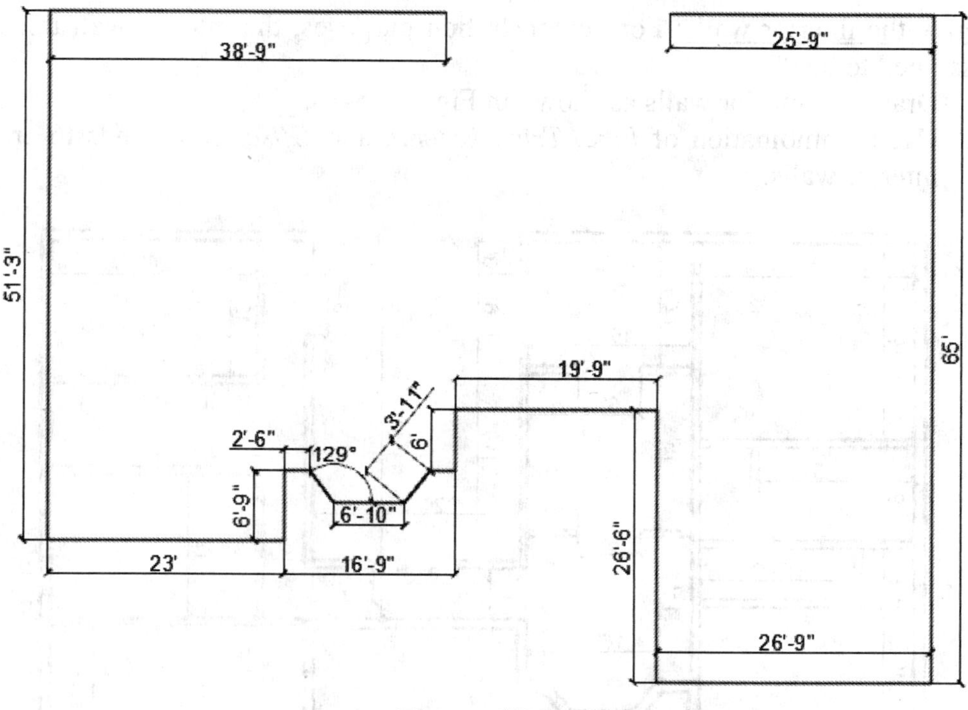

Figure 15-9a

d. For demonstration purposes, the exterior wall thickness is assumed to be 1' foot.

e. Use the *Offset* command with offset distance of 1' to create the interior face of the exterior wall. To create the offset, click inside of the exterior face of the exterior wall, Figure 15-9b.

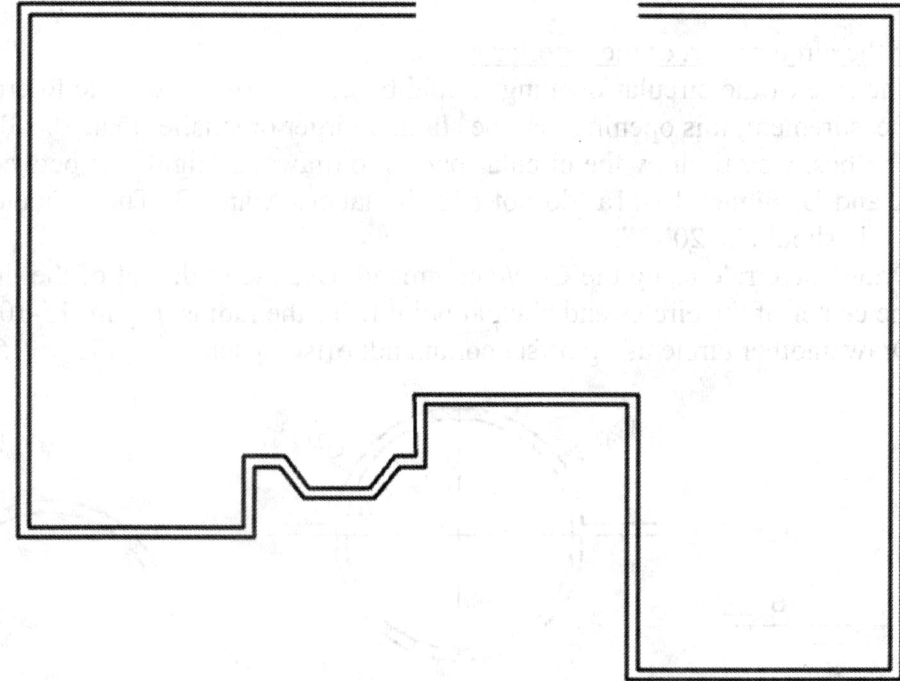

Figure 15-9b

2. <u>Draw the interior walls</u>: For demonstration purposes, the interior wall thickness is assumed to be 9".
    a. Draw the interior walls as shown in Figure 15-10.
    b. Use a combination of *Line, Trim, Extend,* and *Offset* commands to create the interior walls.

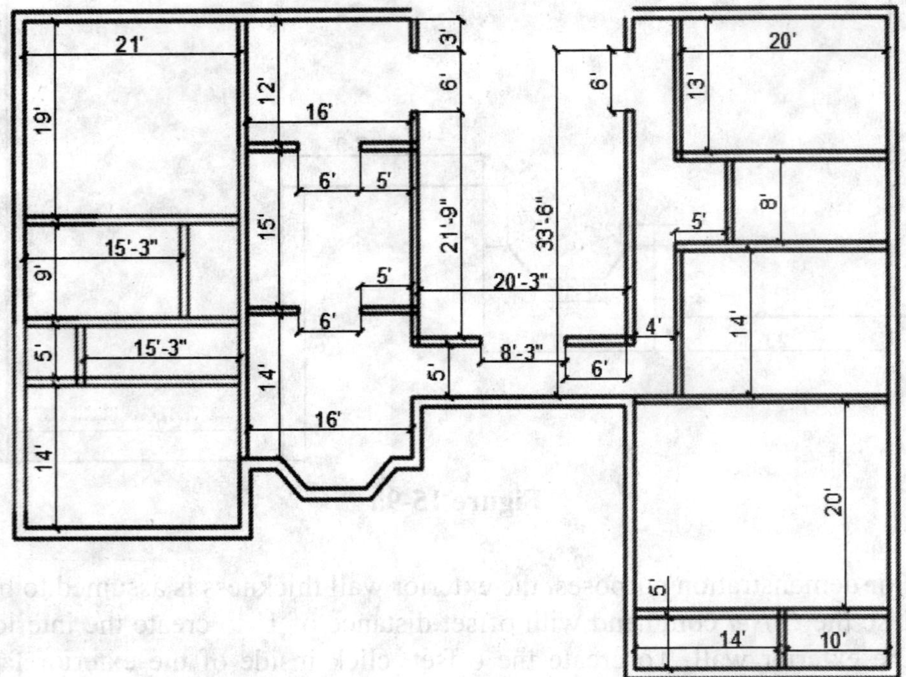

Figure 15-10

3. <u>Draw the circular part of the exterior walls</u>:
    a. The size of the circular opening should be 20'-3". However, due to error in the measurement, this opening may be slightly larger or smaller than 20'-3".
    b. The best way to draw the circular part is to draw a straight line between points A and B, Figure 15-11a; do not add the labels A and B. The diameter of this circle should be 20'-3".
    c. Draw one circle using the *Circle* command. Use the midpoint of the line AB as the center of the circles and click at point B for the radius, Figure 15-10b.
    d. Draw another circle using offset command; offset distance 1', Figure 15-11b.

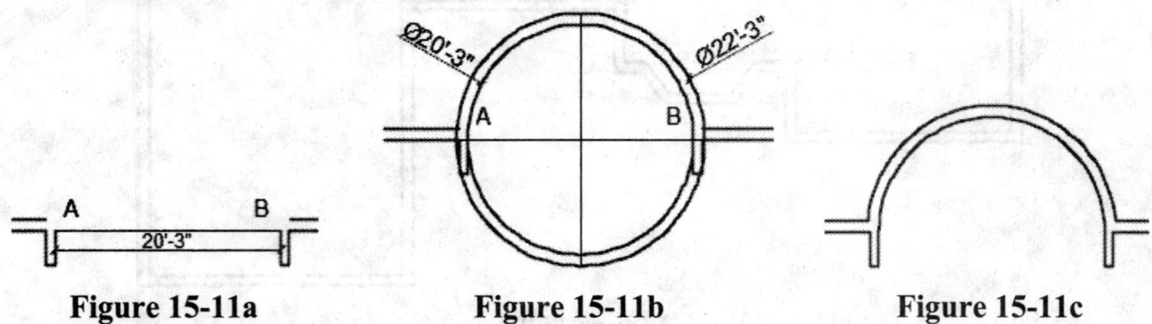

Figure 15-11a   **Figure 15-11b**   **Figure 15-11c**

    e. Activate the *Trim* command and trim the circles to create the shape shown in the Figure 15-11c.

    f. Delete the line AB to complete the circular part of the exterior wall, Figure 15-11c and Figure 15-12.

4. <u>Label various part of the house</u>:

    a. Create a layer, **Room_Label**, for displaying the names of the various rooms.

    b. Make the **Room_Label** layer to be the current layer.

    c. Add the label using the *Text* command, as shown in the Figure 15-12.

    d. In the figure, WIC is the walk-in-closet and the empty space in the study will be closet.

    e. Use the four corner's grip points of the text to match the four corners of the room to place the text in the center.

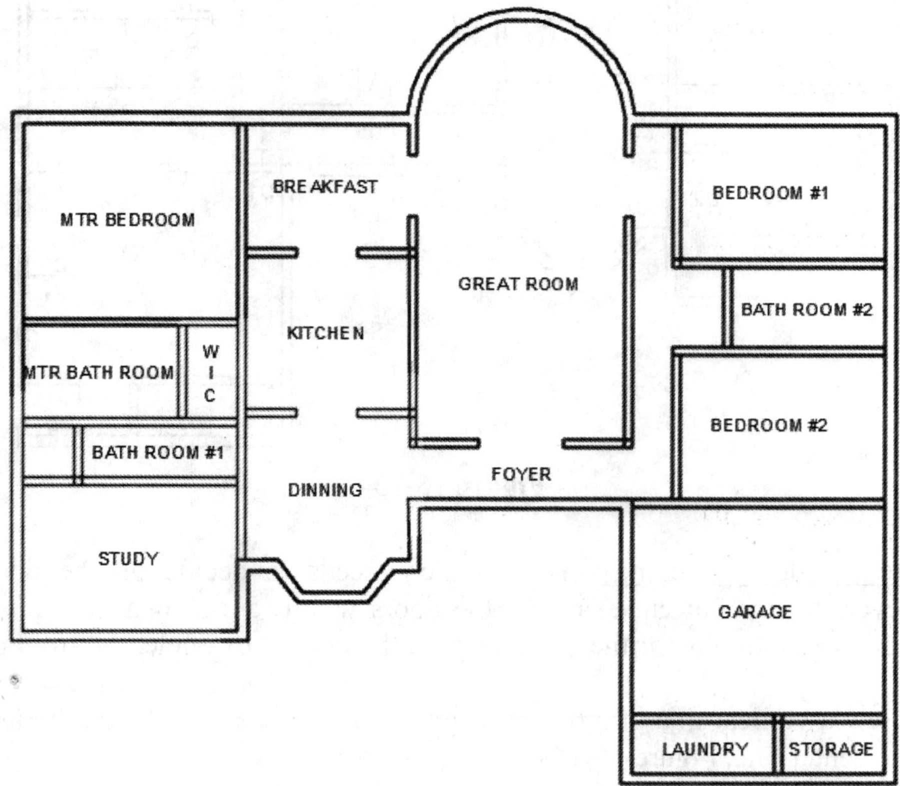

Figure 15-12

5. <u>Locate the center lines for the doors openings</u>: The architect needs to decide on the door location and the distance from the nearest wall. However, for the current example, the door location and the distance from the nearest wall is shown in Figure 15-13.

    a. Load the linetype *Center*.

    b. Create a layer, **DoorCL**, for the center of the doors; set linetype as *Center*.

    c. Make the **DoorCL** layer to be the current layer.

    d. Draw 7'-10" long center lines for the doors' center, Figure 15-13.

6. Add the doors labels:
    a. Create a layer, **DoorLabel**, for the labels of the door.
    b. Make the **DoorLabel** layer to be the current layer.
    c. Using the *Text* command, label the doors as shown in the Figure 15-13.

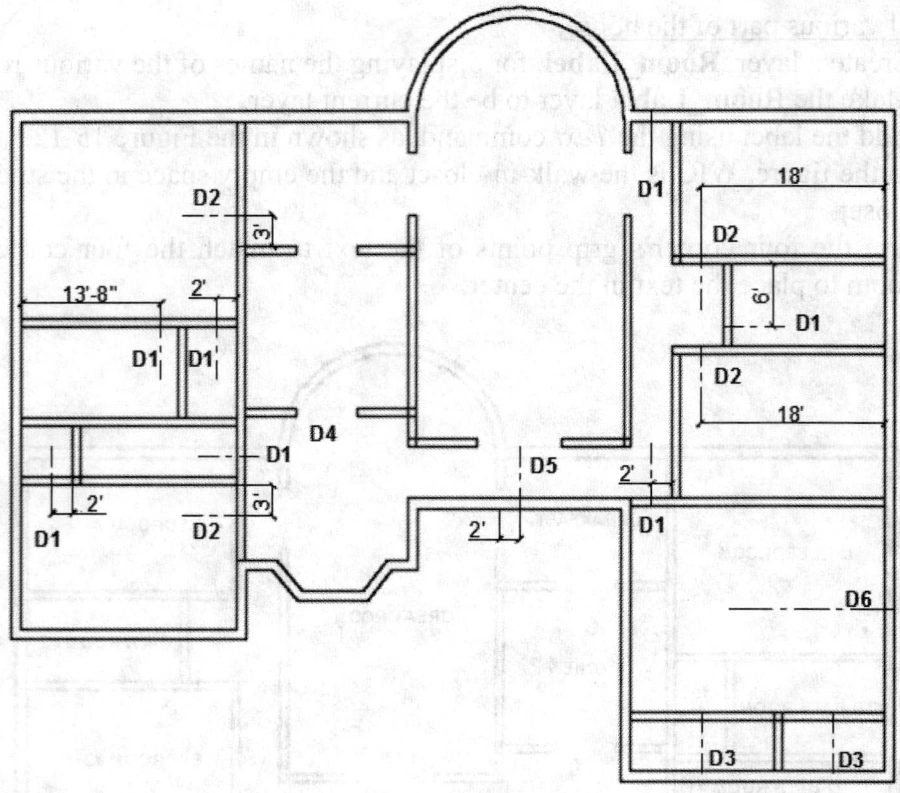

Figure 15-13

7. Create the doors openings: The architect needs to decide on the door width. However, for the current example, the doors widths are shown in Figure 15-14c. This demonstration is for the front door. In the current example, the front door is 4' wide.
    a. Draw a vertical line of arbitrary length at a distance of 2'-0" on the left side of the center line, Figure 15-14a
    b. Use the *Mirror* command to create the similar line on the right side, Figure 15-14b.
    c. Use the *Trim* command to trim the lines representing the wall and extra portion of the two parallel lines drawn in the previous step, Figure 15-14c.
    d. Repeat the process for the other doors, Figure 15-14d. The door widths are shown in the figure, too.
    e. The Figure 15-14d shows D7; these door are sliding doors and will be used for closets.

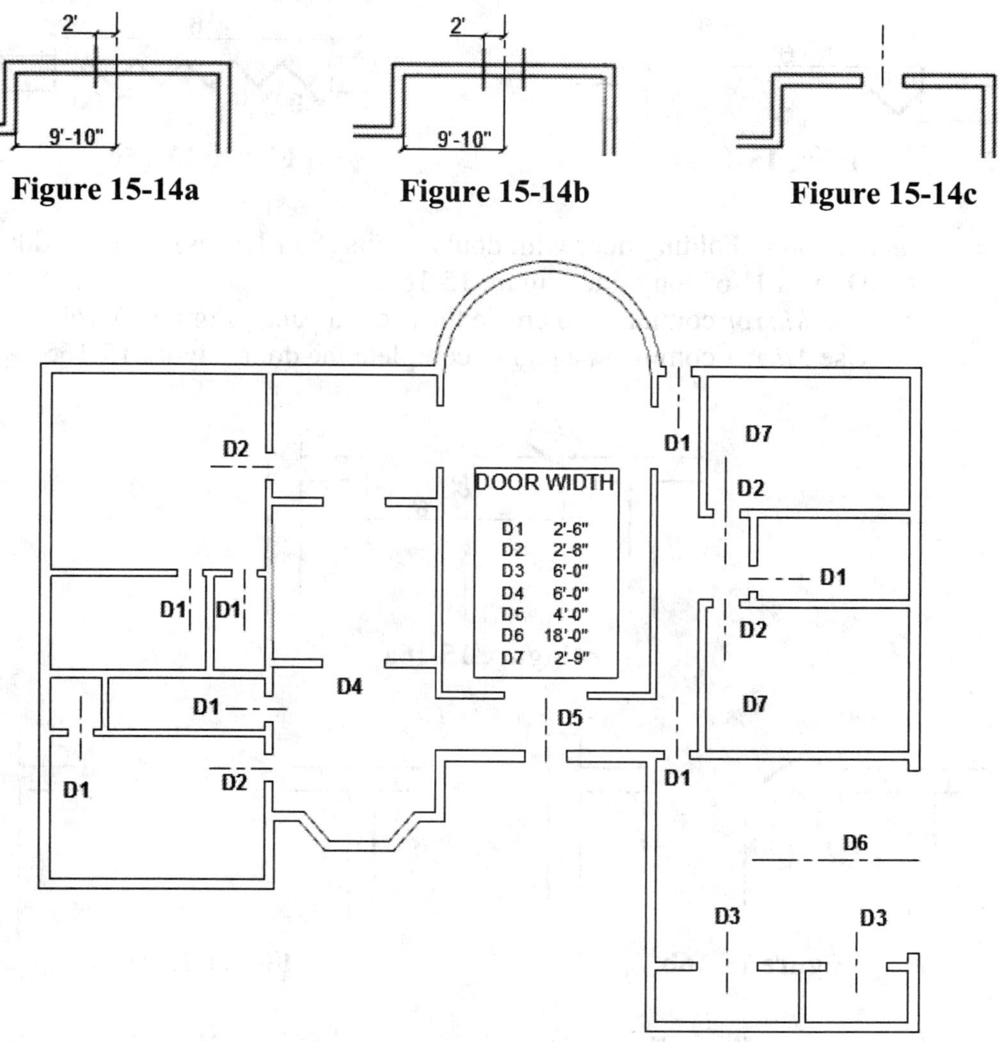

Figure 15-14a   **Figure 15-14b**   **Figure 15-14c**

Figure 15-14d

8. <u>Draw the doors</u>: Figure 15-18 shows the different types of doors used in the building.
   a. Make the **Main_Drawing** layer to be the current layer.
   b. *Opening from dining room to kitchen*: Accordion door, panel width 9".
      - Draw a 9" long line, Figure 15-15a.
      - Use *Mirror* command to create the second panel, Figure 15-15b.
      - Use *Copy* or *Array* command to complete the door, Figure 15-15c.

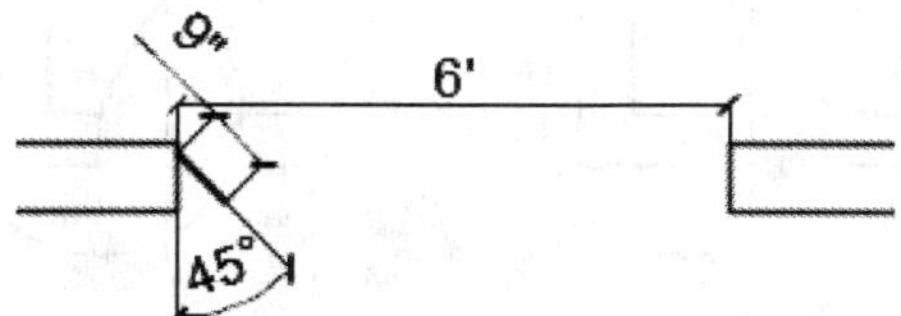

Figure 15-15a

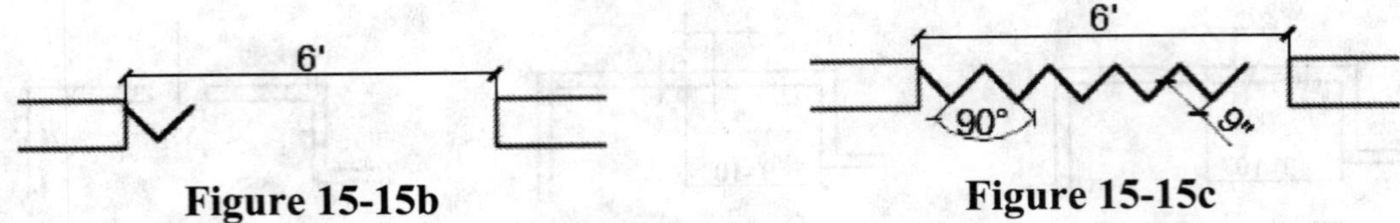

Figure 15-15b   **Figure 15-15c**

c. *Laundry room*: Folding door with double units (four leaves), panel width 1'-6".
    - Draw a 1'-6" long line, Figure 15-16a.
    - Use *Mirror* command to create the second panel, Figure 15-16b.
    - Use *Mirror* command again to complete the door, Figure 15-16c.

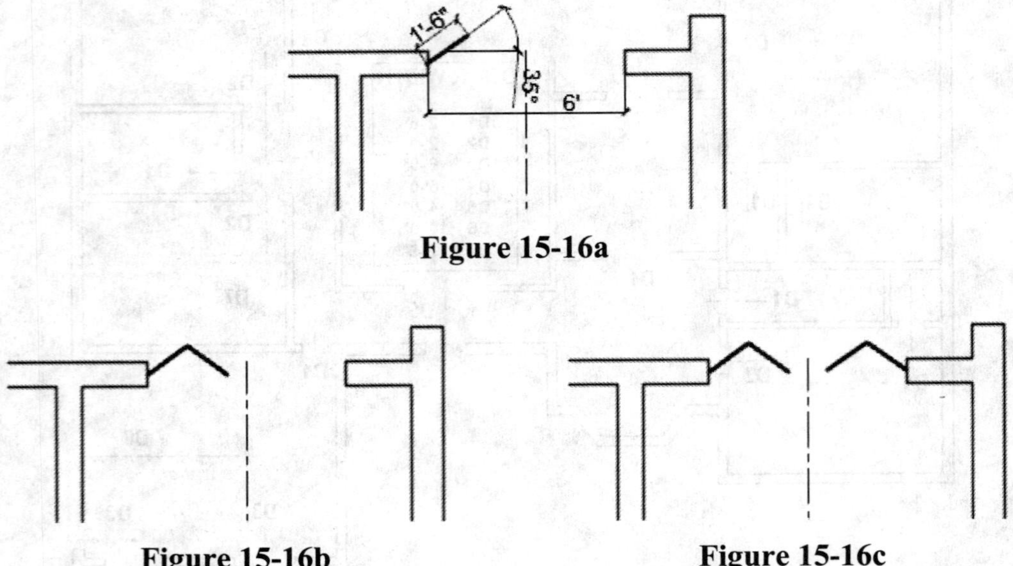

Figure 15-16a

Figure 15-16b   **Figure 15-16c**

d. *Single swing doors*: Figure 15-17a shows an opening for a single swing door.
    This section illustrates step-by-step procedure to draw a single swing door.
    - Draw a circle of radius equal to the door opening and center as shown in
      Figure 15-17b.
    - Draw the door panel using the *Line* command and the *Intersection* option
      in object snap setting. Also change the line's lineweight, Figure 15-17c.
    - Use the *Trim* command to create the desired appearance of the door,
      Figure 15-17d.

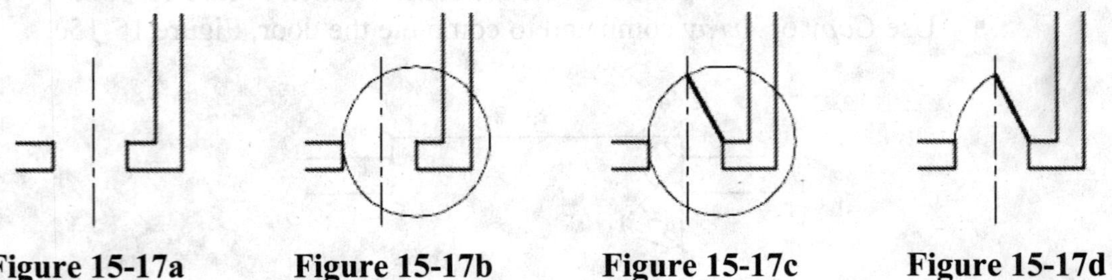

Figure 15-17a   **Figure 15-17b**   **Figure 15-17c**   **Figure 15-17d**

e. *Front door*: Two panel with inward swing. (i) Draw a single swing door.
    (ii) Use the mirror command to create the other panel.

f. *Garage door*: The garage door height is 10'; it is an overhead type door (just draw a polyline and change its linetype).

g. *Other doors*: Use the *Mirror*, *Copy*, and *Move* commands to create the remaining doors.

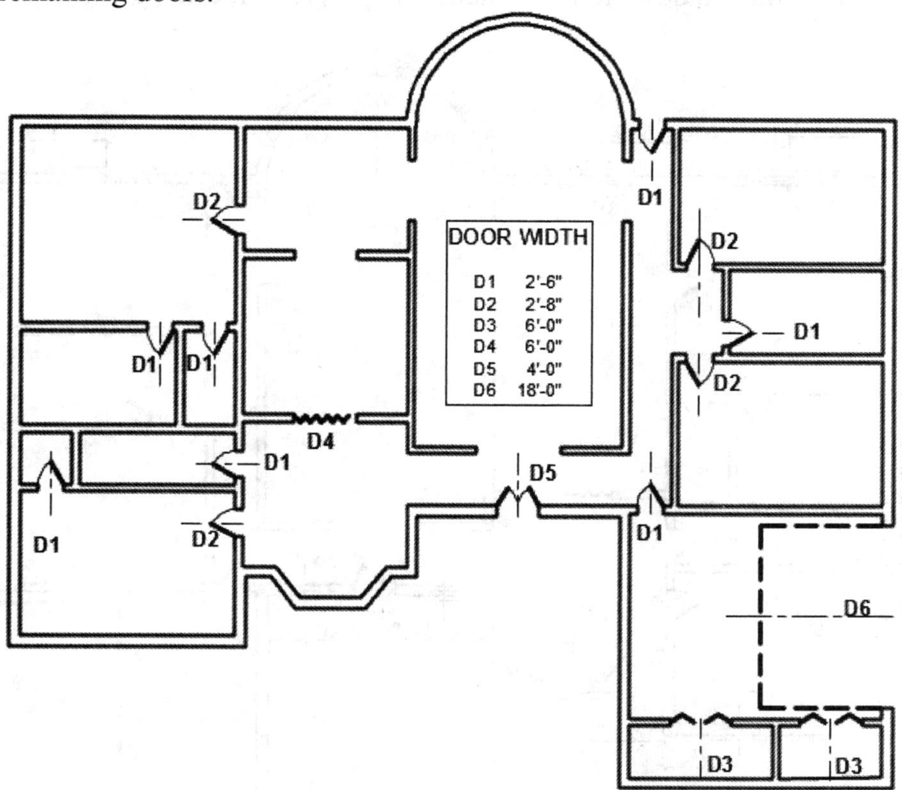

Figure 15-18

9. <u>Locate the center lines for the windows</u>: The architect needs to decide on the window location and the distance from the nearest wall. However, for the current example, the window location and the distance from the nearest wall are shown in Figure 15-19.
    a. Create a layer, **WindowCL**, for the center of the windows; make the linetype as *Center*.
    b. Make the **WindowCL** layer to be the current layer.
    c. Draw the center lines for the windows of length 7'-0", Figure 15-19.

10. <u>Label the windows</u>:
    a. Create a layer, **WindowLabel**, for the labels of the windows.
    b. Make the **WindowLabel** layer to be the current layer.
    c. Using the *Text* command, label the windows as shown in the Figure 15-19.

11. <u>Draw the windows</u>: The detail of the windows labeled as W1, W2, W3, and W4 are shown in Figure 15-20a, Figure 15-20b, Figure 15-20c, and Figure 15-20d, respectively.

a. Make the **Main_Drawing** layer to be the current layer.
b. Draw W1, W2, W3, and W4 in the building, once.
c. Use combination of *Mirror*, *Copy*, and *Rotate* commands to create multiple copies of the windows to place them at appropriate locations.

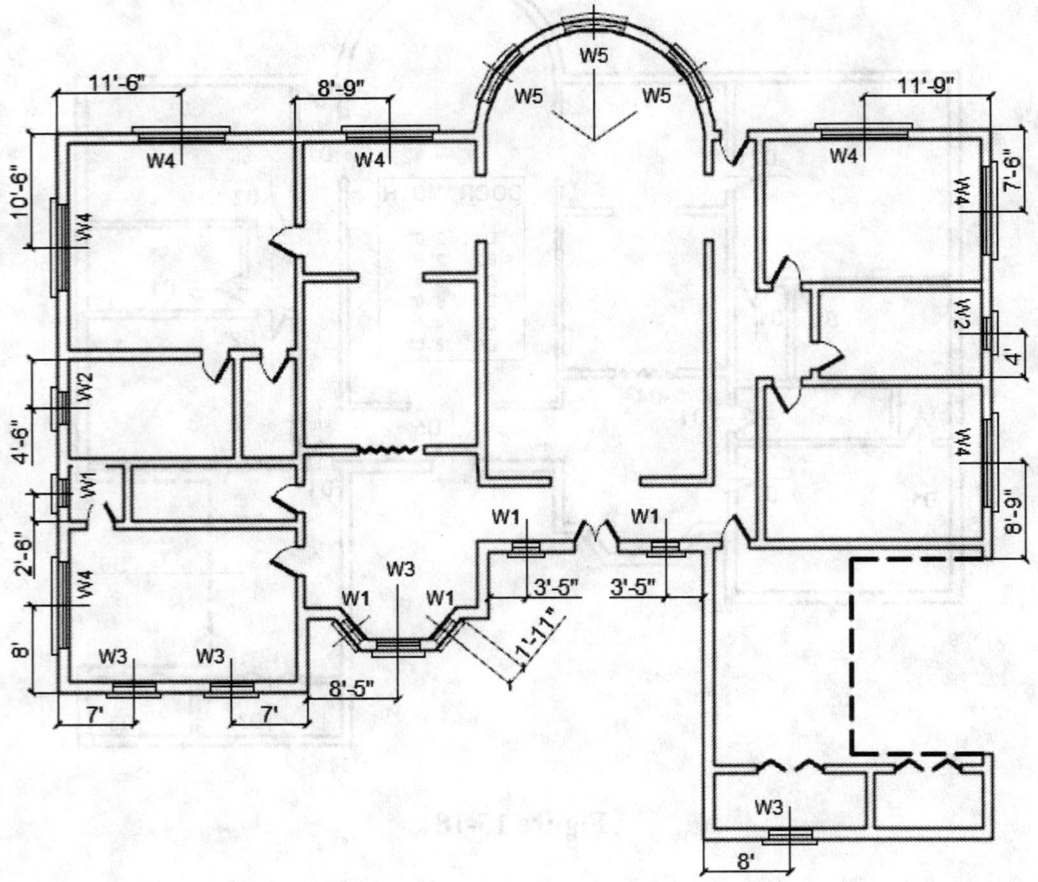

Figure 15-19

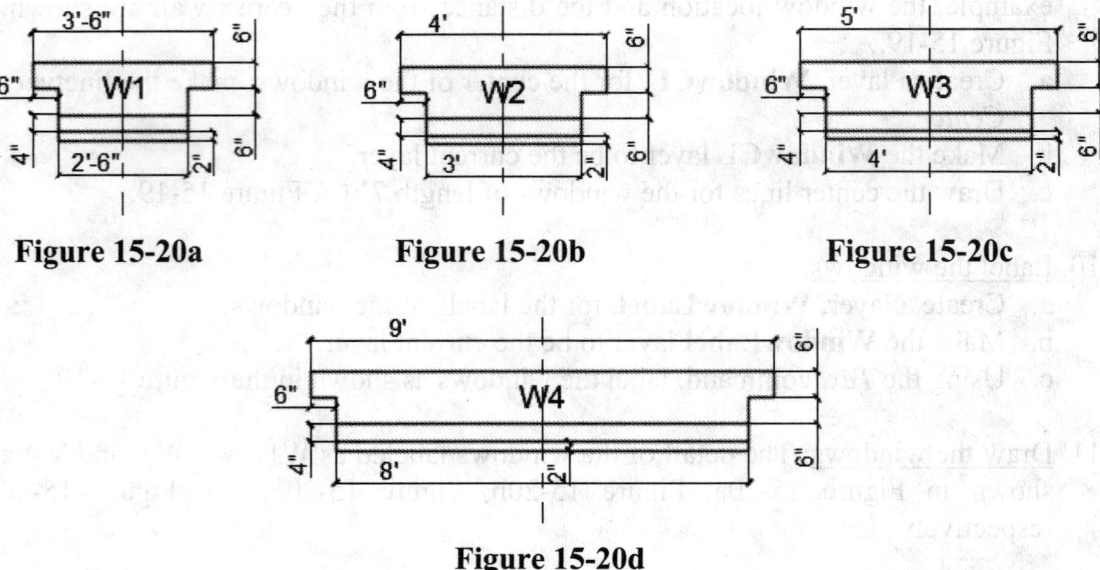

Figure 15-20a   **Figure 15-20b**   **Figure 15-20c**

Figure 15-20d

d. The circular window or W5:
- Draw a horizontal line starting at the center of circle, Figure 15-21a. The center of the circles is the center of the circular window.
- Draw straight lines originating at the center of the circles and terminating at the outermost circle. The angles are shown in the Figure 15-21b.
- Activate the Mirror command; and mirror the three highlighted line, Figure 15-21c, with respect to an imaginary vertical line passing through the center of the circles, Figure 15-21d.
- Draw three circles of diameters 10'- 7", 21'- 3", and 23'- 3", Figure 15-21a. The center of the circles is the center of the circular window.
- Perform the appropriate trimming to achieve the desired result, Figure 15-21e.

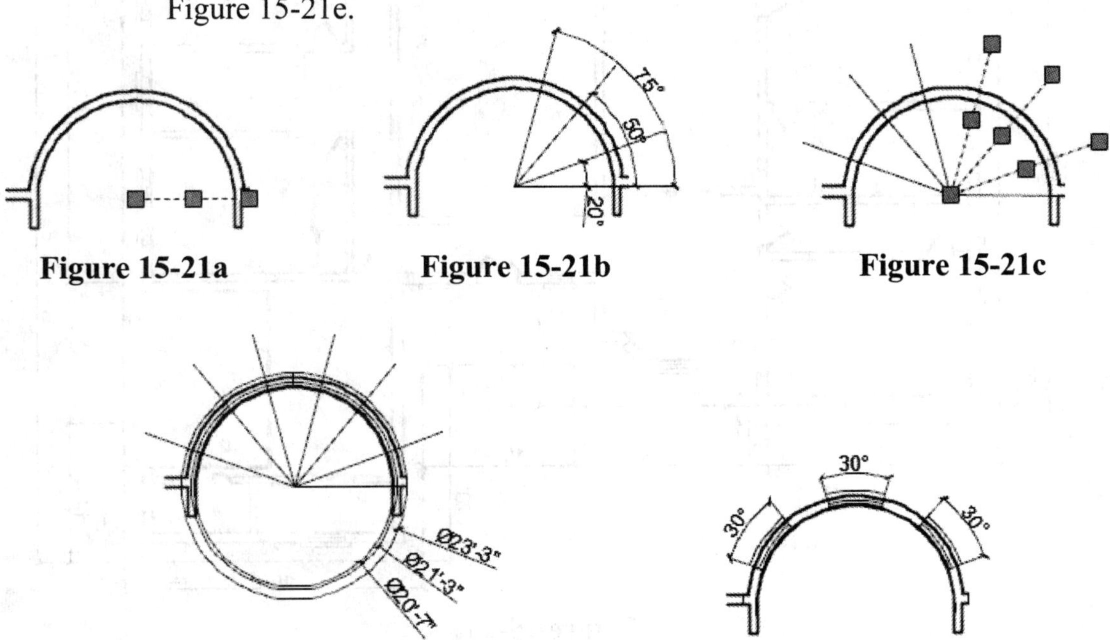

Figure 15-21a   **Figure 15-21b**   **Figure 15-21c**

Figure 15-21d   **Figure 15-21e**

12. <u>Draw the closets</u>: For demonstration purposes, the closet's wall thickness is 4.5". The details of the closets are shown in the Figure 15-22. The closets in the two bedrooms are mirror image of each other, Figure 15-23. Create one of the two closets and then use the *Mirror* command with the imaginary horizontal line passing through the center of the bathroom #2.

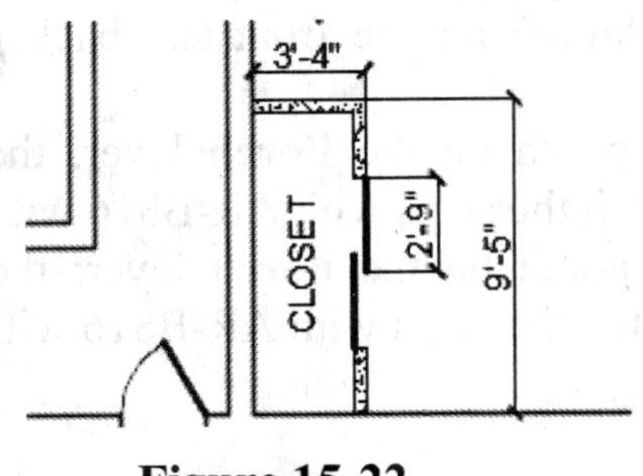

Figure 15-22

13. <u>Add the roof line</u>:
    a. Load *Hidden* linetype.
    b. Create a layer, **RoofLine**, and make it the current layer; set *Hidden* its linetype.
    c. Draw the roof line as shown in Figure 15-23.

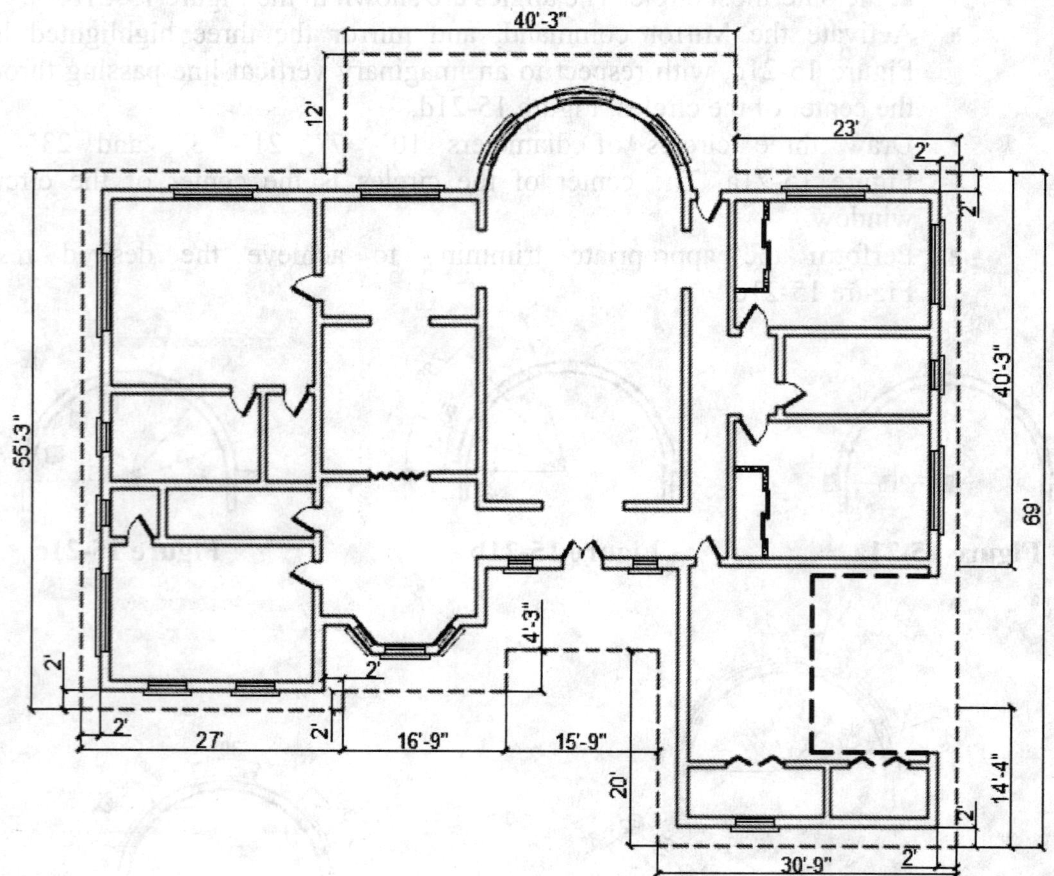

Figure 15-23

14. <u>Hatch the wall</u>:
    a. Create a layer **Wall_Hatch** and make it the current layer.
    b. Activate the *Hatch* command.
    c. Select the *AR-CONC* pattern. The scale factor in the current example is 1.0.
    d. Select the exterior, interior, and the closets walls to hatch, Figure 15-24.

15. <u>Draw the front and back porches</u>:
    a. Create a layer (**Porch**) for the front and back porch, and make it the current layer.
    b. Create the front porch on the **Porch** layer; the dimensions are given in the Figure 15-25. Hatch the steps with AR-B816 with scale factor of 0.8.
    c. Create the back porch on the **Porch** layer; the dimensions are given in the Figure 15-26. Hatch the steps with AR-B816 with scale factor of 0.8 at an angle of 90°.

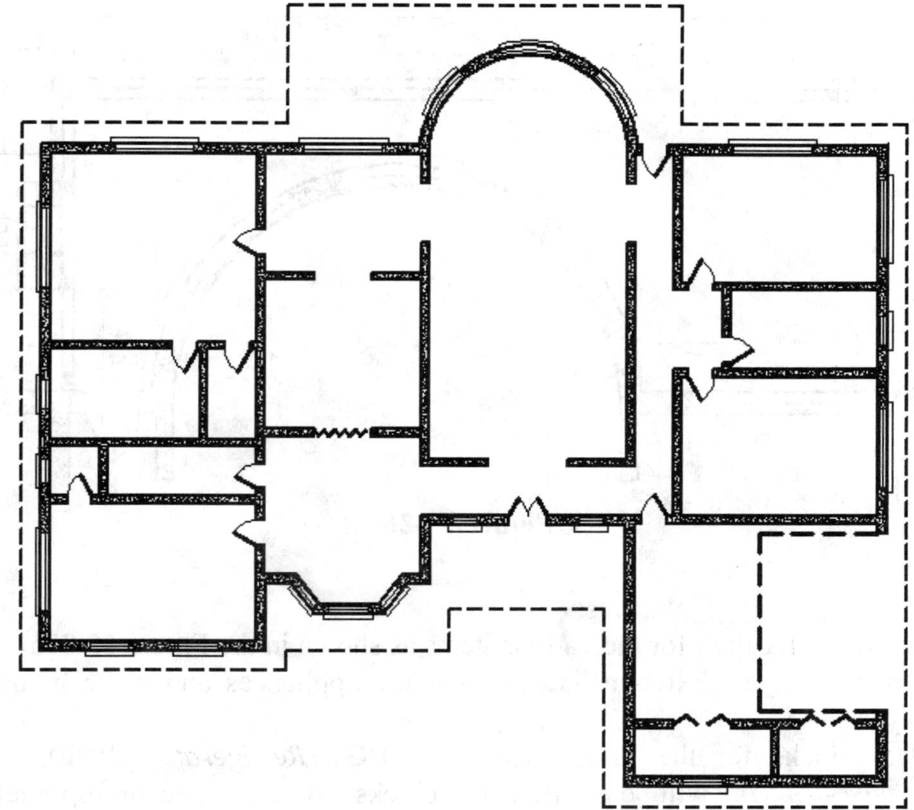

Figure 15-24

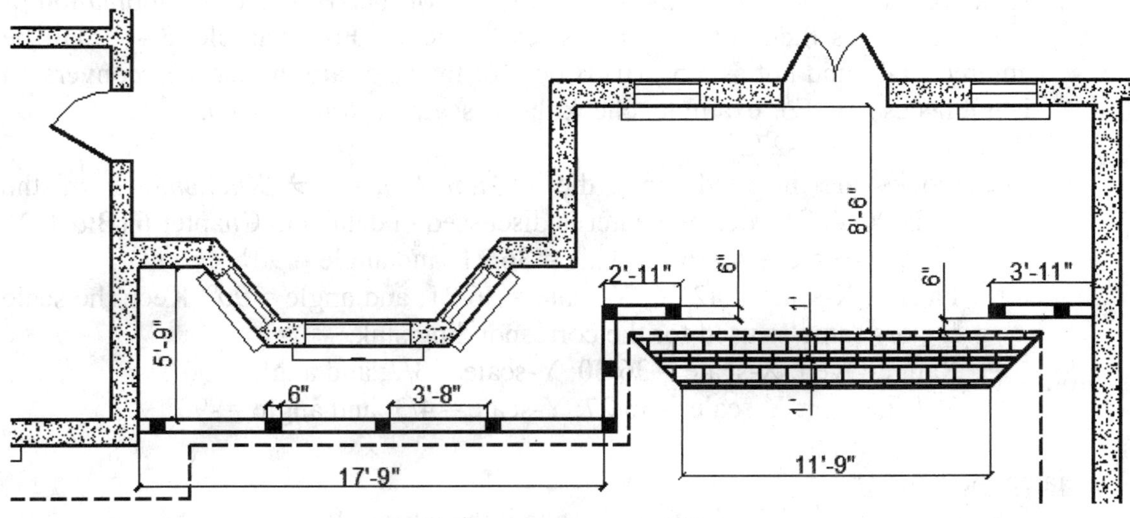

Figure 15-25

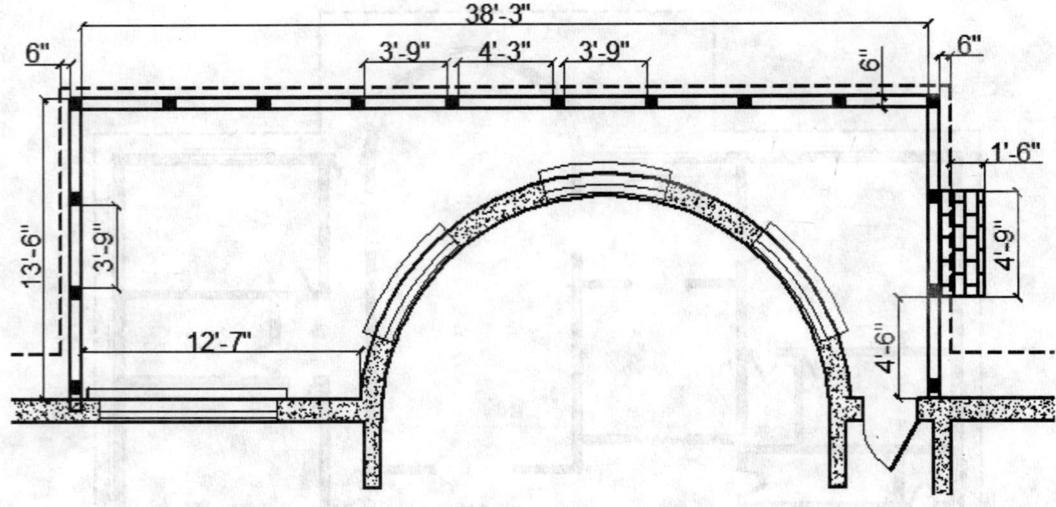

Figure 15-26

16. <u>Draw the kitchen's appliances</u>:
    a. Draw the location for the various items as shown in the Figure 15-27a.
    b. Create a layer (**KitchenFixtures**) for the appliances and make it the current layer.
    c. The blocks for the *Range-Oven-Top* (RG), *Refrigerator* (REF), *Sink*, and *Faucet-Kit-Top*, will be inserted. The blocks must be scaled appropriately.
    d. **Note**: Calculate the scale factor as follow:
        Scale factor in the x-direction = Desired size/Size from the Design Center
    e. However, keep the units consistent. (i) If one of the sizes is the combination of feet and inches then convert both sizes to inches. For example, 3'-6" will be entered as 42 and not as 3.5'. (ii) If both of the sizes are in feet then conversion is not necessary. For example, check the Y-scale of *Range-Oven*.
    f. Refer to Figure 15-27a.
    g. The blocks are inserted from the *Design Center* → *Kitchen.dwg* of the AutoCAD 2014. The design center is discussed in details in Chapter 6 (Blocks).
        - Sink: X-scale = 42/36; Y-scale = 36/21; and angle = 90°.
        - Faucet: X-scale = 42/36; Y-scale = 36/21; and angle = 90°. Keep the scale factors same as used for the corresponding sink.
        - Range-Oven: X-scale = 36/30; Y-scale = 3/2; and angle = 90°.
        - Refrigerator: X-scale = 36/27; Y-scale = 4/3; and angle = -90°.

17. <u>Hatch the Kitchen</u>:
    a. Create a layer **KitchenHatch** and make it the current layer.
    b. Create the boundary of the floor area using *Polyline* command.
    c. Hatch the kitchen floor using *Hatch* command and *HEX* pattern at the scale of 25, Figure 15-27b.
    d. Hatch the counter tops using *Hatch* command and *HEX* pattern at the scale of 9, Figure 15-27b.

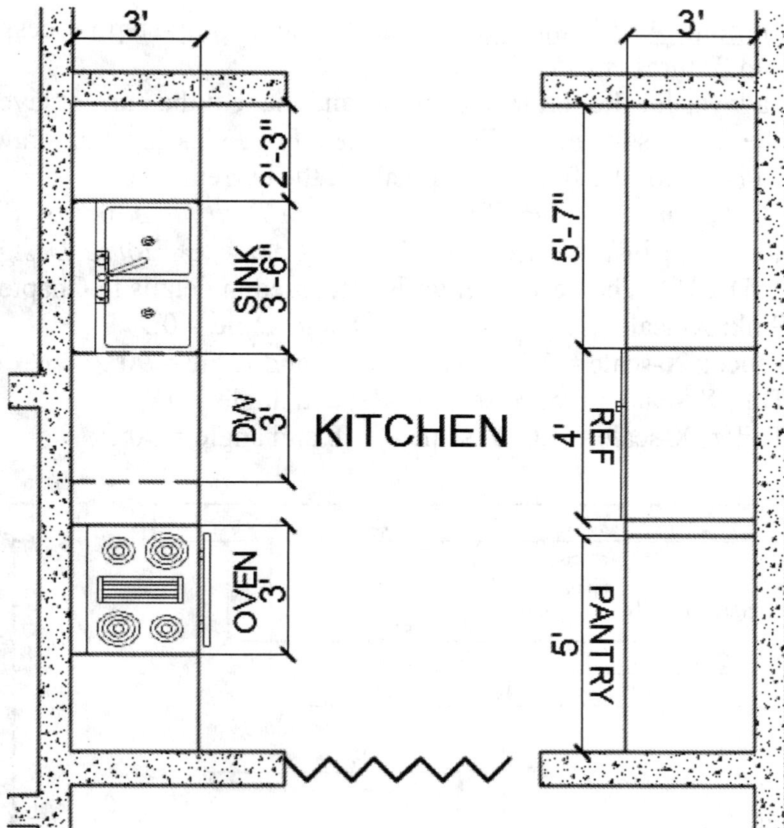

Figure 15-27a

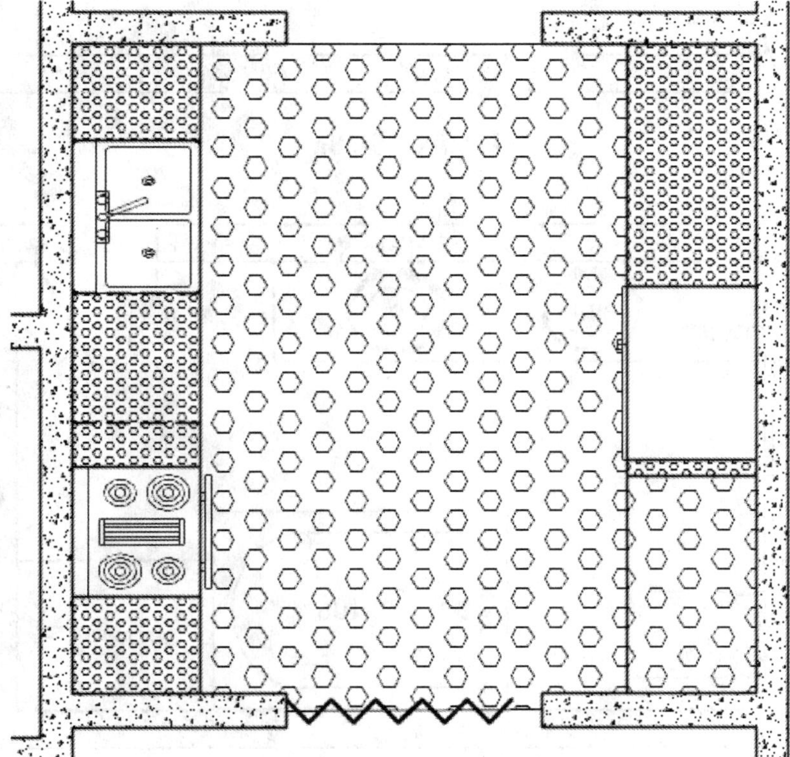

**Figure 15-27b

18. <u>Master bathroom: Add bathrooms' fixtures</u>: The step-by-step process for inserting the bathroom fixtures is listed below.
   a. Create a layer for the fixtures locations and make it the current layer.
   b. Draw the fixtures locations, Figure 15-28a. For a sink location draw an ellipse.
   c. Create a layer for the fixtures and make it the current layer.
   h. Insert *Toilet top*, *Sink-oval Top*, *Faucet*, and *Bath tub*'s blocks, Figure 15-28b. The blocks are inserted from the *Design Center* → *House Design.dwg* of the AutoCAD 2014. The design center is discussed in details in Chapter 6 (Blocks).
      ▪ Sink: X-scale = 1.0; Y-scale = 1.0; and angle = 0°.
      ▪ Faucet: X-scale = 1.0; Y-scale = 1.0; and angle = 90°.
      ▪ Tub: X-scale = 6/5; Y-scale = 4/3; and angle = 0°.
      ▪ Toilet: X-scale = 1.0; Y-scale = 1.0; and angle = 90°.

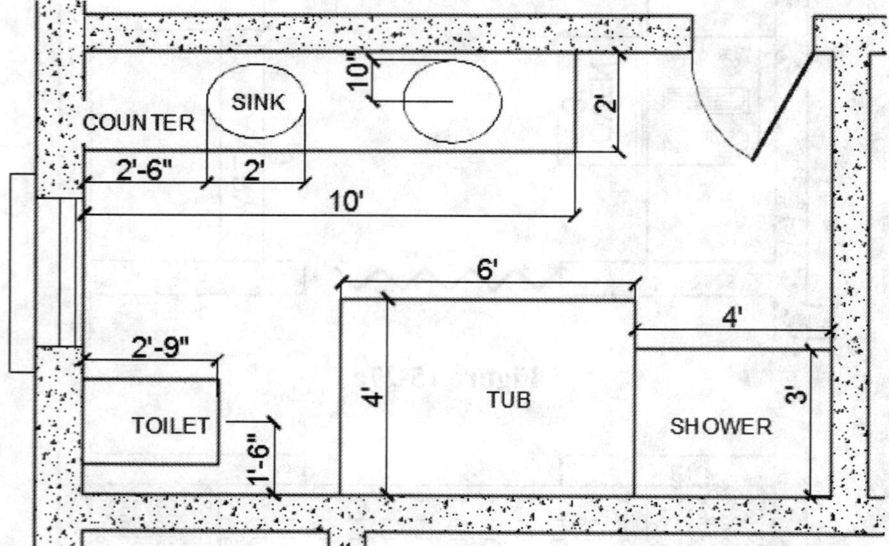

Figure 15-28a

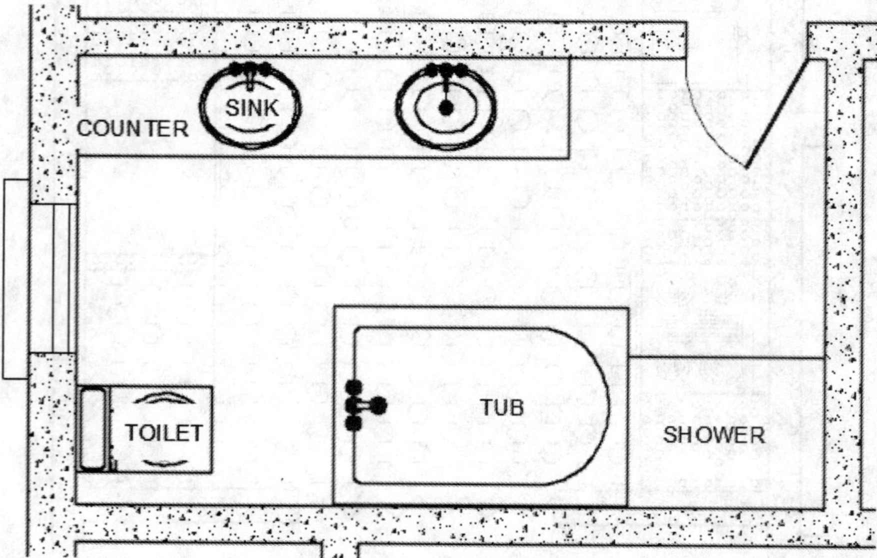

Figure 15-28b

19. <u>Master bathroom: Add the hatch</u>:
   a. Turn off the fixture layer.
   b. Create a layer for bathroom hatch and make it the current layer.
   c. Add the hatch to the counter area, Figure 15-28c. Use the *STARS* pattern at the scale of 10.
   d. Add the hatch to the bathroom floor, Figure 15-28c. Use the *STARS* pattern at the scale of 25.

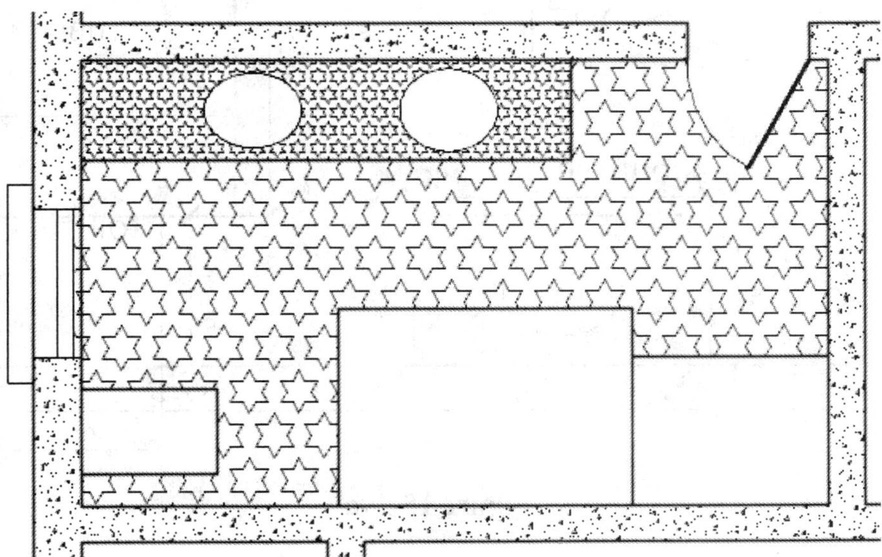

Figure 15-28c

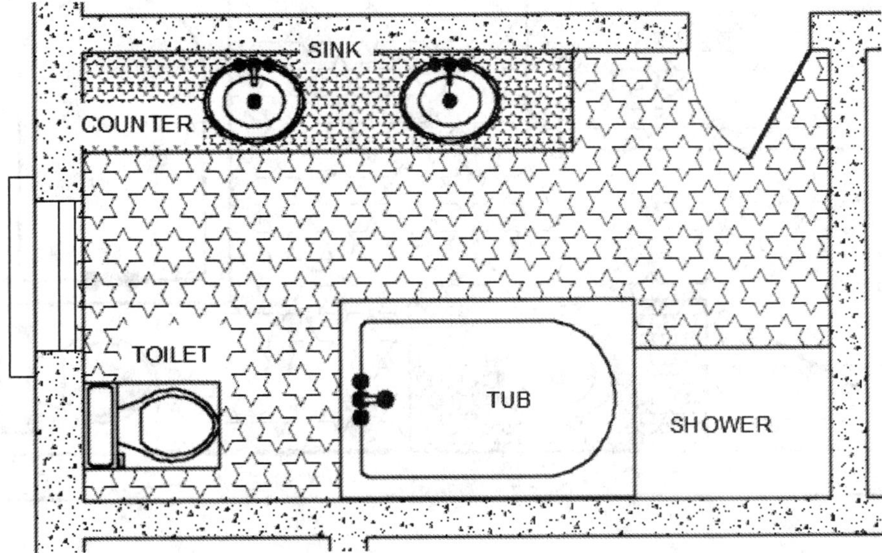

Figure 15-28d

20. <u>Add bathrooms' fixtures to the *Bathroom #2*</u>: Repeat the process of the master bathroom for the *Bathroom #2*. The location for the various items and the fixtures

are shown in Figure 15-29a. The items are added in Figure 15-29b. The user can add sliding or folding doors to the closet.

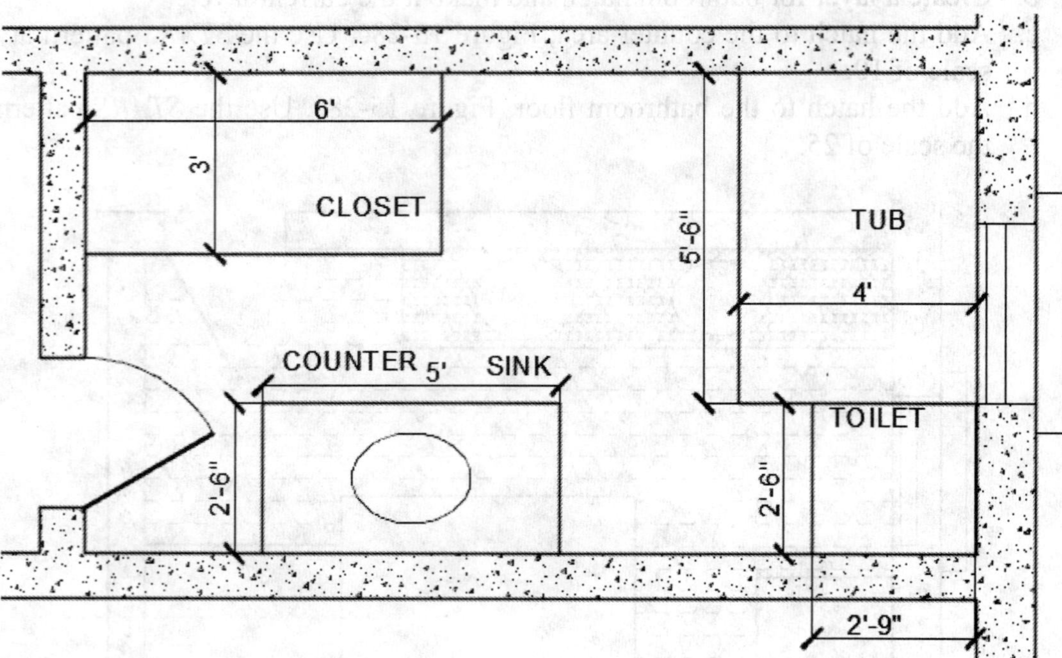

Figure 15-29a

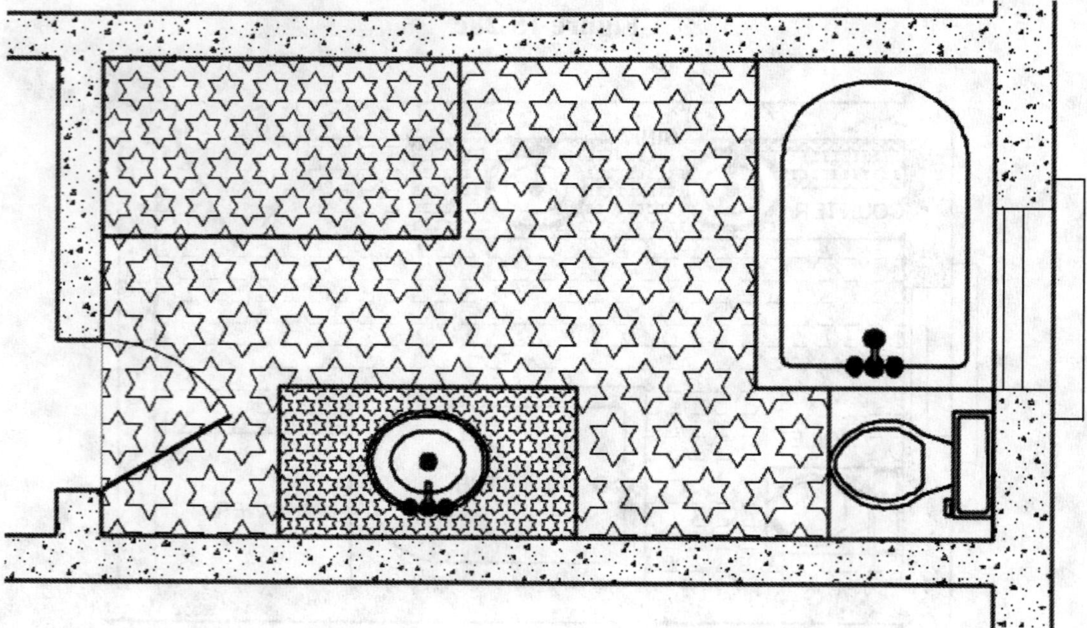

Figure 15-29b

21. <u>Add bathrooms' fixtures to the *Bathroom #1*</u>: Repeat the process of the master bathroom for the *Bathroom #1*. The location for the various items and the fixtures are shown in Figure 15-29c.

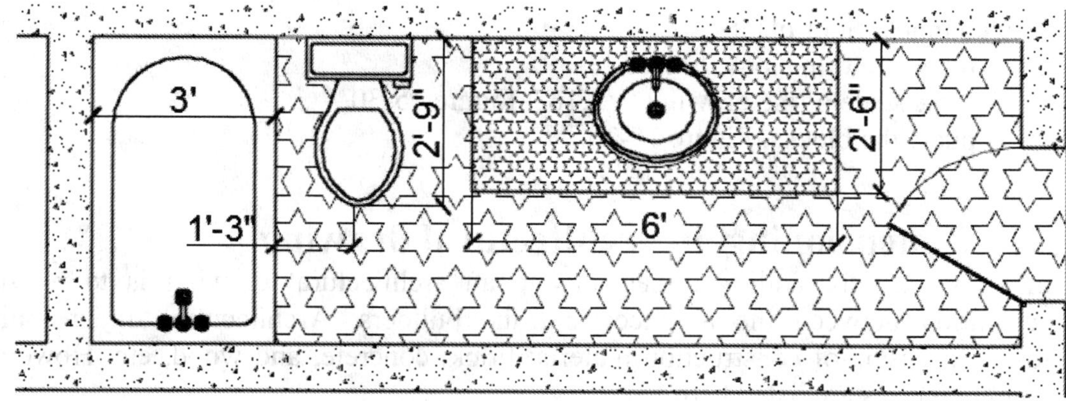

Figure 15-29c

22. <u>The North sign</u>:
   a. Create a layer for the North sign. Make it the current layer.
   b. Insert *North Arrow* block, Figure 15-30 from the *Design Center* → *Landscaping.dwg* of the AutoCAD 2014. The design center is discussed in details in Chapter 6 (Blocks)

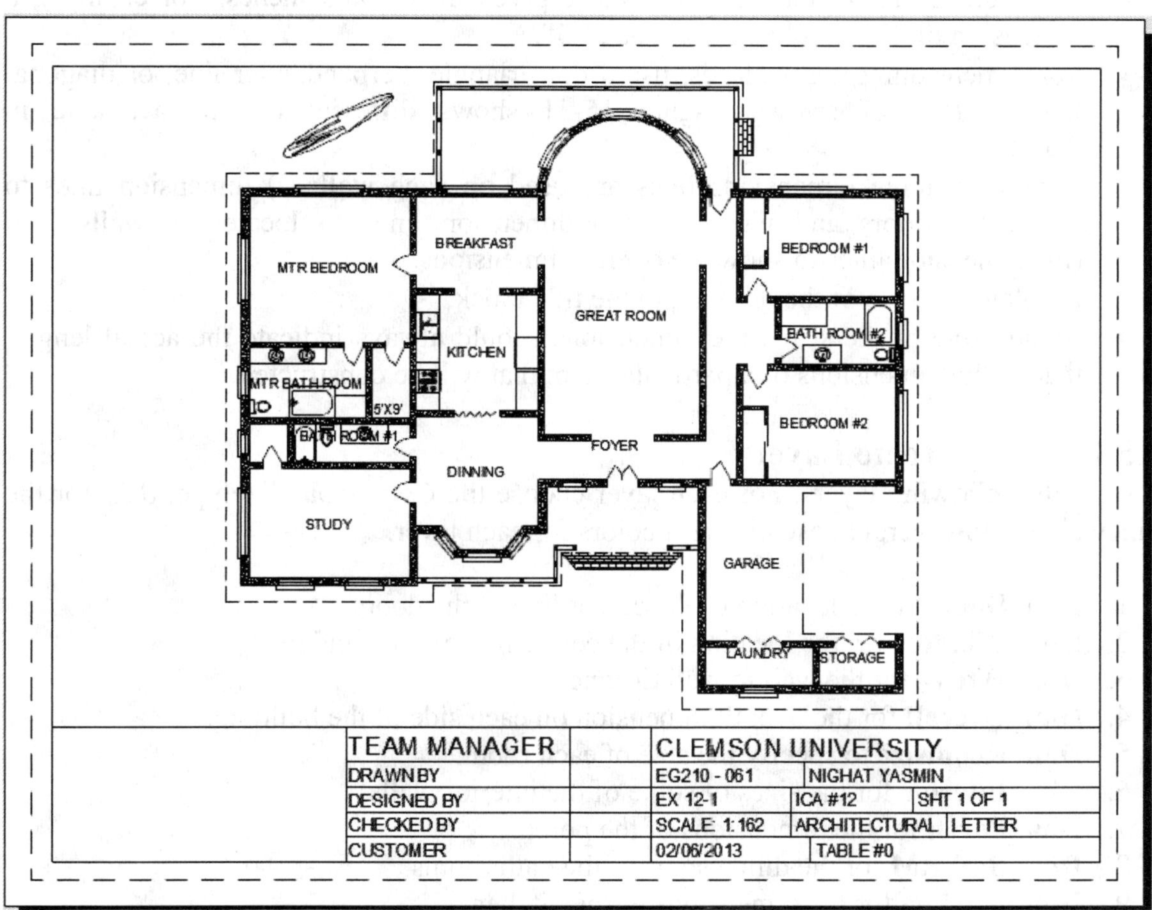

Figure 15-30

23. <u>The complete floor plan:</u>
   a. Update the title block, Figure 15-30.
   b. Set the scale of the drawing to 1:162, Figure 15-30.
   c. Update the blocks, Figure 15-30.

15.11. Dimensioning an architectural drawing

The major reason for adding dimensions to an architectural drawing is to provide communication between the architect and the builders. Architectural dimensioning depends on the type of construction material brick, concrete, and wood, etc. However, some common rules are listed here.

- Avoid the crossing of extension and dimension lines.
- Avoid crowding the dimensions.
- Omit the obvious dimensions, such as the width of side-by-side identical closets, interior doors at the end of hallways, and interior doors at the corner of a room.
- Dimension lines are continuous lines and numbers are placed on top of the dimension lines.
- Dimensions greater than 12" should be given in feet and inches. For example, a dimension of 27" should be given as 2'-3".
- For dimensioning tight places, use a dot, triangle, perpendicular line, or diagonal lines instead of arrows. Figure 15-31 shows different options available in AutoCAD.
- Generally, three dimensions lines are used on each wall: (i) dimension lines to locate the doors and windows; (ii) dimension lines to locate the walls; and (iii) dimension lines to show the overall dimensions.
- Display the scale of the drawing in the title block.
- Irrespective of the scale, the dimensions should always indicate the actual length, that is, the dimensions of a particular item that will be constructed.

15.11.1.   Create Layers

Create the following layers. For each layer choose the *Continuous* linetype, *0.25* for the lineweight. However, choose different colors for each layer.

1. **Dim_Door** for the location of the center line of the doors.
2. **Dim_Window** for the location of the center line of the windows.
3. **Dim_WtoW** for the wall to wall distance.
4. **Dim_Overall** for the overall dimension on each side of the building.
5. **Dim_Roomsize** to specify the size of each room.
6. **Dim_Interior** for the sizes of some of the interior walls.
7. **Dim_Porch** for the dimensions of the porch.
8. **Dim_BathRM** for the dimensions of the bath rooms.
9. **Dim_Kitchen** for the dimensions of the kitchen.
10. **Dim_Schedule** for the door and window schedule.

15.11.2.   Set Dimension Style dialog box

1. Add dimension toolbar to the workspace.
2. Open the *Dimension Style Manager* dialog box by clicking the last button ( ) on the dimension toolbar.
3. Click on the *Modify* button.
4. This will open the *Modify Dimension Style* dialog box.
5. Select the *Symbols and Arrows* tab as shown in Figure 15-31a.
   a. In the *Arrowheads* panel, click on the down arrow under *First* option and select the *Architectural tick* option.
   b. Make sure that the *Architectural tick* option is also selected for the *Second* option.
   c. In the *Arrowheads* panel, set the *Arrowsize* (not shown in the figure).
6. Select the *Primary Units* tab as shown in Figure 15-31b.
   a. In the *Linear dimension* panel, click on the down arrow under the *Unit format* option and select the *Architectural* option.
   b. Set the *Precision* field to 0'-0" (not shown in the figure).

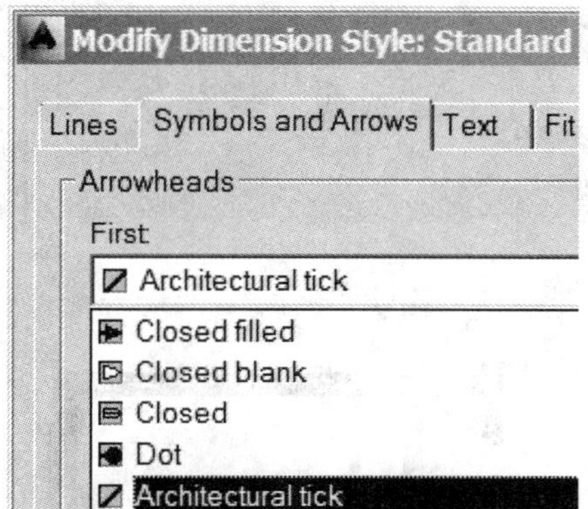

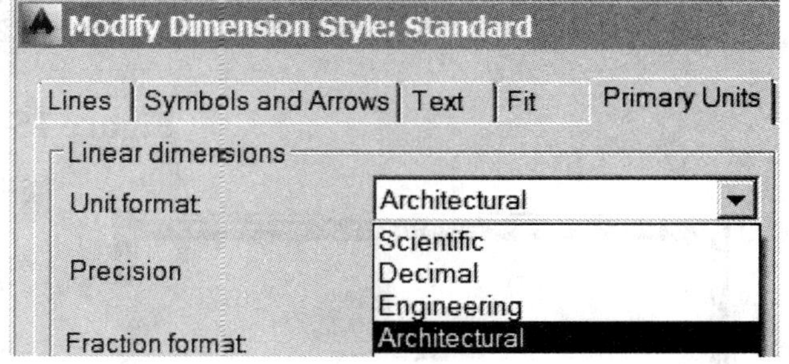

Figure 15-31a   **Figure 15-31b**

7. Select the *Text* tab as shown in Figure 15-31c.
   a. In the *Text appearance* panel, set the *Text height*.
   b. In the *Text placement* panel, click on the down arrow under the *Vertical* option and select the *Above* option.
   c. In the *Text placement* panel, set the *Offset from the dim line*. If the text is too close to the dimension line or too far from the dimension line then increase or decrease this number.
   d. In the *Text alignment* panel, select *Aligned with dimension line* option.

15.11.3.   Add dimensions to the floor plan

1. <u>Doors dimensions</u>:
   a. Turn *On* the door label layer.
   b. Make the **Dim_Door** layer to be the current layer.
   c. Using the *Linear* dimension tool, add the dimensions to the centerline of the doors, Figure 15-32.

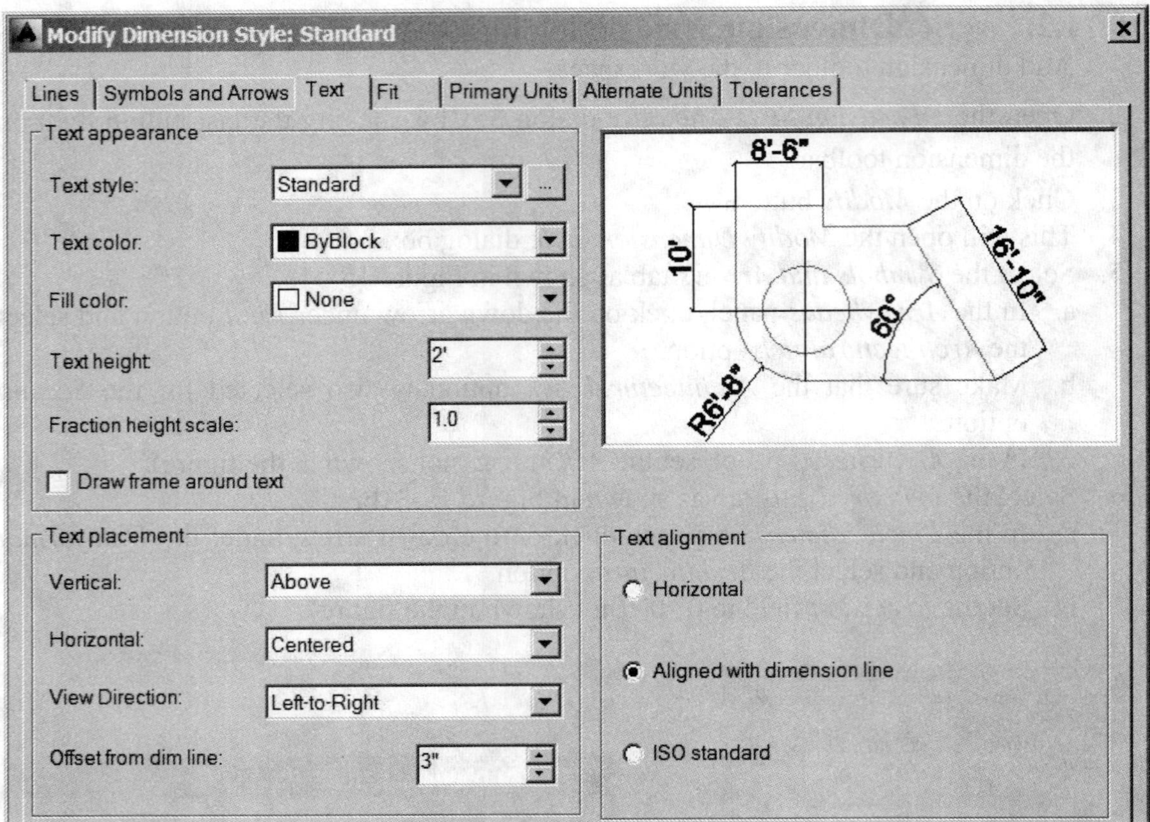

Figure 15-31c

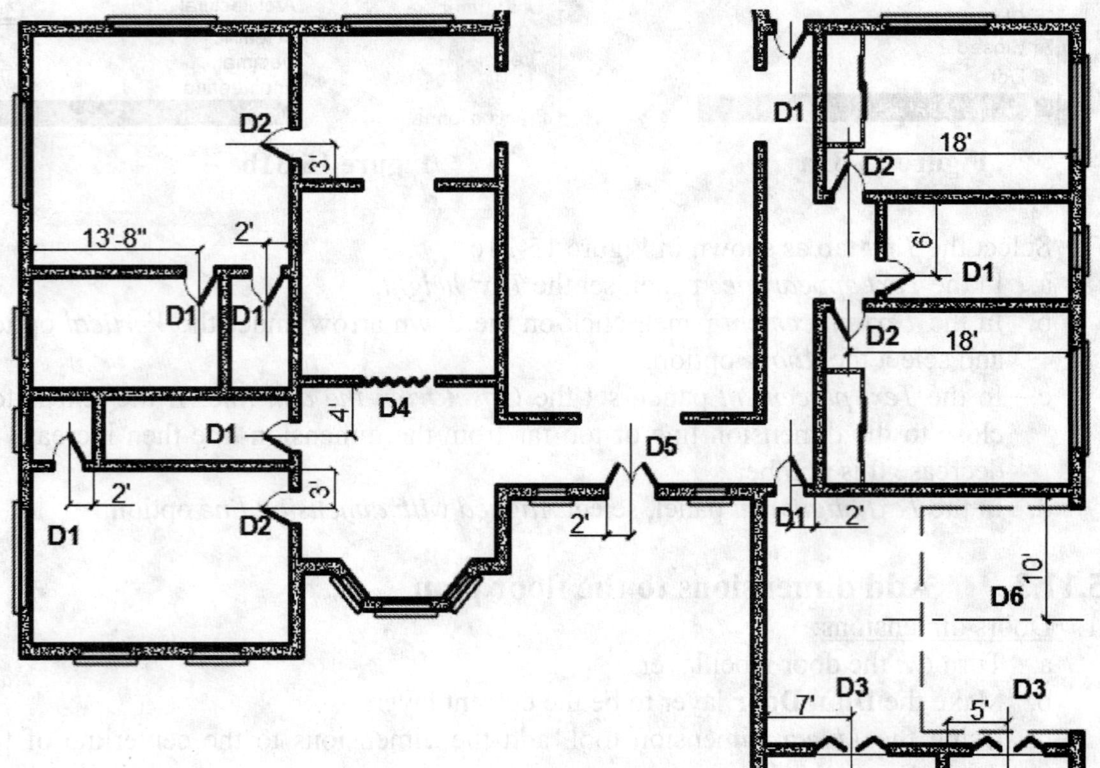

Figure 15-32

2. <u>Windows dimensions</u>:
   a. Turn *On* the windows label layer.
   b. Make the **Dim_Window** layer to be the current layer.
   c. Using the *Linear* dimension tool, add the dimensions for the centerlines of all the windows, Figure 15-33.

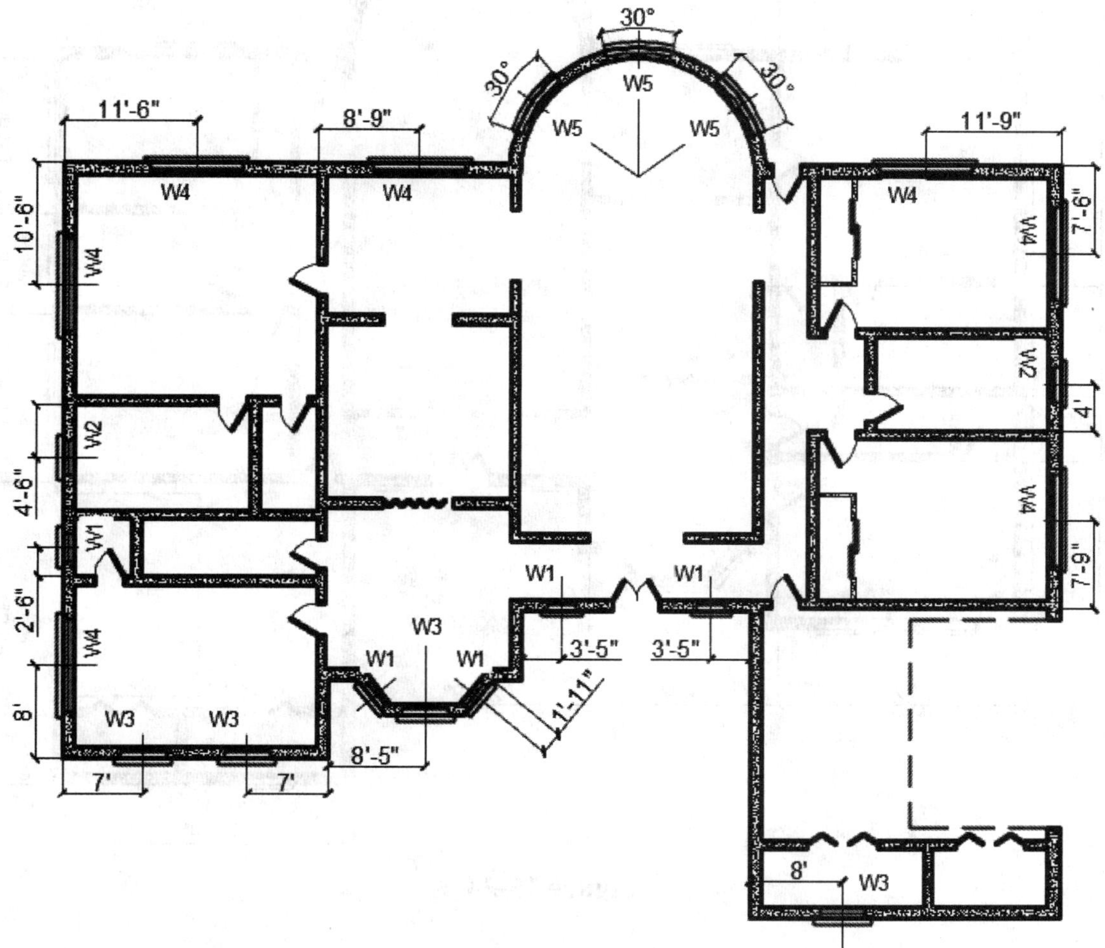

Figure 15-33

3. <u>Wall to Wall dimensions</u>:
   a. Make the **Dim_WtoW** to be the current layer.
   b. Using the *Linear* dimension tool, add the dimensions for the wall to wall distance, Figure 15-34.

4. <u>Overall dimensions</u>:
   a. Make the **Dim_Overall** to be layer the current layer.
   b. Using the *Linear* dimension tool, add the dimensions for the overall distance, Figure 15-35. Some of the dimensions can be calculated from the other dimensions; the overall dimension of the front side, 86'-3", in Figure 15-35 can be obtained by adding 22', 16'-9", 20'-9", 25'-9", and 1'(wall thickness) in

Figure 15-34. However, it is recommended to add the overall dimensions in an architectural drawing and not to omit any useful dimensions.

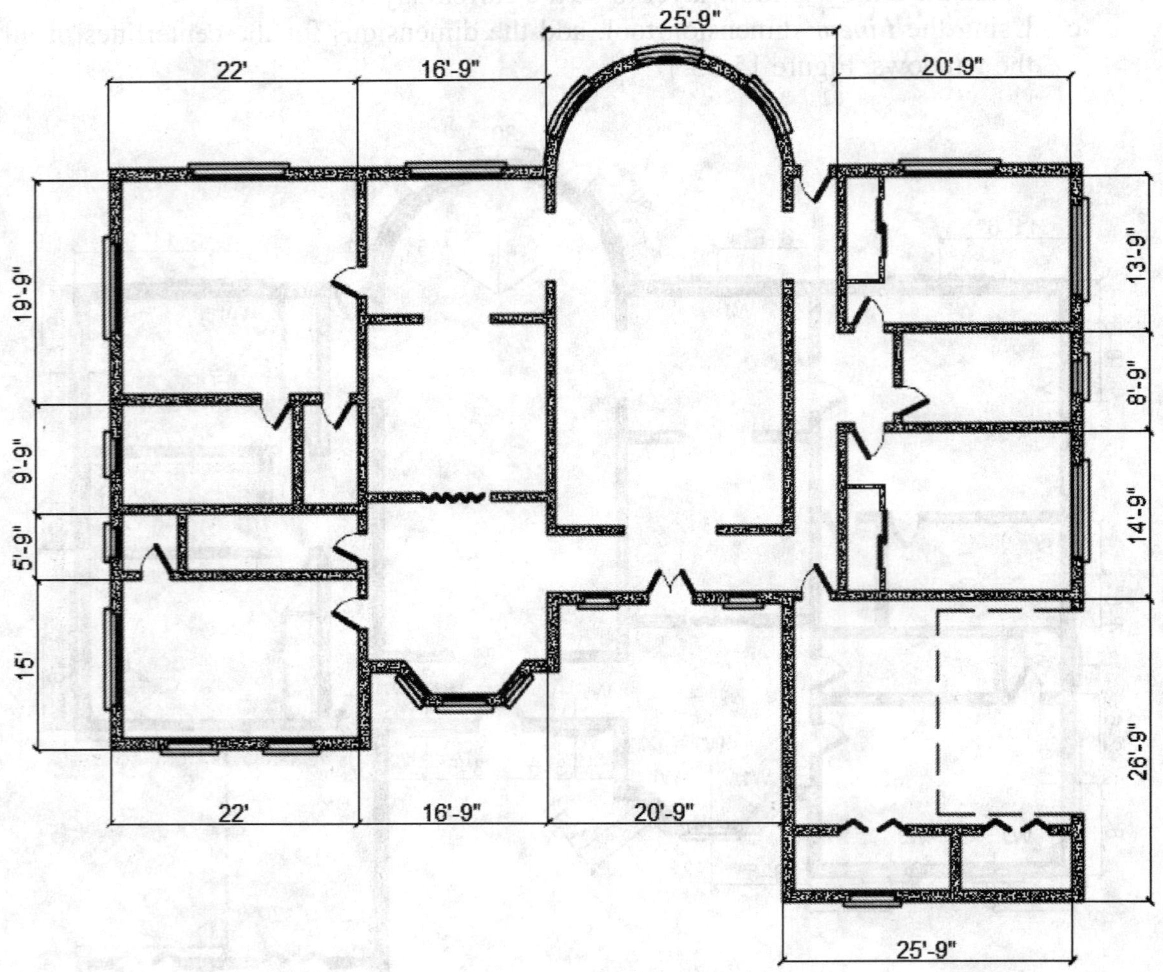

Figure 15-34

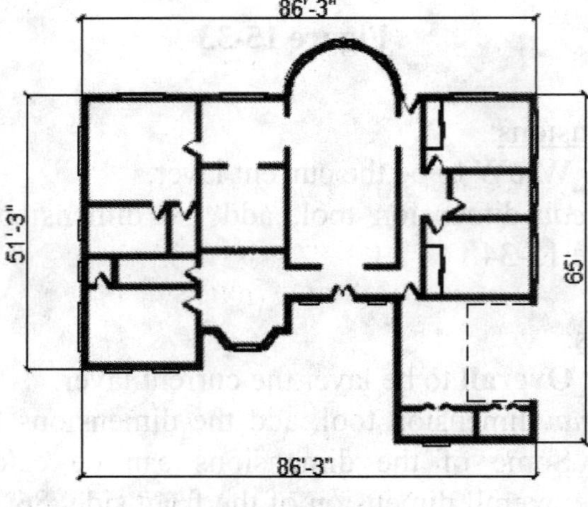

Figure 15-35

5. <u>Room size</u>:
   a. Make the **Dim_Roomsize** layer to be the current layer.
   b. Using the *Text* command, create text boxes for the room size. A room size is written as x-dimension times y-dimension, Figure 15-36.
   c. Use the four corner grip points of the text to match the four corners of the room to place the text in the center.

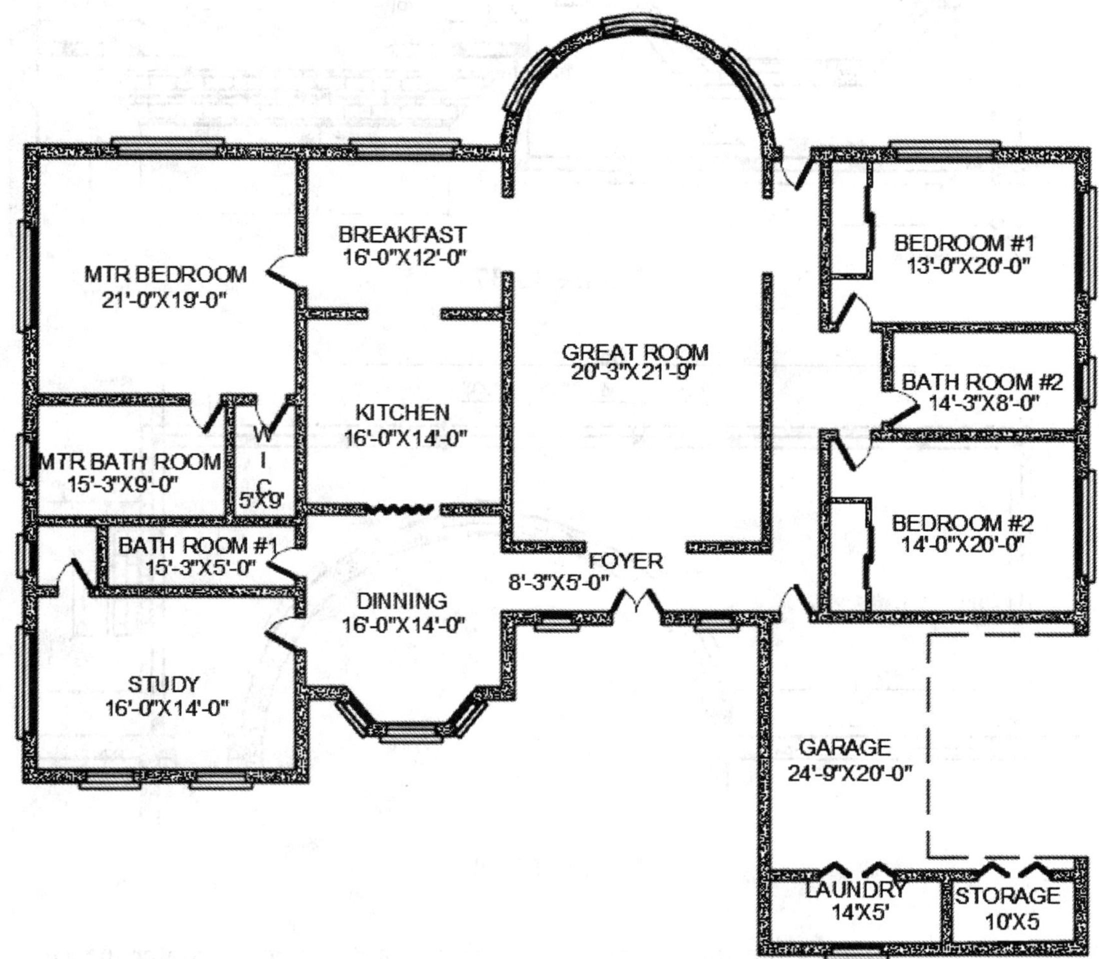

Figure 15-36

6. <u>Interior dimensions</u>:
   a. Make the **Dim_Interior** layer to be the current layer.
   b. Using the *Linear* dimension tool, add the dimensions to the interior walls which are not dimensioned in any of the previous steps.

7. <u>Porch dimension</u>:
   a. Make the **Dim_Porch** layer to be the current layer.
   b. Turn *On* the porch layer
   c. Using the *Linear* dimension tool, add the dimensions to the front (Figure 15-37) and back porch (Figure 15-38).

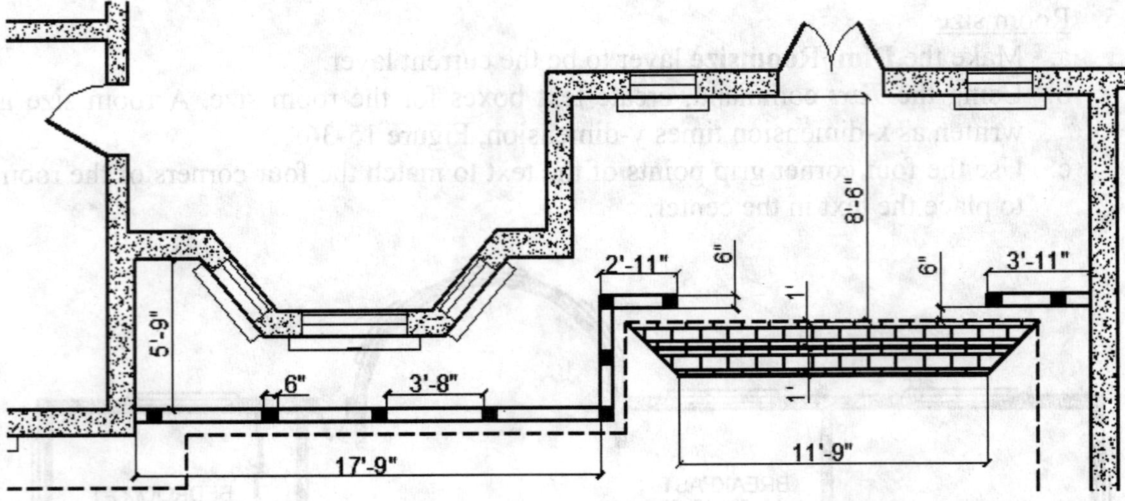

Figure 15-37

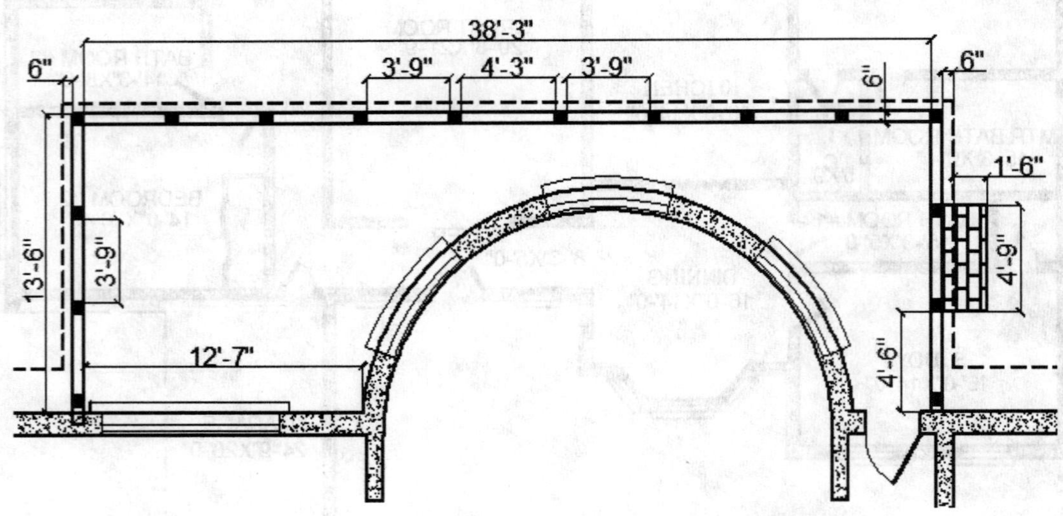

Figure 15-38

8. Figure 15-39 shows the dimensions of the doors and windows centerline (in the exterior wall), wall to wall, overall, and room sizes.

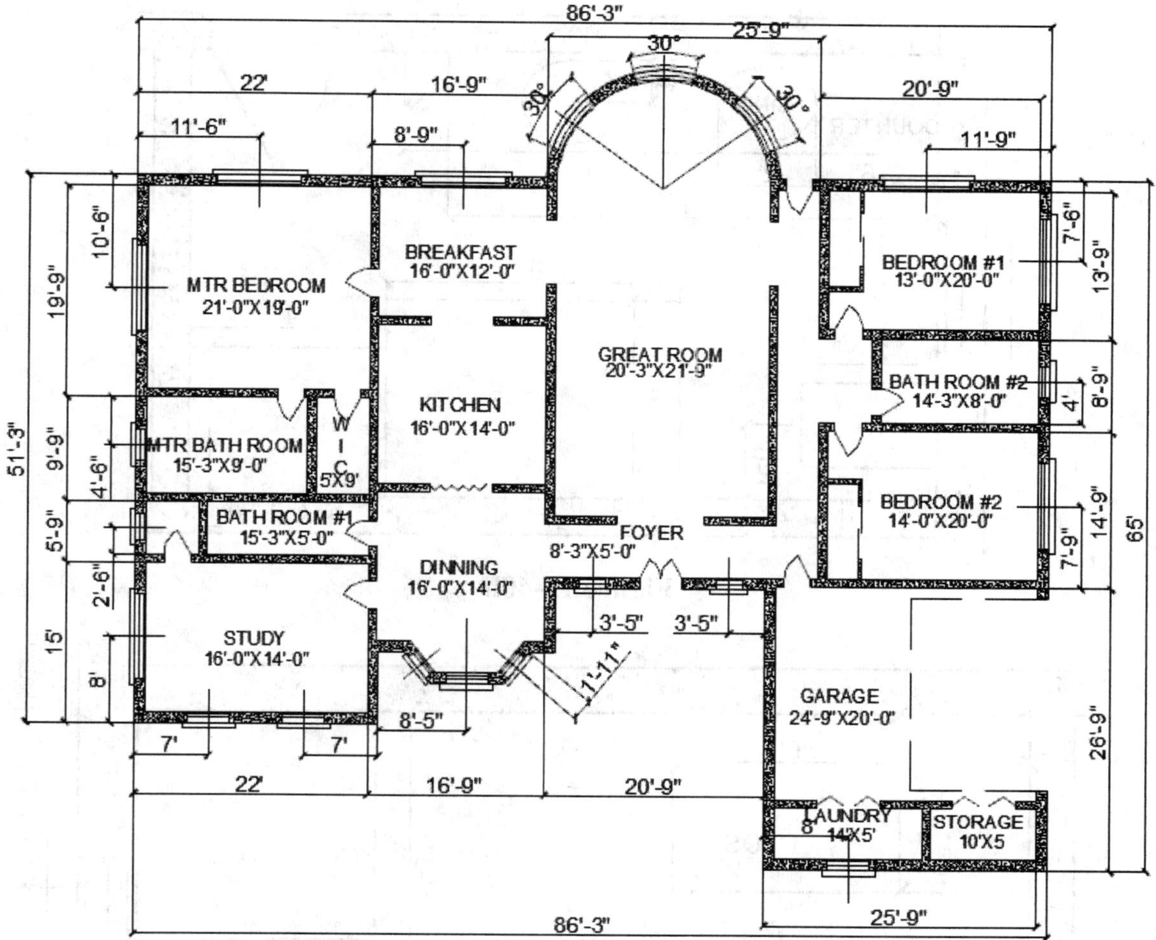

Figure 15-39

9. <u>Bathrooms dimension:</u>
   a. Make the **Dim_BathRM** layer to be the current layer.
   b. Turn *On* the bathrooms fixtures layer
   c. Using the *Linear* dimension tool, add the dimensions to the bathrooms fixtures, Figure 15-40a (bathroom #1), Figure 15-40b (master bath room), Figure 15-40c (bathroom #2).

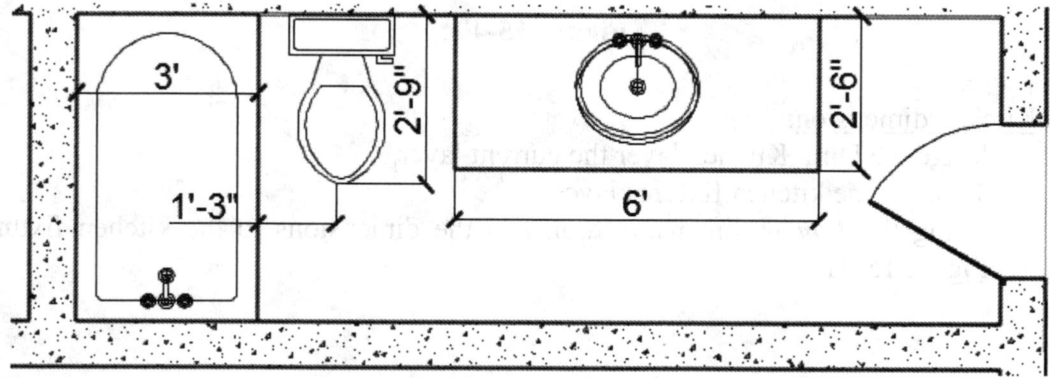

Figure 15-40a

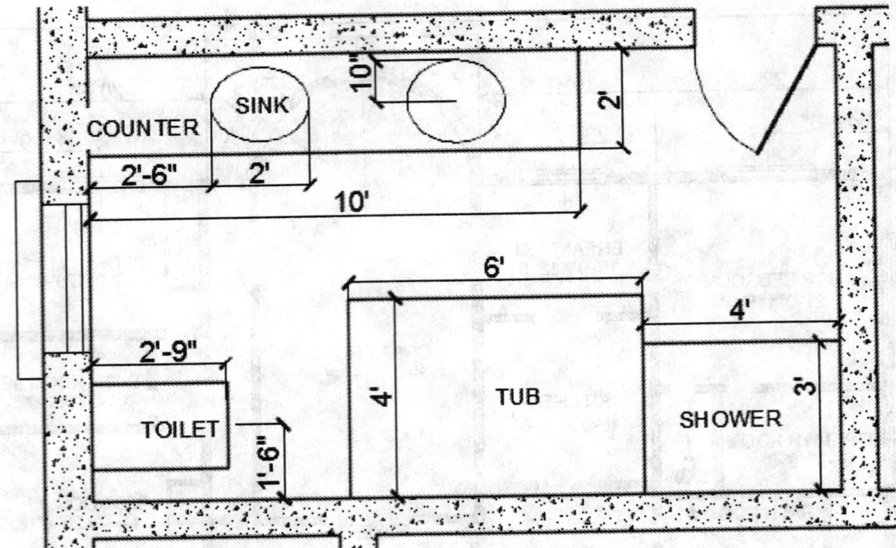

Figure 15-40b

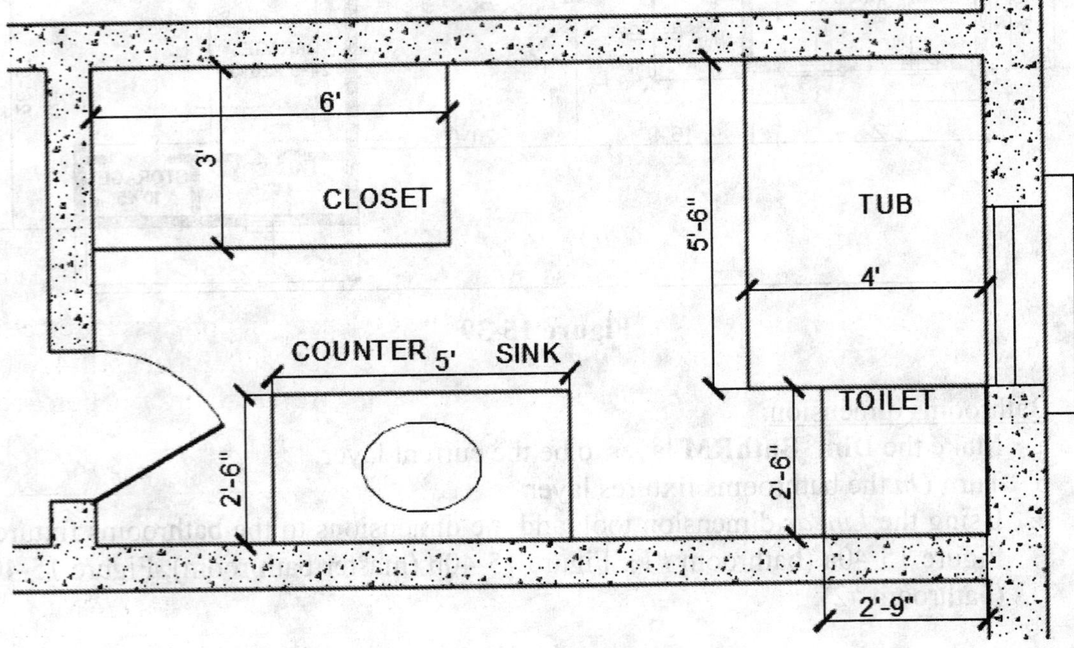

Figure 15-40c

10. <u>Kitchen dimension</u>:
   a. Make the Dim_Kitchen layer the current layer.
   b. Turn *On* the kitchen fixtures layer
   c. Using the *Linear* dimension tool, add the dimensions to the kitchen fixtures, Figure 15-41.

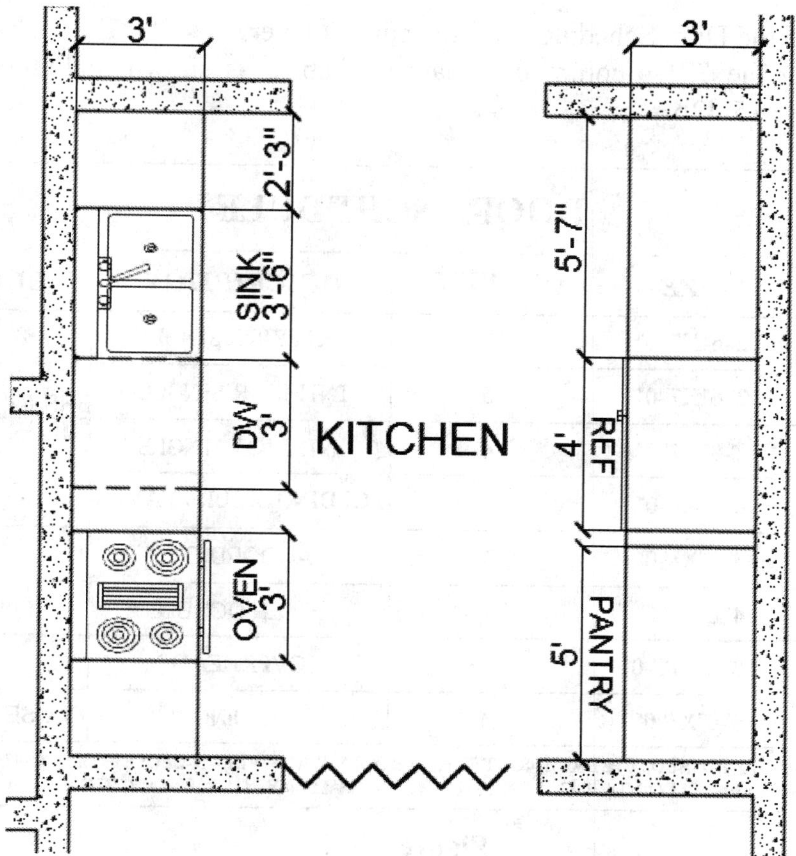

Figure 15-41

11. <u>Door and window schedule</u>: Finally, complete the dimensioning process by creating the schedule for the doors and window, Figure 15-42a and Figure 15-42b. In architectural terminology, schedule is a table displaying the detail information about the doors and windows.

<table>
<tr><th colspan="5" align="center">WINDOWS SCHEDULE</th></tr>
<tr><th>WINDOW NO.</th><th>SIZE</th><th>QUANTITY</th><th>DESCRIPTION</th><th>LOCATION</th></tr>
<tr><td align="center">W1</td><td align="center">2'-6"X2'-0"</td><td align="center">5</td><td align="center">SLIDDING</td><td align="center">FOYER, DNG, CLOSET(STUDY)</td></tr>
<tr><td align="center">W2</td><td align="center">3'-0"X5'-0"</td><td align="center">2</td><td align="center">SLIDDING</td><td align="center">MBH, BH-#2</td></tr>
<tr><td align="center">W3</td><td align="center">5'-0"X3'-0"</td><td align="center">4</td><td align="center">SLIDDING</td><td align="center">DNG, STDY, LD</td></tr>
<tr><td align="center">W4</td><td align="center">10'-0"X5'-0"</td><td align="center">7</td><td align="center">CASEMENT</td><td align="center">STDY, MBD, BFT, BD #1, BD #2</td></tr>
<tr><td align="center">W5</td><td align="center">25°X5'-0"</td><td align="center">3</td><td align="center">CIRCULAR SLIDDING</td><td align="center">GREAT ROOM</td></tr>
<tr><td colspan="5">LEGEND: M: MASTER, BD: BED, BH: BATH, STDY: STUDY, R: ROOM, GRG: GARAGE, LD: LAUNDRY, BFT: BREAKFAST, DNG: DINING, KCN: KITCHEN, CASEMENT* IS THE COMBINATION OF CASEMENT+FIXED+CASEMENT</td></tr>
</table>

Figure 15-42a

a. Make the Dim_Schedule layer the current layer.
b. Using the *Table* command create the tables as shown in Figure 15-42a and Figure 15-42b.

<table>
<tr><td colspan="5" align="center">DOORS SCHEDULE</td></tr>
<tr><td>DOOR NO.</td><td>SIZE</td><td>QUANTITY</td><td>DESCRIPTION</td><td>LOCATION</td></tr>
<tr><td>D1</td><td>2'-6"X7'-0"</td><td>2</td><td>EXTERIOR SINGLE</td><td>STUDY, GRG</td></tr>
<tr><td>D1</td><td>2'-6"X7'-0"</td><td>5</td><td>INTERIOR SINGLE</td><td>BHR #1, MBHR, WIC, BHR #2, BACK PORCH</td></tr>
<tr><td>D2</td><td>2'-8"X7'-0"</td><td>4</td><td>INTERIOR SINGLE</td><td>MBDR, BDR1, BDR2, STUDY</td></tr>
<tr><td>D3</td><td>6'-0"X7'-0"</td><td>2</td><td>FOLDING, FOUR LEAVES</td><td>LD, STG</td></tr>
<tr><td>D4</td><td>6'-0"X7'-0"</td><td>1</td><td>ACOORDION</td><td>DNG</td></tr>
<tr><td>D5</td><td>4'-0"X7'-0"</td><td>1</td><td>FOYER DOUBLE</td><td>FOYER</td></tr>
<tr><td>D6</td><td>18'-0"X10'-0"</td><td>1</td><td>OVERHEAD</td><td>GRG</td></tr>
<tr><td>D7</td><td>6'-0"X7'-0"</td><td>4</td><td>SLIDING</td><td>CLOSETS IN BDI, BDII</td></tr>
<tr><td colspan="5">LEGEND: M: MASTER, BD: BED, BH: BATH, S: STUDY, R: ROOM, WIC: WALK-IN-CLOSET, GRG: GARAGE, BFT: BREAKFAST, DNG: DINING, KCN: KITCHEN, HW: HALLWAY, LD: LAUNDRY, STG: STORAGE</td></tr>
</table>

Figure 15-42b

16. Elevation

16.1.   Objectives

- Learn to draw simple roofs
- Learn to draw the front and right side elevations
- Learn to project from the floor plan to front elevation
- Learn to project from the floor plan and front elevation to create the right side elevation
- Learn to insert windows and doors blocks from the *Design Center*
- Learn to use the *Hatch* command

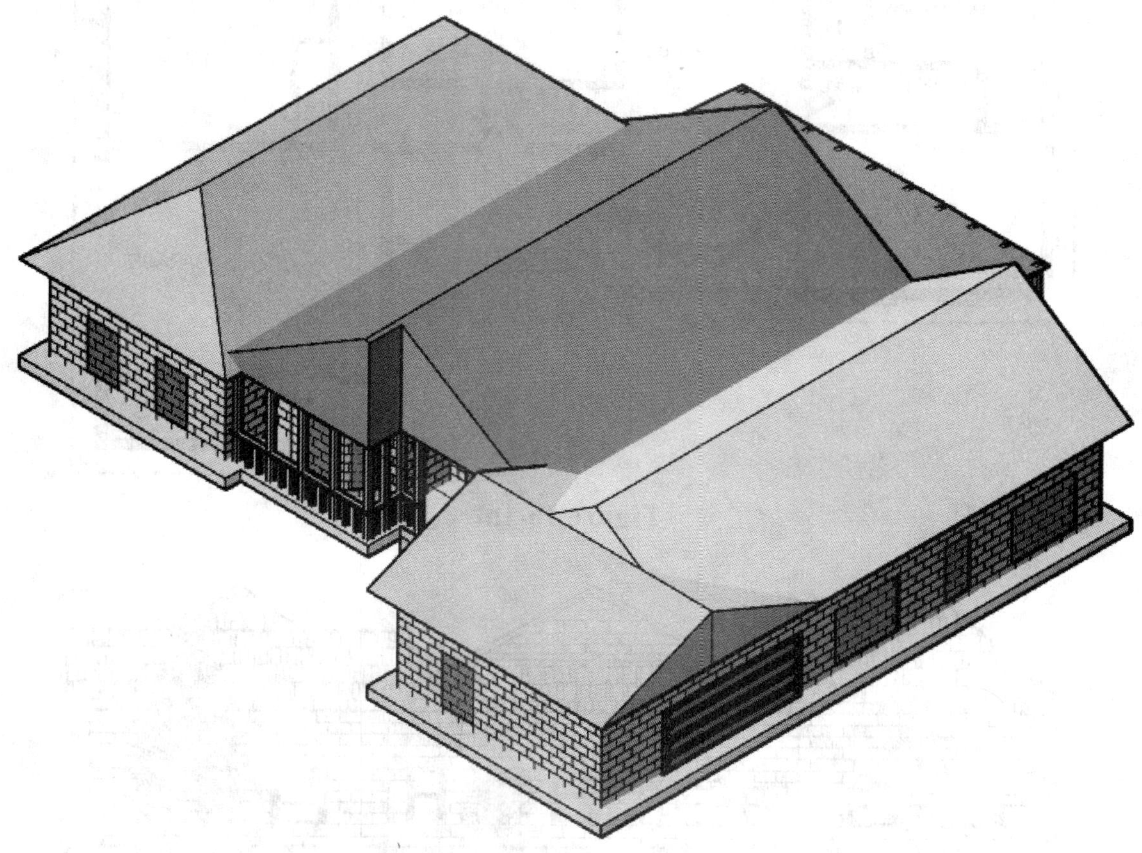

16.2.   Introduction

The exterior elevations are commonly used for conveying the appearance of a building from the exterior. Figure 16-1b shows the front elevation of the residential building of the floor plan, Figure 16-1a, created in the previous chapter. In architecture and building engineering terminology, elevation is an orthographic projection of a building from a side. The elevations can be used to view the building view from all four sides; that is, from the front, rear, left, and right sides. Therefore, the elevation drawings of a building include one drawing for each of the front, rear, left, and right sides of the building.

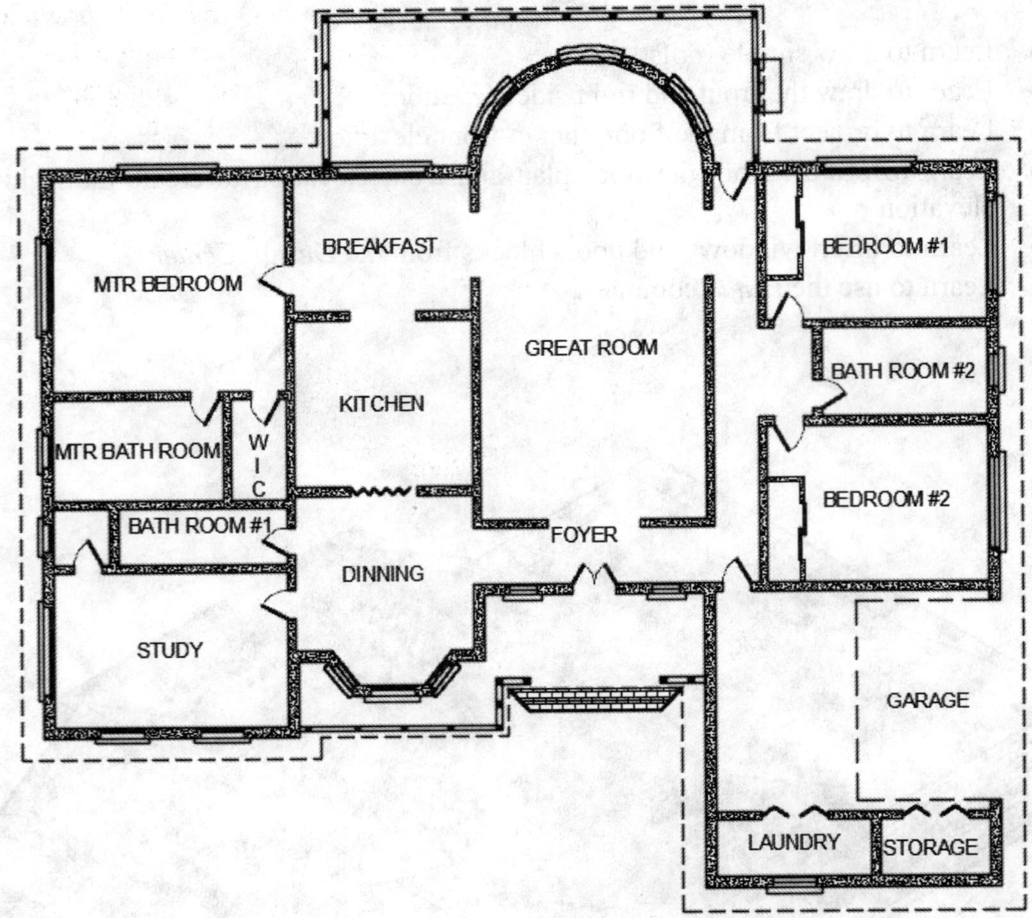

Figure 16-1a

Figure 16-1b

The elevation drawings are simpler than floor plan. The elevation drawings display the height and appearance of the windows and doors, shape of the roof, floor to floor levels (for multistory buildings), and the exterior walls. A single level building's elevation drawing starts with the ground level. In the drawing, objects below the ground level (foundations and crawl spaces) are shown using dashed (*Hidden*) lines. The next step is the drawing of all the floor slab, windows, doors, and walls. Finally, the elevations are finished with the roof. Since the roof is an important part of the elevation design of a building, the next section briefly discusses basics of roofs.

The focus of this chapter is the front and right side views of a building, also known as the front and right side elevations. Consider a simple building shown in Figure 16-1c. The figure shows the south east isometric view of the building. The three orthographic views (top, front, and right side view) of this building are shown in Figure 16-1d.

Figure 16-1c

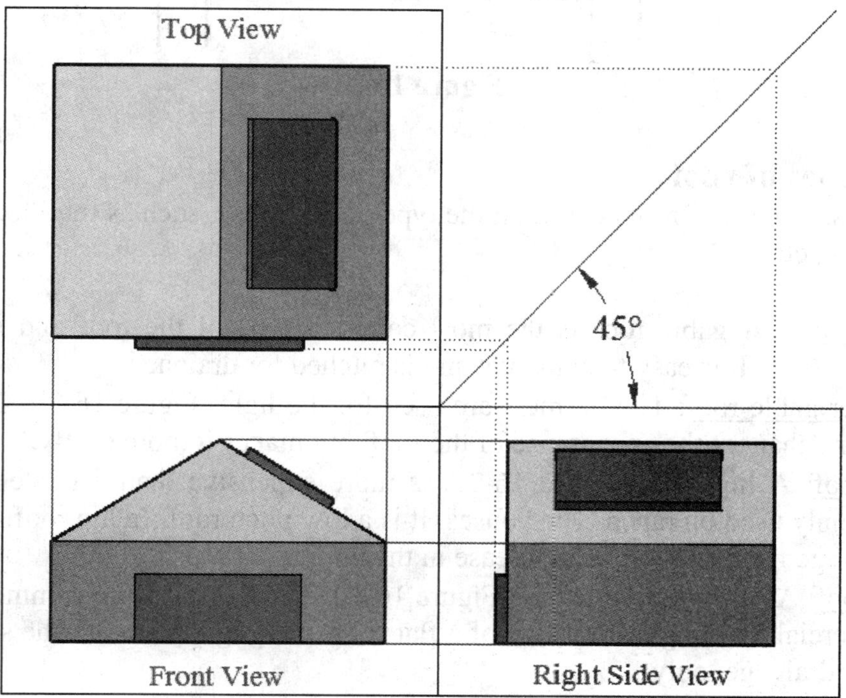

Figure 16-1d

Notice the projection of the skylight (the box in the roof), front door, and the gable roof in the three orthographic views. Vertical lines are used to project information between top (floor plan) and front views. Horizontal lines are used to project information between front and right-side views. Horizontal and vertical lines are used to project information between front and right-side views using 45 degree miter line, Figure 16-1c.

16.3.   Roof

16.3.1. Terminology

Some of the commonly used terms are listed here and are shown in Figure 16-2.

- *Span*: The span of a roof is the horizontal distance covered by the roof.
- *Run*: The run of a roof is the half of the span.
- *Rise*: The rise of a roof is the vertical distance covered by the roof.
- *Pitch*: The pitch of a roof is the slope of a roof. The pitch is the ratio of the rise and the run (*Pitch = Rise/Run*). The steepness of a roof increases as the pitch of the roof increases.

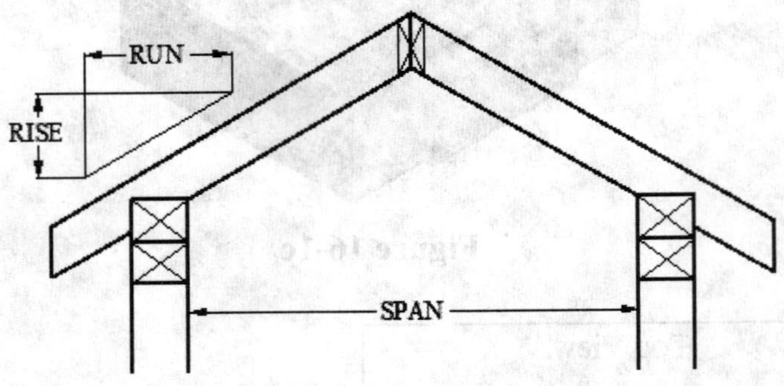

Figure 16-2

16.3.2. Types of roof

There are many types of roofs based on the type of the house, such as traditional, dormer, contemporary, etc.

- Gable roof: A gable roof is the most common type of the roof and is shown in Figure 16-3a. It is easy to construct and is pitched for drainage.
- Dormer gable roof: The dormers are used for the light, Figure 16-3b. The use of a dormer enhances the appearance of the roof, but makes it more costly.
- Hip roof: A hip roof (Figure 16-3c) is more expensive than a gable roof and is commonly used on ranch type houses. It is a low pitch roof. In hip roof, the chances of leakage increases with an increase in the number of hips.
- Flat roof: A flat roof is shown in Figure 16-3d. The flat roofs are commonly used in commercial buildings. The slope of a flat roof is negligibly small. The slope is used for the drainage, only.

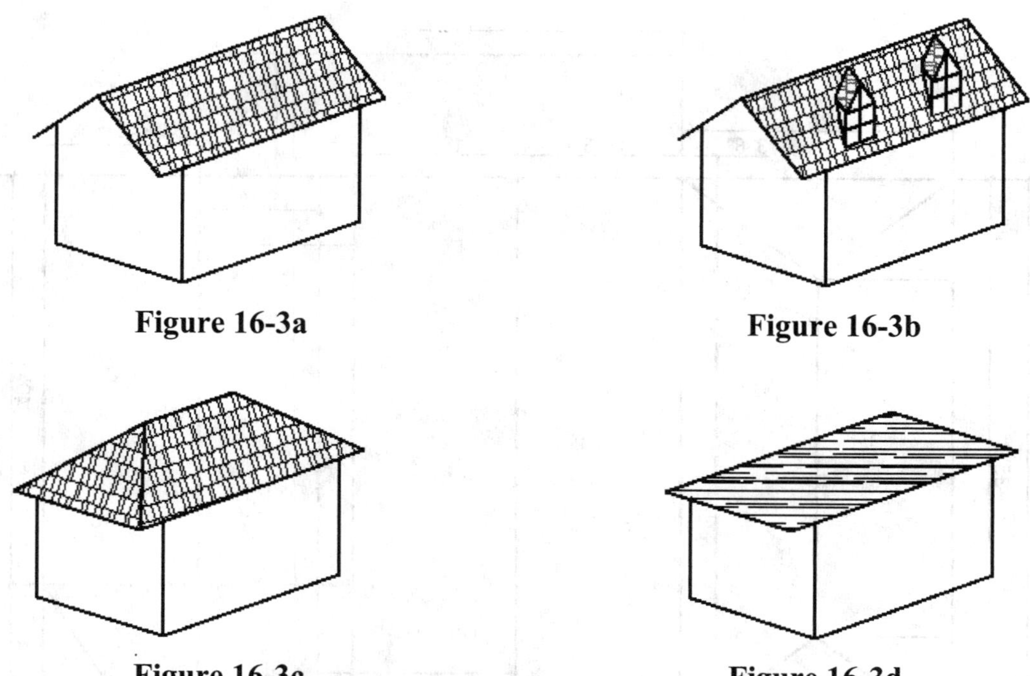

Figure 16-3a   Figure 16-3b

Figure 16-3c   Figure 16-3d

16.3.3. Important points
The selection of a roof type depends on several factors.

- <u>Low pitched verses high pitched roof</u>: Low pitched roofs are cheaper than high pitched roofs. However, a high pitch roof enhances the appearance of the house.
- <u>Color and material</u>: The color and material of the roof should be selected based on the durability and in accordance with the materials used on the exterior of the building. As a general rule, only two types of material should be used in the exterior finish.

16.4.   Roof plan
Before drawing the front elevation, draw the roof plan as shown in Figure 16-4a. In the figure, roof of the master bedroom (the right side of the roof plan) is a hip roof; the garage and the right side of the house are covered by gable roofs. The front porch is also covered by a gable roof. The heights of the three gables are different. However, two of the three gables are in the front of the house and the gable of the garage is on right side of the house (Figure 16-1). The dashed lines show the part of the roof not directly visible from the top of the house.

Figure 16-4b shows the location of hips, ridges, and valleys. In the figure, arrows indicate the direction of the down slope. The ridge and valley labels are created using *Text* command and the enclosing rectangles are created using *Enclose in Object* command from the *Express Tool* tab and *Text* panel (with the offset factor of 0.2). Finally, the text and rectangles are rotated using the *Rotate* command. The arrows are created using the first two clicks of the *qleader* command (press the Esc key after the first two clicks). The bigger and smaller arrow head sizes are 4' and 2', respectively.

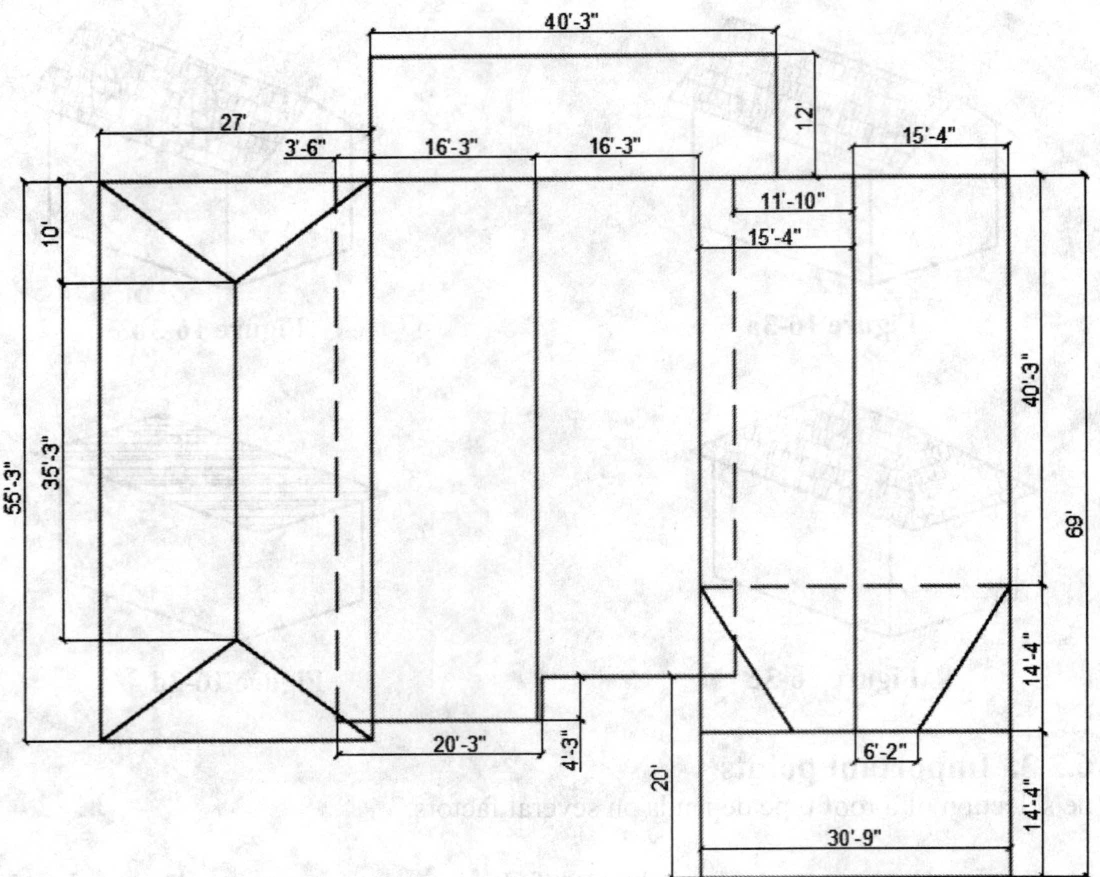

Figure 16-4a

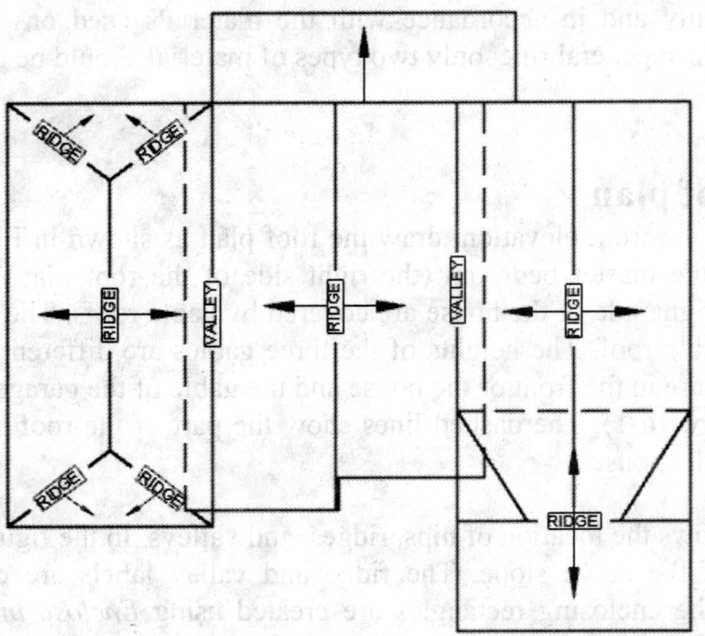

Figure 16-4b

Figure 16-4c shows the roof plan using hatching command with pattern *AR-RSHKE* at the scale value of 1.4. The figure also displays the hatch angles of the various hatches used in the roof plan.

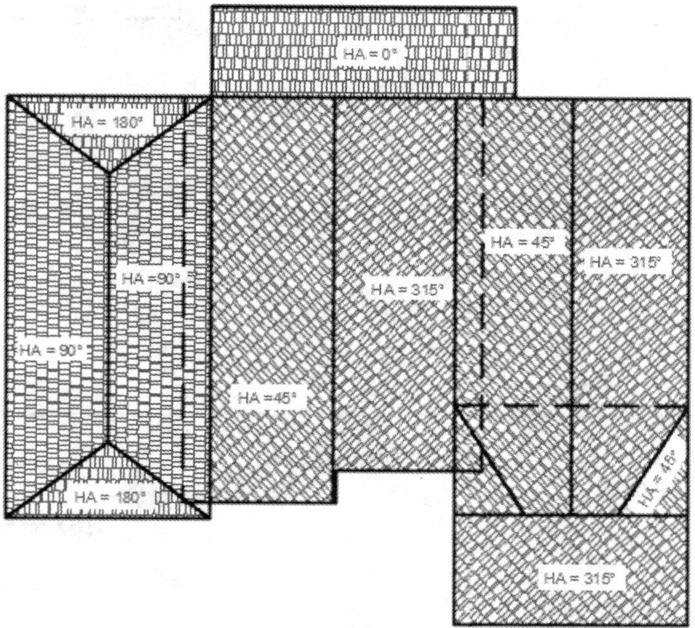

Figure 16-4c

16.5.   AutoCAD and the front elevation

The front elevation drawings of a building depend on its floor plan. This section provides step-by-step instructions for drawing the front elevation of the floor plan of the three bedroom residential building drawn in the previous chapter.

1. <u>Orthogonal lines</u>: Since most of the lines in the front elevation are either horizontal or vertical, turn *On* the *ORTHO* option by pressing the corresponding button ( ) on the status bar.

2. <u>Load linetype</u>: The front elevation will use continuous, dashed, and center lines. Therefore, load *Hidden* and *Center* linetypes (for reference, see Chapter 3 of the book). By default, the continuous linetype is loaded.

3. <u>Ground level</u>:
   a. Create a layer called *Grade_Line* (Linetype: *Continuous*; Line weight: 0.0).
   b. Make the *Grade_Line* to be the current layer.
   c. The grade line is a thick solid line representing the ground level. Draw a horizontal line representing the ground level, 37'-2" below the garage in the floor plan, as shown in Figure 16-5a. Change its lineweight to 0.80.
   d. Draw a 2' wide rectangle, Figure 16-5b.
   e. Hatch the grade line, Figure 16-5c.

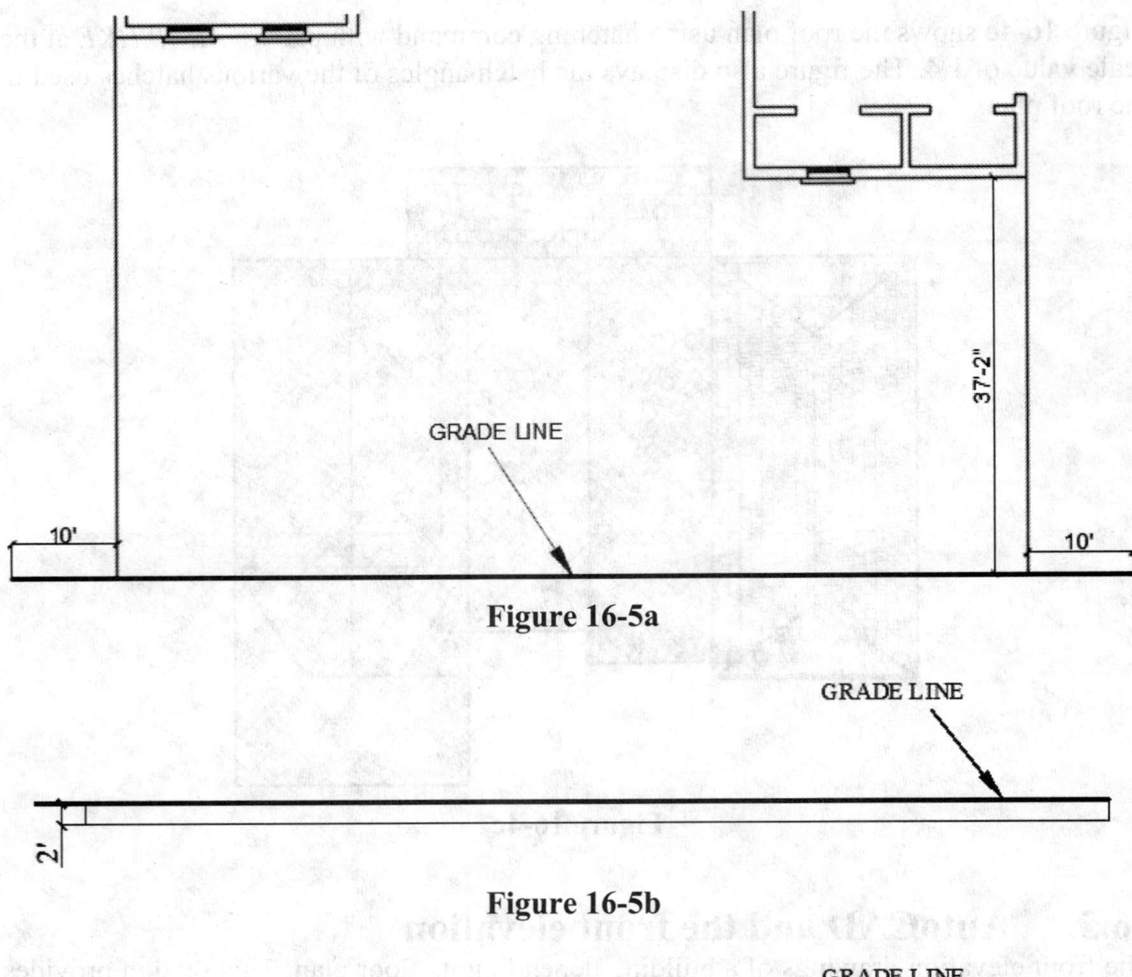

Figure 16-5a

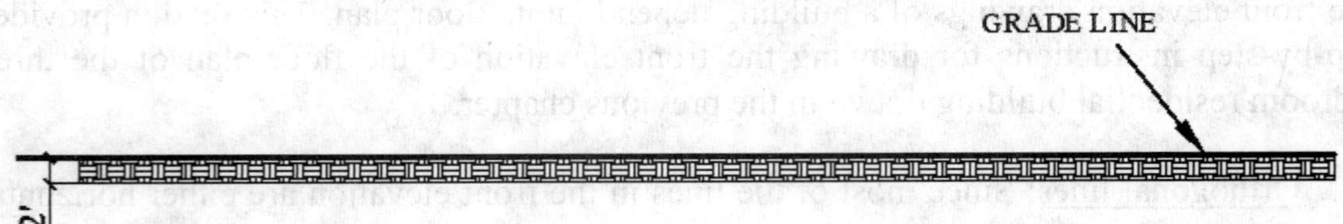

Figure 16-5b

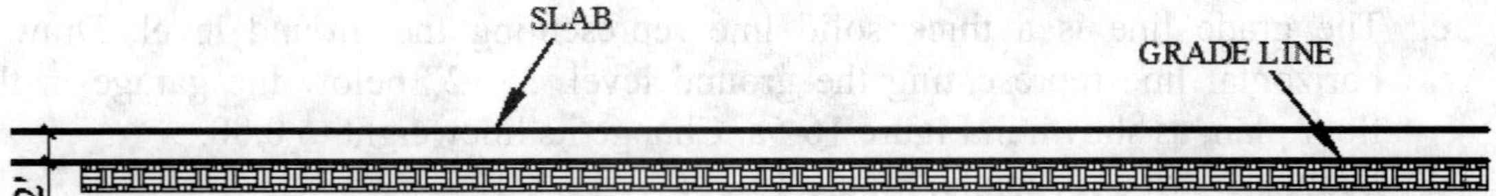

Figure 16-5c

4. <u>Slab level</u>:
    a. Create a layer called *Slab_Line* (Linetype: *Continuous*; Line weight: 0.0).
    b. Make the *Slab_Line* to be the current layer.
    c. The slab surface is shown as a thick solid line representing the main floor level. Draw a horizontal line representing the main level, 2'-0" above the grade line, as shown in Figure 16-6a. Change it lineweight to 0.80.

Figure 16-6a

d. Draw a 2' wide rectangle, Figure 16-6b.
e. Hatch the grade line, Figure 16-6c.

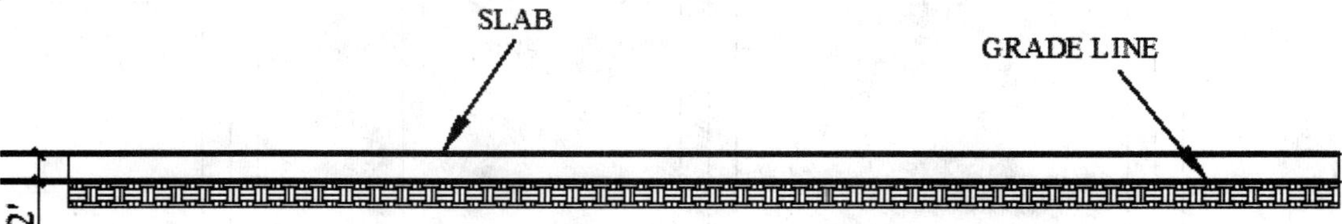

Figure 16-6b

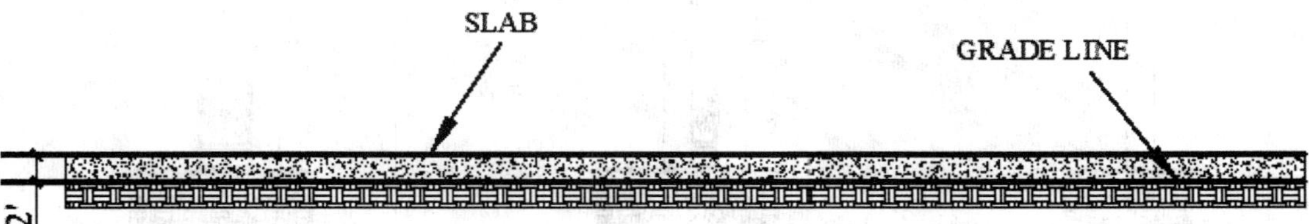

Figure 16-6c

5. <u>Draw the projection lines for the doors</u>:
    a. Create a layer called *Proj_Door*.
    b. Set its linetype to *Hidden*, lineweight: 0.0, and change its color.
    c. Make the *Proj_Door* to be the current layer.
    d. Since the projection lines will be perpendicular to the floor plan, turn *On* the *ORTHO* option by pressing the corresponding button (⬕) on the status bar.
    e. Draw the projection lines starting at the front door in the floor plan and terminating at the slab line, Figure 16-7a. Use the *Trim* or *Extend* commands as necessary.

6. <u>Draw the front entrance door</u>: Assume the front entrance door is 7'-0" high.
    - Create a layer called *Elevation*.
    - Set its linetype to *Continuous*, lineweight: change its color.
    - Make the *Elevation* to be the current layer.
    - Open the *Design Center* from the *View* tab and *Palette* panel by clicking the button.
    - Open the blocks folder of the *House Design.dwg*.
    - Insert the *Door-Fancy 36 inch* block by scaling down to 2/3 in X-direction (because the door width for one panel in the *Design Center* is 3'-0" and in the elevation is 2'-0"), Figure 16-7b. Keep the scale in Y- and Z-direction to be 1.0.
    - Use the *Mirror* command to add the second panel, Figure 16-7c.

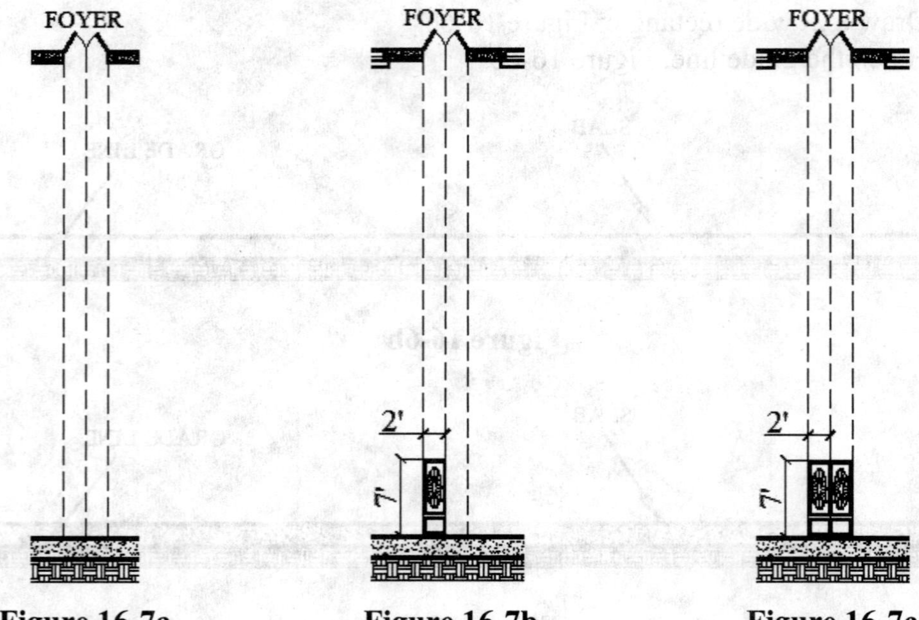

| Figure 16-7a | Figure 16-7b | Figure 16-7c |

7. <u>Draw the projection lines for the windows in the front wall</u>:
   a. Turn *Off* the *Proj_Door* layer.
   b. Create a layer called *Proj_Window*.
   c. Set its linetype to *Hidden*, lineweight: 0.0, and change its color.
   d. Make the *Proj_Window* to be the current layer.
   e. Since the projection lines will be perpendicular to the floor plan, turn *On* the *ORTHO* option by pressing the corresponding button on the status bar.
   f. Draw the projection lines starting at the windows, Figure 16-8a, in the floor plan and terminating at the slab line, Figure 16-8b. Use the *Trim* or *Extend* commands as necessary. The Figure 16-8a shows the starting points of the projection lines for the dining room and foyer's windows.

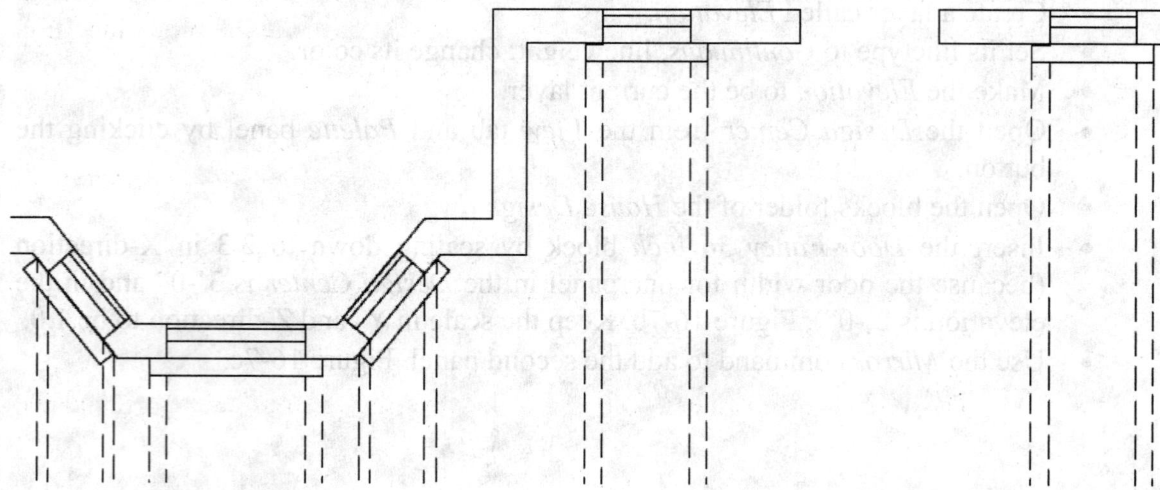

Figure 16-8a

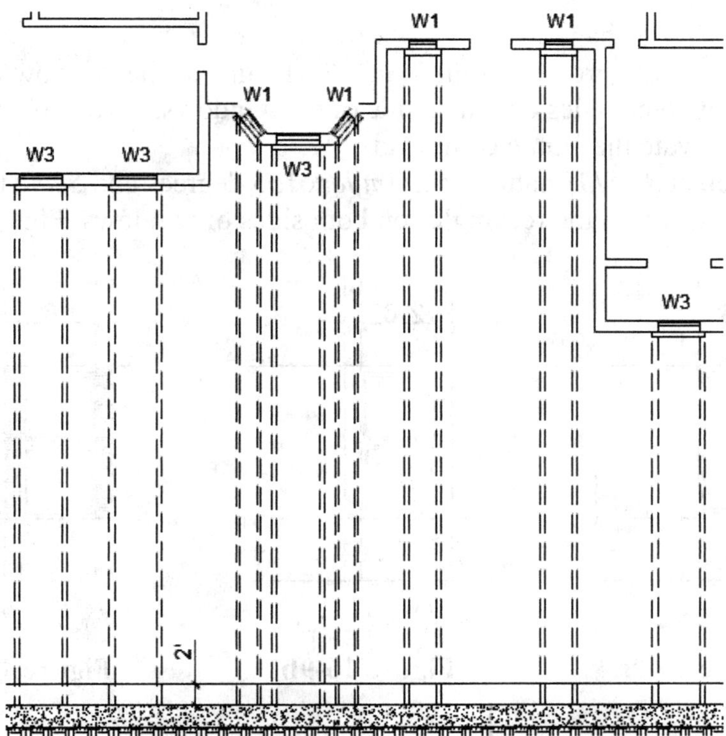

Figure 16-8b

8. <u>Draw the windows in the front wall</u>:
   - Make the *Elevation* to be the current layer.
   - In the front elevation three types of windows are used, Figure 16-7b: W3, W1, and distorted W1. The draftsman can increase the productivity and reduce the drawing generation time, if the multiple occurrence of the windows are created using *Copy* command. This section will create one of each type and then using then using the *Copy* command, create the copies at the desired locations.
   - Every window in the front wall is 2' above the slab level and 5' tall. Draw a horizontal line 2' above the slab level, Figure 16-7b, to make the block insertion and coping process faster. This line will be deleted later.
   - Create W1 main window:
     - For the W1 windows, the *Window Wood Frame 36X36* block would be inserted from the *Design Center* → *House Designer.dwg* as shown in Figure 16-8c.
     - For scaling, convert the desired and the *Design Center* block sizes in same units; either both of them should be in feet or both in inches.
     - The X-direction scale factor is 30/36 because the desired size is 30 inches (2'-6") and the block size is 36 inches.
     - The Y-direction scale factor is 5/3 because the desired size is 5' and the block size is 3'.
     - Using the 2' line as a guide lines, insert the scaled window block, Figure 16-9a.

- Create W1 side panel:
  - o Using the projection lines and the height of the window as a guide lines, draw rectangles on either side of the windows, Figure 16-9b.
  - o Activate the *Hatch* command.
  - o Select *ANSI31* pattern, set *Angle* to 135 degrees and *Scale* to 10.
  - o Now, hatch the rectangles on both sides of windows, Figure 16-9c.

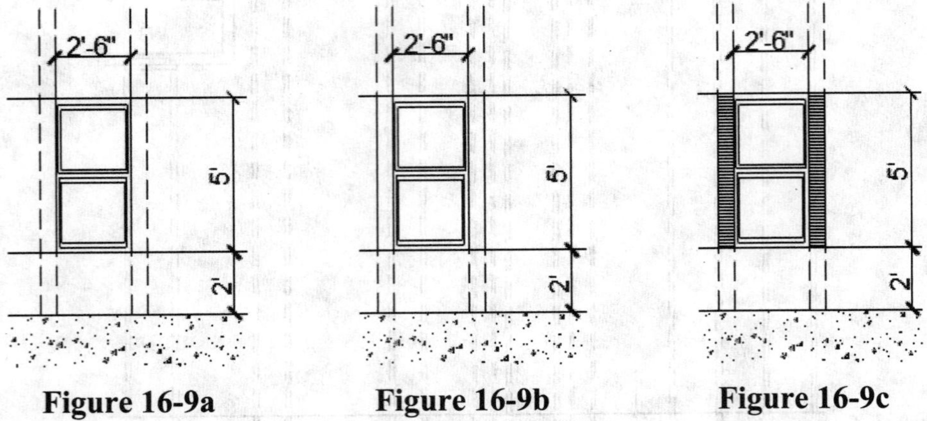

Figure 16-9a   **Figure 16-9b**   **Figure 16-9c**

- Create W3 window:
  - o The front elevation of W3 is shown in Figure 16-9d. This window is created with two blocks and two side panels.
  - o The process of creating the lower middle part is the same as before; the X- and Y-direction scale factor are 4/3 and 42/36, respectively.
  - o For the side panels, repeat the process of W1.
  - o For the upper circular part, insert the *Window Half-circle 36in* block from the *Design Center* → *House Designer.dwg* with the X-and Y-direction scale factors of 4/3 and 1, respectively.

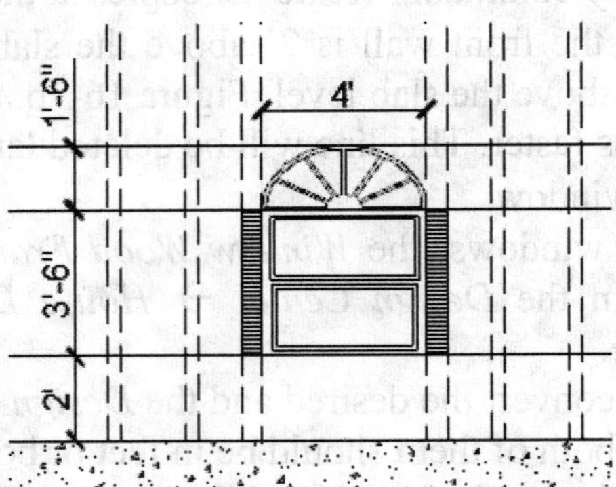

Figure 16-9d

- Create distorted W1 window:
  - o The process of creating the distorted W1 is the same as before, except the W1 width appears to 1'7", and its height will be 3'6", Figure 16-9e.
  - o The X-direction scale factor is 19/36 because the desired size is 30 inches (1'-7") and the block size is 36 inches.

o   The Y-direction scale factor is 42/36.
o   For side panels, repeat the process of W1.

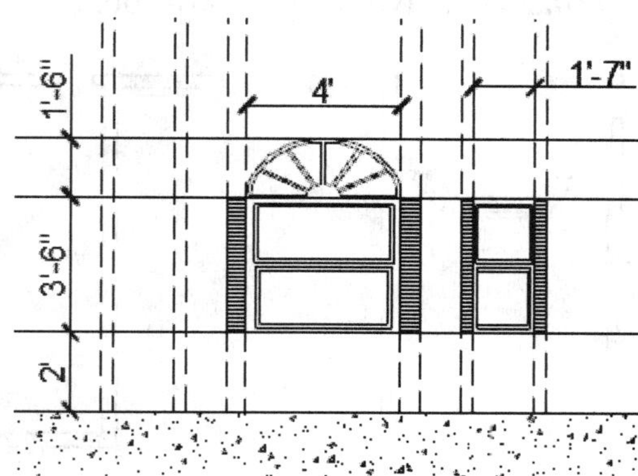

Figure 16-9e

- Three windows are created, Figure 16-9f. Using copy command and the 2' line as a guide line, crate the remaining window, Figure 16-9g.

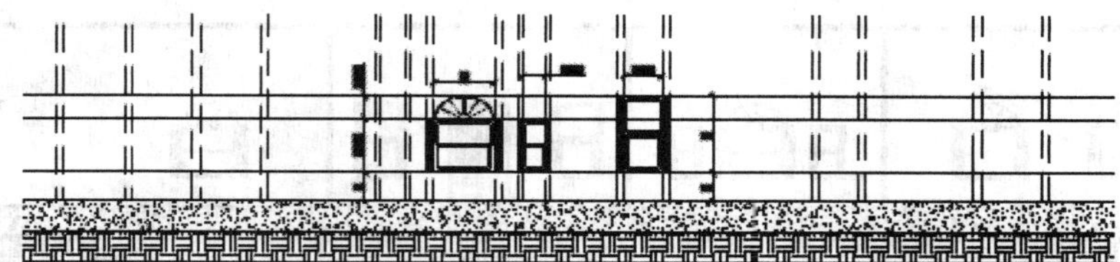

Figure 16-9f

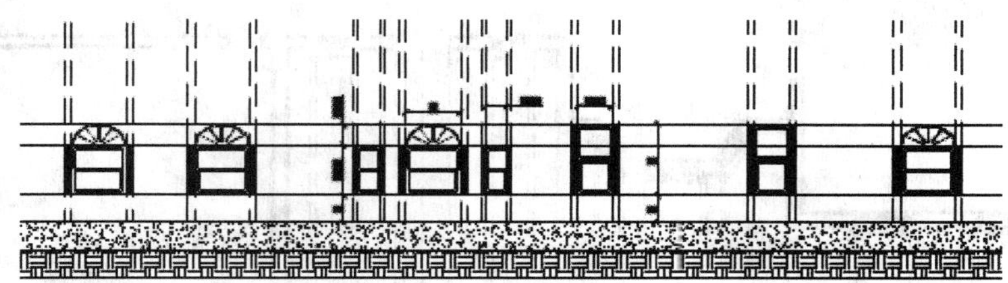

Figure 16-9g

9. Draw the projection lines for the wall:
    a. Create a layer called *Proj_Wall*.
    b. Set its linetype to *Hidden*, lineweight: 0.0, and change its color.
    c. Make the *Proj_Wall* to be the current layer.
    d. Since the projection lines will be perpendicular to the floor plan, turn *On* the ORTHO option by pressing the corresponding button on the status bar.
    e. Draw the projection lines starting at the corners of the wall (that are visible from the outside) in the floor plan and terminating at the slab line, Figure 16-10a. Use the *Trim* or *Extend* commands as necessary.

10. Add the exterior walls and the hatch to the wall:
    - Make the *Elevation* to be the current layer.

- The walls are 12'-0" high.
- Draw the exterior face of the exterior wall, Figure 16-10a.
- Turn *On* the *Proj_Window*'s layer, Figure 16-10c.

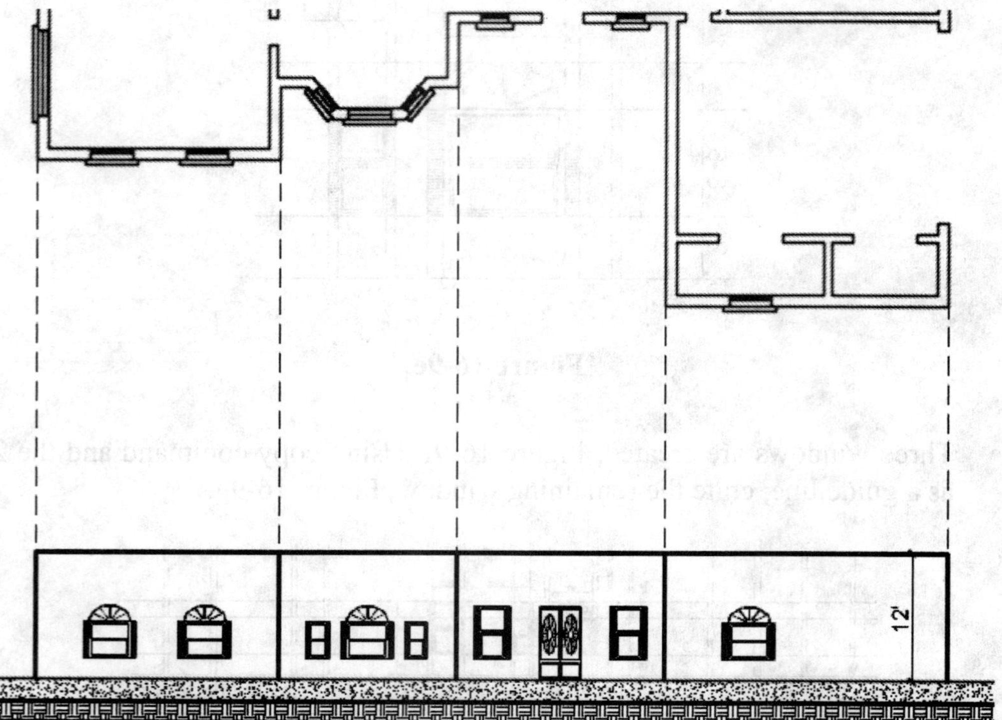

Figure 16-10a

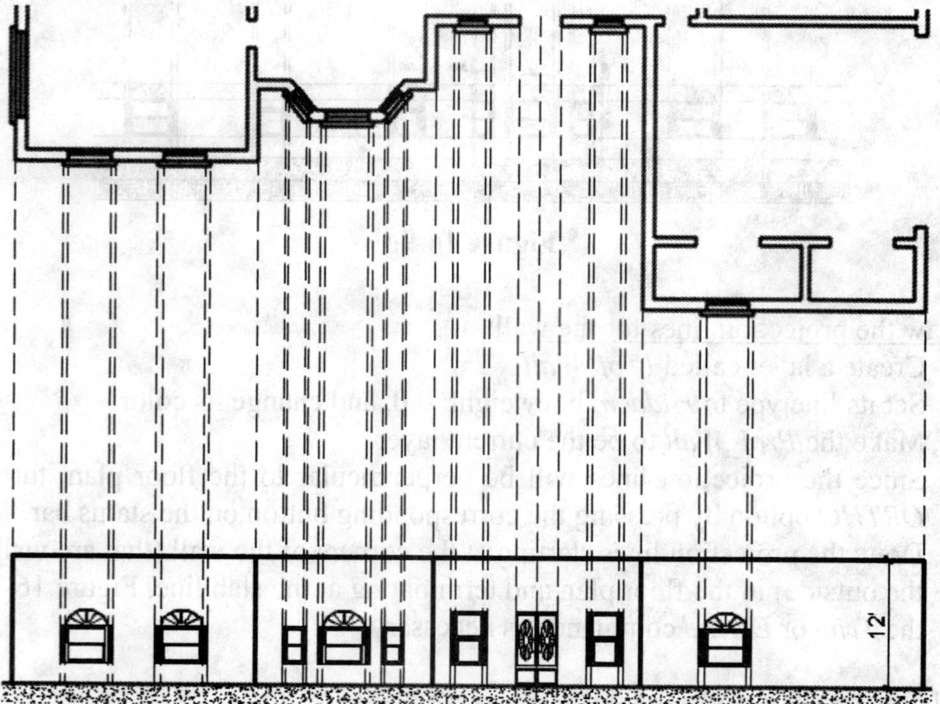

Figure 16-10b

- **Do not create the hatch for the front wall with the door and window's projection lines *Off*. It will take a very long time and the hatch will enter inside the doors and window.**
- Activate the *Hatch* command.
- Select *AR-B816* (brick) pattern, set *Angle* to 0 degrees and *Scale* to 1.
- Now, hatch the rectangles created by the window's projection lines, Figure 16-9c.
- Change the color of the hatched area.

Figure 16-10c

11. <u>Draw the projection lines for the roof</u>:
    a. Turn *On* the layer of the roof plan.
    b. Turn *Off* the layer of the floorplan.
    c. Create a layer called *Proj_roof*.
    d. Set its linetype to *Hidden*, lineweight: 0.0, and change its color.
    e. Make the *Proj_roof* to be the current layer.
    f. Since the projection lines will be perpendicular to the floor plan, turn *On* the ORTHO option by pressing the corresponding button on the status bar.
    g. Draw the projection lines starting at the roof in the roof plan and terminating at the wall height, Figure 16-11a. Use the *Trim* or *Extend* commands as necessary.

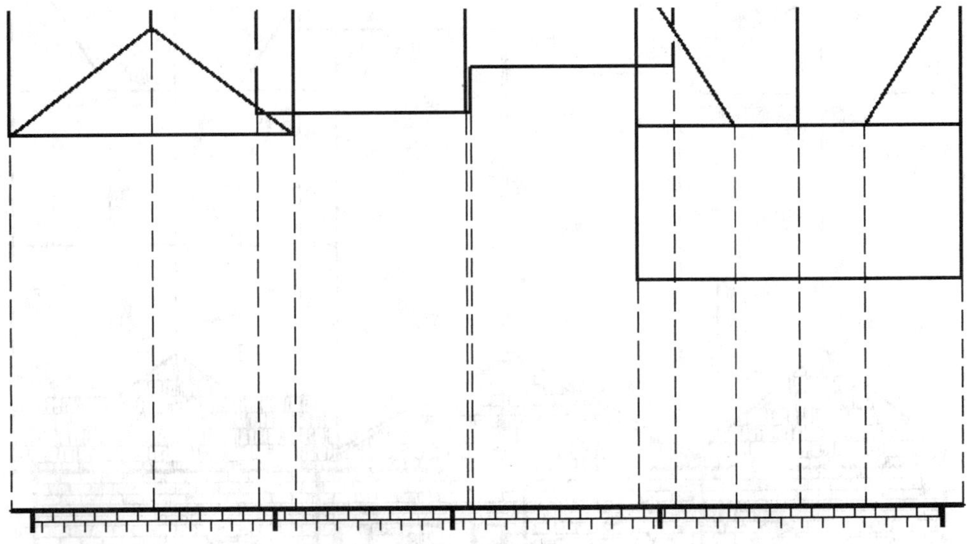

Figure 16-11a

12. <u>Add the main house roof</u>: The roof is a combination of the hip and gable types.
    - Make the *Elevation* to be the current layer.

- Create the lines as shown in Figure 16-11b.
- Use a combination of the *Offset* (set *Offset* distance = 6") and *Trim* commands to create the lines shown in Figure 16-11b.

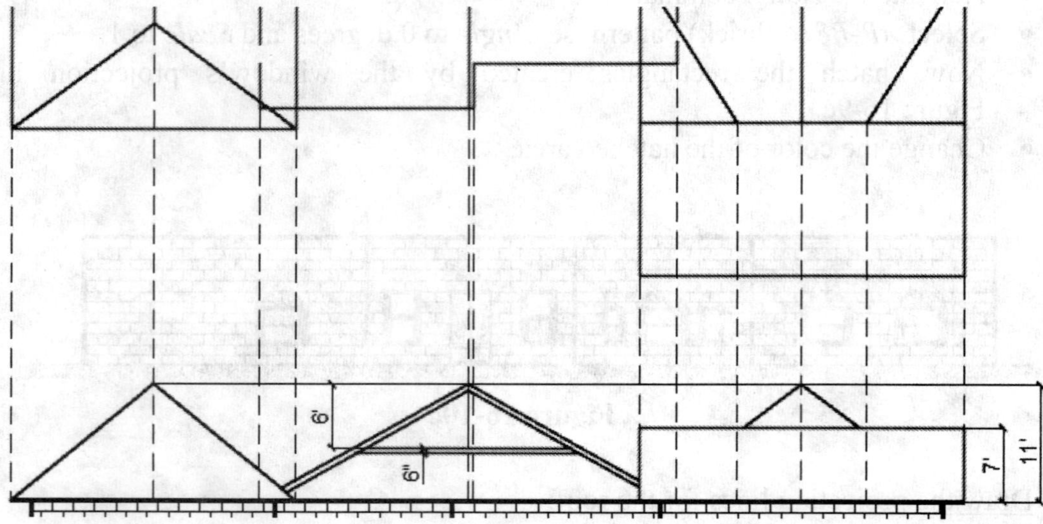

Figure 16-11b

13. <u>Add the hatch to the roof</u>:
   - Turn *Off* the *Projection Line*'s layer.
   - Make the *Elevation* to be the current layer.
   - Use the *Hatch* command to hatch the roof, select *AR-B816* (the brick pattern) and *AR-RSHKE* patterns, set *Scale* to 1 and angles appropriately, Figure 16-11c.

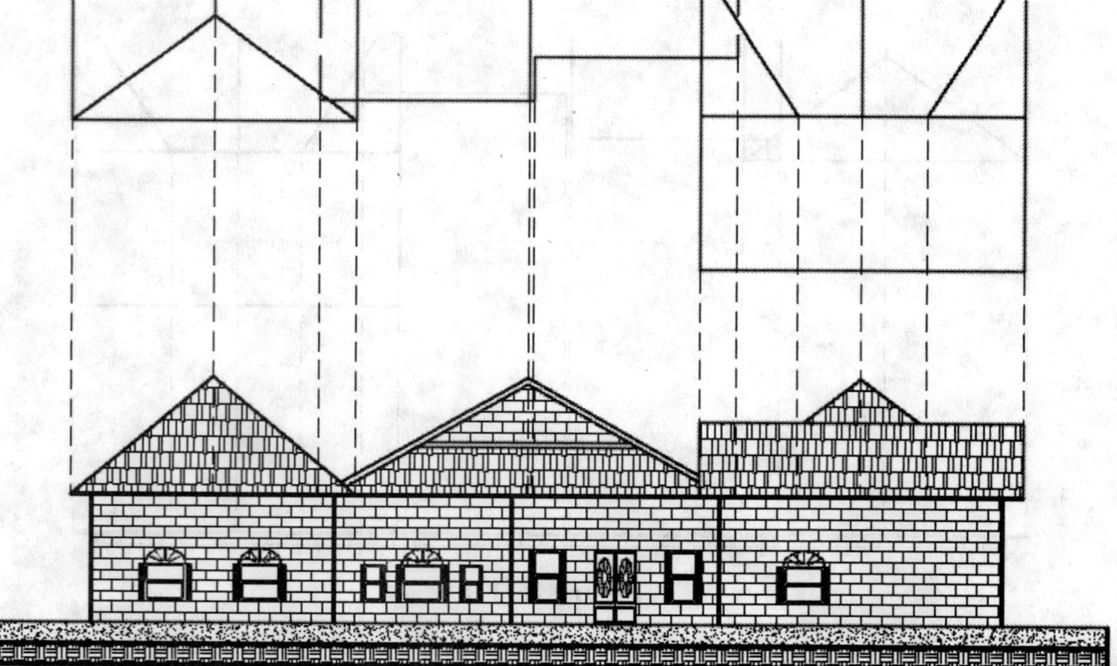

Figure 16-10c

14. <u>Draw the projection lines for the front porch</u>:
   a. Create a layer called *Proj_Porch*.
   b. Set its linetype to *Hidden*, lineweight: 0.0, and change its color.
   c. Make the *Proj_Porch* to be the current layer.
   d. Turn *Off* the roof plan, wall hatch, doors and window projection layers.
   e. Turn *On* the floor plan layer.
   f. Since the projection lines will be perpendicular to the floor plan, turn *On* the *ORTHO* option by pressing the corresponding button on the status bar.
   g. Draw the projection lines starting at the front porch, Figure 16-12a, in the floor plan and terminating at the slab line, Figure 16-12b. Use the *Trim* or *Extend* commands as necessary.

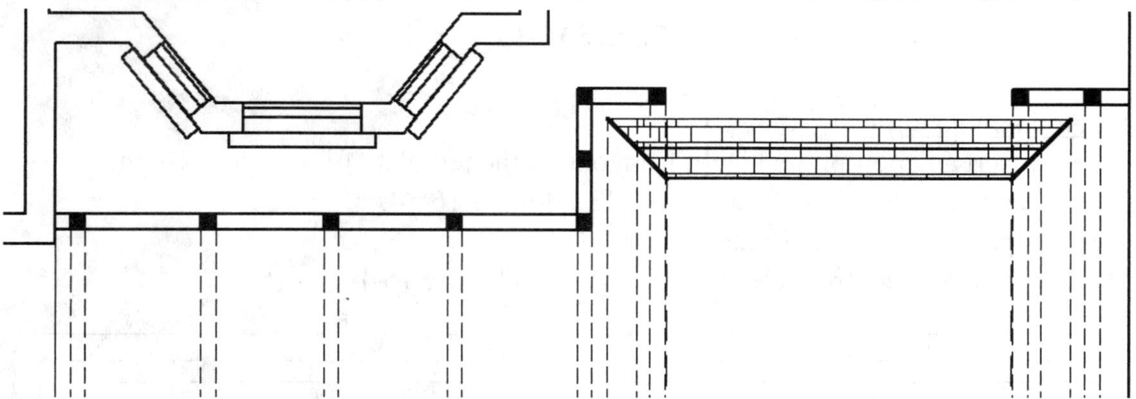

Figure 16-12a

15. <u>Add the front porch</u>:
   - Make the *Elevation* to be the current layer.
   - Draw the columns and create the hatch.
   - Draw steps (the risers are 7" high) and create the hatch, Figure 16-12c.
   - Turn *Off* the *Projection Line*'s layer.
   - Change the color of the hatched area.

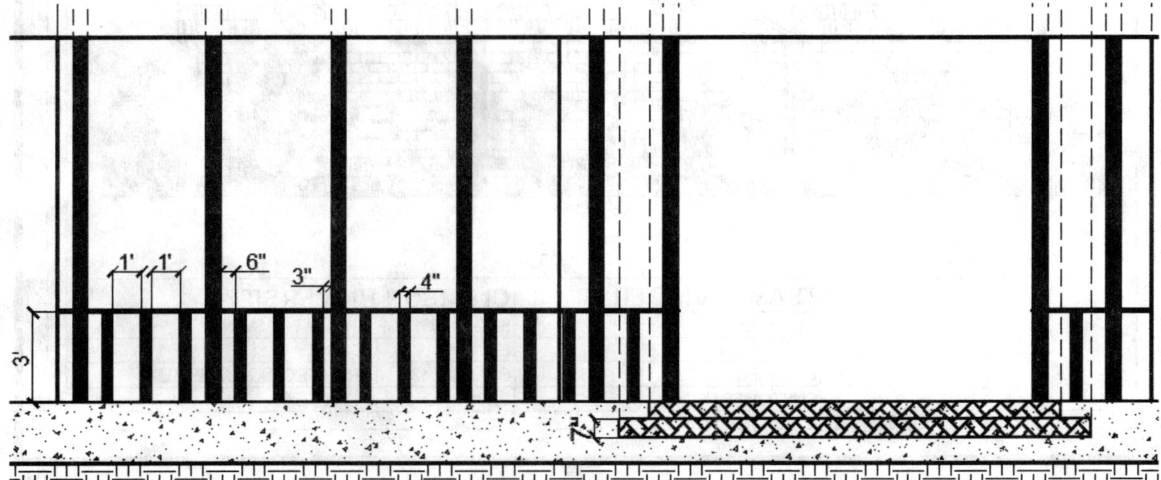

Figure 16-12b

16. <u>Add the landscaping features</u>:
   - Insert the blocks for the trees, bushes, and street lights from the *Design Center* → *House Landscaping.dwg*, Figure 16-13.

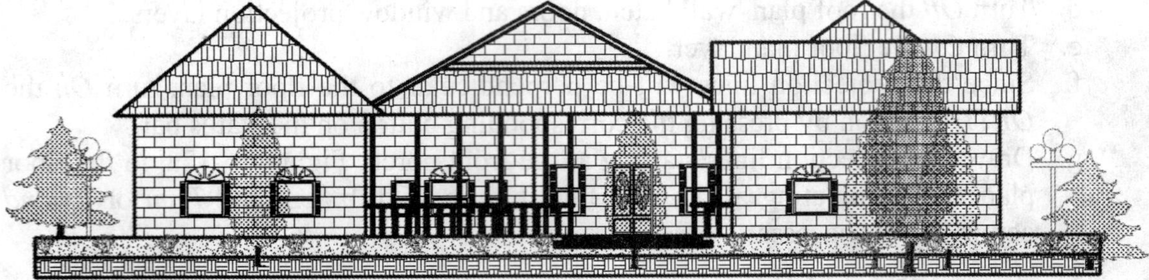

Figure 16-13

17. <u>Add template file</u>:
   - Insert an appropriate layout from one of the template files, Figure 16-14.
   - Set the scale of the drawing to 1:132, Figure 16-14.
   - Update the blocks, Figure 16-14.
   - The complete front elevation is shown in Figure 16-14.

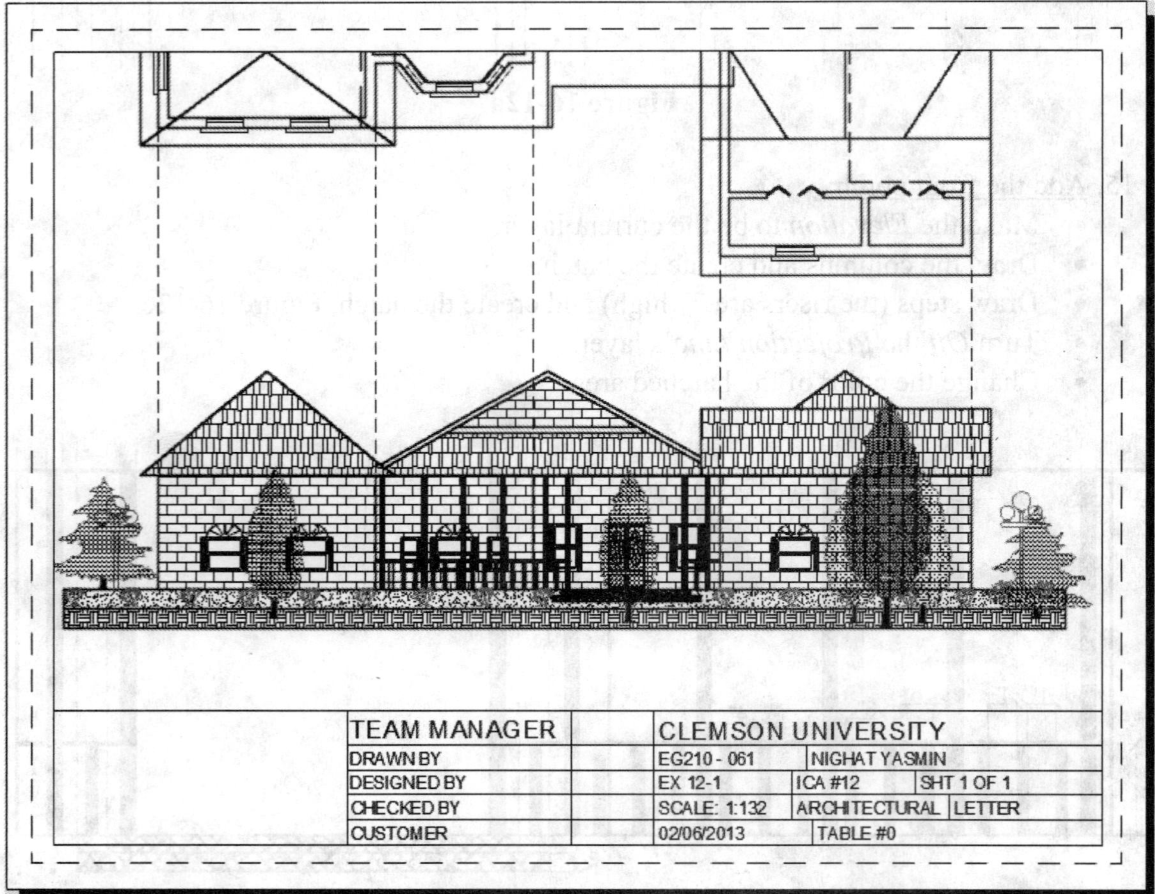

Figure 16-14

16.6.   AutoCAD and the right side elevation

The right side elevation not only depends upon the floor plan, it also depends on the front elevation. The process of drawing the doors and windows appearing only in the right side wall is the same as the process for the front elevation. However, the process of creating the height of the right side wall, the roof appearance, and the doors and windows appearing in both the front and right side elevation is different and will be discussed in detail.

The right side elevation is created by projecting the information from the floor plane using horizontal lines; and by projecting the information from the front elevation to the right side elevation using horizontal, vertical, and 45 degrees miter lines.

1. <u>Load linetype</u>: The right side elevation will use continuous, dashed, and center lines. Therefore, load *Hidden* and *Center* linetypes (for reference, see Chapter 3 of the book). By default, the continuous linetype is loaded.

2. <u>Create layers</u>:
    a. Create four layers and name them as *Proj_45*, *Proj_45_GL_Slab*, *Proj_45_Roof*, *Proj_45_Wall*, and *Proj_45_Wind*.
    b. Set their linetype to *Hidden*, lineweight to 0.0, and change their color.
    c. Turn *On* and *Off* these and previously created layers as necessary.

3. <u>45 degrees miter line</u>: Draw a line at 45 degrees from the lower right corner of the roof line, Figure 16-15. This line will be used to project information from the front elevation to the right side elevation.

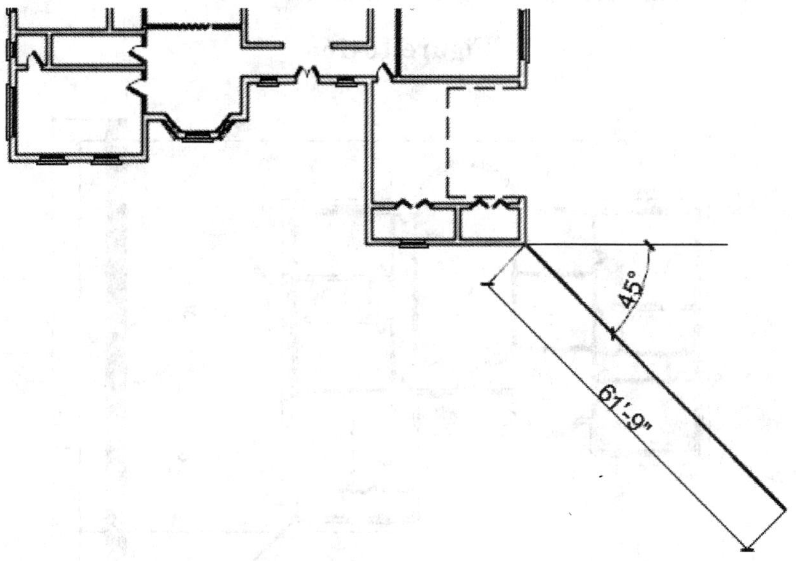

Figure 16-15

4. <u>Orthogonal lines</u>: Since most of the lines in the right side elevation are either horizontal or vertical, turn *On* the *ORTHO* option by pressing the corresponding button ( ) on the status bar.

5. <u>Ground and slab level</u>:
   a. Turn on the *Grade_Line* and *Slab_Line* layers.
   b. Make the *Proj_45_GL_Slab* to be the current layer.
   c. Draw horizontal lines starting at the right end of the grade and slab lines and terminating at the 45 degrees miter line, Figure 16-16a.
   d. Draw 122'-10" long vertical lines starting at the 45 degrees miter line as shown in Figure 16-16a.
   e. Now complete the ground and slab level as discussed in the front elevation, Figure 16-16b.

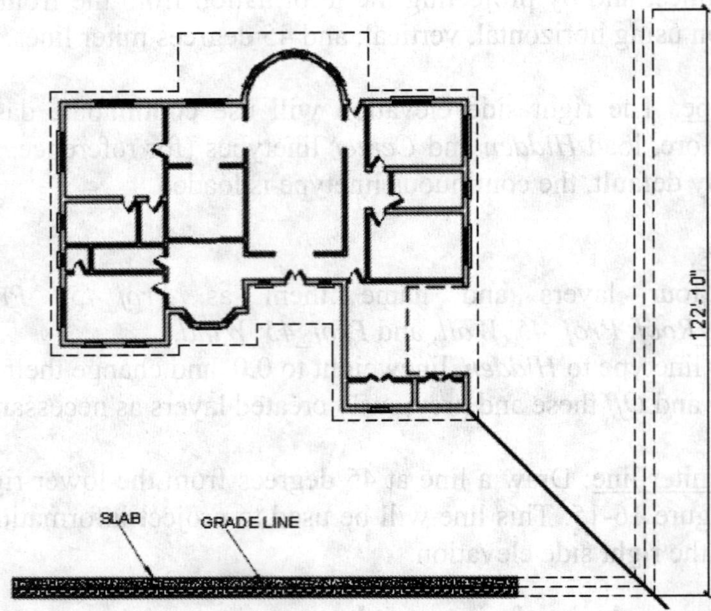

Figure 16-16a

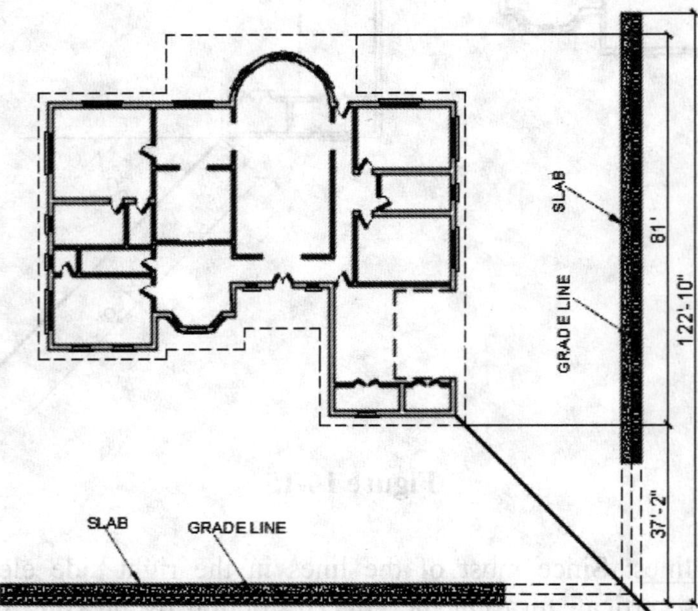

Figure 16-16b

6. The windows:
   a. Turn *Off* the *Proj_45_GL_Slab* layer.
   b. Make the *Proj_Window* to be the current layer.
   c. Draw the projection lines starting at the windows (Bedroom #1, Bedroom #2, and Bathroom #2) in the floor plan and terminating at the slab line, Figure 16-17. Use the *Trim* or *Extend* commands as necessary.
   d. Make the *Elevation* to be the current layer.
   e. *Bedroom #1 window*: The Bedroom #1 window is of type W4; and this window is 8'-0" wide. The bedroom window opening is 2'-0" above the ground level, Figure 16-17. The window has 6 parts: the left and right panels are 2'-6" wide; the central panel is 3'-0" wide (W4 is 8' wide); the semicircular part is   1'-6" tall and 3' wide, and the left and right sidings.
   - For the left and right panels, insert the *Window Wood Frame 36X36* from the *Design Center* → *House Designer.dwg*. For scaling, convert the desired and block sizes in same units; either both of them should be in feet or both in inches. In the example, for both the x- and y-direction scaling, both the desired and the block sizes are in inches. Scale the window by 30/36 in X-direction and 42/36 in Y-direction; and set the rotation angle to be 90°.
   - For the central panel, insert the *Window Wood Frame 36X36* from the *Design Center* → *House Designer.dwg*. Scale the window by 1 in X-direction and 42/36 in Y-direction; and set the rotation angle to be 90°.
   - Add the semi-circle window, *Window Half circle 36 inch* block from the *Design Center*. Scale the windows by 1 in X-direction and 1 in Y-direction. Also, set the rotation angle to be 90°.
   - For the left and right sidings, repeat the process from the front elevation.

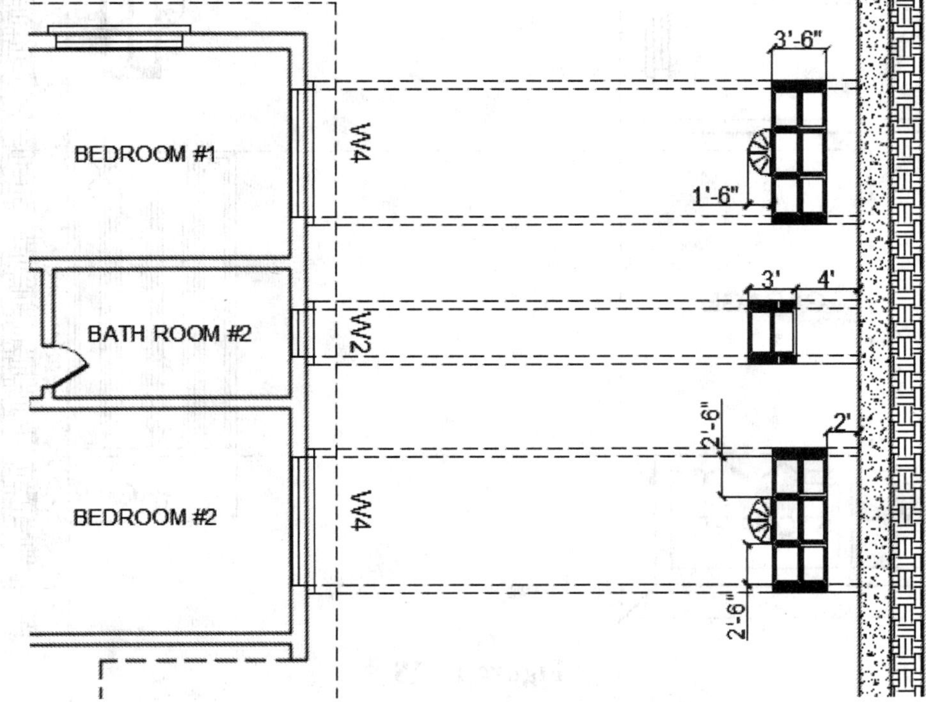

Figure 16-17

    f.   *Bedroom #2 window*: The Bedroom #2 window is identical to the Bedroom #1's window. Hence, repeat the process.

    g.   *Bathroom window*: The bathroom window is of type W2; and this window is 2'-6" wide. The bathroom window opening is 4'-0" above the ground level and the window itself is 3'-0" tall, Figure 16-17. It is a single panel window with left and right sidings. For the drawing process, insert the *Window Wood Frame 36X36* from the *Design Center* with appropriate scale factors and rotation angle of 90°; and create the sidings.

7. <u>The garage door</u>:
    a.   Turn *Off* the *Proj_Window* layer.
    b.   Make the *Proj_Door* to be the current layer.
    c.   Draw the projection lines starting at the garage door in the floor plan and terminating at the slab line, Figure 16-18. Use the *Trim* or *Extend* commands as necessary.
    d.   Make the *Elevation* to be the current layer.
    e.   The garage door is 18'-0" wide and 10'-0: high.
    f.   Insert the *Garage Door – Paneled 10* from the *Design Center → House Designer.dwg*. For scaling, convert the desired and block sizes in same units; either both of them should be in feet or both in inches. In the example, for both the x- and y-direction scaling, both the desired and the block sizes are in feet. Scale the door by 18/10 in X-direction and 10/7 in Y-direction; and set the rotation angle to be 90°.

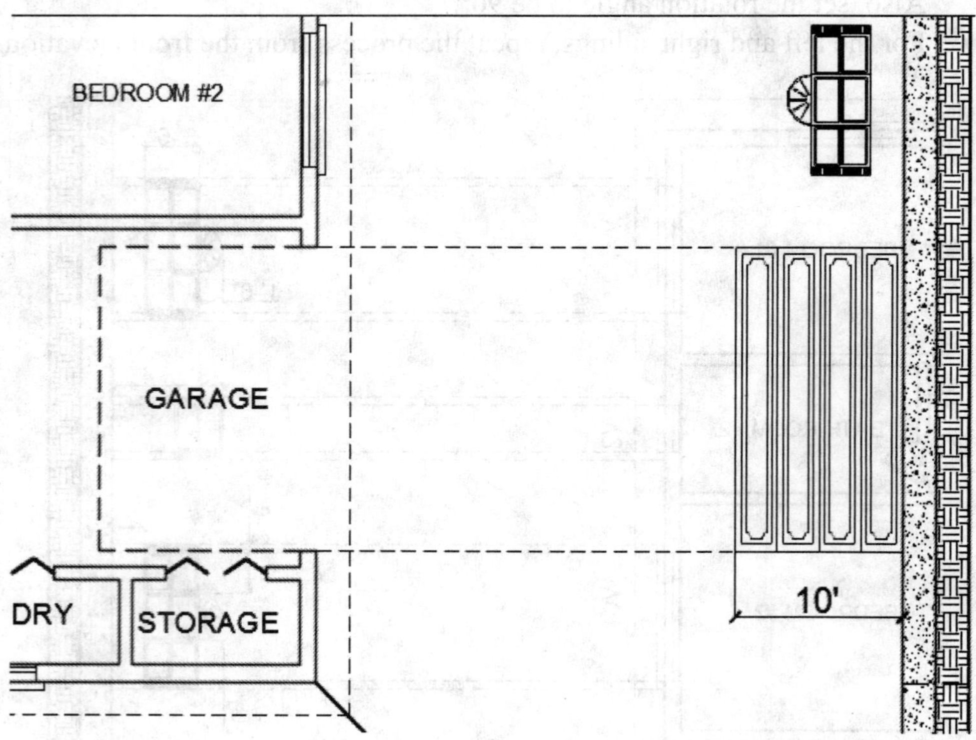

Figure 16-18

8. The wall:
   a. Turn *Off* the *Proj_Door* layer.
   b. Make the *Proj_Wall* to be the current layer.
   c. Draw the projection lines starting at the exterior face of the exterior walls and corners of the roofline in the floor plan and terminating at the slab line, Figure 16-19a. Use the *Trim* or *Extend* commands as necessary.
   d. Make the *Proj_45_Wall* to be the current layer.
   e. Draw the projection lines starting at the wall height in the front elevation and terminating at the 45 degrees miter line, Figure 16-19a. Use the *Trim* or *Extend* commands as necessary.
   f. Draw the projection lines starting at the 45 degrees miter line and terminating at the projection of roof line from the floor plan, Figure 16-19a. Use the *Trim* or *Extend* commands as necessary.
   g. Make the *Elevation* to be the current layer.
   h. Draw the exterior face of the exterior wall, Figure 16-19b.
   i. Turn *On* the *Proj_Window*'s and *Proj_Door*'s layers.
   j. Activate the *Hatch* command.
   k. Select *AR-B816* (brick) pattern, set *Angle* to 90 degrees and *Scale* to 1.5, Figure 16-19b.
   l. Change the color of the hatched area.

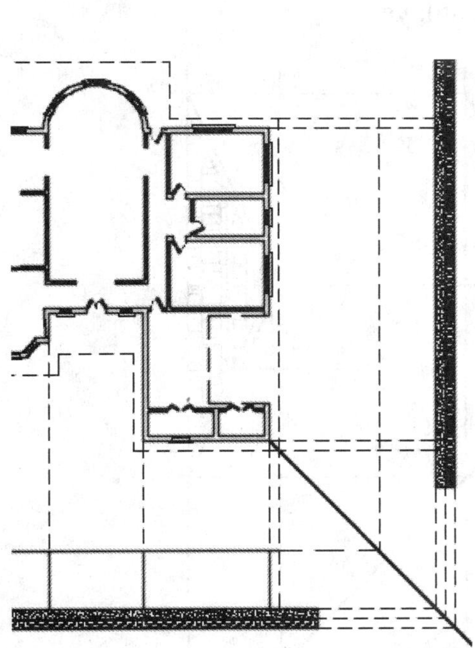

Figure 16-19a

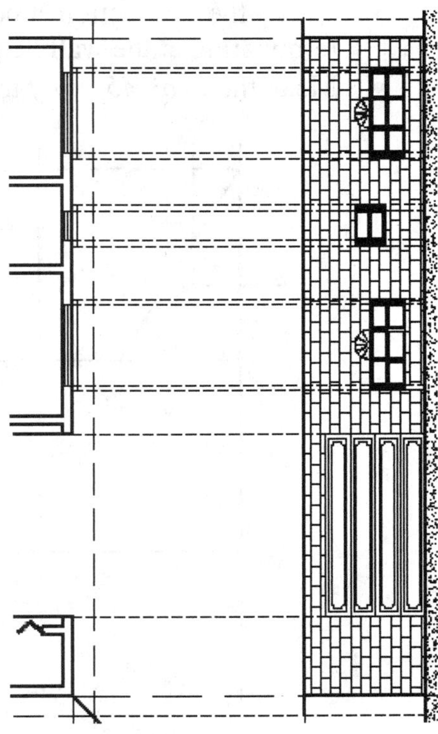

Figure 16-19b

9. The porch:
   a. Turn *Off* the *Proj_Wall* layer.
   b. Make the *Proj_Porch* to be the current layer.

c. Draw the back porch as shown in Figure 16-20 using the method discussed in front elevation.

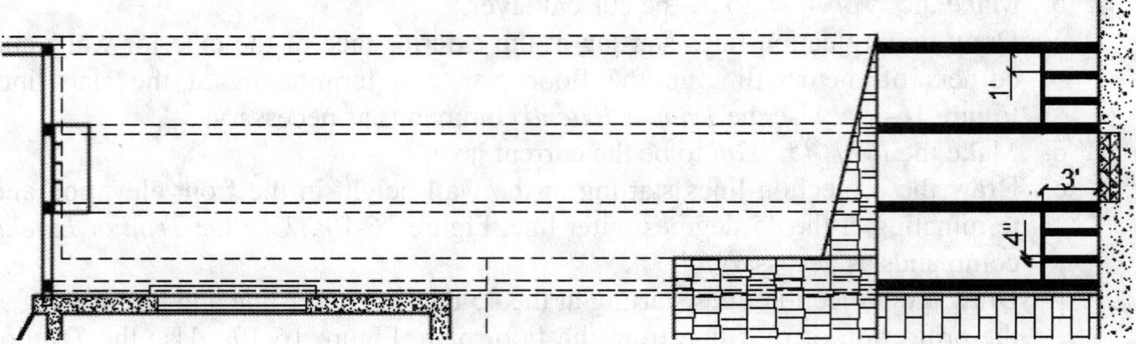

Figure 16-20

10. <u>The roof</u>:
   a. Turn *Off* every projection layer except the *Proj_45* layer.
   b. Turn *Off* the floor plan and turn *On* the roof plan layer.
   c. *Garage's roof*: The master bedroom is covered by a hip roof.
   - Use the *Trim* or *Extend* commands as necessary.
   - Make the *Proj_Roof* to be the current layer.
   - Draw the projection lines starting at the garage in the floor plan and terminating at the wall height line, Figure 16-21a.
   - Make the *Proj_45_Roof* to be the current layer.

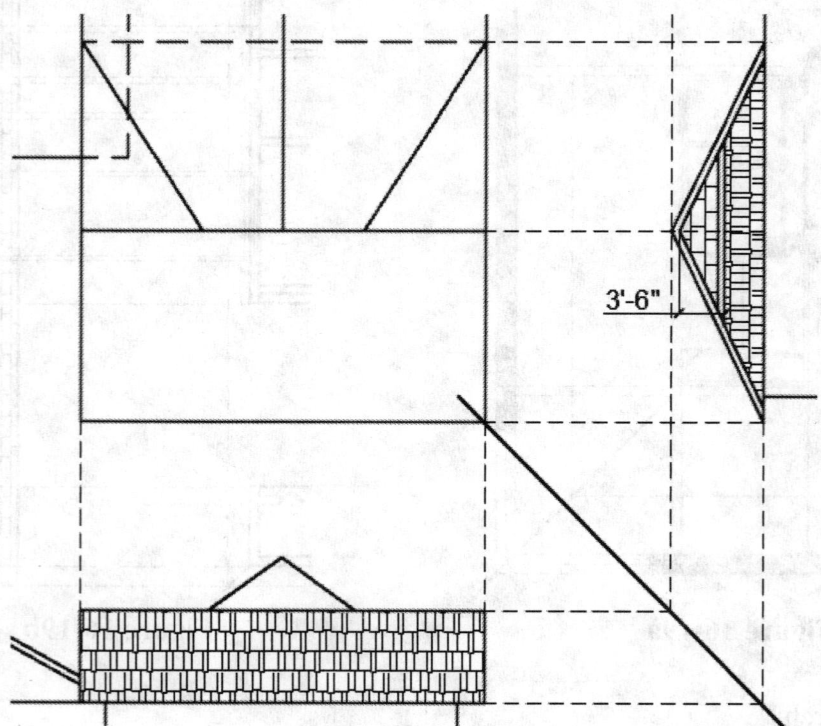

Figure 16-21a

- Draw the projection lines starting at the highest and lowest points (of the garage roof) in the front elevation and terminating at the 45 degrees miter line, Figure 16-21a.
- Draw the projection lines starting at the 45 degrees miter line and terminating at the projection of roof line from the floor plan, Figure 16-21a.
- Make the *Elevation* to be the current layer
- Draw the gable roof and hatch as shown in Figure 16-21a. The offsets are at 6".
- Notice that the right elevation has only one dimension shown in the figure. The remaining dimensions are shown in floor plan or front elevation.

d. *Master bedroom's roof*: The master bedroom is covered by a hip roof.
- Use the *Trim* or *Extend* commands as necessary.
- Make the *Proj_Roof* to be the current layer.
- Draw the projection lines starting at the bedroom roof in the floor plan and terminating at the wall height line, Figure 16-21b.
- Make the *Proj_45_Roof* to be the current layer.
- Draw the projection lines starting at the highest and lowest visible points in the front elevation and terminating at the 45 degrees miter line, Figure 16-21b.
- Draw the projection lines starting at the 45 degrees miter line and terminating at the projection of roof line from the floor plan, Figure 16-21b.
- Make the *Elevation* to be the current layer
- Draw the side of the gable roof and hatch as shown in Figure 16-21b.

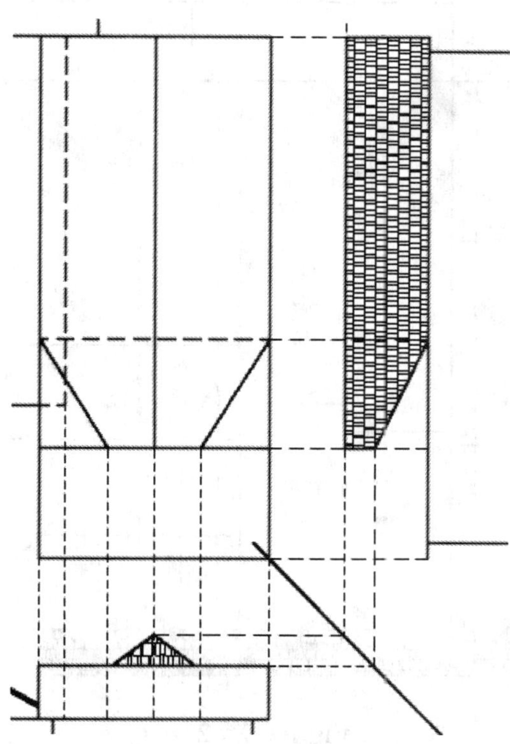

Figure 16-21b

e. *Porch's roof*: The front porch is not visible from the right side. The back porch is covered with a sloping roof.

- Use the *Trim* or *Extend* commands as necessary.
- Use the *Trim* or *Extend* commands as necessary.
- Make the *Proj_Roof* to be the current layer.
- Draw the projection lines starting at the porch roof in the floor plan and terminating at the wall height line, Figure 16-21c.
- The highest point of the porch roof is 3' above the wall height. Complete the roof of the back porch as shown in Figure 16-21c.

f. *Right side roof*: The complete roof is shown in Figure 16-21d.

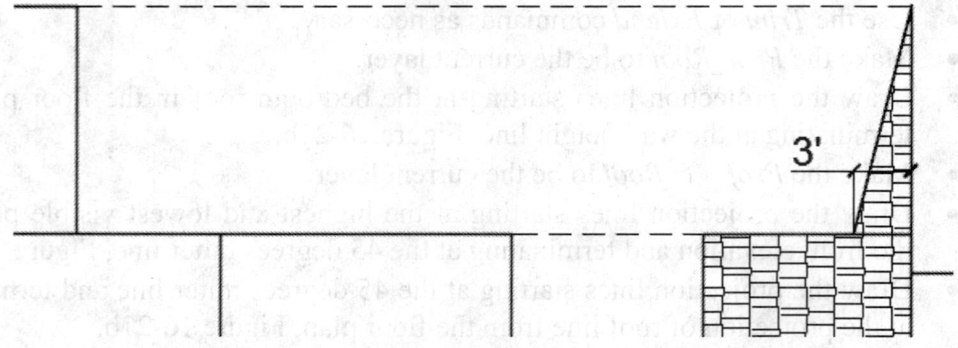

Figure 16-21c

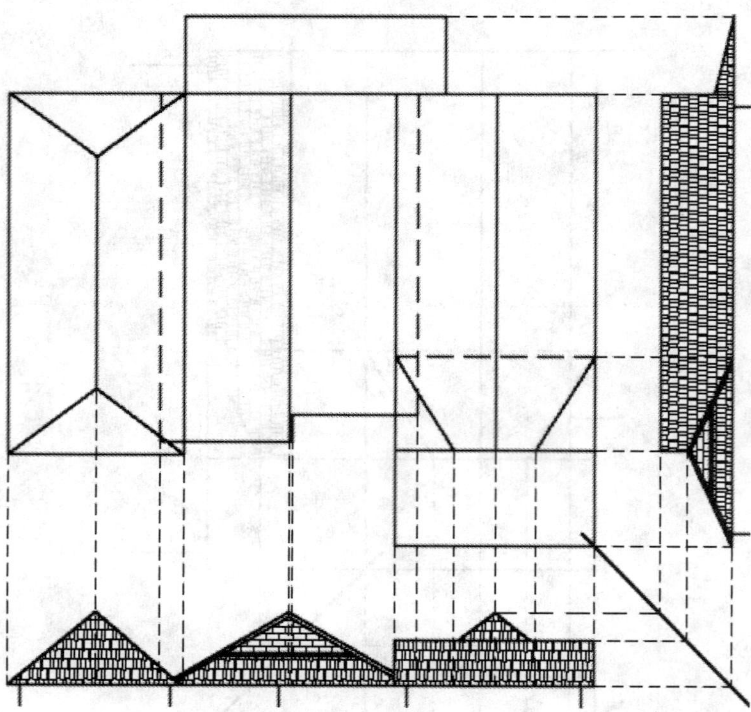

Figure 16-21d

g. Add the landscaping to the elevation.

- Use the *Trim* or *Extend* commands as necessary.

- Make the *Landscaping* to be the current layer.
- Add the landscaping to the elevation.

h. The complete right side elevation is shown in Figure 16-22.

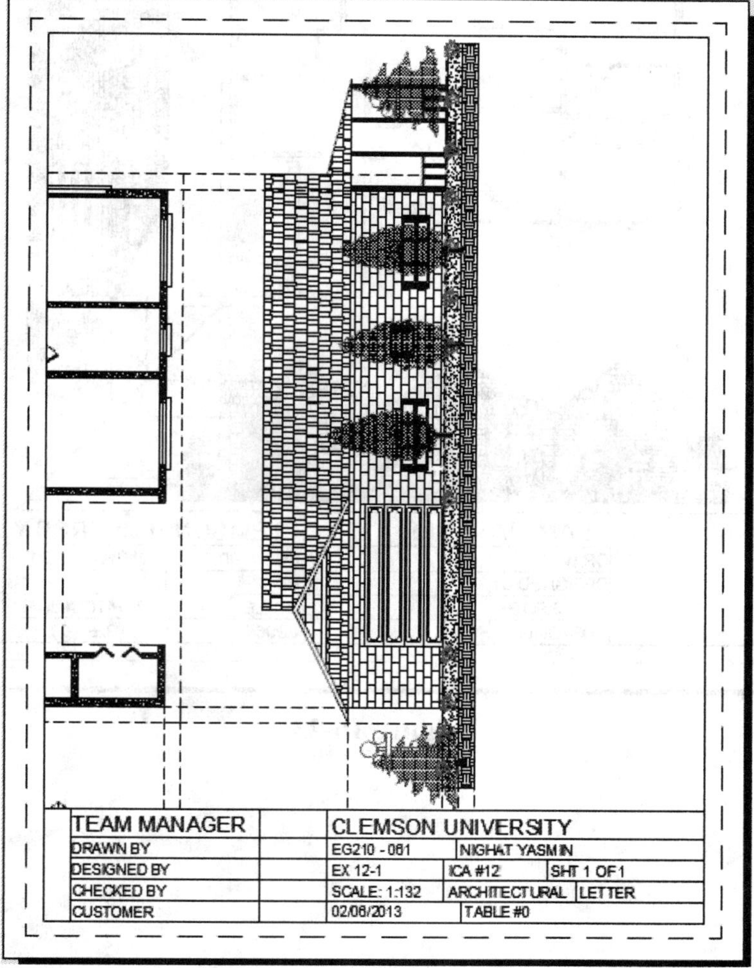

Figure 16-22

The floor plan and the front and right side elevations are shown in Figure 16-23. The rear and the left side elevations are left for the readers.

TEAM MANAGER
CLEMSON UNIVERSITY
DRAWN BY
EG210 - 061
NIGHAT YASMIN
DESIGNED BY
EX 12-1
ICA #12
SHT 1 OF 1
CHECKED BY
SCALE: 1:240
ARCHITECTURAL
LETTER
CUSTOMER
02/06/2013
TABLE #0

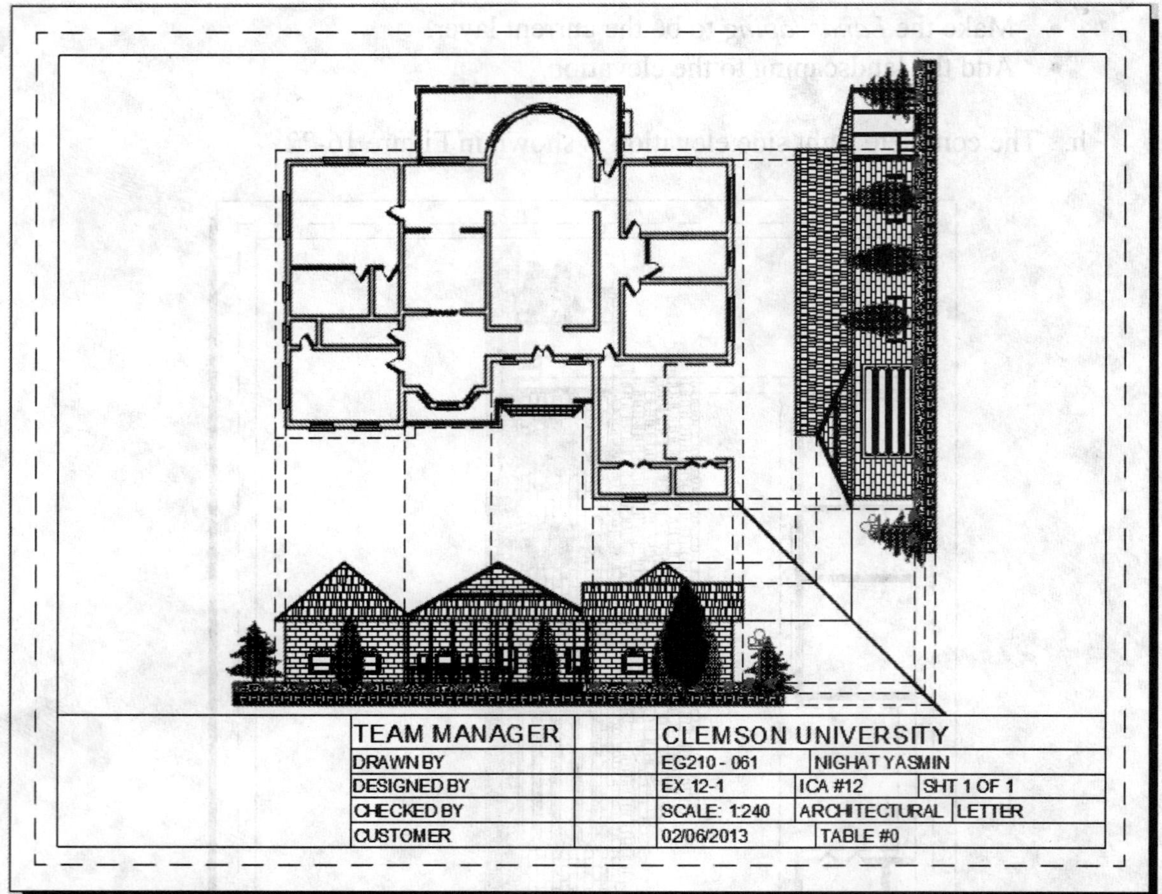

Figure 16-23

17. Site Plan

17.1.   Objectives

- Lear the basics of a site plan using AutoCAD
- Lear to draw a site plan using AutoCAD

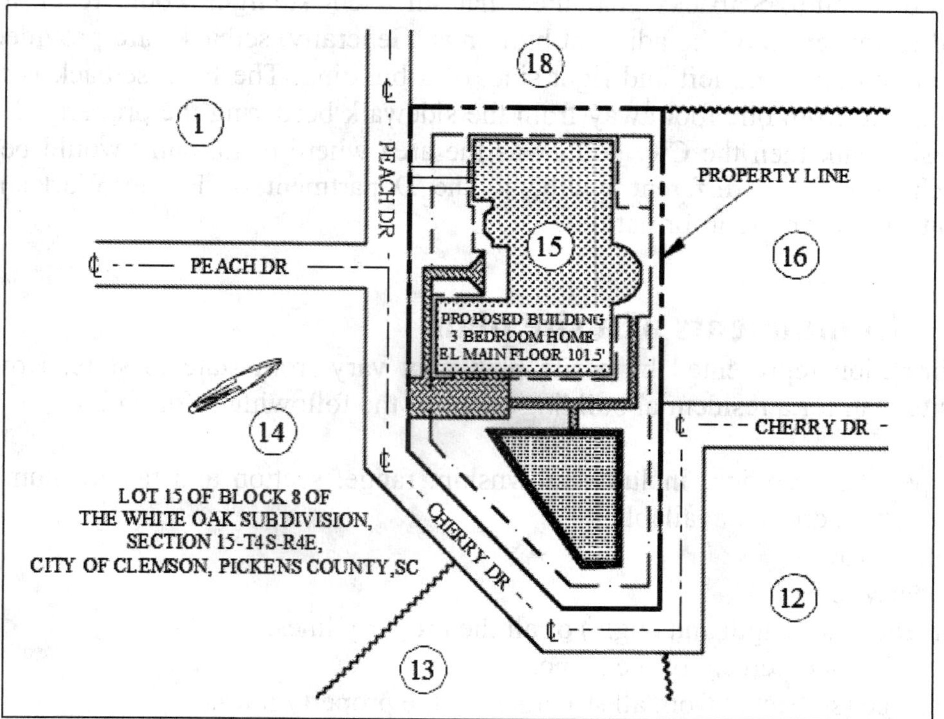

17.2.   Introduction

The map of an individual construction site is known as a site plan, plat, or plot. The site plan not only displays the location of the project, but it also exhibits other key features. A site plan of a typical building shows an outline of the building, utilities (sewer line, water supply, power lines, gas supply, etc.), driveways, walkways, adjacent roads, adjoining building (if any), etc.

17.3.   Terminology

- <u>Property line</u>: A property line is the legal boundary of a parcel of land. The boundary is set using one of the survey method discussed in *Land Survey*'s chapter. The property line is described as a closed traverse using lengths and bearing (or azimuth) of each course.
- <u>Easement</u>: An easement is defined as a right of way or privilege offered by the property owner to a general public or selected users.
- <u>Setback</u>: A setback is the distance from the property line to any structure on the property (site). Setbacks guarantee that sufficient sunlight would reach the street and lower levels of the adjacent buildings. Generally, setbacks are provided on the front and rear, and left and right side, of a building. The front setback is typically measured from one foot away from the sidewalk bordering the property. If there is no sidewalk then the City still owns the area where it normally would be placed. Each street is a different width, so the Department of Public Works must be contacted for more information

17.4.   Components of a site plan

The information represented by a site plan may vary from state to state. However, a typical site plan for a residential building contains the following information.

1. Property description, including township, range, section and tax lot number, and property address if available.
2. North arrow.
3. Property line.
4. Dimensions (length and angle) of all the property lines.
5. Direction and percent of the slope.
6. Distance (setbacks) from all structures to the property lines.
7. Names and locations of all the roads adjacent to the property.
8. Names (or labels) and locations of all other properties adjacent to the property in question.
9. Location, size, and intended use of all structures, existing and proposed.
10. Location of driveways, walkways, or any other roads on the property, existing and proposed.
11. Location of any public utility.
12. Location of all major features (e.g., canals, irrigation ditches, or rock ledges).
13. Location of well or water sources on the property under consideration and adjacent properties.

14. Location of test holes used for the site evaluation during the feasibility process.
15. Height from grade to all shade producing points of roof lines for solar calculation. NOTE: in some cases, plat plans for parcels over 2 acres may need to be scaled for solar purposes.
16. For new septic construction, three elevation shots on each leach line for both the initial and reserve leach field area.
17. Location of proposed septic tank, drain field, and replacement field, showing dimensions and spacing of leach lines. Furthermore, the distance from the septic tank and system to the property lines should be included. NOTE: In some cases, a sanitarian may require the system to be drawn to scale.

17.5.   AutoCAD and site plan

This section will create a site plan for the residential building designed in the previous two chapters (Floor plan and Elevation) using the lot-15 from the lots and blocks drawing created in the chapter named as Land Survey.

1. Launch AutoCAD 2014.

2. Open a file to create the site plan using one of the two methods.
    o   Open a new file (the landscape template file for the ANSI units) and work through all the steps listed in this section.
    o   Open the drawing created for lots and blocks, Figure 17-1a; use the *Trim, Delete,* and *Move* commands to modify the drawing as shown in Figure 17-1b.

3. Create layers and turn them *On, Off,* and freeze, as necessary.

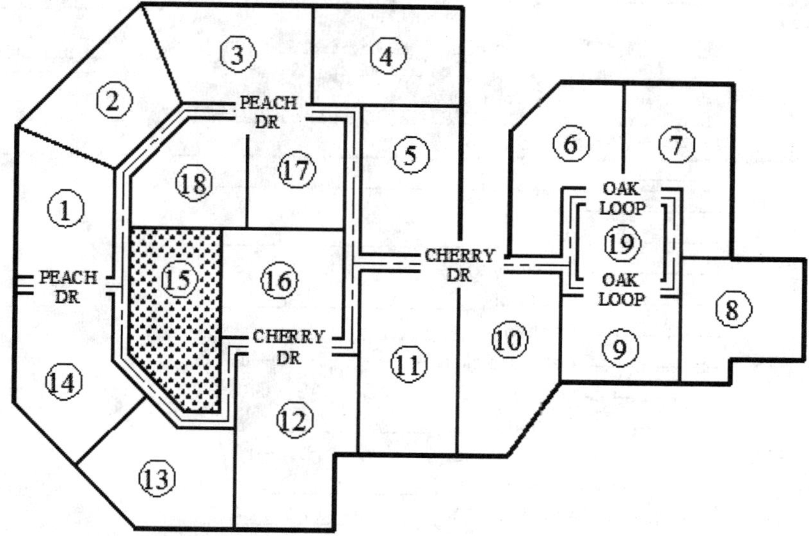

LOT 15 of BLOCK 8 OF THE WHITE OAK SUBDIVISION

Figure 17-1a

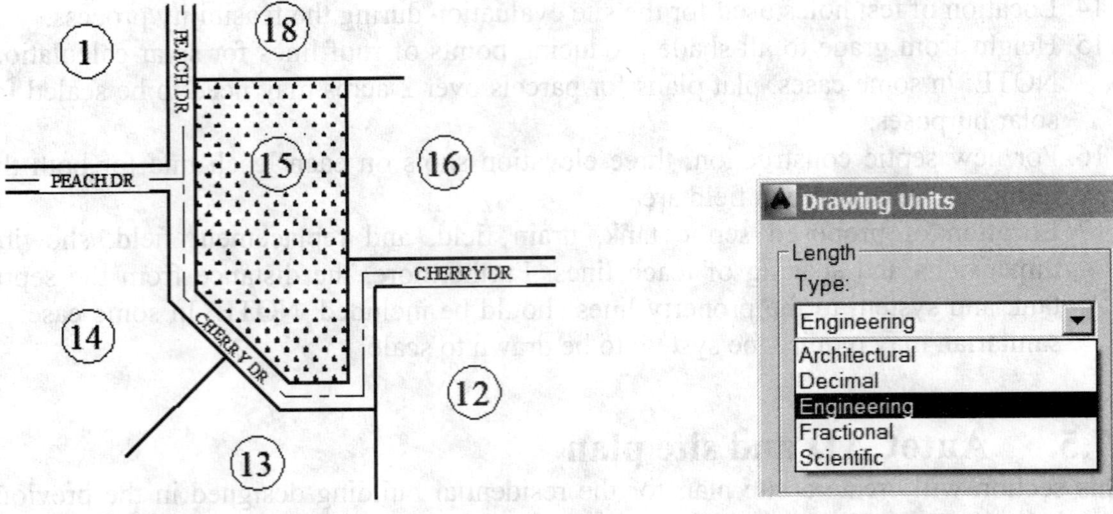

Figure 17-1b   **Figure 17-2a**

4. In case of in Figure 17-1b, the user may skip a step or perform the step partially. For example, for inserting north, the user can skip this step; for the property line, create the layer and move the boundary of lot #15 to the layer.
5. Type *Units* on the command line and press the *Enter* key. This will open the *Units* dialog box, Figure 17-2a. From the Units dialog box, expand *Length* option and select the *Engineering* option.
6. Load the linetypes shown in Figure 17-2b.

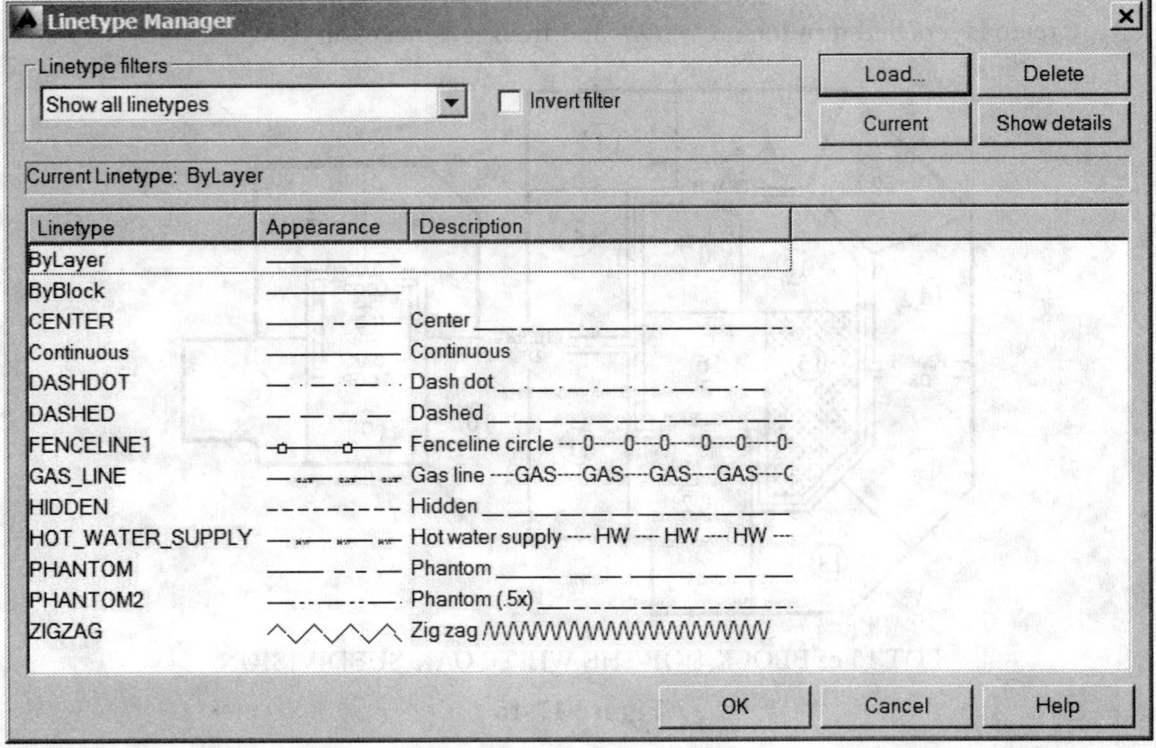

Figure 17-2b

7. <u>North direction</u>: Figure 17-3
   - o Create a layer and name it as *North*. Change its color.
   - o Make the *North* layer to be the current layer.
   - o Insert the *North* block from the *Design Center* → *Landscaping.dwg*.

8. <u>Property line</u>: Figure 17-3
   - o Create a layer and name it as *Property_Line*. Set its *linetype* to *Phantom*, *lineweight* to *0.7*, and change its color.
   - o Make the *Property_Line* layer to be the current layer.
   - o Draw the property's boundary as a closed traverse or trace over the block 15 of the lots and blocks drawing. Make sure the linetype is clearly visible.

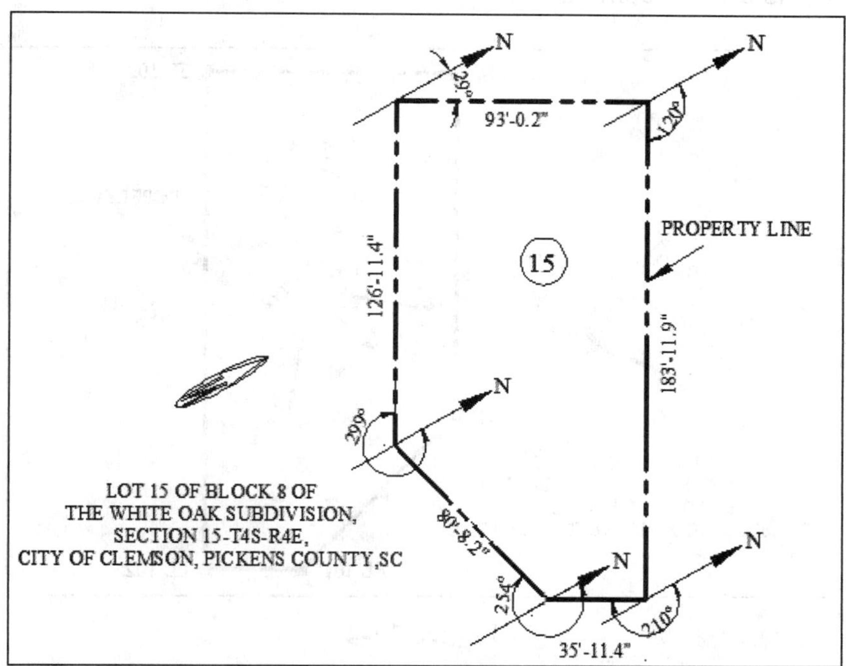

Figure 17-3

9. <u>Property line's dimension</u>: Figure 17-3
   - o Create a layer and name it as *Property_Line_Dim*. Set its *linetype* to *Continuous*, *lineweight* to *default*, and change its color.
   - o Make the *Property_Line_Dim* layer to be the current layer.
   - o Show the dimensions following a closed traverse dimensioning techniques. The angles are represented as azimuths. The dimension and extension lines are turned *Off* for the length of each course.

10. <u>Property's label</u>: Figure 17-3
   - o Create a layer and name it as *Property_ Label*. Set its *linetype* to *Continuous*, *lineweight* to *default*, and change its color.
   - o Make the *Property_Label* layer to be the current layer.
   - o Show the label using the *Text* and *Rotation* commands and arrow using the *qleader* command.

11. <u>Ground slope</u>: Figure 17-4
   o   Create a layer and name it as *Slope*. Set its *linetype* to *Continuous*, *lineweight* to *0.5*, and change its color.
   o   Make the *Slope* layer to be the current layer.
   o   Draw points using the *Point* command as shown in the Figure 17-4. In this example, points are drawn when property line changes its direction. Change the point style and size using *Point Style* dialog box from the *Home* tab and the *Utilities* panel.
   o   Using the *Text* command, label the elevation as shown in the Figure 17-4.
   o   Using the *Text* and *qleader* commands show the direction of slope. (Activate *qleader* command three times to draw three arrows or use combination of *Mirror* and *Copy* commands.)

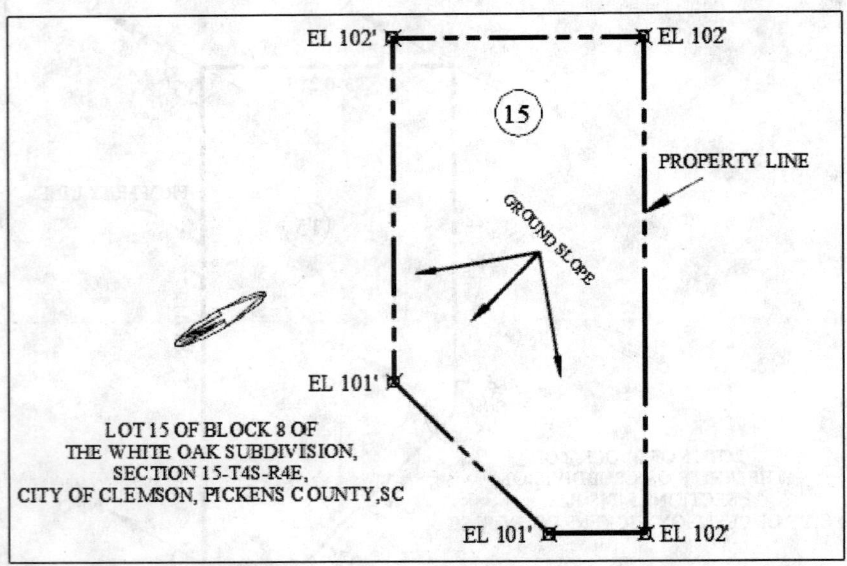

Figure 17-4

12. <u>Setbacks</u>: Figure 17-5
   o   Create a layer and name it as *Setback*. Set its *linetype* to *Dashdot*, *lineweight* to *0.5*, and change its color.
   o   Make the *Setback* layer to be the current layer.
   o   Draw the setbacks from the property lines as shown. In this example, the front setback is 8', the rear setback is 4', and each of the two sides' setbacks is 10'. (Create 3 offsets and perform the necessary trims). Make sure the linetype is clearly visible.

13. <u>Setbacks' dimension</u>: Figure 17-5
   o   Create a layer and name it as *Setback_Dim*. Set its *linetype* to *Continuous*, *lineweight* to *default*, and change its color.
   o   Make the *Setback_Dim* layer to be the current layer.
   o   Show the dimensions.

14. <u>Setbacks' label</u>: Figure 17-5
   - Create a layer and name it as *Setback_Label*. Set its *linetype* to *Continuous*, *lineweight* to *default*, and change its color.
   - Make the *Setback_Label* layer to be the current layer.
   - Add the label using the *Text* and *Rotation* commands.

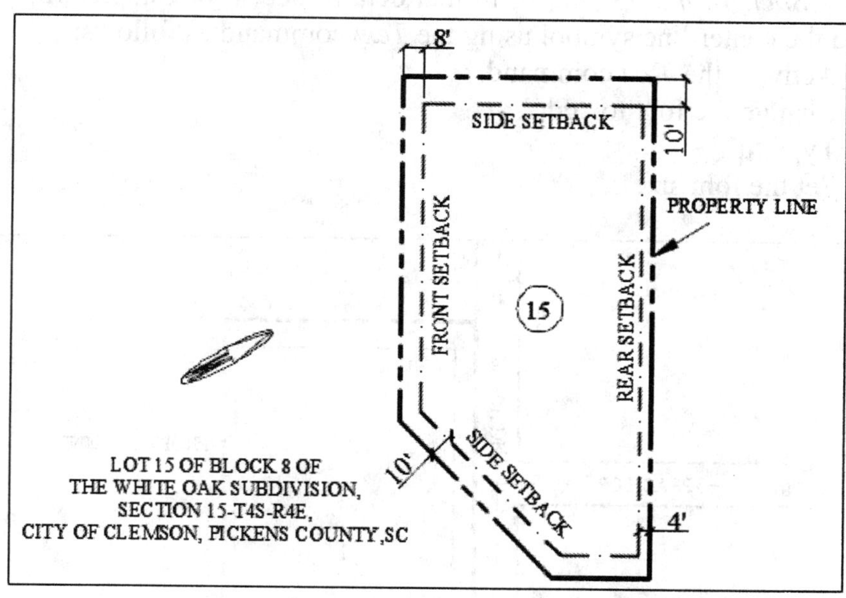

Figure 17-5

15. <u>Roads</u>: Figure 17-6
   - Create a layer and name it as *Road*. Set its *linetype* to *Continuous*, *lineweight* to *0.5*, and change its color.
   - Make the *Road* layer to be the current layer.
   - Draw the roads. The width of the road is shown in the Figure 17-6 or trace over the road given in the lots and blocks drawing.

16. <u>Roads' dimension</u>: Figure 17-6
   - Create a layer and name it as *Road_Dim*. Set its *linetype* to *Continuous*, *lineweight* to *default*, and change its color.
   - Make the *Road_Dim* layer to be the current layer.
   - Show the dimensions.

17. <u>Roads' Center line</u>: Figure 17-6
   - Create a layer and name it as *Road_CL*. Set its *linetype* to *Center*, *lineweight* to *0.5*, and change its color.
   - Make the *Road_CL* layer to be the current layer.
   - Add the center line. Make sure linetype is clearly visible.

18. <u>Roads' label</u>: Figure 17-6
   o Create a layer and name it as *Road_Label*. Set its *linetype* to *Continuous*, *lineweight* to *default*, and change its color.
   o Make the *Road_Label* layer to be the current layer.
   o Add the names of the roads using the *Text* command. Remember to use the *Mask Background* option (for further details, check for Chapter #3).
   o Add the center line symbol using the *Text* command as follows:
      ▪ Activate the *Text* command.
      ▪ Change the font to "gdt".
      ▪ Type 'q'.
      ▪ Set the font size

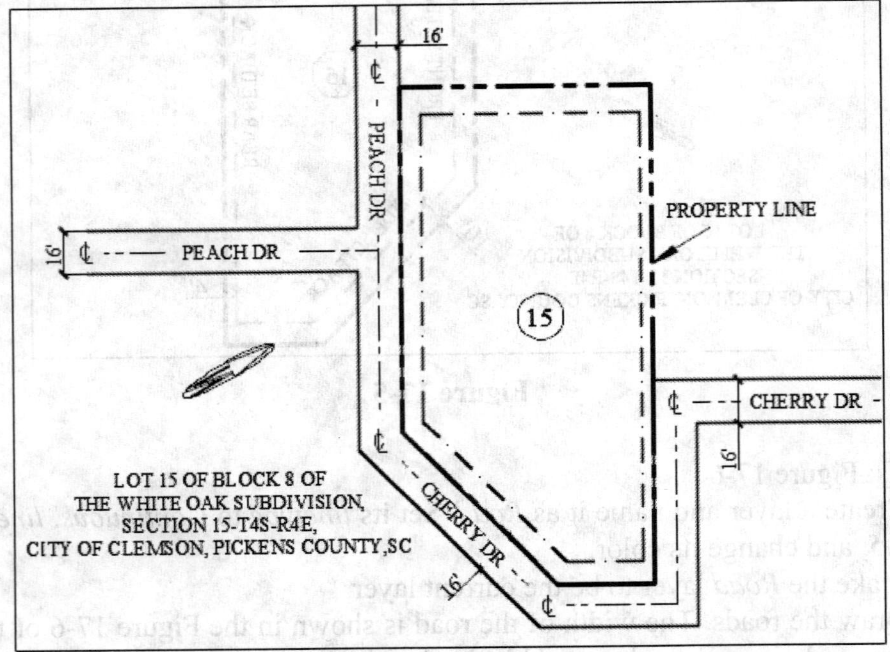

Figure 17-6

19. <u>Adjacent properties</u>: Figure 17-7
   o Create a layer and name it as *AP*. Set its *linetype* to *Zigzag*, *lineweight* to *0.5*, and change its color.
   o Make the *AP* layer to be the current layer.
   o Draw the adjacent properties or trace over the lots and blocks drawing. Make sure the linetype is clearly visible.

20. <u>Adjacent properties' label</u>: Figure 17-7
   o Create a layer and name it as *AP_Label*. Set its *linetype* to *Continuous*, *lineweight* to *default*, and change its color.
   o Make the *AP_Label* layer to be the current layer.
   o Add the names of the adjacent properties using the *Text* and *Circle* commands or transfer to the current layer from the lots and blocks drawing.

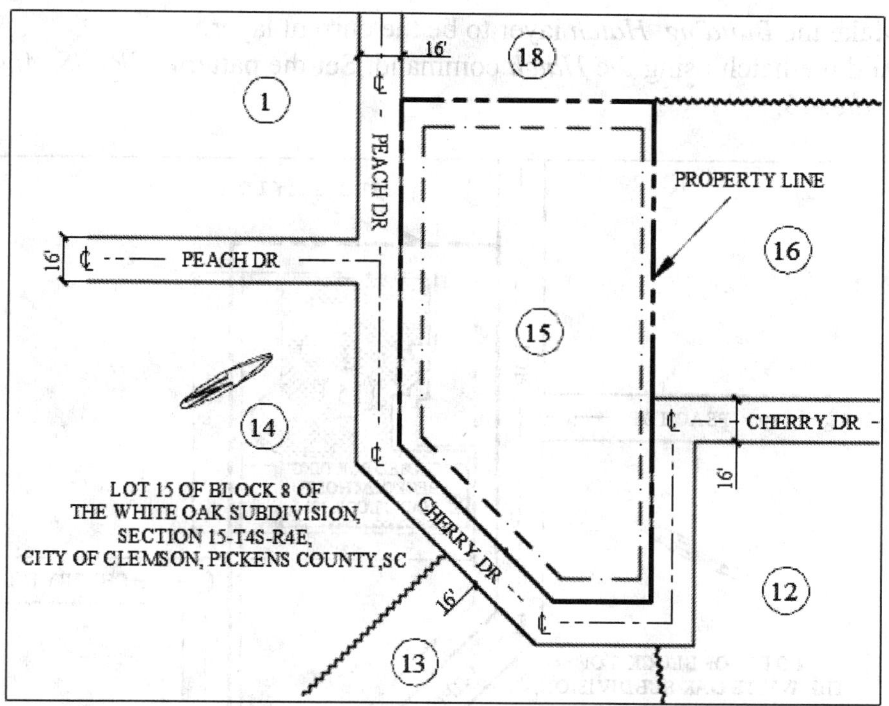

Figure 17-7

21. <u>Structure</u>: Figure 17-8
   - o Create a layer and name it as *Building*. Set its *linetype* to *Continuous* and change its color.
   - o Make the *Building* layer to be the current layer.
   - o Draw the location and size of all the structures. Add the exterior face of the exterior wall of the residential building (drawn in the floor plan chapter). Also, add the roof line. Note that the roof line is drawn inside the setbacks.
   - o Rotate the building to match the block orientation.

22. <u>Structure's dimension</u>: Figure 17-8
   - o Create a layer and name it as *Building_Dim*. Set its *linetype* to *Continuous* and change its color.
   - o Make the *Building_Dim* layer to be the current layer.
   - o Show the dimensions.

23. <u>Structure's label</u>: Figure 17-8
   - o Create a layer and name it as *Building_Label*. Set its *linetype* to *Continuous* and change its color.
   - o Make the *Building_Label* layer to be the current layer.
   - o Add the label using the *Text* command. The label is: PROPOSED BUILDING, 3 BEDROOMS HOME, EL MAIN FLOOR 101.5'.

24. <u>Structure's hatch</u>: Figure 17-8
   - o Create a layer and name it as *Building_Hatch*. Set its *linetype* to *Continuous* and change its color.

- o Make the *Building_Hatch* layer to be the current layer.
- o Add the hatch using the *Hatch* command. Set the pattern: *GRASS*, *Angle*: 0, and *Scale*: 25.

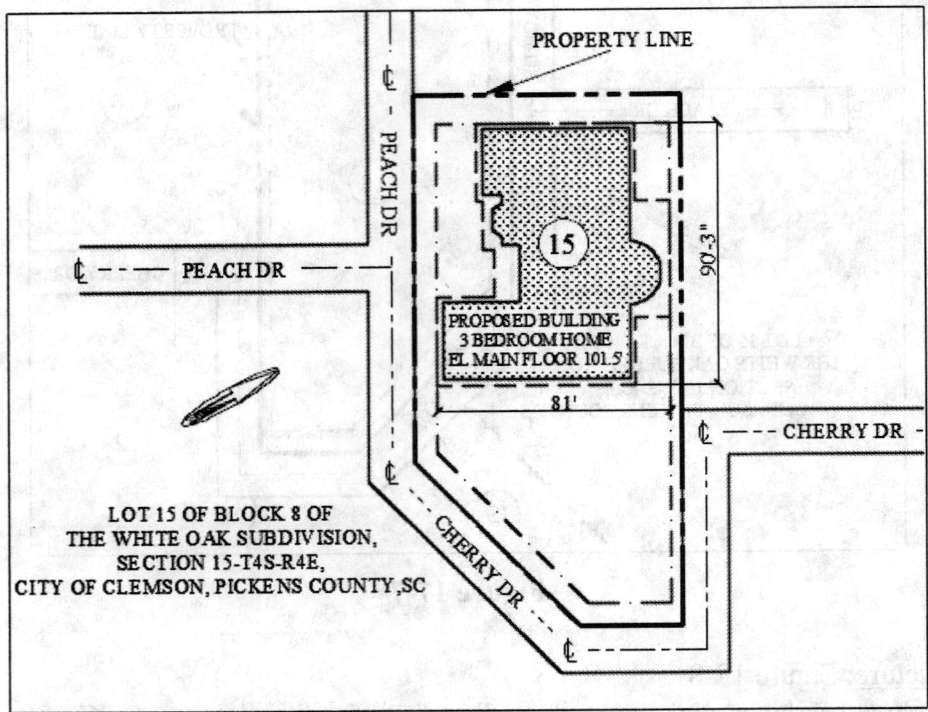

Figure 17-8

25. <u>Driveway</u>: Figure 17-9 and Figure 17-10
- o Create a layer and name it as *Driveway*. Set its *linetype* to *Continuous* and change its color.
- o Make the *Driveway* layer to be the current layer.
- o Draw the driveway as a closed traverse (for dimensions refer to Figure 17-10).

26. <u>Driveway's label</u>: Figure 17-9
- o Create a layer and name it as *Driveway_Label*. Set its *linetype* to *Continuous* and change its color.
- o Make the *Driveway_Label* layer to be the current layer.
- o Add the label using the *Text* command and arrow using *qleader* command.

27. <u>Driveway's hatch</u>: Figure 17-9
- o Create a layer and name it as *Driveway_Hatch*. Set its *linetype* to *Continuous* and change its color.
- o Make the *Driveway_Hatch* layer to be the current layer.
- o Add the hatch using the *Hatch* command. Set the pattern: *AR-HBONE*, *Angle*: 90, and *Scale*: 5.

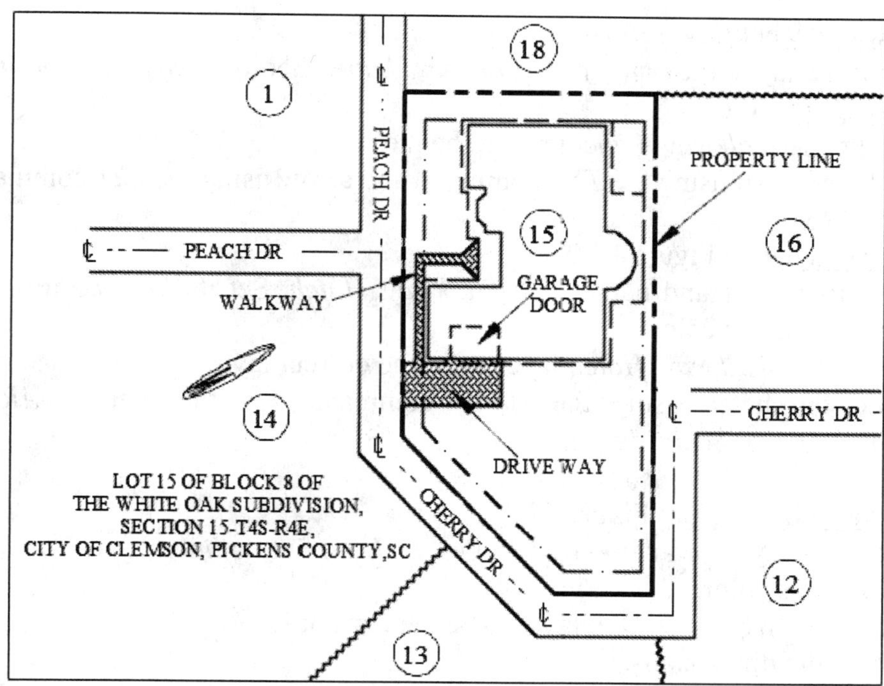

Figure 17-9

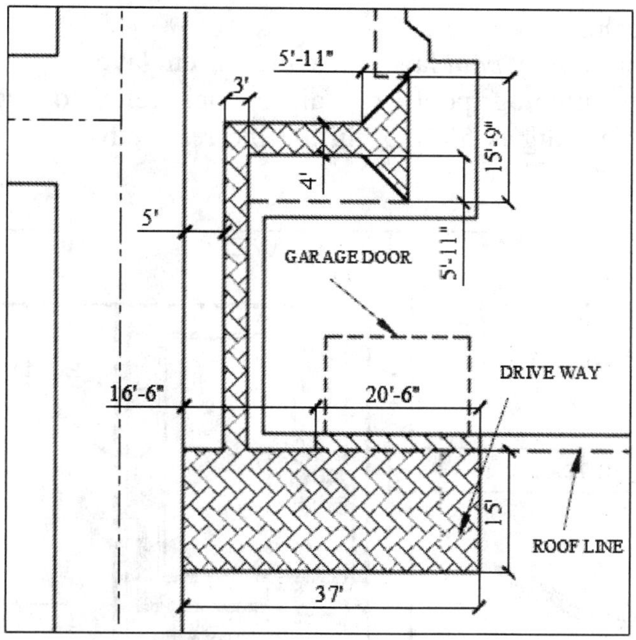

Figure 17-10

28. <u>Walkway</u>: Figure 17-9 and Figure 17-10
   o Create a layer and name it as *Walkway*. Set its *linetype* to *Continuous* and change its color.
   o Make the *Walkway* layer to be the current layer.
   o The walkway's dimensions are given in Figure 17-10.
   o Draw the walkway using the dimensions shown in Figure 17-10.

29. <u>Walkway's label</u>: Figure 17-9
   o Create a layer and name it as *Walkway_Label*. Set its *linetype* to *Continuous* and change its color.
   o Make the *Walkway_Label* layer to be the current layer.
   o Add the label using the *Text* command and arrow using *qleader* command.

30. <u>Walkway's hatch</u>: Figure 17-9
   o Create a layer and name it as *Walkway_Hatch*. Set its *linetype* to *Continuous* and change its color.
   o Make the *Walkway_Hatch* layer to be the current layer.
   o Add the hatch using the *Hatch* command. Set the pattern: *AR-HBONE*, *Angle*: 0, and *Scale*: 5.

31. <u>Walkway's dimension</u>: Figure 17-10
   o Create a layer and name it as *Walkway_Dim*. Set its *linetype* to *Continuous* and change its color.
   o Make the *Walkway_Dim* layer to be the current layer.
   o Show the dimensions.

32. <u>Swimming pool</u>: Figure 17-11a and Figure 17-11b
   o Create a layer and name it as *Swimming_pool*. Set its *linetype* to *Continuous* and change its color.
   o Make the *Swimming_pool* layer to be the current layer.
   o Draw the swimming pool (for dimensions refer to Figure 17-11b). The swimming pool dig is 5'-10.5" inside the rear setback. For the finished pool, make an offset of 2' inside.

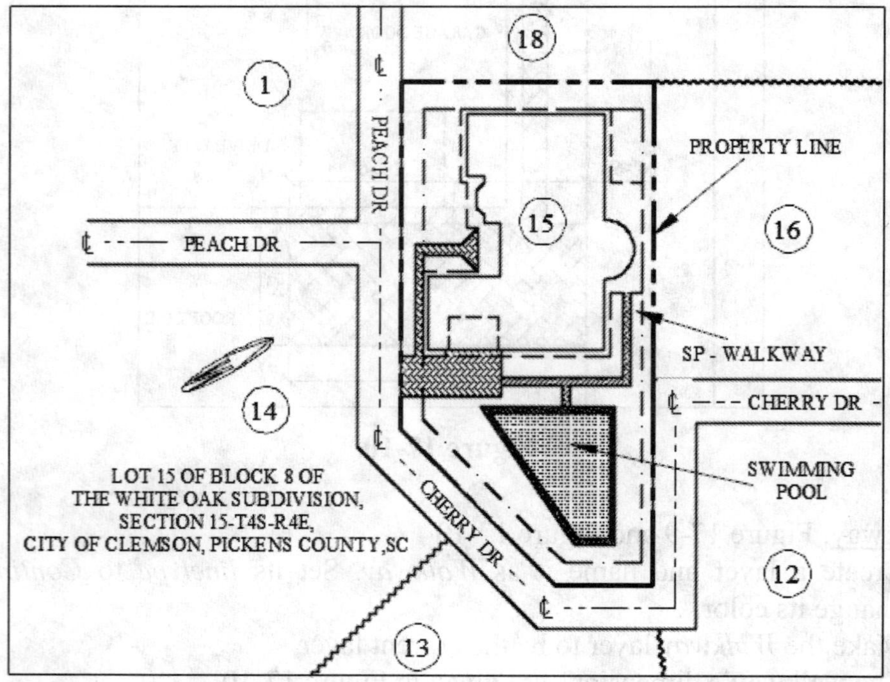

Figure 17-11a

33. <u>Swimming pool's label</u>: Figure 17-11a
   o Create a layer and name it as *Swimming_pool_Label*. Set its *linetype* to *Continuous* and change its color.
   o Make the *Swimming_pool_Label* layer to be the current layer.
   o Add the label using the *Text* command and arrow using *qleader* command.

34. <u>Swimming pool's hatch</u>: Figure 17-11a
   o Create a layer and name it as *Swimming_pool_Hatch*. Set its *linetype* to *Continuous* and change its color.
   o Make the *Swimming_pool_Hatch* layer to be the current layer.
   o For the finished pool, add the hatch using the *Hatch* command. Set the pattern: *MUDST*, Angle: 0, and Scale: 60.
   o For the sides of the pool, add the hatch using the *Hatch* command. Set the pattern: *AR-HBONE*, Angle: 0, and Scale: 2.

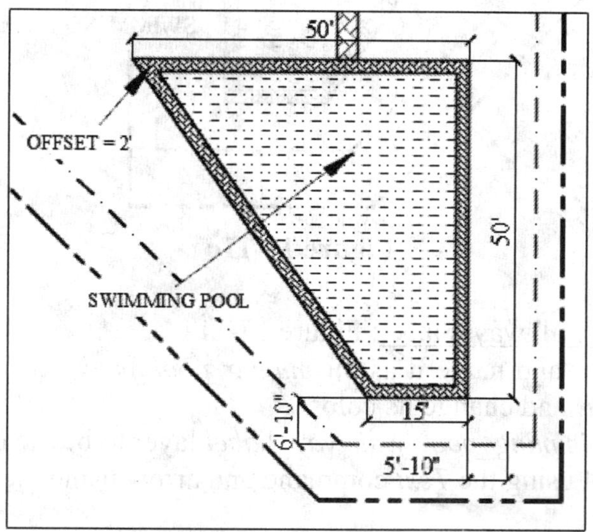

Figure 17-11b

35. <u>Swimming pool's dimension</u>: Figure 17-11b
   o Create a layer and name it as *Swimming_pool_Dim*. Set its *linetype* to *Continuous* and change its color.
   o Make the *Swimming_pool_Dim* layer to be the current layer.
   o Show the dimensions.

36. <u>Swimming pool_walkway</u>: Figure 17-11a and Figure 17-11c
   o Create a layer and name it as *Swimming_pool_walkway*. Set its *linetype* to *Continuous* and change its color.
   o Make the *Swimming_pool_walkway* layer to be the current layer.
   o Draw the swimming pool walkway (for dimensions refer to Figure 17-11c). For the finished walkway, make an offset of 3' outside.

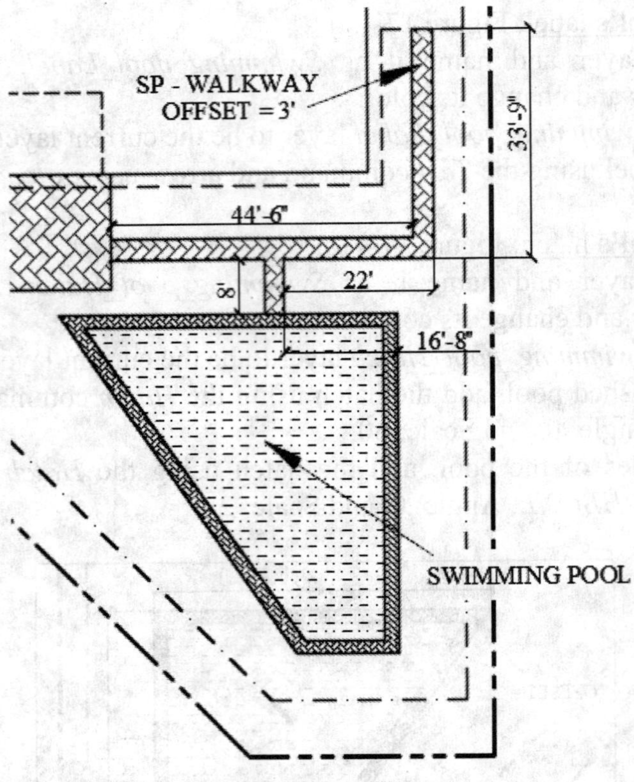

Figure 17-11c

37. <u>Swimming pool-walkway's label</u>: Figure 17-11a
   o   Create a layer and name it as *Swimming_pool_walkway_Label*. Set its *linetype*
       to *Continuous* and change its color.
   o   Make the *Swimming_pool_walkway_Label* layer to be the current layer.
   o   Add the label using the *Text* command and arrow using *qleader* command.

38. <u>Swimming pool-walkway's hatch</u>: Figure 17-11a
   o   Create a layer and name it as *Swimming_pool_walkway_Hatch*. Set its *linetype*
       to *Continuous* and change its color.
   o   Make the *Swimming_pool_walkway_Hatch* layer to be the current layer.
   o   For the finished walkway, add the hatch using the *Hatch* command. Set the
       pattern: *AR-HBONE*, Angle: 0, and Scale: 4.

39. <u>Swimming pool-walkway's dimension</u>: Figure 17-11c
   o   Create a layer and name it as *Swimming_pool_walkway_Dim*. Set its *linetype* to
       Continuous and change its color.
   o   Make the *Swimming_pool_walkway_Dim* layer to be the current layer.
   o   Show the dimensions.

40. <u>Utilities</u>: Figure 17-12a
   o   Create a layer and name it as *Utilities*. In this case, *linetype* will set
       independently for each utility; change its color.
   o   Make the *Utilities* layer to be the current layer.

- o Change linetype to *Fenceline1* and draw the sewer line.
- o Change linetype to *Gas_Line* and draw the gas supply line.
- o Change linetype to *Hot_Water_Supply* and draw the water supply line.

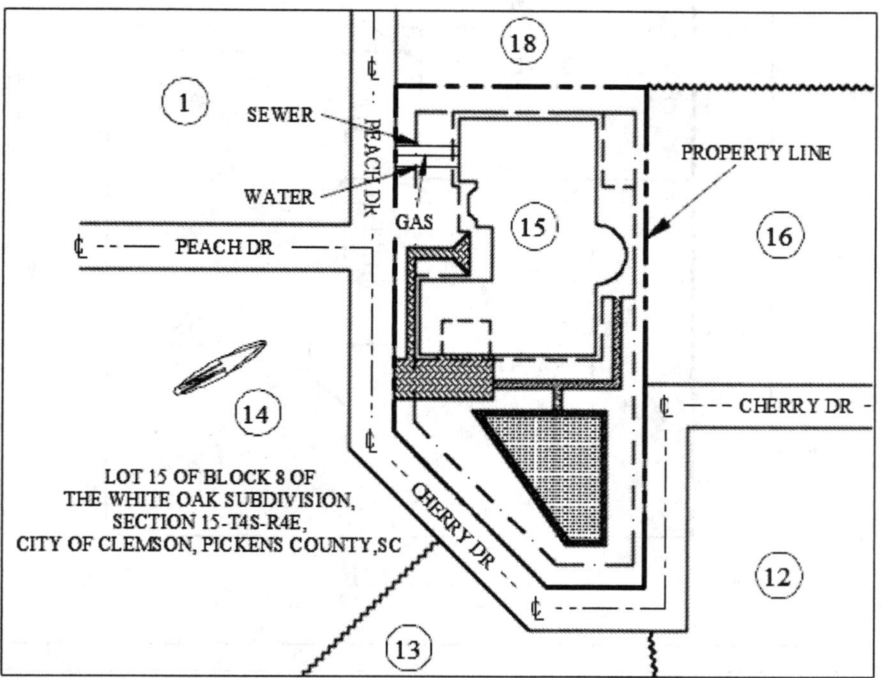

Figure 17-12a

41. <u>Utilities' label</u>: Figure 17-12a
- o Create a layer and name it as *Utilities_Label*. Set its *linetype* to *Continuous* and change its color.
- o Make the *Utilities_Label* layer to be the current layer.
- o Add the labels using the *Text* command and arrows using *qleader* command.

42. <u>Utilities' dimension</u>: Figure 17-12b
- o Create a layer and name it as *Utilities_Dim*. Set its *linetype* to *Continuous* and change its color.
- o Make the *Utilities_Dim* layer to be the current layer.
- o Show the dimensions.

43. <u>Template File</u>:
- o Insert an appropriate layout from one of the template files, Figure 17-13.
- o Set the scale of the drawing to 1: 500, Figure 17-13.
- o Update the blocks, Figure 17-13.
- o The complete site plan is shown in Figure 17-13.

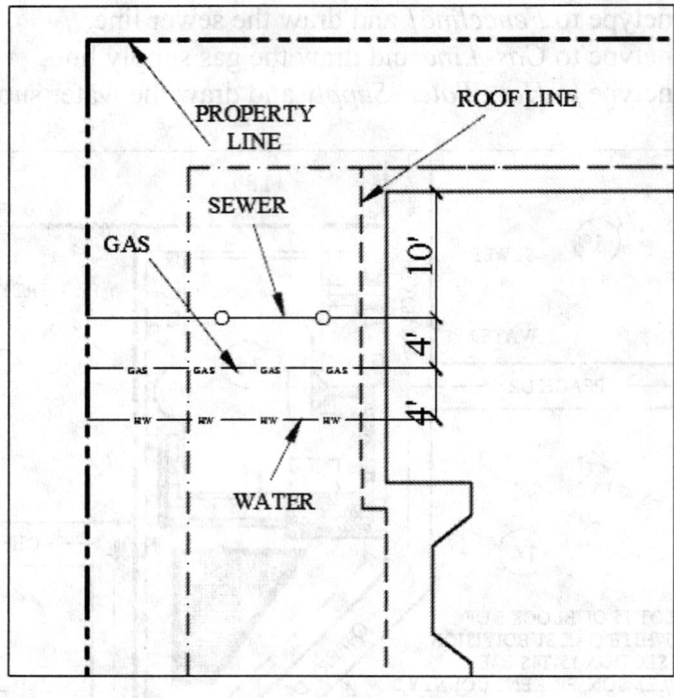

Figure 17-12b

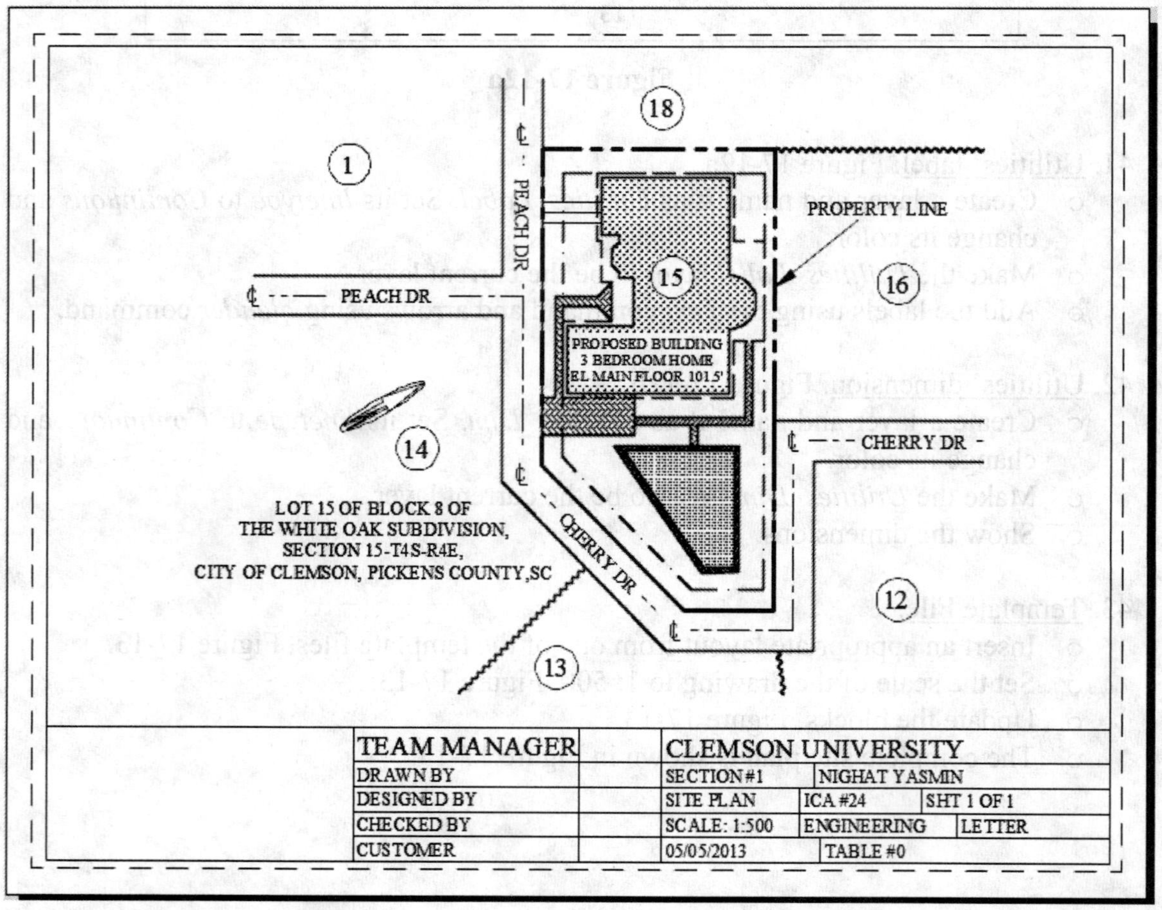

TEAM MANAGER		CLEMSON UNIVERSITY		
DRAWN BY		SECTION #1	NIGHAT YASMIN	
DESIGNED BY		SITE PLAN	ICA #24	SHT 1 OF 1
CHECKED BY		SCALE: 1:500	ENGINEERING	LETTER
CUSTOMER		05/05/2013	TABLE #0	

Figure 17-13

18. Construction Drawings

18.1.   Objectives

- Learn about a family of drawings

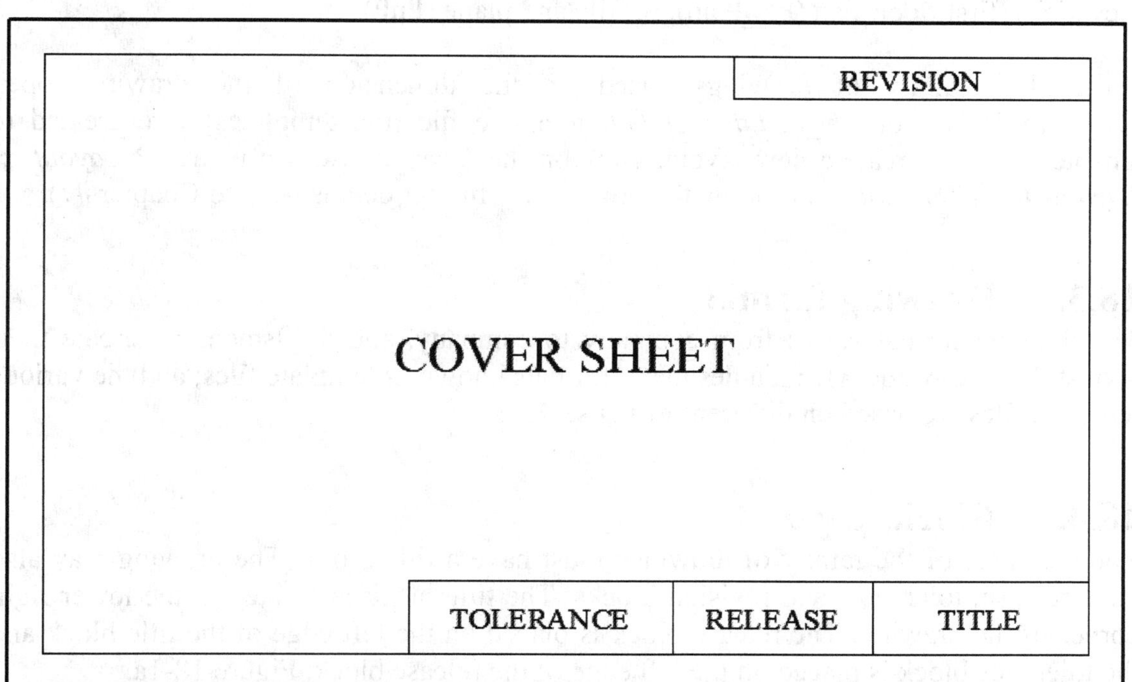

TOLERANCE UNLESS OTHERWISE STATED		TEAM MANAGER		CLEMSON UNIVERSITY		
$x \pm 1$	$0.xxx \pm 0.001$	DRAWN BY		SECTION #1	NIGHAT YASMIN	
$0.x \pm 0.1$	$x° \pm 0.5°$	DESIGNED BY		EX 3-4	LAB #8	SHT 1 OF 2
$0.xx \pm 0.01$		CHECKED BY		SCALE : 1:1	INCHES	LETTER
		CUSTOMER		05/05/2013	TABLE #0	

18.2.   Introduction

Construction drawings are the collection of several drawings that are used to complete a project. The development of working drawing is the last step of the design process. The next step is the construction of the project!

Generally, the arrangement and number of the drawings depend on the client's requirement, company, and project type and size. Some of the commonly used drawings are shown in Figure 18-2. For most of the projects at least one of these sheets is created, and for larger projects, there can be more than one of the same types of drawings. For example, for a single story building, there can be only one floor plan. On the other hands, for a multilevel building there can be as many floor plans as the number of levels. For both of the single and multilevel buildings there can be four exterior elevation drawings (north-, south-, east-, and west-side elevations).

This chapter uses layouts to create different types of the drawing. Hence, to navigate the layouts efficiently, the layouts should be named properly. For example F_Elev (front elevation), first floor plan (FF_Plan), profile and plane (PnP), etc.

To start a family of drawings based on the dimension of the drawing, open *My_acad3D_tmlt* or *My_acadiso3D_tmlt* template file (the templates were created in Chapter #7). To create a new layout, click on the *Insert* pull down menu → *Layout* → *Layouts from Template* and follow the prompt (for further details refer to Chapter #7).

18.3.   Drawing format

The drawing format varies from company to company, and draftsmen can create their own style. The AutoCAD includes many formats known as template files; and the various template files are based on different formats.

18.4.   Blocks used

The members of the family of drawings must have a title block. The drawing may also have release, tolerance, and revision blocks. The title block is located in the lower right corner of the drawing. The release block is placed on the left edge of the title block and the tolerance block is placed on the left edge of the release block, Figure 18-1a.

The title block contains the general information about the company and the drawing. A release block contains a list of approval signatures or initials required before a drawing is released for the production. The contents of these blocks may vary from company to company. A typical title and release blocks are shown in Figure 18-1b and Figure 18-1c, respectively. For further details of these blocks, refer to Chapter #6, Blocks.

Figure 18-1a

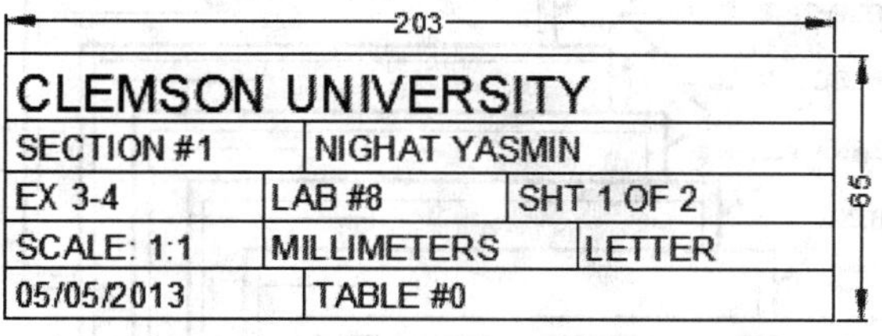

Figure 18-1b

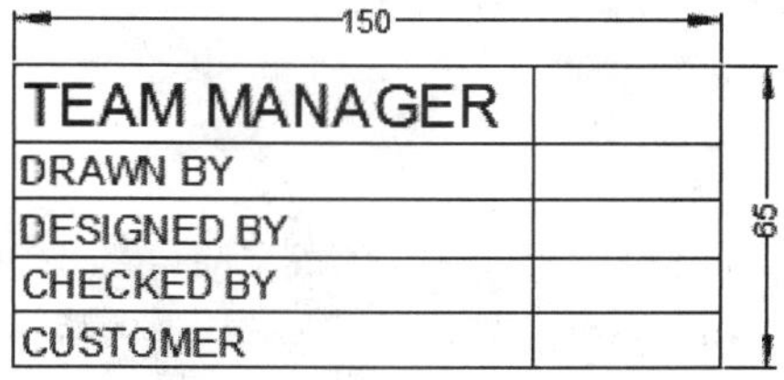

Figure 18-1c

The tolerance block is used to list the standard tolerances. The block is created using line and text commands. In AutoCAD, the plus-minus symbol is created by typing %%p in a text object. The contents of this block may vary from company to company. The tolerance block is placed on the left edge of the release block. A typical tolerance block is shown in Figure 18-1d. The tolerance of "*X plus-minus 1*" implies that if the basic or theoretical dimension of an object is 15 then 16 and 14 are acceptable, too. For further details of blocks in general, refer to Chapter #6, Blocks.

A revision block is used to show the name of the modification made to the drawing, initial or signature of the person responsible for the revision, and the date of the revision. The block is created using line and text commands. The contents of this block may vary from company to company. A revision block is generally located in the upper right corner of the drawing. A typical revision block is shown in Figure 18-1e. For further details of blocks in general, refer to Chapter #6, Blocks.

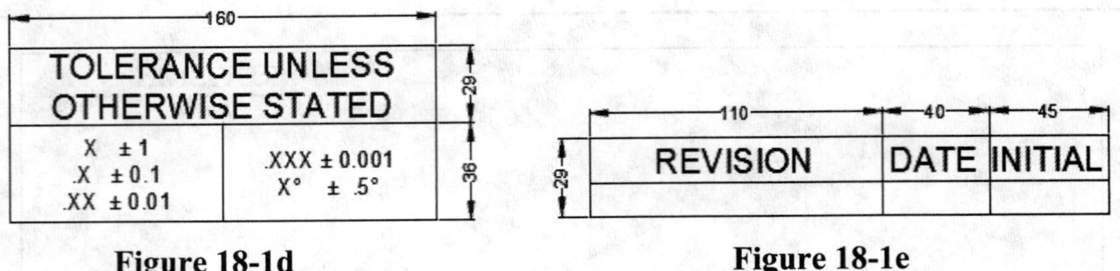

Figure 18-1d　　　　　　　**Figure 18-1e**

18.5.　Family of construction drawing

This section briefly describes the drawings shown in Figure 18-2.

18.5.1.　Cover sheet

As the name suggests, the cover sheet is the title page for the set of the drawings. It is always the first sheet. A cover sheet includes the project's title, number, location map, name of the owner, names and signature and stamps of the designers, index of sheets, legend, survey data, perspective drawing, etc.

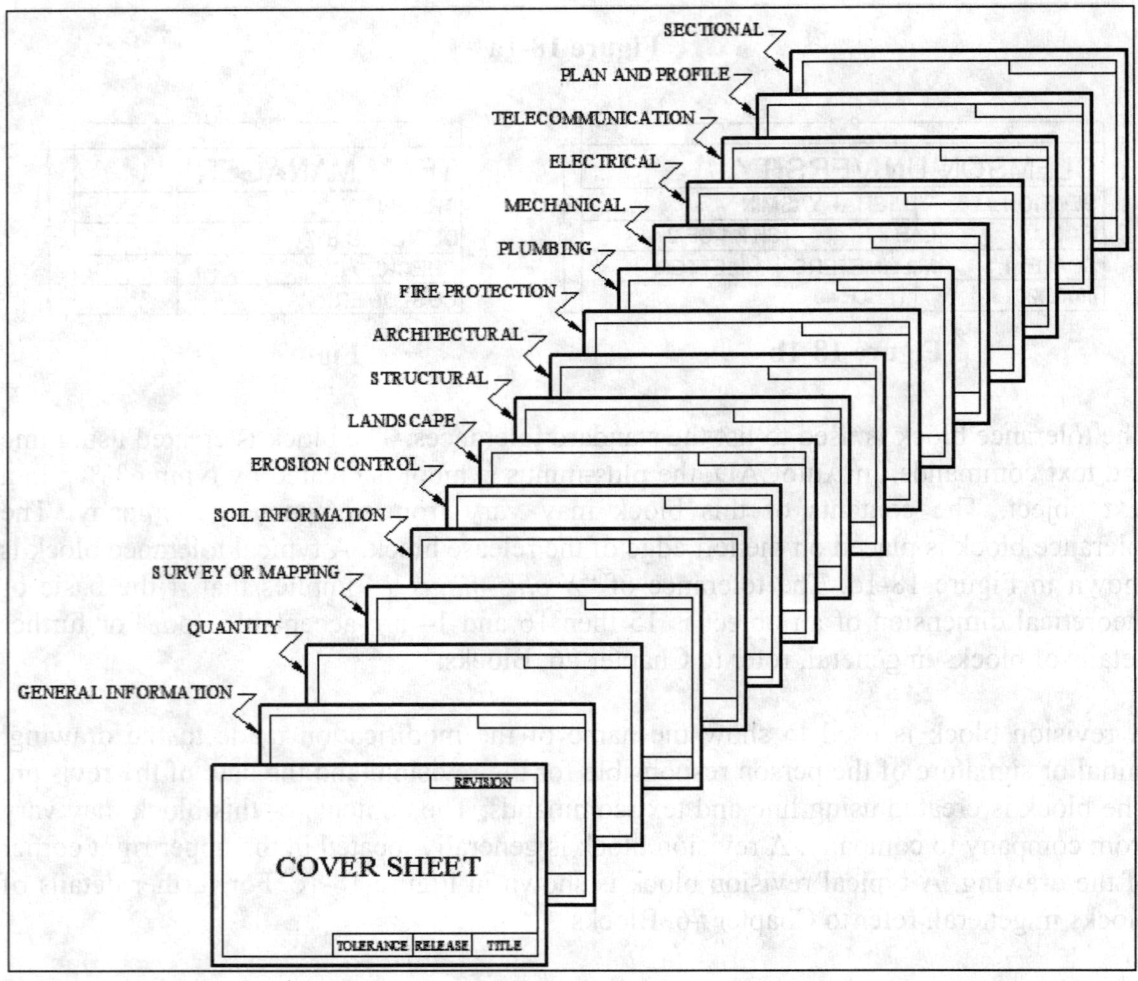

Figure 18-2

18.5.2. General information

The general information sheets are also known as G sheets. These sheets include the site data, location map, abbreviations, index to the other drawings, and building code data. In some projects, the cover and general information sheets are merged into one cover sheet.

18.5.3. Quantity sheet

The quantity sheet represents the estimate of the quantities (sod, concrete, lumber, paint, glass, etc.) and the cost of the activities (clearing, digging, hauling, etc.). That is, it represents the estimated cost of the projects. It includes the cost of everything used in the project, ranging from the cost of buying a pepper clip to renting heavy machinery.

18.5.4. Survey or mapping

The survey or mapping sheets are also known as V sheets. The cover and/or general information sheets include brief data. On the other hand, survey sheets represent the detail information. These sheets are used to represent the real estate information and the vicinity information. These sheets are developed by professionals; however, the data is provided by the owner. The cost of the survey may or may not be included in the estimated cost of the project.

18.5.5. Soil information

The soil information sheets are also known as G sheets. These sheets are used to provide the geotechnical characteristic of the land used for the construction.

18.5.6. Erosion control

The erosion control sheets provide the information on the methods and techniques used in the erosion control of the project site. For example, the first step in the construction process is the clearing of the site (cutting the trees and removal of the top soil). This process will lead to the erosion and environmental effect (the eroded material will end up in the stream, lakes, and rivers). Hence, this sheet should be present in every project.

18.5.7. Landscape drawings

The landscape drawings sheets are also known as L sheets. These sheets are used to provide the landscaping information such as the plant plan, types of plants, irrigation system, fences, benches, walkways, etc.

18.5.8. Structural drawings

The structural drawings sheets are also known as S sheets. In heavy construction, anything composed of parts is called a structure. These sheets provide the information for designing, fabricating, manufacturing, and erecting the structural elements.

18.5.9. Fire protection drawings

The fire protection drawings sheets are also known as F sheets. These sheets are used to provide the fire code, access to site, on-site street width and curvature, location of hydrants, power supply, or any other information that will make the fire fighter jobs effective.

18.5.10.   Architectural drawings

The commonly used architectural drawings are floor plans, site plan, elevations, and sectional views.

- *Plan views*: A plan view is a horizontal orthographic view looking from the top. Site plan is the top view of the proposed or existing building situated in the building site. A floor plan is the top view of a building.
- *Elevation views*: An elevation is a vertical orthographic view looking from the side. For example, they include the front, rear, left, and right side elevations for a building.
- *Sectional views*: Sectional views represent the internal detail of the project. As a rule of thumb, the sectional views should be drawn at the same scale as the plan and elevations. In a building, generally the sectional views of the foundations, beams, column, joints, doors and windows jams, etc. are used to display the internal detail.

18.5.11.   Plumbing drawings

The plumbing drawings sheets are also known as P sheets. These sheets are used to provide the drain waste, hot and cold water supply, and fixtures information for the site as well as for the proposed structure.

18.5.12.   Mechanical drawings

The mechanical drawings sheets are also known as M sheets. These sheets are used to provide the information regarding the location, size, and type of the units used for distributing, filtering, humidifying/dehumidifying, and cooling and heating air.

18.5.13.   Electrical drawings

The electrical drawings sheets are also known as E sheets. These sheets are used to provide the information regarding the electrical services (wiring, metering, main switch), distribution (panel boards and switches), branch work (circuitry), and devices used during the construction and the proposed project.

18.5.14.   Telecommunication drawings

The telecommunication drawings sheets are also known as T sheets. These sheets are used to provide the information regarding how to use computer technology on the site.

18.5.15.   Plan and profile drawings

The plan and profiles drawings sheets are also known as PnP sheets. Theses sheets are used for the water and sewer pipelines, storm drainage system, curbs, sidewalk, and road construction.

- *Plan*: A plan view is a horizontal orthographic view looking from the top.
- *Profile*: A profile is a vertical orthographic view looking from the side.

19. AutoCAD 2014 – Classics Interface

19.1.   Objectives

- Learn the features of the AutoCAD 2014 classics interface
- Learn to use the toolbars
- Learn to add and/or remove a toolbar from the workspace

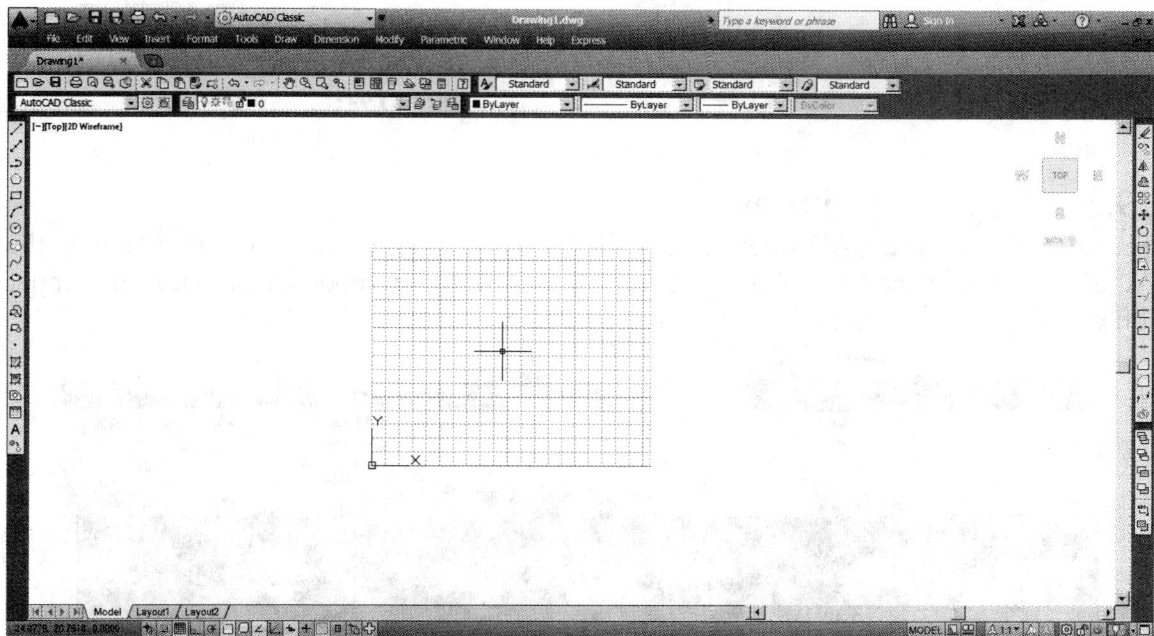

19.2.   Introduction

The focus of this chapter is the *AutoCAD Classic* interface. The various drawing and editing commands work exactly the same both in classics and ribbon interfaces. However, access to the commands is different in the two interfaces. The classics interface mainly uses the toolbars and menus; and the ribbon interface uses ribbon, tabs and panels. The execution of the commands is discussed in great details in previous chapters. This chapter emphasizes on the toolbars and menus and how to start a command from a tool bar or a menu. The user should use the index and table of contents for the details of the commands.

The AutoCAD can be launched by either double clicking on the AutoCAD icon (Figure 19-1a) on the desktop or by clicking *Start* → *All Programs* → *Autodesk* → *AutoCAD 2014* → *AutoCAD 2014*, Figure 19-1b. If the path of the software is different on your computer, then follow that path. Either of the two launching process will result in opening a new drawing. For the first launch of the software, the AutoCAD interface will be in the *Drafting & Annotation* mode, Figure 19-2a.

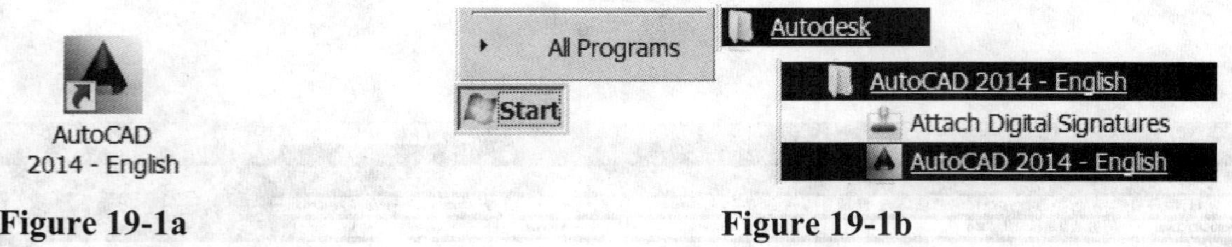

Figure 19-1a   **Figure 19-1b**

19.3.   Typical window screen

Technically, the AutoCAD interface is called a workspace. For the first time launch, the AutoCAD workspace will be in the *Drafting & Annotation* mode as shown in the upper left corner of the Figure 19-2a and Figure 19-2b.

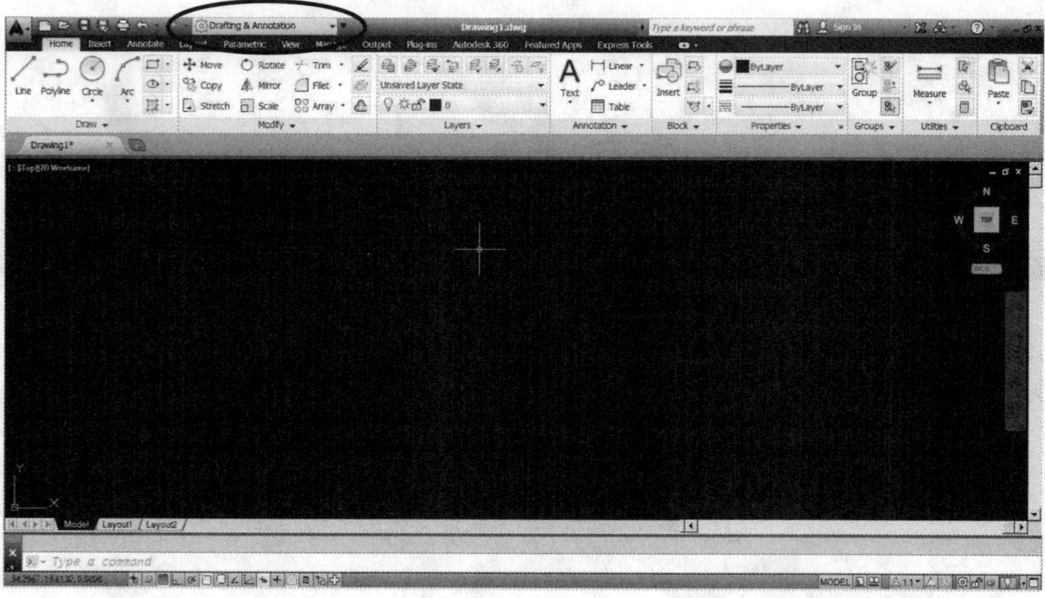

Figure 19-2a

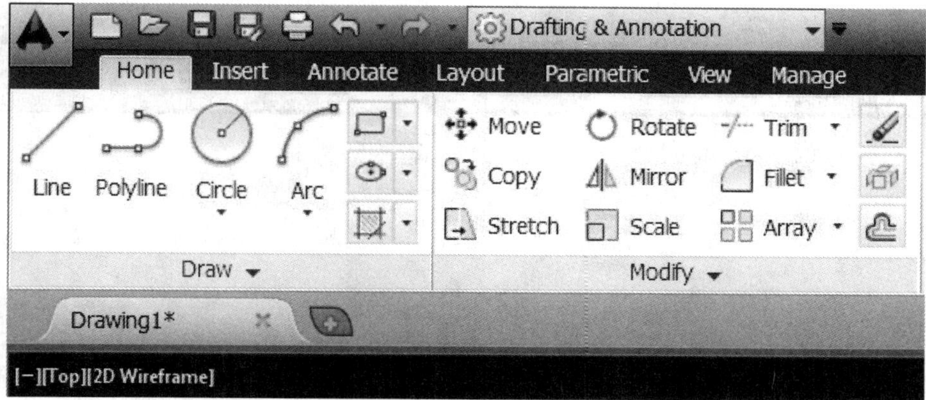

Figure 19-2b

19.3.1. Switch to AutoCAD Classic

The focus of this chapter is the *AutoCAD Classic* workspace. The remaining of this section discusses the process to switch from *Drafting and Annotation* to *AutoCAD Classic* workspace using one of the following two methods.

- (i) Click the small downward arrow to the right of the *Drafting and Annotation* in the upper left corner of the interface, Figure 19-3a. A small window displaying the *Workspace* options will appear on the screen. (ii) Click on *AutoCAD Classic* option and the interface will be switched to the *AutoCAD Classic* format, Figure 19-3c.

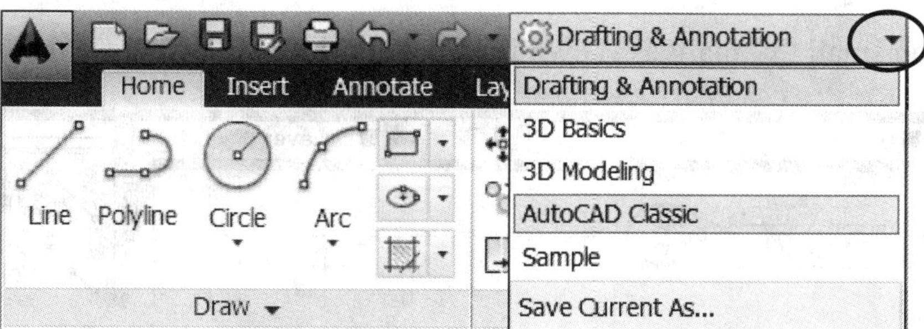

Figure 19-3a

- (i) Click on the small downward arrow on the wheel in the lower right corner of the interface, Figure 19-3b. A small window displaying the *Workspace* options will appear on the screen. (ii) Click on *AutoCAD Classic* option and the interface will be switched to the *AutoCAD Classic* format, Figure 19-3c.

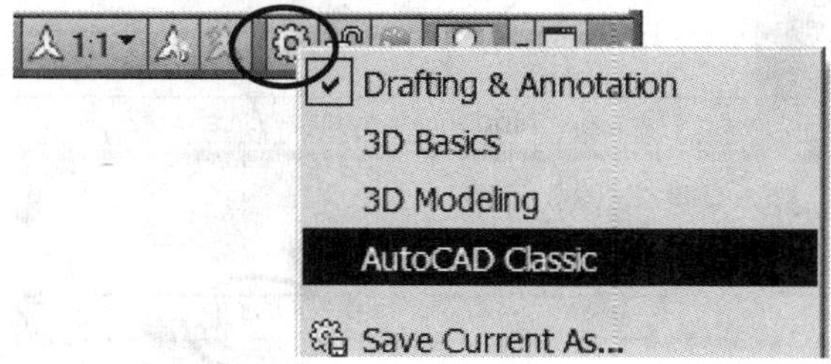

Figure 19-3b

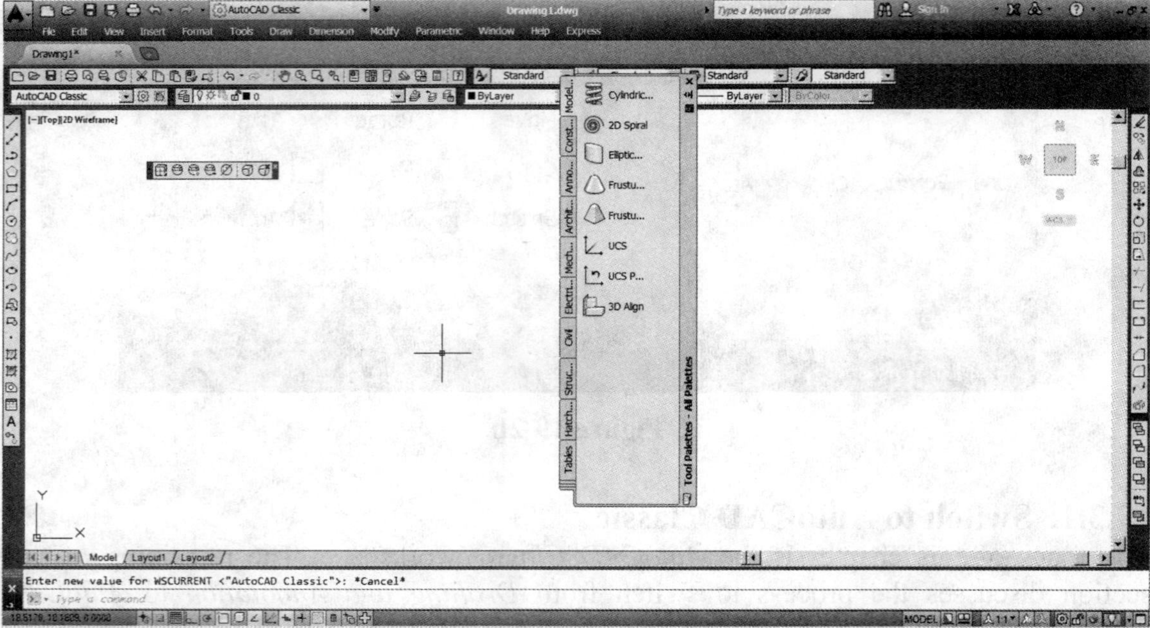

Figure 19-3c

19.3.2. Initial setup

For the demonstration, the background color (of the drawing area) is changed. The drawing area and the color change are discussed in Chapter #2.

- Click on small "x" mark as shown in Figure 19-4a. This will close the two toolbars.

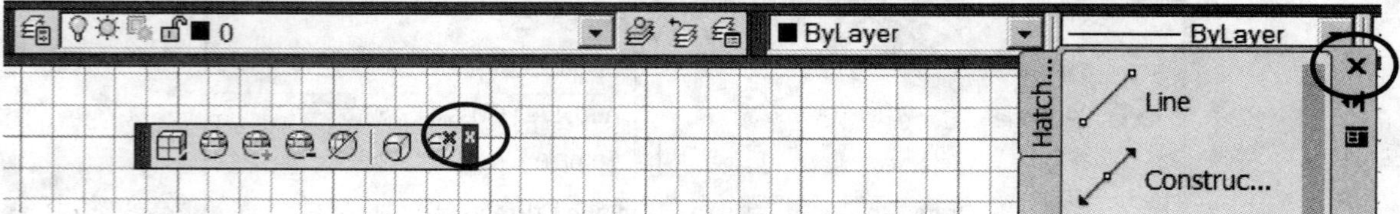

Figure 19-4a

- Turn *Off* the grid by clicking the grid box in the lower left corner as shown in Figure 19-4b.
- The interface is updated to a typical 2D classics workspace, Figure 19-4c.

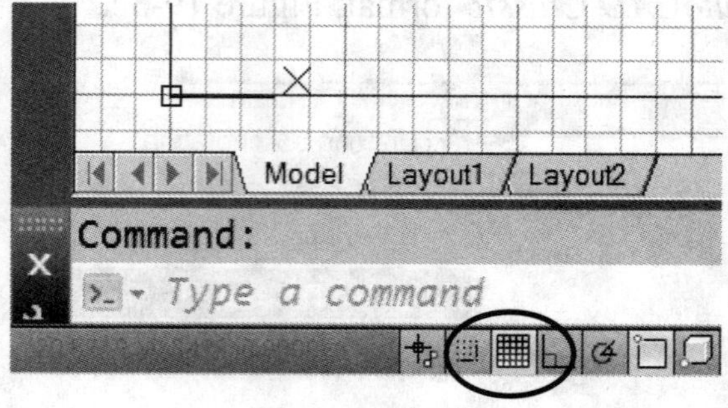

Figure 19-4b

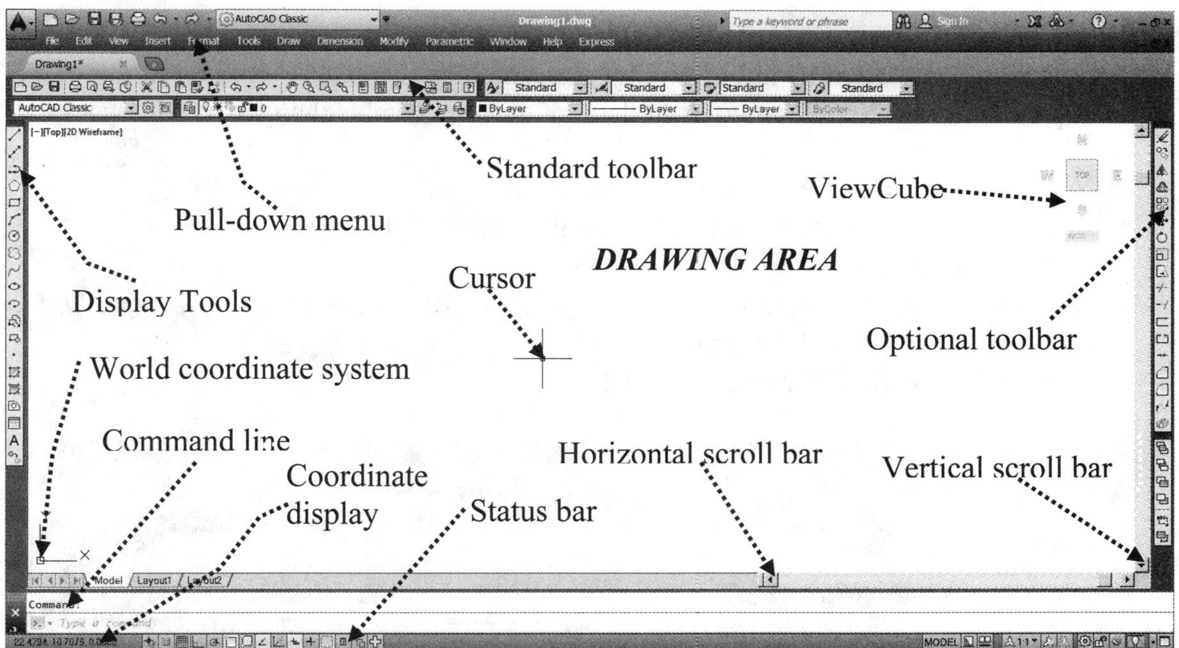

Figure 19-4c

A typical window screen, Figure 19-4c, is a display of the drawing area, cursor, World coordinate system, viewcube, drawing display format, scroll bars, pull down menus, command line, status bar, toolbars, and dockable windows (not shown in the figure). These features are grouped and organized based on the drawing environment and the user requirements.

19.4.   Drawing area

The drawing area (the empty blank area in Figure 19-4c) is a rectangular area used to create a new drawing or modify a previously created drawing. Although the drawing area is unlimited, however, the size of the drawing window depends on various factors such as the size of the computer screen, AutoCAD's window, and number of the toolbars and other elements displayed.

The drawing area is classified as the model space or layout. The user can switch to the model space or a layout by selecting the *Model* or *Layout* (*Layout1* or *Layout2*) tab, respectively, from the lower left corner of the drawing area, Figure 19-5.

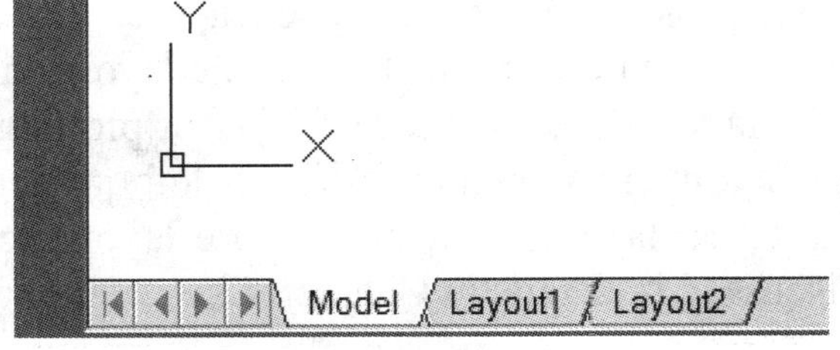

Figure 19-5

19.4.1. Model space

A model is a 2D or 3D drawing of an object. Generally, a model is created in the model (workspace) space. The default color of the model space can be changed as follows:

- Click on the *Tools* menu and select the *Options* option.
- The *Options* dialog box (Figure 19-6) will appear on the screen.
- Select the *Display* tab by clicking on it.
- Press the *Color* button in the *Window Elements* panel to open the *Drawing Window Colors* (Figure 19-6b) dialog box.
- For further details refer to Chapter #2.

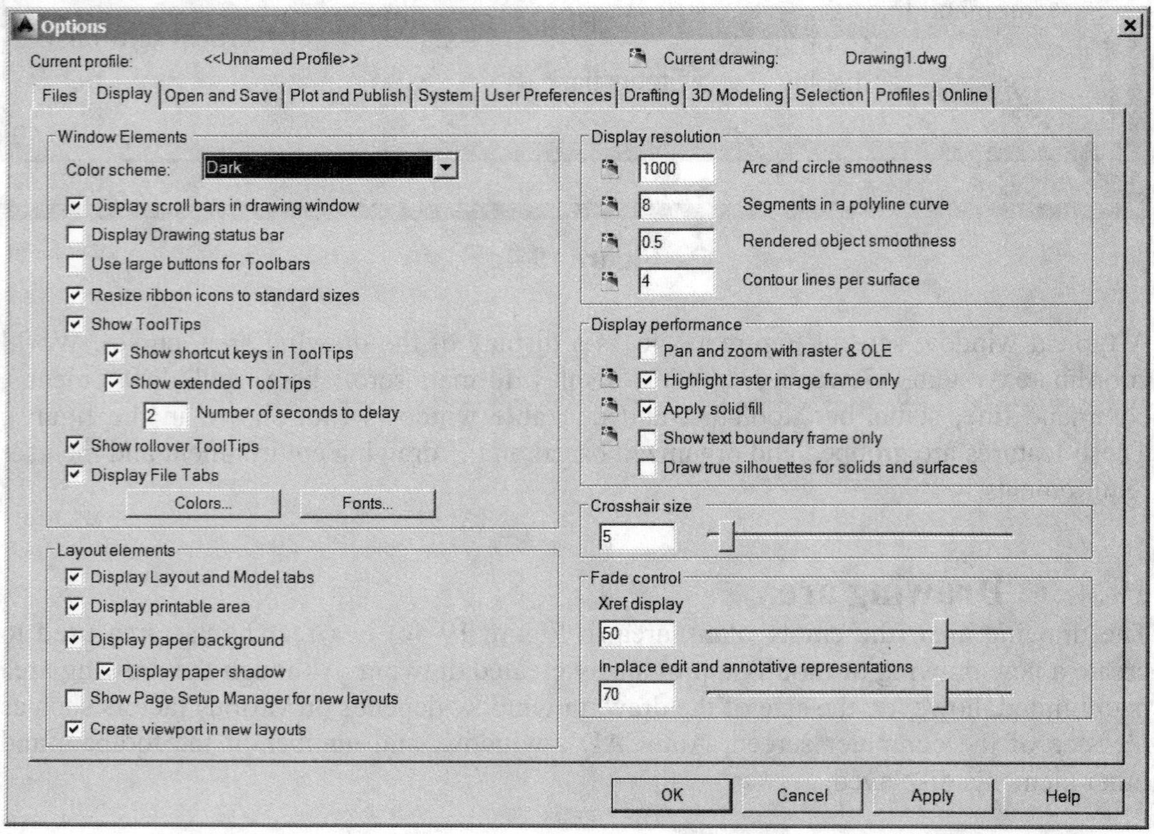

Figure 19-6

19.4.2. Layout

The layouts are also known as paper space. When a user clicks on a layout tab, the drawing area will appear as shown in Figure 19-7a. The layouts are not used for drafting or design work; generally, layouts are used for printing or plotting the drawing. The self-explanatory options for a layout are shown in the lower left quarter of the Figure 19-6. By default, AutoCAD creates two layouts; however, more layouts can be created for each drawing. Layouts are discussed in details in Chapter #7.

A user can display or hide the Model/Layout tab using *Options* dialog box. (i) Open the *Options* dialog box by clicking the *Tools* menu and selecting the *Options* option.

(ii) Select the *Display* tab by clicking on it. (iii) Check or clear the *Display Layout and Model tabs* box shown in the *Layout elements* panel, Figure 19-7b. (iv) Click the *Apply* or *OK* button. The *Apply* button will NOT close the *Options* dialog box but will hide the tabs. The *OK* button will close the *Options* dialog box and hide the tabs.

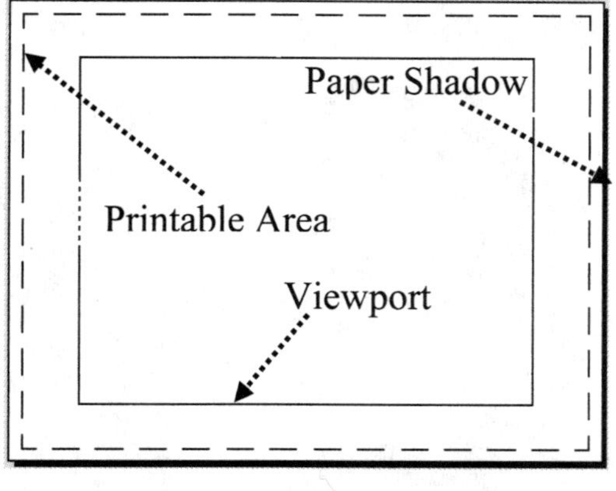

Figure 19-7a

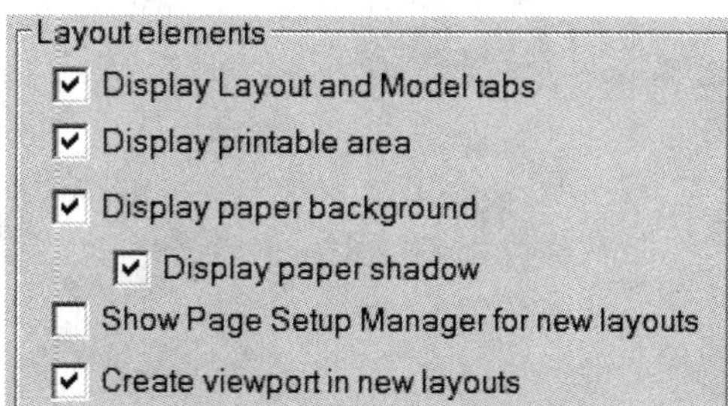

Figure 19-7b

19.5.   Cursor and pointer

In AutoCAD, cursor appears in different format based on the location and status of the cursor. The cursor appears as crosshairs (two intersecting lines and a small square surrounding the intersection point) in the drawing area if none of the command is active, Figure 19-8. The small square at the intersection of the crosshairs is called an aperture.

The size of the intersecting lines and aperture and the color of the cursor can be changed from the *Options* dialog box. The *Options* dialog box can be opened by clicking the *Tools* menu and selecting the *Options* options; this will open the *Options* dialog box. Select the *Display* tab and make the desired changes.

19.6.   ViewCube

The ViewCube is a navigational tool. It is displayed in 2D or 3D visual style, both in model space and layouts. By default, the tool is on, inactive, and semi-transparent. The ViewCube tool contains coordinate system (WCS) and compass (NSWE), Figure 19-9a. It is located in the upper right corner of the drawing area. In 2D model space, the default view is the top view as shown in the figure.

Figure 19-8   **Figure 19-9a**

The ViewCube can be turn *On/Off* by typing NAVVCUBE on the command line and choosing the desired option. The various features of the ViewCube can be changed from the *ViewCube Settings* dialog box; Expand the *View* menu and select the *Display* option followed by the *ViewCube* and *Settings* options, Figure 19-9b.

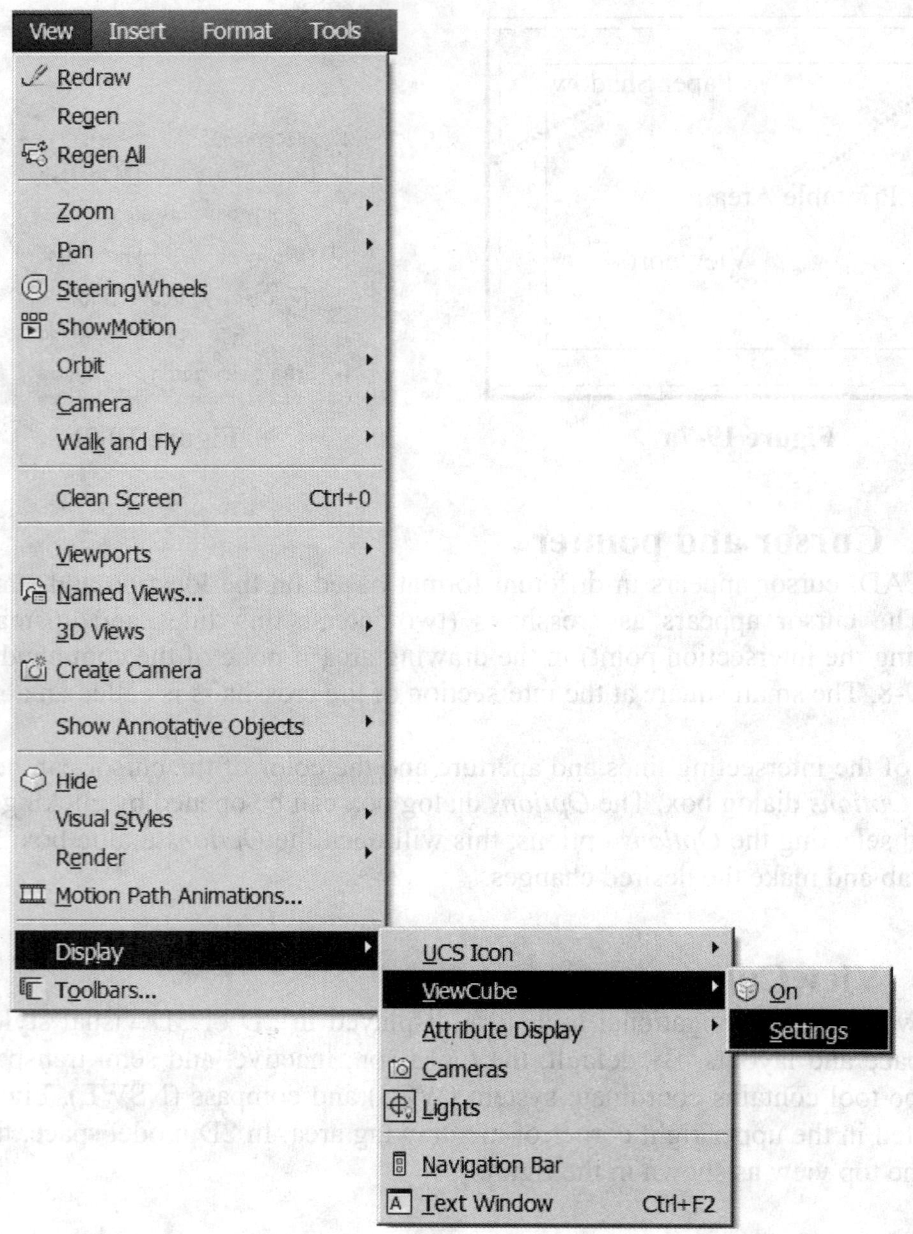

Figure 19-9b

19.7.   Scroll bars

A user can display or hide the scroll bars using *Options* dialog box. (i) Open the *Options* dialog box by clicking the *Tools* menu and selecting the *Options* option. (ii) Select the *Display* tab by clicking on it. (iii) Check or clear the *Display scroll bars in drawing window* box shown in the *Window elements* panel, Figure 19-10. (iv) Click the *Apply* or

OK button. The *Apply* button will NOT close the *Options* dialog box but will hide the tabs. The *OK* button will close the *Options* dialog box and hide the tabs.

Figure 19-10

19.8.   Pull down menus

The pull down menus are important part of the AutoCAD classics interface. In order to find the list of commands available under a menu, click the desired menu with the left button of the mouse. The first click shows the list of accessible commands under the selected menu and the second click will hide the list. After the first click, if the cursor is moved to any other menu heading, then the newly selected menu's options will be revealed. On the list of commands, either click a command or use the down arrow key on the keyboard to move down the list and then press the *Enter* key, Figure 19-11. The figure shows the expansion of the *Format* menu and the selection of the *Scale List...* command.

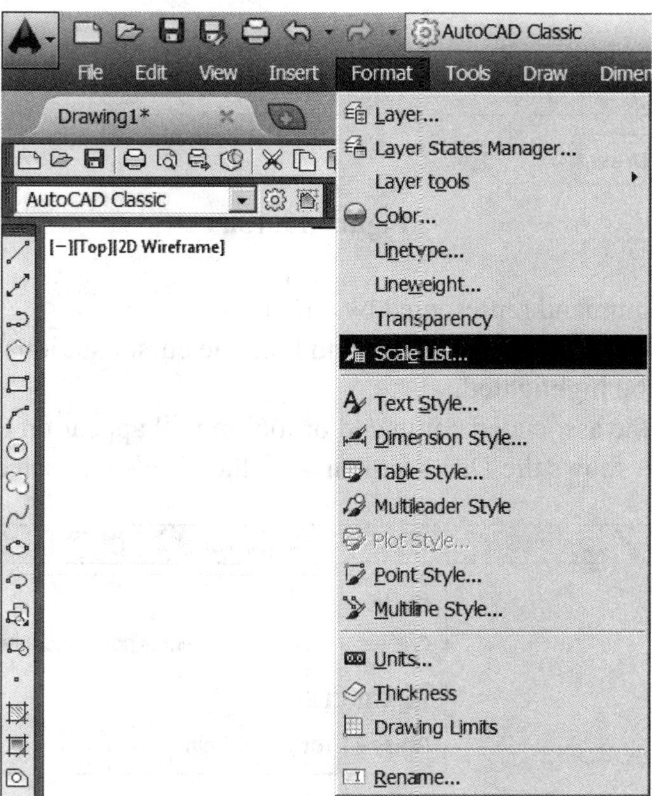

Figure 19-11

19.9.   Command line box

The command line box (CLB) is a text area reserved for the keyboard input, prompts, and messages. The default position of the CLB is at the bottom of the AutoCAD's window.

The user can display the command line box on the interface or hide from the interface using the *Tools* menu. Click the *Tools* menu and select the *Command Line* option, Figure 19-12. For further details refer to Chapter #2.

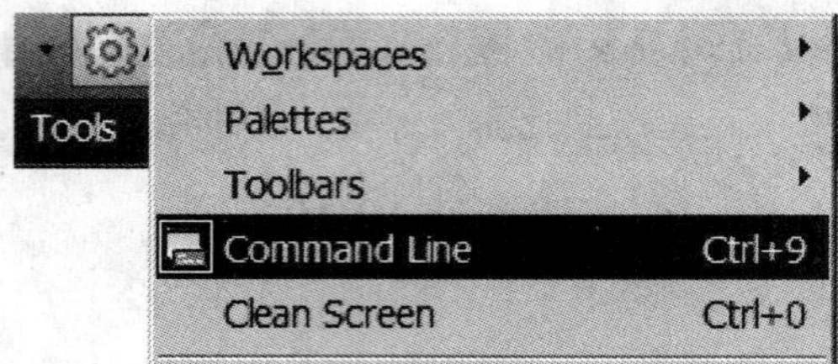

Figure 19-12

19.10.   Toolbars

The toolbars are important part of the AutoCAD's interface. A tool is a pictured icon that represents an AutoCAD command and a toolbar is a collection of tools or a graphical representation of the commands. To view the name of a toolbar, hold the cursor on the grey area at either end of the toolbar. Figure 19-13a shows the *Draw* toolbar. In the figure, the cursor was placed at the left end.

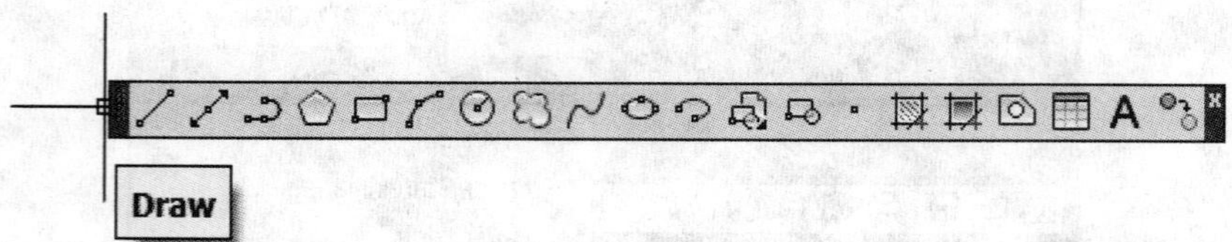

Figure 19-13a

To determine the command represented by a tool:
- Place the cursor on the desired icon and hold the cursor stationary.
- The tool will be highlighted.
- The name of the associated command or tooltip will appear on the screen.
- Figure 19-13b shows the *Draw* toolbar with the *Circle* tool selected.

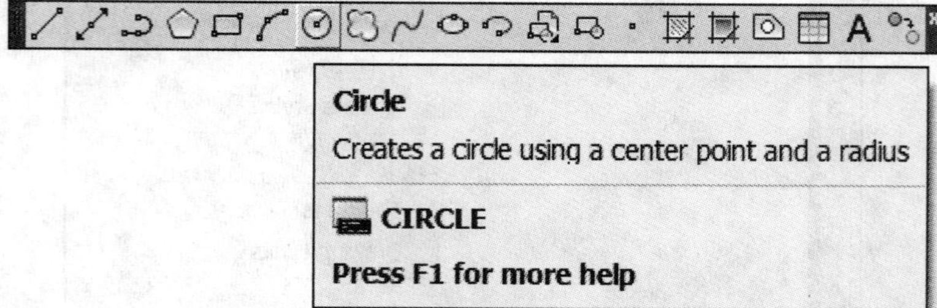

Figure 19-13b

19.10.1.   Add a new toolbar to the workspace

A new toolbar can be added to the workspace using one of the following two methods.

19.10.1.1. Method #1

- Locate the cursor arrow in the toolbars area (in the upper right corner of the interface), and click the right button of the mouse. The options list shown in Figure 19-14a will appear. However, if the arrow is on any part of the toolbar, then the toolbars list shown in Figure 19-14c will directly appear.

- In Figure 19-14a, select the "AutoCAD" option, the selection will be highlighted (Figure 19-14b), and the toolbars list shown in Figure 19-14c will appear. The check mark in front of the *Draw* and *Draw Order* toolbars indicates that these toolbars are previously added to the interface.

- Locate the cursor arrow on the desired toolbar (for example the *Dimension* toolbar), and it will be highlighted, Figure 19-14d.

- Now, press the right or left button of the mouse. The toolbars list will disappear and the selected toolbar will appear on the screen.

- Figure 19-14e shows the *Dimension* toolbar in the drawing area.

- If the toolbars list shown in Figure 19-14c is open again, then the selected toolbar will appear with the check mark in front of it, Figure 19-14f.

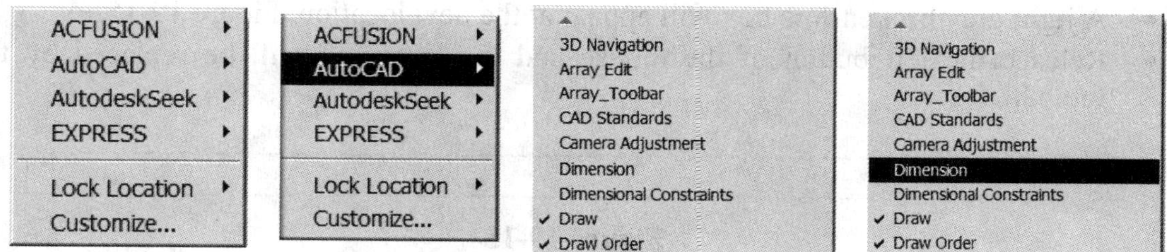

Figure 19-14a   **Figure 19-14b**   **Figure 19-14c**   **Figure 19-14d**

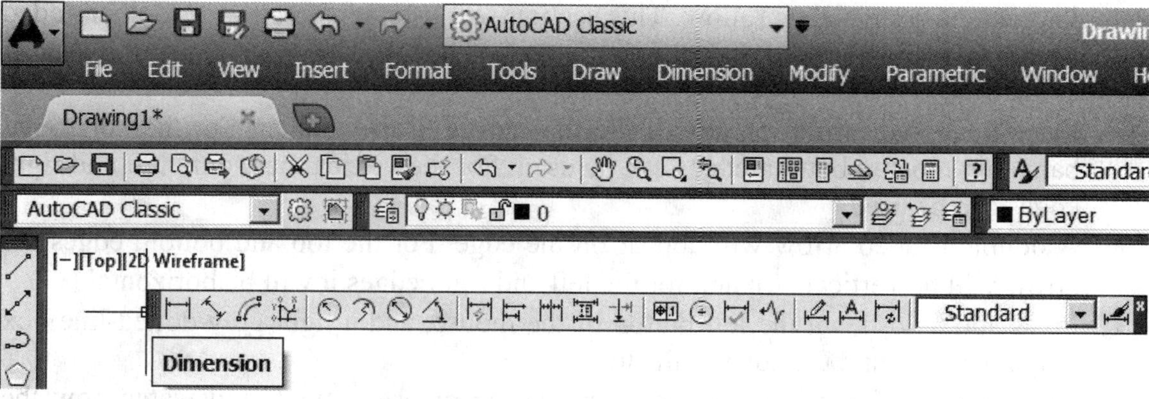

Figure 19-14e

19.10.1.2. Method #2

- From the *Tool* pull down menu click the *Toolbars* option, Figure 19-14f.
- From the *Toolbars* option, select the *AutoCAD* option.
- From the *AutoCAD* option, click on the desired toolbar.

- The check mark in front of the *Dimension* toolbar's name indicates that the toolbar is already added to the workspace.

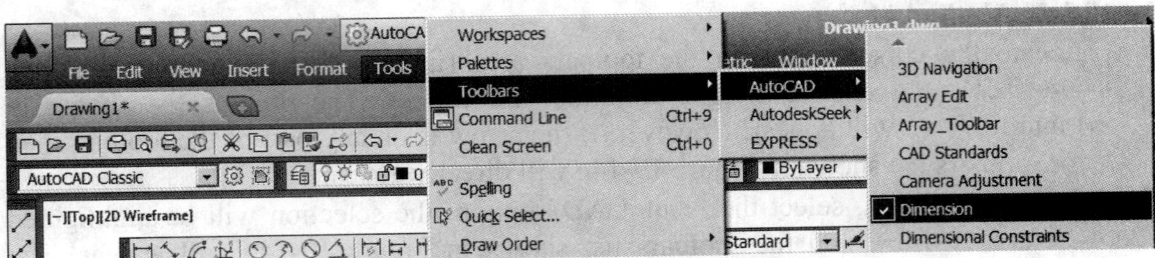

Figure 19-14f

19.10.2.   Move a toolbar

A toolbar can be moved from its default or current location to a new location as follow. This section will use the *Dimensions* toolbar added earlier.

- Select a toolbar by placing the cursor on either end of the toolbar.
- Press and hold down the left button of the mouse.
- Keep holding down the left button and move the cursor to the desired location.
- A light gray broken-line box will appear at the new location, Figure 19-15.
- Release the left button of the mouse and the gray box will be replaced by the toolbar.

Figure 19-15

19.10.3.   Reshape a toolbar

A toolbar can be reshaped as follow. This section will use the *Dimensions* toolbar added in the previous section.

- Place the cursor arrow on any of the four edges of the toolbar. For the horizontal bars only top and bottom edges can be used. For the vertical bars only left and right edges can be used.
- A double headed arrow will appear on the edge. For the top and bottom edges the arrow will be vertical ($\updownarrow$); and for the left and right edges it will be horizontal ($\leftrightarrow$).
- Press and hold down the left button of the mouse, and a light gray dotted-line box will appear around the edge of the toolbar.
- Keep holding down the left button, move the mouse around, and watch how the gray box changes its shape, Figure 19-16a.
- Release the left button when the toolbar is vertical (or of the desired shape).
- A reshaped toolbar will appear as shown in Figure 19-16b.

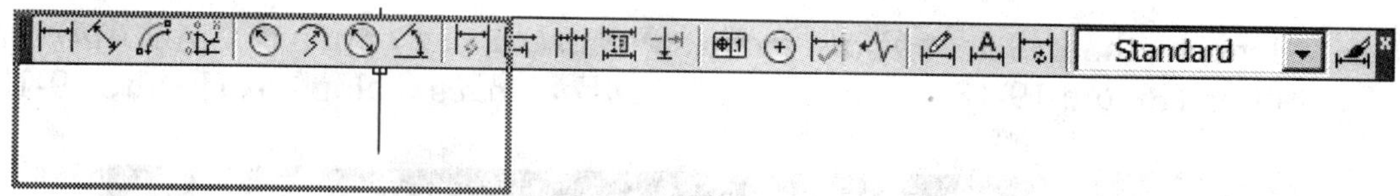

Figure 19-16a

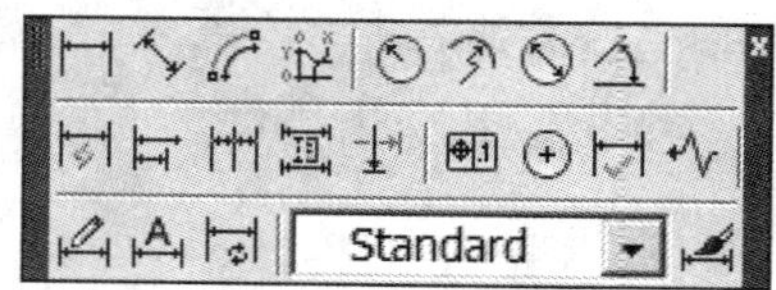

Figure 19-16b

19.10.4.   Remove a toolbar from the workspace
A toolbar can be removed from the workspace using one of the two following methods.

- Click on the "X" at the upper right corner of the toolbar, Figure 19-17.
- Open the option box of Figure 19-14d and click on the name of the toolbar (it must have a check mark in front of it).

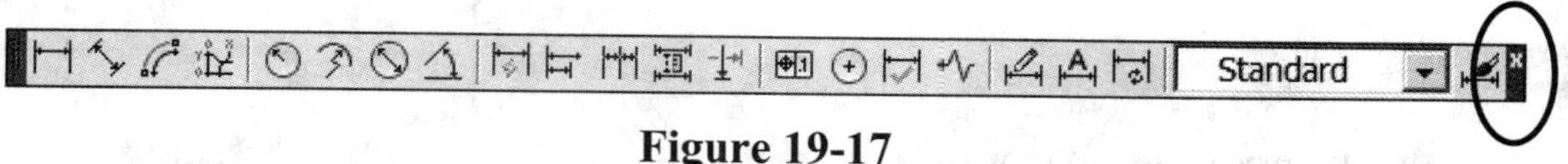

Figure 19-17

19.11.   Workspace
The collection of the drawing area, cursor, World coordinate system, viewcube, drawing display format, scroll bars, pull down menus, command line, status bar, toolbars, and dockable windows is known as workspace. The set of toolbars and menus used in 2D and 3D drawings are different. Hence, to increase the efficiency and productivity, a user can customize the workspace according to the project at hand.

19.11.1.   Save a workspace
A workspace can be saved as follow.
- Open the *Save Workspace* dialog box using toolbar or menu method
  - Toolbar method: Press the down arrow (⏷) on the right side of the *Workspace* toolbar and click on the *Save Current As* option, Figure 19-18a, to open the *Save Workspace* dialog box, Figure 19-18b.

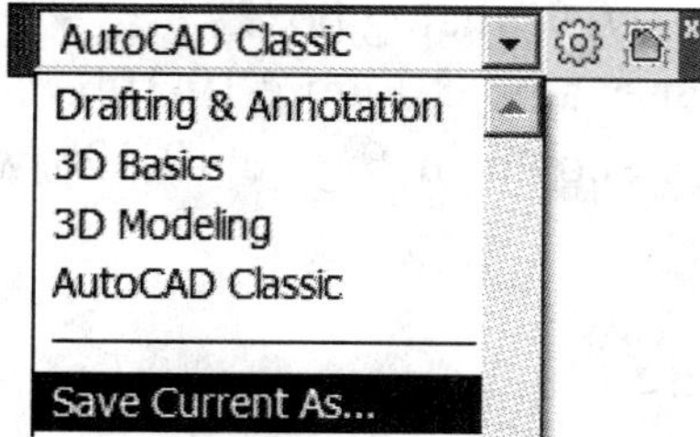

Figure 19-18a

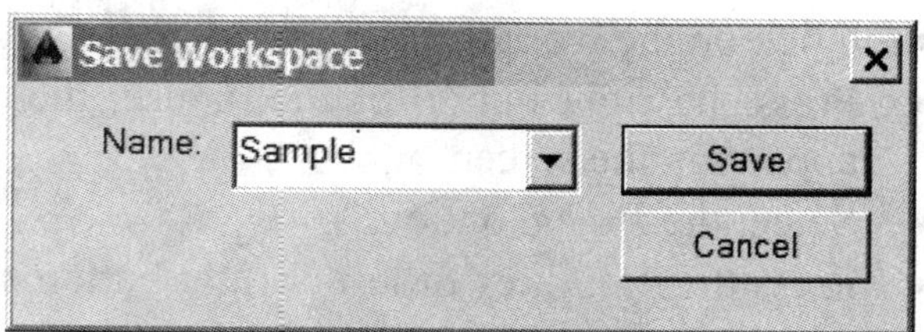

Figure 19-18b

o Menu method: Select *Tools* menu → *Workspaces* option→ *Save Current As* option (Figure 19-18c) to open the *Save Workspace* dialog box (Figure 19-18b).

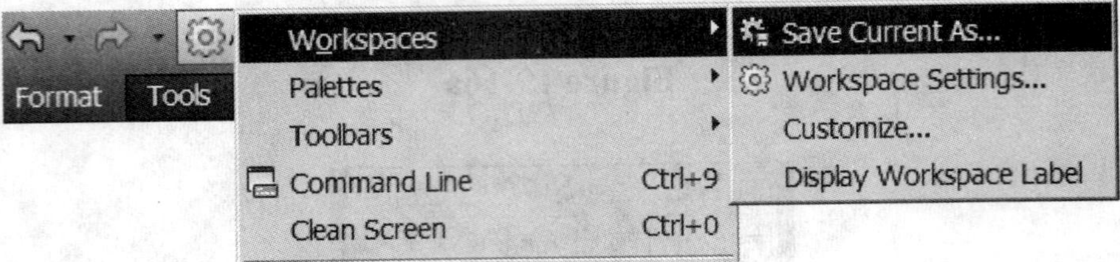

Figure 19-18c

- Specify the name for the workspace and press the *Save* button. The example workspace is saved as *Sample*.
- If a workspace exists with the specified name, then *AutoCAD* warning dialog box will appear, Figure 19-18d. Select *Replace* or *Cancel* as desired.
- The new workspace will appear in the listing of the workspaces, Figure 19-18e.

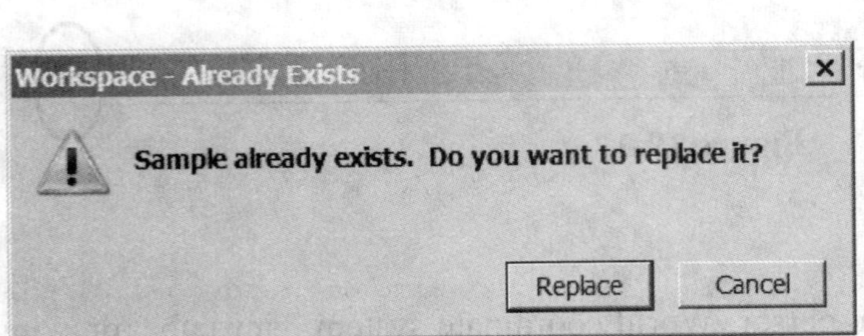

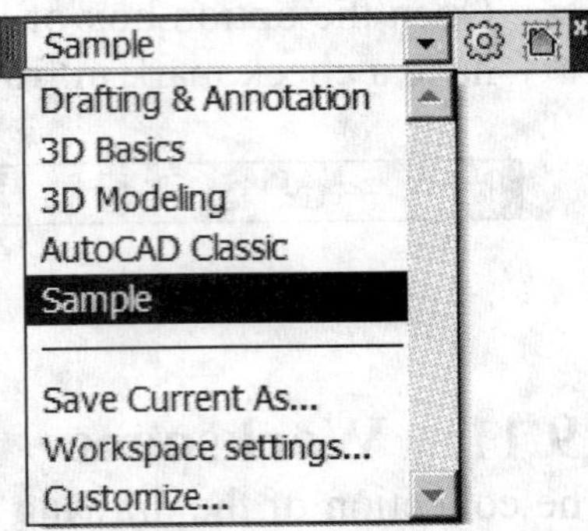

Figure 19-18d   **Figure 19-18e**

19.11.2.   Delete a workspace

A workspace can be deleted as follows.

- Open the *Customize User Interface* dialog box using toolbar or menu method
  - o Toolbar method: Press the down arrow (⯆) on the right side of the *Workspace* toolbar and click on the *Customize* option (Figure 19-19a) to open the *Customize User Interface* dialog box, Figure 19-19b.
  - o Menu method: Select *Tools* menu → *Workspaces* option→ *Customize* option to open the *Customize User Interface* dialog box, Figure 19-19b.
- Click on the *Customize* tab of the *Customize User Interface* dialog box.
- Click on the workspace to be deleted, 'Sample' in our example, Figure 19-19b.
- Press the right button of the mouse, the option box shown in Figure 19-19b will appear on the screen.
- Select the *Delete* option.
- Press the *Enter* key or left or right button of the mouse.

- This will close the option box and open the *AutoCAD* error message box, click the *Yes* button.
- This will close the *AutoCAD* error message box and activate the *Apply* button of the *Customize User Interface* dialog box.
- Click the *Apply* or *OK* button.
- The *Apply* button will NOT close the *Customize User Interface* dialog box but will make the delete operation permanent.
- The *OK* button will close the *Customize User Interface* dialog box as well as make the delete operation permanent.

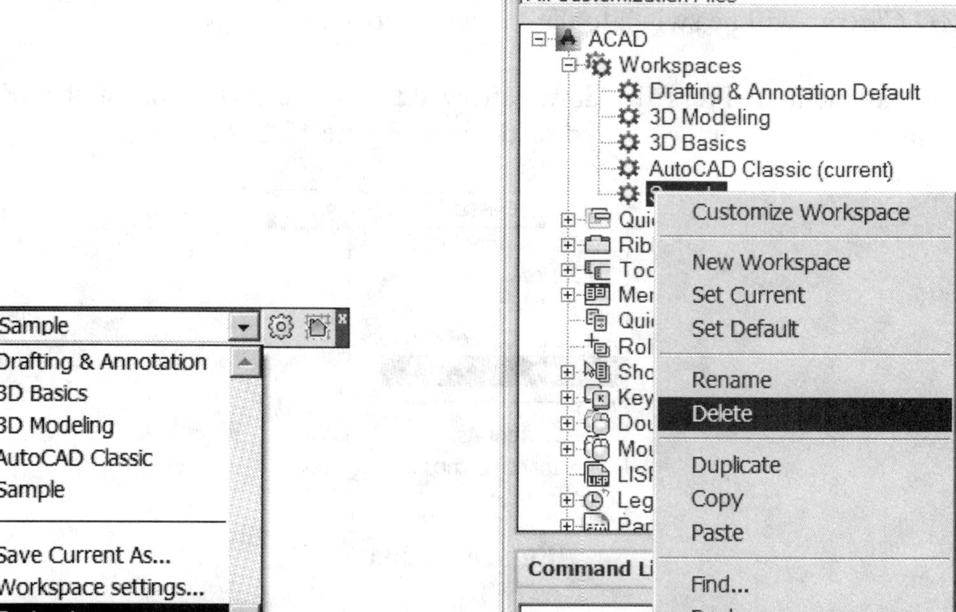

Figure 19-19a　　　　　　　　　　**Figure 19-19b**

19.11.3.　　Rename a workspace

A workspace can be renamed as follows.

- Open the *Customize User Interface* dialog box using toolbar or menu method
  - Toolbar method: Press the down arrow (⏷) on the right side of the *Workspace* toolbar and click on the *Customize* option (Figure 19-19a) to open the *Customize User Interface* dialog box, Figure 19-19b.
  - Menu method: Select *Tools* menu → *Workspaces* option → *Customize* option to open the *Customize User Interface* dialog box, Figure 19-19b.
- Click on the *Customize* tab of the *Customize User Interface* dialog box.
- Click on the workspace to be renamed, Sample in our example.

- Press the right button of the mouse, the option box shown in Figure 19-19b will appear on the screen.
- Select the *rename* option.
- This will close the option box and the name (to be changed) will be highlighted.
- Enter the new name and click anywhere on the screen. This will activate the *Apply* button.
- Click the *Apply* or *OK* button.
- The *Apply* button will NOT close the *Customize User Interface* dialog box but will make the delete operation permanent.
- The *OK* button will close the *Customize User Interface* dialog box as well as make the delete operation permanent.

19.11.4.　　Switch a workspace

A workspace can be switched as follows. In this example, the current workspace, *AutoCAD Classic*, will be switch to the '*Sample*' workspace.

- Toolbar method: Press the down arrow (▾) on the right side of the *Workspace* toolbar and click on the desired workspace, Figure 19-20a.

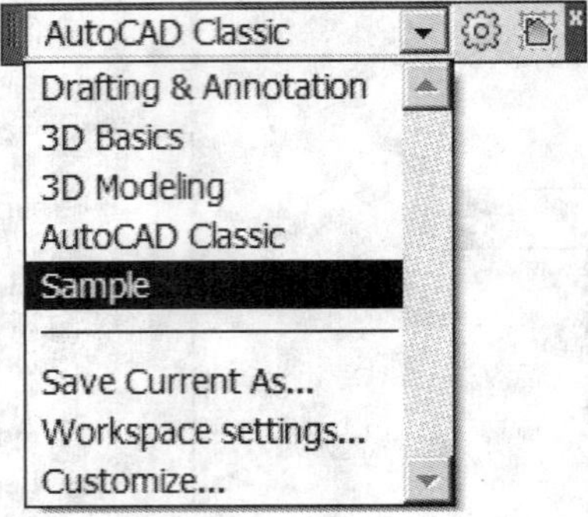

Figure 19-20a

- Menu method: Select the *Tools* menu and select the *Workspaces* option and click on the desired workspace, Figure 19-20b.

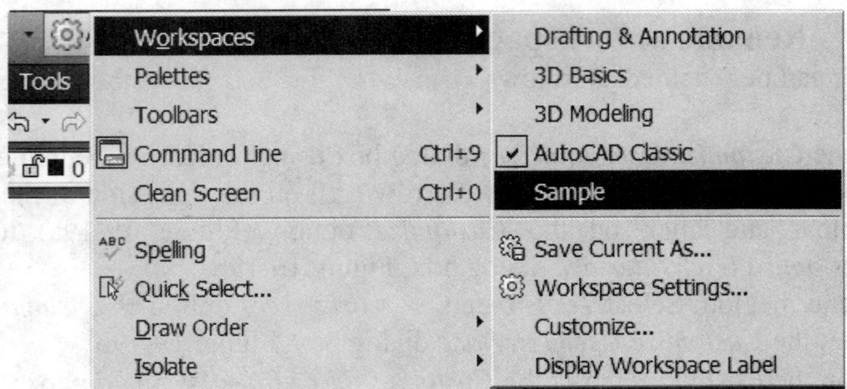

Figure 19-20b

19.12.   File manipulation

19.12.1.   New drawing file 
In AutoCAD, a new drawing can be opened using toolbar or menu method as follow.

1. Toolbar method: Select the *QNEW*, a new drawing tool (⧉) in the standard toolbar, Figure 19-21a
2. Menu method: Select the *File* pull-down menu and then select *NEW*, Figure 19-21b.

The method discussed above will open the *Select template* dialog box. For further details refer to Chapter #2.

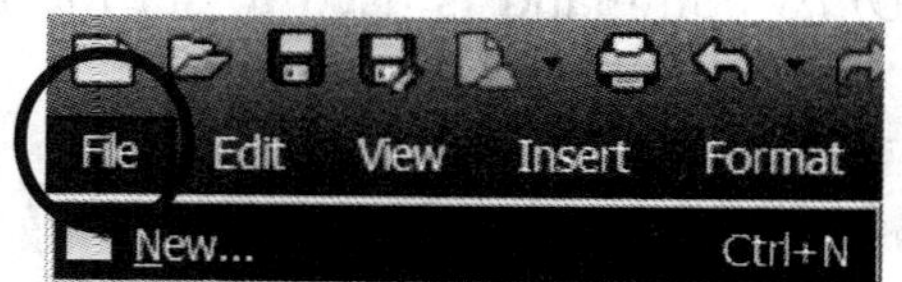

Figure 19-21a   **Figure 19-21b**

19.12.2.   Save a file
In AutoCAD, a file can be saved using the *Save As* or *Save* command.

19.12.2.1. Save As
A newly created file can be saved using the *Save As* command. Activate the command from the *File* menu and follow the prompts.

1. Menu method: Select the *File* dropdown menu and then select the *Save As* option.

19.12.2.2. Save
The *Save* command is also called a quick save. It is mainly used to save previously saved files. Activate the *Save* command using one of the following procedures and follow the prompts.

1. Toolbar method: Press the save (⊞) tool on the *Standard* toolbar.
2. Menu method: Select the *File* dropdown menu and then select the *Save* option.

19.12.3.   Open a pre-existing file
In AutoCAD, a pre-existing file can be opened using the *Open* command. The *Open* command is activated using one of the following procedures. Activate the command and follow the prompts.

1. Toolbar method: Press the open (⧉) tool on the *Standard* toolbar.
2. Menu method: Select the *File* dropdown menu and then select the *Open* option.

19.12.4.   Close a file

In AutoCAD, an open file can be closed via *Close* command. The command is activated using one of the following procedures. Activate the command from the *File* menu and follow the prompts.

1. Menu method: Select the *File* dropdown menu and then select the *Close* option.

19.12.5.   Drawing units

As the name suggests, the drawing units is used to set the input format of the dimensions of the objects to create the drawing; that is, specify the style of the input values. For example, the efficiency of the drafter can be increased if the lengths could be specified in architectural units for drawing a floor plan.

The *Units* command is used to set the input units. The *Units* command can be activated using the menu method.

1. Menu method: Select the *Format* dropdown menu and then select the *Units* option, as shown in Figure 19-22a.

The *Units* command will open the *Drawing Units* dialog box. For further details refer to Chapter #2.

19.12.6.   Drawing limits

Generally, the *drawing limits* is the metaphor for the size of the paper on which the drawing will be printed. It is used to set the boundaries of the drawing or grid display in the current *Model* or *Layout* tab. Generally, limits are set to match the size of the paper (on which the drawing will be printed).

Activate the *Drawing Limits* command using menu method as follow.

1. Menu method: Select the *Format* pull-down menu and then select the *Drawing Limits* option, Figure 19-23b.

The method discussed above will open the *Select template* dialog box. For further details refer to Chapter #2.

19.12.7.   Grid and Snap

The grid and snap properties can be set using the *Drafting Setting* dialog box. The *Drafting Setting* dialog box can be open from the *Tool* pull down menu and then selecting the *Drafting Settings* option. This will open the *Drafting Setting* dialog box. For further details refer to Chapter #2.

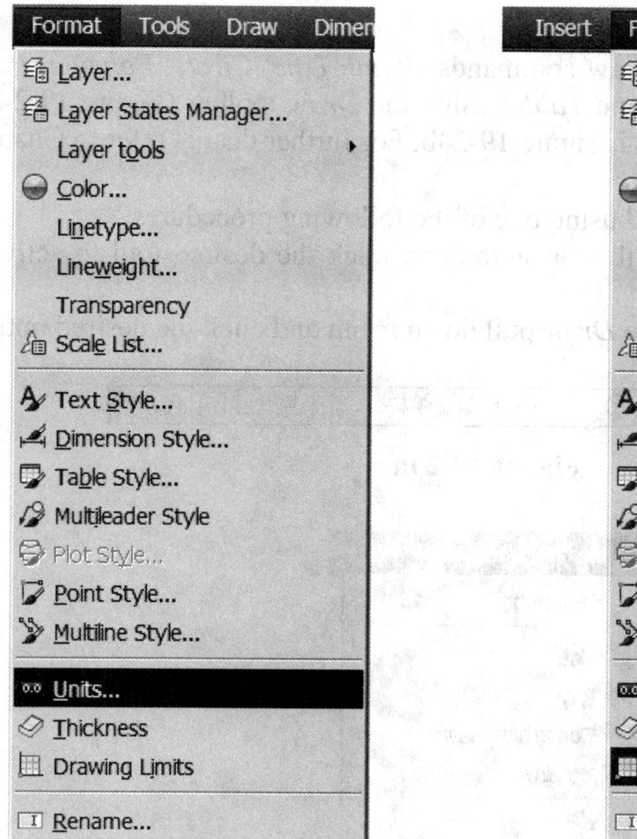

Figure 19-22

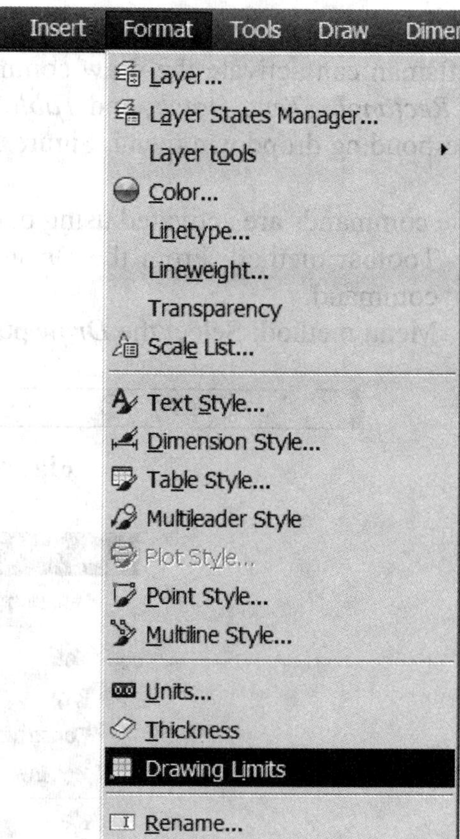

Figure 19-23

19.12.8.   Plot

The *Plot* command is used to output a drawing file. The *Plot* command is activated using one of the following procedures. Activate the command. For further details refer to Chapter #2.

1. Toolbar method: Select the *Plot* tool (⊟) from the *Standard* toolbar.
2. Menu method: Select the *File* dropdown menu and then select the *Plot* option.

19.13.   Exit AutoCAD

The *Exit* command is used to close AutoCAD; it can be activated as follow. Activate the command. For further details refer to Chapter #2.

1. Menu method: Select the *File* dropdown menu and then select the *Exit* option.

19.14.   Basics of 2-Dimensional Drawings

A drafter can create unlimited design by creating new drawings and editing previously drawn drawing. The focus of this section is the AutoCAD capabilities to draw basic 2D objects and change their appearances using the toolbar and the dropdown menu.

19.14.1.   The draw commands

The draftsman can activate the draw commands (*Point, Line, Circle, Polygon, Polyline, Ellipse, Rectangle, Text, Hatch,* and *Table*) using the *Draw* toolbar (Figure 19-24a) and the corresponding dropdown menu, Figure 19-24b. For further details refer to Chapter #3.

- The commands are activated using one of the following procedures.
  1. Toolbar method: From the *Draw* toolbar, click the desired tool to activate the command.
  2. Menu method: Select the *Draw* pull down menu and click the desired option.

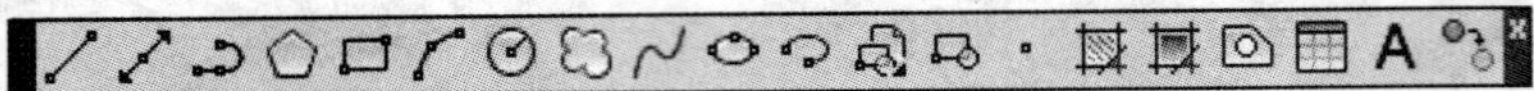

Figure 19-24a

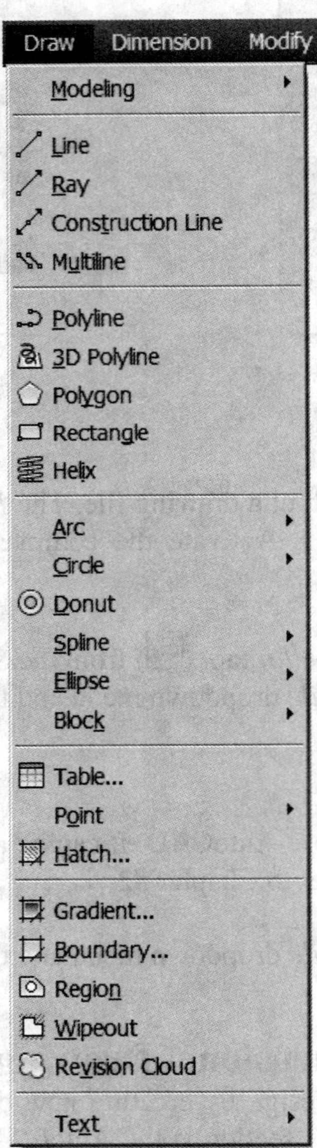

Figure 19-24b

19.14.2.   Object appearance

To make a drawing easily readable, usage of different line style and/or line thickness visually distinguish objects from one another. In order to change the appearance of an object, add the *Properties* toolbar to the workspace. Figure 19-25. Although, the figure shows the multiple selections simultaneously, however, the software provides one selection at a time.

The Figure 19-25 shows the available options under the three controls. It is cleared from the figure that by default all the possible lineweight, some of the colors, and only one linetype is available. The user can load the desired linetype before using it.

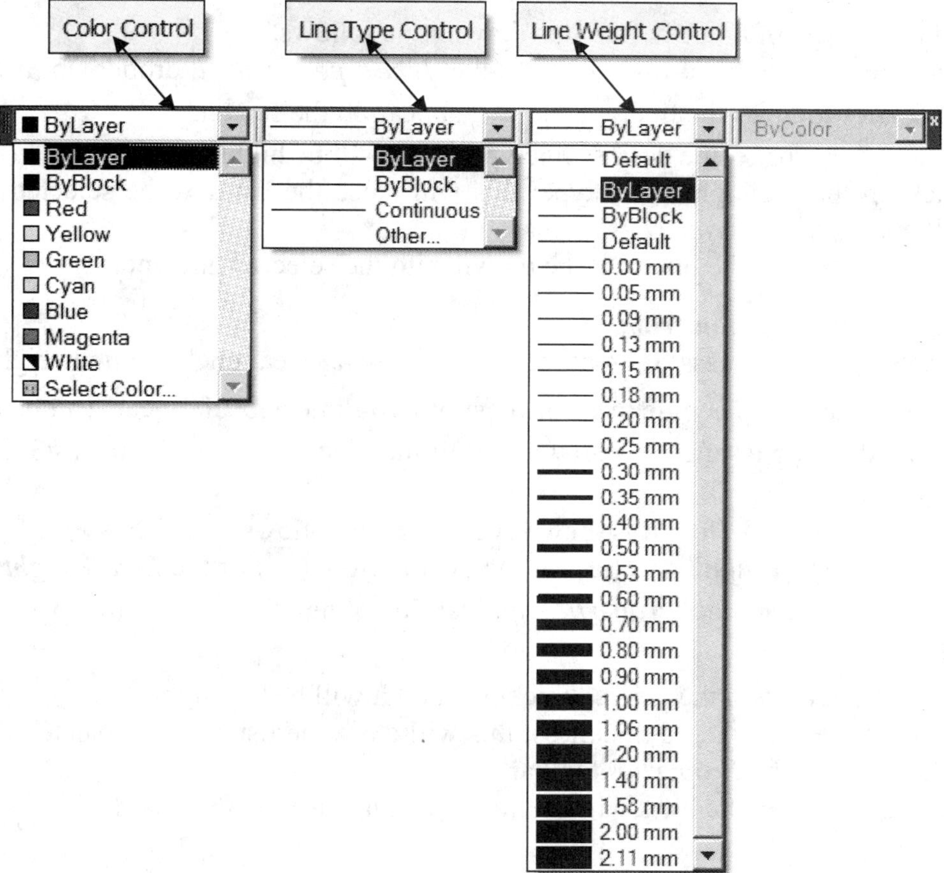

Figure 19-25

19.14.2.1. Color Control

The color of most of two-dimensional objects can be changed either before drawing or after it is drawn. The color of a line before it is drawn is changed as follows. For further details refer to Chapter #3.

1. In the *Properties* toolbar, click on the down arrow (⊡) of the *Color Control*. A dropdown list in the *Properties* toolbar will appear on the screen, Figure 19-25.
2. Bring the cursor on the desired color and it will be highlighted.

3. Click on the highlighted color; this will close the list and the selected color will appear in the *Properties* toolbar.
4. Now draw a line, the lines will be drawn with the selected color.

19.14.2.2. Linetype Control

The line style (linetype) of most of two-dimensional objects can be changed either before drawing or after it is drawn. However, the user needs to load the desired linetype before using it. Load the desired linetype as follow: (i) From the *Format* pull down menu, select the *Linetype* option; this will open a *Linetype Manager* dialog box. (ii) In the *Linetype Manager* dialog box, click the *Load* button; this will open a *Load or Reload Linetypes* dialog box. (iii) For further details refer to Chapter #3.

Change the linetype of a line before it is drawn is as follows.
1. Click on the down arrow (⊡) of the *LineType Control* dropdown list in the *Properties* toolbar; the linetype list will appear on the screen.
2. Bring the cursor on the desired linetype and it will be highlighted.
3. Click on the highlighted linetype; this will close the list and the selected linetype will appear in the *Properties* toolbar.
4. Now draw a line, the lines will be drawn with the selected linetype.

19.14.2.3. Lineweight Control

In order to display thickness of an object in the drawing area, click the lineweight button (⊡) on the status bar. The thickness of most of two-dimensional objects can be changed either before drawing or after it is drawn. For further details refer to Chapter #3.

The thickness of a line before it is drawn is changed as follows.
5. In the *Properties* toolbar, click on the down arrow (⊡) of the *Line Weight Control* dropdown list in the *Properties* toolbar; the lineweight list will appear on the screen.
6. Bring the cursor on the desired thickness and it will be highlighted.
7. Click on the highlighted thickness; this will close the list and the selected thickness will appear in the *Properties* toolbar.
8. Now draw a line, the lines will be drawn with the desired thickness.

19.15.   Basics of 2-Dimensional Editing

A drafter can create unlimited design by creating new drawings and editing previously drawn drawings. The focus of this section is the AutoCAD capabilities to edit 2D objects.

19.15.1.   Grips

The size and color of the grip points can be changed from the *Options* dialog box. Click the *Tools* menu and select the *Options…* option. This will open the *Options* dialog box. In the *Options* dialog box, select the *Selection* tab. For further details refer to Chapter #4.

19.15.2.   Zoom capabilities

The zoom capabilities are used to change the magnification of the objects in the drawing. The user should add the zoom toolbar in the workspace, Figure 19-26. For further details refer to Chapter #4.

19.15.3.   Draw order

The draw order capabilities are used to change the relative position overlapping objects. The user can access the commands through the *Draw Order* toolbar, Figure 19-27. For further details refer to Chapter #4.

Figure 19-26   **Figure 19-27**

19.15.4.   Object Snap

The *Object Snap* command allows snapping at strategic points on the selected objects in the drawing area. Recall that the <u>*Snap* option</u> allows snapping to the <u>snap point points</u>. The *OSNAP* options are also available from the *Object Snap* toolbar, Figure 19-28.

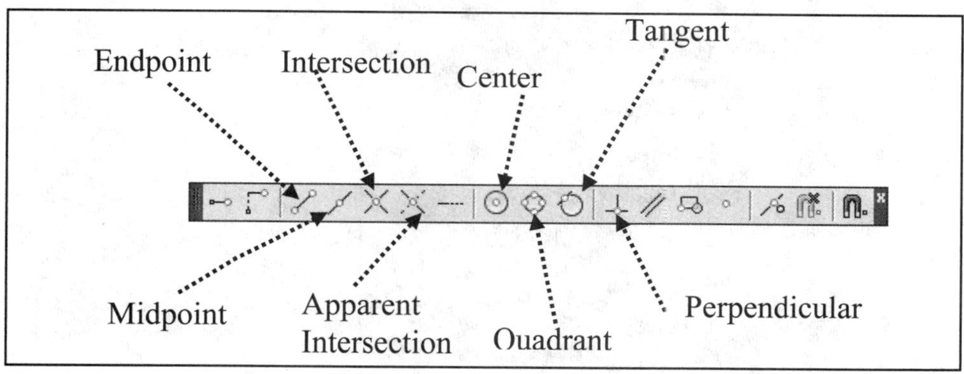

Figure 19-28

The *Object Snap* commands are activated by clicking on the tool in the *Object Snap* toolbar. However, the command's behavior is different depending where it was activated from; that is, through the dialog box or from the toolbar. *If the object snap command is activated by clicking the tool on the toolbar, then it will be effective only once. However, if the object snap command is activated by checking the box in the dialog box, then it will be effective as long as the box is checked.* **Therefore, for the multiple use, always activate the object snap commands from the dialog box**. For further details refer to Chapter #4.

19.15.5.   The edit commands

A drafter can create unlimited design by creating new drawings and editing previously drawn drawings. The focus of this section is the AutoCAD capabilities to edit basic 2D objects. The draftsman can activate the *Erase, Copy, Array, Mirror, Offset, Move, Rotate,*

Scale, Stretch, Break, Break at a point, Explode, Join, Fillet, Chamfer, Trim, and *Extend* commands using the *Modify* toolbar (Figure 19-29b) and *Modify* dropdown menu (Figure 19-29a); the *Rectangular Array, Polar Array,* and *Path Array* commands using the *Array* toolbar (Figure 19-29d); and *Edit Polyline* commands from the *Modify II* toolbar (Figure 19-29c).

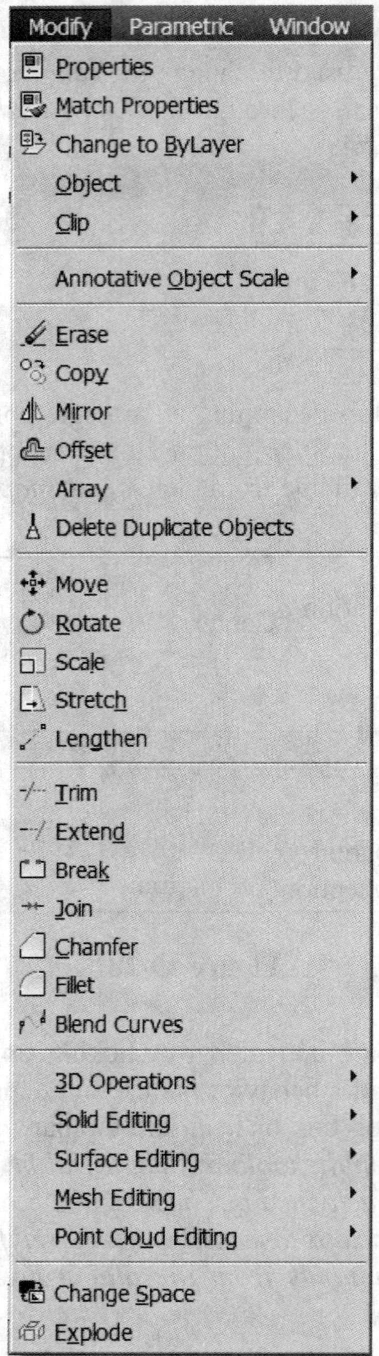

Figure 19-29a

Figure 19-29b

Figure 19-29c

Figure 19-29d

- The commands are activated using one of the following procedures.
  1. Toolbar method: From the *Draw* toolbar, click the desired tool to activate the command.
  2. Menu method: Select the *Draw* pull down menu and click the desired option.

- For further details refer to Chapter #4.

19.16.   Layers

The use of overlays provides a technique of managing, organizing, and controlling the visual layout of a drawing. In AutoCAD, an overlay is replaced by a layer.

The Layers are controlled by the layer properties manager button which is located on the layer toolbar, Figure 19-30. The tools on the toolbar are not the command tool, but the indicator of the status. For example, the light bulb shows that the selected layer is *On* (visible) or *Off* (hidden). The yellow and grey colors of the bulb represent that the layer is *On* or *Off*, respectively.

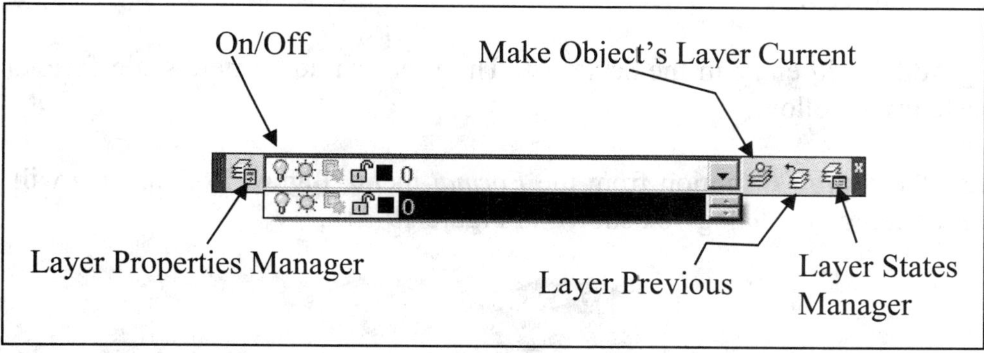

Figure 19-30

The *Layer* command is used to create new layers and modify the existing layers.
- The *Layer* command is activated using one of the following procedures.
  1. Toolbar method: From the *Layers* toolbar click on the *Layer Properties Manager* tool.
  2. Menu method: Select the *Format* dropdown menu and then select the *Layers* option.

- For further details refer to Chapter #5.

19.17.   Blocks

In AutoCAD, block is a general term for one or more objects that are combined to create a single entity. If an object (or group of objects) is used frequently, then time can be saved if the object is created once and inserted as many time as needed in the same or a different drawing.

- A block can be created using the *Make Block* command and the command is activated using one of the following procedures.
  1. Toolbar method: From the *Draw* toolbar select the *Make Block* tool.
  2. Menu method: Select the *Draw* dropdown menu, select the *Block* option, and finally select the *Make* option.

- A block can be inserted using the *Insert Block* command and the command is activated using one of the following procedures.

  1. Toolbar method: From the *Draw* toolbar select the *Insert Block* tool.
  2. Menu method: Select the *Insert* dropdown menu and then select the *Block* option.

- For further details refer to Chapter #6.

19.18.   Add an entry in the scale list

A situation may arise when the user need to use a scale factor not available in the default scale list of AutoCAD.

Example: Add *1:120* entry in the scale list. The user can add a new scale factor in the default scale list as follow.

- Select the *Scale List* option from the *Format* menu, Figure 19-31a. This will open the *Edit Scale List* dialog box shown in Figure 19-31b.

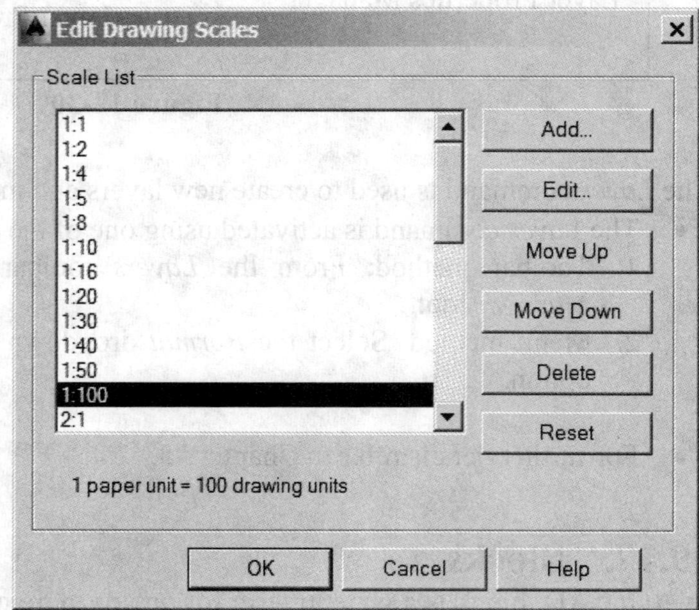

Figure 19-31a   **Figure 31b**

- Select the *Scale List* option from the *Format* menu, Figure 19-31a. This will open the *Edit Scale List* dialog box shown in Figure 19-31b.
- Select the entry labeled as 1:100. This will help in the addition of the new entry at its correct location. (1:120 should be after 1:100.)
- Click the *Add* button of the *Edit Scale List* dialog box. This will open the *Add Scale* dialog box.
- For further details refer to Chapter #7.

19.19.   Dimensioning Techniques

A dimension describes the size and location of the feature of an object. Hence, it is given in the form of a distance, an angle, or a note, irrespective of the type of the drawing and units used in the drawing. To achieve these functionalities, AutoCAD add the dimension to a drawing. The draftsman can activate the dimension commands (*Linear*, *Aligned*, *Angular*, *Radius*, *Diameter*, *Continue*, *Baseline*, *Ordinate*, *Center Mark*, and *Dimension Style*) using the *Dimension* toolbar (Figure 19-32b) and the corresponding dropdown menu, Figure 19-32a. For further details refer to Chapter #8.

- The commands are activated using one of the following procedures.
  1. Toolbar method: From the *Dimension* toolbar, click the desired tool to activate the command.
  2. Menu method: Select the *Dimension* pull down menu and click the desired option.

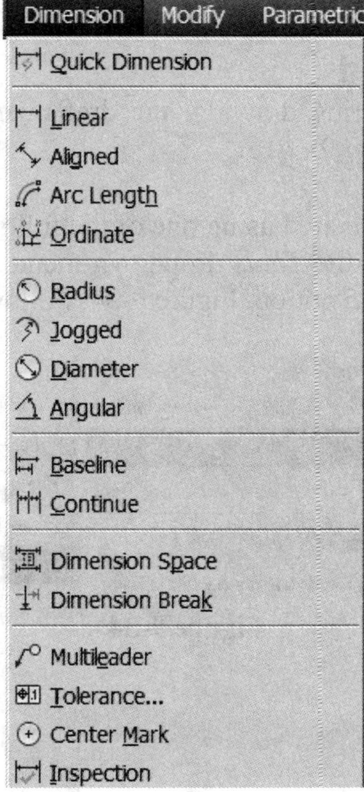

Figure 19-32a

Figure 19-32b

19.20. Drawing units

In an architectural or engineering drawing, the draftsman must set the format of input units. The units can be set as follow:

1. From the *Format* menu select the *Units* option. This will open the *Drawing Units* dialog box. From the dialog box under the length panel, select the *Engineering* units, Figure 9.33a, or select the *Architectural* units, Figure 9.33b. For further details refer to Chapters #9 - #15.

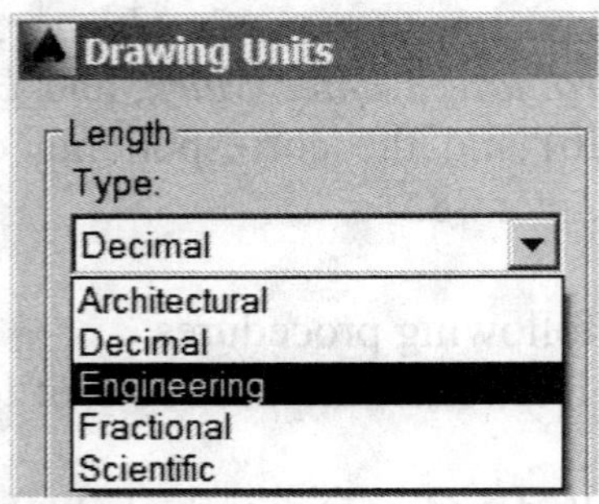

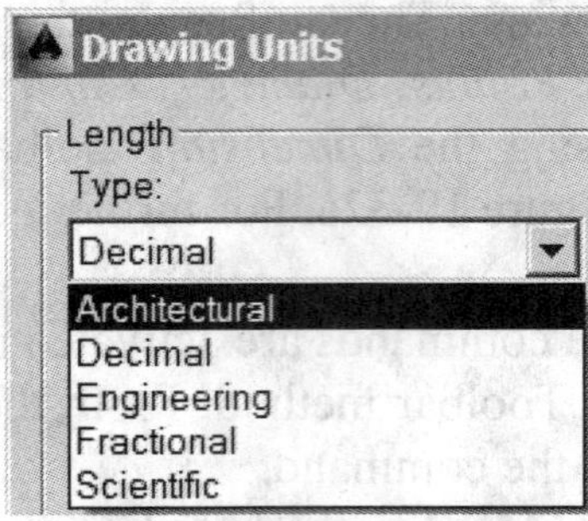

Figure 9-33a   **Figure 9-33b**

19.21. Area command

In an architectural or engineering drawing, the draftsman needs to find the area. For further details refer to Chapters #9 - #15.

- The *Area* command is activated using one of the following procedures.
  1. Menu method: Select the *Tools* dropdown menu, select the *Inquiry* option, and finally choose the *Area* option, Figure 9-34. Follow the prompts.

Figure 9-34

20. Suggested In-Class Activities

20.1.   Introduction

This chapter provides in-class activities (or ICAs). Every ICA begins with its objectives. The next is the hints section (that refers to the corresponding chapter in the text) followed by the ICA description. Finally, the ICA describes the submission method. The ICAs will be submitted using one of the following three methods.
- Students will show the complete drawing in class.
- Student will submit the print from the model space making sure that linetype and lineweight are clearly visible.
- Student will submit the print from the layout making sure that linetype and lineweight are clearly visible. The students will also be asked to scale the drawings.

For some of the initial ICAs, step-by-step instructions to complete the drawing are also given. If an ICA uses a drawing created in one of the previous ICAs or a figure from the text, then a small size (dimensions and text may not be visible) figure is shown at the end of ICA in question. Therefore, students should check the corresponding chapter for the details.

** The user should save the drawing at various stages of the development process.

General Information
- Based on the topic of the ICA, follow the instruction from the corresponding chapter of the book.
- Use the *Erase* command or *Delete* button on the keyboard.
- If need to draw horizontal or vertical line turn *On* the ORTHO option from the status bar.
- If necessary, turn *On/Off* object snap.
- If necessary, show/hide lineweight option.
- If necessary, create layers and manipulate layers in model space and layouts.
- The draftsman may need to change the linetype scale from the *Properties* sheet. Linetype scale depends on the size of the drawing, zooming factor, and drawing environment (model space or layout), and lineweight.
- The lineweight of 0.3mm will create reasonably thick line in the model space. However, in a layout, the same effect will be created by the lineweight of 0.7mm.

20.2. Download AutoCAD 2014

Objectives

- Learn to download AutoCAD 2014
- Get familiar with AutoCAD 2014
- General information about ICAs

Hints

- Refer to Chapter #2 for help

ICA Description

1. Download AutoCAD 2014.
2. Start AutoCAD 2014.
3. If you have provided the licenses number correctly, you should be able to perform step 2, otherwise, take necessary steps to fix the problem.

ICA Submission

1. Launch AutoCAD 2014 in class.
2. Show the default workspace in class to the instructor or TA.

20.3.   Customize a Workspace

Objectives
- Learn to customize and save a workspace

Hints
- Refer to Chapter #2 (ribbon interface) or Chapter #19 (classics interface) for help

ICA Description
1. AutoCAD ribbon users: Create and save the workspace shown in Figure 20-3a.
2. AutoCAD classics users: Create and save the workspace shown in Figure 20-3b.
3. Do not add text boxes or arrows.

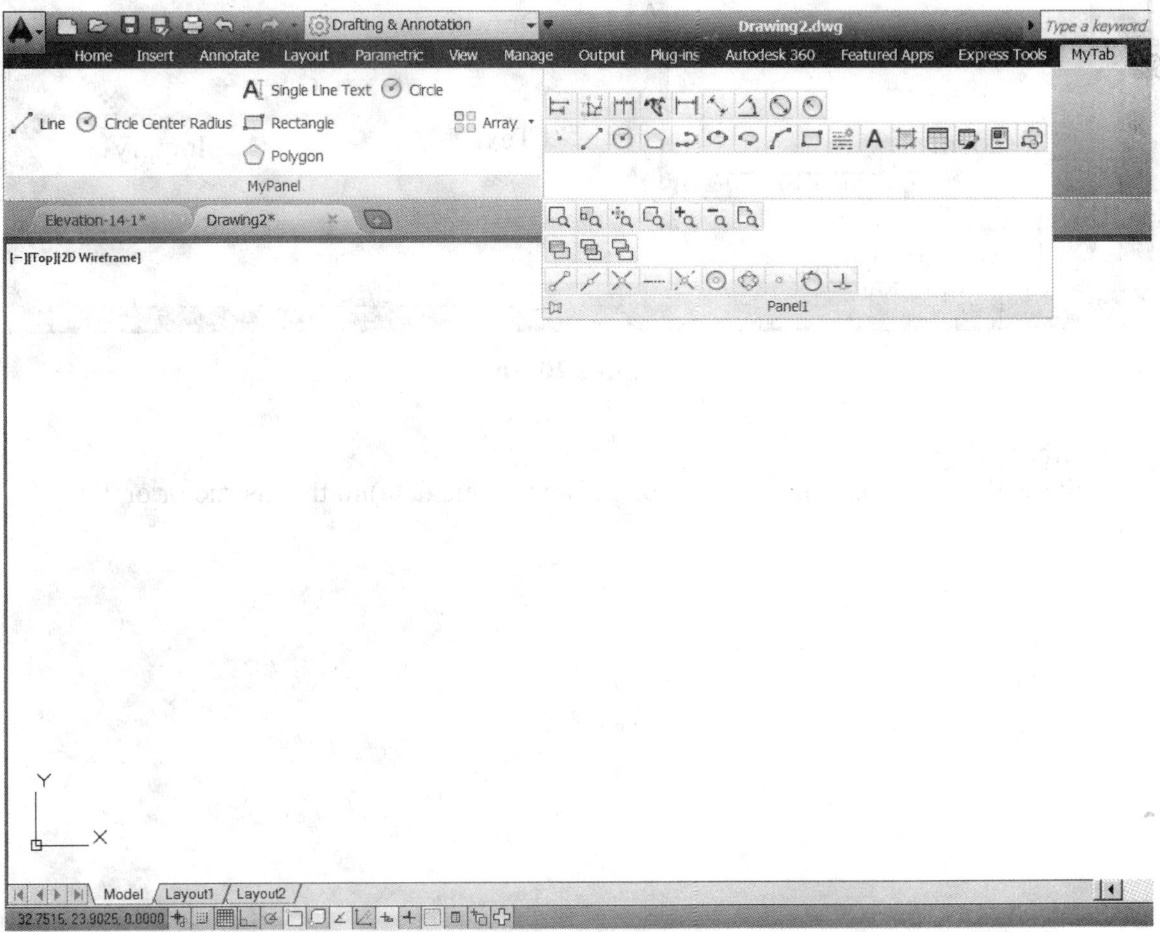

Figure 20-3a

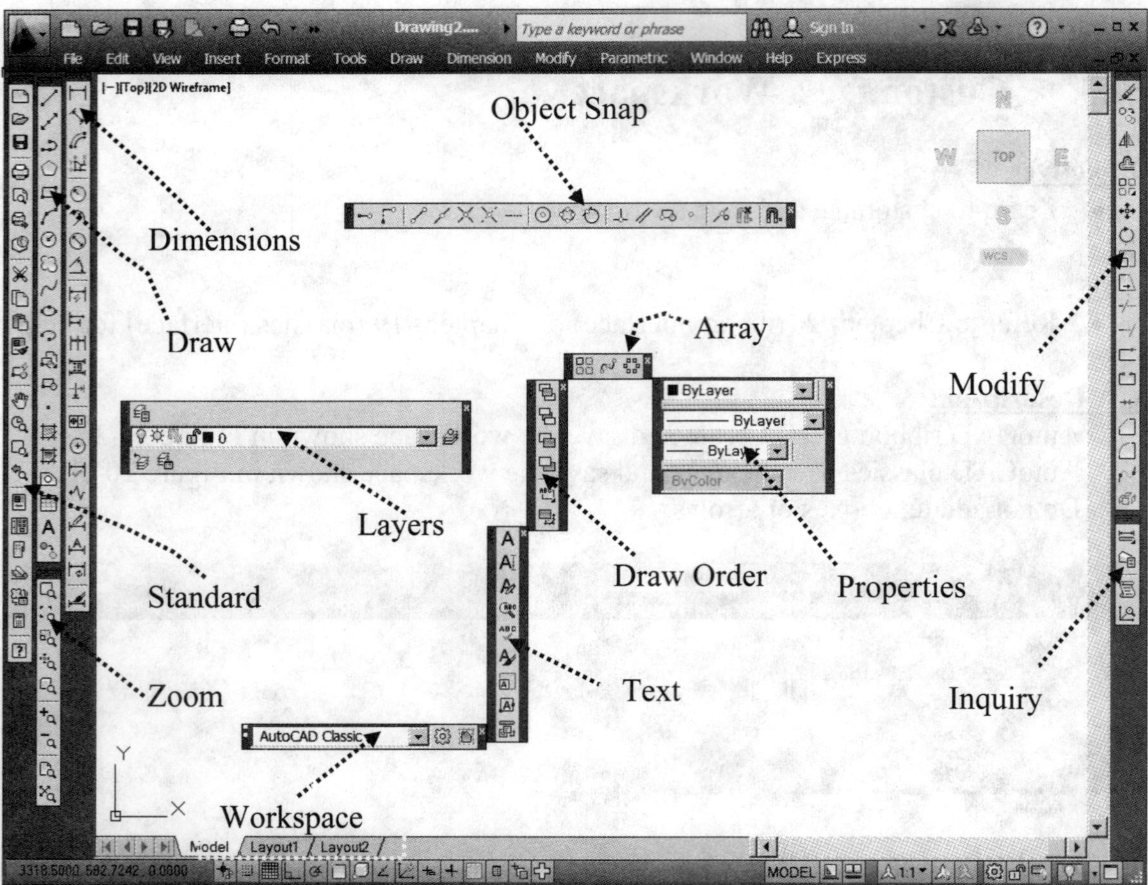

Figure 20-3b

ICA Submission

1. Show the workspace in class (on or before the due date) to the instructor or TA.

20.4.   Grid and Snap Capabilities

<u>Objectives</u>
- How to set and use grid and snap capabilities

<u>Hints</u>
- Refer to Chapter #2 for help

<u>ICA Description</u>
1. <u>Drawing units</u>: Millimeters   <u>Input format</u>:   Decimal units
   <u>Drawing limits</u>: 420, 430   <u>Grid</u>: 10   <u>Snap</u>: 5
   - a. Use the grid created above to create the drawings shown in Figure 20-4.
   - b. Also, save the drawings.

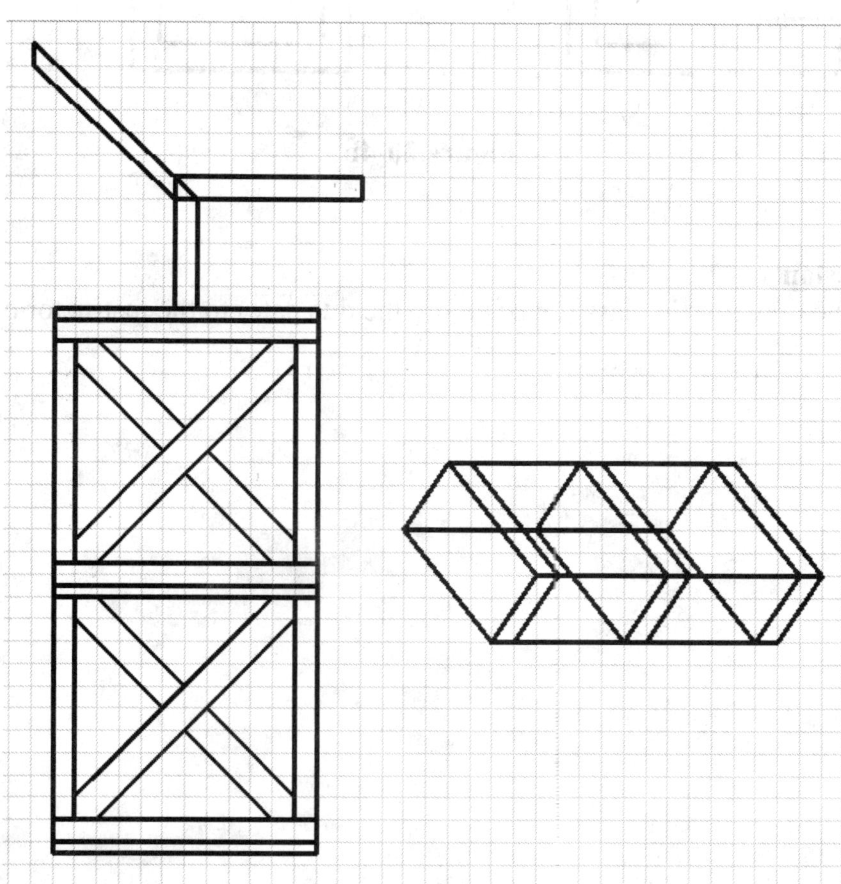

Figure 20-4a

2. <u>Drawing units</u>: Inches   <u>Input format</u>:   Decimal units
    <u>Drawing limits</u>: The user should select reasonable values for the drawing limits, grid, and snap.

      a. Create the drawings shown in Figure 20-4b.
      b. Also, save the drawings.

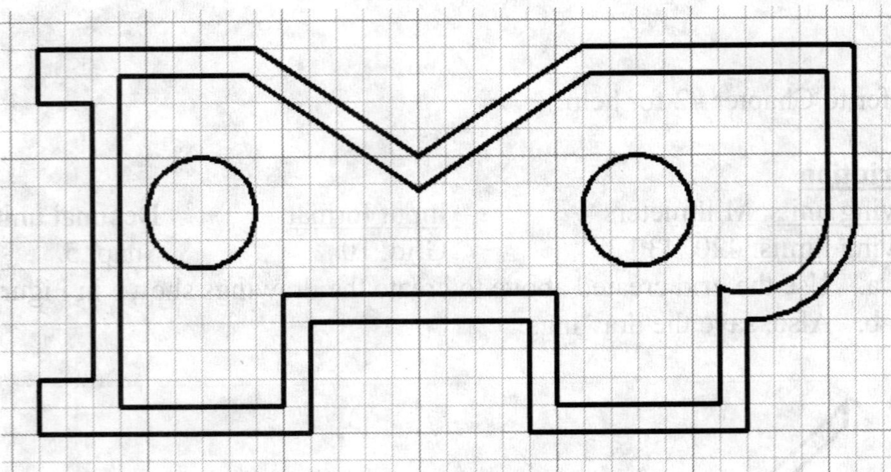

Figure 20-4b

<u>ICA Submission</u>

1. Show the drawings in class (on or before the due date) to the instructor or TA.

20.5. Erase, Line, Polyline and Polyline Edit

Objectives

- Learn to use *Erase*, *Line*, *Polyline* and *Polyline Edit* commands

Hints

- Refer to Chapter #3 and Chapter #4 for help

ICA Description

1. <u>Drawing units</u>: <u>Inches</u>: Create and save the drawing shown in Figure 20-5a using *Line* command and absolute Cartesian coordinates.
   a. Save the drawing.
   b. Do not add labels to the drawing and do not create the table.

ABSOLUTE COORDINATES (INCHES)			
A	(0, 0)	I	(4.5, 9.5)
B	(0, 30)	J	(7.5, 12.5)
C	(22, 5)	K	(7.5, 20.5)
D	(22, 29)	L	(4.5, 17.5)
E	(6, 20)	M	(14.5, 11.5)
F	(16, 22)	N	(17.5, 14.5)
G	(6, 19)	O	(17.5, 22.5)
H	(16, 21)	P	(14.5, 19.5)

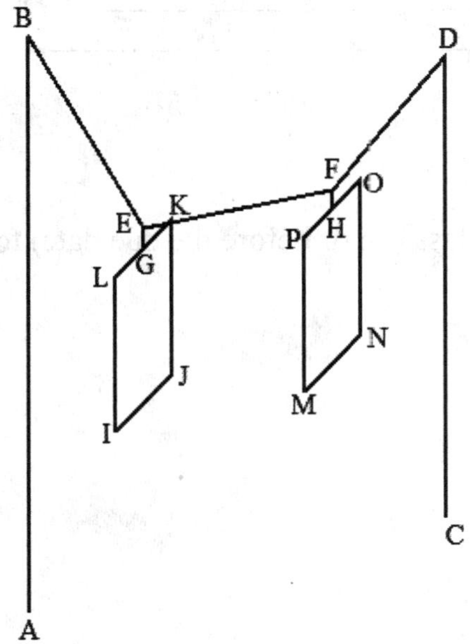

Figure 20-5a

2. <u>Drawing units</u>: <u>Inches</u>: Create and save the drawing shown in Figure 20-5b using *Line* and *Polyline* command and polar coordinates.
   a. Save the drawing.
   b. Do not add dimension.

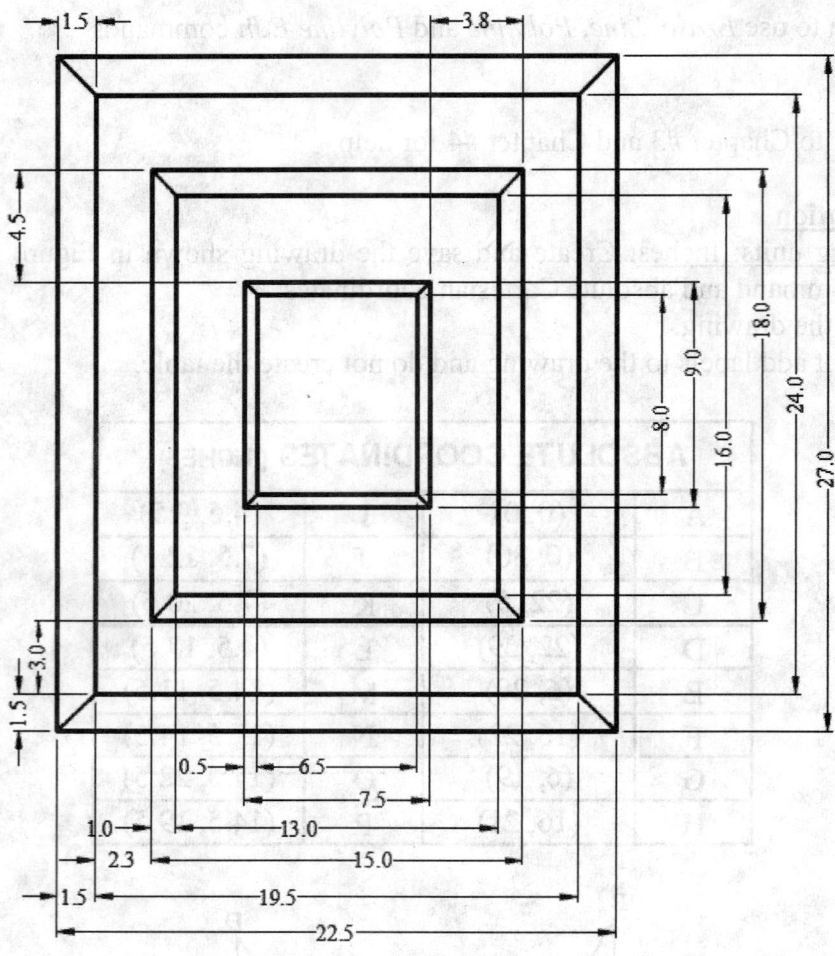

Figure 20-5b

<u>**ICA Submission**</u>
   1. Show the drawings in class (on or before the due date) to the instructor or TA.

20.6.   Point, Circle, Polygon, Offset, Move, Trim, Extend, and Zoom

Objectives
- Learn to use *Point, Circle (radius and ttr), Polygon, Offset, Move,* and *Trim* commands
- Learn to use *Zoom* capabilities

Hints
- Refer to Chapter #3 and Chapter #4 for help

ICA Description
1. <u>Drawing units</u>: <u>Millimeters</u>: Create the light bulb arrangement shown in Figure 20-6a using *Line* and *Point* commands.
   a. Save the drawing.
   b. Do not add dimension.

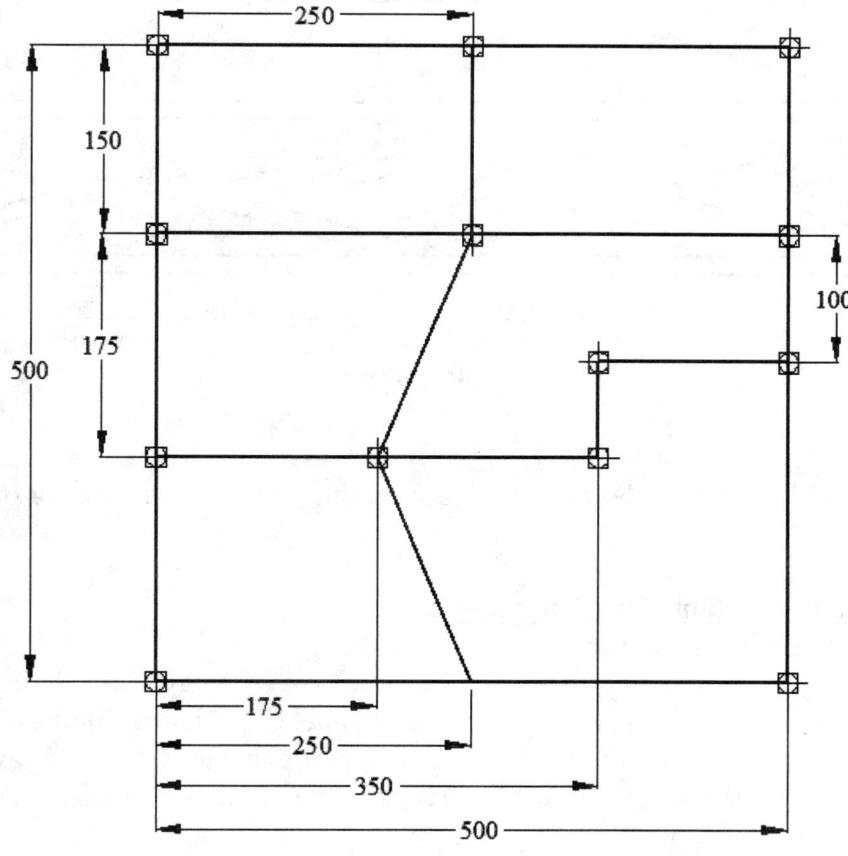

Figure 20-6a

2. <u>Drawing units:</u> <u>Inches:</u> Create and save the drawing shown in Figure 20-6b using *Line*, *Polyline*, *Polygon*, *Circle*, *Offset*, and *Trim* commands.
   a. Save the drawing.
   b. Do not add dimension.
   c. Follow the step-by-step instruction.

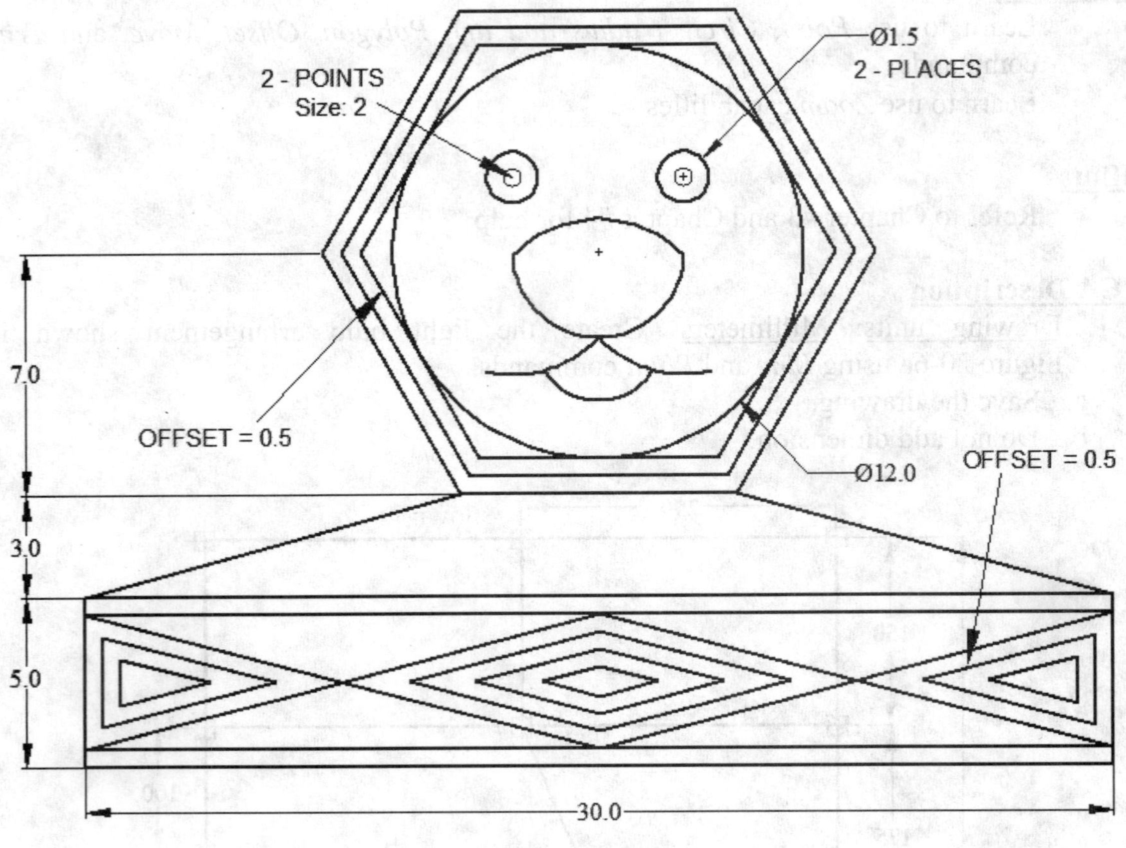

Figure 20-6b

ICA Submission
1. Show the drawings in class (on or before the due date) to the instructor or TA.

Step-by-Step instructions for Figure 20-6b
1. Open an *acad* template file.

2. Draw the circles (ϕ is the symbol of 'diameter'), Figure 20-6ba. (i) Draw a horizontal line of length 5.0. (ii) Draw circles of diameter 1.5. (iii) Draw the circle of diameter 5.0 using TTR option. (iv) Using the center of diameter 5.0, draw another circle of diameter 12.0.

3. Draw circles shown in Figure 20-6bb to Figure 20-6bd. The new circle in the figures is selected to display the grip points. These grip point will help in locating the center of a circle.

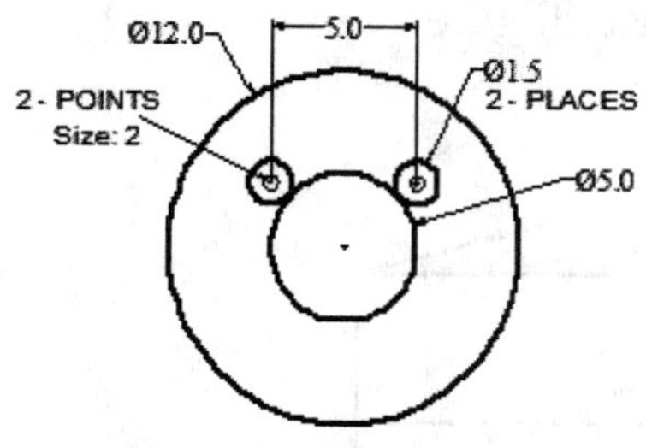

Figure 20-6ba

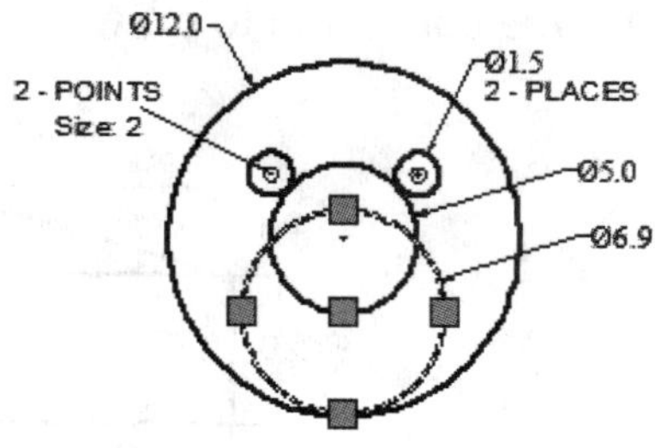

Figure 20-6bb

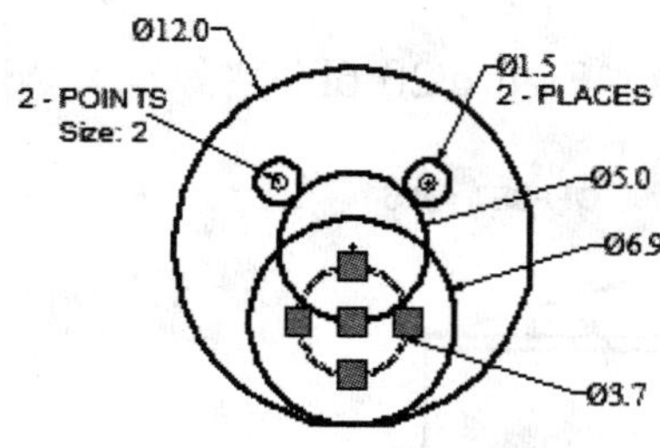

Figure 20-6bc

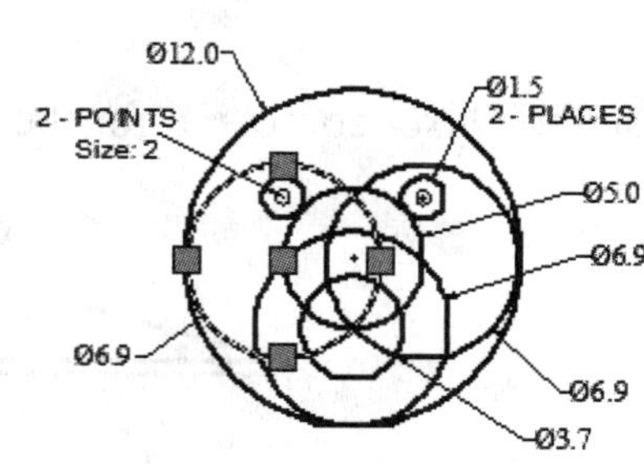

Figure 20-6bd

4. Use the *Trim* command, to create the shape shown in Figure 20-6be.

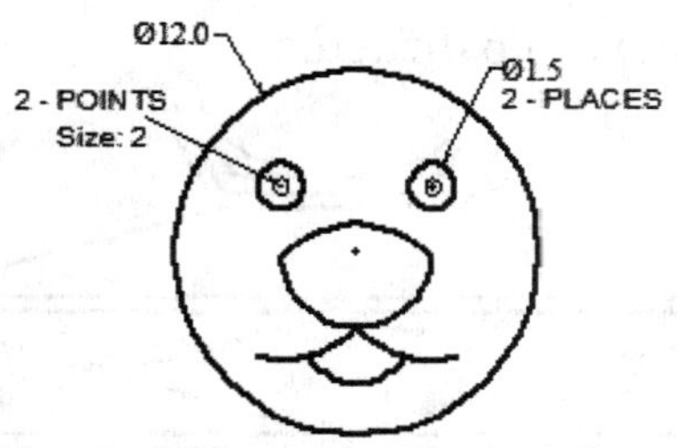

Figure 20-6be

5. Draw the polygon. The center of the polygon is the center of the 12" diameter circle. Select the *Circumscribed about circle* option, Figure 20-6bf.

6. Use the Offset command for the outer polygons, Figure 20-6bg. Set offset distance to be 0.5 inches.

Figure 20-6bf

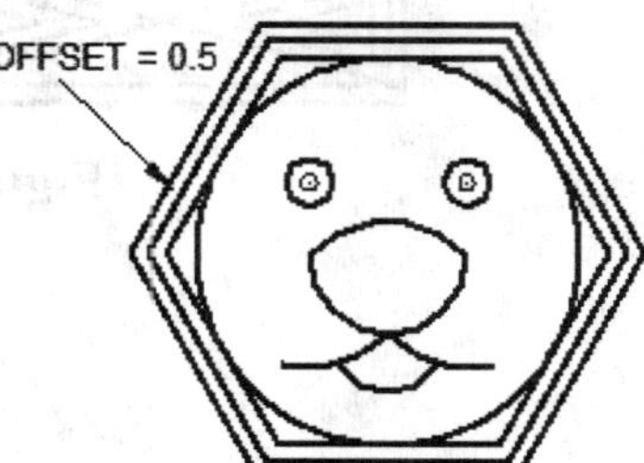

Figure 20-6bg

7. Use *Line* command to draw the outline of the base, Figure 20-6bh.

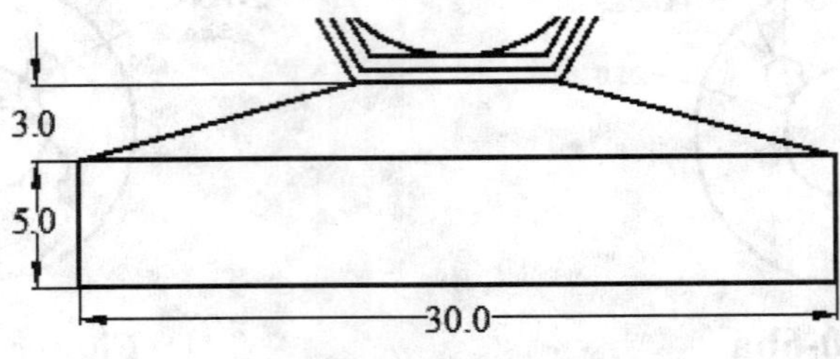

Figure 20-6bh

8. Use the *Offset* command for the inside of the base, Figure 20-6bi.

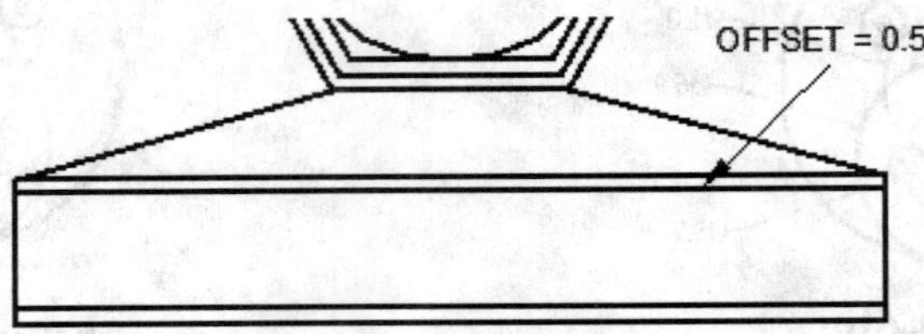

Figure 20-6bi

9. Draw ONE closed polyline of the base, Figure 20-6bj. The line command or several polylines will make the next step difficult.

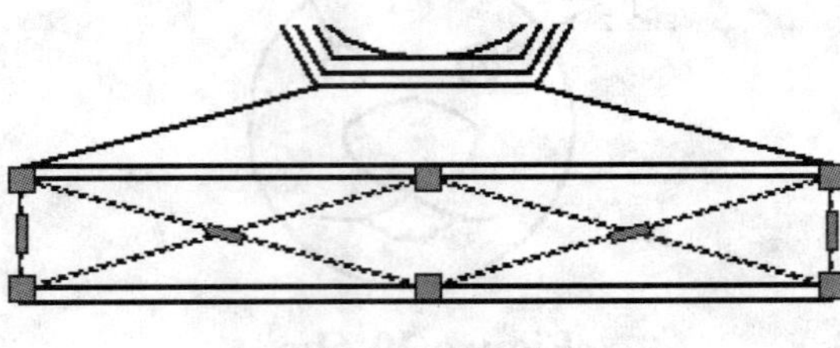

Figure 20-6bj

10. Use the *Offset* command to complete the drawing, Figure 20-6bk

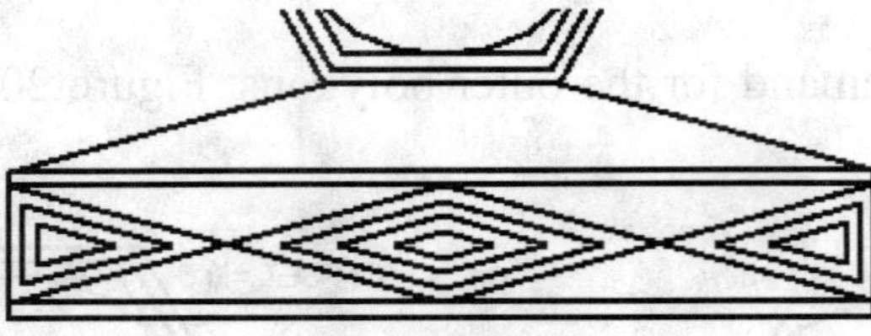

Figure 20-6bk

20.7.   Linetype, Lineweight, Mirror, Copy, and Scale

Objectives

- Learn to use *Circle (ttr)*, *linetype*, *lineweight*, *Mirror*, *Copy*, and *Scale* commands.

Hints

- Refer to Chapter #3 and Chapter #4 for help

ICA Description

1. <u>Drawing units</u>: Inches: Use TTR option of the *Circle* command to create the circle shown in Figure 20-7a.
   a. Save the drawing.
   b. Do not add the dimension or center lines of the circle.
   c. Set the lineweight and linetype shown in the figure.
   d. Set linetype scale (not shown in the figure).

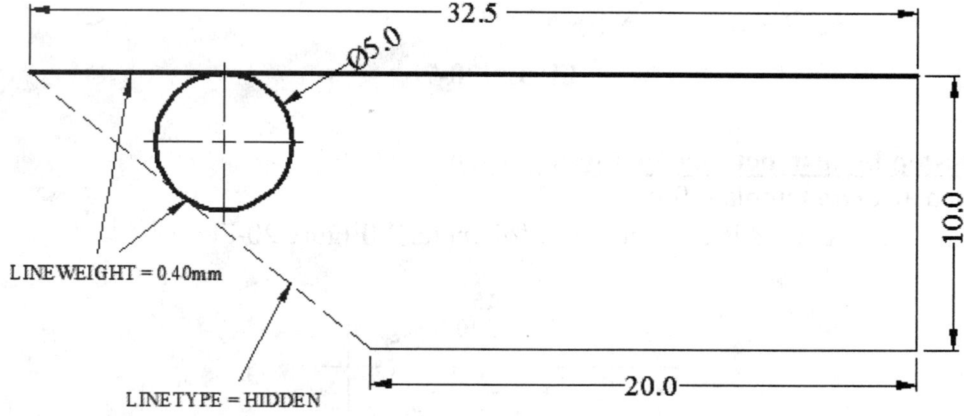

Figure 20-7a

2. <u>Drawing units</u>: Inches: Use TTR option of the *Circle* (TTR), *Mirror*, *Copy*, and *Scale* commands to create the objects shown in Figure 20-7b.
   a. Save the drawing.
   b. Do not add dimension or center lines of the circle.
   c. The smaller object is 60% of the bigger object.
   d. Show the complete drawing on one screen.
   e. Step-by-step instruction starts on the next page.

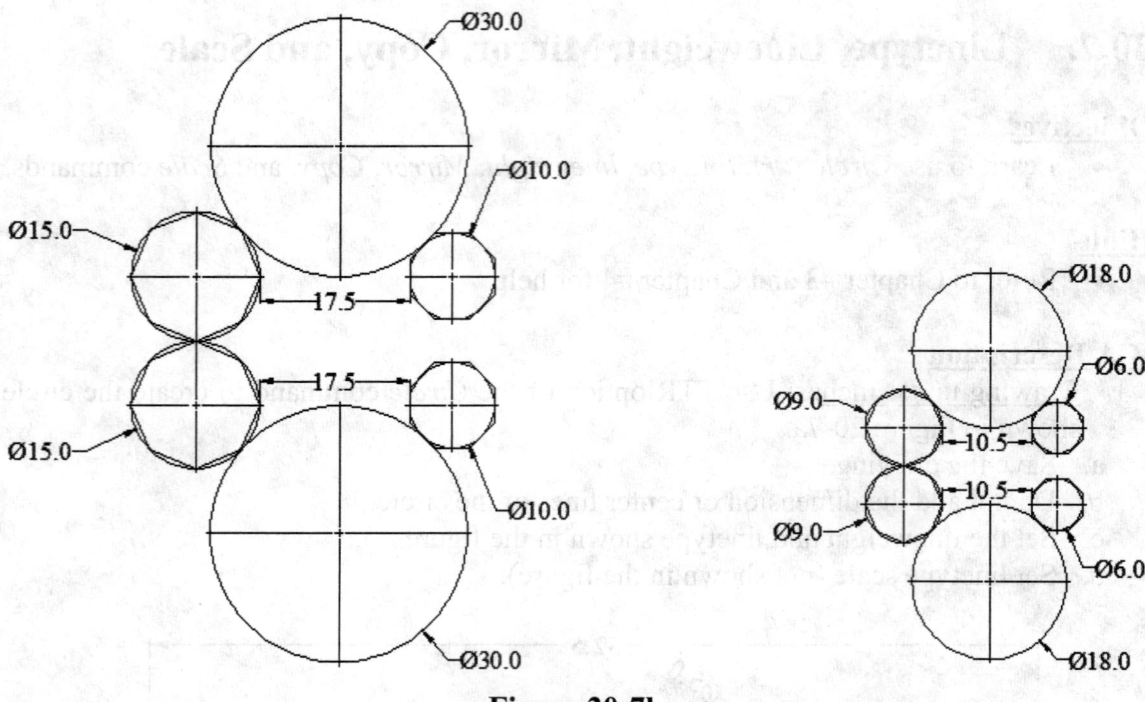

Figure 20-7b

Step-by-Step by instructions for Figure 20-7b

1. Open an *acad* template file.
2. Draw the circles (ϕ is the symbol of 'diameter'), Figure 20-7ba.

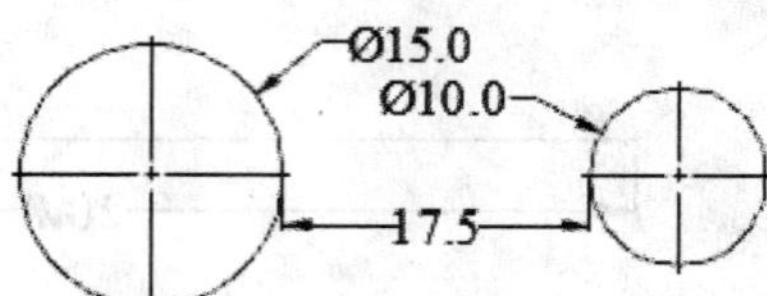

Figure 20-7ba

3. Draw the bigger circles (diameter = 30) using TTR option of the circle command, Figure 20-7bb.
4. Draw the the polygons, Figure 20-7bb. (15-inch circle: *Inscribed* option and 10-inch circle: *Circumscribed* option), Figure 20-7bc.

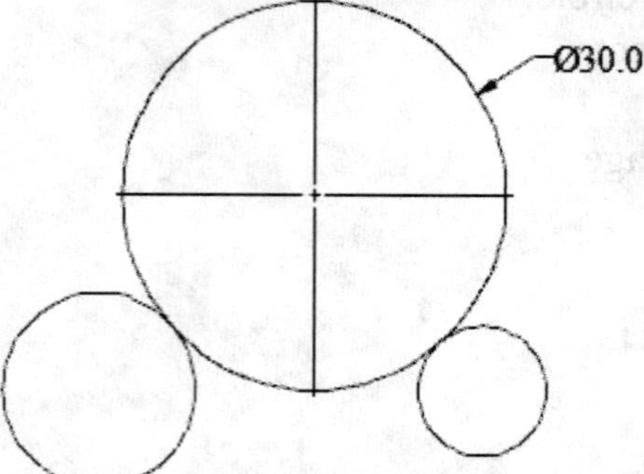

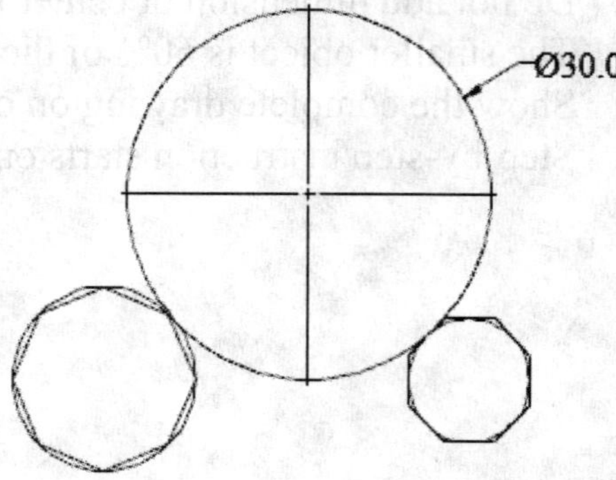

Figure 20-7bb   **Figure 20-7bc**

5. (i) Turn *On* the ORTHO option. (ii) Activate the *Mirror* command. (iii) Use the lower quadrant of the circle of diameter = 15 as the base point and complete the *Mirror* command, Figure 20-7bd.

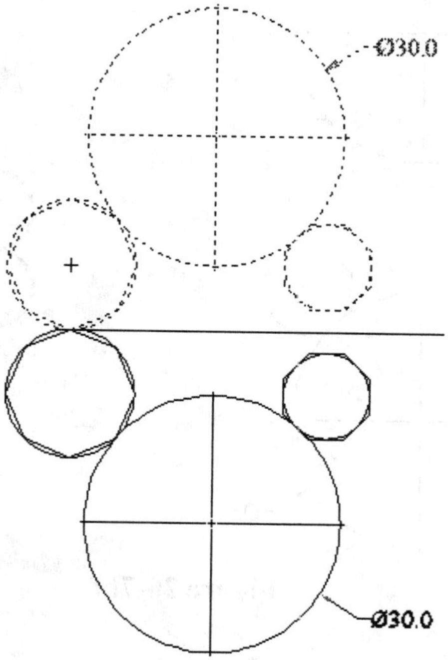

Figure 20-7bd

6. Use the *Copy* command to create the second object, Figure 20-7be.
7. Scale the object: (i) Activate the *Scale* command, (ii) select the copy created in step #6, (iii) select the center of one of the large circle as the base point, (iv) for the scale factor, type the value 0.60, and (v) press the *Enter* key, Figure 20-7bf.

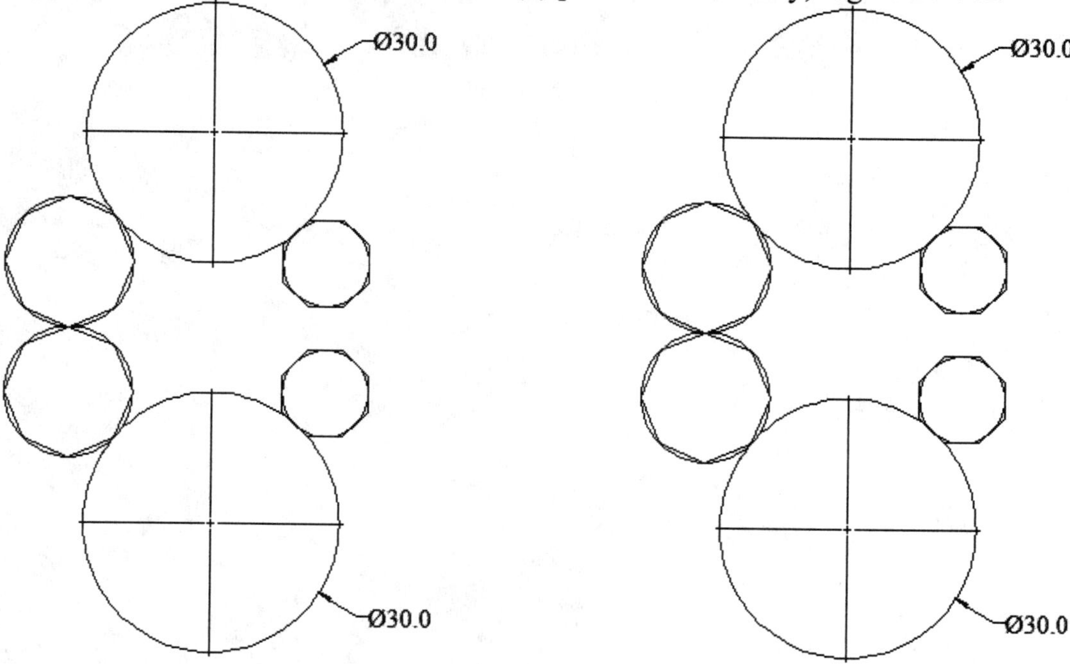

Figure 20-7be

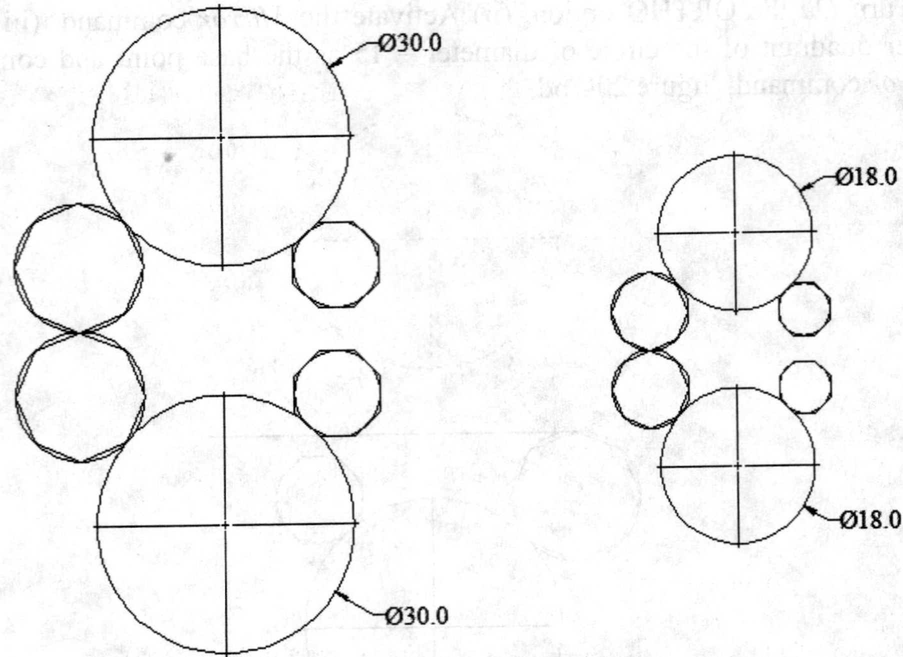

Figure 20-7bf

ICA Submission
1. Show the drawings in class (on or before the due date) to the instructor or TA.

20.8.   Array, Text, Hatch, Ellipse, qleader, and Draw Order

Objectives

- Learn to use *Array Rectangular, Text, Hatch, Ellipse,* and *qleader* commands
- Learn to use *Draw Order* capabilities

Hints

- Refer to Chapter #3 and Chapter #4 for help

ICA Description

1. <u>Drawing units</u>: <u>Inches</u>: Draw the object shown in Figure 20-8b using *Array, Text, Hatch, Ellipse,* and *qleader* commands.
   a. Add the text boxes and arrows.
   b. Save the drawing.
   c. Do not add dimension or center lines of the circle.
   d. Figure 20-8a shows the details of the columns used in Figure 20-8b.
   e. The step-by-step instructions for the left quarter cable are given.
   f. The bridge is symmetrical in the center.
   g. Assume reasonable value for the missing dimensions, if any.

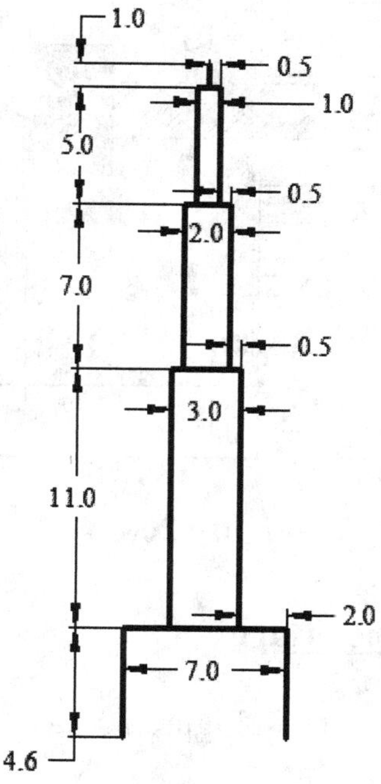

Figure 20-8a

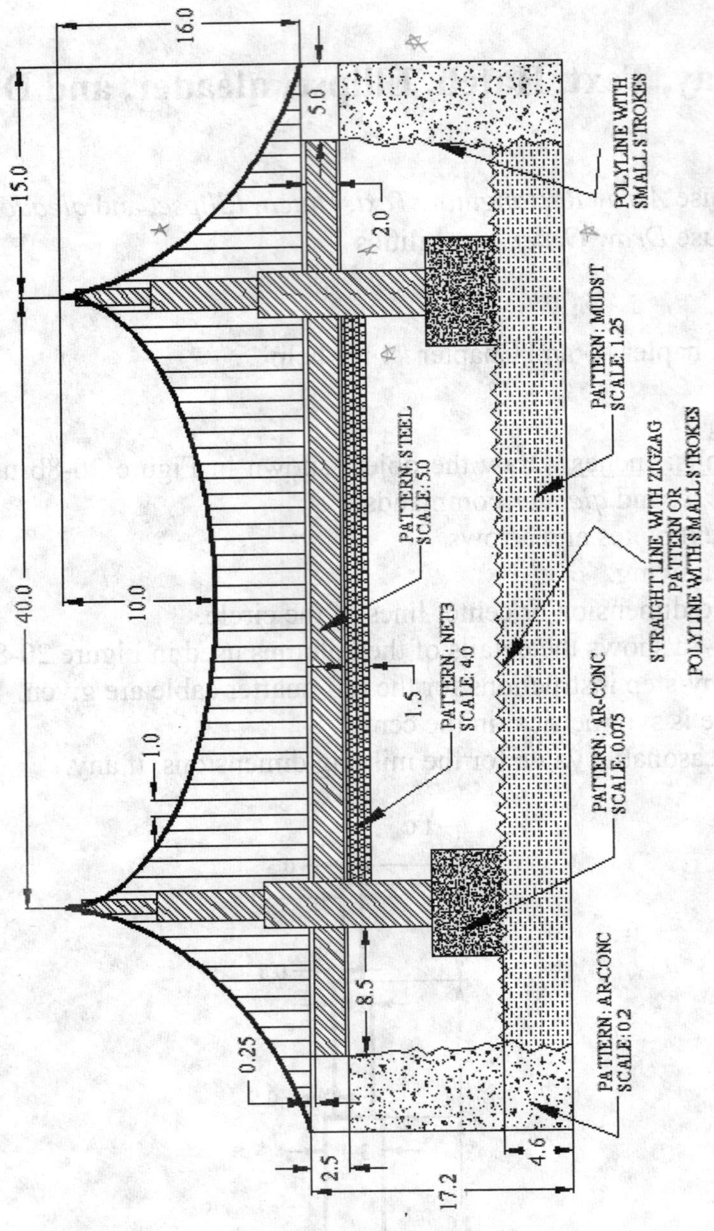

Figure 20-8b

Step-by-Step instructions for the bridge

1. Draw the right column as shown in Figure 20-8a.

2. Draw an ellipse with the major axis is 40.0" and the minor axis 10" for the central cable of the bridge, Figure 20-8b.

3. Draw the cable on the right side of the bridge using step # 4 - #9.

4. Draw a 15.0 inch long line (the line's grip point are shown for the demonstration purpose), Figure 20-8c.

5. Draw an ellipse with the major axis is 40.966" and the minor axis 16.762" as shown in Figure 20-8d. The figure also shows the location of the center of the ellipse. The ellipse's grip points are shown for the demonstration purpose.

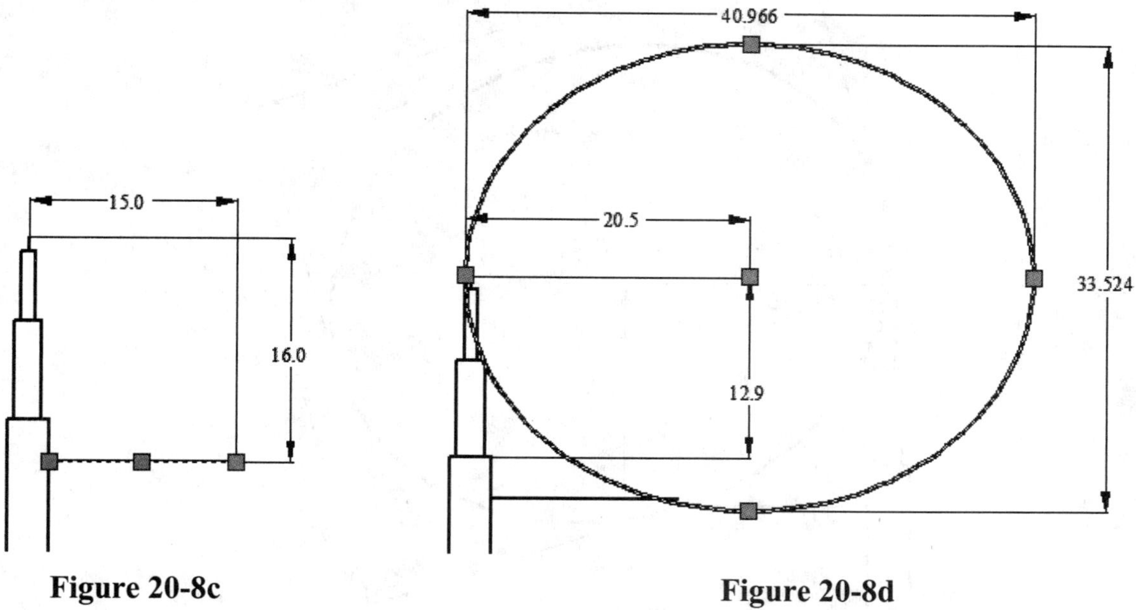

Figure 20-8c   **Figure 20-8d**

6. Rotate the ellipse at an angle of 19° clockwise, with the center of the ellipse selected for the base point, Figure 20-8e. The ellipse's grip points are shown for the demonstration purpose.

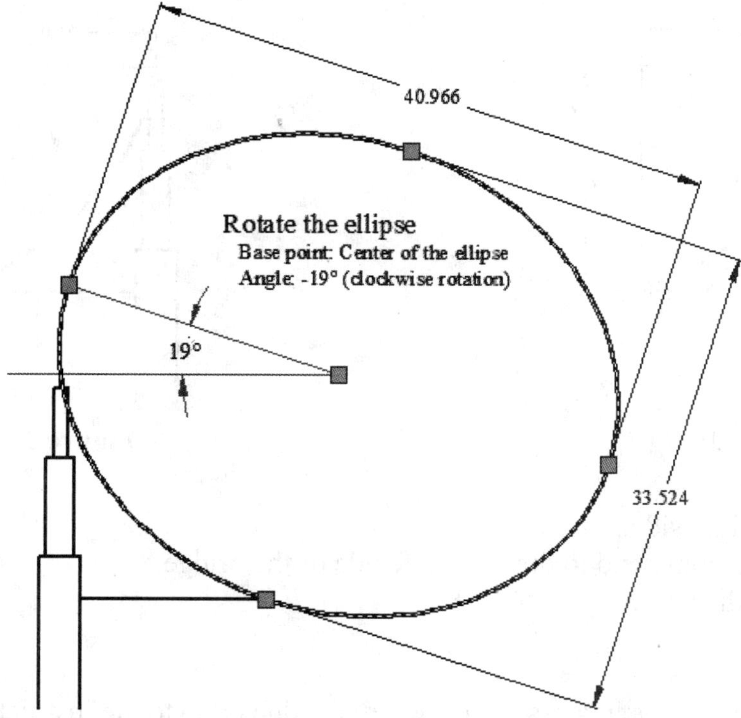

Figure 20-8e

7. Draw a temporary line as shown in Figure 20-8f.

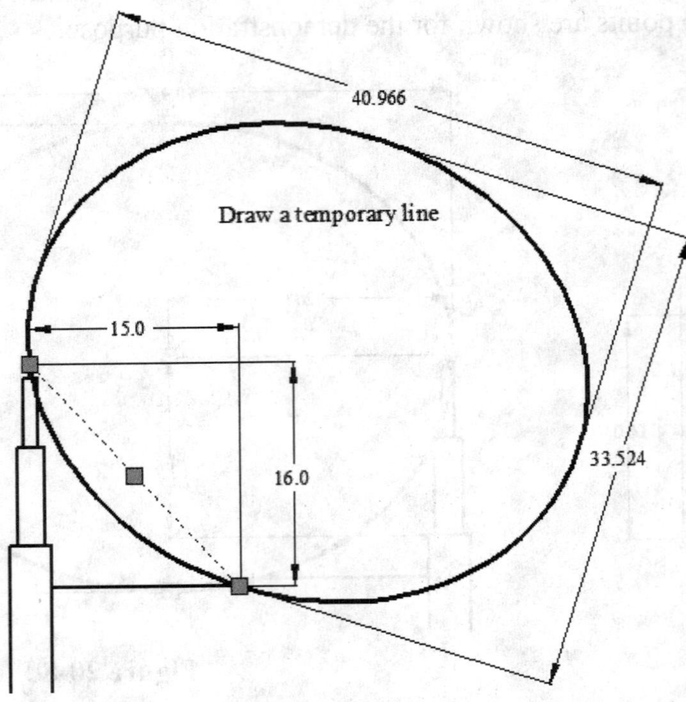

Figure 20-8f

8. Trim the ellipse using the temporary line, Figure 20-8g.
9. Delete the temporary line, Figure 20-8h.

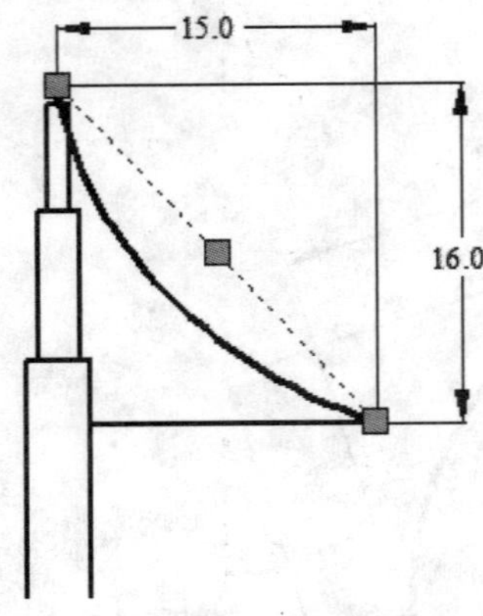

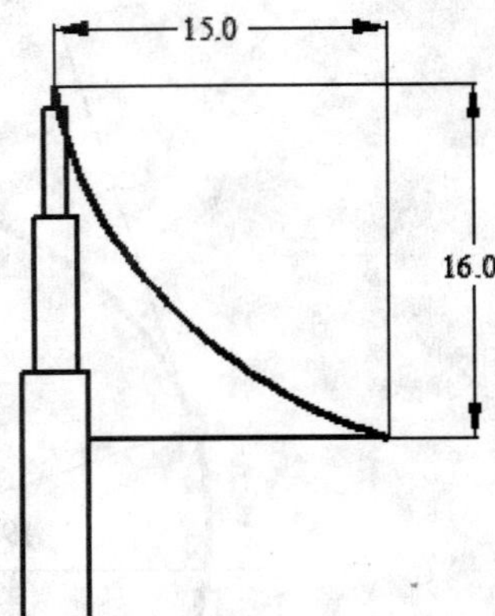

Figure 20-8g   **Figure 20-8h**

10. Draw the right side gravity wall.
11. Use *Mirror* command to draw the left side of the bridge.
12. Complete the bridge.

ICA Submission
1. Show the drawings in class (on or before the due date) to the instructor or TA.

20.9.   Layers

Objectives
- Learn to create *Layer*s commands
- Learn to use *Linetype*, *Linetype Scale*, and *Mirror* commands

Hints
- Refer to Chapter #5 for help

ICA Description
1. Drawing units: Inches: Draw the object shown in Figure 20-9a using *Line, Circle,* and *Mirror* commands
   a. Save the drawing.
   b. Do not add dimension or center lines of the circle.
   c. Create appropriate layers.
   d. Set the lineweight and linetype shown in the figure.
   e. Set linetype scale (not shown in the figure).
   f. Use reasonable value for *linetype scale* in *Properties* sheet.
   g. The step-by-step instructions are given.

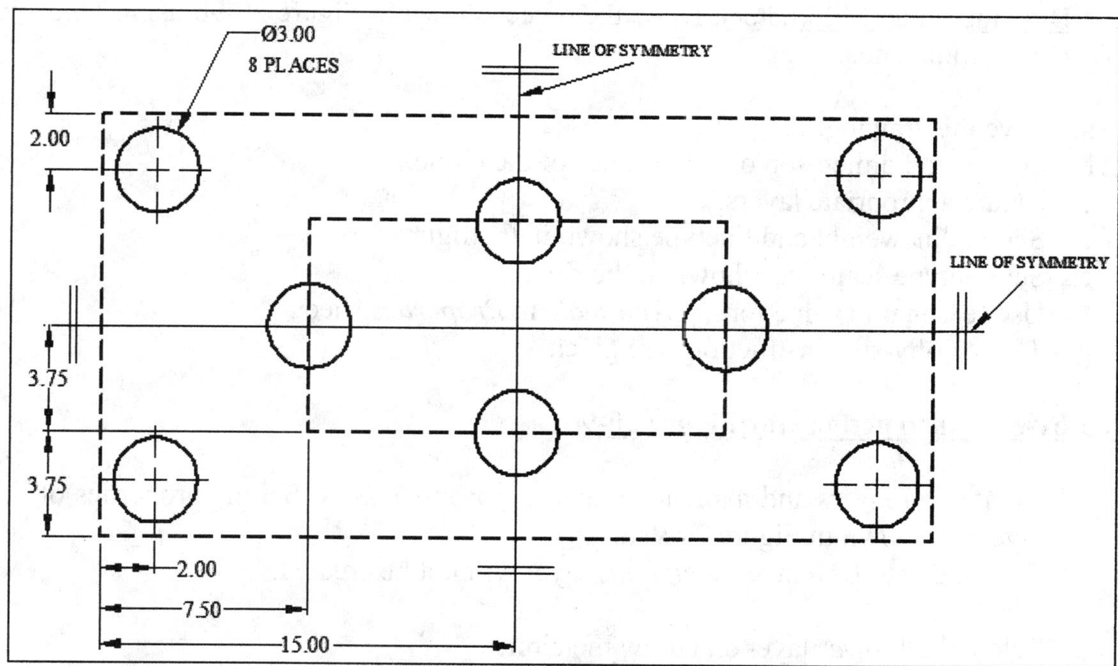

Figure 20-9a

Step-by-Step instructions for Figure 20-9a:
   a. Create two layers and name them as *Circle* and *Rectangle*. Set the properties of the layers as shown in Figure 20-9ab.
   b. Do not create *Dim* layer. *Defpoints* layer will not be created!

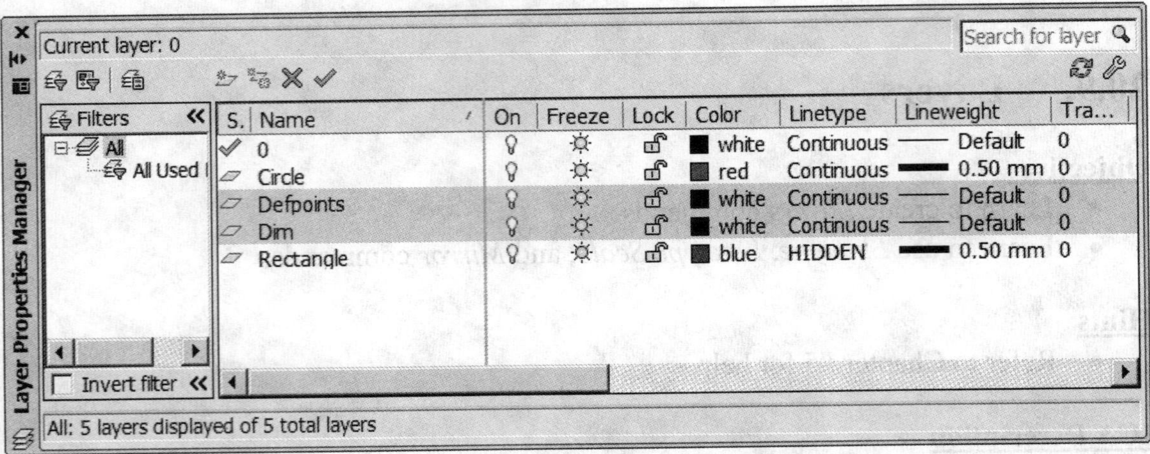

Figure 20-9ab

c. Select the *Circle* layer and draw the circles.
d. Select the *Rectangle* layer and draw the rectangles.
e. Turn *Off* the *Circle* layer, only rectangles will be displayed.
f. Turn *On* the *Circle* layer; both circles and rectangles will be displayed.
g. Turn *Off* the *Rectangle* layer, only circles will be displayed.

2. <u>Drawing units:</u> Millimeters: Draw the object shown in Figure 20-9b using *Line* and *Circle* commands.

a. Save the drawing.
b. Do not add dimension or center lines of the circle.
c. Create appropriate layers.
d. Set the lineweight and linetype shown in the figure.
e. Set linetype scale (not shown in the figure).
f. Use reasonable value for *linetype scale* in *Properties* sheet.
g. The step-by-step instructions are given.

<u>Step-by-Step instructions for Figure 20-9b</u>:

a. Create two layers and name them as *Flower* and *Tracks*. Set the properties of the layers as shown in Figure 20-9ba.
b. Do not create *Dim* layer. *Defpoints* layer will not be created!

c. Select the *Flower* layer and draw the circles.
d. Select the *Tracks* layer and draw the triangles.
e. Turn *Off* the *Flower* layer, only tracks will be displayed.
f. Turn *On* the *Flower* layer; both tracks and flower will be displayed.
g. Turn *on* the *Tracks* layer, only circles will be displayed.

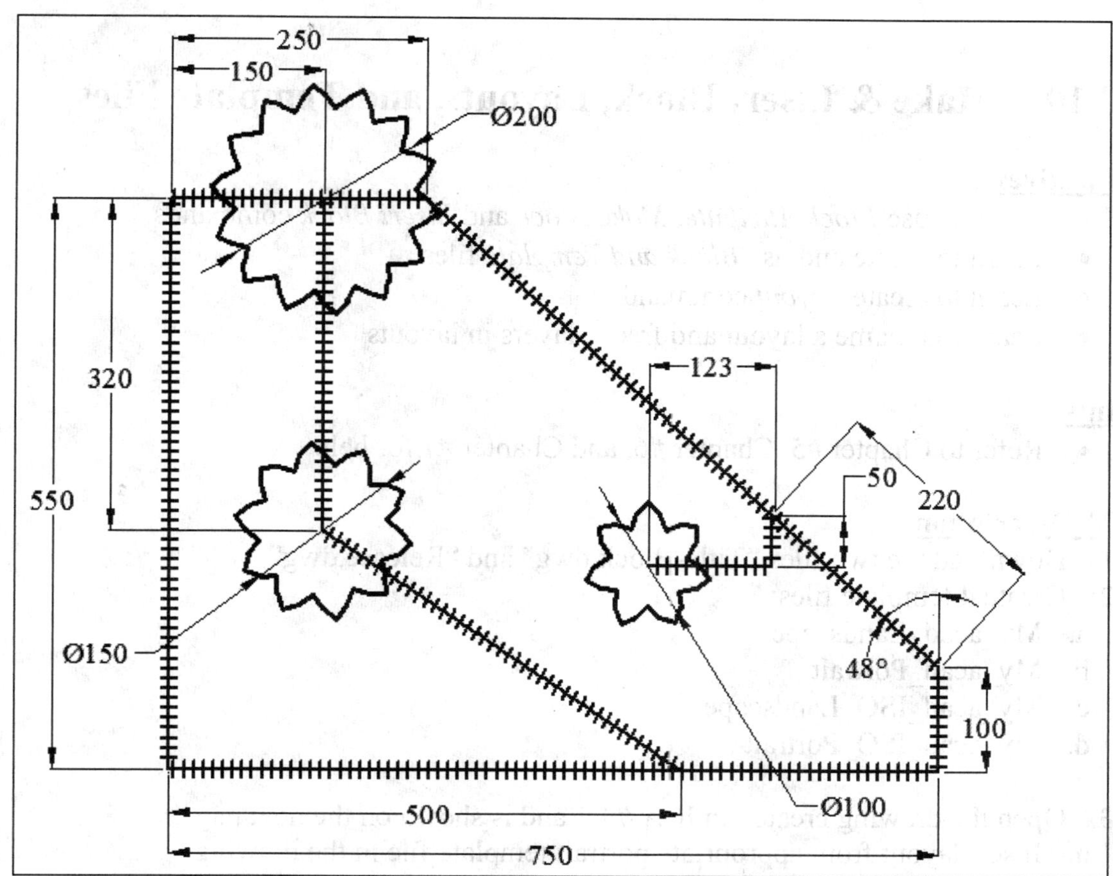

Figure 20-9b

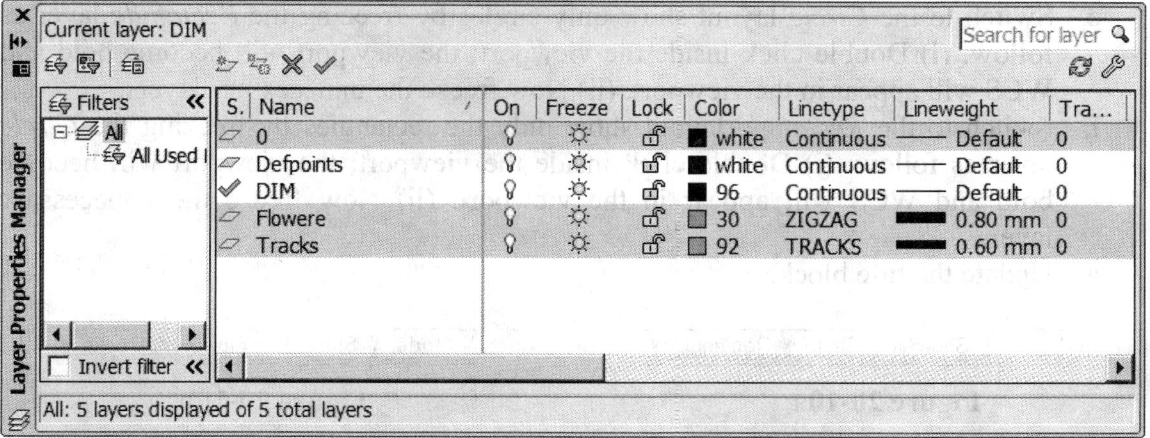

Figure 20-9ba

ICA Submission

1.   Show the drawings in class (on or before the due date) to the instructor or TA.

20.10. Make & Insert Block, Layouts, and Template Files

Objectives
- Learn to use *Block Attribute*, *Make Block* and *Insert Block* commands
- Learn to create and use *Block and Template* files
- Learn to create *Layout* command
- Learn to rename a layout and freeze layers in layouts

Hints
- Refer to Chapter #5, Chapter #6, and Chapter #7 for help

ICA Description
1. Download the two files "Title-Block.dwg" and "Release.dwg"
2. Create 4 template files:
   a. My_acad_Landscape
   b. My_acad_Portrait
   c. My_acad_ISO_Landscape
   d. My_acad_ISO_Portrait

3. Open the drawing created in ICA #9-1 and is shown on the next page.
   a. Insert layout from appropriate portrait template file in the drawing.
   b. Create three layouts and rename them as shown in Figure 20-10a.
   c. In each layout, use reasonable value for *linetype scale* in *Properties* sheet.
   d. Switch to the *ShowAll* layout show circles and rectangles.
   e. Switch to the *Circle* layout show only circles by freezing the *Rectangle* layer as follow: (i) Double click inside the viewport; the viewport will become bold and WCS will appear in the viewport. (ii) Now freeze the unnecessary layers.
   f. Switch to the *Rectangle* layout show only the rectangles by freezing the *Circle* layer as follow: (i) Double click inside the viewport; the viewport will become bold and WCS will appear in the viewport. (ii) Now freeze the unnecessary layers.
   g. Update the title block.

Figure 20-10a	Figure 20-10b

   a. Open the drawing created in ICA #9-2 and is shown on the next page.
   b. Insert layout from appropriate portrait template file in the drawing.
   c. Create three layouts and rename them as shown in Figure 20-10b.
   d. In each layout, use reasonable value for *linetype scale* in *Properties* sheet.
   e. Switch to the *ShowAll* layout show flower and tracks.

h.   Switch to the *Flower* layout show only the flowers by freezing the *Tracks* layer as follow: (i) Double click inside the viewport; the viewport will become bold and WCS will appear in the viewport. (ii) Now freeze the unnecessary layers.

i.   Switch to the *Tracks* layout show only the tracks by freezing the *Flower* layer as follow: (i) Double click inside the viewport; the viewport will become bold and WCS will appear in the viewport. (ii) Now freeze the unnecessary layers.

j.   Update the title block.

ICA Submission

1.   Show the drawing in the viewport and the updated Title block in class (on or before the due date) to the instructor or TA.

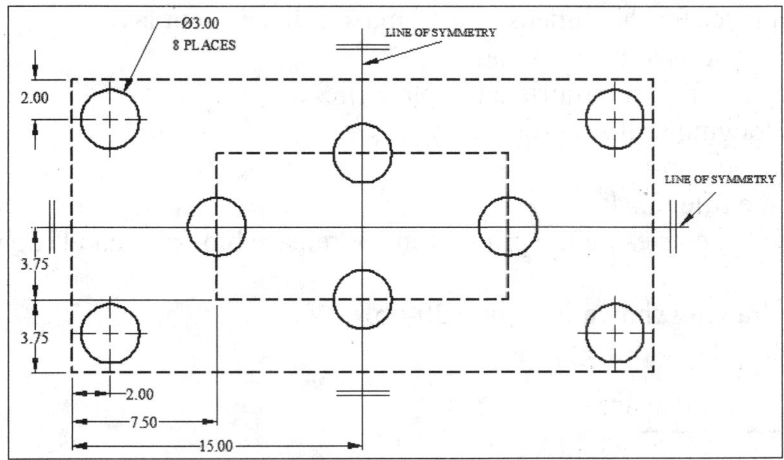

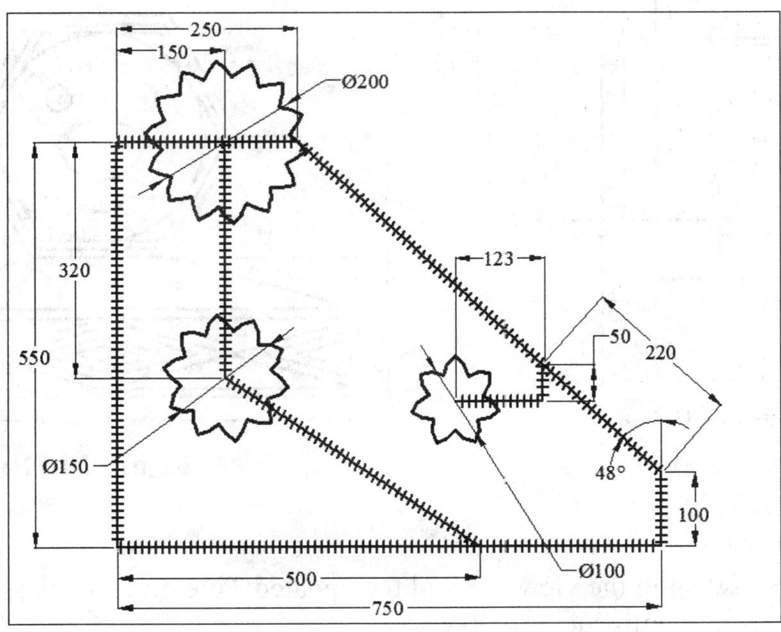

20.11. Dimension

Objectives
- Learn to add *dimensions* to a drawing

Hints
- Refer to Chapter #8 for help

ICA Description
1. Open the drawing shown in Figure 20-5b.
   a. Create a layer for the dimension and make it the current layer.
   b. Add dimensions to the drawing.
   c. Insert layout from appropriate template file.
   d. Set the drawing scale appropriately.
   e. Lock the viewport.
   f. Update the title block.
   g. Initialize the entries on the printout in the release block by hand (do not type).

2. Open the drawing shown in Figure 20-6b.
   a. Repeat the above process.

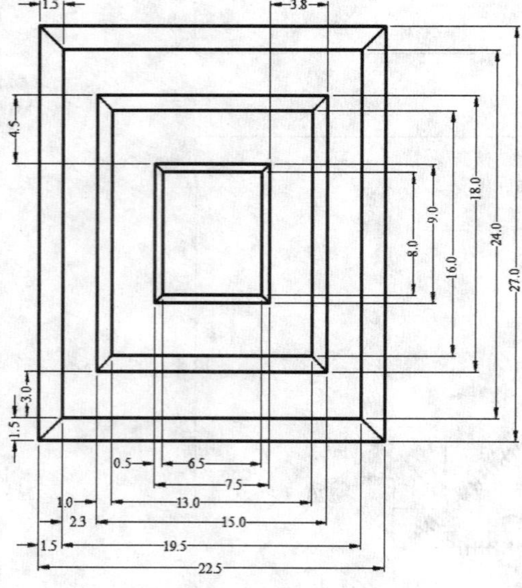

Figure 20-11b

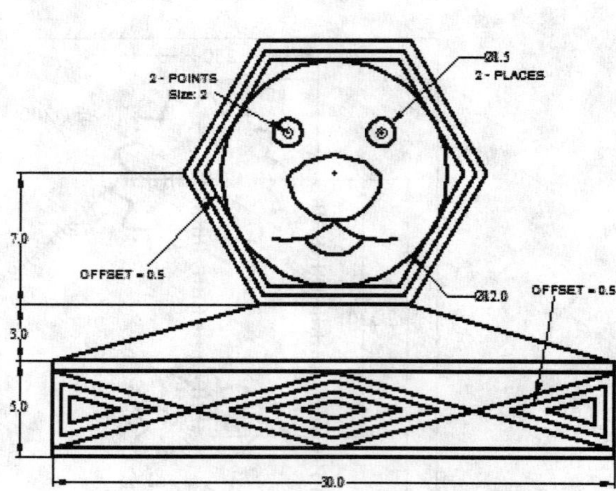

Figure 20-11b

ICA Submission
1. Show the drawing in the viewport and the updated Title block in class (on or before the due date) to the instructor or TA.

20.12.   Azimuths, Bearing, and Closed Travers

Objectives
- Learn to convert an azimuth into a bearing and vice versa.
- Learn to draw closed traverses using azimuths and bearings.

Hints
- Refer to Chapter #9 for details and help

ICA Description
1. Convert bearing to azimuths: N43°W, S23°E, N15°E, and S75°W. Hand written solution is accepted.

2. Convert azimuths to bearing: 123°12'32", 19°47'56", 258°08'01", and 349°15'21". Hand written solution is accepted. **Answers must be in degree, minutes, and seconds format**.

3. Drawing units: Millimeters: Draw the closed traverse shown in Figure 20-12a.
    a. Create appropriate layers.
    b. Add the dimensions as shown in the figure.
    c. Find the length and bearing labeled as **?**.
    d. Save the drawing.

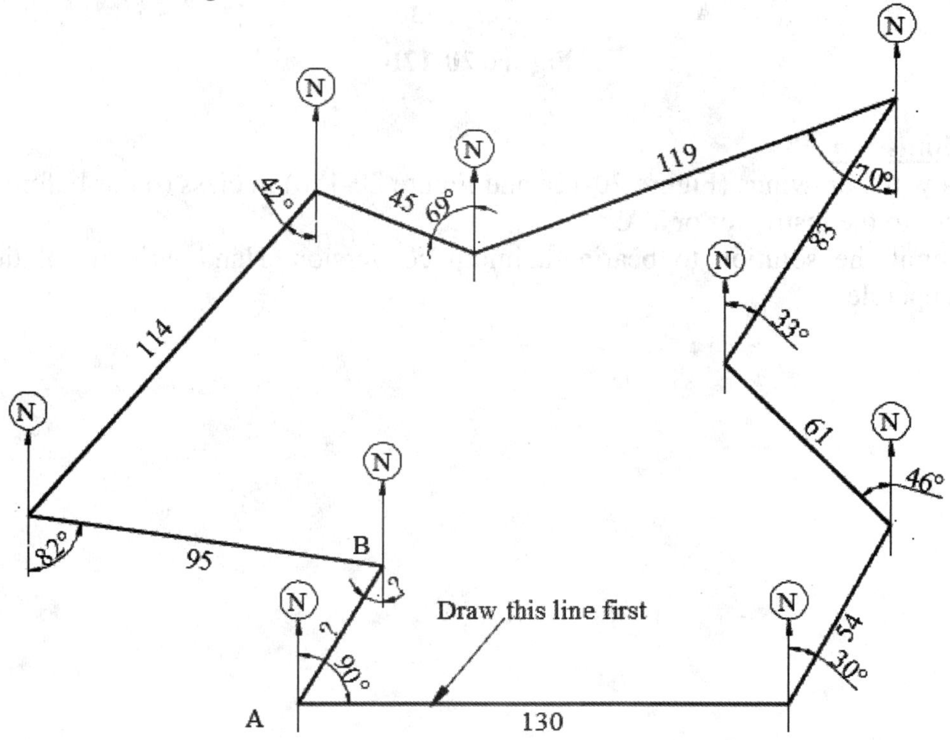

Figure 20-12a

4. <u>Drawing units</u>: <u>Millimeters</u>: Draw the closed traverse shown in Figure 20-12b.
   a.   Create appropriate layers.
   b.   Add the dimensions as shown in the figure.
   c.   Find the length and azimuth labeled as **?**.
   d.   Save the drawing.

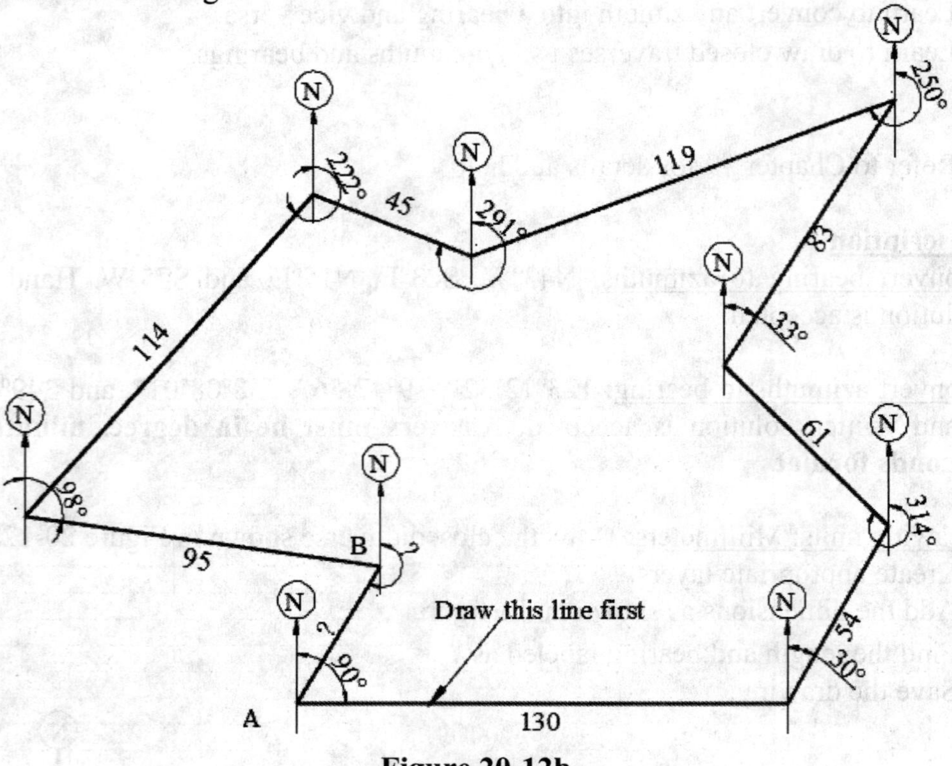

Figure 20-12b

ICA Submission

1. Show the drawings (Figure 20-12a and Figure 20-12b) in class (on or before the due date) to the instructor or TA.
2. Submit the solution to bearing-azimuth conversion. Hand written solutions are acceptable.

20.13.   RSS, Lots and Blocks

Objectives
- Learn to labels subdivision using RSS
- Learn to draw lots and blocks (Text book: Figure 9-13)

Hints
- Refer to Chapter #9 for details and help

ICA Description
1. <u>Range and township</u>: Find SECTION31-T4S-R5E using Rectangular system, Figure 20-13a.Take the printout of this page and submit it in next class.

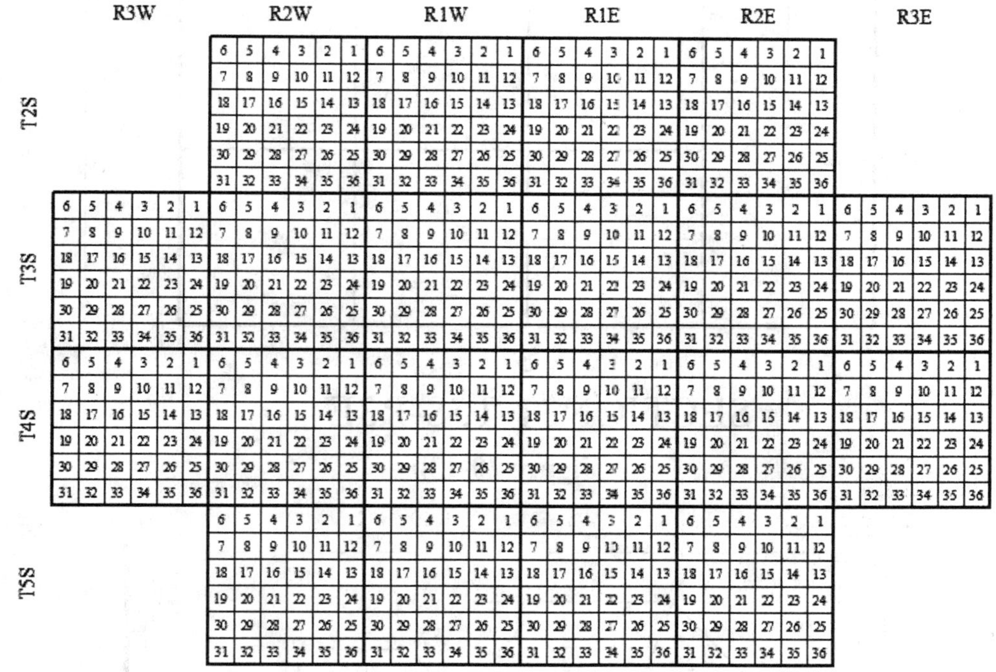

Figure 20-13a

2. <u>RSS</u>: Label the various subdivisions of Figure 20-13b using Rectangular system,. Also, write the area of each subdivision. Hand written solution is acceptable.

3. <u>Lots and Blocks</u>:
   a. Draw the parcel of land and divide it into the lots, Figure 20-13c.
   b. Add the dimensions
   c. Insert layout from appropriate template file.
   d. Set the drawing scale to 1:1320.
   e. Set the drawing units to ENGINEERING.
   f. Update the title block.
   g. Initialize the entries on the printout in the release block by hand (do not type).

ICA Submission

1. Submit the solution of range and township and RSS.
2. Submit the print of lot and block drawing as a HW.

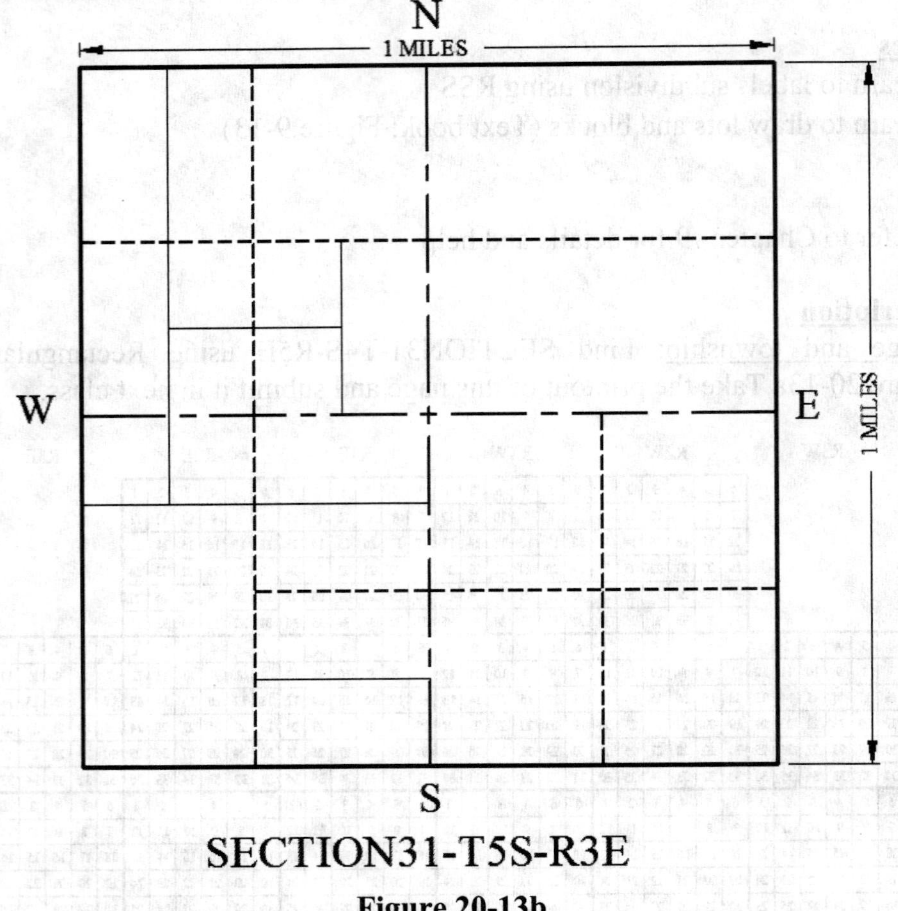

SECTION31-T5S-R3E

Figure 20-13b

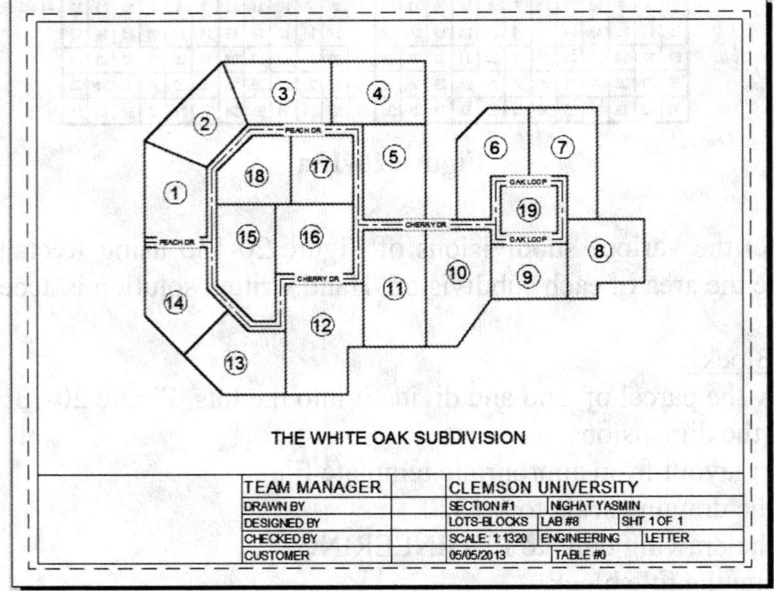

Figure 20-13c

20.14.   Rotate, Text, Background Mask, & Table Command and Contour map

<u>Objectives</u>
- Learn to label a *Contour* map
- Learn to use *Table* command

<u>Hints</u>
- Refer to Chapter #3 and Chapter #10 for details and help

<u>ICA Description</u>
1. <u>Drawing units</u>: Engineering: Create the contour map shown in Figure 20-14a.
   a. Download the contour map file
   b. For the contour map: Label each index contours at 3 different places using *Text* and *Background Mask* commands.
   c. Note: In the sample figure only one index contour is labeled.
   d. In the contour map file, insert the layout from the appropriate template file.
   e. Set the viewport Scale to 1:8.
   f. Set the drawing units to ENGINEERING.
   g. Update the title block.
   h. Save the drawing.

2. <u>Drawing units</u>: Inches:
   a. Create the table as shown in Figure 20-14b.
   b. Update the title block.
   c. Save the drawing.

<u>ICA Submission</u>
1. Show the drawings in class (on or before the due date) to the instructor or TA.
2. Show the contour map with every layer on.

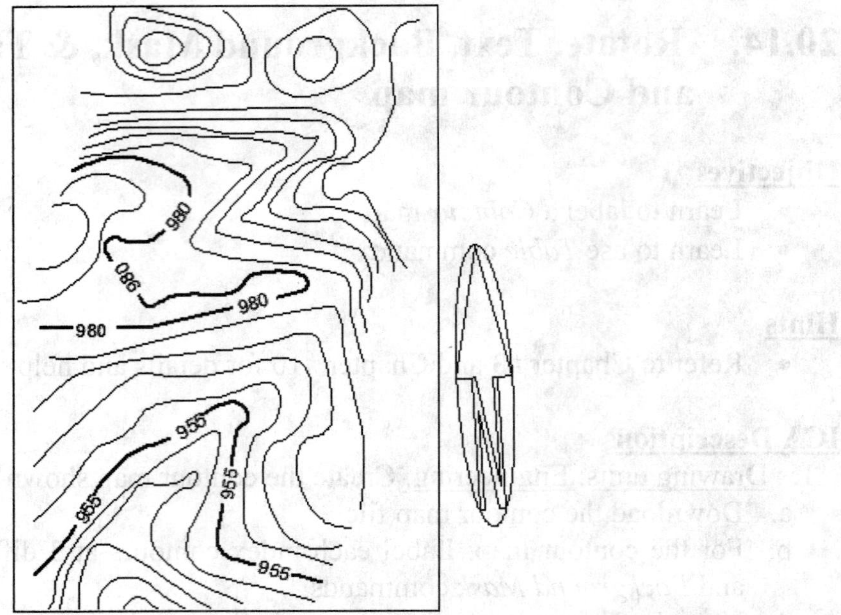

Figure 20-14a

EG210 – TABLE #1

COLORS	DAYS	MONTHS
BLUE	SATURDAY	JANUARY
GREEN	SUNDAY	FEBRUARY
MAGENTA	MONDAY	MARCH
ORANGE	TUESDAY	APRIL
PURPLE	WEDNESDAY	MAY
RED	THURSDAY	JUNE
YELLOW	FRIDAY	JULY

TEAM MANAGER		CLEMSON UNIVERSITY		
DRAWN BY		EG210 – 000	NIGHAT YASMIN	
DESIGNED BY		EX 14–2	ICA #14	SHT 1 OF 1
CHECKED BY		CUSTOM	INCHES	LETTER
CUSTOMER		05/05/2013	TABLE #0	

Figure 20-14b

20.15.   Drainage Basin Delineation

Objectives
- Learn to delineate a drainage basin of a channel

Hints
- Refer to Chapter #3 and Chapter #11 for details and help

ICA Description
1. Drawing units: Engineering:
2. Download the contour file.
3. Label the index contours at three different places.
   a. Contour Interval = 1ft
   b. If the elevation of the first index contour is H1 and the elevation of the next index contour is H2 then H2 = H1 + 5* Contour Interval
   c. If the elevation of the first index contour is 120 then the elevation of the next index contour is: 120 + 5*1 = 125ft
4. Draw the center line of the channel.
5. Show the direction of the flow in the channel.
6. Display the outlet point of the watershed.
7. Delineate the watershed (drainage basin) boundary. (Hint: Connect ridges)
8. Hatch the watersheds.
9. Find the length of the channel in feet.
10. Find the drainage areas in acres.
11. Display the area of the watershed and length of the channel appropriately.
12. Insert an appropriate layout from one of the template files.
13. Set the viewport scale to 1:1200.
14. Set the drawing units to ENGINEERING
15. Update the blocks.

ICA Submission
1. Show the drawing in class (on or before the due date) to the instructor or TA.
2. The printout will be submitted as a HW.

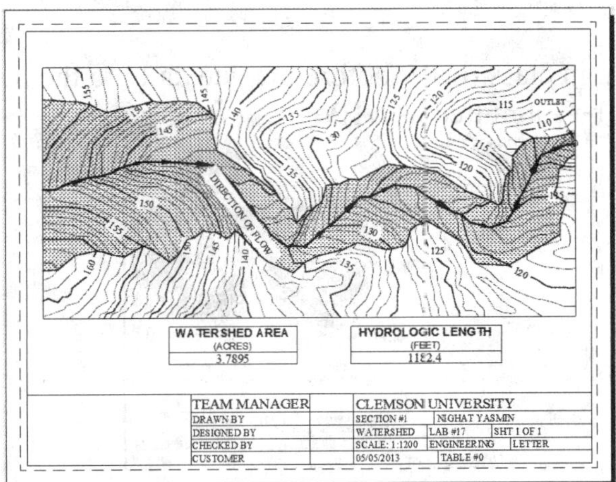

20.16.   Floodplain Delineation

Objectives
- Learn to delineate the floodplain of a channel

Hints
- Refer to Chapter #3 and Chapter #12 for details and help

ICA Description
1. Drawing units: Engineering:
2. Download the contour file.
3. Label the index contours at three different places.
   a. Contour Interval = 1ft
   b. If the elevation of the first index contour is H1 and the elevation of the next contour is H2 then H2 = H1 + 5* Contour Interval
   c. If the elevation of the first index contour is 120 then the elevation of the next contour is: 120 + 5*1 = 125ft
4. Draw the center line of the channel.
5. Show the direction of the flow in the channel.
6. Mark the gauging stations at a distance of 50' interval.
7. Display the main channel using *Offset* command; offset distance is 10'.
8. Display the bankfull using *Offset* command; offset distance is 20'.
9. Draw the perpendicular lines to the direction of flow.
10. Draw a polyline to delineate the floodplains.
11. Hatch the main channel, bankfull, and the floodplains.
12. Find the length of the channel in feet.
13. Find the floodplain areas in acres.
14. Display the area of the floodplain and length of the channel appropriately.
15. Insert an appropriate layout from one of the template files.
16. Set the viewport scale to 1:1200.
17. Set the drawing units to ENGINEERING.
18. Update the blocks.

ICA Submission
1. Show the drawing in class (on or before the due date) to the instructor or TA.
2. The printout will be submitted as a HW.

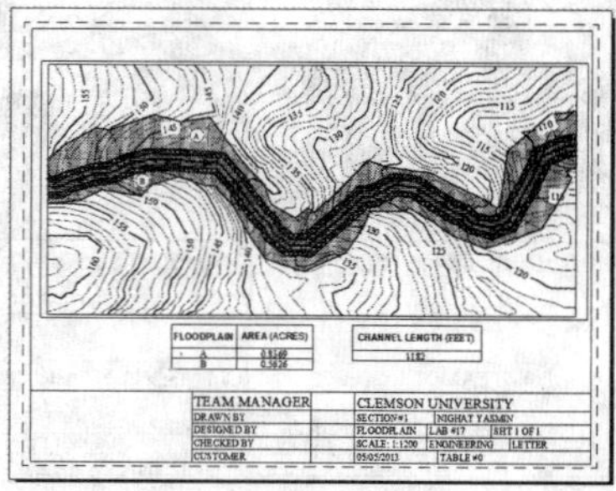

20.17.   Road Design: Plan and Profile

Objectives
- Learn to draw a plan and profile of a road

Hints
- Refer to Chapter #13 for details and help

ICA Description
1. Drawing units: Engineering:
2. Download the contour file from the BB.
3. Use the layers created in the drawing.
4. Draw the center line of the road 59'-10" above the lower edge of the contour map.
5. Draw the road plan; the road is 16' wide.
6. Hatch the road plan.
7. Draw and label the grid.
8. Draw the projection lines.
9. Draw the points on the grid.
10. Draw the profile through the points.
11. Hatch the profile.
12. Label the profile.
13. Insert an appropriate layout from one of the template files.
14. Set the scale of the drawing to 1:360.
15. Set the drawing units to ENGINEERING.
16. Update the blocks.

ICA Submission
1. Show the drawing in class (on or before the due date) to the instructor or TA.
2. The printout will be submitted as a HW.

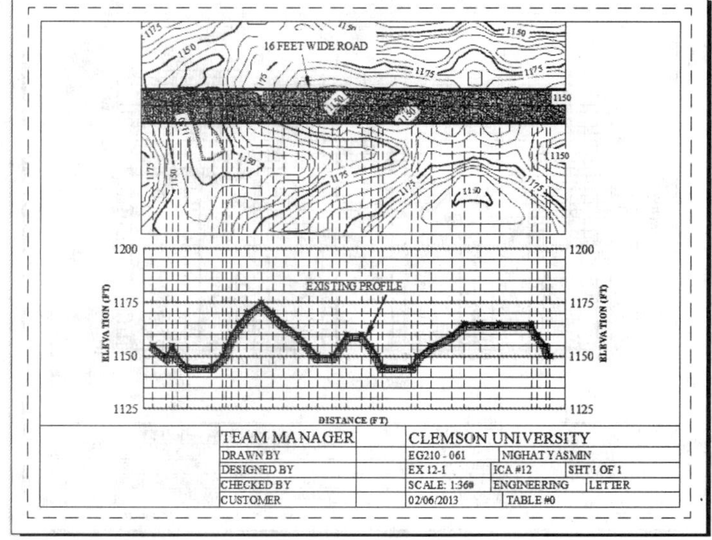

TEAM MANAGER		CLEMSON UNIVERSITY		
DRAWN BY		EG210 - 061	NIGHAT YASMIN	
DESIGNED BY		EX 12-1	ICA #12	SHT 1 OF 1
CHECKED BY		SCALE: 1:360	ENGINEERING	LETTER
CUSTOMER		02/06/2013	TABLE #0	

20.18. Road Design: Cross-Section

Objectives
- Learn to draw cross-sections of a road

Hints
- Refer to Chapter #13 for details and help

ICA Description
1. Drawing units: Engineering:
2. Download the contour file.
3. For the given plan of a road, draw and label the stations.
4. At each station, draw the cross-sections line.
5. Mark the point on the cross-sections lines.
6. Find the distance (for the points of step #5) from the nearest contours.
7. Find the elevation for the points of step #5 (using the distance of step #6 and elevation from the contour map) by interpolation.
8. Draw the grid for the cross-section.
9. Draw cross-sections.
10. Label the cross-sections.
11. Hatch the cross-sections.
12. Insert an appropriate layout from one of the template files.
13. Set the scale of the drawing to 1:216.
14. Set the drawing units to ENGINEERING.
15. Update the blocks.

ICA Submission
1. Show the drawing in class (on or before the due date) to the instructor or TA.
2. The printout will be submitted as a HW.

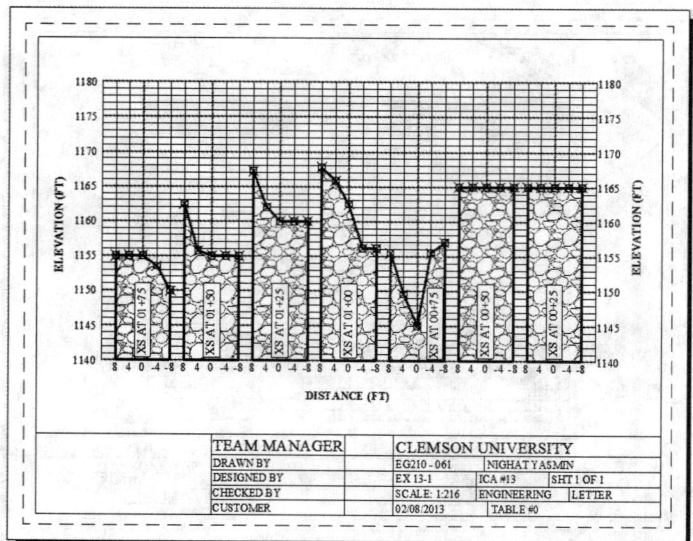

20.19. Road Design: Earthwork

Objectives
- Learn to delineate the cut and fill boundaries

Hints
- Refer to Chapter #14 for details and help

ICA Description
1. Download the contour file from the BB.
2. Use the layers created in the drawing.
3. Draw the road.
   a. Draw the center line of the road 92'-6" above the lower edge of the contour map.
   b. Draw the road plan; the road is 26'-8" wide.
   c. Hatch the road.
4. Draw the existing profile.
   a. Draw and label the grid.
   b. Draw the projection lines.
   c. Draw the points on the grid.
   d. Draw the profile through the points.
   e. Hatch the profile.
   f. Label the profile.
5. Delineate the earthwork.
   a. Draw vertical lines between two profiles.
   b. Delineate cut and fill on the lower side of the road
   c. Extend the projection lines to the other edge of the road.
   d. Repeat the delineation process for the other edge of the road.
   e. Hatch and label the cut and fill.
6. Insert an appropriate layout from one of the template files.
7. Set the scale of the viewport of the drawing as 1:450.
8. Set the drawing units to ENGINEERING.
9. Update the blocks.

ICA Submission
1. Show the drawing in class (on or before the due date) to the instructor or TA.
2. The printout will be submitted as a HW.

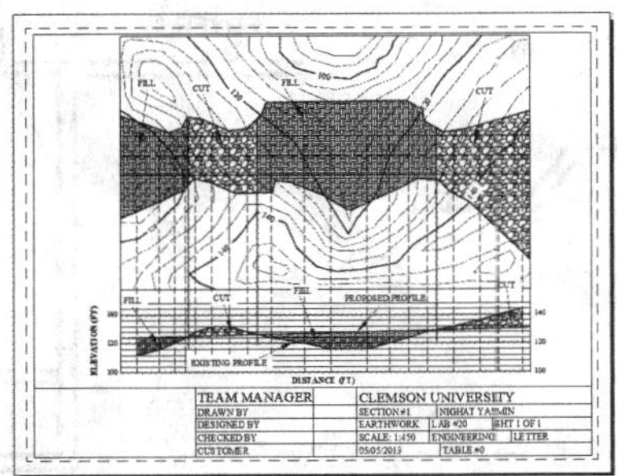

20.20. Floor plan

Objectives
- Learn to draw a floor plan of a residential building

Hints
- Refer to Chapter #15 for details and help

ICA Description
1. Drawing units: Architectural:
2. Open your "*My_acad_Landscape*" template file.
3. Create an entry "1:130" in the scale list.
   a. Set the drawing scale to 1:130.
   b. Set the drawing units to ARCHITECTURAL.
4. Update the Title block.
5. If necessary, create a new layer at each step.
6. Assume a reasonable value for a missing dimension.
7. Now draw the floor plan shown in Figure 15-12 of the text book.
8. Do not add dimension.
9. Set the scale appropriately.
10. Update the blocks.

ICA Submission
1. Show the drawing in class (on or before the due date) to the instructor or TA.
2. The printout will be submitted as a HW.

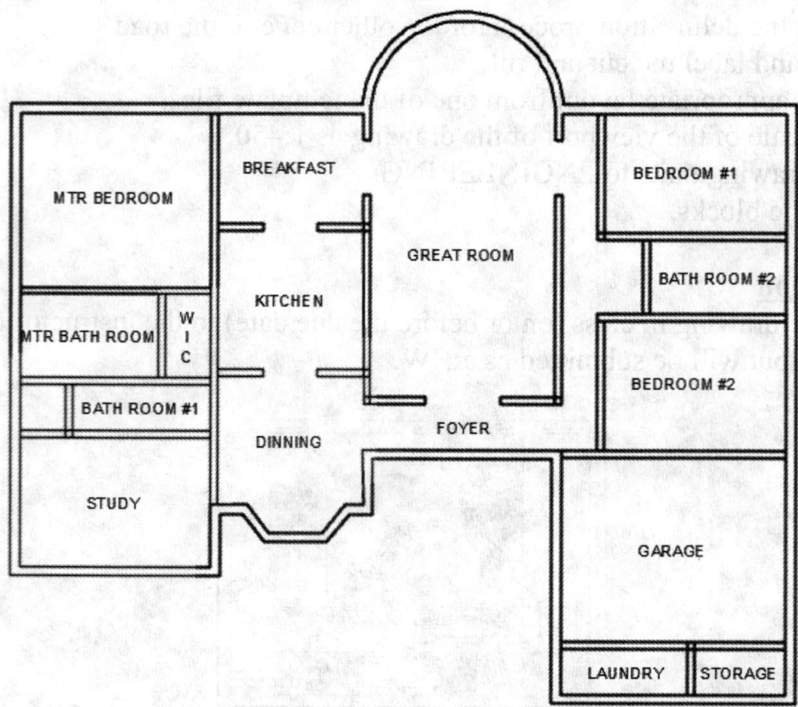

20.21. Floor plan (Cont)

Objectives
- Learn to draw a floor plan of a residential building

Hints
- Refer to Chapter #15 for details and help

ICA Description
1. If necessary, create a new layer at each step.
2. Assume a reasonable value for a missing dimension.
3. Update the floor plan drawn in ICA #20 to the floor plan shown in Figure 15-18 and Figure 15-19 of the text book. That is, add doors and windows to the floor plan.
4. Do not add dimension.
5. Set the scale appropriately.
6. Update the blocks.

ICA Submission
1. Show the drawing in class (on or before the due date) to the instructor or TA.
2. The printout will be submitted as a HW.

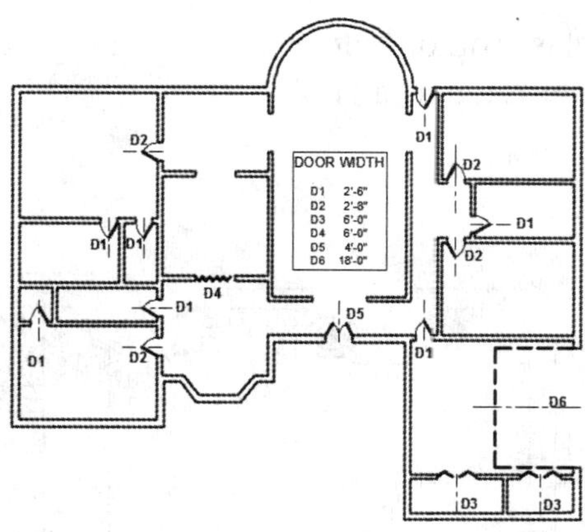

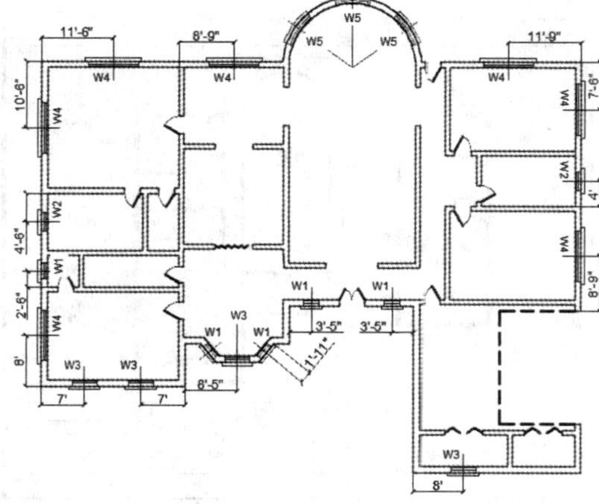

20.22. Floor plan (Cont)

Objectives
- Learn to draw a floor plan of a residential building (Text book: Figure 15-30)

Hints
- Refer to Chapter #15 for details and help

ICA Description
1. If necessary, create a new layer at each step.
2. Assume a reasonable value for a missing dimension.
3. Complete the floor plan (Figure 15-30 of the text book).
    a. Add the kitchen and bathrooms fixtures.
    b. Hatch the kitchen and bathrooms.
    c. Add the roofline.
    d. Add the front porch.
    e. Hatch the walls
4. Set the scale appropriately.
5. Update the blocks.

ICA Submission
1. Show the drawing in class (on or before the due date) to the instructor or TA.
2. The printout will be submitted as a HW.

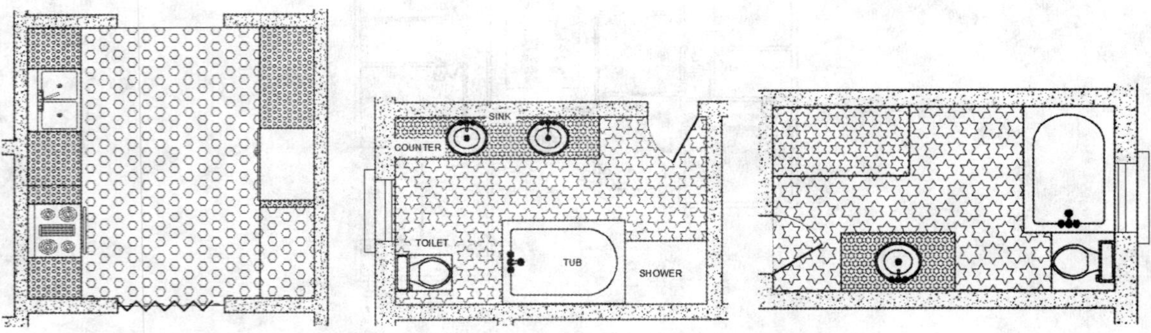

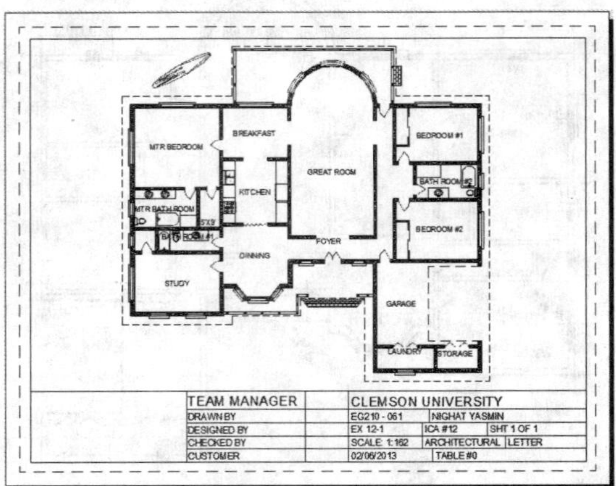

20.23. Dimensions (Architectural drawing)

Objectives
- Learn to add the dimensions to the floor plan

Hints
- Refer to Chapter #15 for details and help

ICA Description
1. <u>Drawing units</u>: <u>Architectural</u>:
2. Create the layers, as necessary.
3. Open the floor plan created in the previous ICA and add the dimensions.
4. Schedules are part of the dimensions.

ICA Submission
1. Submit the following four prints.
2. Set the scale appropriately.
3. Update the blocks.
   a. Floor plan with the dimensions and labels, Scale: 1:144.
   b. Dimensioned and labeled Front porch, Scale: 1:100.
   c. Dimensioned and labeled Kitchen, Scale: 1:50.
   d. Doors' and windows' schedule, any Scale is acceptable.

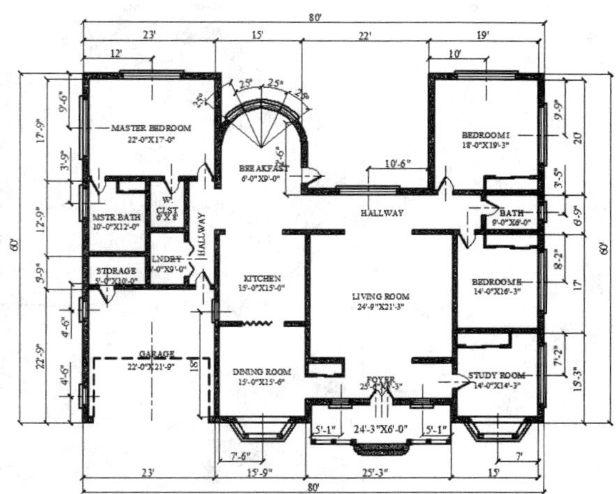

DOORS SCHEDULE				
DOOR NO.	**SIZE**	**QUANTITY**	**DESCRIPTION**	**LOCATION**
D1	2'-6"X7'-0"	2	EXTERIOR SINGLE	STUDY, GRG
D1	2'-6"X7'-0"	5	INTERIOR SINGLE	BHR #1, MBHR, WIC, BHR #2, BACK PORCH
D2	2'-8"X7'-0"	4	INTERIOR SINGLE	MBDR, BDR1, BDR2, STUDY
D3	6'-0"X7'-0"	2	FOLDING, FOUR LEAVES	LD, STG
D4	6'-0"X7'-0"	1	ACOORDION	DNG
D5	4'-0"X7'-0"	1	FOYER DOUBLE	FOYER
D6	18'-0"X10'-0"	1	OVERHEAD	GRG
D7	6'-0"X7'-0"	4	SLIDING	CLOSETS IN BDI, BDII

LEGEND: M: MASTER, BD: BED, BH: BATH, S: STUDY, R: ROOM, WIC: WALK-IN-CLOSET, GRG: GARAGE, BFT: BREAKFAST, DNG: DINING, KCN: KITCHEN, HW: HALLWAY, LD: LAUNDRY, STG: STORAGE

20.24. Roof Plan

Objectives

- Learn to develop roof plan for the given floor plan

Hints

- Refer to Chapter #16 for details and help

ICA Description

1. Drawing units: Architectural:
2. Create the layers, as necessary.
3. Open the complete floor plan file.
4. Create the roof plan shown in Figure 16-4a, Figure 16-4b, and Figure 16-4c of the text book.
5. Set the scale to 1:162.
6. Update the blocks.

ICA Submission

1. Submit the print of the roof plan.

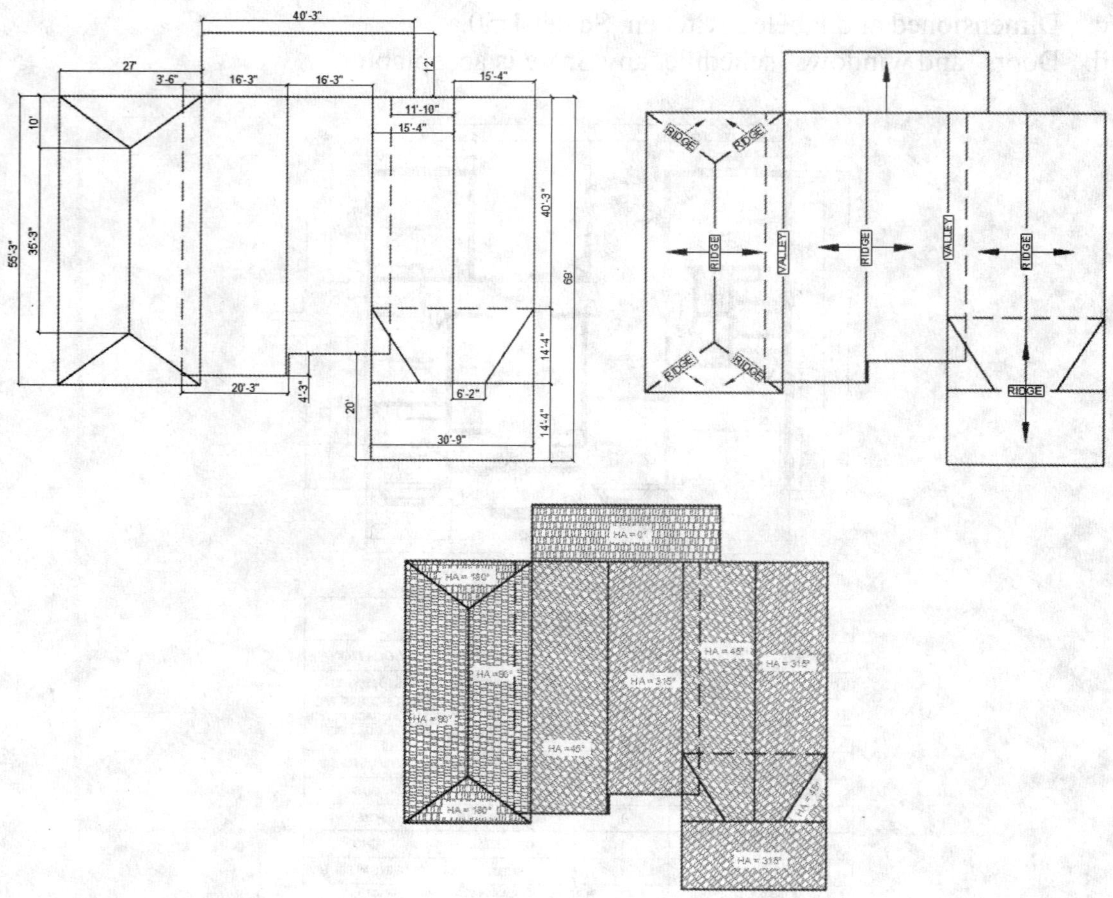

20.25.   Elevation

Objectives
- Learn to insert block from the *Design Center*
- Learn to develop front elevation for the given floor and roof plans

Hints
- Refer to Chapter #16 for details and help

ICA Description
1. Drawing units: Architectural:
2. Create the layers, as necessary.
3. Open the drawing created in the previous ICA (both the floor plan and roof plan in one file).
4. Create the front elevation shown in Figure 16-14 of the text book.
5. Do not add dimension.
6. Landscaping is optional
7. Set the scale to 1:132.
8. Update the blocks.

ICA Submission
1. Submit the print of the front elevation.

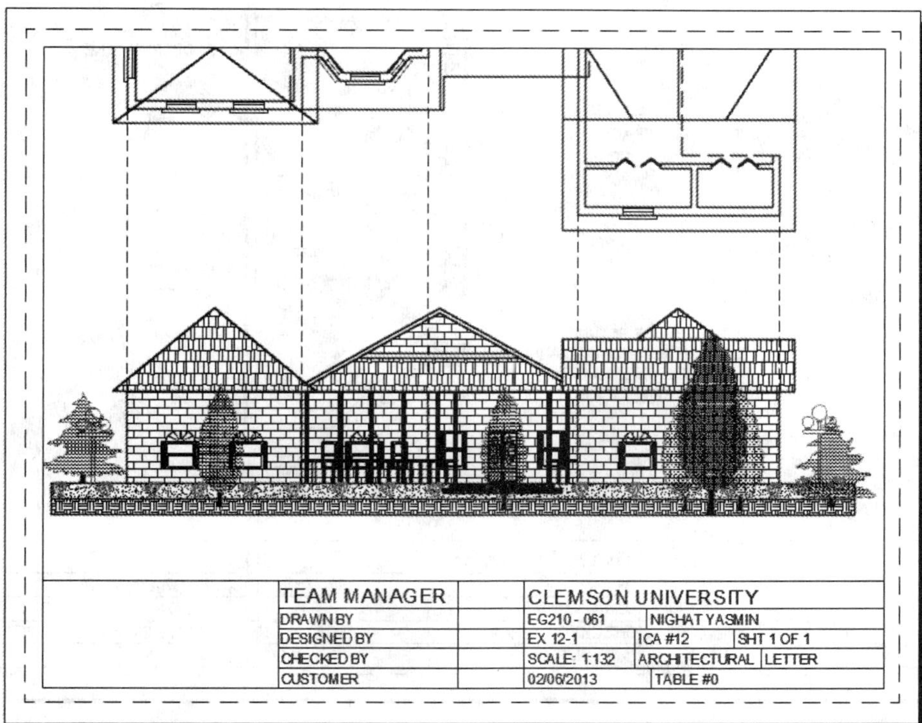

20.26. Site Plan

Objectives

- Learn to develop a site plan (Text book: Figure 17-13)

Hints

- Refer to Chapter #17 for details and help

ICA Description

1. <u>Drawing units:</u> <u>Engineering</u>: Draw the site plan shown in Figure 17-13 of the text book.
2. Add the labels.
3. Add the dimensions.

ICA Submission

1. Submit the print of the site plan, Figure 17-4, Figure 17-5, and Figure 17-13 at the Scale: 1:500.

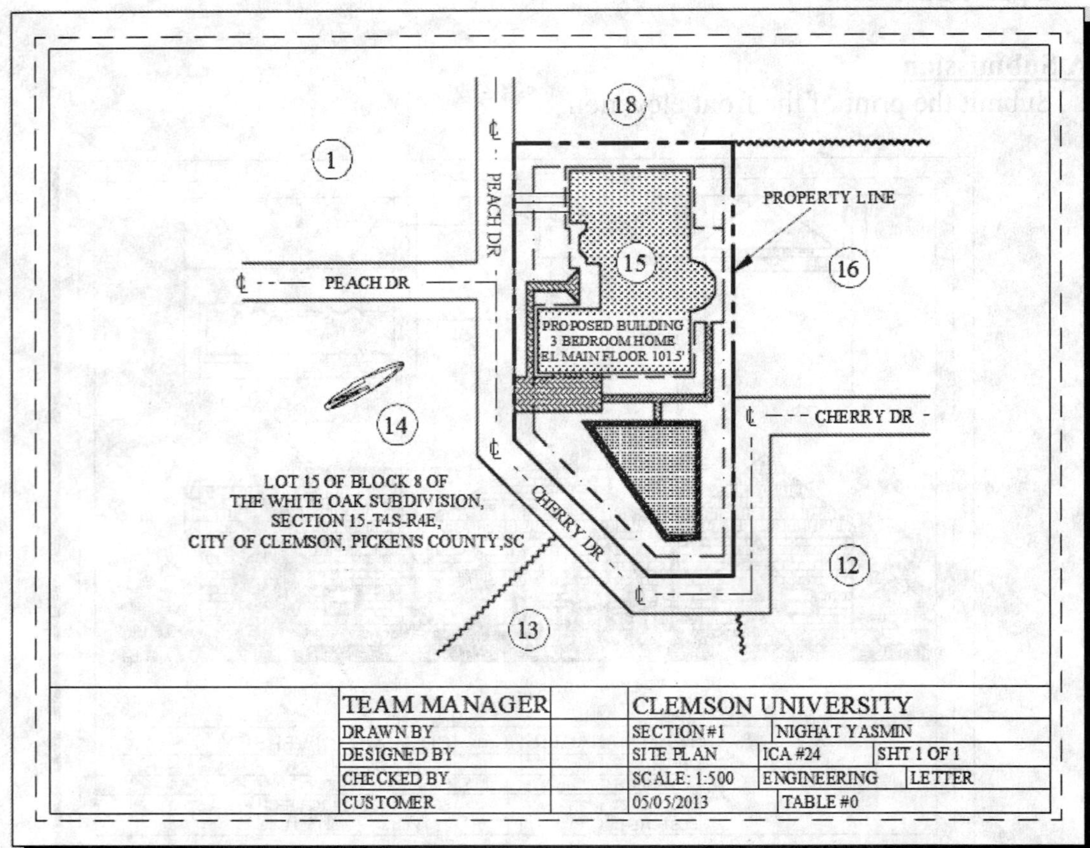

TEAM MANAGER	CLEMSON UNIVERSITY		
DRAWN BY	SECTION #1	NIGHAT YASMIN	
DESIGNED BY	SITE PLAN	ICA #24	SHT 1 OF 1
CHECKED BY	SCALE: 1:500	ENGINEERING	LETTER
CUSTOMER	05/05/2013	TABLE #0	

21. Homework Drawings

21.1. Grid-1 (Units: Inches)

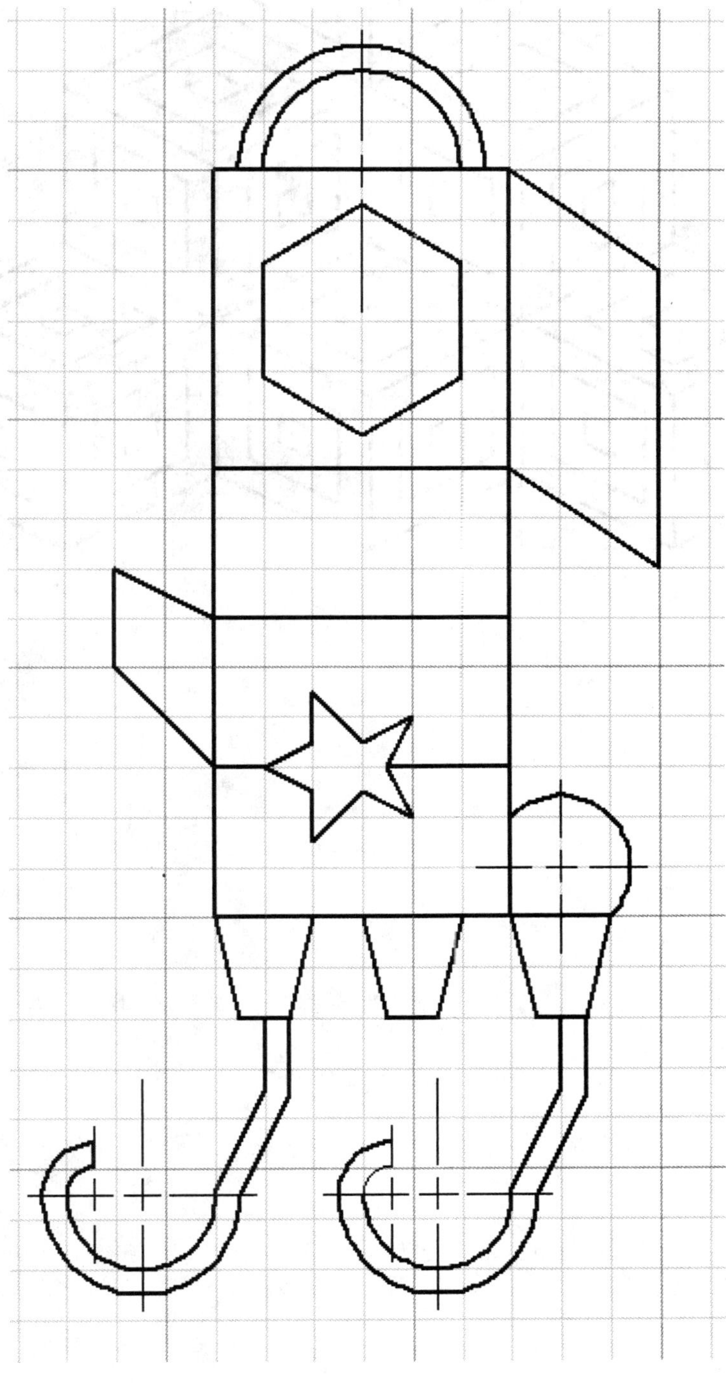

21.2.   Grid -2 (Units: Millimeters)

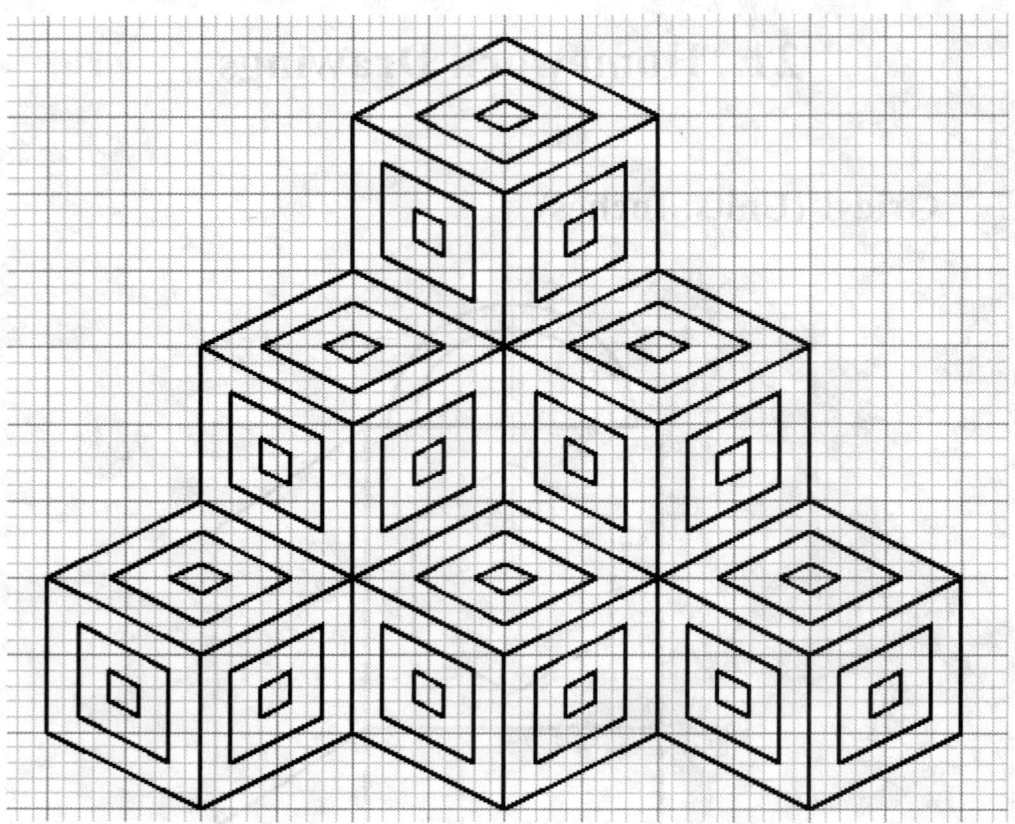

21.3. Light Signal (Units: Inches)

ABSOLUTE COORDINATES (INCHES)			
A	(0, 0)	I	(4.5, 9.5)
B	(0, 30)	J	(7.5, 12.5)
C	(22, 5)	K	(7.5, 20.5)
D	(22, 29)	L	(4.5, 17.5)
E	(6, 20)	M	(14.5, 11.5)
F	(16, 22)	N	(17.5, 14.5)
G	(6, 19)	O	(17.5, 22.5)
H	(16, 21)	P	(14.5, 19.5)

CIRCLES (INCHES)			
DIAMETER = 2.0			
1	(6, 17.5)	4	(16, 19.5)
2	(6, 15.0)	5	(16, 17.0)
3	(6, 12.5)	6	(16, 14.5)

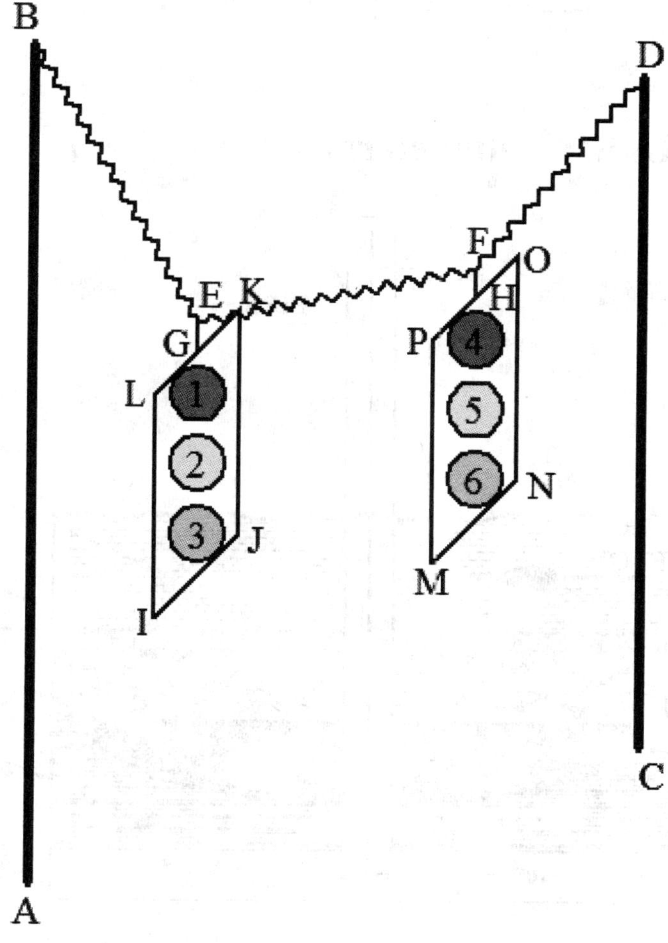

21.4. Plate with holes (Units: Inches)

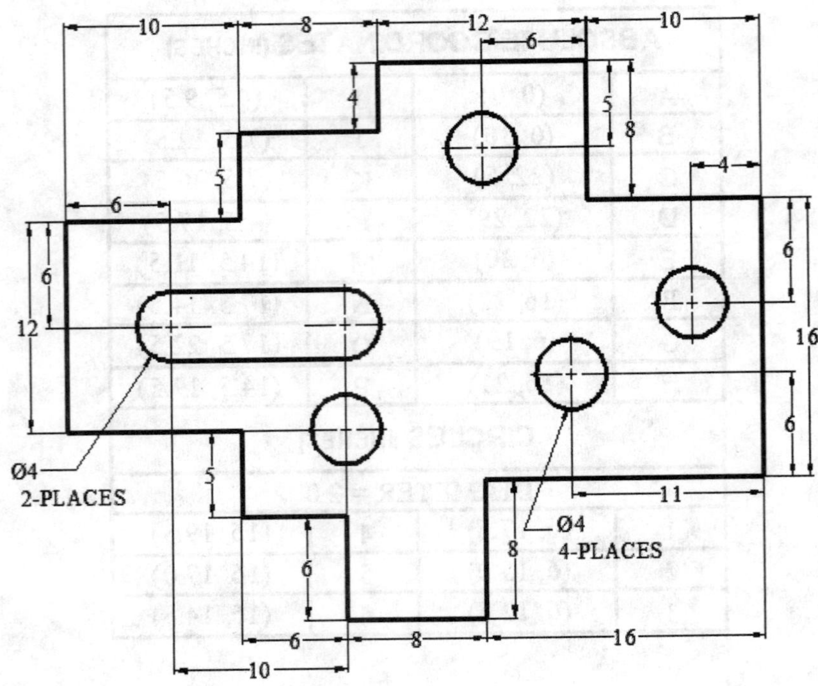

21.5. Pier (Units: Millimeters)

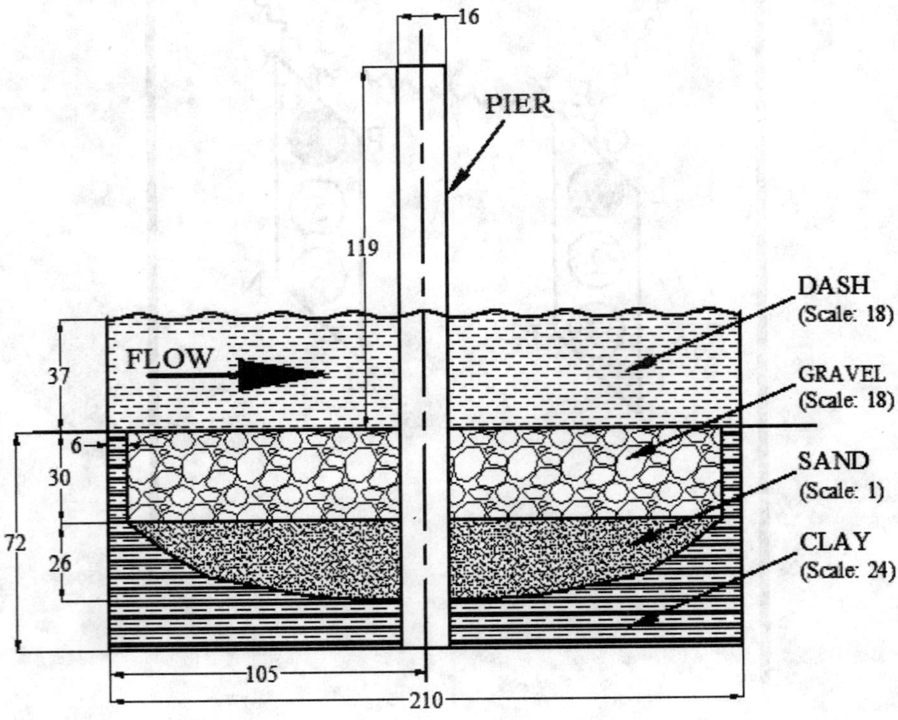

21.6. Pipe Cutter (Units: Millimeters)

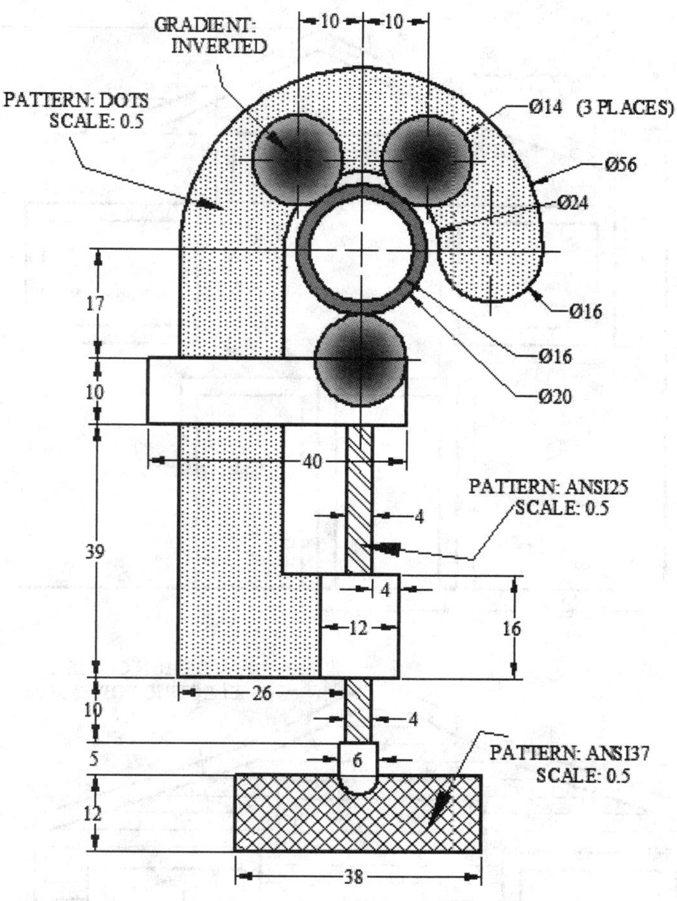

21.7. Circle-TTR (Units: Millimeters)

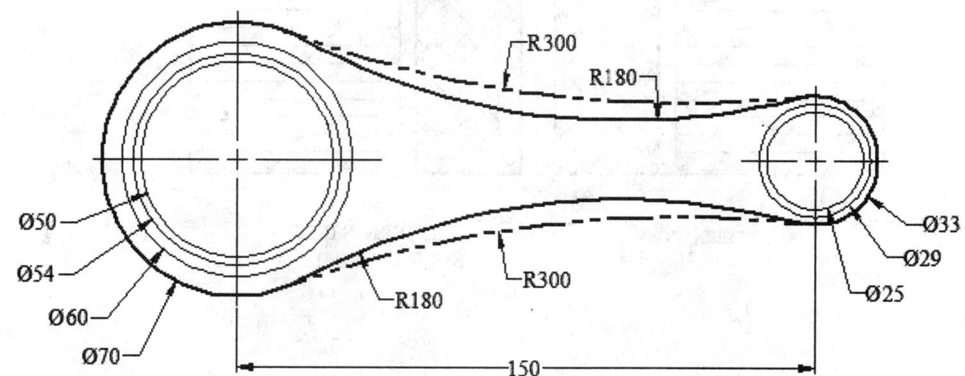

21.8. Barn (Units: Inches)

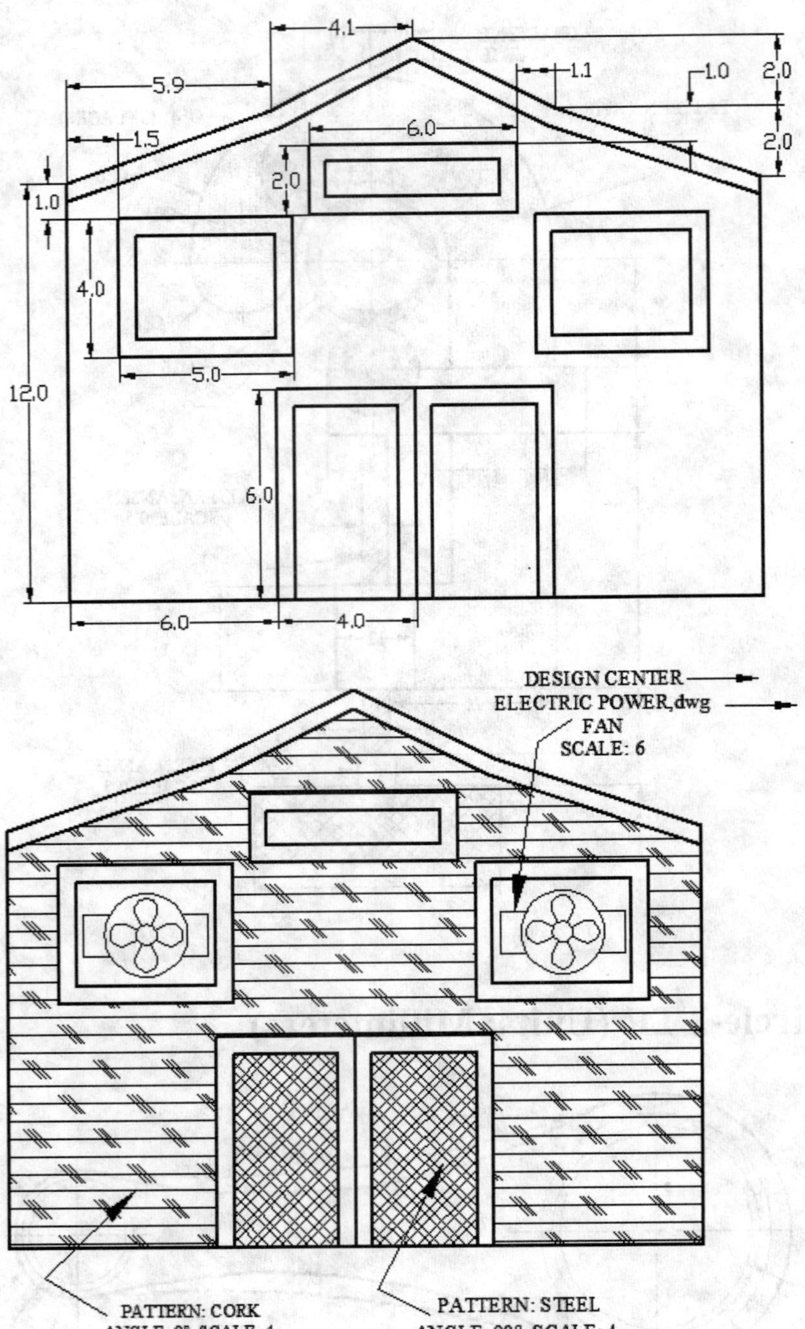

21.9. Geometrical Design in Layout (Units: Inches)

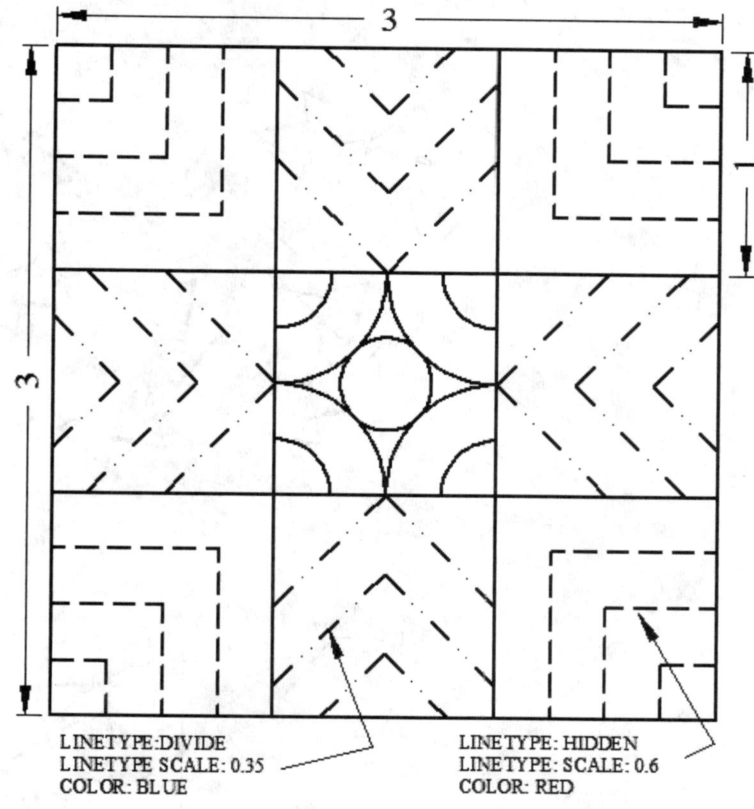

21.10. Rectangular Array (Units: Inches)

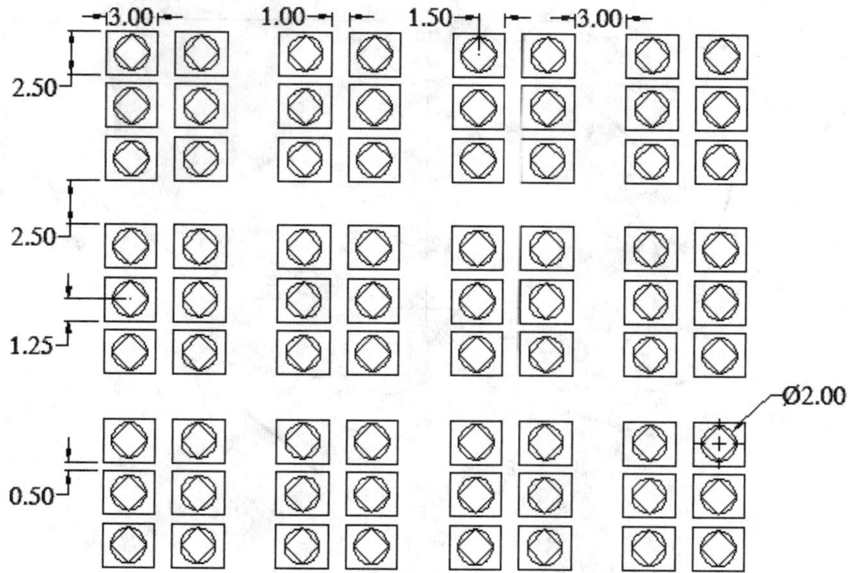

21.11. Polar Array (Units: Inches)

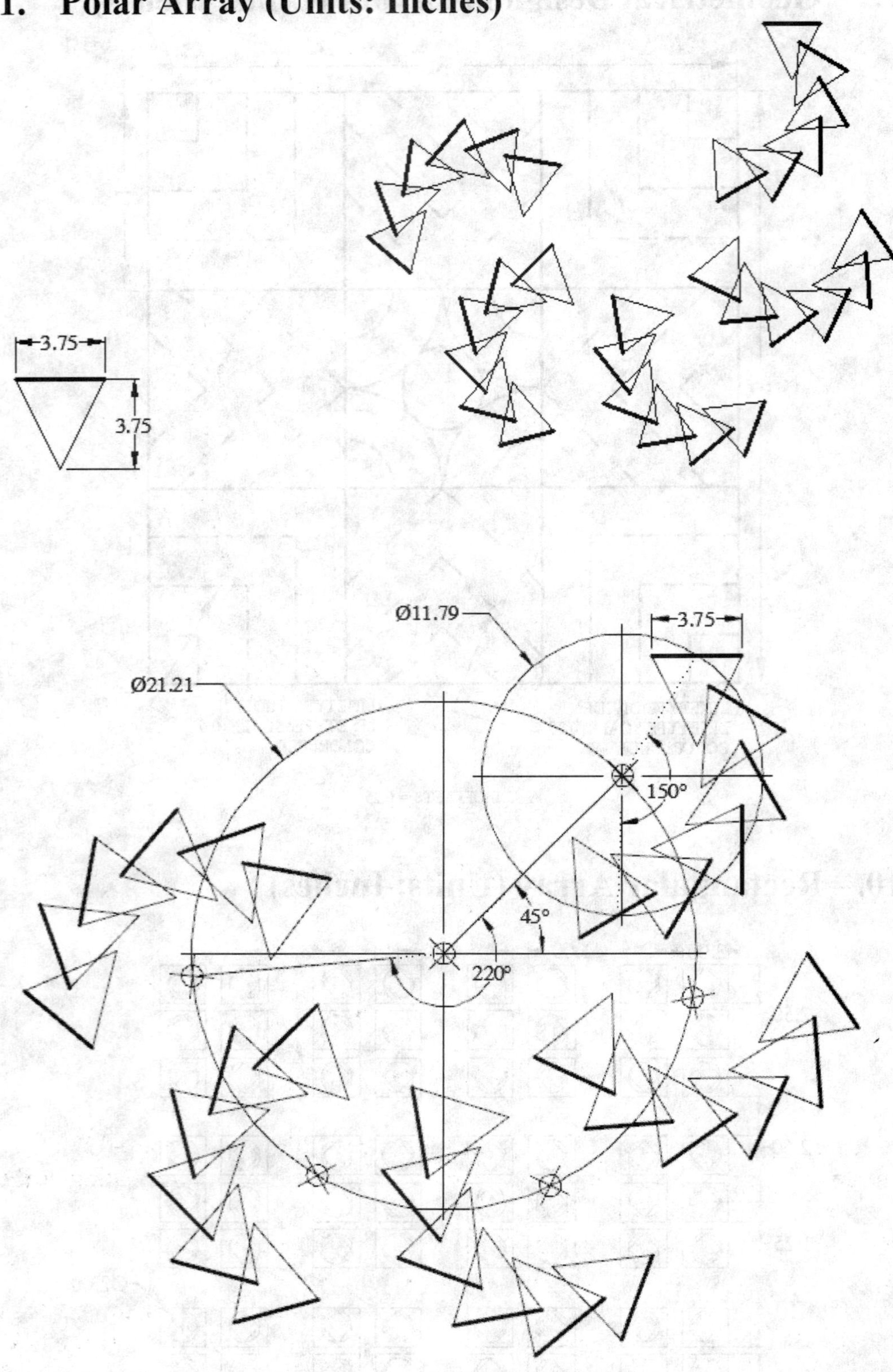

21.12. Spiral of Archimedes (Units: Millimeters)

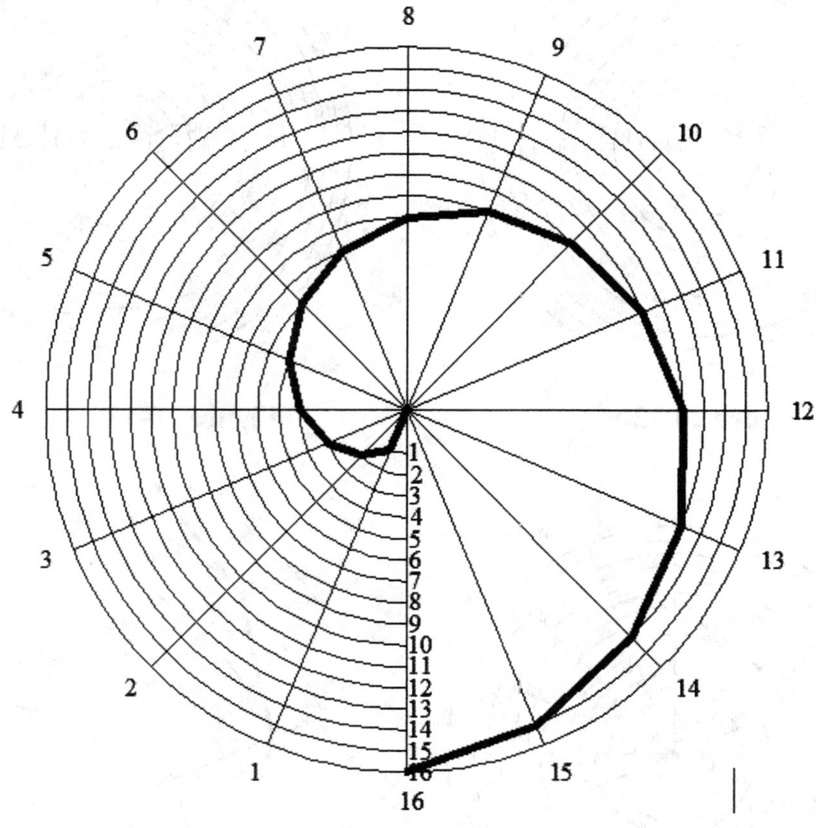

Figure 20-12

<u>Step-by-step instructions for the spiral of Archimedes</u>
1. Draw a circle of the given diameter, Figure 20-12a.

Figure 20-12a

2. Create 16 concentric circles with offset distance = 20mm, Figure 20-12b.
3. Draw a straight line starting at the center of the circles and terminating at the right quadrant of the outermost circle, Figure 20-12c.
4. Create 16 straight lines using *Arraypolar* command, Figure 20-12d.
5. Label the lines created in step #4 as shown in Figure 20-12.
6. Figure 20-12e (i) Activate the polyline command. (ii) Click at the center of the circle. (iii) Click at the intersection of first circle and the first line. (iv) Click at the intersection of the second circle and second line. (v) Repeat the process for the remaining circles and lines.
7. The Figure 20-12f shows the spiral of Archimedes.
8. Finally, trim the part of the circles as shown in Figure 20-12.

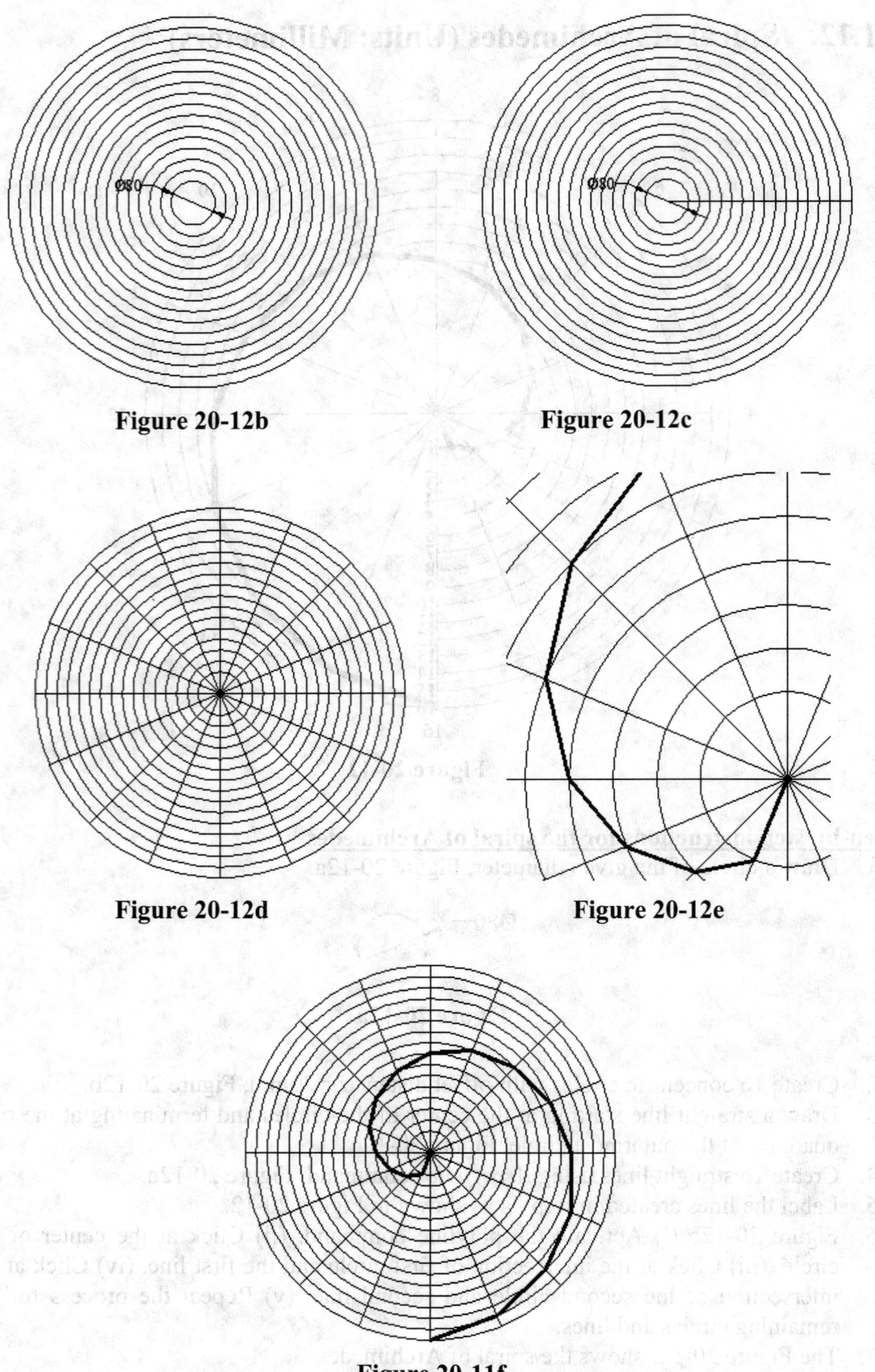

Figure 20-12b

Figure 20-12c

Figure 20-12d

Figure 20-12e

Figure 20-11f

21.13. Elevator system (Units: Millimeters)

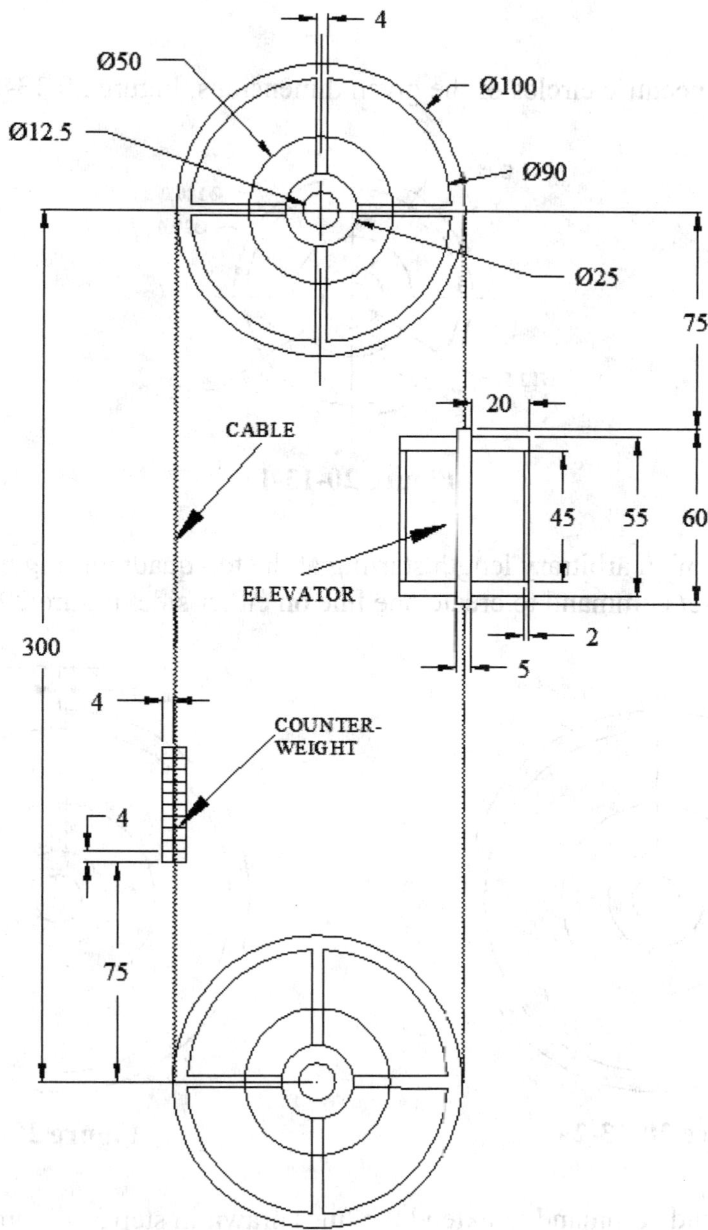

Figure 20-13

Step-by-step instructions for the elevator

First sheave

1. Draw the concentric circles of the given dimensions, Figure 20-13-1.

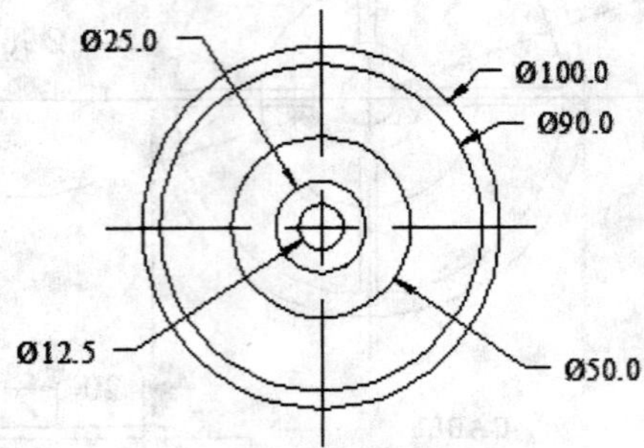

Figure 20-13-1

2. Draw a line of an arbitrary length starting at the top quadrant, Figure 20-13-2a.
3. Use the *Offset* command to create one line on either side, Figure 20-13-2b.

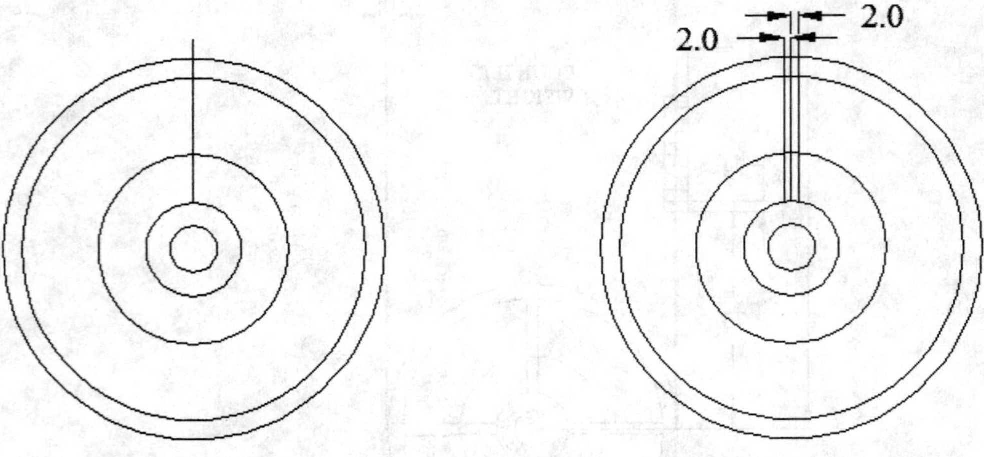

Figure 20-13-2a   **Figure 20-13-2b**

4. Use the extend command to extend the lines drawn in step 3, Figure 20-13-3.

Figure 20-13-3

5. Delete the line drawn in step 2, Figure 20-13-4a.
6. Use the trim command to trim the (two parallel) lines to create the desired shape, Figure 20-13-4b.
7. Use the *Arraypolar* command to create the polar array, Figure 20-13-4c.

8. Use the trim command to trim the part of the circle of the (diameter 90.0) between the two parallel lines to create the desired shape, Figure 20-13-4d

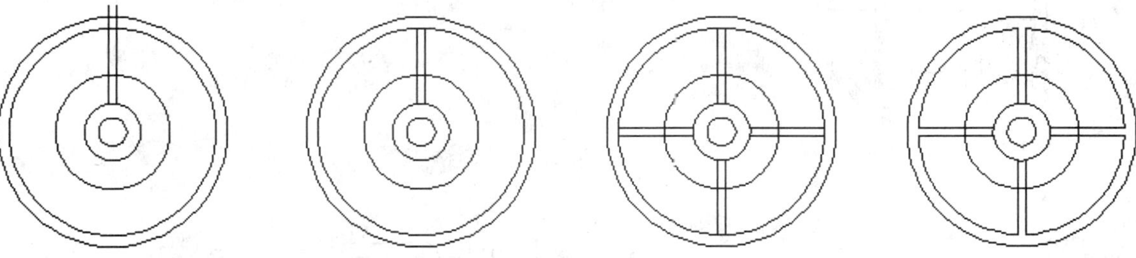

Figure 20-13-4a   **Figure 20-13-4b**   **Figure 20-13-4c**   **Figure 20-13-4d**

Cable
1. Draw the cable by drawing a line of length 150.0 units starting at the right quadrant, Figure 20-13-5a.
2. Change the linetype of the line drawn in the above step to the "Zig-Zag", Figure 20-13-5b.
3. Change the Linetype scale (using properties sheet) of the line to 0.1, Figure 20-13-5c.
4. Use the *Copy* command to create the copy of the modified line at the left quadrant, Figure 20-13-5d.

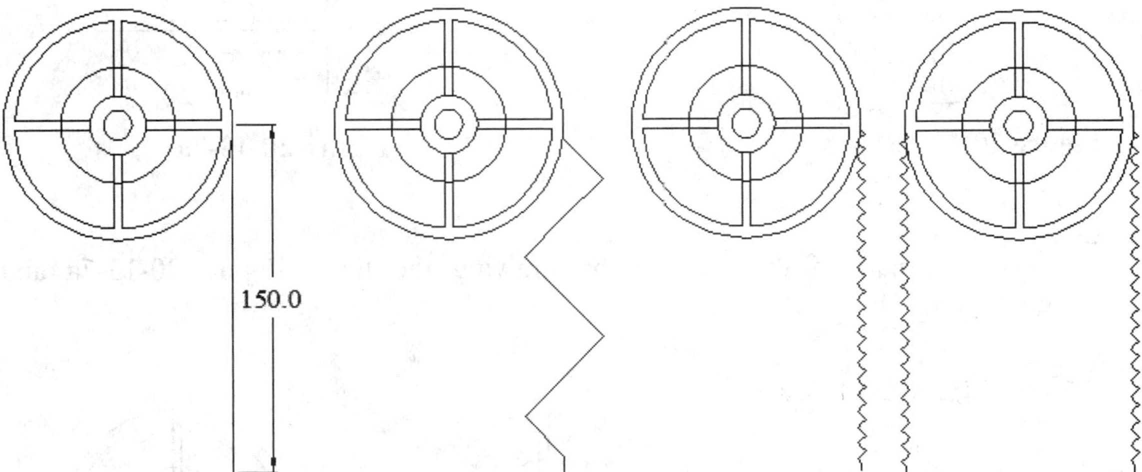

Figure 20-13-5a   **Figure 20-13-5b**   **Figure 20-13-5c**   **Figure 20-13-5d**

Second sheave
1. Use the Mirror command to create the mirror image (second sheave), Figure 20-13.6.

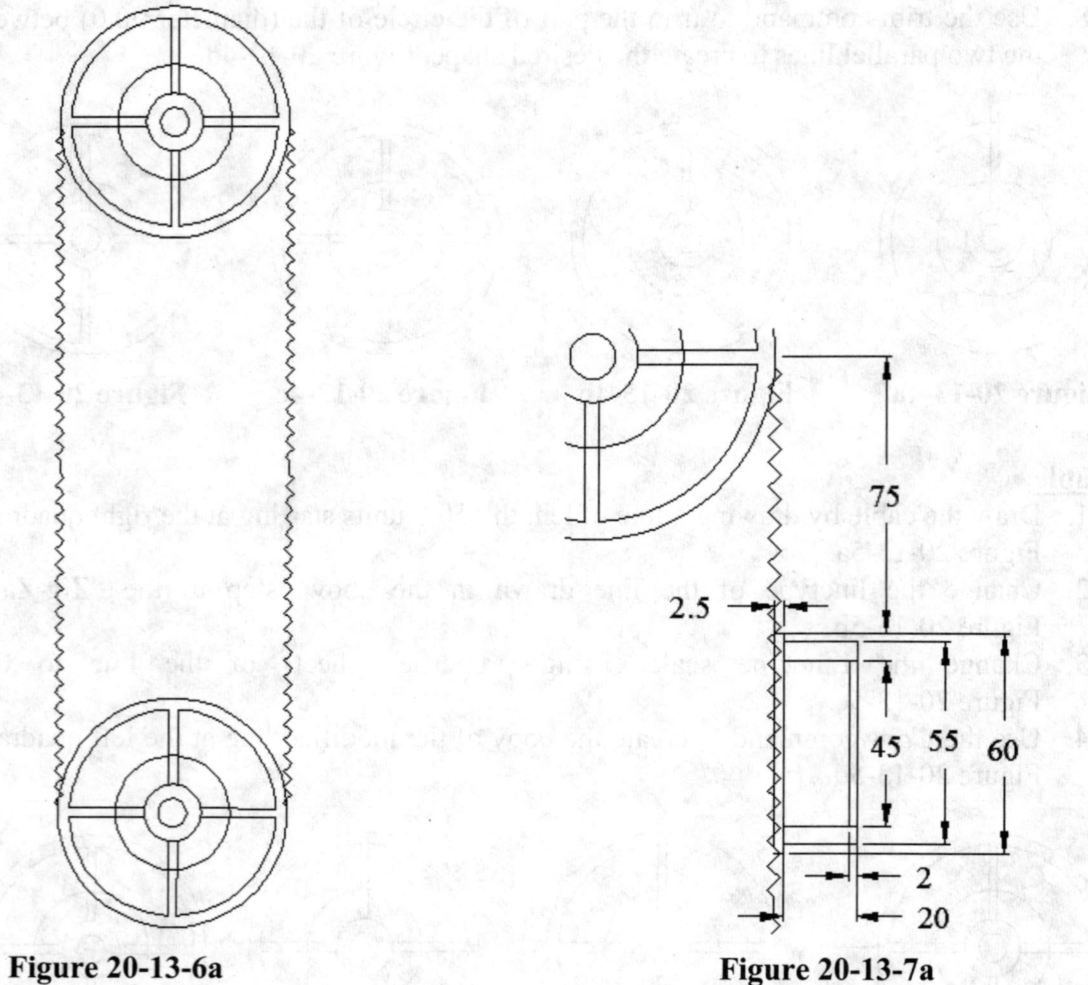

Figure 20-13-6a   **Figure 20-13-7a**

Elevator

1. Draw front half of the elevator by drawing the lines, Figure 20-13-7a and Figure 20-13-7b.

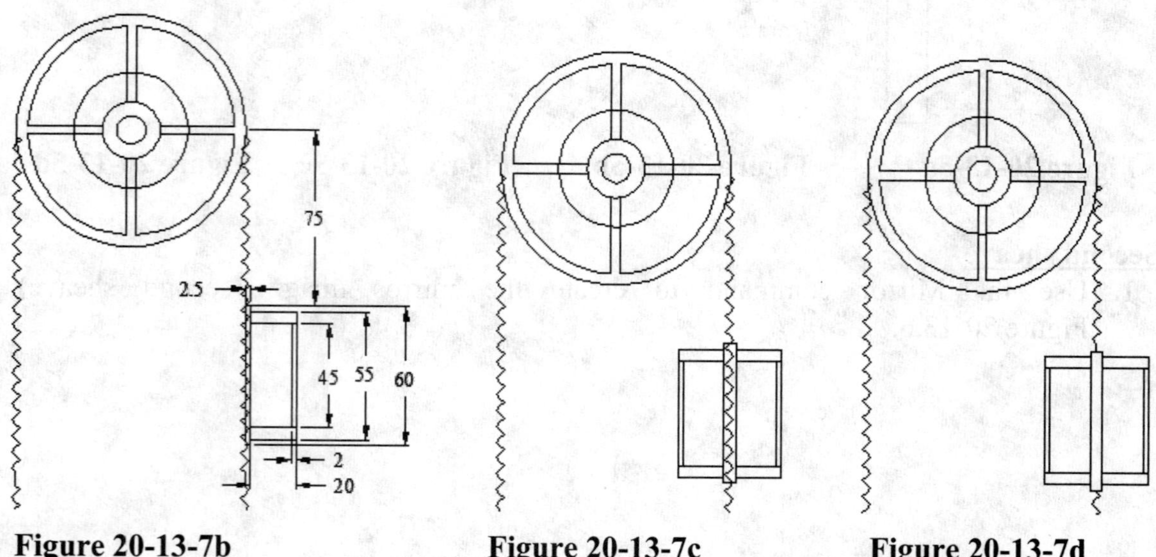

Figure 20-13-7b   **Figure 20-13-7c**   **Figure 20-13-7d**

2. Use the *Mirror* command to complete the elevator, Figure 20-13-7c.
3. Use the *Trim* command to remove the part of the cable from the central part of the elevator, Figure 20-13-7d.

Counter weight
1. Draw a small square by drawing the lines, Figure 20-13-8a.
2. Use the array command to create the rectangular array, Figure 20-13-8b.

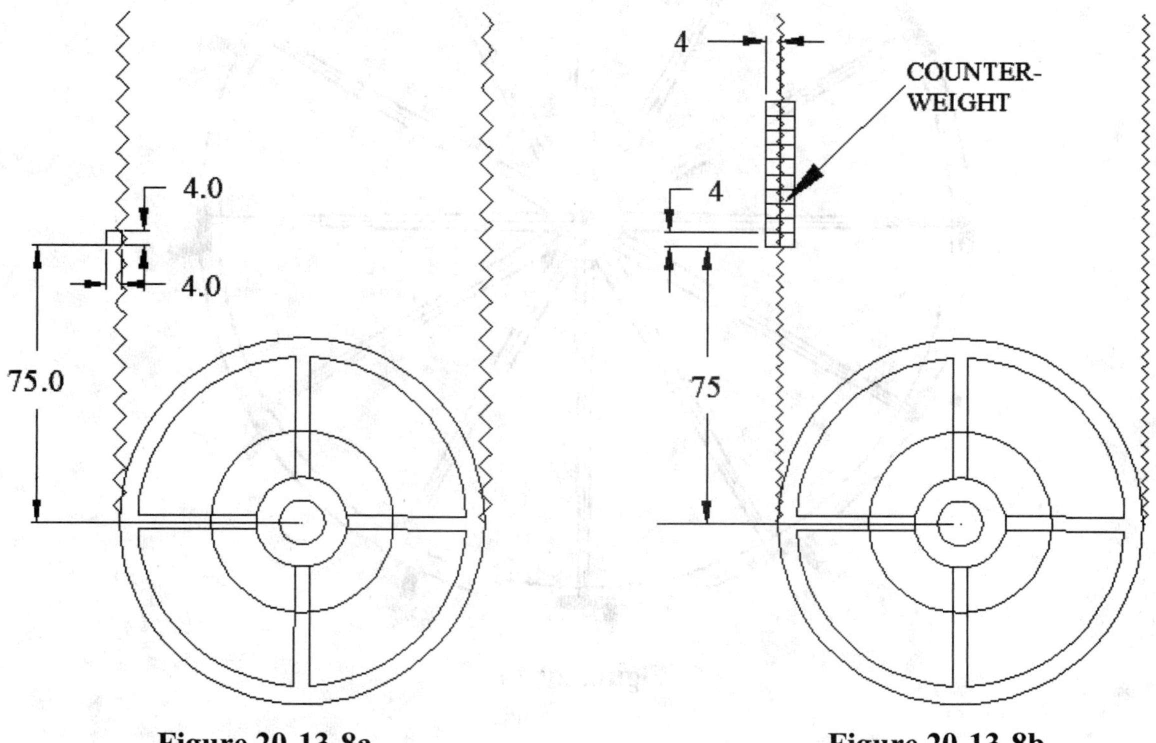

Figure 20-13-8a   **Figure 20-13-8b**

Complete system
1. The complete system is shown in Figure 20-13.

21.14.   Ferris wheel (Units: Millimeters)

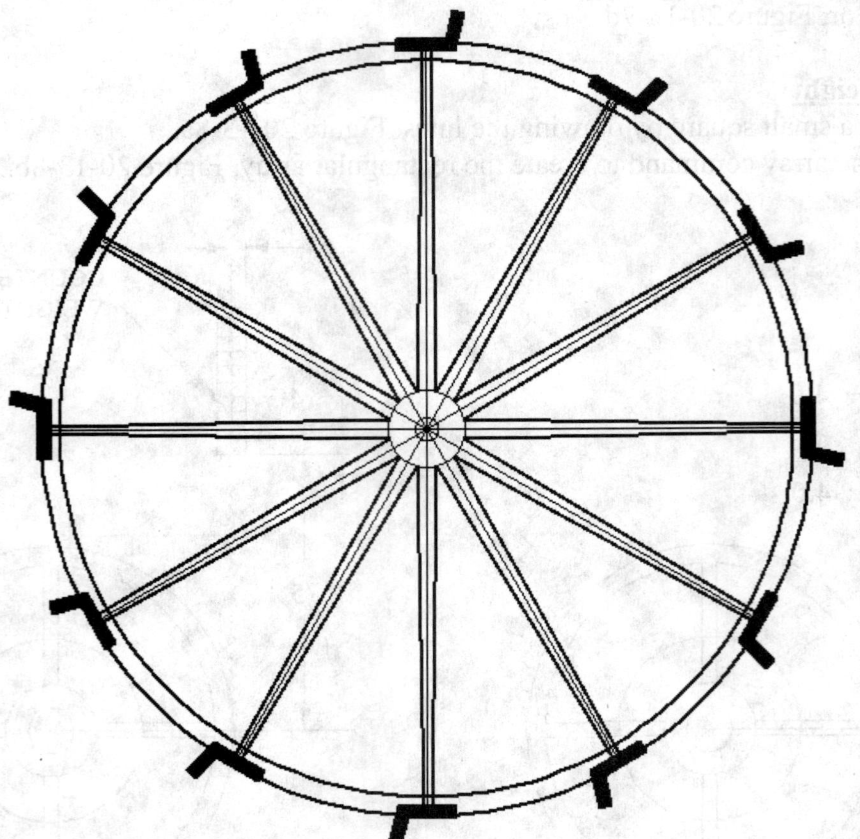

Figure 20-14

Wheel

1.   Draw the concentric circles of the given dimensions, Figure 20-14-1.

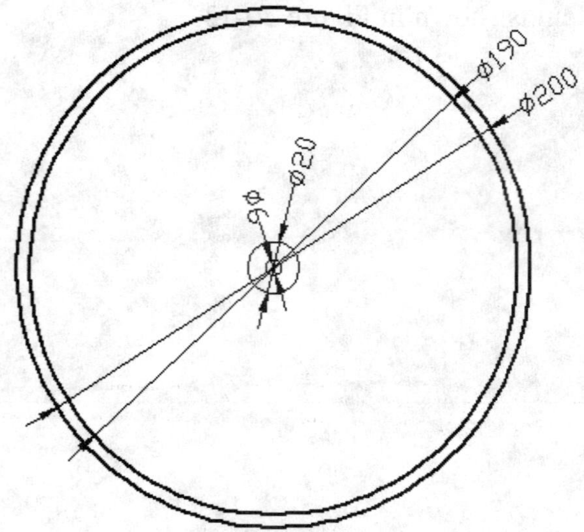

Figure 20-14-1

Spoke

1. Draw a straight line originating at the center of the circles and terminating at the right quadrant of the outermost circle, Figure 20-14.
2. Draw a 0.34mm long horizontal line originating at the intersection of the horizontal line drawn in step #1 and 20mm diameter circle, Figure 20-14-2a.
3. Draw a vertical line originating at the left end of the horizontal line drawn in step #2 and terminating at 20mm diameter circle, Figure 20-14-2a. Label the intersection of the vertical line and the circle as A.

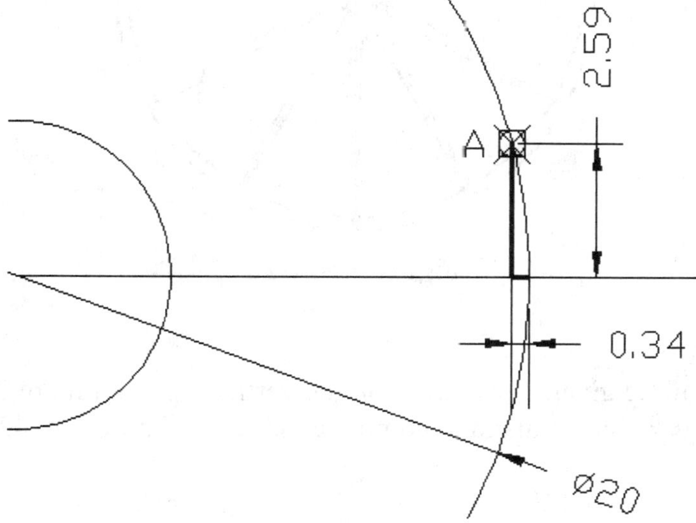

Figure 20-14-2a

4. Draw a straight line originating at point A and terminating beyond the 200mm diameter circle, Figure 20-14-2b.

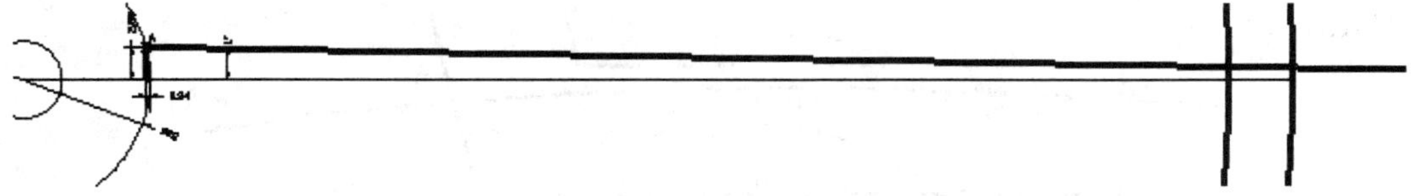

Figure 20-14-2b

5. Trim the line drawn in step #4 with respect the outer most circle, Figure 20-14-2c.
6. Use the *Mirror* command to create a line below the horizontal line, Figure 20-14-2c.

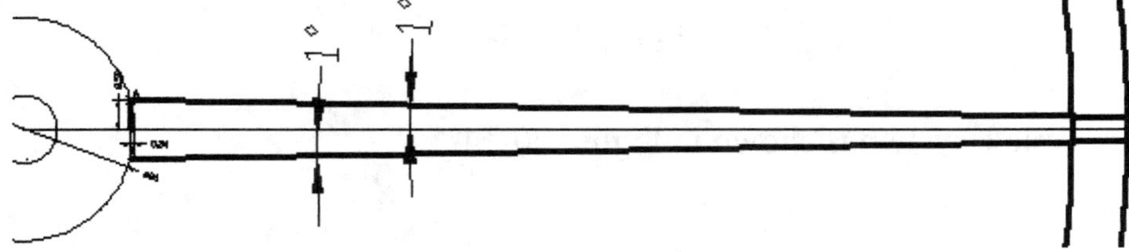

Figure 20-14-2c

7. Use the *ArrayPolar* command to complete the spokes, Figure 20-14-2c.

Figure 20-14-2d

Seats

1. Draw a seat of the given dimensions on the vertical spoke, Figure 20-14-3a.
2. Use the *ArrayPolar* command to complete the seats, Figure 20-14.

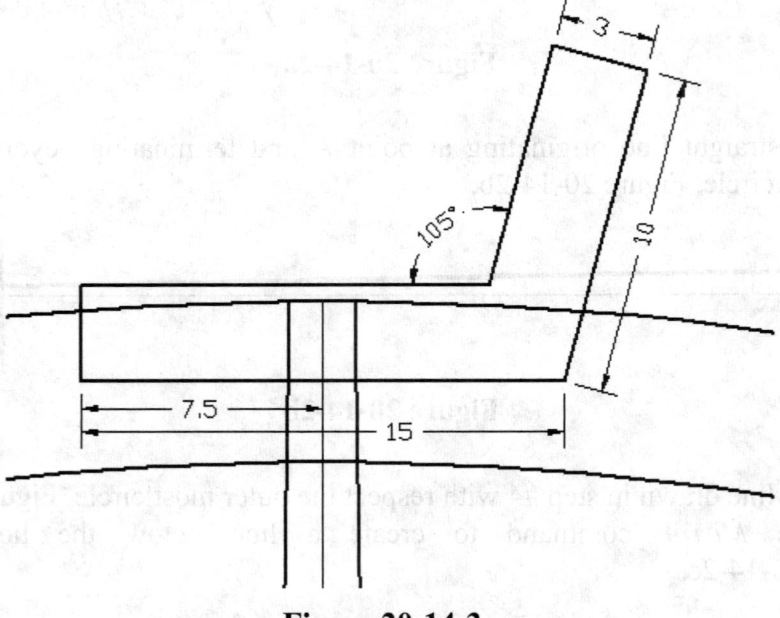

Figure 20-14-3a

3. The complete system is shown in Figure 20-14.

22. Bibliography

Edward Allen and Joseph Iano, "*Fundamental of Building Construction: materials and methods*", John Wiley and Sons, Inc, 4th ed., 2004.

James Ambrose, "*Building Construction and Design*", Van Nostrand Reinhold, 1992.

AutoCAD 2008, Help Documentations.

AutoCAD 2010, Help Documentations.

Gerald Baker, "*Civil Drafting for the Engineering Technician*", Thomson Delmar Learning, 2006.

Gary R. Bertoline and Eric N. Wiebe, "*Fundamentals of Graphics Communication,*" McGrawHill, 5th ed., 2005.

James D. Bethune, "*Engineering Graphics with AutoCAD 2006,*" Prentice Hall, Pearson Education, 6th ed., 2006.

Wilfried Brutsaert, "*Hydrology: An Introduction*", Cambridge University Press, 2005.

David A. Chin, "*Water Resources Engineering*", Prentice Hall, 2nd ed., 1988.

Ven Te Chow, David R. Maidment, and Larry W. Mays, "*Applied Hydrology*", McGraw-Hill Book Company, 3rd ed., 1988.

Mackenzie L. Davis and David A. Cornwell, "*Introduction to Environmental Engineering*", McGraw-Hill, 3rd ed., 1998.

Raymond E. Davis, Francis S. Foote, and Joe W. Kelley, "*Surveying: Theory and Practice*", McGraw-Hill Inc., 5th ed., 1966.

Raymond E. Davis and Joe. W. Kelley, "*Elementary Plane Surveying*", McGraw-Hill Book Company, 4th ed., 1967.

James H. Earle, "*Fundamentals of Graphics Communication,*" Prentice Hall, Pearson Education, 6th ed., 2002.

Stephen V. Estopinal, "*A Guide to Understanding Land Survey*", John Wiley and Sons, Inc, 2nd ed., 1993.

David Frey, "*AutoCAD 2002*", SYBEX, 2002.

Nicholas J. Garber and Lester A. Hoel, "*Traffic and Highway Engineering,*" University of Virginia, Cengage Learning, Toronto, Canada, 4th ed., 2009.

Frederick E. Giesecke, Alva Mitchell, Henry C. Spencer, Ivan L. Hill, and John T. Dygdon, "*Technical Drawing,*" Macmillan Publishing Company and Collier, 8th ed., 1986.

Frederick E. Giesecke, Alva Mitchell, Henry C. Spencer, Ivan L. Hill, John T. Dygdon, and Shawna Lockhart "*Technical Drawing,*" Published by Pearson – Prentice Hall , 13th ed., 2009.

David L. Goetsch, "Structural, Civil, and Pipe Drafting for CAD Technicians", Thomson Delmar Learning, 2003.

David L. Goetsch, "*Technical Drawing*", Macmillian Publishing Company, 8th ed., 2003.

Randolph P. Hoelscher and Clifford H. Springer, "*Engineering Drawing and Geometry*", John Wiley & Sons, INC. New York, 1955.

William J. Hornung, "*Architectural Drafting*", Prentice Hall, 3rd ed., 1960.

Mark Huth, "*Basic Principles for Construction,*" Thomson Delmar Learning, 2004.

Barry F. Kavanagh, "*Surveying Principles and Applications*", McGraw Hill Inc., Prentice Hall, 6th ed., 2003.

Philip Kissam, "*Surveying for Civil Engineers*", McGraw Hill Inc., 2nd ed., 1981.

Philip Kissam and Jerry A. Nathanson, "*Surveying Practice*", McGraw Hill Inc., 4th ed., 1987.

A. S. Levens, "*Graphics in Engineering and Science*", John Wiley & Sons, INC. New York, 2nd Printing, 1957.

Warren J. Luzadder, "*Fundamental of Engineering Drawing for Design, Communication, and Numerical Control*", Prentice Hall, 6rd ed., 1971.

David A. Madsen and Terence M. Shumaker, "*Civil Drafting Technology*", Prentice Hall, 3rd ed., 1998.

David A. Madsen and Terence M. Shumaker, "*Civil Drafting Technology*", Prentice Hall, 6th ed., 2007.

Jack C. McCormac, "*Surveying Fundamentals*", Prentice Hall, 2nd ed., 1991.

Jack C. McCormac, "*Surveying*", Prentice Hall, 4nd ed., 1991.

Richard H. McCuen, "*Hydrologic Analysis and Design*", Prentice Hall, 3rd ed., 2004.

John G. McEntyre, "*Land Survey System*", John Wiley and Sons, Inc, 1978

Edward J. Muller, James G. Fausett, and Philip A. Grau III, "*Architectural Drawing and Light construction*", Prentice Hall, 6th ed., 2002.

Jerry A. Nathanson and Philip Kissam, "*Surveying Practice*", McGraw-Hill Book Company, 4th ed., 1988.

Ralph W. Liebing and Mimi Ford Paul, "*Architectural Working Drawings,*" John Wiley and Sons, 2nd ed., 1983.

William J. O'Connell, "*Graphic Communications in Architecture*", Stripes Publishing Company, 1972.

Dave Rosgen, "*Applied River Morpohology*", Wildland Hydrology, Pagosa Springs, Colorodo, 1996.

Harry Rubey, George Edward, and Marion Wesley Todd, "*Engineering Surveys: Elementary and Applied*", The Macmillan Company, 2nd ed., 1950.

George K. Stegman and Harry J. Stegman, "*Architectural Drafting,*" American Technical Society, 2nd ed., 1974.

Warren Viessman, Jr. and Gary L. Lewis, "*Introduction to Hydrology*", Prentice Hall, 5th ed., 2003.

Harvey W. Waffle, "*Architectural Drawing*", The Bruce Publishing Company, Revised edition, 1962.

Ernest R. Weidhaas, "*Architectural Drafting and Design*", Allyn and Bacon, 6th ed., 1989.

"*Webster's New Collegiate Dictionary*", G. & S. Merriam Co., Publishers, Springfield. MASS, U.S.A.

Notes:

23. Index

Z